ON THE LOOSE IN CALIFORNIA

WITH LAS VEGAS AND THE GRAND CANYON 1993

WRITTEN BY BERKELEY STUDENTS IN COOPERATION WITH THE ASSOCIATED STUDENTS OF THE UNIVERSITY OF CALIFORNIA

ISBN 0-679-02222-8

First Edition

● ● ● ON THE LOOSE IN CALIFORNIA

Editor: Michael Mullen
Managing Editor: Kristina Brooks
Assistant Editors: Belynda Biller, David DeGusta
Creative Director: Fabrizio LaRocca
Cartographer: David Lindroth, Eureka Cartography
Text Design: Tigist Getachew
Cover Design and Illustration: Rico Lins

● ● ● SPECIAL SALES

The Berkeley Guides and Fodor's Travel Publications are available at special discounts for bulk purchases (100 copies or more) for sales promotions or premiums. Special editions, including personalized covers, excerpts of existing guides, and corporate imprints, can be created in large quantities for special needs. For more information, write to Special Marketing, Fodor's Travel Publications, 201 E. 50th Street, New York, NY 10022. Inquiries from Canada should be sent to Random House of Canada, Ltd., Marketing Department, 1265 Aerowood Drive, Mississauga, Ontario L4W 1B9. Inquiries from the United Kingdom should be sent to Fodor's Travel Publications, 20 Vauxhall Bridge Road, London, England SW1V 2SA.

MANUFACTURED IN THE UNITED STATES OF AMERICA
10 9 8 7 6 5 4 3 2 1

Contents

6 THE GOLD COUNTRY 205

7 THE SIERRA NEVADA AND SAN JOAQUIN VALLEY 233

8 THE CENTRAL COAST 277

9 LOS ANGELES 315

10 ORANGE COUNTY 367

11 SAN DIEGO 389

12 PALM SPRINGS AND THE DESERT 429

13 LAS VEGAS AND THE GRAND CANYON 451

What the Berkeley Guides Are All About

Last year, a bunch of Berkeley students set out to write a new series of budget guidebooks covering California, Eastern Europe, Mexico, and the Pacific Northwest and Alaska. Over the course of the summer, our student writers found themselves sleeping in whorehouses in Mexico, landing bush planes in the Arctic Circle, wandering through the deserts of California, and milking cows in Romania in exchange for precious food. The result is *The Berkeley Guides*, a true budget-travel series. We wrote the books because the current crop of guidebooks just doesn't appeal to student travelers like us. It seems to us, the competition has been regurgitating the same old muck for decades. In contrast, *The Berkeley Guides* are written from scratch: The information is fresh, and we're brutally honest about what we found on the road. The destinations covered were slept in, eaten in, boogied down in, and sized up by our writers. If a place sucks, we tell you and recommend something else.

But most of all, these guides are for travelers who want to see more than just the main sights. We find out what the locals do for fun, where they go to eat, play, or just hang out. Most guidebooks concentrate on the touristy stuff, ignoring important local issues, events, and culture. Boring! In *The Berkeley Guides*, we give you the information you need to understand what's going on around you, whether it's gay life in San Francisco or the war on weed in the Lost Coast. We tell you about customs to respect, political and social situations you should be aware of, and your potential impact on the place you're visiting.

It's one of life's weird truisms that the more cheaply you travel, the more you usually experience. You're bound to experience a lot with *The Berkeley Guides* because we believe in stretching a dollar a long, long way. We show you cheap or free ways to live—and live it up—while you're on the road. You won't find much in our guides about the wallpaper pattern in a hotel room or the spices used in a restaurant's duck à l'orange; instead, we tell you if a place is cheap, clean (no bugs), and worth your money.

Most of us are Californians so it's not surprising that we emphasize the outdoors in these guides, including lots of info about hikes and biking trails, as well as tips on low-impact camping and protecting the environment. (As the saying goes: "Take only pictures and leave only footprints.") To further minimize our impact on the environment, we print our books on recycled paper using soy-based inks, and we plant two trees for every one we use. Coming from a community as diverse as Berkeley, it was also important to us that our books be useful to *everyone*, and so we tell you if a place is wheelchair-accessible; where people of color may encounter discrimination; provide resources for gay and lesbian travelers; and recognize the needs of women travelers.

We've done our best to make sure that the information in *The Berkeley Guides* is accurate, but time doesn't stand still, and stuff is going to change. Call ahead when it really matters to you. These books are brand new, and we'd really appreciate some feedback. Tell us about your latest find, a new scam, a budget deal, whatever—we want to hear about it. Write to the editors at 505 Eshleman Hall, University of California, Berkeley, CA 94720.

Thanks to You

Loads of people helped us put together On the Loose in California; some are listed below but many others—whom our writers met briefly on buses, in motels, and in hostels—also helped out. We would like you to help us update this book and give us feedback from the road. Drop us a line—a postcard, a scrawled note on some toilet paper, whatever—and we'll be happy to acknowledge your contribution below. Our address is 505 Eshleman Hall, University of California, Berkeley, CA 94720.

Special thanks go to Candy Acevedo; Laurie Allison of the San Diego Convention and Visitors Bureau; Todd Anderson (Palos Verdes); Diana Askea (Chico/Paradise); John Aune (New York); Debbie Bassett (Sacramento); Michael Barrow (M.I.T.); Renee Basye (Sacramento); the Biller family (Burlingame); Priscilla Bingham (Lemon Grove); Mark Blundell; Cathy Ortega and Joe Vitullo of Budget Rent A Car; Bill Bogert (Hollywood); Bruce and Charlotte Bolinger (Nevada City/Grass Valley); Martin Boscos of the Old Town Travelodge (San Diego); Sarah Brancart of the San Luis Obispo Chamber; John Brattin; Betsy Bromberg and Wendy Grant of Choice Hotels; Bob Bryzman (Redding); California State Park Service (Calaveras Big Trees and Bodie); Bill Cassity (Sacramento); Armando Chacon (Escondido); Jan Chapman (Chico/Paradise); Steve Cilenti (Sacramento); Debbie Clark of the Bartell Hotels (San Diego); Roberta Collier (Redding); Tony and Sue Ann Converse (Brentwood); Charlie Cowart (Ocotillo); Corene Darney (San Luis Obispo); Mr. and Mrs. Darrah (Stockton); the DeGusta family (Sacramento); Robert Deuel of Knott's Berry Farm (Buena Park); Alyce Dudley (Red Bluff); Mr. and Mrs. Eaton at Long Valley Hostel; Dee Dee Fitzgerald (Carpenteria); Martin Foigelman and family (Newport Beach); Linda Furr (Chico/Paradise); Bill Goodyear (Red Bluff); Joel Grande and family (San Diego); Leah Greenblatt (San Francisco); Bernard Griego (Berkeley); Tom Hanscom of the San Diego Wild Animal Park; Chris Harper (Las Vegas); Christine Harper (New York); Maury Hatch (Sacramento); Rob Heggen at the Blackwater Café (Stockton); Hilton Creek Hostel; Monica Hrybko of the Ramada Old Town (San Diego); Heather Hughes (Santa Cruz); Maura Jasper; Errol Lafrenais; Deborah Lavigna (San Diego); Karen and Paul Leib (Santa Barbara); Barbara McClelland of the Anaheim Area Visitor and Convention Bureau; Mike McConnell (Lemon Grove); Susan McKinney (Nevada City/Grass Valley); Sheila Mannix (Napa); Mike Martin (Redding); Chloe May (Chico/Paradise); Drew Monaghan (Berkeley); Deborah Mullen-Lycett (Irvine); Jim Oddo of Atlas Hotels (San Diego); Michael Owyang (Sacramento); Eren Ozker (Hollywood); Victoria Palarea (Long Beach); Carla and Glen Paradise (Ocotillo); Allan Perlmutter (Monterey); Lee Peters (Red Bluff); Linda Pollack (Palos Verdes); Redwood Empire Association (San Francisco); Anne Rowe (Pasadena); the Rubiano Family (New York); Melissa Sheng (Berkeley); Sigma Phi Epsilon, Cal Alpha Chapter (Berkeley); Patty Skinner of the Sports Arena Travelodge (San Diego); Betsy Smith of the Dana Inn and Marina (San Diego); Jay Stephenson; Stockton Econo Lodge; Zackary Stone (Berkeley); Kelly Stevens (New York); Beth Streets of the Hotel St. James (San Diego); Ian Sundly (Long Beach); Ted Taylor (Santa Barbara); Caryl Teplitzky of the Hacienda AYH–Hostel (Fullerton); Val Thomas (Los Angeles); George Thurlow (Chico/Paradise); Vic's Ice Cream Bungee Jumping Team (Sacramento); Joel Vitt of the Corinthian Suites Hotel (San Diego); Walfredo's Fish Palace (Berkeley); Pam Walker (Napa); Arthur Whitman (New York); Lauren C. Wilkins (Monterey); Mark Wilkinson of the Ramada Hotel Bay View (San Diego); Dale Wilson (Redding); Jeremy Wolfe (Berkeley); George Wright (Chico/Paradise); and Jim Herron Zamora (San Fernando Valley). Thanks also to Robert Blake, Ellen E. Browne, Tara Hamilton, Caroline Liou, Marcy Pritchard, and Helayne Schiff, all of the staff of Fodor's in New York.

Berkeley Bios

Behind every restaurant blurb, write-up, lodging review, and introduction in this book lurks a student writer. You might recognize the type—perpetually short on time, money, and clean underwear. Eight Berkeley students spent the summer traveling around the state researching and writing *On the Loose in California.* Every two weeks they sent their manuscript back to a three-person editorial team in Berkeley, who whipped it into shape.

The Writers

The author of the Gold Country and Cascades chapters, **Colleen Cotter** has long been a proponent of the overlooked "North State," the huge but strangely anonymous part of California that lies north of Sacramento flanked by the Coastal and Cascade ranges. She spent eight years in Red Bluff, Redding, and Chico, with stints as a reporter and editor for the *Record-Searchlight* and as a journalism instructor at Chico State. Colleen was thus well acquainted with the region's charms: the stunning mountains, pretty lakes, clear skies, funky towns, friendly people, and busy arts scene. It was tough deciding whether to divulge all the secret locales and local lore in a travel guide, or let the treasures lie with the natives. Since someone was bound to do it, she decided she would—and do it right.

A graduate student in journalism, **Jason Fine** was happiest when no one else was in sight. Covering the North Coast and part of the Gold Country, Jason had plenty of opportunity to get away from the tourist hordes and get back to nature. In a letter to Berkeley he wrote: "There is nothing like the experience of a long hike through the coastal mountains, through dramatic fern-filled canyons where the redwood trees loom like ancient sages, up on ridges overlooking the Pacific Ocean, and through streams and rivers where you can feel (even if you can't see them) the presence of deer, bears, raccoons and mountain lions. Redwood National Park is perfect for this kind of hike, and afterwards you can walk down to any of the miles and miles of undisturbed beach for a fire and a bottle of wine, to rest your feet and marvel that despite all the development, the crowds, the traffic pushing at the edge of this continent, there are still places like this where you can feel a million miles away."

The trouble for **Chris Hallenbeck** started when he crossed an invisible line in the sand on his way to Las Vegas, the Grand Canyon, and the desert. "Real bread ceases to exist about 100 miles east of Los Angeles," he wrote. "So does coffee." Fueled by caffeine withdrawal, Chris's patience sometimes wore a little thin. In a letter from Las Vegas, he let it all out: "I'm surrounded by weirdos: Some guy with a hand puppet won't leave me alone, and another keeps insisting that the government is making test flights of captured UFOs." At the same time, Chris was fascinated by the paradox that is Las Vegas. "Sure Las Vegas is crass," he wrote to the editors, "but what really makes it special is that no other city in the world can be as bad and as good as Las Vegas at the same time." On his travels through the desert, Chris found a bunch of great hostels and some fun characters. He speaks fondly of a pathological liar with whom he traveled for a while (the man claimed to be a soldier, a motorcycle racer, and the son of a mass-murdering Hell's Angel) and a flamboyant hostel proprietor in Kanab, Utah. Apparently, he ribbed the guests so mercilessly that he scared several away, including the *Let's Go* revisor, who happened to be there. Chris, of course, stayed.

A resident of San Francisco, **Leigh Anne Jones** was well placed to write the chapter about the city. Leigh Anne recently graduated with a degree in English, and is going on to graduate school in creative writing at the University of Iowa.

Better known as "Tory," **Mary Victoria M. Robbins** wrote the chapter on Los Angeles. Although she's not a native of the City of Angels, she soon learned how to drive offensively, the difference between eating and doing lunch, what to do in case of smog alerts, and how to hang out in coffeehouses and pretend to be in New York. Among L.A.'s most noteworthy offerings, she says, are the Griffith Observatory, the Bourgeois Pig Café, the lean blond surfer boys, their friends, and their friends' friends. "It's a wonderful city," comments Tory, "even on its knees."

As part of his research for the San Diego chapter, **Michael Rubiano** explored Anza-Borrego Desert State Park, the largest state park in the United States. Most of the park attractions lie in the middle of desert, accessible only in four-wheel-drive vehicles. In his boldness (read stupidity), Mike decided to take his rental car into the sandy inferno. He drove from one site to the next, skidding and sliding over the sand roads. Then, going over a steep sand embankment, he lost control of the car and ploughed into a deep dune. "I desperately tried to dig the desert out from under my car," he confessed in a letter. "After about 20 minutes of grubby digging, rocking the car in and out of reverse, jumping on the hood and trunk and screaming for help, I decided that another course of action might be wise. As the sun was setting over the mountains (is this sounding like a bad B movie yet?), I abandoned the car and walked through the desert to Route S2. During the peak winter months this road would probably be teeming with tourists, but during July the only traffic was tumbleweed. I walked approximately 2 miles along the road in 100° heat before I became so dehydrated that I didn't even have any spit to swallow. Eventually a car came down the road. Standing in the middle of this two-lane road—parched, panicked, and grubby—I must have appeared to be the devil in Gap clothing to the elderly couple who took one look and sped off. Needless to say, I was really beginning to hate life. Some time later, I saw an 18-wheel Mack truck coming over a hill. Determined to either make the truck stop or become road-kill in the attempt, I stood directly in the path of the oncoming behemoth. Screeching to a halt, the driver uttered the sweetest words I had heard in a long time: 'Do you need help?' "

Over the course of the summer, **Shelly Smith** crisscrossed California, covering San Francisco's East Bay, the Sierra Nevadas, and the San Joaquin Valley, with a quick detour to San Diego for good measure. Highlights of the trip: Hitting all the gay bars in Bakersfield with a jovial band of subversive, country music-lovin' townsfolk, and watching a woman in a black leather bra and chaps do country line dancing; sitting by a lake in the Eastern Sierra on June 28 and watching it snow; an amazing motorcycle ride through the high desert of the eastern Sierra with a guy named Rod, who proved that the grasses really do look gold at sunset; and falling literally head over heels in love with a mountain range, the Minarets.

When **Susan Williams** agreed to write the Central Coast chapter, she little suspected that she would have to cope with the worst excesses of New Ageism and wellness groupies. "Determined to experience the California 'thang,' I literally drank it all in," she explained in a letter to her editors. "Standing at a natural-food bar in Half Moon Bay, egged on by hard-core vegetarian and granola types, I ordered a glass of wheat-grass juice. The olive-colored liquid (squeezed from several hundred defenseless greens) was bitter, and I choked as I tried to pound it down. This raised a hearty chorus of boos from the onlookers, triggering flashbacks of tequila shots in Tijuana. At least there you got drunk for your troubles (though the juice probably satisfied my vegetable requirements for the next decade)." Susan recently graduated from Berkeley with a degree in English and Political Science, and is recovering from a health-food overdose in San Francisco.

The Editors

With a B.A. and a M.A. in English literature from U.C. Berkeley, Editor **Michael Mullen** periodically does work on a Ph.D. in the same subject. His area of interest is the 18th century, primarily because of the powdered wigs. And he looks good with a red flower tucked jauntily behind his ear. Michael is originally from Long Beach.

When the stress level in the office got too high, Assistant Editor **David DeGusta** relaxed by covering the People's Park riots for the *Daily Californian* (the school newspaper), bungee jumping (the ultimate California experience—pointless, hazardous, and great fun), and taking long runs in the hills. David, who hails from Sacramento, has now become the project manager of *The Berkeley Guides.*

Fluent in Spanish and German, Assistant Editor **Belynda Biller** earned a double degree in English and Latin American studies. She likes to travel but jobs like this one have prevented her from doing so over the past three years. Belynda, who has been practicing her marriage vows since she was a small child, recently announced her engagement.

A native of Los Angeles, **Scott McNeely** returned from writing the Romania chapter for *On the Loose in Eastern Europe* to edit several chapters of the California book.

Northern California

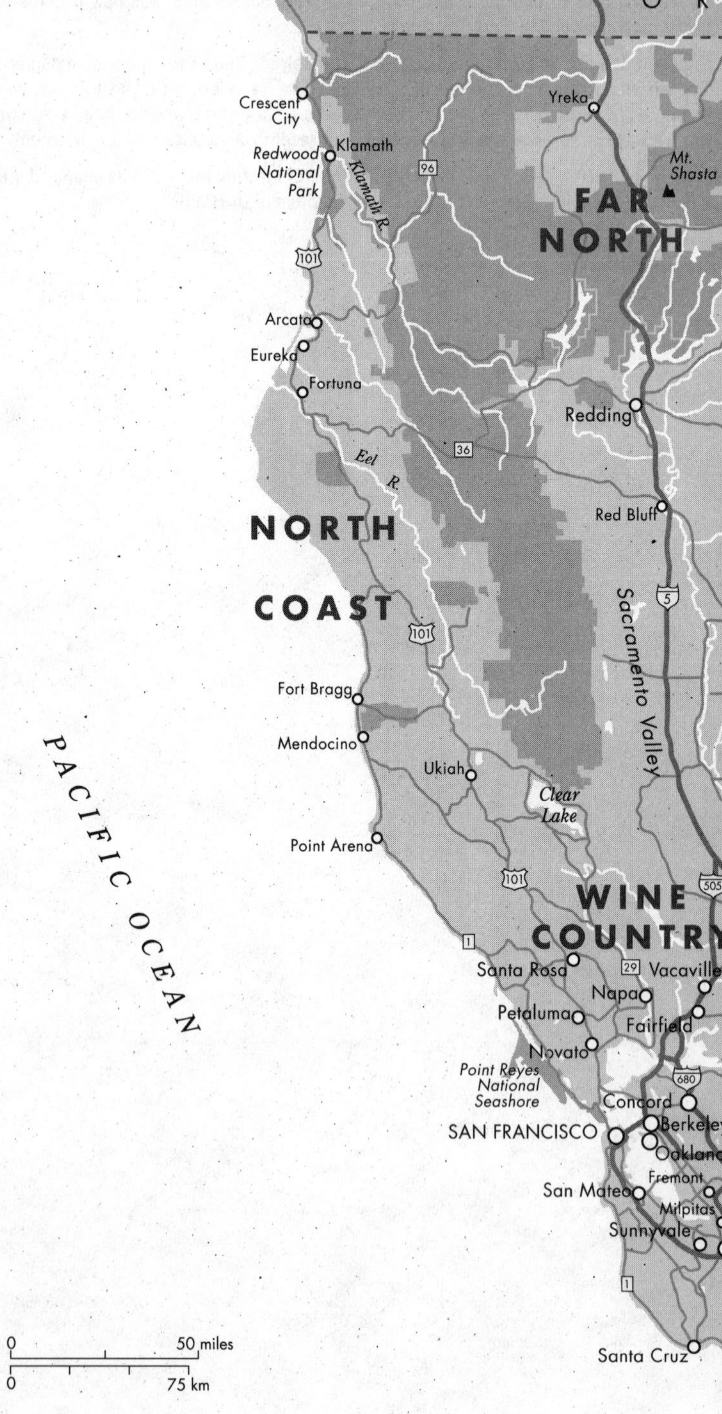

O R
Crescent City
Klamath
Redwood National Park
Klamath R.
96
Yreka
Mt. Shasta
FAR NORTH
101
Arcata
Eureka
Fortuna
Redding
Eel R.
36
Red Bluff
NORTH COAST
5
Sacramento Valley
101
Fort Bragg
Mendocino
Ukiah
Clear Lake
Point Arena
PACIFIC OCEAN
101
505
WINE COUNTRY
1
Santa Rosa
29
Vacaville
Napa
Petaluma
Fairfield
Novato
Point Reyes National Seashore
680
Concord
SAN FRANCISCO
Berkeley
Oakland
Fremont
San Mateo
Milpitas
Sunnyvale
1
0
50 miles
0
75 km
Santa Cruz

Northern California

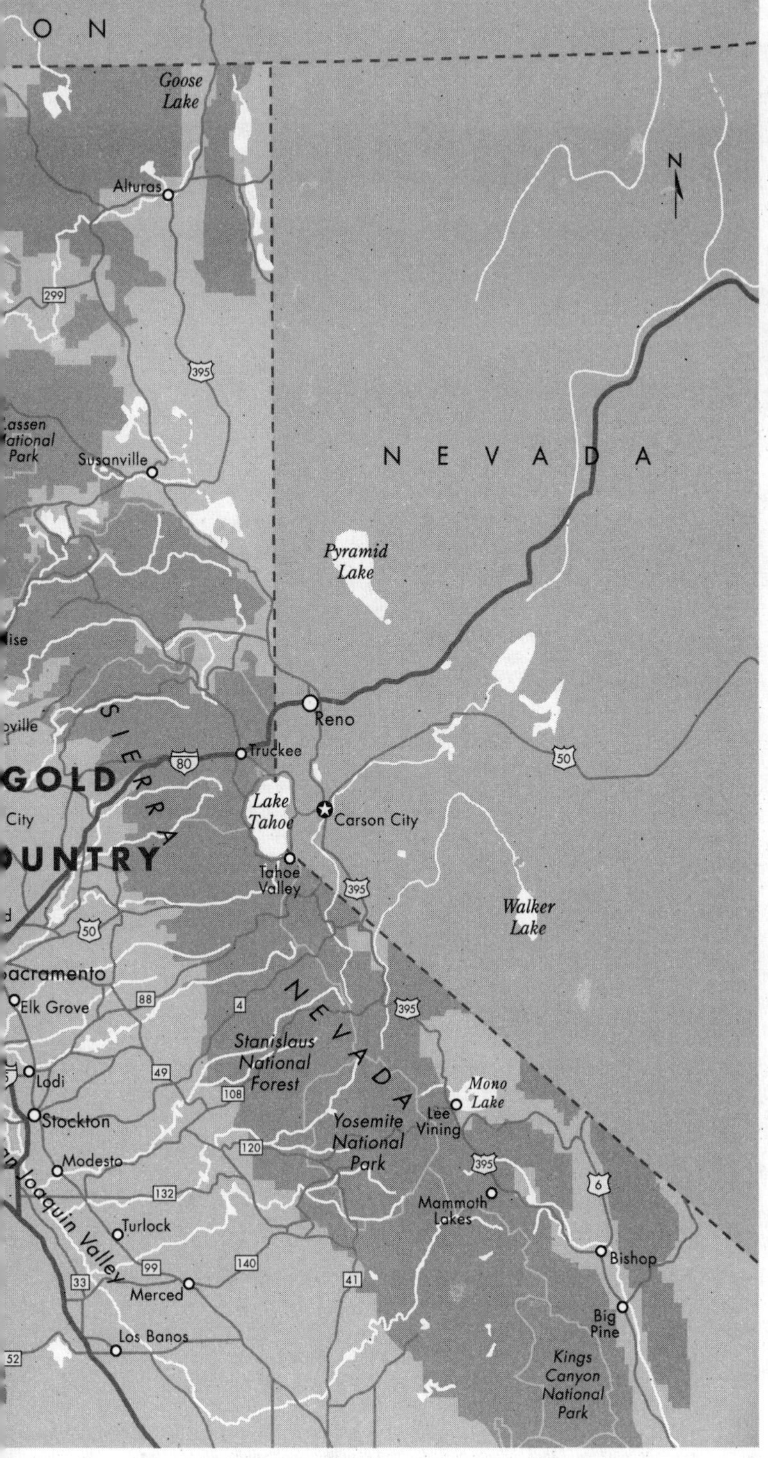

Southern California

Oakland
Yosemite National Park
San Jose
Merced
SAN JOAQUIN VALLEY
Sierra National Forest
SIERRA NEVADA
Big Pine
San Luis Res.
Chowchilla
Gilroy
Los Banos
Madera
Kings Canyon National Park
Santa Cruz
Castroville
Fresno
Salinas
Monterey
Carmel
Soledad
Sequoia National Park
Visalia
Big Sur
King City
Coalinga
Porterville
CENTRAL COAST
Tulare Lake Bed
San Simeon
Paso Robles
Bakersfield
San Luis Obispo
McKittrick
Arroyo Grande
Tejon Pass
Santa Maria
VANDENBERG AIR FORCE BASE
Lompoc
Solvang
Los Padres National Forest
Ojai
Simi Valley
Santa Barbara
Ventura
Oxnard
Santa Barbara Channel
San Miguel
Malibu
Santa Rosa
Santa Cruz
CHANNEL ISLANDS
Santa Catalina
San Nicolas
PACIFIC OCEAN
San Clemente

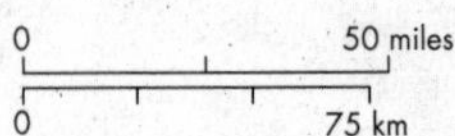

Southern California

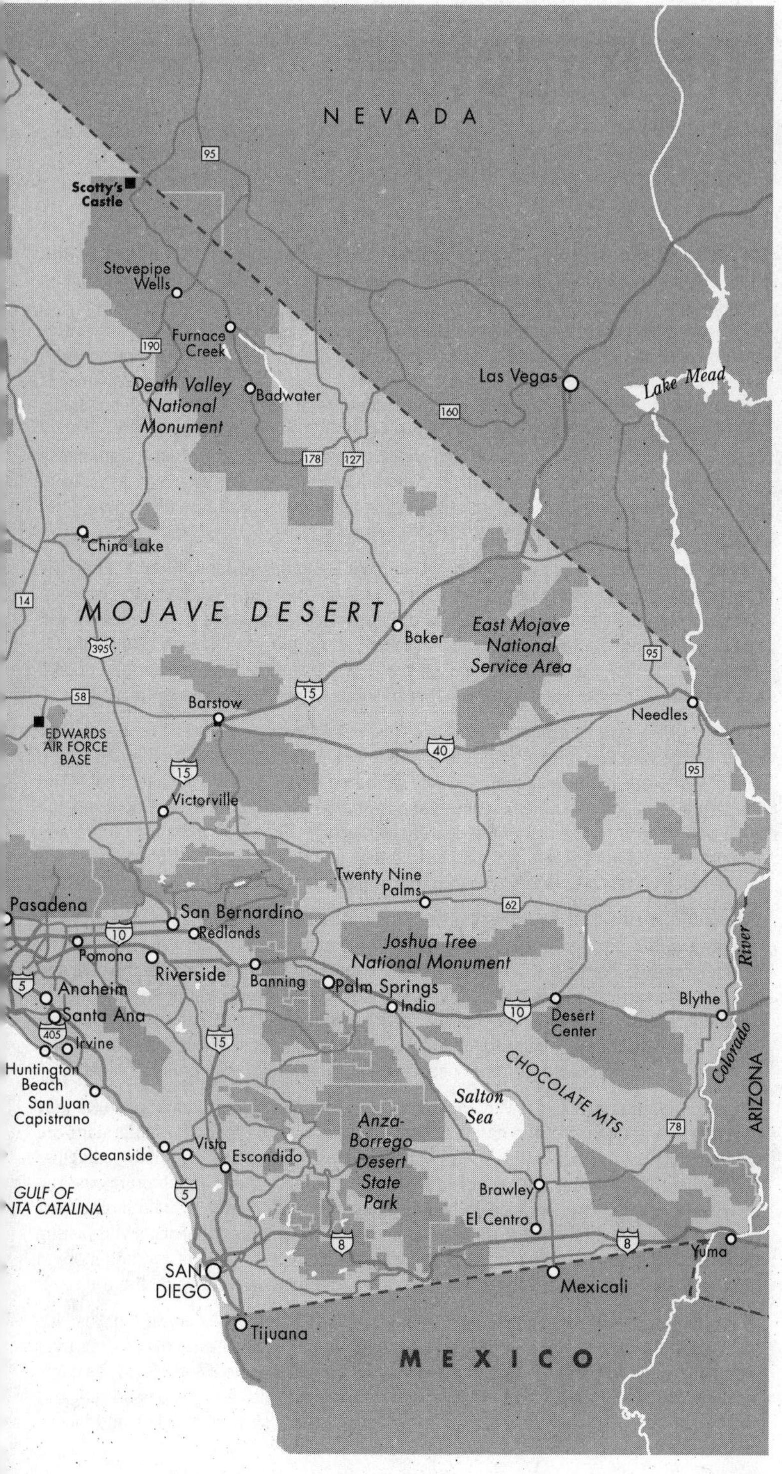

NEVADA
95
Scotty's Castle
Stovepipe Wells
Furnace Creek
190
Death Valley National Monument
Badwater
Las Vegas
Lake Mead
160
178
127
China Lake
14
MOJAVE DESERT
Baker
East Mojave National Service Area
395
95
58
Barstow
15
Needles
EDWARDS AIR FORCE BASE
40
15
95
Victorville
Twenty Nine Palms
62
Pasadena
San Bernardino
Redlands
10
Pomona
Riverside
Banning
Joshua Tree National Monument
Palm Springs
Indio
10
Desert Center
Blythe
River
5
Anaheim
Santa Ana
405
Irvine
15
Huntington Beach
San Juan Capistrano
CHOCOLATE MTS.
Salton Sea
Colorado
ARIZONA
Anza-Borrego Desert State Park
78
Oceanside
Vista
Escondido
GULF OF
NTA CATALINA
5
Brawley
El Centro
8
8
Yuma
SAN DIEGO
Mexicali
Tijuana
MEXICO

Introduction

By Shelly Smith

To much of the world, California is what Hollywood makes it. Images of the state abound in movies, commercials, TV shows, and music videos. California trends in fashion, sport, and language are immediately seized by the movie industry, polished, and packaged. Like most of what Hollywood touches, the likeness is tenuous at best. Of *course* some people say "totally, dude" and "hella cool" and "bitchen waves," of *course* you'll see a lot of blondes who appear to be heading for the world of advanced melanoma, of *course* you'll meet hippies and potheads and budding starlets who can't spell their names right. Hollywood clichés do come from somewhere. But California grants a multiplicity of truths, some of the most profound and indisputable of which stem from its immense geography: It continues to grant, with remarkable aplomb, fist-size strawberries in April, the oldest trees on the planet, the dizzying and relentless proximity of mountains to coastline, and climates so gentle they feel like first love.

It is the land that travelers will probably find most appealing about California. From the foggy cliffs of the Pacific coast to the jagged spires of the Sierra Nevada to the redwood forests of the north and the dizzying heat of Death Valley, the diversity of the terrain will boggle your mind. There's no way you can take it all in, but you'll have a blast trying. It sounds a bit hokey, but at some stage, you will drive around a bend and happen upon a scene so stunning you won't know whether to shout or cry. It's that beautiful.

The 100,000 men who descended on California in 1849 didn't come for the views. They came for the gold that laborer James Marshall found in the foothills of the Sierra Nevada. Life in California in the years that followed was a free-for-all, and the pursuit of gold (and the virtual absence of women) saw social conventions and norms tossed right out the window. Cut off from the rest of the country by nearly 2,000 miles of plains, desert, and mountains, California developed in an atmosphere of unrestrained isolation for nearly 20 years until the last spike was driven into the transcontinental railroad on May 10, 1869.

Even with the arrival of the interstate and airports, however, California has continued to display a willful disdain for social tradition and the status quo. In the minds of millions of Americans, California is still a place where you can discard the baggage of the past and go about the earnest business of re-creating yourself. Just because your entire family is Southern Baptist (or multimillionaires, or circus performers), that doesn't mean you can't move a good two or three thousand miles away and embrace Islam or Buddhism or Sufism, or live on a commune with 10 other people and raise all 25 of your children together.

In California, the emphasis is very much on doing your own thing. On any given Sunday in winter, while the rest of the nation comes together to watch football, Californians are out doing 1001 other activities—rollerblading, biking, skiing, chanting, hiking, hugging, and windsurfing. The cult of the individual has reached its apogee in California, and the body is its temple. Nowhere else do people devote so much energy to maintaining their physical selves, whether they're running up and down mountains or putting awful-tasting things in their body that are supposed to make them smarter, fitter, faster, and more in tune with their inner selves. If all else fails, a nip and tuck can always do the trick.

Unfortunately, the promise of personal regeneration in California also has it flip side. Too many people come here from other states hoping to get a new start, only to drag their mental baggage with them. California has it's fair share of people living life on the edge: Most are harmless—new members for the state's myriad self-help groups and religious communes—but the state also has a long and ugly history of mass murders and bloody rampages.

In a state where the individual and the pursuit of wealth has always meant so much, it's not altogether surprising that history and a sense of community have taken a back seat. Community suggests a common bond—a shared history—but people tend to look to their history only when their future fails to inspire. Since its earliest days, California has barely paused for breath in its headlong rush to a future that has always burned brightly. This is, after all, a place where people still live, die, and otherwise go about their business in towns that were thrown together in the space of a few weeks to accommodate gold prospectors. This is a place that saw a 2000% increase in its population and attained statehood within the space of time it takes for your average jaywalking case to come to trial. Los Angeles is a perfect example of that unlimited, unbridled growth, a fluid city that constantly reinvents itself in response to economic rather than community opportunities. In such an environment, status quo is equated with stagnation, change with success.

For the first time, though, California's future now seems uncertain, and there are signs that Californians may have to undergo some rather severe dream modifications. The state is struggling to cope with a stubborn recession; water is scarce; companies are relocating to states with cheaper land and more plentiful resources; and unemployment is high. The L.A. race riots of 1992 added further proof that the California Dream hasn't worked for everyone, and that without a sense of community, there's no safety net to catch the dispossessed when the economic engine slows down.

For 150 years California has lived by baseballer Satchel Paige's old adage: "Don't look back. Something may be gaining." Despite California's best efforts though, the present has caught up. For some Californians, the answer to the state's problems has a familiar ring—reinvent yourself. In the 1992 primaries, Californians in a few districts voted on an initiative to split the state in half. The initiative was largely symbolic but many residents of the north feel that their half of the state is worlds away from the violence and overcrowding of the southern megalopolis, and that their needs are overlooked by the state legislature.

California remains the most ethnically diverse state in the country, and is projected by the year 2000 to become the first state with a minority population of European-Americans.

The initiative is one indicator of just how different the two halves of the state are. Northern Californians tend to dismiss their southern counterparts as shallow surburbanites forever wedded to their cars, malls, tract homes, and big hair. Northern Californians further resent the fact that most of their water is siphoned off by Southern Californians, who happily irrigate their lawns in the desert while Northern Californians don't flush the can in order to save water (the state is entering its sixth year of drought). But nowhere is the split between north and south so apparent as in politics. The south is one of the most conservative parts of the nation, the rock on which Reagan and Nixon built their presidencies. The north, on the other hand, is generally very liberal. During the Gulf War, San Francisco and Berkeley declared themselves safe havens for deserters while Southern California rooted on the troops with all the fervor of a football game.

As a budget traveler, you probably won't be able to get too worked up about all this, because you'll be too busy dribbling at the unbelievable beauty of the state. If you can afford it, rent a car, rip off the roof, pop in some tunes, and let it all hang out. Soon, you too will find yourself with that slightly dazed look espoused by so many residents. It's a look that comes from the realization that amid all this beauty nothing really matters, that it's okay to lose your shit, and that, yes, that crystal around your neck works just fine.

BASICS 1

By Kristina Brooks and Susan Williams

If you've ever traveled with anyone before, you know the two types of people in the world: the planners and the nonplanners. You also know that travel brings out the very worst in both groups: Left to their own devices, the planners will have you goose-stepping from attraction to attraction on a cultural blitzkrieg, while the nonplanners will invariably miss the flight, the bus, and the point. One way or the other, you're going to end up wanting to bury a large hatchet in the back of your companion's head. And that just won't do. This Basics chapter offers you a middle ground, giving you enough information to help you plan your trip without saddling you with an itinerary or invasion plan. From the minute you decide to take a trip, you're confronted with a seemingly endless series of choices: how to get there, where to stay, where to buy M&Ms. We don't want to make the choices for you, but we hope to provide you with the resources to help you make those all-important decisions yourself. If all else fails, we tell you where to buy the hatchet. Keep in mind that companies go out of business, prices inevitably go up, and, hey, we're only too human; as a Reagan official so eloquently said, "Mistakes have been made."

Planning Your Trip

USEFUL ORGANIZATIONS • • •

TOURIST OFFICES Aside from offering the usual glossy tourist brochures, state and local tourist offices can answer general questions about travel in their areas or refer you to other organizations for more information. If you write for information, you may want to request brochures on specialized interests, such as boating, horseback riding, or biking, which may not be included in a generic information package.

California Office of Tourism (801 K St., Suite 1600, Sacramento, CA 95814, tel. 916/322–1397) is the official state-tourism promotor. Unless you have a specific question, they will give you the toll-free number listed below, which you should call to request a general booklet about California.

California State Department of Tourism (Box 9278, Van Nuys, CA 91409, tel. 800/862–2543 to order booklet) mails out a booklet titled "Discover the Californias" and will send you off to individual chambers of commerce for more information. Foreign visitors who want to get some official tourist information on California can check with the **U.S. Travel and Tourism Administration** (Dept. of Commerce, 14th St. and Constitution Ave. NW, Washington, DC 20230, tel. 202/377–4003 or 202/377–3811). The administration has offices in foreign countries, too: Suite 6106, MLC Centre, King and Castlereagh Sts., Sydney, NSW, Australia, 02/233–4666; Suite 602, 480 University Ave., Toronto, Ont. M5G 1V2 Canada, tel. 416/595–5082; and American Embassy, 24 Grosvenor Sq., London W1A 1AE, England, tel. 071/495–4466.

BUDGET TRAVEL ORGANIZATIONS **Council on International Educational Exchange (CIEE)** (205 E. 42nd St., New York, NY 10017, tel. 212/661–1414) is a nonprofit organization dedicated to the pursuit of work, study, and travel abroad. Through its two subsidiaries, **Council Travel** and **Council Charter** (tel. 212/661–0311 or 800/223–7402), CIEE offers budget travel services, such as discounted air fares, accommodations, guidebooks, I.D. cards, and lots more. Council Travel is an international network of travel agencies that specialize in the diverse needs of students, youths, teachers, and indigent travelers for air, rail, and car transportation. Council Travel also issues the **International Student Identity Card (ISIC),** the **International Youth Card (IYC),** the **International Teacher Card (ITC),** and **Youth Hostel** cards (*see* Student I.D. Cards, *below*). At least 38 Council Travel offices serve the budget traveler in the United States (*see box*), and there are about a dozen offices overseas in Britain, France, Germany, and Japan; university travel centers may also carry CIEE's *Student Travel* magazine, a gold mine of travel tips that details CIEE's services and discounts. *Student Travel* also includes feature articles on a wide range of topics such as studying and working abroad and managing on a low budget. The Council Charter division (tel. 212/661–0311 or 800/800–8222) buys blocks of seats on commercial flights and sells them at a discount. Dates, rates, destinations, and seat availability change yearly.

Educational Travel Center (ETC) (438 N. Francis St., Madison, WI 53703, tel. 608/256–5551) sells tickets for low-cost flights within the continental United States and around the world. Most flights depart from Chicago, and ETC claims it can beat student and charter fares. It also issues **American Youth Hostel** cards (*see* Student I.D. Cards, *below*). For more details, request their free brochure, "Taking Off."

Council Travel Offices

Arizona: Tempe, tel. 602/966–3544. California: Berkeley, tel. 510/848–8604; La Jolla, tel. 619/452–0630; Long Beach, tel. 310/598–3338 or 714/527–7950; Los Angeles, tel. 310/208–3551; Palo Alto, tel. 415/325–3888; San Diego, tel. 619/270–6401; San Francisco, tel. 415/421–3473 or 415/566–6222; Sherman Oaks, tel. 818/905–5777. Colorado: Boulder, tel. 303/447–8101. Connecticut: New Haven, tel. 203/562–5335. District of Columbia: Washington, D.C., tel. 202/337–6464. Florida: Miami, tel. 305/670–9261. Georgia: Atlanta, tel. 404/377–9997. Illinois: Chicago, tel. 312/ 951–0585; Evanston, tel. 708/475–5070. Louisiana: New Orleans, tel. 504/866–1767. Massachusetts: Amherst, tel. 413/256–1261; Boston, tel. 617/ 266–1926 or 617/424–6665; Cambridge, tel. 617/497–1497 or 617/225–2555. Michigan: Ann Arbor, tel. 313/998–0200. Minnesota: Minneapolis, tel. 612/379–2323. New York: New York, tel. 212/666–4177, 212/564–0142, or 212/254–2525. North Carolina: Durham, tel. 919/286–4664. Ohio: Columbus, tel. 614/294–8696. Oregon: Portland, tel. 503/228–1900. Pennsylvania: Philadelphia, tel. 215/382–0343. Rhode Island: Providence, tel. 401/331–5810. Texas: Austin, tel. 512/472–4931; Dallas, tel. 214/363–9941. Washington: Seattle, tel. 206/632–2448 or 206/329–4567. Wisconsin: Milwaukee, tel. 414/332–4740. United Kingdom: London, tel. 071/437–7767.

International Youth Hostel Federation (IYHF) is the grandmammy of hostel associations, offering single-sex dorm-style beds ("couples" rooms and family accommodations are available at certain IYHF hostels) and kitchen facilities (about $4–$19 per night) at more than 5,300 locations in 70 countries around the world. Membership in any national Youth Hostel Association (*see below*) allows you to stay in any IYHF-affiliated hostel at member rates; you also have priority if the hostel is full, and you're eligible for discounts on rail and bus travel around the world. A one-year membership is open to all ages and runs about $25 for adults (renewal thereafter is $15), $10 for those under 18; a one-night guest membership is about $3; family memberships are $35; and a lifetime membership will set you back $250. Lightweight guidebooks listing all current hostels and special offers (like budget cycling and hiking tours) are available from the national associations: Volume 1 covers Europe and the Mediterranean; Volume 2 covers Africa, the Americas, Asia, and Australia ($10.95 each).

Associations aiding and abetting hostel-goers include **American Youth Hostels (AYH,** Box 37613, Washington, DC 20013, tel. 202/783–6161); **Canadian Hostelling Association (CHA,** 1600 James Naismith Dr., Suite 608, Gloucester, Ont. K1B 5N4, tel. 613/748–5638); **Youth Hostel Association of England and Wales (YHA,** Trevelyan House, 8 St. Stephen's Hill, St. Albans, Herts. AL1 2DY, England, tel. 0727/55215); **Australian Youth Hostels Association (YHA,** Box 61, Strawberry Hills, Sydney 2012, New South Wales, tel. 02/212–1266); and **Youth Hostels Association of New Zealand (YHA,** Box 436, Christchurch 1, tel. 799–970). **Student Travel Australia (STA)** has 120 offices worldwide and doesn't serve just Australia anymore. This international travel network offers students low-price airfares to destinations around the globe—including California. STA offers the **ISIC** and their own **STA Travel Card** (about $5) for recent graduates, which proves eligibility for some travel discounts (*see* Student I.D. Cards, *below*). Write or call a national head office for a slew of free pamphlets on services and rates. North American West: 7204½ Melrose Ave., Los Angeles, CA 90046, tel. 213/937–5714; North American East: 17 E. 45th St., Suite 805, New York, NY 10017, tel. 212/986–9470 or 800/777–0112; Australia: 224 Faraday St., 1st floor, Carlton 3053, tel. 61/3–347–6911; New Zealand: 10 High St., Box 4156, Auckland, tel. 64/9–39–9723; U.K.: Priory House, 6 Wrights La., London W8 6TA, tel. 44/71–938–4711. **Travel CUTS (Canadian Universities Travel Service, Ltd.)** (187 College St., Toronto, Ont. M5T 1P7, tel. 416/979–2406) is a full-service travel agency that sells discounted airline tickets to Canadian students and issues the **ISIC, IYC,** and **IYH** cards. Their 25 offices are on or near college campuses. Call weekdays 9–5 for information and reservations.

Y's Way International (356 W. 34th St., New York, NY 10001, tel. 212/760–5856) is a network of YMCA overnight centers offering low-cost accommodations (average overnight rate of $26) in California to travelers of all ages. Their booklet, "The Y's Way," details locations, reservation policies, and package tours. There are large YMCAs in Los Angeles (1553 N. Hudson Ave., Hollywood, CA 90028, tel. 213/467–4161) and San Francisco (220 Golden Gate Ave., San Francisco, CA 94102, tel. 415/885–0460). For more details *see* Where to Sleep in Staying in California, *below*.

WHEN TO GO • • •

Unbeknownst to many, California does have seasons—they're just incredibly subtle. The time to visit So-Cal's oft-filmed beach spots and coastal cities is late May–early October; glorious weather carries a price tag, one that's sometimes doubles the going rate during the off-season. Summer is undoubtedly the hottest and liveliest time of year in southern California, but if you follow the coast north you'll hit thick fog trapped by the coastal mountain ranges. Mid- to late spring and early to mid-fall are the optimum times to travel along the coast, when the fog gives way to sun, tourist crowds are smaller, and prices drop.

Complaining about the rain, if and when it comes, will probably merit you a lecture from environmentally correct Californians: best to shut up and pack an umbrella.

CLIMATE California has it all, from temperatures as high as 134°F in July to lows near -9°F in January at exactly the same place (Death Valley). Coastal areas tend to be shrouded in fog as often as not, and the central valley and other inland areas are hot and dry from May to October. Due to the recent and seemingly endless drought, reservoirs are low, skiing areas are less deeply piled than usual, and the San Francisco area's fabled rainy season (October–February) has all but dried up.

Weather freaks can call *USA Today*'s WeatherTrak information service (tel. 900/370–8728; 95¢ per minute) to hear a taped forecast (up to 10 days in advance) for more than 750 cities around the world. For U.S. cities, the touch-tone access codes are the cities' area codes.

FESTIVALS Festivals and other special events go on year-round in California, but only the major ones (and an occasional little funky one we couldn't resist) are highlighted below. Look in individual chapters for smaller festivals in each particular region; call the state office of tourism (tel. 800/862–2543) for a free copy of the Ethnic Events Calendar; and check out *California Festivals* (by Carl and Katie Landau with Kathy Kincade, Landau Communications, 1032 Irving St., Suite 604, San Francisco, CA 94122, tel. 415/564–5684, $11.95), which lists more than 300 events statewide.

January 1: The Tournament of Roses Parade is a New Year's Day ritual that attracts thousands who not only line the downtown streets of Pasadena but sleep there overnight in order to claim a prime slab of concrete. One of these coveted spots will guarantee a good view of the route where mammoth flower-packed floats glide by at dawn. For more information, contact Pasadena's Tournament of Roses Headquarters (391 S. Orange Grove Blvd., Pasadena, CA 91184, tel. 818/449–4100).

January–April: Whale-watching takes place along the west coast, as gray whales migrate from Arctic feeding grounds in order to mate and calve off the Baja coast. Contact the California Office of Tourism (*see* Useful Organizations, *above*).

February: Chinese New Year is a week-long celebration in San Francisco's Chinatown, culminating with the Golden Dragon Parade, For info, contact the Visitor Information Center (Box 6977, San Francisco, CA 94101, tel. 415/391–2000). Los Angeles also has a parade (contact the Chinese Chamber of Commerce, 978 N. Broadway, Suite 206, Los Angeles, CA 90012, tel. 213/617–0396).

March: The **Academy Awards** ceremony is Hollywood's main event, held in downtown Los Angeles, usually the last week of March. You can't get in without an invitation, but you can freely gawk at the movie stars from bleachers set up outside. Contact the Los Angeles Visitor Information Office (tel. 213/689–8822).

March–July: Catch the **Grunion Run** if you're in southern California, but don't expect a 10k race. This is a nighttime fish-breeding orgy that allows voyeurs to observe the wiggling, ecstatic, silvery grunion fish, the only fish that comes ashore to mate. Not all southern California beaches are turn-ons for the grunion, so check with state beaches or the Cabrillo Marine Museum (tel. 213/548–7562), in San Pedro, which sponsors grunion-peeping programs.

April–May: The **Ramona Pageant,** based on the popular novel *Ramona,* by Helen Hunt Jackson, takes place on an outdoor stage in Hemet. If you go, you might find out what this classic is about. The pageant is usually held the last weekend in April and first two

The Highs and the Lows

Average daily highs and lows stack up as follows:

City	*January High/Low*		*July High/Low*	
Los Angeles	*64°F/44°F*	*18° C/7°C*	*75°F/60°F*	*24° C/16°C*
San Diego	*62°F/46°F*	*17° C/8°C*	*73°F/62°F*	*21° C/11°C*
San Francisco	*55°F/41°F*	*13° C/5°C*	*69°F/51°F*	*21° C/11°C*

weekends in May (tickets are about $15). Contact the Ramona Pageant Association (27400 Ramona Bowl Rd., Hemet, CA 92344, tel. 714/658–3111).

May 5: Cinco de Mayo festivities pop up statewide, as Californians celebrate their Hispanic heritage. Try visiting San Diego's Old Town on the weekend closest to the 5th if you can't make it across the border. For information, contact the Old Town (2461 San Diego Ave., Suite 203, San Diego, CA 92110, tel. 619/291–4903).

May: Bay to Breakers is a San Francisco tradition for thousands of runners, who show up in shorts, G-strings, or wacky costumes to run from, you guessed it, the bay side of the city to the ocean (about 7½ miles). This San Francisco-style athletic extravaganza usually takes place on a weekend near the end of the month. You can get information from the *San Francisco Examiner* (Box 7260, San Francisco, CA 94120, tel. 415/777–7770).

June: The **Gay Freedom Day Parade** in San Francisco's downtown and the **Los Angeles Gay and Lesbian Pride Parade** in West Hollywood are rollicking bashes with costumes and floats. Contact Gay Freedom Day Parade (584 Castro St., San Francisco, CA, 94114, tel. 415/777–7770); or Los Angeles Gay and Lesbian Pride Parade (Santa Monica Blvd., Suite 109–24, West Hollywood, CA 90046, tel. 213/656–6553).

June 21: Santa Barbara's **Summer Solstice Celebration** (tel. 805/965–3396) gives new meaning to the word *counterculture.* The festivities, held each year on the Saturday closest to June 21, feature a parade with no written words or motorized vehicles, just people dressed every which way and acting strange.

July: The **International Surf Festival** features amateurs shredding on raspy waves along Los Angeles's South Bay beaches. Contact Redondo Harbor (415 Diamond, Redondo Beach, CA 90277, tel. 213/318–0631) for information. The **Gilroy Garlic Festival** (Box 2311, Gilroy, CA 95021–2311, tel. 408/842–1625), near the end of the month, is a huge, aromatic celebration and mass gorging of one of the tastiest plants around. The **California Rodeo** (Box 1648, Salinas, CA 93902, tel. 408/757–2951) is a cowpoke's fantasy, complete with chuck-wagon races, square dancin', and chili cook-offs. Yee haw.

August: Old Spanish Days Fiesta (1122 N. Milpas St., Santa Barbara, CA 93103, tel. 805/962–8101) in Santa Barbara is a five-day, community-wide celebration of California's Spanish and Mexican heritage, with shows, markets, and parades. Join the fiesta in early August. The **Steinbeck Festival,** in his birthplace, Salinas, commemorates the author's literary contributions with three days of lectures and tours. Contact the Salinas Public Library (350 Lincoln Ave., Salinas, CA 93901, tel. 408/758–7314) for information.

August–September: For a down-home, rural experience get on down to Sacramento's **California State Fair** (Box 15649, Sacramento, CA 95852, tel. 916/924–6000), which lasts from August through Labor Day. The **Poison Oak Festival** celebrates the dreaded plant by encouraging the foolhardy to sculpt and even cook with it. The festivities take place in late August (sometimes September) in Tuolumne County. Contact the Tuolumne County Visitors Center (tel. 800/446–1333) for dates and location.

September: The **Renaissance Pleasure Faire** is a gathering of fun-loving Elizabethans (suspiciously similar in appearance to modern-day Deadheads), who re-create Shakespearean England in the dusty hills north of San Francisco. The Living History Centre (Box B, Novato, CA 94948, tel. 415/892–0937) provides information.

October: Half Moon Bay sponsors the **Art and Pumpkin Festival** the third weekend of October, with crafts and the Great Pumpkin Parade. Linus never misses it. Contact Mainstreet Beautification (Box 274, Half Moon Bay, CA 94019, tel. 415/726–9652). Pismo Beach throws its annual **Clam Festival** the third weekend in October (usually). You need a fishing license to dig for clams, but watching preschoolers in clam costumes parade down the main street is free. There's also a chowder cook-off. Contact the Pismo Beach Chamber of Commerce (581 Dolliver St., Pismo Beach, CA 93449, tel. 800/443–7778). **October 31: Halloween** night in San Francisco's Castro neighborhood is akin to Mardi Gras in other parts of the world. People dress (and undress); be prepared.

November: The **Hollywood Christmas Parade** (6255 Sunset Blvd., Suite 911, Hollywood, CA 90028, tel. 213/469–2337), held at the end of November, is more than a little tacky, but the opportunity to stare at second-string movie stars makes it a classic Hollywood experience. The creator of Pasadena's **Doo Dah Parade** (Box 2392, Pasadena, CA 91102, tel. 818/796–2591) freely admits that the birth of this Rose Parade spoof occurred over a few beers with friends who were not allowed to participate in the respected flower fest. Today the Doo Dah has grown to alarmingly oddball proportions. Go the Sunday after Thanksgiving just to see the talented and legendary briefcase drill team. The **Death Valley '49er Encampment** in Furnace Creek celebrates those who made it across the Valley of Death in 1849, with seminars, races, and displays. Contact Death Valley National Monument (Box 579, Death Valley, CA 92328, tel. 619/786–2331) for information.

December: Certain coastal cities have **Christmas Boat Parades.** Newport Beach's nautical parade runs for six nights before Christmas in the harbor. Contact the Newport Chamber of Commerce (1470 Jamboree Rd., Newport Beach, CA 92660, tel. 714/644–8211).

● ● ● STUDENT I.D. CARDS

Students traveling around California should not expect big discounts—except possibly on air travel if they purchase tickets through special student-travel agencies (such as Council Travel, Council Charter, or STA). Still, bring your student I.D. card with you for those occasional discounts on bus travel, admission to some museums, theater tickets, and club cover charges. An I.D. card issued by your university or college is almost always sufficient to prove student status for admission discounts; if you purchase a nonuniversity I.D., make sure you're getting your money's worth in travel bargains or in the value of any travel insurance provided. Application costs and processes vary, so contact the issuing agent directly. The **International Student Identity Card (ISIC)** entitles students 12 years and older to special fares on local transportation, rail passes, and admission to museums, theaters, sports events, and many other attractions. If purchased in the United States, the $15 cost for the popular ISIC card also buys $3,000 in emergency medical coverage, limited hospital coverage, and access to a 24-hour international, toll-free hot line for assistance in medical, legal, and financial emergencies. The card can be valid for up to 16 months, depending on your student status when you buy it. International Youth and Teacher I.D. cards are also available. Applicants must submit a photo as well as proof of current full-time student status, age, and nationality. In the United States, apply to CIEE or STA; in Canada, the ISIC is available for C$12 from Travel CUTS (*see* Budget Travel Organizations, *above*). In the United Kingdom, students with valid university I.D.s can purchase the ISIC at any student union or student-travel company.

The **STA Travel Card** is available to travelers 35 and under for $6. With it you'll get discounted student fares and the coupon book, "Discount Counter," that offers dollars-off coupons for a limited number of subscribing businesses' services. Purchase the STA card *before* departing for California (*see* Budget Travel Organizations, *above,* for telephone numbers and addresses).

International Youth Card provides the same services and similar benefits as the ISIC card to travelers under age 26. It is available from CIEE, Council Travel Offices nationwide, and ISE (Europa House, 802 W. Oregon St., Urbana, IL 61801, tel. 217/344–5863). In Canada contact Travel CUTS or the Canadian Hostelling Association (*see* Useful Organizations, *above*).

● ● ● MONEY

Cash is never out of style, but traveler's checks and a major U.S. credit card are usually the safest and most convenient ways to pay for goods and services when you travel. Depending on the length of your trip, strike a balance among these three forms of currency, and protect yourself by carrying cash in a money belt, neck wallet, or front pocket, and keeping accurate records of your traveler's-check serial numbers. It's also a good idea to record your credit-card numbers and an emergency number for reporting the cards' loss or theft; keep these numbers separate from the cards. Carrying a minimum amount of cash is wise. Aside from panhandling, you may be able to replenish your cash supply by cashing personal checks at American Express offices or by having money sent to you while you're on the road (*see* Obtaining Money from Home, *below*).

TRAVELER'S CHECKS Traveler's checks may look like play money, but they work much better. They can be signed for purchases, just as you would sign a personal check, or they can be exchanged for cash at banks, some hotels, tourist offices, American Express offices, and currency-exhange offices. Not all stores and restaurants take them (especially the kind of flea-bag hotels and hole-in-the-wall restaurants frequented by shoestring travelers)—so always ask first. The most widely recognized traveler's checks are American Express, Visa, and MasterCard (Thomas Cook is one brand of MasterCard check). Some banks and credit unions issue the checks free to established customers, but most charge a 1% commission. If you're a member of the American Automobile Association (AAA), you can purchase American Express traveler's checks from them commission-free. Buy most of your checks in small denominations (a pack of five $20 checks is the smallest you can get); many establishments won't accept large denominations, and, even when they do, you'll end up carrying a wad of cash when you have to break large checks for small purchases. **American Express** (in U.S. and Canada, tel. 800/221–7282; in Europe, call Brighton, England, collect 0273/693–555) cardholders can buy checks by phone free of charge with a gold card or for a 1% commission with the basic green card. You can't charge the checks to your account, however; instead you'll be asked for your card number and American Express will contact your bank for an immediate withdrawal. In three to five business days you'll receive the checks—up to $1,000 can be ordered in a seven-day period. If you lose your checks or get ripped off, American Express can give you a speedy refund, often within 24 hours, just like Karl Malden says. At American Express offices (about 1,500 around the world) you can usually buy and cash traveler's checks, write a personal check in exchange for traveler's checks, report lost or stolen checks, exchange foreign currency, and pick up mail. Ask for the **"American Express Traveler's Companion,"** a directory of offices and services. For 45 days from the date you purchase **Citicorp** checks you'll also have access to the **24-hour International S.O.S. Assistance hot line** (in U.S., tel. 800/645–6556; outside U.S., call collect 813/623–1709), which provides English-speaking doctor, lawyer, and interpreter referrals; assistance with loss or theft of travel documents; traveler's- check refund assistance; and an emergency message center. **MasterCard International** (tel. 800/223–7373 in the U.S., 609/987–7300 collect from anywhere outside the U.S., 447/335–02–995 in Europe, or 07/335–02–995 collect from anywhere in Europe) traveler's checks, issued in U.S. dollars only, are offered by banks, credit unions, and foreign-exchange booths. Call for local numbers to contact in case of loss or theft.

Two giants in the traveler's-check universe (BankAmerica Corporation and Barclays) have tied the knot, and their baby was christened **Interpayment Visa Traveler's Cheques** (in U.S. and Canada, tel. 800/227–6811; outside U.S., call collect 415/574–7111), which are imprinted with the name of the financial institution that sells you the checks. Don't worry: you're getting **Visa** traveler's checks, widely known and available in at least 10 currencies. The refund-referral service operates 24 hours a day.

Four Fail-safe Places to Stash Money

- ***Socks (problem: embarrassing, when retrieving damp and smelly balls to pay a dinner tab).***
- ***Orifices (problem: possible health hazard).***
- ***Between pages of your pocket Bible (problem: you don't have a pocket Bible).***
- ***Inside big hair (problem: don't comb or pick in public).***

LOST/STOLEN CHECKS Unlike cash, lost or stolen traveler's checks can be replaced or refunded, and the process can be speeded up if you have a copy of the purchase agreement and a record of the serial numbers of the checks you bought and cashed. Do not carry traveler's checks around without signing them. Unsigned checks are just like cash: Anybody can use them. Sign the checks when you buy them; you'll endorse them a second time when you exchange them for cash or make purchases. One modern translation of "don't keep all of your eggs in one basket" is "keep the purchase agreement in a separate place from the checks, or you could lose both." Those who like to cover their bases twice will even give a copy of their purchase agreement and the checks' serial numbers to someone back home. Most issuers of traveler's checks promise to refund or replace lost or stolen checks in 24 hours, but some cross their fingers behind their backs as they promise this. If you're in a remote area, expect the process to take longer.

CREDIT CARDS They're definitely bourgeois, probably environmentally unsound, and possibly the most convenient invention since sliced bread. If you're willing to ignore the bad points long enough to actually apply for a credit card, you may be disappointed to find that students or those with low incomes are often turned down by major credit-card companies. Check at university bookstores and student unions for special student offers from American Express and other companies. If a more economically able (PC-speak for richer) family member or friend is willing, he or she can apply for a second card for you, which is linked to his or her account. Plastic money is not free. Annual fees for basic credit cards range from zilch to upward of $60, and the interest rate on unpaid monthly balances can be as high as 20%. Diners, hostels, and pool halls will probably not accept credit cards, but restaurants, hotels, and department stores in most cities and towns do—look for the card logo on windows. American Express, Visa, and MasterCard are the safest bets. Credit cards can also be lifesavers in financial emergencies—making a rental-car deposit, reserving a flight, or keeping a roof over your head when your pockets are empty. Most credit-card companies offer lots of extra services, some free, some not (*see below* for details).

If you can put up with multiple junk mailings every month that attempt to push all your consumer buttons, American Express may be the card for you.

American Express (24-hour hot line, in U.S., tel. 800/528–4800) lures students with discount airline coupons and other come-ons. The company pushes its student card: Technically this is not a credit card, as you have to pay your entire balance every month, but there's a special plan, Sign and Travel, in which you can spread out payments for big-ticket items like airline tickets (interest will accrue). For an annual fee of $55 you'll get access to the **Global Assist Hotline,** a toll-free referral service and emergency message

Making the Most of Your Parents' Credit Cards

Even if you have no job, no credit, no credit cards, no little plastic thing to put them in, or nothing, you can still tap the fabulous services offered by the Visa Assistance Center if one of your parents has a Visa Gold or Business card and you are a dependent under age 22 and at least 100 miles from home. Just memorize the card number (or write it down in a safe place), and when you call the Center they can offer emergency cash service, emergency ticket replacement, lost luggage assistance, medical and legal assistance, and emergency message service. Helpful and, we're assured, multilingual personnel await your call 24 hours a day, seven days a week (in U.S., tel. 800/847–2911; outside U.S., call collect 301/265–7700).

center; **emergency card replacement,** a guarantee of replacement (usually) by the end of the next business day if your card is lost or stolen; mail-holding, check-cashing, and check- purchasing services at more than 1,500 **American Express Travel Service Offices** around the world; $100,000 worth of **travel accident insurance;** and lemon assurance, or a **purchase-protection plan,** that refunds or replaces damaged or malfunctioning products you buy with the card (certain restrictions apply).

Individual banks market **MasterCard**; the yellow-and-orange logo was chosen because it inspires you to spend, psychologists tell us. Each bank sets its own annual fee and interest rate and offers different services, so you're on your own. Visit a bank or call 800/999–0454 to find out which banks in your area handle the card. **Visa** offers the same deal as MasterCard; individual banks "enhance" the "core features" of the card (little did you know, there's a whole credit-card lingo), so you may be eligible for emergency cash service, emergency card-replacement service, and other extras. Visa can be used in 90,000 ATMs in 40 countries. Ask your bank's customer-service department for a Visa ATM directory. The **Visa Classic** card is the basic (read: lower minimum-income requirement and lower spending limit) card, which, depending on the issuing bank, may charge no annual fee—look around and compare. The **Visa Gold** card requires a higher income, but some privileges are extended to dependents (*see box*). **Working Assets** offers a **Visa** that satisfies your consumer urges and your desire to make the world a better place (*see box*).

OBTAINING MONEY FROM HOME Provided there's money at home to be had, there are at least three ways to get it: (1) Have it sent through a large commercial bank with a branch in the town where you're staying. Unless you have an account with that large bank, though, you'll have to go through your own bank, and the process will be slower and more expensive. (2) If you're an American Express cardholder you can cash a personal check for up to $1,000 (usually given in traveler's checks rather than cash) at one of their offices. Or an **American Express Moneygram** could be your dream come true if you can call home and convince someone to go to an American Express Moneygram agent (American Express offices, bus stations, airports, convenience stores), fill out the necessary form, and transfer cash to you. Transactions must be in increments of $50 and must be paid for with cash, MasterCard, Visa, or an Optima card. Fees vary according to the amount of money sent but average 8%–10%. You'll need to show identification when picking up the money and know the transaction-reference number. Word is the money will be available in 15 minutes, but don't count on it. For the nearest Moneygram agent and the locations of receiving offices, call 800/543–4080 in the United States; outside the United States, call collect 303/980–3340. (3) Have money sent through **Western Union** (tel. 800/325–6000). Although this has a certain glamorous ring to it, it's really expensive. If your personal economy has gone from bad to worse, beg someone back home to take cash, a certified cashier's check or a healthy MasterCard or Visa to a Western Union office. The money will reach the requested destination in two business days but may not be available for several more hours or days, depending on the whims of local authorities.

A Politically Correct Credit Card?

A P.C. credit card? Yeah, right. Working Assets (230 California St., San Francisco, CA 94111–9876, tel. 800/522–7759) donates $2 of your first Visa purchase and 5¢ from every purchase thereafter to a pool of nonprofit progressive organizations: Amnesty International, the Southern Poverty Law Center, Oxfam America, and the Rainforest Action Network, to name a few. They're for real, but, unfortunately, you also have to have a real income (or convince someone who does to sign you on as a co-applicant) to obtain a Working Assets Visa. After that you can charge it and help save the world at the same time.

CASH MACHINES Virtually all U.S. banks belong to a network of ATMs (automated teller machines), which gobble up bank cards and spit out cash 24 hours a day in cities throughout the country. To receive a card for an ATM system you must apply at a bank and select a PIN (personal identification number). A Visa or MasterCard can also be used to access cash through certain ATMs if you have a PIN for it, but the fees for this service are usually higher than bank-card fees and a daily interest charge accrues on these credit-card "loans," even if monthly bills are paid on time. Check with your bank for information on fees, daily limits for cash withdrawals, and locations of cash machines in a given city.

Express Cash allows American Express cardholders to withdraw up to $1,000 in a seven-day period (21 days overseas) from their personal checking accounts via ATMs worldwide. Gold-cardholders can receive up to $2,500 in a seven-day period (21 days overseas). Each transaction carries a 2% fee, with a minimum charge of $2 and a maximum of $6. Apply for a PIN and set up the linking of your accounts at least two to three weeks before departure. Call 800/CASH–NOW for an application and to find out where these Express Cash machines hide at your destination.

LUGGAGE

Don't bring more luggage than you can comfortably carry; if you can't tote your bag all the way around the block at home, it's going to be worse than a ball and chain on your Big Adventure. Backpacks are the most manageable way to lug all your belongings around, but bring a duffel or large shoulder bag if you want to blend in more with other travelers. Leaving some room for gifts and souvenirs is also wise. Outside pockets on backpacks are especially vulnerable to pickpockets, so don't store any valuables there. Lockers and baggage-check rooms are available in most airports and in train and bus stations, but you'll save time and money if you can easily carry everything with you.

BACKPACKS By distributing the weight of your luggage across your shoulders and hips, backpacks ease the burden of traveling. You can choose among four types of packs: day packs (best for short excursions), external-frame packs (for longer travels and for use on groomed trails), internal-frame packs (for longer travels across rougher terrain), and travel packs (hybrid packs that fit under an airline seat and travel well in cities or the backcountry). External frames achieve the best weight distribution and create an airspace between you and your goodies, but they're more awkward and less flexible than packs with internal frames. Packs are the best luggage for travelers who plan to walk a lot or do any hiking or camping. Be sure to have your pack fitted correctly when you buy it; there shouldn't be any gaps along your back, it should not drag down on your hips, and the frame shouldn't stick up too high above your head. Height specifications are useful, but your torso length is the real deciding factor, so try a fully loaded pack on before investing in it (external-frame packs run $100–$225 and about $50 more for an internal frame). Make sure the pack is waterproof, or bring an extra waterproof poncho to throw over it in downpours. An inside pocket is great for dirty laundry or food storage, and straps for a sleeping mat are good for those who'll be roughing it. The disadvantages of packs are that you can't disguise 'em: You're marked as a budget traveler. In cities, especially on public transportation, you may have a hard time negotiating through doorways and down crowded aisles. Someone behind you could also be merrily stealing your passport and all your traveler's checks unless you pack them *inside* the pack.

SHOULDER BAGS AND SUITCASES Bags with a long strap (preferably wide and padded) can be worn across your body so the weight is distributed somewhat, and you won't be vulnerable to bag-snatching. This method will still result in aching shoulders if your bag is too heavy. Duffels and shoulder bags are less conspicuous than backpacks and suitcases, so if you're the self-concious or wanna-be-native type, this may be the best choice for you. Shoulder bags are not ideal for travelers who plan to camp, hike, or walk a lot or who need instant accessibility to their goods. Straps, zippers, and seams are the most vulnerable points on a bag. Check that straps are wide, adjustable, and padded; check the stitching on zippers and seams, and look for a wide zipper if possible. A zipper that can be locked never hurts.

Basically, suitcases are for those who are staying in resorts, are traveling excusively by car, or would actually use one of those carts with wheels.

WHAT TO PACK

As little as possible. Besides the usual—clothes, toiletries, camera, a Walkman, and the latest Hite Report—bring along a day pack or some type of smaller receptacle; it will come in handy not only for day excursions but also for those places where you plan to stay for only one or two days. You can check your big, heavy, cumbersome bag at a train or bus station (or leave it at your motel/hostel) and just carry the essentials while you go looking for lodging. People planning to visit Los Angeles and San Francisco in summer will find two completely different climates—one hot and dry, the other damp and cold (*see* When to Go, *above*)—so read about your particular destination before packing.

THE SLEEP SHEET DEFINED

Take a big sheet. Fold it down the middle, the long way. Sew one short side and the long, open side. Turn inside out. Get inside. Sleep.

BEDDING Unless you're carrying a tent, you don't need a sleeping bag. But bring a sleep sheet if you plan to stay in hostels—some rent them, some don't. If you have a backpack, consider buying a sleeping mat that can be rolled tightly and strapped onto the bottom of your pack; these make train- and bus-station floors a tad more comfy. For more information on what to bring for camping, *see below.*

CLOTHING If you're really smart (and not terribly fashion conscious), you'll bring two outfits and learn to wash clothes by hand regularly. At the very least, bring comfortable clothes that are easy to clean. Californians are, by and large, casual dressers. Black hides dirt but absorbs heat, so pack a couple of light-colored T-shirts. Light cotton sweaters and pants dry more quickly than jeans and sweatshirts. If you're traveling in summer, pack one pair of pants and a sweater or heavy sweatshirt for colder nights (especially in the mountains and along the coast). Pack a raincoat and/or umbrella for the inevitable. Socks and undies don't take up too much room, so throw in a couple extra pairs even if you think it's easy to spend every evening washing out dirty laundry. Shoes may be your biggest friend or foe: A sturdy pair of walking shoes or hiking boots and a spare pair of other shoes (probably sandals) will allow you to switch off and give your barkin' dogs a rest. Plastic sandals or thongs will protect your feet on communal shower floors that are often rough, wet, and skanky—they're also useful if you'll be camping or beach-hopping.

LAUNDRY In small towns and wilderness areas laundromats may not exist. Play it safe and bring your own laundry service: a plastic bottle of liquid detergent (powder doesn't break down as well), about 6 feet of clothesline, and some plastic clips (bobby pins or paper clips can substitute). **Dr. Bronners** makes scented soap safe for clothes and your bod. Porch railings, shower-curtain rods, bathtubs, and faucets can serve as wet-laundry

The Four Rules of Luggage

- ***You must be able to carry it at least 2 miles.***
- ***You must be able to fit it into a conventional storage locker and on an overhead rack in a train.***
- ***Keep anything you cherish in the middle of your bag. Your heaviest stuff should also be packed in the middle of a pack and whatever you need quick access to (maps, guidebooks, address book) in an outer pocket. Keep money and travel documents on your body if possible.***
- ***Attach a clearly marked luggage tag to your bag and put some identifying paper or tag inside as well.***

hangers if you forget the clothesline. If a sink doesn't have a plug, stuff a sock or plastic bag in the drain. Bring an extra plastic bag or two for still-damp laundry and for the dirty kind.

CAMERAS AND FILM While you're traveling, keep your film as cool as possible, away from direct sunlight and blazing campfires. If your camera is new or new to you, shoot and develop a few rolls of film before leaving home to avoid spoiling your travel footage with prominent thumb shots or miscalculated f-stops. The smaller and lighter the camera the better, if you're not a photo artiste. Pack some lens tissue and an extra battery if you've got a built-in light meter. Invest about $10 in a skylight filter to protect your lens and reduce haze in your photos.

On a plane trip, unprocessed film is safest in your hand luggage, and you can ask security to inspect it by hand. (It helps to keep your film in a plastic bag, ready for quick inspection.) Inspectors at American airports are required by law to honor requests for hand inspection, so don't be afraid to demand your rights (if you've got nothing to hide in your luggage, that is). Airport scanning machines used in all U.S. airports are safe for five to 500 scans, depending on the speed of your film. The effects are cumulative, so you don't have to worry until you pass the five-scan mark.

MISCELLANEOUS Contact-lens wearers should bring a spare set and a pair of glasses and should consider investing in disposable extended-wear contacts (about $30 for six pairs, each lasting two weeks). Travelers from other countries who are bringing their contact-lens cleaning system with them should either check with their eye doctor to make sure the same system exists in California or bring enough supplies to last through their trip.

INFO FOR FOREIGN VISITORS

PASSPORTS AND VISAS

BRITISH You need a valid 10-year passport to enter the United States (cost £15 for a standard 32-page passport, £30 for a 94-page passport). Application forms are available from most travel agents and major post offices and from the **Passport Office** (Clive House, 70 Petty France, London SW1H9BR, tel. 071/279–3434 for recorded information or 071/279–4000). A British Visitor Passport is not acceptable.

You do not need a visa if you are visiting for pleasure and are staying less than 90 days. If you are entering the United States by plane or boat, you must hold a return or onward ticket, enter aboard an air or sea carrier that participates in the Visa Waiver Program (in effect, any airline that flies from the United Kingdom to the United States), and complete visa waiver form I-94W, which is supplied at your point of departure or on the plane or ship. You may now also enter the United States by land from Canada or Mexico without a visa; you must complete the I-94W form at the port of entry.

If you fail to comply with any one of these requirements, you will need a visa. Apply to a travel agent or the **U.S. Embassy Visa and Immigration Department** (5 Upper Grosvenor St., London W1A2JB, tel. 071/499–3443 for a recorded message or 071/499–7010). Visa applications to the U.S. Embassy must be made by mail, not in person. Visas can be given only to holders of 10-year passports, although visas in expired passports remain valid. If you think you might stay longer than three months, you must apply for a visa *before* you travel.

CANADIAN Canadian citizens require proof of citizenship and identity to enter the United States (a passport, birth certificate with raised seal, or voter registration card are preferred). For additional information while in the United States, contact the **Canadian Embassy** (501 Pennsylvania Ave. NW, Washington, DC 20001, tel. 202/682–1740). Consulates are located in Atlanta, Boston, Chicago, Cleveland, Dallas, Detroit, Los Angeles, Minneapolis, New York City, San Francisco, and Seattle.

AUSTRALIAN Australian citizens are required to have a valid passport and visa to enter the United States. Passport applications are available at any post office or at passport offices located in every major city. In addition, details on applying for a passport are listed in public telephone books. A birth or citizenship certificate and photo I.D. are required. For information on obtaining a visa, contact the American Embassy or Consulate nearest you. While in the United States, Australians may obtain additional information from the **Embassy of Australia** (1601 Massachusetts Ave. NW, Washington, DC 20036, tel. 202/797–3000). Consulates are located in Chicago, Honolulu, Los Angeles, and New York City.

NEW ZEALAND New Zealand citizens need a valid passport to enter the United States. Passport applications are available from the **New Zealand Passport Office** (Documents of National Identity Division, Department of Internal Affairs, Box 10526, Wellington, New Zealand). You do not need a visa if you are entering for pleasure and are staying less than 90 days. For more information, contact the American Embassy or Consulate nearest you. In the United States, you can get more information from the **New Zealand Embassy** (36 Observatory Circle NW, Washington, DC 20008, tel. 202/328–4800). The embassy has a second office in Los Angeles.

COMING AND GOING

FROM CANADA BY AIR **Air Canada** (tel. 800/776–3000) and **United** (tel. 800/538–2929) have nonstop flights from Calgary and Toronto to L.A. and San Francisco. **Canadian Airlines International** (tel. 800/426–7000) also serves LAX and SFO. **Northwest** (tel. 800/241–2525) and **American** (tel. 800/433–7300) have flights with one stop on the way to San Francisco. **Delta** (tel. 800/241–4141) flies nonstop from Vancouver to LAX and SFO, and from there can fly you to many other California airports using its Delta's of small airlines. Delta can also fly you from Vancouver to San Diego with a single plane-change or stopover. Travel CUTS (Canadian Universities Travel Service, 187 College St., Toronto, Ont. M5T 1P7, tel. 416/979–2406) arranges cheap flights from Canada.

FROM THE UNITED KINGDOM BY AIR **British Airways** (tel. 800/247–9297), which offers youth fares, sometimes has special fares on its nonstop flights fromHeathrow to L.A. and San Francisco. **United** (tel. 800/538–2929) also flies nonstop from Heathrow to L.A. and San Francisco. **American** (tel. 800/433–7300) flies nonstop from Heathrow to L.A. and via Kennedy Airport in New York to San Francisco. **Delta** (tel. 800/241–4141) flies from Gatwick via Atlanta or Cincinnati to L.A., San Francisco, and San Diego. **TWA** (tel. 800/221–2000) stops in St. Louis on its way to L.A. from Gatwick.

FROM AUSTRALIA AND NEW ZEALAND BY AIR **Qantas** (tel. 800/227–4500) and **United** (tel. 800/538–2929) fly nonstop from Sydney to L.A. and San Francisco and from Auckland to L.A. **Air New Zealand** (tel. 800/262–1234) flies nonstop from Auckland to L.A. **Japan Airlines** (tel. 800/525–3663) flies from Australia and New Zealand to LAX and SFO with a stopover in Tokyo.

CUSTOMS AND DUTIES Visitors 21 and older can bring in (1) 200 cigarettes or 50 cigars or 2 kilograms of smoking tobacco, (2) one U.S. quart of alcohol, and (3) duty-free gifts to a value of $100. Forbidden are meat and meat products, seeds, plants, and fruits. Avoid illegal drugs like the plague.

CANADIAN CUSTOMS Exemptions for returning Canadians range from $20 to $300, depending on how long you've been out of the country: For two days out you're allowed to return with C$100 of goods; for one week out you're allowed C$300 worth. You'll be taxed 20% for items exceeding these limits (more for items you ship home). In any given year you're allowed one $300 exemption. Duty-free limits are: up to 50 cigars, 200 cigarettes, 2 pounds of tobacco, and 40 ounces of liquor—all must be declared in writing upon arrival at customs and must be with you or in your checked baggage. To mail back gifts, label the package "Unsolicited Gift—Value under $40." For more scintillating details, request a copy of the Canadian Customs brochure "I Declare/Je Déclare" from the Revenue Canada Customs and Excise Department (Connaught Bldg., MacKenzie Ave., Ottawa, Ont., K1A OL5, tel. 613/957–0275).

U.K. CUSTOMS Travelers age 17 and over returning to the United Kingdom may bring in the following duty-free goods: (1) 200 cigarettes or 100 cigarillos or 50 cigars or 250 grams of tobacco, (2) 1 liter of alcohol over 22% volume or 2 liters of alcohol under 22% volume, plus 2 liters of still table wine, (3) 50 grams of perfume and 250 milliliters of toilet water, (4) other goods worth up to £32.

AUSTRALIAN CUSTOMS Australian travelers 18 and over may bring back, duty free: (1) 1 liter of alcohol, (2) 250 grams of tobacco products (equivalent to 250 cigarettes or cigars), (3) other articles worth up to AUS$400. If you're under 18 your duty-free allowance is AUS$200. To avoid paying duty on goods you mail back to Australia, mark the package "Australian Goods Returned." For more rules and regulations, request the pamphlet "Customs Information for Travellers" from a local Collector of Customs (Box 8, Sydney NSW 2001, tel. 02/2265997).

NEW ZEALAND CUSTOMS Although you may be greeted with a "Haere Mai" ("Welcome to New Zealand"), you'll face the following restrictions. Travelers over 17 are allowed to bring back, duty-free: (1) 200 cigarettes or 250 grams of tobacco or 50 cigars or a combo of all three up to 250 grams, (2) 4½ liters of wine or beer and one 1,125-milliliter bottle of spirits, (3) goods with a combined value of up to NZ$700. If you want more details ask for the pamphlet "Customs Guide for Travellers" from a New Zealand consulate.

WORKING IN THE UNITED STATES

LEGAL REQUIREMENTS In order to work legally in the U.S. of A., you must have a social-security number, which is the birthright of U.S. citizens. Obtaining a green card, which entitles foreigners to work and reside in the United States, is a long shot for most visitors. Another option is to participate in an **Exchange Visitor Program (EVP)** (*see* Work-abroad Programs, *below*). With a little persistence (and chutzpah), illegal work (i.e., with no papers in hand) can be found, but, because employers are severely penalized if caught hiring illegally, there are fewer opportunities now than in the past and more competition for the same jobs. Be warned that if you're caught working illegally you will be deported and perhaps permanently denied entrance into the United States.

PAYING YOUR WAY Working now and then to keep travel funds flowing is substantially easier if you have a green card. Because you probably will not, your best bet is to find casual service-oriented jobs in restaurants or bars, housecleaning, or child care. Locals can usually help you find these jobs, and some opportunities are posted on notice boards at youth hostels and universities. The **American Institute for Foreign Study** (AIPS, 102 Greenwich Ave., Greenwich, CT 06830, tel. 203/869–9090) has an au-pair program (tel. 800/727–2437, ext. 6123) that places foreign nannies in American households. Seasonal agricultural work, like fruit-picking in California's abundant fields, is sometimes plentiful but often low-paid and far from public transportation.

WORK-ABROAD PROGRAMS Exchange-visitor programs are authorized by the U.S. government to provide foreign students with legal jobs. Most jobs are not big money-makers and come with restrictions, usually on the amount you can earn and the length of time you can stay. For British travelers, **British Universities North America Club** (BUNAC, 16 Bowling Greenland, London EC1R OBD, tel. 071/251–3472) operates in conjunction with CIEE to provide temporary work permits. **Camp America** (Dept. WW 37A, Queens Gate, London, SW7 SHR, tel. 071/589–3223) is run by **AIFS** (*see above*) and places visitors in camps throughout the United States, including some in California. Australians and New Zealanders should look into the **SWAP Program** (SSA/SWAP, Box 399, Carlton South, Melbourne, VIC 3053 Australia).

VOLUNTEER WORK If you can afford to work for nothing, more power to you. CIEE publishes *Volunteer! The Comprehensive Guide to Voluntary Service in the U.S. and Abroad* (CIEE Publications Dept., 205 E. 42nd St., New York, NY 10017, $8.95 plus postage), an extensive list of options, including U.S. work camps with archaeological, environmental, and social foci. Work in the great outdoors as a host or interpretive guide in one of California's many state parks attracts thousands of people each year. Contact the **California Department of Parks and Recreation** (Box 942896, 1416 9th St., Sacramento, CA 94296–0001, tel. 916/653–6995) or call **Sierra Club Service Trips** (730 Polk St., San Francisco, CA 94109, tel. 415/776–2211) for information.

PHONES AND MAIL

INTERNATIONAL CALLS Calls between the U.S. and Canada are not considered international calls and can be dialed as regular long-distance numbers. To call any other country, dial 011, the country code, the city code (dropping the initial zero if there is one), then the actual number. If you get stuck, dial 00 for a long-distance operator, who can help you. The country code for England is 44, New Zealand 64, and Australia 61. When calling, remember to account for time differences from PST (Pacific Standard Time): England is eight hours ahead; New Zealand is 19 hours ahead; and Australia, with three time zones, is 16–18 hours ahead. The cheapest times (PST) to call England are 6 PM–7 AM, New Zealand 11 PM–10 AM, and Australia 3 AM–2 PM. A three-minute call from anywhere in the United States during those bargain times will cost about $2.18 (England), $4.07 (New Zealand), or $3.30 (Australia).

SENDING MAIL HOME International rates for sending letters to destinations beyond the North American continent begin at 50¢ for the first 1/2 ounce and 95¢ for the first full ounce. Add 39¢ per ounce for letters heavier than 1 ounce. Rates are slightly cheaper for mail to Canada (40¢ for the first ounce) and Mexico (45¢ for the first ounce.) You can also stop by any post office and buy ready-to-mail aerogrammes to send anywhere in the world. For 45¢ you get paper, envelope, and postage all in one; the charge for the second ounce is 45¢, and each ounce thereafter is 39¢. Post cards cost 40¢. Allow one to two weeks delivery time for international mail.

RECEIVING MAIL Being in transit does not mean you have to go without that little love note from your squeeze back home. You can receive mail (including packages) in care of General Delivery at any post office. Have the sender indicate the city and zip code of a specific post office within a specific city. Most post offices are open Monday–Friday 9–5 and Saturday morning and will hold mail for up to 30 days before returning it to the sender. **American Express** (tel. 800/847–6242) offices also hold mail (but not packages) for 30 days for cardholders and traveler's-check holders who present cards/checks when claiming their mail. Call American Express to obtain locations.

RESOURCES FOR WOMEN TRAVELERS • • •

Large cities like San Francisco and Los Angeles have bookstores and groups that cater to women's issues and provide a network for the woman traveler. Keep in mind that the liberal bent of the state's urban centers goes only so far, and, true to its stereotype, Californians place great emphasis on looks and weight (especially in Southern California). Physical and verbal harrassment definitely occur here, particularly if you stand out as a foreigner or just someone in the wrong neighborhood. Women and single men should be aware of their surroundings, especially after dark. Women should be informed about areas they venture to alone and should hook up with other travelers when they can. Dangerous spots best avoided are the dark and deserted ones—be they bus stations, streets, seedy bars—use your imagination. Outlying rural areas seem to inspire a certain "cowboy factor": Men may be more forward and aggressive in their attempts to mate. Hitchhiking alone is a bad idea here, and women who stop to pick up roadside hitchers should exercise caution as well.

ORGANIZATIONS California has many women's organizations in the larger cities of San Francisco, Los Angeles, San Diego, and Sacramento. Check in the front of the local phone book's white pages under "Community Service Numbers," or check with universities for student feminist and women's organizations that may be able to refer you to other resources in the area. Also try the *Index/Directory of Women's Media* (Women's Institute for Freedom of the Press, 3306 Ross Place NW, Washington, DC 20008, tel. 202/966–7793), which lists women's periodicals, presses, cafés, what have you. For organizations in specific cities, *see* individual chapters, *below*. The **Center for Women's Studies and Services** (2467 E St., San Diego, CA, 92102, tel. 619/233–3088) assists battered and raped women. The **Commission on Assaults Against Women** (543 N. Fairfax Ave., Los Angeles, CA 90036, tel. 213/655–4235) provides a 24-hour rape-and-battery hotline. **Mama Bears** (6536 Telegraph Ave., Oakland, CA 94609, tel. 510/428–9684) and **Sisterhood Bookstore** (1351 Westwood Blvd., Westwood, CA 90024, tel. 310/477–7300) carry a ton of women-oriented publications and can refer you to other bookstores around the state if they haven't got what you're after. The **National Organization for Women** (NOW, 3543 18th St., San Francisco, CA 94110, tel. 415/861–8880; Los Angeles, tel. 310/657–3894) is a feminist organization committed to equality for women. NOW is also a good resource and referral center for just about any women's issue. **Pacific Harbor Travel** (519 Seabright Ave., Suite 201, Santa Cruz, CA 95062, tel. 408/425–5020) specializes in independent adventure travel with an emphasis on women's travel. The **Women's Alliance** (Box 2154, Oakland, CA 94620, tel. 510/658–2949) offers evening and weekend programs and a week-long summer camp that draws visitors from around the world. The **Women's Needs Center** (1825 Haight St., San Francisco, CA 94117, tel. 415/221–7371) is a medical clinic for women. **Woodswomen** (tel. 612/822–3809) specializes in adventure travel for women of all ages. The **Young Women's Christian Association** (YWCA, 620 Sutter St., San Francisco, CA 94102, tel. 415/775–6502; in Los Angeles, tel. 213/482–3470) offers social-service programs and accommodation referrals to women.

●●● RESOURCES FOR PEOPLE OF COLOR

California has a rich mix of ethnicities, but everyone in this so-called melting pot does not live in harmony. The 1992 riots in Los Angeles provided powerful evidence of that. Cities tend to have mixed African-American, Latino, Asian, and white populations—each of these splintered into many smaller racially identified groups. Smaller towns and more isolated areas (along the coast and in the inner agricultural valleys) tend to have mixed white and Latino populations. Check the white pages of the phone book for groups that cater to the needs of a specific ethnic group, or check with local universities for relevant student organizations.

ORGANIZATIONS Organizations in the state that concentrate on human and ethnic relations and resources can be located by telephoning information (tel. 411) and asking for a particular county or city human-relations commission.

The **Black Women's Resource Center** (518 17th St., Suite 202, Oakland, CA 94612, tel. 510/763–9501) offers information and referrals and publishes a newletter on issues of interest to African-American women and girls. The **National Association for the Advancement of Colored People (NAACP)** is committed to ensuring the rights of minority groups and elimating discrimination. Chapters are located in the state's major cities. Contact the western regional office (4929 Wilshire Blvd., Suite 360, Los Angeles, CA 90010, tel. 213/931–6331). The **Northern California Black Chamber of Commerce** (119 Broadway, Oakland, CA 94607, tel. 510/444–5741) lists businesses operated by African Americans.

●●● RESOURCES FOR GAYS AND LESBIANS

Gay men and women enjoy a certain amount of freedom in the larger Californian cities. San Francisco and Los Angeles have large gay communities served by many organizations, bookstores, cafés, and the like. Despite these supportive environments, gay bashing continues even on the streets of San Francisco, so always try to be aware of your surroundings if you're with your same-sex lover. Outside the big cities, attitudes are definitely more conservative and prejudicial. Publications focusing on gay issues can be found in gay-community bookstores and cafés. San Francisco has the *Bay Times*, a bimonthly, and the *Sentinel* is a statewide weekly. Both offer news and views plus entertainment options. *The Advocate* (Libertation Publications, 6922 Hollywood Blvd., Los Angeles, CA 90028, $3) is the best-known, national bimonthly gay magazine. Guidebooks that cover all of North America include **Bob Darmon's Address Book** ($12.95 plus shipping), which focuses on gay-male travel and lists services and entertainment options; and *The Womens' Traveler* ($10 plus shipping), which lists resources for lesbians. For both publications, write to Box 422458, San Francisco, CA 94142–2458, or call 415/255–0404.

ORGANIZATIONS The best way to locate organizations that center around issues of interest to gays and lesbians is to browse through one of the publications listed above. Many of California's cities have community centers that serve as meeting places for locals; check local phone books and individual chapters in this book. **The Fraternal Order of Gays (FOG) Travel Service** (304 Gold Mine Dr., San Francisco, CA 94131, tel. 415/641–0999) arranges tours and can make bookings. The **Gay Switchboard** (tel. 510/841–6224) is a referral service in the Oakland area that provides crisis support and information on social events and emergency housing for gays. The **International Gay Travel Association** (IGTA, Box 4974, Key West, FL 33041, tel. 800/448–8550) is a nonprofit organization of 387 member travel agencies worldwide; it provides listings of its members. **International Lesbian and Gay Association** (ILGA, 81 Rue Marche au Charbon, 1000 Brussels 1, Belgium, tel. 32/2–502–2471) is a fine source of information about conditions, specific resources, and hot spots in any given country.

RESOURCES FOR THE DISABLED

When President Bush signed the Americans With Disabilities Act in July 1990, implications for travel industries were far-reaching. By 1995 all rail lines must provide at least one wheelchair-accessible car per train. Hotels and motels must make the biggest changes by 1995: Most new and existing hotels must ensure that a percentage of their rooms and bathrooms (around 4%) are wheelchair accessible and that a further percentage are prepared for use by the deaf. Accessibility may soon have an international symbol if an initiative begun by the Society for the Advancement of Travel for the Handicapped (SATH) catches on. A bold, underlined, capital *H* is the symbol that SATH is using to indicate that hotels, restaurants, and tourist atractions have some accessible facilities.

Awareness of the needs of travelers with disabilities increases every year, but budget opportunities are harder to find. Always ask if discounts are available, both for you and for a companion. In addition, plan your trip and make reservations far in advance, since companies that provide services for people with disabilities go in and out of business regularly. Many attractions do not make it their business to accommodate travelers in wheelchairs, so call ahead to make sure they're accessible. The national-park system offers the **Golden Access Passport,** a free lifelong entry pass that exempts travelers with disabilities and their families or friends from all entry fees and 50% of use fees for camping and parking in federal parks and wildlife refuges. You aren't allowed to register by mail or phone, but you can apply in person with medical proof of disability at all National Park Service and Forest Service offices, Forest Service ranger-station offices, national parks that charge fees, Bureau of Land Management offices, and Fish and Wildlife Service offices. For information, contact the Western Regional Information Office (450 Golden Gate Ave., Box 36063, San Francisco, CA 94102, tel. 415/556–6030).

ACCOMMODATIONS Whenever possible, reviews in this book will indicate if rooms are wheelchair accessible. Most of the larger hotel chains, such as **Best Western, Embassy Suites,** and **Radisson,** can accommodate wheelchair users but rarely offer them discounts. The budget chain **Motel 6** (tel. 800/437–7486) has wheelchair-accessible rooms at almost all of its locations: Advance reservations are essential. **Red Roof Inns** (in U.S. and Canada, tel. 800/843–7663) have wheelchair-accessible rooms at almost all locations and are currently installing special alarm systems for their deaf and blind guests.

Hotels of America Reservation Service (501 7th Ave., New York, NY 10018, tel. 212/768–8200 or 800/432–4683), representing about 1,400 U.S. hotels, provides information for the disabled and make reservations free of charge.

GETTING AROUND **The American Public Transit Association** (tel. 202/898–4000) in Washington, D.C., has information on transportation options for travelers with disabilities in all U.S. cities. In addition, many organizations offer accessibility guides for specific areas (*see* Organizations, *below*).

BY PLANE Most major airlines are happy to help travelers with disabilities make flight arrangements as long as they are notified up to 48 hours in advance.

BY TRAIN **Amtrak** (tel. 800/872–7245; hearing-disabled line, tel. 800/523–6590, or, in PA, tel. 800/562–6960) offers a 25% discount on one-way coach fares for travelers with disabilities. However, you must show written verification of your disability from a state or national handicapped organization, a government agency, or a physician. If notified when reservations are made, Amtrak will provide assistance for travelers at stations.

BY BUS **Greyhound/Trailways** (tel. 800/752–4841) allows a traveler with disabilities and a companion to ride for the price of a single fare. No advance notice is required, although you will need to show proof of disability (such as a doctor's letter) to receive the special fare.

BY CAR Some major car-rental companies are able to supply hand-control vehicles with a minimum of 24-hour advance notice. **Avis** (tel. 800/331–1212) will install hand-control mechanisms at no extra charge if given a day's notice. **Hertz** (tel. 800/654–3131; TDD, 800/654–2280) asks for 48 hours advance notice and a $25 cash or credit-card deposit to do the same. **National** (tel. 800/328–4567; TDD, 800/328–6323) and **Thrifty** (tel. 800/367–2277) have hand-control cars only at certain locations and ask for at least two days' notice to serve mobility-impaired renters. **Budget** has a TDD line (800/826–5510) but cannot supply hand-control cars. **Alamo** has diddly.

ORGANIZATIONS The **American Foundation for the Blind** (15 W. 16th St., New York, NY 10011, tel. 212/620–2147 or 800/232–5463) offers *Access to Mass Transit* ($21.95), which covers cities throughout the United States. **Directions Unlimited** (720 N. Bedford Rd., Bedford Hills, NY 10507, tel. 914/241–1700 or 800/533–5343) sets up individual and group tours and cruises.

Disabled Outdoors Foundation (320 Lake St., Oak Park, IL 60302) is a nonprofit organization that works to increase recreational opportunities for outdoors enthusiasts with handicaps. Its executive director also serves as editor and publisher of the quarterly *Disabled Outdoors Magazine* (5223 S. Lorel Ave., Chicago, Il 60638, tel. 312/284–2206), which is full of information on fishing, camping, boating, what have you. Subscriptions are $10 for one year, $18 for two years, $27 for three years.

Evergreen Travel Service (4114 198th Ave. SW, Suite 13, Lynnwood, WA 98036, tel. 206/776–1184 or 800/435–2288) offers "Wings on Wheels" package tours (which include meals, lift-equipped vans, wheelchair-accessible boats, etc.) and bus tours in all sorts of vacation areas.

Flying Wheels Travel (143 W. Bridge St., Box 382, Owatonna, MN 55060, tel. 800/535–6790; in MN, tel. 800/722–9351) arranges cruises, tours, and vacation itineraries.

Information Center for Individuals with Disabilities (Fort Point Pl., 1st floor, 27–43 Wormwood St., Boston, MA 02210–1606; voice and TDD, tel. 617/727–5540; in MA, tel. 800/462–5015) is a resource center for Massachusetts residents who have disabilities or injury-related needs. Those outside Massachusetts can subscribe to the *Disability Issues* newsletter, published six times yearly and free to people with disabilities. Fact sheets on planning a vacation and travel agents and tour operators who cater to travelers with disabilities are about $5 each.

Mobility International USA (MIUSA, Box 3551, Eugene, OR 97403; voice and TDD, tel. 503/343–1284) is an internationally affiliated nonprofit organization that coordinates exchange programs for disabled people around the world and offers information on accommodations and organized study programs for members. Membership ($20 annually) gives you discounts on publications, services, MIUSA travel and educational programs, and a quarterly newsletter. Nonmembers may subscribe to the newsletter for $10.

Moss Rehabilitation Hospital's Travel Information Service (1200 West Tabor Rd., Philadelphia, PA 19141–3009, tel. 215/456–9900; TDD, 215/456–9602) provides information on tourist sights, transportation, accommodations, and accessibility for destinations around the world. You can request and receive information by state or by country for a $5 postage-and-handling fee. They also provide toll-free telephone numbers for airlines with special lines for the hearing impaired.

Outdoors Forever (Box 4811, East Lansing, MI 48823, tel. 517/337–0018) is a new nonprofit organization that works to make the outdoors more accessible to people with physical limitations. Call or write for more information on their magazine, *Outdoors Forever*, and their publications on equipment, techniques, and organizations that plan outings.

Redmond Travel (16979 Redmond Way, Redmond, WA 98052, tel. 206/885–2210) has a disabled-travel division, Wheelchair Journeys, that serves travelers in wheelchairs.

Self Help for the Hard of Hearing (SHHH, 7800 Wisconsin Ave., Bethesda, MD 20814, tel. 301/657–4350; TDD, 301/657–2249) can refer you to a state or local organization that has information on public places (like concert halls or museums) equipped with listening systems for hearing-impaired visitors.

The Society for the Advancement of Travel for the Handicapped (26 Court St., Brooklyn, NY 11242, tel. 718/858–5483) is a nonprofit educational group that works to inform and educate people about travel for the disabled. Annual membership is $45, or $25 for students and senior citizens, and entitles you to receive a quarterly newsletter that details new tours, tourism guides, resources, and late-breaking political advances for the disabled. Members can also request information about a specific destination; send $1 and a stamped, self-addressed envelope.

Travel Industry and Disabled Exchange (TIDE, 5435 Donna Ave., Tarzana, CA 91356, tel. 818/368–5648) publishes a quarterly newsletter and a directory of travel agencies and tours catering to disabled travelers. The annual membership fee is $15.

PUBLICATIONS ***Access to the World: A Travel Guide for the Handicapped***, by Louise Weiss, is highly recommended for its worldwide coverage of travel boons and busts for the disabled. If you can't find it in your local bookstore, contact Henry Holt and Company (tel. 800/247–3912); the order number is 0805001417, and the book costs $12.95. ***The Itinerary*** (Box 2012, Bayonne, NJ 07002, tel. 201/858–3400) is a bimonthly travel magazine for the disabled. It's not available in bookstores; a one-year subscription costs $10.

Twin Peaks Press (Box 129, Vancouver, WA 98666, tel. 206/694–2462; orders only, tel. 800/637–2256) specializes in books for the disabled, such as ***Travel for the Disabled***, which offers helpful hints as well as a comprehensive list of guidebooks and facilities geared to the disabled. Their ***Directory of Travel Agencies for the Disabled*** lists more than 350 agencies throughout the world. Each guidebook costs $19.95 plus $2 for shipping. Twin Peaks also offers the **Traveling Nurse's Network,** which connects travelers with disabilities with registered nurses to aid and accompany them on trips. Travelers fill out an application that Twin Peaks matches to nurses' applications in their files. The rest of the arrangements, such as destination and nurse's pay, are left to the traveler. An application for the network costs $10.

Staying in California

GETTING AROUND ● ● ●

If you've glanced at a map you already know that California is large. With its extensive road system, the easiest way to see as much of the state as possible is by car. However, if you don't plan to travel much off the beaten track, buses can get you between major cities and Amtrak trains will take you up the coast and inland.

BY TRAIN **Amtrak** (tel. 800/USA–RAIL) has two main routes in state. The *Coast Starlight* runs north and south from Los Angeles to Seattle, Washington, stopping at cities in between and offering bus connections to outlying towns. Although the name implies that tracks skim the coastline, in California the *Starlight* does so only south of San Luis Obispo and skips the most spectacular scenery of Big Sur. The other route, the *San Joaquin,* also runs north–south between Bakersfield and Oakland, with stops at cities in the San Joaquin Valley. Feeder bus connections are available north of Sacramento and east of Los Angeles. Fare from San Francisco to Los Angeles runs $75 one-way and $82–$150 round-trip, depending upon availability. Because of the huge distances involved, train travel in the United States is not as speedy, popular, or economical as in Europe. Reservations are not required, but the *Coast Starlight* tends to fill up, so book ahead. Trains have dining cars on board, but it's cheaper to bring food with you.

The **All-Aboard Pass** (tel. 800/872–7245 or 800/USA–RAIL) is good for people who plan their itinerary in advance. The pass, which is actually a booklet of tickets, allows Amtrak riders special fares for three stops made in 45 days of travel within a region. For travel in or through California, request the All-Aboard Pass for the western United States region (about $180) and choose your route. Call Amtrak before purchasing a pass, however, because All-Aboard fares are available in limited quantities, and ticket agents need to know your dates of travel and intended destination for ticketing. Amtrak also provides shuttle services on a limited basis when there is no connecting railway. The shuttle-service cost is included in the purchase price of your pass. **USARailPass** (tel. 800/872–7245 or 800/USA–RAIL) works to the advantage of the foreign budget traveler (it's not available to U.S. or Canadian citizens) because it requires no formal itinerary, works on any of Amtrak's U.S. routes, and allows for spontaneous planning. If you like a particular city or town, then by all means stay there until you feel like leaving, provided, of course, that you complete your travel within the time limit for which the pass is valid. Purchase the USARailPass for $179 at an International Travel Agency before entering the United States. If you are already in the States, you must buy the pass at an Amtrak office at your port of entry, and you must show a valid passport and visa.

BY BUS **Green Tortoise Adventure Travel** (Box 24459, San Francisco, CA 94124, tel. 415/821–0803 or 800/227–4766) is not just a bus ride; it's often the most memorable part of your vacation. It's also *the* cheap alternative to humdrum public transportation. Green Tortoise's buses crawl their way to cities up and down the West Coast and are equipped with sleeping pads, kitchens, and stereos. The company also offers a summer trek to Alaska, winter tours to Mexico and Baja, and other package trips across the continental United States. Reservations are recommended, especially for the weekly trips between San Francisco and Seattle.

Greyhound/Trailways (425 Mission St., San Francisco, CA 94103, tel. 415/495–1569; or 625 8th Ave., New York, NY 10018, tel. 212/971–0492) has bus service along Highways 101 and 5 and to a few offshoot towns. Cheapest fares are offered during low season (January–June and September–November).

Ameripass can be purchased in advance or, for spontaneous folks, 45 minutes before the bus leaves from the terminal. The pass allows purchasers unlimited travel within a limited time period: seven days ($208), 15 days ($289), or 30 days ($389). Foreign visitors can get slightly lower rates on all three passes. You can extend the pass for $10 per day but must do so when you purchase the ticket. Ameripass is valid for all U.S. routes. Certain rules and restrictions apply to each pass, so call or write a Greyhound International Travel office for details.

BY CAR Interstate 5 is the fastest way to go when traveling north–south through the San Joaquin Valley, but the scenery is flat and uneventful—except for the occasional cow. The road is also heavily patrolled by police and scorchingly hot in summer. The speed limit edges from 55 miles per hour up to 65 mph once you get outside the cities, but most people cruise at 70–75. Highway 1 is a beautiful but slow, sometimes literally cliff-hanging, drive that hugs the coast north of Santa Barbara all the way up into Oregon. Highway 101 lies between the two and is a compromise in scenery and time; the rolling hills are pretty but less spectacular than those you'll see on Highway 1, and the route takes about eight hours to travel between Los Angeles and San Francisco (compared to six hours on I–5). The best thing about having a car, however, is that you can opt to jag off on back roads where mass transportation fears to tread. For exploration within California, renting a car is economical, but take your own car if you plan to drive for more than a week or two.

The **American Automobile Association** (AAA, 1000 AAA Dr., Heathrow, FL 32746, tel. 407/444–7000 or 800/222–4357) is the organization to be in touch with if you'll be driving around the state. If you belong to an auto club abroad, AAA may honor your membership; otherwise, consider joining while you're here. Year-long memberships are about $50 and entitle members to free road maps, travel guides (nonmembers can buy them), and on-call emergency roadside service. There are offices throughout California.

CAR RENTALS Renting a car might be the easiest option if you want to come and go as you please. Major car-rental companies charge about $25–$45 a day (often with unlimited mileage) to renters over 25 who have a major credit card. In the off-season, a week's rental with unlimited mileage can be as low as $120. National agencies include **Alamo** (tel. 800/535–1391), **Budget** (tel. 800/527–0700), **Dollar** (tel. 800/800–4000), and **Thrifty** (tel. 800/367–2277). Expect to pay more ($10–15 a day) for the privilege of being under 25 years old; very few companies (except Budget) rent to anyone under 21.

Reserving a car a few days in advance and renting it for a week or more may get you a better guaranteed rate. Some companies charge nothing to return the car to another location, others charge $100–$150 extra; be sure to check. A company like Avis or Hertz may charge more per day but cost less overall with no drop-off charges. Insurance is optional (and will cost you extra, about $9–$12 a day), but it's a very good idea. Some credit cards, such as American Express, provide automatic auto-insurance coverage if you charge your rental, but be sure to read all the small print. Local companies and companies specializing in cheaper, older, and uglier cars, such as **Rent-A-Wreck** (tel. 800/535–1391), sometimes undercut the national companies on rates, but make sure the lower rental cost is not eclipsed by added mileage charges or a limit on how far you can drive the car out of the city. Car-rental companies are listed in local phone books, and some are listed at the beginning of each chapter in this book.

BUYING A CAR Some people try to beat car-rental costs by buying a car and selling it when they leave. Buying does provide an alternative to sinking money into a rental, but unless you plan to stay for a while, or know what to look for, or are willing to risk spending all your money on a lemon, renting may be less costly in the end. Hassles to consider include registration, insurance, and repairs. Registration means enduring long lines at the **Department of Motor Vehicles (DMV),** where you must present the car title, bill of sale, and state-required smog certificate. Registration fees are a percentage of the cost of the car—usually anywhere from 7% to 12%. California also requires proof of an insurance policy that will cover the cost of damages to another driver's car; policy costs vary depending upon the county. Unless you're an amateur mechanic, do not invest in a car needing repair work. Because mechanic labor fees run $50–$80 an hour, even simple repairs will probably top $100.

BY MOTORBIKE To enjoy the open-air and off-road freedom of a bicycle without the hassle of having to pedal, jump on a motorcycle and start exploring the California countryside. But there are problems. First, rentals are few and far between, thanks to enormous

Cool Music to Drive By

"Route 66" (lately covered by DePeche Mode), "Keep on Truckin'" (Eddie Kendricks), "Truckin'" (the Grateful Dead), "Convoy" (C. W. McCall), "Little Red Corvette" (Prince), "Wreck on the Highway" (the Boss—then again, just about all his songs are about driving), "Baby, You Can Drive My Car" (the Beatles), "Driving My Life Away" (Eddie Rabbitt).

liability-insurance costs, and prior riding experience is almost always required. Buying a bike involves registration fees if the bike is not currently registered, transfer fees, sales tax (about 8% of the price of the bike), and insurance costs. California's helmet law requires motorcycle riders and their passengers to wear helmets at all times or face a stiff fine that varies from county to county but can set you back as much as $160. Check free newspapers that specialize in auto and motorcycle sales (usually available around newspaper racks and at garages) for potential wheels.

BY BIKE Bicycling through California is perhaps the cheapest, most environmentally sound, and—depending on your physical shape—most enjoyable way to see the state. Campgrounds cost less for cyclers, and hostels sometimes make room for you even if they're full. Some highways, including stretches on Highways 101 and 1, accommodate bicyclists, but the best routes are the less crowded rural and side roads that parallel or branch off the highways. Bicyclists should be experienced or go with someone who is—perhaps a touring group. Wear a helmet and bring along repair tools and a spare tube or patch kit. **Backroads Bicycling Touring** (1516 5th St., Berkeley, CA 94710–1740, tel. 800/245–3874) offers trips around California, Baja, and the Grand Canyon for $200 and up. If you go on your own and plan on biking only part way, **Amtrak** will transport your bike ($5 handling fee) and you on the *Coast Starlight* route. They provide the bike box but require you to disassemble the bike. A good book that explores the coastal route from Canada to Mexico is ***Bicycling the Pacific Coast*** (The Mountaineers, 306 2nd Ave. W, Seattle, WA 98119, $12.95), by Tom Kirkendall and Vicky Spring.

HITCHHIKING Hitchhiking is illegal in California. Of course, people do it anyway, with most success in Northern California's rural communities, where people often know one another, and the hippie culture, with its ethic of picking up everyone, survives. Travelers may also have luck along parts of Highway 1 and in big parks like Yosemite, but generally Californians are wary of hitchhikers. If you do decide to thumb it, travel with a friend, especially if you're female. Catching rides in campgrounds, diners, or youth hostels is one technique. If thumbing at roadside, make sure the spot allows room for cars to easily pull over, and, needless to say, try to look as unthreatening as possible. Offer gas money and be somewhat destination-flexible, but never accept a ride if you're unsure about the driver. Always be aware of location and other travel options. Do not hesitate to tell a driver to stop if you feel at all unsafe: It's better to be embarassed than sorry. Have a backup plan for emergency situations (faking car-sickness is effective).

HIKING California's Pacific Crest Trail stretches from Mexico to Canada through the Sierra Nevada Mountains, offering prime trails for hikers. This and other major trails are discussed below. Roadside hiking is permitted along Highway 1 but illegal on I–5 and Highway 101. Camping on other than specifically designated lands is illegal and sometimes dangerous. Ask before plopping down on someone's property, or risk a rude awakening. **Wilderness Press** (2440 Bancroft Way, Berkeley, CA 94704, tel. 510/843–8080) publishes excellent guides on hiking in California, including the ***High Sierra Hiking Guide***, complete with topographical maps, for about $10.95. The **Sierra Club Bookstore** (730 Polk

Bikes in Flight

California is a great place to hit the road on two wheels, and most airlines will accommodate by shipping bikes as luggage, provided they are dismantled and put into a box. Call first to see if your airline sells bike boxes (about $10). International travelers can substitute a bike for the second piece of checked luggage for no extra charge; otherwise, it will cost $100 extra. Domestic flights are less gracious and make travelers with bikes pay a $45 fee.

St., San Francisco, CA 94109, tel. 415/923–5660), located at Sierra Club headquarters, also has an extensive selection of guides in addition to information about hiking trips.

BY PLANE If you're short on time and long on desire to see the major cities, air travel is the quickest and cheapest option. If you make reservations 21 days in advance, round-trip tickets between Los Angeles and San Francisco can cost as little as $60; try **Southwest Airlines** (tel. 415/885–1221) or **United** (tel. 800/722–5243).

Many major airlines offer special "See-the-United-States" discounted-fare passes for non-U.S. residents that offer substantial savings depending on destinations; and, with some restrictions, dates of travel are often left up to the traveler's whims. Inquire about these at travel agencies before arrival in the United States because they cannot be bought in the States.

WHERE TO SLEEP

Depending on where you are in California, budget lodgings may be available everywhere or may be nonexistent. The really cheap options are youth hostels, which charge $8–$11 per person, and campgrounds, which charge $10–$18 for a campsite but not always in the most convenient locations. Hotels and motels can start as low as $25 for a double, with $10–$15 for each additional person. Single travelers pay the most, usually the double rate. Hotels and motels are cheapest in the off-season and sometimes offer package deals. The **American Automobile Association** (1000 AAA Dr., Heathrow, FL 32746–5063) publishes a tour book that provides a detailed hotel-and-motel list (including prices) covering the entire state. It's available free to members and for about $9 to nonmembers at AAA locations around the state. Not only do room reservations make life easier, they may be essential in popular areas like the coast. Bed-and-breakfasts are not the money savers they are in Europe; they usually cost just as much, if not more, than nice motels or hotels. The price categories used in this book refer to a double room plus tax, unless otherwise stated.

HOTELS About $40 will buy you a double room with private bath in an average hotel. The hotels featured in this book are generally the cheapest we could find—either the cheap and moderately priced ones with character or the larger, unassuming places with budget deals. Budget chains permeate the state and can be a relatively cheap ($30 and up for a double) and reliable option, although they're usually bland. The major budget chains that operate statewide are **Motel 6** (tel. 505/891–6161), **All Star Inn** (tel. 800/782–7466), and **E-Z 8 Motels** (tel. 619/291–4824 or 800/326–6835).

BED-AND-BREAKFASTS Bed-and-breakfasts are usually out of the budget range, but, if you want to splurge for a homey and more personal touch, spend your money here rather than at a larger, swankier hotel. B&Bs start as low as $45 in some areas but usually average about $80 and up for a double. The room price includes breakfast, which can range from a Danish and coffee to a five-course feast. Rooms are often without telephones and televisions and sometimes have a shared bathroom. Most B&Bs are privately owned homes and/or restored architectural beauties. They vary in size and atmosphere and can be solidly booked most of the year. Many have interesting owners who love talking about their area. **Bed and Breakfast International** (Box 282910, San Francisco, CA 94128–2910, tel. 415/696–1690) is a reservation service for more than 500 B&Bs in California and Nevada, with prices starting at $45 per night and discounts on longer stays. Individual chambers of commerce often list them, too. ***Bed and Breakfast California, A Select Guide*** (Chronicle Books, 275 5th St., San Francisco, CA 94103, $10.95), by Linda Kay Bristow, is a good reference.

HOSTELS Youth hostels are few and far between in California, but those there are often have first-rate facilities and staff. The **American Youth Hostel Association** (AYH, Dept. 801, Box 37613, Washington, DC 20013–7613, tel. 202/783–6161; 425 Divisadero, San Francisco, CA 94117, tel. 415/863–9939; Central CA Council, Box 28148, San Jose, 95115, tel. 408/298–0670; Los Angeles Council, 1434 2nd St., Santa Monica, CA 90401, tel. 310/393–6263; San Diego Council, 335 W. Beech St.,

San Diego, CA 92101, tel. 619/239–2644) accepts travelers of all ages. Facilities vary widely, from lighthouse cabins to small three- to four-bed in-home operations; some are wheelchair accessible. AYH has strict rules: Alcohol, drugs, and smoking are forbidden, curfews (some as early as 10) are enforced, and each visitor is responsible for a simple chore. The maximum stay is three days unless an extension is granted. In season it's a good idea to book ahead. Some hostels allow you to use your sleeping bag, although officially they require a sleep sack that can be rented for about $1 a night. All hostels have a kitchen, common room, and often useful listings detailing cheap things to do in the area. A real pain in the butt is the lockout that most hostels institute from 9 AM to 5 PM, during which all guests must leave the premises. It is usually not necessary to be a member ($25 for one year) to secure a bed, but nonmembers will pay $11 while members pay $8. AYH publishes a U.S. handbook ($1 for members, $5 for nonmembers) that details the location and amenities of each hostel.

The **Young Men's Christian Association** (YMCA, tel. 800/922–9622, and *see* box, *below*) and **YWCA** operate hostels that range from dorms to makeshift high-school-gymnasium setups in summer. Age limits and prices vary, so contact the YMCA in the area you'll be visiting. Some offer special rates for lengthy stays.

UNIVERSITY/STUDENT HOUSING During the summer, universities often rent out dorm rooms by the night or the week; however, it's usually under the pretense that you're there on some sort of school-related business. A good line in such a circumstance is to say you're thinking of attending school there. Generally, universities are not a real bargain. Dorms are dreary and costs high—$30–$40 for a single or double. This book lists, in individual destination chapters, some universities that offer housing. If you're interested in one not listed, contact the university's housing office.

LODGING ALTERNATIVES

ROUGHING IT Crashing somewhere for free is definitely possible in certain areas of California if you're willing to take a few risks. Public places such as bus stations and train stations are rarely open 24 hours and are rarely safe after hours; you would be better off just finding some open ground. Beaches, especially in the north, are often state-owned and rarely patrolled—unlike those near cities such as Santa Cruz or Santa Barbara. Without permission, sleeping on someone's private property is NOT a good idea. Sleeping in your car can be done along certain back roads but can also be dangerous. If you succeed in avoiding police detection, someone else may target and rob you or worse.

According to California state law (and our unnamed sources), all chemistry and engineering buildings on college campuses must have readily available showers (for emergency showering after toxic experiments). Of course, they are free. (Can you imagine groping in your backpack for a quarter while your skin or eye sizzles from an acid spill?) Readers should know that most showers in engineering buildings are in the rest rooms and are private, as opposed to those in chemistry buildings. (HINT, HINT.)

APARTMENT STAYS If you have a group of friends and want to stay in one place for a few weeks, consider renting or subletting an apartment. Contact the area's chamber of commerce for agencies that specialize in vacation apartment stays.

Ys in California

Berkeley Albany YMCA, 2001 Allston Way, Berkeley, CA 94704, tel. 510/848–6800; Hollywood Wilshire International YMCA, 1553 N. Hudson Ave., Hollywood, CA 90028, tel. 213/467–4161; Stillwell Hotel, 838 S. Grand Ave., Los Angeles, CA 90017, tel. 213/627–1151; San Diego ASY, 500 W. Broadway, San Diego, CA 92101, tel. 619/232–1133; San Francisco Central YMCA, 220 Golden Gate Ave., San Francisco, CA 94102, tel. 415/885–0460.

OTHER OPTIONS Formed in the aftermath of World War II, **Servas** (11 John St., New York, NY 10038, tel. 212/267–0252; 229 Hilcrest Ave., Willowdale, Ont. M2N 3P3, tel. 416/221–6434; 55 Jackson Ave., Leeds, Yorkshire LS8 1NS, tel. 0532/665–219; 16 Cavill Court, Vermont S, 3133 Victoria, BC, Canada, tel. 03/803–5004; 15 Harley Rd., Takapuna, Oakland, New Zealand, tel. 09/489–442) is a membership organization that enables you to stay with host families. Servas is dedicated to promoting peace and understanding around the globe. Becoming a member makes you eligible for their host-list directory for any participating country. California listings are plentiful, so you can arrange a stay with a Servas host or host family in advance or try your luck when you arrive. Servas is *not* for tourists or weekend travelers; peace-minded individuals who want more than a free bed can write or call for an application and an interview. Membership is $45 per year, and a one-time deposit of $15 is required.

CAMPING ● ● ●

California is a wonderful place to camp. Most of the state's many forests, mountains, and coastal areas have designated campgrounds and informal backcountry camping. Wildlife abounds and is generally harmless, although potentially harmful bears roam, and snakes slither about in wooded areas. Never feed wild animals. Put your food in containers, or you may find out in the morning just how dexterous a determined raccoon can be. Many designated campsites have food lockers designed to be bear proof. Never sleep with food in your tent or backpack, and remember that any boulder you can climb to secure your food a bear can climb, too. If you're backcountry camping, put food in sealed containers inside of a sleeping-bag sack and hang it from a tree branch at least 20 feet above the ground. Make sure the branch is too thin to support a bear and that the tree is far from where you're sleeping. Rattlesnakes will not eat your food, although they might eat your small dog. If you're in the desert or drier foothills avoid taunting them, because their poisonous bite, while rarely fatal, is seriously painful. Probably the biggest threats you're likely to encounter are the dreaded, rash-inducing poison ivy and poison oak. Poison ivy has oily three-leaf stems that are shiny green in late spring and rich orange and red in fall. The leaves of poison oak are similar but have rounded lobes instead of notches. If you happen to fall into a shrub or vine, wash your skin with soap and water and do not scratch. When you scratch, the toxic oil spreads—and so do the red bumps. For more general, statewide camping information check with the **National Park Service** (Fort Mason, Bldg. 201, San Francisco, CA 94123, tel. 415/556–0560) or **California Parks and Recreation** (Publications, Box 942896, Sacramento, CA 94296–0001, tel. 916/653–6995). The **Sierra Club** (730 Polk St, San Francisco, CA 94109, tel. 415/776–2211)has a good selection of guidebooks and group tours. For a guide to more than 15,000 campgrounds, splurge on a copy of ***California Camping*** (Foghorn Press, Box 77845, San Francisco, CA 94107, tel. 415/241–9550, $16.95), by Tom Stienstra.

If you're hiking where snakes are common, it's a good idea to carry a snakebite kit; it'll buy you the time to find a doctor or ranger.

CAMPING GEAR Before packing loads of camping gear, seriously consider how much camping you will actually do versus the hassle of hauling around a tent, sleeping bag, stove, and accoutrements in the heat. Also consider climate in choosing what to bring. A great place to get equipment, outdoor publications, and free useful pamphlets is **Recreational Equipment, Inc.** (REI, 1338 San Pablo Ave., Berkeley, CA, tel. 510/527–4140 or 800/828–5533), with locations up and down the West Coast. **Patagonia, Inc.** (259 W. Santa Clara Ave., Ventura, CA 93001, tel. 805/643–8616 or 800/336–9090) also puts out a catalog featuring outdoor gear.

Sleeping bags are of primary concern. Both down and synthetic bags (like Qualofil) will keep you snug in cold dry weather. However, down is useless when wet, whereas Qualofil provides warmth (uncomfortable though it may be) when sopping wet, thus protecting you against hypothermia (*see box*). If you do have a down bag, take the precaution of wrapping it in a plastic bag to keep out moisture. Down bags cost more ($150 and up) but are lighter and smaller; synthetics cost $100 and up. Campers who want something between them and the hard ground should buy a sleeping mat. Foam pads are light, cheap ($10–$20), and can be rolled up and tied to your pack, but they soon flatten to feel as hard as the ground itself. Therm-a-Rest pads are self-inflating air mattresses that cushion well but are more expensive ($40–$50). Tents come in cotton- or synthetic-canvas breeds. The synthetic variety is more water-resistant and shelters against wind. Test the weight, trying to imagine yourself toting the tent around on your back. A 7- or 8-pound tent is probably the heaviest that's comfortable to carry. For camping in damp areas, make sure your tent has edges that can be turned up off the ground to prevent water from seeping in, or else bring a plastic tarpaulin. Also check the tent's windows and front flaps for mosquito-proof netting, and make sure the front flap can be completely zipped shut during rain. Self-standing tents are a plus on hard ground—but watch out for high winds.

Avoid camping or reserve ahead during these busy dates: Labor Day, Memorial Day, July 4, and any other summer three-day weekends. Fellow campers are also out in full force during federal and state holidays observed in California: New Year's Day, Martin Luther King Day, Lincoln's Birthday, Washington's Birthday, Good Friday, Easter, Columbus Day, Thanksgiving, and Christmas.

In general, the lighter a tent for a given size, the more expensive, but the cost may be well worth the price, especially if you're traveling by bike or doing a lot of walking. Expect to pay $100–$150 for an average two-person tent, with larger sizes costing more. An alternative to a one-person tent is a bivouac bag, or "bivvy," a water-repellent shell that fits over a sleeping bag. Camping stoves are no longer the huge green tanks you once lugged on family camping trips. You can buy a white-gas-burning mini-stove that provides one amazingly powerful flame and folds up into a little bag, all for about $35. A white-gas-burning lantern costs about $40. Other odds and ends include matches in a waterproof container, a Swiss-army knife, something for banging in tent pegs (your shoe will work if it's sturdy enough), mosquito repellent, a mess kit ($15), a water purifier ($35), and water-purification tablets or iodine crystals ($8). If you feel you'll need a shower, try a solar shower, a thick but smallish bag (holding up to 5 gallons) that can be filled with water and set out in the sun. Within a short time a quick hot shower is ready. The solar shower runs $10–$15. Last but not least, bring sealable plastic bags for garbage and recyclable items.

CAMPGROUNDS Campgrounds in California can be found along the ocean, near cultivated fields, and high in the mountains. Sites range from primitive (meaning no running water and pit toilets) to commercialized private sites overrun by RVs and arcades. Prices vary accordingly—anywhere from $8 to $18 for a public site; usually more for a private one. National-park campgrounds are fairly well kept but often crowded. National forests are considered less spectacular, and the campsites are usually the primitive type but they're often the least crowded. State parks lie somewhere in between with regard to the quality of the scenery and campground maintenance. Many campgrounds do not accept reservations, but those in the most popular spots wlll often take bookings eight

How to Avoid Hypothermia

Hypothermia, which occurs when body temperature falls below normal, kills many campers every year. It usually occurs after exposure to cold water (rain, river, lake) and cold air. The first symptom is an apathetic sleepy feeling, which is followed by confusion, collapse and, finally, death. Precautions to take: (1) Maintain your energy by eating high-calorie foods, and avoid becoming overly fatigued. (2) Wear layered clothing. Wool and synthetics are best. Down is completely ineffective when wet, and wet cotton draws heat from the body. (3) Seek shelter from the wind and rain and stay dry. Put on any extra dry clothing you've had the foresight to stash in a plastic bag.

weeks in advance. In summer, popular spots like Yosemite and coastal campgrounds are always booked exactly eight weeks in advance, so plan ahead. Reservations can be made ($4) by telephoning **Mistix** (tel. 800/444–7275; TDD, 800/274–7275).

OFF-ROAD CAMPING Unfortunately, it's illegal to camp anywhere but at designated campgrounds on state land. Although private landowners may let you camp, it is not common practice in California. The "Official Guide to State Parks" lists certain "on-route" camping spots that basically allow you to pull your vehicle off to the side of the road and sleep inside. Contact the California State Park System (*see* National and State Parks, *below*) to obtain a copy.

FOOD

California has become famous for California Cuisine—light, tasty, and creative dishes characterized by their fresh and native ingredients and attractive presentations. Sadly, this stuff costs bucks. Face the reality: California may consider itself the health-conscious trendsetter, but the burger joints and familiar fast-food chains that are so very American are also liberally splattered along every major route in the state.

The widest variety of cheap, tasty specialties can be found in cities with Mexican, Thai, Chinese, Indian, and other minority populations. Because of its Mexican heritage, California's Mexican food is particularly good and somewhat different from what you'll find in Mexico itself; it includes more fresh vegetables and the much-hallowed burrito. Overpriced restaurants are the norm around state parks and popular tourist destinations such as Big Sur. One way to eat cheaply is to buy your food in markets and cook at youth hostels. If you're hiking or camping, buy food in a supermarket in a well-populated area; you'll inevitably pay more in a country market if it's the only one around. If you do eat out, eat big breakfasts—they tend to be less expensive and will last you through the day. Meat dishes and alcohol can boost restaurant tabs considerably. Vegetarians will have little trouble finding meatless meals. Restaurants charge a sales tax, but markets do not. If you don't want to hit the wagon altogether, do your barhopping in the late afternoon or early evening for happy-hour specials on drinks and (sometimes) free food. The restaurant price categories used in this book are loosely based on the assumption that you are going to chow down a main course, a drink, and a cup of coffee or tea. Antacids are extra.

NATIONAL AND STATE PARKS

VISITOR INFORMATION California's national- and state-park systems encompass millions of acres of diverse natural flora and fauna. The **National Park Service** (Fort Mason, Bldg. 201, San Francisco, CA 94123, tel. 415/556–0560) has information on the five national parks in California: Lassen, Redwood, Sequoia and Kings Canyon, Yosemite, and the Channel Islands. **National monuments,** such as Joshua Tree, Muir Woods, and Pinnacles, also fall within the park service's jurisdiction, as do the three national recreation areas of Golden Gate in San Francisco, the Santa Monica Mountains near Los Angeles, and the Whiskey-Shasta-Trinity area in the northeast corner of the state. National parks are administered federally and tend to have more spectacular scenery than the state

Finding Your Way: This Map's for You

Car campers: Go with a regular road map; AAA puts out a detailed map highlighting car-accessible campgrounds—any AAA office has these babies. Backpackers: Use U.S. Geological Survey maps or Forest Service maps. The selection varies, depending on the area you want to cover. Check directly with the Forest Service or try Wilderness Press Map Center (2440 Bancroft Way, Berkeley, CA 94704, tel. 510/841–6277), which has a wide selection of both kinds.

parks. **National forests** are less protected "multiple-use land" areas, which permit camping and fishing, as well as some lumbering and off-road driving. Wilderness areas inside national forests are largely untouched by humans and offer good backpacking routes. Contact the U.S. Forest Service (Pacific Southwest Region, 630 Sansome St., San Francisco, CA 94111, tel. 415/705–2874).

The **California State Park System** (Dept. of Parks and Recreation, Box 942896, Sacramento, CA 94296, tel. 916/653–6995) is in charge of state parks, which often have either historical or geological significance and are smaller than the national parks. **Big Basin Redwoods** in Santa Cruz, the **Anza Borrego Desert** northeast of San Diego, and **Empire Mines** in the Mother Lode in Grass Valley are some of the most noteworthy.

WHEN TO GO Parks are most crowded in summer and some shut down during winter, so call ahead. The best times to go are late spring and early fall, when crowds are small and the weather is relatively mild. If you do visit in summer, avoid the tourist crunch by going during the week.

WHAT IT WILL COST National parks and state parks charge a $5–$6 entrance fee per car. National forests tend to be more lax; often there's no ranger to collect fees, just a self-pay metal bin that operates on the honor system. The $25 **Golden Eagle Pass,** available through the mail from the National Park Service (*see above*), will get you into any national park during the calendar year. The **Golden Access Passport** is a free, lifelong entry pass that exempts travelers with disabilities (and family and friends who accompany them) from all entry fees and 50% of use fees for camping and parking. With medical proof of disability, you can pick one up in person at most federally run parks and refuges.

The state parks currently sell an annual pass for $75, although the price may soon change. They also offer a 50% discount pass to visitors who are blind or disabled. Contact the California State Park System (*see above*) for an application.

STAYING HEALTHY If you're hiking or camping it's a good idea to bring a first-aid kit with the standard adhesive bandages, sterile gauze, aspirin, infection ointment (Neosporin is a good brand), an elastic bandage, hydrogen peroxide, tweezers, and sunscreen with a protection factor of 15 or more. If you plan on hiking, bring moleskin (thicker than bandages) and tape for blisters. Combat mosquitoes with insect repellent and sturdy clothes that cover as much of your skin surface as possible. Ticks inspire fear because of the Lyme disease they can transmit. Lyme disease is rare in California, but guard against it by tucking your pants into your socks and investing in tick repellent. If a tick does get to your skin, pull it out with tweezers and apply hydrogen peroxide to the wound. See a doctor as soon as possible if you can't get it out. Poison ivy and poison oak blanket much of California with their evil, oily, three-leaf stems, which cause severe itching and rash. Keep a look out for the leaves: poison ivy is shiny green in spring and rich orange and red in fall, and poison oak leaves resemble small white-oak leaves. If you happen to fall into a bush, wash your skin with soap and water and do not scratch. Although drinking water fresh from a stream will not kill you, you may want to die if you contract giardia, a microscopic protozoan that causes excruciatingly painful stomach cramps and diarrhea. Always use a water filter (*see* Camping, *above*) or boil the water for at least five minutes. Water-purification pills do not always kill giardia. Also carry water with you and drink often to avoid dehydration.

EMERGENCIES Notifying rangers of your plans—including a return date—is a good idea if you intend to go backcountry camping. Also bring a piece of extra-bright clothing so you'll be more easily spotted in an emergency. Always come prepared for the unexpected.

PROTECTING THE ENVIRONMENT So many people use (and abuse) the great outdoors that it is necessary to offer some simple guidelines. Always travel on trails and, if possible, camp on previously used sites to avoid trampling vegetation and causing soil erosion. Always pack up the garbage you create, and bury human waste 8 inches deep, at least 200 feet from water, your camp, and trails. To wash anything, use only biodegradable soap and a container. Never wash directly in a stream or lake—do it at least 50 feet from the water's edge.

The danger of forest fires is extremely high in this drought-ridden state, and forests often require that hikers obtain free fire permits at the nearest ranger station if they're bringing a stove with them. Very few allow you to build fires in the wilderness. Check to see what's permitted; policies vary from park to park. ***How to Shit in the Woods*** (Ten Speed Press, Box 7123, Berkeley, CA 94707, $5.95), by Kathleen Meyer, is a good book on a not especially pleasant but important skill.

BACKCOUNTRY PERMITS Wilderness permits are usually required if you plan any backcountry hiking. They are free and obtainable (no more than a day before you plan to hike) at the point of entry to the park. Permits outline backpacking rules and help limit the number of people on the trail.

OUTDOOR ACTIVITIES

HIKING California's beautiful scenery and temperate climate make for some of the nation's best hiking. Many trails have closed during the past year because of budget cuts, but the Sierras, the Mt. Shasta area, Big Sur, the Angeles Mountains, and the North Coast still offer many options, for one day or a month of hiking. Take a look at the ***Hiker's Guide to California*** (Falcon Press, Box 1718, Helena, MT 59624, $12) and the ***High Sierra Hiking Guide*** (*see* Getting Around, *above*).

ROCK CLIMBING In the past few years more and more Californians are trying to learn this difficult, and somewhat scary, sport. Two favorite spots are Stoney Point in Los Angeles's San Fernando Valley and Pinnacles National Monument in the Salinas Valley. For equipment, advice, and names of climbing schools contact **REI** (1338 San Pablo Ave., Berkeley CA, tel. 510/527–4140 or 800/828–5533), **Northface** (180 Post St., San Francisco, CA, tel. 415/433–3223), or the **Northface Outlet** (1238 5th St., Berkeley, CA, tel. 510/526–3530; for catalog, tel. 800/654–1751).

SKIING Assuming the drought lets up and there's some snowfall, skiing throughout the state is excellent. The Cascades and Mt. Shasta to the north, Lake Tahoe and the Sierras in the center, and the Angeles National Forest to the south have downhill and cross-country trails. Skiing is a rich person's sport, with lift tickets costing anywhere from $30 to $40 and equipment rental about $15 a day in the popular areas on weekends. To minimize costs, try going midweek, when lodges offer special deals. For more details check the ***Skier's Guide to California*** (Gulf Publishing Co., Book Division, Box 2608, Houston, TX 77252–2608), by Nadine Nardi Davidson.

In-line Skating

Plain old roller skating is a thing of the past, but shed no tears—flashier and faster in-line skates have cropped up on California bike paths, at the beach, and in parks, as well as on college campuses. The idea orignated with Minneapolis hockey players who wanted to train in the off-season. Since then the speedy skates, also known as Rollerblades, have taken the state by storm, with shops offering lessons as well as rentals. According to aficionados, in-line skating is more stable than ice skating because the amount of wheel surface touching the ground is greater than the amount of blade touching the ice. Of course the real question is: how do you stop? Merely lift the toe of one skate and press the heel-brake pad to the ground, or try the T-stop—drag one skate behind and perpendicular to the other, they say. Sounds easy, right? Good luck!

SURFING Probably one of the hardest activities to learn, surfing is the quintessential California sport, inspiring awe in both those who do, as well as those who merely observe. Beaches up and down the coast offer ample opportunity to catch a wave and a few offer lessons. To find instruction, ask at beachside equipment-renting shops (*see* individual destination chapters). One of California's biggest con jobs has been the image of blonde babes and dudes surfing and swimming in warm Pacific waters. The truth is that the water around some of California's most popular surfing towns (Santa Cruz, for example) is cold enough to freeze the balls off a brass monkey. In fact, many surfers suffer from a condition called surfer's ear in which a bone spur grows across the ear canal to protect the ear from the dangerously cold water.

WHITE-WATER RAFTING Rafting the white-water rivers of the West has become a popular and exciting thing to do in spring and summer on the Tuolumne River in Yosemite and the American River north of Sacramento. Contact the **Tuolumne Visitors Center** (tel. 800/446–1333) for information on outfitters.

● ● ● BEACHES

Ahhhh, finally the real reason to come to California: the beaches. Those who expect the palm-dotted, serene waters of the tropics will be startled to find that the majority of California's beaches have a harsh and violent beauty. Beaches from Santa Barbara to the south uphold the California image of wide and sandy expanses, prominent lifeguard stands, and loads of Beautiful People in skimpy, slinky beachwear. The water is never warm but is nonetheless swimmable in summer at famous Malibu and Newport Beach. Not as many people swim along the beaches farther north (with the exception of Santa Cruz), because water temperatures are low, and the air is often chilly and damp. Beaches along the central coast are few and far between because of the ominous cliffs of Big Sur, but it's here you'll see seals frolic and mate. The northern coast, stretching all the way to the Oregon border, is deserted, peaceful, and downright primitive compared to the south. Summertime is when most people hit the sand, but, unless your only interest is getting a tan, you can enjoy the beaches year-round. In fact, if you're heading to the central coast, summer is often the foggiest and dampest time to visit.

● ● ● CRIME AND PUNISHMENT

California's legal drinking age is 21 and is often strictly enforced in the cities and college towns. It is essential to carry picture identification such as a passport or driver's license, or you may not be allowed into places that serve alcohol. Drinking and driving is a bad idea. In addition to putting yourself and others on the road in danger, you may get pulled over by the police. If the alcohol content in your blood exceeds the legal .08% limit, you'll be arrested, your license will be suspended, and you'll face fines starting at about $400.

The Dope on Dope

Northern California is the pot-growing center of the world—or was until five years ago—but don't expect anyone to talk to you about it. Mum's the word in the Emerald Triangle (Mendocino, Humboldt, and Trinity counties) since the Campaign Against Marijuana Planting (CAMP) came to town. Ask about the Triangle, and people will more likely tag you a narc than a brother/sister in the battle to liberate the world through marijuana. If stopped in a car, you're also more likely to be searched here for possession than in other parts of the state where pot is less prevalent.

Attitudes toward drugs largely depend on the company you keep. One thing is certain: California courts do not have a positive outlook on drug use. Possession or sale of any type of illegal drug is a crime: Carrying 1 ounce of marijauna is a misdemeanor punishable by up to one year in jail. Possession or sale of any other illegal drug, such as hash, cocaine, heroin, or more than 1 ounce of marijuana is a felony and punishable by more than a year in jail, although first-time offenders are often placed in drug-treatment programs in lieu of prison. Much of what happens to you and how strictly the laws are enforced depends on the county in which you're arrested.

FURTHER READING • • •

Reference works on California are legion. *California Coastal Trails* (Capra Press), by John McKinney, covers coastal hikes. *California Coastal Access Guide* (University of California Press), put out by the California Coastal Commission, provides maps and much information on the wildlife along the coast. *The Pacific Crest Trail* (Wilderness Press) is a guide to the southern section of the trail. Also try *Brewery Adventures of the Wild West* (Red Brick Press, Reston, VA 22090), by Jack Erickson. For fictional California, try *Changing Places,* by David Lodge, about an English professor at Berkeley during the 1960s; *Run, River,* by Joan Didion; *Big Sur* and *On the Road*, by Jack Kerouac; *Day of the Locust*, by Nathanael West; *The Joy Luck Club,* by Amy Tan; and *Travels with Charley* and *The Grapes of Wrath,* by John Steinbeck.

SAN FRANCISCO 2

By Leigh Anne Jones

San Francisco, love child of the West, remains a proud oasis for all manner of people and events that diverge from the norm. Located on the tiny tip of a peninsula that separates the Pacific and San Francisco Bay, this hilly, compact, and eminently explorable city continues to go about its business through ubiquitous fog and ever-impending earthquakes, Be-Ins, Love-Ins, and one of the world's most severe AIDS epidemics, with dignity and aplomb. Whatever's hit the streets, from the drinkin' and whorin' of the gold prospectors to the living and loving of the country's largest gay and lesbian population, has left reminders of its presence in nooks and crannies all over the city. You just gotta find them: a task that will be a joy, especially if the weather holds.

Without doubt, San Francisco is one of the most beautiful cities in the world, and almost every traveler already knows what he or she wants to see—the Golden Gate Bridge, Alcatraz, cable cars, windy Lombard Street, and impossibly steep hills—and the city won't disappoint you. The views of the city from its many hills are literally breathtaking. But don't settle for just the coffee-table San Francisco, because it has a whole lot more to offer. To best explore the city, you're going to need to do some legwork and climbing. The compactness and density of San Francisco pretty much beg you to walk it; in an hour or two of wandering you'll pass from high-crime area to high-rent district to industrial wasteland, through several distinct ethnic communities, and hopefully end up somewhere where you can put your feet up and nurse a soothing drink.

You'll no doubt notice in your ramblings that the city embraces and nurtures all of its ethnic selves, which you'll see expressed in its charismatic neighborhoods, festivals, restaurants, and in various and frequent passionate political activities. Take advantage of the density and diversity. Although the genteel face of old, high society San Francisco has its own sort of charm, it's a charm that you can probably afford to indulge in only passively, kind of like reading the society pages while eating a bowl of cereal for dinner. The streets are far too full of animation, too full of goings-on that beg you to participate—from galleries and museums to demonstrations and rallies to performances and poetry readings to plain old hanging out—for you to worry that you don't have a thing to wear to the tea dance at the Sheraton Palace.

Sure, San Francisco is in California but you're going to freeze your buns off in summer unless you bring some warm clothes. As some wag (not Mark Twain) once said: "The coldest winter I ever spent was a summer in San Francisco."

Do yourself one more favor. Resist the urge to compare San Francisco to Paris or New York or Los Angeles or wherever you're from. San Francisco has a beauty, a politic, and a climate all its own, which means you're the only loser if you get all bent out of shape

San Francisco

PACIFIC OCEAN
Golden Gate Bridge
Fort Point
101
Golden Gate National Recreation Area
The Presidio
1
Baker Beach
Phelan Beach
Palace of the Legion of Honor
Land's End
Lincoln Park
Point Lobos
Cliff House
SEACLIFF
Lake St.
Clement St.
Geary Blvd.
Park Presidio Blvd.
8th Ave.
Arguello Blvd.
43rd Ave.
34th Ave.
25th Ave.
19th Ave.
Balboa St.
Turk
RICHMOND
Fulton St.
Golden Gate Park
Kennedy Dr.
Middle Dr.
Stanyan St.
Lincoln Way
Judah St.
28th St.
Funston Ave.
7th Ave.
Lawton St.
Great Highway
Noriega St.
Ortega St.
Clarendon Ave.
SUNSET
41st Ave.
Sunset Blvd.
Quintara St.
19th Ave.
Dewey Blvd.
McCoppin Square
Taraval St.
14th Ave.
Larsen Park
Vicente St.
Portola Dr.
Yerba Buena Ave.
Mt. Davidson
Stern Grove
San Francisco Zoo
Sloat Blvd
STONESTOWN
Monterey Blvd.
Junipero Serra Blvd.
Miramar Ave.
Ocean Ave.
Harding Park
Lake Merced
Skyline Blvd.
Lake Merced Blvd.
San Francisco State Univ.
Font Blvd.
Holloway Ave.
Garfield St.
Plymouth Ave.
Brotherhood Way
N
0
1 mile
0
1 km

San Francisco

San Francisco Bay
Pier 39
Fort Mason
Marina Green
Fisherman's Wharf
MARINA
Bay St.
NORTH BEACH
Coit Tower
Columbus Ave.
TELEGRAPH HILL
RUSSIAN HILL
Hyde St.
Lombard St.
101
(tunnel)
Grant St.
Powell St.
FINANCIAL DISTRICT
San Francisco-Oakland Bay Bridge
80
Broadway
Washington St.
PACIFIC HEIGHTS
California St.
Sacramento St.
NOB HILL
UNION SQUARE
Post St.
Geary St.
Pine St.
Bush St.
Gough St.
Van Ness Ave.
Laguna St.
Divisadero St.
1st St.
2nd St.
3rd St.
Mission St.
4th St.
5th St.
6th St.
Turk St.
JAPAN TOWN
Steiner St.
Franklin St.
Market St.
SOMA
Golden Gate Ave.
Fulton St.
Fell St.
Folsom
Harrison
Bryant
Brannan St.
Townsend St.
280
10th St.
9th St.
7th St.
WESTERN ADDITION
Central Skyway
Buena Vista Park
Duboce Ave.
Castro St.
17th St.
Potrero Ave.
Mariposa St.
Central Basin
3rd St.
Indiana St.
Pennsylvania Ave.
Harrison St.
MISSION
Mission Dolores Park
POTRERO
Market St.
CASTRO
20th St.
Dolores St.
Guerrero St.
Mission St.
Van Ness Ave.
San Francisco General Hospital
Army St.
25th St.
Islais Cr. Channel
India Basin
Diamond St.
Oakdale Ave.
Bosworth St.
Fwy.
Quesada Ave.
Hunter's Point
Silver Ave.
GLEN PARK
Felton Ave.
Excelsior Ave.
Alemany Blvd.
Mission St.
Persia Ave.
Moscow St.
John McLaren Park
Mansell St.
Gilman Ave.
Jamestown Ave.
South Basin
Candlestick Park
France Ave.
Geneva Ave.
TO COW PALACE

because you can't find a good Philly cheese steak or because the water's too cold to swim in or the fog is obscuring your view. This is the city that offered the world the first fortune cookie, the Beat generation, the United Nations, *and* topless dancing—so whaddaya have to be homesick about?

"I have seen purer liquors, better seegars, finer tobacco, truer guns and pistols, larger dirks and bowie knives, and prettier cortezans, here in San Francisco than in any place I have ever visited; and it is my unbiased opinion that California can and does furnish the best bad things that are obtainable in America."—Hinton Helper, in *Land of Gold,* 1855.

ORIENTATION Let's begin in a most unlikely spot, one every visitor should know about: the **Tenderloin District,** an area also known as the crime capital of San Francisco, roughly bordered by Van Ness Avenue and Market, Post, and Powell streets. **Union Square** (San Francisco's premier shopping and luxury hotel district), the **Theater District,** and the **Financial District** all sit to the north and northeast, while the **Civic Center** sits just southwest, like several precious gems clustered around a chunk of coal. To the north of downtown are **Chinatown** and the Italian neighborhood of **North Beach.**

Heading north from Union Square are **Nob Hill** and **Russian Hill,** two well-established, upscale San Francisco neighborhoods where at least the views are still free. **Pacific Heights** and the **Marina District,** to the west, provide the land for the homes of San Francisco's nouveau riche—Pacific Heights is reputedly the neighborhood most densely populated with professionals in the country. (That's probably why you came here, right?) The famous tourist attraction **Fisherman's Wharf** takes up the northern waterfront of the city, and **Fort Mason** and the **Army Presidio** lie to the west of that. To the south span the hipper and more diverse neighborhoods you'll probably want to wander around and explore, areas like **SOMA** (the South-of-Market area), the **Mission** and **Castro** districts, and **Noe Valley.**

To the west of downtown and the aforementioned districts lie the **Western Addition,** home to low-income housing projects and Japantown, the enormous and lush **Golden Gate Park,** and the perennially counter-cultural **Haight-Ashbury.** Here, too, are the neighborhoods known as **"the Avenues"**—the vast Richmond District to the northwest and Sunset District to the southwest (where you probably won't go much unless you get lost).

Basics

A good all-purpose source of information is the front matter of the San Francisco Yellow Pages, called the **Access Pages,** which feature listings for different community organizations, public transit information, maps, famous attractions, etc. The best map of the city, available at most bookstores, convenience stores, liquor stores, and MUNI stations, is the **MUNI Street and Transit Map,** which shows all transit lines and labels all the neighborhoods in the city.

AMERICAN EXPRESS American Express has four offices in San Francisco that offer travel services, including personal check-cashing for members. *Main Office: 237 Post St., tel. 415/981–5533. For lost or stolen American Express traveler's checks, tel. 800/968–8300.*

DOCTORS AND DENTISTS

REFERRALS If you need help choosing a doctor, call the **San Francisco Medical Society Physician Referral Service** (tel. 415/567–6230). Dentist referrals are available through the **San Francisco Dental Society** (tel. 415/421–1435).

CLINICS **The Haight-Ashbury Free Medical Clinic** offers medical service with fees based on your ability to pay. *558 Clayton, tel. 415/431–1714. Open weekdays 1–4 and Mon.–Thurs. 6–8:30.*

Access Health Care offers drop-in medical care with no membership required at three San Francisco locations: *Davies Medical Center, Castro St. and Duboce, tel. 415/565–6600; 26 California St., in the Financial District, tel. 415/397–2881; 1604 Union St., in Pacific Heights, tel. 415/775–7766. Clinic Information: tel. 415/922–2377.*

St. Luke's Neighborhood Clinic (3555 Army St., tel. 415/641–6500) will treat uninsured outpatients at low cost.

Planned Parenthood clinics administer pregnancy tests, gynecological exams, birth control, and abortions; treat sexually transmitted diseases (STDs); and offer free, anonymous AIDS tests. Clinics are located throughout the Bay Area, with Civic Center (815 Eddy St., tel. 415/441–5454) and Financial District (582 Market St., tel. 415/982–0707) locations in San Francisco. Sliding-scale fees are based on ability to pay; the clinics accept Visa and MasterCard.

EMERGENCIES Dial 911 for all emergency **police, fire, ambulance** and **paramedic** services. For a **24-Hour Crisis Line,** dial 415/777–9696. Several San Francisco hospitals operate 24-hour emergency rooms, including **San Francisco General** in the Mission District (1001 Potrero Ave., tel. 415/821–8111; TDD/TTY 415/621–0953.)

Emergency shelter and clothing are available from the Central City Hospitality House in the Tenderloin (146 Leavenworth St., tel. 415/776–2103). Free meals are served to the needy by St. Anthony's Dining Room (45 Jones, tel. 415/241–2690).

LUGGAGE STORAGE In the city, you can store your bags on the third floor of the **Transbay Bus Terminal** at First and Mission streets (tel. 415/495–1569) for $1.50 per day. You pay for one day up front, then pay for subsequent days when you pick up your luggage.

You can also store your bags at the San Francisco Airport in the International terminal, near the Air France ticket desk (tel. 415/877–0422). Charges are based on the size of the luggage (an average bag runs $3.50 per day). There are also lockers available in the airport that cost $1 (four quarters). These are 15 by 24 inches, and 31 inches deep. Though technically just for 24-hour use, you can use them longer if you put $2 in the locker, with your luggage, for each additional day you need. Remember to do this before you lock it, since it'll cost you another dollar to reopen the locker.

PHARMACIES To get prescriptions filled after hours, head for one of the chain stores. **Walgreens** offers 24-hour prescription service at two San Francisco locations: 498 Castro St., tel. 415/861–3136; 3201 Divisadero St., tel. 415/931–6417.

PUBLICATIONS San Francisco's only daily morning newspaper is the ***Chronicle;*** its afternoon "competition" is the ***Examiner.*** The two produce a single Sunday edition, which you may want to purchase if only for the "pink pages"—the "Datebook" section that lists a vast number of the cultural events taking place in the Bay Area in the coming week.

Alternative free papers include ***S.F. Weekly,*** an arts and entertainment guide, and the San Francisco ***Bay Guardian,*** another useful compendium of cultural listings, general-interest features, political commentary, and personal ads that can provide hours of entertainment for you and your friends.

TELEPHONES The area code for San Francisco is 415. The East Bay—Alameda County, including Oakland and Berkeley, and Contra Costa County—uses 510. The San Jose area uses the 408 area code and the wine country, 707. A list of area codes, country codes, time differences, etc., is printed in the front matter of the telephone book white pages.

HELPFUL NUMBERS **Time** (tel. 415/767–8900). **Highway conditions** (tel. 415/557–0305). **Movie listings** (tel. 415/777–FILM).

TOURIST INFORMATION **San Francisco Convention and Visitors Bureau.** Write in advance of your trip to receive free information about hotels, restaurants, and shopping. *201 3rd St., 3 blocks from Montgomery BART, Suite 900, 94103, tel. 415/974–6900. Open weekdays 8:30–5.*

Once in San Francisco, stop in for maps and brochures at the city's **Tourist Information Center** in the lower level of Hallidie Plaza, next to the Powell Street BART station at Powell Street and Market Street. *Tel. 415/391–2000. Open weekdays 8:30–5:30.*

Also try **Traveler's Aid,** which gives transportation directions, information on housing, and other special services for the traveler. *201 1st St. at Mission, inside the bus terminal, tel. 415/255–2252; 1049 Market St., Suite 500; and at the airport, tel. 415/877–0118.*

● ● ● COMING AND GOING

BY PLANE The major air hub is **San Francisco International Airport (SFO)** (tel. 415/761–0800), although you can also come in to Oakland International (OAK) (*see* Coming and Going, under Oakland in Chapter 3, San Francisco Bay Area), or San Jose Municipal (SJC). San Francisco International is about 10 miles south of San Francisco on U.S. 101. Major carriers to SFO include **United, Delta, USAir, Continental,** as well as many national airlines from all over the world. Contact individual carriers for specific flight information. The airport has luggage storage (*see* Luggage Storage, *above*) and two currency exchange offices, both located in the International Terminal: **Bank of America** (tel. 415/877–0264; open daily 7 AM–11 PM) and **Thomas Cook** (tel. 415/583–4029; open daily 6:15 AM–10:45 PM).

AIRPORT TRANSPORT A metered taxi from SFO to downtown San Francisco costs about $30 and takes 35–45 minutes. ***The Airporter*** (tel. 415/673–2432), a private shuttle

Gay Publications

***Bay Times*, the most articulate of San Francisco's free newspapers, comes out biweekly and has a left-of-center orientation. It's exclusively for the gay, lesbian, and bisexual communities, and serves as an information network for different groups that cater to gays, lesbians, and bisexuals. It lists clubs, 12-step meetings, political clubs, dance clubs, gay locksmiths, mechanics, lawyers, dentists, chiropractors, etc., and, of course, personal ads.**

***Bay Area Reporter*, San Francisco's left-of-center gay newsweekly, appears on Thursdays, and has excellent political reporting, personals, a good arts and style section, and several excellent columnists, including Rachel Pepper.**

***The Sentinel*, the Bay Area's right-wing queer newspaper is owned and operated by Ray Chaulker, who also owns and operates the Rawhide II, a country-and-western bar. The paper often serves as Chaulker's own forum. A recent series of articles titled "Is Feminism Hurting Gay Men?" illustrates the politics of the publication. The paper is known for better fact-checking than most free newspapers in San Francisco, has a "This Week in Leather" column, and a complete listing of dance clubs and bars. It's published every Thursday.**

Besides these comparatively mainstream publications, you also have access to a wide variety of queerzines, published by special-interest groups (that can consist of as few as one member) for a special-interest audience. A Different Light (489 Castro St., tel. 415/431–0891), San Francisco's premier queer bookstore, has an impressive queerzine section, including such titles as Brains, the magazine for men turned on by intellect; Up Our Butts, On Our Rags, On Our Backs, the lesbian porn mag; Bear, the magazine for big, hairy, husky men and the men who love them; and Pomo Momo Homos, the magazine published by Queer Nation Utah.

bus service, runs between downtown San Francisco and the airport stopping at several hotels along the way; it runs about every 20 minutes between 5:30 AM and 10:30 PM for around $8 one-way, $12 round-trip. Another option is to take one of the private shuttles that pick you up or drop you off right at your door. These minivans leave frequently, usually when they're full, from the upstairs level at the airport. One-way fare is about $11. Shuttle companies include **Super Shuttle** (tel. 415/558–8500), **Yellow** (tel. 415/282–7433), and **Franciscos Adventure** (tel. 415/821–0903).

The way to cut your travel costs between the airport and the city by about 90% is to take the **SamTrans** (tel. 800/660–4287) bus lines **7B** and **7F.** Both travel from the airport to the Transbay Terminal in downtown San Francisco. They stop every half-hour from about 5:45 AM to 1:15 AM; you can catch them outside Delta or United on the departure level of the airport. Bus 7B costs 85¢ and takes 55 minutes; while Bus 7F is an express line that costs $1.75 and takes 35 minutes. On Bus 7F, you are restricted to only a small, carry-on bag, but there is no luggage restriction on Bus 7B.

BY TRAIN Several **Amtrak** (tel. 800/USA–RAIL) lines, including the *Zephyr* from Chicago via Denver, and the *Coast Starlight,* traveling between San Diego and Seattle, as well as local trains to Sacramento and the San Joaquin Valley, stop at the Oakland station (1807 Wood St.), across the bay from San Francisco. From here you can catch a connecting Amtrak bus that will drop you at the Transbay Terminal at First and Mission streets in San Francisco. Sample fares: Seattle–San Francisco: $153 one-way; Los Angeles–Oakland: $75 one-way.

REGIONAL TRAIN LINES ***CalTrain,*** a commuter train that runs daily between San Francisco and San Jose, stops at a number of peninsula cities along the way such as Mountain View, Sunnyvale, and Santa Clara. During noncommuting hours, you can wait an hour or two for a train, so definitely call in advance for the schedule (tel. 415/557–8661 or 800/558–8661). CalTrain runs from 5 AM to 10 PM, and the CalTrain Station is at Forth and Townsend streets.

BY BUS **Green Tortoise Adventure Travel** (Box 24459, San Francisco, 94124, tel. 415/821–0803 or 800/227–4766) is *the* cheap, fun alternative to humdrum bus travel. Only on Green Tortoise is your trip to Seattle accompanied by a cookout and skinny dipping on their own private piece of land. Green Tortoise's buses are equipped with sleeping pads, kitchens, and stereos to make the ride comfortable as they crawl their way to cities up and down the West Coast. Reservations are recommended, especially for the weekly trips between San Francisco and Seattle ($59 one way).

Greyhound-Trailways buses travel to and from San Francisco all day long; major destinations include Seattle (three times daily, $110 one-way), Los Angeles (eight times daily, $43 one-way), and Portland (five times daily, $93 one-way). The area around the station is dark and deserted at night, so it's probably not a bad idea to plan to arrive during the day. It's on the third floor of the Transbay Bus Terminal (1st and Mission Sts., tel. 415/558–6789).

REGIONAL BUS LINES **AC Transit** (tel. 510/839–2882) buses travel between San Francisco and the East Bay (Alameda and Contra Costa counties) 24 hours a day, while **SamTrans** (tel. 800/660–4287) services San Francisco from San Mateo County, south of San Francisco. **Golden Gate Transit** (tel. 415/332–6600) comes in from Marin and Sonoma counties, across the Golden Gate Bridge. Fares and schedules vary.

BY CAR From the north, you'll reach San Francisco via U.S. 101, which will shoot you right over the Golden Gate bridge (for the low, low price of $3) and into the city. From the south, you can either head up I–5 to Route 580 west, up U.S. 101, or up Route 1, the Pacific Coast Highway. From the east, you'll take either Route 580 or I–80 west, over the Oakland Bay Bridge.

COMMUTER LANE HITCHHIKING Since car pools of three or more don't pay tolls on the Bay Bridge, wily types hang out at **Park and Ride** locations in the East Bay or the Emeryville bus nexus at Yerba Buena and San Pablo avenues during the rush hour, and catch a ride with commuters, paying nothing or only a small amount. It's a win-win situation.

GETTING AROUND

If you're sticking around for a long time, consider getting a **Fast Pass,** which allows you unlimited travel within San Francisco on MUNI and AC Transit buses, the cable cars, and on BART, the subway system. The $30 pass is good for one calendar month and is available from any Safeway grocery store in the city.

BY SUBWAY Relatively clean and quiet, **BART** (Bay Area Rapid Transit, tel. 415/788–BART or 510/465–2278) is a smooth subway system somewhat reminiscent of Disneyland's Monorail. It serves San Francisco and Daly City as well as parts of the East Bay on a four-prong line that reaches 34 stations. BART runs daily until midnight and starts up again at 4 AM on weekdays, 6 AM on weekends. Schedules are available at the stations, or you can call ahead to plot your journey. Expect trains every 15–20 minutes. The cost of a ticket depends on the length of the journey. A half-hour ride from Civic Center to Berkeley costs $1.80. Tickets discounted by 10% are available for children, seniors, and the disabled.

BY BUS **MUNI** (tel. 415/673–MUNI), the main bus and streetcar service, covers the city with 78 lines. It runs as often as every five minutes in certain well-traveled parts of town. Between 1 AM and 5 AM, service is cut back to just 12 lines. As of this writing, the adult fare was 85¢, but the mayor had proposed a hike. Ask for a transfer when you get on, as it's good for two additional rides within 90 minutes. Short-term "Passport" passes are available that allow unlimited access to MUNI for one day ($6), three days ($10), and one week ($15).

BY TAXI You can hail a cab in San Francisco, but you may end up standing in the street for hours. Most residents phone for cabs. All taxis are metered, but you may be able to negotiate a flat rate to the airport at the discretion of the driver. **Veteran's Cab** (tel. 415/552–1300), for example, charges $1.70 at the drop, 30¢ every 1/6 mile thereafter, and 30¢ for every minute of waiting time or traffic delay. Don't forget to tip the driver.

BY CABLE CAR Cable cars are pretty and fun, and you should take them at least once if only to feel like you're in a Rice-A-Roni commercial. They run at a pace right out of the early 1900s, however, so if you're into zooming around the city you'd better take the bus. At $2 a ride, the fare is somewhat prohibitive, but you can ride for free using many of the discount passes available. Cable cars are useful only for getting around central San Francisco. For great views, take the California Street cable car or the Hyde and Powell Street line. On the latter, you get a good gander at Alcatraz and pass right by Lombard Street, the crookedest street in the world. Don't be surprised if the conductor stops his car at the corner of Hyde and Jackson to run in **U-Lee Restaurant** (tel. 415/771–9774) to place an order for Chinese food.

Slip Slidin' Away

In New York, you curb your dog; in San Francisco, you curb your car. If you park on a grade of 3% or more, you must "curb" your tires—block them against the curb—and set the emergency brake or you'll get a ticket. The idea is to keep the car from rolling down the hill and wreaking serious havoc. Here's how to do it: If the front of your car is going uphill, "heel" your front wheels by turning them out so that the back of the tire hits the curb. Parking downhill, the wheels should be "toed"—turned in so the front of the tire is against the curb.

BY CAR Common frustrations of driving to or around the city include, among other things, continuously rising tolls on the Golden Gate and Bay bridges, traffic jams at any time of the day or night, and a notable lack of places to leave the damn thing once you've miraculously arrived with nary a scratch or a nervous breakdown to your name. If you learned to drive just about any place else, the combination of hills and traffic will present a formidable challenge to both your driving skills and your bravado. You would not be the first individual to shudder visibly as you sit at a stop light on the very crest of a steep hill in a temperamental stick shift, staring in the rear-view mirror at the car you expect to cream as soon as you lift your foot off the brake. If you ever find a parking space, it's likely to be on the side of a sheer precipice. If you manage to park parallel to the slope, congratulations—now just open the door and you will fall out of your car. If you are faced with the hideous prospect of parallel parking on a slope that looks like the north Face of the Eiger, look at your insurance policy and then panic. Once you have succeeded in wedging your car into the space, curb your wheels and (if you're in a stick shift) leave the car in gear (see info box). If this all seems too much for you, there are many garages and lots that offer parking by the hour, or all day. Pay close attention to the rates, as they can get quite steep—especially around prime tourist country like Fisherman's Wharf. For the Union Square area, you can expect to find a parking place at the large **Sutter-Stockton Garage** (330 Sutter St., tel. 415/982–8371). They charge a graduated rate—$2.50 for three hours, $8 for five hours, and $17.25 for all day. Welcome to California.

Where to Sleep

On average, hotel rooms in San Francisco cost more than $100 a night but, depending on your standards, you should be able to find a bed for anywhere between $10 (at one of the youth hostels) and $50 (for a basic but well-located motel room). Try to make reservations if you're especially concerned about saving money, especially from July through September. Many of the lowest-priced hotels are located downtown and in the Tenderloin. The many budget motels that line Lombard Street in the Marina District are better suited for travelers with cars, although they're only about a 15-minute MUNI ride (Bus 76) from downtown. Rates usually go up during the tourist season; off-season travelers should not hesitate to ask for a lower or weekend rate, especially if the place looks deserted (check the number of cars in the parking lot).

DOWNTOWN

UNDER $35 **Olympic Hotel.** A good, good deal in a good, good location near the Powell Street BART station and Union Square. The clean, smallish rooms are basic and functional. Reserve at least a week in advance in the summer. Single or double with hall bath: $30 plus tax; with private bath, $40 plus tax. *140 Mason St., at Ellis, tel. 415/982–5010.*

Temple Hotel. Small, tidy rooms located a few blocks south of North Beach. Singles with hall bath are $30, doubles $35; rooms with private bath also available for $10 more. *469 Pine St., between Montgomery and Kearny, tel. 415/781–2565. Montgomery BART.*

UNDER $50 **Adelaide Inn.** This is a homey place that's popular with Europeans. Guests share hall baths. Rates include a Continental breakfast, and some kitchen facilities are available. Singles run $32–$38, doubles $42–$46, depending on size of room and availability. *5 Isadora Duncan La., off Taylor St., tel. 415/441–2261. Bus 38 or 38 L from Montgomery St. BART.*

Grant Plaza. Situated near the entrance to Chinatown, this hotel offers a true bargain for a group of four: two double beds for $62. That's comparable to hostel rates, but these admittedly small rooms have private baths, color TVs, and phones. Otherwise you'll pay $45 for one person, $49 for two. *465 Grant Ave., tel. 415/434–3883, 800/472–6899, or 800/472–6805 in CA. From 3rd and Market walk up Kearny to Bush, turn left to Grant.*

Pensione San Francisco. This well-located establishment near the Civic Center has managed to retain some character without getting all bougie and expensive. Rooms

Downtown San Francisco Lodging

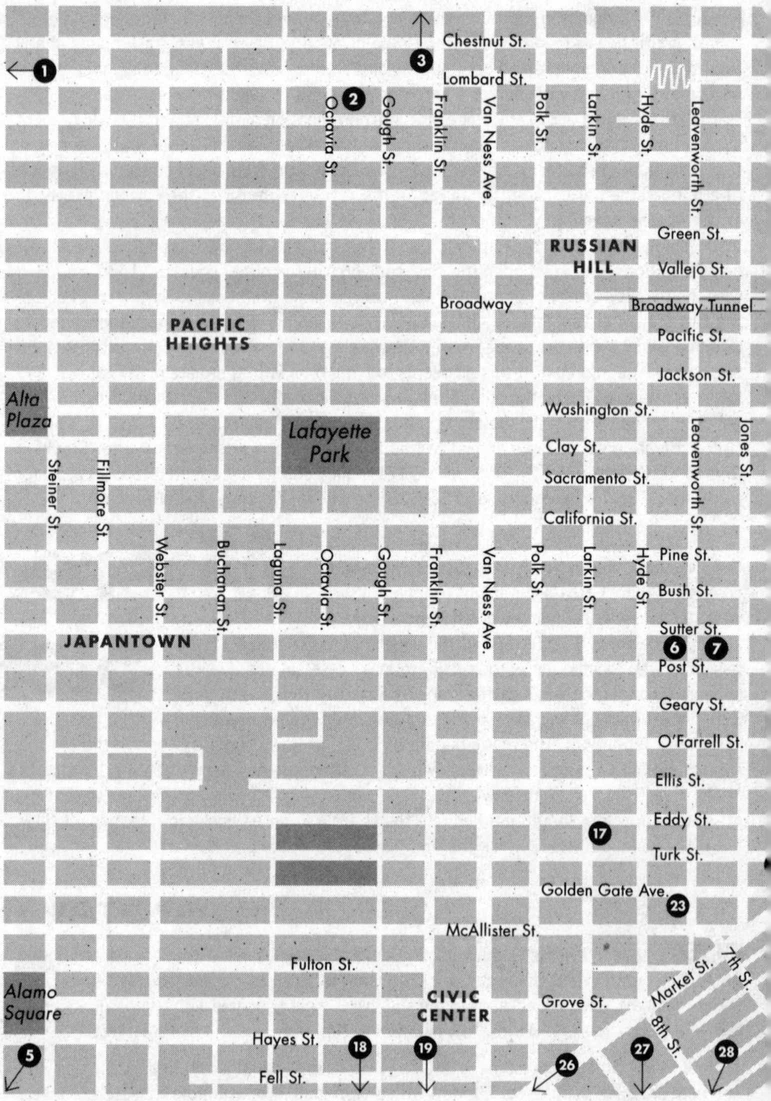

Chestnut St.
Lombard St.
Octavia St.
Gough St.
Franklin St.
Van Ness Ave.
Polk St.
Larkin St.
Hyde St.
Leavenworth St.
Green St.
Vallejo St.
RUSSIAN HILL
Broadway
Broadway Tunnel
PACIFIC HEIGHTS
Pacific St.
Jackson St.
Alta Plaza
Lafayette Park
Washington St.
Clay St.
Sacramento St.
California St.
Jones St.
Steiner St.
Fillmore St.
Webster St.
Buchanan St.
Laguna St.
Pine St.
Bush St.
Sutter St.
JAPANTOWN
Post St.
Geary St.
O'Farrell St.
Ellis St.
Eddy St.
Turk St.
Golden Gate Ave.
McAllister St.
Fulton St.
Alamo Square
CIVIC CENTER
Grove St.
Market St.
7th St.
8th St.
Hayes St.
Fell St.

Adelaide Inn, **14**
The Alexander Inn, **20**
Amsterdam, **11**
Beresford Arms, **7**
Budget Inn, **18**
Campton Place Hotel, **30**
Cornell Hotel, **12**
David's Hotel, **16**
European Guest House, **27**
Fairmont Hotel, **8**
Grand Hyatt San Francisco, **29**
Grant Plaza Hotel, **22**
Holiday Inn Financial, **13**
Hyatt Regency Hotel, **34**
Interclub Globe, **19**
Marina Motel, **1**
Mark Hopkins Hotel, **9**
1906 Mission, **28**
Olympic Hotel, **24**
Pensione International, **6**
Pensione San Francisco, **26**
Phoenix Hotel, **17**
San Francisco International Youth Hostel, **3**
San Francisco Marriott at Moscone Center, **31**
San Francisco RV Park, **35**
San Remo Hotel, **4**
Sheehan, **15**
Sheraton-Palace Hotel, **33**
Stanford Court Hotel, **10**
Temple Hotel, **32**
Town House Motel, **2**
University of California, San Francisco, **5**
The Westin St. Francis Hotel, **21**
YMCA Central Branch, **23**
Youth Hostel Centrale, **25**

Downtown San Francisco Lodging

feature little decorative touches and refrigerators, and the shared bathroom facilities are clean. Continental breakfast is served in a sunny eating area that has a TV. Reserve at least a week in advance during the high season. Rates are $49 for a single, $55 for a double; $10 less October–March. *1668 Market St., tel. 415/864–1271.*

YMCA Central Branch. The Golden Gate YMCA offers functional, clean single rooms downtown in the Tenderloin, with a complimentary Continental breakfast and use of the gym facilities included. Bathrooms are shared. Singles are $31.70; doubles $45. Four less expensive beds are reserved for students as a "hostel" type of thing, but these are often booked up so don't count on getting one. A 10% discount is available to ISIC card holders. *220 Golden Gate Ave., tel. 415/885–0460. From Civic Center BART walk up Hyde to Golden Gate, turn right. Café, TV room, wheelchair access.*

Pensione International. You'll find small, clean rooms with character here and the management is very helpful. It's about a 10-minute walk from Union Square. Rates range from $45 to $55 for a single or double with a private bath, $35–$40 for a shared bath; about $10 cheaper during the low season. *875 Post St., tel. 415/775–3344.*

Budget Inn. A good solution to the parking dilemma around the Civic Center; here, there's free parking for all. $45 for a single, $55 for a double. *111 Page St., at Gough St., tel. 415/626–4155. Civic Center BART.*

UNDER $75 **The Alexander Inn.** This clean, well-located establishment two blocks from Union Square offers relatively sunny rooms, all with private bath, color TV, and a coffee maker for $60–$70 for a single/double, $79 for a triple. Starting in about April, you should reserve at least a week in advance. *415 O'Farrell St., tel. 415/928–6800 or 800/843–8709.*

Amsterdam. For a bed-and-breakfast in a Victorian that's two blocks from Nob Hill, this is a sweet bargain: $65 for two people, $59 for one. Rates are lower off-season. Rooms have cable TV and most have private baths, although you pay less to share a bath. There's a cozy reading room. *749 Taylor St., tel. 415/673–3277. Take Bus 2, 3, or 4 from Montgomery St. BART.*

Beresford Arms. This is a nice Victorian hotel with extras. Some rooms have kitchenettes, though these go for $95; standard rooms ($69 single; $79 double) have queen-size beds and refrigerators. They even allow dogs with prior approval and a security deposit. *701 Post St., tel. 415/673–2600. Take Bus 2, 3, or 4 from Montgomery St. BART, get off at Jones St., walk 1 block to Post.*

Cornell. This place is like a small, family French-style hotel. Singles are $55–$65, doubles $65–$80. A few rooms with a shared bath go for even less: $45 for one person, $55 for two, and they include breakfast. They also offer weekly rates that include five dinners and seven breakfasts for $385 for one, $465 for two. The elevator is very small. *715 Bush St., tel. 415/421–3154. Take Bus 81X from Transbay Terminal.*

Sheehan. Most guests share a bath, since only 20 of the 65 rooms have private baths. The building was formerly a YWCA, so guests have free use of a gym and swimming pool. $55 for a single, $65 for a double, $75 for a triple. *620 Sutter St., at Mason St., tel. 415/775–6500 or 800/848–1529. Take Bus 2, 3, or 4 from Montgomery St. BART.*

UNDER $100 **David's Hotel.** The rooms are small but spotless, bright, and tasteful; the best part of staying at David's, however, is undoubtedly the free breakfast-and-dinner deal from the Jewish delicatessen downstairs. And this is some good food: Breakfast is all you can eat—any item on the menu—and dinner is your choice of several entrées, all of which makes the room rates seem extraordinarily economical. Single: $79 plus tax, double: $89 plus tax. Located on Theater Row across from the Four Seasons, David's also provides free airport transportation if you stay two nights or more. One floor of the hotel is reserved for nonsmokers. *480 Geary St., tel. 415/771–1600 or 800/524–1888. From Powell St. BART walk up Powell to Geary, turn left. Wheelchair access.*

Phoenix Hotel. Located in the nether regions of the Tenderloin, the Phoenix has built a reputation among young hipsters. Bands like the Red Hot Chili Peppers, NRBQ, Simple Minds, and Living Colour stay here, and despite the vague, "tropical Southwest" design scheme, the rooms feature original work by Bay Area artists. A special legal exemption had to be obtained for the Phoenix's swirling black-tile pool bottom. In-room massage/body work is available, and the hotel is joined at the hip, as it were, to Miss Pearl's Jam House (*see* Food, *below*). High-season rates: $84 for a single, $89 for a double. Rates go down as much as $20 in the winter, depending on demand. Some bathrooms are not wheelchair accessible; call ahead with wheelchair dimensions. *601 Larkin St. at Eddy St., tel. 415/776–1380. Take Bus 31 from Embarcadero, Montgomery, or Powell BART, get off at Larkin St.*

SURROUNDING NEIGHBORHOODS

UNDER $15 **1906 Mission Hotel.** This shabby but clean pension-turned-residential-hotel in the Mission District has a limited number of rooms for tourists from April to September. Solo women travelers should stay elsewhere: The area, which is a lot of fun during the day, can be intimidating after dark. Here's the good part: Singles are $12, doubles $20, weekly $85. *1906 Mission St., tel. 415/864–3629.*

UNDER $55 **San Remo Hotel.** Close to the Wharf and North Beach, this is the cheapest place you'll find in this price-inflated area. You save by taking a smaller room than average and sharing a bathroom. Singles are $45; doubles $55. Super-bargain weekly rates (for individuals only) are $100–$115; for weekly rates you must fill out an application in advance. *2237 Mason St. at Chestnut and Bay St., tel. 415/776–8688. From 4th and Market, take Bus 30 to Mason St.*

Marina Motel. A standout bargain among Lombard Street motels, it has a Spanish-style stucco facade. Singles are $44.50, doubles $49.50; prices are slightly higher during the peak season. About half the rooms have kitchens. *2576 Lombard St., between Broderick and Divisadero Sts., tel. 415/921–9406. Take Bus 76 from Montgomery St. BART. Parking.*

Town House Motel. With low rates, free parking, and pleasant surroundings, this is a good bet in the Marina District. Singles are $50, doubles $55. *1650 Lombard St., tel. 415/885–5163 or 800/255–1516. Take Bus 76 from Montgomery St. BART.*

HOSTELS

You should definitely make reservations before you arrive in San Francisco. American Youth Hostel-affiliated hostels offer a certain welcome predictability.

San Francisco International Youth Hostel. This is the only AYH-affiliated hostel in San Francisco, and it's in a beautifully scenic setting near the waterfront. The rules and regulations are tedious and complex, however, so pay close attention: It's almost impossible to stay here unless you reserve in advance, but no in-person reservations are accepted. If space is available, you can register between 7 AM and 2 PM (get here early). The cost is $12 per person, $6 for those under 18 with parent. By phone, you may charge your first night's stay as a nonrefundable deposit on Visa or MasterCard at least 48 hours in advance. By mail, send the cost of your first night's stay at least two weeks prior to the date of your arrival and include the names and gender of the people in your party, as well as the dates you intend to stay. During the summer there is a five-night maximum stay. Rooms are inaccessible between 10 AM and 4:30 PM, although there is limited access to the hostel between 10 and 2. Curfew is midnight (lights out), but guests are admitted to the hostel until 2 AM. You are expected to perform a chore each day, and smoking is not allowed. There are also AYH hostels nearby in Sausalito and Point Reyes, and further south in Montara and Pescadero. *Bldg. 240, Box A, Fort Mason 94123, tel. 415/771–7277. From Transbay Terminal take MUNI Bus 30. Midnight curfew, laundry, free bike and luggage storage, kitchen, common room.*

Interclub Globe Hostel. Reserved for international travelers (you can be American, but there should be fresh ink on your passport, i.e., you've just been overseas), this South-of-Market hostel has fewer rules and a warmer, more relaxed atmosphere than some of the others. It's four to a room, and each room has a bathroom. Cost is $12 per person with a $10 key deposit. There's no preset maximum stay, and there's one no-smoking floor. You can bring in your own groceries to cook in the kitchen, but they also provide low-cost meals (about $2–$4). *10 Hallam Place near Folsom St., between 7th and 8th Sts., tel. 415/431–0540. Civic Center BART. No curfew, laundry, kitchen.*

European Guest House. It's dorm-style living here at $12 per person, so expect to share your area with three other people. *763 Minna St., near Mission St. between 8th and 9th Sts., tel. 415/861–6634. From Civic Center BART walk down 8th for 2 blocks, take a right. No curfew, laundry, kitchen.*

Youth Hostel Centrale. If you look up the word "dive" in the dictionary, you'll find a definition of this hostel. A bright new awning only amplifies the surrounding squalor, so weigh carefully the pros and cons of spending $20 for one person, and $27 for two. The rooms are private, but you share a bath. Wash your hands after you touch the doorknob. *166 Turk St., tel. 415/346–7835. Powell St. BART.*

● ● ● CAMPGROUNDS

San Francisco RV Park. This is as close as you'll get to a campground, though its South-of-Market location is more concrete jungle than KOA. You can't pitch a tent here, but you can hook up your recreational vehicle at one of the 200 sites. *250 King St., tel. 415/986–8730. 200 sites. Store, laundromat, propane, city tours, and car rental available.*

Food

San Francisco, city of more than 4,000 restaurants, beckons gourmands and garbage gums alike. Visitors and locals are offered quality, diversity, reasonable prices, and a seemingly endless selection of restaurant reviews, dutifully pasted up in the window of almost every restaurant in the city. Don't assume that this little strip of paper means that the restaurant is any good, however. A large number of them are authored by Herb Caen, a local gossip columnist whose forte is gossip about old rich people and reminiscences about dead rich people, thus making his authority about culinary matters somewhat suspect. You'll have better luck following the advice of local reviewers like Jim Wood, who writes for the *Examiner.* Be sure to check the date of the review, since these writers frequently update their impressions, and restaurants regularly change hands and chefs. A restaurant owner is unlikely to replace that good review with a later one if it's bad: Ten-year-old praise tells you only that the restaurant was good 10 years ago.

Those who don't have anything better to do will argue endlessly about which is the best restaurant in San Francisco, "the best" being gauged by criteria like attentive service, pleasant ambience, and aesthetically pleasing presentation. Among those vying for this title: **Masa's** (648 Bush St., tel. 415/989–7154; dinner for two: about $175), **Postrio** (545 Post St., tel. 415/776–7825; dinner for two: about $95), and **Stars** (150 Redwood Alley tel. 415/861–7827; dinner for two: about $90). Just think, you'd only have to sell about a gallon of plasma to take your sweetie to dinner the right way in San Francisco.

Just one San Francisco neighborhood is likely to boast more good restaurants than exist in many American cities. Variety abounds—you'll be able to sample ethnic cuisines you've never tasted before, in addition to local specialties like nouvelle and California cuisines. One way to keep dining costs low is to make lunch the biggest meal of the day, and thus take advantage of the cheap lunch specials available all over town.

● ● ● DOWNTOWN

Downtown abounds with the old, classic restaurants that evoke S.F.'s Golden Years and lunch counters that still feature Blue Plate Specials and chocolate malts. There are, of course, new yuppified haunts sprinkled in that cater to a high-rolling Financial District clientele.

UNDER $5 **International Food Fair.** It's a small world after all in this busy lunchtime cafeteria, where Persian, Greek, Burmese, Korean, Mexican, Japanese, Chinese, and American fast-food concessions rub shoulders. Most offer $3–$5 lunch specials. On your way out, pick up a frozen yogurt to go and some postcards to send home. *24 Ellis St., at Market St. Wheelchair access. Closed Sun.*

Sears Fine Foods. Known for breakfasts—especially large bowls of fresh fruit and servings of 18 small pancakes—this cafeteria offers inexpensive food within jumping distance of Union Square. Good Swedish pancakes, egg waffles, strawberry shortcake. *439 Powell St., tel. 415/986–1160.*

UNDER $10 **101 Restaurant.** A news clipping in the window touts this Tenderloin Vietnamese restaurant as a favorite of the Chez Panisse kitchen staff. This is no small praise for any restaurant. Try the *Canh Chua Tom* (shrimp and vegetable soup), *Chao Tom* (shrimp and sugarcane), *Banh Joi Bo Nuong* (lemongrass and barbecued beef), *Ga Ngu Vi* (five-spice BBQ'ed chicken), or *Ga Xao Lang* (coconut chicken curry). *101 Eddy St., tel. 415/982–4490.*

Tu Lan. This place welcomes adventurous, poor, street-smart gourmands with terrific Vietnamese food in a really seedy location. The menu is expansive and the items are unusual, authentic, and cheap, with plenty to offer the vegetarian. Sit at the counter and

How to Eat for Free, Get Sloshed, and Network All at the Same Time

That ritual observed by working stiffs all over the country—Happy Hour—which offers free hors d'oeuvres to anyone who buys a drink (you were probably going to order one anyway, weren't you?) is of course commemorated in San Francisco, too. You can obtain some pretty wonderful food in these places, including pizza, chicken wings, nachos, tacos and tostadas, egg rolls, hamburgers, and fried calamari. On occasion you'll encounter some slightly less fabulous hors d'oeuvres, more reminiscent of what June Cleaver might have served at those sex toy parties she hosted when Ward was out of town: Yup, Triscuits and Velveeta are still around, yum yum. Of course, what did you expect when you shelled out that $1.25 for a beer in a paper cup: pâté?

Some of the happiest hours in town include The Starlight Roof in the Sir Francis Drake Hotel (at the corner of Powell and Sutter, tel. 415/392–7755), Achilles Heel (1601 Haight St., tel. 415/626–1800, weekdays 5–7), Cadillac Bar (1 Holland Ct., tel. 415/543–8226, weekdays 4–7), La Barca (2036 Lombard St., tel. 415/921–2221, weekdays 4–6), The Gold Coin Lounge (in the Holiday Inn, 750 Kearny St., tel. 451/433–6600, weekdays 5:30–7), Bull's Texas Café (25 Van Ness Ave., tel. 415/864–4288, weekdays 4–6), and New Bruno's (2389 Mission St., tel. 415/641–1145, daily 4:30–6:30). Dewey's (in the St. Francis Hotel in Union Square, tel. 415/397–7000) charges $1.99 for a chance to graze weekdays 4–7. Two cautions: The drink prices themselves can get quite expensive—they range anywhere from $2 to $6—and your name may end up in some Rolodexes that you'll later regret.

watch the kitchen staff prepare your food, including addictive Imperial rolls and chicken with five herbs. *8 6th St., at Market St., tel. 415/626–0927.*

UNDER $15 **David's Delicatessen.** A longtime fixture on Theater Row, David's dishes up humongous kosher meals, including pastries, blintzes, and potato pancakes with apple sauce. Sometimes there's a line after the shows let out; a celebrity corner shelters performers from the crowd. *474 Geary St., tel. 415/771–1600. Wheelchair access.*

Lori's Diner. A witty, friendly staff serves traditional American diner food (breakfasts, burgers, hand-cut fries) in this earnestly nostalgic '50s diner. Great $3 milkshakes are even better at 4 in the morning. *336 Mason St., at Geary St., tel. 415/392–8646. Open 24 hrs.*

Yank Sing. Great choice for dim sum in a pleasant, modern setting. Dim sum are small dumplings filled with all kinds of different goodies that you choose from carts as they pass by; you're charged by the number of plates left on your table. Just watch out... those little plates can add up! *427 Battery St., at Clay St., tel. 415/362–1640; 380 Market St., between Pine and Front Sts., tel. 415/392–3888; 53 Stevenson Place, between 1st and 2nd Sts., tel. 415/495–4510.*

UNDER $25 **Bix.** Another theme restaurant, Bix bills itself as a "supper club" that celebrates the Jazz Age and Art Moderne. Order a manhattan or a martini at the bar, but expect the food to be postmodern American. *56 Gold St., at Montgomery St., tel. 415/433–6300. Reservations advised.*

●●● CIVIC CENTER

Along with museums and theaters, this area also offers a number of good restaurants from the highly touted **Stars** to the predictable **McDonald's.**

UNDER $5 **Tommy's Joynt.** "Decorated" with beer ephemera, this lively cafeteria-style hofbrau and bar is a long-time San Francisco fixture. The specialties include buffalo stew ($5.45) and bean-and-beer soup ($1.50). Go easy on the sinus-clearing horseradish. They also serve inexpensive carved-meat sandwiches ($3.49) and dinner platters. The corner television is sure to be tuned to a game while patrons roll dice at the end of the bar. *1101 Geary St., tel. 415/775–4216. Wheelchair access.*

UNDER $15 **Golden Turtle.** Some of the best Vietnamese food in San Francisco is created here, and consumed in style with the help of the elaborate, attractive decor. A second location in the Richmond District is smaller and cozier than the Van Ness site. *2211 Van Ness Ave., between Broadway and Vallejo St., tel. 415/441–4419; 308 5th Ave., tel. 415/221–5285.*

Max's Opera Café. It's no big secret that the food at Max's is not particularly good, but—perhaps to partially make up for it—the portions are huge. The staff are all trained singers (some are better trained than others), and they perform throughout the day and night. (No, they don't let you sing for your supper.) Expect long lines after performances. Most go for the deli sandwiches and ample desserts, including gargantuan slices of cake. *601 Van Ness Ave., tel. 415/771–7300. Wheelchair access. Open late.*

Phnom Penh. With its lace curtains and dainty table settings, this little place looks like the setting for an elaborate tea party. Despite the rawness of the neighborhood, expect excellent Cambodian food and friendly service. *631 Larkin St., near Eddy St., tel. 415/775–5979.*

Racha Café. An exceptional Thai choice, both for the food and the service, in the city of a 100,000 Thai restaurants. Try the spicy mint chicken for around $6, or one of the tasty vegetarian dishes. If you come for lunch you can browse at the excellent used bookstore or visit the headquarters of the Sierra Club, both located in the same building. *771 Ellis St., at Polk St., tel. 415/885–0725. Wheelchair access.*

Stars Café. Located next door to the flagship restaurant, this spinoff could be called Stars *(see below)* Junior (for the gourmand in training, the poor gourmand, or the smart shopper.) Like the big Stars, the menu changes daily, but the inventive entrées run about half the cost of those next door, and since they don't take reservations, you'll have a better chance of getting in as well. Save room for dessert. *555 Golden Gate Ave., between Van Ness Ave. and Polk St., tel. 415/861–4344.*

UNDER $25 **California Culinary Academy.** How'd you like to eat someone's homework assignment? You can at the Culinary Academy, where fledgling chefs prepare food under the watchful eyes of their instructors. The results vary, but for the adventurous, it's worth a shot. The Academy actually encompasses three restaurants, with **Careme** a more formal (and expensive) option than either **Cyrill's** or **The Grill.** *625 Polk St., at Turk St., tel. 415/771–3500.*

Miss Pearl's Jam House. This place caters to a young crowd in a loud (in both senses of the word) atmosphere. Eat poolside or pretend you went down with the *Titanic* in the downstairs dining room. The Caribbean food is better described as California exotic, flavored in high style. In addition to regular entrées, Miss Pearl's prepares a good selection of interesting appetizers. Attached to the Phoenix Hotel, Miss Pearl's is owned by Julie Ring, who also owns the popular South-of-Market diner, Julie's Supper Club. Their jerk chicken (Jamaican-style chicken) is famous in these parts. *601 Eddy St., at Larkin St., tel. 415/775–5267. Open for lunch Wed.–Sat. 11:30–2:30, Sun. 10:30–2:30; dinner Tues. and Wed. 6–10, Thurs.–Sat. 6–11, and Sun. 5:30–9:30.*

UNDER $50 **Stars.** This place is one of the very best. Far from stuffy, the atmosphere is meant to suggest a Parisian bistro, and the place is full of laughter and loud voices. It's expensive, but not beyond the reach of budget travelers who are ready for a big splurge. How much it'll cost depends on how carried away you get; the average entrée runs around $22, but you mustn't skip your appetizer and dessert, and if you get wine. . . . *150 Redwood Alley, off Van Ness Ave. between McAllister St. and Golden Gate Ave., tel. 415/861–7827.*

JAPANTOWN ● ● ●

When in search of good Japanese food, take this advice and stay away from the expensive restaurants in the Japan Center. Instead, explore the surrounding streets for the older, more divey places.

This Pearl Is No Ugly Duckling

Everybody should be made to eat at the Swan Oyster Depot (1517 Polk St., tel. 415/673–1101) once a month just to give them a sunny disposition. This place makes you feel **that** ***good. Politicians can open their mouths wider than this place, which consists of nothing more than a lunch counter, a few stools, a tiled floor, and the best damn seafood in town. Doubling as a fishmongers and a lunch room, the Swan Oyster Depot is run by a genial bunch of beefy guys, who really seem to enjoy their work and are actually glad to see you. They know many of their customers by name and enjoy nothing more than putting a bowl of New England clam chowder in front of you, with an Anchor Steam beer and a plate of sourdough bread. That'll cost you about $5, but don't be surprised if you find yourself ordering a half-dozen oysters from Point Reyes and a half-cracked Dungeness crab. Such gluttony will set you back $20 but you just won't care. The Depot closes at 5:30 and is shut on Sunday.***

UNDER $15 **Sanppo.** Japanese restaurants, like Japan, have a reputation for costliness. But Sanppo, a longtime Japantown fixture, has good Japanese food at prices that won't break the bank, including vegetable tempura for $7.95, grilled salmon for $8.95, and a six-piece California roll (vegetarian sushi with avocado) for $3.50. *1702 Post St., at Buchanan St., tel. 415/346–3486.*

● ● ● NORTH BEACH

This old-time Italian neighborhood beckons the hungry visitor with strong coffee, fresh pasta, spicy sausages, and the most densely packed restaurants in the city. Both Columbus Street and Grant Avenue north of Columbus are lined with good and reasonably priced restaurants from which you can pick and choose. If you overindulge, go to the nearby Church of Saints Peter and Paul to atone.

UNDER $10 **Capp's Corner.** Come for lunch, when former boxing manager Joe Capp himself, wearing fedora, sunglasses, and trench coat, seats the customers. The soup, salad, and pasta lunch plate ($7.50) is the perfect precursor to an afternoon siesta. A complete five-course dinner, including the spumoni ice cream, will set you back $9.50–$11.50. *1600 Powell St., tel. 415/989–2589.*

Gira Polli. *Polli* means chicken and Gira Polli serves some of the best roast chicken in San Francisco, cooked on a unique rotisserie they promise is the only one in the United States. Their Gira Polli Special, the most expensive thing on the menu, is half a roasted chicken with Palermo potatoes, salad, vegetables, and roll for $11.95. But you can get a lunch for only about $5. They also serve Italian-style salads, appetizers, and pasta dishes. You'll find them in a prime location across from Washington Square and the Church of Saints Peter and Paul. *659 Union St., across from Columbus Ave., tel. 415/434–4472.*

Hunan. This old favorite in North Beach, which serves painfully hot but delicious Chinese food, resembles a big warehouse, perfect when you and 20 of your closest friends want to get obnoxious. *924 Sansome St., near Broadway, tel. 415/956–7727.*

Il Pollaio. The grilled chicken at this place gives Gira Polli a run for its money, and is even less expensive. You can get a terrific half-chicken with salad, bread, *and* wine for less than $10; without the wine it's around $7. *555 Columbus Ave., near Washington Sq., tel. 415/362–7727. Closed Sun.*

UNDER $15 **Helmand.** This new favorite serves Afghan food—an unusual speciality, even for San Francisco—and presents a perfect opportunity to budget travelers to experience a new cuisine in an elegant restaurant without going broke. Excellent vegetarian dishes are served along with lamb and chicken specialties. *430 Broadway, between Kearny and Montgomery Sts., tel. 415/362–0641.*

The Stinking Rose. Take a moment and guess at this restaurant's raison d'être. A recent addition to the glut of Italian restaurants lining Columbus Avenue, it distinguishes itself by its unwavering dedication to garlic: "We season our garlic with food," the menu boasts. Every dish on the menu is garlic-based, save for the few exceptions designated "vampire fare." Specialty entrées, like the 40 Clove Garlic Chicken, and a garlic-roasted Dungeness crab, run $12–$20, but the pasta dinners are only $8–$13. A carrot on the menu denotes vegetarian entrées. A garlic brunch on weekends (just the thing to kill that hangover) is $6. *325 Columbus Ave., tel. 415/781–ROSE.*

UNDER $25 **Buca Giovanni.** You'll find this rustic, bricked-in cave (*buca*) at the bottom of a short stairway. Often rated the best Italian restaurant in North Beach, it features solid Northern Italian food in an area sadly lacking in it—especially when you consider the number of Italian restaurants within spitting distance of here. Definitely get in on the *salsa rosa. 800 Greenwich St., at Mason St., tel. 415/776–7766.*

FISHERMAN'S WHARF/PIER 39 ● ● ●

The best dining experience you could have here would involve a loaf of sourdough, some shrimp or perhaps a crab, a bottle of wine, a perch on the pier, and a tantalizing dining partner. And remember to eat with your fingers.

UNDER $5 **Eagle Café.** Lifted whole from its former location two blocks away and dropped onto the upper story of Pier 39, this bar/food joint is authentically rustic, unlike the rest of this area. Windows and patio tables offer a view of the waterfront, Fisherman's Wharf, and Alcatraz. A good place to stop, rest, look, eat, and plan how you're going to escape Fisherman's Wharf without a single $40 neon-yellow California sweatshirt. *Upper level, Pier 39. Wheelchair access.*

UNDER $10 **Buena Vista Café.** This often-packed bar also serves food; and while the tourists throng in here, it manages to retain its dignity, claiming strenuously to have served the first Irish coffee in America. *2765 Hyde St., tel. 415/474–5044.*

CHINATOWN ● ● ●

Finding something to eat in Chinatown will probably be one of your easiest and most pleasurable projects. Steer clear of the glaringly tourist-oriented restaurants (i.e., the places where you have to ask for chopsticks, those with ketchup on the tables, those with a clientele that looks as if it could have stepped off the *Mayflower,* if only they were dressed a little differently). For extra adventure, go to a place with no English on the menu, close your eyes, and point to something.

UNDER $5 **Sandy's.** Yes, it's a hole in the wall. But order the lunch special for $2.95 and eat what food critics claim is the best roast duck in Chinatown. *1040A Stockton St., tel. 415/989–0477.*

UNDER $10 **Hong Kong Tea House.** This is the original source for dim sum in San Francisco, and one of the least expensive. It's a large, bustling place, especially on the weekend. *835 Pacific Ave., at Stockton St., tel. 415/391–6365.*

House of Nanking. This place offers excellent Shanghai home cooking at lower-than-usual Chinese food prices. Ask for the delicious shrimp cakes in peanut sauce—they're not on the menu—and then get the chicken Nanking, which is what General Tso's chicken is supposed to taste like. A big, big favorite in Chinatown; there's often a line stretching out the door. *919 Kearny St., between Jackson and Columbus Sts., tel. 415/421–1429.*

The R&G Lounge. This place serves what is arguably some of the best Chinese food in Chinatown. The sauces are incredibly delicate. Order anything featuring the melt-in-your-mouth tender greens (bok choy). If you order in English the staff may steer you away from anything they consider "too Chinese." Go for a hearty lunch and watch women preparing egg rolls (vegetarian!) in the dining room. *631B Kearny St., tel. 415/982–7877.*

SOUTH OF MARKET ● ● ●

If you eat down here, you'll see lots of youthful club goers getting an early start on their evening and youthful Financial District workers trying to create a pleasant end to their day.

UNDER $10 **Hamburger Mary's.** The messy hamburgers and the cluttered decor go together wonderfully. These may well be the best hamburgers in San Francisco. Come by at 2 in the morning to hang out with the clubbers in various states of drunkenness and undress. *1582 Folsom St., at 12th St., tel. 415/626–5767.*

UNDER $15 **Chevy's.** "Fresh-Mex" cuisine is served in a boisterous atmosphere popular with well-scrubbed young Americans networking away, whether for business or pleasure. Part of a local chain, this location is distinguished by neon and a sheet-glass exterior. Most locals agree that the food's pretty good for a chain restaurant. Try the mesquite-broiled fajitas. *150 4th St., at Howard St., tel. 415/543–8060. Additional locations in the Embarcadero Center and Stonestown Galleria.*

South Park Café. This French-style bistro opens at 8 AM for fresh croissants and coffee, and stays open for country-cooked lunches and dinners. Lunch will cost between $5 and $10 and dinners between $6 and $15. *108 South Park Ave., tel. 415/495–7275.*

● ● ● RICHMOND DISTRICT

Some people travel all the way out to this residential neighborhood a bit north of Golden Gate Park just to eat at one of these highly recommended restaurants.

UNDER $5 **Acropolis Deli.** Despite the Greek name, this is a Russian deli with Chinese owners that serves some of the best deli fare in San Francisco. Make up your mind and order something, already. *5217 Geary Blvd., at 16th Ave., tel. 415/751–9661.*

UNDER $15 **Khan Toke Thai House.** This attractive restaurant serves good, spicy Thai cuisine, and, as added bonus, makes you sit on the floor to eat it. What fun. *5937 Geary Blvd., at 24th Ave., tel. 415/668–6654.*

Angkor Wat. The flavorful food and pleasant surroundings are enough of a draw, but if you come at the right time you'll also catch a special Cambodian dance performance. *4217 Geary Blvd., at 6th Ave., tel. 415/221–7887.*

UNDER $25 **Hong Kong Flower Lounge.** Make the trek for the succulent, authentic Cantonese food here that's artfully prepared and wonderfully flavored (there's an emphasis on seafood). Try the dim sum for lunch. The lush red surroundings will make you feel imperial, at least as imperial as it's possible to feel in a Yankees cap and Reebok's. *5322 Geary Blvd., between 17th and 18th Aves., tel. 415/668–8998.*

● ● ● CASTRO DISTRICT

You can easily find something on your own in the dense, colorful area on upper Market and along Castro Street; real restaurants are interspersed with smaller food stands that offer such frivolous extras as espresso, muffins, and ice cream.

UNDER $15 **La Méditerranée.** This small, personable, and tastefully decorated restaurant across the street from Café Flore serves good Middle Eastern and Greek food including dolmas, salads, quiche, hummus, baba ghanoush, and levant sandwiches. *288 Noe St., tel. 415/431–7210. Other locations: 2210 Fillmore St. and 2936 College Ave. in Berkeley. Open for lunch and dinner.*

Siam Grill. Delicious Thai food—the unusual curries are especially good—and *cheap*. Try such exotica as red duck curry with coconut milk, tomatoes, spinach, and pineapple for $6, or one of nine vegetarian dishes that range from $3.50 to $6. *4248 18th St., 2 blocks from Castro, tel. 415/552–1174.*

No-Name (Nippon) Sushi. Everybody just calls it No-Name Sushi, but the proprietors did eventually put up a tiny cardboard sign in the window, officially dubbing it "Nippon." This tiny restaurant always has a line out the door and serves huge, delicious sushi combos for $6–$10. No liquor is served so if you want to drink, you have to bring it in a paper bag and swig it under the table. *314 Church, at 15th, no phone.*

● ● ● HAIGHT-ASHBURY

The Haight abounds with good breakfast places that are full to the brim with the "youth of today"—in case you can't tell, they're the ones who're generally smoking, wearing black, looking like hell, and sucking on that coffee like it's the primal life force.

UNDER $15 **Cha Cha Cha.** If you're willing to wait a long time, by San Francisco standards, and endure well-intentioned but slow service from the overworked staff, you'll enjoy the skillfully prepared *tapas,* salads, and grilled sandwiches served in this small, festive restaurant with crazy pseudo-Catholic icons on the walls. Entrées range from $10 to $15, but tapas start around $5. The sangria will make your potential two-hour wait fly by in a veritable blur. *1805 Haight St., at Stanyan St., tel. 415/386–5758.*

Indian Oven. This places serves a San Francisco rarity: fairly cheap and interesting Indian food, including many vegetarian appetizers and curries. *237 Fillmore St., at Haight St., tel. 415/626–1628.*

Thep Phanom. In the lower Haight, this place serves the best Thai food in the city—its regulars claim anyway—and has good service to boot. *400 Waller St., at Fillmore St., tel. 415/431–2526.*

MARINA DISTRICT/COW HOLLOW

UNDER $15 **Doidge's Kitchen.** If anyone asks if you want to "do breakfast," Doidge's is likely to be the spot they pick. A San Francisco tradition, Doidge's serves up great morning comfort foods, although it does often seem like the staff got up on the wrong side of the bed or something (which is not always all that comforting). Or maybe they're just into that negative attitude thing. *2217 Union St., at Fillmore St., tel. 415/921–2149. Reservations advised.*

Vlasta's. If you're seeking out old-fashioned, hearty Czechoslovakian meals served in a friendly surrounding, come here. Try the house special, Bohemian duck with herbs, and apple strudel for dessert. *2420 Lombard St., tel. 415/931–7533.*

UNDER $25 **Angkor Palace.** Excellent Cambodian food served in a fantasy-blue dining room by waiters dressed in traditional Cambodian clothing. This is one of those places where you take off your shoes and sit on the floor, or, if you wimp out, you *can*

Vegetarian Restaurants

Vegetarians needn't fear dining in the city: There are so many vegetarians in the Bay Area that virtually every San Francisco restaurant has at least one or two vegetarian entrées on the menu, often more. The following eateries, however, will offer the picky vegetarian a veritable cornucopia of meatless options.

Amazing Grace. A favorite spot among local vegetarians. 216 Church St., tel. 415/626–6411.

Counter Culture. Hip vegetarian with gourmet pretensions. 2073 Market St., tel. 621–7488.

Greens. Haute vegetarian, somewhat expensive. Fort Mason, tel. 415/771–6222.

Just Like Home. Excellent Lebanese and Mediterranean fare. 1924 Irving St., tel. 415/681–3337.

Kowloon Vegetarian. Chinese, with an extensive menu. 909 Grant Ave., tel. 415/362–9888.

Real Good Karma. Macrobiotic and other vegetarian food. 501 Dolores St., tel. 415/621–4112.

Shangri-La. Chinese vegetarian. 2026 Irving St., tel. 415/731–2548.

request to be seated on chairs. *1769 Lombard St., at Octavia St., tel. 415/931–2830. Wheelchair access.*

UNDER $25 **Greens.** After a long day of museums and cultural enrichment, or on your way back to the hostel at night, or if all the restaurants in Fisherman's Wharf turn you off, head here instead. This place will make you entirely reevaluate your notion of vegetarian food. Nope, no Kraft macaroni and cheese or carrot sticks here. Greens serves state-of-the-art vegetarian food in a lovely, gallery-like setting (belied by the warehouse exterior of Fort Mason) with a romantic view. Soups, salads, and bread by the Tassajara Bakery are all highly recommended, but bring Band-aids for the waiters' noses that inexplicably seem to be forever dragging along the ceiling. *Bldg. A, Fort Mason, tel. 415/771–6222.*

● ● ● MISSION DISTRICT

The Mission is one area where you could wander from taqueria to café to bookstore to taqueria again in a chilé-induced state of bliss. All of the following places, including the taquerias listed in the info box, are accessible from either the 16th and Mission Street BART or 24th and Mission Street BART stations.

UNDER $5 **Korean Cabin.** At this terrific Mission District bargain for Korean barbecue and other specialties, you'll order tasty, spicy dishes with no-nonsense names like "Noodle" and "Pork." The special "Monk's Food" menu is all vegetarian. *2170 Mission St., between 17th and 18th Sts., tel. 415/626–6236.*

A Cheap Trip South of the Border

Taquerias are reliable places to go for inexpensive, quality fast food. Authentic Mexican and Central American burritos, tacos, and tortas (sandwiches) are served up cheap from scores of storefront kitchens all over the Mission District.

- **La Cumbre** ***is a long-standing favorite with locals. The carne asada (marinated beef) burritos here are so good they can bring a vegetarian back to the herd—so to speak. They have good quesadillas, too. 515 Valencia St., tel. 415/863–8205.***
- **Los Panchos.** ***They have Mexican and Salvadoran food, including pupusas. 3206 Mission St., tel. 415/285–1033.***
- **Taqueria San Jose.** ***Is this the Mission's best burrito? You decide. 2830 Mission St., tel. 415/282–0203; 3274 24th St., tel. 415/282–7018.***
- **La Taqueria.** ***High-quality, authentic burritos and a great taco al pastor. 2889 Mission St., tel. 415/285–7117.***
- **El Tazumal Taqueria.** ***Located next door to El Tazumal restaurant, you can get many of the same items here for less. 3530 20th St., tel. 415/550–1928.***
- **El Toro.** ***The land of choice: Black beans or pinto, and 10 choices of meat for your burrito, including lengua and cabeza (tongue and head). You'll have plenty of time to study the menu, since the line often trails out the door. It's a good place for gringos as the burritos are a bit on the bland side. 598 Valencia St., tel. 415/431–3351.***

UNDER $10 **Dusit.** Inexpensive, impressive Thai specialties, including notable vegetarian offerings. You can dictate the level of spiciness. Try the garlic prawns. *3221 Mission St., tel. 415/826–4639.*

Mom Is Cooking. It ain't much on looks and the service is slow, but back in the kitchen Mom sure knows what she's doing. The highlight of any meal is the *boquitas* (meat or vegetarian nacho-style appetizers); stay away from the nasty margaritas. A good choice for inexpensive, sit-down Mexican meals. *1192 Geneva Ave., tel. 415/586–7000. No credit cards.*

Nicaragua. Try one of the fried plantain and cheese dinners, and take the advice of a helpful Nicaraguan: "Put a bit of everything in your mouth all at once for an explosion of flavors!" This is a bad neighborhood, so take precautions (or order to go!). *3015 Mission St., near Army St., tel. 415/826–3672.*

UNDER $15 **Angkor Borei.** A great neighborhood Cambodian place that serves original, distinctive meals to an appreciative following. Order the *Bangkea Ahng* ($8.25) and you'll get prawns served in an elaborate aluminum foil bird. *3471 Mission St., tel. 415/550–8417.*

La Rondalla. A strolling mariachi band passes by the iron-haired waitresses serving up good, cheap Mexican dinners in a room decorated with Christmas ornaments year-round. If that isn't enough of a draw, it's open until 3:30 AM. *901 Valencia St., tel. 415/647–7474. No credit cards.*

Late-Night Restaurants

So many occasions call for a big meal at 3 AM. . .

- ***Bagdad Café. Castro District eatery good for late-night people-watching. Open 24 hours. 2295 Market St., tel. 415/621–4434.***
- ***Clown Alley. Burgers, fries, and shakes in North Beach. Open until 3. 42 Columbus Ave., tel. 415/421–2540.***
- ***Church St. Station. Your basic cheap American joint in the Castro District. Open 24 hours. 2100 Market St., tel. 415/861–1266.***
- ***Grubstake. Burgers and breakfasts in Polk Gulch. Open until 5. 1525 Pine St., tel. 415/673–8268.***
- ***Lori's Diner. Diner food downtown. Open 24 hours. 2336 Mason St., tel. 415/392–8646.***
- ***Pine Crest. If Lori's is full or you don't like its ersatz '50s look, walk across the street to this more authentic '50s ('40s? '30s?) coffee shop. Open 24 hours. 401 Geary St., tel. 415/885–6407.***
- ***Sparky's. A menu with shades of Denny's, but the atmosphere is much trendier. In the Castro District. Open 24 hours. 240 Church St., tel. 415/621–6001.***
- ***Zim's. The type of laminated-menu coffee shop/restaurant so familiar in the American landscape. Open 24 hours. 1498 Market St., at Van Ness Ave., tel. 415/931–5890; 1090 Van Ness at Geary Ave., tel. 415/885–2620; 901 Taraval St., at 19th Ave., tel. 415/681–4743.***

Manora's Thai Cuisine. More good Thai food at Mission and South-of-Market locations. The fresh, attractive dishes are worth the wait. *3226 Mission St., at 29th St., tel. 415/550–0856; 1600 Folsom St., at 12th St., tel. 415/861–6224.*

CAFÉS

As reliable as the sunrise, as stimulating as a spring rain, the San Francisco café will welcome you with new friends/a hundred ideas for that new poem you've been trying to write/painting you've been trying to get going/love affair you've been trying to cultivate/addiction you've been nursing. And when you leave, if you leave, you'll never go back to Folgers again.

Café Beano/The Marsh. Find out what's going on culturally and otherwise in the Mission District over coffee or tea. At night the performance area in the back (The Marsh) features alternative, often one-person performances. It's new, it's hip, it's literally in your face. *878 Valencia St., tel. 415/285–2728. 16th and Mission St. BART.*

Café Flore—also known as Café Bore, Café Hairdo, Café Hairdon't, Café Hairspray, Café Gel, Café Cruisemart, and Café Le Pretense—is a hotbed of hippies and punks, students from S.F. State and strays from U.C. Berkeley, every stripe of artist, pseudo-artist, and political activist, and don't forget the trendy young men parading their latest fashions. It's crowded and the music's loud, but you can usually find a place at one of the outside tables, or strike an attractive pose and loiter until someone makes room for you. Sharing tables here is de rigeur. The café has a restaurant that operates during the day only, and serves light alcohol. Expect noise and commotion and, in the middle of it all, an incredibly attractive someone sipping a camomile tea and pretending to read Genet. *2298 Market St., in the Castro District, tel. 415/621–8579. Take Bus 8 from Embarcadero, Montgomery, Powell, or Civic Center BART.*

Café International. Locus for recovering Deadheads going through patchouli withdrawal and those who can stand to be around them, this place serves sandwiches, salads, and falafel, along with coffees. In the lower Haight. *508 Haight St., tel. 415/552–7390. Take Bus 6 or 71 from any point on lower Market St.*

Café Picaro. This large, cheerful, unpretentious café in the Mission District nurtures artists, writers, and bohos young and old. You can watch the people, eat good meals, drink coffee, find a place to sit without too much difficulty, make phone calls, read novels, write poetry, and otherwise hang out for hours; in other words, a little slice of heaven. You can't leave until you've generated at least one fantasy romance about a fellow patron. Across the street from the Roxie Theater. *3120 16th St., tel. 415/431–4089. 16th and Mission BART.*

Café Puccini. This small, sophisticated North Beach Café offers the perfect refuge on a rainy day. The jukebox plays opera, and one imagines that Puccini would approve. If you're hungry, try the simple, hearty sandwiches made with *focaccia* bread. *411 Columbus Ave., tel. 415/989–7033. Take Bus 15 from Transbay Terminal.*

Café Trieste is a legendary North Beach café, its history entwined with the Beat movement. Kerouac and the gang used to expend a lot of energy being members of the Beat generation here. Trieste means sadness, which will fuel that angst-ridden diary entry you're writing all the more. *601 Vallejo St., at Grant, tel. 415/392–6739.*

Ground Zero. The Official Café of the Apocalypse. Don't you dare come in here with a smile on your face, unless you're smiling bitterly at the irony of our petty lives. They mainly serve coffee and pastries, the two official food groups of the apocalypse generation. *783 Haight St., tel. 415/861–1985.*

Exploring San Francisco

The best way to get around, at least in certain areas of the city, is on foot. Only with a little hill climbing and wandering around, and even getting lost, will you really get a clear idea of San Francisco's density and diversity. Another way to familiarize yourself with a large chunk of it is to take MUNI Bus 22 from Fillmore Street in the Marina District, just west of Fort Mason. This magic bus heads south on Fillmore, and will touch neighborhoods as diverse as the extremely wealthy Pacific Heights, the extremely impoverished Western Addition, the Lower Haight, the Castro district, and the Mission.

ALCATRAZ ISLAND ● ● ●

Known as the Rock, Alcatraz Island served as the nation's most notorious federal penitentiary until 1963, holding prisoners thought to be special risks in its isolated maw. Some were well known in their own right, like Al Capone, Robert Stroud ("The Birdman of Alcatraz"), and "Machine Gun" Kelly. In 1969, a group of Native Americans occupied the island in an attempt to reclaim it, saying that a federal treaty of 1868 allowed Native Americans to use all federal land that wasn't actively being used by the government. After almost two years of occupation, the U.S. government forced them off. Today the island is part of the national park system and tourists visit its grounds in hordes. The **Red and White Fleet** (tel. 415/546–2896) ferries you to the island, and you have as much time as you want to explore (the average tour is about 2½ hours). You can take guided tours with park rangers, or an individual tour by renting a pre-recorded tape (available in several languages) and a personal cassette player with headphones. Alcatraz is one of San Francisco's most popular tourist attractions, so you'll probably want to hit the ferry ticket office at Pier 41 early to guarantee your visit. To get there take Bus 32 from the Ferry Building, near downtown.

CASTRO DISTRICT ● ● ●

Twin Peaks, one of the few places in the city where you can see both the bay and the ocean, and all of the city in between, is naturally one of the prime make-out spots in San Francisco. If you surface long enough to look at the view, you will have to admit that it's truly spectacular. When the Spanish came to this area in the 18th century, they named the peaks "Los Pechos de la Choca," or "The Breasts of the Indian Maiden." Just another

The NAMES Project

Drop by the NAMES Project (2362 Market St., tel. 415/863–5511), where panels from the now famous NAMES Quilt—a tribute to those who have died of AIDS—are displayed. The project started in 1987 when a man named Cleve Jones organized a meeting with several others who had lost friends or lovers to AIDS, in hopes that they could create a memorial. They decided on a quilt that was to feature panels dedicated to individuals who have succumbed to the disease, each panel to be created by a loved one of the deceased. The idea caught on big and people from all over the country sent in quilt panels. To date, the entire quilt has been displayed in front of the White House three times (it now contains more than 14,000 panels). There are always some on display in the San Francisco office, as well as in other offices all over the world.

Downtown San Francisco

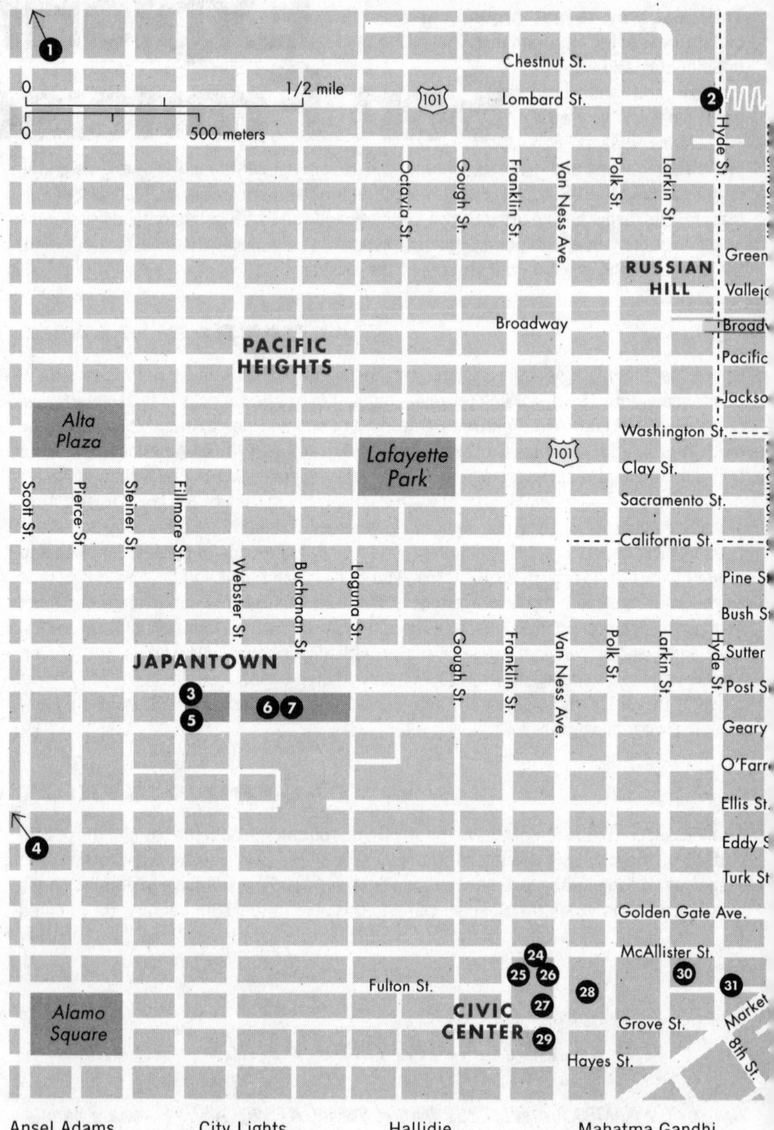

Ansel Adams Center, **47**
Bank of America World HQ, **37**
Cable Car Museum, **10**
Cartoon Art Museum, **48**
Chinese Cultural Center, **21**
Chinese Historical Society Museum, **22**
Circle Gallery, **35**
City Hall, **28**
City Lights Bookstore, **12**
Coit Tower, **8**
Condor Club, **9**
Colombarium, **4**
Embarcadero Center, **42**
Exploratorium, **1**
Fairmont Hotel, **16**
Ferry Building, **44**
Golden Gate Fortune Cookie Factory, **13**
Grace Cathedral, **11**
Hallidie Building, **38**
Herbst Recital Hall, **26**
Hyatt Regency Hotel, **45**
Japan Center, **7**
Justin Herman Plaza, **41**
Kabuki Hot Springs, **5**
Kabuki Theatre, **3**
Lombard Street, **2**
Louise M. Davies Symphony Hall, **29**
Mahatma Gandhi Statue, **43**
Mark Hopkins Hotel, **17**
Museum of Modern Art, **25**
Old Chinese Telephone Exchange, **15**
Old San Francisco Mint, **34**
Pacific Stock Exchange, **40**
Peace Plaza, **6**

Downtown San Francisco

Portsmouth Square, **20**
Public Library, **30**
Rincon Center, **46**
S.F. Centre, **33**
Sheraton Palace Hotel, **39**
Stanford Court Hotel, **18**
Stockton Street Tunnel, **19**
Tin Hou Temple, **14**
Transamerica Pyramid, **23**
U.N. Plaza Promenade, **31**
Veteran's Building, **24**
Visitors Information Center, **32**
War Memorial Opera House, **27**
Wells Fargo Bank History Museum, **36**

example of missionaries hard at work converting the heathens. To reach Twin Peaks, take MUNI Bus 37 from Castro and Market streets.

The biggest gay neighborhood in the world, the Castro is close-knit and always bustling. It's a great area for window shopping, with lots of offbeat shops lining Market and Castro. The flagship of the region is probably **Café Flore** (2298 Market St., tel. 415/621–8579), where the eyes turn and the gossip mills churn. The **Castro Theatre** is an impressive repertory house that hosts the San Francisco Lesbian and Gay Film Festival each summer. This is the area to head for information on gay and, to a lesser extent, lesbian resources, to read literature, and to hit the bars and make a friend or two. If you happen to be in San Francisco around the end of June or on Halloween, come to the Castro to witness two of the craziest parties in the city—the **Gay and Lesbian Freedom Day Parade** (held on the last Sunday in June) and the Castro Street **Halloween party,** in which thousands of gorgeous men in drag perform cabaret shows for onlookers roaming Castro Street. Both events attract tens of thousands of participants.

● ● ● CHINATOWN

You'll know you've stumbled into Chinatown when the street signs are in Chinese, but the best way to enter is through the ornamental dragon gateway on Grant Avenue at Bush Street, when the sense of being in a different world is quite suddenly palpable. Or enter through **Portsmouth Square,** on Washington Street (at Kearny Street). Though only 16 blocks, Chinatown contains the largest Chinese community outside of Asia; a large

Areas Where You Can Get Lost and Still Have a Good Time

There are certain places in a city where you can just put the map in your pocket and surrender to the whims of the streets; you won't need to look for places to check out because they will emerge spontaneously in the course of your wanderings. There are other neighborhoods, usually those that contain a preponderance of used car dealerships and 7-Elevens, where no amount of romantic spirit or lightheartedness will make your exploring interesting, that is, unless you're looking for a used car. Here are a few suggestions for neighborhoods that are good to get lost in and for finding hidden treasures.

The Mission District/Noe Valley/The Castro. Get off the BART at 16th and Mission, and head west on 16th or south on Mission or Valencia, or a little bit of both. Either direction will guarantee that you'll see scenes of neighborhood life, funky shops, galleries, and enough cafés and restaurants to keep you sufficiently fueled up.

The Castro to the Haight. Take MUNI K, L, M, or MUNI Bus 8 up Market Street, and get off at Castro Street station. South will take you through the Castro district and north, over the hill to the Haight-Ashbury district. If you feel especially athletic head north to the Haight and then west to Golden Gate Park. Someone will send for help if they haven't heard from you by next week.

North Beach/Chinatown. From Montgomery Street or Powell Street BART station, head north. See if you can find at least one of the following: Union Square, Coit Tower, Chinatown, North Beach. Don't look too hard or you might miss everything.

population of Southeast Asians have immigrated here as well. Today, though, many Chinese and other Asians are moving away from the cramped conditions in Chinatown in favor of more residential neighborhoods like Richmond and Sunset. Don't miss the week-long, huge, colorful Chinese New Year's festival (during the first new moon in February)—especially the parade that features a massive dancing dragon.

Grant Avenue is the main thoroughfare in Chinatown, crowded with tourists, souvenir shops, Chinese restaurants, and intricate red, green, and gold lampposts. The old **Chinese Telephone Exchange** building, now the Bank of Canton, stands at 743 Washington Street at Grant Avenue. It's both architecturally and historically interesting; operators here had to memorize the names of all their customers, and speak English and five Chinese dialects. **Stockton Street** is the main street for residents, packed with grocery stores, bakeries, and trade and service shops. In between these two main drags, narrow alleys peel away, carrying with them the secrets of Chinatown, not the tourist Chinatown, but the real neighborhood, where the Chinese people you see working in restaurants and bustling in the streets, eat and sleep and live out their lives.

Among the most interesting streets are Waverly Place (you may remember the name from *The Joy Luck Club*), known as the **"street of painted balconies,"** and Ross Alley, home of the **Golden Gate Fortune Cookie Factory** (56 Ross Alley), where you can get risqué fortunes to slip to whomever you'd like to see blush. There are Chinese temples along Waverly Place, including the oldest in the country, the **Tien Hau Temple** (125 Waverly Pl.). At the end of Ross Alley is Jackson Street, home to several Chinese **herbal medicine shops,** the walls of which are lined with drawers containing the magic herbs.

CIVIC CENTER AND VAN NESS AVENUE

The **Civic Center** is the locus of the city government and home of many of the city's cultural events, including dance, opera, and theater. It's also where a good percentage of the city's homeless sleep, and have slept since as far back as the 1940s. **City Hall,** built in classic baroque style, dominates the scene with its bronze rotunda. It was here in 1978 that conservative ex-City Supervisor Dan White shot and killed Mayor George Moscone and Supervisor Harvey Milk, the first openly gay elected official in the United States. In the early '60s, protesters were washed down the City Hall central stairway with giant firehoses while inside Senator Joseph McCarthy led hearings of the House Un-American Activities Committee, all of which is depicted in the amusing government propaganda effort (now a cult film), *Operation Abolition.* And last but not least, Joe DiMaggio and Marilyn Monroe got married here on January 15, 1954. Has this building seen some crazy times or what?

Surrounding City Hall are many of the city's cultural mainstays. The **Louise M. Davies Symphony Hall** and the **War Memorial Opera House** host some of the city's offerings of high culture. The **San Francisco Public Library** (Larkin St., tel. 415/557–4567), which will move around the corner upon the completion of a new Asian Art Museum (*see* Museums, *below*), has a fine collection of books, records and CD's, and San Francisco memorabilia. The **Veterans Building,** at Mc Allister and Van Ness, houses the **Museum of Modern Art** (*see* Museums, *below*) and the **Herbst Recital Hall,** where you can catch a variety of cultural events, including concerts, readings, and lectures. Across from City Hall on the south side is a large plaza, the ultimate destination of many protest marches, including a couple of 200,000-plus ones during the Persian Gulf War, and the site of countless rallies and occasional riots. Leading away from City Hall toward Market Street is the **United Nations Plaza promenade,** overlooked by a dramatic statue of Simón Bolivar and commemorating the founding of the United Nations in San Francisco in 1949.

Van Ness is a wide avenue flanked by a themeless hodgepodge of businesses grouped in uncanny multiples: steak houses, electronics stores, bakeries, movie theaters, car dealerships. The street is notably drab from Lombard Street all the way to Civic Center.

● ● ● COIT TOWER

Though built to memorialize San Francisco's volunteer fire fighters of the 1850s and '60s, the 542-foot concrete observation tower with the panoramic bay view is perhaps more reminiscent of the woman who left the funds to build it, Lillie Hitchcock Coit. An eccentric San Francisco legend in her own time, heiress Lillie Coit was a cross-dresser (in men's clothes she could gain access to the most interesting realms of San Francisco) who literally chased fire engines around town. The walls inside the lobby are covered with Depression-era murals by local artists, undertaken as a Public Works of Art project. The elevator inside the tower will take you to the top and some great views of the Golden Gate Bridge, the Bay Bridge, and Alcatraz Island. *Tel. 415/982–2648. Admission: $3. Take Bus 30 or 45 from the corner of Kearny and Geary downtown; get off at Washington Square. Open Mar.–Sept., daily 10–5:30; Oct.–Feb. 9–4:30.*

Tumbling down the hill from Coit Tower is the **Grace Marchant Garden,** carefully cultivated for 30 years by a certain Grace Marchant—and transforming a former dump into a hidden treasure of the city. Look also for **Napier Lane,** a quaint wooden street just off the Filbert Steps.

● ● ● EMBARCADERO

The Embarcadero, which is Spanish for "wharf," more resembles, well, *office buildings* than anything vaguely maritime. At least they're office buildings on the water. In the center of it all, at the end of Market Street, stands the **Ferry Building.** The 230-foot clock tower and terminus for transbay ferries before the Bay Bridge was built, is now merely a convenient and attractive landmark. This is where you can catch the ferry for Sausalito or Larkspur (*see* Coming and Going by Ferry under Marin County in Chapter 3, San Francisco Bay Area). Even if you don't want to go out on the bay, you can still get a hot dog at the stand in front of the Ferry Building, admire the new statue of **Mahatma Gandhi** in the Ferry Building Plaza while munching away on your little tube of sacred cow, and take a breather on the observation deck. Every 20 minutes or so, you'll witness the docking

Great San Francisco Views

- ***Treasure Island. A slightly different angle reinvigorates a postcard-familiar night view of San Francisco. The Bay Bridge, dramatically draped in lights, frames the panorama. By car, take the Treasure Island exit from the Bay Bridge and park at the water's edge.***
- ***Coit Tower. A 360° view of San Francisco. 1 Telegraph Blvd., tel. 415/274–0203.***
- ***The 49-Mile Drive. Start at the Civic Center and head north on Van Ness, following the blue-and-white signs with seagulls on them to see many of the scenic and historic draws of San Francisco.***
- ***Portola. Where Portola Street ends and Market Street begins, near Twin Peaks, you'll find a gorgeous vision of the city and the East Bay.***
- ***Top of the Mark. At the top of the Mark Hopkins Hotel—accessible only to those in proper attire or willing to pay dearly for a drink with a great view.***
- ***Tank Hill. Take 17th Street to Twin Peaks Boulevard Park at the fork of Twin Peaks and Clarendon, find the steps to the right of the house at 192 and climb until you spot a concrete area. Cross it and climb the slope.***

of yet another ferry and yet another colorful parade of passengers disembarking. This would be the ideal place to read Jack London's *The Sea Wolf,* or at least its opening pages, which vividly portray the capsizing of a ferry boat going from Sausalito to San Francisco in the days before the Golden Gate Bridge. The view of the waterfront used to be obstructed by the elevated **Embarcadero Freeway,** but after the 1989 earthquake rendered it wobbly, beauty-loving San Franciscans garnered enough clout to have it razed.

EMBARCADERO CENTER Dominating the Embarcadero area is a concrete monster, the **Embarcadero Center.** The center is a conglomeration of four nearly identical office towers connected to each other by bridges, with shops and restaurants below that cater to a corporate crowd. From a distance they look like rectangular pancakes planted in an unnaturally tidy row; they get prettified in December when they're festively lit. The fifth tower you'll see is the **Hyatt Regency Hotel,** which offers occasional tea dances (finally a place to wear your Easter hat and little white gloves!) and an elevated, revolving bar with an incredible view of the city and the bay. Unless you're going through Benetton withdrawal, save your shopping expeditions for other areas of town.

Between the center and the Ferry Building stretches **Justin Herman Plaza,** a favorite haunt of the office bag-lunch crowd and young skateboarders who favor long expanses of brick and concrete. Here, Jean Dubuffet's mammoth stainless-steel sculpture, *La Chiffoniere,* poses like a Napoleonic Pillsbury doughboy, and Armand Vallaincourt's huge building-block fountain looks just a little too much like prehistoric plumbing. Though the pipes are often dry during drought years, you can gambol amid the girders even when the water is streaming through. During a free, unannounced concert by the Irish band U2 in the plaza in 1988, lead singer Bono spray painted the fountain, earning the ire of city officials who were waging a war against graffiti at the time. Bono later apologized, but the "anarchistic" gesture is recorded for posterity in the movie *Rattle and Hum.*

Another water adventure awaits nearby at the stately, restored **Rincon Center.** The outside of the building is unassuming—you'll recognize it by the raised blue dolphins on its sides—but inside there's a newly restored 1930s lobby and a stately atrium into which a tall shimmering column of rain descends. The social realist murals in the lobby depict the history of California, including the oppression of American Indians and the exploitation of workers by capitalist overlords. *121 Spear St., at Mission, tel. 415/543–8600.*

FINANCIAL DISTRICT

San Francisco is the financial capital of the west coast, and the center of San Francisco's Financial District is Montgomery Street, "the Wall Street of the West," where the towers of wealth block all sun at street level. Traffic lights here stop vehicles in all four directions to allow busy office workers to cross diagonally and bicycle messengers to cheat death. A concentration of San Francisco's architectural landmarks are here, including the **Transamerica Pyramid** (600 Montgomery St.), *the* distinguishing and pointy feature of the San Francisco skyline, whose perky spire locals studiously ignore. The 1917 **Hallidie Building** (130 Sutter St.) has the dubious distinction of being the first edifice ever constructed with a glass-curtain wall. The **Sheraton Palace Hotel** (633–65 Market St.), one of the most luxurious in the city, has come out of its $135-million renovation lookin' fine. Check out the insanely opulent, glass-domed **Garden Court Restaurant,** where good boys and girls get to have lunch after they die. The north plaza of the glowering **Bank of America World Headquarters** is graced with a black granite shard of public art officially called *Transcendence,* but popularly known as *The Banker's Heart.* Worthwhile historical exhibits include the **Old Mint** (5th and Mission Sts.), original birthplace of many a buffalo nickel, and the **Wells Fargo History Museum,** interminably celebrating the short-lived but picturesque pony express (*see* Special Museums, *below*).

While you're in the Financial District, gaze through the plate-glass window at the memento-encrusted office (720 Montgomery St.) of celebrity attorney Melvin Belli, famous for initiating high-profile palimony suits on behalf of jilted live-in lovers. On occasion, you can actually watch the octogenarian at work.

Two giant sculptures, *Earth's Fruitfulness* and *Man's Inventive Genius,* attempt to inject some life and soul into probably one of the least fruitful, least inventive places in the city, the **Pacific Stock Exchange,** on the south side of Pine Street at Sansome.

FISHERMAN'S WHARF

This is San Francisco's prize tourist trap, specially designed to make you spend money. The astounding thing about the Wharf is that it seems to be a tourist attraction that attracts tourists solely on the basis of being a tourist attraction. There's no there there. Go, by all means, just don't let this be your main—much less your only—memory of San Francisco. You'll find a semblance of an authentic experience only if you arrive in the misty early morning hours to watch the fishing boats unload. Once the sole domain of Italian, mainly Sicilian, fishermen, Jefferson Street is now studded with seafood restaurants, markets, and stands; souvenir shops; and tourist "museums" like the **Wax Museum, Ripley's Believe It or Not!, Guinness Museum of World Records,** and the **Medieval Dungeon,** which features graphic recreations of torture devices from the Middle Ages. Buy clam chowder in a "bowl" of sourdough bread, or a half pound of shrimp and a loaf of bread, eat on the pier, and then hightail it out of there to catch a ferry to Alcatraz, Angel Island, or to take a cruise of the entire bay.

Up Jefferson Street at the Hyde Street Pier stands the **National Maritime Museum,** (tel. 415/929–0202), which features all sorts of artifacts from the maritime history of San Francisco. Docked nearby is the ***Balclutha,*** a 100-year-old square-rigged ship, along with other ships of interest. Nearby, the **American Carousel Museum** (633 Beach, tel. 415/928–0550) tells the history of the merry-go-round.

Just in case you're gathering tidbits of San Francisco lore, Jonathan Winters was once briefly institutionalized after he climbed the mast of the Balclutha and hung from it, shouting: "I am the man in the moon!"

Three shopping complexes girdle the wharf: **Pier 39,** the **Cannery,** and **Ghirardelli Square.** Owned by the billionaire Bass brothers of Texas, Pier 39 is a bland, trivial imitation turn-of-the-century seaport village that more resembles the shopping mall that might surface in your worst nightmares. Its one redeeming quality is the swarms of sea lions who took over several of the marina docks next to the development a few years ago and have refused to leave. For an ersatz history lesson there, you might take in **The San Francisco Experience** (tel. 415/982–7394; admission: $6), a 28-minute movie that lets you "feel" a San Francisco earthquake—in Sensurround. To shake off that lingering "I'm-being-ripped-off" feeling, eat at the **Eagle Café** (*see* Food, *above),* and take a moment to read the yellowed newsclippings describing how the establishment was lifted whole from its former location in 1978 and plunked down on the upper level of Pier 39.

A former Del Monte peach-canning facility, **the Cannery** (Jefferson, Leavenworth, Beach, and Hyde Sts., tel. 415/771–3112) is now a gallery of chic boutiques. Chocolate is no longer made on-site at **Ghirardelli Square,** but you can buy it there in bars or topping an ice-cream sundae. Across the way, stop in at **The Sharper Image** to see the latest in high-tech toys for grown-ups. If the word "crafts" makes you think of dolls with crocheted dresses fitted over toilet paper rolls, check out the impressive cutting-edge contemporary crafts at the small **California Crafts Museum** (tel. 415/771–1919). Squeeze into the **Buena Vista Café** (Beach St., at Hyde St.), which claims to have served the first Irish coffee in the U.S., and stroll down to **Lahaina Gallery** (645 Beach St.) to see Larry Yung's **Chinois Pop Art.** The easiest way to get there from downtown is on Bus 32 from the Ferry Building, near downtown.

FORT MASON

Once an army command post, this series of warehouses built on piers is now a nexus of artistic, cultural, and environmental organizations as well as small specialty museums, including the **African American Historical and Cultural Society,** the **Mexican Museum,** the **San Francisco Craft and Folk Art Museum,** and **Museo ItaloAmericano,** which features Italian and Italian-American art (*see* Museums, *below*). The renowned vegetarian restaurant **Greens** (*see* Food, *above*) is also tucked into one of the warehouses, as is the **Book Bay Bookstore,** run by the Friends of the San Francisco Public Library, where you can still get a book for a quarter, and few items cost over $3. On a crest above the piers is the **San Francisco International Youth Hostel** (*see* Where To Sleep, *above*). *General information: tel. 415/441–5706. MUNI Buses 22, 28, 30, 42, 43, 47, and 49.*

GOLDEN GATE BRIDGE • • •

It's that big orange thing that you can't actually see from that many places in the city, but when you do catch a glimpse your heart sort of goes pitter pat. Nearly 2 miles long, this baby has come to symbolize San Francisco to the rest of the world more than any other single monument. Its Art Deco design has withstood many a high wind and a 7.3 earthquake, as well as several hundred thousand revelers who turned up to celebrate its 50th birthday in 1987. You absolutely must cross it once (or more likely twice) while you're here, whether by car or on foot; you can take MUNI Bus 28 to the toll plaza and hoof it or hitch a ride with other bridge lovers from there. In addition, the bridge is one of the most preferred spots from which to commit suicide. What a way to go.

GOLDEN GATE PARK • • •

The western keyhole into San Francisco is Golden Gate Park, a strip of nature 4 miles long but less than a mile wide. With over a thousand acres, it's a peaceful, lovely place to spend time, with plenty of activities, gardens, museums, and performances to enjoy. Hippie historians should note that Ken Kesey and friends celebrated the first **Human Be-In** here on January 14, 1966.

Once a collection of sand dunes, Golden Gate Park was designed in 1868 by a 24-year-old civil engineer with no prior experience (his bid was the lowest) and landscaped by John MacLaren. The park is the largest of its kind and much prettier than New York's Central Park, despite the claim of that park's designer, Frederick Law Olmstead (who also designed the Stanford University campus), that beautiful trees could not be made to grow in San Francisco. Today, blue gum eucalyptus, Monterey pine, and Monterey cypress trees, not to mention one of the world's foremost horticultural displays, all proudly inhabit the park.

The **Strybing Arboretum and Botanical Gardens** (tel. 415/661–1316) is 70 acres of plants, featuring some 5,000 specimens arranged by country of origin, genus, and fragrance. With its koi fish ponds and 18th-century Buddha, the **Japanese Tea Garden** (tel. 415/666–7201) is the country's oldest. Other flowery attractions include the **Shakespeare Garden,** which features all the types of plants that are mentioned in Shakespeare's works (just don't eat the nightshade), **Rhododendron Dell, Fuchsia Garden,** and the **Queen Wilhelmina Tulip Garden,** with its nearby **Dutch Windmill.** The park's oldest building is the delicate Victorian **Conservatory,** a knock-off of London's Kew Gardens that houses a tropical garden and exotic orchids.

The park's fixtures also include three world-class museums. The **Asian Art Museum** boasts the **Avery Brundage collection,** the western world's largest assemblage of Asian art (John F. Kennedy and Tea Garden Drs., tel. 415/668–8921), while the **M.H. de Young Memorial Museum** (between John F. Kennedy Dr. and 8th Ave., tel. 415/750–3600; recorded message 415/863–3330) is notable for its 21-gallery survey collection of American art. The **California Academy of Sciences** (between John F. Kennedy and Martin Luther King, Jr. Drs., tel. 415/750–7000) is a complex of natural science facilities including the **Morrison Planetarium,** the **Natural History Museum,** and the **Steinhart Aquarium.** Golden Gate Park is bordered by Stanyan Street, the Great Highway, Lincoln Way, and Fulton Street. To get there from downtown or Civic Center, take Bus 5, 71, or 73.

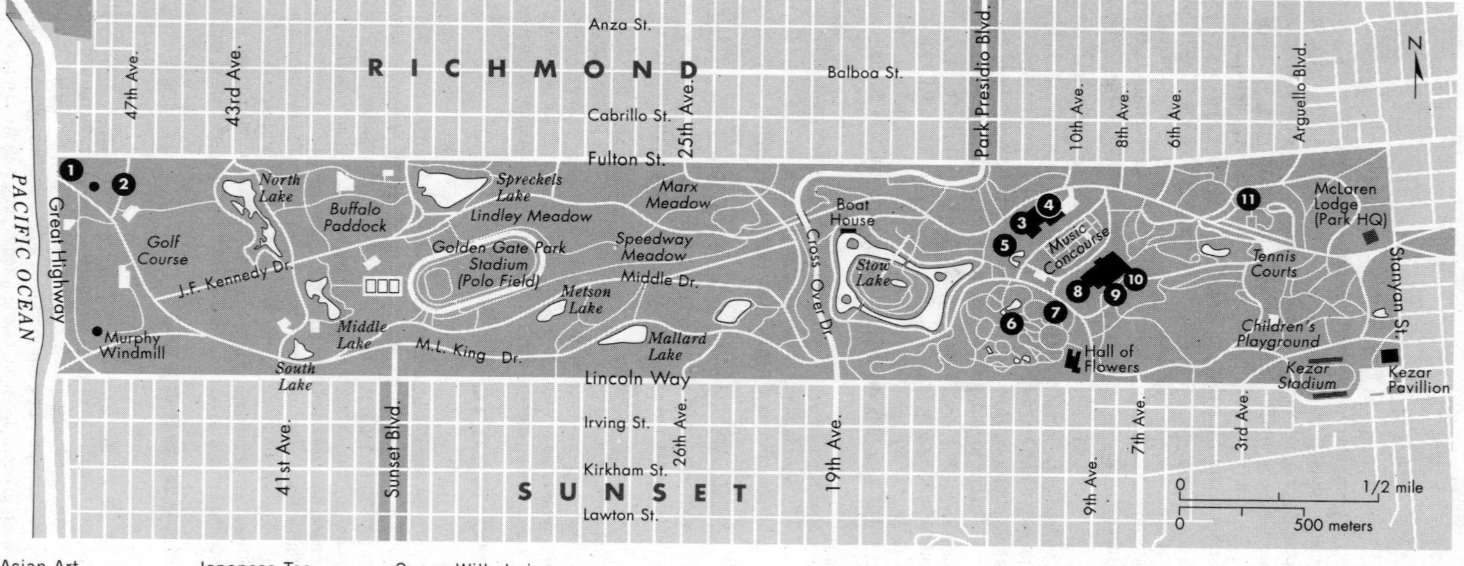

Asian Art Museum, **3**
California Academy of Sciences, **8**
Conservatory, **11**
Dutch Windmill, **1**
Japanese Tea Garden, **5**
M.H. de Young Memorial Museum, **4**
Morrison Planetarium, **10**
Queen Wilhelmina Tulip Garden, **2**
Shakespeare Garden, **7**
Steinhart Aquarium, **9**
Strybing Arboretum, **6**

Golden Gate Park

THE HAIGHT-ASHBURY DISTRICT • • •

East of Golden Gate Park sits the Haight-Ashbury district, the name of which still strikes fear in the hearts of suburban parents everywhere. The Haight began its career as a center for the counterculture in the late-50s and early 60s, when the Victorians deserted their Victorians for homes in the suburbs, and some of the Beat writers, several illustrious fathers of the drug culture, and bands like the Grateful Dead and Jefferson Airplane moved in. There went the neighborhood. Soon thereafter several hundred thousand blissed-out, drugged-out teenagers were converging on the Haight to drop their body weight in acid, play music, sing renditions of "Uncle John's Band" for days at a time, and generally do things for which they would feel incredibly silly 20 years later—thus continuing that tradition of youth since time immemorial.

HOME SWEET HOME FOR PARAGONS OF THE COUNTERCULTURE

Janis Joplin: 112 Lyon St. between Page and Oak • The Grateful Dead: 710 Ashbury at Waller St. • The Manson family: 636 Cole St. at Haight St. • Jefferson Airplane: 2400 Fulton St. at Willard North.

Since those golden days, the Haight has gone through various stages of increasing and decreasing seediness and gentrification, to rest uneasily at its current status of The Place Where Alienated Upper-Middle-Class Youth Move and Shop and Get Their Hair Cut. It's still sort of countercultural, but now most of the youth are wearing black and riding motorcycles and piercing body parts, and it just costs more than it used to.

Rest easy, however: The Haight-Ashbury of the '60s isn't dead, it just relocated. The "lower Haight" picks up where the '60s and '70s left off at around Haight and Fillmore, with an authentic collection of hippies, drugs, and bedraggled Victorians (houses, that is). In the *International Café* you can hear those old Donovan songs you thought you'd finally rid yourself of, see an American flag hanging upside down from an iron window grate, and pick up a copy of the *Hair* soundtrack at a yard sale, cheap. The addition of a few beatniks and punks makes it a veritable time capsule; you'd almost think it was a theme park celebrating the second half of the 20th century, except that it's too dirty. Buses 6, 7, 66, 71, and 73 will get you to Haight-Ashbury from near the Civic Center. They ain't the Magic Bus but what the hell.

JAPANTOWN • • •

The modern Japantown, which spans the area north of Geary Street between Fillmore and Laguna streets, is mostly comprised of a shopping complex called the **Japan Center,** or **Nihonmachi.** The community was once much larger, until it dispersed during World War II when California made a practice of dumping Japanese-Americans in concentration camps.

The **Peace Plaza** and five-story **Pagoda** still remain, however, designed by architect Yoshiro Taniguchi in a gesture of goodwill from the people of Japan. The plaza is landscaped with traditional Japanese-style gardens and reflecting pools, and is the site of many traditional festivals throughout the year. There are several shops selling Japanese wares, as well as a number of good restaurants in the area. To relax after a day of sightseeing, try a Japanese steam bath at the **Kabuki Hot Springs** (1750 Geary Blvd., tel. 415/922–6000), a single-sex steam bath where you can use the steam room, sauna, and hot and cold baths for $10, or get a half-hour shiatsu massage and unlimited bath use for $35. The bath is reserved for women on Sunday, Wednesday, and Friday; men the rest of the week. Also in the same area, the **Kabuki Theatre** (1881 Post St., tel. 415/931–9800) shows first-run films in a high-tech octoplex. Buses 2, 3, and 4 will deposit you in Japantown from the BART Montgomery Street Station.

● ● ● MISSION DISTRICT

Unplagued by fog, the sunny Mission District once represented San Francisco's prime real estate, first to the Ohlone Native Americans and then to the Spanish missionaries. Over the years, various predominantly European populations—Scandinavians, Germans, Irish, and Italian—have given way to those of Central and South American descent.

Named after the Spanish Mission Dolores *(see below)*, the district stretches from South of Market to Army Street, and is served by two BART stations (one on Mission at 16th St. and the other at Mission and 24th). The community is low-income and ethnic, most notably Latino, but also includes a significant contingent of bohemians, artists, and radicals. The Mission is colorful and friendly, a great place to hang out, but it can also be dangerous. Women won't feel comfortable walking alone here at night, and while you can actually find a parking space, you might think twice about leaving your car here. The streets of the Mission are crowded and the pace brisk—great for daytime walking. Probably the best place for a stroll is on Valencia and Mission between 16th and 24th, and 24th between Mission and Potrero, where the scene is most densely Hispanic.

Much of the artsy scene, with its bookstores, cafés, and theaters, is concentrated in the northern half of the Mission, while the southern half is predominantly Latino-oriented businesses. A good place to find out about the offbeat side of the Mission is on **Valencia Street** (a block west of Mission St.) between 16th and 24th streets. This low-key street is lined with cafés, second-hand furniture and clothing stores, a few odd bars, and galleries. The **New College** (766 Valencia St.), a center for alternative education with a renowned degree in Poetics, has a campus on Valencia near 18th. Around the corner is the **Women's Building** (3543 18th St., tel. 415/431–1180), a meeting place for progressive and radical political groups. Valencia Street is also the site of several good used and new bookstores, including the leftist **Modern Times** (968 Valencia St., tel. 415/282–9246) and the feminist **Old Wives Tales** (1009 Valencia St., tel. 415/821–4675). Women may want to check out **Good Vibrations** (1210 Valencia St., tel. 415/550–0827), a user-friendly vibrator store run by lesbians.

Though made of humble adobe, **Mission Dolores** has survived San Francisco's great earthquakes and fires, and today is the oldest structure in the city. It was commissioned by Juniperro Serra to honor San Francisco de Asis (St. Francis of Assisi). The Spanish nicknamed it Dolores after a nearby stream, Arroyo de Nuestra Senora de los Dolores ("Stream of Our Lady of the Sorrows"), and the name stuck. Mission Dolores is both the simplest architecturally and the least restored of all the California missions, with a bright ceiling painted by local Costanoan Indians. The mission bells still ring on holy days, and the cemetery next door is planted with a few California celebrities, including San Francisco's first mayor, Don Francisco de Haro. *16th and Dolores Sts., tel. 415/621–8203. Admission: $1. Open daily 9–4.*

The Mission provides a bounty of cheap food, especially in the form of huge Mexican burritos and succulent tacos made up fresh in the numerous storefront taquerias. You'll quickly grow to learn the distinction between real Mexican fast food and Taco Bell, if you don't already. The area also abounds with specialty bookstores and a lively, relatively inexpensive alternative theater scene.

● ● ● NOB HILL AND RUSSIAN HILL

The most classically elitist of San Francisco's many elitist districts is Nob Hill, the locus for all sorts of establishments that cater to San Francisco high society, and all sorts of great views that anyone of any class will enjoy. A steep walk north from Union Square, the area was once the site of the hilltop estates of four of the city's biggest entrepreneurs and now holds some of its poshest hotels. Ignore the looks of suspicious doormen as you nose around the lobbies of the **Fairmont Hotel** at California and Mason streets, the **Mark Hopkins,** across California Street from the Fairmont, and **Stanford Court Hotel,** at California and Powell streets. Also up here you'll find the **Cable Car Museum** (Washington and Mason Sts., tel. 415/474–1887; admission free), which exhibits photographs, scale models, and other memorabilia from the cable car's 115-year history.

Right on Nob Hill, **Grace Cathedral** is a nouveau Gothic structure that took 53 years to build; it's basically a poured-concrete replica of an old European-style cathedral. The gilded bronze doors at the east entrance were taken from casts of Ghiberti's *Gates of Paradise* on the baptistery in Florence. For a truly sublime experience, come for the singing of the **Vespers,** every Thursday at 5:15 PM; an all male choir will lift you out of the muck of your petty little world and leave you feeling almost like you have a little gold halo over your head. Guided tours of 15th-century artifacts are free, but donations are accepted. *Tel. 415/776–6611.*

Farther north is **Russian Hill,** originally the burial ground for Russian seal hunters and traders, and today one of the city's most elite addresses, featuring a combination of old Victorian homes and new high rises. Along with some spectacular views of the Bay and Alcatraz Island, Russian Hill is home to the crookedest street in America, **Lombard Street,** which runs between Hyde and Leavenworth. Take your Rollerblades off for this one.

NORTH BEACH • • •

The neighborhood that starts at the intersection of Columbus Avenue and Broadway and heads north on Columbus comprises the well-established, and much-loved Italian district of San Francisco. Nowadays North Beach offers an incredible selection of restaurants, delis, and cafés, not to mention a lingering aura of the alternative or "beat" culture that thrived here during the 1950s. Poets and writers like Jack Kerouac, Lawrence Ferlinghetti, and Allen Ginsberg came to North Beach from New York around 1953 to write, play music, and generally live and promote a lifestyle that emphasized eastern religions, free love, free thinking, drugs, and crazy new means of artistic expression. From this movement sprung Ferlinghetti's **City Lights Bookstore** (261 Columbus Ave.), which to this day continues to publish and sell alternative forms of literature as well as stuff by the Beats, who have since been anthologized to high heaven, and who are now only vaguely more alternative than the half-time show at the Rose Bowl. One indication of this new mainstream status is the recently renamed **Jack Kerouac Lane,** which is right next to the store.

Although the number of Italian-Americans living in the area is diminishing, and the Beats reached their peak back in the late-1950s, the neighborhood remains one of the most interesting to explore, with its innumerable shops, galleries, and watering holes—some which have been catering to the same clientele for the last 40 years. Washington Square, at the intersection of Broadway and Union, is the heart of North Beach. Bordered by great bakeries and coffee shops, the square attracts an eclectic crowd of old-time Italian residents, noisome bums, and tourists. Come early in the morning to see dozens of old Chinese men practicing tai chi in the mist.

POLK GULCH • • •

Once the gay heart of San Francisco, Polk Gulch is now the second most prominent gay neighborhood, after the Castro District. The Gulch is part yuppie neighborhood, part urban blight. It's a good place to buy stick-to-your-ribs roasted coffee (at the two **Royal Ground** locations) as well as heavy-metal leather and spandex for cousin Bob back home. Two of its big industries, drug sales and prostitution, don't exactly make it a prowling ground for tourist buses. Rumor has it that the call boys get more expensive by the block, with the most expensive block being from Bush to Pine streets, and the bargain basement around Geary Street. Once you get past the sleaze, Polk Street makes a nice walk to Aquatic Park and the Wharf area. Stop in at **Les Croissants** (between Pine and California Sts.) for coffee, sandwiches, and loitering. **Hot 'n' Hunky** serves good hamburgers with a Menage A Trois (fried mozzarella, mushrooms, and zucchini) on the side.

● ● ● THE PRESIDIO

Founded in 1776, the Presidio is one of the oldest military installations in the country. The base is slated for closure in the '90s, which has launched a huge debate about what to do with the land, which occupies a prime position above the Golden Gate and is some of the most beautiful real estate in the city. Whatever happens the base is open to the public, and you should take some time to wander through the 1,500 acres of rolling hills, forests, and attractive old military buildings. The views out over the bay are terrific. The

Gay and Lesbian San Francisco

San Francisco actually promotes the fact that it is a gay city, the gayest in the world, even. In most cities, gays and lesbians are one of a number of special-interest groups clamoring for attention; in San Francisco, homosexuals are the most prominent special-interest group, and they are visible everywhere. You see couples holding hands and kissing and getting in fights and flirting, just as couples do everywhere. Depending on the neighborhood you visit, the population can be as much as 95% gay—it really is feasible for a lesbian woman or a gay man to go about her/his life in San Francisco and deal exclusively with other gays and lesbians, both in business and in pleasure.

Gay people populate all of the neighborhoods in San Francisco, but the most concentrated gay neighborhood is the Castro District, followed closely by Polk Gulch. There is not really a lesbian neighborhood per se, but many lesbians gravitate to the Mission District, Bernal Heights, and Noe Valley. The Mission is home to the Old Wives' Tales bookstore and the Women's Building, a community resource center.

You'll find a vital club scene, but if you're not into the clubs there are lots of other features to hold your interest. There's usually a good movie playing at the Castro Theatre (see After Dark, below), and there's a thriving café scene, the flagship of which is probably Café Flore (see Food, above). San Francisco also features a good number of gay theater productions, poetry readings, and comedy shows that provide new insights into the dilemmas, issues, and hilarities facing the gay community, whether you're gay or straight or bisexual or asexual or transsexual or. . . . Such events are listed in gay-oriented publications like Bay Times and The Sentinel.

While gay people are the victims of violence everywhere, in San Francisco a lot of such cases are well documented and prosecuted. This poses the question of whether more instances of gay bashing actually occur here, or whether the gay population is stronger, more vociferous, and more effective in assuring their rights—and whether the law and court system is better versed in civil rights in the Bay Area or whether persistent efforts on the part of gay political organizations and politicians alike have forced them to stand up and take heed.

easiest way to get there is to drive toward the water on Van Ness, turn left on Lombard, and then follow the signs. Otherwise, take Bus 41 from the Embarcadero.

SOUTH OF MARKET ● ● ●

The South-of-Market area, or SOMA, leads a Jekyll-and-Hyde kind of existence: By day it's the mild-mannered, sprawling home of large factory outlet stores that cater to suburbanites in neat sportswear (the outlet merchandise ranges from high-quality goods to schlock; *see* Shopping, *below*). By night the area magically transforms into a neon landscape of clubs and bars that indulge fun-seekers, disparate and desperate. Some clubs cater to bright-eyed boys and girls from bedroom communities all dressed up for a night of partying, some lure in tattooed leatherettes of varying genders who, in some cases, really are as tough as they look. If you like clubbing at all, you're bound to find a place that suits you. The music ranges from post-industrial house to a variety of live bands to mainstream pop country and western to eccentric live cabaret music. Some of the hottest clubs only happen once a week or even once a month, and they change their locations (*see* After Dark, *below*).

Other features to check out: The new **Ansel Adams Center** (250 4th St., tel. 415/495–7000) has the best photography museum around, and the **Cartoon Art Museum** (Print Center Building, 665 3rd St., at Townsend St., tel. 415/546–3922) will teach you everything you ever wanted to know about the history of the cartoon. You can pick up a guide to all of the area's offerings, including maps and discount coupons, for $2 at most of the outlet stores.

UNION SQUARE ● ● ●

Union Square might be considered the center of the city if it weren't so soulless. The square was named in honor of rallies held prior to the Civil War in support of the Union, but some San Franciscans will tell you the name more appropriately refers to the huge demonstrations held here in the '30s by labor organizations, which at one point effectively shut down the city for a week. Today, Union Square is encircled by a ring—make that a solid gold band—of the most elegant stores and boutiques in the city, including I. Magnin, Neiman-Marcus, Saks, Chanel, Tiffany, Cartier, Hermés, and Gumps. Gumps, a major importer of goods from the far East, originated in San Francisco and is known for its jade collection; visit the upper floors if you want to feel like you're in a museum and have people glare at you like you're going to make off with the *Mona Lisa.*

MAIDEN LANE A short alley off the east side of Union Square, Maiden Lane was once the lair of the "cribs" or brothels that formed the center of a world-renowned and extremely violent red-light district. Now it's a shopping arcade for the thick-walleted, and the site of San Francisco's only Frank Lloyd Wright building, the **Circle Gallery,** which served as the prototype for the Guggenheim Museum in New York. Wright also designed the gorgeous teak cabinets. And just a note, the bubble ceiling costs $4,000 to clean. The gallery's collection includes paintings by artists as incongruous as fashion illustrator René Gruau, Yaacov X, and Donna Summer. (Yes, that Donna Summer). *140 Maiden La., tel. 415/989–2100. Wheelchair access.*

POWELL STREET Everyone passes through the intersection of Market and Powell streets: proselytizers, street musicians, artists, punks, young professionals, flower vendors, protesters, dogs, pigeons, and tourists in matching jogging suits. Especially tourists in matching jogging suits. All converge around the cable-car turnaround, the Powell BART station, the **Tourist Information Center** tucked below the street in the submerged Hallidie Plaza, and a Woolworth's with astonishingly inflated prices. Along Powell and Market are a string of cheap fast-food joints, including **Blondie's** (or, according to locals, "Blandie's") **Pizza.** Across Market Street are the Emporium department store and, adjoining it, San Francisco's latest monument to the shopping gods, the **San Francisco Centre** (corner of 5th and Market, tel. 415/495–5656). The open interior of the building is seven stories high, and surrounded by a vertiginous spiral of escalators that lead up to

Nordstrom's department store. Riding the escalators to the top is like being shrunk to an infinitesimal size and given a tour of a DNA helix: Guaranteed to produce a flashback, even if you've never taken acid.

● ● ● MUSEUMS

On a rainy day, you should take a look at some of the most diverse museums on the West Coast. Although the big ones, especially the Asian Art Museum, compare to those found anywhere else in the country, you should check out the little, free, funky ones, too, for tastes eclectic and perverse. To save a little money on the big three, you can buy one ticket at the De Young Museum, Asian Art Museum, or the Legion of Honor, and use it for admission to the other two.

African American Historical and Cultural Society Museum fulfills a number of purposes, all of them aimed at exploring and disseminating African-American culture. It encompasses a contemporary art gallery that features works by African and African-American artists, an intriguing gift shop that sells jewelry and artifacts, and a historical archive and research library. In addition, the museum provides other services to the community, such as performing-arts classes and lecture series. *Building C, Room 165, Fort Mason Center, tel. 415/441–0640. Donation requested. Open Wed.–Sun. noon–5.*

Ansel Adams Center. If you're even remotely interested in serious photography, come here, the place where art photographs go to die. The largest repository of art photography on the West Coast, the Ansel Adams Center has five rotating exhibits, one of which is devoted to Adams's work. Born of the Friends of Photography, a national group founded by Adams, the center serves photographers with publications, awards, and an educational series taught by famous shutterbugs. They also have an incredible bookstore. *250 4th St., between Howard and Folsom Sts., tel. 415/495–7000. Admission: $4, $3 students; free first Tues. of month. Open Tues.–Sun. 11–6.*

Asian Art Museum. The western world's largest collection of Asian art is here, and what you'll see on a single visit constitutes just a small fragment of it. In an attempt to showcase it all, the museum rotates the exhibits year-round. The first floor is given over to Chinese art; the second floor holds treasures from almost every country in Asia (including South Asia and Southeast Asia). Notable features include the Jade Room and the Indian Gallery. *John F. Kennedy and Tea Garden Drs., Golden Gate Park, tel. 415/668–8921. Admission: $5; free first Wed. of month, first Sat. of month until noon. Open Wed. 10–8:30, Thurs.–Sun. 10–5.*

California Academy of Sciences is a huge natural-history complex that actually houses several separate museums, the **Steinhart Aquarium,** and **Morrison Planetarium.** The biggest draw is the Aquarium's **Fish Roundabout,** which places you in an underwater world of 14,500 different creatures. The living coral reef, with fish, giant clams, tropical sharks, and a rainbow of hard and soft corals, is beautiful and unusual. Go mid-morning so you can watch the penguins and dolphins at feeding time. If earthquakes are inextricably linked with San Francisco in your imagination, try the trembling earthquake floor in the Space and Earth Hall of the **Natural History Museum.** Other halls of interest include the Life Through Time Hall, which chronicles evolution from the dinosaurs through early mammals, and the Wattis Hall of Man, which presents lifelike habitat scenes that range from the icy terrain of the Arctic Inuit to the highlands of New Guinea. There's even a Far Side Gallery for Gary Larson fans. *Between John F. Kennedy and Martin Luther King, Jr. Drs., Golden Gate Park, tel. 415/750–7000, laser shows at planetarium: 415/750–7127. Admission: $6. Open daily 10–5.*

California Palace of the Legion of Honor is a fine-arts museum that features a permanent collection of European—especially French—paintings, sculptures, tapestries, and 18th-century household treasures in its 14 galleries, as well hosting occasional special exhibits. You'll find Auguste Rodin's ***The Thinker*** thinking in the courtyard, and you can see more of Rodin's work inside. The largest collection of prints and drawings in the West is housed in the Achenbach Foundation for the Graphic Arts, modeled on the Palace of the Legion of Honor in Paris, and built as a memorial to San Francisco's World War I dead. *Clement St. and 34th Ave., Lincoln Park, tel. 415/863–3330 (recorded information message) or 415/750–3600. Admission: $5; free first Wed. of month, and first Sat. of month 10–noon. Open Wed.–Fri. 10–5.*

Chinese Historical Society Museum features artifacts relating to the history of Chinatown, as well as the Chinese immigrant experience in California and San Francisco. This is the largest collection of its kind anywhere. *650 Commercial St. between Kearny and Montgomery Sts., tel. 415/391–1188. Donation requested. Open Tues.–Sat. noon–4. Closed major holidays.*

Come to the **Exploratorium** for the ultimate fourth grade field trip you never took—it's a fun place for children and grown-ups to learn about science and technology in a big, drafty warehouse. In the more than 650 exhibits, many of them computer-assisted, a strong emphasis is placed on interaction with the senses, making it especially popular with people on hallucinogenic drugs. Reservations are required for the crawl-through Tactile Gallery. *3601 Lyon St. between Marina Blvd. and Lombard St., tel. 415/561–0360. Admission: $7, students $5, disabled $3; free first Wed. of month. Closed Mon. except for most holidays.*

Galeria de la Raza. Founded in 1970 by artists of the Chicano Arts movement, this was the first Mexican Museum in the United States and it remains a strong and influential cultural resource. Eight major exhibits are presented each year along with numerous community arts programs. *2851 24th St., at Bryant, tel. 415/826–8009. Admission free. Open Tues.–Sat. noon–6.*

Jewish Community Museum is a handsome, small museum with revolving exhibits that trace important moments in Jewish history. *121 Steuart St., at Mission St., tel. 415/543–8880. Admission: $3, $1.50 students. Open Sun., Tues.–Fri. 10–4. Closed Jewish holidays.*

M.H. de Young Memorial Museum is a large museum most impressive for its substantial, 21-gallery survey collection of American art, from paintings and sculpture to decorative arts, textiles, and furniture that goes as far back as 1670. Artists represented include Sargent, Whistler, Church, and Wood. The de Young also puts up the kind of international traveling exhibit that draws the art lovers out of the suburbs: Past exhibits have included the King Tut exhibit, the Helga paintings, and the Dutch Masters. There are also displays of classical and tribal arts. And don't miss the great gift shop and garden café. Tours of the American collection are offered Wednesday through Sunday at 1:30 and 2:30. *Between John F. Kennedy Dr. and 8th Ave., Golden Gate Park, tel. 415/750–3600 or 415/863–3330 (recorded message). Admission: $5. Open Wed.–Fri. 10–5.*

The Mexican Museum is a unique center for Mexican and Chicano culture in the United States, with an impressive 9,000-object permanent collection. It's a relatively snug space, but they have had scored the likes of Diego Rivera and Frida Kahlo exhibits; an excellent recent show concentrated on Chicano graffiti art. *Building D, Fort Mason Center, tel. 415/441–0404. Admission: $4, $2 students. Free first Wed. of month, noon–8. Open Wed.–Sun. noon–5.*

Museo ItaloAmericano celebrates Italian and Italian-American cultural contributions in a large gallery space. There is often a special exhibit on display, in addition to the permanent collection. *Building C, Room 100, Fort Mason Center, tel. 415/673–2200. Admission: $2. Open Wed.–Sun. noon–5.*

San Francisco Museum of Modern Art was the West Coast's first museum devoted to 20th-century art. Founded in 1935, SF MOMA is significant among modern art museums despite its small size. The permanent collection contains paintings and sculpture that represent the major modernist and postmodernist movements. It was one of the first museums to showcase art photography, and its collection of contemporary photos is vast. Newer pursuits include architecture and design and video installations. There's an excellent bookstore on the ground floor. It has long been located on the third and fourth floors of the Veterans' Building, but a move is planned for 1993 to put the museum in a much larger space, designed by Mario Botta, in the South-of-Market area. *401 Van Ness*

Ave., at McAllister St., tel. 415/252–4000 or 415/863–8800 (recorded message). Admission: $4, students $2; free first Tues. of month, 10–5. Thurs. admission: 2 adults $4, individuals $3, students $1, 5–9 PM.

● ● ● CHEAP THRILLS

Black-clad hipster though you may be, San Francisco is such a beautiful city that you just have to do a few of the touristy things that would otherwise make you gag. For starters, you should take a **ferry** to Tiburon or Sausalito from the Ferry Building. The views of the city are great. Similarly, check out the view from atop **Twin Peaks;** from up there you realize just how small the city is. Nothing can compare to a bottle of Napa wine at **sunset** on Ocean or Baker Beach; failing that, watch the sunset from the **Marina Green** with the Golden Gate Bridge in the foreground. And, last but not least, walk across the **Golden Gate.** But, for God's sake, take a sweater.

FESTIVALS AND SEASONAL EVENTS

JANUARY In addition to the ballet and chamber orchestra seasons, January opens **whale-watching season,** which runs through April.

FEBRUARY Definitely check out February's **Chinese New Year,** celebrated by the largest Chinese community in North America and culminating in the justly famous **Golden Dragon Parade.**

MARCH The Irish take over on **St. Patrick's Day,** which revolves around drinking alcoholic beverages, a special San Francisco activity.

APRIL Japantown hosts the **Cherry Blossom Festival,** a Japanese cultural festival that extends over two weekends and incorporates a variety of activities. Also at the end of April through the beginning of May is the **San Francisco International Film Festival.** For info, call 415/567–4641.

MAY World-class runners compete against costumed centipedes and huge safe-sex condom caravans in the **Bay to Breakers** race, a 7.5-km race that stretches from the bay to the ocean and which draws costumed revelers, spectators, and a few serious runners in a successful San Francisco combination of partying and fitness. The Mission District comes alive with **Cinco de Mayo** celebrations on the days surrounding the 5th of May.

JUNE Summer brings out all the neighborhood celebrations, including the Mission District's **Carnaval** celebrations (tel. 415/826–1401), the **Union Street Fair,** the **Haight Street Fair,** the **North Beach Fair,** and the **Polk Street Fair,** all of which stretch over a weekend and feature craft booths, music, food, and other cultural activities. On the last Sunday in June, attend the huge, high-spirited **Lesbian and Gay Freedom Day Parade,** preceded by Gay Pride Week, which features such special-interest celebrations as Let It

Ways to Spot a Tourist in S.F.

- ***Tourists are the ones dressed in shorts and T-shirts in summer at the Golden Gate Bridge when the temperature is 50° and the wind is singing in the wires.***
- ***Tourists are the ones driving down windy Lombard Street, steering through the viewfinder of the videocamera.***
- ***Tourists are the same people trying to balance accelerator and clutch on the hill leading up to Lombard Street. Notice the smell of burning oil and the dents in front and rear bumpers.***
- ***Tourists are anyone at Fisherman's Wharf.***

All Hang Out Day: Fat Dykes on Castro—an annual street dance party for large lesbians. Watch for rainbow flags displaying gay pride.

JULY The **Fillmore Street Fair** usually takes place over a weekend in late June or early July. The Fourth of July **fireworks** at Crissy Field in the Presidio are a San Francisco tradition, drawing tens of thousands.

SEPTEMBER The **San Francisco Blues Festival,** which draws some mighty big names, is held at Fort Mason. Also in the fall are other, smaller music festivals, including a reggae festival and a jazz festival. Also check out the **Folsom Street Fair,** one weekend in September, and the **Japantown Festival for the Viewing of the Moon.**

OCTOBER This is the best month to be in the Castro District, which begins with the **Castro Street Fair,** a huge, fun street fair, and winds up with the **Castro Street Halloween** celebration, with beauties in drag performing for onlookers in drag.

DECEMBER December brings traditional and hugely popular San Francisco performances of **The Nutcracker** and **The Messiah.**

Shopping

Even if you can't afford to do any other kind of shopping, you can still do some good window shopping in San Francisco. Sophisticated emporia ornament Union Square, chic boutiques flourish on Union Street, souvenir shops crowd Fisherman's Wharf, bizarre bazaars line Haight Street, and outlet stores are scattered south of Market Street. Though brimming with pricey boutiques, San Francisco doesn't neglect budget shoppers; off-price department stores, outlet stores, and thrift and second-hand stores abound. Bargain hunters also flock to the South-of-Market area's outlet stores, usually clustered in out-of-the-way places and carrying new merchandise not sold in regular retail stores—sometimes because of small flaws, but often solely because the product is a season out of date, didn't sell well, or has been discontinued. Other specialty stores there carry leather, silk, exercise, large-size, and bridal apparel. There's even an outlet for teddy bears. The *Factory Outlet Shopping Guide,* a helpful listing and map of the area's offerings, is available at most of the outlet stores for $2. For a more extensive account of the Bay Area's discount shopping opportunities, locals use Sally Socolich's book, *Bargain-Hunting in the Bay Area.*

SPECIALTY STORES **Adolph Gasser.** Simply the best source for photography and video equipment in San Francisco, and the largest inventory in northern California. *181 2nd St., at Howard St., tel. 415/495–3852; 5733 Geary Blvd., at 22nd Ave., tel. 415/751–1045.*

Condomania. The first store in the Bay Area devoted wholly to that symbol of modern sexuality and prudence-without-being-a-prude. They come in all shapes, sizes, flavors, and textures, and you can also obtain information on creative safe sex as well. *Corner of California and Fillmore Sts.*

Dudley Perkins Harley-Davidson. The oldest Harley-Davidson dealership in the world. *66 Page St. between Franklin and Gough Sts., tel. 415/431–5323.*

FAO Schwarz Fifth Avenue. Remember in the movie *Big* when Tom Hanks plays in that humongous toy store and then performs "Chopsticks" by jumping around on an enormous piano keyboard? That store was FAO Schwarz, and you too can wreak this much havoc if you try hard and have a lot of money to pay for the damage. *48 Stockton St., tel. 415/394–8700.*

Global Village Bazaar. Politically correct products from Third World countries and related to environmental concerns. A quarter of the profits go to ecological organizations. *1659 Haight St., tel. 415/864–4415.*

Good Vibrations. A lesbian-owned, user-friendly vibrator store with a large selection of vibrators and adult literature. Don't be afraid. *1210 Valencia St., tel. 415/550–0827.*

Image Leather. They'll accommodates all of your intimate leather needs, with a wide variety of cock rings, harnesses, whips, collars, and boots to choose from. *2199 Market St., at Sanchez, in the Castro, tel. 415/621–7551.*

Kit Shickers. Gorgeous handmade Western boots, shoes, and belts in colorful, exotic leathers. *442A Haight St., tel. 415/431–5487; 509 Columbus Ave., tel. 415/433–5487.*

Magri Motorcycles. The motorcycle enthusiast and historian will appreciate emphasis on hard-to-find British and American bikes, including Vincent, Indian, Norton, and BSA. *1220 Pennsylvania Ave., tel. 415/285–6735.*

North Beach Leather. Ignore the snippy staff and browse to your heart's content through the intricately designed and richly colored expensive leather and suede garments. *190 Geary St., tel. 415/362–8300; 1365 Columbus Ave., tel. 415/441–3208.*

Perestroika Store. With the breakup of the Soviet Union, this store provides a last chance to pick up Soviet memorabilia. *Pier 39, tel. 415/788–7043.*

OUTLETS **Esprit Factory Outlet.** You too can look like the fresh scrubbed and slightly artsy young American (Joe/Jill normal but with gel in your hair), and now at a substantial savings!!! *499 Illinois St., tel. 415/777–5558.*

Aca Joe Factory Outlet. Men's sportswear (also suitable for women). *148 Townsend St., tel. 415/541–9192.*

New York Cosmetics & Fragrances. *318 Brannan St., tel. 415/543–3880; 674 8th St., tel. 415/621–4445.*

Basic Brown Bear Factory and Store. Tour one of the few remaining teddy bear factories in the United States on Saturdays at 11 and 2. *444 DeHaro St., at Mariposa St., tel. 415/626–0781.*

THRIFT AND SECOND-HAND STORES **Aardvark's Odd Ark.** Keeps the thrifty crowd coming back with a good selection of used clothing. A good source for basics, like men's cotton dress shirts and vintage Levi's. *1501 Haight St., tel. 415/621–3141.*

American Rag Compagnie. This store mixes old and new, and while none of it is cheap, the dreck has already been filtered out, the clothes are in good shape, and everything is sanitized for your protection. Possibly the best selection of vintage little black dresses in San Francisco. *1305 Van Ness Ave., tel. 415/474–5214.*

Buffalo Exchange. A popular, offbeat source of used (and some new) clothing and accessories for men and women, especially young people. *1555 Haight St., tel. 415/431–7733; 1800 Polk St., tel. 415/346–5726.*

One Moment In Time. Gals—forget to pack your formal? Consider renting (or buying) designer evening gowns, cocktail dresses, or fake fur coats here. They also have purses, jewelry, and other accessories. You can even rent a wedding dress, if the occasion calls for it. *278 Post St., #404, tel. 415/788–1980.*

Thrift Town. A large, traditional thrift store, and sometime repository of decades-old designer clothing and accessories. It's a good source for anything from spectator pumps to acrylic sweaters to used cribs. A fine selection of bric-a-brac. *2101 Mission St., at 17th St., tel. 415/861–1132.*

Wasteland. T.S. Eliot probably wouldn't shop here, but it's a great place for eccentrics who dress like he did. All natural fibers and lots of black, plus the grooviest selection of bell bottoms and other fashion items you hoped to never see again. A good source for vintage costume jewelry. *1660 Haight St., tel. 415/863–3150.*

Worn Out West. San Francisco can be counted on to supply what you can't find back home, and this Castro District store does its part by providing second-hand western wear to budget-conscious cowboys manqué. *582 Castro St., tel. 415/431–6020.*

BOOKSTORES **A Clean Well-Lighted Place for Books.** A very pleasant bookstore with lots of nice, new, clean books. Attend regular readings by well-known authors. *601 Van Ness Ave. in Opera Plaza, tel. 415/441–6670.*

Bound Together Book Collective. Anarchist literature from all over the world, as well as nifty stickers declaring you vehemently anti-establishment. *1369 Haight St., tel. 415/431–8355.*

City Lights. The most famous bookstore in San Francisco, mother and home to the Beat generation. Owned by poet Lawrence Ferlinghetti, the store was busted on obscenity charges for selling Allen Ginsberg's poem *Howl*—which City Lights also published. The store is still the source for Beat literature, much of which it publishes under its own imprint, as well as a wide selection of other poetry and literature. *261 Columbus Ave., tel. 415/362–8193.*

European Book Company. European language materials, including magazines and newspapers. Foreign language dictionaries and travel guides. *925 Larkin St., between Geary and Post Sts., tel. 415/474–0626.*

Modern Times. Good selection of titles on progressive political issues and international fiction. *968 Valencia St., tel. 415/282–9246.*

Old Wives' Tales. Primarily women's issues and women authors; also a good feminist-information resource. *1009 Valencia St., tel. 415/821–4675.*

After Dark

San Francisco nightlife leans toward the casual, though you can wear incredibly expensive clothes and sneer at your fellow patrons over $10 martinis if you really want to. You can choose to see a funky old movie or have a drink in any one of about 10,000 neighborhood bars, see a performance art piece where actors in blue body paint throw carrot peelings and Jell-O into the audience, or don a floppy flower hat and ingest some illegal substances and dance all night and all day and all night long. Look in the *San Francisco Weekly* (the city's free weekly entertainment guide) for possibilities; you should be able to find somewhere between two and 100 different things to do on any given night, costing from next to nothing to a whole lot of money. The *Bay Times* is the best source for gay and lesbian-oriented entertainment listings. Bars and clubs (and liquor stores!) are all supposed to close by 2 AM, but several clubs stay open after hours for those who just can't stop dancing.

BARS **The Albion.** Catering to a young disaffected crowd, this place has a fine pool table, a nice bar, and music that will make you feel more disaffected, all in the glow of pink neon lights that will only make you feel nauseated. *3139 16th St., between Valencia and Guerrero, tel. 415/552–8558.*

Cafe du Nord. Recently heralded by the local press as an "in" spot, this place, which features live jazz, and a hip, smoky and friendly atmosphere, will probably be out by the time you read this, but renaissances do happen. *2170 Market St., near Church St., tel. 415/861–5016.*

Edinburgh Castle. A wannabe British pub in the Tenderloin where you can play darts, eat fish-n-chips, imitate Monty Python movies, smoke pipes, etc. *950 Geary, tel. 415/885–4074.*

The Elbo Room. Filled with a couple pool tables and an artsy young crowd listening to a variety of rock music, this place has a mellow atmosphere conducive to conversation. *647 Valencia St., near 17th, tel. 415/552–7788.*

The Golden Cane. With very little in the way of atmosphere, and the cheapest drinks on the street, this is a good place to pound a few cold ones before heading to the Haight Street clubs. *1569 Haight St., tel. 415/626–1112.*

Murio's John Trophy Room. The biker bar for the new generation of Harley riders and those who wish they were, with the standard pool table, jukebox, TV showing cult porn films, etc. etc. Fun and grungy. *1811 Haight St., tel. 415/752–2971.*

The Noc Noc. This bar has an interior that looks like a postmodern cave, music that sounds like a postmodern complaint, and a crowd that looks like it was born sometime after disco, and learned how to use eyeliner about 10 minutes after that. *557 Haight St., tel. 415/861–5811.*

Pierce Street Annex Drinking Establishment. One of the bars in the "Triangle," an area in the Pacific Heights/Marina area known for its clonelike bars in close proximity to each other, that serves yuppies, fraternity and sorority people, and innocent out-of-towners who get sucked in. This particular one has a dance floor and karaoke nights. *3138 Fillmore, tel. 415/567–1400.*

Savoy-Tivoli. A North Beach institution that caters to those who have strolled up from a hard day in the Financial District. They open the front doors when the weather's nice, making it prime territory to drink wine, watch the world go by, and generally feel like you're in Italy. *1434 Grant Ave., tel. 415/362–7023.*

Specs'. One of the classic, longtime North Beach hangouts for the perennially half-sloshed, this is a jovial, divey, no-attitude sort of place where even if your company sucks, you can still gaze at the memorabilia on the walls all night and stay entertained. *12 Saroyan, in the alley across the street from City Lights Books, tel. 415/421–4112.*

The Toronado. A narrow, dark dive in the Haight with lots of folks in leather and lots of beer on tap. Good casual hangout—boisterous and loud compared to the generally cool climate of the Haight. *547 Haight St., tel. 415/863–2276.*

GAY AND LESBIAN **Café San Marcos.** This large, fairly plush bar caters mainly to lesbians and those who hang out with them; play pool, or go out on the patio and watch Castro Street go by. *2367 Market St., tel. 415/861–3846.*

The Detour. Minimally decorated with a chain link fence and pool table. The urgent techno-house music causes the sexual frustration level in the room to skyrocket, since there's no dance floor. A youngish leather queen wannabe crowd with goatees predominates. Friday and Saturday nights are dollar beer nights. If you forget to bring the address, listen for the music, since the black-on-black sign is impossible to see at night. *2348 Market St., tel. 415/861–6053.*

The only straight bar in the Castro is named Dick's, at 290 Sanchez Street off Market.

Midnight Sun. Three video screens help alleviate the need for conversation in this crowded vanilla bar, showing a mix of weird TV and current music videos. *4067 18th St., tel. 415/861–4186.*

QT. Stands for "quick trick." Legend has it that the owner gave Anita Baker her start. Cozy up to the hustlers and drag queens and the "appreciative older gentlemen." The unassuming decor (read: mirrors) is reminiscent of the cover of a Traffic album from 1971.

Two Loads of Laundry and You Might Get the Spins

Although you may have to lug your laundry a ways to get to the Brainwash Laundromat (1122 Fulsom St., tel. 415/861–FOOD), once the clothes are in the machine you can drink a beer or a glass of wine, relax over a pizza or sandwich, and listen to some live music that happens four nights a week. A fine place to exchange your deepest thoughts about powder vs. liquid, and to generally air your dirty laundry.

Live music Thursday, Friday and Saturday. Strip shows Sundays and Tuesdays for men. *1312 Polk St., tel. 415/885–1114.*

CLUBS Nightclub life ranges from the cheap, local, and casual to the expensive, pretentious, and trendy. For the most eclectic and underground of the clubs, keep eyes and ears open for the one-night extravaganzas that take place in changing locations; the most common way to find them is by word of mouth, or by going to a regular club and looking cool enough to get handed a little card by a roving club publicist who wants to keep his/her club filled with interesting/rich-looking people. The *San Francisco Weekly* has listings for lots of clubs gay, straight, and mixed.

STRAIGHT **Big Heart City.** This big, funky space hosts a variety of semi-underground clubs both gay and straight including the aptly named **Love.** Curious? *836 Mission St., tel. 415/957–1825.*

Cesar's Latin Palace. Cesar's Latin All-Stars play salsa most nights, with occasional guest artists. Open until 6 AM weekend nights. *3140 Mission St., near Army St., tel. 415/648–6611.*

Clubhouse. A smaller dance spot way over on the casual end of the spectrum where you can catch everything from reggae dance nights to acid-techno-modern-house nights to Faster Pussycat (*see below*), the sometimes lesbian club on Wednesdays. Cheap. *3160 16th St., tel. 415/621–1617.*

DNA Lounge. This reliable standby for late-night dancing ('til 4 AM nightly) and eclectic live shows, from music to tattoo/piercing shows, will always be around and you'll always find somebody interesting to talk to or dance with, no matter whether you come today or in 10 years. *375 11th St., tel. 415/626–1409.*

Rave Culture

By the time you read this it may be unbearably mainstream or snuffed out of existence by overzealous law enforcement officials with misplaced priorities. But if it's not, you may get a chance to sample the latest trend to hit the shores of San Francisco and be embraced by the perennially youthful culture here—it's the rave, the enormous, ecstatic techno-shamanic trend that has permeated nightclub life and fashion all over the city. The rave basically consists of a few thousand people dancing in a large space to thumping techno-house music (wave after wave of undulating sound) with looks of utter bliss on their faces for six to eight hours straight. Boys, girls, genderfucks, straight, gay, bi, and others indulge, and claim that within the parameters of that timespan, everyone is created equal by their love for the music. Everyone who can afford the $10–$20 cover charge plus the cost of drugs or drinks, that is. Ravers are members of the technology generation: They grew up on TV—lost their virginity in front of MTV in fact—and now they mostly just want to dance all night in floppy hats and baggy clothes and lots of flower accessories. Another important component of the rave movement in many people's minds is the drug MDMA, also known as Ecstasy, which creates a state of euphoria, a sense of being at peace with the world, and general blissed-outedness—all for the low, low price of about 20 bucks and a vicious hangover (loveover?) the next day.

Mister Five's. The best place in town to dance to hip hop, soul, dance-hall reggae, and jazzy grooves in an attractive, open space. *30 Rose St., tel. 415/864–7336. Open Wed.–Sun.*

Nickie's Haight St. Bar and Grill. Red vinyl booths and Christmas lights decorate this hole in the wall entirely lacking in pretension and low on cover charge ($2). Excellent dance music, including funk, rare groove, soul, hip hop, reggae, and African/Latin/Arabic mixes. Eclectic, cheap, fun, racially mixed, and mostly straight. *460 Haight St., tel. 415/621–0249.*

Nightbreak. Trendoid, straight rock-and-roll gothic, both live and recorded. *1821 Haight St., tel. 221–9008.*

1015 Club. Hosts various clubs on a nightly basis, including the vastly popular **Colossus** (*see* Gay and Lesbian Clubs, *below*) and the vastly popular **Martini,** which encapsulates the history of disco into three little rooms: deep funk in the basement, 70s disco in the gold room, and High House in the main dance room. Dress up for this one and plan to wait outside a bit, but it'll be worth it once you start dancing. *1015 Folsom St., tel. 415/431–0700.*

Townsend. Hosts various nightly club happenings in a wide, open, neo-industrial warehouse space. *177 Townsend St., tel. 415/974–6020.*

MIXED **The Box.** Hardcore hip hop, funk, and house; less attitude than most young places because everybody's sweating on the dance floor. Go-go boxes mounted on the wall showcase dancers with breathtaking bodies at full throttle. This is technically a gay club, run by lesbians, but the multi-cultural crowd includes straights. Simply put, it's a very popular club and everybody wants to go. The most accomplished DJs and club dance troupes in the city, including Page Hodel, SF's most-famous queer DJ on Thursday nights at the Kennel Club. *628 Divisadero St., tel. 415/931–1914.*

GAY AND LESBIAN **Club Q,** a lesbian club on Friday nights at the I-Beam, caters to a variety of ages and styles. Low on pretension, with go-go dancers and house music. *1748 Haight St., tel. 415/668–6006.*

Colossus. Many beautiful boys dancing to loud, deep house music till all hours of the night. A San Francisco institution. *1015 Folsom, tel. 415/431–0700.*

The End Up hosts different clubs catering to different crowds different the week. The mixed **Club Uranus** (say it out loud for maximum impact), on Sunday night, is a good place to dance to techno-house music in your underwear or your harness and G-string or your dashiki and pearls. Be sure to check out the variously gendered go-go dancers and the party games featuring said go-go dancers, such as "Crisco Twister," which inevitably end in activities that will make the casual visitor blush and giggle. Fridays is **Decadence** (one patron describes it as Uranus on a bad night), the place to go by default since there's not much happening elsewhere on Friday nights. For the gals, there's **The Girl Spot** on Saturday night, featuring mixed house music, gorgeous girl go-go dancers who will turn you out right there on the stage, and a minimum of attitude. The bar has a pool table, a patio with an elevated deck, and a waterfall surreally situated almost underneath U.S. 101. Admission to the clubs is usually $5–$10. *401 6th St., at Harrison, tel 415/543–7700.*

Esta Noche, tucked away in the Mission, plays a good mix of Latin, house music, and '70s disco. Most often frequented by young Latinos and the men who love them. European-American patrons are respectfully requested to refrain from doing the cha cha cha. *3079 16th St., between Mission and Valencia, tel. 415/861–5757.*

Faster Pussycat, on Wednesday nights at the Clubhouse, is a primarily lesbian dance space where other cats can play as long as they're cool. Look for events such as erotic short story readings with titles like "The Wet Seat of her Harley," and of course the ubiquitous go-go dancers. *3160 16th St., tel. 415/621–1617.*

The Phoenix. This is a good pick-up joint for beginners, admission is free, and it's the only bar in the Castro with a dance floor. *482 Castro St., tel. 415/552–6827.*

Pleasuredome. The Colossus crowd 10 years later. At Townsend *(see above)* on Sunday nights. *177 Townsend St., tel. 415/974–6020.*

Rawhide. Country and western with free swing dance lessons early on some weeknights. Owner Ray Chalker, who also publishes the San Francisco *Sentinel,* roused the ire of gay political activists when he rented the club as a set for the film *Basic Instinct. 280 7th St., tel. 415/621–1197.*

The Stud is a San Francisco legend and a good standard watering hole any night of the week. A good place to dance for a few hours to unwind after work and pick up on innocent out-of-towners (that's you!). Dress up or come as you are. *399 9th St., tel. 415/863–6623.*

MUSIC

ROCK

Club Chameleon. Catch truly alternative up-and-coming local acts at this small space in the Mission. Bonus: It's cheap and grungy and unpretentious. *853 Valencia St., tel. 415/821–1891.*

Kennel Club. A variety of excellent hip-hop and thrash-funk acts, along with the occasional multimedia performance art gig, come through this midsize venue that caters to a mixed, young crowd. Cover usually $5–$10. *628 Divisadero St., tel. 415/931–1914.*

I-Beam. A small, loud room with a very high ceiling and a variety of live music, mostly along the lines of rock/punk/funk. Only for the young and alienated. Cover $5–$10. *1748 Haight St., tel. 415/668–6006.*

Paradise Lounge. The quality of music varies widely, to put it kindly at this cocktail lounge/cabaret, which also has poetry readings from time to time. *11th St., at Folsom St., tel. 415/861–6906.*

The Stone. Heavy metal to thrash funk. Sweaty, pissed-off teens and those who wish they still were, throw their bodies around in wild abandon. *412 Broadway, tel. 415/547–1954.*

The Warfield. Big acts in a medium-size performance hall for $15–$20. Past acts have included the Red Hot Chili Peppers and Public Enemy. *982 Market St., tel. 415/775–7722.*

JAZZ

El Rio features live Latin jazz and samba in a casual and entirely unpretentious setting. *3158 Mission, tel. 415/282–3325*

Jazz Workshop. Small, dark, intimate venue for jazz. *473 Broadway, tel. 415/398–9700*

Kimball's. This very sharp club/restaurant, with tables and all, hosts jazz greats on a regular basis. Skip dinner unless you have money to burn. *300 Grove St., tel. 415/861–5555.*

Slim's. This club, owned by Boz Skaggs, features all types of American Roots music. A great variety of blues and jazz acts come through, plus the occasional funk, gospel, reggae,

When You Just Can't Get Enough

Go dancing at The End Up on Saturday or Sunday morning, because you never stopped partying the night before, or because your mom won't let you stay out late, or because you're doing a documentary on the countercultural elements of the city, or because you want to see people in various states of dishevelment and in the coming down stages of various drug trips. It opens at 6 AM and keeps going and going and going. A perfect way to mess up your internal clock for life. Call ahead to make sure something's going on before you get all decked out in your finest to go dancing at 8 AM.

and rock. Personable and fun for all ages—that is, all ages over 21. *333 11th St., tel. 415/621–3330.*

CLASSICAL **San Francisco Symphony.** The city's most stable performing arts organization plays from September to May. Special events include a Mostly Mozart Festival in the spring; a Beethoven Festival in the summer; a New and Unusual Music Series, also in the spring in Herbst Theater; and summer pops concerts in the Civic Auditorium. *Davies Symphony Hall, Van Ness Ave., at Grove St., tel. 415/431–5400.*

Stern Grove Concerts. This is the nation's oldest continual free summer music festival, offering 10 Sunday afternoons of symphony, opera, jazz, pop music, and dance. The amphitheater is in a eucalyptus grove. *Sloat Blvd., at 19th Ave., tel. 415/398–6551.*

Don't get bowling ball wax on your leather jacket at the Park Bowl (1855 Haight St., tel. 415/752–2366) on their Rock 'n' Bowl nights, which feature that quintessentially American pastime accompanied by that quintessentially American music, all in one alley.

ECLECTIC AND AVANT-GARDE MOVIE THEATERS **The Castro.** The most beautiful place to see a film in San Francisco, this theater shows a wide selection of rare, foreign, and offbeat films that change anywhere from nightly to weekly, and specializes in Audrey Hepburn flicks and other cornerstones of gay culture. The little man who comes up out of the floor playing the Wurlitzer organ is guaranteed to make you giggle for the sheer kitschiness of it all. *429 Castro St., tel. 415/621–6120.*

Kabuki Cinemas. High-tech octoplex that gets all the current release films before anybody else does. *Post and Webster Sts., tel 415/931–9800.*

The Red Vic. The only theater in town with couches. How cool. Besides this little perk, the films range from the artsy to the cultish to the rare, and you can drink herbal tea or coffee, too. *1659 Haight St., tel. 415/863–3994.*

The Roxie. This theater in the Mission District shows political, cult, and otherwise bent films. The audience can get raucous, probably because they need to lighten up after looking at all their black clothing all day. Movie Snobs Unite. *3117 16th at Valencia. tel. 415/863–1087.*

The Strand. Foreign films and classics in a shabby theater, perfect for a matinee. Be careful in this area at night. *1127 Market St., tel. 415/621–2227.*

CABARET **Beach Blanket Babylon.** This wacky talent show is the longest-lived musical revue in history and features high production values, impeccable timing, well-practiced musicians, polished performers, extra-large headgear, and a zesty, zany script that changes often to incorporate topical references and characters. For $20-plus, it's a great $8 show. Ba-dum-*dum.* BBB is notable for spending significant amounts of its profits on local charities. Under 21 admitted to Sunday matinees only. *Fugazi Hall, 678 Green St., tel. 415/421–4222. Shows Wed.–Sun., call box office well in advance for reservations.*

THEATER While it doesn't carry the national reputation of New York, Los Angeles, or Chicago, the Bay Area has a diverse and affordable theater scene. Nearly everyone should find something to enjoy. The most mainstream, Broadway-type musicals and dramas come to town in the **Best of Broadway series. ACT** and **Berkeley Repertory Theater** occupy the high end of the local repertory scene, but many smaller companies do excellent work, too. The area is also notable for experimental theater, with a particular emphasis on multi-media visual theater and solo performers. These events appear regularly at venues like **Theater Artaud.** If you've just arrived in town, it's best to look through the *SF Weekly, Bay Guardian,* or the Sunday *Chronicle-Examiner*'s "Pink Pages" for special events.

Eureka Theater (2730 16th St., tel. 415/558–9898) and **Magic Theater** (Fort Mason, tel. 415/441–8822) are the city's principal medium-size repertory houses. Both have been around since the '70s and feature well-mounted productions leaning toward the moderately experimental and ethnic/sexual/political-minority concerns.

Theater Artaud (450 Florida St., tel. 415/621–7797) is the largest local venue that regularly programs the avant-garde in terms of dance, drama, and multimedia work.

Theater Rhinoceros (2926 16th St., tel. 415/861–5079). Gay theater is their charter.

Life on the Water (Fort Mason, tel. 415/885–2790), **Intersection for the Arts** (446 Valencia St., tel. 415/626–2787), and **Climate Theater** (252 9th St., tel. 415/626–9196) are all smaller venues that handle local and touring work of both an experimental and multicultural nature including monologues, political satires, and performance art.

Lorraine Hansberry Theatre is another alternative theater that specializes in productions by African Americans. *620 Sutter St., at Mason, tel. 415/433–9500.*

Outdoor Activities

Residents of San Francisco enjoy some of the most spectacular scenery in the country right on their doorstep. Within a few hours' drive are ski resorts, famous national parks, and that stunning coastline. If you can't join 'em—not everyone can just take off in the ol' 4x4 Pathfinder—fear not. Have another cup of coffee, smoke another cancer stick, and plan a more civilized day of activity right in the city. You can probably work up a good sweat just looking at some of the hills.

BIKING ● ● ●

Unless you're some kind of weirdo who aspires to ride in the Tour de France, don't rent anything except a mountain bike for San Francisco hills. Otherwise, you will have a coronary, fall off your bike, and get hit by a tourist in a rental car. A bunch of places on Stanyan Street rent bikes. Two places worth checking are **Presidio Bicycle Shop** (5335 Geary Blvd., between 17th and 18th Aves., tel. 415/751–3200) and **Park Cyclery** (1865 Haight St. at Stanyan, tel 415/751–RENT). Golden Gate Park is a great place to ride. Kennedy Drive is closed to traffic on Sundays from 6 to 5, which allows you to ride all the way through the park to the Great Highway, another great ride fronting Ocean Beach. Perhaps the most interesting ride, through, starts at Fort Mason, runs along Marina Green, and then follows the water through the Presidio all the way to the Golden Gate Bridge. From there you have the option of riding across the bridge (totally cool) or continuing along the bike path all the way to the Cliff House at the entrance to the bay. The views on this ride are among the best in the city. Obviously, you can do all this on foot, too.

GOLF ● ● ●

Not many budget travelers will have packed their plus-fours with the yellow and blue whales on them, but don't let that stop you from playing one of the cheapest, most scenic municipal courses in the country. For just $13 you can play 18 holes at **Lincoln Park Golf Course** (34th Ave. and Clement, tel. 415/221–9911). Even if you barely know how to swing a mashie, rent some clubs and start hacking. The course is right on the headlands and has some views of the ocean and bay that the bozos down at Pebble Beach are paying $200 for. The par-three 17th, running along the cliffs above the ocean and overlooking the Golden Gate Bridge, is so beautiful you are almost guaranteed to whiff.

BEACHES ● ● ●

Hot sun, rad surf, blond babes. Think again. In summer on the coast near San Francisco, the only chillin' you're going to be doing is when hypothermia sets in. Fog plagues the beaches for the entire summer and the water is colder than a witch's tit. Sea lions aren't fat for nothing, you know. The beaches *are* beautiful though; bundle up and go for a stroll and watch the sun set.

BAKER BEACH At the base of the Presidio, with great views of the Golden Gate Bridge and the Marin Headlands, Baker Beach is San Francisco's most interesting stretch of silicon. You can park up high near the Presidio and descend a mountainous sand dune to the beach or follow the road to the bottom of the hill and park like every other fat slob. The city end of the beach is popular among gays, nudists, and nudist gays. The other end is deserted except for the occasional fisherman or couple throwing a tennis ball for their dog. The surf here is big and dangerous—don't even think of swimming. To get to the beach, follow the seagull signs (for the 49-mile scenic drive) from Fort Mason. Otherwise, take Bus 41 from the Transbay Terminal to the Presidio and transfer to Bus 29.

OCEAN BEACH This beach faces the Pacific and stretches for miles and miles. Surfers love the place and international surfing competitions are often held here. Sadly, the beach isn't all that clean and some of the butt-ugliest houses are the beach's uninspiring backdrop. Still, it's a great place to watch the sunset or to collect sand dollars. To get there, follow the seagull signs from Fort Mason or take Bus 38 from the Transbay terminal. At the northern end of Ocean Beach is the Cliff House, a restaurant popular with package tours; beyond that is Land's End, the northwestern tip of the San Francisco peninsula. Part of the Golden Gate National Recreation Area, Land's End is a great place to watch the waves crashing on the rocks and watch the ships coming in and out of the bay. Hiking trails wind through the wind-blown trees.

SAN FRANCISCO BAY AREA 3

By Shelly Smith, Leigh Anne Jones, and Jason Fine

You're standing on Telegraph Hill, maybe even perched on the phallic tip of Coit Tower. It's a sunny day, there's a light wind off the bay, and San Francisco looks like the center of the world. "Ah," you say to yourself like so many before you, "beautiful San Francisco. There's no other." Yet something is amiss. You've been to Fisherman's Wharf and the Ripley Museum. You've cruised North Beach and made your pilgrimage to City Lights. You've driven down Lombard Street, had a burrito on the Mission, and snapped a photo of the Haight-Ashbury street sign. You've got some great stories to tell future grandkids, but at the moment you're asking yourself somewhat anxiously: What am I going to do now?

Luckily, the diversity of the San Francisco Bay Area is only a stone's throw away—extending from **Marin County** to the north, **Berkeley** and **Oakland** to the east, and **Half Moon Bay** and **San Jose** to the south. These areas may be clustered around San Francisco and immensely influenced by it, but each has its own unique character and identity, and each a different appeal for visitors. There's no doubt "beautiful San Francisco" is, well, just that, but there are a few things the city just doesn't have—from the hip-hop Oaktown beat and the hippie parade in Berkeley to the wild beauty of Marin and the sleepy seaside charm of Half Moon Bay. And whether you're looking for a day on the beach or a week in the mountains, a New Age healing session, or a grungy blues band, odds are good that you'll find it somewhere in the surrounding Bay Area. Most of the places covered here are within easy reach of San Francisco—both by car and public transportation—and can be covered in day trips or short overnight forays.

Marin County

Just across the Golden Gate Bridge, Marin thrives as the state's richest county and perhaps most relaxed suburban community—an odd combination of hippie ideals and yuppie wealth. Everywhere you turn there are expensive estates buffered by ragged log cabins, Porsches and BMWs parked next to aging Volvo station wagons and VW vans. Both Grateful Dead member Jerry Garcia and film maker George Lucas live in the area, and yet if these cultural-heroes-turned-millionaires have helped transform Marin into an upscale playground, legions of young people continue to carry on the altruistic values of the '60s. Reggae music pours out of cafés and hole-in-the wall clubs; crystals, patchouli oil, and colorful Guatemalan wear are the equivalent of a fashion statement; and the free-spirited good life is definitely in the air. Marin may have gained the stamp of respectability, but

The Bay Area

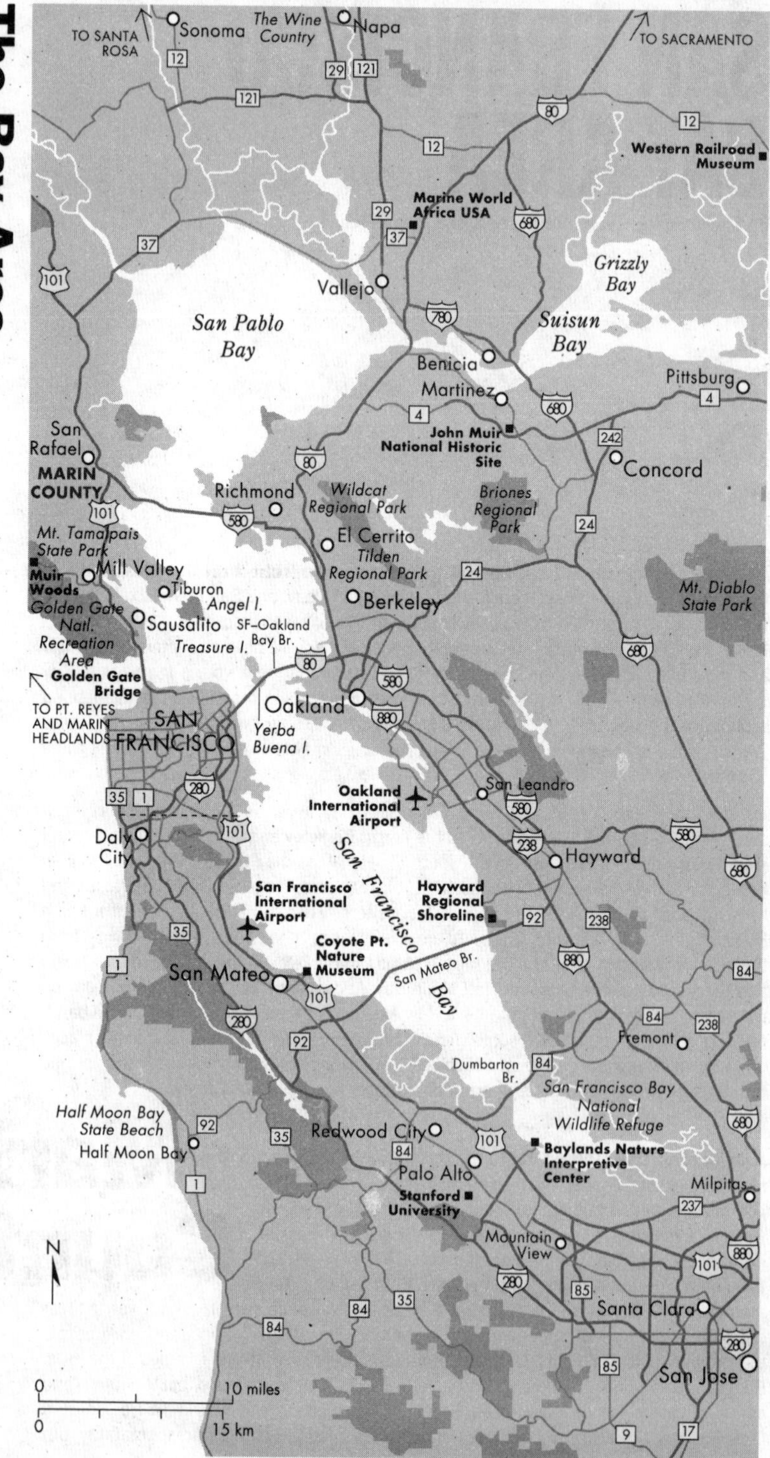
TO SANTA ROSA
Sonoma
The Wine Country
Napa
TO SACRAMENTO
12
29
121
80
Western Railroad Museum
Marine World Africa USA
37
680
101
Vallejo
Grizzly Bay
San Pablo Bay
780
Suisun Bay
Benicia
Pittsburg
Martinez
4
242
John Muir National Historic Site
San Rafael
MARIN COUNTY
Concord
Richmond
Wildcat Regional Park
Briones Regional Park
580
24
Mt. Tamalpais State Park
El Cerrito
Tilden Regional Park
Muir Woods
Mill Valley
Tiburon
Berkeley
Mt. Diablo State Park
Angel I.
Golden Gate Natl. Recreation Area
Sausalito
SF–Oakland Bay Br.
Treasure I.
Golden Gate Bridge
Oakland
880
TO PT. REYES AND MARIN HEADLANDS
SAN FRANCISCO
Yerba Buena I.
280
35
1
Oakland International Airport
San Leandro
238
Daly City
San Francisco Bay
Hayward
San Francisco International Airport
Hayward Regional Shoreline
92
Coyote Pt. Nature Museum
San Mateo
San Mateo Br.
84
Fremont
Dumbarton Br.
San Francisco Bay National Wildlife Refuge
Half Moon Bay State Beach
Half Moon Bay
Redwood City
Baylands Nature Interpretive Center
Palo Alto
Stanford University
Milpitas
237
Mountain View
N
85
Santa Clara
San Jose
0
10 miles
15 km
9
17

it's still the spiritual center of the New Age, heralded by 20-year-old rebels and middle-aged business people who remember Woodstock as if it were yesterday.

Whether your bag is hiking, camping, café-sitting, or strolling its picture-perfect hamlets, Marin—despite the price tag—is a place you don't want to miss. It encompasses jagged coastlines, thick redwood forests, and a sleepy collection of small, untroubled towns. In its western reaches, rural back roads crisscross a series of coastal mountains and cliffs that offer stunning ocean vistas, tempered by the occasional sheep ranch or country farm. Spend a lifetime hiking in **Muir Woods** and the **Point Reyes National Seashore,** or grab a beer and a taco in **Stinson Beach** or **Inverness,** two of West Marin's popular small-town hideaways. In East Marin, bayside cities like **Tiburon** and **San Rafael** serve as weekend escapes for city-weary San Franciscans, while **Sausalito**—an upscale resort town just across the Golden Gate Bridge—is a great place to get away without having to go too far.

Exploring Marin doesn't have to be frustrating for the budget traveler. Despite the ostentatious show of wealth that surrounds you, loads of college students and young adults have found ways to make the area affordable by shopping at organic grocery stores, sipping mug after mug of free coffee refills, and playing hacky sack in the warm Marin sunshine. Many of its best sights are well off the beaten path, but even Marin's most rural corners are little more than two hours from San Francisco (except during rush hour, when it can take you nearly an hour just to cross the bridge). Having a car is helpful for day trips, but if you don't mind sleeping in a forested youth hostel high in the hills, you can cover the area by bus on short overnight hauls. Either way, once you cross the bridge you'll feel days away from the urban grind.

BASICS ● ● ●

TOURIST INFORMATION **Marin Chamber of Commerce** distributes a free monthly, "MariNITE Entertainment Guide," which lists live music events in the area. *30 N. San Pedro Blvd., San Rafael, tel. 415/472–7470. Open weekdays 9–5.*

Point Reyes National Seashore's Bear Valley Visitors Center has exhibits on park wildlife, topographical and hiking maps, and loads of information on exploring the peninsula. Look for a sign marking the turnoff for this center half a mile past Olema. *Tel. 415/663–1092. Open weekdays 9–5, weekends 8–5.*

Muir Woods Visitor Center. *Muir Woods, tel. 415/388–2595 or 415/388–2596. Open daily 8 AM–sunset. Take U.S. 101 north to the Rte. 1/Stinson Beach exit. Follow the signs to Muir Woods.*

West Marin Chamber of Commerce has a free newsletter, "The Coastal Traveler," with great information on out-of-the-way beaches, bike rides, and backpacking trips. *Box 1045, Rte. 1, Point Reyes Station, tel. 415/663–9232. 2 mi north of Olema on Rte. 1.*

COMING AND GOING

BY BUS All north–south Greyhound buses that travel on U.S. 101 stop at San Rafael's **Greyhound station** (at 3rd and Tamalpais Sts. in downtown San Rafael, tel. 415/453–0795). Routes include San Francisco ($10), Oakland ($14), and San Jose ($18). The **Marin Airporter** (300 Larkspur Landing Circle, tel. 415/461–4222) runs shuttle buses every half-hour between San Rafael and the Oakland ($15) and San Francisco ($10) airports.

Otherwise, **Golden Gate Transit** (*see* Getting Around, *below*) travels regularly to Sausalito ($2) and Marin from First and Mission streets in San Francisco.

BY CAR From San Francisco, head north on **U.S. 101** and cross the **Golden Gate Bridge** (no toll this direction). For Sausalito, take the Sausalito exit then go south on Bridgeway to the municipal parking lot near the center of town. To reach **Route 1** and West Marin, continue north on U.S. 101 to the village of Muir, Stinson Beach/Route 1 exit. Follow Route 1 north and, as it winds uphill, you will see a turnoff for Muir Woods. Keep going to get to the village of Muir, Stinson Beach (one hour), and the Point Reyes National Seashore ($1^1/_2$ hours).

Traffic is a problem year-round, especially on summer weekends and holidays. The Golden Gate Bridge turns into a gigantic parking lot every weekday from 7 to 9 in the morning and from 4 to 6 in the afternoon. The Sunday traffic on Route 1 reminds you of what "painfully slow" and "brain-numbing headache" really mean.

BY FERRY If you're sick of Bay Area traffic, or just in the mood for a change of pace, ferries travel regularly between Marin (Larkspur Landing, Tiburon, or Sausalito) and San Francisco, from 6 AM to 8 PM. Fares are $2.20 to Larkspur, $3.50 to Sausalito, $4.50 to Tiburon, and include free transfers for GGT public buses (*see* Getting Around, *below*). **Golden Gate Ferry** (tel. 415/332–6600) crosses the bay to Sausalito and Larkspur from the Ferry Building at Market Street and the Embarcadero; **Red and White Fleet** (tel. 415/546–2896) leaves from Pier $43^1/_2$ at Fisherman's Wharf for Sausalito and Tiburon. Either way, the trip takes 15–30 minutes.

GETTING AROUND

BY BUS **Golden Gate Transit** (tel. 415/453–2100 or 415/332–6600) provides excellent service almost everywhere in Marin County. Rates range from 75¢ to $3.75, and monthly discount cards can be purchased from drivers or at the depots in **San Rafael** (at Fourth and Heatherton) or **Larkspur** (Larkspur Ferry Terminal, East Sir Francis Drake Blvd). Buses connect San Francisco with San Rafael, Larkspur, Tiburon, Mill Valley, and Sausalito every half-hour during the week. Buses travel between San Rafael, Inverness, Point Reyes, Olema, and Stinson Beach on weekends only.

HITCHHIKING Hitchhiking is difficult along U.S. 101, primarily because of congestion and the fact that most Marinites just don't have time to stop. Yet if you can somehow cross the Golden Gate Bridge and find your way onto one of Marin's quiet back roads, rides are not hard to come by, especially from Petaluma to Point Reyes and along Route 1 between Stinson Beach and Tomales Bay.

OUTDOOR ACTIVITIES

BIKING Despite a long brewing controversy over trail usage, Marin is still a haven for mountain bikers. Particularly popular are the Marin Headlands, with trails skirting the wide ridges and canyons of its coastal cliffs, and Mount Tamalpais, the highest peak in the area with loads of biking trails. Route 1 itself is really too treacherous until you get beyond Stinson Beach, when the road flattens out and the traffic lightens up.

FISHING Compared to lakes and rivers of Sonoma and Mendocino counties, there's not much in the way of freshwater fishing in Marin. Even the fairly isolated lakes along the Point Reyes Coastal Trail have been fished out and not amply restocked. Surf fishing is popular along many beaches, as is clamming and mussel gathering. However, always be on the look out for Red Tide, a poisonous substance found in clams and mussels along the northern coast. It forced a quarantine on these shellfish for much of the past year, so ask around at any sporting-goods shop before consuming shellfish. You can also call the Point Reyes Visitors Center (tel. 415/663–1092) for current advisories.

HIKING It would take years to learn all the trails just in Point Reyes, let alone in Muir Woods and the Marin Headlands, and each trail you walk will make you hunger for more. The diversity of landscapes—from breathtaking ocean views and old-growth redwood forests to white-sand beaches and ragtag grazing land—make Marin a hiker's dream come true. Everyone has their favorite trails, and hikers throughout the county are happy to share information. Perhaps the best way to choose, though, is to look at a trail map, decide how long a trail you'd like to hike, and pick at random; you can't go wrong. As in most areas, the longer the trail and the harder it is to access, the fewer people you'll find. A good resource for beach walks is the *California Coastal Access Guide*, available at most local bookstores and the Point Reyes Visitor Center.

MARIN HEADLANDS ● ● ●

As you head north across the Golden Gate bridge, look for the spectacular Marin Headlands to the left, accessible via the Alexander Avenue exit on U.S. 101 and a short drive up Conzelman Road. Perched on a small bluff overlooking the San Francisco Bay and the Pacific Ocean, these undeveloped, 1,000-acre headlands are a great place to snap a few photos or while away a sunny afternoon. Hundreds of hiking and bicycle trails meander along the wind-beaten hills and cliffs, and the views are stunning, encompassing downtown San Francisco, much of the East Bay, and even Point Reyes to the north. The headlands were used as a military camp during the late 19th century, and during World War II emplacements were dug for huge 16-inch naval guns to protect the approaches to the bay. The guns were never installed but you can still see the bunkers. Most weekends—especially in summer—the area is crawling with locals, but the farther north you hike, the fewer people you'll encounter. With this is mind, the unmarked coastal cliff trail is one of the most scenic and least traveled; drive all the way through the headlands to the Marin Headlands Visitors Center at Fort Cronkhite (you can't go any farther); walk as far out to the ocean as possible, then turn north and look for a small dirt path. It ends 1½ miles farther on.

If you're headed into San Francisco during rush hour, come here for a traffic-free respite (and laugh at all the foolish people held hostage in their cars). If things get really bad, check in at the **Golden Gate AYH-Hostel,** only five minutes away in historic Fort Barry. Set amid the beaches and forest of the headlands, the hostel, built in 1907, has a common room with fireplace, a communal kitchen, laundry room, and a tennis court. Beds cost $8 a night. Reservations suggested two weeks in advance. If you're coming from San Francisco on Golden Gate Transit, catch the Sausalito bus and ask to be left off at the bottom of the off-ramp for the Alexander Avenue exit; from there it's a long hike to the headlands. *Fort Barry, Bldg. 941, Sausalito 94965, tel. 415/331–2777. From U.S. 101, take Alexander Ave. exit, cross under freeway, and make first right after Marin Headlands sign. 1 mi farther, turn right on McCullough Rd., left on Bunker Rd., and follow signs to hostel, 1½ miles ahead. 66 beds.*

SAUSALITO ● ● ●

Only a few miles north of San Francisco, Sausalito used to have a "tough" reputation—the sort of place where sailors and riffraff could hang out, get drunk, and cause a lot of trouble on the docks. During the 1880s and '90s it flourished as a small whaling town, infamous for its saloons, gambling dens, and bordellos. Even after it became suburbanized in the 1940s, Sausalito continued to attract an offbeat and raffish element, both as an artists' colony and seaside playground. Over the years, however, Sausalito's fishing trawlers have been slowly replaced by sailboats and houseboats, its wharf rats by lawyers and investment bankers. As a result, Sausalito has turned into an upscale resort town, popular with yachters and San Francisco's upwardly mobile crowd. If you have limited time to explore the Bay Area, Sausalito is definitely worth a gander, but prepare yourself for expensive seafood restaurants and a slew of forgettable gift shops.

Bridgeway is Sausalito's main thoroughfare, bordered on one side by waterfront restaurants and the bay, on the other by pricey antiques shops, a few hotels, and a handful of Victorian-era, hillside homes. At the south end of Bridgeway is the Sausalito Ferry Terminal, a 10-minute walk from the center of town. Farther south—near the end of Bridgeway at Richardson Street—is Sausalito's oldest restaurant, originally known as **Valhalla.** Built in 1893, it was used as a backdrop in the classic 1940s film, *The Lady of Shanghai.* Today, unfortunately, it's just a Chart House restaurant.

If you head north on Bridgeway, look for the **Village Fair** (777 Bridgeway), a four-story warehouse that's been converted into a surprisingly tasteful shopping area, with clothing, crafts, and gift stalls. Another half-mile north look for the **Bay Model** (2100 Bridgeway, tel. 415/332–3871), a 400-foot-square re-creation of the San Francisco Bay Area. It's used by the U.S. Army Corps of Engineers to reproduce the rise and fall of the tides, and it's open to the public weekdays 9–4, weekends 10–6. It sounds absurd—and is—but it shouldn't be missed.

Once the sun goes down, there isn't much to do here, unless you're loaded with cash. One thing that's usually free though is jazz. In particular, the **No Name Bar** (757 Bridgeway, tel. 415/332–1392) and the **Seven Seas** (682 Bridgeway, tel. 415/332–1304) attract some of the Bay Area's most talented musicians, and their weekend jazz sessions are packed with both Sausalito's hip, middle-aged set and beret-clad bohemians. It's mostly an over-25 crowd, and the music is top rate.

COMING AND GOING

BY CAR Sausalito is only a stone's throw from San Francisco, 8 miles north of downtown across the Golden Gate Bridge. Take U.S. 101 north to the Sausalito exit, then go south on Bridgeway to the municipal parking lot near the center of town. In a perfect world, the trip would take 30 minutes; if there's traffic, plan on at least an hour. If you just want to drive through Sausalito, take the Alexander Avenue exit off U.S. 101 and follow it down the hill; the road enters Sausalito from the south, takes you along the waterfront, and then puts you back on U.S. 101.

BY BUS **Golden Gate Transit** (tel. 415/453–2100 or 415/332–6600) has daily bus service to Sausalito ($2) that leaves from Mission and First streets in San Francisco six times daily.

BY FERRY The best way to come is by ferry. Not only do you beat the crowds, but the 20-minute boat ride ($3) has great views of the bay. **Golden Gate Ferry** (tel. 415/332–6600) leaves from the Ferry Building at Market Street and the Embarcadero; **Red and White Fleet** (tel. 415/546–2896) leaves from Pier 41 at Fisherman's Wharf. Either way, they both dock at Sausalito's Ferry Terminal, at the southern end of Bridgeway, a 10-minute walk from downtown.

WHERE TO SLEEP Don't even bother. Unless you have $80–$100 to blow on a room, Sausalito is a budget traveler's nightmare. The only reasonable alternative is the **Golden Gate AYH-Hostel** (*see above*), 15 minutes away in the Marin Headlands.

FOOD Restaurants and cafés line Bridgeway, Sausalito's main street, but they're generally overpriced and touristy. Most specialize in seafood and waterfront vistas, but expect to pay $10–$15 for one of these "picture-perfect" meals. Your best bet is to pack a lunch and picnic on the docks or at the Marin Headlands (*see above*), where the views are equally stunning.

The Lighthouse Coffee Shop. Open at the crack of dawn seven days a week, the Lighthouse has surprisingly cheap (and good) omelets, burgers, and sandwiches, generally priced under $6. For dinner, try their barbecue chicken ($6), seafood pasta ($8), or roast turkey ($6). This is a no-frills sort of place, popular with just about everybody. *1311 Bridgeway, tel. 415/331–9221. Open weekdays 6 AM–3 PM, Sat. 7 AM–3 PM, Sun. 7:30 AM–3 PM.*

Winship Restaurant. On the Bridgeway shopping strip, it has moderately priced ($6–$12) seafood, pasta, steaks, and burgers—nothing to scream about, but fine in a pinch. The bad news: It's decorated like a ship, with flotsam and fishing nets on the walls, and popular with families of six who think it's cute. Breakfast and lunch are served daily, dinners Wednesday–Sunday. *670 Bridgeway, tel. 415/332–1454. Open winter, Mon.–Thurs. 8 AM–3 PM, Fri.–Sun. 8 AM–10 PM; summer, daily 8 AM–10 PM.*

● ● ● TIBURON

Although Tiburon is an expensive seaside resort, one look at the tranquil bay from the foot of **Main Street** and you'll understand why this city has become a popular weekend getaway for both tourists and Bay Area locals. Some come to ride bikes along the picturesque streets and promenades, some to sit on the grass and eat picnic lunches, others to just lounge around and work on their tans. Whatever the reason, it's the view that draws people here, a dreamy panorama of sailboats, mountains, and beach. Of course, Tiburon has its expensive boutiques and tacky seafood restaurants, but it's only 15 miles north of San Francisco—an easy and recommended day trip. Simply hop on U.S. 101 north, cross the Golden Gate Bridge and, 3 miles past Sausalito, take **Route 131** south. Otherwise, Golden Gate Transit (tel. 415/453–2100 or 415/332–6600) offers weekend service from San Rafael, Sausalito, and San Francisco for under $3. If you want to go by ferry, **Red and White Fleet** (tel. 415/546–2896) runs across the bay from Pier 43½ at Fisherman's Warf. The fare is $4.50.

If you're hankering for some satisfying food and a good view, head downtown to **Old Sam's Anchor Cafe** (27 Main St., tel. 415/435–4527), the best of Tiburon's waterfront eateries. It's packed on weekends with people sipping Bloody Marys and gin fizzes. Old Sam's specializes in fresh fish ($8–$15), crab omelets ($8), and fish stew ($7), but budget diners might want to stick to the fish-and-chips ($5.50) or vegetable sautée ($6).

SAN RAFAEL ● ● ●

Ten miles north of Sausalito on U.S. 101, San Rafael is a rather dull, working-class town. But even though it may not be as aesthetically appealing as nearby Sausalito, Tiburon, or Mill Valley, San Rafael is still refreshing in its own way. You won't find Marin's glamour-set here, just a bunch of folks who know how to drink beer and have a good time. It's also cheaper than the rest of Marin, and along San Rafael's bustling **Fourth Street**—the main shopping drag—you'll find everything from discount department stores to cheap restaurants and dimly lit cocktail lounges. For a slice of local life, grab a beer at **New George's** (842 4th St., tel. 415/457–1515); it has live music six nights a week that ranges from local thrash to big-name rock bands. During the day it's popular with slackers and Nam vets.

North of downtown—take North San Pedro Road exit off U.S. 101—the **Marin Civic Center** (3501 Civic Center Dr., tel. 415/499–7407) has guided tours of its impressive complex, designed by architect Frank Lloyd Wright. Concerned with preserving the natural contours of the site, Wright integrated the buildings into the surrounding landscape, which are built around, in, and under its three principal hillocks. It looks a lot like a bloated whale from the outside, but the inside has been heralded as one of the most functional and offbeat office spaces ever conceived. Tours are available by reservation, but there's a well-stocked information kiosk in the lobby (open weekdays 9–5) for walk-in visitors. For information on dance and drama performances in the adjoining theater, call 415/472–3500.

If you're tired of suburbia and minimalls, drive 4 miles east on San Pedro Road to the **China Camp State Park,** a beautiful 1,600-acre wilderness area on the fringe of civilization. Most people are surprised to find such a pristine slice of nature so close to a big city, and somehow it's remained undeveloped and unpublicized—making it easy to get away without going too far. Remnants of an old Chinese fishing village are still visible, and the oak knolls and saltwater marshes are great for both hiking and camping (*see* Where to Sleep, *below*).

At **Guide Dogs for the Blind** (350 Los Ranchitos Rd., tel. 415/499–4000), west of downtown, you can play with the 100 or so puppies in training and learn how they're taught to navigate their blind owners. Free tours are available weekdays at 10:30, 1:15, and 2:30. The 2-mile drive (take N. San Pedro Rd. exit off U.S. 101, head west and turn right on Los Ranchitos Rd.) meanders through quiet meadows and a handful of '30s-era farm houses scattered among old orchards.

The small town of **Fairfax,** 2 miles northwest of San Rafael on Sir Francis Drake Boulevard, is the most hippied-out spot in Marin county. Cafés and bookstores abound in Fairfax's two-block-long center, but **Patrick's Books & Café** (15 Bolinas Rd., tel. 415/454–2428) is a real retreat from the Marin sunshine, with dim lights, dark wood, big tables, and a casual atmosphere.

COMING AND GOING

BY CAR San Rafael is only 15 miles north of San Francisco; take U.S. 101 north across the Golden Gate Bridge and keep going. You'll see the "Welcome to San Rafael" sign before you know it.

BY BUS **Golden Gate Transit** (tel. 415/453–2100 or 415/332–6600) offers daily service between San Francisco (First and Mission Sts.) and San Rafael (4th and Heatherton Sts.). Other destinations include Tiburon, Mill Valley, Stinson Beach, Point Reyes, and Inverness. Buses run weekdays 6–6, less frequently on weekends.

There's daily service from San Rafael's **Greyhound station** (3rd and Tamalpais Sts., tel. 415/453–0795) to San Francisco ($10), Oakland ($14), and San Jose ($18). The **Marin Airporter** (300 Larkspur Landing Circle, tel. 415/461–4222) runs shuttle buses every half-hour between San Rafael and the Oakland ($15) and San Francisco ($10) airports.

WHERE TO SLEEP Camping is your only budget option in San Rafael, but if you're desperate, try one of the chain motels near the freeway. **The National 9 Inn** (855 Francisco Blvd., tel. 415/456–8820) has generic doubles for $30, a swimming pool, and hot tub. The **San Rafael Inn** (865 Francisco Blvd., tel. 415/454–9470) has clean, simple rooms for $50, some with kitchenettes.

CAMPING Only 4 miles northeast of San Rafael, the trappings of civilization quickly fade as you enter the 1,600-acre **China Camp State Park,** perched on the banks of San Pablo Bay. It has 30 walk-in campsites nestled in an oak forest; they're $13 per site. Reservations are advised on summer weekends, but otherwise China Camp is generally empty. *Tel. 415/456–0766. Take San Pedro Rd. exit from U.S. 101 in San Rafael, head east and follow the signs. Flush toilets, hot water, showers, and fire pits.*

FOOD Most of San Rafael's restaurants are concentrated along Third and Fourth streets, in the town center. Besides the usual fast-food chains, there are plenty of casual and inexpensive Asian, Mexican, and American eateries to choose from. **Royal Thai** (610 3rd St., tel. 415/485–1074) serves no-frills seafood and curry dishes for under $6 in a restored Victorian mansion decorated with Thai wood carvings and art. Head to the **Mayflower Inne** (1533 4th St., tel. 415/456–1011), a dark, English-style pub that's lit by candles even in the daytime. You'll find such things as shepherd's pie ($6), Cornish pastries ($5), and heaping plates of sausage-and-chips ($5). Wash it all down with one of nine rotating tap beers.

In Fairfax, **Spanky's** (1900 Sir Francis Drake Blvd., tel. 415/456–5299) is the place for sandwiches and salads. For $6, try their house-size BLT Deluxe with avocado, grilled onions, and a half-pound of bacon. Afterwards, grab an ice cream in the adjoining parlor.

● ● ● MILL VALLEY

Accessible from U.S. 101 via the Stinson Beach/Route 1 exit, Mill Valley is a mecca of mansions and millionaires set amid the California redwoods—a laid-back,. sleepy town where people have paid dearly for their solitude and want to keep it that way. There aren't any official tourist sights, but a drive through the hills and forested canyons will explain why this is some of the Bay Area's most coveted real estate. Afterwards, have coffee at the **Depot Cafe** (87 Throckmorton Ave., tel. 415/383–2665), which faces Mill Valley's small central plaza. The Depot has salads and pita sandwiches ($4–$6), as well as espresso drinks, teas, and a motley selection of paperbacks and magazines.

If you're hungry, **Jennie Low's** (38 Miller Ave., tel. 415/388–8868) Chinese food is locally famous, especially the spicy eggplant ($6) and Hunan prawns ($8). For breakfast, however, **Mama's Royal Cafe** (393 Miller Ave., tel. 415/388–3261) is unbeatable. Mama's specialties include incredible *huevos rancheros* (Spanish eggs, $5) and *huevos con nopales* (eggs with cactus, $6). This funky café is full of thrift-store artifacts and psychedelic murals, with plenty of outdoor seating.

Once the fog starts creeping through the forest after sunset, locals mosey over to the **Sweetwater** (153 Throckmorton Ave., tel. 415/388–3820), where on any given night bluesman Roy Rogers, Huey Lewis, or even Jerry Garcia himself might show up to jam. This club is a Bay Area institution and, even though it's tiny, attracts some of the finest blues and R&B talents in the country.

MUIR WOODS • • •

Judging from the crowded parking lot and tacky gift shop, the **Muir Woods National Monument** looks like just another overtouristed attraction to be avoided. This 550-acre park, however, contains one of the most majestic groves of redwoods in the world, some more than 250 feet tall and 1,000 years old. It's crowded, to be sure, but within minutes you can find rugged, unpopulated trails that wander along cool, fern-filled ridges high above the overrun canyon below. The **Panoramic Trail,** which begins just beyond the gift shop and is rarely crowded, leads 1½ miles to **Fern Creek Trail,** which returns to the gift shop after an easy mile-long descent. Along the way, you'll pass the Bohemian and Cathedral groves—two of the park's most impressive stands of redwoods.

Neither picnicking nor camping is allowed in the park, but snacks are available at the gift shop, along with every type of redwood souvenir imaginable. The **visitor center** (tel. 415/388–2595) organizes free nature walks through the woods; call for current schedules. The weather here is usually cool and often damp, so dress warmly. *Off U.S. 101, 17 mi northwest of San Francisco. Take the Stinson Beach/Rte. 1 exit and follow the signs. Open daily 8 AM–sunset. Free parking.*

If you stick to Route 1 instead of following the turnoff to Muir Woods, you come to **Muir Beach,** a quiet strip of sand cluttered with odd-shaped pieces of driftwood and hundreds of tidal pools. It's strikingly scenic and tends to attract folks looking to get away and relax—not the Budweiser and volleyball crowd you'll find at Stinson, 6 miles farther on.

Muir Beach's other attraction is the **Pelican Inn** (Rte. 1 at Muir Beach, tel. 415/383–6000 or 415/383–6005). Its restaurant serves everything from fish-and-chips ($7) to prime rib ($11) and Yorkshire pudding ($9), along with a healthy sampling of British ales and bitters. There's a stone fireplace in its wood-paneled dining room and, for after dinner sport, a dart board in the adjoining pub. Upstairs, there are six Tudor-style rooms ($75 a night) filled with antiques and canopied beds—about as atmospheric and rustic as they come.

If you really want to get a feel for life in Marin, park your car at Muir Beach and hike the coastal trail, which leads up a steep hill overlooking the ocean and crawls around a series of deserted coves and valleys. Return the same way and reward yourself with a pint of beer and ploughman's lunch in front of the fire at the Pelican Inn. Ah, heaven.

The Towering Legacy of John Muir

One hundred fifty million years ago, redwood trees grew throughout the United States. Today, the Sequoia sempervirens can be found only in a narrow, cool coastal belt that stretches from Monterey to Oregon. Muir Woods has been preserved by the Federal government since 1908, primarily as a result of John Muir's campaign to save old-growth forests from destruction. His response: "This is the best tree-lover's monument that could be found in all of the forests of the world. Saving these woods from the axe and saw is in many ways the most notable service to God and man I have heard of since my forest wandering began."

● ● ● STINSON BEACH

Six treacherous miles north of Muir Beach on Route 1, Stinson Beach is one of the most popular coastal towns in northern California. It's loaded with rickety wooden houses and friendly general stores, and its beach—the longest in Marin County—has a beach-bum and barbecue appeal that's hard to find north of Santa Cruz. Despite Stinson's isolated location, its chilly water temperatures, and the threat of sharks lurking offshore, hordes of surfers and sun worshippers descend upon this city of 1,200 people—along with a healthy dose of tourists and the Bay Area party crowd.

Even if you're not planning to surf or swim, and even if it's a rainy and foggy day, the 45-minute drive from Muir Woods to Stinson is incredible. Etched along the side of towering cliffs and jagged granite peaks, this 10-mile stretch of road is one of the most breathtaking in the state. Traffic can be a problem on summer weekends, but there are plenty of bars, restaurants, and scenic overlooks along the way to cushion the blow of bumper-to-bumper traffic.

The **Stinson Beach Surfshop** (3450 Rte. 1, tel. 415/868–0333) rents body boards ($8 a day), wetsuits ($12 a day), and surfboards ($12 a day) year-round; just look for the building with a surfboard on the roof. If you're hungry, stop off at the **Sand Dollar** (Rte. 1, tel. 415/868–0434), a pleasant pub that serves great hamburgers and sandwiches ($5–$8) for lunch, and mediocre seafood ($8–$14) for dinner. Grab a table on the outdoor dining deck and while away a sunny afternoon. Cash only.

Along Bolinas Lagoon, just north of Stinson on Route 1, you'll find the **Audubon Canyon Ranch** (tel. 415/868–9244). On weekends between mid-March and mid-July, this 1,000-acre bird sanctuary and ranch (and its 10 or so hiking trails) are open to the public, offering bird lovers the chance to watch blue herons and egrets close up. There's a small museum ("donation" required) with geological and natural history displays, a bookstore, and picnic area.

COMING AND GOING From San Francisco, take U.S. 101 north across the Golden Gate Bridge, and exit at the Stinson Beach/Route 1 exit. Continue on this curvy road for 27 miles. **Golden Gate Transit** (tel. 415/453–2100 or 415/332–6600) offers semiregular service to Stinson from San Francisco, but call for current schedules.

WHERE TO SLEEP Stinson Beach is full of the quaintest of quaint bed-and-breakfasts that cost upwards of $80 a night. Instead, head to **Steep Ravine Cabins** (2 mi south of Stinson on Rte. 1, tel. 800/444–7275), rustic and comfortable cabins that look right over the ocean. They're only $25 a night, and each sleeps up to four people. Make reservations early though, because they book up quickly. Otherwise, the **Stinson Beach Motel** (3416 Rte. 1, tel. 415/868–1712) has generic doubles starting at $50, all with private bath. The **Ocean Court Motel** (18 Arenal St., tel. 415/868–0212) is pricier (doubles $65 with private bath and kitchen), but all its rooms have pleasant ocean views. Take a left (toward the ocean) at the only stop sign in Stinson; the hotel is 1/4-mile ahead.

● ● ● BOLINAS

Bolinas may not be the "zen-purity, earth-magnet, long-hair, free-to-do-what-you-want place to be, man," as one local described it, but even so, the town manages to preserve a few relics from its wacked-out past.

A few miles beyond the Audubon Canyon Ranch (*see above*), at the end of an unmarked road running west from Route 1, Bolinas works hard to avoid notice. Every time the state tries to post street signs and mileage markers, the raffish residents tear them down. They seem to want this sleepy town to retain its reputation as a center for alternative and communal living, but a walk through town reveals million-dollar homes and a slew of upscale seafood restaurants—so much for championing the ideals of the '60s.

Despite its yuppification, you'll still find a few VW buses and bearded hippies strumming their guitars on street corners. The **Bolinas People's Store** (14 Wharf Rd., tel. 415/868–1433) is famous for its fresh, high-quality local produce, grown by the same sweaty hippies who once gave Bolinas so much of its character. The only nightlife in town is **Smiley's Schooner Saloon** (41 Wharf Rd., tel. 415/868–1311), where huddled around its pool table and jukebox you'll find an odd combination of the suit-and-tie professional and the tie-dyed alternative fringe.

If the smell of patchouli is fraying your nerves, take Mesa Road 4½ miles north to the **Point Reyes Bird Observatory** (tel. 415/868–0655), a sanctuary that harbors 225 species of birds. It's open year-round, and admission is free. On your way, make the mile-long detour to **Duxberry Reef,** a peaceful breaker that's littered with hundreds of tidal pools. To get there go left on Overlook Drive and left again on Elm Avenue.

Serious hikers should consider the **Palomarin Trail,** which stretches from Bolinas to the edge of the Point Reyes National Seashore. The trailhead is at the end of Mesa Road, just past the bird observatory, and can be used as a day hike to **Bass Lake** (5½ miles round-trip) or **Pelican Lake** (7 miles round-trip). Either way, it's a great hike carved along the edge of the cliffs that overlook the Pacific Ocean and meanders through eucalyptus groves and untamed wetlands.

POINT REYES NATIONAL SEASHORE ● ● ●

Exploring the Point Reyes National Seashore—a 70,000-acre jumble of marshes, ferocious cliffs, and undisturbed beaches—you'll feel a lot farther than 30 miles away from San Francisco. With its lush grazing land and rambling farms, Point Reyes could easily pass for the Scottish Highlands or Western Ireland—minus the pubs. Even though it's isolated, Point Reyes is a manageable day trip from San Francisco, about 1½–2 hours each way. There are hundreds of hiking trails on the peninsula and, if you want to spend the night, four campgrounds (backpackers only) and an excellent hostel that's just off Route 1. No matter what your interests, the beauty of this wilderness is worth your time. Crowds are a problem on summer weekends, but otherwise it's generally deserted and unblemished: An ideal escape for nature lovers and misanthropes alike.

Twelve miles north of Bolinas on Route 1, you'll pass the block-long town of Olema; just a little farther, look for a sign marking the turnoff for **Point Reyes National Seashore's Bear Valley Visitor Center** (tel. 415/663–1092). This is the best place to begin your exploration; you can check out the exhibits on park wildlife, the ranger-led interpretive hikes, and get trail maps and camping permits here. A short walk away, look for the reconstructed **Miwok Indian Village,** built on the ruins of a 400-year-old Miwok farming settlement. Also nearby is the **Bear Valley Trailhead,** a lightly traveled, 4-mile hike that wanders through the woods and down to a secluded beach. If you can't make it to Point Reyes Lighthouse, the Bear Valley trail offers a good overview of the peninsula.

Two miles farther on Route 1 you'll pass through the quiet town of **Inverness,** an offbeat place that overflows with Czech restaurants and architecture. Coming across one of its motley colored, intricately carved wooden houses can be somewhat disorienting. After miles of trees and uncluttered coast, Inverness looks more like a Disney-type theme world than anything else, but its East European–flavor is definitely real. In 1935, after a freighter ran aground in San Francisco Bay, a number of its Czech deck hands jumped ship and ended up here. Ever since, dozens of Czech families have settled in Inverness, bringing both their culture and cuisine. For some of the best dumplings this side of Prague, head to **Vladimir's** and **Manka's**—two of the town's pricey but outstanding Czech restaurants (*see below*).

West of Inverness, at the end of Sir Francis Drake Boulevard, there's a massive stretch of white sand known as **Drake's Beach.** It's often windy and too rough for swimming, but it's great for a relaxing day in the sun. Check with the Point Reyes Visitor Center for current regulations; if they give the okay, there's plenty of driftwood on the beach for an early evening campfire.

A quarter-mile north of Drake's Beach, there's a sign directing you to the **Point Reyes Lighthouse,** 6 miles to the west. Even if you hate lighthouses, the best part of the trip is the drive itself, which winds through some downright incredible scenery. From the small parking lot there's a steep trail that leads down to the lighthouse (admission free; open weekdays 9–5, weekends 8–5), and a dozen or so trails etched into the surrounding cliffs. The hike to **Chimney Rock,** 3/4 mile away, is one of the most scenic; look for the trailhead in the parking lot.

COMING AND GOING

BY CAR From San Francisco, take U.S. 101 north and cross the Golden Gate Bridge. If speed is more important than scenery, exit at Greenbrae and follow Sir Francis Drake Boulevard 21 miles to the coast. Eventually, you'll end up 2 miles north of Olema on Route 1. Otherwise, take the Stinson Beach/Route 1 exit and enjoy the curvy, 29-mile scenic drive along the coast.

BY BUS **Golden Gate Transit** (tel. 415/453–2100 or 415/332–6600) offers daily service to Olema, the Point Reyes Visitor Center, and Inverness. On weekdays only, Bus 24 leaves in the late afternoon from San Francisco (First and Mission Sts.) and returns every morning at 9; on weekends only, Bus 64 leaves at 9 from San Rafael (4th and Heatherton Sts.) and returns the same day by 6 in the evening.

WHERE TO SLEEP

Dozens of B&Bs line Route 1 near Point Reyes, but expect to pay anywhere from $85 to $120 in one of these excessively charming cottages. There are a few hotels in the area, but they, too, charge upward of $70 a night.

Instead, head straight for the **Point Reyes AYH-Hostel,** 8 miles west of the Point Reyes Visitor Center. Popular both with foreign travelers and local college kids, it's a great base camp for excursions onto the peninsula. There are hundreds of hiking trails nearby, and its two common rooms have wood-burning stoves and loads of reading material. Dorm-room beds cost $8 per night. Reservations are advised, but they're not accepted over the phone; either write (enclose a check or money order) or show up in person as early as possible. Golden Gate Transit (*see* Coming and Going, *above*) stops at the visitor center, but you'll have to hitch or walk the remaining 8 miles to the hostel. *Box 247, Point Reyes Station 94956, tel. 415/663–8811. From Olema, turn left (west) on Bear Valley Rd., 1 block beyond the town's only stop sign. 1 1/2 mi farther, turn left at the Lighthouse/Beaches/Hostel sign, go for 6 mi and turn left on Crossroads Rd. The hostel is 1/2 mi farther. Office open daily 7:30 AM–9:30 AM and 4:30 PM–9:30 PM. 44 beds. Communal kitchen, linen rental, on-site parking.*

CAMPING The Point Reyes National Seashore has four campgrounds that are open to backpackers only and located in isolated wilderness areas. You may have to hike in as much as 6 miles to reach one, but that's part of their appeal. All are free, but reservations are required; call the Point Reyes Visitor Center (tel. 415/663–1092) up to one month in advance on weekdays between 9 AM and noon. Trails to the campgrounds leave from the visitor center; they all have picnic tables and pit toilets, but none has running water or allows fires, so bring plenty of supplies and warm clothing.

Coast Camp. It's a 2-mile hike from the visitor center to this secluded campground on the beach—it's within a stone's throw of the water. 15 sites.

Glenn Camp. People tend to avoid this one because it's 5 1/2 miles from the nearest road. It's great though, if you don't mind the hike; nestled among the trees in a quiet valley, it's miles away from the reek of civilization. 13 sites.

Sky Camp. Because it's only a 2-mile hike from the visitor center, this is Point Reyes most popular campground. Perched on the ridge of a small mountain, there's an outstanding view of the peninsula and seashore from all vantage points. 16 sites.

Wildcat Camp. It's a 6 1/2-mile hike from the nearest road, accessible only to the rugged, and sites are scattered in a dense thicket, so privacy is never a problem. 14 sites.

FOOD

There aren't too many places to eat inside the Point Reyes National Seashore, so stock up in San Francisco or at the **Bovine Bakery** (11315 Rte. 1, 2 mi north of Olema, tel. 415/663–9420). They have excellent, reasonably priced sandwiches, pastries, and breads—the perfect makings for a picnic. The most popular stop, however, is in Inverness's **Perry's Delicatessen** (12301 Sir Francis Drake Blvd., tel. 415/663–1491).

For under $6, brown bag one of their shrimp or crab sandwiches and a freshly made garden salad. Also in Inverness is the **Gray Whale Inn** (12781 Sir Francis Drake Blvd., tel. 415/669–1244), a good pit stop for home-style pizzas, pastries, sandwiches, coffee, and beer. It's more expensive than Perry's, but the sunny patio is a good place to watch one day fade into the next.

Manka's. This rustic, wood-paneled Czech restaurant offers a large selection of hearty stews and soups, smoked pork with sauerkraut and dumplings, and homemade strudels. A full meal runs $12–$18, but the longer you sit by its fireplace and the more Pilsen Urquell you drink, the less you seem to care. *30 Calendar Way, Inverness, tel. 415/669–1034. Reservations recommended in summer. Open Thurs.–Mon. for dinner. Sun. brunch.*

Vladimir's. Manka's has more style and charm, but Vladimir's is certainly cheaper. It has many of the same Czech dishes (variations on the roast pork and dumpling theme), but a full meal costs only $7–$12. *In the center of Inverness on Sir Francis Drake Blvd., tel. 415/669–1021. Reservations recommended in summer. Open Tues.–Sun. 5–10 PM.*

The Wine Country

The wine country is only 60 miles northeast of San Francisco—an easy and highly recommended day trip if you have a car. Most of the vineyards are concentrated in the **Napa** and **Sonoma valleys,** but the wine country actually stretches north to Santa Rosa and all the way into Lake and Mendocino counties. Vintners have been making wine here for well over a 100 years, but it was only in 1976, when a locally produced cabernet sauvignon won a blind taste test in Paris, that Californians began boasting and people all over the world began buying. Since then, production has skyrocketed. Twenty years ago there were only about 25 wineries, now there are more than 200. Napa Valley has the largest concentration of wineries, but also the most expensive and pretentious. Once upon a time, visitors were greeted with open arms—and flowing bottles—by jolly vintners thankful for even a trickle of business. These days, unless you're wearing a sport jacket and driving an expensive car, you're likely to get a semichilly, if not impertinent, reception. If so, hop in the car and make a beeline for Sonoma Valley or **St. Helena,** home to the more rustic and unassuming wineries.

The best time to go is in spring or fall, when mustard and wildflowers bloom amid the lush vines scattered across hill after hill. In summer, unfortunately, it sometimes feels as if each and every one of the 2.5 million annual visitors is backed up along Route 29, each impatient for another glass of zinfandel. If you have to go in summer, stay off Route 29

Just 'Cause the Pros Spit It Out Doesn't Mean You Have to

Wine tasting is generally free, but you may have to take a tour or watch a film at the bigger wineries before you can get to the good stuff. Luckily, the tours are usually interesting and, after a few glasses of free wine from the previous place you stopped at, completely painless. Of course, there is a complicated etiquette for sampling wine, but don't worry: This isn't France, so you're allowed to be ignorant and ask a lot of questions. Just don't ask for ice. One hint: You should move from light wines to dark so as not to "clutter your palate," as a vintner might say. You will undoubtedly be tempted to buy some of the wine you try, but don't buy in volume until you check the local supermarkets, which may have it for less.

The Wine Country

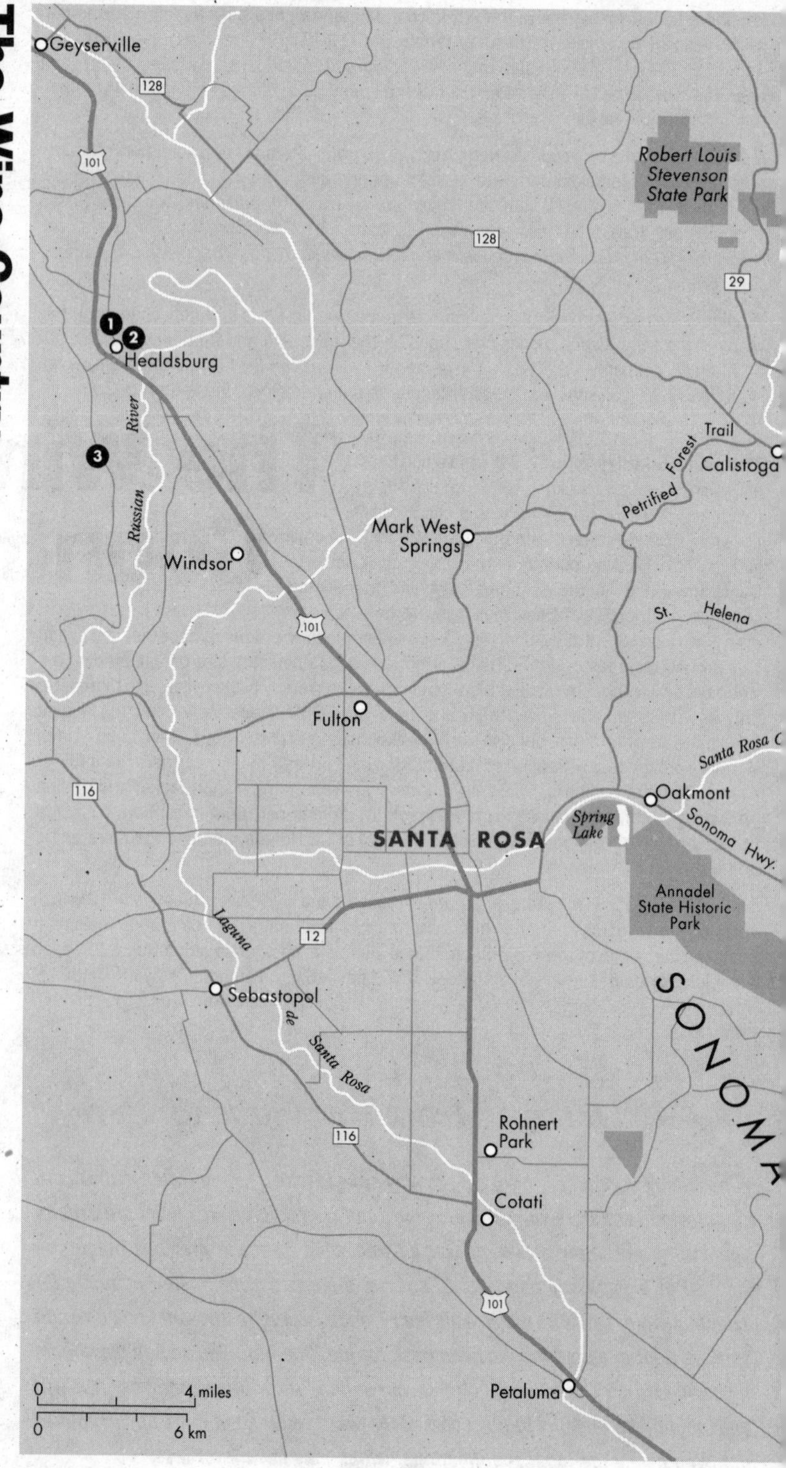

The Wine Country

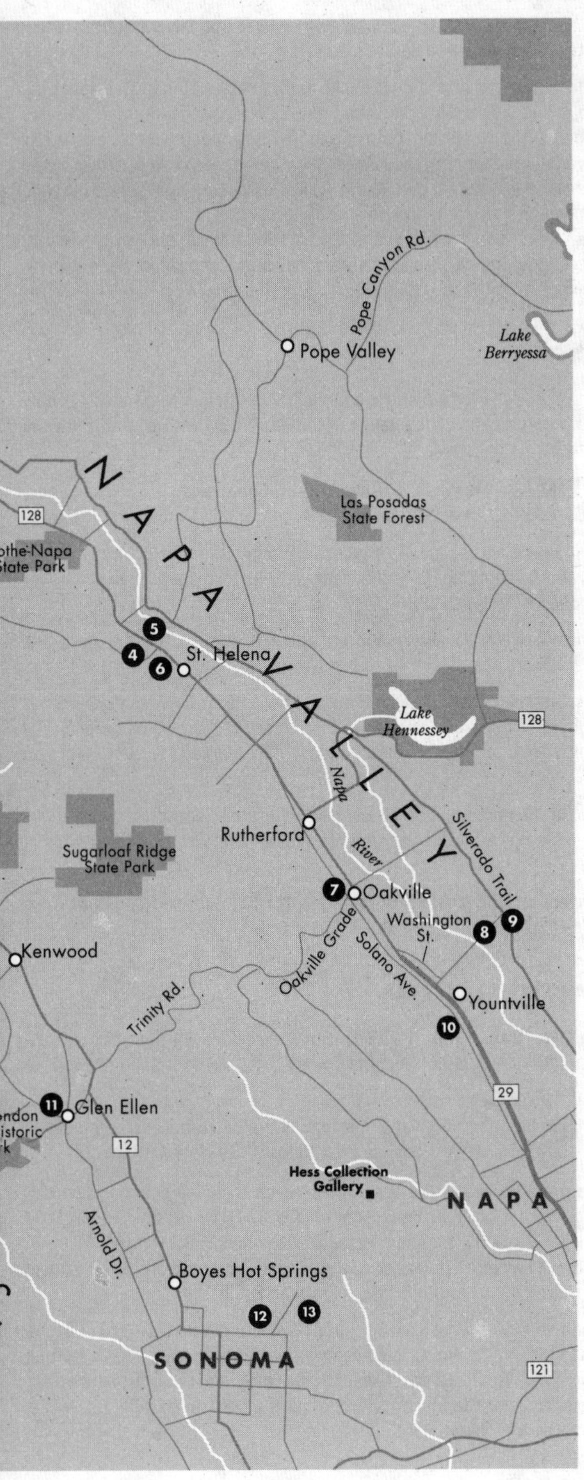

Beringer, **6**
Buena Vista, **13**
Charles Krug, **5**
Christian Brothers, **4**
Clos du Bois, **2**
Domaine Chandon, **10**
Glen Ellen, **11**
Hop Kiln, **3**
Robert Mondavi, **7**
S. Anderson Vineyards, **8**
Sebastiani, **12**
Simi, **1**
Stag's Leap Winery, **9**

as much as possible and explore the less crowded and more scenic **Silverado Trail,** which runs parallel to Route 29 a mile to the east.

If you absolutely detest wine, there are mud packs and mineral baths in **Calistoga;** the Spanish mission and old adobes of **Sonoma;** small museums devoted to former residents Jack London and Robert Louis Stevenson, both of whom wrote about the area; and the city of **Santa Rosa,** a convenient base for day trips east to the wine country or west to the rugged Sonoma Coast. Be forewarned, though, that unless you camp, an overnight stay in the wine country will take a monster-size bite out of your budget. Lodging tends to be even more expensive than in San Francisco, and food is pricey as well. You can survive cheaply by eating at roadside produce stands, drinking free wine, and sleeping in a state park. Otherwise, expect to pay through the nose.

● ● ● BASICS

TELEPHONES The area code for the entire area is **707.** Although Napa Valley is only 35 miles long, a call from one end of the valley to the other can cost up to 75¢ for the first three minutes from a pay phone.

TOURIST INFORMATION **Healdsburg Chamber of Commerce.** *217 Healdsburg Ave., 95448, tel. 707/433–6935 or 800/648–9922.*

Napa Chamber of Commerce. They can help organize a trip into the wine country (though they won't say a word about nonmembers) and provide you with more maps than you'll ever need. *1556 1st St., 94559, tel. 707/226–7455.*

Napa County Historical Society, Research Library and Museum. *1219 1st Ave., tel. 707/224–1739.*

Redwood Empire Association. Grab a copy of their "Redwood Empire Visitor's Guide" if you're headed into Marin or the Wine Country, available free at their office or for $2 by mail. It lists all the wineries and major tourist sights. *785 Market St., San Francisco 94103, tel. 415/543–8334.*

St. Helena Chamber of Commerce. They have useful information about "up valley" wineries for those headed north toward Sacramento. *1080 Main St., Box 124, 94574, tel. 707/963–4456.*

Sonoma County Convention and Visitors Bureau *10 4th St., Suite 100, Santa Rosa 95401, tel. 707/575–1191.*

● ● ● COMING AND GOING

BY BUS **Golden Gate Transit** (tel. 415/332–6600) provides 24-hour bus service from San Francisco to towns throughout Sonoma County. The fare from San Francisco to Santa Rosa is about $4.

Greyhound runs from San Francisco (7th and Mission Sts., tel. 415/558–6789) to Napa ($11) twice daily, Sonoma ($9) once a day, and Santa Rosa ($9) four times a day.

BY CAR Though traffic is heavy, the best way to reach the wine country is by car. Several routes are possible. From San Francisco, take **U.S. 101** over the Golden Gate Bridge and connect with **Route 37 east** near Ignacio. From here, take **Route 121** north for Sonoma; **Route 12** east for Napa. Traffic is heaviest on weekends and during rush hours (7–9 AM, 4–6 PM), but even so it shouldn't take more than two hours.

Santa Rosa is less than an hour's drive from San Francisco straight up U.S. 101, but the trip can take twice as long during morning and evening rush hours. Instead, make the trek to Sonoma and then join with **Route 12** east toward Santa Rosa. It's a beautiful drive (i.e., green hills, cattle pastures, quiet farms) and, except for the occasional pickup or horse trailer, traffic shouldn't be a problem.

GETTING AROUND ● ● ●

BY BUS If you can't afford to rent a car, there are ways to see the wine country by bus. It'll require some creativity on your part, but hey—that's half the fun. In particular, **Sonoma County Transit** (tel. 707/576–7433) connects all cities in Sonoma County. Buses run weekdays 6 AM–6:30 PM, Saturday 8 AM–6 PM, and limited hours on Sunday. Fares run under $2, and buses can generally get you within walking distance of a few wineries.

Otherwise, **Bear Flag Express** (tel. 707/255–7631) offers service between Napa and Yountville, while **Santa Rosa City Bus** (tel. 707/524–5306) has bus service in and around Santa Rosa, Monday–Saturday 6 AM–8:30 PM, Sunday 10–5.

BY BIKE Biking is perhaps the best way to see the wine country. You may not want to make the long haul from Sonoma to St. Helena by bike, but within a particular region the wineries tend to be huddled close together, making them easy to see on two wheels. Even better, the terrain is generally flat and lush. In St. Helena, **St. Helena Cyclery** (1156 Main St., tel. 707/963–7736) rents bikes for $5 per hour, $20 per day, or $100 per week. **Bike Tours of Napa Valley** (4080 Byway East, tel. 707/255–3380), at the northern end of Napa, rents bikes starting at $4 per hour, or $15 per day. **Calistoga Bike Rentals** (1227 Lincoln Ave., tel. 707/942–0421), in downtown Calistoga, rents bikes for $7 for the first hour and $3 for each additional hour, or $24 for the whole day. All offer biking maps and tour suggestions, so squeeze as much information from them as possible before heading out.

BY TRAIN Established in 1989, the **Napa Valley Wine Train** infuriates many locals who see it as Disneylike entertainment that pollutes the valley and brings too many tourists. Proposals to stop at various wineries have not been approved, so for the moment the wine train remains an overpriced way to get from Napa to St. Helena and back again. Despite this and the outrageous prices ($59 round-trip with "gourmet" lunch), nearly every three-hour trip is booked during summer. Relaxing it may be, but the wines aboard are overpriced and the route no more scenic than Route 29. For a lot less money you could have a rental car of your very own, so save your money. *1275 McKinstry St., Napa, tel. 707/253–2111 for reservations.*

BY CAR One of the most popular drives is unofficially known as the Napa–Sonoma loop. Start on Route 29 in Napa, head 12 miles north to Yountville, and then cross over to Route 12 and Sonoma via Glen Ellen. The drive is spectacular and, without any stops, easily navigated in under two hours. Depending on your final destination, you may have to backtrack to take in Calistoga, St. Helena, or Santa Rosa, but don't panic: All are easily accessed from Routes 12 or 29.

For the grand tour, however, take Route 29 north from Napa to Calistoga, head west for 12 miles toward Fulton and U.S. 101, drive 4 miles south on 101 to Santa Rosa, and then join with Route 12 south. Twenty-six miles later, you'll be in Sonoma. This semicircular drive takes four hours without any stops, but it passes through the wine country's major towns and vineyards.

BY BALLOON If you have some money to burn, a number of companies offer balloon tours of the wine country. They're expensive ($80–$150 for up to four people), but where else can you sip champagne while swaying beneath a helium-filled balloon, high above California's vineyards? In particular, try **Balloons Above the Valley** (tel. 707/253–2222 or 800/233–7681 in CA) in Napa, **Napa Valley Balloons** (tel. 707/253–2224 or 800/253–2224) in Yountville, and **Once in a Lifetime** (tel. 707/942–6541 or 800/722–6665 in CA) in Calistoga. All are competitively priced, and all recommend reservations at least one to two weeks in advance.

WHERE TO SLEEP ● ● ●

Budget travelers be warned: Unless you camp at Lake Berryessa or at one of the nearby state parks, expect to pay at least $40 a night in the wine country. Unfortunately, this area is geared for an upscale crowd, and even the generic motels charge a ridiculous price for ramshackle accommodations. If you are willing to splurge, though, this is a good place to indulge yourself. The area is crawling with small inns and bed-and-breakfasts, some offering splendid service in beautiful surroundings.

NAPA VALLEY Not surprisingly, the most expensive lodging is in the posh Napa Valley. If you're on a tight budget, don't even attempt to stay overnight unless you're camping. The cheapest place around is **Motel 6** (3380 Solano Ave., tel. 707/257–6111), off Route 29 at Redwood Road, but even their generic-looking doubles start at $35. The only nice thing is its swimming pool, perfect after a long day at the wineries—many of which are within biking distance. All 58 rooms here are booked during the summer, so call ahead.

On the upper-end of the scale is **Tall Timbers Chalet** (1012 Darms La., tel. 707/252–7810), 4 miles north of Napa off Solano Avenue. It has deluxe cabins with kitchens and is an ideal starting point for bike trips through the wineries. Proprietor Mary Monte is full of stories about the valley and can help arrange a tour that fits your interests. Cabins are (don't scream) $100–$125 a night, but they sleep up to four people. Reservations are required during summer and, annoyingly enough, full payment is required one week in advance. Needless to say, you won't find many budget travelers here.

SONOMA VALLEY In Sonoma, call to see if the comfortably rustic **Swiss Hotel** (18 Spain St., tel. 707/938–2884) has reopened after earthquake repairs and if the prices are comparable to what they were before closing: $18 for a room with shared bath. Otherwise, your best bet is camping.

SANTA ROSA Santa Rosa may be a convenient base for day trips east into the wine country, but its lodging ranges from extremely to outrageously expensive. If you're desperate, try the motels along U.S. 101 north of downtown for rooms in the $45–$50 category, or head to the **Heritage Inn** (870 Hopper Ave., tel. 707/545–9000), off U.S. 101 at Mendocino Avenue, 2½ miles north of downtown. It has clean, simple rooms ($35 a night) and a heated swimming pool.

CAMPGROUNDS Camping is your only budget option in the wine country. Unfortunately, though, they're generally located way off the beaten path—good news for nature lovers, but bad news for those intent on visiting the wineries. To make matters worse, there isn't any public transportation to the campgrounds; unless you have a car, you may have to hitchhike, walk, or bike back to civilization.

If you're getting desperate and don't mind driving, head 20 miles east from Rutherford on Route 128 to Lake Berryessa. The lake is divided into three campgrounds: **Pleasure Cove** (tel. 707/966–2172), **Spanish Flat** (tel. 707/966–2101), and **Camp Lake Berryessa** (tel. 707/966–2111). All together there are 771 campsites near the water (225 tent sites and 546 RV sites), for generally around $15 a night. Because it's 1½ hours away from Napa's wineries, crowds are never a serious problem, but this relative solitude does have its price. The area around the lake is barren, dusty, and very hot during the summer—more of a place to crash cheaply for a night than to discover nature.

Bothe-Napa Valley State Park. This is the wine country's nicest campground, situated in the Napa foothills amid redwoods, madrone, and tan oaks. The campsites are reasonably private, and the park is one of the few with a swimming pool, much used on hot summer days. The clean bathrooms have hot showers and flush toilets. There is a $14 camping fee and reservations are suggested in summer, especially on weekends. *3801 St. Helena Hwy. N, Calistoga, tel. 707/942–4575. From St. Helena, go 5 mi north on Rte. 29. 48 sites. Wheelchair access, no kitchen facilities.*

Spring Lake Park. Though it's only a few miles from downtown Santa Rosa, the park is secluded and thickly wooded, with 31 campsites ($15 a night, no hookups) on a bluff overlooking Spring Lake. Swimming and motorboating aren't allowed in the lake, but you can row or fish year-round. The road to the park winds through some new tract housing developments, but don't let that deter you. *5390 Montgomery Dr., tel. 707/539–8092. Off Rte. 12 at Hoen Ave., turn left on Newanga Rd. to park. Reservations advised.*

Sugarloaf State Park. Only 8 miles north of Sonoma on Route 12, Sugarloaf has 50 creekside campsites nestled in a shady meadow. There are 25 miles of trails for hiking and horseback riding, and plenty of wildlife (including giant crows and deer who are not afraid to walk right up to a quiet campfire). Campsites cost about $14. *2605 Adobe Canyon Rd., Kenwood, tel. 707/833–5712. From Sonoma, take Rte. 12 north to Adobe Canyon Rd. exit. Reservations a good idea in summer and on weekends. Flush toilets, running water.*

FOOD ● ● ●

If wine tasting is Napa Valley's main attraction, gourmet cuisine runs a close second. Many of the wineries, most notably **Domaine Chandon** (California Dr., Yountville, tel. 707/944–2280), serve elegant meals at steep prices. The best way to eat well without losing your shirt, however, is to stock up at one of the area's makeshift farmers' markets, where you'll find a bevy of fresh produce at reasonable prices. Otherwise, there's a standard array of fast-food stands and moderately priced restaurants in Santa Rosa and the other large towns.

Many of the wineries provide picnic grounds free of charge; grab your lunch box and thermos and pull over at any winery for a leisurely lunch in the sun.

NAPA

UNDER $10 **The Diner.** Several good restaurants line Washington Street in Yountville, but this is the best for the price. You can get huge plates of American or Mexican food for lunch and dinner, or specialty eggs and pancakes for breakfast. Most meals are under $6, so there's almost always a line on weekends. *6476 Washington St., tel. 707/944–2626. Open Tues.–Sun. 8 AM–3 PM, 5:30 PM–9 PM.*

The Red Hen Restaurant/Cantina/Antiques. Tired of rushing from one winery to another? Pull into the Red Hen for a plate full of *chimichangas* (deep-fried burritos, $8.25) or one of its hefty à la carte dishes, starting at about $3. There's an odd pleasure in sipping one of the Cantina's locally famous margaritas on the large outdoor patio overlooking a huge valley, as people race by to wineries on nearby Route 29. The Red Hen also features a long list of Mexican beers. *5091 St. Helena Hwy., tel. 707/255–8125. 5 mi north of Napa off Oak Knoll Rd. Open daily 11 AM–9 PM.*

Willett's Brewing Company. The brewery is a better pub than restaurant, but it's a great place to relax over beer or late lunch after a long afternoon bike ride. Enjoy a burger or sandwich ($4–$6) with a pint of freshly made Tail Waggin' Ale on the patio overlooking the Napa River. Expect a line on weekends. *902 Main St., tel. 707/258–2337. Open Mon.–Sat. 11 AM–10 PM.*

MARKETS AND DELICATESSENS **Napa Valley Farmers' Market—St. Helena.** *Old Railroad Depot, Railroad Ave. and Pine St., St. Helena, tel. 707/963–7343. May–Nov., every Fri. 7:30 AM–noon.*

Oakville Grocery and Post Office. This country store has all the makings for a great picnic. The wide selection of meats, cheeses, breads, cakes, and pastas can be pricey, but you can get enough supplies for $15 to feed four easily. *7856 St. Helena Hwy., Oakville, tel. 707/944–8802. Open 10–6.*

Pometta's Deli. This place is famous for its barbecued chicken platters ($7), but you can also get box lunches to go ($5–$12). Especially good is the vegetarian sandwich (about $4) stuffed with avocado, provolone, zucchini, and jalapeños. *Rte. 29 at Madison Road, Oakville, tel. 707/944–2365. Open Wed.–Sat. 10–6 (sandwich bar closes at 4), Sun. 10–4.*

Yountville Market. This unpretentious market/deli is across from Yountville's upscale shopping center. Pick up some hefty sandwiches (about $4), some wine, fruit, and freshly baked bread and head for a field, or eat on the front porch where local winery workers gather to relax in the shade and talk about their crops. *6770 Washington St., Yountville, tel. 707/944–1393. Open daily 7:30–6.*

SANTA ROSA Unlike the rest of the wine country, Santa Rosa has plenty of interesting restaurants that offer good food at affordable prices. On Fourth Street, both east and west of the freeway, something is bound to meet your fancy.

Omelette Express. Locals pack this place for its 40 varieties of omelets (served all day), good burgers, and sandwiches—all priced under $9. Housed in an old brick building on Old Railroad Square, this restaurant has something the locals call "gosh dern country charm." *112 4th St., tel. 707/525–1690. Open weekdays 6:30 AM–3:00 PM, weekends 7 AM–4 PM.*

Fonseca's. Also on the historic Old Railroad Square, Fonseca's offers a wide selection of inexpensive, American-style Mexican food served in an atmosphere heavy on wrought-iron grillwork and Mexican knickknacks. Their tasty *menudo* (tripe soup) will cure any hangover for around $6. Less adventurous diners might want to stick to the fresh cactus salad ($5) or Volkswagen-size burritos ($4.50). *117 4th St., tel. 707/576–0131. On Old Railroad Sq. Open Mon.–Thurs. 10–9, Fri. 10–10, weekends 9–9.*

SONOMA As in Napa, the best way to eat well in Sonoma is to picnic. For a healthy sit-down meal that won't empty your pocketbook, **Zino's on the Plaza** (420 E. 1st St., tel. 707/996–4466) serves good pasta lunches and dinners for under $10. Go to the nearby **Old Sonoma Creamery** (400 1st St. E, tel. 707/938–2938) for great deli sandwiches and ice cream.

WORTH SEEING

NAPA VALLEY Although Napa Valley is one of the biggest tourist attractions north of Fisherman's Wharf, the town of **Napa** retains a cozy, rural feel. The streets are lined with Victorian houses and California bungalows, and the old shopping district is full of antiques shops and neighborhood restaurants. Most tourists are in a hurry to get to the wineries, but a quiet stroll through Napa is a worthy prelude to the hectic wine stomp ahead. Like the rest of the valley, however, Napa is going upscale. Plans for a riverfront marina and shopping district are underway, and the new stucco buildings springing up in the downtown area are already diluting Napa's old-time charm.

WINERIES With literally hundreds of wineries crammed into the 35-mile-long Napa Valley, it's difficult to decide which ones to visit. Some, like **Robert Mondavi,** pour the wine only after visitors have taken a full 45-minute tour. Others, like the charming and unpretentious **Sequoia Grove** (known for its fabulous Chardonnay), wait for you to ask the questions. For a complete listing, stop by any tourist office (*see* Basics, *above*); they have brochures detailing each and every winery.

How to Prate About the Grape

If you want to pass yourself off as someone who really knows about wine (as opposed to a freeloading swiller), you need to know the form. First, stick your snoot in the glass, inhale, and then look reflective; swish the wine around the glass and make appreciative comments about the "tails" of alcohol running down the sides. Having done that, take a sip and do everything short of gargling with it. If you're really pretentious, spit it out in the handy bucket; otherwise, swallow. Now you have to rate the wine. You can't go wrong by identifying the flavor of various fruits and berries—black currant, red currant, cherry—or spices like pepper. To make your tasting complete, look poised and self-assured and make some completely asinine summation. The present favorite: "It's a cheeky little wine, reminiscent of running naked through verdant pastures."

You can avoid the crowds by taking the **Silverado Trail** (parallel to Route 29, 1 mile east), which passes through many of the finest vineyards without the hectic traffic of the main road. Exit Route 29 at any point and follow the Silverado Trail signs. Otherwise, head north from Napa on Route 29; this will take you into the heart of wine country.

Domaine Chandon. One of the largest producers of sparkling wines, this elegant, modern winery offers free hors d'oeuvres and tours, but sampling their wines costs $3 a glass. Tours leave every hour on the hour. *California Dr., Yountville, tel. 707/944–2280. Open Wed.–Sun. 11–5.*

Hess Collection Gallery. High above Route 29, the Hess Collection doubles as a top-rate winery and art gallery, with an outstanding collection of contemporary European and Latin American art. After contemplating the artwork, you can observe several stages of the wine-making process, from its fermentation in stainless-steel vats to bottling. There's a slide show about the process, after which wine tasting begins ($2/person). *4411 Redwood Rd., Napa, tel. 707/255–1144. Take Redwood Rd. exit off Rte. 29. Open daily 10–4.*

S. Anderson. Tours are given twice daily of their "Stone Wine Caves," which hold over 400,000 bottles of sparkling wine. Reservations are generally required, but their excellent tours and generous tastings (free) are worth the hassle. In spring, you may even hear the strains of Bach or Mozart emanating from the murky caves—the site of evening concerts between March and June. *1473 Yountville Crossroad (off the Silverado Trail), Yountville, tel. 707/944–8642. Open daily 10–5.*

Stag's Leap Wine Cellars. Many people credit Stag's Leap with putting Napa Valley on the international map: In 1976, its cabernet sauvignon rated higher than any other in a blind taste test in Paris. Luckily, success hasn't ruined this comfortably small and unpretentious place. Wine tastings cost $2. *5766 Silverado Trail, tel. 707/944–2020. Open daily 10–4.*

ST. HELENA Sixteen miles north of Napa on Route 29, this quiet town with plenty of grocery stores, pharmacies, and no-frills rural appeal is a good rest stop on your way up the valley. This modest boondock town is also home to the **Christian Brothers Greystone Cellars** (2555 Main St., tel. 707/967–3112) and **Charles Krug** (2800 N. Main St., tel. 707/963–5057). Both offer tours and wine tastings ($2 a person) throughout the year. The Nestlés-owned **Beringer Winery** (200 Main St., tel. 707/963–4812), perhaps the most interesting in town, has been open continuously since 1876. A government license to make sacramental wine kept them in business during the prohibition era, when most wineries were shut down. Tours and tastings are available year-round, but reservations are advised on summer weekends.

CALISTOGA Most tourists come to this funky, offbeat town for mineral baths, not as a last stop on the wine tour. The bubbling mineral spring on which the town verges became a spa in 1859, when entrepreneur Sam Brannan slurred together the word California with New York's Saratoga Springs resort. Calistoga has been attracting health seekers ever since.

For the best workover in town, go to **Dr. Wilkinson's Hot Springs** (1507 Lincoln Ave., tel. 707/942–4102) and ask for "the Works"—a $59 treatment that includes mud bath, mineral bath, sauna, steam wrap, and massage. If you're strapped for cash, an "à la carte" massage runs $25–$30. The comfortable hotel rooms at Dr. Wilkinson's aren't cheap ($64–$94 in summer, less in off-season), but they're less expensive than most places in the valley. Luckily, it isn't necessary to stay overnight to get a massage or a mineral soak. After your treatment, stroll down Lincoln Avenue, full of funky shops and good delis like **Fellion's** (1359 Lincoln Ave., tel. 707/942–6144). For hundreds of titles in New Age, erotica, and winemaking, head to the **Calistoga Bookstore** (1343 Lincoln Ave., tel. 707/942–4123).

Nearby is **Robert Louis Stevenson State Park** (Rte. 53, 3 mi northeast of Calistoga). Romantic literati will want to hike to the bunkhouse of the Silverado Mine, where the impoverished Stevenson honeymooned with his wife, Fanny Osbourne, in the summer of 1880. The stay inspired Stevenson's *The Silverado Squatters.* The park is perched at the top of Mt. St. Helena, which is said to be the model of Spyglass Hill in *Treasure Island.* The 3,000-acre park is largely undeveloped, but picnicking is permitted.

SONOMA VALLEY The town of **Sonoma** has recently grown into an upscale bedroom community for San Francisco commuters, so watch out for the trendy restaurants and chic clothing boutiques that beset the city. Sonoma has a rich history, though, and retains the feel of old California. It was here that Father Serra built the last and northernmost of the missions, **Mission San Francisco Solano** (1st and Spain Sts., tel. 707/938–1519), now a museum housing a collection of 19th-century watercolors by Chris Jorgenson. The area around the mission is like a living ghost town. Many adobe buildings remain from the days of Spanish and Mexican rule, including the old army barracks and **Lachryma Montis,** the ornate home of the last Mexican governor, General Vallejo.

Sonoma Valley's wineries are still its biggest draw, however, and have the advantage of being more relaxed and less crowded than those in nearby Napa. You can easily spend a leisurely day driving up Route 12 through the 17-mile-long valley, stopping at **Sebastiani** (389 4th St. E., tel. 707/938–5532), **Chateau St. Jean** (8555 Rte. 12, Kenwood, tel. 707/833–4134), the **Smothers Brothers Winery** (Rte. 12 at Warm Springs), and the **Glen Ellen Winery** (1883 Jack London Ranch Rd., Glen Ellen, tel. 707/996–1066). All offer tours and tastings year-round, and walk-in visitors are embraced with open arms.

Nearby in Glen Ellen, look for the **Jack London State Historic Park.** Tired of drinking and brawling on the Oakland waterfront, Jack London (1876–1916) began building his dream home on the 800-acre Beauty Ranch. The house was torched by an arsonist before it was finished, but a few stubbly ruins remain. The title of London's book, *Valley of the Moon,* has become an alternate name for the Sonoma Valley, despite the fact that the Native American word *sonoma* actually means "many moons." A gorgeous ½-mile walk takes you from the Jack London Museum to his grave and the ruins of his home. *Box 358, Glen Ellen, tel. 707/938–5216. Small parking fee. Museum open daily 10–5, park open daily 8 AM–sunset. Picnic tables.*

SANTA ROSA When residents of Sonoma County refer to "the city," they no longer mean San Francisco. Once a small farming community, Santa Rosa has become one of California's fastest-growing suburban areas, with shopping malls, minimarts, and housing tracts sprouting at an alarming rate. Most of old Santa Rosa was destroyed in the 1906 earthquake, but a section at the west end of Fourth Street called **Old Railroad Square** has been preserved. Here you'll find Santa Rosa's old train depot (now closed) and the pleasant Railroad Park, as well as a battalion of cafés, restaurants, and antiques stores. Four blocks farther east is the Fourth Street Mall and Santa Rosa Plaza Shopping Center where every retail chain imaginable can be found. To get a real whiff of modern Santa Rosa, check out **Cafe Aroma** (95 5th St., at Wilson, tel. 707/576–7765), the happening place for coffee and conversation. Live jazz on Friday nights and Sunday afternoons draws an excitable, intriguing, and mostly local crowd.

The **Luther Burbank Home** (corner of Santa Rosa and Sonoma Aves., tel. 707/576–5115; admission: $1) is where influential horticulturist and Santa Rosa resident Luther Burbank

The Bear Flag Republic

For a short period in 1846, Sonoma belonged not to Spain, Mexico, or the United States, but to the lesser-known Bear Flag Republic. The Republic was the brainchild of Captain John C. Fremont and a ragtag group of Yankee trappers who decided to resolve tensions between the Mexican government and non-Mexican immigrants by throwing the Mexican commander in prison and creating their own country. The republic evaporated a few months later when the U.S. Navy arrived, but the bear remains on the California state flag.

spent his life breeding hybrid plants. On Wednesdays and Sundays during spring and summer, you can tour his home, full of original furnishings and memorabilia. The beautiful gardens are free and open year-round. Across the street is one in the chain of **Ripley Museums** (492 Sonoma Ave., tel. 707/524–5233), a place generally devoted to the tacky and absurd but not so in this case. Believe it or not, Ripley was another Santa Rosa native, and the museum here is filled with almost heartwarming childhood memorabilia and photographs. In back, there's a church carved out of the trunk of a single redwood tree—the largest such structure in the world. Tickets are only $1.50.

COTATI This funky farming community 8 miles south of Santa Rosa is a popular hangout with students from nearby Sonoma State University—the sort of town that doesn't ever vote Republican. **El Sol** (8197 La Plaza St., tel. 707/792–0807), on the west side of its central plaza, serves great cheap burritos and beer. Check the schedule for the **Cotati Cabaret** (85 La Plaza, tel. 707/545–5483), which has live music nightly, sometimes by famous rock and jazz bands.

PETALUMA Petaluma, 17 miles south of Santa Rosa on U.S. 101, doesn't look like much from the freeway (tract homes, minimarkets, and gas stations), but old Petaluma remains intact, its streets lined with '30s-era bungalows and storefronts. The **Petaluma Area Chamber of Commerce** (215 Howard St., at Washington, tel. 707/762–2785) sells maps ($1) that detail the city's historic buildings, including **McNear's Feed Mill,** now a café; the **Palace Theater;** and the stately homes along nearby Kentucky Street. Old Petaluma, concentrated in a six-block area along Petaluma Boulevard North, also includes interesting antiques shops, bookstores, and cafés.

If Petaluma looks eerily familiar, don't panic. The city was used as a backdrop for the film American Graffiti.

SEBASTOPOL Long famous for its Gravenstein apples, Sebastopol still has the look of a slow-moving agricultural town despite its suburbanization in the last 10 years. Its proximity to Santa Rosa (only 7 miles east on Route 12) and San Francisco has turned it into a dull bedroom community, but even so its **Main Street** has a few cafés, bookstores, and restaurants that are worth a gander. For a taste of the local apples, check out the **Gravenstein Apple Fair** in early August, or visit one of the nearby commercial apple farms. Complete listings are available at the **Chamber of Commerce** (265 S. Main St., tel. 707/823–3032). **Hallberg's Apple Farm** (2500 Gravenstein Hwy., tel. 707/829–0187) is one of the most popular, offering over 40 varieties.

For food, try the hip and trendy **East-West Cafe** (128 N. Main St., tel. 707/829–2822), with a menu full of adventurous tofu and egg dishes. For more down-home cooking, the **Pine Cone Cafe** (162 Main St., tel. 707/823–1375) has top-rate pancake, egg, and bacon breakfasts ($4); burgers and sandwiches ($3–$5); and shish-kebab dinners ($8). For summer fruit and berries, be on the lookout for many come-and-go roadside stands, or stop by the local **farmers' market,** held every summer weekend across from Tuttles Drugs on McKinley Street, just behind Main Street.

Berkeley

Berkeley and the University of California may not be synonymous, but it's difficult to tell where one stops and the other begins. You won't find many knapsack-toting students in the upscale neighborhoods that buffer the north and east sides of campus, but for the most part Berkeley is a student town, dominated by the massive U.C. campus and its 30,000 enrollees. Because of its offbeat, counterculture reputation, the university attracts every sort of person imaginable—from artists, anarchists, and hypergenius intellectuals to superjocks, sorority girls, and fashion slaves, not to mention the stubbornly apathetic and the piously ideological, and of course the food snobs, intellectual snobs, and people whose only professed prejudice is against snobbishness itself. The city's liberal bent has led detractors to describe it as the People's Republic of Berkeley or Berzerkly, but this is perhaps more of a compliment than anything else. Berkeley thrives on being different and on the cutting edge, which has helped keep

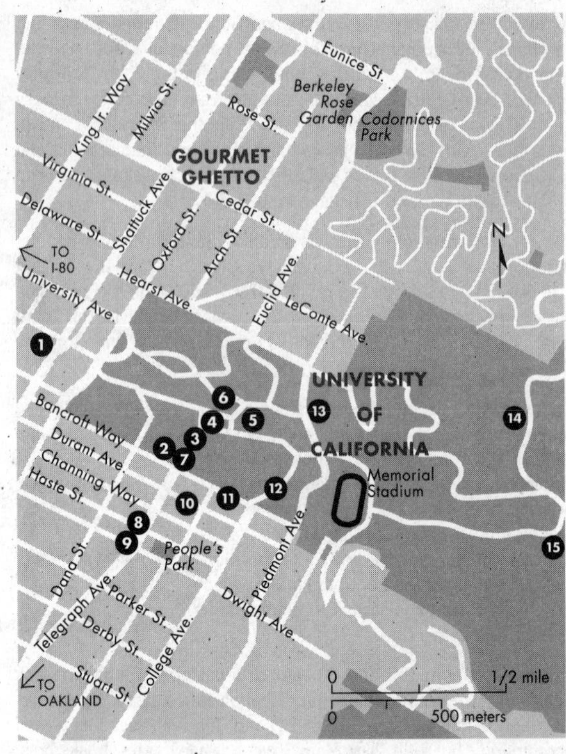

Berkeley BART Station, **1**
Botanical Gardens, **15**
Campanile, **5**
Cody's Books, **8**
Greek Theatre, **13**
Lawrence Hall of Science, **14**
Leopold Records, **10**
Main and Bancroft Libraries, **6**
Museum of Anthropology, **12**
Moe's Books, **9**
Sather Gate, **3**
South Hall, **4**
Sproul Plaza, **7**
Student Union Building, **2**
University Art Museum, **11**

it culturally diverse and politically adventurous—a breeding ground for social trends and all things alternative.

To visitors, it may seem as if Berkeley citizens exude a tiny bit of moral superiority—nowhere else does the cashier at the store make the question "Paper or plastic?" sound like a political interrogation. Yet this attitude merely reflects the typical transformation of someone faced with so many *choices* all the time. Am I a poet, dysfunctional, or merely someone coping with tarnished karma? What is my current political cause, my preferred sexual orientation, and do I want Thai or Burmese for dinner? The beauty of Berkeley—and the reason why it attracts such a diverse cross section of society—is its ability to be whatever you require of it. It sounds a bit hokey, but the

Homeless—and Voiceless—Even in Berkeley

Berkeley may treat its homeless better than most cities its size, but for those faced with sleeping in doorways and parks every night the City Council's "brotherly love" attitude rings a bit hollow. The national problem of homelessness, particularly visible here, forces visitors and denizens alike to confront a sector of society that is generally ignored, so ease up on your pursuit of personal betterment every once in a while to tune into some pressing social issues. If you're interested, Julia Vinograd (a.k.a. the Bubble Lady) has published a number of street poem anthologies, available at most Berkeley bookstores.

attitudes of the 1960s still flourish here and encourage people to drop their defenses and be the sort of person they always knew they could be. In the words of one of Berkeley's residents: "Life's too short, man, to worry about the things you shouldn't worry about anyway, so don't worry about it. Man, just be whatever it is you are."

Berkeley's major sights are located in three areas—along **Telegraph Avenue** on the south side of campus, **Euclid Street** on the north side, and **Shattuck Avenue** on the west—that encompass the city's walkable downtown area. No matter what part of town you're in, though, there are cafés and restaurants catering to student budgets, movie houses and bookstores geared toward the young and ideological, and a smattering of upscale shops popular with Berkeley's middle-aged huppie (hippie/yuppie) crowd. Except for the occasional droves who come to Berkeley with hopes of getting tear gassed, arrested, or just stoned out of their minds, tourists don't come over much, which makes it all the more enjoyable for the real folks. This said, don't be afraid to make the easy journey over from San Francisco to load up on some caffé latte, organic produce, and alternative literature. Even better, let down your hair, grab a guitar, and sing Dead covers on a street corner. Whatever your pleasure, though, be careful: People who hang out in Berkeley too long look up from their granola 20 years later only to realize they forgot to pursue the American Dream.

COMING AND GOING

BY CAR From San Francisco, cross the Bay Bridge and take **I–80** east. The easiest way to reach downtown is via the University Avenue exit, which eventually dead-ends at the west side of campus near the Shattuck Street/downtown area. For Telegraph Avenue and the traditional campus entrance, turn right on Shattuck Avenue, left on Durant Avenue, and then look for parking; Telegraph Avenue is ¼ mile ahead. Unless there's heavy traffic, the trip takes 30 to 40 minutes. Parking is a serious problem on weekends, but there's a **parking garage** on Durant just south of Telegraph; look for it on the right side of the street. The rate is 75¢ per hour.

BY BART Take BART (Bay Area Rapid Transit, tel. 510/788–2278) from San Francisco or Oakland to the downtown Berkeley station on Shattuck Avenue. Fares range from $1.50 to $3, and the trip takes anywhere from 20 to 35 minutes. From here, you can make the 10-minute walk to Telegraph up Bancroft Way (to the south), or the five-minute walk to the campus's west entrance via University Avenue (to the north). Otherwise, Humphrey GoBart shuttles make the 10-minute drive to campus daily between 7 AM and 8 PM; look for the stop across the street from BART. Fares are 50¢, and shuttles leave every 15 minutes or so.

BY BUS BART is the easiest way to reach Berkeley. If crossing under the bay gives you the creeps, however, **AC Transit** (tel. 510/839–2882) offers daily service from both Oakland and San Francisco. The last F bus from San Francisco's Transbay Terminal (First and Mission Sts.) doesn't leave until 2:32 AM and is a good place to meet friendly, if inebriated, Berkeley students.

WHERE TO SLEEP

Lodging in Berkeley is either pretty shabby or downright expensive, and sometimes both. West of campus, along **University Avenue,** a string of budget motels caters to a mixed crowd of prostitutes, drug fiends, and scared-looking parent types. Your life isn't in danger here, but don't expect much more than a vibrating bed, red velvet curtains, and the reek of cheap perfume. One of the less seedy ones is the pink **California Motel** (1461 University Ave., tel. 510/848–3840), set away from the noise of the street. The fairly spacious rooms are decorated with furniture probably purchased at a garage sale, but at least the rooms are clean. Singles are $35; doubles $40. From Berkeley BART, take Bus 51 west down University Avenue.

There are no youth hostels in Berkeley, but—for men only—the **YMCA** (2001 Allston Way, tel. 510/848–6800) is cheap and within easy reach of Berkeley's sights. There's a common bathroom, and its 86 dorm-style beds go for $22 per night, available on a first-come, first-served basis. There's a maximum stay of 14 days.

The Berkeley Motel. Shabby but centrally located, this place is three blocks from Berkeley BART. Its dank rooms ($33 a night) have no phones, but you're within an easy walk of Shattuck Avenue's stores and restaurants. Reservations are required. *2001 Bancroft Way, at Milvia, tel. 510/843–4043.*

The Golden Bear Motel. The nicest budget lodging in town is on the periphery of Berkeley. All its rooms are clean, sunny, and decorated with a modicum of good taste. The surrounding neighborhood isn't very safe though, so be wary walking around at night. Singles are $41, doubles (two queen-size beds) $49. *1600 San Pablo Ave., tel. 510/525–6440. Take Bus 51 west on University from Berkeley BART, transfer to Bus 2 going north on San Pablo Ave.*

UNIVERSITY HOUSING **University Guest Housing** offers summer dorm accommodations on the Berkeley campus for $30–$40 per night. Different dormitories are used each year, so call for current listings. Reservations are required; before June 1 call 510/642–4444, after June 1 call 510/642–5925.

● ● ● FOOD

Berkeleyites take their food very seriously. California cuisine, designer fuel for the yuppie generation, got its start in Berkeley, born of the idea that fresh, home-cultivated ingredients are vital to the success of a dish, and that portions are to be savored, not shoveled in. This concept has reached its apex at the world famous restaurant **Chez Panisse,** which serves visually and viscerally pleasing five- to six-course meals for upwards of $65 per person. If this exceeds your budget for the month, Berkeley has hundreds of intriguing restaurants worth a visit, from no-frills soup kitchens to exotic holes-in-the-wall, mostly concentrated on Telegraph Avenue between Dwight Way and the U.C. campus. Berkeley prides itself on being one of the most ethnically diverse cities in the country, and this is reflected in its tremendous variety of restaurants and offbeat groceries.

On the south side of campus (Bancroft Blvd. between Telegraph and College Aves.), there are no less than 15 food stands that cater to student budgets and Berkeley eclecticism. For less than $5, load up on some Middle Eastern, Mexican, Thai, Vietnamese, Chinese, American, or Japanese delicacies, then find a bench or shady tree. For entertainment, look up and watch the street musicians, the Hate Man, the krishnas, zealots, prophets, Rick Starr, and the Spirit of '29 all doing their thing.

UNDER $5 For pizza with an "eat it or screw you" attitude, stop by Berkeley's infamous **Blondie's Pizza** (2340 Telegraph Ave., tel. 510/548–1129), popular with street freaks and bleary-eyed students in need of a 1 AM pepperoni fix. This stand-up pizza counter is loud and always packed, its deranged and rude employees always entertaining, but for $2 you'll get a filling, greasy slice. Look for their daily pesto and whole-wheat vegetarian specials. For cheap hot dogs and Polish sausage, make the short walk to **Top Dog** on Durant Avenue, 200 feet east of Telegraph (toward the hills). Across the street, there are 10 small restaurant-type places, inside the **Durant Food Court,** that range from Chinese and Mexican to Ethiopian. For the ultimate budget meal, however, walk down Telegraph to the **Soup Kitchen.** It has no sign—it's on the northwest corner of Telegraph and Dwight Way—but it does have exceptionally cheap soups, salads, and sandwiches served by street urchins with nose rings.

Cafe Intermezzo. Head here if you're hankering for a quality salad for under $5. They also have a good selection of delicious soups and sandwiches, and everything is wholesome and homemade. The walls are adorned with changing artwork, and there are wooden tables and booths: It's an affable, cozy pace. *2442 Telegraph, at Haste, tel. 510/849–4592.*

Panini. This is a gourmet sandwich, soup, and dessert spot, one block west of campus. Featured are such unusual specialties as the chicken-avocado-cilantro sandwich ($5.50) and the garbanzo-garlic-Monterey Jack sandwich ($5.50). Their sandwich menu changes weekly, so be daring. *In the plaza at 2115 Allston Way, tel. 501/849–0405. 1 block east from Berkeley BART.*

UNDER $10 **Blue Nile.** This is Berkeley's best Ethiopian eatery, serving everything from lemon-basted chicken tips and pepper-cooked beef to honey wines and freshly blended fruit shakes. The restaurant itself is small, dark, and intimate, decorated with wicker furniture and Ethiopian knickknacks. As with most restaurants along Telegraph Avenue, the Blue Nile attracts an eclectic crowd of students and locals. Silverware is available, but bring someone you enjoy feeding with your fingers and who enjoys feeding you. Dinners run $6–$8, lunches $4–$5. *2525 Telegraph Ave., tel. 510/540–6777. Open daily 11:30 AM–10 PM.*

Cha-am. In a city that abounds with Thai restaurants, Cha-am is among the best. In particular, try the magical *Pam-Ka Gai* (chicken and coconut soup, $6) or mixed seafood plate with chili, garlic, and vegetables ($8.50). Cha-am's crowd is eclectic, but the restaurant itself looks rather bland. *1543 Shattuck Ave., tel. 415/848–9664. 1 block north on Shattuck from Berkeley BART. Open daily for lunch and dinner.*

China Station. Near the Berkeley Marina, it's housed in a former railroad station in homage to the Chinese laborers who built Southern Pacific's railroad in the mid-1800s. You can sit and enjoy exceptional Chinese food and watch the trains go by. Prawns with black bean sauce, $6.50; nasal-sizzling Szechuan chicken, $6.25. Reservations recommended. *700 University Ave., tel. 510/548–7880. Take Bus 51 from Berkeley BART. Open daily 11:30 AM–1 AM. Wheelchair access.*

Juan's Place. This unassuming Mexican restaurant has a small but devout following of Berkeley students and Mexican-American locals. It's stuck on the fringe of Berkeley, surrounded by steel factories and warehouses, but it serves some of the best home-style Mexican food in the East Bay. Lots of cast-iron grill work and family photographs adorn its wood paneled walls; there's an adjoining bar. *941 Carlton, at 9th St., tel. 510/845–6904. Open daily 11 AM–10 PM.*

Pasand Madras Cuisine. Reasonably priced and authentic South Indian food accompanied by live sitar music. Enormous six-course meals run between $8 and $11, or pick and choose from the extensive (and cheaper) appetizer menu. The adjoining lounge features live jazz nightly. *2286 Shattuck Ave., tel. 510/549–2559. 1 block south of Berkeley BART. Open daily 11:30 AM–10:30 PM.*

UNDER $15 **Anna's.** A changing dinner menu accompanies a changing menu of live music on the weekends, from folk to mellow jazz. The chef borrows from cuisines from all over the world, and on any night the menu might include Kenyan coconut chicken with plantain ($10), gumbo with shrimp and andouille sausage ($10), or braised Middle Eastern lamb with lentils ($9). Several vegetarian dishes are also featured on a nightly basis. *6420 Shattuck Blvd., tel. 510/655–5900. 1 block north of Alcatraz Ave.*

UNDER $25 **Chez Panisse Cafe.** The trendy restaurant may be out of reach, but the café upstairs serves many of the same dishes for half the price, and there's less silverware to contend with. The lunch and dinner menu changes daily, but expect exotic pizzas, little salads with flowers in them, and various pasta dishes with long names. Even if the atmosphere is a bit stuffy, the food is phenomenal. Vegetarian dishes also served. *1517 Shattuck Ave., tel. 510/548–5049. 5 blocks north of Berkeley BART on Shattuck. Open Mon.–Sat. 11:30 AM–3 PM and 5–11:30 PM.*

Ristorante Venézia. Dinner here can be as romantic as a gondola ride: There's laundry hanging from the ceiling, a painted second-story balcony, and a mural of Venice on the walls for that "outdoor" feel. Luckily, the food measures up to the decorations, ranging from excellent seafood pastas ($11) and lasagnas ($8–$10) to risotto with artichokes, leeks, and fontina ($11), and grilled homemade sausages with polenta ($13). A popular night to come is Tuesday, when live opera accompanies your meal. *1902 University Ave., tel. 510/644–3093. 2 blocks down University from Shattuck and Berkeley BART. Open Tues.–Thurs. 6–10, Fri. and Sat. 5–10:30, Sun. 5:30–9.*

MARKETS Berkeley is enamored with European-style specialty markets, but even these come with a Berkeley twist (i.e., heavy on organic and pesticide-free produce, light on butcher shops). On Shattuck Avenue north of University, look for the area known as **Gourmet Ghetto,** filled with patisseries, wine and cheese shops, coffee emporiums, fresh-fish markets, and gelato stands. **The Cheese Board** (1504 Shattuck Ave., tel. 510/549–3183) is one of the only successful collectives remaining in Berkeley, and features an incredible selection of cheeses and freshly baked breads. On the south side of Shattuck is **Berkeley Bowl** (2777 Shattuck Ave., tel. 510/843–6929), alternative grocery shopping at its best. The organic produce selection is endless, the bulk granola and other grains cheap, and the "environmentally friendly" selection stunning. For Twinkies, pork skins, white bread, and efficiency, head across the street to **Safeway.**

CAFÉS Without its cafés, Berkeley would collapse: Students would have nowhere to see and be seen while "studying," 15-year-old skate punks nowhere to hang out while cutting school, artists and poets no place to share their angst. Luckily, within a square mile of the U.C. campus, no less than 55 cafés peacefully co-exist, sustaining coffee achievers with every type of coffee concoction imaginable (not to mention the plethora of teas and other assorted beverages available). They're generally grouped in three areas: on or around Telegraph Avenue and the south side of the U.C. campus; between Shattuck and Oxford Street, on the west side; and those on the north side of Euclid Street, on the north side.

Caffe Mediterraneum. Featured in the film *The Graduate,* and the place where Allen Ginsberg wrote many of his best poems (*Howl, America*), the Med has nurtured countless bursts of inspiration, the occasional failed revolution, and countless be-ins. It survives today as a relic of '60s-era Berkeley, but it's still one of the best places to hang out and ponder humanity. Because it's located away from campus at the south end of Telegraph, it's somewhat less frequented by students and more popular with hardened, life-long Berkeleyites. Besides espresso drinks and desserts, Cafe Med has a small grill that serves up breakfasts, burgers, and pasta dishes all day long. It's wheelchair accessible, but the rest rooms aren't. *2475 Telegraph Ave., between Haste and Dwight, tel. 510/841–5634. Bus 40 from Berkeley BART. Open daily 7 AM–midnight.*

Tune up that guitar, let down your hair, free your spirit, and escape for a while into the past. Strange as it sounds, there are those who have been doing this for 20 years. The summer of love may be over, but in Berkeley it seems like only yesterday.

Caffe Strada. There's very little indoor seating, but the sprawling outdoor patio attracts an eclectic mixture of architecture students, fraternity and sorority members, and foreigners. It's a social café, so don't expect to get much work done. Instead, bring a newspaper and relax in the sun for a few hours, eavesdropping and sipping espresso. Even if you hate coffee, try the iced, white chocolate mocha ($1.50), more a member of the milk-shake family than the coffee family. *2300 College Ave., at Bancroft, tel. 510/843–5282. Open daily 6:30 AM–11 PM.*

The Musical Offering. With its airy interior and constant stream of classical music, this café caters to a more tweedy and ponderous mature crowd. Smoking is forbidden. Sandwiches, coffees, and soup are served in front, classical CDs and cassettes sold in back. Shopper's hint: If you buy something on a composer's birthday, you get a 20% discount. *2430 Bancroft Way, tel. 510/849–0211. Café open 8–6, music store 10–9.*

••• WORTH SEEING

Berkeley is dominated by the University of California campus. No matter how hard you try, it's difficult to get away from the fact that this is a student town, so why even bother? Instead, start on **Telegraph, Shattuck,** or **University** avenues and just take in the sights, meandering along the streets and in and out of shops that border campus. You never be too far away from a smoky café, a used clothing shop, a top-rate bookstore, or an excellent restaurant. Every day of the week, Telegraph is lined with dozens of merchants, offering everything from crystals and incense to tie-dyed T-shirts and hand-crafted jewelry. Sit down and have your tarot cards read or your past life explored, then make your way to **People's Park** (east of Telegraph between Haste St. and Dwight Way) for an afternoon rally on the green. This was the center of student protests in the 1960s, and on most days it looks as if this era still lives.

UNIVERSITY OF CALIFORNIA CAMPUS After you've soaked up this important piece of American culture and history, head over to campus itself, established in 1868 as the first of the statewide University of California system. It retains some of the beauty and gentility of its early years (especially in the old brick and stone buildings scattered about campus), some of the fire of the revolutionary 1960s (Sproul Plaza at noon), and some of the apathy and complacency of the 1980s (also Sproul Plaza at noon). On a walk through campus you'll find peaceful glades and other resting spots, imposing academic buildings created in the style known as brutalism, and battalions of musicians, dogs, zealots, and students "on their way to class" (i.e., napping in the sun). For a tour, stop by the **Student Union Building,** just north of the Telegraph and Bancroft intersection. Inside the lobby there's a small visitor center (tel. 510/642–5215) that has maps and brochures for self-guided tours and a sign-up sheet for free student-led tours, held on Monday, Wednesday, and Friday at 10 AM.

Sproul Plaza, the area of campus situated where Telegraph Avenue meets Bancroft Way, is widely known as the spot where the Free Speech Movement began in 1964. Look inside Sproul Hall (the nearby administration building) for a display of photographs from this first demonstration in which 3,000 students surrounded a police car that was holding a man arrested for "disturbing the peace" and distributing political flyers. Both the man and car were released after 32 hours, but Berkeley's activists had found a worthy cause.

Farther north, you'll pass through **Sather Gate** (1909), formerly the main entrance to campus until expansion in the 1960s. The second building on your right, **Doe Library,** is worth a look for its cavernous and beautiful reference room and the cozy Morrison Reading Room (*see* Cheap Thrills, *below*). Adjacent to Doe on the east side is the **Bancroft Library,** which houses an amazing collection of historical documents, rare books, and old photographs. On permanent display is a gold nugget purported to have started the California Gold Rush when it was discovered on January 24, 1848.

Directly east of Bancroft Library is the **Campanile** (1914), a 307-foot clock tower modeled after the one in Venice's Saint Mark's Plaza. The carillon is played three times daily, and

People's Park

It was over this university-owned plot of land that students erupted into protest in 1969, after the university tried to replace the park with a dormitory. Within a few days, thousands of students and locals converged here and refused to leave, preferring instead to celebrate people's power with music and generous doses of LSD. The university reacted by erecting a chain-link fence around it, and the protests that ensued resulted in nasty battles with the police, the death of one man, the dropping of tear gas on Sproul Plaza, and the 17-day occupation of Berkeley by the National Guard. Over the years, the university has attempted to regain control of the land several times. In 1991, the university decided to beautify the park and build a few volleyball courts, but many residents saw this as a pathetic attempt to dislocate the homeless and hippies who call the park home. After several riots, the Berkeley police stood 24-hour guard at the park, mostly to protect the handful of volleyball-loving students from hecklers. At press time, the park continued to sport the volleyball courts (albeit vandalized). Many residents would prefer that the park become a historical landmark open to everyone (including the homeless).

you can watch the performance (at 9 AM, noon, and 3 PM) from the 175-foot observation deck; take the elevator to the top (50¢). Even if you miss the performance, the views from here are stunning, encompassing all of Berkeley, Oakland, and San Francisco. From the campanile, walk east toward the hills and you'll pass the **Hearst Mining Building,** a masterpiece of Beaux Arts architecture designed by John Galen Howard. If you continue up this road, you'll eventually run into Piedmont Avenue and the **Greek Theater** (1903). This is a good place to catch concerts or run around at midnight. Designed by Julia Morgan, it's a replica of the theater in Epidaurus, Greece.

Continue south on Piedmont to the intersection at Bancroft Way. On your left is the **International House,** a dormitory that houses international students and hosts cultural events. One block farther down Bancroft (at College Avenue) is a small plaza containing the **Law School. Wurster Hall** (a brutalist monstrosity that houses the architecture and environmental-design schools, a fact which many find very highly ironic); and **Kroeber Hall**, which contains the **Hearst Museum of Anthropology** (tel. 510/642–3681). This is one of Berkeley's best museums, with rotating exhibits that cover everything from ancient America to neolithic China. Also on display are artifacts used by Ishi, the lone survivor of California's Yahi tribe, brought to live at the museum in 1911 after gold miners slaughtered the rest of his tribe.

Another half-block down Bancroft is the **University Art Museum,** a low-key cement block with balcony galleries and an outdoor sculpture garden. It houses the largest university-owned collection in the country, mostly contemporary European and American works. On the ground floor is the **Pacific Film Archive** (tel. 510/642–1124), which offers daily programs of offbeat and generally obscure art films. *2626 Bancroft Way, tel. 510/642–0808. Admission free. Museum open Wed.–Sun. 11–5.*

THE BERKELEY HILLS The hills east of campus offer incredible views of San Francisco and the bay, as well as access to Berkeley's Tilden Park (*see* Outdoor Activities, *below*). **Grizzly Peak Boulevard,** a curvy two-lane road etched into the hillside, is a great place to get an overview of the city and campus. It can be reached near the Memorial football stadium via Centennial Drive (look for the signs), and leads far up into the hills past some of the area's nicest homes. Around sunset, large numbers of Berkeley students hang out and drink beer in the turnoffs, sunning themselves and enjoying the view. Along the way, nestled in Strawberry Canyon, you'll pass the 30-acre **Botanical Garden,** with 25,000 species of plants collected from around the world. Admission is free, and there are benches and picnic tables good for a quick breather. *Take Bus 65 from Berkeley BART, or walk 15 min from Memorial Stadium. Open daily 9–5.*

In October 1991, a brush fire in the Oakland-Berkeley Hills went out of control, fanned by high winds and years of drought. Hundreds of homes were burned to the ground and several people were killed. In addition, several U.C. professors lost their life's work, as did many graduate students. As rebuilding continues, restrictions are being placed on the kinds of materials people can use and the kinds of flora they can plant.

On Centennial Drive, a half-mile beyond the Botanical Gardens and just before Grizzly Peak, is the **Lawrence Hall of Science,** perched on a cliff overlooking the East Bay. It's named for Ernest O. Lawrence, who received a Nobel Prize for creating the first cyclotron and helping to design the first atom bomb. Inside are a number of scientific and educational exhibits; most of them are hands-on and geared for those without Ph.D.s. One of the best is the massive dinosaur display, popular with children of all ages. On weekends there are additional films, lectures, and demonstrations on topics from "The Limits of Fractal Geometry" to "The Evolution of Sentient Life." Look over the observation deck for the long, slender pipes sticking out of the ground. These are wind chimes, and if you sit next to them you can hear the eery, aphrodisiac tones they emit. *Tel. 510/642–5132. Drive east (toward the hills) on Hearst St. and follow the signs, or take Bus 18 from Berkeley BART to the end. Open Mon.–Sat. 10–4:30, Sun. noon–5.*

NORTH BERKELEY Grad students, professors, and over-30 locals tend to frequent the area north of campus, generally referred to as "The Northside," lending it a more quiet and refined tone. The neighborhoods here are architecturally diverse and date mostly from the 1920s, which makes this an especially pleasant part of town to explore on foot. Cutesy cafés and restaurants line a three-block-long section of **Euclid Street,** where it dead-ends at the periphery of the campus. Otherwise, head for the area around Shattuck and Vine streets, known as the **Gourmet Ghetto** by locals (*see* Markets in Food, *above*). Here you'll find specialty stores, cafés, bookshops, and hoards of restaurants.

TELEGRAPH AVENUE When most people think of Berkeley, they think of Telegraph, which begins at campus and runs south into Oakland. Whether you love it or hate it, this congested and colorful avenue is the spiritual heart of Berkeley—a five-block-long jumble of cafés, bookstores, art shops, students, long-haired hippies, homeless buskers, lunatics (let out of institutions to save money back when Ronald Reagan was governor), metaphysical warriors, and wide-eyed tourists. Every day—rain or shine—troops of street vendors hock handmade and imported crafts along the "Ave," as its called, while New Age prophets offer tarot and numerology readings to uninterested passersby. If you're lucky, you may even cross paths with the Bubble Lady (poet and bubble maker), Rare (lunatic and sports trivia fiend), the Hate Man (high heels, lipstick, and an eye for style), or any one of the wacked-out denizens who give Berkeley its odd appeal.

Shops along Telegraph come and go, but neighborhood landmarks include **Rasputin's Records** (2333 Telegraph Ave., tel. 510/848–9005), **Leopold Records** (2518 Durant Ave., tel. 510/848–2015), both of which feature that rare medium: vinyl. Book lovers should check out **Cody's Books and Cafe** (2454 Telegraph Ave., at Haste, tel. 510/845–7852), **Moe's** (2476 Telegraph, tel. 510/849–2087), and **Shakespeare & Co.** (2499 Telegraph Ave., at Dwight Way, tel. 510/841–8916). Cody's hosts regular readings and has probably the largest selection of new books in the area, while Moe's and Shakespeare specialize more in used and rare books. For candles, incense, black-light posters and, er, any other recreational needs, stop by Berkeley's only remaining head shop, **Annapurna** (2416 Telegraph Ave., tel. 510/841–6187).

UNIVERSITY AVENUE University stretches all the way from I–80 and the bay to the U.C. campus, providing easy access to (or a quick escape from) downtown Berkeley and the university. It's the least crowded and student-oriented part of town, but it still teems with budget ethnic restaurants, cafés, and offbeat clothing stores. In case you missed the first-run of *Brazil* or the *Festival of Animation,* the **U.C. Theater** (*see* After Dark, *below*) shows an incredibly diverse range of classics, film noir, art, and 3-D porno flicks, along with weekly midnight performances of *The Rocky Horror Picture Show.*

Near I–80 at the far end of University, **Takara Sake**—one of only three makers of *sake* (Japanese rice wine) in the United States—has daily tours and tastings. Admission is free, but reservations are advised during the summer. *708 Addison St., tel. 510/540–8250. ½ block from University Ave. Open weekdays noon–6.*

Warm windy days were meant to be spent at the **Berkeley Marina,** on the water a half-mile west of I–80. The views of San Francisco and the Golden Gate Bridge are stunning, and you can even arrange a free spin around the bay with the **U.C. Sailing Club** (tel. 510/527–7245). Otherwise, flop down on the grass and watch local kids flying their dragon kites. *Take Bus 51 west from Berkeley BART.*

CHEAP THRILLS ● ● ●

For a cheap thrill guaranteed to last a lifetime, get a tattoo; there are several reputable and clean artists in the Berkeley area. The **Tattoo Archive** (2804 San Pablo Ave., tel. 510/548–5895) abounds with potential design ideas, while **The Blue Buddha** (1959 Ashby Ave., across from BART, tel. 510/540–9860) offers a more zen-like tattooing experience. If this seems too permanent, get something pierced along Telegraph Avenue instead.

Sometimes, the incessant flow of people in summer or the heavy rains in winter can make you crazy. If you want to curl up somewhere and recuperate, Doe Library's **Morrison Reading Room** (tel. 510/642–3671) was designed for exactly this purpose. It's on the U.C. campus and overrun with students, but anyone is welcome to peruse its international newspapers and magazines, classical and jazz records, or to just plant themselves in a lush leather easy chair. The subdued brass lamps, oak paneling, and ornate tapestries will make you nostalgic for living rooms which—at least until now—you could find only in Jane Austen novels.

Berkeley is a haven for street musicians and buskers. In particular, look for the **Spirit of '29,** one of the best Dixieland blues and jazz ensembles in the world—honestly. They're not very punctual, but look for them on the corner of Telegraph and Bancroft where they haphazardly set up and let it loose. On a sunny afternoon, sit down and let these cats blow you away with their groovy beat. As always, a small donation is encouraged. Otherwise, every weekend evening a rag-tag group of **bongo drummers** jam in Lower Sproul Plaza on the U.C. campus. Bring your own pot and kettle and join in, or just hang and listen.

A source of endless entertainment for locals and tourists alike is **Sproul Plaza,** where some of Berkeley's most famous loonies get a chance to clash wits. Watch a man in a bra and high heels heckle a Jew for Jesus who's preaching damnation and hellfire to fornicators and sodomites. Engage in a debate on foreign policy or on the existence of God with philosophers of all stripes. Listen to an endless stream of bad show tunes sung by the immortal Rick Starr, a man who apparently believes his unplugged Mr. Microphone reaches a national audience.

"Watch a man in a bra and high heels heckle a Jew for Jesus preaching damnation to fornicators and sodomites."

A flea market is held every weekend at the **Ashby BART station** (intersection of Ashby Ave. and Adeline St.), a mecca of treasure and trash. Most things fall into the can't-use-it-don't-want-it category, so don't feel obliged to buy. Occasionally, though, you'll come across an odd lamp or knickknack worth the $2 investment. Get here early for the best selection, late for the best prices, and don't be afraid to bargain for that dreamy macramé plant hanger. Just in case you have a doctor's office or bordello to decorate, there are upwards of 10 upscale antiques stores across the street from BART.

● ● ● AFTER DARK

Like everything else in Berkeley, nightlife is eclectic and casual, and you don't have to mingle with millions of drunken university students if you don't want to. However, chances are good that at least one will step on your foot no matter where you are.

The campus paper, *The Daily Californian,* regularly lists all student-oriented events, most of which are free or dirt cheap. The free weekly *East Bay Express* contains a complete events' calendar for the East Bay, including films, lectures, reading, and musical events.

If you don't want to drop any cash, attend a reading at **Cody's** (2454 Telegraph Ave., tel. 510/845–7852) or **Black Oak Books** (1491 Shattuck Ave., tel. 510/486–0698). Some big name authors and poets travel through town now and again, comparing stanzas and the size of their NEA Grants. Otherwise, get your karma healed at the **Berkeley Psychic Institute** (2436 Haste St., tel. 510/548–8020). They offer free weekly psychic readings and healing seminars from 7:30 to 10 PM. The atmosphere is friendly and informal, popular with all sorts of New Agers and alternative enthusiasts.

BARS **The Albatross.** This no-nonsense, no-attitude pub attracts a relaxed mix of students and working folk. Besides cheap beers and drinks ($1.25–$3), the Albatross has free popcorn, a cozy fireplace, and dart boards. Even better, the bartender puts together one of the best mixes of music in town. *1822 San Pablo Ave., tel. 510/849–4714.*

Le Bateau Ivre. This elegant bar is attached to an equally upscale restaurant. Neither is cheap, but both are beautifully decorated in a French chateau–style. There's a fireplace in the back room and a candle on every table—perfect for a romantic bottle of wine with your significant other. A small appetizer menu is available in the bar, ranging from cheese and fruit plates ($6) to decadent slices of cheesecake ($3.50). Le Bateau Ivre also serves one of the creamiest pints of Guinness west of Dublin. Dress ranges from formal to blue jeans and sweaters. *2629 Telegraph Ave., tel. 510/849–1100. Open daily 9 AM–11 PM.*

Bison Brewing Company. This is one of Berkeley's more interesting hangouts, noted for its innovative architecture and hearty pints of homemade stout, ale, and cider. It's generally crawling with students and local bohemians, and there's free live music Thursday through Sunday. Bands range from blues to Irish folk. *Friday afternoon happy hour features $1 pints. 2598 Telegraph Ave., tel. 510/841–7734. 5 blocks south of U.C. Wheelchair access.*

Brennan's. This bar is woefully nondescript, but its specialty drinks are worth the trip. Try the Irish coffee ($2.50) or a white Russian ($3), guaranteed to put a spark in your step. Popular with bar scum and heavy drinkers, this is as far from student Berkeley as you can get. *720 University Ave., near the Marina, tel. 510/841–0960. Take Bus 51 from Berkeley BART to the intersection of University and 4th St.*

Cafe Bistro. Nightly background jazz to accompany your Gitane and glass of brandy, low lighting, and a smokey European feel makes this place popular with the beret-and-spectacles set. *2271 Shattuck Ave., tel. 510/848–3081. 4 blocks south of Berkeley BART at Durant.*

The Pub. This unpretentious hole-in-the-wall is great for cheap pints and thick coffee—the sort of place where barflies blend into the woodwork and don't bother you. Its over-stuffed sofas, oak tables, and pipe-tobacco aroma nicely complement that novel you're reading or writing. If you forget your book, borrow one of theirs. It teams with students on weekend nights, but during the week it's generally quiet. *1492 Solano Ave., tel. 510/525–1900. Bus 43 north from Berkeley BART.*

The Starry Plough. Another Berkeley standby, this Irish-style pub caters largely to an older, politically left crowd. It has pints of Guinness, Bass, and Anchor Steam at the bar, and darts and chit chat in the seating area. There's live music most nights that ranges from ska and rock to blues and Irish folk. Visit on Mondays for free Irish dance lessons at 7 PM. *3101 Shattuck Ave., tel. 510/841–2082. Bus 40 south along Shattuck from Berkeley BART. Wheelchair access.*

Triple Rock Brewery. This microbrewery is decorated with '50s-era posters and knickknacks, and is popular with just about everybody. On weekend nights, look for grad students talking shop, frat and sorority types pounding homemade ale (it comes in light red or dark), and office workers having a good time. Loud and raucous in a collegiate sort of way, but the crowds are friendly. During the day, there's excellent pub food (nachos, grilled sandwiches, and the like) on the outdoor patio. *1920 Shattuck Ave., tel. 510/843–2739. 3 blocks north of Berkeley BART. Wheelchair access.*

MUSIC

BLUES **Larry Blake's.** This restaurant and jazz joint was opened in the late 1940s, and since then it's become a Berkeley legend. The upstairs dining room serves decent food to a yuppie crowd, so head straight for the cramped bar downstairs—a sawdust-covered, no-frills basement that hosts some of the best blues acts in the area. Covers are $5 and up; thumb through the *East Bay Express* or call for current listings. *2367 Telegraph Ave., tel. 510/848–0886. 1½ blocks south of campus.*

ROCK **The Berkeley Square.** For a long time this was the hippest venue for alternative music, both local and big name. Changes in ownership and focus—and some trouble with the law—have sullied the Square's good name, and today it's closed more often than open. It still attracts some national bands on a haphazard basis, though, and hosts weekend hip hop dancing. In general, the Square caters to the young and fashionable, and people with fake IDs. Call for current schedules. *1333 University Ave., tel. 510/841–6555. Take Bus 51 west from Berkeley BART.*

924 Gilman Street. This all-ages, alcohol-free cooperative features local garage bands and occasional big-name acts. The music is generally loud and aggressive, the crowd young, sweaty, and not afraid to throw themselves around. *924 Gilman St., tel. 510/525–9926.*

FOLK Berkeley sustains a thriving (and gradually aging) folk-music community. The best place to catch a wide variety of folk and bluegrass is at **The Freight and Salvage.** On a given night, look for world-class accordionists and harpists accompanied by any locals who care to join in. Even if you hate folk, this is a great place to mingle with interesting and friendly locals. *1111 Addison St., tel. 510/548–1761. Wheelchair access.*

WORLD MUSIC **La Peña** (3105 Shattuck Ave., tel. 510/849–2568), a Latin American cultural center, offers a wide selection of live music, political lectures, and films on Central and South American issues.

Ashkenaz (1317 San Pablo Ave., tel. 510/525–5054) offers something it calls "world music and dance." Essentially, this means there's a different beat every night, from African and Cajun to Bulgarian folk. Lessons are available, but most people come just to watch others perform. You won't find any brain-dead ravers here, only a devoted group out to broaden their cultural horizons. Vegetarian lunches are served Tuesday–Sunday. *Take Bus 51 west on University from Berkeley BART. At San Pablo Ave., transfer to Bus 72 northbound.*

CLASSICAL The **Berkeley Symphony Orchestra** periodically plays at Zellerbach Hall on the U.C. campus. Under the innovative direction of internationally renowned Kent Nagano, the symphony has delved into some very unorthodox but intriguing areas, including a Frank Zappa piece complete with life-size puppets. Call Cal Performances (tel. 510/642–9988) for the orchestra's current schedule. Otherwise, the **U.C. Music Department** (tel. 510/642–4864) hosts free noontime concerts during the school year, generally on Wednesdays. Most of the performers are students, but then again, most of the students are incredibly talented.

MOVIE THEATERS Along with several big cinema complexes that show first-run releases, two Berkeley theaters specialize in the rare, the old, and the avant-garde. The **U.C. Theater** (2036 University Ave., tel. 510/843–6267), which has been in operation since 1917, specializes in foreign films and classics that change nightly; double features are juxtaposed with great care and creativity. The theater is cavernous, the seats are lumpy, and the popcorn refreshingly cheap. In case you've never seen a real performance of *The Rocky Horror Picture Show,* it has midnight performances on Friday and Saturday.

The Pacific Film Archive, in the U.C. art museum, caters to hard-core film enthusiasts with its collection of rare titles. Films change nightly and often center around a certain theme (past offerings include film portrayals of people with disabilities and an evening of Clint Eastwood films). No popcorn or drinks allowed. *Entrance at 2625 Durant Ave., tel. 510/642–1124.*

THEATER Surprisingly, Berkeley doesn't have a strong theatrical tradition. There are a number of good companies in town, but not enough to sustain innovative drama on a regular basis. This said, the **Berkeley Repertory Theater** (2025 Addison St., tel. 510/845–4700) is an extremely diverse and popular ensemble, performing everything from Beckett and Brecht to Corneille and Mamet. Get half-price tickets for the otherwise expensive ($21–$27) performances after noon for that night's show. Other Berkeley area companies include **The Black Repertory Group** (3201 Adeline St., tel. 510/652–2120), whose performances address all aspects of the African American experience, and **The Blake St. Hawkeyes** (2019 Blake St., tel. 510/849–3013), whose offbeat and casual shows gave birth to Whoopi Goldberg's career. For information on student performances—many of which are quite good—call **Cal Performances** (tel. 510/642–1677).

● ● ● OUTDOOR ACTIVITIES

Even if you have to borrow your friend's cousin's brother's uncle's car, head into the hills above Berkeley for some stunning views of the East Bay. Despite urban development in the lowlands, the hills are inspiring, beautiful, and unspoiled, and loaded with miles of hiking and biking trails. **Tilden Park,** the only regional nature area accessible by public transportation, has more than 2,000 acres of forests and meadowland, perfect for a

Sunday drive or picnic. Camping isn't allowed, but there's no one to stop you from hiking deep into the woods and swimming in nearby Lake Anza. *Tel. 510/843–2137. Follow Spruce St. to Grizzly Peak Blvd. and follow the signs to Tilden Park. From Berkeley BART, take Bus 67 to the end.*

U.C. Berkeley has hundreds of sport and recreational facilities, but they're generally closed to nonstudents. However, you may be able to pick up a basketball game or racquet match at the student sports facility, **RSF** (2301 Bancroft Way, tel. 510/643–8038).

MOUNTAIN BIKING Inside Tilden Park, **Nimitz Way** is popular with local mountain bikers because of its spectacular views of the bay. It's a steep and moderately difficult ride, with access to more difficult and rugged fire trails. *Take the Canyon Dr. entrance into the park and go right on Central Park Dr. Follow the signs for the Brazilian Bldg., make a left turn onto Grizzly Peak Blvd. and continue to Inspiration Point. The gate at the west end of the lot marks the beginning of the trail. Bus 67 makes the trek on weekends, and every other bus is equipped to accommodate bicycles.*

For hot tips on less populated trails, hang out at any of the numerous bike stores in Berkeley and see if you can get the guy in neon hot pants to share his secrets. In particular, try **Velo Sport** (1650 Martin Luther King Jr. Way, tel. 510/849–0497) or **Pacific Bicycle** (2701 College Ave., tel. 510/644–3751).

SWIMMING In Tilden Park, Lake Anza has swimming for a fee of $2 during the summer. The water is clean and the beaches sandy, but you may have to compete with a Girl Scout troop or two for precious towel space. On hot summer days, Lake Anza is packed. Otherwise, U.C. Berkeley allows the public access to its pools for $3–$5 an hour. It's the best way to rub elbows with students and the water polo team. For pool availability, call the **Department of Recreational Sports** (tel. 510/643–7144).

Oakland

If you expect Oakland to dazzle you like San Francisco, save the $2 train fare for a cup of coffee. If, on the other hand, you approach Oakland with an open mind and a taste for the simple and offbeat, you may well have found a new favorite town. Oakland isn't glitzy or chic, so just enjoy it for what it is—a predominantly working-class community where people go about their business and have a hell of a good time on Saturday night. Nobody's out to entertain you (there isn't a single wax museum within the city limits), and yet that's what makes real entertainment all the more possible. Okay, so it's a bit dirty, ugly, and slummy, but in an odd way, that's the root of Oakland's appeal.

Even though they live in the shadow of San Francisco, Oaklanders are still proud of their city. In particular, Oakland is the home of West Coast Blues, and downtown there are hundreds of seedy clubs doin' the blues on a Saturday night—the sort of places where cool pool sharks named Shorty and Moe hang out. More recently, Oakland has nurtured the

Marching to a Different Beat

Like San Francisco and Berkeley, Oakland has a reputation for being a center of alternative culture and revolutionary politics. The militant and still widely debated Black Panther Party began in Oakland. In the 1970s, the city was headquarters for the Symbionese Liberation Army who kidnapped Patty Hearst (aka Tania) and demanded as part of her ransom that food be distributed to Oakland's poor. Even the city's most famous literary figure, Jack London, was steeped in controversy—an ardent socialist and debauched trouble maker, he wanted California to form its own country (although that's hard to detect in those two novels about dogs).

Oakland

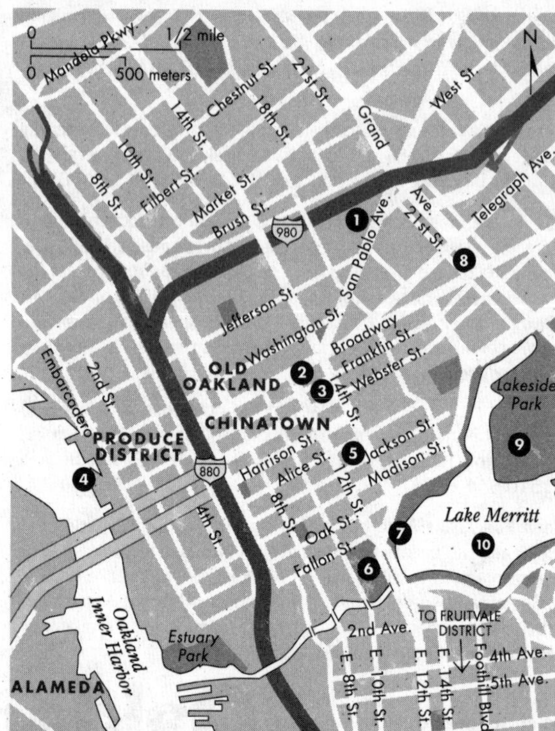

Camron-Stanford House, **7**
Greyhound Bus Station, **1**
Jack London Square, **4**
Lake Merritt, **10**
Lakeside Park Garden Center, **9**
Oakland Museum, **6**
Paramount Theatre, **8**
Post Office, **5**
Tribune Tower, **3**
Visitors Center, **2**

Oaktown school of rap and funk whose practitioners include local artists Hammer, Digital Underground, Too Short, Tony Toni Tone, Oaktown 3-5-7, and 2 Pack. Even if you're a devoted Bon Jovi fan, there's something exciting about sipping beers in a dive bar, listening to top-rate blues or funk, and dancing to the hip-hop beat until 4 in the AM.

On the downside, Oakland is one of the main shipping ports in the United States and a major West Coast rail terminus. The city has had its economic ups and downs, and for years has been notorious for its high crime rate. You'll see a depressing number of drunks and crack addicts on the streets, but don't let that deter you from a visit. To judge Oakland by its worst neighborhoods would be like judging New York solely on the basis of the South Bronx. Much of Oakland is at least as safe as other urban areas, and the downtown area has benefited immensely from a slew of urban renewal projects. That's not to say you should feel safe walking the streets alone at 3 in the morning, but with a little caution and sense of adventure, you'll be surprised how hip/cool/funky Oakland is. If you have the time, take a drive through the spectacular Oakland Hills. Many of the multimillion-dollar homes were destroyed in the October 1991 fire, but even so the area retains the feel and look of the 1930s, when this city was mostly a cluster of ranches, farms, and lavish summer estates.

● ● ● BASICS

TELEPHONES Oakland and the East Bay used to be in the 415 area code, but recently it's been changed to **510.** Luckily, it's still only 20¢ to call anywhere in Oakland and San Francisco from a pay phone.

TOURIST INFORMATION **East Bay Regional Parks District** has maps and information about the 46 parks and 13 regional trails in the Oakland hills. *2950 Peralta Oaks Ct., at 106th St., tel. 510/635–0135.*

Northern California Black Chamber of Commerce. *5741 Telegraph Ave., Oakland, tel. 510/601–5741.*

Oakland Chamber of Commerce. *475 14th St., tel. 510/874–4800.*

Oakland Convention and Visitors Bureau is geared more toward convention goers, but the staff is happy to answer all inquiries. Pick up a copy of their small pamphlet, "The Official Visitors Guide," which lists dozens of museums, historical attractions, and community events. *1000 Broadway, Suite 200, tel. 510/839–9000. Take BART to 12th St. Station, walk down Broadway to 11th St. Open weekdays 8:30–5.*

COMING AND GOING • • •

BY BART BART is the Bay Area's version of a subway. It's neither quick nor cheap, but it does stop conveniently in downtown Oakland. From any BART station, take the train to the 19th Street or Lake Merritt stations. Fares range from $1.80 to $3 (*see* Getting Around, *below*).

BY BUS There are hourly buses from San Francisco's Transbay Terminal (First and Mission Sts., tel. 415/673–6864) to Oakland. The fare is $2.80, and all buses stop downtown (*see* Getting Around, *below*).

BY CAR From the Bay Bridge, take I–580 to the Grand Avenue exit for Lake Merritt; the Waterfront and Downtown exits for, well, the waterfront and downtown. Depending on traffic, the trip takes 30–45 minutes.

BY PLANE The **Oakland International Airport** (tel. 510/577–4000) is a small, convenient airport, readily accessible by public transportation from points throughout the Bay Area. It's less hectic and crowded than San Francisco International Airport, and often much cheaper to fly into. For $2, the **Air-Bart Shuttle** (tel. 510/444–4200) runs every 15 minutes from the airport to Coliseum BART, where you can catch a BART train (*see* Getting Around, *below*) into Oakland proper, Berkeley, and San Francisco. The shuttle runs daily 6 AM–midnight.

The **Bay Porter Express** (tel. 415/467–1800) has door-to-door service from both Oakland and San Francisco Airport for $16. By car, take the Oakland Airport exit off I–880 and follow the signs. The airport is 15 minutes from downtown Oakland; 45 minutes from San Francisco.

BY FERRY Pack a thermos of coffee, some pastries and fruit, and a warm jacket and hop on one of the commuter ferries from San Francisco. **The Blue and Gold Fleet** (tel. 510/522–3300) leaves from both Pier 39/Fisherman's Wharf and the Financial District ferry building as early as 6 AM on weekdays, 10 AM on weekends, and arrives 30 minutes later at Jack London Square. One-way fare is $4.50.

GETTING AROUND • • •

The city is served by an extensive and efficient mass transit system, which includes BART (Bay Area Rapid Transit, a sleek subway system that stops at eight points in Oakland) and AC Transit, the much more thorough and wide-reaching bus service.

Although Oakland covers a huge geographical area, certain neighborhoods are best explored on foot. In particular, Downtown/Lake Merritt, Grand Avenue, Piedmont Avenue, and the Rockridge neighborhood in North Oakland all warrant bipedal exploration. However, you might want to view the areas in between through the window of a bus or car.

BY BART Oakland has eight BART stations, but the only ones near downtown are 12th Street, 19th Street, and Lake Merritt. All four BART Lines (Concord to San Francisco, Richmond to Fremont, Fremont to San Francisco/Daly City, Richmond to San Francisco/Daly City) pass through Oakland, so getting around the Bay Area is extremely easy. Tickets can be purchased at any station; the farther you travel, the more expensive the ticket (a one-way trip costs $1–$3). Trains run every 15–20 minutes, 6 AM–midnight, Sun. 9 AM–midnight. For more information, call 510/465–2278.

BY BUS The East Bay bus system, **A.C. Transit,** provides extensive service to Oakland and the entire East Bay, with several lines to San Francisco's **Transbay Terminal** (First and Mission Sts.). BART closes at midnight, but the N bus runs hourly, all night, between San Francisco and Oakland ($2.50). If you're transferring from BART to the A.C. Transit system, get a bus transfer before leaving the BART paid area. They're dispensed by machines near the exit and will allow you to ride the bus for 60¢; otherwise, the bus fare is $1. Stop by the AC Transit office for schedules and an excellent map of all routes. *1600 Franklin St., Oakland, tel. 510/839–2882.*

BY TAXI Taxis are expensive, but they're a good idea if you plan to explore the nether regions of Oakland at night. Unless you're headed for some bar next to a BART station, it's a lot safer to travel by cab. Both **Friendly Cab** (tel. 510/536–3000) and **Yellow Cab** (tel. 510/444–1234) offer competitively priced service within Oakland ($10 cross town), to Berkeley ($8–$15), and San Francisco ($20–$30).

● ● ● WHERE TO SLEEP

Most of Oakland's hotels are geared toward business people of one kind or another. If you're desperate, hundreds of faceless chain motels ($50–$75 a night) can be found in downtown Oakland and around the airport. Along West MacArthur Boulevard, near the MacArthur BART station in North Oakland, there's a string of motels used for more illicit, after-hours business transactions. Women should not stay here alone. On West MacArthur Boulevard east of Telegraph are a few reasonably priced motels in semisafe surroundings. Check out the **Imperial Inn** (490 W. MacArthur Blvd., tel. 510/653–4225) or the **Town House Travel Inn** (444 W. MacArthur Blvd., tel. 510/653–9032). Both offer mediocre singles for $30; doubles for $35. Sad to say, there are no youth hostels in Oakland, nor any campgrounds.

The Civic Center Lodge. This is the only reasonably priced option in downtown Oakland within walking distance of the waterfront, Lake Merritt, and the downtown bars and restaurants. It offers basic, no-frills doubles for $35. *50 6th St., tel. 510/444–4139. From Lake Merritt BART, walk down Lakeside to 6th St. and turn left.*

The Broadway Motel. It's a grimy dirt bag of a place, but at least it's in a reasonably safe neighborhood. Singles run $25, doubles with or without kitchen facilities $35. *4140 Broadway, at 41st St., tel. 510/653–0458. From downtown, take Bus 51 up Broadway, get off at 41st St.*

● ● ● FOOD

From Southern-style barbecue shacks to Salvadoran holes-in-the-wall, Oakland is loaded with cheap and colorful eateries. Because the population is so diverse, you can find just about every type of cuisine imaginable, so explore this area with eager taste buds and an open mind.

Breakfast with a Vengeance: Three Outstanding Breakfast Spots

- ***Mama's Royal Cafe (4012 Broadway, tel. 510/547–7600).***
- ***Lois the Pie Queen (851 60th, tel. 510/658–5616).***
- ***The Oakland Grill (3rd and Franklin, tel. 510/835–1176).***

FRUITVALE DISTRICT This district, which encompasses the neighborhoods around the Fruitvale BART station, has dozens of cheap Mexican and Central American restaurants. If you're using public transportation you should restrict your visits here to the daylight hours, since you'll have to walk several blocks from BART or the nearest bus stop (even if you drive, be cautious). **El Taco Zamorano,** a silver truck parked at the corner of East 14th and High streets, serves delicious burritos ($2), tacos ($1), tortas, and drinks. This is a carnivore's paradise; burrito and taco fillings include beef head, beef tongue, and pork skins, as well as spicy pork, chicken, and *carne asada.* Vegetarians can go across the street to **Taqueria Moralia** (4481 E. 14th St., tel. 510/261-6360) for one of the best quesadillas around. Next door is the **Talk of the Town,** a dive bar with cheap beer, a good jukebox, and a pool table.

Los Cocos. This is Fruitvale's best Salvadoran restaurant, famous for its fried bananas and tender carne asada. It may not look like much from the outside (nor inside, for that matter), but its food is incredible. A full meal runs less than $7. *1449 Fruitvale Ave., tel. 510/536-3079. From Fruitvale BART, head north on E. 14th St. to Fruitvale Ave. Open daily 9 AM–10 PM.*

Otatez Mexicatessen. This authentic Mexican grocery and restaurant is a good place for a sit-down meal. Nothing is more than $5, and the jukebox is loaded with your favorite salsa tunes. On Sundays after church, Otatez is popular with families of 10; expect a short wait. *3872 E. 14th St., tel. 510/536-0909. About 3 blocks from the Fruitvale BART station at the corner of 38th St.*

CHINATOWN The center for Asian food is **Chinatown,** a more authentic and less touristy version of its counterpart across the bay. Downtown between Seventh, Tenth, Harrison, and Franklin streets, Chinatown offers increasing numbers of Southeast Asian restaurants and markets, as well as the older and more established Chinese ones. **Tin's Teahouse** (701 Webster, tel. 510/832-7661), open daily 8–4, serves great dim sum for about $5. Try **Pho Hoa** (326 8th St., tel. 510/893-0124) for a huge bowl of Vietnamese noodle soup ($4).

Nin Yang. Although it's in Chinatown, Nin Yang serves authentic Burmese cuisine. The atmosphere is less than intimate, but the service is fast and cordial, and the food is delicious. Concentrate on Burmese specialties rather than the supplementary Chinese dishes. Especially tasty are the Burmese curry chicken noodle soup ($5), the ginger salad ($5.50), and the Burmese curry fish ($8.75). They also serve vegetarian entrées. *301 8th St., at Harrison St., tel. 510/465-6924. Open Tues.–Sun. 11 AM–9 PM.*

NORTH OAKLAND There are several East African restaurants along Telegraph and Shattuck avenues in North Oakland, and **Asmara** (5020 Telegraph Ave., tel. 510/547-5100) is possibly the best. It offers traditional Ethiopian specialties (from seared chicken strips to honey pork) in the $5–$8 range. This is true communal dining; don't make the mistake of asking for a plate or a fork. Otherwise, head to **Flints** (6609 Shattuck Ave., tel. 510/653-0593), widely regarded as the best barbecue shack in the world. It's a bit pricey ($7–$11), but Flints serves up ribs, chicken, and potato salad better than anybody else. It's open daily 11 AM–2 AM, weekends until 3 AM.

PIEDMONT AND COLLEGE AVENUES Maybe the lining of your stomach has dissolved. Maybe you need a weekly burger fix. Whatever the reason, sometimes you want to have a meal that isn't necessarily an adventure. There are two long avenues in Oakland offering a wide selection of delis, burger joints, and gringo burrito shops. From downtown, Bus 59 or 59A will take you north on Broadway to **Piedmont Avenue,** where you can wander among the shops and cafés and munch on a burger or slice of pizza. There are several gourmet specialty shops here as well; this is a good area to explore if you want to go on a picnic.

College Avenue is longer and more diverse than Piedmont. Take Bus 51 north on Broadway from downtown, or take BART to Rockridge and disembark right in the middle of it. Try **The Burrito Shop** (5359B College Ave., tel. 510/658-7646) or **Cactus Taqueria** (5525 College Ave., tel. 510/547-1305) for a cheap burrito. Farther north, you'll find **Zachary's**

Pizza (5801 College Ave., tel. 510/655–6385), renowned all over the Bay Area for its stuffed spinach and mushroom pizza. Zachary's may have lines going out the door, but it's definitely worth the wait.

MARKETS Another alternative for cheap eating is to stock up at one of Oakland's hundred or so markets, and downtown you can find a variety of ethnic ones. **G.B. Ratto and Company** (821 Washington St., tel. 510/832–6503; open Mon.–Sat. 8–5) is your source for delicacies like buffalo-milk mozzarella, as well as more standard picnic fare. There are 15 top-rate ethnic food stalls two blocks down at the enormous **Housewives Market** (8th St. and Jefferson, tel. 510/444–4396; open Mon.–Sat. 9–6), including a Creole and African counter. On Seventh Street between Franklin and Clay, **Mi Rancho** (464 7th St., tel. 510/451–2393) sells incredible tacos and burritos made with their own fresh tortillas.

CAFÉS AND COFFEEHOUSES **Peet's Coffee and Tea.** The granddaddy of them all. People come from miles around for a cup (or pound) of their java, arguably the strongest in town. Peet's has a few tables, but good luck getting one on a Sunday morning. *4050 Piedmont Ave., tel. 510/655–3228.*

Royal Coffee Exchange. It doesn't look like much, but this is a good place for chit chat and an afternoon read. Good coffee, chess-playing locals, and a heap of colorful atmosphere. *307 63rd at College, tel. 510/653–5458.*

The Edible Complex. Popular with teenage street kids and the weekend brunch crowd, the Edible serves potent espresso drinks and a large menu of light meals. Outdoor seating available. *5600 College Ave., tel. 510/658–2172. 2 blocks south of Rockridge BART station.*

● ● ● WORTH SEEING

After you've strolled around **Lake Merritt,** toured some interesting Victorian buildings and an art gallery or two, hit the downtown area. You could easily spend a week wandering wide-eyed through the untouristy **Chinatown** (downtown between 7th, 10th, Harrison, and Franklin Sts.), through the barrios and food stands in **Fruitvale** (near Fruitvale BART), or in the recently restored **Old Oakland.** Afterwards, grab a coffee along Grand Avenue, College Avenue, or Piedmont Avenue or head for a blues club when evening rolls around (*see* After Dark, *below*). If the city is fraying your nerves, Oakland's many parks offer a gorgeous respite from downtown's slummy craziness. The parks in the hills east of the city are rugged and undeveloped, and give an idea of what the topography was like when the Ohlone Native Americans first lived here 2,000 years ago. You'll need a car to really explore the hills, but most everything else is within reach of a BART station.

Oakland has its share of tourist sights, but it's the small things that make Oaktown interesting—its '30s-era apartment buildings and churches; a handful of drunks shooting dice on a corner; its grungy storefronts and alleyways; its dark pool halls and smoky bars.

Several walking tours are available from **Oakland Walking Tours** (tel. 510/273–3234) and, for those interested in a historical perspective, from the **Oakland Heritage Alliance** on weekends in July and August (tel. 510/763–9218); they're free. For those with a soft spot for shipping, the popular and free **Port of Oakland Tour** (tel. 510/839–7493 for reservations) ferries people around the bay between May and August.

LAKE MERRITT AND LAKESIDE PARK Lake Merritt, a 155-acre oasis in the middle of urban Oakland, is filled with shady trees, meandering paths, and lots of old men feeding the ducks. Lakeside Park (tel. 510/273–3091), on the north shore of Lake Merritt, has picnic facilities, boat rentals, Japanese and herb gardens, and frequent music events. Each June, this is the site of Oakland's "Festival by the Lake" (*see* Festivals, *below*). The lake itself was created in 1860, when a tidal saltwater lake was dammed. Man-made though it may be, Lake Merritt has the distinction of being the first national wildlife refuge in the United States. It's a nice place for an afternoon nap or stroll and easily reached from downtown; walk 1/4 mile southwest from the 12th Street or 19th Street

BART station, or go directly to the Lake Merritt BART station. Nearby, you can tour the **Camron-Stanford House** (1418 Lakeside Dr., tel. 510/836–1976), the only remaining Victorian building in this formerly bourgeois neighborhood. Tours ($2) are offered Wednesday 11–4 and Sunday 1–5.

JACK LONDON SQUARE Although born in San Francisco, Jack London spent his early years in Oakland before shipping out on adventures that inspired *The Call of the Wild, The Sea Wolf,* and *The Cruise of the Snark.* In an effort to make a buck and draw a Fisherman's Wharf–type crowd, Oakland created the Jack London Square, a collection of boutiques and restaurants on the waterfront. In particular, look for **Heinhold's First and Last Chance Saloon** (56 Jack London Sq., tel. 510/839–6761), one of Jack's debauched hangouts. Next door is a reassembled Klondike cabin that he once spent a winter in—when it was in Alaska. Keep in mind that the square is mainly for drinking, dining, and spending money, so patronize the specialty shops and upscale eateries in the adjoining **Jack London Village** with care. If you're interested in Jack the writer, check out the collection of letters, manuscripts, and photographs in the Oakland public library's **Jack London Room** (125 14th St., tel. 510/273–3134). *Jack London Sq. is on the Oakland Embarcadero, at the end of Broadway west of downtown.*

MORMON TEMPLE It's hard to tell whether this is a place of worship or a forgotten Disneyland attraction. The Mormons have received a lot of flak for believing the Garden of Eden may be in Mississippi; for building their temples near major freeways to attract distraught souls; for reportedly having more guns per capita than the U.S. Army; for reportedly owning a controlling share in a major U.S. soft drink firm; for barring women from many church services; and for spending millions of dollars on elaborate, marble-covered temples. Well, come see for yourself. Free tours are given daily between 9 AM and 8 PM, but of the outside only. Pick up a souvenir in the visitor center, or watch their 15-minute video about Mr. Smith and the gang. *4770 Lincoln Ave., tel. 510/531–1475. Take Lincoln Ave. exit off Warren Freeway (aka Rte. 13), or Bus 46 from Oakland Coliseum BART.*

OLD OAKLAND When you view the rows of Victorian houses in Old Oakland, it's hard not to imagine a young Gertrude Stein getting deep with the bohemian crowd. This is the 1920s East Bay style—all the houses have been restored and decorated with period furniture, and some are open to the public on a seemingly random basis. The neighborhood also contains several interesting art galleries, including the increasingly popular **PRO-ARTS** (461 9th St., tel. 510/763–4361). East Bay artists pay a small fee to exhibit one piece of their work in this gallery. Then, for two weekends in June, artists open their studios to the public. *Old Oakland is between 7th, 10th, Broadway, and Jefferson Sts., about 3 blocks south from 12th St. BART.*

PARAMOUNT THEATER First-time visitors to Oakland are generally surprised by the Art Deco architecture around the 19th Street BART. Some buildings have fallen into disrepair, but the Paramount Theater remains an operating venue for concerts and performances, and is an architectural masterpiece. If you can't attend a show, you'll still be able to afford the 1½-hour tour ($1), offered the first and third Saturday of each month at 10 AM. For concert information, thumb through the free weekly *East Bay Express,* or call the box office. *2025 Broadway, tel. 510/465–6400.*

MUSEUMS Oakland has a number of excellent museums. In particular, stop by the **Northern California Center for African American History and Life** (5606 San Pablo Ave., tel. 510/658–3158), which focuses on the history of Africans in North America, and includes a library and display of artifacts. Admission is free, and it's open Tuesday–Friday, 12:30–5:30. Take the Bus 72 north on Broadway from downtown. The **Ebony Museum of Art** (1034 14th St., tel. 510/763–0131) features work by African and Afro-American artists in a restored Victorian mansion. It's open Tuesday–Saturday 11–6, and admission is free. Also free is the **Creative Growth Art Center** (355 24th St., tel. 510/836–2340), which displays arts and crafts by disabled artists and is open Tuesday–Sunday 10–4.

OAKLAND MUSEUM For those with California culture shock, the Oakland Museum's historical wing puts today's multicultural population into context. Its extensive mixed-media exhibits document the rise and fall of the Ohlone people (the region's first inhabitants), and tackle the issues of urban violence and Oakland's subsequent deterioration. Other exhibits include Spanish-era artifacts, a fire truck that battled San Francisco's 1906 fire, and some hokey relics from the 1969 "summer of love." The wing of natural sciences offers a simulated walk through the state's eight biotic zones and a view of the plants and animals of each. The changing shows in the art wing feature work by California artists. Be sure to visit the museum's rooftop gardens and the nearby Estuary Park, a 22-acre sculpture garden. *1000 Oak St., tel. 510/273–3401. 1 block east of Lake Merritt BART. Admission free. Open Wed.–Sat. 10–5, Sun. noon–7. Wheelchair access.*

● ● ● CHEAP THRILLS

When sitting under a shady tree sounds like nirvana, head to the **Mountain View Cemetery,** a peaceful place to get your emotional and metaphysical bearings (and contemplate the meaning of death, if you want to). Interspersed among the acres of tombstones are dozens of gaudy chapels and morbid funerary pyramids—the final garish homes of people like Ghirardelli and Crocker (of Crocker Bank). Bus 59 from downtown will drop you a block away. When you're ready to rejoin the land of the living, head down Piedmont Avenue (which intersects the south boundary of the cemetery) for a nice lunch, a new dress, or a stiff drink. *5000 Piedmont Ave., tel. 510/658–2588. Gates open daily 8–5.*

Believe it or not, locals get a kick out of wandering around at 3 AM in the **Produce District** (between Broadway, Webster, 2nd, and 3rd streets, a block up from Jack London Square) to watch the vendors setting up shop. It's kind of reassuring to see all this excitement in the wee hours of the morning, when most of Oakland looks like a ghost town. After you've had your fill, walk down to the 24-hour **Jack London Cafe** (on Embarcadero and Broadway) for some pancakes.

FESTIVALS The *Official Visitors Guide,* distributed by the Oakland Convention and Visitors Bureau (*see* Basics, *above*), has a comprehensive listing of sights and annual events in Oakland. If possible, make it to the annual **Festival at the Lake** (tel. 510/464-1061), a three-day music, food, and arts extravaganza held at Lake Merritt in June. Also in June at Lake Merritt is the **Oakland Juneteenth Celebration** (tel. 510/273–3090), celebrating the anniversary of the signing of the Emancipation Proclamation. Every September, Estuary Park hosts the **Oakland Arts Explosion** (tel. 510/444–5588), and in February a myriad of events occur in celebration of **Black History Month,** including the Black Film Makers' Oscar Micheaux Awards (tel. 510/465–0804) at the Paramount Theater.

● ● ● AFTER DARK

Music, especially the blues and jazz, is an integral part of the Oakland scene. For this reason, you may want to venture into that seedy bar or unassuming nightclub down the street—you know, the kind of places mom warned you about. There's no telling what kind of magic may be going on inside. For a complete listing of cultural events, thumb through the *East Bay Express* calendar section, a free weekly available at most newsstands, cafés, and major street corners.

Harley enthusiasts might cruise by the **Hell's Angels Clubhouse** (4000 block of Foothill Ave., east of Lake Merritt) on a Friday or Saturday night. Leather, long hair, and tattoos galore, but don't let anybody catch you sizing up their bike too closely; you're liable to end up in a nasty brawl. This isn't the safest place in town, and those sporting Nikes and college sweat shirts should definitely stay clear. Otherwise, grab your pool cue, rev up the hammer head, and pound a few beers with the boys. They're awfully nice once you get to know them.

BARS Did your last evening in San Francisco end in a conversation about Wim Wenders? The merits of Treasury bills versus mutual funds? Heidegger and the who of

Dasein? Don't be overwhelmed, don't get discouraged, the bars in Oakland are much cheaper, more sincere, and just generally rougher around the edges.

The Alley. Along Grand Avenue east of Lake Merritt, this is the only bar in Oakland where you can sit at a piano and sing along with your drunken compadres. It's been in business since the late 1940s, and it has the clientele to prove it. Dark, musty, and unassuming, this is a great place to hang out with low-key locals. Live piano music begins at 9 every night; drinks are $2–$5. *3325 Grand Ave., tel. 510/444-8505. 2 blocks south of Piedmont Ave.*

Chalkers Billiard Club. Looking for a game of snooker or pool? Chalkers is one of the nicest pool halls in town, decorated in a "Miami Vice" color scheme and loaded with dozens of well-maintained tables. It's a yuppie hangout (their motto is "for civilized fun"), but there's a full bar and reasonably priced café (i.e., snack counter) in front. 21 and over. *5900 Hollis, at 59th St., tel. 510/658-5821. 1 block north of Powell off I-80.*

The Kingfish. No-nonsense drinking and camaraderie in a dark, lively sports bar. Order yourself an ice-cold beer and bide your time: It's only a matter of minutes before someone starts talking about the As. Drinks $2–$4. *5227 Claremont Ave., tel. 510/655-7373. Take Bus 40 north on Telegraph Ave. from MacArthur BART, get off at Claremont.*

The Lobby. With its soft couches, low lights, and live jazz (Thurs.–Sat.), this is a good place to seduce somebody. Drinks are $3–$4. *5612 College Ave., tel. 510/547-9152. 1 block from Rockridge BART Station.*

McNally's Irish Pub. This place has the smell and feel of a real Dublin pub. Grab a pint of Guinness, Bass, or Harp and warm yourself by the stone fireplace. There's a decent jukebox and bumper-pool table in back. *5352 College Ave., tel. 510/654-9463.*

Pacific Coast Brewing Company. In Old Oakland, this brew pub serves three kinds of homebrew and 16 others on tap. It's popular with the 30-something crowd and a bit yuppie-ish, but their beers are top rate. Lunch is available from 11:30–3, dinner Tuesday–Saturday until 9. The burgers, grilled specialties, and salads range from $3 to $10; drinks $2 to $4. *906 Washington, tel. 510/836-2739. 3 blocks down Broadway from 12th St. BART, then 1 block west to Washington.*

Walt and George's. A stylish place filled with pool tables and comfortable booths. It's popular with Berkeley students and locals, and generally packed on weekend nights. One block away from McNally's (*see above*). *5445 College Ave., tel. 510/653-7441.*

DANCING The dance scene is much sparser here than in San Francisco. In a pinch, stop a fashion victim on the street and ask about the floating clubs that sometimes surface in East Oakland warehouses.

The Caribee Dance Center. Dancing to reggae, salsa, and African music five nights a week with occasional live shows and daily dance classes. A fun place to lose your inhibitions. Drinks are $2–$5. *1408 Webster St., tel. 510/835-4006. 2 blocks east on 14th St. from Broadway; 12th St. BART. Open Wed.–Sun. 9 PM–2 AM.*

The White Horse Inn. On the Oakland–Berkeley border, this is a very unpretentious place to get down under a gleaming disco ball. Most of the clientele are gay and lesbian, but other assorted fun-seekers are welcome as long as they behave themselves. DJ nightly after 9 PM, bar open daily 11 AM–2 AM. *Corner of 66th St. and Telegraph Ave., tel. 510/652-3820. Take Bus 40 north on Broadway from downtown.*

MUSIC

BLUES In the years following World War II, Oakland gave birth to the gritty, grungy, hurts-so-bad-I'm-gonna-die soulful movement known as the West Coast blues. Luckily, even after 50 years, it still flourishes in clubs and bars all over Oakland. Dedicated to the preservation of blues, jazz, and gospel, **The Bay Area Blues Society** (tel. 510/836-2227) sponsors shows and festivals year-round, and is a wellspring of information about West Coast blues. Hardcore fans will want to visit the society's **West Coast Blues Hall of Fame** (1925 Broadway) in Old Oakland, scheduled to open in late 1993.

A consistently good bet for blues is **Eli's Mile High Club** (3629 Martin Luther King Jr. Way, tel. 510/655–6661)—the reputed birthplace of West Coast blues. It's a small, basic club with a pool table, soul food, and music Wednesday to Sunday. The kitchen opens around 6:30, and music starts by 9; cover $3–$8. Otherwise, check out the tiny **Your Place Too** (5319 Martin Luther King Jr. Way, tel. 510/652–5837). Besides nightly blues shows (and the occasional hardcore band), there are 50¢ beers and an uneven pool table. Watch out for Shorty, though, the local pool shark. He plays a mean game of eight-ball.

JAZZ Jazz greats come through Oakland on a regular basis, so catch a show at one of Oaktown's two main jazz clubs. In downtown, **Koncepts Cultural Gallery** (480 3rd St., off Broadway, tel. 510/451–9072) hosts a variety of jazz events, lectures, films, and poetry readings. Prices vary according to event; call for the latest listings. North Oakland's **Yoshi's** (6030 Claremont Ave., tel. 510/652–9200), part jazz club and part Japanese restaurant, has nightly jazz concerts and occasional salsa, calypso, and blues bands. Depending on the act, covers vary between $5 and $25.

In Emeryville, a small community tucked in between Berkeley and Oakland, look for **Kimball's East,** a fine jazz and supper club. It hosts music Wednesday to Sunday; the cover ranges from $12 to $25. *5800 Shellmound St., Emeryville, tel. 510/658–2555. From MacArthur BART take Bus 6 or 57 west on 40th St.*

ROCK Oakland's music scene can't compete with San Francisco's, but check out **The Omni** (4799 Shattuck Ave., tel. 510/547–7655) in North Oakland. It hosts bands across the rock-and-roll spectrum, from glam rock to heavy metal, with the occasional thrash, funk, or hip-hop show thrown in to keep the neighbors confused; cover $5–$15. Otherwise, lace up your Doc Martins and head downtown to **Merchant's Lunch** (401 2nd St., tel. 510/465–8032), a haven for thrash garage bands.

The South Bay

Just south of the San Francisco International Airport, you'll notice a subtle change in scenery. It doesn't exactly hit you over the head, but as you tread farther into the nether reaches of San Francisco you'll notice a proliferation of shopping malls and industrial parks, of tract homes, quiet suburbs, and fast-food restaurants. Before you realize it, you'll be deep into the South Bay, surrounded by cities with names like **Palo Alto, Santa Clara,** and **San Jose.** The windy streets and frenetic energy of San Francisco will seem miles away, and you'll pull off the freeway at some greasy roadside diner wondering to yourself, "Where did I go wrong?"

Of course, not all forays into the South Bay—stretching from San Mateo in the north to San Jose in the south—need be so disorienting, but preparing for the worst may save you a dose of disappointment. The South Bay is largely residential and suburban. It encompasses a number of interesting sights and cities, but these are best handled as day trips from San Francisco—not as places for in-depth exploration. If you have a car or don't mind a 45-minute train ride, you can navigate your way around quite easily.

The original thoroughfare of the Spanish monks, **El Camino Real** runs through the middle of the South Bay, but it's not what you'd call a scenic drive. **I–280,** however, is one of the most pleasant freeways around, featuring unblemished mountain vistas and a 50-foot statue of Father Junipero Serra pointing west near San Mateo—a far better choice than either El Camino Real or industry-laden **U.S. 101** (aka the Bayshore Freeway).

Only on El Camino Real, however, can you visit **Acres of Orchids** (1450 El Camino Real, South San Francisco, tel. 415/871–5655), the world's largest orchid source with over 1 million square feet of greenhouse cultivation. Also worth stopping for is the **Museum for Environmental Education** within the pristine **Coyote Point County Park** (tel. 415/342–7755), off U.S. 101's Poplar Avenue exit heading south, or Peninsula Avenue heading north. Inside are hundreds of South Bay ecology exhibits, many of them hands-on and geared for children between 18 and 50. Bring a picnic lunch and soak in the bay views, or spend an afternoon hiking in the park. Either way, it's a nice escape from South Bay suburbia.

Farther south along I–280, communities like Hillsborough, Atherton, and Woodside have long benefited from the great fortunes made in the Bay Area, and San Francisco magnates have built their mansions here ever since there were San Francisco magnates. A testament to this is **Filoli** (Cañada Rd., Woodside, tel. 415/364–2880), a 43-room Georgian mansion with an intricate 16-acre garden open to the public. The name is a hybrid of the original owner's motto, "Fight, Love, Live." The estate, designed by Willis Polk, is decorated with turn-of-the-century antiques, aging photographs, and a large collection of hand-painted oil lamps. If you've ever watched *Dynasty,* you may recognize this as the home of Blake and Krystal Carrington. It's only open a few days each month, though, so call ahead for tour information.

Four miles south, couched between I–280 and U.S. 101, is the quiet suburb of **Palo Alto,** best known as the home of Stanford University. Beyond this is the amorphous realm of **Silicon Valley,** a collection of Santa Clara and San Jose suburbs marked by large-scale, high-tech architectural anonymity. Keep going and you'll end up in **Santa Clara** itself, much appreciated for its **Great America Theme Park**—home to roller coasters with names like Vortex and the Demon. Ten minutes farther east on the interstate you cross into **San Jose,** the most populous and unwieldy city in northern California. Not the sort of place people go out of their way for, it nevertheless boasts a richer cultural life than most South Bay cities, with its art museums, symphony, and opera.

If you need a place to crash, there are two excellent youth hostels in the area, both located in the mountains far away from the suburban sprawl. Otherwise, the South Bay is accessible by car and public transportation, which makes it an easy day trip from San Francisco, only 45 minutes north.

BASICS ● ● ●

TOURIST INFORMATION Among Bay Area newspapers, the daily *San Jose Mercury News* is considered the best. It lists local events along with world news, and its hefty "Eye" section can navigate you through the South Bay's nightlife. **Convention and Visitors Bureau of Santa Clara.** *2200 Laurelwood Rd., Santa Clara, tel. 408/296–7111.*

San Jose Convention and Visitors Bureau. *150 W. San Carlos, San Jose, tel. 408/283–8833.*

San Jose Events Hotline. Call during regular business hours for a listing of community events and after-dark diversions. *Tel. 408/295–2265, ext. 411.*

San Mateo County Convention and Visitors Bureau. *111 Anza Blvd., Burlingame, tel. 415/348–7600.*

When People Die, They Move to the Suburbs

If you're driving to the South Bay on I–280, be sure to drive through the small city of Colma, a modern-day necropolis filled with cemeteries and macabre graveyard art. In the 1920s, San Francisco decided its land was too valuable for the dead, and nearly every grave was relocated to Colma. Since then, nobody's been buried within San Francisco's city limits. The Colma Town Hall (1198 El Camino Real, at Serramonte Blvd., tel. 415/997–8300) offers a self-guided tour ($2.50) of the city's cemeteries, from the prestigious Cypress Lawn to the eerie Pet's Rest, littered with flea collars and dog toys. Individual grave sites of interest include Dodge City's Wyatt Earp and Lefty O'Doul.

COMING AND GOING

BY CAR **I–280** (aka the Junipero Serra Freeway) is more scenic than the industry laden **U.S. 101,** but both connect San Francisco with Palo Alto, Santa Clara, and San Jose. Avoid rush hours (weekdays 7–9 and 4–6) when traffic is bumper to bumper, especially on 101.

From Oakland or Berkeley, take **I–880** south for San Jose; I–880 south to **Route 84** and the Dumbarton Bridge for Palo Alto and Santa Clara.

BY TRAIN The easiest way to explore the South Bay is by **CalTrain** (tel. 800/558–8661), which offers regular service from San Francisco (4th and Townsend Sts.) to downtown San Jose (65 Cahill St.) with stops at Palo Alto and Santa Clara. One-way fare costs $3.50, and trains leave hourly between 5 AM and 10 PM.

BY BUS San Francisco's BART trains don't travel beyond Daly City, but **SamTrans** (tel. 800/660–4BUS) buses run regularly throughout San Mateo County (last stop Palo Alto and the Stanford shopping center). They leave daily from the Daly City BART station, downtown San Francisco, and the San Francisco International Airport.

It's possible to take **Greyhound** (tel. 408/297–8890) from San Francisco to San Jose ($9), but the train is cheaper and more convenient.

WHERE TO SLEEP The South Bay is filled with nondescript chain motels, concentrated around freeway off-ramps and the larger cities. A room here will run you $40–$50 a night, but don't expect much more than a bed and HBO. You're much better off heading to one of the region's two excellent hostels.

The **Sanborn Park Hostel** is possibly the most beautiful in the world, located in a wooden cabin that dates from 1908 and surrounded by a dense redwood forest. This hostel is perfectly situated for avid hikers and easily reached by public transportation. Also available to hostelers are a volleyball court and barbecue grill, in addition to the standard AYH kitchen with pots and pans. A nature museum is nearby. The cost is a mere $7 for AYH members; $10 for nonmembers, and half price for those under 18. It's a busy place, but they'll try to find room for anyone who shows up on their doorstep. You'll need to bring your own food, though, as the only restaurants and grocery stores are in Saratoga, 4 miles away. *15808 Sanborn Rd., Saratoga, tel. 408/741–0166. Take I–280 south to Saratoga/Sunnyvale exit, turn right and continue for 5½ mi. At Saratoga's only stoplight, turn right onto Rte. 9 (toward Big Basin) and follow for 2½ mi. Turn left at the Sanborn Skyline County Park sign, go 1 mi farther and make first right. You can catch Bus 54 from the Sunnyvale CalTrain station, or Bus 22 in downtown San Jose and transfer to Bus 54 at El Camino and Hollenbeck. Get off in Saratoga, in front of the post office, and call the hostel to arrange a ride. Office open daily 5–11 PM only.*

The **Hidden Villa Hostel** is in the Los Altos hills between Palo Alto and San Jose. Nestled in a 1,500-acre canyon, it has easy access to hiking trails and peaceful dirt roads. Large rustic cabins that hold up to 45 people each dot the canyon, each with communal bathroom facilities. Bring your own food. Unfortunately, public transportation doesn't come anywhere near here. *Moody Rd., Los Altos, tel. 415/949–8648. Take I–280 south from San Francisco past Palo Alto. Take El Monte/Moody Rd. exit, turn right on El Monte West, then left on Moody Rd. at stop sign. The hostel is 1.7 miles ahead. Office open 8–9:30 AM and 4:30–9:30 PM. Reservations advised during summer.*

OUTDOOR ACTIVITIES At 4,062-feet, **Mt. Hamilton** is the highest point in the Bay Area, and the site of the Lick Observatory (*see* San Jose, *below).* You can drive right to the top and wander around on the rugged fire trails or make the short but steep hike to the summit. Bikes aren't allowed technically, but none of the locals seems to care. On weekends, you'll find hundreds of people enjoying an afternoon picnic or putting their mountain bikes to the test. From San Jose, take Route 130 (Mt. Hamilton Road) to the peak.

A good source for state-of-the-art hiking equipment, information, and advice is **Western Mountaineering** (840 Town & Country Village, at Stevens Creek and Winchester Blvds.,

San Jose, tel. 408/984–7611). They rent hard-to-find mountaineering supplies, including rock-, alpine-, and ice-climbing shoes, down sleeping bags, and cross-country skis. Otherwise, **Action Sports** rents mountain bikes ($26 a day) from three locations: in San Jose (1777 Hillsdale Ave., tel. 408/978–8383), Mountain View (791 Castro St., tel. 415/968–7723), and Palo Alto (401 High St., tel. 415/328–3180).

PALO ALTO • • •

If it weren't for **Stanford University,** Palo Alto would probably fade into urban oblivion. A few bars and collegiate-type restaurants line downtown, along with shopping malls and upscale clothing boutiques, but nothing to lose much sleep over. If you're curious what a $20,000-a-year education would look like, swing through the Stanford campus and check out the sights. Otherwise, stay on the freeway and save your strength.

Palo Alto is a wealthy community filled with lush homes and ranch-style estates, but on the excitement scale it falls somewhere between late-night "infomertials" and cutting your toe nails.

Needless to say, Stanford University's 8,200-acre campus—nicknamed "the Farm" because the land was once a stud farm (that's certainly not the case anymore)—is Palo Alto's star attraction. Designed by Frederick Law Olmstead, its look-alike, mustard-colored buildings combine Romanesque squatness with the ranchy feel of a Spanish mission, giving the campus an austere and refined (if not unfriendly) flavor. **Palm Drive** is the entrance to the campus, and leads past the **Museum of Art** (Museum Way and Lomita Dr., tel. 415/723–4177) to the quad, a popular hangout with students. Check out the **university bookstore,** the **Memorial Church,** and, thrusting mightily into the sky, the 280-foot **Hoover Tower,** home of the Hoover Institution for the Study of War, Revolution, and Peace. For an overview, climb up to the tower's pleasant observation deck where you can get an excellent 360° view of campus and parts of Palo Alto.

Even if you're only moderately interested in science, make the short trek to nearby Menlo Park and the **Stanford Linear Accelerator Center** (2575 Sand Hill Rd., at Wickham Pl., Menlo Park, tel. 415/926–2204). This 2-mile-long atom smasher is amazing: Thousands of house-size machines, dials, diodes, and mussy scientists who get excited when you mention n-orbits and electrons. If you can, reserve space in advance for the free two-hour tour that includes a slide show and lecture; it's geared for lay people and is extremely interesting.

SANTA CLARA • • •

The city of Santa Clara lies just north of San Jose, sandwiched between the suburbs of Sunnyvale and Saratoga. Most Bay Area locals stay away from this part of the peninsula except when they get the itch to propel themselves upside down at 60 miles per hour. **Great America,** a pastel-colored amusement park loaded with roller coasters and hokey gift shops, is probably the best "spin 'til you vomit" park north of L.A.'s Magic Mountain. Besides the new stand-up, $5 million **Vortex,** its most popular ride is the **Edge,** simulating all too vividly a high-speed, free-fall drop from the top of a cliff. Unfortunately, after these two death-defying experiences, the remaining rides are a little bit of a let down, consisting of tamer loop-de-loops (**The Revolution**) and a handful of water rides. The park is expensive ($22) and somewhat Republican in tone (a sign at the entrance admonishes visitors to behave in a manner supportive of family values), but even so it's a great place to let off some steam and put your stomach to the "chili dog and roller coaster" test. Whatever you do, though, avoid the park's Lawrence Welk-esque variety shows and bring your own lunch. Food in the park is both expensive and unsavory. *Great America Parkway, Santa Clara, tel. 408/988–1800 or 408/988–1776. Take the Great American Pkwy. exit off U.S. 101, 50 mi south of San Francisco. Open spring and fall, weekends; summer, daily 9 AM–11 PM.*

The city's other main attraction is **Mission Santa Clara** (tel. 408/554–4023), located on the Santa Clara College campus. It's been rebuilt and refurbished a number times but it's still a great Spanish-era relic, surrounded by 200-year-old olive trees and a grapevine reputedly planted by the mission's original founders. Take U.S. 101 to the De La Cruz exit and follow the signs to campus. Nearby, the **Santa Clara Cemetery** (490 Lincoln Blvd., tel. 408/296–4656) is a good place for a picnic. It's one of the older (and more macabre) graveyards in northern California, filled with looming tombstones and marble-covered chapels. It's open Monday–Saturday dawn–dusk.

Five miles south, in the hills behind Saratoga, is the 176-acre **Villa Montalvo.** Named for the Spanish writer who apparently coined the name "California" in a novel, this vast estate was created by James Phelan, a one-time U.S. senator and three-term mayor of San Francisco. Upon his death, Phelan's estate was transformed into a rent-free refuge for writers, artists, and musicians. Besides the artists' quarters (currently there are five very lucky artists in residence), there's a multimedia gallery inside the villa, open Thursday–Sunday 11–4. Behind is a lush arboretum and bird sanctuary, interspersed with hiking trails and streams. Admission is free, so bring a picnic lunch and spend the afternoon hiking in the hills. On weekends between April and October, the Villa also hosts a variety of evening concerts, attracting some big-name conductors and symphonies from around the world. These, though, aren't free; call for current schedules and prices. *15400 Montalvo Rd., Saratoga, tel. 408/741–3421. Take I–280 to Saratoga Rd./Sunnyvale exit, and continue west for 7 mi following the Montalvo Arboretum signs.*

In downtown Saratoga, 15 minutes from Villa Montalvo, the **Country Store Cafe** (14577 Big Basin Way, tel. 408/867–2440) serves up darn fine coffee and sandwiches in a laid-back atmosphere. There's a small restaurant upstairs, but most people prefer to hang out in the café and wine bar below, popular with the long-haired/chess-playing set. Most evenings the Country Store features live blues and folk bands that attract people all the way from San Francisco.

● ● ● SAN JOSE

In one sense, northern California's largest city is really just a big, overgrown town, marked by the sort of minimall sprawl you'll find all over America. Emphatically middle-class, ugly, and smoggy, San Jose is generally seen as a burgeoning Los Angeles—the sort of charmless suburbia everyone loves to hate. Despite these criticisms, however, San Jose has an oddly comfortable and metropolitan feel to it. Encircled by mountain ranges, buffered by city parks and gardens, San Jose is home to wineries as well as industrial parks, computer companies, and corporate headquarters. Like San Francisco, San Jose has openly encouraged ethnic diversity and, though race relations aren't always good, its large Japanese, Portuguese, Latino, Filipino, and Chinese populations contribute to its appeal. In reality, of course, it's nothing more than a rag-tag jumble of residential neighborhoods and convenience stores. Yet if you can look beyond this fact, you'll find an intriguing city that's more than just the sum of its suburban parts.

California Doesn't Have a Second to Waste

If you're coming from Oakland, stop by the Garbage Museum in Milpitas, 5 miles north of San Jose on I–880. Californians generate more garbage per capita than any other group of people in the world. This fact is brought to life in the massive "Wall of Garbage" exhibit, which represents one second of what the state is continually throwing out. In the Recycling Hall, you can also play with a huge magnet that separates steel and iron from a mountain of tin cans. 1601 Dixon Landing Rd., Milpitas, tel. 408/262–1401. The museum is visible from the freeway; take the Dixon Landing exit off I–880. Admission free. Open Mon.–Sat. 7:30 AM–3:30 PM.

The new, billion-dollar downtown is a good place to start exploring. Hop on the light rail that connects San Jose State University on one end with the Center for Performing Arts on the other; with numerous stops in between, it will give you a good overview of the city center. Whatever you do, though, don't miss the **Rosicrucian Egyptian Museum and Planetarium** (1342 Naglee Ave., at Park Ave., tel. 408/287–2807), off I–880 at the Alameda exit. It houses one of the most impressive collections of Egyptian, Assyrian, and Babylonian artifacts west of the Nile, including animal and human mummies, an underground tomb, textiles, jewelry, and decorative wall reliefs. Admission is a paltry $4, and it's open Tuesday–Sunday.

Another popular attraction is the **Winchester Mystery House** (525 S. Winchester Blvd., between Stevens Creek Blvd. and I–280, tel. 408/247–2001), advertised as the "World's Strangest Monument to a Woman's Fears!" This 160-room Victorian mansion was built by rifle heiress Sarah Winchester, reportedly to appease those killed by her father's world-famous rifles. A fortune teller told Winchester that as long as she continued to build her house, she wouldn't die. As a result, the mansion underwent continuous construction—24 hours a day for 38 years, from 1884 until 1922. She died nevertheless, which doesn't exactly do wonders for one's confidence in fortune tellers or U.S. foreign policy under Reagan. There are a number of bizarre, inexplicable additions, such as a door that opens onto a brick wall and a stairway leading nowhere. Tiffany stained-glass windows brighten the rather dreary woodwork, and a continuing motif is the use of the number 13 (Winchester even wrote a 13-part will that she signed 13 times). Sarah might not approve, but there's a firearms museum on the grounds, along with a "Winchester Antique Products Museum" in the gift shop. Admission is $11, and includes a guided tour.

More traditional sights include the **San Jose Historical Museum** (Kelley Park, 635 Phelan Ave., tel. 408/287–2291), a fun re-creation of San Jose's first Main Street. Lining the dusty avenue is a candy store where, according to locals, California's first ice-cream sodas were served, as well as A. P. Giannini's Banca d'Italia building, which didn't take off until renamed "Bank of America." Also look for the Old West–style hotel, blacksmith's shop, print shop, and restored firehouse. Take the Tenth Street exit of I–280 and follow the signs to Kelly Park. Afterwards, to complete your tour of Americana kitsch, stop by the nearby **American Museum of Quilts and Textiles** (766 S. 2nd St., tel. 408/971–0323), which displays some amazing examples of Pioneer-era needlework.

San Jose also has one of the world's largest **flea markets** (12000 Berryessa Rd., tel. 408/453–1110), housing some 2,600 vendors over a 120-acre area. It's open dawn to dusk Wednesday to Sunday, off U.S. 101 at the 13th Street exit. In the hills surrounding San Jose are a number of good wineries, among them **Mirassou Vineyards** (3000 Aborn Rd., tel. 408/274–4000) and **J. Lohr** (1000 Lenzen Ave., tel. 408/288–5057). Both have tasting rooms, tours, and picnic grounds. East of San Jose, the **James Lick Observatory** (tel. 408/274–5061) has one of the world's largest telescopes, which sits atop the summit of Mt. Hamilton. Visitors can use it on Friday evenings in July and August; call well in advance to reserve space. The observatory also features a seismograph station that is open for tours, if you ask someone in a white overcoat very politely. From San Jose, drive 12 miles east on Route 130 and follow the signs.

If you're stuck in San Jose after dark, head downtown to the **Cactus Club** (417 S. Hearst St., tel. 408/280–1435), which features local and big name bands on a regular basis. It's 18 and over and has a small bar in back. **Marsugis** (399 S. 1st St., tel. 408/286–8345), two blocks away, also features live music but less regularly. This place is more of a bar (21 and over), loaded with ragged booths, professional drinkers, and a darn fine jukebox.

FOOD San Jose and its suburbs are infested with fast-food chains and generic sit-down restaurants. If you're in a hurry, pull off the freeway and grab a burger and fries or stock up at any one of the hundreds of grocery stores in the area.

UNDER $5 **Crisper's.** It's a short walk from the Winchester Mystery House, and you'll pay by the pound for make-your-own salads and sandwiches, stuffed baked potatoes, ice cream, frozen yogurt, soups, muffins, and beer. The salad bar spread is truly vast, and the average cost is around $4.25. It's somewhat generic looking, but a good stop for a quick and healthy lunch. *813 Town and Country Village, San Jose, tel. 408/985–9103. Open weekdays 10:30–6:30, Sat. 10:30–3. Wheelchair access.*

Taco Al Pastor. This no-frills restaurant has been serving good, cheap Mexican food for more than 15 years. Nothing is priced over $5, so fill up on its excellent homemade burritos and tacos. There's a large dining room in back, but most people prefer their tacos to go. *400 S. Bascone Ave., San Jose, tel. 408/275–1619. Open daily 10–10.*

UNDER $10 **Chez Sovan.** Every weekend, carloads of North and East Bay locals make the 45-minute trek to Chez Sovan for its incredible Cambodian cuisine. The menu changes on a weekly basis but generally includes a selection of ginger-cooked meats and vegetables, coconut and leek soups, and other traditional Cambodian specials. It's always crowded, so call ahead. *923 Oakland Rd., at Madera, tel. 408/287–7619. 1 block north of Heding and 13th Sts. Open weekdays 11 AM–3 PM and 5 PM–10 PM, weekends 5 PM–10 PM.*

The Flying Lady. This huge restaurant—supposedly one of the largest in the world—is part of a complex that includes an airport, a museum, and a saloon. Collections abound, from jukeboxes and carousel horses to telephones and license plates. You can eat while radio-controlled model airplanes fly overhead, then visit the "Wagons to Wings" Museum to view full-scale versions. The cuisine is primarily Americana, including prime rib and steak ($8–$10), pastas ($5–$7), and a healthy selection of burgers and sandwiches ($4–$6). Unfortunately, it's located in the middle of nowhere, 16 miles south of San Jose in Morgan Hill. *15060 Foothill Ave., near Tennant Ave., Morgan Hill, tel. 408/779–4136. Take the San Martin exit off U.S. 101, 20 min. south of San Jose.*

UNDER $15 **El Maghreb.** This place can't be beat for atmosphere: The dining room is under a tent, the food is Morroccan, and belly dancers perform nightly. Unfortunately, though, expect to pay $12 for a plate of couscous and roast lamb. Popular with just about everyone in town, it's packed on weekend nights. *145 W. Santa Clara St., at San Pedro St., tel. 408/294–2243. Reservations are advised. Open Mon.–Sat. 6–10 PM.*

Half Moon Bay

Famous for growing Halloween pumpkins and Christmas trees, Half Moon Bay is an easygoing seaside town 29 miles south of San Francisco. With its small-town rural feel, it's also the most inviting of San Francisco's nearby coastal communities. Its **Main Street** is lined with crafts shops, health-food cafés, and flower gardens; its small downtown with cluttered antiques shops and unpretentious burger joints. Venture out to **Pillar Point Harbor** to watch rickety old men fishing, or study them at closer quarters in the bars near the wharf. If lolling on the beach interests you, follow Kelly Avenue west to the popular **Half Moon Bay State Beach** or, 2 miles south of town, to the quiet and undisturbed **San Gregorio Beach.** North of downtown on Route 1 is the privately owned **Gray Whale Cove,** one of northern California's most popular (and secluded) nude beaches (parking here costs $5).

If it's too cold near the water, trek 2 miles inland along Route 92 to taste the local wine at **Obester Winery** (tel. 415/726–9463; open daily 10–5). If you're headed south to Santa Cruz, stop in at the **San Gregorio General Store,** 1 mile east of Route 1 on Route 84, 8 miles south of Half Moon Bay. This funky store has been serving the ranch and farming community since 1889, and has everything from a saloon-type bar to cast-iron pots and pans, used books, and antiques. Definitely worth the stop if you're anywhere in the vicinity; on weekends, you might hear some Bulgarian bluegrass or Irish R&B.

One of the best reasons to visit Half Moon Bay, though, is for the drive itself. The 45-minute trip from San Francisco on coastal Route 1 is incredibly scenic, and a great way to escape the bustle of city life on a sunny afternoon. Traffic can be a problem, especially on summer weekends when gaggles of motorcyclists and families of 12 pile onto the road. But if you need a break, there are dozens of sandy beaches and sleepy bars along the way, not to mention the cliffside overlooks begging for a few picnickers. One of the nicest pit stops is **Moss Beach Distillery** (Beachway and Ocean Blvd., tel.

415/728–5595), off Route 1 a few miles north of Half Moon Bay. The restaurant is fairly expensive, but grab a beer on its outdoor patio and soak up the amazing ocean view.

BASICS ● ● ●

TOURIST INFORMATION **Half Moon Bay Chamber of Commerce.** *225 S. Cabrillo Hwy., in a green caboose, tel. 415/726–5202. Open weekdays 9–5.*

Half Moon Bay State Parks, District Office. *Tel. 415/726–6203.*

COMING AND GOING ● ● ●

Half Moon Bay is 29 miles south of San Francisco, 55 miles north of Santa Cruz, and easily reached on **Route 1** (aka Cabrillo Highway) from either direction. For downtown, turn off Route 1 at Kelly Avenue and keep your eyes peeled for Main Street, half a mile ahead.

Route 92, which starts in Hayward and passes through the city of San Mateo, enters Half Moon Bay from the east, providing access to San Jose and the East Bay. If you're coming from San Francisco, **San Mateo County Transit** (tel. 800/660–4287) has daily buses between Half Moon Bay and the Daly City BART station; the fare is $1.

WHERE TO SLEEP ● ● ●

A visit to the Half Moon Bay coast can be relatively cheap if you camp or stay in a youth hostel. Otherwise, hotels and motels start at $60 per night in winter, $75–$100 in summer. If you can afford it, the **Old Thyme Inn** (779 Main St., tel. 415/726–1616) is the nicest B&B in town. Built in 1899, this seven-room cottage has been restored by its British owners and sits a few blocks past the shops on Main Street. Each cozy room is named and decorated after a different herb, and each has a private, old-fashioned claw-foot bathtub. Rates start at $65 for two and peak at $110, and include breakfast (juice, scones, meats, cheeses, and homemade flan). Reservations are required.

HOSTELS **Point Montara Lighthouse Hostel.** This functioning lighthouse and adjoining hostel sit 4 miles north of Half Moon Bay, perched on a cliff in the small artisan community of Montara. The living room has a fireplace, and there's a dining area and outdoor redwood hot tub ($5 for half an hour). Beds cost $8 for members, $11 for nonmembers, and everyone must do one small chore. Check-in is 7:50–9:30 AM and again at 4:30 PM. If you're taking a coastal bus from San Mateo or Daly City, tell the driver you're going to the hostel and he or she will drop you off within 100 feet. *16th St. and Rte. 1, tel. 415/728–7177. 8 rooms, sleeps 45. Laundry, kitchen, shared bathrooms. Reservations recommended for summer weekends.*

Pigeon Point Lighthouse Youth Hostel. The hostel is 20 miles south of Half Moon Bay, but it's one of the nicest in California. Perched on a small bluff overlooking miles of unblemished beach and the (sometimes) dreamy Pacific Ocean, the Pigeon Point hostel tends to enchant its guests and destroy their will to leave—perhaps that's why there's a 3-night maximum here. A bed in one of its 4 bungalows (with names like "Seal" and "Whale") costs $8 per night; rooms for couples, $5 more. After a hard day on the beach, slide into the outdoor, ocean-viewing hot tub ($3 per half hour). Guests get a free tour of the lighthouse the morning after their stay. Check-in is 7:30–9:30 AM, 4:30–9:30 PM. *Pigeon Point Rd. and Rte. 1, Pescadero, tel. 415/879–0633. From Daly City BART, take San Mateo Bus 96C; it stops in front. 54 beds. 11 PM curfew, wheelchair access, dryer but no washer, $1 linen rental. Reservations recommended.*

CAMPING **Francis Beach at Half Moon State Beach.** 53 barren sites ($14 a night) sit at the base of a small sand dune. Because of its proximity to downtown, this place attracts teenage partyers and a lot of weekend-warrior types. Good in a pinch, but hardly the great outdoors. Reservations—highly recommended in summer—can be made through MISTIX (tel. 800/444–7275) for an additional $6 fee. *95 Kelly Ave., tel. 415/726–6238. Outdoor beach showers only. Pit toilets. No open fires permitted.*

Memorial Park Campground. Most of its 163 sites are scattered in a thick forest—quiet, private, and peaceful—in the mountains 25 miles south of Half Moon Bay. All have picnic tables and fire pits, and are extremely popular with car campers. Summer crowds are a headache, but otherwise this wooded campground is lightly visited. *Tel. 415/879–0212; for reservations, tel. 415/363–4021. Take Pescadero Rd. exit off Rte. 1, follow east for 11 mi.*

● ● ● FOOD

Half Moon Bay has everything from expensive seafood restaurants to reasonably priced health-food counters. Despite its chain-restaurant exterior, **3 Amigos** (200 N. Cabrillo Hwy. at Kelly Ave., tel. 415/726–6080) has tasty, cheap Mexican food, including veggie burritos for under $3. A good place for breakfast or lunch is **Cosmic Charlies** (510 Kelly Ave., tel. 415/726–0239), noted for its omelets ($7), hearty tofu burgers ($5), and New Age atmosphere. Every table has a crystal encased in a glass pyramid, part of owner Judy Johnson's healing philosophy. Upstairs she has a small store, the Crystal Clutter (tel. 415/726–7644), chock-full of soothing stones, incense, and literature. For picnic supplies, stop by the 24-hour **Safeway** (junction of Rtes. 1 and 92) or **Cunha's Country Grocery** (corner of Kelly Ave. and Main St.).

● ● ● OUTDOOR ACTIVITIES

HERB WALKS AND BERRY PICKING Ask Suzanne Elliott at **The Healing Moon Natural Foods Market and Cafe** about the spring herb walks ($12 a person) she leads through nearby Hatchwoods and the James V. Fitzgerald Marine Reserve. *523 Main St., tel. 415/726–7881.*

For the freshest fruit in town, head to **Coastways Ranch,** where you can pick olallieberries in summer, pumpkins in October, and kiwifruit and Christmas trees in November and December. You generally pay for your pickings by the pound, but the prices are reasonable. *640 Rte. 1, 30 mi south of Half Moon Bay, tel. 415/879–0414.*

HIKING AND MOUNTAIN BIKING Recently converted into a state park, the **McKnee Ranch** remains undeveloped and relatively uncrowded. A four- to five-hour hike will take you up **Devil's Slide** where, on a clear day, you can see the whole bay area. Mountain bikes are allowed, but trails to the top are fairly steep and sometimes treacherous. There's also a heap of poison oak in the hills, so don't romp in the foliage too much. *8 mi north of Half Moon Bay. From Rte. 1, take Farallon View Rd. north until it ends. Admission free.*

HORSEBACK RIDING If you want to spend an hour racing a steed along the strand, contact **Sea Horse Ranch** or **Friendly Acres Ranch** (tel. 415/726–2362); expect to pay $20 per hour for a guided ride. The two ranches—owned by the same people—are just north of Half Moon Bay on Route 1, about 500 yards from each other.

KAYAKING **Jim Wilcox's Aquatic Adventures** (tel. 415/728–0125) offers kayaking trips as well as scuba and scupper-kayak instruction. Rentals cost $8 an hour, $40 a day. An introductory class, which includes one hour of paddling and a half-hour beach lecture, is $20.

SPORT FISHING If you have a yen to sail out of Pillar Point Harbor in search of rock cod and salmon, **Captain John's** (on the harbor, tel. 415/728–3377) offers expeditions starting at $34, tackle and license $10 extra. Two doors down, **Huck Finn Sportfishing** (tel. 415/726–7133) has trips for about the same price.

WHALE-WATCHING December through April is the prime time to catch sight of the California Gray Whale migration. **Huck Finn Sportfishing** (tel. 415/726–7133) at Pillar Point Harbor offers boat trips for $17.

NORTH COAST 4

By Jason Fine

Rugged shoreline, lush mountains, ancient redwood forests, and rural towns stretch for some 400 miles between San Francisco and the Oregon border. It's difficult to describe just how spectacularly beautiful the coast can be, but picture yourself in the shade of an 800-year-old, 100-foot-tall tree at the top of a cliff with waves crashing in the boulder-strewn Pacific below, and you'll get a sense of the region at its dramatic best. There are opportunities for sportfishing, scuba diving, and river rafting here, but you can keep yourself quite busy just combing the beaches or hiking in the mountains. Many first-time travelers find they haven't done any of the things they'd planned and had a great trip just the same.

North of San Francisco, Route 1 and U.S. 101 separate in Marin County to become the two main routes through the region. **Route 1** winds up the coast past Stinson Beach, Point Reyes, Bodega Bay, Mendocino, and Fort Bragg. This is some of the most dramatic and spectacular coastline in the United States, with the highway usually within diving distance of the Pacific—although some of the cliffs are so steep you might not dare to look over the edge. Virtually anywhere along the rocky shoreline you can find perfect places to sit and watch for whales or quiet stretches of beach to picnic on as seals play on the rocks nearby. Great surfing beaches are concentrated in Sonoma County between Jenner and Bodega Bay. However, this is no Malibu-type paradise: the icy-cold waters are treacherous, and if sharks don't get you, the riptides might.

The towns along the coast are small and funky, with a mixed population of old-timers and urban expatriates. If the town is big enough to have a post office, chances are it also has a New Age bookstore, an organic grocer, several art galleries, and a pub brewing up an ale popular with the locals. Though Mendocino, Gualala, and Bodega Bay are full of pricey restaurants and bed-and-breakfasts geared for yuppie getaways, there are enough taverns, pizza joints, campgrounds, and nearby beaches (where you can covertly camp if you hide your car well enough) to satisfy those of us on a tight budget.

North of Rockport, Route 1 abruptly leaves the Pacific and heads east to join U.S. 101. The land for the next 73 miles is so rugged that the state has never extended the highway along the coast. This isolated region, known as the **Lost Coast**, is accessible only by a series of windy, treacherous roads—some paved, some not—that meander through virgin (never logged) redwood forests and open grazing lands overlooking black-sand beaches. Even the sleepy seaside towns of Mendocino and Fort Bragg seem like overcrowded tourist traps in comparison to the Lost Coast.

U.S. 101, which runs parallel to Route 1 farther inland, is a faster route that takes you through turn-of-the-century farming towns, vineyards, and the impressive **Avenue of the**

The North Coast (Rockport to Oregon)

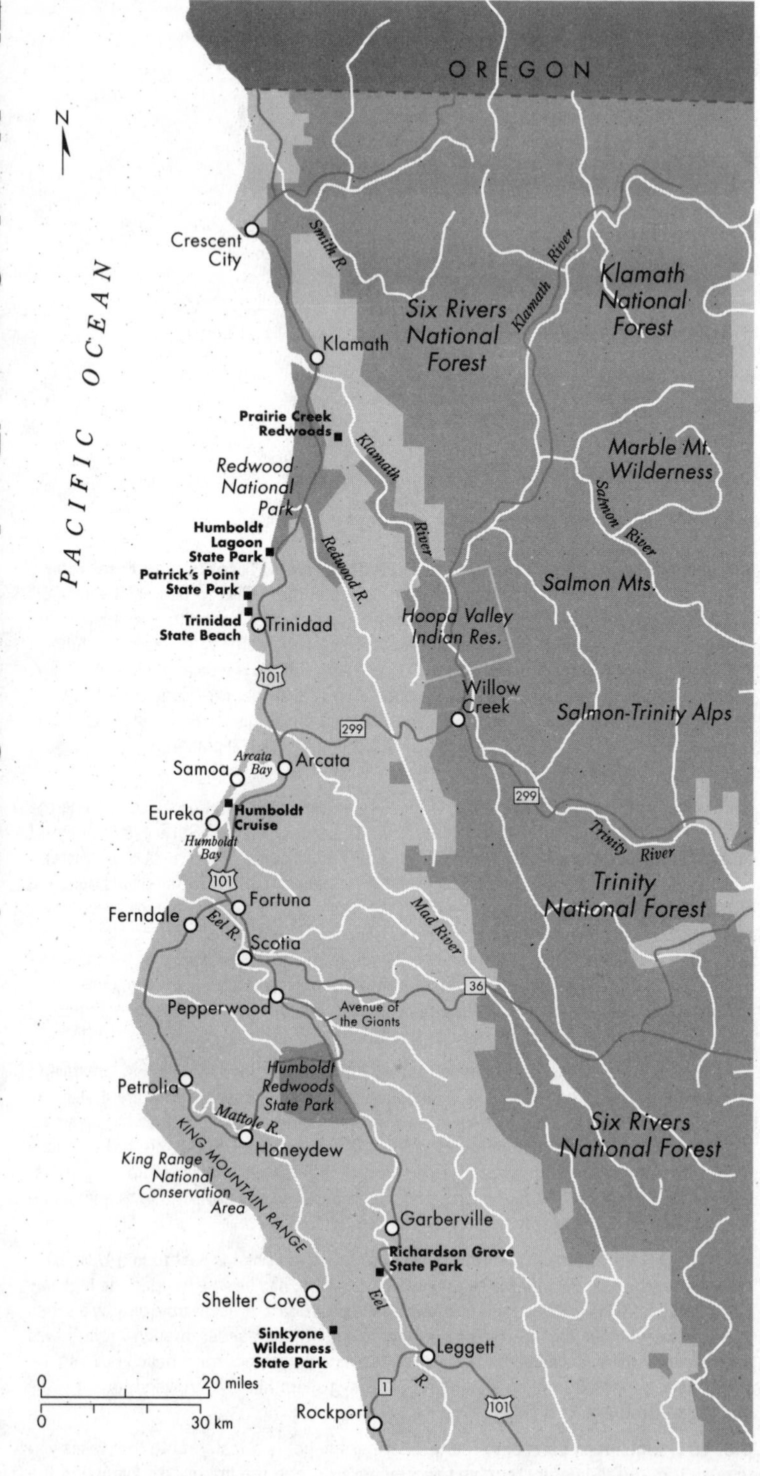
OREGON
N
PACIFIC OCEAN
Crescent City
Smith R.
Klamath River
Klamath National Forest
Six Rivers National Forest
Klamath
Prairie Creek Redwoods
Klamath River
Marble Mt. Wilderness
Salmon River
Redwood National Park
Humboldt Lagoon State Park
Redwood R.
Patrick's Point State Park
Salmon Mts.
Trinidad State Beach
Trinidad
Hoopa Valley Indian Res.
101
Willow Creek
Salmon-Trinity Alps
299
Samoa
Arcata Bay
Arcata
299
Eureka
Humboldt Cruise
Humboldt Bay
Trinity River
101
Trinity National Forest
Fortuna
Ferndale
Eel R.
Mad River
Scotia
36
Pepperwood
Avenue of the Giants
Humboldt Redwoods State Park
Petrolia
Mattole R.
Honeydew
KING MOUNTAIN RANGE
King Range National Conservation Area
Six Rivers National Forest
Garberville
Richardson Grove State Park
Shelter Cove
Eel R.
Sinkyone Wilderness State Park
Leggett
0
20 miles
0
30 km
1
Rockport
101

The North Coast (San Francisco to Rockport)

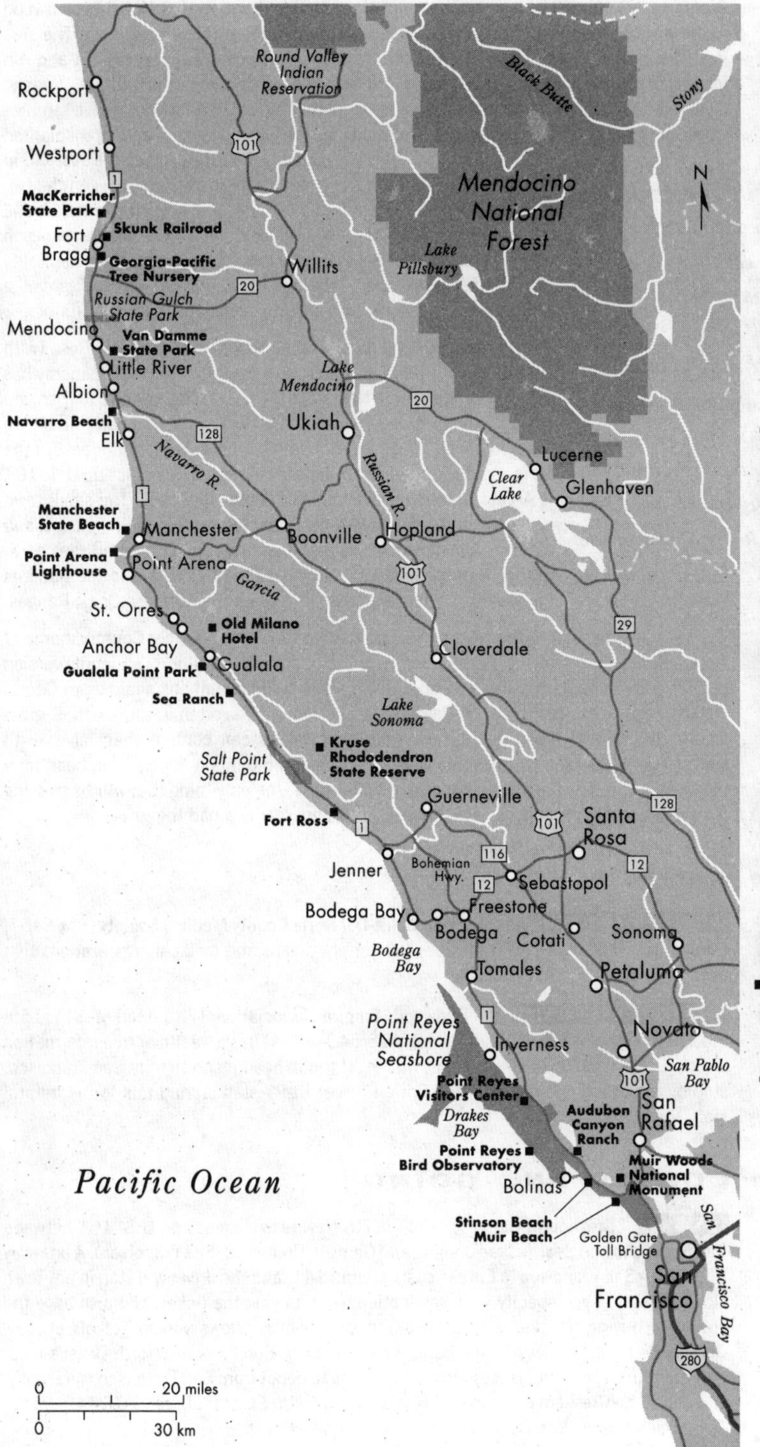
Round Valley
Indian
Reservation
Black Butte
Stony
Rockport
Westport
101
1
MacKerricher
State Park
Fort
Bragg
Skunk Railroad
Georgia-Pacific
Tree Nursery
Mendocino
National
Forest
Lake
Pillsbury
N
Willits
20
Russian Gulch
State Park
Mendocino
Van Damme
State Park
Little River
Albion
Lake
Mendocino
20
Navarro Beach
Ukiah
Elk
128
Navarro R.
Russian R.
Lucerne
Clear
Lake
Glenhaven
1
Manchester
State Beach
Manchester
Boonville
Hopland
Point Arena
Lighthouse
Point Arena
101
Garcia
29
St. Orres
Old Milano
Hotel
Anchor Bay
Cloverdale
Gualala Point Park
Gualala
Sea Ranch
Lake
Sonoma
Kruse
Rhododendron
State Reserve
Salt Point
State Park
Guerneville
128
Fort Ross
101
Santa
Rosa
1
116
Jenner
Bohemian
Hwy.
12
12
Sebastopol
Bodega Bay
Freestone
Bodega
Cotati
Sonoma
Bodega
Bay
Tomales
Petaluma
1
Point Reyes
National
Seashore
Novato
Inverness
San Pablo
Bay
101
Point Reyes
Visitors Center
San
Rafael
Drakes
Bay
Audubon
Canyon
Ranch
Point Reyes
Bird Observatory
Muir Woods
National
Monument
Pacific Ocean
Bolinas
Stinson Beach
Muir Beach
Golden Gate
Toll Bridge
San
Francisco
San
Francisco Bay
280
0
20 miles
0
30 km

Giants near **Garberville.** Here you can touch the Dyerville Giant, the fourth-largest redwood in the world, which fell in 1990 and stretches across the fern-filled forest floor. The area is still a center for the state's rich timber industry, but post–World War II cut-and-run logging practices have destroyed much of the once-abundant redwood and pine forests. Now most of the rustic inland hamlets are populated by a strange mix of native families who for generations have made their living through logging, and transplanted environmentalists who are working hard to protect the last virgin redwood forests. There's an unmistakable tension between the two factions that can be felt in the tone of newspaper articles, the undercurrents of bar conversation, or just the looks people give each other in restaurants. Both groups have an us-against-them mentality that underscores the immense problem facing the area: a timber-based economy and a nearly exhausted supply of timber.

In the 1980s, a marijuana boom temporarily pumped up the economy; but since the inception of CAMP (Campaign Against Marijuana Planting) in 1984 and the onset of the area's worst drought in 20 years, the economy is stagnant and no one seems to know what to do about it.

Though **Eureka** is the biggest metropolis north of Santa Rosa (with a population of 24,000), the town's once-thriving mill economy has suffered irreparably in the last 20 years, and fishing and tourism are having a tough time picking up the slack. Still, you can find cheap seafood meals—the oysters from Humboldt Bay are the best in the state—and the cheapest motels in the region. Six miles up U.S. 101 is **Arcata**, the home of Humboldt State University. The small town is like a mini-Berkeley, with tofu burritos, repertory film houses, and plenty of live music. It's a great launching point for adventures north to the stunning **Redwood National Forest** or east into the national forests and wilderness areas that cover the Northern Coast Ranges.

Once you head east into the Northern Coast Ranges, you enter **Bigfoot Country,** home of the legendary (or merely shy) Sasquatch. The 7-foot apeman, California's friendly version of Tibet's abominable snowman, supposedly resides in the mountains near Happy Camp. Hikers who've explored the northern Klamath Mountains often return with Bigfoot sightings that fuel the mystery. Less ambitious hikers can content themselves with sightings of redwoods, fir trees, black bears, deer, and mountain lions. If you head for a place as isolated as the **Marble Mountain Wilderness,** the only thing that will be missing is *other people*—and that, as we all know, isn't necessarily a bad thing.

● ● ● BASICS

DOCTORS AND DENTISTS **Humboldt-Del Norte County Medical Society** (Box 6457, Eureka, tel. 707/442–2367) provides lists of physicians and medical organizations that accept various insurance policies.

TOURIST INFORMATION **Redwood Empire Association** (785 Market St., 15th Floor, San Francisco 94103–2022, tel. 415/543–8334) has a wealth of free information on attractions, activities, and regional history. If you're heading north from San Francisco, stop by the office, located near the Powell Street BART station, and talk to the helpful staff.

● ● ● COMING AND GOING

BY BUS **Greyhound** (tel. 415/834–3070) travels twice a day on U.S. 101 between San Francisco and Seattle (*see* Coming and Going in Chapter 2, San Francisco). A one-way ticket from San Francisco to Eureka costs around $41, and the driver will stop in any town along the way if you specify your destination when buying the ticket. You also have the option of buying a ticket with a specified stop, which allows you to get off at, say, Garberville for a few days before continuing up north. Eureka is the North Coast's most important transport hub. Buses arrive at the **Eureka depot** from San Francisco twice daily, and depart for Crescent City three times daily. *1603 4th St. at P St., tel. 707/442–0370. Open weekdays 6:30 AM–10 PM; fewer hours on weekends.*

Greyhound also travels up and down the coast on Route 1 twice daily, and will stop in any town along the way. Schedules and additional information are available at the Fort Bragg depot, located at **Looking Good Women's Fashions** (262 N. Main St., tel. 707/964–0877).

Redwood Empire Lines (tel. 707/443–9923) buses connect Eureka with Redding, a stop for both **Amtrak** trains and **Green Tortoise** buses (*see* Chapter 1, Basics). Buses go once a day in each direction, and use the Greyhound terminals in both cities. The bus line also serves Weaverville and other stops along Route 299 in the Shasta-Trinity and Six Rivers National Forests. The one-way fare for trips between Eureka and Redding is around $18; slightly less for other destinations on Route 299.

BY TRAIN North of San Francisco, **Amtrak** (tel. 800/872–7245) trains turn inland and follow approximately the same route as I–5. If you're determined to go by train, take Amtrak as far as Redding (around $51 one way) and then find other transport to the coast. Reservations should be made one week in advance.

BY PLANE The nearest major airports are **San Francisco International Airport** and **Oakland International.** From either, you can catch a shuttle to a Greyhound depot or rental car agency. Within the region, the Eureka-Arcata airport is served by **American Eagle** (tel. 415/398–4434 or 800/433–7300), but fares are high.

BY CAR The best way to explore the North Coast is by car, particularly if you want to stray from Route 1 and U.S. 101. Much of the region is mountainous and remote, and the distances you'll cover are tremendous. A car gives you the freedom to travel from the rocky shoreline of Mendocino to the Marble Mountains in a matter of hours, a trip that could take days if you were using mass transit or hitchhiking.

CAR RENTAL If you don't rent a car in San Francisco, you're best off looking for a weekend or week-long deal at one of the agencies in the Santa Rosa area. Try **Bay Area Rentals** (3264 Santa Rosa Ave., Petaluma, tel. 707/763–2900), which rents cars, pickups, and passenger vans; or **U-Save Rentals** (1426 Petaluma Hill Rd., Santa Rosa, tel. 707/571–1711) in Santa Rosa, which offers free mileage and accepts cash deposits (no credit card required). **Hertz** (tel. 800/654–3131) rents cars at the Eureka-Arcata airport. In general, rentals in small towns are more expensive; you're best off with one of the large chains, which offer the option of drop-off in another city.

GETTING AROUND

BY BUS **Greyhound** provides regular service to towns along U.S. 101, but fares are expensive for short hops (*see* Coming and Going by Bus, *above*). If you're not under severe time constraints, you can get around on the local bus systems, but be forewarned that no single system comprehensively covers the region, and making connections from one transit district to another can be a frustrating experience. For more information, contact: **Sonoma County Transit** (tel. 707/576–7433), **Mendocino Transit Authority** (tel. 707/462–1422), and **Humboldt Transit Authority** (tel. 707/443–5826).

BY BIKE Nearly all of U.S. 101 from Ukiah to the Oregon border is bikeable, though you'll have to share the road with RVs, passenger cars, and logging trucks. During the summer, a tail wind makes pedaling south through Humboldt County on U.S. 101 easy and fun, and you'll find a parade of other riders in day-glo colors out to enjoy the amazing scenery. The rainy season here can last up to eight months, so plan a summer trip unless you don't mind getting very, very wet. Also, don't even think of riding on Route 1 unless you're extremely confident and an experienced rider. The cliff-hugging road can be terrifying even for motorists.

It's hard to bike into the Clear Lake area, but once you get over the surrounding mountains you'll find a wide choice of good routes. There are lots of campgrounds along both Route 1 and U.S. 101, and plenty of opportunities for heading off the main road to beautiful forest groves or deserted beaches. On **Avenue of the Giants**, you can even ride your bike through the center of a carved-out redwood. Unfortunately, some of the most tempting side roads are dirt and gravel, and therefore inaccessible to all but the hardiest bikes. Still, it's easier to stow a bike than a car if you have a sudden urge for backpacking. Bring along a good lock.

The best source of information for biking the North Coast is the **District 1 Bicycle Touring Guide**, available through Caltrans (Box 3700, 1656 Union St., Eureka 95501). The pamphlet contains routes, information on campgrounds, bike shops, and attractions.

BY CAR The roads along the north coast and in the coastal mountains can be treacherous, but the scenery is spectacular. Make sure you have decent tires, and be prepared for rock slides, hairpin turns, road work, and intimidating logging trucks. Your car can take you to areas that simply aren't accessible by public transportation, but make sure you abandon it periodically or you'll miss out on some great hiking and backwoods camping experiences.

Driving is by far the easiest way to see Route 1, and gives you the freedom to stop for ocean views and short hikes up rivers or down to beaches. On summer weekends when tourists are out in force, you can spend up to 90 minutes traveling 20 miles on the narrow and often difficult roads. On U.S. 101, traffic is usually not too bad once you're north of Santa Rosa. If you're an experienced motorcyclist, this is a brilliant way to see the coast, especially during the summer. You'll find many other riders on the road, all whom seem to exude an extreme satisfaction in riding the curves. The roads are rough, though, and often wet or fogged in, so this isn't a good place for your fledgling road trip.

HITCHHIKING Hitching is always risky business in California, but along the north coast you'll still find some of the "hail fellow, well met" spirit that made hitchhiking the hippies' favorite form of transportation. In fact, quite a few of the residents are hippies who hitchhiked north from Los Angeles or San Francisco years ago and haven't left. You might have a hard time getting a ride out of San Francisco or Santa Rosa, but it gets easier once you leave the major urban areas behind. Hitching is part of the culture here, and a good way to explore the coast. Have fun, but don't be lulled by friendly overtures or good sinsemilla into a situation you'll regret. The best places to get picked up are in the small towns near the entrances to Route 1 or U.S. 101. You can also check the ride boards at Sonoma State University in Santa Rosa or Humboldt State University in Arcata, or the various kiosks and bulletin boards in grocery stores and cafés.

●●● WHERE TO SLEEP

If you have a bit of money to throw around, there are some really great places to stay on the north coast, including bed-and-breakfasts—the sort that travel guides call quaint—and charming old wooden hotels dating from the 19th century. Other than that, you'll find the usual, forgettable modern hotels, which can be quite expensive here, and lots of cheap roadside motels good for a desperate late-night rest and shower, if not much else. In most towns, the best choices are away from the highway. Everything costs more during the summer and on holiday weekends, but even at other times prices can vary greatly, so shop around before checking in.

There are a number of health spas in the region around Ukiah and Clear Lake, where deep springs of warm, clear waters bubble to the surface. The waters have long been used for medicinal purposes by Native Americans, and now attract a wide range of New Age-types, hippies, yuppies, and health enthusiasts. Though many of the resorts are expensive, a few, like the quintessentially "West Coast" Harbin Hot Springs (*see* U.S. 101, *below*), offer camping and a wide range of recreational possibilities at very reasonable prices. In small mountain towns, you can often rent cabins in the $40–$60 range—a real bargain if you're traveling with four people or so. Many cabins have two beds and a pull-out couch, and most include kitchens. Check chambers of commerce and kiosks in towns for listings. A good source of information for lodging in the whole area is the **Redwood Empire Association** (*see* Tourist Information, *above*).

Unless you're going during the rainy season, consider camping. California has a great range of campgrounds—from rustic backcountry reserves to veritable camping Disneylands. Though state parks fill up fast, most are increasingly adding hike-in spots on a first-come, first-serve basis. Even if the sign says "full," it always pays to ask the ranger. Although beach camping is most often illegal, you can almost always tuck yourself neatly behind some driftwood on the wide-open beaches of the North Coast. Just bring plenty of blankets, and don't leave a car parked nearby on the highway; you're easily found that way.

FOOD • • •

The economy here is depressed, and most residents do their eating at home. As a result, many of the restaurants along the coast cater primarily to tourists, and are accordingly expensive. You'll do best to find the few places where locals do go. Since the '60s, the North Coast has been drawing enterprising, counterculture-type new residents, so expect to find restaurants serving food made with seriously healthy ingredients—organic vegetables, unprocessed flour, and lots of grains. Conversely, in restaurants frequented by loggers, you'll find large portions of food that're unambiguously filling, and you'll probably have to put up with excessive amounts of smoke. In Eureka, you can get good cheap seafood, especially Humboldt Bay oysters and clam chowder. If you're camping, the cheapest place to get your food is at supermarkets in major towns, or at the open-air produce markets you'll find along the road during spring and summer. It helps if you have a cooler and a camp stove. Many backcountry campsites don't allow open fires in the summer.

When you get tired of good vibes and want to see your mellow waiter lose his or her cool, just light up a cigarette in one of these health-food places—you'll probably be treated like Bigfoot on a rampage.

OUTDOOR ACTIVITIES • • •

Not surprisingly, outdoor activities along the North Coast are centered around water—but remember, beaches in this region aren't known for good swimming. Except in the mouths of rivers, the water is too cold for all but the Polar Bear Club. What the coast does offer is wide sandy beaches and wooded inlets; tide pools filled with starfish, sea anenomes, and crabs; and rocky cliffs where you can see pelicans, sandpipers, and seagulls. Surfing is good at Miwok and North Salmon Fork beaches. If you're truly hydrophobic, head inland to the Northern Coast Ranges for secluded camping in the many wilderness areas, but don't be surprised if it rains on you after all.

Coastal Route 1

After it crosses the Golden Gate Bridge, Route 1 follows the rugged northern California coast for close to 200 miles before turning inland and joining U.S. 101 in Leggett. The dramatic shoreline here has nothing to do with popular conceptions of sunny California beaches. The highway is windy and dangerous, and the weather nearly always foggy—especially in the summer. Some of the most beautiful little spits of sand lie at the base of jagged cliffs nearly impossible to scale, and the forest extends right to the shore in many places. Huge rocks tower out of the surf, and every few miles a river snakes out of the forest and pours into the sea. With a little calculated ignoring of logging equipment, you can imagine what California was like before it had the name. If you want hot fun in the summertime, though, look elsewhere; this is where you'll find natural beauty of the moody variety—the kind that Alfred Hitchcock captured in *The Birds,* filmed in Bodega Bay.

The road passes through a number of carefully maintained and extremely quaint towns before reaching Fort Bragg, pretty much the only place on the coast that doesn't look like storybook land. A quite feasible day trip is to set out from San Francisco in the early morning, drive up the coast for a late lunch in alluring Mendocino, and return to the Bay Area in the evening on U.S. 101. Take your time, though. Nearly every turnoff has its riches to yield, and a night spent camping in any of the coastal state parks could be the most memorable on your trip. The forested hillsides and rough cliffs make for great hiking, and in the oceanside lagoons you have a chance of a close-up visit with our friends the whales.

Of course, you can't exactly hide this kind of beauty from the more than 3 million people living in the San Francisco Bay Area. The slow-moving traffic over windswept switchbacks on summer weekends testifies to the area's popularity with RV trekkers and snapshot-shooting families. Nearly all of the campgrounds in state parks along the coast are heavily used in the summer and booked up in advance. Even greater changes have been wrought by wealthy urbanites from the Bay Area, who have developed some of the best-situated property. The coast on Route 1 has been tamed by city dollars, or so it seems in comparison to the pristine "Lost Coast" farther north. Still, if you're in a position to splurge on a night in a rustic inn or a bed-and-breakfast, this is one of the best places in California to do it, and it's quite possible that the desk clerk will be knowledgeable about karma and bodywork, too.

● ● ● BASICS

TOURIST INFORMATION **Fort Bragg and Mendocino Coast Chamber of Commerce** (332 N. Main St., tel. 707/961–6300 or 800/726–2780) has maps, brochures, and lodging referrals for the Mendocino County coast from Gualala to Sinkyone Wilderness State Park.

● ● ● WHERE TO SLEEP

Lodging is generally expensive along the coast, and camping is the only real solution. Swanky inns and bed-and-breakfasts are the main attraction, and most charge upwards of $90 in the summer, slightly less off-season. Generally speaking, lodging gets cheaper the farther away you get from the San Francisco Bay Area. Fort Bragg has the widest selection of economy motels; in Sonoma County to the south, you'll be hard-pressed to find even a dive for under $60 per night.

You'll find a dazzling array of camping options along the coast, some of them really spectacular, although you might have to look a bit if you want something primitive and isolated. Campsites are close together, beach access is restricted to certain hours for day use, and trails are well-marked and well-worn—all signs of a fragile area that's overused. Luckily, most of the campgrounds are state parks, and the park rangers are working to preserve the fragile ecosystems. Private campgrounds geared toward recreational vehicles are also available. The RV parks are sometimes less crowded than the state parks, but with prices approaching those of inexpensive motels, they're generally only worth it in a pinch. Cold winds whip the coast at night, even during the summer, so bring extra blankets and use the abundant driftwood on the beach to build a toasty fire.

Some of the best campgrounds include: **Salt Point State Park, Manchester State Beach, Navarro Beach, Van Damme State Park, Russian Gulch State Park,** and **Mackerricher State Park.** For more information about camping in California state parks and about these parks in particular, *see* Chapter 1, Basics.

Salmon Creek Ranger Station (tel. 707/875–3483), on Route 1 just north of Bodega Bay, has information on campgrounds and day-use beaches along the coast in Sonoma County. For information about state parks in Mendocino County, contact **Mendocino State Park Headquarters** (Box 440, Mendocino 95460, tel. 707/937–5804) or consult the publication *Northwind,* available at any ranger station.

BODEGA BAY There are some places to stay here, but the nice ones tend to be very expensive. **The Bodega Bay Lodge** (103 Rte. 1, tel. 707/875–3525) is a beautiful, spacious, wood-shingle affair with pool, spa, sauna, and weight room—but rooms start at $108 in the summer.

CAMPING **Doran Park.** On a narrow spit of sand extending into the southern end of Bodega Bay, this Sonoma County–run park offers free camping at several decent campgrounds on barren beaches with little privacy. Entrance to the park is $3. For tent-camping, try **Shell Campground** where sites are set in the dunes and scrub brush, or better yet the sites lettered A–J on the beach. Running water and toilets are provided and you can fish from the jetty at the end of the park. *Turn off Rte. 1 at the sign just south of the prominent Bodega Bay Lodge.*

Bodega Dunes Campground. Part of Sonoma Coast State Beaches north of Bodega Bay, Bodega Dunes has 98 campsites. Most are in the open, but if you look around you can find some secluded sites set off behind the sand dunes or in patches of trees. The campground has running water, showers, and beach access.

FORT BRAGG You'll find a wealth of nondescript motels that are generally less expensive than lodgings elsewhere on the coast. Try the **Fort Bragg Motel** (763 North Main St., tel. 707/964–4787) or the **Colombi Motel** (647 Oak St., tel. 707/964–5773). Both are plain but clean, and wheelchair accessible. Rooms start at around $30.

GUALALA If you can't camp, try the standard **Surf Motel** (S. Rte. 1, tel. 707/884–3571), where rooms start at $65.

THE RUSSIAN RIVER In Guerneville, it's almost impossible to find a room during the summer without reservations. If you're out of luck, try camping on the beach. **Johnson's Resort** (16241 1st St., tel. 707/869–2022) has cabins on the river for around $30 a night. Some of the cabins have kitchens, but the operation closes down from October to May. **Fife's Lodge** (16467 River Rd., tel. 707/869–0659) is a well-known private gay resort, with cabins renting for $45–$115 a night.

CAMPING **Willow Creek.** Near the Russian River are 11 "environmental" campsites set in meadows against a backdrop of willow and alder thickets only a 1/4-mile hike from the road. The campground ($6 per night) is not well known yet and may have sites available even on crowded Russian River weekends. You can't gather wood yourself, but you can purchase it down the coast at Bodega Dunes or at small grocery stores in the area. From Route 1 heading north from Bodega Bay, turn right on Willow Creek Road, then left on the first dirt road (impassable after storms). You'll reach the parking area after a half-mile drive—be sure to close the two livestock gates after you pass through.

FOOD ● ● ●

Unfortunately, most of the good restaurants in the towns along Route 1 cater to well-heeled tourists looking for a slice of the good life and willing to pay for it. Though seafood is abundant, prices aren't cheap and most meals are out of a budget traveler's range. There are a few roadside diners, but the best way to eat cheaply is to shop at either the great selection of health food–oriented grocery stores or at the Safeway supermarkets you'll see along the way.

ALBION South of Fort Bragg and near Mendocino Headlands State Park, the **Albion Grocery** (tel. 707/937–5784) has a good selection of meat and picnic items—perfect if you're on your way to one of the beaches in the area. The delicatessen across the highway, despite its inviting deck, serves disappointing overpriced fare.

BODEGA BAY Most of the seafood restaurants in Bodega Bay are overpriced and the seafood is no great thrill, despite it's freshness. If you want good value for your money, skip **Lucas Wharf** (595 Rte. 1, tel. 707/875–3522) and **The Tides** (800 Rte. 1, tel. 707/875–2251), the two most popular spots in town, and go to **Lucas Wharf Deli** (595 Rte. 1, tel. 707/875–3562) for a pint of crab cioppino ($4) or the fish and chips ($5) and choose from a good selection of wine and beer. Though it's mainly a sportfishing center, the **Boat House** (1445 Rte. 1, tel. 707/875–3495) serves up good clam chowder ($2.50) and fried fish, and it's open late.

FORT BRAGG The most workaday town on Rte. 1, Fort Bragg has a number of low-heeled restaurants catering to tourists on a budget and local working people. Of course, this *is* northern California, so expect a few twists.

Egghead Omelettes of Oz. The waitresses dress like Dorothy and the yellow brick road leads to the bathroom. Try the delicious vegetarian omelette stuffed with peppers, onions, mushrooms, and cheese ($6.50) or the bacon, avocado, sprouts, tomatoes, and onion sandwich ($5.50). Expect to wait in line on weekend mornings. *326 N. Main St., tel. 707/964–5005. Open until 2 PM. Wheelchair accessible.*

North Coast Brewing Company. To accompany their regionally celebrated beer, the Brewing Company cooks up good burgers, sandwiches, and fish and chips. During the lively happy hour from 4 PM to 7 PM, a glass of beer costs only about $1 ($2.50 a pint in the evenings). The airy bar, with wood-burning stoves, stuffed elk, and wood floors, also features live jazz several nights a week and a pricey dinner menu in the restaurant next door. Tours of the brewery can be arranged by appointment, and will probably yield some free samples. *444 Main St. at Pine St., tel. 707/964–2739.*

GUALALA The restaurant in **The Gualala Hotel** (39301 S. Rte. 1, tel. 707/884–3441) serves good breakfasts and lunches in a casual atmosphere. For a big Sunday brunch, try the bacon and eggs with hot biscuits and home fries ($5). A couple of doors down, the **Upper Crust Pizza** (39331 S. Rte. 1, tel. 707/884–1324) has good, cheap pizza ($5–$10) and a salad bar. Another Upper Crust is located north in Point Arena at the Wharf (790 Port Rd., Point Arena, tel. 707/882–3254).

MENDOCINO You'll find better restaurants at cheaper prices nearby in Fort Bragg, but you'll manage just fine with the deep-dish pizza at the **Mendocino Bakery** (10483 Lansing St., tel. 707/937–0836) or a burger at **Mendocino Burgers** (tel. 707/937–1111) on the bakery's back patio. Entrées run close to $20 at the renowned **Café Beaujolais** (961 Ukiah St., tel. 707/937–5614), but at the adjacent "brickery," which supplies the café's bread, you can get a tasty pizza for one (around $6) and eat it in the peaceful herb garden. If you want to buy your own supplies, stop downtown at **Corners of the Mouth Natural Foods** (45015 Ukiah St., tel. 707/937–5345), where there's a wonderful selection of organic produce, juices, pasta, nuts, and baked goods.

RUSSIAN RIVER AND GUERNEVILLE In Guerneville it's easy to eat good food on the cheap, but stopping at just that would miss the point—restaurants here are great places to hang out, listen to music, and talk to strangers.

The Coffee Bazaar. Put together a customized feast from the great selection of coffees, bagel sandwiches, and ice cream. The $2 pizza bagel is a meal in itself. Locals lounge here for hours reading the papers, browsing the bulletin board for information about town events, or listening to impromptu jam sessions in the gallery space just behind the main café. *In the Cinnabar Mall, 14045 Armstrong Woods Rd., tel. 707/869–9706. Wheelchair accessible.*

El Taco Rio. Across from the riverside beach, this hole in the wall has plenty of character and serves plenty of food. Try one of their huge burritos with fresh salsa, guacamole, and your choice of meat stuffed into 14-inch tortillas ($4.50), or the two-enchilada dinner with rice and beans ($6). *16225 1st St., tel. 707/869–3125. Wheelchair accessible.*

Jirk's Pizza Café. Pizza, beer, and loud rock 'n' roll are the hallmarks of this pizzeria. The pizza is great old-style New York ($2 a slice), the beer is reasonable ($5 a pitcher), and the local drunks are the most interesting part of the atmosphere. *16205 1st St., Guerneville, tel. 707/869–0651. Wheelchair accessible*

Rocco's. Although the building used to house a gas station, chef Rocco takes pride in his work of serving up huge, tasty burgers with just the basics ($5–$6). If you want to get fancy, ask for sharp cheddar cheese and an order of wedge-cut fries. *At the intersection of Rte. 12 and the Bohemian Hwy. in Freestone, tel. 707/823–7756. Open till 10 PM.*

● ● ● EXPLORING ROUTE 1

North of San Francisco, Route 1 travels through Marin County past Mill Valley, Muir Woods, Stinson Beach, and Point Reyes (*see* Marin County in Chapter 3, San Francisco Bay Area). We pick up the route at Bodega Bay, about 25 miles north of Point Reyes Station and 50 miles north of San Francisco. If you don't wish to travel all the way up the coast on Route 1, there are three roads connecting it to U.S. 101, a faster and less arduous drive. Route 116 west from Santa Rosa takes you through the Russian River resort area, and joins

Route 1 at Jenner. Route 128 passes through the interesting hamlet of **Boonville** (*see* U.S. 101, *below*) and a lush redwood forest before joining Route 1 south of Albion. Route 20 connects Fort Bragg with Willits on U.S. 101.

The drive on Route 1 from San Francisco all the way to its end in Leggett takes a minimum of seven hours, but will take longer in foggy weather, on summer weekends, and if you're big on stopping.

BODEGA AND BODEGA BAY With its rusty schooners, crooked streets, and old wooden houses, Bodega Bay looks at first sight like a crusty old harbor town, the kind of place that should be full of wizened fishermen, fresh seafood, and the smells and sights of the sea. So it is, to a certain extent, but don't expect to run into Billy Budd. Instead of old saloons, cheap grub, and tales of the sea, you're more likely to find real estate agents, overpriced seafood, and developers doing their best to transform this outstanding natural harbor into a top-notch resort. Luckily, developers can't take credit for the place's abundant natural beauty. The town of Bodega Bay hugs the bay itself, cut off from the rest of the Pacific by the **Bodega Head,** which juts dramatically into the ocean toward the Point Reyes Peninsula to the south. A walk out on the headland will lead you through tall grasses and wildflowers (in spring and summer) to rocky cliffs where, on a clear day, you'll swear you can see all the way to Mount Fuji. If you're wearing sturdy shoes, climb down the rocks along the ocean trail to check out the tide pools full of anenomes, star fish, crabs, snails, and fish, and watch tiny sea palms (a delicate form of kelp) hang tough to the rocks in a big swell.

A few miles inland from Bodega Bay is the even cozier town of **Bodega** (Rte. 1 south to Rte. 12), where you can visit an old-fashioned saloon and wander around interesting antique stores, a small market, and an organic outdoor nursery that sells vegetables, flowers, and herbs.

SONOMA COAST STATE BEACHES Between Bodega Bay and Jenner to the north stretches a line of broad, bare, windswept cliffs leading down to some of California's finest white-sand beaches. The beaches are collectively administered by the California Department of Recreation under the name **Sonoma Coast State Beaches,** and although some of the rules may seem rigid (no dogs, gates closed at sunset, etc.), they're needed to keep the popular beaches in more or less their natural state. In the south, you can camp at **Wright's Beach** or watch the surfers fight for waves at **Miwok Beach** and **North Salmon Creek Beach.** Even on weekdays, it's not unusual to see 15–20 surfers, although they're sometimes mistaken for seals by passing motorists and the occasional hungry shark. Heavy surf and strong undertows make swimming here dangerous, but most people are sufficiently deterred by the freezing water. The hiking is wonderful, though, and the many tide pools endlessly fascinating. If you stop in only one place, make it **Goat Rock State Beach** at the northern end of the recreation area, where a paved road leads down about a mile to Goat Rock, a massive terraced granite hill with grass on top. You can't climb the hill, but the beach itself is one of the least-used and most beautiful in the park. Entrance is free, dogs are allowed, and toilets are provided—yes, it's heaven.

JENNER On the other side of the Sonoma Coast State Beaches is the tiny town of Jenner. The Russian River empties into the Pacific here, often under the close observation of coastal seals. Jenner is the start of one of most dramatic stretches of Route 1, a series of dizzying switchbacks that take you rapidly up and down coastal mountains and to the brinks of some really frightening cliffs. You'll pass by sharp precipices, wild surf, and craggy boulders rising from the seething whitewater of the Pacific. Passengers, take a video camera so the driver can see what you were all gasping about while she was busy keeping a steely eye on the road.

On foggy days even the passengers are petrified and stare steadily ahead with hopes that the more eyes on the road the better in keeping the car between the lines.

GUERNEVILLE AND THE RUSSIAN RIVER Just south of Jenner is the start of Route 116, which heads east along the Russian River through the resort town of Guerneville, and eventually joins U.S. 101 at Santa Rosa. Even when the coast is wrapped in fog (as it is nearly year-round), it'll probably be sunny in Guerneville, and folks from the San Francisco Bay Area and the north will be swimming in the Russian River's warm waters. The river attracts a wide range of visitors, but is especially popular with gays and lesbians. Several of the most popular resorts, notably **Fife's** and **The Willows,** have a largely gay clientele and are owned and operated by people in Guerneville's sizable gay community.

Guerneville is a great place to just hang out. Head to one of the friendly local cafés to read a paper, listen to music, or strike up a conversation. There are a number of good, inexpensive restaurants in town, and a surprising number of cultural events. Every year in September, the two-day **Russian River Jazz Festival** (tel. 707/869–3940) attracts more than 6,000 people who come to hear some of the world's finest jazz musicians. To keep up with it all, cruise by **Bobbi's Last Word Newsstand** (14045 Armstrong Woods Rd., tel. 707/869–0571) next to Cinnabar shopping mall, which carries a wide range of magazines and periodicals, including several gay publications as well as the latest reggae, jazz, and New Age cassettes and CDs.

FORT ROSS Back on Route 1, after driving 12 dramatic miles north from Jenner, you arrive at Fort Ross—not a town, but a historical park with a reconstructed fort as its centerpiece. Perched dramatically above the ocean, the fort was originally built by Russians in 1812 to serve as an outpost for Russian hunters seeking valuable pelts on the California coast. In 1841, when the supply of seals and otters had begun to dwindle, the Russians sold the fort to John Sutter, who also owned the mill where the California gold rush would begin seven years later. In addition to the stockade, barracks, and blockhouse, the carefully reconstructed fort includes a Russian Orthodox chapel. Fort Ross is a great place in which to imagine that California is not part of the United States—an activity beloved by Californians. *Fort Ross Historical Park, 19005 Rte. 1 at Fort Ross Rd., tel. 707/847–3286. Day use: $3. Open daily 10–4:30. Closed Dec. 25 and Jan. 1*

SALT POINT STATE PARK This 3,500-acre reserve immediately north of Fort Ross is an ocean lover's delight, full of white-sand coves, tidal pools, windswept sandstone cliffs, and headlands. A good place to start exploring is **Fisk Mill Cove** where you'll find wonderful picnic spots (and toilets, too). If you park on the highway, you can avoid the $5 day-use fee. Intrepid swimmers (that's to say, people as cold-blooded as dinosaurs) enjoy the clear waters at nearby **Stump Beach,** and there's an underwater park for divers. **Grestle Cove** has fully equipped campsites and hot showers near the ocean, as does **Woodside** on the east side of Route 1. The state park is the area's most popular day-use and camping spot. *Tel. 707/847–3221. Day use $3; camping $10. Open daily.*

KRUSE RHODODENDRON STATE RESERVE To the north is **Kruse Rhododendron State Reserve,** where you can wander on 5 miles of trails through second-growth redwood, fir, and oak. From May through early June, the 20-foot-tall rhododendron plants are in lavish, pink bloom. Consult your copy of *Through the Looking Glass* before accepting any food from hookah-smoking caterpillars.

GUALALA Several miles farther north, winding Route 1 calms down in time to enter Gualala, the southernmost town in Mendocino County. The one-street town overlooking the ocean is much frequented by far-flung coastal residents for its two well-stocked supermarkets and several restaurants. South of Gualala, the 5,200-acre vacation-home development of **Sea Ranch** provides the ultimate getaway for people who can realize their dreams of a second or third home. The development continues to be controversial because it allows public access to the state-owned beaches at only six spots (up from zero spots before 1985). The beaches are open only from sunrise to sunset, and there's a $2 day-use fee per car. At least the boxy homes of weathered wood fit neatly into the landscape, and leave lots of open space.

POINT ARENA Sixteen miles north of Gualala is the tiny fishing village of Point Arena, a good place for a break from driving. Take an inexpensive tour of the **Point Arena Lighthouse** (tel. 707/882–2777). The 115-foot structure is the second lighthouse to stand at this location. The first, built in 1870, did its job efficiently until it was knocked down by the 1906 earthquake (the famous one, starring Clark Gable).

MANCHESTER STATE BEACH If you have a penchant for the primitive, stop 8 miles north of Point Arena at Manchester State Beach (tel. 707/937–5804), a grassy park with wind-twisted Monterey cypress trees and sand dunes. Water runs through the park via Bush Creek and Alder Creek, but be sure to boil it before you use it. A stroll along the beach can yield some wonderfully gnarled pieces of driftwood.

NAVARRO BEACH About 14 miles north of Point Arena, you'll pass through the blink-and-miss-it town of **Elk,** with its old grocery store and saloon (closed most of the time) and the cozy Elk Café. Shortly thereafter, Route 1 begins a series of hair-raising ascents and descents. Near the Navarro River Bridge just south of the town of Albion is the unmarked turnoff for Navarro Beach, the only place on Route 1 where you can **camp for free** legally. It's a scruffy spot where people drive 4x4's across the beach and, when the wind picks up, there's nowhere to hide. Popular with homeless folks and those unwilling to pay to camp, it can be an interesting place to meet travelers and get away from the tourist grind.

VAN DAMME STATE PARK Located 3 miles south of Mendocino just across from the beach, Van Damme's 74 sites are often crowded, but you can slink off by yourself to a walk-in campsite in the dewy coastal forest only $1^3/_4$ miles away. From the park's main entrance, a very popular, wheelchair-accessible trail leads to the naturally freaky **Pygmy Forest,** where trees that are decades old stand only three and four feet tall. Highly acidic soil and poor drainage work together to stunt the trees' growth, but you could probably fool quite a number of your fellow campers with a more imaginative explanation of your own. Ask for a map at the Ranger Station.

MENDOCINO The picturesque town became a popular artists' retreat in the '50s and '60s, but tourists and collectors bought up art faster than artists could produce it, and today the galleries and crafts shops import much of their wares from outside the area. Like a number of other California towns billed as artists' retreats (Laguna Beach and Ojai come to mind), the original bohemian impulse has gotten a bit lost in the shuffle to make money off the tourists. Each summer, thousands pour in to stay at the town's many bed-and-breakfasts or eat at such excellent but expensive restaurants as **Café Beaujolais** (961 Ukiah St., tel. 707/937–5614). Happily, many artists remain and more are arriving yearly, and it's a real pleasure to browse through their weather-beaten wooden studios. In summer, Mendocino is the only town on the north coast where you'll have trouble parking or have to wait in line for a table at a restaurant. If you want a slice of real Mendocino life, visit in the winter, fall, or spring, when the tourists have left and the town feels like it must have 30 years ago.

RUSSIAN GULCH STATE PARK At this small 30-campsite park just north of Mendocino and 8 miles south of Fort Bragg, you can dive or surf-fish in the ocean, fish for trout in a stream, or (if the drought ever ends) hike up Falls Loop Trail to the 36-foot **Russian Gulch Falls.** Campers on horseback can hitch up at nearby **Jackson State Forest,** where you can ride on old logging roads and choose your sleeping quarters from among 20 campgrounds (for information, contact California Department of Forestry, 820 N. Main St., Box 1185, Fort Bragg 95437, tel. 707/964–5674). For information on horse camping, contact Mendocino District Headquarters (tel. 707/937–5804).

FORT BRAGG If you're almost to the point of overdosing on quaintness, Fort Bragg will be a welcome change. This is just about the only "real" town on this make-believe coast. People have jobs here (there's a huge military base), and spend their locally earned money in working-class bars and restaurants. Even an influx of T-shirt shops and other tourist-oriented businesses hasn't seriously compromised Fort Bragg's integrity. The largest city on this stretch of the coast, Fort Bragg is the place to go for camping and outdoor supplies, as well as reasonable motels, good food, and entertainment. In nearby Caspar, the **Caspar Inn** (tel. 707/964–5565) has been booking great jazz and blues bands for years, and continues to feature some of the best live music on the north coast. Best of all are the "open microphone" Sunday nights, when you can hear some serious acoustic jam sessions by local talents for no cover charge. It's easy to strike up a conversation with one of the friendly regular customers.

A ride on Fort Bragg's biggest attraction, the **Skunk Train,** will give you a close-up look at snaking streams and redwood-covered hills, along with some areas of clear-cut forest, on a route that logging trains have been covering since 1885. The full-day train excursions take you 40 miles inland to **Willits,** with stops on the way to drop off mail and groceries to settlements inaccessible by car. During summer, you can also take a three-hour round-trip to **Northspur,** an old logging camp now featuring an overpriced concession stand selling food and trinkets. Train buffs will be delighted by the Skunk, but the best way to get a view of the terrain is simply to hike into the redwoods on any of the area's trails. *California Western Railroad, tel. 707/964–6371. Trains leave from the Laurel St. Station downtown twice daily for ½-day trips and once in the morning for full-day trips. Tickets cost $18.50 for ½ day, $23.50 for full day.*

MACKERRICHER STATE PARK Only 3 miles north of Fort Bragg are Mackerricher State Park (tel. 707/964–9112) and the nearby freshwater Lake Cleone, where you can fish for trout or watch flocks of ducks who migrate in from Mono Lake each summer. (The trail that encircles the lake is partially submerged from winter to late spring.) There's a blacktop promenade along the beach that's good for biking. Only a short walk north of the campground you can see seals relaxing on the rocks at low tide. The easily hiked **Coast Trail** begins at the popular **Pudding Creek Beach,** also to the north, and offers spectacular views of the ocean as it winds its way for 8 miles until it reaches the **10-Mile River.**

Mackerricher's campground has 142 sites crammed closely together. All "family" or "developed" campgrounds have running water and hot showers. The best camping can be had at the walk-in sites that are only 50 yards from the parking lot but are still fairly secluded. Reservations are recommended in the summer, but you might be able to find a decent place at the walk-in sites if you arrive early. For more information, contact the Department of Parks and Recreation, Mendocino Area (Box 440, Mendocino 95460, tel. 707/937–5804).

After leaving Fort Bragg, Route 1 hugs the coast for another 25 miles before turning inward near **Rockport** and snaking around the **King Range,** a stretch of rugged mountains that the road builders found impassable. The coastal area to the north of Rockport and south of Eureka is generally referred to as the Lost Coast (*see* U.S. 101, *below*). From Rockport, Route 1 goes northeast for 17 miles to **Leggett** on U.S. 101, deep into the heart of redwood country.

● ● ● OUTDOOR ACTIVITIES

ABALONE DIVING Abalone diving is great along the coast, and **Mendocino Coast Adventures** (tel. 707/937–1703) offers local dives daily from June to September, as well as rafting trips on local rivers.

FISHING

MENDOCINO COAST Surf fishing is popular at beaches up and down the coast and any of the local bait and tackle shops can advise you on where to go and what bait to use. Try **Coast to Coast** (300 N. Main St., Fort Bragg, tel. 707/964–2318) or **Noyo Fishing Center** (32450 N. Harbor Dr., Noyo Harbor, tel. 707/964–7840). For deep-sea fishing, try **Matlick's Tally-Ho** (1184 N. Main St., Fort Bragg, tel. 707/964–2079).

SONOMA COAST Sportfishing is very popular in **Bodega Bay,** and there are plenty of charter services ready to take you out in the bay. You can also rent your own skiff, but be sure not to power yourself beyond the mouth of the bay; sneaker waves have killed many people in small boats. Several charter services also offer **whale-watching trips** from January to April. For a friendly charter try the **Boat House** (1445 Rte. 1, tel. 707/823–5786) with daily outings for salmon and rock cod on 55- and 65-foot modern fiberglass vessels.

RAFTING AND CANOEING

MENDOCINO COUNTY **Mendocino Coast Adventures** (Box 1930, Mendocino 95460, tel. 707/937–1703) arranges rafting trips on local rivers, including the Navarro and the Eel. The rivers meander through the thickly forested coastal mountains and wide-open valleys before spilling into the ocean. Depending on the time of year, drought conditions, and your own level of experience, you can have a relaxing float or an intense shoot through rapids. The **Navarro River,** just south of Albion, is good for relaxed, do-it-yourself kayaking and canoeing. Access to the mouth of the river is easy and free, but you'll have to bring your own equipment.

RUSSIAN RIVER Though **Johnson's Beach** in downtown Guerneville is packed solid on summer weekends, during the week you can park for free, rent canoes ($5/hour, $10/day), and paddle lazily up and down the river, stopping to sunbathe at several spots along the way. **Burke's Canoe Trips** (tel. 707/887–1222) in nearby Forestville offers guided half-day canoe trips that are well worth the minimum $30 cost.

WHALE WATCHING From December through March, California gray whales pass the California coast on their annual migration from the Arctic Ocean and Bering Sea to Baja California (and you thought the logging trucks on Route 1 were bad!). Not only can you spot some of the whales as they pass, but you can learn about them from nature talks at **Mendocino Headlands State Park** and **Mackerricher State Park** on Saturday and Sunday at 10 AM in season, or any day during the Mendocino/Fort Bragg Whale Celebration Weeks in March. For more information, contact the Department of Parks and Recreation, Mendocino Area (Box 440, Mendocino 95460, tel. 707/937–5804 or 707/964–9112).

U.S. 101

Once you're north of Santa Rosa (see The Wine Country in Chapter 3, San Francisco Bay Area), California seems to unfold into a more natural, peaceful place. This is where you begin to leave the crowds behind, where the land starts to open up and you find yourself among dilapidated barns, 19th-century vineyards, old loggers' taverns, and redwood trees more than 1,500 years old.

While Route 1 follows the coast north of San Francisco, U.S. 101 takes the inland route, passing through the Wine Country and the Russian River before rejoining Route 1 at Leggett. From here, the road skirts the **Lost Coast,** a region so rugged that the state gave up attempts to extend Route 1 along the shoreline. Just south of **Eureka,** the most populous town on the North Coast, U.S. 101 meets the Pacific again for the first time since crossing the Golden Gate Bridge 280 miles to the south. Past **Eureka** and the nearby college town of **Arcata** (home of Humboldt State University), there are still more than 100 miles of dramatic coastline and tremendous redwood forests before U.S. 101 passes into **Oregon** on its way to the Olympic Peninsula in **Washington** state.

The towns along U.S. 101—**Cloverdale, Hopland, Willits, Leggett, Garberville**—were stagecoach stops over a hundred years ago, and still retain a bit of their pioneer spirit. People with strong ties to the left and the environmental movement have been relocating here since the '60s, and their presence is widely felt. A case in point is the quaint one-street town of **Boonville,** halfway between Ukiah and the Pacific in the center of Anderson Valley (on Rte. 253). Like small towns everywhere, it has a few markets and restaurants. The tip-off that you're not in an average American small town is the presence of a comfortable brew pub, the **Buckhorn Saloon,** offering home-brewed ales. More surprising still is the town's continued support of the local **Anderson Valley Advertiser,** a radical, independent newspaper that takes on issues ranging from local pot raids to international politics and, notwithstanding its shoestring budget, manages to attract top leftist contributors like Alexander Cockburn, who also writes for *The Nation.* Now *that's* northern California!

For the first hundred miles or so, U.S. 101 follows the path of the **Russian River,** rolling toward the sea from **Lake Mendocino,** and most of the points of greatest interest are off the main highway. East of Cloverdale are a number of geysers and health resorts. Stop by the *très* New Age **Harbin Hot Springs** for nude sunbathing and meditation, or the **Hopland**

Brewery for some of the best microbrewed beer in California. Also to the east is peaceful **Clear Lake,** an ideal spot for languorous lakeside activity. From **Ukiah** on, state parks and forests, both east and west of the highway, offer a dazzling array of camping options, some in very isolated spots.

After joining Route 1 at Leggett, U.S. 101 begins to wind through stunning redwood forests, where you can camp among some of the oldest living things on earth. Starting just south of Garberville, the highway follows the course of the **Eel River,** great for fishing. To the west is the **Lost Coast** and the stunning, isolated **Sinkyone Wilderness** where the redwoods meet the sea. The drive between **Arcata** and **Crescent City** is dominated by the massive and spectacular **Redwood National Park.** Here you'll find the world's tallest trees (the tallest redwood in **Tall Tree Grove** was last measured at 367 feet), as well as the rare Roosevelt elk and thousands of other species of plants and animals rarely seen elsewhere. The 80-mile stretch of road winds between the windswept shoreline, lovely deserted beaches, rugged forests, and several of the state's finest parks. It's a great swath of wilderness, and one of the few such places in the state that haven't been overrun by crowds.

● ● ● BASICS

TOURIST INFORMATION

UKIAH The **Greater Ukiah Chamber of Commerce** puts out a yearly tourist tabloid brochure in July (distributed in the *Ukiah Daily Journal* around July 15 and on request throughout the year) with comprehensive listings of motels, restaurants, and attractions in the Ukiah area. The office also has brochures to help you plan excursions. *495-E Perkins St., ½ mi west of the freeway exit, tel. 707/462–4705. Open Mon.–Sat.10–5.*

CLEAR LAKE AND LAKE COUNTY The **Lake County Visitor Information Center,** located on a hill overlooking Clear Lake, has loads of information on everything from bird-watching to boat rentals; if the staff doesn't know the answer to a question, they'll find out for you. They also have information about nearby **Mendocino National Forest.** *875 Lakeport Blvd., just off Rte. 29, Lakeport, tel. 707/263–9544. Open Mon.–Sat. 10–5.*

EUREKA **Eureka/Humboldt County Convention and Visitors Bureau** (1034 2nd St., tel. 707/443–5097 or 800/338–7352) has brochures on where to stay and what to do in Eureka and Humboldt County. Their yearly guide *Eureka! Come and Find It...* is available at the office.

Eureka Chamber of Commerce (2112 Broadway, tel. 707/442–3738) provides good walking-tour maps and the opportunity to talk with knowledgeable locals.

CRESCENT CITY **The Crescent City–Del Norte Chamber of Commerce** (1001 Front St., off U.S. 101, tel. 707/646–3174) provides detailed maps of Crescent City.

● ● ● WHERE TO SLEEP

For the most part, lodging options along U.S. 101 are limited to standard American motels in the $30–$40 range, and some lovely bed-and-breakfasts which, unfortunately, usually cost twice that much. The possibilities for camping, though, are nearly infinite, ranging from full-service RV campgrounds to family-oriented state parks and more remote hike-in sites. Between Willits and Leggett, south of Garberville on U.S. 101, are plenty of private campgrounds for recreational vehicles. Once you pass north of Leggett, you're better off in one of the many state parks scattered along the Eel River, most of which are set among groves of virgin or second-growth redwoods and Douglas firs (*see* Exploring U.S. 101, *below*). Be warned, though: It's hard to prepare for the weather along the coast and in the coastal mountains—surprise rains and even hail are common from fall to spring, and mist and fog are completely normal even in summer, especially along the coast. Luckily, the region's two hostels are both beautifully located, one in Mendocino National Forest and one in Redwood National Park. Information about many of the area's other campgrounds is included in the Exploring U.S. 1 section, *below.*

ARCATA Arcata doesn't have much in the way of accommodations, and your best bet is to stay in Eureka or head for the campgrounds to the north. Locals are known to invite travelers back to their homes, though this is not the most reliable plan. Several motels are north of town on U.S. 101 at Janes Road. As always, **Motel 6** (4975 Valley West Blvd., tel. 707/822–7061) is one of the cheapest, with rooms starting at $34. The **Coast Inn** (4975 Valley West Blvd., tel. 707/822–4861) is also a good deal, with rates starting at $44.

If you can muster the money, consider staying in the stately old **Hotel Arcata** (700 9th St., tel. 707/826–0217) right on the plaza, where rooms start at $70 in the summer, and $55 other times of the year. Many rooms feature views of the plaza and all have TV, beautiful wood furniture, and antique tubs. The hotel was renovated several years ago and recently opened under new management. It also has a fine restaurant serving breakfast, lunch, and dinner, and a full service bar.

CLEAR LAKE AND LAKE COUNTY Don't even bother with motels: This is an outdoors paradise with relatively mild temperatures year-round that can best be appreciated with a tent and a sleeping bag. If you're determined to sleep indoors, consider staying at one of the several natural hot springs in the Ukiah area (*see* Harbin Hot Springs in Exploring U.S. 101, *below*). Prices at the standard motels along U.S. 101 can be quite steep in the summer, but are substantially less at other times of the year.

CAMPING **Clear Lake State Park.** Set on 500 acres on the western edge of the lake near Soda Bay, Clear Lake State Park has meadows, forests, a rocky beach, and a grungy looking slough that rangers say is one of the best fishing spots around the lake. The park has 147 sites, and if you get there early you can pick from campgrounds in the meadow, near the water, or on the bluff overlooking Soda Bay, where hot springs surface on an off-shore island. There are also several hiking trails, including one that takes you on a self-guided tour of herbs and plants used by the native Pomo tribe. Though **Clear Lake State Park** fills up fast, there is no shortage of private campgrounds around the Lake, as well as cheap rustic camping on nearby rivers and in the **Mendocino National Forest** nearby. *3½ mi northeast of Kelseyville on Rte. 53, tel. 707/279–4293. Reservations advised 8 weeks in advance during summer.*

Indian Valley Reservoir. The sparse, treeless campsite is about 20 miles east of Clear Lake on Route 20. The land bakes all summer, but wildflowers bloom amazingly from cracks in the granite and the reservoir is a quiet place for rugged camping and trout fishing. A store near the dam at the south end of the lake sells some supplies, but bring enough to tide you over as the store often runs low. *From Rte. 20, follow the dirt Walker Ridge Rd. to the dam. Camping is $5, no reservations needed. Campsites include fire pits.*

CRESCENT CITY Several reasonably inexpensive motels ($30–$35) are strung out along the highway in **Crescent City**—try the **Motel Trees** (15495 South Klamath Blvd., tel. 707/482–3152) with a tennis court and movies for about $34, or the more down-at-the-heels **Totem Motel** (1055 U.S. 101, tel. 707/464–7312) for about $25.

EUREKA Eureka has a wide range of reasonably priced lodgings catering to everyday people and families. Motels are concentrated on Broadway and Fourth Street near U.S. 101. Most are little more than noisy (but clean) places to crash: For the money they can't be beat. On the south entrance to Eureka along Broadway, try **Ranch Motel** (2109 Broadway, tel. 707/443–6751) or **The National 9 Inn** (2846 Broadway, tel. 707/443–9381). Single rooms at both cost around $30. Closer to Old Town along Fourth Street, **Christie's Motel** (1420 4th St., tel. 707/444–3011) and the **Townhouse Motel** (4th and K Sts., tel. 707/443–4536) offer comparable rooms for comparable prices.

A little nicer and a little pricier than your average motel is the **Royal Pacific Lodge** (1304 4th St. at N St., tel. 707/443–3193), with large, comfortable rooms, cable TV, an indoor heated pool, Jacuzzi, and sauna. Prices range $65–$89 in the summer, $42–$58 in the off-season. Eureka is also the home of many elegant, and accordingly expensive, bed-and-breakfasts, to which the Chamber of Commerce will be happy to direct you.

GARBERVILLE Garberville is a convenient stopping point if you're heading north to Eureka or west to the Lost Coast, and there are a number of relatively cheap, relatively generic motels in town. The comfortable, roomy **Motel Garberville** has singles going for around $46 and doubles for $52 during the summer—one of the best bargains in town. Prices are less off-season ($38 for a single, $42 for a double). *948 Redwood Dr., tel. 707/923–2422.*

HEALDSBURG **Lake Sonoma,** near Geyserville between Healdsburg and Ukiah, is a good place to pitch a tent or just stop for a swim. Since this manmade recreation area first opened in 1984, it's become a favorite spot for fishing, boating, hiking, and horseback riding. There are drive-in campsites, or you can camp at a primitive site by the lake. *Lake Sonoma Recreation Area, 3333 Skaggs Spring Rd., Geyserville, tel. 707/433–9483.*

THE LOST COAST For every cheap motel in Garberville, there's a pricey bed-and-breakfast in Ferndale. All of the lodging is expensive in Ferndale. Unless you're set on a night of luxury, either camp or push on to Garberville or Eureka—you can eat breakfast for weeks on what you'll save.

If you can afford luxury and want to act out your favorite Hansel and Gretel fantasy, try **The Gingerbread Mansion,** a lavish bed-and-breakfast in Ferndale. After being used for everything from a hospital to an American Legion Hall, the mansion was "Victorianized" into its present form in 1981. The two parlors, dining room, and each of the nine suites (from $75–$135, but less in the winter) are exquisitely decorated, very formal, and a bit stuffy. Tea and cake is served between 4 PM and 6 PM, your bed sheets are pulled back for you, and chocolates placed on the nightstand. Those with a low tolerance for being pampered won't be comfortable here, but it's free to admire it from the outside. *500 Berding St., Ferndale, tel. 707/786–4000. Reservations are suggested 8 weeks in advance for summer weekends.*

CAMPING **Sinkyone Wilderness State Park.** The best primitive back-country camping in the Lost Coast is in Sinkyone. Stop at the **Needle Rock Visitor Center** (tel. 707/986–7711), an old ranch house, to check in and figure out the best camping area. In case of foul weather, you can rent a room here for $14 and try camping in the Great Indoors. To reach Sinkyone Wilderness State Park, take the Briceland-Whitehorn Road from Garberville through Whitehorn to Four Corners, where you head west on a rough unpaved road for 2½ miles to the ranch house. All the campsites are short (¼–½ miles) walk-ins. The only drive-in campsites are at **Usal Beach** to the south, 3 miles north of Rockport off Route 1 (take the rugged and unpaved County Road 431 for 6 miles). The campgrounds at **Jones Beach** and **Needle Rock** are close to the ranger station and good for beachcombing. **Bear Harbor,** at the trailhead of the Lost Coast Trail, is not much frequented except by wild elk, who often bed down in the meadows next to the beach.

More-developed and less-scenic campsites, operated by the Bureau of Land Management (555 Leslie St., Ukiah, tel. 707/462–3873), are available at **Wailaki Camp** and **Wadelos Camp** at the foot of Chemise Mountain near Shelter Cove. The hour-long hike to the top of the mountain will reward you with a view of the entire Lost Coast.

For all campsites bring water or boil stream water before drinking. Firewood (driftwood) can be gathered at *some* beaches; pit toilets, picnic tables, and fire pits are provided. Store food in airtight bags and hang them in trees at night to prevent bears from getting at your necessities.

MENDOCINO NATIONAL FOREST **Eel River Redwoods AYH-Hostel.** Located 2 miles north of Leggett on U.S. 101 in Mendocino National Forest, this is one of the most beautiful hostels in California. You'll feel like a first-class vacationer here, no matter how tight your budget: Beds are $10 for AYH members, $11 for non-members. Set on a stretch of the Eel River, the wooded, 10-acre facility has a 15-foot, warm-water swimming hole and dorm space for 43, including four beds in an outdoor tepee. Also on the premises are several bed-and-breakfast cottages that aren't part of the hostel. Owner Gene Barnett, a former aerospace engineer who bought the hostel in 1985, opens a pub in the evenings and trades travel stories with the many foreign travelers who pass through on foot, by bus, car, bike, and motorcycle. At the center of the grounds is a pond with a gazebo, surrounded by a rose garden. A bed in the hostel also entitles you to free use of bikes, innertubes for the river, and a well-equipped kitchen. Though the hostel fills up quickly on weekends, Barnett has been known to find room for just one more weary traveler. *70400 South U.S. 101, Leggett, tel. 707/925–6469. $1 sheet rental. Reservations advised 2 weeks in advance. Not wheelchair accessible.*

CAMPING **Lake Pillsbury.** This isolated lake in the southern part of Mendocino National Forest is a lush, cool getaway for summer campers craving peace and quiet. Fishing is good both in the lake and in the Eel River drainage to the west. Try **Oak Flat Campground** for free sites or the more developed nearby **Sunset Campground** ($5), both right on the water. Recreational vehicles should stay off the narrow, winding, rough road that leads to the lake, and all drivers should proceed slowly with an eye out for deer, snakes, and doughboys crossing the road. *From Rte. 20, take the road to Potter Valley. For information about reservations and recreational activities, contact Mendocino National Forest Headquarters, 420 E. Laurel St., Willows 94988, tel. 916/934–3316.*

SCOTIA **The Scotia Inn.** Pacific Lumber considered tearing down this elegant hotel, built in 1922, but instead leased it to Gerald Carley in 1985 for renovation. Rooms are filled with antiques, and the bathrooms feature large porcelain bathtubs. Carley has preserved the hotel's stately charm and renovated the formal dining room, where dinner is served Wednesday through Sunday evenings. The pub downstairs is open nightly. Singles start at $55, but the rates, which include Continental breakfast, go up in summer. *Corner of Main and Mill Sts., tel. 707/764–5683. Reservations advised on weekends. Not wheelchair accessible.*

UKIAH If you're not up to camping at nearby Cow Mountain or Lake Mendocino, Ukiah offers a fairly wide range of choices. Most of the low-rate motels are clustered along State Street. **The Cottage Inn** (755 S. State St., tel. 707/462–8509) has double units with kitchens for about $32. The motel is clean and simple with TVs and a swimming pool. Nearby, **The Lantern Inn** (650 S. State, tel. 707/462–6601) has double rooms for around $38.

For a relaxing splurge, you could do worse than checking into **Vichy Springs,** a spa that was purportedly Jack London's favorite retreat. The 12 rooms have patios and are finely appointed with antiques. Best of all, a large swimming pool, eight warm-water outdoor tubs, and a 24-hour Jacuzzi are filled with water from a spring reputed by Native Americans to heal physical ailments ranging from poison oak to arthritis. Massage is also available. Most folks use the pools as a stress-release for city pressures and the resort is popular with families and couples from the Bay Area. Rooms start at $75, private cottages cost $140, and breakfast is provided. *2605 Vichy Springs Rd., Ukiah, tel. 707/462–9515.*

CAMPING **Cow Mountain Area.** The area is run by the Bureau of Land Management, which provides trail maps and information about the four campgrounds with 34 sites, water, and pit toilets (*see* Exploring U.S. 101, *below*). *BLM Headquarters, 555 Leslie St., Ukiah, tel. 707/462–3873. 4 campgrounds, 34 sites with water, pit toilet.*

Lake Mendocino. The most accessible camping near Ukiah is in the rugged wilderness near Lake Mendocino, popular with families, jet-skiers, and anglers after striped bass, crappie, bluegill, and perch. The 300 first-come, first-served sites cost around $10 per night. *1160 Lake Mendocino Dr. at N. State St., tel. 707/462–7581. From U.S. 101 north of Ukiah, take Rte. 20 east 2 mi to Marina Drive.*

REDWOOD NATIONAL PARK

HOSTEL **Redwood AYH-Hostel.** Perched high above the ocean in Redwood National Park, this turn-of-the-century logger's mansion is a great base from which to explore the beaches and mountains of the park. Open since 1987, it's clean, with new furniture, a well-equipped kitchen (separate stoves for vegetarian and meat cookers) and two showers. It has more rules than most California hostels and closes during the day, but the atmosphere is friendly. In the evening, guests gather for conversation on the redwood deck or around the wood-burning stove in the living room. Reservations suggested in summer.

14480 U.S. 101, Klamath, tel. 707/482–8265. $8 per person, $1 sheet rental. 11 PM curfew, no smoking, kitchen.

CAMPING *See* Exploring U.S. 101, *below.*

FOOD

ARCATA Arcata has a wide range of inexpensive restaurants catering to the student community. **Los Bagels** (1061 I St., tel. 707/822–3150) is something of an Arcata institution, with outdoor tables, reggae music on the stereo, and a basketball court in back. Expect to see lots of students. At **Casa de Que Pasa** (854 9th St., tel. 707/822–3441), you can get decent chili rellenos and vegetarian burritos (about $5.50) or just have some nachos ($3.50) and a beer. Regardless of when you were born, you can greet the rising sun at the **Gemini Café** (854 9th St., tel. 707/822–3223) with good breakfast specials ($3–$6) and espresso.

If you're passing through town on your way to camp up north, stop by the **Co-Op Food Store** (corner of 8th and I Sts., tel. 707/822–5947) for its great bakery and excellent selection of produce, cheeses, bulk foods, and locally produced tofu. The Co-Op is open most evenings until 9.

CLEAR LAKE Considering that most of the restaurants around the lake cater to tourists, there are a surprising number of places where you can eat cheaply and well, especially in **Lakeport.** In good weather, pull up a chair on the outside deck of one of Lakeport's several lakeside hangouts.

UNDER $5 **Cottage Coffee Shop.** This pleasant indoor-outdoor café serves nourishing home-cooking of the bland variety. Still, the friendly waitresses treat everyone like regular customers. With a little Tabasco sauce, the Spanish omelet ($5) hits the spot for breakfast, and the $3 chicken-salad sandwich will keep you going until dinner. The coffee shop opens at 5 AM to serve local fishermen and campers who can't bear another meal in the wild. *1090 North Main St., Lakeport, tel. 707/263–5071.*

UNDER $10 **Park Place.** Perhaps the lake's most popular restaurant, Park Place serves Italian food in a "California cuisine" format. The pasta is made fresh daily, and the restaurant serves lots of meatless dishes, a great Mediterranean salad ($6.50), and good local beer and wine. Best of all is the restaurant's lakeside location. Sitting on the open-air deck at sunset, you have a great view of huge, colorful birds fishing for their dinners. If you're in a boat, you can dock right in front of the restaurant. *50 3rd St., tel. 707/263–0444. Next to Library Park on the lake in downtown Lakeport. Open daily 11–10:30. Wheelchair accessible indoors only.*

EUREKA The restaurants here aren't as trendy and health-conscious as those in nearby Arcata, but you should have no difficulty finding something to suit your taste and budget among Eureka's fish grottos, coffeehouses, diners, and home-style Italian restaurants. A walk through Old Town will give you a wide range of options, and restaurants in areas less frequented by tourists are even more reasonably priced.

UNDER $10 **Eureka Seafood Grotto.** The Grotto's no-frills but delicious seafood lunches and dinners have made it one of Eureka's best-loved restaurants among locals and tourists alike. Sit down to the tasty oyster stew ($6) or a healthy crab meat sandwich ($9), or just stop in for a pint of clam chowder to go ($2). *605 Broadway, tel. 707/443–2075. Open Mon.–Sat. 11–10, Sun. noon–9. Wheelchair accessible.*

Lost Coast Brewery. With beer brewed on the premises and good food, this relatively new establishment looks like it may wind up being a Eureka landmark. The rustic restaurant has hardwood floors and live acoustic music several nights a week, and serves hearty sandwiches, chili, and great Cajun stew ($8.50). *617 4th St., tel. 707/445–4480. Kitchen and bar open daily 11–10. Bar open weekends until midnight or later. Wheelchair accessible.*

Samoa Cookhouse. Because cutting trees is very hard labor, logging companies prudently used to supply loggers with lots of fresh, nourishing food. Across the bridge at the north end of town in Samoa (a five-minute drive), the last bona fide lumberman's cookhouse still serving three hearty meals a day. These days the cookhouse is a stop for tour buses, but that hasn't changed the policy of good, plentiful food. Take your seat at one of the hundred or so long redwood tables, and enjoy an all-you-can-eat meal consisting of soup (one huge bowl per table), salad, vegetables, bread, an entrée, and dessert. The menu changes daily. Lunches are around $6; dinners are slightly more expensive. Expect to wait for a place on summer weekends. *445 W. Washington St., on Samoa Peninsula, tel. 707/442–1659. Take Samoa Bridge to the west and follow the signs. Open Mon.–Sat. 6 AM–10 PM.*

GARBERVILLE Given the general division of the Garberville citizenry into two camps, it's hardly surprising that half the restaurants cater to ethereal health-food enthusiasts and the other half to loggers looking for a meat-and-potatoes kind of meal. If you think the loggers have the right idea, try the **Plaza Café** (770 Redwood Dr.), where a plate of pork chops and apple sauce with soup, potatoes, vegetables, and dessert costs around $7. Right across the street is the **Woodrose Café** (911 Redwood Dr., tel. 707/923–3191), where pretty much everyone shows up for breakfast and lunch. The Woodrose serves huge omelettes, bowls of oatmeal, and lunch sandwiches starting at $3.50. If none of this is rarefied enough for your tastes, you can assemble your own meal from the wide selection of organic fruits, juices, and other healthful foods at the **Chataqua Market** (436 Church St., tel. 707/923–2452).

THE LOST COAST Apart from a few places to eat in Ferndale, the only restaurants in the Lost Coast are a couple of pricey seafood joints in the growing retirement community of Shelter Cove. If you're planning anything longer than a day trip, bring your own food and cooking supplies. The **Petrolia General Store** on the Petrolia Road usually has a good supply of fresh local seafood—the salmon, prawns, and oysters are all excellent. **The Honeydew General Store** on the Honeydew Road has a decent selection of vegetables, breads, and drinks. The porch outside is a great place to sit and pet neighborhood dogs (and billy goats) and talk to the locals. It'll help you get a sense of what it's like to live out here, so close to the main highway but so far from life in the fast lane.

UKIAH Don't bother with the fast-food chains near U.S. 101. If you're willing to take the time to head downtown, you'll find that Ukiah has some decent and reasonably priced restaurants with menus that weren't planned by a corporation.

UNDER $5 **The Mutt Hutt.** The Hutt's on the busiest street in town and isn't exactly a charmer inside, but who can resist a restaurant that has both corn dogs and "bowl of grains" on the menu? Other dishes are bizarre culinary mongrels in their own right: for example, a baked potato stuffed with mushrooms, carrots, broccoli, and cauliflower; or the burrito filled with rice, grains, tofu, sprouts, and avocado (both around $4). The unadventurous can enjoy a simple sandwich or salad on the enclosed patio. *732 S. State St., tel. 707/468–5376. Open Mon.–Sat. 8 AM–9 PM. Wheelchair accessible.*

EXPLORING U.S. 101

From San Francisco, U.S. 101 crosses the Golden Gate Bridge and proceeds through Marin County and the Wine Country to **Santa Rosa** 57 miles to the north (*see* The Wine Country in Chapter 3, San Francisco Bay Area). From Santa Rosa, you can take Route 116 west to the resorts on the **Russian River**, eventually meeting Route 1 at **Jenner** on the Pacific (*see* Exploring Route 1, *above*), or continue north on U.S. 101 through the golden, rolling California hills, interspersed with vineyards and hot springs.

HEALDSBURG At Healdsburg, 14 miles north of Santa Rosa, the southward-moving Russian River crosses U.S. 101 for the last time before heading west to the ocean. In hot summer weather, this is a good place to stop for a quick dip. Get off U.S. 101 at the Central Healdsburg Avenue exit, make a right at Healdsburg Avenue, cross the bridge and park. You can even rent a canoe at **Bob's Rentals** (20 Healdsburg Ave., no phone).

The whole region around the central Russian River has long been home to Pomo and Wappo Native Americans, but the town is named after Ohio-born forty-niner Harmon Heald, who settled in what is now the town's central plaza in 1852. The redwood-lined plaza is a great place for a serene picnic or nap. Several nearby stores like the **Salame Tree Deli** (304 Center St., tel. 707/433–7224) stock a good selection of meats, cheeses, and dried and fresh fruits, many of which are locally grown.

Healdsburg has produced wine since the early 1900s, but only recently has it become a stop on tours of the wine country. Among the established wineries are **Simi** (16275 Healdsburg Ave., tel. 707/433–6981), **Clos Du Bois** (5 Fitch St., tel. 707/433–5576), and **Hop Kiln** (6050 Westside Rd., tel. 707/433–6491), known for its stone hop-drying house and excellent zinfandel.

Near Healdsburg, you can get a glimpse of the geysers that blow natural dry steam out of molten earth, used as a clean source of energy by the Pacific Gas and Electric Company. Take Dry Creek exit off U.S. 101, head north on Healdsburg Avenue and east on Alexander Valley Road. Go left onto Route 128 until you hit Geyser Road, which takes you 16 miles to Vista Point. North of Healdsburg and west of U.S. 101, **Lake Sonoma** is a good place to pitch a tent or just stop for a swim (*see* Camping under Where to Sleep in Healdsburg, *above*).

HARBIN HOT SPRINGS A real California treat, Harbin Hot Springs is a clothing-optional, 1,200-acre resort that's well worth the 38-mile detour from U.S. 101. Run by the Heart Consciousness Church, a New Age group that advocates holistic health and spiritual renewal, the resort has three natural mineral pools of varying temperatures and a cold stream-fed "plunge" pool. Sunbathers (mostly nude) relax on redwood decks by the pool, but that's only the beginning—there's also a massage school, a cozy restaurant (with vegetarian meals), nightly movies, and meditation groups. Anyone who wishes to visit must pay $5 for a one-month membership or $15 for a year. Dorm rooms start at $20 during the week, $32 on weekends; endless camping sites are available along the creek and in nearby meadows ($12 a week or $20 on weekends, per person). Despite the continuous round of events and programs, no one pressures you to do anything. If you're feeling adventurous, you can take off for a steep hike up one of the nearby ridges. *From U.S. 101 in Geyserville, take Rte. 128 east to Calistoga, then Rte. 29 north to Middleton. At the stop light, turn left, then right at Barnes St., go for 4 mi. For reservations call 707/987–2477. Greyhound travels daily from San Francisco to Middletown, where a ride to Harbin can be arranged.*

HOPLAND BREWERY It's off U.S. 101 in the middle of nowhere (about 45 miles north of Santa Rosa in the town of Hopland, to be precise), but the Hopland Brewery is one of the best-known "brew pubs" in California. On summer weekends, the beer garden is crowded with bicyclists coming down from Oregon, motorcyclists out for a ride in the country, and day-tripping Deadheads from the San Francisco Bay Area. Inside, the woodsy pub is decorated with beer-making equipment and local artifacts, including customers who might have had a few too many. Four types of beer are brewed on the premises: Peregrine Pale Ale, Blue Heron Pale Ale, Red Tail Ale, and Black Hawk Stout, in order of ascending potency. To give you strength to hoist another pint, there's a good selection of food, too, including oysters and sandwiches, of both the meaty and tofu varieties (around $6). The beer-sausage sandwich is a favorite. Blues bands entertain the crowd several nights a week, giving the maudlin an excuse to cry into their beers and everyone else an excuse to raise hell. *1335 U.S. 101, tel. 707/744–1015. Open in summer 11–11, Sat. 11–2* AM. *Winter hours are shorter.*

The loggers and activists may be in a longstanding, mostly unspoken feud over land use and lifestyle, but it's not uncommon to see them drinking next to each other at Ukiah bars. In fact, sometimes it's quite difficult to tell them apart.

UKIAH Thirteen miles north of Hopland is the sensible town of Ukiah. Originally a rough and rugged lumber town, in recent years Ukiah has become an agricultural center specializing in prunes, apples, and grapes. It's also one of the southernmost outposts of northern California's "green belt," a band of forest that stretches to Oregon and is the home of both loggers and the environmental activists who have been moving to the area since the '60s. Though it's no traveler's paradise, Ukiah is a good place to buy supplies or spend a last night in a bed before striking out for the rugged Mendocino coast to the west or Clear Lake, Cow Mountain, and Mendocino National Forest to the east.

COW MOUNTAIN East of Ukiah, the Cow Mountain area has 50,000 acres of steep chaparral-covered slopes—up to elevations of 4,000 feet—and small stands of fir, pine, and oak. The area attracts backwoods campers (*see* Camping, in Ukiah in Where to Sleep, *above*), but it's especially popular with hunters after deer, bear, and wild pig, so stick to one of the designated campgrounds if you insist on wearing your antler hat (if you do decide to stomp around the wilderness, do your best to find something bright to wear to distinguish yourself from the hunted beasts). No info about cows available at press time. *From Hopland on U.S. 101, take Rte. 175 to Scotts Valley Rd.; from Calpella on U.S. 101 north of Ukiah, take Rte. 20 east to Mill Creek Rd.; tel. 707/462–3873.*

CLEAR LAKE Lake Tahoe dangles traitorously into Nevada . . . and the Salton Sea was created by an engineering error. That makes **Clear Lake,** with over 100 miles of shoreline, the largest natural lake within the borders of California. It's also a great place for fishing and boating, and the centerpiece of watery **Lake County.** The northwestern shore of Clear Lake is about 30 miles east of U.S. 101 on Route 20, which eventually joins I–5 in Williams.

On a map, Clear Lake looks like it's been squeezed around the middle, so don't be surprised when locals direct you to places on "Upper Lake" (the northwestern part, where Lakeport is) or "Lower Lake" (the southeast). Once you turn off U.S. 101 to reach the lake (on Rte. 75 from Hopland or Rte. 20 north of Ukiah), you may feel as if you've stumbled into some mythical bucolic scene—say, in Minnesota. **Lakeport,** the town on the lake with the best services and most reasonable prices, is especially midwestern.

On warm summer evenings, long-time residents mingle with recent retirees in the downtown park along the lake, kids play hackysack in the gazebo, and weary travelers sip wine in nearby open-air cafés.

The lake is great for boating, water skiing, jet skiing, and even parasailing. If high-speed adventure isn't your forte, the fishing for crappie, catfish, and largemouth bass is good year-round, and there are plenty of quiet inlets wonderful for watching grebes, egrets, cormorants, and other birds. The truly sedentary can take their time admiring the view of Mt. Konocti, a volcano rising 4,200 feet above the southern part of the lake. Campgrounds are plentiful near Clear Lake and the other lakes and rivers of Lake County, including **Blue Lakes** on Route 20 and **Indian Valley Reservoir** on Walker Ridge Road off Route 20, both of which are popular with anglers (*see* Camping under Where to Sleep, Clear Lake and Lake County, *above*). With a map, a car, and a sense of adventure, you can find some of California's most beautiful scenery in Lake County, and avoid the crowds of tourists that flock to nearby Mendocino and Sonoma counties. For more information, contact Clear Lake State Park in Kelseyville (tel. 707/279–4293).

MENDOCINO NATIONAL FOREST East of U.S. 101 and directly north of Clear Lake on Route 20 is the southern edge of the huge Mendocino National Forest, which has mountains soaring to more than 7,000 feet, lots of lakes and rivers, and unspoiled wilderness ideal for a quiet retreat. Here you can fish, hike, and camp under pines, fir, and scrub oaks that remain green even in the heat of summer. Campgrounds range in price from free to around $5 per night, and you don't have to worry about crowds, reservations, or noise from recreational vehicles, as rough roads prevent all but the most determined Winnebago warriors. If you're up to navigating the rough 20-mile dirt road (closed much of the winter) that leads to **Lake Pillsbury,** you'll find marshy inlets great for trout-fishing and bird-watching, and plenty of tranquil sites for free camping (*see* Camping under Where to Sleep in Mendocino National Forest, *above*).

STANDISH-HICKEY STATE RECREATION AREA Beyond Ukiah, U.S. 101 moves into increasingly rugged land. From the logging town of Willits, 33 miles to the north, you can take the **Skunk Train** to **Fort Bragg** on the coast (*see* Exploring Route 1, *above*).

Approximately 50 miles north of Willits, U.S. 101 joins Route 1 at Leggett. This is redwood country. From here on all the way to Crescent City, you'll be faced with the choice of *which* stupendously beautiful grove of ancient (or second-growth) trees you want to visit.

First in line is the Standish-Hickey State Recreation Area, with plenty of areas for fishing and swimming in the South Fork of the Eel River, and several hiking trails, including the 3-mile **Lookout Trail** that climbs 1,600 feet above the river. First established in 1922 by Edward R. Hickey, the park expanded in 1956 when Miles Standish (no, not that Miles Standish) donated 512 acres of mostly second-growth redwoods to the Save-the-Redwoods League. Campers have a choice between 162 sites on three campgrounds, many with huge stone fireplaces and all with tables, food cupboards, and nearby bathrooms with hot showers. Across the highway from the campgrounds is a stand of virgin redwoods. *1 mi north of Leggett on U.S. 101, tel. 707/925–6482. Open all year.*

RICHARDSON GROVE STATE PARK When the cool ocean breezes meet the inland heat, the result is fog as thick as, yes, pea soup. On most mornings Richardson Grove State Park (tel. 707/946–2311), less than 20 miles north of Standish-Hickey and 7 miles south of Garberville, is socked in with the stuff, making for either a gloomy or a mystical stay, depending on your disposition. Besides the usual skunks, lizards, chipmunks, and deer, you can observe bats hunting for mosquitos on summer evenings, and occasionally catch a glimpse of black bears. The 170 family sites have fire rings, picnic tables, and food lockers. Hot showers and toilets are available. *See* Camping in Chapter 1, Basics, for information on camping in California state parks.

BENBOW LAKE Two miles south of Garberville on U.S. 101, the exposed, meadow-filled Benbow Lake Recreation Area (tel. 707/946–2311) has 75 family campsites, many on the shore of the lake. Benbow Lake is a popular swimming spot and also the site of the **Summer Arts Fair** and **Shakespeare at Benbow Lake** (tel. 707/923–3238) each summer.

GARBERVILLE Two hundred miles north of San Francisco and 65 miles south of Eureka, the much-beleaguered town of Garberville has seen logging, fishing, and marijuana booms go bust, and has managed to survive despite frequent periods of desperate economic depression. It was in this area in the '70s that backwoods botanists first produced world-famous *sinsemilla* (Spanish for "seedless") marijuana, and soon succeeded in turning a form of personal recreation into the basis of the local economy. That era began nearing its end in 1984 with the arrival of CAMP (Campaign Against Marijuana Planting) and Operation Greensweep—the federal government's domestic Grenada invasion. Since then, there have been no more outlandish harvest parties at local motels, the bars have emptied out, and the local travel agent, Astral Travel, has had to "go mail order" to make up for the revenue once garnered from pot growers who paid for exotic vacations with wads of hundred-dollar bills.

More than in perhaps any other California town, you can feel the tension here between loggers whose families have been in the area for generations and back-to-the-landers who moved here from the cities in the wake of the '60s. In the summer, the streets fill up with a lively mix of people and, for two days each August, thousands flock to the Eel River, just south of town, for **Reggae on the River,** maybe the best reggae festival in the world aside from Reggae Sunsplash in Jamaica.

In the spring of 1992, a massive earthquake hit the North Coast around Eureka and the Lost Coast. Several people were killed, houses slid off their foundations, and a huge shopping mall burned to the ground. Rescue operations were hampered by the sheer remoteness of the area, but we can only guess at the damage if the quake had hit in a major metropolitan area.

THE LOST COAST Because of the rugged terrain, the state of California abandoned hope of extending Route 1 along the Pacific between Rockport and Eureka, and now the whole region west of U.S. 101 between Leggett and Humboldt Bay goes by the name of the Lost Coast. It's true that, in California terms, lack of proximity to a major highway is ample reason for a place to be considered "lost," but this strange, isolated region earns its name in other ways, too. While other California coastal regions have been the sites of major building and development, the Lost Coast remains in a virtually pristine state. It's comparable in beauty to Big Sur, but not nearly so explored, since most tourists head to places that better accommodate their automobile addiction. Redwood trees perch on cliffs 200 feet above the rocky shores. Black-sand beaches give way to tide pools brimming with marine life. Black bears, mountain lions, and bald eagles thrive here; in most other areas of California they were killed off long ago. Hiking the beautiful **Lost Coast Trail** (*see* Outdoor Activities, *below*) or pitching a tent in the backcountry or on the beaches of **Sinkyone Wilderness State Park** (*see* Camping under Where to Sleep in The Lost Coast, *above*), you can feel like you're in another time as well as out of view of the nearest gas station.

The only way to enter the Lost Coast is from U.S. 101 at Garberville or Redway in the south, or Eureka in the north. **Greyhound** travels to Garberville (*see* Coming and Going by Bus, *above*), but there is no public transportation in the region itself. You'll need either a car with a strong engine, reliable brakes, and good tires, or a willingness to stick out your thumb (hitchhiking being a fairly reliable means of transport here). The Trails of the Lost Coast map put out by Sinkyone Wilderness State Park is the best guide to car and foot travel.

Only about 700 people live in the whole region, and many of them moved here as part of the late-'60s, early '70s hippie migration to northern California. This is one of the world's most celebrated pot-growing regions. As the price of a pound of quality pot rose from $200 to about $2,000 by 1980, the economic boom that hit the area was big enough to replace the prosperous timber industry that died out due to the clear-cutting practices of local loggers. During the '80s, huge pot farms sprang up all over the Lost Coast and an outrageous cash-crop economy paid for elaborate new ranch homes, BMWs, and exotic winter vacations. Locals remember that the economy was so flooded with hundred-dollar bills that the stores ran out of small change. So much for the hippie ethos. Since CAMP started weeding out pot crops all over California, with a major emphasis in Humboldt County, the once-proud pot farmers have become secretive and suspicious of outsiders. You may even feel uncomfortable with the suspicious glares you receive in some of the back-country towns: this is rural, "frontier" California.

The stories of gun-toting growers shooting at innocent hikers mistaken for garden raiders are largely false, but don't expect to hear anyone talking about marijuana on the porch of a small town market in the Lost Coast.

In addition to the natural beauty of the area, the entire town of **Ferndale** is a state historical landmark because of its Victorian homes and storefronts. Most of the Victorians were originally owned by wealthy dairy families and were either passed on unchanged from generation to generation or were preserved by city folks looking for a hideaway. It's a strange fairy-tale town, painted up pink, blue, and yellow, and—judging from pictures taken in the early part of the century—its look hasn't changed much at all. Instead of grain stores, open markets, and saloons, the town is now full of antiques shops, touristy boutiques, candy stores, and bookstores. There are several restaurants in town, but aside from the so-so (and overpriced) Mexican restaurant on Main Street, it's best to eat in Eureka. For a look at Ferndale's history, which began in 1852 when the first farmers arrived to use the lush pastures for dairy cattle, stop by the **Ferndale Museum.** *Corner of Shaw and 3rd Sts., tel. 707/786–4466. Admission: $1. Open Wed.–Sat. 11–4, Sun. 1–4. Closed in Jan.*

AVENUE OF THE GIANTS This 31-mile drive winds between the world's largest concentration of coastal redwoods—and, yes, they are giants. The road runs roughly parallel to U.S. 101 between Phillipsville, just a few miles north of Garberville, and Pepperwood. Many of the groves of redwood are up to 1,500 years old—you remember, when Justinian was emperor—and are named after individuals and organizations who donated money to protect them. With luck, the trees will still be standing long after their names are forgotten.

Part of the Avenue of the Giants runs through **Humboldt Redwoods State Park**, where you can hike along trails, fish in the Eel River, and camp. It's amazing that this large park of spectacular redwood forests isn't nearly as crowded as Yosemite. There are 244 campsites spread out along the Avenue of the Giants, and campers should pick up a map at the

Visitors Center between Myers Flat and Weott. All campgrounds have running water and toilets, tables, and fire rings, and the setting is like nowhere else on earth.

You could easily keep yourself busy and amazed here for weeks without ever visiting such predictable tourist traps as **Confusion Hill,** where water appears to flow uphill, and the schlocky shops that sell redwood carvings and slabs of burl. Take a self-guided tour of **Founders Grove** and visit the **Dyerville Giant,** which fell down in March 1991. At 362 feet, it was the fourth-tallest tree in the world when it was last measured in 1972, and some believe it surpassed the 367-foot record before it toppled. Also, don't miss the **Rockefeller Forest**—almost 13,000 acres of breathtaking virgin redwoods, with many trails through the grove. If you feel the need for further convincing that these trees are huge, you can visit the **One Log House** or the **Drive-Thru Tree,** both of which live up to their names if not the splendor of their surroundings.

Even if you can't stay amid the redwoods for more than an afternoon, pack a lunch and make your way to the stand of 300-foot trees, it shouldn't be missed. Sure you're a puny mortal, but life... life is sublime. Take U.S. 101 to Avenue of the Giants, at the Phillipsville exit. For maps and information about camping and other activities, contact the Visitor Center in Weott, near the Burlington Campground (tel. 707/946–2263).

SCOTIA Just a few miles north of Avenue of the Giants and looking like a movie set is **Scotia,** a town that has been completely owned by **Pacific Lumber Company** since 1869. Taking the role of Big Brother, Pacific Lumber runs the churches, the school, and the medical clinic. It provides housing for 270 families and leases space in the town shopping center to privately operated businesses. The largest lumber mill in the United States, Pacific Lumber sprawls from one end of town to the other and blows its whistles twice at the beginning of the work day and twice at the end. The effect is eerie, but the town's close-knit residents don't seem to mind. The mill offers a self-guided tour that's worthwhile for even the most staunch opponent of lumber companies. You see the logs unloaded from trucks, moved through the log pond, stripped of bark with hydro-jets and whittled into usable lumber—in short, the whole process. All along the tour are explanation cards with pro-timber industry information designed to sway visitors to the "jobs first" school of thought and promote the idea that Pacific Lumber is a redwood's best friend. Passes for the hour-long tour can be obtained at the **Scotia Museum** (tel. 707/764–2222, ext. 247) near the center of town. Look across the street at the old **Cinema,** a spectacular 1930s movie house owned and operated by . . . well, it ain't the Lorax.

FORTUNA Fortuna is another old logging town, but without the neat and tidy appearance of the planned community of Scotia, 8 miles to the south. After all that law and order, you may be just in the mood for Fortuna's ramshackle Victorian storefronts and several taverns, where thirsty Scotians come to drink out of earshot of the factory whistle. Be prepared for lots of proudly waving American flags and signs on shops announcing "We support the timber industry."

EUREKA Seven miles north of Fortuna and about 280 miles north of the San Francisco Bay, U.S. 101 returns to the coast at Humboldt Bay, and arrives at Eureka, the most populous city on the north coast. When whaler James T. Ryan in 1807 screamed "Eureka!" (Greek for "I've found it!") upon finding his way through the narrow entrance to the bay, he succeeded in giving the future state of California its motto, but failed to be the first European-American on the premises. That distinction belonged to Russian sailors who had taken a brief peek at the largest natural bay north of San Francisco the year before. Later, the gold miners of 1849 traveled here to search the Trinity River for gold, but Eureka's distinction came as a whaling and logging town, and as a Native American lookout post where soldiers were known to go crazy with boredom. In fact, it was in **Fort Humboldt** (3431 Fort Ave., tel. 707/443–7952) that pre–Civil War Ulysses S. Grant's drinking escalated to the point that he quit his post and returned to the Midwest to become a farmer. (Besides a display of early logging equipment and some nice views, there's not a whole lot to see in the fort today; a six-month stay there could probably *still* make the inside of a bottle look appealing.)

Eurekans have a proud sense of local history, and have impeccably preserved some of the state's finest Victorian homes and storefronts. In the last decade, the city's once seedy waterfront district has been transformed into **Old Town** (1st, 2nd, and 3rd Sts. between C and M Sts., tel. 707/442–3738), a neighborhood of gentrified homes, boutiques, restaurants, antiques stores, and craft shops. A walk through Old Town will give you a good sense of where Eureka's been and where it's headed. Maps and free guide books for walking tours are available at the Eureka Chamber of Commerce (*see* Tourist Information, *above*).

For a more in-depth view of Eureka, head to the fascinating **Clarke Memorial Museum,** housed in a marble and granite edifice that used to be the Bank of Eureka. The building was purchased by local high-school teacher and historian Cecilia Clarke in 1959 and operates now as a privately funded non-profit organization. As the museum brochure says, "the history of Humboldt County is the history of the working man," and this work ethic is vividly expressed in the museum's many displays, ranging from Native American baskets and deer-hide clothes to the trade tools of rugged outdoorsmen who came west to hunt bear and elk for profit. *240 E St., Eureka, tel. 707/443–1947. Open Tues.–Sat. noon–4.*

Walk all the way north on Second Street to glimpse the amazingly green **Carson Mansion** (near the corner of 2nd and M Sts.), one of the most ornate Victorian homes you'll ever see, where lumber baron William Carson once looked down over his sprawling mill. You can't go inside, because today it's an exclusive, all-male club, but the outside view is impressive. A less-sanitized version of old Eureka can be found along First Street, in the form of sea-weathered winos and collapsing warehouses.

If you have the time and the fare, head to the pier at the foot of C Street downtown and board the *Madaket* for the **Humboldt Bay Harbor Cruise** (tel. 707/445–1910; or call the Humboldt Bay Maritime Museum at 707/444–9440). This isn't your typical harbor cruise, thanks largely to *Madaket's* skipper, Leroy Zerlang, a Eureka native and tour guide for 17 years. Zerlang gives you a fascinating look at the history of Humboldt Bay, complete with amusing anecdotes. From the decks of the *Madaket*, which has been in continuous operation since 1910, you can see harbor seals, Canadian geese, cormorants, lumber mills, and shipwrecks. The *Madaket* sails daily in summer; after October 15 you may have to arrange a charter. Fare for adults is $8.50.

Eureka has an airport (*see* Coming and Going at the beginning of the chapter) and a wide assortment of relatively cheap restaurants and lodgings. **Eureka Transit Service** (133 U St., tel. 707/443–0826) buses serve the town of Eureka from 6 AM to 6 PM (50¢ fare) and make trips to Arcata and back roughly once an hour ($1).

ARCATA Eight miles north of Eureka and surrounded by trees is beautiful Arcata, the kind of town that makes you feel instantly at home. Most shops, restaurants, and services are within easy walking distance of the town's grassy central plaza, where you can get perhaps the world's only tofu hot dog from a stand and listen to street musicians who are often quite good. Just outside town, **Cal State Humboldt** (Plaza Ave. off L.K. Wood Blvd., tel. 707/826–4402) has a deserved reputation as a hotbed of environmentalism, and has attracted a lot of students interested in alternative lifestyles.

Smiles and hellos are exchanged routinely on the streets, and seem quite sincere, if occasionally pot-induced.

Cafés, bookstores, and cheap restaurants catering to the student population are all over town, and nicely accommodate the budget traveler as well. Head to the local bagel shop for long political discussions or to watch people comparing the sizes of their healing crystals. For simpler pleasures, go out for brews and live blues and folk music at the **Jambalaya** (915 H St., tel. 707/822–4766) or the **Humboldt Brewing Company** (856 10th St., tel. 707/826–2739). The town even has *two* discount repertory movie houses, the **Arcata** (1036 G St., tel. 707/822–5171) and the **Minor** (1015 H St., tel. 707/822–5174).

Arcata is the gateway to Redwood National Forest to the north and the mountainous national parks to the east on Route 299 (*see* The Northern Coast Ranges, *below*), which continues on to Redding. Easy travel to and from Eureka is provided by **Arcata Transit** (735 F St., tel. 707/823–5951 ext. 318).

MAD RIVER, CLAM, AND TRINIDAD BEACHES U.S. 101 hugs the coast north of Arcata, passing by a number of wide windswept beaches great for camping. You can't camp at the first of these, **Mad River Beach County Park** (tel. 707/445–7652), but it's close enough to Arcata to head there for a brisk morning walk or an afternoon weenie roast. The wide Mad River meets the Pacific here, cheered on by a colorful array of wildflowers in July. Write to your friends that you've seen something mad swallowed by the sea (or something mad become pacific), and let them draw their own conclusions. To get there, take U.S. 101 to Guintoli Lane.

From here on the coast is untamed, with wide sand dunes and rough surf. **Clam Beach County Park** (tel. 707/445–7652) is—surprise!—a great place for clamming during low tides. Beach camping costs $8 per vehicle, but some campers arrive on foot and avoid the fee. Pit toilets are provided. Another 8 miles or so north is **Trinidad**, whose idyllic natural harbor was the first supply link between San Francisco and gold miners along the Trinity River. Today it's a sleepy little resort town (population 432) with an assortment of renovated beach houses, RV parks, and redwood burl shops that are typical of this stretch of coast.

PATRICK'S POINT STATE PARK AND HUMBOLDT LAGOONS STATE PARK Patrick's Point State Park (tel. 707/677–3570) and Humboldt Lagoons State Park (tel. 707/488–5435), several miles to the north, are fantastic parks with access to stretches of wide sandy beaches and rocky coves.

Patrick's Point is a forested plateau almost 200 feet above the surf—an ideal spot for whale and sea lion watching. The nimble-footed can explore the tide pools, and a small museum offers natural history exhibits. Day use is $3; all other fees are normal state park rates (*see* Camping in Chapter 1, Basics).

Aside from developed campsites with fire rings, tables, and food lockers, Humboldt Lagoons offers walk-in environmental campsites (only about 100 yards from the parking lot) where you can get away from the family-oriented campsites and experience more isolated stretches of beach. The lagoon is especially good for bird-watching. Humboldt Lagoons' environmental sites cost $7 per night and reservations can be made at the park office (tel. 707/488–5435).

REDWOOD NATIONAL PARK Just past the town of Orick, a few miles north of Humboldt Lagoons, you arrive at the jewel of the north coast—Redwood National Park, where majestic stands of ancient redwoods meet the Pacific Ocean. The national park and the contiguous **Jedediah Smith Redwoods State Park** (tel. 707/458–3310), **Prairie Creek Redwoods State Park** (tel. 707/488–2171, and **Del Norte Coast Redwoods State Park** (tel. 707/464–9533) offer superb opportunities for camping in spectacular settings and close proximity to a dazzling array of animals, birds, and sea life. U.S. 101 moves in and out of the park all the way from Orick to Crescent City, 44 miles to the north. If you're determined not to lose sight of the Pacific and you have a sturdy vehicle, take the Coastal Drive just north of Orick, which returns to U.S. 101 near Klamath approximately 22 miles later.

Though the redwood park is confusingly divided between state and federal jurisdiction, it's easiest to approach the whole as one long continuum, making forays off the highway to whatever appeals. For information about both national and state parks, stop at **The Redwood Information Center** (tel. 707/488–3461), off U.S. 101, 1 mile south of Orick near the southern entrance of the park. This impressive wood-and-glass structure serves as the central office and the more-than-helpful staff will gladly suggest hikes and campsites to suit your interests. If you're heading into Redwood Park from the north, a more convenient information stop is **The Redwood National Park Headquarters** in Crescent City (1111 2nd St., Crescent City 95531, tel. 707/464–6101). For information about campgrounds and reservations, call 800/444–7275.

Redwood Creek and the **Klamath River** both meet the Pacific in the park, the first near Orick and the second near Klamath (both on U.S. 101). Rafters and kayakers will enjoy the park's rivers, but anyone can take a hike or just enjoy the outdoors. Even if the serenity of the magical redwood forests gets old, you can spend days watching the park's 370 species of birds, or gazing at **Roosevelt elk** from U.S. 101 at **Prairie Creek Redwoods State Park.** For birding, try the **Bald Hills** in the Orick district for red-tail hawks, red-shouldered hawks, and turkey vultures; the **Coastal Trail** for chickadees, orange-crowned warblers, and dark-eyed junkos; and in the summer, visit **Lost Man Creek** to see the rare marbled murrelet, a small sea bird that researchers believe nests only in coastal forests between Alaska and central California.

There are a multitude of trails in **Redwood National Forest.** The **Lady Bird Johnson Grove,** a 1-mile loop that features a self-guided nature trail, and the **Tall Trees Grove,** a 3-mile round-trip hike to the site of three of the world's tallest Redwood trees, are two relatively easy hikes in the southern area of the park. Redwood National Park provides a shuttle twice daily in summer (once in the off-season) from the Redwood Information Center to the Tall Trees trailhead, where you can head out on backcountry trails. The 17-mile drive to the trailhead is closed during summer and visitors must take the shuttle. Another fascinating short hike is the easy ¾-mile jaunt across shallow creeks to **Fern Canyon,** a 60-foot ravine covered with maidenhair, five-finger, and sword ferns (off U.S. 101 at Davison Rd. north of Orick). The hike to **Flint Ridge** will take you through lush coastal growth into a quiet redwood forest—the trailhead is 1 mile south of the Klamath River, heading west on the Coastal Drive road. There are many other short hikes in the park, and your first step should be to pick up a map at either visitor center.

Whether you want the facilities of state park camping or the solitude of the backcountry, you've come to the right place. You can camp along the **Redwood Creek Trail** on the way to the Tall Trees Grove, or on Flint Ridge. For free camping, no crowds, and tide-pooling, head for **Nickle Creek,** a half-mile walk from Endbert's Beach Road near Crescent City. Before camping in these or any backcountry locations, get a permit from the visitor center. Whatever you do, savor it: This park is the pay-off you get for traveling nearly to the edge of the map.

CRESCENT CITY Coming out of the Redwood National Park is like entering an American nightmare. Fast food, cheap motels, mini-malls, and greasy-spoon diners—Crescent City is bereft of any of the charm its name suggests. More than anything, Crescent City is a travel hub through which visitors pass to reach other places. U.S. 101 crosses the Oregon border about 20 miles north of Crescent City, and then proceeds along the coast toward **Coos Bay.** Route 199 heads northeast through **Six Rivers National Forest** into Oregon, and joins I–5 at **Grants Pass.**

OUTDOOR ACTIVITIES

BIKING In the **Clear Lake** area, the **Lake Cycling Club** (Box 1062, Lakeport 95453, tel. 707/263–1200) has route recommendations and organizes regular club rides. You can rent a bike for around $25 per day from **The Bicycle Rack** (350 N. Main St., Lakeport, tel. 707/263–1200).

FISHING Starting just south of Garberville, U.S. 101 basically follows the course of the **Eel River** until the river empties into the Pacific south of Eureka. This stretch of the river is good for steelhead trout fishing, although over-fishing, erosion from logging, and several years of drought have depleted the supply. Farther up the Eel, in **Mendocino National Forest,** you can catch your fill of rainbow trout.

The lakes and reservoirs of the **Clear Lake** area in Lake County are some of California's best waters for bass, trout, and catfish. **Pete's Sporting Goods** (690 S. Main St. Lakeport, tel. 707/263–4413) offers good advice, and several fishing guides are available through the Lake County Visitor Information Center (*see* Tourist Information, *above*).

HIKING A number of the best places for hiking have already been mentioned. *See* Cow Mountain, Mendocino National Forest, Standish-Hickey State Recreation Area,

Avenue of the Giants, Patrick's Point State Park and Humboldt Lagoons State Park, and Redwood National Park in Exploring U.S. 101, *above*.

THE LOST COAST From Hidden Valley Trailhead (accessible from Wailaki and Wadelos Camps) at the base of the Chemise Mountain, the **Lost Coast Trail** is an increasingly popular three-day to one-week trip that heads south through Bear Harbor to Usal Beach. The trail, best hiked in the spring or fall when the days are warm and the evenings cool, alternates between ridges with ocean views and lush, dark, fern-filled canyons. Five miles along the trail is **Wheeler**, where you can camp among the remnants of an old mill town before hiking down Jackass Creek to Usal Beach.

The Northern Coast Ranges

The Northern Coast Ranges are "Bigfoot Country," where the legendary man-ape is sometimes sighted. With 8,000-foot mountain peaks where the snow doesn't melt until July, glacial lakes and salmon-filled rivers, the mountainous regions of the Six Rivers, Klamath, and Shasta-Trinity national forests are some of the state's most spectacular and unpopulated wilderness. There are more birds and wild animals than anywhere else in the state, and in early summer the roadsides blaze with colorful wildflowers. You'll find lots of opportunities for fishing, rafting, hunting, kayaking, and mountain biking here as well, but best of all is the chance for days of solitary and challenging hiking in wilderness areas that haven't been touched by logging.

In the northern part of the Klamath National Forest, **Happy Camp** makes a good launching pad into the Siskiyou Mountains or Marble Mountain Wilderness, or just a good roadside stop on your way east to Yreka or southwest to the coast. Still an active gold-mining town, Happy Camp has the feel of the old California frontier. There's a helpful ranger station and modern conveniences in the center of town, but the charming part of town is the west side, where you'll find abandoned wood-front houses and old hotels, remnants of California's colorful past.

If you're heading south from Happy Camp into Six Rivers National Forest, you might want to stop in **Willow Creek** along the Trinity River to catch a last glimpse of sunlight before continuing into the foggy mountains. Just north of Willow Creek is the 89,000-acre Hoopa Valley Indian Reservation, the first land granted to Native Americans in California after the northern California gold rush in 1864. The land is shared by Hoopa and Yurok tribes, and despite the spectacular forested peaks and rushing Trinity River, both Willow Creek and the town of Hoopa, 12 miles to the north, retain a dusty, desperate feel. In the Hoopa Shopping Mall off Route 96, the **Hoopa Tribal Museum** (tel. 707/625–4110; open Mon.–Sat. 9–5) has a display of Hoopa baskets and weapons (the bingo parlor next door is far livelier!).

For information on adjacent areas, including Weaverville, Clair Engle (Trinity) Lake, Trinity National Forest, and the Yolla Bolly Middle Eel Wilderness, *see* Chapter 5, The Cascades.

● ● ● BASICS

It's possible to send away for trail maps and make camping reservations in advance through all of the branches of the National Forest Office Headquarters. Plan ahead if you're the type, but don't count on the weather to comply (*see* When to Go, *below*).

TOURIST INFORMATION

KLAMATH NATIONAL FOREST **Happy Camp Ranger District Office** (Box 377, Happy Camp 96039, tel. 916/493–2243) has information on Northern Klamath trails.

Scott River Ranger District Office (11263 S. Rte. 3, Fort Jones 96032, tel. 916/468–5351) provides trail information, back-country permits, and a map of the Marble Mountain Wilderness.

SIX RIVERS NATIONAL FOREST **Six Rivers Headquarters** (500 5th St. at F St., Eureka, tel. 707/442–3543) has maps, books, and displays about the forest, and several rangers on hand. The district ranger office for the specific area you're headed has more detailed information, so consider stopping there as well.

Six Rivers Gasquet District Office (Box 228, Gasquet 95543, tel. 707/457–3131) provides information on Smith River National Recreation Area, the South-Kelsey Trail, and other remote sites.

TRINITY NATIONAL FOREST **Lower Trinity Ranger Station** (Box 68, Willow Creek 95573, tel. 916/629–2118) has information on river rafting and camping in the southern section of Trinity National Forest. For information on other parts of Trinity National Forest, *see* Weaverville in Chapter 5, The Cascades.

FEES Compared to state parks, which generally charge $5 for day use and $14 for camping, national forests are a bargain. Day use is free, and camping prices range from nothing—all campgrounds with no running water are free—to $8 for areas equipped with running water and bathrooms. Free campgrounds have pit toilets.

WHEN TO GO Rain (50–70 inches per year), sleet, and hail soak the unprepared, even in summer. Despite the occasional summer precipitation, wildfires periodically serve up Wilderness Barbecue-Style. Fall and spring bring more rain, mud slides, and the occasional flood. A few areas are accessible in winter, but the weather is really nasty then. The up-side of all the climatic bluster is the cooler summer temperatures, which make long backpacking treks much more pleasant. Late spring, summer, and early fall are the best times to visit; by September you're likely to be all alone on the trail; by October you're likely to be all alone and freezing to death.

Be ready for an almost-biblical onslaught of strange weather.

WHAT TO PACK Aside from the usual camping gear, do bring the means to secure your supplies from hungry bears (*see* Chapter 1, Basics). Make sure you have a good tarp to lay under your tent in case of rain and spikes to hold your tent down in heavy wind. Wood is generally abundant, but bring some kind of easy fire starter in case the wood is wet (charcoal works, or fire-starter sticks can be purchased at most hardware stores). You probably aren't planning on a close encounter with a rattlesnake, but pack a snake-bite kit with your first-aid supplies in case you are so honored.

COMING AND GOING

The Northern Coast Ranges stretch south from Oregon through northern California, skirted by U.S. 101 and Route 5. The major route through the forest is Route 299, which you can reach by turning east from U.S. 101 north of Arcata or west from Route 5 at Redding. **Greyhound** (in Redding, tel. 916/241–2531) travels to both Arcata and Redding. **Redwood Empire Lines** (tel. 707/443–9923) buses travel once a day between the Greyhound depots in Eureka and Redding for around $17 one way, and you can arrange to have the bus let you out at a town along Route 299 for slightly less. You might consider renting a car in Eureka or Redding. From Route 299, you can tour all three forests, with the option of detouring off into the backcountry, by making a loop on Route 3 and Route 96. It's important to have good tires and a spare, because many of the forestry-service roads are gravel and not maintained, and rock slides can make for some rough going. Read the fine print on your rent-a-car agreement to see if you can get away with Indiana Jones–like driving without taking a direct hit in the wallet.

WHERE TO SLEEP

Most visitors to the area camp, but a range of accommodations is available. One popular and affordable travel plan is to camp out several nights and then retreat to a lodge or motel for a hot shower and comfortable bed. One convenient place for lodging not listed here is Weaverville (*see* Chapter 5, The Cascades). For information about campgrounds, *see* Exploring the Northern Coast Ranges, *below*.

HOOPA If you're not camping, the selection of lodgings is very limited. A good option is the **Best Western Tsewenaldin Inn** (Box 219, Rte. 96, tel. 916/625–4294) down the street from the Hoopa Tribal Museum and facing the Trinity River. The inn has large, comfortable rooms starting at about $40, a heated swimming pool, and a 24-hour Jacuzzi.

FOOD

HAPPY CAMP **Indian Creek Café** (106 Indian Creek Rd., tel. 916/493–5180). It's concrete front isn't much to look at, and the cafeteria-style furnishings give the place a stodgy institutional atmosphere. Even the menu is textbook size (21 pages) and comes with a table of contents guiding you through "chapters" on seafood, vegetarian dishes, omelettes, sandwiches, and more. The six-piece chicken in German beer batter is enough for two and a bargain at $7. The grilled crab and cheddar sandwich at $5 is tasty, too.

EXPLORING NORTHERN COAST RANGES

The "Greenbelt" that extends from the Oregon border all the way down to Clear Lake is comprised of several mountain ranges, national forests, and wilderness areas. Six Rivers National Forest in the northwest and Klamath National Forest and Marble Mountain Wilderness to the northeast are covered here. To the south is Mendocino National Forest (*see* Exploring U.S. 101, *above*). To the east are Shasta-Trinity National Forest, Salmon Trinity Alps Wilderness, and Yolla Bolly Middle Eel Wilderness (*see* Chapter 5, The Cascades). This is all confusing, even on the map, but don't be discouraged. Just talk to one of the rangers, and then point yourself in the direction of the greatest beauty.

SIX RIVERS NATIONAL FOREST The Six Rivers National Forest stretches like a long finger south from Oregon to the Trinity County line. Unless you're on an extended expedition you probably won't be able to explore the whole forest. In the north, east of Gasquet on Route 199, the **Smith River National Recreation Area** is an easily accessible area of rugged mountains, streams, and lush canyons along the crystal-clear waters of the Smith River. Campgrounds dot the roadside and many offer walk-in sites right next to the river. Try **Patrick Creek,** with 17 sites, or **Cedar Rustic**; both cost $8 per vehicle, less for bikers or hikers, and have pit toilets and drinking water. For more information on campsites, or pamphlets on local plants, birds, and wildlife, stop by the **Gasquet Ranger Station** (Box 228, Gasquet 95543, tel. 707/457–3131) on Route 199 just east of town. The southern part of the forest is good for car camping, while the Trinity River provides opportunities for fishing, kayaking, and swimming. The scenery here isn't as spectacular as in the rest of the Northern Coast Ranges, and its proximity to the coast and warm summer weather draw more people. **Tish Tang Campground,** 8 miles north of Willow Creek on Route 96, offers camping or day-use in a beautiful river-cut canyon. **Hawkins Bar,** 10 miles east of Willow Creek on Route 299, has great fishing and is popular with inner-tubers content to float around for hours in the sun.

KLAMATH MOUNTAIN NATIONAL FOREST Like the other forests that surround it, the Klamath Mountain National Forest offers a range of activities from white-water rafting to the solitude of back-country mountain travel. The 250,000-acre **Marble Mountain Wilderness** is held by many to be the most pristine area in California. This is where the wild things are. Bears, mountain lions, quail, foxes, deer, red-tail hawks, bald eagles, and maybe even Bigfeet make their home here. Marble Mountain itself is 8,925 feet tall, and its marble and limestone peak is hidden under snow year-round. Though the "real" way to see the Marble Mountains (and not see other people) is to set out on a major week-long trek, a weekend or over-night stay might be more enjoyable for those with limited time and/or outdoor expertise.

In summer, most of the forestry-service roads in the northern part of the Klamath National Forest near Happy Camp are well-maintained (despite warning signs that advise against use) and lead to many rarely used trails. For a beautiful and obscure camping spot, head for the small and shallow **Kelly Lake,** surrounded by grassy meadow and forests. To get there, set off from the Westbranch Campground, 14 miles north of Happy Camp. Take Indian Creek Road 1/4 mile to Forestry Service Road 18N27 on the left and follow the signs hidden on the left side of the dirt road for about 6 miles.

OUTDOOR ACTIVITIES • • •

The Northern Coast Ranges, while primarily a haven for those seeking solitude and wilderness hiking, are also full of opportunities for those who prefer to travel by horse, bicycle, boat, kayak, or jet ski. Trail erosion and varying water levels change conditions drastically each year, so talk to rangers and other outdoors people before setting out.

HIKING

SIX RIVERS NATIONAL FOREST The South-Kelsey Trail was constructed in 1851 as an army supply artery from Crescent City to Fort Jones, and was also used to transport gold for shipment to San Francisco. Today, it provides over 16 miles of rugged hiking through the **Siskyiou Wilderness,** along the south fork of the Smith River and onto the 5,775-foot Baldy Peak, from which you can view the rugged Siskiyou Backbone, the Marble Mountains, and Mount Shasta to the east. There's plenty of water along the way (boil stream water before drinking) and lots of good fishing spots. You can cover the whole trail in a great 3- to 4-day hike. To reach the trail, turn off Route 199 onto County Road 427, then onto Forest Service Road (F.S.R.) 15N01, and finally to F.S.R. 15N39.

MARBLE MOUNTAIN WILDERNESS For information about the Marble Mountain Wilderness, consult with the rangers at either **Fort Jones Ranger Station** (11263 S. Rte. 3, tel. 916/468–5351) if you're approaching the area from the east or **Ukonom Ranger Station** (tel. 916/627–3291) in Orleans if you're approaching from the west. A popular, spectacular, and easily accessible trail sets off from Lover's Camp. Take Route 3 to Scott River Road, then to Indian Scotty over the bridge, and then follow signs. That trail hooks up with paths to the murky, misnamed Paradise Lake, the remote Wright Lake, and—if you have the time—20 or 30 other outstanding spots for camping amid awesome beauty.

A detailed trail map costs $2, and is a dirt-cheap way to avoid that terrible, oh-shit-I'm-lost feeling you can get in the middle of a forest (see The Brothers Grimm).

FISHING

You'll find great fishing for salmon and steelhead trout in the Trinity and Klamath rivers and year-round trout fishing in the lakes of the Marble Mountains and Trinity Alps wilderness areas. For more information, *see* Outdoor Activities for Weaverville and Trinity National Forest in Chapter 5, The Cascades.

RAFTING AND CANOEING

The Trinity, Klamath, and Smith rivers snake through deep gorges and valleys with stretches of both calm, glassy waters and wild, churning rapids suitable for rafting. The Forest Service rates each section of the rivers from Class I, for beginning rafters and kayakers, to Class VI, for experts only. The Smith River, from Grey Falls to Hawkins Bar, is about a three-hour trip through 300-foot gorges and sunny, open spots that is rated Class I. A more challenging trip is in the Southern Six Rivers area from Willow Creek along the Trinity River to **Tish Tang,** about a four-hour trip. For a guided white-water adventure in the Shasta-Trinity National Forest, try the **Trinity River Company** (Trinity River Inn, Rte. 299 in Big Flat, tel. 916/623–3033), which offers trips of varying difficulty down the Trinity River. A half-day guided trip is $39 for Class III, and $29 for Class II waters. Both include snacks and the Class II trip has stops for swimming. Class III runs through some of the most enticing rapids, including "Hell Hole," "Zig-Zag," and "Fish-tail." The company also rents rafts for self-guided Class II tours for $19 per half-day, and $29 per full day. **Bigfoot Outdoor Company** (Box 729, Willow Creek, tel. 916/629–2263) offers a wider selection of guided tours, including an overnight kayak trip down the Klamath River for $140. Bigfoot also rents kayaks, rafts, wet suits, and other gear by the day and has a shuttle service to and from the river. Reservations suggested.

BIRD-WATCHING From ospreys and falcons to red-tail hawks and the rare bald eagle, the Northern Coast Ranges are a haven for birds of prey. Best spots to engage in avian voyeurism are high mountains, peaks, canyons, and hillsides overlooking meadows. Many books are available or pick up the free pamphlet on birds of the Trinity area at the Weaverville Ranger Station (*see* Chapter 5, The Cascades).

BIKING Bicycles are not allowed on trails in the designated wilderness areas, but most backcountry trails in the three forests are great for mountain biking. For a Wilderness Biathlon, try biking down one of the dirt and gravel forestry roads to a trailhead and then hike to a river or lake. As with motor bikes, follow the forest's "tread lightly" rules and avoid grown-over trails, stream banks, and new forests and meadows. Be careful of wildlife and erosion near water sources. In the summer many bicyclists use Route 3 and Route 96 as take-off points for bike trips. The roads are not crowded and cycling along rivers and through picturesque mining towns such as Callahan, Etna, Seiad Valley, and Somes Bar is a wonderful way to travel. Many rest stops and campgrounds along the road are free to bikers.

THE CASCADES 5

By Colleen Cotter

A conceptual map of California, like those New Yorker pastel drawings of the Big Apple that swallow the Midwest and give a brief nod to the West Coast, would include Los Angeles, San Francisco, Yosemite, and possibly the state capital. Chances are the north inland expanse of pine forests, alpine mountains, dormant volcanoes, and bald eagles would be overlooked.

The "anonymous" part of the state from Sacramento north on I–5 to the Oregon border is by no means an unpeopled paradise. To the east the Sierra Nevada Mountains gradually melt into the Cascade Range, to the west the forests and mountain lakes of the Coast ranges play host to Bigfoot, and looming over all is the mystical Mt. Shasta, whose white shadow stretches across the Sacramento Valley. In between, however, you'll find charming towns, ramshackle towns, towns overrun by franchises, towns with great restaurants, towns with colorful characters, towns with great civic pride, towns with fascinating historical backgrounds—and a small city or two.

These places have been built by people who bring the pride of a pioneer past and those who have fled the San Francisco Bay Area and Los Angeles, by people who preserve and those who develop, who fancy Merle Haggard or love Pavarotti, who like Kentucky Fried Chicken or can't live without Cajun and sorbet, who may not mind newcomers but still want to keep the secret of this north-state good life to themselves, who distrust intellectuals but lobby to get a four-year university: The contradictions of the California character are felt more intensely here in this rural setting.

Perhaps the pervading sense of relaxation and good humor is what makes this area so engaging. Chico might well be a good first stop on your way north from Sacramento. It's known for its hot, Mediterranean-summer climate, abundant trees and orchards, and university-town liveliness. Chico is a good pivotal point for turning east along Route 70 and driving through the dramatic rock corridors of the Feather River Canyon (especially in the fall when the leaves are turning), to the friendly mountain town of Quincy with its subtle inclinations toward fine food, art, conversation, and community.

Northwest of Chico is the small Victorian town of Red Bluff. Both Red Bluff and Redding, a half-hour north, are good points from which to explore the Lassen Volcanic National Park area. Within an hour or so you've gone from a dusty, hot valley to cooler, fresher, higher elevations. Route 36 runs from Red Bluff to the south entrance of the park and continues east toward Susanville and other playgrounds, natural and otherwise, like Eagle Lake, Lake Almanor, and Reno. Along Route 36 are a number of lodges and motels that may (or may not, unfortunately) be open. Route 44 from Redding will take you to Manzanita Lake,

The Far North

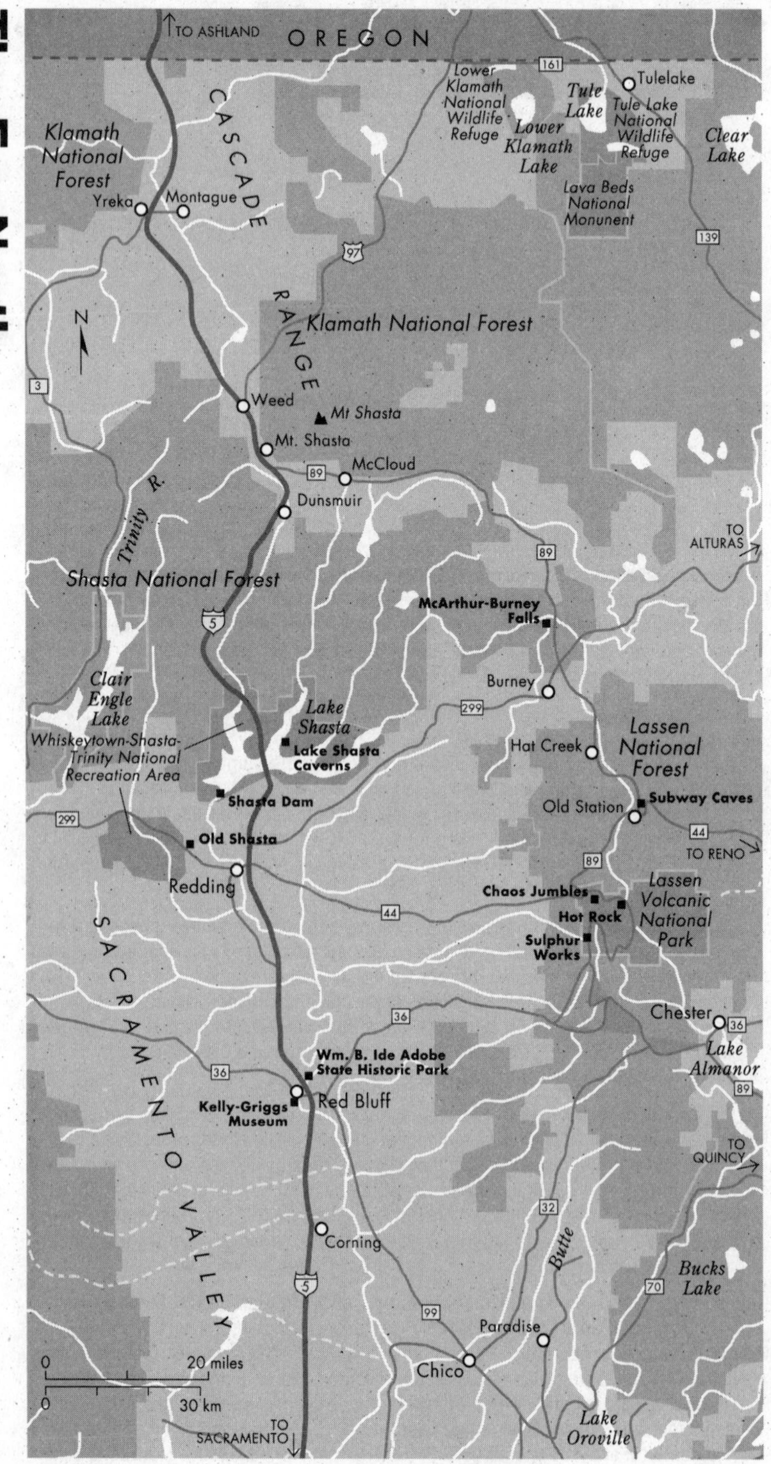
TO ASHLAND
OREGON
161
Lower Klamath National Wildlife Refuge
Tule Lake
Tulelake
Tule Lake National Wildlife Refuge
Lower Klamath Lake
Clear Lake
Lava Beds National Monunent
139
Klamath National Forest
CASCADE RANGE
Yreka
Montague
97
N
Klamath National Forest
3
Weed
Mt Shasta
Mt. Shasta
89
McCloud
Dunsmuir
Trinity R.
TO ALTURAS
89
Shasta National Forest
McArthur-Burney Falls
5
Burney
Clair Engle Lake
Lake Shasta
299
Lassen National Forest
Whiskeytown-Shasta-Trinity National Recreation Area
Lake Shasta Caverns
Hat Creek
Shasta Dam
Old Station
Subway Caves
299
44
Old Shasta
TO RENO
Redding
89
Lassen Volcanic National Park
Chaos Jumbles
Hot Rock
44
Sulphur Works
SACRAMENTO VALLEY
Chester
36
36
Lake Almanor
Wm. B. Ide Adobe State Historic Park
36
89
Red Bluff
Kelly-Griggs Museum
TO QUINCY
32
Corning
Butte
Bucks Lake
5
70
99
Paradise
0
20 miles
Chico
0
30 km
TO SACRAMENTO
Lake Oroville

the north entrance of the park, and allow you to link up with Route 89 and the Hat Creek and Burney Falls areas.

Upstart Redding grew fast and somewhat awkwardly with the building of Shasta Dam in the '30s and '40s. Woody Guthrie wrote "This Land Is Your Land" while he was in Redding working on the dam. The small city of about 60,000 is now the transport hub of northern California, with outlet stores, cheap groceries, inexpensive motels, nice parks, and a surprising number of cultural attractions.

To the west on Route 299 is Old Shasta Historical Park, Whiskeytown Lake (the locals' swimmin' hole), the gold-rush town of Weaverville, and the Trinity Alps. To the north on I–5 is Mt. Shasta, the peak, and Mount Shasta, the city, as well as old lumber towns, bird refuges, and the volcanic formations at "the top of the state." Take the opportunity to customize your trip. Everybody goes to Disneyland, but how many people do yoga on the slopes of Mt. Shasta or send postcards from the caves of Lava Beds National Monument?

BASICS

TOURIST INFORMATION Each town has its own travel office (*see* individual listings). The national parks and recreation areas also have information centers with well-informed staff. The U.S. Forest Service's **Shasta Lake Information Center** on I–5 north of Redding is particularly well stocked, and is open daily 8:30–4:30.

The Red Bluff-Tehama County Chamber of Commerce has information for the whole area. If you're heading west off I–5 toward Weaverville, north toward Mt. Shasta, or east toward Mt. Lassen, stop here for brochures and details about what the mountainous expanse has to offer. *100 Main St., tel. 916/527–6220. Open Mon. 8:30–4, Tues.–Thurs. 8:30–5, Fri. 8:30–5.*

COMING AND GOING

Although buses, trains, and planes travel through the area, your best chance for mobility and flexibility is with a car. **Greyhound** serves the area, but buses come infrequently most days and may be full in summer. **Green Tortoise** (*see* Chapter 1, Basics) makes a stop in Redding. Redding is a good base and a convenient place to rent a car. Redding also has good bus connections to Eureka on the coast (*see* Chapter 4, The North Coast). From several towns in this region you can get cheap transportation to Reno on casino bus tours.

BY BUS **Greyhound** (tel. 916/241–2531 in Redding) buses serve Chico, Red Bluff, Redding, and other towns along I–5 en route to Sacramento, San Francisco, Seattle, and points beyond. **Mt. Lassen Motor Transit** (22503 Sunbright Ave., Red Bluff, tel. 800/822–9660) offers open charters from Red Bluff to Reno, Nevada, several times a week. It's $22 to get to Reno where you can spend six hours in the casinos, and then return to Red Bluff; $40 for an overnight trip that also includes a motel room. Call for schedule updates.

BY TRAIN **Amtrak** (tel. 916/243–4104 in Redding; or 800/872–7245) travels between San Francisco and Seattle and stops in Marysville, Chico, Redding, Dunsmuir, and Yreka. Trains arrive and depart in the dead of night, and are often delayed, but the stations along the line are safe places to wait. The four- to six-hour trip between San Francisco and Redding costs $77 one way, $102 round-trip. A cheaper but more tedious way to get to Redding from San Francisco is to take the train to Stockton and then pick up an Amtrak bus from there to Redding; cost is $58 round-trip. Reservations are advised in all instances. Call for schedule updates.

BY CAR I–5 is the West Coast's main highway, traveling from the Mexico border just south of San Diego all the way to Seattle and on to Canada. Give yourself about four hours to drive from the San Francisco Bay Area to Red Bluff (I–80 to Rte. 505 to I–5), and about three hours from Sacramento. Red Bluff is 520 miles from Los Angeles, 220 miles from Reno, and 440 miles from Portland. Redding is a half-hour's drive to the north; Mt. Shasta

Highway Highlights: The Best of I–5

Dunnigan Safety rest stop (just north of 505 turnoff): Get out and smell the eucalyptus trees.

Williams: A quintessential Sacramento valley town near Route 20 on the way to Clean Lake and Mendocino. Travelers stop here for the franchise restaurants and chain motels fronting the town along the interstate. Try Louis Cairo's ("the talk of the valley," its menus have proclaimed for decades) for great Italian food and steaks.

Arbuckle: Notice how the indefatigably straight interstate curves first to the right, and then the left, and then right again. The flowering greenery in the center divider is a welcome sight if you're punching it up the freeway on a summer's day, when the heat overexposes the sky and the distant horizons to a bleached and blotchy white.

Sutter Buttes: Even on a hazy day in the flat valley you can always see Sutter Buttes, jutting into the sky to the east like some AWOL piece of mountain range. It's private land, rich in Native American, geologic, and botanical lore. If you're going to spend any time in the area, make sure to find out when the Sierra Club, the UC-Davis Extension, or Chico State's Adventure Outings is planning a permitted visit—they're your only ticket in.

Corning: Taste olives at The Olive Pit off I–5. Stock up on 'em—Napa Wine, Texas Chili, and Cajun are some of the more exotic flavors—and on almonds.

Red Bluff: Stop at Pronto Market on Antelope Boulevard for $4 pinatas, great homemade tamales or burritos, and lots of other Mexican food, spicy or sweet.

If it's late August or September, drive 20 minutes west on orchard-lined Route 99 to Dairyville. Inhale. It's the aroma of the prune harvest, and fruity, sun-warmed, delicious California.

When you pass Cottonwood, notice to your right the Shasta Livestock Auction Yard, the biggest auction yard west of Amarillo, Texas. Have lunch with cattle ranchers at the adjacent restaurant frequented by locals. "The ambience is really bovine," said one fan who brings her out-of-town friends up for some good beef and hopes the wind is blowing the right way.

The Collier Rest Stop: They saved the prettiest rest stop in California for last, the last stop before you enter Oregon. Walk down to the Klamath River, which runs through the rest area. Save your picnic for here. It'll taste better.

another hour from Redding; and the Oregon border is slightly less than an hour north of Mt. Shasta.

I–5 shoots through the middle of the Sacramento Valley, straight as an arrow and at times so monotonous that you may feel like strapping the steering wheel into place and taking a nap in the back seat.

CAR RENTALS Redding offers the biggest selection of car rental agencies, including **Avis** (tel. 800/331–1212), **National** (tel. 800/227–7368), **Hertz** (tel. 800/654–3131), **Rent-A-Wreck** (tel. 916/222–8304, closed Sunday), **Harrison's** (tel. 916/221–6343), and **King Richard's** (tel. 916/222–2755). **California Compacts Rent-a-Car** has outlets in Montague (tel. 916/459–3456), **Mt. Shasta** (tel. 916/926–2519), **Weed** (tel. 916/938–2729), and **Yreka** (tel. 916/842–7379). Agencies in Redding are concentrated at the Redding Municipal Airport and near the corner of Cypress and Hilltop avenues.

BY PLANE Although you can fly into Redding or Chico, you'll have a wider range of choices if you fly into Sacramento (*see* Chapter 7, The Sierra Nevadas and San Joaquin Valley). **Redding Municipal Airport** (tel. 916/225–4124), southeast of town, is served by **American Eagle** (tel. 800/433–7300) and **United Express** (tel. 800/241–6522), with flights to and from San Francisco. **Chico Municipal Airport** is served by **United Express** (tel. 916/893–1394) and **American Eagle** (tel. 916/898–9801).

WHERE TO SLEEP

Lodging is relatively cheap in the northern part of the state. Finding a room for $30–$35 a night isn't difficult, and rooms even less expensive are available in some of the smaller towns. There are plenty of mom-and-pop motels of varying quality and comfort, a number of national budget-chain offerings such as **Motel 6**, and some big city–style hotel complexes (especially in Redding). The area also has lots of unique bed-and-breakfasts, starting at around $40 a night, and ranging from stone cottages to converted operating rooms.

Camping is widely available and often free. You can camp on the slopes of a dormant volcano, near the shores of the Sacramento River, or high in the Trinity Alps or secluded Cascades. It's easy to rough it—just meander down a logging road off the state highways. For good quality at a low price, try the public **U.S. Forest Service, Pacific Gas and Electric Co.**, and **State Park Service** campgrounds. Residents say that for women, camping in areas away from I–5, or in national parks where there are more people around, such as Mt. Lassen, is probably safer than camping alone. The ranger station personnel will tell you which campgrounds have rougher reputations.

FOOD

There's no shortage of pizza places, burger joints, taco stands, and delis, especially in the more populated areas along I–5. You won't have to travel far for a great steak (this is cattle country); and seafood is as fresh as a short three-hour trip from the coast can provide. There are also gourmet dinners to be had ($10–$15) that you would pay double or more for in San Francisco. Uncovering these finds may give you a greater sense of satisfaction than eating at the standard trendy spots elsewhere. If you happen upon a town-sponsored picnic or barbecue, count on Western-style beans and hot peppers. No matter where you are, the dress code is casual.

OUTDOOR ACTIVITIES

Name your thing, and you can probably enjoy it here a bit more cheaply and with fewer crowds than elsewhere. The **Sacramento River**, from its source on Mt. Shasta all the way down the valley, affords rafting, fishing (salmon trolling near Anderson is especially fruitful), inner-tubing, picnicking, summer riverside concerts, and incredible sunsets. **Shasta Lake**, looking a bit rough from the drought years, is still a draw for out-of-towners and locals who want a houseboat vacation. **Trinity (Clair Engle) Lake**, west of Redding, is a less populous, less expensive houseboating alternative.

Avid hikers consider the **Trinity Alps** to be among the most beautiful mountains in the world. Take just a one-day trip to **Coffee Creek** (*see* Near Redding, *below*) and you'll be converted. The area is also great for fly-fishing, hunting, waterskiing, sailing, hiking, camping, and bicycling. The National Forest lands of Trinity, Shasta, Tehama, and Siskiyou counties (which cluster around I–5 in the far north of the state) are positively deserted by Yosemite standards.

Since the decline of the lumber economy, many communities along I–5 are now supported by tourism and recreation. And no matter where you go, you'll be rubbing elbows with the locals who invest a lot of time in the legacy of the great outdoors. In addition to the beautiful, obscure spots you might find along your way, **Lassen Volcanic National Park**, **Mt. Shasta**, and **Lava Beds National Park** are all wonderful, relatively untouristed, and fiercely loved.

Chico

A simple trip on Route 99 north from Sacramento or south from Red Bluff will allow you to dodge the monotony of I–5. Better yet, it will deliver you to the friendly town of Chico (east of I–5 on Route 32), home of one of the liveliest branches of the California State University system and gateway to **Quincy** and the **Plumas National Forest** high in the Sierras. The whole area from Chico east to Plumas National Forest recalls days when America's troubles didn't bother the soul. Residents from the San Francisco Bay Area have recently been moving here in droves.

Chico is anything but a major tourist destination, but that doesn't mean it's not an interesting place to hang out, meet people, and have a lot of fun. Besides agriculture and handling the almost unkempt population growth of the past decade or so, the town revolves around Cal State Chico, which has one of the best public relations departments in the state.

The town is revved up during the school year and slow and sleepy in the hot summers, although more students are tending to stay between semesters, livening things up a bit. The current state budget cuts are expected to make serious inroads on student numbers.

The life of a town rests to a certain extent on its roots, and the people of Chico come from sturdy, independent stock. The town's "parents" are John and Annie Bidwell, free-thinking and far-seeing pioneers with a strong sense of culture, fairness, and sensitivity. John planted lots of trees in the area and instituted modern agricultural practices on his vast land holdings, and Annie employed and taught the local Indians. In 1887 Annie donated choice land to the city for what is now the university. **Bidwell Mansion State Historic Park** is one of the more interesting historical mansions in northern California, primarily because the Bidwells were so interesting themselves (two presidents were among their guests at their 1868 Washington, DC, wedding). The pink Italian villa–style mansion is worth seeing on one of the $2 tours that start on the hour till 4. Probably the most fascinating tour is given by a blind woman who has worked here for years; she has memorized the positions of all the furniture. You might want to stop for just 20 minutes to walk around the grounds and pore over the exhibit in the museum foyer. It's free. *Corner of 1st Ave. and The Esplanade, tel. 916/895–6144. Admission free. Open weekdays 10–5 (noon–5 in winter).*

The "California look"—well-coifed, tanned, muscled, and surfer-garbed—is the predominant mode of dress, somewhat baffling given the ocean is nowhere near.

The Bidwell legacy of trees is all around you—it's what gives Chico its expansive, leafy look even in the midst of a hot, 110° summer day. Here you'll find **Bidwell Park**, "the largest municipal park west of the Mississippi." The park has much-used bicycle and running trails, and you can swim in the tree-lined **Big Chico Creek** not far from downtown. Locals know to go swimming in the creek at One-Mile (1 mile) or Five-Mile (5 miles) but the water at One-Mile tends to be gross. The park gets dry, craggy, rugged, and pleasantly secluded as you head toward Five-Mile. The Upper Park may be the best part of all—unspoiled and secluded. Skinny- dippers head for Bear Hole, known locally as Bare

Hole. Back in town, the **Rose Garden** at Chico State blossoms roughly from March through December. There are paths among the bushes, and strategically located benches. Bring your lunch and maps, and plan the rest of your trip here.

BASICS ● ● ●

TOURIST INFORMATION **Chico Chamber of Commerce** (Corner of 5th and Main Sts., tel. 916/891–5556) stocks "The Visitor Guide," a seasonal listing with map, hot spots, sights, and strolls in the area. .

The *Chico News and Review*, free every Thursday and available everywhere (gas stations, grocery stores, etc.), provides an excellent weekly calendar, as well as well-written movie, theater, and concert reviews.

GETTING AROUND ● ● ●

Both **Greyhound** and **Amtrak** have stations in Chico (*see* Basics at the beginning of the chapter), but if you want to travel around the area, you're better off in a car. From Sacramento, take I–5 north to Orland, and head east on Route 32 into Chico). Your chances of catching a ride out of Chico are pretty good when Cal State Chico is in session (end of August to mid-May). Many of the students are from the San Francisco Bay Area, and have no problem making the three-hour drive home for the weekend. Check the ride board on campus, or make some new friends.

Within the city of Chico, you can get by okay in the downtown and university areas on foot, though the heat of a summer day might have you seeing mirages on the sidewalks. Chico is also a great town for bicycling, largely because it's pretty flat. Just carry plenty of water in the summer, and walk your bike on the campus or the bike police get ornery (a ticket is guaranteed).

The **Chico Area Transit System** (tel. 916/893–5252) can take you away from downtown to the shopping malls and the outer reaches of Bidwell Park, as well as to some of the neighboring towns.

WHERE TO SLEEP ● ● ●

Chico has the standard motel fare and a few bed-and-breakfasts. You could always try to make friends with some students, most of whom live off-campus or in Greek-system houses (Nord Avenue and the area south of campus are high-density student spots). In commercial establishments, add 9% tax to the room price.

The best of the average motel scene includes **Econo Lodge** (630 Main St., tel. 916/895–1323), **Safari Garden Motel** (2352 Esplanade, tel. 916/343–3201), **Motel Orleans** (655 Manzanita Ct., tel. 916/345–2533), and **Motel 6** (665 Manzanita Ct., tel. 916/345–5500). All offer rooms for $40 a night or less.

For nicer, pricier accommodations try the **Music Express Inn** (1091 El Monte Ave., east off Rte. 32, tel. 916/891–9833), which still serves as a music school. There are eight rooms in this modern and pretty house, $55–$95. A well-organized group could rent out the entire house.

For that bed-and-breakfast charm, try the homey **O'Flaherty House Bed and Breakfast** (1462 Arcadian Ave., tel. 916/893–5494) near the university. It has four rooms that cost $45–$72 (each room shares a bath). The cottage outside is $99, $125 on Fridays and Saturdays. Reservations "definitely recommended."

CAMPING You'll find a pleasant place to camp for the night about a half-hour away, off Route 99 toward Corning at Woodson Bridge, right on the Sacramento River. Call MISTIX for reservations. (*See* also Where to Sleep in Red Bluff, *below.*)

● ● ● FOOD

If you don't eat well in Chico, it's your own fault. Besides many cheap burrito spots, there are numerous complimentary buffets and happy hours—try **La Fonda's** (downtown, corner of 2nd St. and Salem Ave., tel. 916/345–5289) or **Lollipop's** (2201 Pillsbury, tel. 916/343–2267). Breakfast downtown is a very Chico thing to do. Three highly popular, under-$5 spots are: **Cory's** (230 W. 3rd St.) for the homemade bread, baked goodies, ambience, and coffee (closed mid-afternoon); **Oy Vey Café** (146 W. 2nd St.) for bagels and the hefty $3 Early Bird Special of omelette, bacon, home fries, and bagel; and **Perche No!** (119 W. 2nd St.) for incredible Belgian waffles and fresh fruit ($4) and espresso (open weekdays 8:30 AM–11 PM, till midnight weekends). Another Chico institution is **Al's Drive-In** (1844 Esplanade, tel. 916/342–2722), which serves thick, creamy milk shakes to die for (open daily 10 AM–10:30 PM). Cafés and bakeries are well frequented, and there are more frozen yogurt places catering to students than there are copy shops. Many restaurants are closed on Sunday nights.

UNDER $5 **The Madison Bear Garden**. Just off campus, "The Bear" is a popular watering hole, hamburger joint, dance spot, student hangout, and bastion of rowdiness. Check for the food and drink specials, such as Burger Madness ($3 for burger and fries). *326 W. 2nd St., tel. 916/891–1639.*

Speedy Burrito. Listen to this: grilled steak tostada salad for around $4; grilled-steak, rice-and-bean, or stir fried-veggie burrito for less than $3; black bean soup and tortilla chips for $1.50. The ingredients are fresh and the food is good—not the burrito mush you might associate with cheap Mexican food. The Nord Avenue location delivers. *300 Broadway, tel. 916/894–1178; and 1031 Nord Ave., tel. 916/896–0141.*

UNDER $10 **Scotty's Boat Landing**. For a real Chico experience, head to Scotty's on the Sacramento River and have weekend brunch on the deck along the water. Scotty's is extremely in with inner-tubers, who congregate here for burgers and brews after a day of floating down the river and basking in the sun. *River Rd., tel. 916/893–2020. Take Rte. 32 a few mi toward Orland and turn left on River Rd., or head west on Sacramento Ave. and turn right on River Rd. Open 10 AM–midnight.*

UNDER $15 **R. Fish & Co.** This popular and crowded restaurant, with attractive lighting and casually elegant decor, is also a market and oyster bar. The seafood specialties, like pasta jambalaya, average about $14 ($4 less if you skip the salad bar), but you can get the seafood buffet, a seafood salad, or a seafood sandwich for $5–$8. Buy yourself a colorful T-shirt with a fishy pun. *Corner of East Ave. and The Esplanade, tel. 916/895–3474. Open Sun.–Thurs. 11 AM–9:30 PM, Fri.–Sat. 9 AM–10 PM.*

● ● ● AFTER DARK

It's so hot at night in summer that everyone hangs out outside. Teenagers cruise the Esplanade, hormones revving. If you go 28 mph, you'll hit all the lights just right.

Chico has a reputation for exciting collegiate nightlife. The vastly popular Friday night **Concerts in the Downtown City Plaza** during the summer and fall feature excellent jazz, rock, bluegrass, and classical musicians. **The Topflight Ballroom** (303 Main St., tel. 916/342–5131) has live music Tuesday through Saturday, and a comedy club Friday through Sunday. **LaSalle's** downtown has live bands. Stop by **Panama Café** (177 E. 2nd St.) for Cajun munchies. You can go on a pub crawl from **Riley's** to **The Oaks** to **The Graduate**, or just try to infiltrate one of the many frat keggers. A ways from campus you'll find the **Sierra Nevada Brewery** (1075 E. 20th St., tel. 916/345–2739) with its taproom and restaurant. **Tower Books** (211 Main St., tel. 916/893–2665), open daily until midnight, is where everyone hangs out late night, thumbing through magazines, checking out new releases, running into friends. It's a post-movie, post-dinner, post-Concert in the Park thing to do. The **Pageant Theater** (352 E. 6th St., tel. 916/343–0663) has a good schedule of foreign and domestic films, as well as real popcorn and a nostalgia-inducing $3.50 admission price.

OUTDOOR ACTIVITIES ● ● ●

Favorite outdoor activities are inner-tubing and swimming in **Bidwell Park**, and bicycling, bicycling, bicycling. For bike information and rentals contact: **Chico Velo Cycling Club** (Box 2285, tel. 916/343–8356); **Mountain Sports** (176 E. 3rd St., tel. 916/345–5011); or **Campus Bicycles** (Corner of 5th and Main Sts., tel. 916/345–2081).

Only a half-hour drive away, **Lake Oroville** has a full range of recreational activities—boating, waterskiing, swimming, camping, picnicking, hiking (*see* Near Chico, *below*). **Chico State's Adventure Outings** (tel. 916/898–6116) plans day-long and overnight hiking, skiing, and rafting trips. Chico State students get a great bargain; non-students can sign up if space is available. **Lassen Volcanic National Park** (*see* Mt. Lassen, *below*) is less than two hours away. In the winter, fine cross-country skiing is just a short drive east near the small, interesting towns of Paradise and Inskip.

Near Chico

PARADISE ● ● ●

Easily 10° F cooler than Chico in the summer, and just 20 minutes east of Chico on a road called the Skyway, you'll find Paradise (what else?). Many young families and retired people have moved to this little well-kept town, which used to have the less celestial name "Pair o' dice." The town is a great base for cross-country skiing in winter, and has a small symphony, the well-regarded **Theater on the Ridge**, the **Gold Nugget Museum**, and the **Feather River Canyon** nearby. It also has restaurants that Chicoans drive here for, such as **Peter Chu's**. For more information, contact the **Paradise Chamber of Commerce** (tel. 916/877–9356).

The **Covered Bridge/Honey Run Road** off the Skyway to Paradise is a favorite bicycling destination and a pretty place to romp in the water (with everyone else). Follow the signs; it's well-marked.

If you've an inclination to get a tattoo, look up Ronita Yvarra, a born-again Christian who is serious about body art, and won't tattoo anything demonic or names of significant others ("too iffy").

OROVILLE ● ● ●

The center of government in Butte County, Oroville has a picturesque old-time downtown, a Chinese temple, and a fish hatchery. Contact the **Chamber of Commerce** (1789 Montgomery St., tel. 916/533–2542 or 800/655–4653) for information about the town or activities on nearby **Lake Oroville** (*see* Outdoor Activities, *above*). To get to Oroville from Chico, take Route 99 south for about 20 miles.

QUINCY AND THE FEATHER RIVER CANYON ● ● ●

Less than two hours from Reno to the east and Chico to the west, and smack in the center of Feather River country, you'll find the pleasant town of Quincy—a great place for a rest or even an overnight stay. Wander around the friendly, mountainous town (elevation 3,500 ft.) and check out the **Quincy Historical Museum** downtown, where you'll find friendly volunteers, postcards, and quilts that might make you wish you knew your great-grandmother better (open weekends 10–4; free). In September, Quincy hosts the **Annual Northern Sierra Indian Days** at Feather River College. The event includes films, storytelling, food, drum groups, dancers, and a pow-wow.

Quincy is on Route 70, which climbs past **Lake Oroville** and into **Plumas National Forest.** (To reach Rte. 70 from Chico, take Rte. 99 south to Rte. 149.) The drive takes you by moderately striking rock cliffs, the clear, tumbling North Fork of the Feather River, interesting bridges, a number of side roads that lead to campsites in Plumas National Forest, and dozens of excellent spots to pull over and go swimming, sunning, or fishing.

The highway is a bit crowded on summer weekends, but not anything like what you'll find just an hour to the south around Lake Tahoe.

WHERE TO SLEEP If you choose to stay in town, try the **Gold Pan Motel** (Rte. 70W, tel. 916/283–0166) where you can soak in one of four Jacuzzis. Most of the comfortable pine-and-blue rooms have a microwave oven and a small refrigerator. Single rooms are $31, doubles $38–$40, and three of the 48 rooms are wheelchair accessible. Other options include the comparably priced **Spanish Creek Motel** (Rte. 70W, tel. 916/283–1200) or one of the motels east of town on Route 70.

FOOD **Morning Thunder Café.** This place serves up great breakfasts. A single blueberry pancake ($2) just might do it. It's huge. Or, try the breakfast burrito ($4), the 3-egg omelet ($6), or one of the scrumptious sandwiches ($5). The atmosphere is friendly and relaxed, and you can chase your breakfast with an espresso. *557 Lawrence St., tel. 916/283–1310. Open for breakfast daily 7:30 AM–2 PM.*

Moon's. Locals are wild about this wonderful, Italian-flavored restaurant with a verdant outdoor patio. House specialties, such as mushrooms St. Thomas (Italian sausage, spinach, mushrooms, and Mornay sauce), are $7–$9; or you can get an extra-large "full moon" vegetarian pizza for $14. *497 Lawrence, tel. 916/283–0765. Reservations advised.*

The Airport Steakhouse. Vegetarians will want to avoid the big, beefy meals at this joint out at the small, local airstrip. Small planes are tethered nearby, some belonging to people who have flown in for a meal. Dinners run $10–$17. *Rte. 70, tel. 916/283–4999. Open daily for lunch and dinner (closed 3–5), Sunday brunch 8 AM–1 PM.*

● ● ● PLUMAS NATIONAL FOREST

In the huge Plumas National Forest, the Sierra mountain range to the south gradually merges with the Cascade range to the north. Though Plumas isn't as uniformly spectacular as national forests in the Sierras, you're bound to get your beauty fix from the massive granite domes in the Feather River canyon, rocky stretches of the river forks, and a number of dramatic waterfalls (the tallest of which, **Feather Falls**, is 640 feet high). The **Bucks Lake Recreation Area** (at an elevation of 5,155 feet) is especially popular with Plumas County residents for its fishing, and winter sports (especially snowmobiling), as well as its lake-side resorts and camping. The Plumas County fall foliage tour is much touted—"the closest thing to New England this side of Vermont," a brochure says. Most people will be satisfied with the color of the leaves turning on Route 70, but real autumn enthusiasts may want to make digressions on Route 89, Bucks Lake Road, and LaPorte Road.

There are 41 campgrounds in the forest, those at lower elevations open from mid-May through October. A forest map ($1) and several leaflets are available from **Park Headquarters** (Box 1500, Quincy 95971, tel. 916/283–2050) or the **Quincy Ranger District** (Box 69, Quincy 95971–6025, tel. 916/283–0555). From Quincy, take Bucks Lake Road west for 14 miles.

Red Bluff

Like many northern California towns built on ranching, mining, or logging, Red Bluff retains a mix of Victorian gentility and Old West roughness. Unlike some of the towns around it, though, Red Bluff got its start as a shipping center. Steamer service on the Sacramento River between San Francisco and Red Bluff continued until after the turn of the century. It's still a pretty little town of about 20,000 people with streets full of well-maintained Victorians. A tour map is available at the Chamber of Commerce (*see* Tourist Information, *below*) or the Kelly-Griggs House Museum. Each historic home is marked with a placard announcing the date it was built. Residents can get their homes on the tour after the structure turns 100, and the tour is a relaxing way to while away a late summer evening and recover from daytime temperatures that all too frequently turn 100°.

If you want to catch just one historical house museum in the northern state, the **Kelly-Griggs House Museum** is a good choice. The informative docents lead you through renovated rooms with interesting antique furnishings and Victorian-garbed mannequins. The Ishi Room contains artifacts about Ishi, the last of the Yahi Native Americans of eastern Tehama County. The **Kelly-Griggs Ice Cream Social** (tel. 916/527–1127) in mid-August features an old-fashioned social and band concert. *311 Washington St., tel. 916/527–1129. Voluntary donation. Open Thurs.–Sun. 2–4.*

William B. Ide Adobe State Historic Park celebrates the man who briefly ruled the short-lived nation of California. In 1846, Ide led a group of settlers against the Mexican government and for a few weeks was president of the Bear Flag Republic. U.S. government troops soon put an end to that, and Ide settled on a bend in the Sacramento River 2 miles north of what would become Red Bluff. The park has a reconstruction of Ide's adobe house, some outbuildings, a small museum, and a donkey named Lucy who's really friendly. Try to catch **Ide Adobe Day** in August, when they make a festival out of it. *3040 Adobe Rd., tel. 916/527–5927. Follow signs from the north Red Bluff I–5 exit. Admission free. Open daily 8–5.*

Red Bluffers are reserved but friendly with strangers. Drop in at **Moore's Blacksmith Shop** near downtown and watch some horses being shod. Walk over to Ash Street and chat with Bob Grootveld, who carves carousel horses and has an "electric camel" in his workshop: it's a precursor to the exercise bike and was actually in the exercise room on the *Titanic*. Browse through the antique shops on Main and Washington streets. During the summer, catch an old-fashioned city band concert on the little stage near the river (Mondays at 8 PM).

BASICS ● ● ●

TOURIST INFORMATION The **Red Bluff-Tehama County Chamber of Commerce** is well stocked with regional information. The Chamber office is next to a grassy riverside park. Save your picnic for here. *100 Main St., tel. 916/527–6220. Open Mon. 8:30–4, Tues.–Thurs. 8:30–5, Fri. 8:30–5.*

GETTING AROUND ● ● ●

Red Bluff is to the west of I–5. The center of town is around the intersection of Main Street, which runs north–south (paralleling I–5), and Antelope Boulevard, which runs east-west. Antelope Boulevard heads east toward Route 36, the main route to Mt. Lassen. The town's famed Victorian neighborhoods are to the west of Main Street, and mostly within walking distance of the business district. **Mt. Lassen Motor Transit** (22503 Sunbright Ave., tel. 800/822–9660) offers open charters from Red Bluff to Reno several times a week (*see* Chapter 7, The Sierra Nevadas and San Joaquin Valley). At the **Greyhound** station you can catch one of five buses running daily to Sacramento or one of the three to San Francisco. Seven buses head northbound. *1023 Main St., tel. 916/527–0434. Open weekdays 9–3 and 6–8, weekends 9:30 AM–12:30 AM.*

WHERE TO SLEEP ● ● ●

You can go the budget motel route (about $30–$50) or try a bed-and-breakfast ($45–$85). The motels are mostly clustered along Antelope Boulevard, and all those listed below have pools. Try **King's Lodge** (38 Antelope Blvd., tel. 800/426–5655) or **Motel Orleans** (5 John Sutter Sq., tel. 916/527–6131) for under $30 a night. For around $40, check into **Super 8** (203 Antelope Blvd., tel. 916/527–8882) or **Value Inn** (Gilmore Rd. off Antelope Blvd., tel. 800/621–2028). Room tax is 8%.

BED-AND-BREAKFASTS Red Bluff has three equally hospitable and charming B&Bs on quiet, tree-lined streets: The **Faulkner House** (1029 Jefferson St., tel. 916/529–0520), a Queen Anne built in 1890 with four rooms for $55–$80 a night; **Buttons and Bows** (427 Washington St., tel. 916/527–6405), an estate Victorian built in the 1880s, with three rooms for $50–$65; and The **Jeter Victorian Inn** (1107 Jefferson

St., tel. 916/527–7574), built in 1881, with four rooms for $45–$85. Reserve in advance.

CAMPGROUNDS You're getting into RV country, so there'll be lots of spots for you to park your Winnebago. Pick up a comprehensive listing of RV and regular campgrounds at the Chamber of Commerce (*see* Tourist Information, *above*). The 24 sites at **Red Bluff Diversion Dam** (tel. 916/824–5196) have no services but are quiet and out-of-the-way, with nice views of Mt. Lassen. Take Antelope Boulevard to Gilmore Road south and follow the signs.

South of Red Bluff, near the town of Corning, **Woodson Bridge State Recreation Area** is a pretty and well-equipped spot with $14-a-night campsites among the oaks along the Sacramento River; good fishin'. *On South Ave. Call MISTIX, tel. 800/444–7275, for reservations. Near Corning off I–5 or off Rte. 99S from Red Bluff. Open end of May–end of Sept.*

● ● ● FOOD

Food in Red Bluff is a great bargain—tasty, varied, and inexpensive. You can get away with breakfast and lunch for under $5, and dinner for under $10, depending on your appetite. Dining is informal. Your cowboy boots, jeans, belt buckle, or bolo tie won't snag a second glance.

UNDER $5 **Countryside Deli.** Punch in a Randy Travis hit at your table-side jukebox and settle down for one of the deli's "gourmet sandwiches" ($3.50 for the vegetarian, $4.50 for the Reuben) or filling daily specials (around $5). Don't forget a slice of fresh pie. A two-egg breakfast with hash browns and toast is $3, a short stack of pancakes is $2. 1007 Main St., tel. 916/529–3869. Located next to the Greyhound station. *Open Mon.–Sat. 7 AM–8 PM, closed Sun.*

The Feedbag. Here's another option for a quality, filling breakfast where "they kill you with food," as one Red Bluff resident put it. Ask for apricot syrup for your pancakes. *200 S. Main St., tel. 916/527–3777.*

Great Wok Restaurant. This being beef country, vegetarians might want to take advantage of no-meat selections among the Great Wok's Szechuan and Mandarin meals; they also have a $3 lunch special. *490 Antelope Blvd., tel. 916/529–5558.*

The Snack Box. The reassuringly down-home Snack Box serves one of the best breakfasts around—expect to wait on weekends. Omelets go for $5–$6; a stack of buttermilk pancakes (which hang over the plate) is $3; a breakfast of eggs, meat, and toast is around $4. The lunch menu includes hot or cold sandwiches ($4–$5), soup and chili ($2), salad, and homemade pies. The decor reflects the Victorian house-proud side of Red Bluff, with blue geese stenciled on the walls and dried flowers. *257 Main St., tel. 916/529–0227. Open daily 7 AM–2 PM.*

UNDER $10 **Francisco's.** With meals from $4 to $7 and two locations, Francisco's is a local favorite for Mexican food. Try the Memo Special—a quesadilla topped with lettuce and chili or the Cuco Special, a tostada with spiced beef, chicken, or chili. *914 Walnut St., tel. 916/527–1138; 480 Antelope Blvd., tel. 916/527–5311.*

UNDER $15 **The Green Barn.** A local favorite that's great for dinner or lunch. The steak sandwiches ($5) are succulent, and the prime rib ($14) Thursday–Saturday gets lots of repeat customers. The menu also includes seafood, chicken, salads, and mock abalone ($7). *Corner of Antelope Blvd. and Chestnut Ave., tel. 916/527–3161.*

● ● ● CHEAP THRILLS

At the **Red Bluff Diversion Dam Salmon Viewing Plaza** during summer and fall you can watch king salmon jumping up a fish ladder (an ascending series of pools) on their way to upstream spawning grounds. The best viewing time is between 10 AM and 2 PM;

otherwise, you may have to rely on the exhibits telling you all about the fish. *Follow signs down Gilmore Rd. after turning off Antelope Blvd. Admission free.*

FESTIVALS Locals are most proud of the **Red Bluff Round-Up**, the world's largest two-day rodeo, which is held annually during the third weekend in April. The town also hosts an annual **Arabian Horse Show** and a famous (in some circles) four-day bull and gelding sale in January.

The Sun Country Fair, overrun with 4-H-ers (wearing green and white) and Future Farmers of America, runs for nearly a week in late July.

OUTDOOR ACTIVITIES

FISHING AND BOATING Trout, steelhead, salmon, catfish, and bass are here for the casting. Call the **Chamber of Commerce** (tel. 916/527–6220) for a list of fishing guides. The Sacramento River north of Red Bluff is prime rafting and canoeing country.

HOT-AIR BALLOONING If a hot-air balloon ride over the Napa Valley wine country is too much of a cliché, try taking a ride over this part of the state. Call **Red Bluff's Adventures Unlimited** (tel. 916/527–8786) for details.

Near Red Bluff

The Tehama County Museum in the nearby town of Tehama is where interesting old-time families in the area donate their interesting old things. *Corner of C and 3rd Sts. Admission free, but donations accepted. Take County Rd. A8 south of Red Bluff for a few mi to the town of Tehama. Open weekends 1–4.*

The Yolla Bolly-Middle Eel Wilderness is where you can get away from it all (but remember to check in at a ranger station first). This nearly inaccessible wilderness area—take Corning Road west through Paskenta—is a favorite of solitude-loving locals. Contact the Corning Ranger District (tel. 916/824–5196).

Lassen Volcanic National Park

There are still folks living in Shasta and Tehama counties, sons and daughters of pioneer families, who say they can remember when Lassen Peak erupted in a huge steamy 4-mile high mushroom cloud in 1915. It's a natural event that doesn't often happen in your own backyard. The mystique of the awakening volcano captured the imagination of the national press, whose accounts of the eruption are considered to be somewhat fanciful, and is incarnated in one of the park's current-day marketing slogans, "Go Climb a Volcano." People who live in its shadow don't seem to care that it might spit and spew again one of these decades.

Clambering around the volcano is something a lot of people do, winter and summer. Walk the trail to the top of the peak and you're bound to find someone—even grandmas in tennis shoes—who has been doing it every year for the past umpteen. The park is filled with evidence of volcanic devastation, and bubbling, steaming geothermal areas. Its geologic attributes are matched by its natural endowments: wildlife, crystalline mountain lakes, vast panoramas, and sweet piney air (except when you're around the malodorous geothermal Sulphur Works). Mt. Lassen was made a national park shortly after it blew its top (if only we were all so lucky). The park marked its 75th anniversary on August 9, 1991.

● ● ● BASICS

TOURIST INFORMATION All visitors receive the "Park Guide," which includes detailed seasonal information on camping, fishing, hiking, backpacking, the naturalist program schedule, and wheelchair-access information. The guide also describes the 67 road markers that dot the 35-mile scenic road through the center of the park, and tells you about early settler Peter Lassen, after whom the park is named. **Lassen Park Headquarters**, on Route 36 west of the park's main entrance, (tel. 916/595–4444) is open weekdays 8–4:30, (open on weekends in summer). It's your source for general information and up-to-the minute reports on campground availability and hiking conditions. Near the north entrance to the park is the **Manzanita Lake Ranger Station** (tel. 916/335–7373) and the **Manzanita Lake Visitor Center** (tel. 916/335–7575; open June 15–Sept. 2, 8 AM–6 PM). For information on road conditions call 916/225–3028.

FEES The entrance fee, good for two weeks, is $5 per vehicle. The park's seven campgrounds, available on a first-come basis, are $6–$8 a night. Backcountry camping is free with a wilderness permit.

WHEN TO GO Lassen is open year-round. In winter, snow closes the road through the park, making for great snowshoeing and skiing (both downhill and cross-country). In summer, hiking, camping, water recreation, and naturalist activities predominate. Spring wildflowers and autumn leaves round out the seasons.

WHAT TO PACK Pack for warm days and cool mountain nights. Even when it's boiling outside, you'll want a jacket if you climb to the top of the peak. Huge snow drifts are present year-round at the higher elevations.

GENERAL STORES The **Lassen Summer Chalet** (tel. 916/595–3376), just inside the south entrance, has a gift shop selling "Go Climb a Volcano" T-shirts and a restaurant with an outside deck for burgers and sandwiches. Small lockers are available for 50¢ a day. **Manzanita Lake Camper Store** (tel. 916/335–7557), at the north end of the park, stocks groceries, camping supplies, gasoline, propane, soup, and sandwiches. Expect to pay a bit more for the convenience. You can also shower and wash your clothes here.

● ● ● COMING AND GOING

There is some bus service from Red Bluff to Mineral (west of the park entrance) and from Susanville. A car is your best bet. From Red Bluff, take Route 36 east to Route 44 north, which leads to the park's main entrance. From Redding, take Route 44 to the park's north entrance at Manzanita Lake.

● ● ● WHERE TO SLEEP

MOTELS AND LODGES Most visitors who don't camp stay in nearby towns like **Red Bluff** and **Redding**, off I–5; Burney on Route 299; and Chester and Susanville, on Route 36. The only place to stay within the park itself is the **Drakesbad Guest Ranch** (tel. 916/529–1512). It's a bit steep ($54–$81 per person), but the price includes meals and access to great swimming.

UNDER $40 **Hat Creek Resort.** This well-known and meticulously tended fishing resort has been around for decades. In winter there's cross-country skiing across the road, and in summer Hat Creek bubbles through. You can stay in the seven-room motel ($32 for 1–2 people, $42 for 2–4) or rent a cabin that will remind you of the places you've seen in black-and-white photos of your grandparents in the '20s and '30s ($32 a day or $192 a week for two people). Reserve ahead: Some regulars have booked rooms three years in advance. *11 mi east of park's entrance on Rte. 89, tel. 916/335–7121.*

UNDER $50 **The Lassen Mineral Lodge.** This 20-room motel has a swimming pool, tennis courts, restaurant, bar, general store, and a ski shop that are open 7:30–5 when there's snow. Some of the lodges and cabins clustered along Route 36 wax and wane with the economy, but the Mineral Lodge has been open a long time. According to the owner, 30% of the guests are European. Singles start at $35, doubles at $45. Reservations are recommended. *9 mi from park's south entrance on Rte. 36; tel. 916/595–4422. Wheelchair accessible. Reservations recommended.*

CAMPGROUNDS

INSIDE THE PARK There are seven campgrounds (for $6–$8 a night; first-come, first-served) in the state park, not all suitable for trailers. Depending on the campground, there's fishing, swimming, fireplaces, flush toilets, garbage collection, piped water, and boating without motors. Camping outside the established sites is prohibited. A free wilderness permit is required to camp in Lassen's extensive backcountry, and can be obtained from ranger stations, visitor centers, park headquarters, or park campground hosts. The maximum stay is two weeks.

OUTSIDE THE PARK In **Lassen National Forest**, which surrounds the park, there are a number of campsites near creeks, under trees, and next to pleasant meadows—all fairly close, but not too close, to the highway. Fees are under $10. Contact the **Hat Creek Ranger District** (tel. 916/336–5521) in Fall River Mills for sites along Hat Creek on Route 89, and the **Almanor Ranger District** (tel. 916/258–2141) in Chester for spots along (and away from) Route 36. All campgrounds close in winter, except the Southwest Campground off Route 36. Restroom facilities are available at the Lassen Chalet nearby. Backcountry exploration is allowed, but wilderness permits are required for overnight stays, and campers should keep an eye on the unpredictable winter weather and heed avalanche warnings.

The Mt. Lassen KOA (tel. 916/474–3133) on Route 44 in Shingletown is 14 miles west of Manzanita Lake. Amenities include a grocery store, laundromat, showers, and a pool. *Full hook-up sites $17.50, tent sites $13.50. Reservations recommended for holidays, weekends, and during the summer. Open year-round.*

FOOD

INSIDE THE PARK You're better off bringing your own food and letting the fresh mountain air make it taste like the best sandwich you've ever sunk your teeth into. Otherwise, the **Lassen Summer Chalet** (*see* General Stores, *above*) offers burgers, sandwiches, and breakfasts for under $5. It's open from May to October from 9 to 6. The **Manzanita Lake Camper Store** (*see* General Stores, *above*) has a self-service food area in the best mini-mart tradition, at mini-mart prices.

NEAR THE PARK Besides the restaurants in the slightly more distant towns of Red Bluff, Chester, Susanville, and Redding, there are a few places to eat closer to the park that are filled with locals, such as the **Mineral Lodge Restaurant** on Route 36 west of the park entrance (the bar serves "the best Bloody Marys ever," according to one enthusiastic tippler), and the **Black Forest Lodge Restaurant** on Route 36 east of the park entrance near Chester (sauerbraten and wienerschnitzel for $13 are among the German specialties). In Shingletown on Route 44 (15 miles northwest of the park's Manzanita Lake entrance) are **Auntie Bo's Bakery** (tel. 916/474–3173; open daily 7–6), famed for its baked goods, and **Big Wheels Bar and Restaurant** (tel. 916/474–3131; open daily 7 AM–10 PM).

EXPLORING MT. LASSEN

NATURALIST PROGRAMS The park offers many naturalist programs to teach you about the stars, volcanic activity, Native American ways, and flora and fauna (*see* Tourist Information, *above*). The guided tours, hikes, and nature walks really do contribute significantly to your understanding of the park. This isn't school; the naturalists do their best to make the programs relevant and fun. One of the programs, "Ooze and Ahs," has you baring your feet and squooshing through some soft, gooshy mud near a mountain lake.

HIKING A number of the park's popular hiking trails (as well as 150 miles of backcountry hiking trails) take you past some of the volcanic phenomena. The most spectacular is the **Lassen Peak Hike**, a 5-mile, five-hour uphill walk to the top of the peak. The panorama is breathtaking—Mt. Shasta looks different from this vantage point—and worth the exertion. The trail near the top can be snowy even in July. Do it if you possibly can! Also fascinating is the 3-mile **Bumpass Hell Trail**, which takes three hours to hike and features the park's largest thermal areas, hot springs, steam vents, and mudpots. One of the easiest is the scenic **Manzanita Lake Hike**. Figure 1½ hours for the 1-mile walk along the south shore of the lake.

CAR TOUR Driving through the park is strictly a summer activity, as snow closes the north-south road through the park in the winter. If anyone tells you it's just a bunch a scenery, drive through anyway. It's just a bunch of scenery, but what scenery! The "Park Guide's" list of road markers points out the peaks, lakes, and volcanic topography. The power of the volcanic earth beneath you might make you shudder—it's not something you can sense on a city sidewalk.

● ● ● PARK ACTIVITIES

Besides biking, bird-watching, horseback riding, swimming, picnicking, hiking, camping, and scenery-seeing, there's also fishing and boating, but a California fishing license is required of anyone over 16. **Manzanita Lake** is being managed as a natural fishery, and a catch-and-release policy is in effect. The catch limit at **Reflection Lake** and elsewhere is five per day. Non-motorized boating is permitted on all park lakes except Emerald Lake, Lake Helen, Reflection Lake, and Boiling Springs Lake.

SNOWSHOEING This is a favorite in the winter. Naturalist-led snowshoe walks, which emphasize the park's winter ecology and geologic history, are held at 1:30 in the afternoon Saturday and Sunday throughout the winter, and daily during holiday periods. Snowshoes are provided free of charge, although a donation is requested for their upkeep.

SKIING The winter "Park Guide" lists touring routes for nordic skiers and snowshoers, rated for different levels of ability. Especially popular with Redding and Red Bluff residents is the **Manzanita Lake Area** off Route 44 at the north end of the park.

The **Lassen Park Ski Area** is located at the southwest entrance to the park. All-day chair lift tickets are $20 for adults, half-day tickets $13. College students with a valid ID and AAA card-holders get $3 off on Fridays and non-holidays. Skiers with disabilities pay $12 for the day. Surface tows are cheaper. *Ski Area Operations: tel. 916/595–3376; the* ***Snowfone****: tel. 916/595–4464. Snow permitting, open Nov. 15–Apr. 7, Thurs.–Sun., daily during holiday periods. Rental shop opens at 8:30 AM; lifts run 9–4:30.*

SNOW TUBING Outside the park, the hill in Mineral on Route 36 is frequented by locals in the winter. Buy your tubes for $6 from the Chevron station (they'll buy them back for $4). There are spots along Route 44, as well.

Near Lassen

● ● ● LASSEN NATIONAL FOREST

The 1.2 million-acre Lassen National Forest that surrounds the park supports three significant wilderness areas: **Caribou Wilderness** to the east, **Ishi Wilderness** to the south, and **Thousand Lakes Wilderness** to the north. For maps, trail descriptions, and other details, contact the Hat Creek or Almanor ranger district offices or Lassen National Forest Supervisor's Office (55 S. Sacramento St., Susanville 96130, tel. 916/257–2151).

HAT CREEK, OLD STATION, AND BURNEY FALLS

North of the park on Route 89, you'll find world-class stream fishing along **Hat Creek**. Bring a flashlight and explore nearby **Subway Caves**, long subterranean corridors that were once rivers of molten lava. The lava on the surface cooled and hardened from contact with the air, while the lava underneath continued to flow, leaving the caves in its wake.

Farther north on Route 89, **Uncle Runt's Place** in the town of **Old Station** is a popular local restaurant and hangout. Clint Eastwood stops in from time to time. The **Mt. Lassen Inn** at Old Station has four rooms ($55–$95) in a very pretty, meadow-side location (tel. 916/335–7006). Nearby, **Rim Rock Ranch** (tel. 916/335–7114) rents one- and two-bedroom and group cabins for $32–$36. If you've come this far, don't turn back before **McArthur-Burney Falls Memorial State Park** (farther north on Rte. 89). Take the hiking trail to the base of the 129-foot falls—go there *now.* Camping in the park is $14 (reserve through **MISTIX**, tel. 800/444–7275); entry per vehicle is $5. The place is hot and popular in summer. It's chilly in the winter, but a beautiful place for a lonesome picnic.

CHESTER

Just 'cause it's a little lumber town in the mountains (population 2,500), don't think they'll have a room ready for you when you blow in late in the day. Chester is accommodation-central for hunters, anglers, and loggers, so reserve early. It's one of those towns that bulge out a little bit along the highway—in this case, Route 89 east of Mt. Lassen. The youth of Chester on a summer's night park their pickups on Main Street and hang out.

Options in motels, which are very basic and done in vintage '70s earth tones, include **Cedar Lodge** (tel. 916/258–2904) on Route 36 just west of Chester, where a single runs $28–$36, a double $35–$39. In town on Main Street there's the **Seneca Motel** (tel. 916/258–2815), charging $27 for a single and $3 for each additional person; or the 13-room **Antlers Motel** (tel. 916/258–2722) with rooms for $30–$40.

If you want to splurge, try the **Cinnamon Teal Bed and Breakfast** (227 Feather River Dr., tel. 800/676–8325), which features European-style feather beds and four rooms from $65–$95, or the larger and historic **Bidwell House** (1 Main St., tel. 916/258–3338) for about the same price.

Food prices in Chester aren't exactly small town: Breakfasts run about $6, sandwiches $4–$6, and dinners $7–$12. Your best bets are **The Knot Bumper**, with deck-seating and deli foods and sandwiches; the historic **Timber House** for steak and prime rib dinners; the **Kopper Kettle Cafe**, popular with hunters, for a breakfast pancake that hangs off the edge of the plate; the **Old Chester Saloon** for Italian fare; the **Pizza Factory** for good pizza; and the **Lassen Drugstore**, for soda-fountain specialties.

SUSANVILLE

Founded by Isaac Roop and named after his daughter Susan, Susanville is the Lassen County seat. It's bigger and more populated than Chester to the west on Route 36. If you've been holing up at Lassen Park and need provisions for your journey on to Reno, you'll find a full complement of franchise drugstores, grocery stores, and fast-food places on your way out of town. **Historic Uptown Susanville** is the distinct and unique end of town (this is where the post office, museum, and Chamber of Commerce can be found). According to one resident, the people who live in Susanville, many affiliated with the state correctional facility, Lassen Community College, or the logging industry, fall into two extremes: "people on the real conservative end and people who remember the '60s."

For fun, the locals head for the hills, angle for trout on the river or bass in nearby **Lake Almanor**, or hike and bike along the very popular 27-mile **Bizz Johnson Trail**, which used to be a rail bed and still has tunnels. In the fall, the leaves change color dramatically. In addition to Lake Almanor to the southwest, there's **Eagle Lake** to the north of Susanville.

Boating, fishing, camping, picnicking, and resort accommodations are available. Annual events include the **Sagebrush Round-Up**, a rodeo and chili cook-off, and the **Lassen County Fair** the third week in August.

Susanville has a number of motels in the $30–$40 range, most of them located at the franchise end of town. Uptown options include the historic, western-flavored **Motel Mt. Lassen** (28 South Lassen, tel. 916/257–6609), with 16 rooms ($35 for one person; $38 for two); and **The Roseberry House** (609 North St., tel. 916/257–5675), a bed-and-breakfast with four delightful rooms ($45–$65; one person, $40).

For breakfast, locals recommend **The Frontier, The Grand Café**, and **Walker's. The Aardvark** has a good salad bar and pizza. **Josefina's** and **Mi Casita** serve Mexican food; **T&A's** stirs up Chinese. **The Mahogany Room** is recommended for its steaks and full bar. All are located at some point along Main Street; prices are middle-of-the-road.

Redding

After the straight-as-an-arrow monotony of I–5, many weary travelers are seduced by the array of fast-food joints, gas stations, drugstores, and motels that beckon from the Hilltop Drive/Cypress Avenue exit. Then the town is seared into their memory by the heat that shoots past 100° F nearly all summer long.

As it happens, there's more to Redding than that exhaust-clogged intersection. It's a county seat, the major population (and shopping and transport) center for the north state, and no stranger to culture. Not many towns this size have two symphony orchestras (the recently organized Redding Symphony is giving the established Shasta Symphony a run for its money). You can rent bikes, boats, fishing gear, rafts, and just about anything else here. Annual events such as the **Redding Airshow, Shasta Dixieland Jazz Festival,** and **Redding Rodeo** draw tens of thousands.

The Redding Museum of Art and History, the largest museum in California north of Sacramento, is in Caldwell Park near the Sacramento River. Exhibits change about 10 times a year and the curators consistently snag high-quality shows. In the permanent exhibits (and the attached **Shasta Historical Society**) you can explore the history of the area and the culture of California Native Americans. The museum store has interesting jewelry, art glass, and native crafts. *56 Quartz Hill Rd., tel. 916/225–4155. Admission free. Open June–Aug., Tues.–Sat. 10–5, Sun. noon–5; Sept.–May, Tues.–Sat. noon–5.*

A short walk away, in Caldwell Park, is the fun **Carter House Natural Science Museum** whose energetic staff oversees 37 species of live animals, changing natural history exhibits, interactive displays, and a little store. The free museum also sponsors wildflower walks, nature hikes, birding expeditions, and raft trips. *48 Quartz Hill Rd., tel. 916/225–4125. Open Tues.–Sun. 10–5.*

Ask someone who lives elsewhere in the state about Redding and they'll probably say, "Redding. Yeah. I got a taco/went to the bathroom/got gas there once—and it was hot."

Stargazers should head to the **Shreder Planetarium** (1644 Magnolia Ave., tel. 916/244–4600). A cheap and thrilling date for a weekend night. Call for program details.

Because of its rapid growth in recent decades, Redding itself has a sense of sprawl, rather than of architectural continuity. Most of the older buildings still standing date from the '30s in the WPA (Works Project Administration) Moderne style. The **1939 Redding Fire House** (1335 Shasta St.) is a striking example of Streamline Moderne, in sharp contrast with the 1907 Old City Hall around the corner. **Old City Hall Gallery** (1313 Market St., tel. 916/241–7320) houses exhibits by local artists and has concert space for local musicians and touring performers. The oldest church is the **1894 African Methodist-Episcopal Zion Church** (1090 California St.), a stucco-and-wood Classic Revival building.

BASICS

TOURIST INFORMATION The **Redding Convention and Visitors Bureau** (777 Auditorium Dr., tel. 916/225–4100), is a better source of information about Redding than about the surrounding area. It's open daily until 5.

COMING AND GOING

BY BUS The **Greyhound Station** (1315 Butte St., tel. 916/241–2531) is downtown at the corner of Butte and Pine streets. Small, coin-operated lockers are available. For more information, *see* Coming and Going, *at the beginning of the chapter.*

BY TRAIN The **Amtrak Station** (tel. 916/243–4104) is located on the west side of the mall downtown at Yuba and California streets. For more information, *see* Coming and Going, *at the beginning of the chapter.*

BY PLANE **Redding Municipal Airport** (tel. 916/225–4124), southeast of town, has flights to and from San Francisco. Airport bus service to and from downtown is around $8; cab fare is about $20. For more information, *see* Coming and Going, *at the beginning of the chapter.*

BY CAR Redding is about 3 hours north of Sacramento on I–5, 4 hours from San Francisco (I–80E to U.S. 505 to I–5), and 2½ hours south of the Oregon border.

GETTING AROUND

Just remember that I–5 is your best compass, pointing north to Mt. Shasta. Lassen Peak looms far to the east and the nearer Coast Ranges hover to the west. Most locals give directions by compass point and distance, not by city block. The Sacramento River winds through the center of town, where you'll find Caldwell Park and a few museums. From I–5, the main drag, Cypress Avenue, will take you to Pine and Market streets, which comprise downtown; Lake Boulevard winds westerly to Shasta Dam in Central Valley. Parallel to I–5 to the east is Hilltop Drive, a major motel strip that eventually gets to the Mt. Shasta Mall.

BY BUS **The Ride**, administered by the **Redding Area Bus Authority**, serves Redding and Central Valley, the town to the north. *Dial-a-Ride: tel. 916/241–8295 for route information. Fare: 60¢–75¢. Service weekdays 6:30 AM–7:30 PM; Sat. 9:30 AM–7:30 PM.*

WHERE TO SLEEP

A good number of the motels in town have pools. Listed prices don't include 10% tax. On and near **Hilltop Drive** you'll find a good selection of standard national chain motels. Try the friendly **Allstar Inn** (2385 Bechelli La., tel. 916/221–0562), where you can get a room (some wheelchair accessible) for $23–$27. Other possibilities under $40 include **Colony Inn** (2731 Bechelli La., tel. 916/223–1935), which also has some wheelchair-accessible rooms; **Motel Orleans** (2240 Hilltop Dr., tel. 916/221–5432); or **Monterio Inn** (2059 Hilltop Dr., tel. 916/221–6530).

There's also a concentration of motels on **Market Street**, but they vary greatly in quality and price. Motels in nearer downtown on Market and Pine streets tend to be better run than the places farther up (and a few dollars cheaper than the Hilltop spots). For $25–$35, you can get a room in the **American Lodge** (1250 Pine St., tel. 916/241–7020); the **Budget Lodge** (540 N. Market St., tel. 916/243–4231); or the **Shasta Lodge** (1245 Pine St., tel. 916/243–6133). Comparable in quality but slightly more expensive are the **Econo Lodge** (2010 Pine St., tel. 916/243–3336) and the **Thunderbird Lodge** (1350 Pine St., tel. 916/243–5422).

CAMPGROUNDS There's good camping a half-hour drive west at Whiskeytown Lake and a half-hour or more north at Shasta Lake (*see* Near Redding, *below*). **KOA Kampgrounds of Redding** (280 Boulder Dr., tel. 916/246–0101) has 123 sites and rates ranging from $16 for a tent with one or two people to $21 for a full hookup with water and electricity and $3 for each additional person. Reservations are recommended in summer. From I–5, take the Lake Boulevard exit and drive west about a mile.

FOOD

Of course there's the pizza-parlor-on-every-corner view of Redding cuisine, but the town really does have some great (and inexpensive) restaurants. **Serendipity** (236 Hartnell Ave., tel. 916/223–4497) is the place to go for a café-like coffee experience (espressos, au laits, pastries, muffins, light lunches). Don't leave without trying a raspberry mocha ($1.50). **The Shack** (1325 Eureka Way, tel. 916/241–5126) is a favorite breakfast ($3–$9) and dinner ($7) spot for longtime locals. **DJ's Bar-B-Q-Pit** (5 Hilltop Dr., tel. 916/243–3001) serves breakfast ($4–$5) as well as their "famous" ribs ($9). **Pio Loco** (491 Lake Blvd., tel. 916/246–2111) features fine Mexican and California cuisine, and the seafood specials are just the best. **C.R. Gibbs' Alehouse** (2300 Hilltop Dr., tel. 916/221–2335) features 99¢ appetizers (quesadillas, fish tacos, fajitas, spicy french fries) and $1 margaritas during happy hour, 4:30–7 every day. Shrimp are 15¢ apiece.

A unique restaurant is **Slender Treat** (2633 Park Marina Dr., tel. 916/243–8830), which serves low-calorie, heart-healthy, and vegetarian food, from appetizers to specialty sandwiches to baked potato entrées ($4–$6). **Orchard Nutrition Center** (221 Locust St., tel. 916/244–9141) is a small restaurant attached to a natural foods grocery store and features sandwiches for $4 and bowls of frozen yogurt for $3 or $4. On your way to Whiskeytown Lake, stop at **Harpo's Deli** (1970 Eureka Way, tel. 916/241–2490) for sandwiches and picnic stuff (check out the turkey cranberry sandwich, about $4).

UNDER $5 **The Brown Bag**. Sandwich-loving locals make a habit of this place for its "feast-on-'em sandwiches" (about $4). Homemade soup is about $1 a cup, $3 for a large bowl. If you're really hungry, try the Brown Bag Special, a triple-decker French roll with all the accoutrements. *2704 Hartnell Ave., tel. 916/221–7306. Open Mon.– Sat. 9–9, closed Sun.*

Gene's Drive–In. A Redding institution—try to make it here on Thursdays when the classic car enthusiasts gather. The Geneburger, with double patty and cheese, is an old–fashioned $1.19. *2515 S. Market St., tel. 916/241–4381. Open Mon.–Sat. 10 AM–11 PM, Sun. 10–10.*

UNDER $10 **Andy's Cow Patty Palace**. More than just a breakfast and lunch place—here you get jokes, quotes, flourishes, and Shakespeare over-easy with your homemade biscuits or chili. Locals hang around over their coffee and shoot the breeze with Andy (a former Hollywood actor with a penchant for the piquant). You won't find anything quite like it anywhere. Breakfasts are $4–$5; burgers and sandwiches are about $4. *2105 Hilltop Dr., tel. 916/221–7422. Open weekdays 6 AM–2:30 PM, Sat. 7 AM–1 PM, closed Sun.*

Buz's Crab. This restaurant's casual, breezy, pier–side ambience (this is downtown, mind you) belies some seriously great food. Besides the fish and chips ($2–$7.50), there are seafood pocket sandwiches ($3 for a half–portion big enough for lunch), and seafood burritos and tacos ($3). Pick up a loaf of Buz's "almost famous" sourdough bread, or buy some fish at the attached market to bring home to grill. *2159 East St., tel. 916/243–2120. Open daily 11–9.*

UNDER $15 **Jack's Grill**. People drive for hours to have a steak here, and the place is always crowded, so wander in before 9 or 9:30 to get a table. The procedure is to put in your name and then hang out around the crowded bar and gab with your friends. It looks a bit like a dive (despite the plastic grapes on the wall) and it's dark, packed, and friendly. The waitresses have made Jack's their lifetime career. A small filet (with baked potato or fries and unlimited salad) is $13, a brochette is $9. *1743 California St., tel. 916/241–9705. Open Mon.–Sat. 5–11, closed Sun.*

UNDER $20 **Nello's Place.** This popular Italian restaurant promises a night of "pasta, amore, and vino." Favorite menu items are the veal and scampi combo ($17) and the scampi house special ($18). Less voracious diners can get something for under $10. The best deal is the soup and salad (served with bay shrimp and bleu cheese) for about $4. A full bar and a large selection of wines will help you wash it all down. *3055 Bechelli La., tel. 916/223-1636. Open Mon.–Sat. 5–10, closed Sun.*

AFTER DARK • • •

For a comprehensive listing of movies, theater, special events, live music, dancing, happy hours, and other nightlife, read the **"Spectrum"**, which the city's newspaper, *Record Searchlight*, publishes every Thursday. A safe bet for the bar scene are the lounges at the larger Hilltop Drive motels. At the north end of Hilltop Drive (near Lake Boulevard) is **Doc's Hilltop Skyroom** (10 Hilltop Dr., tel. 916/241-3673), a beacon to top entertainers back in the days when big bands could afford to go on the road and audiences weren't affixed to their home-entertainment centers). The **Redding Convention Center** schedules top-name performers today. If it's a warm summer night, hang out with the young folks along "the cruise" (which roughly circumnavigates the Downtown Mall on Pine and Market streets).

OUTDOOR ACTIVITIES • • •

Sacramento River rafting or canoeing is particularly inviting on a hot summer's day while an hour's drive to **Lassen Volcanic National Park** (Route 44 takes you to the Manzanita Lake entrance) puts you in range of snow during the winter. You can rent your gear at: **High Adventure Sports** (2643 Bechelli La., tel. 916/222-4606), **Redding Raft Rentals** (2275 Park Marina Dr., tel. 916/243-6400), **Alpine Outfitters** (950 Hilltop Dr., tel. 916/221-7333, 24-hour snow phone tel. 916/221-7669), **The Bike Shop** (3331 Bechelli La., tel. 916/223-1205), or **Wilderness Adventures** (Box 938, tel. 916/243-3091).

HIKING AND BIKING Put on your walking shoes or rent a bike and hit the **Sacramento River Trail**, which stretches from the west end of Lake Redding Drive to the south end of Diestelhorst Bridge (Caldwell Park is in the middle). You can walk on either side of the river, and cross between the two on a curious bridge that's part of the trail. In summer, the tree-lined path is mercifully cooler than the rest of town, and it feels like you've left asphalt and traffic far, far behind. Women tend to hike in pairs for safety.

SWIMMING For a standard approach to water, head for the municipal pool (tel. 916/225-4095) in Caldwell Park downtown. But if slithering down a waterslide seems like the best way to combat the valley heat, head for **Waterworks Park**. *152 N. Boulder Creek Dr., tel. 916/246-9550. From I-5, turn west after getting off the Burney/Alturas exit. $10.95 per day. Open Memorial Day–Labor Day, 10 AM–8 PM.*

Near Redding

WHISKEYTOWN LAKE • • •

Eight miles west of Redding on Route 299 is **Whiskeytown Lake**, the locals' mountain-ringed swimmin' hole, fishin' hole, and boating area. Find your own place to plunge in or drive to **Brandy Creek** (a sandy swimming beach and picnic area) or **Oak Bottom** (with a boat launch and marina for rentals). The **Whiskeytown-Shasta-Trinity National Recreation Area Visitor Center** (off Rte. 299, tel. 916/246-1225) has hiking and camping information and an incredible view of the sailboat-flecked lake. National Park Service rangers organize a number of activities like gold-panning and boat tours. Gold-panners must register at the visitor center or park headquarters. John F. Kennedy dedicated Whiskeytown Dam just a few months before his assassination in 1963, and there's a plaque to that effect at the dam.

On the way to Whiskeytown Lake from Redding, stop at the tiny town of Shasta and visit the **Old Shasta Historic Site** and **Shasta State Historic Park**. Check out the hanging tree at the **Courthouse Museum** (admission $2), the handicrafts at the little store, and the fascinating turn-of-the-century set up in **Litsch General Store** (free, but open only on weekends). Clamber among the brick ruins of what was once the Queen City of the north during its gold-rush heyday. If you're just passing through, at least stop at the **Courthouse Museum** and press the button on the outside wall for a taped summary of the area's wild and woolly history.

Several miles past Whiskeytown Lake on Route 299 is the turnoff to **French Gulch**, once a lively gold-rush town. If you have the time, drive past the trailer park on the outskirts and take a look at some of the original buildings. A short hike into the hills (starting across from the historic Catholic Church) will bring you to a pioneer cemetery.

● ● ● SHASTA LAKE

Sprawling **Shasta Lake**, 15 minutes north of Redding on I–5, can look a little ragged in drought years. The dropping water levels sometimes expose the artifacts of old gold-mining towns normally submerged under the lake. No matter what the water level, the lake's four main arms and many inlets afford miles of scenery, privacy, and fishing for rainbow trout, brown trout, and salmon. Shasta Lake supports 12 pairs of resident bald eagles, the largest nesting population of bald eagles in California, and also Merle Haggard's houseboat. You can rent houseboats ($900–$2,200 a week for a huge group of people), patio boats, fishing boats, jet skis, canoes, and parasailing gear at the 11 marinas and resorts around the lake. Two water-ski schools are also in operation.

Trails abound for the casual hiker: **Samwel Cave Nature Trail** is especially good and many, such as **Fish Loop Trail**, lead to good fishing areas. There are nearly 20 campgrounds at Shasta Lake in the **Whiskeytown-Shasta-Trinity National Recreation Area** and miles and miles of free shoreline camping (with permit). Campground fees vary from nothing to $7. Many are open all year and some are accessible only by boat. In addition, there are a number of private campgrounds. To sort all this out, visit **Shasta Lake Information Center** (off I–5 north of Redding). It's open daily 8:30–4:30.

The drive to **Shasta Dam** (take Lake Boulevard from Redding or the Central Valley exits from I–5) affords great views of the second largest dam in the United States (finished in 1945) with a backdrop of the lake and the celebrity mountain. The informative **Shasta Dam Visitor's Center** (tel. 916/275–1587) shows what it took to build the dam and how it fits into the whole power-generating scheme of the Central Valley Project.

If you're hungering for an old-fashioned tourist trap, take the two-hour **Lake Shasta Caverns** tour (tel. 916/238–2341). It starts at the store (with snack bar and all manner of gaudy souvenirs), continues by boat across the lake and by bus up a genuinely scary narrow road, and includes a walk through some fascinating limestone and marble caverns. The tour is marred only by inane commentary; nature's own work seems eloquent enough. Take the O'Brien exit from I–5 and follow signs; the tours run daily throughout the year and cost around $12.

Weaverville and Trinity County

Trinity County's entire population—less than 14,000—is smaller than many universities, and instead of occupying cramped and crowded city blocks, it's spread out over 3,222 forested, lake-dotted, snowy-peaked square miles. The people who live here (50 miles west of Redding on Route 299) are longtime residents who are particular about what happens to their county; artists who find the locale inspirational (there's lively support for theater, music, and the visual arts); loggers and miners; environmentalists; ex- and neo-hippies who want to live their lives without urban stress; and retirees. You won't find a stoplight or parking meter anywhere. The county seat, **Weaverville**, is a historic, gold-rush town with a brick- and wood-fronted Main Street. Elsewhere in town you'll find ingredients for a macrobiotic diet, clothes to wear while you're working your river dredge for gold, and friendly folks willing to talk about their good fortune to be living in such a pristine, comfortable place.

Hidden away in the **Trinity Alps** (as beautiful in their own way as their European counterparts) are uncrowded hiking trails, backpacking Shangri-las, and lonely lakes. The **Trinity River**, which flows along Route 299 as you go west from Weaverville, is prime for rafting, gold-dredging, and trout, salmon and steelhead fishing. The houseboats for rent on **Lewiston** and **Clair Engle (Trinity)** lakes are more secluded and less expensive than those on other north state lakes. There are also resorts, cabins, and campgrounds, as well as horseback riding and llama touring (*see* Lewiston, *below*). If you travel north on Route 3 from Weaverville, you'll notice Scenic Byway signs along the road referring to sites of regional historical importance (e.g., old logging operations) and directing you to scenic vistas. A free, interpretive map is available at the Trinity County Chamber of Commerce in Weaverville (*see* Tourist Information, *below*).

BASICS ● ● ●

TOURIST INFORMATION **Trinity County Chamber of Commerce** is a great source of information for the whole area. If possible, talk to Dale Lackey, an expert angler who writes books on the great outdoors and knows all about fishing, hiking, and rafting in the Trinity Alps. *317 Main St., Weaverville 96093, tel. 916/623–6101. Open weekdays 9–5 and varied hours on summer weekends.*

Weaverville Ranger District Office on Route 299 in Weaverville has very helpful trail maps and pamphlets about bird-watching, wildlife, flowers, and trees. You can obtain permits for camping in wilderness areas here. *Box 1190, Weaverville 96093, tel. 916/623–2121. Open summer, daily 8–4:30; rest of the year, weekdays 8–4:30.*

WEAVERVILLE ● ● ●

The most interesting sight in this town is the **Joss House State Historic Park** (Oregon and Main Sts., tel. 916/623–5284), otherwise known as "The Temple of the Forest Beneath the Clouds." Originally built by and for Chinese pioneers, this is the oldest Taoist temple in California still in use. The building was constructed in 1874 to replace a 20-year-old structure destroyed by fire. Back in the late 19th century, Weaverville's Chinese community numbered 2,500, and had its own restaurants, bakeries, barbershops, and the Golden Gate Saloon with 17 gambling tables and tea as the only beverage. A free exhibit shows the history of the Chinese in California and in Trinity County.

The **J.J. (Jake) Jackson Memorial Museum** also explores Trinity County's past in interesting ways, including a display of jail cells covered with graffiti dating back as far as the 1880s. *508 Main St., tel. 916/623–5211. Admission free. Open Apr.–Oct., daily 10–5; Nov.–Mar., daily noon–4.*

At the **Highlands Art Center** you can see what Weaverville's active arts community is up to these days. *503 Main St., tel. 916/623–5111. Open Tues.–Sat., 10–5.*

Though it's a tiny town, Weaverville's location at the junction of Route 299 and Route 3 makes it a hub for travel through the Coastal Ranges and between Redding and Eureka. In addition to historical sites, the Trinity County seat has grocery stores, motels, restaurants, and a hospital—you'll find just about everything you'll need along Main Street (Route 299). The walking-tour brochure of historical Weaverville lists an amazing 116 sites of historic interest. The **Hays Book Store** on Main Street has topo maps, hiking guides, written instructions on how to be a redneck, and postcards. Check out the spiral staircases leading to upstairs porches on Main Street. All historic buildings are marked by plaques. The **Ranger District Office** provides gold-panning instruction, and you can buy the necessary equipment (for about $10) at either J. J. Jackson Memorial Museum (*see above*) or a hardware store.

WHERE TO SLEEP Budget motels cost about \$30–\$40 (\$8 more a night than in Redding). Most are on Main Street (Route 299), including **Motel Trinity** (tel. 916/623–2129), **Weaverville Hotel** (tel. 916/623–3121), and **The 49er** (tel. 916/623–4937). **The Old Yellow House** (tel. 916/623–2274) and **Granny's House** (tel. 916/623–2756) are bed-and-breakfasts in the \$55–\$75 range. There are a number of small-scale resorts in the area, and you can rent a cabin in the Trinity Alps at **Ripple Creek Cabins** (Rte. 2, Box 3899, Trinity Center 96091, tel. 916/266–3505) for about \$65 a night, \$400 for a week. On Lewiston Lake, try **Lakeview Terrace Resort Cabins and RV Park** (Star Rte. Box 250, Lewiston 96052, tel. 916/778–3803).

The cheapest option is camping in the **Shasta-Trinity National Forest**, either in improved campgrounds in the Big Bar, Hayfork, Weaverville, and Yolla Bolla ranger districts which converge in Trinity County, or in wilderness areas. The required campfire and wilderness permits are free at ranger district offices. Call 916/246–5338 for current 24-hour recreation information.

If you prefer the back seat to the backcountry, **Trinity Lake** has lots of car campgrounds that cost \$5–\$8 and offer running water, flush toilets, and boat ramps. **Bush Trail**, about 15 miles north of Weaverville, has plenty of firewood and a decent swimming beach. The popular **Tannery Gulch** (with more than 50 campsites) is closer to Weaverville and also has good lake access. You can also head for one of the many RV parks in the area, such as **Pinewood Cove RV Park and Campground** (H.C. Rte. 1, Box 500, Lewiston 96052, tel. 916/286–2201); **Del Loma Village RV Park and Store** (Star Rte. 1, Box 54, Del Loma, Big Bar 96010, tel. 916/623–2834), which also offers on-site trailer reservations for \$40 a night; and **Bigfoot Campground RV Park** (Box 98, Junction City 96048, tel. 916/623–6088).

FOOD The area's few restaurants, concentrated in Weaverville, are favorite spots for north-staters traveling to and from Trinity Alps wilderness areas. Most meals cost \$4–\$10. Within a stone's throw of each other on Main Street in Weaverville are **The Mustard Seed** for breakfast and lunch (open Mon.–Sat. 7–3, Sun. 8–3); **Pacific Brewery** for substantial meals (open daily 6 AM–9 PM); and **Mountain Market Place** for natural deli sandwiches, salads, organic foods, and Guatemalan clothes (open Mon.–Sat. 9–6). **The Confectionery** (open at 7 for breakfast, lunch, and soda fountain goodies) serves parfaits named after local peaks and road conditions: Weaver Bally, Bully Choop, Salyer Mud Slide (all \$3.75).

● ● ● LEWISTON

Even if you're sick of exploring dinky, little, historic California towns, drive a few miles north from Route 299 to Old Historic Lewiston. On **Old Lewiston Bridge**, one of the oldest one-way bridges in California, you earn right-of-way simply by being the first to arrive. You can picnic along the Trinity River, poke around the antiques and collectibles in **The Country Peddler**, take a walking tour of the **Deadwood Road Historic Area**, and finish off the day with a beer or dinner at the **Lewiston Hotel** (Deadwood Rd., tel. 916/778–3823). The hotel has served the travel-weary since 1863 when it started as a stagecoach stop, but its restaurant has only recently begun serving pesticide-free vegetables and free-range beef. Man-made sounds in Old Lewiston are so few that you can hear Nature between the spaces. **The Old Lewiston Inn Bed and Breakfast** (on Deadwood Road, tel. 916/778–3385) promises—in its brochures, at any rate—to be "romantic as all get out!"

OUTDOOR ACTIVITIES Besides good fishing, especially in the spring and fall, **Clair Engle (Trinity) Lake** has two swimming beaches, three picnic sites, five boat ramps, and many private and public campgrounds. With more than 50 lakes and miles and miles of gee-whiz scenery, the **Trinity Alps** and **Coffee Creek** are great for mountain climbing, backpacking, camping, fishing, and pack trips with horses, mules, or llamas. For information on pack trips, contact **Trinity Outfitters Inc.** (Box 1973, Weaverville 96093, tel. 916/623–2476); **Coffee Creek Ranch** (Star Rte. 2, Box 4940, Trinity Center 96091, tel. 916/266–3343); or **Shasta Llamas** (Rte. 1, Box 183-A, Mt. Shasta 96067, tel. 916/626–3959).

The helpful rangers at the Weaverville Ranger Station (*see* Tourist Information, *above*) can issue wilderness permits and recommend various hikes and camping areas suited for the length of your stay and your tolerance for exertion and heat. One popular hike begins 30 miles north of Weaverville near **Trinity Center** and goes 2 miles to **Big Boulder Lake**, and then 1 more mile to **Little Boulder Lake**. The lakes are surrounded by virgin forests and granite cliffs, and, although you're not likely to be alone out here, there are plenty of quiet places to pitch a tent. You have to leave your car behind to get to the dozens of lakes in the **Salmon-Trinity Alps Primitive Area**, where it'll probably be just you and Bigfoot, the huge, hairy manlike animal that is reputed to live in these parts (and no, we're not talking about the lead singer of ZZ Top).

For up-to-date fishing information and guides, contact **Brady's Sport Shop** (tel. 916/243–3121) in Weaverville or **Trinity Alps Angling Experiences** (tel. 916/623–6757) in Lewiston.

Mount Shasta and the Top of the State

The very top of California seems to be more familiar to Oregon and Washington residents than folks from the Golden State. Looming over all is **Mt. Shasta**. Western writer Joaquin Miller said it best in 1873: "Lonely as God and white as a winter moon, Mount Shasta starts up sudden and solitary from the heart of the great black forests of Northern California." The forests may not be as pristine now, hacked away by wood-hungry settlers and loggers and, more recently, by people engaging in recreational activities that Miller and his Modoc friends never dreamed of. But somehow, none of this has really made a dent in the mystic mountain. On a clear day, you can see the white shadow of the 14,162-foot, dormant volcano from a couple hundred miles south. Native Americans valued the mountain for its spiritual force, which was central to their interpretation of the universe. The mountain is also reputed to be home to the legendary Lemurians, as well as to a number of human types with cabalistic inclinations (the place was a "power point" during the world-wide Harmonic Convergence in the summer of 1987).

Mt. Shasta is the centerpiece of Siskiyou County, where you'll also find the railroad town of **Dunsmuir**, the logging town of **Weed** (named after one Abner Weed), the former mining and current transport hub of **Yreka**, scenic **Scott Valley** west of Yreka, and **Shasta Valley** to the east. The **Oregon Shakespearean Festival** is over the border and through the mountain pass in Ashland. If you really want to launch yourself into the unknown, head east on highways 89 and 161 to **Tulelake** and the **Lava Beds National Monument** where the birds, marshes, and caves in the spare but richly detailed, high-desert landscape may thrill you more than the state's more famous attractions.

BASICS • • •

COMING AND GOING Many of the towns mentioned below lie along I–5 (including Castella, Dunsmuir, Mount Shasta, Yreka, and Ashland). **Amtrak** has a station a half-hour south of Mount Shasta in Dunsmuir (5750 Sacramento Ave.) with arrivals and departures in the early morning. **Greyhound** passengers can arrange to get dropped off in Mount Shasta, but can be picked up for destinations north or south only in Weed to the north or Dunsmuir to the south (service twice daily).

A car or bicycle is imperative if you want to venture very far to the east or west of I–5. It's less than a two-hour drive from Yreka to Tulelake through land that will evoke all the plaintive melodies you ever heard on steel guitar. Of course, it could take considerably longer, depending on how often you stop to watch the great blue herons, western grebes, pelicans, and cormorants in the **Klamath Basin National Wildlife Refuge**. It's 1½ hours from Tulelake to Alturas, and another three to Reno.

OUTDOOR ACTIVITIES You can take your pick of activities around Mt. Shasta. Rafters can contact **Turtle River Rafting Company** (Box 313, Mount Shasta 96067, tel. 916/926–3223). Backpackers can hook up with **Mount Shasta Mountain Guides** (1938 Hill Rd., Mount Shasta 96067, tel. 916/926–3117). If you'd rather be up in the air, contact **Silent Flight** (Box 1206, Mount Shasta 96067, tel. 916/938–2061) for hang gliding or **Montague Aviation** (Box 128, Montague 96064, tel. 916/459–3456) for motorized flying.

Mt. Shasta is a peak that comes with its own folklore. "Little people" of lofty legend—the Lemurians—are said to live in the mountain. Some humans—particularly those that don't think Waterford when you say crystal—claim to have espied the friendly critters.

SKIING At **Mt. Shasta Ski Park**, all-day ski tickets are $25; $17 half-day; $16 night. There are multi-day passes, weekly specials, and group and private lessons. Ski rental is $16 all day, $13 half-day or night. Snowboard rentals are $15–$19. Chairlift rides ($7), mountain bike rentals ($8 for two hours), and other activities are available in summer. *Tel. 916/926–8610; for info on snow conditions: tel. 916/926–8686. Take Everitt Memorial Hwy. out of town and follow the signs.*

Cross-country skiing is very popular near Castle Lake, Lake Siskiyou, and on Mt. Shasta. **Fifth Season Mountaineering Shop** (tel. 916/926–3606) rents equipment ($9 a day) and other mountaineering gear as well.

WATER SPORTS **Lake Siskiyou** is where Mount Shasta locals go—for a drive and sunset after work, a picnic on a Saturday, a swim anytime, and camping, fishing, and boating. There's a park access fee. Campsites are $10, $13 for full hookup; hourly boat rentals range from $3 for a kayak to $25 for a 28-foot patio boat. For reservations and details, contact **Lake Siskiyou Camp-Resort** (tel. 916/926–2618). From I–5, take the central Mount Shasta exit, go west on Hatchery Lane to Old Stage Road, and then head left on W.A. Barr Road. Ten miles southeast of Lake Siskiyou is alpine **Castle Lake**, where fishing, swimming, camping, cross-country skiing, and picnicking are free.

● ● ● MOUNT SHASTA

At the foot of the mountain, the town of Mount Shasta embraces both the Good Old Boys and the funky New Age-ers. This is "green" territory as much as it is redneck. In places like the **Bagel Cafe** and the **Golden Bough Bookstore**, you'll find a bit of Madison, Cambridge, Eugene, Austin, and other college towns. One tourist brochure lists "metaphysical points of interest," such as the Buddhist monastery, Shasta Abbey, and "Panther Meadows and other locations you are led to" on the mountain. The bulletin board in the Bagel Cafe (*see below*) is a good source of flyers and posters for activities such as **Clairvoyant Lightwork** (tel. 916/926–6623), **Ascension Power Weekends on Mt. Shasta** (tel. 916/926–4176), and various massage services.

One of the best views of Mt. Shasta is from **Black Butte**, which sits next to it like some smaller, darker alter-ego. John Muir once called the 6,325-foot dome Muir's Peak. It'll take you about three hours to hike the trail to the top. To get here, you can take Everitt Memorial Highway and do your best to follow the confusing signs, or ask for more detailed instructions at the visitor center.

The **Sisson Museum** (1 N. Old Stage Rd., tel. 916/926–5508) features changing exhibits about Native Americans, old-time school days, geology, and weather. You can observe the latest tremors on a seismograph, and see a piano (once owned by pioneer Elda McCloud) that traveled by ship around Cape Horn, by boat to Red Bluff, by freight train up the Sacramento Valley, and finally by mule team to Siskiyou County. Next door at the **Mount Shasta Fish Hatchery** (tel. 916/926–5508) you can walk among the hatching and rearing ponds out back to see (and smell) trout in all stages of development (open Mon.–Sat. 10–5, Sun. 1–5).

The popular **Alpenfest Carnival** is the first weekend in February. Mt. Shasta's **Fourth of July** celebration draws thousands of people from miles around. It has a parade, a run, and fireworks at nightfall that splay out across Lake Siskiyou. **Mount Shasta Convention and Visitor Bureau** (300 Pine St., tel. 916/926–4865) has a helpful staff and lots of information. Pick up a copy of the invaluable **Siskiyou County Scene**. From I–5, take central Mount Shasta exit.

To get to downtown Mount Shasta, take the central Mount Shasta exit off I–5.

WHERE TO SLEEP There are a number of motels in the $25–$40 range, many with outdoor spas and pools. Most are located along South Mt. Shasta Boulevard. The Visitor Bureau has a current listing. **Strawberry Valley Inn** (1142 S. Mt. Shasta Blvd., tel. 916/926–2052) is a newly renovated, 1950s-style motor court with friendly management and decent furnishings. Two of the 15 rooms are wheelchair accessible (single, $37; double, $29–$49; free coffee, tea, and wine). The **Evergreen Lodge** (1312 S. Mt. Shasta Blvd., tel. 916/926–2143) has 20 rooms (most wheelchair accessible), kitchen suites, a pool, and a spa (single, $24; double $30–$36). Other good options include **Swiss Holiday Lodge** (2400 S. Mt. Shasta Blvd., tel. 916/926–3446), which has a pool and a hot tub, and **Finlandia Motel** (1612 S. Mt. Shasta Blvd., tel. 916/926–5596).

Bed-and-breakfasts are at least $55, but run $15–$30 cheaper in nearby McCloud (*see* McCloud, *below*).

HOSTEL **Alpenrose Cottage Hostel** (AYH) is a brand-new, aesthetically pleasing, and very friendly place with dorm-style bunk rooms for 12, wood-burning stove, shared kitchen and family room, laundry, a deck with a prime view of Mt. Shasta, and a trailer for families. *204 E. Hinckley St., Mount Shasta 96067; tel. 916/926–6724. From downtown, walk north 20 min. on N. Mt. Shasta Blvd., take a right at the KOA sign on E. Hinckley St. Members, $8.50; non-members, $11.50; showers/day use: $2; $1 linen rental. Open year-round.*

CAMPING Camping costs from nothing to about $8 at the 13 recreation sites in the McCloud and Mt. Shasta ranger districts. Try **Ah-Di-Na**, 4 miles south of Lake McCloud off Route 89 (and notice the remains of a Native American settlement and William Randolph Hearst's 1930s homestead); **McBride Springs**, 4½ miles northeast of Mount Shasta on Everitt Memorial Highway; or **Sims Flat**, 7½ miles south of Castella (south of Dunsmuir) off I–5. For information, call 916/926–3781. Another option is to head to **Lake Siskiyou**—as the natives do (*see* Outdoor Activities, *above*).

If you don't want to rough it quite that much, check into the **Mt. Shasta KOA RV Park and Campground**. The KOA is just up the street from the Alpenrose hostel and within easy striking distance of downtown and its attractions. *900 N. Mt. Shasta Blvd., Mount Shasta 96067, tel. 916/926–4029; for reservations, 800/736–3617. Tents, $15; extra people, $3; horse or llama stalls, $7; showers only, $5; "kamping kabins," $25 for two (bring your own bedding); weekly and monthly rates available. Reservations recommended.*

FOOD At the **New Age Mt. Eddy Bagel Cafe** (105 E. Alma St., tel. 916/926–2800), you can have a healthy evening meal for $5–$6. The fairly new **White House** (1013 S. Mt. Shasta, tel. 916/926–2988) or **Marilyn's Restaurant** (tel. 916/926–2720), right across the street, serve great breakfasts (and other meals) for $5–$10. **Pancho and Lefty's** and **Subs 'n Such** on West Lake Street will do you for a fast and cheap lunch ($2–$5).

For a spaghetti-after-you-slalom-type Italian meal, try the well-established **Piemont** (1200 S. Mt. Shasta Blvd., tel. 916/926–2402); or **Mike & Tony's** (501 S. Mt. Shasta Blvd., tel. 916/926–4792), where you can get a meal for under $10. Then there's the slightly more chic, slightly more expensive **Bellisimo** (204-A W. Lake St., tel. 916/926–4461). There's also Mexican (**Lalo's**), German (**Willy's Bavarian Kitchen**), Franchise (**Round Table Pizza** or the **24-hour Jerry's**), and Fish (**Avalanche Fish Company**). If nothing but bean sprouts will do, head for **Mountain Song Natural Food Market** (134 Morgan Way).

NEAR MOUNT SHASTA

MCCLOUD This small town east of Mt. Shasta on Route 89 used to be owned entirely by McCloud River Lumber Company. If they didn't like you, they'd take up your section of wooden sidewalk until you behaved (so says a long-time north state resident). Nowadays, the pleasant and quiet town is known for hosting a number of popular square-dance events. **McCloud Heritage Days** in late August features logging contests. Ask the locals for the best way to get to **McCloud Falls** (or follow the signs for Fowlers Campground) for excellent swimming and rock diving.

McCloud has several interesting and relatively inexpensive bed-and-breakfasts. **Stoney Brook Inn Bed and Breakfast** (309 W. Colombero, tel. 800/369–6118), in a restored historical building, offers restorative New-Age programs such as therapeutic massage and programs through the Awakening Heart Retreat Center that emphasize yoga, healing, and bodywork. The inn has 18 rooms (single, $22; double, $30 for shared bath, about $10 more for private bath) and five kitchen suites ($48–$65). Work exchange is available. The gracious **Joanie's Bed and Breakfast** (417 Lawndale Ct., tel. 916/964–3106) is tucked away in the pines with incredible views of Mt. Shasta. Its four rooms cost $45–$55. **Hogin House Bed and Breakfast Inn** (424 Lawndale Ct., tel. 916/964–3125) was built in 1905 with McCloud River Lumber Co. lumber. All rooms are $40 for 1–2 people; $10 for each additional person.

For a good meal, head to **Dance Country Restaurant** (424 Main St., tel. 916/964–2225). Breakfast and lunch sandwiches cost $4–$6; dinners range from steamed veggies with lemon-herb dressing ($6) to prime rib ($13).

DUNSMUIR This long, snaky town along the upper Sacramento River canyon is home to a large number of retirees who say they've found "a little piece of paradise" as if the phrase were coined especially for this place. The town originally flourished with the coming of the railroad, and its life seemed charmed until the summer of 1991 when a train car carrying chemicals used in making pesticides jumped the tracks and landed in the Sacramento River. The resulting chemical spill has polluted the pure water, of which residents had been justly proud, and killed many a fish far down river. The disaster's long-term effects aren't yet known. In the meantime, Dunsmuir remains a tidy town with interesting historical buildings, a pleasant city park, and a municipal swimming pool right next to the Chamber of Commerce.

The **Dunsmuir Museum** (4101 Pine St., tel. 936/235–2177) holds one of the largest assortments of train-related memorabilia in northern California, in addition to a curious collection of various old-time items that aren't interpreted or placarded for the unenlightened visitor. The old telephone switchboard was actually used until 1983. During the annual **Dunsmuir Railroad Days**, there's usually a Sacramento River Run, mule-drawn wagon rides, a Rotary Club pancake breakfast, street dances, softball tourney, carnival, parade, a Lions Club chicken barbecue, model railroad display, and whatever else they can think of to occupy about four days in late June.

The **Chamber of Commerce** (tel. 916/235–2177) is filled with helpful citizens and who will help you customize a drive, a hike, or a fishing trip. The **Mumbo Basin-Castle Crags Loop** is popular with car-trekkers.

The **Railroad Park Resort, Restaurant,** and **Caboose Motel** gives you the chance to sleep or eat in a railway car. The motel experience, at $60–$70 a night, may or may not be what you want (rooms look the same with your eyes closed), but the dining experience is worth it. The cars are antique and elegant and softly lit. Patrons hop aboard for the seafood and prime rib ($12.95). Adjacent is a popular RV park and campground (tent campsites are $10; RV hookup is $14). *100 Railroad Park Rd., tel. 916/235–4611 (restaurant), 916/235–4440 (motel/cabin), 916/235–9983 (campground). Take the marked exit south of Dunsmuir. Restaurant open Wed.–Mon. 5 PM–9:30 PM; reservations strongly advised.*

The Dunsmuir Inn (5423 Dunsmuir Ave., tel. 916/235–4543) is a very friendly bed-and-breakfast (look for the porch swing). The place was built in 1925 as a hospital, with the surgery located in the adjacent ice-cream parlor. One guest remembered how as a boy he used to climb a tree and watch the surgical proceedings through the window. Rates are $50–$60, and the decor is simpler than most B&Bs.

Joaquin Miller's Restaurant also gets raves from locals. The entrees, billed as Early California Cuisine, run $8–$12. Try lemon-and-chive Red Snapper ($8), or abalone-and-scallop Steak ($11.50). *5740 Dunsmuir Ave., tel. 916/235–0414. Open Wed.–Sun. 6–10 PM.*

CASTLE CRAGS/CASTELLA **Castle Crags State Park** (Box 80, Castella 96017, tel. 916/235–2684) is home to magnificent, soaring granite crags that can actually startle you as you drive north on I-5. Hiking on the crags is popular with north-staters. "You can spend a lifetime up there," one regular said. You'll get awesome views of Mt. Shasta and the upper Sacramento River valley, and there are picnic areas and ranger-led hikes and talks during the summer. The park is an access point for the Pacific Crest Trail. Day use is $5 (free if you're on foot); the campground fee is $14 a night. Call MISTIX for reservations (*see* Chapter 1, Basics).

There's an unexpectedly attractive place to stay in the nearby riverside community of Castella—**The Castle Stone Cottage Inn** (tel. 916/472–3617), built in 1926, has cozy, lace-curtained stone cottages for $65–$85 a night (you'll eventually sleep through the wailing of the trains). The 33 campsites of **Cragview Valley** (tel. 916/235–0081) just down the road, are open year-round ($15 full hookup, $10 tents, reservations advised).

YREKA • • •

The town of Yreka, north of Mt. Shasta on I–5, was begot during the gold rush. It was first called Thompson's Dry Diggins, then Shasta Butte City, then Shasta Plains, then Ieka, and then Wyreka. The Historic Walking Tour, offered through the tourist center, will give you a sense of the town's origins. Historic Miner Street was once said to be the "richest square mile on earth." In 1887, after the gold rush ended, the town got another boost from the Southern Pacific Railroad. Yreka is also the Siskiyou County seat (see the free gold nugget display at the courthouse).

Those who wish to "Waltz Across Texas" or do the "Tush Push" should find out when the next country line dance class is being held. Classes cost about $4 and information is available at the tourist center.

The free **Siskiyou County Museum** has well-presented exhibits on pioneer history, gold mining, and fur trapping, among other things; an outdoor museum features logging exhibits and replicas of a miner's cabin, a mine shaft, and a church. *910 S. Main St., tel. 916/842–3836. Open Tues.–Sat. 9–5, Sat. 10–4.*

If you're curious about old steam engines and have an itch for a slow-moving, 3½-hour journey with some great views of Mt. Shasta, take a ride on the **Blue Goose Excursion Train**. You'll squeal as the train chugs through the mountain-edged hinterlands of Shasta Valley to the little town of **Montague**, which has not yet become jaded by the hundreds of train travelers who disembark several days a week during the summer. Montague is a historic old mining town which has stayed small and sleepy (and inexpensive) despite the train traffic because of its distance from I–5. You'll have an hour's stopover for lunch and browsing. The train conductors are hospitable and interesting, and even the loudspeaker commentary manages to avoid being overly effervescent and superfluous. *Yreka Western Railroad Depot, 300 E. Miner St., tel. 916/842–4146. From I–5, turn east at the Central Yreka exit. The Blue Goose runs June–Aug., Wed.–Sun., with some weekend runs in Sept. and Oct. Departs 10 AM. Fare: $9. Reserve in advance.*

Mt. Shasta Ranger District office is on Alma Street (off N. Mt. Shasta Blvd.). **Yreka Chamber of Commerce** (1000 S. Main St., tel. 916/842–1649) is at the corner of Turre Street, near the Siskiyou County Museum. For the **Yreka Tourist Information Center** take the central off-ramp to Miner Street and follow the signs.

WHERE TO SLEEP There are a number of motels in the $25–$35 price range, which means more choice and better prices than in Ashland, Oregon, 45 minutes to the north. Those listed below are fairly basic, clean, and comfortable. Add 8% tax.

Gold Pan Motel (801 N. Main St., tel. 916/842–9918) has a pool and 18 slightly worn rooms, some wheelchair accessible, starting at $25 (doubles, $28–$32). **Heritage Inn** (305 N. Main St., tel. 916/842–3365) has 22 rooms, with singles costing $32, doubles $35. **Motel Orleans** has two locations (south at 1806B Ft. Jones Rd., tel. 916/842–1612; and north at 136 Montague Rd., tel. 916/842–5781) with a total of 117 rooms. The well-managed motels have pools and some wheelchair-accessible rooms, starting at $32 for a single, $37–$39 for a double. **Thunderbird Lodge** (526 S. Main St., tel. 916/842–4404) has a pool and 44 rooms for those of you who love orange floral motifs. Singles go for $31; doubles $38.

FOOD Mark Twain was one of the first to notice that "yreka bakery" spelled backwards is "yreka bakery." The food at the **yrekaBakery café** is more straightforward and a very good deal. Breakfasts (served 'til 10:30) range from $3.50 for two eggs, home fries, toast, and fresh fruit to $5 for the 4-H Club omelet. For dinner you'll pay $8–$10 for lasagna, linguini (with feta and sun-dried tomatoes), or chicken marsala. Also open for lunch. *322 Miner St., tel. 916/842–7440. Open Mon.–Sat. 7–2 and 5–9. Reservations recommended for dinner.*

Both I–5 travelers and residents (including the California Highway Patrol) frequent the big and sturdy **Grandma's House** (123 E. Center St.), located right off the highway. Breakfasts (including biscuits and gravy) range from $2 for a short stack of pancakes to around $5 or an omelet; lunches are about $4; and dinners $6–$10. "Grandma's lite meals" are about $5.

NEAR YREKA

SCOTT VALLEY The 28-mile-long Scott Valley (off Rte. 3, west of Yreka) gives you one mountain-valley-river landscape after another, and a chance to poke around historic buildings, gold mines, museums, and ranches (which you can visit—ask around in Fort Jones and Etna). The **Etna Brewing Company Inc.** (131 Callahan St., Etna, tel. 916/467–5277) has tours and tasting on Saturdays (1–9 in the summer, 1–5 in the winter.)

ASHLAND The **Oregon Shakespearean Festival**, held from mid-February through October, has turned Ashland into a staging area for theater of all kinds from experimental to traditional, including the same outdoor Elizabethan productions that spawned the festival more than a half-century ago. The flat, pale-green hills make a pretty backdrop for this town. Oregonian sensibilities have prevented "Disneyfication," but you'll find Puck's Donuts, Romeo Inn, and other allusions to the Bard.

Festival productions sell out quickly, but there are always people standing near the box office trying to sell tickets, and the box office does get returns. Standing-room tickets ($7) for the play of the night on the Elizabethan Stage are a good bet if you're blowing through town and need a Shakespeare fix. For ticket information, call 503/482–4331.

Lodging rates can climb $10–$18 during the summer and holidays. For something in the $30–$50 range, try **Super 8** (tel. 503/848–8888), **Manor Motel** (tel. 503/482–4226), or **Columbia Hotel** (tel. 503/482–3726). Call the **Ashland Bed-and-Breakfast Clearinghouse** (tel. 503/488–0388) for a room in a private home. The **Glenyan KOA Campground** (on Rte. 66, tel. 503/482–4138) is $14–$18 a night; reservations strongly recommended.

The eating in Ashland is good, whether you're picnicking among the swans in Lithia Park or splurging at one of the town's quality restaurants. Try **Ashland Bakery-Cafe** (38 E. Main St.) for breakfast ($5–$7), lunch, or dinner ($3.50 for tofuburgers). A short walk in either direction will give you a choice of steak, at **Beasy's Back Room**; vegetarian, at **North Light Vegetarian Restaurant**; Mongolian, at **ChinaKorea**; and much more. For post-play prandials (and dessert), try the liqueur-tinged steamed milks at **Chateaulin** on East Main Street—they're warm and wonderful on a rainy autumn night.

TULELAKE

Tulelake is the only significant outpost of civilization east of I–5 (besides Klamath Falls, Oregon, 45 minutes to the north), and it's a small one at that. The town has a curious mixture of ingredients: only a thousand people; more millionaires (according to one resident) per capita than you would think possible (their fortunes built on horseradish); hundreds of geese in the blue autumn skies; one flashing red traffic light; and a high percentage of higher education among the populace. The University of California does genetic crop experiments up here, sometimes amidst controversy.

The town itself sits in the middle of land that is at once both desolate and magnificent, with its wide-open skies and gray-blue hues. Once you leave I–5 (take Highway 97 and Route 161 to Route 139) the sense of the place will hit you. As you're driving on Route 139, keep your eyes open for an inconspicuous little monument commemorating the site of a **Japanese-American internment camp**. Some of the camp buildings, known locally as "Jap Houses," still stand in the Klamath Basin, sold off to private citizens for various uses. While the monument doesn't draw crowds, you may spot a former internee looking around at the flattened, windswept land, trying to place where she lived as a teenager.

During World War II, the internment camp (one of 10 in the west and southwest) was the home of 18,789 Japanese-Americans, forcibly detained here by the U.S. government in an outstanding show of paranoia and bigotry after the bombing of Pearl Harbor.

Although the town's economy is based on horseradish, Tulelake is pushing tourism these days. The nearby **Klamath Basin** is on the Pacific Flyway—the main north–south migration route for myriad waterfowl species—and the birds draw avid naturalists, birders, and photographers, as well as hunters. (A "tule," pronounced toolie, is a type of bulrush found in marshes, by the way.) The **Tulelake Horseradish Festival** is held each June, and the **Waterfowl Festival** is in October.

Before leaving town, don't forget to stock up on horseradish products at the tiny but potent **Tulelake Horseradish Co.** (by the flashing red light), or find a soft cushion at the **Tulegoose Pillow Company** (347 Modoc Ave.). The town's bakery (open weekdays 6 AM–7 PM, Sat. 2–7) is on the same block as the library, thrift store, and antiques shop, and serves breakfast (about $4) all day, as well as soup and sandwiches ($2–$4). **Mike and Wanda's** coffee shop downtown (open daily 6 AM–10 PM) is also recommended. Five miles south of Tulelake on Route 139 is **Captain Jack's Stronghold Restaurant**. The town has two unexceptional lodgings: **Ellis Motel** (tel. 916/667–5242) and **Park Motel** (tel. 916/667–2913), both on Route 139.

KLAMATH BASIN

The **Klamath Basin National Wildlife Refuge**, which extends well into southern Oregon, has three distinct areas in northern California. The 47,600-acre **Lower Klamath National Wildlife Refuge** spreads south from the state line on Route 161 and includes Lower Klamath Lake. It was established by Theodore Roosevelt in 1908 as the nation's first waterfowl refuge. The area is a mix of marshes, lakes, and grassy uplands used by marsh birds and waterfowl. An interpretive auto tour route passes through.

The Tule Lake National Wildlife Refuge, at the southern edge of Lava Beds National Monument, off Route 139, encompasses open water and croplands, which help feed the migrating and wintering waterfowl. A self-guided canoe trail is open July–September (the refuge headquarters has a leaflet but there are no canoe-rental facilities).

The **Clear Lake National Wildlife Refuge**, east of Tulelake and Route 139, is comprised of 20,000 acres of water surrounded by upland vegetation. Small islands provide nesting sites for pelicans and cormorants. Waterfowl and antelope hunting is plentiful in season. This refuge is closed from spring through fall because of the fragility of the habitat.

For information on self-guided tours, canoe trails, and seasonal wildlife activity, contact: *The Refuge Manager, Klamath Basin NWRs, Rte. 1, Box 74, Tulelake 96134; tel. 916/667–2231.*

● ● ● LAVA BEDS NATIONAL MONUMENT

With its lava-scarred vistas and Native American petroglyphs, this 46,000-acre park is worth visiting even if you only have time to drive through. The park, west of Highway 139 south of Tulelake, was the site of the Modoc Indian War, where for five months in 1873 Modoc leader Captain Jack used the rough terrain and maze-like lava trails, known as the Stronghold, to fend off a well-fortified U.S. Army. It also has some fascinating lava beds above ground and some 300 caves to explore. For more information, contact **Lava Beds National Monument** (Box 867, Tulelake 96134, tel. 916/667–2282.)

You can explore the caves by yourself (check in at the visitor center, where you can borrow lights for free) or hike and climb in the lava wonderland outside. Walk up **Schonchin Butte**, a volcanic cinder cone. Hike to the **Thomas-Wright Battlefield**, one of the sites of the Modoc War, or visit where the U.S. Army Headquarters were during the war. On **Captain Jack's Stronghold Historic Trail** you can learn about the Modoc's impressive resistance. The Monument has accessible campsites, picnic tables, rest rooms, trails, and caves.

The Visitor Center (open in the summer daily 9–6, in the winter daily 8–5, except Christmas and Thanksgiving) has excellent handouts and the staff is friendly and knowledgeable. Just outside the door is the lighted **Mushpot Cave**, where you can form an acquaintance with basic lava tube formations. The park entry fee is $3. Pick up the newsletter "**Stronghold**" for current schedules and information on ranger-guided activities and tours, hikes, and other programs. There are worse souvenirs than the $4 Lava Beds mugs.

The campground at Lava Beds has 40 sites, suitable for tents or trailers. For $6 a night, the rangers promise: "No showers, hookups, dump-station, store, gas, fast food, or pop machine! Plenty of clean air, crystal-clear cold drinking water, and beautiful open space." It's free in the winter, but water is turned off.

There's plenty of unspoiled backcountry camping at Lava Beds year-round, but keep in mind the hardships of the terrain and the unpredictability of the weather. Register first at the visitor center, and bring your own water. Rattlesnakes are common.

NEAR THE LAVA BEDS

MEDICINE LAKE HIGHLANDS AREA Don't come here if you're not self-sufficient; it'll be just you, the trees, the rock formation, and the lava flow on this shield volcano, 36 miles south of Tulelake (10 miles from the Lava Beds). No stores, no gas stations, no one to borrow a jacket from. There is a U.S. Forest Service ranger station at the west end of Medicine Lake that's open during the summer. The lake is a good place to camp, swim, and picnic.

MODOC COUNTY Stuck in the northeastern corner of the state, Modoc County harbors a million acres of the **Modoc National Forest**, as well as lakes, valleys, and rocks (the stuff of junior-high science classes: obsidian, bloodstone, agate, pumice, etc.). The county is rich in birds and Native American history, and scattered with teeny towns.

Some might say the area is boring—the Chamber of Commerce brochure promises "placid, unruffled enjoyment," while a young Alturas resident said that whenever possible she and her cohorts head off to Reno or Klamath Falls for "unplacid, ruffled activities." If you want to be entertained, don't bother driving here. But if you're self-sufficient and like poking around—well then, why not?

The county seat of **Alturas** prides itself on its history: The **Chamber of Commerce** puts out a list of historical buildings and homes and an historic walking and driving tour of Alturas. *522 S. Main St., tel. 916/661–8434. Open weekdays 8:30–noon and 1–5.*

There's also the well-tended **Modoc County Museum** (600 S. Main St., tel. 916/233–2944). If you're just driving through, note all the murals on the commercial buildings downtown, and stop for a look inside the interesting old Niles Hotel.

Nipa's California Cuisine (1001 N. Main St., tel. 916/233–2520) in Alturas is a surprisingly good restaurant. You'll get a well-prepared Thai meal for about $50.

Alturas is a small oasis of 24-hour gas stations and convenience stores and many $25–$30 motels. For starters, try **Hacienda Motel** (201 East 12 St., tel. 916/233–3459); **Rim Rock Motel** (Rte. 395, Lakeview Hwy., tel. 916/233–5455); or **Wagon Wheel Motel** (308 W. 12th St., tel. 916/233–5166).

Twenty minutes away on Route 299 in the Warner Mountains is **Cedar Pass Ski Lodge**. Daily lift prices are a very low $10 for adults, and $6 for students up to age 18. Cross-country area use fee is $3. Rental available for children; lessons available on request. *Tel. 916/233–3323. Lifts operate Wed. and Fri. noon–4:30; Sat., Sun., and holidays 10–4:30.*

THE GOLD COUNTRY 6

By Colleen Cotter, with Jason Fine

In the land of yogurt and honey, the choicest color is gold. Its glint beckoned thousands of adventurers and seekers of fortune during the famous Gold Rush of 1849 (a population infusion that led to California's statehood). That patina of gold is always somewhere in the landscape, from the golden California poppies, to the burnished yellow hills, to the molten sunlight in the height of summer. And modern-day prospectors can head toward Lake Tahoe and Reno for a taste of the glitter of the casinos.

Most of the early pioneers and prospectors came through Sutter's Fort, the town that grew into Sacramento, the state capital. The city is worth exploring, especially for the history imaginatively preserved in its many lively museums. A center for the Pony Express and the western terminus of the first Transcontinental Railroad, Sacramento was once the most important city in California. Nearby, to the southwest, is the Sacramento River delta, with its miles of green lazy waterways and sleepy little towns, some of which were settled by the Chinese immigrants who labored on the railroad. And to the east of Sacramento is the Gold Country itself, a 350-mile stretch of friendly, quirky old mining towns where shootouts and hangings were commonplace—an area that was booming when L.A. hardly existed, and perhaps the only area of California where the towns were more populous a century ago than they are today.

There's a lingering sense of the Old West, both in towns that have been lovingly restored and those that are no more than a fading, ghostly memory of what they once were.

At the eastern border of the state is Lake Tahoe, threatened by overdevelopment, but still drawing millions of visitors each year to the natural beauty that transcends the condos. Many Northern Californians also frequent casinos in the Nevada town of Reno, a paler, plainer, less exciting version of Las Vegas that nevertheless has its own glitzy attractions. Besides the gold in the hills, there's plenty of first-class skiing in the Sierra Nevada mountains that stretch down the border past Tahoe. The 1960 Winter Olympics were held at Squaw Valley, and there are more than a dozen other ski venues to choose from, depending on your attitude and style.

COMING AND GOING • • •

BY TRAIN **Amtrak** serves Sacramento, Truckee, and Reno and some points in between (*see* Coming and Going in Sacramento, *below*). From there, you'll have to travel by car, bicycle, or bus to reach the small, poky towns of the Gold Country. Stations in the larger cities have 24-hour lockers.

BY BUS **Greyhound** serves most of this region, but is most reliable and frequent to and from the main population areas (*see below*).

HITCHHIKING Hitchhiking is not a common mode of transportation here, so expect to be viewed with suspicion. With summertime temperatures often soaring past 100° F, you may not want to spend a hard-earned vacation languishing at the side of the road. As always, exercise extreme caution (*see* Chapter 1). Your best bet is to find a lift from the ride board at **California State University at Sacramento** (look for flyers posted on the round kiosks), or in the Memorial Union building at **UC Davis** (15 minutes west of Sacramento).

BY CAR You can get along without a car in Sacramento, and even in Reno, Lake Tahoe, and Truckee, but to explore the Gold Country and the many national forests in the area, you'll probably want some wheels.

BY BICYCLE A bike will get you around Sacramento, and is a popular way of exploring Lake Tahoe (roadside trails make it easy). But to cover the entire hilly region by bicycle, especially in the heat of the summer, really isn't practical.

BY PLANE The Sacramento and Reno airports are the largest in this region (*see below*).

● ● ● OUTDOOR ACTIVITIES

Biking is big, especially in Sacramento, and mountain biking is gaining converts daily, especially in the Gold Country. Rivers course through the region, offering great opportunities for rafting, canoeing, and swimming. The national forests that blanket the region afford all sorts of unforgettable hiking and climbing opportunities and Northern Californians themselves flock to Truckee, Tahoe, and Reno for fine Sierra skiing. Some of the choicest fall colors can be found in the upper elevations north and east of Sacramento—try I–80 East or Route 49.

Sacramento

It's been the seat of state government since 1854, but most Californians consider Sacramento a sleepy backwater town. Its location at the confluence of the Sacramento and American rivers, near the gold-bearing foothills, made it a major destination for pioneers from the East. Later, as the western terminus for both the Pony Express and the Transcontinental Railroad, Sacramento continued to play a dominant role in the state's development, a heritage preserved in a lively way in Old Sacramento, the California State Train Museum, and Sutter's Fort. "Sacra-tomato," as locals sometimes call their city, is also an important center for agriculture which, though less exciting than the movie business, is what the state is still really all about. Unlike the folks in San Francisco and Los Angeles, most Sacramentans don't rant about the character of their city, they just go about their lives, and leave the philosophizing to people like native daughter Joan Didion (whose essays on California are good background reading; try *The White Album* or *Slouching Towards Bethlehem*). There are lots of parks and trees (some call it the allergy capital of the world), and the long shady streets provide a certain psychological respite from the long, hot summers. Sacramentans are into softball—a fact that must say something about their character, but we're not sure what—and generally embrace anything that has to do with the outdoors. As a rule, they're friendlier to strangers than either hardened urbanites or xenophobic small-towners. It's enough of a city that there's room for an active arts community, a gay and lesbian neighborhood, and a lousy NBA basketball team (the Kings).

● ● ● BASICS

Travel Service Office. This is a full-service travel agency, but you have to be an American Express cardholder to get your mail here. *515 L St., Sacramento, CA 95814, tel. 916/441–1780. Open weekdays 9–5.*

Sacramento

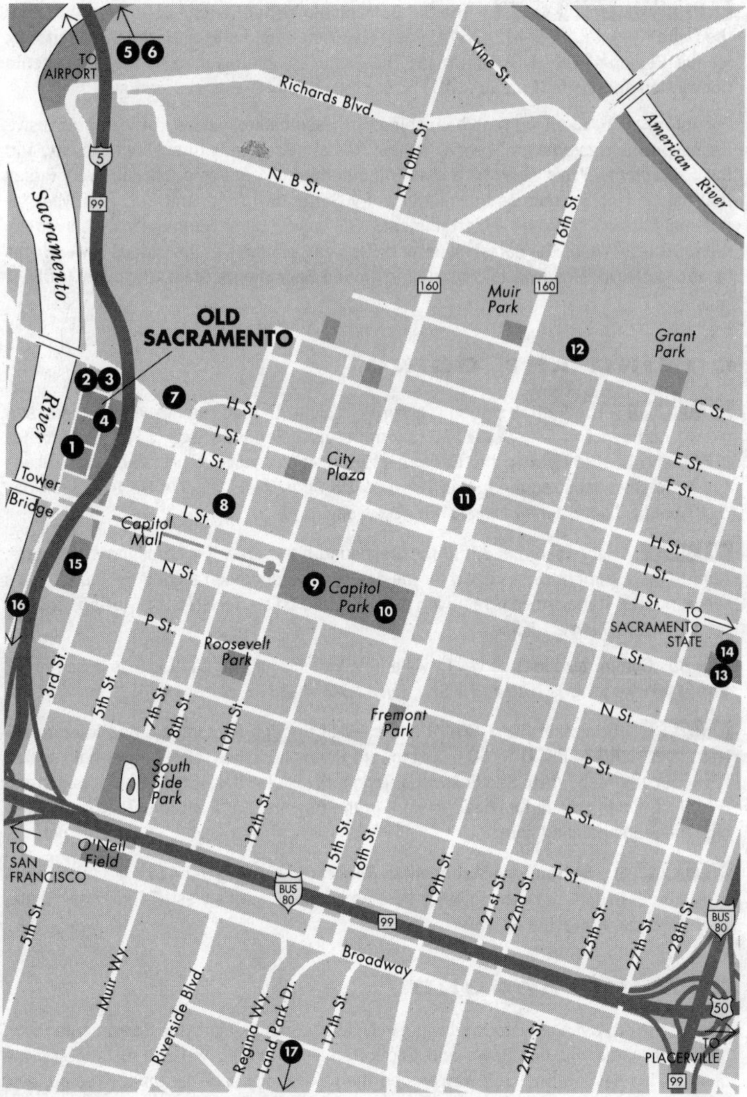

Almond Plaza, **12**

Amtrak Train Station, **7**

B.F. Hastings Building, **4**

California State Railroad Museum, **3**

California Vietnam Veterans Memorial, **10**

Crocker Art Museum, **15**

Discovery Park, **5**

Garden Highway, **6**

Governor's Mansion, **11**

Greyhound Bus Station, **8**

Sacramento History Center, **2**

State Capitol, **9**

State Indian Museum, **14**

Sutter's Fort, **13**

Towe Ford Museum, **16**

Visitor's Center, **1**

William Land Park, **17**

TOURIST INFORMATION **The Old Sacramento Visitor Center** (1104 Front St., near the Delta King, tel. 916/442–7644) has a few useful brochures and a helpful staff. Ask for the Regional Transit System map. The center is administered by the **Sacramento Convention and Visitor Bureau** (1401 K St., tel. 916/449–6711) downtown.

For information about current happenings in Sacramento, check the comprehensive listings in the *Sacramento News & Review,* free at newsstands throughout the city, and the *Sacramento Bee's* "Ticket," a weekend entertainment guide published every Friday that lists hot night spots and restaurants. Try *Suttertown News* and *Sac This Week* for non-mainstream arts and entertainment. The gay/lesbian community is served by *Mom...Guess What?,* the *Latest Issue,* and *Patlar,* all available at the various **Tower Books** locations (1600 Broadway is central) and around **Sacramento State University** (6000 J St.).

● ● ● COMING AND GOING

BY TRAIN The **Amtrak** station is a worn classic, with high ceilings, chandeliers, and old wooden benches. The *Coast Starlight* train serves San Francisco ($17), Los Angeles ($74), and Seattle ($141); the *California Zephyr* runs east to Reno ($51) and Truckee ($40). Reservations required. *Downtown at 4th and I Sts., tel. 916/444–9131. Open 5:30 AM–11:15 PM. Small lockers are 75¢ a day.*

BY BUS Sacramento is a hub for **Greyhound** buses traveling throughout the state. After the government closes down for the day, the neighborhood around the station feels seedy, but the station itself is relatively safe. *7th and L Sts., tel. 916/444–5655. Lockers are $1 a day. Open 24 hours.*

Yolo Bus Commuter Lines serves Davis and Woodland for just $1. Express buses (#43, #44, #45) are $1.50. *10th and N Sts., tel. 916/371–2877. Buses run 6:30 AM–7:30 PM.*

BY CAR **Interstate 80** (I–80) runs east–west through Sacramento and **Interstate 5** (I–5) goes north-south. **U.S. 50** heads toward Reno and Tahoe (about a two-hour drive). It's about 1½–2 hours to San Francisco. Try not to take I–80 west from Sacramento from 6 to 9 AM, when commuters head to work in the Bay Area; or from 4 to 7 PM, when they clog the roads heading home.

BY PLANE **Sacramento Metropolitan Airport** (tel. 916/929–5411), 12 miles north of Sacramento on I–5, is served by United, American, America West, Continental, Delta, Northwest, Southwest, and USAir.

● ● ● GETTING AROUND

Most of the city's major historic sites are in Old Sacramento, along the Sacramento River, and in the adjacent downtown and Capitol area—all within walking distance of one another. It's easy to find your way around the central city area: Lettered streets bisect numbered ones. Bus lines crisscross the city, and a light rail connects the suburbs, although the system is not as extensive as in many major cities. Biking's a good option.

BY BUS Buses and the Metro, better known as **Light Rail** (Regional Transit, tel. 916/321–2877), start rolling at 6 AM and continue till around midnight, depending on the route. Basic one-way tickets are $1, but rides are only 25¢ in the Central Business District from 9 AM to 3:30 PM. A $2.50 daily pass, available from the bus driver, is good for unlimited rides from 4:30 AM to 1:30 AM the following day. You can take your bike on buses and the Metro with a valid permit (get them at 1400 29th St. or 1013 K St.; cost is $5, valid for three years), but you can't use it weekdays 6–9 AM and 3:30–6 PM. The Regional Transit System map, available at the visitor center and at the above addresses, has all the latest information.

BY CAR Parking can be hard to find, especially around the Capitol and Old Sacramento. The two-hour meters there take quarters only, and meter readers will ticket you repeatedly as they cruise by. Consider parking in one of the two garages on either end of Old Sac (off 2nd St.) for only about 50¢ an hour.

BY BICYCLE With its flat broad streets, Sacramento is great for biking, and the city has begun a campaign to encourage bicycle commuting. The summer heat can be daunting, however, and thoroughfares leading out of the central city are clogged with traffic. The well-marked **American River Bike Trail** extends 26 miles from Discovery Park to the town of Folsom. For more information, including bike rental outlets, *see* Bicycling under Outdoor Activities, *below.*

WHERE TO SLEEP

Reservations are advised because of the city's heavy convention schedule. Your best bets are the national-chain motels on **Richards Boulevard,** off I–5, just north of town, or the streets closest to the Capitol and Governor's Mansion **downtown.** Spots farther afield are in somewhat suspect neighborhoods. Several older motels straddle **16th Street** downtown, but check them out first—some are a bit suspicious. There are some other budget options across the river in **West Sacramento,** the cheapest around $30. There are also a number of somewhat older, but generally cheaper motels on **West Capitol Drive,** one of which is **Capitol Travel Inn** (817 W. Capitol Dr., tel. 916/371–6983) where singles run $28–$30 and doubles $34–$40; to get here, take Yolo (West Sacramento is actually in Yolo County, across the river) Buses 40, 41, or 42 from the L Street station; otherwise, it's about a half-hour walk from downtown. Some motels hike their rates during special events. If money is no object, try ***The Delta King*** (tel. 916/441–4440), a paddle wheeler on the river, or the historic **Sterling Hotel** (1300 H St., tel. 916/448–1300). Don't forget to figure in the 11% room tax.

DOWNTOWN Staying near the Capitol will give you easy access to Sacramento's main attractions. A stone's throw from the Governor's Mansion and a short walk from Old Sac is the **Americana Lodge** (818 15th St., tel. 916/444–3980), a bit worn but clean and decently maintained, with a pool. Singles are $35 and doubles $40. Most of the 41 rooms have showers only. **Capitol Center Travelodge** (1111 H St., tel. 916/444–8880) is one of the better deals in the area. It's clean, convenient to downtown, safe, and comfortable enough for the price. Some of the 72 rooms have showers, some tubs. Singles run $36–$46 and doubles $40–$54. Some are wheelchair accessible. **The Mansion View Lodge** (711 16th St., tel. 916/443–6631), across from the posh Clarion Hotel and the Governor's Mansion, has 40 pleasant, well-maintained rooms. Singles are $36, doubles $40–$42. It's within walking distance to everything, security cameras survey the premises, and the management will give you coffee and a downtown map.

RICHARDS BOULEVARD Motels here are a little more expensive than downtown, but there's more security, the bathrooms are less scuzzy, and the decor, if you want to call it that, is more up-to-date. Best bets for under $45 are the **Allstar Inn** (227 Jibboom St., tel. 916/441–0733) at $35 and **Motel Orleans** (228 Jibboom St., tel. 916/443–4811) at $44. Nicer, though more expensive ($60) is the **Discovery Inn** (350 Bercut Dr., tel. 800/952–5516). A walking path, which is safe during the day, runs from this area to Old Sacramento. Discovery Park and the start of the American River Bike Trail are nearby.

HOSTEL **Gold Rush Home Hostel (AYH).** Reservations are required as the nine beds are always booked. Members $7, non-members $10. *1421 Tiverton Ave., tel. 916/421–5954. From downtown, take Bus 62 to Florin Rd. and Amherst, then go 1/2 block south on Amherst to Tiverton. Lockout 9 AM–6 PM.*

CAMPGROUND **KOA Campground.** Full hook-up for two is $23, no hook-up, $19. Additional adults are $4 ($2 if you're under 18). There's a lake for fishing. Reservations are recommended at least three weeks ahead. *4851 Lake Rd., W. Sacramento, tel. 916/371–6771. Take Bus 42 and get off near Eppie's Restaurant. 150 sites. Pool, showers.*

● ● ● FOOD

Wander through shady Midtown, a neighborhood centered around Capitol Avenue, N, L, and J streets, and along the mid-teen streets, and you'll find cafés and coffee shops with sidewalk seating. There are plenty of hot-dog and burrito stands around the Capitol, K Street Mall, and downtown. Old Sacramento is somewhat pricey, but worth it. If the weather's nice, treat yourself to a picnic in one of Sacramento's many parks—Capital Park (bordered by 10th, 15th, L, and N streets) is a local favorite.

DOWNTOWN Locals suggest **Pennisi's Deli** (1216 J St., tel. 916/448–5610) for a patio meal, **Ambrose Heath** (924 J St., tel. 916/448–4526) for "designer sandwiches," **Harry's Bar and Grill** (400 L St., tel. 916/448–8223) for its bar, live music, and food, or **The Earl of Sandwich** (631 16th St., tel 916/444–0919) for great burgers and a secret sauce. **The Torpedo Place** (300 12th St., tel. 916/443–7118) is a little out of the way, but has great burritos for under $5.

OLD SACRAMENTO You'll find a number of fine (read: expensive) restaurants in Old Sac and several fast-food outlets, but little in between. So unless you're prepared to deal with grease or expensive meals, eat elsewhere. Of the nice restaurants, **California Fat's** (1015 Front St., tel. 916/441–7966) is the most reasonable (under $15) and serves excellent "California/Pacific" fare in a lavish setting. More traditional European dishes are featured at the **Firehouse** (1112 2nd St., tel. 916/442–4772), the local "traditional," fancy restaurant (over $20). Also notable in the $10–$15 range are **Fulton's Prime Rib** (900 2nd St., tel. 916/444–9641) and the **Art of Pasta** (1107 Firehouse Alley, tel. 916/441–6726), which draws in the crowds but the food occasionally disappoints.

MIDTOWN The cafés and restaurants in midtown serve up atmosphere in addition to healthy food. Vegetarians, and anyone partial to brown rice, exotic cheeses, and all things soya will be very happy grazing here. Many places have sidewalk seating—a pleasant experience on warm summer evenings.

Greta's Café. This deli and bakery has a mouth-watering selection of desserts—both the healthy kind and the gooey kind. The place is bustling, with a great coffee scent in the air, friendly servers, and a progressive clientele. Try any of the salads ($3.50–$5); brown rice and gouda is a good one. Sandwiches, made with everything from pâte to cheese and pesto, cost about $3.50. The baked goods, all made from scratch, start at $1. *1831 Capitol Ave., tel. 916/442–7382. Open Sun.–Thurs. 6:30 AM–9 PM, Fri. and Sat. 6:30 AM–10 PM.*

Rubicon Brewing Company. This is a favorite hangout among locals, attracting a mix of jocks, ski bums, nine-to-fivers after work, and students. Order a homemade beer—a pint of India Pale Ale is about $2—and stick with the salads and burgers ($4–$6). *2004 Capitol Ave., tel. 916/448–7032.*

The Lucky Café. With its 50s-diner look—requisite Formica lunch counter and all—the café attracts a loyal clientele from the offbeat Midtown neighborhood. Breakfasts cost $4–$8. The steak and eggs and omelettes are good bets. Sandwiches—try the sourdough toast—cost about $8. The donuts are the best in town. *1111 21st St., tel. 916/442–9620. Open weekdays 7–3, weekends 8–2.*

BROADWAY The restaurants on Broadway, the southern "border" of Downtown and Midtown, are inexpensive but a bit short on atmosphere. For Vietnamese food, **Andy Nguyen's** is a top choice. *2007 Broadway, tel. 916/736–1157.*

Vic's Ice Cream. For great ice cream, grilled sandwiches, and a good sense of the Land Park area (one of Sacramento's older, nicer neighborhoods), this is the spot. It's definitely a neighborhood place, where everyone seems to know each other and families run in packs. *3199 Riverside Blvd., tel. 916/448–0892.*

DESSERT/COFFEE HOUSES Besides **Greta's Café** and **Vic's Ice Cream** (*see above*), popular spots include **Tower Café** (1518 Broadway, tel. 916/441–0222), **Rick's Dessert Diner** (2322 K St., tel. 916/444–0969), **Java City** (1800 Capitol Ave.), and **Terra Roxa** (2262 J St., tel. 916/448–8327).

Sacramento's history is not of the archival and dusty sort: The guides at the various sights do their best to give you a feel for what life was like in California's early days. At the Railroad Museum, someone in striped overalls and red scarf will take you to a replica of a railroad station agent's office, complete with telegraph equipment and leather mail pouch. At the B.F. Hastings building in Old Sacramento, a Park Service employee explains why you see brick only on the backs of the old buildings (it was considered too declassé to go up front). At Sutter's Fort, a historical character tries to seem appropriately puzzled when you point out the jet flying above as she dips candles in tallow and wax. Because most major sights are supported by municipal funds, entry fees are usually minimal. Old Sacramento is worth just walking around in—no charge for soaking up the ambience. Nearly all of the buildings are wheelchair accessible (the Railroad Museum has a lift into an old mail car).

OLD SACRAMENTO **The B. F. Hastings Building.** The building is an Old Sacramento gem, and houses a free exhibit on old-time communications. If it's uncrowded and the guide is willing, he or she will show you how to make quill pens. *2nd and J Sts., tel. 916/324–0539. Hours vary due to budget crunch.*

California State Railroad Museum. This immensely popular museum successfully conveys the magnitude of what went into building the first transcontinental railway that linked the east coast with the west—and it doesn't gloss over the loss of human lives and the petty squabbling that occurred. The railroad was completed in 1869, and it's easy to do a little time traveling as you walk through the antique railway cars, which include a sleeper that sways as if it's still running the rails. *125 I St., tel. 916/448–4466. Admission: $5. Open daily 10–5.*

Sacramento History Center. Housed in a building that was once the mayor's office, jail, and policemen's quarters, the museum offers a lively introduction to the history of Sacramento, complete with gold pans that you can work yourself, memorabilia from the World Wars (including the Japanese internment camps), and interactive computer videos. There's so much to look at, it's more like three-dimensional MTV than a stodgy historical museum. Find out what your weight in gold is worth. *101 I St., tel. 916/449–2057. Admission: about $3. Open daily 10–4:30, closed Mon.*

DOWNTOWN **Crocker Art Museum.** A few blocks from Old Sacramento is the oldest art museum on the West Coast, with a collection of European, Asian, and Californian art. The Victorian building in which it's all housed is impressive in itself. Most compelling are the works by California artists. *3rd and O Sts., tel. 916/449–5423. Admission: $2.50. Open Wed.–Sun. 10–5, Tues. 1–9, closed Mon.*

California State Capitol Building. The 1869 structure was extensively restored in the early 1980s with a sumptuous interior rotunda. Walk through replicas of historic rooms, hobnob with men in dark suits waiting for the elevator, and learn 58 different ways (one for each county) to say "boosterism." You're welcome to sit in on the legislative sessions. Trees from all over the world grow in the adjacent **Capitol Park,** the site of the **Vietnam Veterans Memorial.** *10th St. and Capitol Mall, tel. 916/324–0333. Open weekdays 9–5, weekends 10–5. Free guided tours hourly 9–4 (reserve in advance).*

Governor's Mansion. The mansion was home to 13 California governors until Ronald Reagan chose to live elsewhere in 1967. The guided tour gives insight into 19th-century California. *16th and H Sts., tel. 916/323–3047. Admission: $3.50. Tours daily every hour 10–4, closed Mon.*

Sutter's Fort. This is the settlement from which Sacramento grew. It was founded in 1839 by immigrant John Augustus Sutter who fled debts and a family back in Switzerland. The fort's white adobe walls were the destination of many a pioneer crossing desert and mountain. Try to arrive on a Thursday, when well-prepared schoolchildren from throughout the state assume the dress, persona, and even chores (like butter churning) of pioneers. The students will resist like anything getting out of character when you talk with them. Several times a year, the museum has "living history days," which elevate this role-playing to a fine art. Ironically located right next to Sutter's Fort is the **California State Indian Museum,** a small museum that is as long on impact as it is short on actual exhibits. The 10-minute film explores what California was like before the freeway, Hollywood, or the vineyards, and is worth the price of admission alone. *Sutter's Fort: 27th and L Sts., tel. 916/445–4422. Admission: $2. Open daily 10–5, last tour at 4. California State Indian Museum: Sutter's Fort, tel. 916/324–0539. Admission: $2.50. Open Wed.–Sun. 10–5, Tues. 1–9, closed Mon.*

● ● ● CHEAP THRILLS

The original **Tower Records** (corner of Broadway and 16th St.) is still a good place to get your music. The neon-topped old **Tower Theater** across the street features art films with freshly popped popcorn and real butter. The **Tower Cafe,** next to the theater, is a great people-watching spot (you name it, you watch it). **Tower Books** (1600 Broadway) is where you'll find students, punks, activists, hobbyists, old-car aficionados, and avid readers of everything from Danielle Steele to Noam Chomsky. Stop here for information on non-mainstream activities. Pretty much every city-related, special-interest publication is available here.

The world's largest almond-processing factory, **Blue Diamond** (1701 C St., tel. 916/446–8587) provides free tours, including a short cinematic masterpiece, *The Amazing Almond.* Almond treats come at the end. The tour gives a sense of the Sacramento Valley's agricultural tradition, which is not immediately apparent in the city. The factory is downtown in Blue Diamond Almond Plaza, and the building's air-conditioning is a pleasant respite in the summer.

FESTIVALS **Dixieland Jazz Jubilee,** known far and wide, is held in Old Sac and its environs every **Memorial Day weekend.** It attracts world-class Dixieland and thousands of loyal fans. Be warned: Room rates go up during the jubilee.

The California State Fair at the **end of August** is also popular. After a glitzy spell, the fair is returning to its agricultural roots—to the delight of most residents. Agriculture is still California's number-one business, and the agricultural exhibits are fascinating. Did you know almonds and prunes are harvested by machines that throttle the tree trunk and violently shake the fruit loose? (Lots of free samples.)

● ● ● AFTER DARK

Sacramento's busy nightlife scene is best explored in the *Sacramento Bee*'s Friday publication, "Ticket," which includes information on dress codes, cover charges (usually under $3), clientele, and type of entertainment. In Old Sacramento, try **Fanny Ann's Saloon** (1023 2nd St., tel. 916/441–0505) for music, dancing, crowds, and noise or **Popeye's Place** (910 2nd St., tel. 916/446–7206). **The Delta King** (1000 Front St., tel. 916/441–4440) on the river has entertainment and a bar. Young Sacramentans frequent **Paradise Beach** (7942 Arcadia Dr., Citrus Heights, tel. 916/722–8993) and **Yucatan Liquor Stand** (1696 Arden Way, tel. 916/922–6446), a prime pick-up place. For jazz, **On Broadway Bar and Café** (1827 Broadway, tel. 916/443–8492) has a regional reputation. Country-and-western dancing is featured at a number of bars including **Yellow Rose** (5809 Auburn Blvd., tel. 916/332–7062) and **Denim 'n' Diamonds** (6063 Sunrise Blvd., Citrus Heights, tel. 916/961–5701), where free classes are given on Monday nights. Comedy fans frequent **Laughs Unlimited** (1124 Firehouse Alley, tel. 916/446–5905).

● ● ● OUTDOOR ACTIVITIES

BICYCLING **The American River Bike Trail** starts near Discovery Park, not far from Old Sacramento, and stretches some 30 miles to Folsom. Some parts are amazingly pretty. The trail is one of the city's most popular attractions, but it hasn't been trouble-free; don't go on it at night and be smart on the remote parts. If you join the trail around Sac State, you'll avoid some questionable areas on earlier sections. Solar phones are located along the trail.

You can rent bikes for about $5–$10 an hour, $10–$20 a half day, and $20–$25 a full day at **Surrey Cycle Rentals Inc.** (916 2nd St., Old Sac, tel. 916/441–3836) and **City Bicycle Works** (2419 K St., tel. 916/447–2453).

RAFTING Rafting on the American River during the long hot summer is a Sacramento tradition. Call **American River Raft Rentals** (11257 Bridge, Rancho Cordova, tel. 916/635–6400), or look up "River Trips" in the Yellow Pages.

Near Sacramento

SACRAMENTO RIVER DELTA

The Delta is a lazy labyrinth of a thousand or so miles of rivers, streams, and canals connecting Sacramento and Stockton with the San Francisco Bay. Most of the region has a laid-back feel, as if it were part of the Old South. Some folks come to the Delta to fish, some for vacations aboard the many rentable houseboats, some for waterskiing or jetskiing up and down the waterways, some to explore the eerie remnants of the old Chinese settlements of Isleton, Locke, and Walnut Grove. Whatever your reason for coming here, you'll feel like you've traveled much farther than the 30–40 miles from Sacramento or San Francisco. The Delta is a strange, unique slice of California life.

Broken-down tractors sit abandoned by the side of winding levee roads; sweet corn and Bartlett pears grow tall across lolling fields; and migrating waterfowl fish lazily along the grassy banks of quiet sloughs.

In **Rio Vista,** you'll find grocery stores, laundromats, banks, reasonable motels, and the **Chamber of Commerce** (60 Main St., tel. 707/374–2700). Like most places in the Delta, it's very relaxed and you may need to ask lots of questions to get the information you want.

Rio Vista has the services and supplies, but **Isleton** and **Locke** have the charm. Both towns were settled in the early 1900s by the Chinese workers who built the dams and levees that control the flow of water through the Delta. The result is a curious but authentic mix of Far East and Old West. The streets of the two towns are quieter than they once were, but you can still wander among buildings that once housed raucous barrooms and gambling houses, cheap cafeterias, and boarding houses. Except during the Crawdad Day Festival every June, Isleton is mostly a ghost town, with boarded-up buildings and "For Sale" signs. Locke has its share of boarded up buildings as well, but is more actively keeping its history alive. Pick up a walking tour map of Locke at the Rio Vista Chamber of Commerce, which will lead you from the old **Star Theater** (which once hosted performances of traditional Chinese theater), to the **Yuen Chong Market,** a grocery store established in 1916, to **Al's Place,** a lively bar and restaurant. In the center of town, the **Sacramento River Delta Historical Society Museum** has a Chinese history exhibit ($1 admission) and a reconstructed gambling house. Scattered among the abandoned tin buildings are several boutiques and antique shops.

GETTING AROUND The only ways to really see the Delta are by car, boat, or bicycle. You can drive or cycle from town to town, over drawbridges and on ferries, to many of the 70 islands that make up the region. From downtown Sacramento, take I–5 south to the turnoff for Route 160, which follows the Sacramento River through the most interesting Delta towns and sights. From San Francisco travel over the Bay Bridge and east on Route 80. Near Hercules, take Route 4 toward Antioch, then take the turnoff for Route 160. There are no buses or taxis here, but you can rent boats of every variety, from fishing dinghies to speedboats and houseboats (*see* Outdoor Activities, *below*). The free ferries that take motorists across the Cache and Steamboat sloughs are also ideal for bikers who want to cycle on the uncrowded levee roads on the less crowded islands.

WHERE TO SLEEP The most popular place to stay in the Delta is on a rented houseboat—a sort of RV on the water—and cruise up and down the waterways. Prices are steep, but with a large group of people you can manage to spend less in a week aboard a comfortable houseboat than at area motels. At **Herman and Helen's Marina** (tel. 209/951–4634) in Stockton, you can rent a 32-foot houseboat that sleeps six comfortably and includes a kitchen with dishes and silverware, a propane barbecue, and all other equipment, for $900 a week during summer, $450 during winter. If your houseboat won't clear a drawbridge, just signal with one long and one short toot of the horn and the bridge operator will open it for you. You can also camp at one of 102 sites (with flush toilets and drinking water) in **Brannan Island State Park,** near Rio Vista on Route 160. The campground is set in a dry meadow with oak and willow trees near a beach, where you can swim in the slough, and a free boat launch. At **Vieira's Resort** (15476 Rte. 160, Isleton, tel. 916/777–6661) on Route 160 between Rio Vista and Isleton, you can rent a one-bedroom cabin for $40 per night or a two-bedroom cabin for $60. Cabins come with kitchens (but you have to bring your own dishes), and there's a private beach with a bait shop, boat ramp, and dock, all set around a quiet, grassy picnic area.

FOOD The Delta is no great culinary center. If you have cooking equipment or just want to picnic, **Don Quick's Superette** (609 Rte. 12, Rio Vista, tel. 707/374–5399) has a good selection of meats, cheeses, wine, bread, fruit, and vegetables. For a Delta specialty, head for **Ernie's Bar and Restaurant** in Isleton, across the street from the pleasingly decrepit Hotel Del Rio, for a heaping plate of crawdads fresh from the river ($6 appetizer plate, $10 for a full plate—enough for 2). The crawdads look like mini-lobsters and taste more gamey. All the meat's in the tail, and after spending an hour or so getting at those few precious bites, you may wonder if it was worth it. Also in Isleton, **Rogelio's** (34 Main St., tel. 916/777–6606) serves both Chinese and Mexican food; the lunch special, either Szechuan beef or chicken tostada, goes for around $4. The best spot for a cheap, hearty breakfast is **Granny's** (310 Rte. 12, Rio Vista, tel. 707/374–2019), a drive-up joint with a 25¢ cup of coffee and a good bacon and egg sandwich ($2).

OUTDOOR ACTIVITIES The Delta's many waterways are popular with anglers out for striped bass, sturgeon, catfish, bluegill, perch, and an occasional salmon. **The Trap** (660 Rte. 12, Rio Vista, tel. 707/374–5554) has everything you'll need to get started. If you want to hire a guide, try **Jolly Jay Guide Service** (766 Elain Dr. in Stockton, tel. 209/478–6645). Waterskiing is also popular, and many Delta marinas rent all the equipment you'll need to get your thrills in the docile Delta water. Try **Vieira's Resort** (*see* Where to Sleep, *above*) or **Delta Marina Yacht Harbor** (120 Marina Dr., Rio Vista, tel. 707/374–2315) for boat and equipment rentals.

● ● ● DAVIS

Set among miles and miles of flat farmland, the neat and trim college town of Davis has cafés, bookstores, music clubs, and record stores. The town is centered around the University of California at Davis, once a school mainly for agriculturalists and veterinarians that in the last 20 years has become an excellent liberal arts school. This is a prime place to get a degree in the fine art of oenology—wine making. There's not much to do in Davis, but a walk around the downtown area will give you a chance to meet some interesting people. Stop by **Barney's Records** (203 G St., tel. 916/758–0740) for the best selection of new and used rock and jazz in town, and pick up a list of who's playing at **The Palms** (726 Drummond Ave., tel. 916/756–9901), "your cultural oasis," which hosts touring and local rock and blues bands. Browse among the fresh fruits and vegetables at the **Davis Farmers' Market,** held every Wednesday evening, June through August, on Second Street between C and E streets. Pick up an offbeat magazine from the massive selection at **Newsbeat** (231 E St., tel. 916/756–6247), and read it at the popular **Café Roma** (tel. 916/756–4444) next door.

WHERE TO SLEEP Lodging is easier to find and cheaper in nearby Sacramento, but if you simply must stay in Davis, try the **Davis Motel** (1111 Richards Blvd., tel. 916/756–0910) next to the freeway on-ramp, with rooms starting at $42. The motel has satellite TV and a swimming pool, and some rooms are wheelchair accessible. A little more expensive, but more centrally located, is the **Ramada Inn** (110 F St., tel. 916/753–3600), with clean, large rooms starting at $56 for a single, $60 for a double. Both suggest reservations year round.

FOOD The **Paragon Bar and Grill** (2nd and G Sts., tel. 916/758–7550) serves hearty meat-and-potato lunches every day and a decent dinner on Fridays. The full, dark-wood bar is open until 2 AM every night and you can easily make new friends among the regular beer-drinking crowd. For something a little different, try **The Crêpe Bistro** (234 E St., tel. 916/753–2575), which specializes in crêpes with an odd assortment of fillings, such as spinach and white wine ($6). Or go for the rich **Russe Aux Blintzes** with vanilla-flavored ricotta cheese, sour cream, and preserves ($6). The plain cafeteria-style restaurant is nothing to write home about, but outside tables with umbrellas and candles give the place the "touch of Paris" the owners are so proud of.

The Gold Country

Like most things in California, the Gold Country is bigger and more varied than a first glance might suggest. In a 350-mile swath following Route 49 from Sierra City nearly down to Yosemite, the Gold Country stretches through nine counties, more than a half-dozen restored or preserved historical parks, several wine regions, and countless recreation areas. You can visit dozens of 7-Eleven-less towns, either spruced up for tourists or enticingly in decay, and mine more history per inch than all the gold ever found in the Mother Lode.

The only way really to cover the Gold Country is by car, but it's not an area you just want to barrel through. You'll probably be most rewarded by what you find on your own, poking and walking and browsing around. Think of it as prospecting; who knows what treasures you'll find. James Marshall didn't expect to find gold in 1848 while building Sutter's Mill on the American River in Coloma, but he set loose the Gold Rush of 1849.

One way to handle the Gold Country is to drive until you find a town you like, then jump out and explore it until you've had enough. The towns can vary from the gussied-up, user-friendly (and slightly expensive) Sutter Creek, to the take-us-as-we-are Mokelumne Hill. Or, you could take a more focused approach along the lines of "I'm going to stop at all historical markers" (and they are numerous), or, "I'm going to sample all the town bakeries" (and almost every town has one).

Cool, dark, wooden-floored saloons, and other places steeped in Western lore (from the Old Timers Museum in Murphys to Chaw-Se Indian Grinding Rock State Historic Park near Pine Grove), are also characteristic of these old-time towns. "Everybody up here's a quasi-history buff. It's a local pastime," said one resident. There's a museum or history center in almost every town—and the saloons are fun in themselves. If you're used to the big city, think a little differently. Again, remember you're prospecting, and you might hit some entertaining pay dirt.

The going through the yellow, dusty Sierra foothills can be mighty hot in the summer, all the more reason to take your time, duck into a saloon, and quaff some sarsaparilla (its scent hangs in the air in Columbia). The towns still retain much of the character from that period of California's history, a quality that hasn't gone unnoticed by the film industry. Hundreds of movies and commercials have been filmed in Tuolumne County, including *High Noon* and *Back to the Future III*.

Mark Twain and Bret Harte hung out in these parts, and undoubtedly drank something or other in these very saloons.

As for lodging, B&Bs often try to capture the essence of the region, with some priced no higher than a standard motel, but most lean toward the expensive side. Call the chamber of commerce offices for listings (*see* Tourist Information, *below*).

Considering how rural most of the region is, the arts community is surprisingly lively. You can find out about music events in the southern Gold Country at **The Aeolian Harp** (147 Main St., Murphys, tel. 209/728–2852), a store with an eclectic collection of harmonicas, Native American drums, earrings, and other creative curios. In the north,

The Gold Country

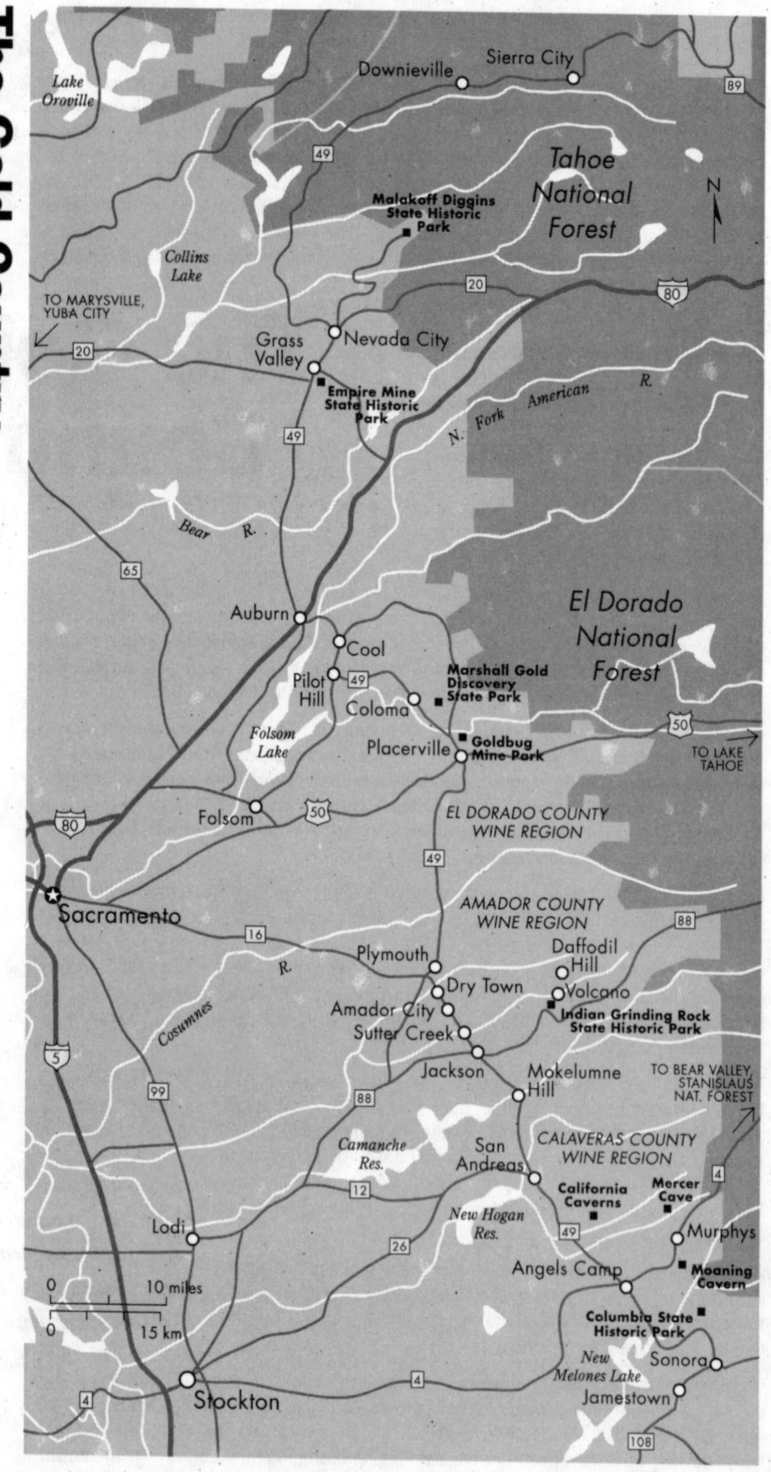

Foggy Mountain Music (104 W. Main St., Grass Valley, tel. 916/273–6676) has information on Nevada County's thriving bluegrass scene. Live drama is presented by several professional theater companies, including **The Foothill Theatre Company** (Box 1812, Nevada City, tel. 916/265–8587), the **Sierra Repertory Theatre** (13891 Mono Way on Rte. 108, East Sonora, tel. 209/532–3120), and the **Columbia Actors' Repertory** (at Fallon Theatre, Columbia, tel. 209/532–4644). For information on nightlife, square dancing, regional music, and theater offerings in the southern half of the region, check out the weekend guide in the Friday edition of the *Sonora Union-Democrat.* In the north, check *The Nevada County Voice* or the weekend entertainment magazine in the *Union.*

BASICS • • •

TOURIST INFORMATION **Amador County Chamber of Commerce** (6048 Rte. 88, Suite 3, in the Amador Plaza Shopping Center, Martell 95642, tel. 209/223–0350). **Auburn Area Chamber of Commerce** (601 Lincoln Way, tel. 916/885–5616 or 800/433–7575). **Calaveras County Chamber of Commerce** (Main St., Angels Camp, tel. 209/736–4444 or 800/999–9039). **El Dorado County Chamber of Commerce** (542 Main St., Placerville, tel. 916/621–5885). **Nevada City Chamber of Commerce** (132 Main St., tel. 916/265–2692). **Tuolumne County Visitors Bureau** (55 West Stockton, Sonora, tel. 209/533–4420 or 800/446–1333).

FESTIVALS Consider planning your trip around one of the many Gold Country music festivals—especially the Annual Father's Day Weekend Bluegrass Festival, held on the third weekend in June. There are also free concerts featuring regional artists at Courthouse Park in downtown Sonora every Friday evening at 6:30 in July and August. Contact the local chambers of commerce to find out whether you've arrived in time for the latest quilt show, cooking competition, fishing derby, or fair.

MAY **Sierra Festival of the Arts** (Contact Foggy Mountain Music, Grass Valley, tel. 916/273–6676).

JUNE **Annual Father's Day Weekend Bluegrass Festival,** Grass Valley-Nevada City (Contact Foggy Mountain Music, Grass Valley, tel. 916/273–6676).

JULY **The Sierra Storytelling Festival** (tel. 209/265–2826).

High Sierra Music Festival at Leland Meadows (tel. 209/965–3662) features names like Alex de Grassi and Jesse Colin Young. The festival is held in Strawberry, east of Sonora on Rte. 108.

Music from Bear Valley (tel. 209/753–2574; in northern California tel. 800/432–1812) is a nationally recognized mid-summer classical series in Bear Valley.

SEPTEMBER **Annual Midsummer Bluegrass Festival** on Labor Day Weekend (contact Foggy Mountain Music, Grass Valley, tel. 916/273–6676).

COMING AND GOING Route 49 is the north–south backbone of the Gold Country, with Placerville (east of Sacramento on east–west U.S. 50) roughly in the middle. The route is divided into the North Gold Country (Placerville and points north) and the South Gold Country (points south of Placerville).

North of Placerville on Route 49 are Grass Valley, Nevada City, and the more obscure Downieville. The northern route takes you along the Yuba River into the Sierras and is the way to go if you want to follow a meandering, scenic route toward Truckee or Reno. Head south from Placerville over rolling, golden hills to Sutter Creek, Jackson, Columbia and Sonora. From there you can continue south toward Yosemite. With Route 49 as your axis, you can take side trips on Routes 50, 108, 4, or 88 to tiny, historic towns like Murphys, Fiddletown, Volcano, Copperopolis, and Cool.

OUTDOOR ACTIVITIES Campers, hikers, and anglers can have a high old time along the many Gold Country rivers. Cross-country skiers head for the Sierras, often setting off from the **Alpha Omega** rest stop east on Route 20. People with disabilities can get information about activities in the area from **Sequoia Challenge** (tel. 916/272–3459). There's plenty of waterskiing, fishing, and other water sports at **New Melones Lake** (*see* Angels Camp, Southern Gold Country, *above*).

BICYCLING **Stevenot Winery** (2090 San Domingo Rd., Murphys, tel. 209/728–3436) has an annual triathlon. Contact **Sierra Cyclery** (tel. 209/532–3654) in Sonora for the inside scoop on the many rides that head out from Sonora. Mountain-biking possibilities abound in the foothills; the best (and only) way to find good trails is to ask around.

CAVING The Mother Lode has three caves to explore, all within close proximity of each other: **California Caverns** (tel. 209/736–2708), at Cave City north of Angels Camp, is open year-round with occasional winter and spring closures; **Moaning Cavern** (tel. 209/736–2708), 9 miles north of Columbia State Park on Parrotts Ferry Road, is also open year-round; and **Mercer's Caverns** (tel. 209/728–2101), a mile north of Murphys just off Route 4, is open Memorial Day through September.

RAFTING For rafting trips on the three forks of the American River, the North Fork of the Yuba, and the Truckee, contact **Tributary Whitewater Tours** (tel. 916/346–6812) in Grass Valley.

WATER SPORTS Parking just about anywhere along Route 49 and plunging into one of the many rivers in the area is the local version of the urban municipal pool. However, swimming in the American and Yuba rivers is not recommended until mid-June due to the swift currents and high waters caused by snowmelt. Check with National Forest offices or local or state recreation departments.

● ● ● THE NORTHERN GOLD COUNTRY

PLACERVILLE Back in the bad old days, Placerville was known as **Hangtown** in honor of the notorious brand of frontier justice practiced here. Today, the largest town on Route 49 hangs its hat on this reputation, which some find morbid and others find intriguing. Many restaurants serve the Placerville breakfast staple: Hangtown Fry (eggs and oysters). You can visit the site of the lynchings on Main Street and collect background info at the **El Dorado County Historical Museum** at the fairgrounds west of town (open weekends 10–4). A half-mile north of downtown on Bedford Avenue, you can take a self-guided tour of the tunnels of the old **Goldbug Mine,** which continued to operate until World War II. The mine is in Goldbug Park, where you can picnic beside a winding stream after your subterranean excursion. *Tel. 916/642–5232. 50¢ for self-guided tour of mine. Park open daily 8 AM–sunset; mine open April–Oct.*

COLOMA Ten miles north of Placerville is the town of Coloma, where James Marshall first discovered gold in 1848. The tiny town had 2,000 new residents within six months, and the population grew to 10,000 before the gold began to run out. Today, most of the town is within **Marshall Gold Discovery State Historic Park,** which has an interpretive center, a museum, and exhibits along the American River, including a replica of **Sutter's Mill.** Dedicated historians can take the 1½-mile Monument Loop Hike leading to Marshall's grave, while others can picnic, follow the nature trail, or fish and raft in the American River. *On Rte. 49, tel. 916/622–3470. Day use: $3 per car. Park open daily 8 AM–sunset; museum open in summer, daily 10–5.*

AUBURN If you're traveling from Sacramento or the Bay Area toward Reno on I–80, this hilly, cobbled town will be your first taste of the Gold Country. The entrance to this town, the oldest of the gold-rush towns, is marked by a much-larger-than-life statue of a prospector bent over his gold pan, while the village itself is a good place to get a feel of the spirit of the Gold Rush, and the grandiose expectations of the miners.

Most of the buildings along the highway are thoroughly modern enterprises (fast-food outlets, auto shops, etc.), however, so venture into town and spend a few lazy hours browsing through the town's intriguing antiques shops. Visit the **Gold Country Museum** and the **Bernhard Museum Complex** (built as a hotel in 1851) to get a well-rounded view of mining and frontier life in the 19th century. *Gold Country Museum: 1273 High St., Auburn. Admission: $1. Open daily 10–4; closed Mon. Bernard Museum Complex: 291 Auburn-Folsom Rd., tel. 916/889–4156. Admission: $1. Open Tues.–Fri. 10–3; weekends noon–4.*

Among the most reasonably priced bed-and-breakfasts in the area are **Victorian Manor** (482 Main St., Newcastle, tel. 916/663–3009) with rooms for $50–$55; **Stone House Inn** (off I–80 in Dutch Flat, tel. 916/389–8353), with rooms for $45, reservations suggested; and **Lincoln House** (191 Lincoln Way, Auburn, tel. 916/885–8880), with rooms for $50–$75, single rates available.

EMPIRE MINE STATE HISTORIC PARK You'll need to drive several of the 23 miles from Auburn to Grass Valley to shake the less-than-inspiring vista of fast-food franchises and shopping centers that hover around modern Auburn before you can begin to enjoy the rolling hills of the countryside. Just outside Grass Valley is the site of the Empire Mine, once the biggest and richest gold mine in the state. The mine, with 367 miles of underground passages, operated from 1850 to 1956—much of what was unearthed immediately being stuck back under the ground at the federal government's treasure hoard in Fort Knox. Included in a tour of the mine is the **Bourn Mansion,** a classy stone cottage built by William Bourn Jr., who saved the mine from financial ruin in the early 1880s. The 784-acre park surrounding the mine is a good place for picnics, horseback rides, and hikes. *10791 Empire St., tel. 916/273–8522. Take the Empire St. exit south from Rte. 49. Admission: $2, $1 for dogs. Open daily 9–6.*

GRASS VALLEY AND NEVADA CITY The neighboring towns of Grass Valley and Nevada City are both friendly, with meandering streets and interesting architecture. But, with only 4 miles between them, they're light years apart in ambience. Grass Valley is much more laid back, the town having evolved naturally around its historical center. The residents of Nevada City, on the other hand, have preserved the old town to within an inch of its former self—this is the only town west of the Mississippi with real gas lights. It all comes off as more peculiarly quaint than authentic; after all, the carriage-drawing horses sport diapers.

In Nevada City, the art-deco **courthouse** is worth a short walk from downtown. The **Nevada Theatre,** on Broad Street, is the oldest California theater in continuous use, and the **Miner's Foundry** behind it is the site of plays, concerts, and an annual teddy bear convention.

If you want a full lunch or dinner in Grass Valley for under $10, or just a quick nosh, try the friendly **Main Street Café and Bar** (213 W. Main St., tel. 916/477–6000). At **Marshall's Pasties** (203 Mill St., tel. 916/272–2844), for less than $3 you can sample the delicious pasties popular with the Cornish miners who settled the area. Fillings include apples, broccoli, cheese, beef, and turkey.

In Nevada City, follow the smell of coffee to **Sierra Mountain Coffee Roasters** (316 Commercial St., tel. 916/265–5282) for a cheap, tasty meal (under $5) in a congenial setting—a small, cozy café with an outdoor patio. **Earth Song Market and Café** (727 Zion St., tel. 916/265–0302) is a natural-food lovers' paradise, with lots of vegetarian and macrobiotic dishes for $5–$8.

If you want to spend the night without spending too many of your own gold pieces, camp at the nearby **Nevada County Fairgrounds,** or else drive 40 minutes west to Marysville or Yuba City where you'll find the usual el cheapo motels (such as a serviceable TraveLodge and many mom-and-pop, low-slung, '50-style motels).

MALAKOFF DIGGINS STATE HISTORIC PARK Sixteen miles north of Nevada City on the snaking Tyler Foote Road, you'll find this 600-foot-deep canyon left from an old hydraulic gold-mining operation. Inside the park, the original buildings of the town of North Bloomfield are being restored or reconstructed. You can set up quarters in the 30-site campground (reserve through MISTIX, tel. 800/444–7275), a group camping area, or in three bare-bones rental cabins open year-round (no water in winter). Rangers conduct tours along the hiking trails in summer, but you can always wander around on your own. *Tel. 916/265–2740. Take Tyler Foote Rd. off Rte. 49 north of Nevada City.*

DOWNIEVILLE Route 49 winds its way up into the stands of broad-leafed trees that cover the landscape here. You don't have to get very far north of Nevada City to appreciate the rustic quiet, but if you continue some 50 miles, you'll come to the tiny gold-rush town of Downieville. The center of town is thick with trees, and narrow bridges span the Yuba River that runs right through town. Chairs line the sidewalks, and most days you'll find people just sitting around chatting. The friendly guides in the tiny **Sierra County Museum** are at least as interesting as the museum itself. Main Street is wider at one end than the other because back in the old days stagecoaches needed room to turn around. The **Downieville Bakery** is great—try the citron-tinged raisin bread. For fun, folks here like to "goof off, fish, swim, mine...," according to one resident, but they used to like to hang people, too. The gallows still stand next to the jail. If you're hot and bothered, go past the last bridge on Main Street and take a swim in the boulder-strewn pools of the Yuba River.

Crandell's Riverside Motel (Commercial St., tel. 800/655–2500) has eight rooms along the river for $35–$50, 20% less during the winter. **Downieville Motor Inn** (Main St., tel. 916/289–3243) has 11 rooms (some wheelchair accessible), with room numbers painted on gold pans; $30–$35.

● ● ● THE SOUTHERN GOLD COUNTRY

Once you head south from Placerville (*see* The Northern Gold Country, *above*), you'll find yourself in refreshing, rolling countryside, passing through modest villages that were once the scenes of thriving mining activity.

SUTTER CREEK The first major town on Route 49 south of Placerville is Sutter Creek, about 30 miles down the road. You'll find bed-and-breakfasts here that pride themselves on detail, streets lined with carefully restored houses, good places to eat, a rich history, and quaintness coming out of the woodwork. This is the Mother Lode all spruced up—for the benefit of both tourists and residents.

JACKSON From Sutter Creek, Route 49 winds south to the Amador County seat, Jackson. With a good range of reasonable lodgings, this town would serve as a good base for this stretch of the drive, except that it's less picturesque than most towns in Gold Country (the town center is pleasant, though). East of Jackson, Route 88 heads into the Sierras to **Chaw-Se Indian Grinding Rock State Historic Park** (tel. 209/296–7488), where you can visit a Miwok village and cultural center, and view petroglyphs and thousands of limestone mortars—small depressions the Miwok carved into boulders to grind acorns into flour. The 30-minute drive from Jackson is worth it for those who want to get a better sense of what Native American life was like. Good information is provided at the **State Regional Indian Museum.**

One mile north is the dwindling town of Volcano, situated in a wee crater. In its heyday, Volcano had 35 saloons that catered to thirsty miners working in the area. Although the population has shrunk to village proportions, you can still whet your whistle here after a walk through streets that have changed very little in the last 100 years. During the spring, **Daffodil Hill** just north of Volcano erupts with colorful flowers, descendants of a few bulbs planted here by Dutch colonists in the last century. To get there, take Ram's Horn Grade 3 miles from Volcano. Prepare yourself for a profusion of picnickers and automobiles, as well.

MOKELUMNE HILL If the restored Sutter Creek pleases with its tidiness, the unfancified Mokelumne Hill pleases with its lack of pretension. To reach the town, turn east on Route 26 about 7 miles south of Jackson. Although it's barely out of sight of Route 49, sleepy "Moke Hill" has all the ingredients of a gold-rush town: old, historic buildings like the Hotel Leger, and the requisite saloon and history repository (that's a museum, not a spittoon). For a view of the surrounding area, head past the town proper to the Protestant cemetery, established in 1850.

ANGELS CAMP Drive 20 miles south to Angels Camp, if only to see the green frogs painted at regular paces on Main Street's sidewalks. Mark Twain set his popular short story "The Celebrated Jumping Frog of Calaveras County" here, an event celebrated annually with a popular frog-jumping contest, during which thousands of spectators root for these confused and not naturally competitive amphibians. When the contest isn't hopping, you can relax on benches between barrels of flowers in the center of town. A few miles out of Angels Camp, south on Route 49, is a small sign that points you up a road to **Mark Twain Cabin,** where Twain was staying when he wrote the story. While the spirit of the frog lives, the cabin decays. The deteriorating wood shack is surrounded by a sturdy wrought-iron fence (but there's a picnic table under a nearby oak). It's a 10-minute detour.

Locals in Calaveras and Tuolumne counties head for **New Melones Lake,** south of Angels Camp on Route 49, for camping (tel. 209/536–9094), waterskiing, sailing, and fishing. If you're happiest on the water, consider renting a houseboat (tel. 209/378–2441). For a fishing-condition report, call **Glory Hole Market** (tel. 209/736–0736) at the **Glory Hole Recreation Area** on the lake.

COLUMBIA If you have only one day and want to get a real feel for the Gold Country, head for **Columbia State Historic Park** on a well-marked turn-off leading from Route 49, south of Angels Camp. Within the park is the early mining town of Columbia, the "Gem of the Southern Mines." Everything in this "living" gold-rush town is calculated to aid your imagination: Stagecoaches clop through shady streets lined with restored buildings and shops, while all motor vehicles are hidden outside city limits. The smell of sarsaparilla hangs in the air around the **St. Charles Saloon.** Grizzled, bearded miner-types wander around (are they for real, or part of the act?). You can stay within the historic park at the **Fallon Hotel** or the **City Hotel,** hop a stagecoach for $4 ($5 if you ride shotgun), or hire a horse from the **Columbia Riding Stable** (tel. 209/532–0663). **Hidden Treasure Gold Mine Tours** leave the Matelot Gold Mine Supply Store daily (tel. 209/532–9693 or 209/533–4819). If you're counting pennies, pick up groceries at the **Columbia Mercantile** and make yourself a picnic. Special events are held throughout the year, including the Victorian Easter Parade, Admission Day (Sept. 7) celebration, Harvest Festival, Christmas Lamplight Tour, and A Miner's Christmas.

SONORA Sonora is at the junction of Route 49 and Route 108, 18 miles south of Angels Camp. It's larger, more crowded, and more modern than most other towns on Route 49, but it still has the feel of the area, and most of the buildings on the town's main street, Washington, have Western-style fronts and awnings and second-story porches. The smell of potpourri and dried flowers mingles with more down-home odors. The park by the courthouse is green, shady, languorously pleasant, and has a designated hacky-sack area.

The Miner's Shack (157 S. Washington St., Sonora, tel. 209/532–5252) is the place for a $3–$5 breakfast, daily until 3 PM. For an under–$10 lunch, **Good Heavens** (49 N. Washington St., tel. 209/532–3663) has a good rep for its burgers, salads, sandwiches, and inventive daily specials.

You won't have trouble finding a decent dinner in Sonora, but consider heading to **The Smoke Café** (18191 Main St., tel. 209/984–3733), a lively restaurant in nearby Jamestown with Mexican dishes for around $7.

The 1850 Gunn House (260 S. Washington St., tel. 209/532–3421) has 24 antique rooms (doubles starting at $40, no wheelchair access), all furnished differently, in the first two-story building constructed in Sonora. Reservations are recommended for this popular hotel: It has a pool, cocktail lounge, refrigerators in some rooms, and free Continental breakfasts.

The standard but clean **Rail Fence Motel** (19950 Rte. 108, tel. 209/532–9191) has eight wheelchair-accessible rooms with showers (no bathtubs!). The azaleas outside may help to compensate for the noise of traffic on Route 108. Singles are around $30 during the week, $40 on weekends.

JAMESTOWN Jamestown, just south of Sonora, boomed twice—once for the gold, and then again in 1897 with the coming of the railroad. *High Noon* was filmed here.

Railtown 1897 is a Historic State Park with exhibits, a tour of the old roundhouse, museum, gift shop, picnic grounds, and one-hour excursions in the foothills on the **Mother Lode Cannon Ball** for $9, March through November. Catch the train at **The Sierra Railway Depot** (tel. 209/984–3953) on Fifth Avenue.

The National Hotel (Box 502, Jamestown 95327, tel. 209/984–3446) on Main Street is one of the oldest hotels in the area and a good base for exploring. Rooms with shared bath are $45–$65; private bath, $55–$75. Breakfast is thrown in, and there's a restaurant and saloon.

Lake Tahoe

Straddling the borders of California and Nevada in the Sierra Mountains, Lake Tahoe is one of the West Coast's most popular playgrounds, in summer and winter. The lake, when the weather is right, defines the word "blue." Everything attendant on the lake defines the word "frenetic," regardless of the weather. There's lots of traffic, hordes of noisy people in an I'm-on-vacation-now frame of mind, tacky casinos, and 7-Eleven-type stores at annoyingly predictable intervals as you drive the road around the lake. But there are also plenty of quiet, secluded places where you can commune with nature, many hiking and riding trails, good camping, and plenty of escape hatches into the surrounding Tahoe, Eldorado, and Toiyabe national forests. You just have to will yourself past the chaos.

In addition to being deep blue, the lake is also just plain *deep*—1,645 feet at its deepest, with the Sierra Nevada Mountains rising 4,000 feet above it. Sixty-three streams flow into it, but only the Truckee River flows out, and it never reaches the ocean. The lake itself is 6,000 feet above sea level, 22 miles long, and 12 miles wide. It's about a four-hour drive east from San Francisco.

California's six-year drought has had a dramatic effect on Lake Tahoe. In many places, boat jetties and piers no longer even reach the water, which has receded many yards.

Given the array of pleasures, natural and man-made, it's no wonder that Lake Tahoe draws up to 100,000 tourists at peak periods. On weekends, the traffic on I–80 between the Bay Area and Lake Tahoe has to be seen to be believed. Tahoe's magnetic effect isn't a recent development, either—for centuries it was the summer gathering place and sacred site for the Washoe Native Americans. By the 1860s, less than 20 years after Kit Carson and John C. Fremont first set foot here, hotels and resorts had supplanted the indigenous people of the area. And development has never ceased being an issue—residents remember only too clearly how a development-induced growth of algae threatened the lake's legendary clarity, which eventually lead to a moratorium on all lakeside building.

The lake's temperature will daunt the person intent on swimming (most visitors just like to chill their feet and scamper back to shore). July and August air temperatures reach only into the 70s, with lows getting into the 40s at night. In the winter, the average daytime high is 36°, with a low at night of 18°. Ski resorts open at the end of November, and sometimes operate until May, courtesy of machine-made snow.

A common way to explore the lake is to drive around its 72-mile perimeter. It's said to take three hours, but plan on a lot of traffic congestion slowing you down. What makes the trip memorable is stopping at a few of the scenic lookout points (especially Emerald Bay on the West Shore), picnicking, and disappearing down a hiking path or two. You'll drive along Route 28 on the north and northeast sides of the lake, U.S. 50 on the south, and Route 89 on the southwest and west.

The main town on the north shore is **Truckee,** rearing out of the Sierras and looking (if you squint) like a chunk of the Old West, complete with the requisite board sidewalks and wood-frame storefronts—it even has a railroad steaming through town. You won't get too lost in reverie, though, thanks to the non-stop downtown traffic and the glut of tourists on the streets. In the summer, Truckee is a link between Reno (less than an hour's drive to the east) and the north and west sides of Lake Tahoe. In the winter, it's a warm, congenial

Lake Tahoe

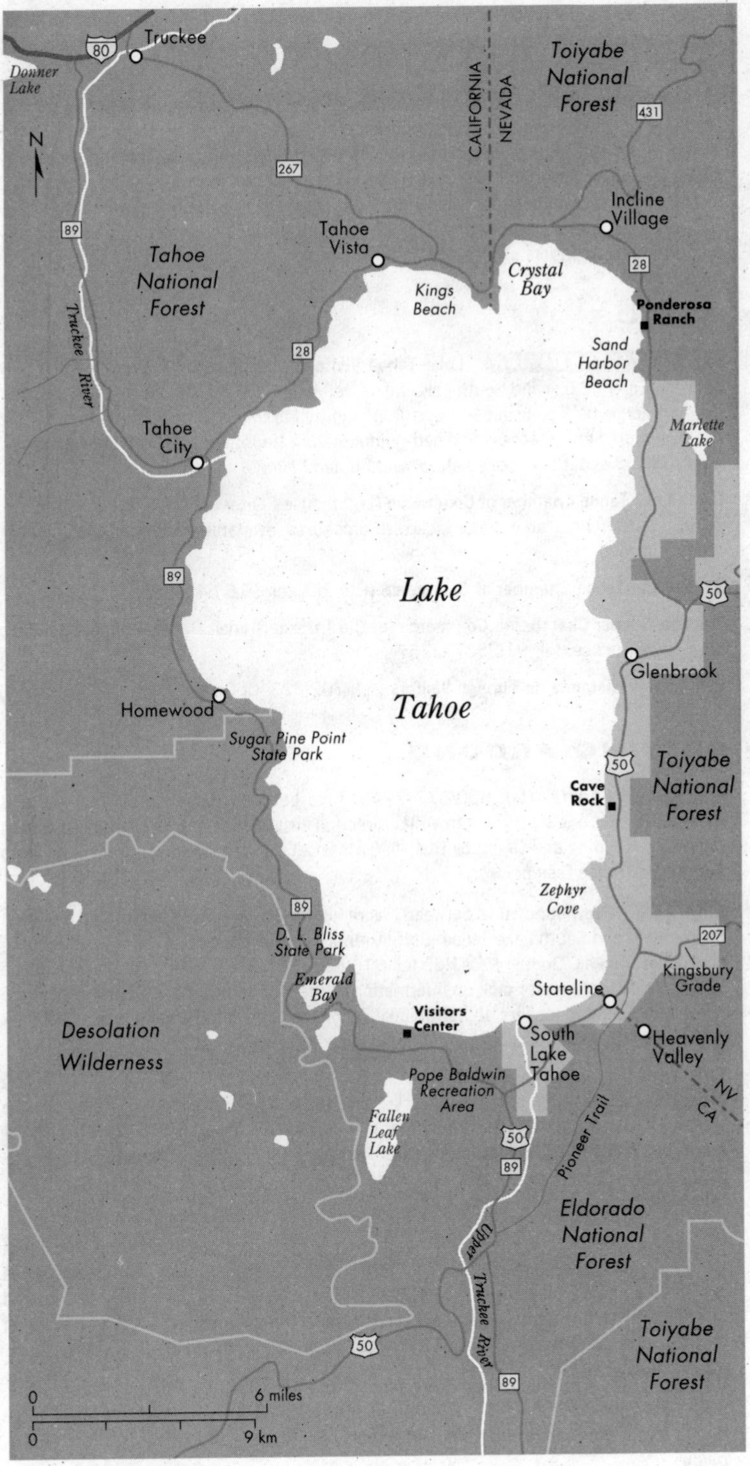

Truckee
80
Donner Lake
Toiyabe National Forest
CALIFORNIA
NEVADA
431
N
267
89
Incline Village
Tahoe Vista
28
Tahoe National Forest
Crystal Bay
Kings Beach
Ponderosa Ranch
Truckee River
28
Sand Harbor Beach
Marlette Lake
Tahoe City
89
Lake Tahoe
50
Glenbrook
Homewood
Sugar Pine Point State Park
50
Toiyabe National Forest
Cave Rock
Zephyr Cove
89
D. L. Bliss State Park
207
Kingsbury Grade
Emerald Bay
Stateline
Visitors Center
South Lake Tahoe
Heavenly Valley
Desolation Wilderness
Pope Baldwin Recreation Area
NV
CA
Fallen Leaf Lake
Pioneer Trail
50
89
Eldorado National Forest
Upper Truckee River
Toiyabe National Forest
50
89
0 6 miles
0 9 km

ski town—a pleasant place for a hot drink or meal. Truckee has a walkable downtown area, and two shopping center complexes west of town (accessible by bike or car). In short, it's a good base for your explorations.

To the south, **South Lake Tahoe** is the center of activity. It butts up against the town of Stateline in Nevada, where casinos flourish. The pace never seems to flag, even in the winter, when a number of downhill ski areas nearby keep the town jumping. Book way ahead if you want to spend New Year's Eve here. Events on the south shore are covered in *Lake Tahoe Action,* a free weekly entertainment magazine put out by the *Tahoe Daily Tribune,* available at most motels. The town's main attraction, however, is its proximity to the natural splendors of the Lake Tahoe area.

● ● ● BASICS

TOURIST INFORMATION **Lake Tahoe Visitor Center** (on Taylor Creek off Rte. 89 between Emerald Bay and South Lake Tahoe, tel. 916/573–2674), open daily 8–5:30 in the summer, is both pleasant and useful. In addition to the usual tourist information, the center features beach access and self-guided nature trails. The staff will tell you all you want to know about the lake's natural and human history.

North Lake Tahoe Chamber of Commerce (Lighthouse Center on Rte. 89, Tahoe City, tel. 916/583–2371) has an outdoor rack with brochures, available even when the chamber office is closed.

South Lake Tahoe Chamber of Commerce (Rte. 50, tel. 916/541–5255).

Truckee-Donner Chamber of Commerce (at the Truckee Transit Depot, Donner Pass Rd., downtown Truckee, tel. 916/587–2757).

Language Assistance for Foreign Visitors (tel. 702/323–0500).

● ● ● GETTING AROUND

BY TRAIN **Amtrak** (tel. 800/872–7245) runs between Sacramento, Truckee, and Reno. Generally, one train going in either direction arrives each day at the Truckee Transit Depot (*see* Coming and Going by Bus, *below*). Local buses can get you from Truckee to South Lake Tahoe (*see below*).

BY BUS **Greyhound** runs between Sacramento, Truckee, and Reno, and between Sacramento and South Lake Tahoe. Both **Amtrak** and **Greyhound** use the Transit Depot in downtown Truckee (Donner Pass Rd., tel. 916/587–3822), a safe and comfortable place to wait for connections or pick up information at the tourist information office. There are a few coin-operated lockers. In South Lake Tahoe the Greyhound station is at 1099 Park Avenue (tel. 916/544–2241).

Tahoe Area Regional Transit or **TART** (tel. 916/481–6365 in CA or 800/325–8278 in NV) has buses, some equipped with ski racks, that serve the north and west shores of Lake Tahoe. The **South Tahoe Area Ground Express** or **STAGE** (tel. 916/573–2080) runs 24 hours within the city limits of South Lake Tahoe.

BY CAR From Sacramento, there are two ways to get to Lake Tahoe (and on to Reno), both taking roughly two hours, depending on traffic. I–80 goes through Truckee, where you can take Route 89 or Route 267 south to the lake or continue on to Reno. The direct route from Sacramento to the lake is U.S. 50, which passes through South Lake Tahoe and (after a name change to Rte. 395) Carson City in Nevada. In the winter, be prepared to drive with chains, as the mountain roads can be treacherous. Try to avoid driving on Friday and Sunday evenings when traffic is at its most nightmarish.

BY PLANE The small **South Lake Tahoe Airport** is served by American Airlines (tel. 800/433–7300) and American Eagle (tel. 800/433–7300). However, there are more flights into **Reno Cannon International Airport** (*see* Coming and Going by Plane, Reno, *below*).

It's hard to pin down motel managers on room rates; they'll try to charge whatever the traffic will bear. Prices jump on weekends and holidays throughout the year. You stand a better chance of getting a good rate by reserving in advance. Bargain hunters usually do best on Route 89 (also called Emerald Bay Road) just outside South Lake Tahoe, and sometimes in Stateline. Don't forget to check with casinos for package deals. The cheapest accommodation in the area, other than camping, is the AYH hostel in Truckee.

Because the whole area is so popular and busy, it's hard to find a place to camp without making reservations. If you try to camp on one of the lake's beaches, there's a good chance you'll be rousted by the well-organized rangers.

SOUTH LAKE TAHOE AREA (ROUTE 89) The rustic **Pine Cone Acre Motel** (735 Emerald Bay Rd., tel. 916/541–0375) is tucked away beneath the pines, with pleasant management and a pool. The 20 rooms (no wheelchair access) run $40–$50 on weekdays, $50–$60 on weekends. Also shielded by shady pines is the well-kept, nine-room **Emerald Motel** (515 Rte. 89, tel. 916/544–5515), with rooms starting at $35 on summer weekdays, and special rates for longer stays. The comparably priced **Crystal Range Motel** (941 Emerald Bay Rd., tel. 916/541–1866) has clean, wheelchair-accessible rooms and winter weekly rates of $95–$150. Slightly rundown, but cheaper, the **Manzanita Motel** (532 Emerald Bay Rd., tel. 916/541–6400) has friendly management, its own coin laundry, and 17 rooms, six with kitchen facilities.

In downtown South Lake Tahoe the 21-room **El Nido Motel** (2215 Rte. 50, tel. 916/541–2711), has a hot tub and a "socializing room" with fireplace. Winter ski packages include breakfast and lift-ticket discounts. Regular rates are $35–$45 weekdays, $45–$55 weekends (shower only, reservations recommended). Closer to the Nevada border, try the **Shenandoah Motel** (4074 Pine Blvd., tel. 916/544–2985), which has some rooms with kitchens (but no utensils) and rates starting around $35 on summer weekdays; or the **Tahoe Country Inn** (4085 Pine Blvd., tel. 916/544–5015), which has 11 attractive rooms starting at around $60 ($40 off-season), free shuttle service to the beach, and private beach passes.

NORTH SHORE In winter, the modern **Best Western Truckee Tahoe Inn** (11331 Rte. 267, tel. 800/824–6385) offers package deals for around $50 that include skiing and lift discounts. Six of the 100 rooms are wheelchair accessible. There's also a weight room, microwaves in some rooms, and bike-rack-equipped bus service to Lake Tahoe.

HOSTELS **The Star Hotel** (10015 West River St., Truckee, tel. 916/587–3007) is both an International Youth Hostel and a hotel. Hostel members pay $10 for a dorm-style room and shared bath or $25 for a private room. Hotel guests pay $45–$80, depending on the season, and get pleasantly furnished rooms with antiques and private bath. The bottom floor rooms are wheelchair accessible. Winter is the busiest time. The management is new and enthusiastic, but the hotel itself has been around since the last century; if you're in the right mood, its creakiness and rumored ghosts are charming.

CAMPING There are seven public campgrounds in the South Shore area ($12–$17 per night) and 10 in the West Shore area ($7–$14 a night). The North Shore/Truckee area has about two dozen campgrounds, private as well as public. There's plenty of campground space, but also plenty of contenders, so reservations are recommended. For details, call the **Lake Tahoe Visitor Center** (tel. 916/573–2600) or the **Tahoe National Forest** (tel. 916/265–4531 in Nevada City, CA). (*See* Chapter 1 for information about camping in state-run campgrounds.) If you want to get away from it all, try the backcountry. Contact any of the ranger districts in the vicinity; the **Truckee Ranger District** (tel. 916/587–3558) is a good place to start.

● ● ● FOOD

Your best bet in the South Lake Tahoe area is to head over to Stateline in Nevada. Ask a resident which is his or her favorite casino buffet, and you're in business. If you want to prepare your own food, try **Grass Roots Natural Foods** at the intersection of U.S. 50 and Route 89, or one of the other large grocery stores on U.S. 50. In Truckee, you'll find a concentration of restaurants downtown and in outlying shopping complexes, which also have large grocery stores.

SOUTH LAKE TAHOE AREA The loyal customers at **Ernie's Coffee Shop** (1146 Emerald Bay Rd., tel. 916/541–2161) keep their personalized coffee mugs hanging on the wall. Breakfasts range from $3 for two eggs to $6 for a tostada omelet (open 6 AM–2 PM). **Chris's Red Hut Waffle Shop** (2723 Lake Tahoe Blvd., tel. 916/541–9024) has a great selection of waffles and wonderful blueberry pancakes ($4). **Los Tres Hombres Cantina** (765 Emerald Bay Rd., tel. 916/544–1233) is a favorite local hangout for Mexican food, music, and drink specials during "Fiesta Hours" (weekdays 4–6). Entrees range from $7 to $14. **Fresh Ketch Lakeside Restaurant** (2435 Venice Dr. E, tel. 916/541–5683) has some dishes for under $10, but you'll be tempted to splurge on the excellent seafood dinners, which start at $13.

WEST SHORE The friendly, airy, and relaxed **Uncle Fudd's Little Tahoe Diner** (6821 West Lake Blvd., Tahoma) is open daily 7:30 AM–2 PM. Settle down at the rustic pine counter for a bowl of chili, a milk shake, or a killer brownie. **Rosie's Café** (571 N. Lake Blvd., Tahoe City, tel. 916/583–8504) is always hopping, no matter when you arrive. Expect to pay $4–$7 for breakfast (the Cajun eggs are good), $6–$7 for lunch, and $5–$13 for dinner. Chow down on jambalaya, pesto chicken, veggie stir fry, or chicken salad. Rosie's has a bar, and live music Tuesday nights.

● ● ● OUTDOOR ACTIVITIES

A checklist of places to explore around the lake should include Emerald Bay, Eagle Falls, Sugar Pine Point, Lake Forest Beach, and King's Beach. And that's just for starters. The free *North Tahoe/Truckee Week* has a great deal of information about the "scenic qua non." Around the shores of the lake are 23 boat ramps and 20 public beaches (access to both available for a small fee). There's also fishing, mountain biking, skiing, hiking, horseback riding, and snowmobiling. For information about the miles and miles of hiking trails, call the **Lake Tahoe Basin Management Unit** (tel. 916/573–2600). In general, your best source of information is the nearest ranger district.

BICYCLING Bicyclists have a variety of paths to choose from, some more challenging than others. The **Pope-Baldwin Bike Path,** a nearly flat 3.4-mile stretch on the south end of the lake, parallel to Route 89, offers longer scenic side trips and is exceptionally popular in the summer. Mountain bikes are gaining in popularity, so don't expect complete solitude on the better-known trails. The U.S. Forest Service prohibits their use on the Pacific Crest Trail and in wilderness areas, but recommends cross-country ski trails, abandoned logging roads, and non-wilderness trails. At **Bear Valley** (tel. 209/753–2834) on the lake, you can rent a mountain bike for $25 a day and compete in "Biking the Sierras," a mountain-bike race series held on successive summer weekends at Tahoe-area ski resorts (contact **Sports Marketing Concepts** in Truckee, tel. 916/582–1426).

Near Lake Tahoe

● ● ● DONNER LAKE

Most families eat away at each other in one way or another, but the Donner family went all the way. For grisly details about the ill-fated Donner party, half of whom perished trying to cross the pass in the winter of 1842, head for **Donner Memorial State Park** (a few miles west of Truckee off Route 80). Don't be embarrassed: Everybody else wants to hear about death, starvation, double-crossing, and cannibalism, too. The short movie shown at the Visitor Center (for a small fee) is always well attended. A stone's throw away is the Donner Monument that stands 22-feet high to mark the depth of the snow that fateful winter. Motels and gas stations have sprung up where 42 would-be pioneers died, and semis and RVs zip by on Route 80.

Nearby is **Donner Lake,** with private cabins, homes, and motels crowding the lakefront. The **Truckee-Donner Recreation and Park District** has a public boat-launch facility ($5 for daily launch; parking $2, RVs $3) and the public **West End Beach** ($2.50). The lake is nice for swimming, but the chilly water takes some getting used to.

ELDORADO NATIONAL FOREST

The **Eldorado National Forest Information Center,** on U.S. 50 east of Placerville (open 7–6; Sundays 8–5 in the summer), has information on trails and campgrounds, maps, and a great view. **Mokelumne Wilderness** is an excellent area for backpacking, as is **Desolation Wilderness,** a 63,473-acre preserve of granite peaks, glacial valleys, subalpine forests, and more than 80 lakes, with hiking, fishing, and camping aplenty. Other areas of striking beauty, as well as quality hiking and camping, include **Crystal Basin, Bear Valley, Tahoe National Park,** and the **Toiyabe National Forest** (North NV Unit).

Reno

Across the Nevada border, Reno makes its living from other people's losses. Gambling is the city's raison d'être, just as it is farther south in Las Vegas. Although you can drop a bundle in Reno in no time flat, it's a better city than Las Vegas for gamblers who still have their training wheels: The minimum stakes are lower; the blackjack dealers don't roll their eyeballs when you ask for another card on 20; and you're less likely to be beaten up by an old woman with blue hair and curlers protecting her turf at the slot machines. Reno is also a whole hell of a lot more attractive than Las Vegas. After you've lost your money, your shirt, and been forced to post your girlfriend as collateral, the beauty of Lake Tahoe and the Sierras helps put it all in perspective. But even if you don't gamble, consider using Reno as a base from which to frolic on Lake Tahoe or ski: Room rates in the city are low because casinos want to lure gamblers, and the casino buffets are cheap, cheap, cheap. Behind the facade, though, there's a real town with real people—and that has its attractions, too.

BASICS

AMERICAN EXPRESS **Deluxe Travel Ltd.** is a representative for American Express (and will hold mail for card members). *Two locations: Reno-Cannon International Airport, Main Terminal, tel. 702/322–0927. Open weekdays 6:30 AM–10 PM, weekends 8–8. 102 California Ave., Reno 89509, tel. 702/323–4644. Open weekdays 9–6.*

TOURIST INFORMATION The **Reno Tahoe Visitor Center** (135 N. Sierra St., tel. 702/348–7788) has the usual brochures as well as tickets for casino shows, concerts, and special events, and a "Downtowner" discount coupon booklet. You can also arrange to go on a $5 "Behind the Scenes" casino tour.

COMING AND GOING

BY TRAIN **Amtrak** (tel. 800/872–7245) heads west to Sacramento in the morning, and comes into Reno in the late afternoon. The station is at East Commercial Row and Lake Street. Trains also stop in Truckee.

BY BUS The 24-hour **Greyhound** terminal (155 Stevenson St., tel. 702/322–4511) is active all day, but the most economical way to get to Reno, whether you're coming from Sacramento, San Francisco, Red Bluff, or Redding, is on a gambling tour bus. From the San Francisco Bay area, fares are usually around $20 (round-trip), and you sometimes also get gambling scrip that you can either wager in the casinos or cash in. Some package

Reno

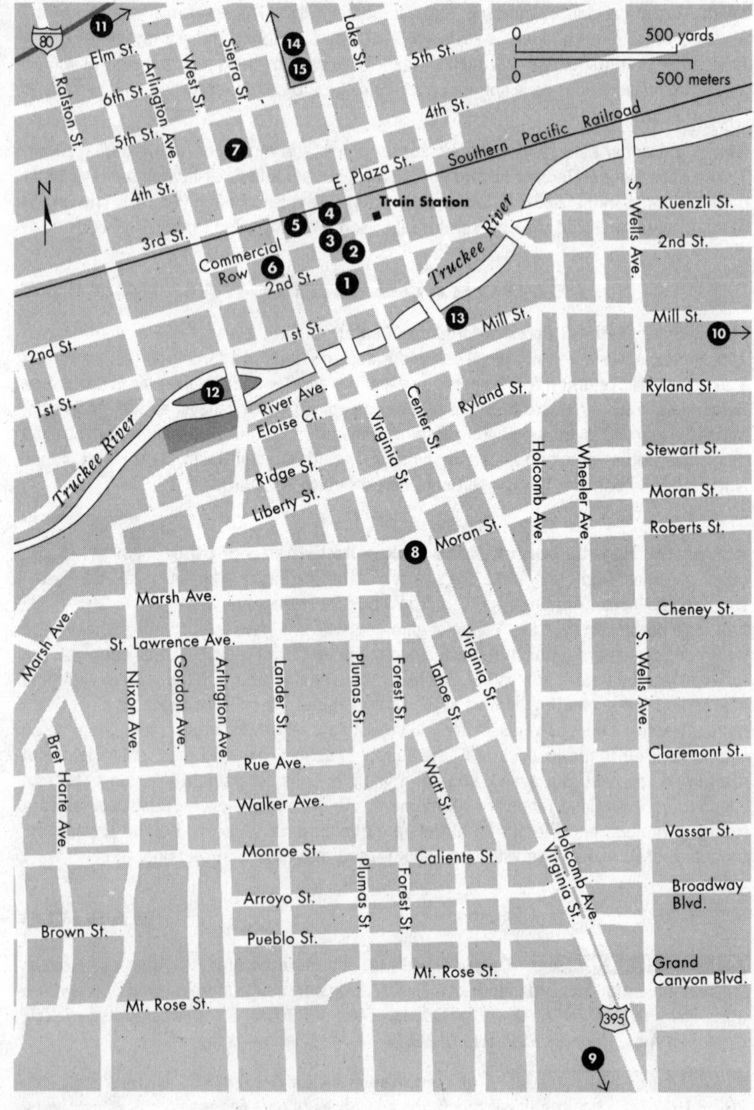

Bally's, **10**
Circus Circus, **7**
Club Cal-Neva, **1**
Fitzgerald's, **5**
Flamingo Hilton, **6**
Fleischmann Planetarium, **14**
Harold's, **4**
Harrah's, **2**
John Ascuaga's Nugget, **11**
Nevada Club, **3**
Nevada Historical Society, **15**
Peppermill, **9**
Ponderosa, **8**
William F. Harrah Foundation National Automobile Museum, **13**
Wingfield Park, **12**

deals include lodging. Check ads in the Sunday travel sections of the *San Francisco Chronicle* or *Sacramento Bee.* One ubiquitous company is **Lucky Reno Tours** (2250 Mission St., San Francisco, tel. 415/864–2545).

BY CAR Reno is at the junction of I–80 (east–west) and Route 395 (north–south). If you want to rent a car in Reno, rates are reasonable: At last look, **Apple Rent-a-Car** (550 W. 4th St., tel. 702/329–2438) had economy cars at $18.50 per day, medium-size at $27.50, and mileage was free. Another cheap option is **Lloyd's International Rent-A-Car** (2515 Mill St., tel. 702/827–4400 or 800/654–7037), which rents economy cars for around $20 per day, medium-size ones for around $27.

BY PLANE **Reno Cannon International Airport** is served by American, American West, Canadian Air, Continental, Delta, Northwest, USAir, and United. Travel agents can advise you about air/land packages to Reno. The airport is east of town off I–80. *2001 E. Plumb La., tel. 702/328–6499.*

GETTING AROUND

It's easy to find your way around Reno, and you don't really need a car if you're staying in one of the many centrally located motels. The splashy casino lights are concentrated downtown. If you have a car or bicycle, head north into some pretty, residential areas to remind yourself that real people live here, too. Walking around the well-lit downtown area is fairly safe at night, but a bad idea in the surrounding areas, particularly east of Virginia Street. The Reno campus of the **University of Nevada** is 1½ miles north of downtown on Virginia Street. Reno's local public transit system, **Citifare** (tel. 702/348–7433), has some 24-hour routes.

WHERE TO SLEEP

On the up side, casinos and some motels offer some really great deals; on the down side, managers have a tendency to raise rates whenever it suits them. Weekend visits at most motels require a two-night minimum; mid-week prices tend to be lower. Some of the best lodging deals come through the casinos, especially mid-week and during the winter. Contact the casinos or the visitor center for leads. The 9% room tax is not included in prices below. For room-reservation referral, call the **Reno-Sparks Convention and Visitor Authority** (tel. 800/367–7366). Reno gets a lot of tourists and conventions, so reservations are advised, particularly during the summer and around holidays.

Downtown, the **Windsor Hotel** (214 West St., tel. 702/323–6171) is a great deal: around $20 for a single with shared bath on weekdays; $24–$35 on weekends. The hotel is a bit run-down, but pleasantly so, and the management is friendly. Close to the University of Nevada and removed from the downtown hubbub is the **Miners' Inn** (1651 N. Virginia St., tel. 702/329–3464). It's slightly more expensive, but there's a pool and you can get a room that sleeps four for around $55. Near I–80, the **Silver Dollar Motor Lodge** (817 N. Virginia St., tel. 702/323–6875) is a decent place to crash ($35–$50 weekdays), and wash your clothes in the coin-operated laundry.

If all you want is a good night's sleep in a cheap motel (around $30; $6 per additional person), try **Motel 6.** The chain has locations in Carson City (2749 S. Carson St., tel. 207/885–7710) and Sparks (2405 B St., tel. 702/358–1080), as well as three locations in Reno (Reno West, 1400 Stardust Ave., tel. 702/747–7390; Reno South, 1901 S. Virginia, tel. 702/827–0255; Reno Central, 866 N. Wells Ave., tel. 702/786–9852).

FOOD

Casino meals are notoriously good deals (*see* Food in Chapter 13): you can walk away entirely sated for $2–$7. You'll find supermarkets, such as Safeway and Raley's, on every major road leading into or out of Reno, but most tourists (for some reason) go downtown to **J.J.'s Market** (445 N. Virginia St.). Inside is a **Port of Subs** (tel. 702/323–2189) with sandwiches from $2.75 to $5.

DESSERT/COFFEEHOUSES **Java Jungle** (246 W. 1st St., tel. 702/324–5282) is the local hangout for caffe latte and cappuccino, as well as sandwiches on croissants ($5), and desserts. With its trendy decor, the café is a welcome respite from the typical Naugahyde schmooze palaces that inundate Reno. Open weekdays till midnight and weekends till 2 AM.

● ● ● WORTH SEEING

The bottom line in Reno is gambling, and most repeat visitors have their favorite casino, which they seem to return to faithfully. **Bally's-Reno** has the best race and sports gambling; **Circus Circus** has circus acts, carnival games, and stuffed animal prizes; **Harrahs, Eldorado, Cal-Neva,** and all the others, have their own appeal. The best orientation is the **Behind the Scenes Gaming Tour** (*see* Tourist Information, *above*), which will help you choose a game that suits your taste and budget.

In any case, there's more to Reno than downtown. The city sprawls over miles of drab, scrubby high desert, and is home to many people whose livelihoods have nothing to do with dice or odds. The presence of the **University of Nevada** at Reno lends a certain intellectual and cultural patina to things. Next door is the **Nevada Historical Society Museum,** which has an intriguing exhibit on the settling of Nevada, including a sobering display on the destruction of the native ecology and the disruption of Native American culture. *1650 N. Virginia St., tel. 702/789–0190. Admission free. Open Tues.–Sat. 10–5.*

Taking one of the free gambling classes offered by many of the casinos is a bit like taking a cooking class from a cannibal: You find out how you're going to be seasoned before being tossed into the pot.

On the campus itself is **Fleischmann Planetarium** (tel. 702/784–4812 or 702/784–4811) where you can view the night sky through a telescope (*see* Cheap Thrills, *below*), tour the free exhibit on matters astronomical, or attend one of the daily star-gazing shows ($5). Car lovers should zoom over to the **National Automobile Museum** (10 Lake St. South, tel. 702/333–9300), which is open daily 9:30–5:30; admission $7.50. **Wilbur May Museum and Arboretum** (1502 Washington St., tel. 702/785–5961) is a historical museum and garden in Rancho Rafael Park north of downtown that is open Tuesday–Sunday. 10–5; admission: $2. Both museums are wheelchair accessible.

Reno is only a two-hour drive from Sacramento and a 3 1/2-hour drive from San Francisco, so Northern Californians who want to gamble head to Reno rather than the glitzier Las Vegas to the south. Many locals, however, avoid the downtown area, and instead take their guests on drives to the nearby towns of **Virginia City**—home of the **Bucket of Blood Saloon,** famous from the big silver-rush days around the Comstock Lode—and **Carson City,** the state's capital.

● ● ● CHEAP THRILLS

Go window-shopping at one of the many **pawn shops** downtown, where you'll find plenty of guitars and other items that gamblers decided they could "temporarily" dispense with in order to finance another round at the tables. Check out the big selection of wedding rings. Quite a few of them probably belong to people who are still married.

During the summer, the **Reno Municipal Band Summer Concert Season** sponsors free concerts noon–1 PM at Wingfield Park downtown and on Wednesday evening from 6 to 8 at Virginia Lake Park on Lakeside Drive.

Better yet, call the "current events" number at **Fleischmann Planetarium** (tel. 702/784–1759) to find out what's happening up above in the nighttime sky. Then drive out of town into the desert and check out the stars.

FESTIVAL Reno's annual **Hot August Nights** (tel. 702/829–1955) is a major nostalgia festival, celebrating cars and rock 'n' roll from the 50s and early 60s. Visitors drive their classics in from all over the United States and join in a 2,500-car parade.

There's a prom, concerts, and rockin' at the 24-hour **Hamburger Haven** soda fountain, among other attractions catering to 50s buffs. Room occupancy is high (as are rates) during this annual early-August festival.

AFTER DARK • • •

The casinos and nightclubs attract top-name entertainers such as Jay Leno, Bill Cosby, and Frank Sinatra, and also feature cabaret shows, comedy, and rock bands. Consult the "Best Bets" section in the Friday issue of the *Reno Gazette-Journal*. If you want to plan ahead, check the Sunday entertainment sections of the *San Francisco Chronicle* or the *Sacramento Bee*, or write the **Visitor Center** (*see above*) for an entertainment lineup.

Near Reno

VIRGINIA CITY • • •

A few miles south of Reno, the scenic Route 341 turns off Route 395 and heads for the heart of silver-mining country. After passing through dry, sagebrush-filled terrain that looks *exactly* like the Old West is supposed to look, the road climbs toward spectacular views of Virginia City, once a rip-roaring silver town widely known as "The Queen of the Comstock." In the 1870s, Virginia City was the largest town between Reno and San Francisco, and the source of incredible wealth. Those days are long gone, but the town's 700 residents have restored the old town into a gaudy reflection of its prosperous heyday.

The spiritual center of Virginia City is the **Bucket of Blood Saloon** (1 S. C St., tel. 702/847–0322) where a huge sign screams "Mark Twain was Robbed Here!" Other signs, all done in serif-typeface with hyperbolic language, order you to visit every last tourist attraction and to learn about every event of the slightest historical importance that ever happened here. Oddly enough, all this hype is not so much a modern technique to lure gullible tourists as it is an extension of the same audacious energy that built the town in the first place. Have an open mind and you just may sort of love it. "Live and kickin' since 1859," they say. Take the fun, 35-minute, narrated **Virginia and Truckee Railroad** ride from Virginia City to historic Gold Hill from May through September for $4. You can also tour **Piper's Opera House** and the mansions of old silver moguls, or just sit down at a picnic table and admire the view from the hill. Take the time to visit the **pioneer cemetery**—you'll see it on a nearby hill. For information about activities, call **Virginia City Attractions** (tel. 702/847–0311). Farther down Route 342 you'll pass through **Silver City,** with its wood-frame Victorians, shacks, and brick storefronts. Set the camera to "moody" and have a field day.

The small and friendly **Virginia City Motel** (675 S. C St., tel. 702/847–0277) has double rooms for $36–$42 (reserve in advance, 1 room wheelchair accessible). The motel is painted white with red trim, and the wagon wheels outside are a nice touch.

CARSON CITY • • •

Down the road, about a half-hour drive south from Reno on Route 395, Carson City is somewhat bland compared to glittery Reno and garish Virginia City. It's the state's capital, and has casinos and lodging if the Reno area is booked. Visit the **Stewart Indian Museum** (5366 Snyder Ave., tel. 702/882–1808, open daily 9–4) and the **Nevada State Railroad Museum** (2180 S. Carson St./Rte. 395, tel. 702/687–6953; admission: $1; open Wed.–Sun. 8:30–4:30). You can also tour the **Nevada State Capitol** (1191 S. Carson St., tel. 702/882–1565), **Brewery Arts Center** (449 W. King St., tel. 702/883–1976), and **Nevada State Museum** (600 Carson St., tel. 702/885–4810); or attend the annual **Nevada Day Parade** in October or the **Kit Carson Rendezvous** in June. For a schedule of events, contact the **Carson City Convention and Visitor Bureau** (1900 S. Carson St., Suite 200, tel. 800/634–8700).

THE SIERRA NEVADA AND SAN JOAQUIN VALLEY 7

By Shelly Smith

The mountains? Who wants to go to the mountains? I've seen mountains before—big deal. If that's what you're thinking, guess again. The Sierra Nevada, the largest continuous mountain range in the United States, is one of the most spectacular natural settings in the world. Looking to reaffirm your belief in the overwhelming oneness of life? Well, trade in those minimalls for mile-high panoramas and lush alpine scenery; motel swimming pools for crystal-clear mountain lakes; parking lots for wind-swept meadows; and faceless high rises for towering peaks and granite cliffs. It sounds a bit Zen—perhaps even like a bad television commercial—but so what. If the pressures of city life are turning you into a neurotic monster, escape from the smog and attitudes of suburban California and flee to the hills. Only four hours east of San Francisco and three hours north of Los Angeles, **Yosemite National Park,** the **Inyo National Forest,** the **Sequoia and Kings Canyon national forests,** and the **Sierra National Forest**—an unparalleled collection of natural wonders—are within easy striking range.

Even if you're not in the mood to abandon civilization for a month-long hike in the backcountry, there's plenty to explore from the confines of your car or on short day hikes. The most eye-opening experience in the Sierra Nevada, in fact, is that of simply getting out of the car. Turn off the motor and walk away from it all for an hour, a week, a month, or eternity. In all seriousness, you'll be a better person for it. Honestly.

The desert doesn't seem so empty when a troop of prairie dogs is howling at sunset; granite doesn't seem so imposing when tempered by the babble of a gentle stream.

Granted, the Sierra Nevada's national parks are difficult to explore without a car, but then no one said traveling on a shoestring was going to be easy. You may have to do some creative planning with buses and trains, but it seems fitting—considering the enormous amount of energy these mountains have expended getting to where they are today—that you, too, should burn a few calories getting here.

Yosemite National Park

There's no other way to say it: Yosemite is simply stunning—a pure and pristine natural wonder that enchants and beguiles like no other in the world. Yes, it's overdeveloped in places; yes, it's crowded; and yes, of course, it can be expensive. But in the scheme of things none of this really matters. There's no doubt that Yosemite has its problems, yet there's also no doubt that Yosemite measures up to its praises. For almost everyone, Yosemite is a striking reminder of what "breathtaking" and "spectacular" mean. Slightly smaller than the state of Rhode Island, it's packed with raging waterfalls, sheer granite cliffs, lush forests, and generous expanses of alpine meadows. **Yosemite Valley,** the central and most easily accessible portion of the park, stretches more than 20 miles from the **Wawona Tunnel** in the west to **Curry Village** in the east. In between, you'll find miles of virgin forests and undisturbed wildlife, interspersed with hiking trails and campgrounds. The valley's other sights include **Half Dome** and **El Capitan**—two stunning but treacherous granite formations—and the **Yosemite** and **Vernal Falls.**

Yet because the valley is surrounded by so much hype, it can be hard to step back and let the beauty soak in. It comprises a meager 7 of the park's 1,200 square miles, but for some reason most people never leave its congested confines. Even worse, it looks rather like a shopping mall with its tacky hotels and unsightly gift shops, and it tends to attract people whose idea of communing with nature involves a case of Budweiser and the Van Halen brothers. It's almost impossible to avoid the valley, but consider it more as a place to stock up on supplies rather than as a destination in itself.

The best words of advice are to visit during the winter, and/or to avoid the touristy valley whenever possible. **Crane Flat** and **Tuolumne Meadows** (accessed via Route 120), **Glacier Point** (near Badger Pass), and the **Hetch Hetchy Reservoir** (north of Big Oak Flat) are perhaps the most popular "non-valley" sights, and it's here that you'll want to spend most of your time. These areas are most accessible to backpackers and horseback riders, but even so there are numerous turn-outs and hiking areas that are easily reached from the highway.

May, June, July, and August are the warmest months, and definitely the most popular. Of the 3.5 million people who visit each year, 70% come during the summer, when temperatures reach a high of 70° F and a low of 40° F. This is Yosemite at its nicest, when the wildflowers are in bloom, the trees thick and lush, and the sunny days peaceful and long. The winter season runs approximately from early November through March, when the valley typically receives 10–20 inches of snow. Temperatures drop to a chilly 45°F by day and to a downright frigid 15°F by night. You may not be able to explore the park as freely as you'd like during winter, but when dusted with a light blanket of snow—and minus the crowds—Yosemite will definitely sneak its way into your heart.

To the Ahwahnee people, Yosemite was the sacred belly of the world—the divine embryo where nature's wonders were spewed forth in infinite perfection.

For centuries, Yosemite was inhabited by the Ahwahnee people who lived in settlements that were scattered up and down the surrounding mountains (look for the Miwok-Paiute village behind the valley visitor center). Some rangers claim that the Ahwahnee word for the land, *Yosemite,* was the same as their word for "soul" and "spirit," something to be as loved and respected as life itself. Unfortunately, the Mariposa Battalion, the first group of whites to enter the area, saw Yosemite as a prime hunting and fur-trapping spot. By 1850, they had settled (i.e., conquered) the Ahwahnee and established a lucrative lumber trade and trading outpost. Thankfully, John Muir, a shepherd and naturalist, formed the Sierra Club in 1892 in order to secure federal protection of the land that even then was showing signs of overdevelopment. Yosemite's other famous associate is Ansel Adams, the world-renowned photographer who somehow captured the untamed majesty of this park on film.

TOURIST INFORMATION Yosemite has two well-stocked visitor centers, one in **Yosemite Valley** (tel. 209/372–0299, open daily 9–5) at shuttle bus stop #6 or #9; and one at **Tuolumne Meadows** (tel. 209/372–0263, open May–Oct., daily 9–5), toward the east end of the park on Route 120. Neither has an address, but both are well marked. Just follow the VISITOR CENTER signs. Besides maps and tourist brochures, both distribute free wilderness permits (required for overnight camping in the backcountry).

The **Park Information Service** (Box 577, Yosemite National Park 95389, tel. 209/372–0265) can answer most questions about Yosemite. Send them a self-addressed, stamped envelope for free brochures and maps, or call them weekdays between 9 and 5. It doesn't have much of a tourist desk, but the **Wawona Ranger Station** (tel. 209/375–6391), at the south end of Yosemite on Route 41, does have wilderness permits. Otherwise, the **Big Oak Flat Information Station,** located at the Route 120 west entrance, is open Friday to Sunday year-round.

FEES The fee for one week is $5 per car, or $2 per hiker, bicyclist, or bus passenger. No daily passes are sold, but you can purchase annual passes for only $15 that entitle you to a one-time $10 rebate on lift tickets at **Badger Pass** (tel. 209/372–1330), Yosemite's downhill ski area.

PUBLICATIONS When you enter the park, the guard will give you a current copy of *Yosemite Guide,* which contains current lodging, dining, tour, recreational, and safety information. To receive a free catalogue, write to the **Yosemite Association Bookstore** (Box 230, El Portal 95318, tel. 209/379–2648).

WHAT TO PACK If you go in winter—and unless you plan on sleeping in Yosemite's expensive hotels—you'll need to bring warm clothing, a sub-zero sleeping bag, and a water-proof (or least water-resistant) tent. Hiking boots are a must for exploring Yosemite's backcountry and, yes, snowshoes would be a good idea if you want to blaze your own trail. Most of this stuff can be purchased in the valley's sporting-good shops, but prices tend to be outrageous. So that you don't end up spending $100 for something like a tube of sun block, bring them with you.

Rain gear is important year-round. Even if the sky is royal blue, thunderstorms often sneak up unexpectedly and drop buckets of rain on the park. Leg gaiters and water-repellant jackets are a smart idea, along with a pair of boots that can stand up to repeated doses of heavy-duty mud. You may never have to battle one of Yosemite's summertime tempests, but unless you want to be stuck sipping hot chocolate in a dreary coffee shop, it pays to be prepared.

GENERAL STORES **Yosemite Village,** 5 miles east of Route 41, in the middle of the park, is well-stocked with grocery and camping stores. This is also the center of Yosemite's god-awful souvenir trade (i.e., "I Luv Yosemite" sweat shirts for only $25). The **Village Sport Shop** (tel. 209/372–1286, open spring to fall, daily 9–9) has fishing, recreational, and camping gear. The **Village Store** (tel. 209/372–1253, open year-round, daily 8–10) offers groceries, film, camping supplies, and a generous selection of El Capitan place mats. Both can be reached via the Yosemite shuttle #3 or #10 (*see* Getting Around, *below*).

Next to the **Wawona General Store** (tel. 209/375–6574, open daily 8–8), which stocks groceries and camping supplies, there's a **post office** at the southwest corner of the park on Route 41.

Badger Pass Sport Shop has ski clothing and equipment, lotions, waxes, and picnic supplies. It's near the Badger Pass ski slopes and Wawona, off Route 41 on the southwest side of the park. *Tel. 209/372–1330. Take Rte. 41 into park and follow* BADGER PASS *signs. Open Oct.–Mar., daily 10–5.*

In Yosemite Valley's Curry Village, 8 miles past the point where Routes 41 and 140 end, look for the **Curry Village Mountain Shop.** You can purchase rock-climbing, backpacking, and camping supplies here. *Tel. 209/372–1296. Shuttle stop #13. Open daily 8–8.*

Yosemite National Park

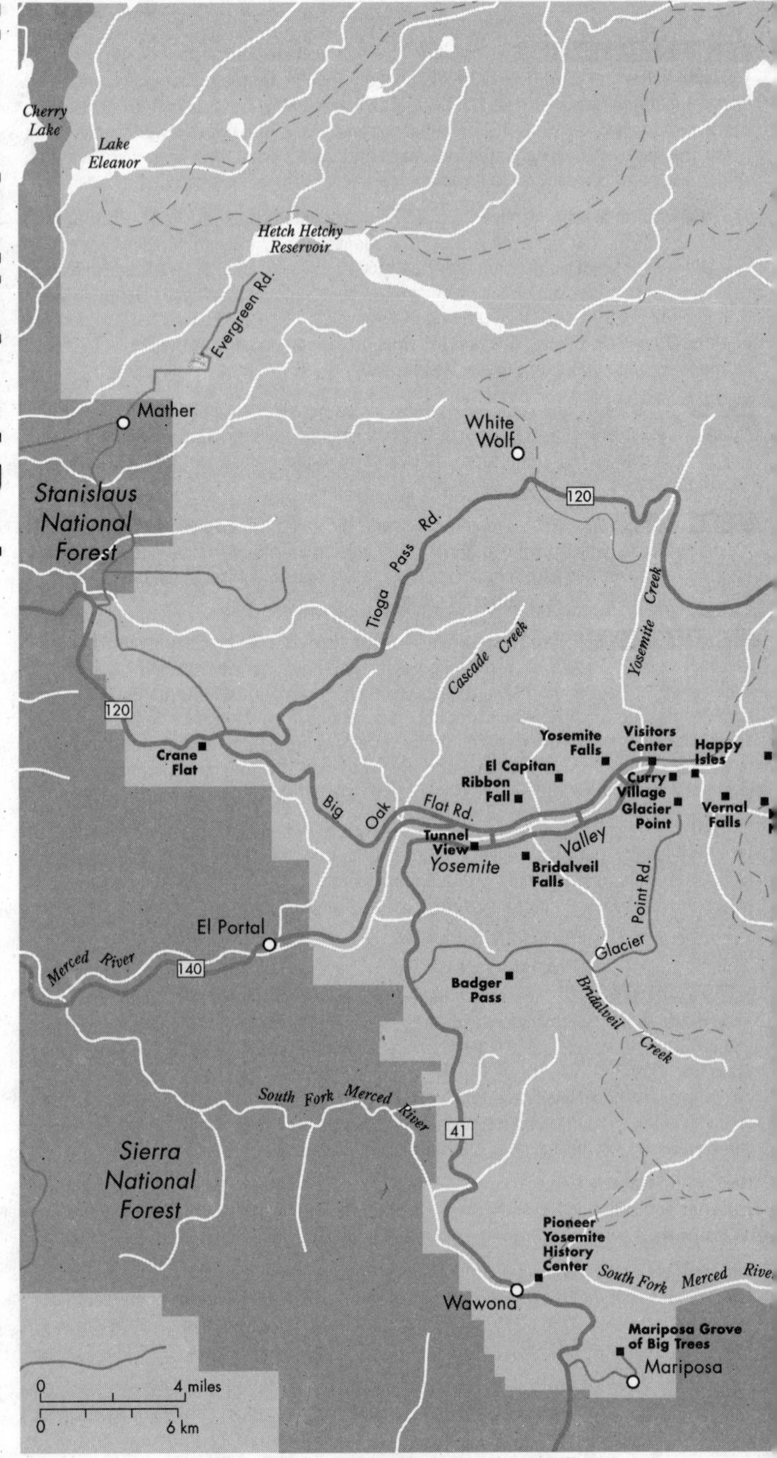
Cherry Lake
Lake Eleanor
Hetch Hetchy Reservoir
Evergreen Rd.
Mather
White Wolf
Stanislaus National Forest
120
Tioga Pass Rd.
Cascade Creek
Yosemite Creek
120
Crane Flat
Yosemite Falls
Visitors Center
Happy Isles
El Capitan
Ribbon Fall
Curry Village
Glacier Point
Vernal Falls
Big Oak Flat Rd.
Tunnel View
Yosemite Valley
Bridalveil Falls
Glacier Point Rd.
El Portal
Merced River
140
Badger Pass
Bridalveil Creek
South Fork Merced River
41
Sierra National Forest
Pioneer Yosemite History Center
South Fork Merced Rive
Wawona
Mariposa Grove of Big Trees
Mariposa
0
4 miles
0
6 km

Yosemite National Park

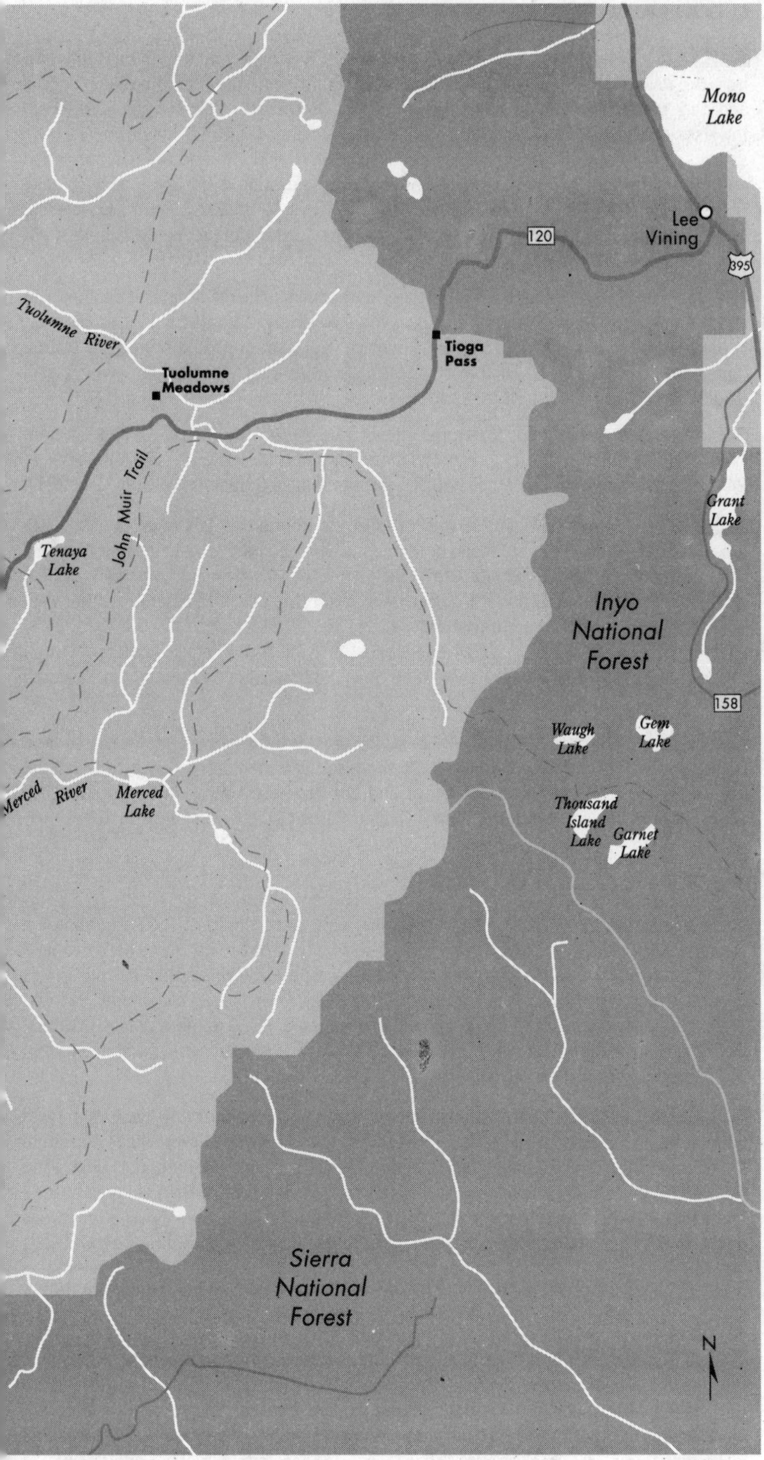

Mono Lake
Lee Vining
120
395
Tuolumne River
Tioga Pass
Tuolumne Meadows
John Muir Trail
Tenaya Lake
Grant Lake
Inyo National Forest
158
Waugh Lake
Gem Lake
Merced River
Merced Lake
Thousand Island Lake
Garnet Lake
Sierra National Forest
N

COMING AND GOING

BY CAR Yosemite is accessible via three routes: **Route 41** from the south, **Route 140** from the west (Merced), and **Route 120** from San Francisco. There are information kiosks and park rangers stationed at all three entrances. Route 120 (a.k.a. Tioga Pass Road) traverses the park from west to east, while Routes 41 and 140 terminate in Yosemite Valley. In winter, Route 120 is closed because of snow and ice, and the recommended entrance to the park is Route 140, as it has the lowest elevation. From San Francisco, take Route 580 east to 205, and connect to 120 (total time: 4½ hours). From Los Angeles, take I–5 north to Route 99, and then join with Route 41 north of Fresno (total time: eight hours).

From late fall to early spring, you should carry snow chains. The roads can get treacherous, and the California Route Patrol often closes the highways to all traffic without snow gear. If you get stuck, you'll have to buy an expensive ($60) set of chains from a gas station (and boy, do they love when that happens). For road and weather information, call 209/372–4605.

Gas is available year-round in Yosemite Valley (8 AM–9 PM), Wawona (9–6), and El Portal (7–6); during the summer at Crane Flat and Toulumne Meadows (9–6). Auto service, 24-hour towing, and repair can be had at **Yosemite Village Garage** (tel. 209/372–1221).

BY BUS There is no direct service to Yosemite from either Los Angeles or the Bay Area; all buses stop in either Fresno or Merced, where you may have to change coaches. The cheapest option is **Yosemite Gray Line** (tel. 209/443–5240 or 800/640–6306), which makes daily runs for under $15 between Fresno, Merced, and Yosemite. Otherwise, buses leave from the Merced **Greyhound** station (710 W. 116th St., tel. 209/722–2121) at 8 AM and 3 PM for Yosemite, $14 one-way, $28 round-trip. There is no depot, but all buses stop in Yosemite Valley, a short walk from the hotels and restaurants in Yosemite Village.

BY TRAIN **Amtrak's** (tel. 800/872–7245) #708 train from San Francisco and Oakland arrives each morning in Merced, where you can then catch Yosemite Gray Line (*see above*) to the park. From San Diego and Los Angeles, Amtrak #703 goes daily to Fresno, where you can catch the Amtrak Thruway Bus ($12) or Gray Line to Yosemite.

GETTING AROUND

The curvy **Route 120** runs the entire 60-mile, east–west length of the park, climbing through 2,000 feet of elevation. There are also plenty of dirt roads and small, two-lane highways to explore inside the park—fit for both cars and bicycles. Bike permits aren't generally required for highway travel, but stay away from places like Crane Flat and Toulumne Meadows. Roads that traverse these jagged peaks rise more than 4,000 feet from the valley floor and are often treacherous and poorly maintained—navigable by car, but not recommended on two wheels.

BY PARK SHUTTLE Free **shuttle buses** operate throughout the year, the most popular being the **East Valley Loop.** It travels year-round between Curry Village, Yosemite Village, and the Yosemite Lodge (*see* Where to Sleep, *below*) every half hour. During the ski season, free shuttles also leave Yosemite Lodge for the **Badger Pass** ski area at 8 AM and 11 AM, returning at 1 PM, 3 PM, and 5 PM. Another shuttle (summer only) runs four times daily between Yosemite Lodge and **Glacier Point** (*see* Exploring Yosemite, *below*). Stops are well marked; just look for the Shuttle Bus signs along the main roads. Depending on demand, shuttles occasionally run between Yosemite Lodge and Crane Flat during the summer; call 209/372–0265 or 209/372–1240 for current schedules.

BACKPACKING There are hundreds of possible day hikes in Yosemite, but to beat the crowds you'll need to do some serious backpacking in the wilderness, miles away from the stench of civilization. All trails, however, are limited to a certain number of backpackers to prevent overuse, and **wilderness permits** (free) are required. Reserve one by mail by writing the **Backcountry Office** (Box 577, Yosemite National Park 95389), or appear in person between 8 AM and 4 PM at the Yosemite Valley or Toulumne Meadows visitor centers, or at the Wawona Ranger Station (*see* Tourist Information, *above*). Arrive early, though, as some trails sell out within five minutes.

Once you have a permit, you can take any one of 70 trails that crisscross Yosemite's outback. Anywhere from 5 to 20 miles long, they often involve strenuous climbs along jagged paths that are no more than a foot wide, and some trails take upwards of a week to complete. Fire rings are interspersed every 2 miles or so along the way, but you'll need to bring your own tent and provisions as there are no shelters. You can order maps and a pamphlet of hiking suggestions from the **Yosemite Association Bookstore** (Box 230, El Portal 95318, tel. 209/379–2648).

WHERE TO SLEEP ● ● ●

Camping is the only real way to "experience" Yosemite. Not only are the hotels completely characterless and packed with tourists, but they also charge handsomely for the privilege of four walls and a sagging bed. Camping can be a challenge, but at least crowds are less of a problem. Either way, reservations are strongly recommended at all times; call the **Yosemite Park Curry Company** (tel. 209/252–4848) to reserve a hotel room, or **Ticketron** (tel. 800/452–1111), no more than eight weeks in advance, to reserve a campsite. If all else fails, call the Curry Company to put your name on a waiting list between 10 AM and 4 PM on the day you want to stay. After 4, all cancellations are distributed to those on the list.

HOTELS AND CABINS Hotel reservations can be made up to 366 days in advance and, believe it or not, most places actually fill up that far ahead. If you're not quite sure where you're going to be a year from now, call for reservations with several dates in mind, or come during the off-season (November–March) when cancellations and vacancies are more common. Because Yosemite is so mobbed, you probably won't have a choice when it comes to your hotel accommodations. If you can find a single vacancy, consider yourself lucky.

This said, most people prefer the **Yosemite Lodge** (5 mi east of Rte. 140 entrance, tel. 209/372–1274), which has pleasant, "European–style" rooms (i.e., the bathroom's down the hall). Doubles run $46 a night, and uncomfortable cots are available for an additional $10. Simple, two-person cabins are available in **Curry Village** (25 mi east of Rte. 140 entrance, tel. 209/372–1233), also in Yosemite Valley. Peak season rates are $41, off-season $30.

Otherwise, look for the campground/shanty-town called **Housekeeping Camp** (tel. 209/252–4848), which has 282 identical units huddled close together in Yosemite Valley, separated by paper-thin walls and covered with canvas. They're not particularly comfortable, but each bare-bones structure houses up to four people for only $33 per night. The camp is open between mid-March and late October, with laundry, bathrooms, shower facilities, and a grocery store nearby.

"Population density in the campgrounds is higher than in Calcutta's most crowded neighbor-hoods."

CAMPGROUNDS Be sure to pick up a copy of *The Complete Guidebook to Yosemite Valley,* available at the park's entrances or in most gift shops. In it, you'll find these words of wisdom about camping in the summer: "Population density in the campgrounds is higher than in Calcutta's most crowded neighborhoods." The only difference, it seems, is that here you have to make a reservation at least eight weeks in advance. You may get lucky and find an open site during the off-season, but otherwise reservations are a must. Once again, call the Curry Company (tel. 209/252–4848) or Ticketron (tel. 800/452–1111). Sites generally run $12–$14 per night.

Luckily, there are a few first-come, first-served campgrounds in the park. In particular, try **Sunnyside Walk-In** (Yosemite Valley), **Wawona** (Route 41 in Wawona), **Bridalveil Creek**

(Glacier Point Road), **White Wolf** (Route 120 east), or the **Tenaya Lake Walk-In** (Route 120 east).

Lower Pines. This is the only valley campground open year-round, with 173 tent and RV sites. *Shuttle stop #19. 173 sites. Fireplaces, picnic tables, piped water, and flush toilets nearby.*

Lower River. Its proximity to Housekeeping Camp makes it somewhat loud. But hey, at least there's a laundromat nearby. In Yosemite Valley. *Shuttle stop #2. 139 sites. Open Apr.–Nov. Fireplaces, picnic tables, piped water, and flush toilets.*

North Pines. It's near the stables, which means occasional equine smells wafting your way. The sites are for tent camping or RVs under 30 feet long. In Yosemite Valley. *Shuttle stop #18. 86 sites. Open May–Oct. Fireplaces, picnic tables, piped water, and flush toilets.*

Upper Pines. This tent and RV campground is the biggest in the Valley, conveniently located near trailheads to Mirror Lake and Vernal Falls. Misanthropes be warned, however: this place gets extremely crowded. *Shuttle stop #15. 240 sites. Open Mar.–Nov. Fireplaces, picnic tables, piped water, and flush toilets.*

Upper River Campground. Located between Curry Village and Yosemite Valley, this is the only valley campground for tents only. It features some sites near the Merced River. *Shuttle stop #2. 124 sites. Open Apr.–Oct. Fireplaces, picnic tables, piped water, and flush toilets.*

FOOD

Yosemite offers a dull variety of Americana eateries, from fast-food cafeterias to expensive sit-down restaurants. Nothing is particularly outstanding or interesting, though—the Curry Company has a virtual monopoly in the park and can charge as much as they like for greasy burgers and other cardboard-tasting meals. Also note: Most restaurants don't have an address, so follow the signs or ask around if you're having trouble.

If you plan on camping, bring as much food as possible. Prices in Yosemite's small grocery stores are generally 50% higher than in the towns outside the park.

YOSEMITE VILLAGE The Yosemite Village complex, 7 miles east of the Route 140 entrance, has the largest selection of food in the park. **The Loft** (open year-round, daily 11 AM–10 PM), on the second floor of the mall, serves mediocre dishes in a cafeteria setting. The menu looks impressive, ranging from chef salads ($6.50) to grilled trout ($11) and vegetarian lasagna ($10), but taste is strangely absent. This place is popular with locals because cocktails are served all day until closing. Reservations are not accepted, so expect a 30- to 45-minute wait in summer. **Degnan's Deli,** on the ground floor of the complex, serves sandwiches ($4) and salads ($4), and also has picnic supplies. Next door is a small **pizza parlor** run by the Curry Company (small cheese pizza $5; large with 2 toppings $11). Both are open year-round from 10 AM to 9 PM daily.

CURRY VILLAGE There's a **cafeteria** and small **pizzeria** inside the Curry Village Hotel (tel. 209/372–1233), 25 miles east of the Route 140 entrance. Neither is particularly appetizing, but the cafeteria does have surprisingly cheap burgers, sandwiches, and breakfasts—all for under $5; open April–October, 8 AM–11 PM. The pizza place is open year-round 11 AM–8 PM, but don't go out of the way for its merely tolerable slices ($2 apiece).

EXPLORING YOSEMITE

It can take anywhere from a day to the rest of your life to familiarize yourself with Yosemite. Realistically, you'll need at least a few days so you can venture beyond the crowds. To get a good overview, drive along **Route 120,** a 60-mile paved road that runs east–west through the park. There are numerous windy, one-lane dirt roads that crisscross the highway, so don't be afraid to take a detour. More often than not, this is where you'll find the best views.

Also don't be afraid to take a walk or a hike wherever you're inclined. There are hundreds of trails meandering through the valley, ranging from relaxing strolls to extremely demanding backcountry excursions. Many are easily reached by shuttle bus (*see* Getting Around, *above*) if you don't have a car.

ORIENTATION PROGRAMS The **Yosemite Valley** visitor center (6 mi east from the Rte. 140 park entrance, tel. 209/372–0299) offers a good slide program on the park's geography and history. The free, 20-minute show runs every half hour from 9:30 to 4, Monday through Saturday. Also look for the center's two documentaries about John Muir and Ansel Adams (call for current schedules) and its evening question/answer programs with a Yosemite ranger. They only last 20 minutes, but you'll learn more about Yosemite's flora and fauna here than you would in a semester at most colleges. The free lectures start at 8, followed by coffee and chit-chat.

GUIDED TOURS All kinds of guided tours are available in Yosemite, from two-hour excursions along the valley floor ($14) to the day-long Grand Tour ($38) that takes you to Mariposa Grove and Glacier Point. Buses also shuttle hikers to Toulumne Meadows or Glacier Point during the summer. For reservations contact the visitor center (tel. 209/372–1240).

Otherwise, the **Yosemite Association** (Box 230, El Portal 95318; tel. 209/379–2646) organizes one- to three-day excursions into the backcountry, with hands-on field courses in forestry, geology, animal life, and astronomy.

SHORT HIKES **Yosemite Falls** is the highest waterfall in North America and the fifth-highest in the world. It may look continuous from the valley floor, but actually it's divided into the upper falls (1,430 feet), the middle cascades (675 feet), and the lower falls (320 feet). From the parking lot, there's a 1/5-mile trail to the base and a 2-mile trail to the lower falls. To reach the top, head to Sunnyside Campground and its strenuous, 3.5-mile **Yosemite Falls Trail,** which rises over 2,700 feet. Get off at shuttle stop #7 and follow the signs.

The popular 3-mile trail around **Mirror Lake** offers some of the best photo opportunities in the park, but the strenuous 6-mile trail to **Vernal Falls** (317 feet) and **Nevada Falls** (594 feet) is a great place to soak yourself on a hot day. The first half is aptly named **Mist Trail** (bring a bathing suit or rain gear, and kiss your hairdo goodbye), and the second half **Nevada Trail.** It'll take two to three hours each way, but the view from the top is phenomenal.

If you arrive in Yosemite via the Wawona Road, your first view of the valley will include **Bridalveil Fall**—a ragged, 620-foot cascade that's often blown as much as 20 feet from side to side by the wind. The Ahwahnee called it *Pohono* ("puffing wind"). There's a 1/5-mile trail leading to its base that starts from the parking lot.

LONGER HIKES **Hetch Hetchy,** one of California's largest reservoirs, has irked conservationists ever since it was built in the 1920s. Environmentalists like John Muir argued that the damming of the Toulumne River would irreparably harm the region's wildlife (and leave one of Yosemite's nicest valleys under 300 feet of water), but politicians in San Francisco wanted mountain-fresh drinking water. Can you guess who won? Today, despite the massive Hetch Hetchy dam, the area still retains much of its beauty, and there's a wonderfully isolated and lightly traveled trail along the northern shore. Mornings and evenings, it's possible to walk for hours without meeting another living soul. No swimming or boating is allowed in the reservoir, but you can camp in the nearby **Stanislaus National Forest** (*see* Near Yosemite, *below*). Hetch Hetchy is 40 miles north of Yosemite Valley, 15 miles east of Route 120 on Evergreen Road.

The area north of **Tuolumne River** is wild and relatively untraveled—a good place to get away from it all. There are numerous trailheads near Tuolumne Meadows, but they're recommended only for determined backpackers who want to spend a week in the wilderness. In particular, try the **Pacific Crest Trail,** which eventually leads to Canada.

Serious hikers should also consider the **Tuolumne Grand Canyon Trail,** accessed from Tuolumne Meadows on one side and Tanaya Lake on the other. There's a harrowing switch-back trail leading 2 miles down the canyon, 8 miles across, and another 2 miles up the far side—a strenuous hike requiring at least two full days.

SCENIC DRIVES AND VIEWS **Glacier Point** offers a spectacular view of the valley and the surrounding mountains—probably one of the most all-encompassing panoramas in the park. During the summer you can drive up to it; the 16-mile road starts at **Chinquapin** (accessible from the south by Route 41 or the west by Tioga Road). Afterwards, park your car and make the easy four-hour (8.5-mile) hike down to the valley. A shuttle (*see* Getting Around, *above*) will then take you back up to the parking lot.

Tuolumne Meadows, the largest subalpine meadow in the High Sierras and site of several backcountry trailheads, is on the Tioga Pass Road (a.k.a. Route 120), 25 miles east of Lee Vining and Route 395. This is a gorgeous and pristine part of Yosemite, with delicate meadows surrounded by huge granite formations. And it's usually much less crowded than the valley. There's also a campground, grocery store, visitor center, and ranger station here. Route 120 is closed during the winter, but it's usually opened by mid-May.

● ● ● PARK ACTIVITIES

BICYCLING Yosemite Valley has 8 miles of mountain trails devoted to bicyclists. Permits are not required, so grab your mountain bike and head for the backcountry. During the summer, you can rent from **Curry Village** (tel. 209/372–1200) daily between 9 and 6, or year-round from **Yosemite Lodge** (tel. 209/372–1208), also open daily between 9 and 6.

BIRD-WATCHING The National Park Service offers weekly bird walks in conjunction with the visitor center. BYOB (Bring Your Own Binoculars). The walks are free, and they generally last two to three hours. Call 209/372–0265 for times.

FISHING The Park Service no longer stocks Yosemite's lakes, but it's still possible to catch rainbow trout and steelheads if you're patient. You'll need a California fishing license, available at any visitor center or sporting-good store. The only stocked waters near Yosemite are **Tioga** and **Ellery lakes,** just outside the park on Route 120, east of the Tioga Pass.

HORSEBACK RIDING Yosemite Valley, Wawona, White Wolf, and Toulumne Meadows all offer hour-long ($12), half-day ($20), full-day ($35), and overnight ($60–$100 per day) horseback trips between Easter and mid-October. For reservations, call 209/372–1248.

ICE SKATING Curry Village (tel. 209/372–0265) operates an outdoor skating rink during the winter, and has skate rentals, a warming hut, and a snack bar.

RAFTING It ain't exactly white water but it's still kind of fun. Curry Village (tel. 209/372–0265) rents rafts, life jackets, and paddles during the summer for $14 a day—perfect for a lazy float down the Merced.

ROCK CLIMBING Take a look around for about two seconds and you'll understand why Yosemite is a mecca for world-class rock climbers. Rock-climbing lessons for all levels are offered year-round by the **Yosemite Mountaineering School and Guide Service** (tel. 209/372–1296 or 209/372–1335). In summer, they organize trips from Toulumne Meadows; in winter, from Curry Village. Also in Curry Village is the **Curry Village Mountain Shop** (tel. 209/372–1200) that has a complete line of gear and clothing.

SNOWSHOEING National Park rangers lead daily tours of Yosemite during the winter months. Tour lengths and difficulty levels depend upon demand. You can rent equipment from most lodges, but the tours themselves are free. See the *Yosemite Guide* for current schedules, or call 209/372–0265.

SKIING

CROSS-COUNTRY Yosemite has 90 miles of cross-country trails through the Badger Pass Ski area to Glacier Point. A free shuttle from the valley runs to and from the Badger Pass slopes three times a day. Lessons are available through the **Cross-Country Ski School** (tel. 209/372–1244). There are also trails out of Crane Flat, a few miles east of the Big Oaks Flat entrance station.

DOWNHILL Yosemite has a small ski area, **Badger Pass** (tel. 209/372–1330), that won't pose much of a challenge to accomplished skiers. It's a good place to learn, however, and there are enough groomed trails to keep intermediate skiers entertained. It's open daily in winter between 9 and 4:30, lift tickets are around $25. Other services here include ski rentals, a warming hut, and a sports shop. Look for Badger Pass 6 miles east of Route 41, on Glacier Point Road.

Near Yosemite

STANISLAUS NATIONAL FOREST ● ● ●

Because it's only a three-hour drive from San Francisco and the Bay Area, the Stanislaus National Forest is one of the most heavily visited parks in California, especially during the summer season. Part of the reason is that camping is allowed almost anywhere within the Stanislaus Forest. Just pick up a wilderness permit (available at any ranger station), pull your car over to the side of the road, then walk 100 feet and pitch a tent wherever your heart desires. This is good news for campers looking to commune with nature, but this also means Stanislaus receives a heap of over-flow campers who couldn't find a space in Yosemite. Crowds are particularly vexing around the resort communities of **Pinecrest, Strawberry,** and **Lake Alpine,** which should be avoided at all costs between June and September.

During the winter, Stanislaus has cross-country and downhill skiing and snowmobiling, but unfortunately you'll have to stay in a hotel or on the side of the road; Stanislaus' developed campgrounds are open only between May and October. Before you venture into the park, pick up a copy of the *Summit Passage,* available at the Sonora Visitor Bureau or the Summit Ranger Station in Pinecrest. This small newspaper gives a detailed description of activities and programs within the Stanislaus forest.

BASICS

TOURIST INFORMATION All ranger stations offer camping/lodging suggestions, hiking and road maps ($2), and wilderness permits. The central station is in **Sonora** (19777 Greenby Rd., tel. 209/532–3671). Otherwise, contact the **Summit Ranger Station** (tel. 209/965–3434) on Route 108 in Pinecrest; the **Calaveras Ranger Station** (tel. 209/795–1381) on Route 4 in Hathaway Pines; the **Groveland Ranger Station** (tel. 209/962–7825) at Buck Meadows; or the **Mi-Wok Ranger Station** (tel. 209/586–3234) on Route 108 in Mi-Wok Village.

GENERAL STORES The town of **Sonora,** about 10 miles from the border of Stanislaus on Route 108, has a few mountaineering and hardware stores that sell camping gear. For general supplies, head down Washington Street (Sonora's main thoroughfare) and turn left on **Mono Way,** where you'll find two shopping centers, a 24-hour Safeway, and a Payless drug store.

Be sure to get gas before heading into the forest—prices seem to go up in direct correspondence with elevation.

COMING AND GOING Three highways traverse Stanislaus: **Route 4** to the north, **Route 108** to the south, and **Route 120,** which connects Stanislaus with San Francisco and Yosemite. Before heading to the high country, check road conditions at the ranger station in Sonora or Calaveras Big Trees—the mountain passes are sometimes closed until late June because of ice and snow. Driving time from San Francisco to Stanislaus (via Route 120) is 3½ hours; two hours from both Stockton (via Route 4) and Modesto (via Route 108).

WHERE TO SLEEP Hotels and motels in the park start at $40 during the summer, $50–$75 during the winter ski season. The majority of visitors, however, prefer to camp. Once you get a wilderness permit (available at any ranger station), you're free to pitch a tent wherever you like. If this sounds like too much trouble, Stanislaus also has developed campsites with grocery stores, showers, and laundromats. Fees for these range from nothing to $15 a night.

HOTELS **Mi-Wok Motor Lodge.** This is the nicest place in the park, hidden within 20 acres of majestic pine trees. The rooms are rustic and comfortable, decorated with brass beds and antique pine furniture. Rooms that sleep two–six range from $40 to $60 (with kitchen). Even better, there's a gift shop, a pool, a barbecue, and a laundry room on the premises. Reserve as far in advance as possible. *Rte. 108 (Box 70), Mi-Wok Village 95346, tel. 209/586–3031 or 800/341–8000. 17 rooms.*

DORM ROOMS **Columbia College** opens its student housing to the public from June until the end of August. Most dorms have kitchen and laundry facilities and private baths; they're $25 per single, $15 per person for a double. The college is in Sonora (11800 Columbia College Dr.), but call **Western Empire Management** (11 S. San Joaquin, Suite 400, Stockton 95202, tel. 209/948–8102) for reservations and availability.

CAMPGROUNDS Camping in Stanislaus is plentiful and, for the most part, cheap. All sites are available on a first-come, first-served basis except at Pinecrest, one of the most developed and popular areas. Call MISTIX (tel. 800/365–2267) for reservations here. Otherwise, the ranger stations can tell you whether a specific campground is full or not.

Mill Creek Campground. This free campground, 14 miles east of Pinecrest on Route 108, is small and quiet and set next to a stream. *Tel. 209/965–3434. 17 sites. Picnic tables, stoves, and pit toilets.*

Middlefork Campground. This is another small campground next to a stream. Twenty-five miles from Groveland on Route 120 and another 5½ miles north on Evergreen Road. Middlefork offers easy access to the Toulumne River and Hetch Hetchy Reservoir. All sites are free. *Tel. 209/962–7825. 25 sites. Picnic tables, stoves, and vault toilets. No drinking water.*

FOOD Expect to encounter the standard burger and steak joints within the park; they're nothing to write home about. Along Route 4, look for the **Bear Valley Deli** (tel. 209/753–2301) at Bear Valley Resort, which serves homemade soups ($5) and sandwiches ($3–$5). On Route 108 west of Dardanelle, try the **Dardanelle Resort** (tel. 209/965–4355), famous locally for its monster-size breakfasts (biscuits and gravy $3, three-egg scrambles $4).

Outside the park, Sonora's Washington Street teems with good restaurants. Try **Caffeine Marys** for cleverly named sandwiches ($3–$5) and espresso ($2–$3). Afterwards, browse through its selection of paperbacks. *52 S. Washington St., tel. 209/532–6261. Open weekdays 8–5, weekends 10–10.*

EXPLORING STANISLAUS Route 4 traverses the 77-mile, east–west length of Stanislaus, offering numerous pull-offs and hiking opportunities along the way. You may be better off, however, buying a map at any ranger station and heading into the backcountry, either by car or on foot. There are hundreds of dirt roads and unimproved highways winding through the forest that offer broad vistas and secluded picnic spots.

Of the three wilderness areas in Stanislaus, the **Emigrant Wilderness** (113,000 acres) is the most crowded, especially during the summer. Gaggles of fishermen and hikers are attracted by its serene subalpine forests, clear lakes, and jagged volcanic formations, while hoards of overflow campers are attracted by its proximity to Yosemite. Despite all this, the wilderness has a number of scenic and relatively uncongested hiking spots. Along Route 108 there are major trailheads at **Bell Meadow, Crabtree Camp, Giarelli Cabin, Coyote Meadow,** and **Kennedy Meadows;** and along Route 120 at **Cherry Lake.**

The **Garson Iceberg Wilderness,** nestled between Routes 108 and 4 in the eastern corner of the park, offers greater solitude but fewer lakes. Major trailheads are located along Route 108 at **Wheat's Meadow, Disaster Creek,** and **Clarkfork;** and along Route 4 at **Lake Alpine, Stanislaus Meadow, Pacific Valley,** and **Highland Lakes.**

The **Calaveras Big Trees State Park,** on Route 4 about 10 miles from the park entrance, is devoted to the preservation of Sierra redwoods. The park offers eight different hiking trails, from the 600-foot-long, children-oriented **Discovery Trail,** to the 8-mile (four-to-six hour) **North Grove Trail,** which meanders along the edge of the Stanislaus River. There's also a visitor center here with guide books and displays, including one dedicated to the now-extinct Mi-Wok Indians.

OUTDOOR ACTIVITIES

BIKING **Bear Valley Mountain Bikes** (tel. 209/753–2834), on Route 4 in Bear Valley, has rentals for $7 an hour ($25 a day) and sponsors free group rides during the week. If you'd rather blaze your own trail, any ranger station can provide information on legal mountain biking trails in the Stanislaus National Forest.

FISHING Pick up a copy of the pamphlet "Fishing Tips" from any ranger station. It lists 23 fishing areas inside the Stanislaus Forest, and provides up-to-date regulations about size limits. All anglers must have a California fishing license ($7), available at ranger stations and sporting-goods stores.

The Eastern Sierras and Inyo National Forest

Whether you approach from Yosemite or Los Angeles, you're bound to be startled by the dramatic and austere beauty of the Eastern Sierra Mountains. The **Inyo National Forest,** which engulfs the Sierras from Mono Lake in the north to Bakersfield in the south, is perhaps one of California's most diverse and unique national monuments—a striking combination of desert and cool aspen groves. Driving through the region, you could conceivably cover several vegetation zones in under an hour, from the piñon trees and sage of the lower elevations, through mixed coniferous forests at mid-mountain, and finally to the lakes and meadows that abound above timberline. The Eastern Sierras are also popular because they're pitted with volcanic craters and explorable caves, especially around **Mono Lake**—one of the strangest-looking bodies of water in the world.

Most visitors are drawn not by the scenery, however, but by the resort towns that lie along **Route 395,** the main north–south route through the Eastern Sierras. During the summer, hikers flock to **Mammoth Lakes** for excellent backpacking and fishing, while in winter skiers congregate at **Mammoth Mountain,** an amazingly popular and trendy resort that boasts some of California's best ski runs. **Bishop,** on the other hand, one hour away from Mammoth, is straight out of a Merle Haggard song—a boondock hick town where cowboy hats, country music, and pick-up trucks are the norm. You're life isn't in any danger, but don't expect much from the Bishop locals. Despite their dependence on tourist dollars, they're not particularly fond of city slickers. The only other towns of note are **Lee Vining,** a three-block-long metropolis consisting of a few motels and greasy diners, and the small town of **Lone Pine,** 61 miles from Bishop. Except for a few gas stations and truck-stops, there's not much to detain you in Lone Pine. This city exists solely for occasional tourists passing through on their way to **Mt. Whitney**—the highest peak in the lower 48 states, 12 miles to the east.

The hiking-camping season generally begins around May 1, when Route 120 and the **Tioga Pass** open. The best time to visit, however, is during the fall when the forests turn amber and the people are scarce. Unless you're an avid "alpinist," stay away from the Sierras during ski season. Not only are accommodations hard to come by and the roads treacherous, but prices generally rise 15% to 50%.

● ● ● BASICS

TOURIST INFORMATION **Inyo National Forest, Main Station.** *873 N. Main St., Bishop 93514, tel. 619/873-5841. Open weekdays 8–4:30.*

Lone Pine Chamber of Commerce. *126 S. Main St., tel. 619/876-4444. Open weekdays 9–5.*

Mammoth Lakes Ranger Station. *Rte. 203, Box 148, Mammoth Lakes 93546, tel. 619/934–2505. 2 mi west of Rte. 395 on Rte. 203.*

Mono Lake Ranger Station. *Rte. 120, 1 mi east of Lee Vining, tel. 619/647–6525.*

Mt. Whitney Ranger Station. *Box 8, Lone Pine 93545, tel. 619/876–5542.*

White Mt. Ranger Station. *798 N. Main St., Bishop 93514, tel. 619/873–4207.*

Among the dignitaries who have attended the Mule Days Festival is Ronald Reagan—actor, denture wearer, and former president.

FESTIVALS Summer is one big festival in Mammoth. In particular, check out the annual **Jazz Jubilee,** held over the Fourth of July weekend. Local bars and ski lodges are transformed into drunken jazz halls, graced by some of the biggest names in contemporary jazz, ragtime blues, and Dixieland. Schedules and venues change from year to year, so call 619/934–2478 for this year's offerings. On a more formal note, the annual **Sierra Summer Festival** is a three-week-long celebration of the arts, where craftspeople and artists from around the state gather to exhibit and sell their latest works. It's held sometime in June or July (depending on when the local chambers of commerce can agree on a date), and each city offers its own calendar of events. Call 619/934–2172 or 800/367–6572 for current listings.

In Bishop, look for the **Mule Days** celebration on Memorial Day weekend, at the end of May. This three-day extravaganza features mule rodeos, mule chariot racing, and—believe it or not—a mule parade. Yee-haw. If that's not enough, take a gander at Bishop's **Wild West** weekend, held on Labor Day, which features rodeos, a chili cook-off, the crowning of the Bishop Rodeo Queen, and cowboy poetry readings. Once again, yee-haw. For a complete listing of activities, call 619/934–2505.

GENERAL STORES **Lee Vining** has a small market and sporting-good store on Main Street, but for more serious provisions you should head to **Mammoth Lakes.** On Old Mammoth Road you'll find a shopping center and a 24-hour **Von's** supermarket. **Kittredge Sports** (tel. 619/934–7566), in the center of Mammoth Lakes on Route 203, rents a staggering selection of outdoor equipment, from tents ($10 first day, $2 each additional day) to mountain bikes ($7 per hour, $25 per day) and fishing gear. They also sell ski clothing and fishing permits.

In **Bishop,** there are two 24-hour Von's supermarkets, one on the north side of town on Route 395 (a.k.a. S. Main Street), the other on Route 395 at Eastline Street. **Wilson's Eastside Sports** (206 N. Main St., tel. 619/873–7520) sells all types of sporting goods and is a good place to find out about the region's best fishing holes, hikes, and camping sites.

In **Lone Pine,** groceries are available at **Joseph's Bi-Rite Market** (119 S. Main St., tel. 619/876–4378). **Slater's Sporting Goods** (130 S. Main St., tel. 619/876–5020) sells equipment and fishing licenses.

● ● ● COMING AND GOING

BY CAR **Route 395** runs north–south through the Inyo National Forest from Lone Pine to Lee Vining and beyond, providing year-round access from both L.A. and Reno. **Route 120** and Tioga Pass are generally closed to winter traffic, but once the roads clear they provide easy access to Lee Vining and northern Inyo from the San Francisco Bay Area. The most scenic route, however, is a little-known country road the drops into Inyo from Sherman Pass and the Sequoia National Forest. It's labeled **Sherman Pass** from the west, **Nine Mile Canyon Road** or **Route J41** from the east.

BY BUS **Greyhound** has two semi-staffed depots in the region at Mammoth (tel. 619/934–7548) and Bishop (tel. 619/872–2721). Buses run once daily between L.A. and Reno, making stops on Route 395 at Lone Pine, Bishop, Mammoth, and Lee Vining. From July 1 to Labor Day, Greyhound also has daily buses ($12) between Lee Vining and **Yosemite.** Lee Vining doesn't have an official station, but there's a Greyhound stop on its small Main Street. Call Greyhound's Reno office (tel. 209/372–1241) for current schedules.

GETTING AROUND

Between June 15 and September 15, Mammoth Lakes offer a **shuttle bus** (tel. 619/934–2505) between the Mammoth Mt. ski area and Red's Meadow, which stops at all the campgrounds and trailheads along the way. It runs daily from 7:30 AM to 5:30 PM every 15 minutes, but it unfortunately costs $6. Look for the Shuttle Bus signs in either the Mammoth Mt. parking lot or along the highway.

During winter, the free **Mammoth Area Shuttle** (tel. 619/934–0687) runs every 20 minutes between Mammoth Village and the mountain; the free **Tamarack Shuttle** (tel. 619/934–2442) runs between the Mammoth Village and Tamarack Lodge. From Bishop, **High Sierra Limousine** (tel. 619/873–4453) provides minivan transportation to trailheads all over Inyo, including Lake Sabrina ($35 for four people) and (try not to choke at the price) Yosemite ($120 for four).

WHERE TO SLEEP

For cheap accommodations, head straight for Inyo's campgrounds or its two youth hostels, on the outskirts of Mammoth Lakes. Wilderness permits ($3) are not required for day trips, but they are required for overnight and trail camping. Fortunately, your $3 permit entitles you to sleep wherever you like—literally. Except where posted, the Inyo National Forest allows campers to pitch a tent anywhere in the forest, just so long as it's 100 feet from the nearest road. To build a fire or use a camping stove, $5 fire permits are also available. Pick these up, along with a handful of trail maps and tourist brochures, from any ranger station. Otherwise, prepare for a pricey room in a drab hotel. Most are concentrated in the northern half of Inyo National Forest, around Lee Vining, Mammoth, and Bishop.

HOTELS AND MOTELS In the small town of Lee Vining, look for the **Blue Skies Motel** (Rte. 395, tel. 619/647–6440), a backpacker-friendly establishment that offers standard rooms (with coffee pots, TV, private bath) for $35. Please note, however: Blue Skies is open only between April and October, when the snow on Tioga Pass has melted. Otherwise, the **King's Inn** (tel. 619/647–6300), also on Route 395 in the center of Lee Vining, is open year-round. Some units have kitchen facilities, but all are clean and comfortable. Doubles fetch $32.

In Mammoth Lakes, the **VLLR Lodge** (5920 Minaret Rd., Box 53, Mammoth Lakes 93546, tel. 619/934–2454) rents several types of accommodations; private rooms with private baths ($35), private rooms with communal baths ($30), and a dorm room that sleeps eight ($15). It also has a communal kitchen and common area with a fireplace and a sauna—very popular with skiers.

In Bishop, the **El Rancho Motel** (274 Lagoon St., tel. 619/872–9251), one block from Bishop's make-shift Greyhound station, has spacious rooms for $38, some with kitchens and refrigerators ($45). The management is friendly and knowledgeable about the area—a real bonus in a town where striking up a conversation with a local can be like pulling teeth. The **Village Motel** (286 W. Elm St., tel. 619/873–3545) may have a few rooms available, but they're often rented to long-term customers (i.e., the sort of people who look like extras from *The Twilight Zone* or *Barton Fink*). It's still worth a shot for the cheapest room in town, however: $30 in winter, $35 in summer.

HOSTELS When you feel the need to hang out for a few days somewhere communal and friendly, there are two hostels south of Mammoth on Route 395 within 3 miles of each other. **Long Valley Hostel** (tel. 619/935–4377) is a small, summer-only hostel 7 miles south of Mammoth (take the Lake Crowley Dr. exit off Rte. 395). It has only 10 beds ($10 each), but the owners of this mom-and-pop place are extremely friendly and will go out of their way to help orient you in the Mammoth area. There's also a communal kitchen and bath here. Three miles farther south on Lake Crowley Drive is **Hilton Creek Hostel** (Rte. 1, Box 1128, Crowley Lake 93546, tel. 619/935–4989), a converted cowboy bunkhouse set right up against the mountains with spectacular views. This hostel is oriented toward hikers and mountain bikers, and the management seems to know every hidden trail and secret hot spring in the area. There are 22 beds ($8–$11), a communal kitchen, and a TV room loaded with maps and literature on the Eastern Sierras. It's open year-round.

CAMPGROUNDS Camping outside developed campgrounds (called "dispersed" camping) is permitted in much of Mono Lake, the June Lake Loop, the Lee Vining Canyon, north of Route 203, and east and west of Route 395. Dispersed camping is not allowed, however, in Big Pine Creek Canyon, Rock Creek Canyon, Bishop Creek Canyon, or in the area around the Bristlecone Pine Forest. For a detailed map of dispersed camping areas, and for wilderness and fire permits, stop by any ranger station (*see* Basics, *above*). Otherwise, head to one of Inyo's developed campgrounds.

Sabrina Campground. This is one of the most scenic and unblemished campgrounds in the forest, located in Bishop Creek Canyon only a stone's throw away from Lake Sabrina and hiking trails that lead into the John Muir Wilderness. All 18 of its free sites are shaded by aspens and nestled on the banks of a tranquil stream. *From Bishop, follow Rte. 168 south for 17 mi; you can see the campground from the road. Tables, fire pits, vault toilets, but no drinking water. Open July 15–Sept. 7.*

Coldwater Campground and Trailhead. In the Mammoth Lakes Basin by Coldwater Creek, this place provides access to Lake Mary, the Pacific Crest Trail, the John Muir Wilderness, and several other lakes. The sites are nothing to scream about, but at least there are 79 of them (for $8 a night). *Head west on Rte. 203, go 4 mi down Lake Mary Rd. to entrance. Picnic tables, stoves, pit toilets, drinking water. Open June 12–Sept. 29.*

Lundy Lake Campground. This campground is nestled in the trees near Lundy Lake, at the edge of the Hoover Wilderness. It provides a good spot from which to fish, day hike, or start on a backpacking trip. There are 100 sites ($7 a night). Bring your own food and water as there's none to be found here. *Head north from Lee Vining on Rte. 395 to the LUNDY CANYON sign; go west 7 mi; tel. 619/647–6525. Pit toilets, picnic tables. Open May–Oct.*

Mosquito Flat. Don't let the name scare you: At 10,000 feet, there's hardly a mosquito to be found. In Rock Creek Canyon, this small, stream-side campground is surrounded by granite formations and lodgepole pines—perfect for a day hike. Nearby is the Mosquito Flat trailhead, another great place to spend the afternoon exploring. Because of its elevation, you need to check weather conditions in advance. Snow and tempestuous winds are common, even in August. You'll find 25 sites at $8 a night. *Take the Tom's Place exit off Rte. 395 (15 mi south of Mammoth exit), turn south on Rock Creek Rd. and go for 7 mi. Fire pits, picnic tables, pit toilets, drinking water. Open July 15–Sept. 7.*

Reds Meadow Campground. The sites are standard and not particularly scenic, but they're located near the Devil's Postpile National Monument, Rainbow Falls, the Ansel Adams Wilderness, and a horse stable that offers rentals. There are 56 sites for $7 a night. *Near Mammoth Lakes, at the very end of Minaret Rd. off Rte. 203; tel. 619/934–2505. Open June 15–Sept. 15. Picnic tables, stoves, pit toilets, drinking water.*

If you're looking for groceries, stop at Mammoth's **Vons** (481 Old Mammoth Rd., tel. 619/934–4536), probably the cheapest grocery store for miles. Look for it in the Minaret Village Shopping Center, at the intersection of Meridian and Old Mammoth roads; open daily 7 AM to midnight. In Bishop, try **Schat's Bakkery** (763 N. Main St., tel. 619/873–7156), a huge Dutch bakery that has homemade sheepherder's bread, pastries, and sandwiches. Stock up before heading into the hills. Also check out **Holmes Health Haven** (192 West Line St., one block west of Main St.), Bishop's only health-food store. It's pricey, but it's the only place within a 100-mile radius that sells organic lettuce and pesticide-free fruit.

UNDER $5 **Matsu.** Matsu is great for huge portions of Chinese and Japanese food, including a large choice of vegetarian dishes. Most of their entrées are a little bland, but they'll satisfy your psychological need for something sort of healthy. *3711 Main St. at Joaquin Rd., Mammoth, tel. 619/934–8277. Open daily 11:30–9.*

Unless you're fond of truck-stop diners and mediocre coffee shops, do most of your eating in Bishop or Mammoth.

Bishop Grill. This diner is strictly meat and potatoes—the sort of place where the waitress calls you "hon" while refilling your coffee mug for the 10th time. Even if you're sick of greasy spoons, try their homemade cherry pie. "Damn fine," as Dale Cooper might say. Even better, it's dirt cheap: Burger and fries go for $2.75, turkey sandwiches are $2.50, and pie $1.25. *281 N. Main St., Bishop, tel. 619/873–3911. Open daily 6 AM–8 PM.*

The Pyrenees. This small lunch counter has delicious homemade soups, sandwiches, and salads at rock-bottom prices. Soup of the day with bread costs $2.80, a roast beef or turkey sandwich with soup is $5. Open for lunch only. *150 N. Main St., Bishop, tel. 619/873–7275. Open Mon.–Sat. 10 AM–3 PM.*

UNDER $10 **El Charro Avita.** Authentic Mexican food in an atmosphere notable for lots of black iron grillwork and plastic flowers. Lunch specials start at $5, flautas $6, homemade tamales $3. Their specialty, however, is breakfast—huge portions of Mexican sausage and eggs for $5. *970 N. Main St., Bishop, tel. 619/872–5516.*

Lee's Kitchen. This small, family-owned restaurant serves excellent Chinese food. Try their chicken salad ($4), sweet-and-sour chicken or pork ($4), or tempura shrimp ($7). *285 N. Main St., Bishop, tel. 619/872–2189. Open Mon.–Sat. 11 AM–2 PM and 4–8 PM.*

Nik and Willie's Pizza. They don't cook 'em, but they sure know how to make 'em. Their ovens can accommodate only two pizzas at a time, so most people call in their order and cook it at home. Nik and Willie can bake your pizza if you don't have an oven, but bring a good book for the wait. If you're having trouble deciding what you want, try their "Atomic" pizza—olive oil, mushrooms, tomatoes, mandarin oranges, and basil (small $6.50, large $11.95). *In Ivy Sq. on the corner of Tavern and Old Mammoth Rds., Mammoth, tel. 619/934–2012. Open daily noon–9.*

Roberto's Cafe. Top-rate Mexican food for hungry backpackers and skiers, including homemade specialties like *chorizo con huevos* (Mexican sausage and eggs; $6), chicken fajitas ($7.50), burritos ($3), and enchiladas ($2.50). *271 Old Mammoth Rd., Mammoth, tel. 619/934–3667. Open daily 9–8.*

UNDER $15 **Anything Goes.** The name of the restaurants reflects the impossible task of trying to describe the food, a unique combination of Italian, Thai, Mexican, French, and more ("everything but Icelandic and African," the owner says). Lunch specials and the dinner menu change regularly, but look for things like Singapore shrimp ($14, dinner) or pesto with tomatoes ($5, lunch). Vegetarian dishes are also featured. *In Sherwin Plaza on Old Mammoth Rd., Mammoth, tel. 619/934–2424. Open daily 8 AM–9 PM.*

● ● ● EXPLORING INYO

The best way to capture the absolute vastness of Inyo National Forest is by car, along Routes 395, 120, and 168. Remember, though, that this forest (and, in particular, the Mammoth Lakes region) fits the definition of nirvana for most hikers, so get out, breathe, and explore the area as much as possible on foot. With the radio blasting and the windows rolled up, it's hard to appreciate how stunning this place really is.

MONO LAKE At the end of the 6.5-mile, 2,700-foot drop from Tioga Pass on Route 120 sits one of the eeriest-looking bodies of water in the state. Even if you're short on time, Mono Lake is small enough to cover in two hours. Start at **South Tufa Grove,** 5 miles south of Lee Vining on Route 395. It has chemical toilets, picnic tables and—best of all—a self-guided nature trail. You can wander among the spiny and fantastically colored tufa columns, formed when calcium in Mono's freshwater springs encounters carbon in its salty and alkaline lake water. Normally, they would remain underwater and out of sight, but since 1940 the level of Mono Lake has dropped 40 feet—good news for hikers who enjoy the bizarre look of the lake, but bad news for local wildlife. Once an isolated sanctuary, Mono's **Negit Island** is now an accessible peninsula, allowing predators to cross the dry lake bed and wreck havoc on its avian nesting grounds. Some effort has been made to replenish the waters (look for "Save Mono Lake" stickers on cars throughout the state), but it's been too little, too late. Environmentalists argue that Mono was irreparably damaged by Angelenos who have depleted upwards of 80% of the water for drinking purposes. They also claim it will be centuries before Mono can once again sustain a hearty population of animal life.

"This forest fits the definition of nirvana for most hikers."

In the meantime, pay a visit to the **Mono Basin National Forest Scenic Area Visitor Center** (north end of Lee Vining, tel. 619/647–6572). It has exhibits about the ecology, geology, and volcanic formations surrounding the lake, as well as lectures, slide shows, an art gallery, and a small gift shop. The **Mono Lake Foundation** (tel. 619/647–6595) offers hour-long canoe trips of the lake ($10) on weekends from June 14 through September 29. For the most buoyant, salty swimming anywhere, check out **Navy Beach,** a half mile east of South Tufa Grove. Otherwise, ramble through the half-mile-wide **Panum Crater,** a dormant volcano on the south shore of Mono Lake.

South of Mono Lake, look for **Lundy Canyon, Glass Creek Meadow,** and the **Obsidian Dome**—all of which are popular hiking spots. The **Hoover Wilderness,** accessible from Lundy Canyon, has perhaps the nicest trails in the area, winding along alpine lakes, deep canyons, and jagged mountain ridges. **Crestview,** a small rest area on the south shore of the lake, has easy access to hikeable volcanic craters.

BODIE Dry, desolate, and unforgiving, ghost-town country lies just outside the Inyo National Forest, north of Mono lake on Route 395. Some of California's oldest mining outposts and gold-rush-era settlements can be found here. As you begin to ascend Bodie Pass and you round the first switchback (where the road takes a 180° turn), look to the right for a small dirt road. Follow it for half a mile, park your car, and walk to the deserted **Rattlesnake Gulch,** a mining town that went bust in the 1890s. This is a do-it-yourself exploration—no brochures, no tours, just a chunk of history, some startling rock formations and decrepit buildings, and a great view of Mono Lake.

A few miles farther north on Route 395 you'll stumble across **Route 270.** Follow it east for 13 miles to reach the **Bodie Ghost Town and State Park** (tel. 619/647–6445). It costs $5 to enter, but it's one of the better-preserved ghost towns in the state, complete with a small Chinatown and abandoned mine shaft. There's also an excellent gold-mining history museum (open May–Sept., daily 10–5). For $1, pick up a copy of the museum's detailed driving guide to Bodie State Park.

MAMMOTH LAKES The **Mammoth Lakes Basin** is a series of glacially formed lakes with fishing, boating, and trail access to the **John Muir Wilderness.** Hundreds of trails here wind amid the lakes, trees, and granite formations, but you may want to head farther south on Route 395 for the **Ansel Adams Wilderness,** which has the ancient and jagged **Minarets**—the oldest mountains in the Sierra Nevadas. **Devil's Postpile National Monument,** another unique geological feature, lies at the eastern border of the Ansel Adams Wilderness. It provides access to the Pacific Crest Trail, **Rainbow Falls** (a 101-foot waterfall), and **Red's Meadow.**

WHITE MOUNTAIN RANGER DISTRICT It's hard to miss the looming and somewhat barren White Mountains, south of Mammoth Lakes on Route 395. Because no water runs through the range, you have to bring your own—which means they're sparsely populated and accessible only to the heartiest of hikers. The landscape doesn't explode with life, with the exception of the **Ancient Bristlecone Pine Forest.** Inside, look for the 4,800-year-old "Methuselah," the oldest-known living tree in the world. **Rock Creek Canyon,** west of Route 395 on Rock Creek Canyon Road, provides access to another series of glacial lakes and canyons. Even if you're not an avid hiker, make the mile trek to the canyon's rim: The ensuing view of Mono Basin is spectacular.

Bishop Creek Canyon, west on Route 168 from Bishop, provides trail access to the numerous lakes that riddle a nearby portion of the John Muir Wilderness. Fishing here is plentiful, as are wildflowers and small meadows. The main feature of **Big Pine Canyon,** 10 miles west of Big Pine on Crocker Street, is the **Palisade Glacier**—the largest and southern-most glacier in the Sierras. Trails from the road lead to **Third Lake,** whose waters appear turquoise because of the mineral-rich, glacial runoff.

MT. WHITNEY The big attraction in the Inyo Forest is **Mt. Whitney,** the highest peak in the continental United States at 14,495 feet. Every year hundreds of hikers make the strenuous 10.7-mile trek to the summit, but reservations and wilderness permits are required between May 20 and October 15. Written applications (name, number in group, dates of arrival and departure) and a $3 fee must be postmarked between March 1 and May 31; send them to the Mt. Whitney Ranger Station (*see* Basics, *above*).

If a 10-mile hike up Mt. Whitney sounds like a nightmare, check out **Taboose Creek** and the **Owens Lake Bed,** two popular day-hiking areas. **Horseshoe Meadows,** 20 miles southwest of Lone Pine—take Whitney Postal Road 3 miles to Horseshoe Meadows Road, go south to the end—provides access to the lush meadows and conifer forests of the **Golden Trout Wilderness,** which extends south into Sequoia National Forest.

FOREST ACTIVITIES • • •

BIKING Mountain-biking is big here—very big. As a result, the Mammoth Mt. ski lodge converts its downhill slopes into a **bike park** (tel. 619/934–0606) during the summer. Lift tickets cost $15, but this gives you access to all ski lifts and miles of rugged mountain-bike trails. Popular routes include the easy "Paper Route" to the intermediate "Beach Cruiser" and the treacherous "Kamikaze." The park is open daily from 9:30 to 6, from Memorial Day to October 1.

If you prefer to strike out on your own, most trails outside the wilderness areas (including logging and forest service roads) are open to mountain bikers. Check with a ranger station for restrictions and recommendations. If you need to rent, contact **Mammoth Adventure Connection** (tel. 619/934–0606 or 800/228–4947) for mountain bikes at $30 a day.

SKIING **Mammoth Mountain** (tel. 619/934–2571) and **June Mountain** (tel. 619/648–7733) are two of the most popular and crowded ski resorts in the state, particularly if there's a good snow pack. Unfortunately, the resorts are not cheap. Plan to spend $35 for a lift ticket, and at least that much on lodging in the area. If you can, rent your skis in town rather than on the mountain and don't eat at the ski area, as prices are outrageous. Cross-country skiers should contact the Mammoth Ranger Station (*see* Basics, *above*); they groom miles of various trails in the backcountry and have detailed maps of popular cross-country routes.

SWIMMING What do you get when you cross volcanic magma with water? **Hot springs!** Dozens exist in the flatlands, many of which are kept secret by the locals. One well-known spot is **Hot Creek Geologic Site,** north of the Mammoth Lakes airport on Route 395. Take the paved road to the Hot Creek fish hatchery, go south on the road behind the airport, then turn left on the dirt road leading to Hot Creek. For smaller, lesser known sites, George Williams' book, *Hot Springs of the Eastern Sierras,* is a must; it's available at most ranger stations and sporting-good stores in the region. If hot springs aren't your thing, there's regular old-fashioned swimming at **June Lake** and **Horseshoe Lake,** both near Mammoth Mountain.

Sierra National Forest

The proximity of Sierra National Forest to the city of Fresno seems a miracle of sorts. After one hour of driving, the landscape is transformed from a vast expanse of car dealerships and tract housing into lakes and coniferous forests, a blessing to valley residents and visitors alike. Unfortunately, this stroke of geological good fortune has resulted in heavy use and extensive development around the bigger lakes and reservoirs—specifically **Bass Lake, Mammoth Pool, Lake Shaver,** and **Lake Huntington.** Even so, the Sierra National Forest is still a great place for a day trip or weekend getaway, nestled between Yosemite and the Sequoia/Kings Canyon national parks, only 1½ hours east of Fresno. These latter parks are definitely more inspiring than the Sierra Forest, but if you're traveling on Route 41 you have no choice but to traverse its western edge. Admission to the Sierra Forest is free, so why not take a peek?

The areas at lower elevations, including Pine Flat Reservoir, the Upper Kings River, and Kerckhoff and Redinger Lakes, have camping and hiking opportunities year-round. Temperatures climb into the 90s during the summer, so try to hit the Sierra National Forest in spring or fall, when both crowds and the blistering sun are less of a problem. The higher elevations (above 5,000 feet) are generally closed between November and March because of snow, but by mid-May the camping season is in full swing. The best time to visit the high country is between July and early September when the snow has melted and the wildflowers are in bloom.

● ● ● BASICS

TOURIST INFORMATION All ranger stations issue **wilderness permits,** free of charge, required for all overnight excursions. Also check at ranger stations for current fire restrictions and to obtain campfire permits (also required for dispersed camping). The main office for the **Sierra National Forest** is in Clovis, west of Fresno. If you can, stop here before breaching the forest's borders as they have information on the entire area (forest maps, campground listings, etc.), while the other offices provide information only for their specific districts. Send them a self-addressed, stamped envelope, and they'll return it full of information. *1600 Tollhouse Rd. (on Rte. 168), Clovis 93612, tel. 209/487–5155. Open weekdays 8–4:30.*

Bass Lake Chamber of Commerce. *Box 126, Bass Lake 93604, tel. 209/642–3676.*

Kings River Ranger Station. *34849 Maxon Rd., Snager 93657, tel. 209/855–8321. At the north end of Pine Flat Reservoir near Trimma Marina. Open weekdays 8–4:30.*

Minaret Ranger Station. *North Fork 93643, tel. 209/877–2218. Open weekdays 8–4:30.*

Oakhurst/Mariposa Ranger Station. *41969 Rte. 41, Oakhurst 93644, tel. 209/683–4665. 15 mi from Yosemite's south entrance on Rte. 41. Open weekdays 8–4:30.*

Pineridge Ranger Station. *Box 300, Shaver Lake 93664, tel. 209/841–3311. At the junction of Rte. 168 and Bretz Mill Rd. Open daily 8–4:30.*

Shaver Lake Chamber of Commerce. *Box 58, Shaver Lake 93664, tel. 209/841–3350.*

GENERAL STORES **Shaver Lake** and **Bass Lake,** two overdeveloped resort areas, have a high concentration of sporting-goods shops and grocery stores, as well as restaurants, gas stations, and lodging. In the backcountry, you can find small stores in **Dinkey Creek** and **Mono Hot Springs.** Save money and lower your stress level by shopping in Fresno or other valley towns (Oakhurst, Clovis) before coming to the mountains. Prices generally double once inside the Sierra National Forest.

COMING AND GOING

There is no public transportation into the forest, so forget about it if you don't have a car. Otherwise, **Route 168** is the forest's main artery connecting Fresno and Clovis with Shaver Lake, Big Creek, and the Sierra Forest's central section. From Yosemite and the north, take **Route 41** south and follow the signs to Bass Lake or Mammoth Pool. **Route 180,** which runs east–west between Fresno and Kings Canyon National Park, also traverses the forest's southern edge, including Paine Flat Lake and the Upper Kings River. Be warned, though, that if you're traveling along Route 395 in the Eastern Sierras, there's no through road into the area; the Sierra National Forest is accessible only from the west.

WHERE TO SLEEP

Dispersed camping is your best option here; not only will you save heaps of money, but you'll also escape the tedious party atmosphere that infests most towns along the highway. This national forest is popular with weekend-warrior types, so even in the developed campgrounds it's hard to get a good night's sleep because of the noise. Wilderness permits (required for dispersed camping) are available free of charge from any ranger station, but it's a good idea to call a week or two in advance to reserve one.

If all else fails, there are a few hotels in Shaver Lake and Bass Lake in the $25–$40 range. Unfortunately, they're mostly owned and operated by realty companies, which means you must call the Shaver or Bass Lake chambers of commerce (*see* Basics, *above*) to make a reservation. **Camp Fresno** (main office: 4522 E. Cortland, Fresno 93726, tel. 209/226–5449), 13 miles east of Shaver Lake in Dinkey Creek, is one of the only privately owned resorts in the park. They rent rustic cabins with electricity and running water for an amazingly reasonable price: One-bedroom cabins that sleep six go for $19 a night, $115 a week; two-bedroom cabins that sleep eight fetch $33 a night, $210 a week. They're not particularly clean or comfortable, but no one seems to mind at these prices. Reservations must be made at least a week in advance, and non-Fresno residents can reserve a space only after May 1.

CAMPGROUNDS The Sierra National Forest offers a variety of camping experiences, from dispersed wilderness camping to crowded and loud developed campgrounds. The most popular (and annoying) areas for the latter are on the banks of Shaver and Bass lakes, but they require advance reservations year-round (mostly because they're always jam-packed). Call MISTIX (tel. 800/283–CAMP) for reservations and information. If you have no specific reason to be next to the water, head for one of the smaller and less crowded campgrounds in the high country. It's well worth the extra 15-minute drive to escape the din of RV-camper generators and speed boats.

KINGS RIVER RANGER DISTRICT The southern portion of this district lies at a low elevation and gets frightfully hot in the summer (specifically at Pine Flat Lake Reservoir and along the Kings River); dispersed camping here would be best in the spring or fall. To the northeast, the elevation increases and the temperatures drop as you make your way toward the Dinkey Lakes Wilderness. Camping is especially good near the two high-country reservoirs: Wishon and Courtright. The **Lily Pad Campground,** on Wishon Reservoir, has 15 sites ($8 a night) with piped water, picnic tables, and fireplaces. It's beautifully situated on the water and is surrounded by trees (open June through September). Call the Kings River Ranger Station (*see* Basics, *above*) for reservations.

PINERIDGE RANGER DISTRICT Secluded campgrounds and dispersed camping opportunities abound in the Pineridge area. The Kaiser Pass Road, which starts at the east end of Huntington Lake, leads high into remote, but car-accessible, country that's dotted with campgrounds. For true seclusion try the campgrounds on **Florence Lake,** 17 miles northeast of Lake Huntington, reserved via Pineridge Ranger Station (*see* Basics, *above*). It gets more crowded as you head farther east toward Mono Hot Springs and Thomas Edison Lake, but even so, the **Jackass Meadow Campground** is a beautiful spot surrounded by unblemished wilderness. Its 15 sites have tables, stoves, toilets, and piped water; they're $6 per night. Otherwise, all four sites at **Bastillo,** 15 miles northeast of Huntington Lake on Kaiser Pass Road, are available on a first-come, first-served basis—free of charge. They're generally occupied, but during the fall and spring you may find an open space.

MINARETS RANGER DISTRICT Unless you want to stay in the crowded Mammoth Pool area, head straight for **Clover Meadow** and **Granite Creek**—two wonderfully secluded and relatively quiet campgrounds on the edge of the Ansel Adams Wilderness. They offer a total of 17 sites with tables, stoves, and toilets. Plan to stay a few days; the drive is too long to make comfortably for one night's lodging. From the town of North Fork, drive southeast on Mammoth Pool Road, turn north on Minarets Road, and continue for another 20 miles. Total driving time from North Fork is a little more than an hour. Both are open June through October, and both are available on a first-come, first-served basis. Admission is $3 to Clover Meadow; it's free at Granite Creek.

MARIPOSA RANGER DISTRICT This area is ideal as a base camp for excursions—by foot or car—into Yosemite. Dispersed camping is allowed everywhere except around Bass Lake, the main resort in the area, making Mariposa a good backup in case Yosemite is booked solid. A series of primitive campgrounds line **Sky Ranch Road,** which leads east from Route 41, about 5 miles north of the town of Oakhurst. In particular, try Big Sandy, Greys Mountain, Soquel, Little Sandy, Fresno Dome, and Kelty Meadow. All lie from 8 to 15 miles east of Oakhurst on Sky Ranch Road, and all provide tables, toilets, and stoves (but no water). Even better, they're all free.

● ● ● FOOD

Shaver Lake has the **Sierra House Restaurant** (Rte. 168, tel. 209/841–3576), which serves excellent pizzas ($8–$10), hickory smoked/grilled chicken ($9), pasta dishes ($7–$8), and monster-size burgers ($5). In Bass Lake's Pine Village, look for **Ducey's On The Lake** (tel. 209/642–3131), which specializes in seafood and prime rib. An average meal runs $8–$12, but the portions are huge and the ambience comfortable. Otherwise, head for any one of the diners or truck-stops along the major highways. They're all pretty much the same, offering slight variations on the burger, fries, and black coffee theme.

● ● ● EXPLORING SIERRA NATIONAL FOREST

The **Kings River Ranger District** encompasses the southern portion of the forest, extending as far north as Shaver Lake in the west and bisecting the Dinkey Lakes Wilderness in the east. The terrain varies widely. Chaparral and woodland vegetation surround **Pine Flat Reservoir** and the **Kings River,** two popular water recreation spots that form the southern border of the forest. Farther north the elevation increases, and the vegetation changes to ponderosa, black oak, and sugar pine, making for shadier and cooler summer camping. Courtright and Wishon reservoirs lie in the eastern portion of this district; many trails that head east into the high, alpine terrain of the John Muir Wilderness begin here.

The **Pineridge Ranger District** cuts a wide swath through the middle of the forest, extending from Shaver Lake to Redinger Lake in the west and extending northeast to the John Muir Wilderness. **Shaver Lake** and **Huntington Lake,** two developed resort areas within 20 miles of each other on Route 168, offer excellent opportunities for water sports, but they tend to be packed with the worst sort of weekenders. The scenery gets dramatically better, as do the hiking opportunities, as you head northeast on **Kaiser Pass Road** into the high country, a region dominated by daunting granite formations, windswept pastures, small lakes, and incredible views. Trailheads at Florence and Edison lakes lead into the John Muir Wilderness, perfect for an extended day hike.

The **Minarets Ranger District,** which includes the northeast portion of the forest from the Ansel Adams Wilderness to the edge of Redinger Lake, also varies greatly in terms of landscape and elevation. The low-altitude **Redinger Lake** (1,400 feet) is a popular spot for year-round recreation, but temperatures hover in the 90s during the summer. Mammoth Pool, another popular spot for connoisseurs of water sports, is better suited to summer exploration. Its 4,000-foot elevation keeps it cool year-round, and it's well shaded by acres of thick, towering pine trees. Trailheads from **Clover Meadow** in the northeast lead into the Ansel Adams Wilderness, an extraordinary, untouched, wild region that's popular with hard-core campers and misanthropes.

ORIENTATION PROGRAMS The Pineridge ranger station (*see* Basics, *above*) offers campfire programs and nature walks out of the Huntington Lake Recreation Area during the summer. The programs are generally free, but call ahead to reserve a space on weekends, when they sometimes fill up.

HIKING

NATURE WALKS The **Shadow of the Giants Trail** in Nelder Grove is a mile-long, self-guided hike lined with signs describing the ecology of the giant sequoia trees. It's an easy and enjoyable way to learn about the forest, and it shouldn't take more than an hour to complete. The **Mono Wind Nature Trail,** near the town of North Fork, is devoted to the culture, history, and gruesome extermination of the Mono tribe that once inhabited the area. Along the way you'll find examples of plants used by the Monos for food and medicinal purposes, and replicas of the structures in which they lived. The trail is privately owned, however, and the manager asks that visitors call the trail office in advance before coming (tel. 209/877–2710).

LONGER HIKES All ranger stations offer detailed maps and pamphlets of hiking trails in their area, but serious hikers should grab their tents and head to the **Pineridge Ranger Station.** Its pamphlet details more than 20 day hikes (between 2 and 16 miles round-trip) from Huntington Lake all the way east to Florence and Edison lakes. From here, you can continue your journey into the John Muir Wilderness, since a number of trailheads start at Edison Lake. Dispersed camping is allowed and highly recommended; pick up a wilderness permit at the ranger station.

SCENIC DRIVES AND VIEWS The **Sierra Vista Scenic Byway** is an inspiring loop that starts in North Fork, heads way up into the high country as far east as Clover Meadow, and then returns to North Fork via Bass Lake. The whole loop takes about five hours to drive, and the road is narrow and windy. If this seems too long, there are numerous places to camp along the way, as well as well-marked shortcuts that lead back to North Fork and the main highways. Otherwise, inquire at any ranger station for the most scenic drives in their area; depending on whom you speak with, you're likely to get a different—but equally worthwhile—suggestion each time.

FOREST ACTIVITIES • • •

ALL-TERRAIN VEHICLES (ATVS) This is very popular in the Sierra; there are probably as many off-road-vehicle trails as hiking trails, and they cover all types of terrain. The ranger stations distribute pamphlets with details and regulations for specific areas.

BIKING Biking is allowed on all ATV trails, but contact specific ranger stations for mountain-bike restrictions on hiking trails. Unless you carry them on your back and don't ride them (yeah, right), all bikes are prohibited in wilderness and dispersed camping areas.

BOATING AND FISHING **Sierra Marina** (tel. 209/841–3324), at the north end of Shaver Lake, rents pontoons ($80, for up to eight people) and fishing boats ($35) between April and September. They also rent tackle and sell bait and permits (required for all people who will be fishing). Otherwise, head to any of the sporting-good stores in the major towns (Bass Lake, North Fork, Shaver Lake). Besides the usual selection of tackle and fishing gear, they sell permits and maps of the "best" fishing spots in the area—places where you won't get your line caught on a speedboat.

HORSEBACK RIDING Depending on demand, at least three different companies offer horse rides into the wilderness. A day trip will run you $50–$75; overnight odysseys with food and supplies will be $100–$120 per day. For reservations and availability, write to the **High Sierra Packers Association** (Box 1362, Clovis 93613), or call any ranger station.

RAFTING Upper Kings River offers 10 miles of Class III and IV (on an ascending scale of difficulty from I–IV) rapids from Garnet Dike to Kirch Flat Campground. Most trips are organized by Kirch Flat's three rafting companies: **Kings River Expeditions** (tel. 209/253–4881), **Spirit White Water** (tel. 707/795–7305), and **Zephyr River Expeditions** (tel. 209/532–6249).

SKIING

DOWNHILL **Sierra Summit,** near Huntington Lake, is a challenging medium-size resort (five lifts) with rentals, a ski school, and your typical, ski-oriented visitor facilities. Advanced skiers may find the slopes a bit disappointing, but beginners and intermediates should thoroughly enjoy themselves. Lift tickets are $30 on weekends, $22–$25 during the week. For more information, contact the **Sierra Summit Ski Area** (tel. 209/893–3316).

CROSS-COUNTRY **Goat Meadow,** near the town of Fish Camp, has trails that enter the southernmost part of Yosemite National Park. Detailed maps and trail suggestions can be obtained at the Oakhurst Ranger Station (tel. 209/683–4665). **Tamarack Meadow,** on Route 168 between Huntington and Shaver Lakes, offers miles of marked trails and a plowed parking area. It's managed by the Pineridge Ranger Station (tel. 209/841–3311), and they sell detailed maps ($3) of the area.

SWIMMING Unsupervised swimming is allowed in Pineflat Reservoir, Shaver Lake, Mammoth Pool, Redinger Lake, and Bass Lake. By July, the water in the lower elevations is pleasantly warm.

Sequoia and Kings Canyon National Parks

The Sequoia and Kings Canyon national parks have some kind of nebulous affiliation that allows you to get into both for the price of one ($5). They share the same highways and administrative facilities, so seeing both parks in one trip is generally quite easy. Once inside their collective boundary, you'll find the world's second-largest living thing (a giant sequoia fondly named "General Sherman"), the deepest canyon in the United States (Kings Canyon), and the highest mountain peak in the 48 contiguous states (Mt. Whitney). Most of the wooded areas are covered with virgin timber and most of the park is without roads, making it an exquisite place to do either day hiking or some serious wilderness camping. Best of all, Sequoia and Kings Canyon retain a rustic feeling even in their most developed areas, a pleasant contrast to their more famous and congested neighbor, Yosemite.

Aside from the extensive redwood groves and spectacular alpine scenery, these two parks encompass land that ranges from less than 1,200 feet to more than 14,000 feet high, combining the miles of low-elevation chaparral and semi-desert environments with cool, forested high country. Both are only one to two hours by car from Fresno and Visalia—perfect for an extended day trip or weekend getaway.

Sequoia and Kings Canyon National Parks

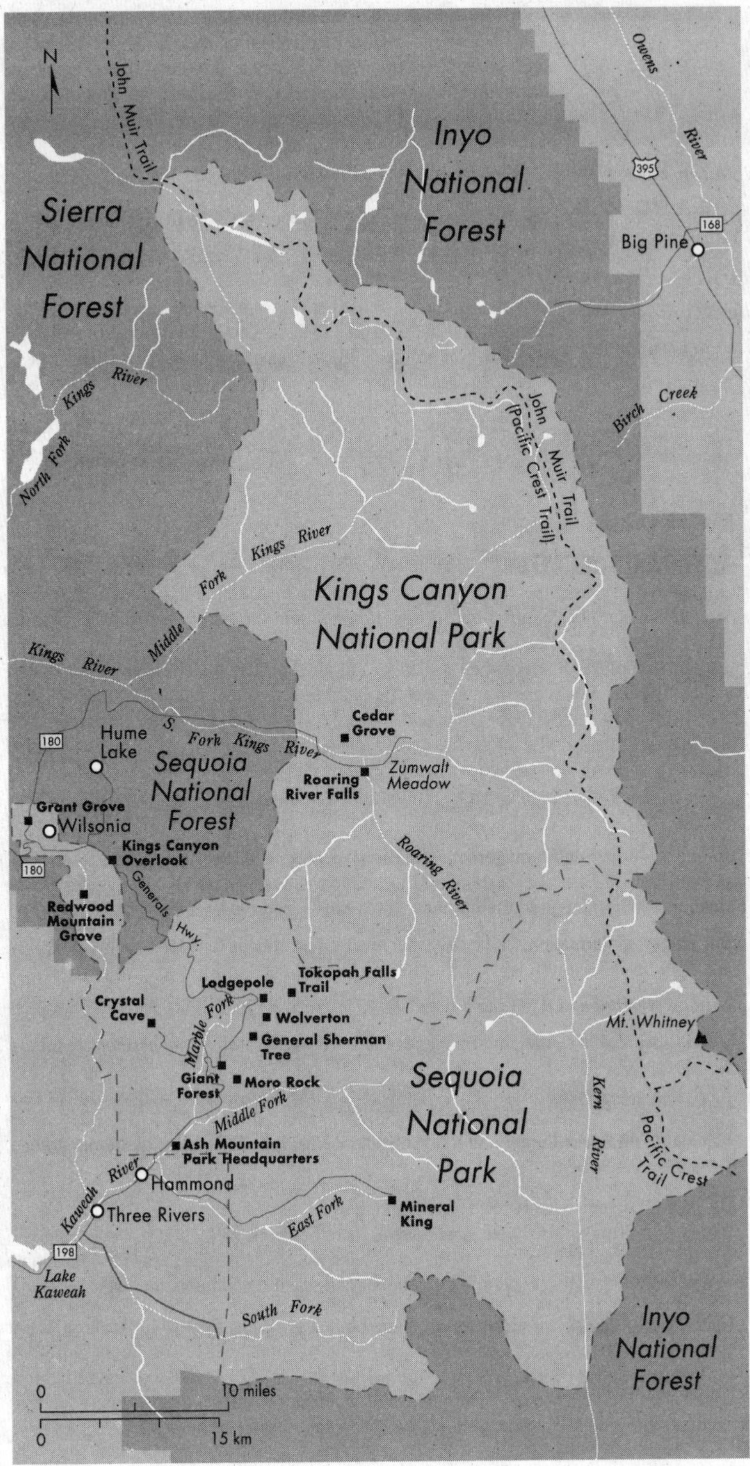
N
John Muir Trail
Inyo National Forest
Owens River
395
168
Big Pine
Sierra National Forest
North Fork Kings River
Birch Creek
John Muir Trail (Pacific Crest Trail)
Middle Fork Kings River
Kings Canyon National Park
Kings River
S. Fork Kings River
180
Hume Lake
Sequoia National Forest
Cedar Grove
Roaring River Falls
Zumwalt Meadow
Grant Grove
Wilsonia
Kings Canyon Overlook
180
Roaring River
Generals Hwy.
Redwood Mountain Grove
Tokopah Falls Trail
Lodgepole
Crystal Cave
Marble Fork
Wolverton
General Sherman Tree
Mt. Whitney
Giant Forest
Moro Rock
Sequoia National Park
Kern River
Middle Fork
Ash Mountain Park Headquarters
Pacific Crest Trail
Kaweah River
Hammond
Three Rivers
East Fork
Mineral King
198
Lake Kaweah
South Fork
Inyo National Forest
0
10 miles
0
15 km

The Generals Highway, running 46 miles from Route 180 in Kings Canyon National Park to the Ash Mountain entrance in Sequoia, is one of the most scenic drives in the state and offers dramatic views and easy access to both parks.

Most people visit between June and October, when the weather is warm and the roads clear. Summer in the high country (above 9,000 feet) is characterized by mild days, occasional afternoon thundershowers, and nights that can dip below freezing. In the foothills (1,500–3,000 feet), summers are usually hot and dry. Crowds are a problem during the summer season, especially in late-August when the residents of Fresno and Visalia swarm up here to escape 100°F temperatures in the Central Valley. But even then it's much less crowded than Yosemite. Fall is the best time to visit; the rivers will not be as full, but the weather is still warm and crisp and there are fewer visitors.

During winter, most of the park is blanketed with snow and virtually deserted, and both the road to Cedar Grove (Route 180) and Mineral King (east of Route 198) are closed. Yet even in the thick of December and January, much of the parks remain open—the best time to come if you're really looking for a solitary experience. Be prepared for freezing temperatures and snow-bound camp sites, however, and don't forget your snow chains.

● ● ● BASICS

TOURIST INFORMATION Upon entrance, all visitors are given a free copy of *Sequoia Bark,* a small newspaper that contains a detailed map and a list of park activities. **Wilderness permits,** required for overnight camping in the backcountry, are sold at all visitor centers ($5). Keep in mind that permits are issued only for the trails within a particular center's district; when in doubt, call ahead. After March 1, permits must be reserved at least two weeks in advance. After October 1, they're available on the spot. Send a brief itinerary and $5 to: Sequoia and Kings Canyon National Parks, Three Rivers, CA 93271. Don't despair if you forget to make a reservation, as 30% of all permits are handed out on a first-come, first-served basis. Simply appear in person at a particular visitor center and sign up. A lot of people try this strategy, so arrive early (between 7 and 10 AM) if you can.

To reach a particular **ranger station/visitor center,** call the general dispatch (tel. 209/565–3341) and they'll transfer your call to the appropriate office. If you're having trouble getting through to the numbers listed below, call the general dispatch.

Backcountry Information. Call for weather and trail conditions, and for permit availability. *Tel. 209/565–3306.*

General Weather and Road Conditions. *Tel. 209/565–3351.*

Grant Grove Visitor Center and Ranger Station. *Rte. 180, 10 mi from northern entrance, tel. 209/335–2315.*

Lodgepole Visitor Center and Ranger Station. *Generals Hwy., tel. 209/565–3341.*

Ash Mountain Visitor Center and Ranger Station. *Rte. 180, 3 mi from southern entrance, tel. 209/565–3456.*

FEES The entrance fee is $5 per vehicle or $2 per person by bus, foot, bicycle, or motorcycle. This entitles you to one week in either park (or both), but you'll need a wilderness permit ($5) to camp in the backcountry. A Golden Eagle pass ($25), available at any entrance, will get you into all national parks and monuments for a year.

PUBLICATIONS Trail guides detailing day hikes in Cedar Grove, Mineral King, Grant Forest, and Lodgepole are available at any visitor center for $1. The **Sequoia Natural History Association** (Box 10, Ash Mountain, Three Rivers 93271) sells extensive literature on the area, including books, pamphlets, maps, and video and audio cassettes. If you drop them a postcard, they'll send you a catalog and some free information on the park.

GENERAL STORES Food, gas, fishing tackle and licenses, and camping gear are available at stores in Giant Forest Village, Lodgepole, Stony Creek, Grant Grove, and Cedar Grove in the summer; and at Giant Forest and Grant Grove in winter. Try to stock up on groceries and camping supplies in Fresno or Visalia before coming to the park, however, where you'll find better prices and greater selections.

COMING AND GOING • • •

BY CAR **Route 198** runs between Visalia and Sequoia National Park (two hours), eventually intersecting with **Route 180** and Kings Canyon. Both highways also intersect Route 99, which runs north–south through the Central Valley. From Los Angeles, take Route 65 north from Bakersfield to Route 198. Traveling between the two national parks is fairly easy; besides the 198–180 route, there's also a scenic, windy road connecting Sequoia's Ash Mountain with Giant Forest in Kings Canyon. Known as the **Generals Highway,** this 46-mile road, open year-round (chains required in winter), rises more than 5,000 feet through twisting turns and harrowing passes and affords spectacular views of the high country. Service stations and limited mechanical service are available in Lodgepole, Grant Grove, and Cedar Grove. For current road conditions 24 hours a day, call 209/565-3351.

BY BUS **Greyhound** (tel. 209/268–9461) can get you as far as Visalia and Fresno, but from here you're on your own. There's no public transportation to the park from either city, so your only option is to contact **Visalia K.O.A.** (tel. 209/651–0100). They offer minivan and bus tours ($10–$15) of Sequoia from both Visalia and Fresno.

WHERE TO SLEEP • • •

All hotels and cabins in Sequoia and Kings Canyon are managed by **Sequoia Guest Services** (Box 789, Three Rivers 93271, tel. 209/561–3314), the concessionaire for both parks. To reserve any room, you must call this number directly, and advance reservations are strongly recommended (most hotels and cabins are booked 6–10 weeks in advance during summer). Giant Forest, Stoney Creek (on the Generals Highway), and Cedar Grove have the heaviest concentrations of motels, but they're way overpriced at $40–$80 a night. The cheapest accommodations in the park are known as **"the Rustics"**—cabins with no carpets or decoration, pit toilets, and kerosene lamps instead of electricity. They do have wood-burning stoves for heat, a roof, and real beds, however, and they're reasonably priced ($20 for the first person, $6–$10 for each additional, up to eight). Look for them in Grant Forest (November–May), Grant Grove (year-round), and Giant Forest (June–October). More elaborate and comfortable cabins with real toilets and electricity are available in Grant Grove and Grant Forest between June and October for $40–$60. For availability and reservations, contact the Sequoia Guest Services.

CAMPGROUNDS From mid-May to Labor Day, the **Lodgepole** campground in Sequoia accepts reservations through Ticketron (tel. 800/452–1111) up to eight weeks in advance. Sites are $10 per night, plus a small service charge. All other campgrounds in Sequoia and Kings Canyon are available on a first-come, first-served basis and cost $4–$8 per night.

South Fork is the smallest campground in Sequoia and Kings Canyon, and definitely one of the nicest. RVs and trailers are not permitted, so you won't be bothered with families of 12 and the noise of generator-powered televisions. The sites are nestled amongst a grove of pine trees, and all have tables and fire pits. There's also a bathroom facility (pit toilets and showers) near the entrance. Sites fetch $4 a night between mid-May and October, after which the water is turned off and camping is free. *13 mi from Rte. 198 on South Fork Dr. Open year-round.*

Mineral King has two campgrounds: **Atwell Mill** and **Cold Springs,** 20 miles up Mineral King Road from Route 198, open from spring (when the roads are cleared) to mid-November. The extremely curvy road prevents RV and trailer use, making this area quieter and more lightly used than the central campgrounds. Sites have pit toilets, tables, stoves, and water from late-May through September only. **Silver City Resort,** on the same road but 5 miles farther, has showers, phones, and a restaurant; it's $4 per night until the water is turned off in November, then it's free.

Sentinel, Moraine, and **Sheep Creek** offer a total of 300 sites in the Cedar Grove area of Kings Canyon. Sites cost $8 per night and have toilets, fire pits, and tables. There's a pay phone and water spigot in the main parking lot. *Rte. 180, Cedar Grove. Open mid-May–mid-Oct.*

There are two small but free campgrounds on the road leading north to Hume Lake. **Upper Tenmile Campground,** 6 miles north of Route 180 on Hume Lake Road, has five sites with tables, stoves, and vault toilets. **Landslide Campground,** another mile north, has six sites with tables, stoves, and vault toilets. A grocery store is available at Hume Lake. Otherwise, stick it out 3½ miles more on Route 180 and turn on the road marked "Big Meadows." Four miles in you'll stumble across the **Buck Rock Campground,** with five sites, tables, fire pits, and toilets. Two miles more and you'll hit the **Big Meadows Campground,** with 25 sites, tables, stoves, and vault toilets.

● ● ● FOOD

Food in the parks ranges from greasy and cheap to greasy and expensive. Most resorts have both a cafeteria and a dining room, the former with food for under $5 and the latter for under $15, but save your money. You're better off eating outside the parks or bringing your own food in. If you're desperate, there are a few restaurants and sandwich counters nestled around Bass Lake, Lodgepole, Giant Forest Village, and Grant Grove. But once again, you'll pay handsomely for a mediocre meal unless you make it yourself. The **Cedar Grove Snack Bar** (tel. 209/565–3617) is the only restaurant in Cedar Grove. A three-egg omelette with toast and hash browns fetches $5, a cheeseburger and fries $5, a cup of chili $2.50. It's next to the market in Cedar Grove. On Route 180 in Grant Grove, the **Grant Grove Coffee Shop** (tel. 209/335–2314) serves basic American fare, from burgers and fries ($5) to eggs and hash browns ($4). Box lunches with a sandwich, fruit, and dessert are available for $7 per person—ideal for a picnic lunch outdoors, if you're not up for making your own. Give them at least eight hours' notice, however.

UNDER $10 **Lodgepole Deli.** Perhaps the best find in the park. It's small and essentially characterless, but it serves good food at rock-bottom prices. Hearty egg-and-sausage breakfasts run $4, hot and cold sandwiches $4, fried chicken $5, and pizza $6. Even better, there's an ice-cream parlor next door. *Generals Hwy., Lodgepole, tel. 209/565–3301. Open mid-May–mid-Sept., daily 8–7.*

Giant Forest Cafeteria. They serve three meals a day cafeteria-style with about five daily choices of entrées. A full breakfast goes for $4–$5, lunch and dinner $5–$7. *Rte. 198, Giant Forest Village, tel. 209/565–3381. Open mid-May–mid-Sept., daily 8–8.*

UNDER $15 **Giant Forest Lodge.** Come here for a more formal dinner. It offers a huge salad bar ($7) and top-rate daily specials ($12–$18). Also try their grilled trout ($14). *Rte. 198, Giant Forest Village, tel. 209/565–3381. Open mid-May–mid-Sept., daily 8–8.*

● ● ● EXPLORING SEQUOIA AND KINGS CANYON

Much of the two parks isn't accessible by road, so your best bet is to get out of the car and hike through the backcountry. Even if you're short on time, there are hundreds of easy, one- to three-hour day hikes in the area, concentrated around Grant Grove and Cedar Grove. Otherwise, stick to Route 180 and the Generals Highway. Both are extremely scenic and easy to navigate.

PARK SETTLEMENTS

GRANT GROVE Grant Grove lies at the western boundary of the parks; you'll pass through it if you come east on Route 180 from Fresno. It's one of the most highly developed sections of Kings Canyon, but even so the mile-long **Big Stump Trail** is a decent place to start. It's not the most scenic hike (it gets its name from the numerous stumps left by loggers), but it contains a grove of giant sequoias that includes the **General Grant Tree**—the nation's official Christmas tree and the third-largest sequoia in the world. Also of interest is the **Gamlin Cabin,** one of several pioneer-era dwellings that's open to the public. On the more practical side, Grant Grove has a gas station, public showers, a visitor center, and three campgrounds.

CEDAR GROVE Cedar Grove, the other major destination in Kings Canyon, is about an hour's drive (32 miles) farther east on Route 180. It's on this road, built by convict labor in the 1930s, that you can actually see how stunning Kings Canyon really is, particularly its glacier-carved valley tempered with jagged cliffs and roaring waterfalls. An added bonus: This road retains a rustic, uncongested feel, making it ideal for an extended drive. In Cedar Grove, named for the incense cedars that blanket the area, there's a campground, ranger station, cafeteria, snack bar, grocery store, and gas station. Everything is closed November–April because of the threat of rock slides, but during summer you'll find the trailheads for **Zumwalt Meadow** and **Roaring River Falls** here.

Route 180 clings to the mountain side and traverses some dramatic overlooks along the way, passing the remnants of turn-of-the-century forests obliterated by loggers.

LODGEPOLE At the south end of the Generals Highway coming from Grant Grove, Lodgepole is a developed area with a campground, grocery store, gas station, deli, ice-cream parlor, and visitor center. A short nature trail leads from behind the visitor center down to the nearby river. A little farther on, there's a makeshift "beach" of sorts (consisting of small rocks and pebbles). You won't want to play beach volleyball here, but it'll do for a few hours of sunbathing. The river is generally ice cold, but if this doesn't bother you, go ahead and take a swim. A few miles east of Lodgepole, the 2-mile **Tokopah Falls Trail** leads up into the hills, tracing the banks of the river. It's a steep hike, but at the end you can bask in the misty air that surrounds the falls.

Two miles south of Lodgepole (just off the Generals Highway) is the **General Sherman Tree**—the second-largest living thing in the world (a mushroom in Michigan covers 30 acres). It's 275 feet tall and 102 feet around at its base, and its first branch is nearly 130 feet up. If you head 2 miles farther south look for the **Giant Forest,** an over-developed resort that has hotels, cafeterias, and a slew of convenience stores. The only reason to bother with this place is to access the trailheads leading from Giant Forest. In particular, **Round Meadow** is an easy 1/4-mile hike that empties into a lush, peaceful field. **Tharp's Log,** at Log Meadow, is a small pioneer cabin built in a fallen sequoia. There's also a log cabin at Huckleberry Meadow, 1 1/2 miles from the visitor center.

Nine miles northeast of General Forest is the **Crystal Cave,** the only one of Sequoia's many caves that's open to the public, and then only on guided tours ($3). It's crowded during the summer, but the one-hour tour will appeal to cave-buffs and amateur spelunkers. You hike half a mile from the parking lot down to the cave. It's only 50° inside, so bring a jacket. It's at the end of a rough, 6-mile spur road off Generals Highway; follow the signs from Giant Forest. Total driving time: 45 minutes. *Tel. 209/565–3341, ext. 732. Open June–Aug., daily 10 AM–3 PM; May–Sept., Fri.–Mon. 10 AM–3 PM.*

MINERAL KING The southernmost attraction in Sequoia is Mineral King, a secluded and relatively uncongested valley that's accessible only in the summer. Numerous trails lead from Mineral King to the surrounding peaks, meadows, and high lakes, as well as to the campgrounds and a small ranger station. From the town of Hammond (on Route 198), a windy, narrow road leads 25 miles east to Mineral King; plan on at least an hour and a half each way.

ORIENTATION PROGRAMS AND NATURE WALKS Grant Grove, Cedar Groves, Ash Mountain, Lodgepole, and Mineral King offer numerous daily activities in the summer that focus on the ecology, wildlife, and geology of the national parks. A complete list of activities and times appears in the *Sequoia Bark,* or ask at the visitor centers. In winter, evening programs are offered on Friday and Saturday at Grant Grove and Lodgepole; if conditions permit, ranger-guided snowshoe walks are also offered on weekends and holidays. Reservations are recommended; call the Grant Grove (tel. 209/335–2315) or Lodgepole (tel. 209/565–3341) visitor centers.

Don't miss **Hospital Rock,** 5 miles north of Ash Mountain's visitor center. It has an outdoor display devoted to the history of the Native American population of the Sierra Nevada, and a series of murals painted by Nanache tribes more than 150 years ago.

HIKING Kings Canyon has incredible hiking opportunities, from short day hikes to extensive trips into the backcountry. For $1 you can obtain trail guides for both Grant Grove and Cedar Grove. These include maps of the area and a detailed description of the hikes. One of the most popular trails is in Cedar Grove, known as the **Paradise Valley Trail.** It eventually winds up in Mist Falls, and features views of the canyon and an intimate encounter with the falls themselves. It's 8 moderately strenuous miles from beginning to end; the trailhead is at Road's End, a small dirt road about 5 miles east of Cedar Grove Village. The **Baldy Trail,** which begins at Little Baldy Saddle (11 miles north of Giant Forest Village on the Generals Highway), climbs 700 feet in 1.7 miles and ends with a stunning view of the surrounding countryside.

BACKCOUNTRY TRIPS The John Muir and Pacific Crest trails merge in Sequoia, roughly following the eastern border of Kings Canyon before heading northwest into Sierra National Forest. Cedar Grove has several trailheads that are about a day's hike from the John Muir/Pacific Crest Trail. Otherwise, consult the visitor centers and ranger stations for maps, trail suggestions, and wilderness permits.

SCENIC DRIVES AND VIEWS Aside from the Generals Highway, the drive to Cedar Grove along **Route 180** is perhaps the most spectacular in the parks. The windy descent into Kings Canyon provides excellent up-close views of the daunting cliffs as well as vistas of the entire canyon. Be sure to pull over onto the shoulder before becoming too enthralled by the landscape. Kings Canyon also offers a motor nature trail—a 3-mile dirt road reminiscent of the original highway into the canyon that runs beside the Kings River. A booklet available at Cedar Grove Visitor Center details points on the trail where you can stop to observe different aspects of the canyon environment.

Between Ash Mountain and Giant Forest, **Route 198** climbs dramatically for more than 5,000 feet, allowing a firsthand look at the stunning topographical differences between the dry, chaparral-covered foothills and the high, moist sequoia groves. On a clear day, you also get excellent views of the valley, hills, and surrounding peaks.

● ● ● PARK ACTIVITIES

BIKING Bike riding is allowed only on paved roads, *not* on hiking or fire trails. Roads in the park are generally hilly and narrow, so be careful and ride defensively.

BIRD-WATCHING Free bird walks are periodically offered by the visitor centers, depending upon demand. Contact the Ash Mountain office for specifics.

CAVE EXPLORATION The Sequoia Natural History Association offers tours several times daily of **Crystal Cave,** which is filled with marble formations, stalactites, and stalagmites (*see* Exploring Sequoia and Kings Canyon, *above*). The 6-mile drive from the Generals Highway takes about 45 minutes on a rough, narrow road. Tours are $3.

FISHING Fishing licenses ($7 a day) are required for all anglers and available at sporting-good stores and ranger stations. Also grab a copy of the pamphlet "Park Fishing Regulations" for other regulations including size constraints and limits, both of which vary year to year. Tackle and rental equipment are available at Lodgepole, Stony Creek, Grant Grove, and Cedar Grove.

HORSEBACK RIDING Guided horse rides are available in Sequoia at the **Wolverton Pack Station** (between Lodgepole and Giant Forest, tel. 209/565–3445) and **Mineral King Pack Station** (tel. 209/565–3404); in Kings Canyon at the **Cedar Grove Pack Station** (tel. 209/565–3464) and **Grant Grove Stables** (tel. 209/335–2482). Most stables open in mid-May and close at the end of September. Rates range from station to station, but expect to pay around $12 per hour, $40 per day, and $100 per day for overnight trips (including food).

SKIING

DOWNHILL The **Wolverton Winter Use Area** (tel. 209/565–3435), 3½ miles north of Giant Forest, is a small, family-oriented ski area that's open—weather permitting—on winter weekends and holidays. Ski rentals and instruction, a snack bar, and a retail shop are available. Lift tickets are $27 a day.

CROSS-COUNTRY The **Sequoia Ski Touring Center** (tel. 209/565–3435) offers rentals and tours of the parks' limitless backcountry. Similar services are provided by the **Grant Grove Ski Touring Center** (tel. 209/565–2314). There are 52 miles of cross-country trails at **Montecito-Sequoia** (tel. 800/227–9900), off the Generals Highway between the two parks. In Grant Grove and Giant Forest, you'll also find miles of marked, sometimes groomed, cross-country routes. Pick up a trail map at any visitor or ski center.

Near Sequoia and Kings Canyon

SEQUOIA NATIONAL FOREST

The Sequoia National Forest is yet another stunning and pristine national wilderness, offering a bevy of outdoor opportunities year-round. Its main advantage, however, lies in its proximity to the Central Valley and the Sequoia and Kings Canyon national parks. Even if you're on a tight schedule, the forest is linked by main highways to Bakersfield, Visalia, and beyond—ideal if you're coming or going to Los Angeles, the Bay Area, or even Yosemite. Of course, Sequoia's proximity to the Central Valley also means crowds are a serious problem during the summer, but mostly around Lake Isabella and the Kern River. As long as you avoid these areas between May and September, the weekenders from Bakersfield shouldn't get in your way.

The **Tule River Ranger District** lies directly south of Sequoia National Park, extending south to Dome Rock and west to the Kern River. The **Greenhorn Ranger District** (which contains Lake Isabella) and the **Hot Springs Ranger District** (which engulfs the western portion of the forest) are characterized by grassland and oak woodlands at the lower elevation (3,000–5,000 feet), and mixed conifer and sequoia groves higher up. Because of their accessibility by paved roads, they're also quite popular in the summer. For greater solitude and easy access to the wilderness areas, head east to the **Cannell Meadow Ranger District.** From here you'll have access to the **South Sierra** and **Golden Trout wilderness areas,** as well as to the scenic **Sherman Pass Road**—the only route (besides Route 120 in Yosemite) that traverses the towering Sierra Nevadas.

BASICS

TOURIST INFORMATION Wilderness permits, maps, and a list of park activities are available from all ranger stations. They also can help plan backcountry excursions and offer suggestions for scenic day hikes.

Cannell Meadow Ranger District Headquarters. *Box 6, Kernville 93238, tel. 619/376–3781. 10 mi north of Lake Isabella.*

Hot Springs Ranger Station. *Route 4, Box 548, California Hot Springs 93207, tel. 805/548–6503. 20 mi east of Route 65.*

Hume Lake Ranger District. *36273 E. Kings Canyon Rd., Dunlap 93621, tel. 209/338–2251. On Rte. 180 near Fresno.*

Tule River Ranger District. *32588 Rte. 190, Springville 93265, tel. 209/539–2697.*

GENERAL STORES Before heading into the backcountry, stock up on supplies in Porterville (18 miles west of Springville on Route 190), Fresno, Bakersfield, or Dunlap. Inside the park, there are small stores in Pine Flat, Kernville and Kennedy Meadows. Don't expect to find your favorite brands, however: Count your blessings if you can find a six-pack of generic beer and a loaf of stale bread.

COMING AND GOING Unless you have a car, save yourself the trouble and turn the page. It's unfortunate, but public transportation does not exist into the Sequoia National Forest. Otherwise, it's accessible from Porterville and other points west via **Route 190**; from the north or south via the **Western Divide Highway.** For the Cannell Meadow area, take the **Sierra Way** north from Kernville (and be sure to stop at the ranger station in Kernville before leaving town). This will provide access to **Sherman Pass Road,** where many wilderness trailheads originate. The Hot Springs area is accessible from the west by **Route J22;** and from the south and east from Kernville and the Sierra Way. However you go, fill up the gas tank outside the park. Once inside, gas prices are criminally high.

WHERE TO SLEEP Looking for a hotel? If so, stop what you're doing and make a beeline for Fresno, Bakersfield, or Visalia. It's hard to believe, but hotels and motels are on Sequoia's endangered species list. Camping—either developed or dispersed—is your only option, so don't forget to pack the tent and cooking stove. Dispersed camping is allowed throughout the Hot Springs and Cannell Meadow ranger districts, and is especially popular in the relatively secluded Sherman Pass area. You'll need a wilderness permit, though, available from any ranger station. One nice thing about Sequoia is that all developed camping is first-come, first-served. If you're having trouble finding a spot, drive along Route 190 in the Tule River District where there are six relatively quiet campgrounds. One of the nicer ones is **Quaking Aspen,** 27 miles east of Springville, which has 32 sites (at $5 a night), toilets, tables, and water. Its proximity to the Golden Trout Wilderness makes it a great base from which to explore the mountains, while its high altitude (7,000 feet) means it stays cool year-round. Farther west in the foothills, **Coffee Camp** is nestled on the banks of a small river. You can swim in pools carved into the face of huge granite formations or hike in the nearby, low-elevation (2,000 feet) chaparral. It's open year-round and has 18 sites ($5 a night) with toilets, water, tables, and stoves.

In the Hot Springs Ranger District, look for **Leavis Flat** in California Hot Springs. It's open year-round, but the water is turned off in the winter. **Lower Peppermint,** 10 miles north of Johnsondale via Lloyd Meadow Road, is a popular but more isolated area offering 17 sites, pit toilets, and piped water. Because it's isolated, only tent campers are allowed. This is a good jumping-off point for hikers, as several trails meander into the Golden Trout Wilderness from here.

The Cannell Meadow Ranger District offers two main camping areas, one along the Kern River north of Kernville, and another near the Sherman Pass Road. All the campgrounds along the river are indistinguishable (dry, peppered with oak trees, and boiling-hot in summer), and all cost $5. Those near Sherman Pass are at higher elevations (which means they're milder in August) and free.

EXPLORING THE SEQUOIA NATIONAL FOREST The Hot Springs Ranger District features two main groves of giant sequoias, both located just off Route M50: the **Deer Creek Grove,** near California Hot Springs, and the wheelchair-accessible **Trail of 100 Giants.** Also check out the dilapidated California Hot Springs Resort which, although still in operation, seems like it's seen better days.

The Cannell Meadow Ranger District provides trail access to three wilderness areas: the Dome Land Wilderness, South Sierra Wilderness, and the Golden Trout Wilderness. The **Dome Land Wilderness,** southernmost in the Sierra Nevada, is comprised of dry and generally rugged terrain covered by piñon pines on the eastern slope and jeffrey pines on the western. Alpine lovers will also appreciate the region's large, and exposed, dome-like granite formations. Trailheads are at Big Meadow (on Cherry Hill Road, off the Sherman Pass Road from Kernville) and Taylor Meadow, which is southeast of Big Meadow. The **South Sierra Wilderness,** just north of the Dome Land Wilderness, is notable for its meadows, granite formations, and diverse topography (from gentle hills to steep peaks). To access its trailheads, take the Sherman Pass Road to State Mountain Route 99 and follow the signs. The **Golden Trout Wilderness** lies north of the South Sierra Wilderness and south of Sequoia National Park. Its pine forests, streams, and meadows are accessible from trailheads at the Black Rock Information Station on Sherman Pass Road. Ask about the popular trek to Jordan Hot Springs, an excellent reward for a long day of hiking.

The rugged and dramatic trails in the Jennie Lakes Wilderness ramble through a seemingly endless series of virgin forests and undisturbed valleys, tracing the edge of the Kings Canyon and Sequoia national parks.

On the Western Divide Highway in the Tule Lake District, look for **Dome Rock**—a massive granite monolith that provides a spectacular view of the surrounding countryside and the eastern portion of the Golden Trout Wilderness. Hikers should head for the Peppermint and Quaking Aspen campgrounds, where you'll find a number of trailheads.

The Hume Lake District offers easy access into the **Jennie Lakes Wilderness,** one of the most uncrowded and unblemished retreats south of Yosemite. The trailhead begins on Big Meadows Road, off Generals Highway, or you can see the wilderness by car if you drive along Route 180 east into the Kings River Canyon.

FOREST ACTIVITIES

BIKING Bicycles are allowed on almost all roads in the park, including the fire trails and unimproved dirt roads. The heaviest concentration of trails is in the Hot Springs ranger district; ask at the station for maps, tips, and any restrictions.

FISHING Fishing—particularly trout fishing—is popular along the Fule River, in the high lakes and streams of the Golden Trout and Jennie Lakes Wilderness, and at Hume Lake. Year-round fishing is possible near Coffee Camp on the Tule River. Licenses are required, available at any ranger station.

HORSEBACK RIDING Day rides ($30–$50) and overnight backcountry trips ($85–$100 per day) are organized by the **Horse Corral Pack Station** (Box 135, Sequoia National Park 93262, tel. 209/565–3404) and, in the Tule River area, by the **Quaking Aspen Campground** (tel. 209/542–2816).

RAFTING Several companies run raft trips along the Kings River, which boasts class III and IV rapids. It is also possible to canoe or kayak the area beginning 3½ miles above Mill Flat Campground and heading toward Pine Flat Reservoir. Above this take off point, the rapids are very dangerous. For specific information on raft trips, contact the **Hume Lake Ranger District** (tel. 209/338–2251).

The San Joaquin Valley

The San Joaquin Valley is something of a California enigma—the sort of place most Californians have heard of, but also the sort of place most Californians probably couldn't find on a map. What's even more inexplicable is the fact that this sprawling and characterless basin, jam-packed with tract homes and minimalls, is one of the fastest-growing regions in the state. Drawn by affordable real estate and the valley's relative proximity to Los Angeles (via Bakersfield) and the Bay Area (via Stockton), many Californians are looking at the Central Valley as an escape route from the evils of urban living. Ironically, the valley has the potential to become the next Los Angeles in 50 years' time, a massive and unsightly metropolis where freeways and smog reign supreme.

San Joaquin Valley's status as a huge string of bedroom communities is a surprisingly recent development for an area that has long been recognized for its agricultural attributes alone. The richness and fertility of the valley has always made it an important supplier of agricultural goods to the rest of the country.

Of course, if you're not looking to relocate you and your family permanently, there isn't much here to detain you. Most travelers treat the San Joaquin Valley, which stretches from Redding in northern California to Bakersfield in the south, as a giant pit stop on their way somewhere else. Since the enormous Central Valley is an inevitable part of trans-California travel you may have no choice but to "discover" its dual overdeveloped-backwater charm. Odds are good that you won't fall in love with the place, but at least you'll get an opportunity to experience the pure and unadulterated rural heartland of California. With a healthy sense of the absurd and an impulse to create your own adventures, you can make your stay here an interesting one as you zip along **I–5** and **Route 99,** the region's principal thoroughfares, on your way to San Diego, Los Angeles, San Francisco, or northern California. The desolate and—to be honest—rather ugly I–5 may not be a nature lover's idea of nirvana, but don't despair if you somehow find yourself in **Stockton, Merced, Fresno, Bakersfield,** or in any number of the small outposts along the highways between L.A. and Stockton. Grab a six-pack and a cheeseburger, put on your cowboy boots and "I Luv Merced" baseball cap, and count the number of semitrailer trucks thundering down the highway. You'd be surprised how much fun this can be.

● ● ● STOCKTON

You almost have to go out of your way to visit this urbanized riverfront town, 75 miles east of San Francisco and 62 miles south of Sacramento. I–5 cuts through the center of town, but unless you're coming from Sacramento and northern California there are a few reasons to take a detour through Stockton when traveling the Los Angeles–San Francisco circuit.

High crime rate, bored teenagers, proud elders…Stockton is worth visiting if only for its resemblance to about 90% of the rest of the United States. This is the other California.

Stockton sits on the east side of the **Delta,** a 1000-mile expanse of waterways that once submerged much of the area before levees were built in the late 1800s. Old-timers proudly recall the town's history as a major inland seaport. Now the waterways are a prime site for boating, fishing, waterskiing, and any other water-related activity you may wish to indulge in (*see* Outdoor Activities, *below*). However, most of these activities take place outside Stockton proper, and about the only things of interest in Stockton itself are its two public parks. **Victory Park,** located right off I–5 at the Pershing exit, is an ideal place to stop for a picnic in the shade or a swim in its public pool. On the grounds you'll also find the **Haggin Museum** (tel. 209/462–1566), with a small collection of antique farm equipment and Native American baskets. Admission is free, and the museum is open daily (except Monday) between 1:30 PM and 5 PM. **Oak Grove Regional Park,** accessed via the Eight Mile Road exit off I–5, offers a view of what Stockton supposedly looked like before the first European farmers settled here 150 years ago. It has one of the last groves of native oak trees in the state, but the adjoining nature center is worth a visit only if you're really bored.

In town you'll find a number of liquor stores, video rental shops, and fast-food restaurants along **Pacific** and **Pershing** avenues, the city's principal streets. Both are lined with signs that declare NO CRUISING, so overcome your urge to join the thousands of teens and UOP students (University of the Pacific) who slowly drive their cars up and down the avenues night after night to check each other out and look as cool as humanly possible. Sad to say, this is probably the most exciting thing to do in Stockton. If you're feeling really courageous spend a day at Stockton's semi-famous **Asparagus Festival** (tel. 209/477–1803) when 75,000 people descend on the city (held every April) for the week-long event. Asparagus cook-offs and tastings, along with a vintage car show, arts-and-crafts booths, and live entertainment are featured. In Stockton, asparagus is a very big deal.

BASICS

AMERICAN EXPRESS Stockton does have its own AmEx office where you can cash traveler's checks, exchange currency, and pick up a few tourist brochures. If you're really lucky, they may even be able to book you a place on the next bus out of town. *2321 March La., tel. 209/952–6606. Open weekdays 8:30–5:30.*

DOCTORS AND DENTISTS **Valley Dental Center.** They welcome walk-in patients who are seen on a first-come, first-served basis. Unfortunately, they do ask that all patients pay in cash for services rendered. *10 E. Charter Way, tel. 209/946–0680. Open daily 8 AM–3 PM.*

LUGGAGE STORAGE There are lockers in the Greyhound station (*see below*), a two- to three-block walk south on South Center Street from downtown. Lockers cost $3 for 24 hours, and must be renewed in person each day.

TOURIST INFORMATION **The Stockton/San Joaquin Convention and Visitor's Bureau.** They have information on the entire region, including maps, brochures, and budget lodging/dining facilities. *46 W. Fremon St., tel 209/243–1987. Open weekdays 8–5.*

COMING AND GOING

BY TRAIN **Amtrak** offers three trains daily from Los Angeles to Sacramento with stops in Stockton. Stockton also lies on the San Francisco–Oakland–Bakersfield line; four routes daily each way. Fares to Los Angeles are $58 one way, $65 round-trip; to San Francisco/Oakland $16 one way, $23 round-trip. Watch your belongings at the station and spend as little time here as possible; the threat of someone making off with your purse or wallet is all too real here. *735 S. San Joaquin, tel. 209/946–0517. Open daily 8:30–8:30, closed 5–6 PM. To reach downtown or the UOP from station take Bus 10 north.*

BY BUS Stockton lies on **Greyhound's** Reno–Sacramento–Los Angeles–San Diego route; nine or 10 buses run daily in both directions. Two buses run daily to and from the Bay Area ($10), Santa Cruz ($16), and Monterey ($20); fares to Los Angeles and San Diego are $25 one way, $40 round-trip. Lockers at the station (121 S. Center St., tel. 209/465–5781) are available for $3 per 24 hours, but you must renew them in person each day. Downtown Stockton is only four blocks away. Bus 2 will take you from downtown to UOP.

HITCHHIKING Two freeways and three state highways run through Stockton, so this is, geographically, a good spot to hitch from. However, be wary of the lunatic fringe around here, and also of "hicks" who may not appreciate foreigners in *their* town. Even if you speak perfect English you may come across some good ol' boys who don't take kindly to strangers—especially if you're not wearing cowboy boots and a "Ford" baseball cap.

BY CAR I–5, which runs all the way from San Diego to the Canadian border, cuts through the center of Stockton. From San Francisco take the 580 east to the 205, and then cut over to I–5. From Stockton, plan on at least an hour's drive to Sacramento, 1½ to San Francisco, and 6½ to Los Angeles. If you're headed east into the Sierra Nevada from the Bay Area, you might also want to stop in Stockton to get supplies and gas while they're still cheap.

GETTING AROUND

Few tourists breach Stockton's borders and most locals have cars, the public transportation system here is less than great. If you don't have a car, buses run through town every half hour with service beginning at 5:30 AM and ending at 10 PM. The Convention and Visitor's Bureau (*see* Tourist Information, *above*) sells schedules; fares are 50¢, transfers 5¢. Some buses are wheelchair accessible. For more information, call the **Stockton Metropolitan Transit District** (their acronym is SMART, which makes you wonder) at 209/943–1111 between 8 AM and 5 PM.

WHERE TO SLEEP

Your cheapest option in Stockton is to rent a room from the housing office at the **University of the Pacific** (2nd floor, Bannister Hall, UOP, tel. 209/946–2331). Since they're usually used by parents and friends of students, you might say you're visiting a friend. Doubles with a private bath run $15 a night, $15–$20 with kitchen facilities. Otherwise, prepare yourself for a lackluster experience at the local **Motel 6** (1625 S. French Camp Rd., tel. 209/467–3600), accessed via the French Camp exit off I–5. Standard rooms with that "Sanitized for Your Comfort" feel fetch $22 per single, $29 per double.

CAMPING The closest thing to camping in Stockton is the **Dos Reis Campground,** 5 miles south of the city on I–5, west of Lathrop on Dos Reis Road. Twenty-six campsites with RV hookups, water, sewer, showers, picnic tables, and barbecue pits. Tent campers are welcome, but the noise of generators and portable televisions sort of ruins the "great outdoors" experience. There is, however, some good fishing along the San Joaquin River, 1/4 mile from the campground. All sites are $11 a night. *Dos Reis Rd., tel. 209/953–8800 or 209/331–7400.*

FOOD Large Mexican-American and Southeast Asian populations have helped Stockton spice up its standard selection of fast-food chains with cheap, hearty ethnic eateries. Besides McDonald's, Burger King, and Carl's Jr., look for the numerous taco stands and chow mein restaurants in the city center—unquestionably worth the extra few dollars. One should not live on Western bacon cheeseburgers alone. If you're in the mood to splurge head to **The Alder Market** (151 W. Alder St., tel. 209/943–1921), a small gourmet market, café, and restaurant, all in one. Their menu changes on a daily basis, but they always feature one pasta dish, one chicken dish, one seafood dish, and one vegetarian dish from $10 to $15. The food is excellent, but if you're strapped for cash try the Alder's less pricey café where you'll find a large selection of sandwiches and salads. Otherwise, there's plenty of fresh produce at Stockton's **Farmers' Market,** one of the largest in the state, held between 7 and 11 every Saturday morning beneath the Crosstown Freeway that connects I–5 and Route 99.

UNDER $5 **Arroyos Cafe.** This place downtown serves one of the best burritos ($3) in Stockton. Other highlights include Arroyos' soft tacos ($3), huevos rancheros ($4.50), and its nachos plate ($3.75). Arroyos may not rank high in the "ambience" category—in fact, it's a bit run-down and filled with seedy looking locals—but its food is worth the trip. *324 S. Center St. (at Lafayette), tel. 209/462–1661. 3 blocks from Greyhound station. Open daily 9 AM–midnight; closed Mon.*

The Blackwater Cafe. The place where Stockton's young and hip congregate. It has a cool jukebox, a wide selection of espresso drinks ($2–$3), a light snack menu ($3–$5), and a good selection of beers ($2–$5). If anything is going on in Stockton you'll probably find out about it here. *912 N. Yosemite, tel. 209/943–9330. Open weekdays 7 AM–midnight, weekends 10 AM–midnight.*

LeKim's. This is the place for great Vietnamese food, located in the Stockton Traveler's Motel. LeKim's seven-page menu features such delicacies as sizzling rice seafood soup ($5) and sautéed chicken with coconut and curry ($5); they also have 21 vegetarian dishes. It's depressing and generic-looking, mostly because of its location, but the food is top-rate. *631 N. Center St., tel. 209/943–0308. 5 blocks from Greyhound station. Open daily 9–9.*

Ye Olde Hoosier Inn. Try here for a cheap breakfast that will permanently raise your cholesterol level, in a setting that resembles an old-fashioned bordello. Enjoy your country sausage, eggs, muffin, toast, and hash browns for $4 while admiring the red velvet wallpaper and the platitudes written across the ceiling. What could make for a more pleasant breakfast companion than the constant reminder: "Prefer loss over unjust gain—for that brings grief but once." Lovers of kitsch, you have arrived. *1537 N. Wilson Way, tel. 209/463–0271. Open weekdays 6:30 AM–8:30 PM, Sat. 7 AM–9:30 PM, Sun. 7 AM–8:30 PM.*

AFTER DARK Those folks looking for a sports bar or a wet T-shirt contest will have no trouble in Stockton. Just head for any of the bars with a flashing Girls! Girls! Girls! neon sign. If that's not quite your speed, hop in your jalopy and go cruising on **Pacific Avenue** (yup, where it says NO CRUISING ZONE). If you tire of teenage mating rituals, visit the UOP campus and look for a frat party. Failing that, the **Shamrock Bar** (602 E. Market, tel.

209/462–2120) downtown has strong Irish coffee, pool tables, and regular Jaegermeister nights. **The Paradise Club,** on Lower Sacramento Road at Bear Creek Plaza, is Stockton's only full-time gay bar, with DJ, dance floor, and pool table. For you hipsters out there, rumor has it that the dance club **Stockton Rocks** (tel. 209/952–3474), at March and Pershing, features alternative music on Sunday nights.

OUTDOOR ACTIVITIES Temperatures in Stockton can hover in the low 100s during the summer, and it'll take a lot of doing just to avoid sun stroke. Fortunately, the California Delta is located within easy reach of Stockton, where swimming, fishing, boating, and even water skiing are easily come by. There aren't many places to rent equipment in Stockton, but the **California Delta Chambers** (Box 177, 49 Main St., Isleton 95641, tel. 916/777–5007) can supply you with maps and brochures of the region. If you send them a self-addressed, stamped envelope, along with a $3 check, they will mail you every brochure you could ever want about the Delta. Fishing is popular along the south fork of **Motelumne River,** near Lodi, as well as from the public piers in **Antioch** and **Rio Vista.** Closer to Stockton, you may fish at the Dos Reis Campground (*see* Camping, *above*) or Oak Grove Regional Park. For the cheapest of thrills, grab an inner tube and a six-pack and spend the day whoopin' and hollerin'. Tubing is mainly done on the Motelumne River.

NEAR STOCKTON • • •

PIXIE WOODS Pixie Woods is a very strange kids' park on the outskirts of Stockton, in the west section of **Louis Park.** For $1 you can spend a surreal afternoon with big cement replicas of all your favorite fairy tale characters, set in a very shady, green park near the San Joaquin River—fun for both the young and twisted at heart. *Take the Pershing exit off I–5, turn left on Monte Diablo Ave., tel. 209/944–8371. Open daily dawn–dusk.*

LODI Seven miles north of Stockton on Route 99, Lodi boasts no less than 10 top-rate wineries, several of which have tastings, tours, and picnic areas. The **Lodi Chamber of Commerce** (215 West Oak St., Lodi 95240, tel. 209/334–4773) distributes a brochure with the names and addresses of all wineries in the area. **Lodi Lake Park** and the **Motelumne River,** near Turner and Lower Sacramento roads, offer swimming, boating, and fishing. **Micke Grove Park,** 2 miles south of Lodi on Route 99 at the Armstrong exit, is a pleasant place to spend an afternoon, complete with a lush rose garden, a Japanese Garden, and a small zoo.

MANTECA Another sub-suburb of Stockton, Manteca's main (and formidable) attraction is **Oakwood Lake Resort,** the largest water-slide park on the West Coast. Spend a day careening down twisty chutes and near-vertical slides with thousands of screaming pre-teens busily cutting into line in front of you. Admission to the park is $14, but it's well worth the price if it's a hot day in Stockton. The slides are open daily June through August, weekends only in May and September. For some reason, Oakwood also has camping and picnic facilities; the campground is open year-round, but don't expect much more than a plot of exposed dirt and a few ramshackle tables. Sites run $15 a night, most with RV hookups. For camping information call 209/239–9566. *Woodward Ave., Manteca, tel. 209/239–2500. Located between I–5 and Rte. 99; take Rte. 120 to Airport Way, exit south, then west on Woodward Ave.*

MERCED Merced, 69 miles south of Stockton and 55 miles north of Fresno on Route 99, might be one of the more important towns to familiarize yourself with in the Central Valley, primarily because of its proximity to Yosemite. Lots of people head eagerly up to Yosemite in the morning and eventually end up in Merced by nightfall, stuck for an evening in Merced's Motel 6. If you're traveling to Yosemite on public transportation you may also end up with a layover in Merced, as all evening trains don't connect with buses to Yosemite until the next day.

Merced isn't the most interesting of towns, but there are a few stores and 50s-era diners along **Main Street.** Otherwise, head straight for the **Yosemite Gray Line** bus depot (tel. 209/384–1315) in the **Amtrak** station (324 24th St., tel. 209/383–1563). Gray Line offers one Yosemite-bound bus daily, leaving Merced mid-morning and arriving in

Yosemite by early afternoon. Fares are $15 one way, $28 round-trip. **Greyhound** (710 W. 116th St., tel. 209/722–2121) offers service to Yosemite twice daily at 8 AM and 3 PM, $14 one way and $28 round-trip. If you get stuck here for the night, however, do not fear. Merced handles much of the Yosemite overflow, and cheap rooms are plentiful. **Motel Drive,** just south of town (take the Motel Drive exit off Route 99) has an ample selection of budget hotels. Merced also has a small **hostel.** Its location changes every year, and only AYH members are accepted. For reservations and directions contact the **Central California Council** (Box 3645, Merced 95344, tel. 209/383–0686).

● ● ● FRESNO

"Fresno is all the home towns in America rolled into one."

Fresno, 55 miles south of Merced and 103 miles north of Bakersfield on Route 99, is the "crown jewel" of the San Joaquin Valley. Not surprisingly, Fresno also has a severe image problem. Part backwater town and part affluent suburbia, Fresno is not quite certain what kind of city it really wants to be. Its rich agricultural industry has made fortunes for the area's conservative, white, upper-middle-class residents while simultaneously providing work for one of the largest immigrant populations in the state. Even as it is made the butt of jokes throughout California (e.g., "What do you say to someone from Fresno with a job? Give me a burger and a small coke."), Fresno tries to cultivate highbrow art galleries, chili cook-offs, and strip-bars, all with equal unease. Yet Fresno has provided the world with such diverse gifts as the first raisins, the first McDonald's, writer William Saroyan, and that dynamic and wacky entertainer, Cher. Believe it or not, Fresno even had its own miniseries once—the creatively named "Fresno," starring Vicki Lawrence (don't look for it in the video store). Fresno is all the home towns of America rolled into one.

For budget travelers just passing through, the bars and restaurants downtown are probably the city's prime attraction. But if you've got some time, also look for the **Kearney Mansion Museum** (Kearney Blvd., 7 mi west of downtown, tel. 209/441–0862), built by raisin mogul M. Theo Kearney in the early 1900s. Open on weekends between 1 PM and 4 PM, the house has been restored and decorated with period furniture. The **Meux Home Museum** (at the intersection of Tulare and R Sts., tel. 209/233–8007), the last example of Victorian architecture in Fresno, has been refurbished to show how the wealthy folks used to live in the 1880s, when Fresno was one of California's most exclusive and affluent farming communities. **Roeding Park** (tel. 209/264–5988), one of the last bastions of natural beauty in urban Fresno, is an excellent place to wile away a few hours. In the park you'll find **Storyland,** an insipid and surreal fairy-tale playground, and the **Zoological Gardens,** which features a tropical rainforest and reptile house. Otherwise, head to the **Tower District,** an artist district of sorts that's filled with coffee houses, bookstores, and art galleries. The central attraction is the **Tower Theater** (815 E. Olive, tel. 209/485–9050), a restored playhouse that now features big-name musical acts. The Tower District is at the west end of Fresno (take Route 41 to the Blackstone off ramp).

BASICS

CURRENCY EXCHANGE Fresno's **Bank of America** exchanges foreign currencies at reasonable rates. *101 Van Ness St., at Tulare St., tel. 209/442–2800. Open Mon.–Thurs. 9–4, Fri. 9–6.*

DOCTORS AND DENTISTS Call Fresno's **Medical Referral Service** (tel. 209/224–4277) for information on doctors in the area, or the **Dental Referral Service** (tel. 209/225–5111) for similar assistance with dentists.

TOURIST INFORMATION The **Fresno Convention and Visitors Bureau** distributes a useful booklet that includes important phone numbers, attractions in the area, public transportation routes, and cheap dining/accommodation options. If you send them a S.A.S.E., they'll mail you more Fresno brochures than anyone could ever want. *808 M St., Fresno 93721, tel. 209/233–0836. Open weekdays 8–5.*

COMING AND GOING

BY TRAIN Three trains on their way to and from Los Angeles ($38) and San Francisco ($45) stop daily in Fresno's **Amtrak** station (corner of Tulare and Q Sts., tel. 209/486–7651 or 800/USA–RAIL), downtown. Luggage lockers are available for $1 for 24 hours, and have to be renewed each day in person. The Amtrak depot is open daily from 6 AM to 1 AM.

BY BUS **Greyhound** (1033 Broadway, tel. 209/268–9461) offers nine buses a day to and from San Francisco ($22); 12 buses a day to and from Los Angeles ($28). The station is open 24 hours, and there are lockers and a small waiting area inside. **Yosemite Gray Line** (2233 Ventura Blvd., tel. 209/443–5240) has daily service between Fresno and Yosemite National Park. Tickets cost $8 one way and $12 round-trip.

BY CAR **Route 99,** Fresno's main north–south lifeline, diverges from I–5 at the Grapevine and passes through Fresno and Sacramento on its way north to Chico, where it once again meets up with I–5. **Route 41** links Fresno with I–5 at Kettleman City, 50 miles south, and also with Yosemite National Park, 90 miles northeast. **Route 180** connects Fresno to Sequoia and Kings Canyon national parks, while **Route 168** leads east from Fresno to the Shaver Lake area in the Sierra National Forest.

BY PLANE Six airlines serve the **Fresno Airport** (5175 E. Clinton Way, tel. 209/498–4095): America West (tel. 800/247–5692), American Airlines (tel. 800/433–7300), American Eagle (tel. 800/433–7300), Delta (tel. 800/221–1212), and United and United Express (tel. 209/252–5711). Surprisingly, these carriers offer competitive rates both to and from Fresno, so it may not be a bad idea to bypass the Los Angeles and San Francisco airports and fly directly here if you're bound for many of California's national parks. The airport is located 4 miles northeast of downtown; public buses marked "Downtown" also make the trip every 15 minutes or so. Otherwise, **Airport Van Service** (tel. 209/453–1234) offers 24-hour door-to-door transportation to and from the airport for $6.

GETTING AROUND Downtown Fresno is the only area easily accessible by foot from the train and bus stations, but there's not much to see here besides a few boarded up buildings. You'll want to spend most of your time in the Tower District, and luckily **Fresno Area Express** (FAX) offers 15 routes connecting it with downtown. Buses run every 30 minutes and the fare is 60¢. Schedules that include route maps and time tables are available at the Convention and Visitor's Bureau (*see* Tourist Information, *above*) or from FAX. If you have your own car, take Route 41 to the Blackstone exit, where you'll find the eminently walkable Tower District. *FAX Office: corner of Fresno and Van Ness Sts., tel. 209/498–1122. Open weekdays 7 AM–6 PM.*

WHERE TO SLEEP The Convention and Visitor's Bureau (*see* Tourist Information, *above*) distributes a comprehensive guide to lodgings in the area. If you can't get your hands on this there's a string of budget motels off Route 99 at the **West Olive Street** and **Belmont** exits. Try the **Allstar Inn** (1240 N. Crystal St., at W. Olive St., tel. 209/237–0855) or the **Econo Lodge** (1804 W. Olive St., tel. 209/442–1082). To reach this area by bus from downtown, catch Bus 20 heading north (a convenient stop is at Van Ness and Fresno), and transfer to the westbound Bus 33 at Belmont or Olive.

Another cluster of cheap motels is on **N. Blackstone Drive,** north of downtown among the malls and car dealerships. Offerings are fairly sparse in downtown itself, but if you've reached the sleep-or-die state after 22 hours on a Greyhound bus try **Motel 7** (888 Broadway St., between Tulare and Inyo, tel. 209/485–7550), one block from the station. Fresno is not a hopping tourist town, so thankfully you won't be forced to pay through the nose for a sleazy room. Crowds are never a problem and most hotels have plenty of vacancies throughout the year. The bad news, unfortunately, is that Fresno has no other accommodation options. No youth hostels, no campgrounds—nothing. In Fresno, it's Motel Generic or bust.

FOOD Because of its large Mexican-American, Southeast Asian, and Armenian populations, Fresno has a number of good and reasonably priced ethnic restaurants. **Belmont Avenue,** east of Broadway Street, is the best place for Thai and Cambodian food, while **West Bullard Avenue** boasts a number of top-rate Armenian eateries. In particular try the **Hye Deli** (3083 W. Bullard, tel. 209/431–7798) for filling and cheap Armenian-esque sandwiches, or **Armenian Cuisine** (742 W. Bullard at Palm, tel. 209/435–4892) for a sit-down meal. If you're looking for livelier and trendier places, the Tower District has an ample supply of bistros, grills, and upscale French restaurants. Strangely enough, you won't find any produce for sale at Fresno's **Farmers' Market,** downtown at the intersection of Divisadero and Tulare streets. Instead, you will find a wide selection of Indian, Thai, Armenian, Vietnamese, Chinese, and Mexican food stands here, generally priced under $6.

UNDER $10 **Butterfield Brewing Company.** The Butterfield serves surprisingly good food to accompany its home-brewed beers. They have excellent chili ($5), stuffed chicken wings ($10), a monster-size Oriental chicken salad ($6.50), and a mouth-watering vegetarian pasta primavera ($8). Pints of their homemade stouts and ales fetch a somewhat pricey $3.50. The Butterfield is popular with the art and business crowds, and its dining room is generally packed come 6 PM. There's almost always a place in the Butterfield's bar, in case you can't get a table immediately. It's in the Tower District. *7777 Olive Ave., tel. 209/264–5521. Open daily 11 AM–2 AM, kitchen closes at 9.*

Livingstone's Restaurant and Pub. American-based cuisine with an international flair. In particular, Livingstone's apricot-ginger chicken ($10) and cajun burger ($6) are quite good. This place doubles as a restaurant and trendy bar so it's packed like a sardine can with libidinal locals on weekend nights. Also in the Tower District. *831 E. Fern Ave., tel. 209/485–5198. Open daily 11 AM–2 AM.*

Rafael's Mexicatessen. Part Mexican deli, part restaurant, and part tortilla factory, Rafael's serves some of the best and cheapest eats in all Fresno. Pay a visit before 6 PM and watch Rafael's cooks lovingly prepare tortillas by hand—Dios mio, it's a beautiful sight. Even better, most meals are under $6. *94 E. Belmont (at Palm St.), tel. 209/264–1684. Open 7:30 AM–8 PM.*

DESSERT AND COFFEEHOUSES **City Cafe.** Offering espresso drinks, muffins, desserts, and heartier specialties like sandwiches, salads, and soup, the City Cafe is a favorite power-breakfast spot for the car phone/BMW set. At night, however, it's transformed into a hangout for the young, bored, and angst-filled. Located north of downtown. *5048 N. Blackstone, tel. 209/224–4399.*

Java. In the heart of Fresno's artsy Tower District, this café has become the city's hippest hangout in the last few years—the unofficial meeting place for Fresno's mods, long-hairs, and the poetically inclined. Espresso drinks fetch a pricey $2–$4, but it's worth it just to watch the antics of the hardcore mods who give Java its wacked-out charm. *805 E. Olive, tel. 209/237–5282. Open daily 7 AM–11 PM, Fri. and Sat. till 2 AM.*

AFTER DARK Fresno has a large population of artists, musicians, clubbers, and hip-hop bozos. As a result, Fresno's club and live music scene is pretty decent, especially if you're into the mod (i.e., bomber jacket, Doc Martin boots, and Vespa) thing. Ask the folks at **Ragin Records** (639 E. Olive St., tel. 209/485–9926) for advice on how to make the most of your Saturday night if you're having trouble finding something to do. The walls are covered with flyers listing the city's upcoming and alternative events.

Ever since the teenage pastime of cruising was abolished (a conviction of cruising now carries a fine of up to $250), cheap thrills in Fresno have been hard to find. However, ask around to see if free weekly movies are still being screened on the wall of the **Chicken Pie Shop** (861 E. Olive St., tel. 209/237–5042) in the Tower District. Bring a lawn chair and take a seat right there in the parking lot. Otherwise, head to the Fig Garden Shopping Mall (at Shaw and Palm streets) and its Thursday night **Fig Gig,** a free weekly jazz concert also held in a parking lot.

BARS AND CLUBS Thirsty? If you can drink all 90 of **Goodbodies** (2915 N. Maroa Ave., tel. 209/229–2355) tap beers in one month—that's three a day—you get your name immortalized on a plaque. Needless to say, Goodbodies caters to the heavy-drinking crowd and on weekend nights it's absolutely packed with sociable locals. The **Butterfield Brewing**

Company (*see* Food, *above*) serves four kinds of homemade beer and offers live music Wednesday through Sunday. **Nettwork** (50 E. Heindon Ave., tel. 209/436–8703) has dancing to hip-hop, house, and industrial music as well as live local bands. Their recent acquisition of a liquor license, however, may mean that a more mainstream sound is in the works. The cover is around $5. In the Tower District, the **Wild Blue** (1145 N. Fulton, tel. 209/268–1379) hosts a wide variety of local bands, some good and some bad. On a typical night you'll find Chili Pepper-esque funk and grungy rock. There are also two predominantly gay clubs in town: **Express** (708 N. Blackstone, tel. 209/233–1791), a popular weekend-only dance club, mostly for men; and **Shades** (1616 N. Cedar Ave., tel. 209/251–2797), a women's dance club that has a full bar and weekly country-and-western dance lessons.

BAKERSFIELD

In Bakersfield, the street named "Panoramic Way" overlooks not golden hills and blue sky but a vast expanse of destitute fields and grimy oil derricks. In Bakersfield, short hair and rap music are signs of moral turpitude; long hair and heavy-metal music signs of a proper upbringing. In Bakersfield, people still proudly display "Saddamize Iraq" bumper stickers on the back of their 4-by-4 trucks.

Eighty-six miles north of Los Angeles, the city of Bakersfield remains stubbornly insulated not only from southern California's trendiness, but also from its own abundant ironies. Its proximity to farm land and oil fields has caused it to grow dramatically as families move here for work and affordable housing, but even so, Bakersfield tries hard to retain its small-town feel. Fiercely loyal to its heritage of country music, country cooking, and conservative country values, Bakersfield is the sort of place where gay bashing and racism are quite common. Of course not everyone here fits into the mold, but steer clear if you're not prepared for closed minds and a "good ol' boy" mentality. Except for its proximity to **Kern River** and **Lake Isabella** (*see* Near Bakersfield, *below*), Bakersfield doesn't have much to offer. There aren't any official tourist attractions here, only a few bars and greasy truck stops to distract you on your way somewhere else. If you're traveling on Route 99 toward Fresno or Yosemite, you may want to stop for some gas and a quick bite to eat, perhaps at one of its excellent Basque restaurants.

BASICS

TOURIST INFORMATION **Kern County Board of Trade.** Information about the entire county, including guides for lodging and regional transit, is available here. The staff is knowledgeable and helpful. *2101 Oak St., tel. 805/861–2367. Open weekdays 8–5.*

Greater Bakersfield Visitors Bureau. Only use this place as a secondary resource; their information is sparse and the staff seems confused. *1033 Truxtun Ave., tel. 805/327–4421. Open Mon.–Thurs. 8:30–5, Fri. 8:30–4.*

COMING AND GOING

BY TRAIN Bakersfield is the terminus for Amtrak's San Joaquin line; trains travel daily from Bakersfield to Oakland ($45) and Sacramento ($60), with stops in Fresno and Stockton. If you're headed to or from Los Angeles and San Bernardino, Amtrak has chartered buses that make the trip three times a day for a small additional fee. There's a motel three blocks away from the station (*see* Where to Sleep, *below*), or walk west on Truxtun to Oak Street where Bus 8 bus will go by a Motel 6 to the south or an E-Z 8 Motel to the north. There are no lockers at the depot, but you can deposit your bags for overnight storage at the Amtrak annex next door. Bakersfield's **Amtrak station** (at the corner of 15th and F Sts. downtown, tel. 800/872–7245) is open daily from 4:30 AM to midnight.

BY BUS Greyhound offers comprehensive service to Bakersfield; nine buses a day from Los Angeles ($18) and six per day from San Francisco ($26) and Sacramento ($29). Three blocks north of the Amtrak station in the center of town, the **Greyhound depot** (18th and F Sts., tel. 805/327–7376) is open around the clock. Lockers here are available for $1 per 24 hours.

BY CAR Route 99 runs north–south through town, connecting Fresno (89 miles north) with I–5 and Los Angeles (85 miles south). **Route 178** will take you east through the Kern River Canyon toward Lake Isabella and Sequoia National Forest. **Route 58** runs southeast, connecting Bakersfield with the town of Mojave (63 miles east) and Route 101 (114 miles west). **Route 65** heads north toward Porterville and Sequoia National Park.

GETTING AROUND Bakersfield sprawls around the main highways in a vast expanse of unremarkable shopping malls and housing developments. **Downtown Bakersfield,** roughly the area between F Street and M Street and 15th Street and 24th Street, encompasses the train station, the bus station, and any remnants of character that the town might once have possessed. Downtown is easily managed on foot and is kind of interesting in a '50s sort of way. The main office of the **Golden Empire Transit District** (GETD: tel. 805/327–7685) is at the corner of 21st and Chester; transit maps and bus schedules are available here. GETD operates 14 lines within Bakersfield and several routes to Lake Isabella and Kernville (*see* Near Bakersfield, *below*).

WHERE TO SLEEP **Union** and **South Union avenues** are lined with cheap motels that vary in degrees of seediness; there is very little to distinguish between them so don't bother trying. North of town along Route 99 you'll come across another cluster of budget motels, once again unworthy of note. If you're having trouble deciding which fleabag to spend the night in, the Kern County Board of Trade (*see* Tourist Information, *above*) distributes a guide to all of the hotels and motels in the area that includes addresses, phone numbers, cost, and a breakdown of facilities.

The **Downtowner Inn** (301 Chester Ave., tel. 805/327–7122) is the only motel within easy reach of the Amtrak and Greyhound stations; it's also located near several restaurants and has a microwave and refrigerator for guest use. Even better, all rooms have 26-channel cable TV for free. Adequate doubles run from $30 to $42. Otherwise, **Motel 6,** a cheap and reliable favorite, has three locations in Bakersfield: one near downtown on Oak Street between California Avenue and the Stockdale Route (350 Oak St., tel. 805/326–1222); one near nothing in particular (5241 Olive Tree Ct., tel. 805/392–9700); and another near Route 99 (2727 White La., tel. 805/834–2828).

STUDENT HOUSING **Bakersfield College** sporadically offers housing during the summer depending on demand. When available, two- to three-bed dorm rooms run $10 per person. All guests must provide their own linen, but at least all the rooms have decent bathroom facilities. Reservations are recommended. *1801 Panorama Dr., Bakersfield 93305, tel. 805/395–4356.*

CAMPGROUNDS **Kern River County Park,** located 15 minutes away by car on the banks of Lake Ming, offers sites with fireplaces, picnic tables, piped water, toilets, and access to showers. Both RV and tent spaces fetch $10 per night, pets $2 extra. Lake Ming isn't particularly scenic, but it's less depressing than downtown Bakersfield. Depending on drought conditions swimming is sometimes allowed in the small lake. *Alfred Harrell Hwy., tel. 805/861–2345 or 805/872–3179. Drive east on Rte. 178 from town; turn north on Alfred Harrell Hwy. and follow the signs to Lake Ming.*

FOOD Bakersfield abounds with two very disparate types of cuisine: that of the greasy, truck-stop sort and—believe it or not—that of the Basques. Little remains of Basque culture in Bakersfield, but you should at least try a Basque meal while you're here—a hearty combination of garlic, tomato salsa, spiced meat, beans, and bread. Even better, the raucous communal dining experience you'll find in these Basque restaurants is just like eating with the peasants in the Old Country, except for the Merle Haggard playing on the radio. If you're looking to save a few bucks head downtown to **Happy Jack's** (20th and G Sts., tel. 805/323–1661), a popular greasy spoon that offers slices of homemade pie ($1.25) and monster-sized burgers ($2.65). For the ultimate, however, grab a burger at **Zingo's** (3201 Pierce Rd., tel. 805/324–3640), a small, 24-hour truck stop off Route 99. For dessert, **Dewar's** (1120 Eye St., tel. 805/322–0933) is an old-fashioned soda fountain and candy shop that's been a Bakersfield institution since 1909. Near 12th and California streets, this is a good place to kill time while waiting for an Amtrak train.

UNDER $10 **The Garden Spot.** When you need a roughage fix to counteract the effects of one too many chicken-fried-steak dinners, make a beeline for this place. Specialties include homemade soups, fresh muffins, fruit plates, and a phenomenal all-you-can-eat salad bar ($7). *3320 Truxtun Ave., at Oak St., tel. 805/323–3236. Open Mon.–Sat. 11 AM–8 PM.*

The hills around Bakersfield are filled with sheep and their Basque-speaking shepherds who settled in the area more than 100 years ago.

Lorene's South-West Coffee Shop. Down home Okie food in a cutesy atmosphere; there are lots of quilted things with duck motifs hanging on the walls. Try their biscuits-and-gravy breakfast ($4.10) or three-alarm chili ($2.70), guaranteed to set your mouth on fire. Lorene's is popular with truck drivers and locals. *2500 New Stine Rd., tel. 805/832–5396. Open daily 6 AM–9 PM.*

UNDER $15 **Noriega Hotel.** Built in 1899, this hotel is the unofficial meeting place of Bakersfield's Basque shepherds; in the afternoon they gather at the bar to play *Mus* (a Basque card game), in the evening to eat, drink, and reminisce about the old country. Food is served family style, and it's "all you can eat." Diners sit at elongated picnic tables, elbow to elbow, and help themselves to a little of this or a little of that as heaping plates of top-rate Basque food are passed from person to person. The Noriega Hotel offers two sittings daily, one at noon and the other at 6:30; $10 for lunch, $16 for dinner. *525 Summer St., at Baker St., tel. 805/322–8419. Closed Mon.*

The Woolgrowers. A family-style Basque restaurant that offers mounds of food at reasonable prices. If you aren't hungry enough for the standard five-course meal you can order "the setup," an à la carte entrée with everything (beans, bread, salsa, french fries, and vegetable) but no meat ($5). Otherwise, a complete meal runs $8 to $12. If you're ordering à la carte, be sure to try the hearty pork stew served on a bed of rice ($7). *620 E. 19th St., tel. 805/327–9584. Open Mon.–Sat. 11:30 AM–2 PM, 6:30–9:30 PM.*

AFTER DARK Cruising **Chester Avenue** is the big activity among the under-21 set, and a fascinating cultural phenomenon for everyone else. If you tire of cruising, you and your honey can go up to **Panoramic Way** to make out. The vista of oil derricks may just inspire a romantic frenzy. If not, there's a cocktail lounge and piano bar in the old, wonderfully decrepit **Padre Hotel** (18th and H Sts., tel. 805/322–1419), where college students congregate for cheap drinks and Frank Sinatra tunes. **Guthrie's Alley Cat** (in the alley of Eye St., between 18th and 19th Sts., tel. 805/324–6328) attracts a crowd that one patron described as "a lot of recently divorced people trying to look just out of college." The atmosphere is progressive and offbeat, at least by Bakersfield standards. At the **Casablanca** (20th and N Sts.), gay culture and country-western culture merge with an ease that's befuddling. If you're lucky you'll get to see a square dance performed by people wearing, among other things, black leather and studs. Even better, most everyone in Casablanca is friendly and unassuming—a rarity in Bakersfield.

NEAR BAKERSFIELD

KERNVILLE AND LAKE ISABELLA The Kern River, which originates near Mt. Whitney and runs through Sequoia National Forest before draining into irrigation canals outside Bakersfield, has excellent white-water rafting opportunities. Five rafting companies operate out of nearby **Kernville** that offer half-day to week-long trips for all levels of experience. The **Cannell Meadow Ranger District** (Box 6, Kernville 93238, tel. 619/376–3781) in Kernville has information about rafting, hiking, and camping in the area.

Lake Isabella, the largest freshwater lake in southern California, is a popular spot with locals on the weekend. Its setting isn't gorgeous but it does beget year-round fishing, swimming, and boating. Unless you have a boat, however, you should base yourself near Kernville and just come to the lake for a swim. The lake is also managed by the Cannell Meadow Ranger District, so call them with any questions. From Bakersfield, take Route 178 east to Lake Isabella; or head north from Isabella along Route 155 to Kernville. It's only an hour drive from Bakersfield, but if you'd prefer to spend the night in something that resembles the great outdoors **Paradise Cove** (10700 Route 178, tel. 619/379–8484) in Lake Isabella offers the cheapest rooms around. Singles start at $25, doubles at $30.

THE CENTRAL COAST 8

By Susan Williams

The California coast reaches all the way from Mexico to Oregon, but the Central Coast area is by far the most popular stretch—running from **Santa Cruz,** 75 miles south of San Francisco, to **Santa Barbara,** a large and affluent beach community 90 miles north of Los Angeles. From the misty redwood forests to the stark mountains and wilderness of **Big Sur,** the Central Coast is one of California's most evocative and cherished retreats. Hikers will appreciate the miles of trails that twist their way through the sprawling **Los Padres National Forest,** a thriving refuge for California's diverse wildlife. Harried students will forget their troubles on seemingly endless stretches of sand—sunning, scuba diving, surfing, or just gazing at the seals, otters, and pods of grey whales offshore.

Route 1 will lead you on a somewhat perilous journey along California's jagged shore—the very edge of the earth, it seems. In addition to the towns of Santa Cruz, Monterey, and Carmel, you can explore Big Sur's forests and hiking trails or head down the coast for a peak at the garish, gaudy, and awesome **Hearst Castle,** perched high on a hill in **San Simeon.** Routes 1 and 101 merge briefly at **San Luis Obispo,** one of the coast's larger and more charming cities. Two hours farther south you'll find yourself in the small, obscenely wealthy community of Santa Barbara—an upscale playground for L.A.'s weekend refugees and the site of former President Reagan's summer ranch.

Surprisingly, the best time to visit the Central Coast is not during the summer months, when the seaboard is blanketed with fog, but in the fall or early spring, when the fog rolls away and temperatures linger in the 70s. Also keep in mind that camping is often the only cheap option—under $25—along the coast.

Santa Cruz

Originally founded as a mission town, Santa Cruz has come to embrace several identities. The old-time residents, many of Italian descent, still look askance at the liberal students and hippies who have been migrating to the town ever since the University of California opened its "alternative, no-stress" branch here in the 1960s. The carnival-like boardwalk is downtown Santa Cruz at its flashiest, drawing legions of hormone-crazed teenagers from Salinas and San Jose every weekend. The boardwalk's most popular attraction is the **Giant Dipper,** one of the best and oldest wooden roller coasters in the world, a harrowing ride that affords you a brief panorama of the Monterey Bay before plunging you down toward the beach. If your stomach's not quite up to such antics, Santa Cruz's picture-perfect coast is a great place to escape the weekend bustle. The rocks off the craggy shore are favored perches for seals

Santa Cruz

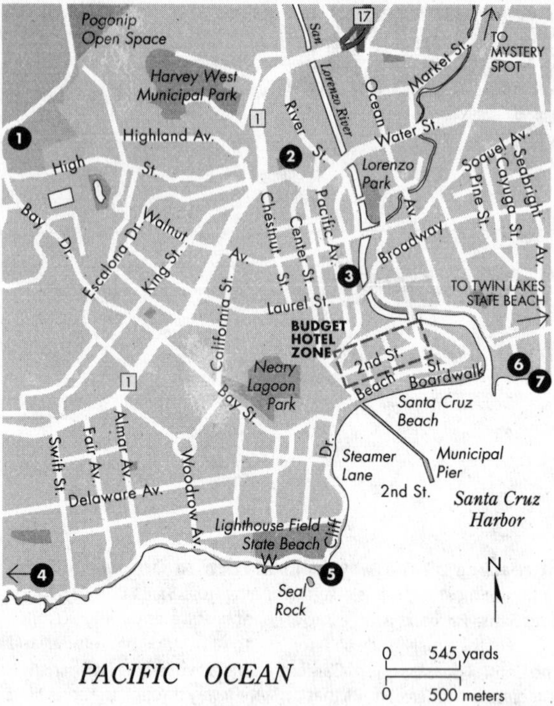

Greyhound and Metro Center, **3**
Mission Santa Cruz, **2**
Natural Bridges State Beach, **4**
Santa Cruz City Museum of Natural History, **6**
Santa Cruz Surfing Museum/ Lighthouse, **5**
Seabright Beach, **7**
University of California at Santa Cruz, **1**

and sea lions, the beaches are thronged by surfers and their retinue, and the hills surrounding the town fade into redwood forests ideal for hiking or reveled musing.

No matter where you wander in Santa Cruz, you're never far from a healing circle, a channeling class, or a workshop about how what you did when you weren't really you is causing trouble for the real you now.

Santa Cruz is also a center for all things New Age. There's something gothic about Santa Cruz's version of the New Age—perhaps it's the presence of those sublime stands of redwoods brooding over the town like something out of a Brothers Grimm story; perhaps it's the incessant winter rain and summer fog that cast a subtle gloom over the city; or perhaps it's the easy access to hallucinogens and the number of soul-seekers wandering the streets. On a good day, Santa Cruz is resplendent and joyful—pure magic. On a bad day, however, it's positively sinister. According to some locals, Santa Cruz is an epicenter of powerful but often undirected energy that can be used for both positive or negative purposes—perhaps it's New Age mumbo-jumbo, but there may be more than a grain of truth in it all. That would explain why people who move here tend to fall into one of two categories: those who remain forever, beguiled by the area's overpowering natural beauty and alternative, altruistic lifestyle, and those who flee with their lives in shambles.

Unfortunately, when the 7.1-magnitude Loma Prieta earthquake struck on October 17, 1989, it tore the heart out of Santa Cruz. Parts of the historic **Pacific Garden Mall,** center of the thriving downtown area, were leveled and nearly 100 people killed. While the world looked at endless film footage of a few collapsed houses in San Francisco's Marina district, the most extensive damage was really done in Santa Cruz and the neighboring towns of Watsonville and Capitola, only a few miles from the earthquake's epicenter. Santa Cruz still looks a bit shell shocked, and rebuilding in the downtown area has been slow. Some of the town's most popular stores are still housed in tents, whose semi-permanent appearance and euphemistic designation as "pavilions" give Santa Cruz even today a strange, apocalyptic sort of feel—just another part of Santa Cruz's brooding appeal.

BASICS

AMERICAN EXPRESS American Express doesn't have an office in town, but **Riordan-Winnett Travel** (903 Pacific Ave., tel. 408/438–1130) is an AmEx representative.

DOCTORS AND DENTISTS **Dentist Referral Hotline.** *Tel. 800/336–8478; call weekdays 7–7, Sat. 8–6.*

Maple Street Clinic, billed as a center for alternative health care, offers chiropractic treatment, acupuncture, and massage therapy. *115 Maple St., tel. 408/423–3713. Between Pacific Ave. and Center St. downtown. Appointments necessary. Open weekdays 9–6.*

Santa Cruz Dominican Hospital. *1555 Soquel Ave., tel. 408/462–7700. Take Bus 71 on Soquel Ave. from Metro Center. Open 24 hrs.*

LUGGAGE STORAGE Lockers are available at the **Greyhound** station for $1 a day, and $3 for each additional day. *425 Front St., tel. 408/423–1800. Next to Metro Center. Open weekdays 7:45 AM–8:25 PM, weekends 7:45–10:45 AM, 1–3:50 PM, 6:30–8:25 PM.*

TOURIST INFORMATION **The Visitor Information Center** has a friendly staff and tons of free pamphlets, including the mediocre *California Coast* tourist magazine. They can't help with room reservations, however. Maps will set you back $1 each. *701 Front St., tel. 408/425–1234. 2 blocks north of Metro Center. Open daily 9–5.*

COMING AND GOING

BY TRAIN You can't get to Santa Cruz directly by train, but **Caltrain** (tel. 408/291–5651 or 800/558–8661) offers daily train service between San Jose and San Francisco for $4. From the San Jose Caltrain station (Cahill and W. San Fernando St.) take the **Santa Cruz Caltrain Connector** (tel. 408/423–1214) to the **Metro Center** (920 Pacific Ave.) in Santa Cruz. The bus leaves every two hours on weekdays, less often on weekends; it takes an hour and costs $5.

BY BUS **Green Tortoise** touring buses (tel. 408/462–6437) pass through Santa Cruz on Monday and Friday. Catch up with the whimsical "tortoises" in the Safeway parking lot on the 2000 block of Mission Street, near Younglove Avenue. Fares are $10 from San Francisco to Santa Cruz, and about $20 from Santa Cruz to Los Angeles. Otherwise, **Greyhound** (425 Front St., tel. 408/423–1800) makes three runs daily between San Francisco and Salinas that stop in Santa Cruz. There's direct service between Santa Cruz and San Francisco ($10) four times a day. **Highway 17 Express Bus** (tel. 408/425–8600 or 408/688–8600) has hourly service, and, at $1, is the cheapest way to travel between San Jose and Santa Cruz during the week. Buses stop in Santa Cruz at the intersection of Soquel Drive and Route 1, and in San Jose at the corner of Third Street and San Fernando Avenue, one block from San Jose State University.

HITCHHIKING Despite its "mellow vibes," Santa Cruz is a dangerous place to hitchhike. Slightly embarrassed locals will regale you with stories of mass murders and abducted women whose bodies were found in the hills. If you're still foolhardy enough to try it, a good spot to catch a ride north out of town is at the corner of Route 1 (Mission Street) and Swift Street by the "Litter Removal" sign (no kidding!). Hitching northeast along Route 17 toward San Jose or south along Route 1 is more difficult. Try standing at the Ocean Street on-ramp on 17. Otherwise, head to the **UCSC rideboard** at Bay Tree Books, the college bookstore, located in the center of campus. The availability of rides varies with the time of year, and some money to cover the cost of gas is appreciated, if not expected.

BY CAR You can get to either San Francisco or Monterey in about 1½ hours on Route 1. San Jose is about 45 minutes away along Route 17, but watch out for traffic tie-ups on weekends when the entire Silicon Valley heads for the beaches.

● ● ● GETTING AROUND

Santa Cruz is perched on the edge of Monterey Bay, cut in half by the San Lorenzo River. The town is full of crooked and confusing streets, so keep a sharp eye on a map (unless you're *looking* to lose yourself). Route 1 becomes **Mission Street,** the town's main thoroughfare, when it enters Santa Cruz, and resumes its old identity on the way out. **Bay Street** and **High Street** both funnel into UCSC, while the Boardwalk is on **Beach Street** just west of the river. Downtown Santa Cruz, the Boardwalk, and the pier are all within comfortable walking distance of each other, and if you're feeling energetic the walk along **West Cliff Drive** from the boardwalk to the lighthouse is wonderfully scenic. Biking is the best way to get around Santa Cruz. Many of the streets have wide bike lanes and the weather is quite moderate, especially in spring and summer. Bring your wheels from home if you can, since renting can be expensive. If you have to, **Surf City Rentals** (46 Front St., near the boardwalk, tel. 408/423–9050) has bicycles for $18 for half a day.

BY BUS Bus service is efficient and fairly easy to use. The **Santa Cruz Metropolitan District Transit (SCMDT)** operates from the **Metro Center.** Any bus in town will eventually take you to the Metro Center, where you can pick up a copy of *Headways,* a free pamphlet that lists all bus routes. The fare is about $1, but you can purchase a special all-day pass for $2 on any bus or at the Metro Center. Exact change is required and buses will not take dollar bills; change machines are available at the Metro Center. *920 Pacific Ave., tel. 408/425–8600 or 408/688–8600. Open daily 7 AM–9 PM. Information booth open in lobby weekdays 8–5, weekends 10–4.*

BY CAR Except on summer weekends, driving and parking are not difficult in Santa Cruz, even downtown. Free two-hour parking is available along Front and Cedar streets; on weekends, some of the parking lots are free all day. Other possible parking spots are the Santa Cruz County Building (701 Ocean St.) and the River Street Parking Garage, which runs shuttles to the beach on weekends.

● ● ● WHERE TO SLEEP

Santa Cruz is a resort town and, as such, it isn't cheap. The local youth hostel is probably the best deal around if you can get a room. Camping in the area is great, but campgrounds fill up quickly in the summer months. Hotels and motels charge $40–$50 per night during the summer, but at other times—ironically the best times to visit Santa Cruz—most hotels drop their prices $10–$30. Behind the boardwalk on Second Street, Third Street, and Riverside Avenue are some rather cheesy hotels that rarely fill up, but you'll find comparably priced motels clustered on Mission and Ocean streets that are much more comfortable. In particular, try the **Sunset Inn** (2424 Mission St., tel. 408/423–3471), a semi-expensive establishment that offers clean rooms in a pinch. Their room rates range from $45 (one person, one bed) to $55 (two people, two beds). For a special treat try one of several good B&Bs. One to check out is the downtown **Babbling Brook Inn** (1025 Laurel St., tel. 408/427–2437) where rooms come complete with private bath and a fireplace or Jacuzzi. The rates, which include a full breakfast, range from $85 to $135 per night for two. If you want to be pampered go to the **Darling House** (314 Westcliff Dr., tel. 408/458–1958), near the beach, which has rooms that range from $95 to $225 for two, including a full breakfast.

UNDER $30 **American Country Inn.** It's a ways out of town and sits on the remains of a mobile-home park, but this inviting inn has pleasant, antique-filled rooms and rates as low as $25 per night during the week, $35 on weekends. If you're sick of charmless Holiday Inns and Motel 6s head here. Call ahead, however, as it's often full. *645 7th Ave., tel. 408/476–6424. Take Bus 65, get off at 7th Ave. and Brommer St. and then walk west* *on 7th for about 10 min. 19 rooms, some with bath. Reservations recommended in summer.*

UNDER $40 **Best Inn.** The rooms are very ordinary at this hotel run by a friendly Texan, but at least they're clean. Free coffee is served all day in the lobby, and all rooms have a TV and phone. Winter rates start at $29; summer rates at $50. Reservations are recommended. *370 Ocean St. at Broadway, tel. 408/458–9220. Take Bus 68 or 69 to corner of Ocean St. and Soquel Ave., then walk south along Ocean. Wheelchair access.*

Villa del Mar Motel and **Peter Pan Motel.** These two motels share the same office, the same rates, the same address, and (surprise! surprise!) the same management. They're both a bit rundown, and the rooms in both places are dark and musty, but at least they're well located in downtown Santa Cruz. *Riverside Ave., tel. 408/423–9449 or 408/423–1393. Across street from Budget 8 Motel. All rooms with bath.*

HOSTELS **Santa Cruz Youth Hostel.** This friendly hostel has small, clean rooms with white-washed walls and bunk beds. You have to be a member to stay, but you can sign up on the premises for $25. The hostel has two communal bathrooms and a kitchen facility, and beds for 20 people. Check-in is at 5 PM, but rooms fill up earlier, especially in summer—if you can, stop by early in the morning (before 9) to make a claim. A decent, comfortable bunk bed will run you $10–$15 a night, depending on the season. *511 Broadway, near Ocean St., tel. 408/423–8304. 10-min walk from downtown: Take Soquel Ave. to the east side of the San Lorenzo River, turn right on Ocean St. and left on Broadway Ave.; or take Bus 68, which stops in front of hostel.*

CAMPGROUNDS **Big Basin Redwoods State Park.** An hour's drive outside Santa Cruz, this is a great place to camp and hike in virgin redwood forests. The park has 144 tent and RV campsites and a number of undeveloped trail camps. In particular, try the 11-mile **Skyline-to-Sea Trail** where you'll find fire pits scattered every 2 miles or so. Bus 40 runs from Waddell Creek, where the trail ends, to Santa Cruz. All campsites—including the trail camps—hover around $12 per night throughout the year. *Tel. 408/338–6132. Take Rte. 98 north to Rte. 236 and continue north. Bus 35 leaves twice daily from Metro Center on weekends.*

Henry Cowell Redwoods State Park. Fifteen miles north of Santa Cruz, this 111-site campground is buffered by a redwood forest and a stunning series of rocky cliff faces. Things get a little out of hand here during the summer when RV homes and screaming teens overrun the place, but otherwise this is a camper's paradise. Communal showers and toilets on site. Reservations are accepted March–October. Both tent and RV sites are around $15 a night. *101 N. Big Trees Park Rd., Felton 95018, tel. 408/335–4598 or 408/438–2396. Take Graham Hill Rd. from Rte. 1, or Bus 30 from Metro Center (about 45 min away).*

New Brighton State Beaches. It's located high above the ocean on a large cliff, and almost every site has an incredible view of the coast. Spaces are available for tent and RV campers, but most have little privacy. Reservations required March–November; sites generally cost $15 throughout the year. *1500 Park Ave., tel. 408/475–4850. Bus 71 goes from the Metro Center to the corner of Soquel Ave. and Park Ave., but leaves you with a long walk.*

ROUGHING IT Santa Cruz has a reputation as a mellow, easy-going town, but the police nevertheless frown on people sleeping in public places. Lots of homeless people try it anyway, even though the cops periodically patrol the beaches and parks and issue waves of citations. If you're willing to take the risk, try one of the small beaches south of town, along Route 1. As long as you don't light a campfire or make a lot of noise you may be left alone.

● ● ● FOOD

To say that Santa Cruzians are health conscious doesn't quite do justice to the situation. Needless to say, there are plenty of cafés, delis, and small restaurants downtown—bordered by Front Street, Pacific Avenue, and Cedar Street—that offer health-oriented menus. If your system is too delicate for health food, look for the markets, fast-food chains, and greasy-spoon coffee shops along Mission Street. For an informal dining experience, try **Uppercrust Pizza** (2415 Mission St., tel. 48/423–9010), popular with Santa Cruz students, or **Tacos Moreno** (1053 Water St., tel. 408/429–6095), a small hole-in-the-wall that sells the best tacos ($3) in town. On the U.C. Santa Cruz campus look for **Sluggo's** (Porter College, 1156 High St., tel. 408/429–6807), a small but popular coffee shop that serves cheap pizza and beer to bleary-eyed UCSC students.

This is a town where even Rick's Charbroiler Pit has a vegetarian menu.

UNDER $5 **The Bagelry.** This deli warehouse specializes in funky bagel spreads. If you're tired of dull bagels that pack no punch, try the homemade "Pink Flamingo" spread (blended cream cheese, lox, and dill, $2.50) or the "Luna" spread (pesto, ricotta, and almonds, $3). A plain bagel with cream cheese costs $1.30, but plain bagels are for the taste bud-timid only; they have some great stuff here you won't find at home, so go on—be bold! If you're short on cash try the "three-seed slug"—a flat, wide bagel without the hole for 60¢. There are two Bagelrys in Santa Cruz, both downtown. *320-A Cedar St., tel. 408/429–8049; 1636 Seabright Ave., tel. 408/462–9888. Open weekdays 6:30 AM–5:30 PM, Sat. 7:30 AM–5:30 PM, Sun. 7:30 AM–4 PM.*

Dolphin Restaurant. Work your way to the end of Santa Cruz's pier and grab an order of fish-and-chips ($5) from the outside window of the Dolphin Restaurant. If you'd rather sit, head to the adjoining restaurant where in addition to the fried fish you'll find burgers ($2) and hearty clam chowder ($2.95). *End of the pier, tel. 408/426–5830. Open daily 9 AM–9:30 PM, weekends until 10 PM.*

King Chwan. Around the corner from the youth hostel, King Chwan has an amazing lunch deal—soup, side dish, tea, Chinese entrée, and fortune cookie for $3.95. The lighting is bright, the decor tacky, and the place looks like a large tract house, but for $3.95 you can't complain. Even better, the food isn't half bad. *415 Ocean St., across bridge from Front St., tel. 408/429–5898. Open daily 11:30 AM–10 PM, weekends until 11 PM. Wheelchair access.*

UNDER $10 **Gamil's.** Entering this place is like stepping into an ancient Egyptian living room. It's musty, dark, and cluttered with knickknacks and tacky souvenirs from the Nile Valley. The Egyptian and Middle Eastern cuisine, however, is phenomenal. Try the vegetable *maza* plate or the excellent falafel. Even more exotic is the *tammera hindi,* a sourberry fruit drink, and *sah'lab,* a sweet rice drink made by Gamil himself. Dishes cost about $8 and are large enough for two to share. There's another, more touristy Gamil's at the end of the wharf, which is definitely to be avoided. *316 Pacific Ave., 2 blocks from pier, tel. 408/426–9377. Open daily 5 PM–9 PM.*

Saturn Cafe. This restaurant, serving hearty and cheap food in a neo-cosmic atmosphere, is a great place to eat, read, and watch the interstellar locals. If it's warmth you need, try the lentil chili for $3. For greens connoisseurs, the Titan salad ($7) is big and satisfying. Wash it all down with Bargetto's (a local winery) Ollalieberry wine. You can sip coffee here while your wash tumbles at the laundromat behind the café. *1230 Mission Blvd., near Laurel, tel. 408/429–8505. Open weekdays 11:30 AM–12:30 AM, weekends noon–12:30 AM.*

Zachary's. This is *the* place to go for breakfast. The huge stack of pancakes and the family-size omelets are definitely worth the $5 price. The eating area is small and crowded—usually packed like a sardine can—but the outstanding food is worth the hassle. Try to stay away on weekends, however, as it often takes up to an hour to get a table. *819 Pacific Ave., tel. 408/427–0646. Open Tues.–Sun. 7 AM–2:30 PM.*

DESSERT/COFFEEHOUSES The café scene is a small but integral part of the city's social life, especially on weekend nights. This may be because of the absence of nighttime diversions for the under-21 set in a college town.

True to the Santa Cruz health dogma, smoking is forbidden in many cafés.

Caffé Pergolesi. In a big rambling house downtown that's graced with a large outside deck, the Perg has all the trappings of a good café—potent house coffee ($1), double-potent espresso drinks ($2), and a large selection of herbal teas (95¢). Try *chai,* a milky Indian spice tea ($1.90). They also have a small food menu that includes veggie lasagna, bagels, and croissants. The crowd is somewhat eclectic, ranging from UCSC students to New Age prophet types. *418A Cedar St., tel. 408/426–1775. Open weekdays 7 AM–midnight, weekends 7 AM–1 AM.*

Jahva House. Located in a big warehouse, the Jahva House feels open, airy, and comfortable. Big oriental rugs are strewn on the floors and ficus trees stand among the wood tables. The incredibly long coffee bar furnishes zillions of different kinds of coffee and teas, each packing a mighty punch of caffeine. Good banana bread and slices of pie cost about $2; specialty coffees are $1–$2. There's live music Monday nights. *120 Union St., tel. 408/459–9876. Walk down Cedar St. toward Mission St. and follow your nose. Open weekdays 6 AM–midnight, Sat. 6 AM–midnight, Sun. 10–6.*

Ultramat. The hippest "fluff and fold" around eases the pain of doing laundry with the comfort of coffee and assorted noshes. Sip and munch while you watch your clothes dance. *501 Laurel St., tel. 408/426–9274. Open daily 7:30 AM–midnight; last wash at 10.*

WORTH SEEING • • •

Most of Santa Cruz's sights are downtown, all within easy walking distance of each other. To explore the jagged coastline, though, you'll definitely need a car or one heck of a mountain bike. Downtown, Santa Cruz's **Pacific Garden Mall** is slowly recovering from the 1989 earthquake; the **Vision Santa Cruz** (1543 Pacific Ave., tel. 408/459–0900), an informal tourist information center, documents what happened that fateful day and exhibits earthquake recovery plans and models. Also downtown, at the corner of Cedar and Lincoln streets, are the temporary pavilions (i.e., tents) that house stores that were destroyed in the quake, including the worthwhile **Bookshop Santa Cruz** (Cedar and Union Sts.). Across from the bookstore the off-beat **Wild Earth** sells strange and cavorting ceramic creations. Also of interest is the **Mission de Exaltación de la Santa Cruz** (126 High St.), built between 1857 and 1931. It's not California's most interesting mission, but its grounds are overrun with colorful gardens and fountains—the perfect place for a leisurely afternoon walk. If you'd rather spend a day on the beach, head to the **Natural Bridges State Beach,** next door to a Monarch butterfly colony. Parking is $5—or avoid the charge and leave your car along Delaware Avenue, which borders the park on the east; from downtown, follow East Cliff Drive until you see the signs. On the beach, downtown, look for the **Boardwalk,** a little Coney Island by the Pacific with carnival rides, cotton candy, and lots of teenage nervous angst. Admission to the boardwalk is free, but the rides cost. If you do nothing else, ride the **Giant Dipper,** a fabulous wooden roller coaster with a spectacular view from the top.

The **University of California at Santa Cruz** (UCSC), just north of downtown, is also worth a quick tour. The **information center** (tel. 408/459–0111; open weekdays 9–5) at the campus entrance has maps and tours. Be sure to investigate the spectacular **limestone quarry** near the campus bookstore, and take a self-guided tour of the organic growing system at the **Farm and Garden Project** (tel. 408/429–2321). It's probably a good idea to park along Meder Avenue at the far west end of campus and catch the free shuttle at Bay and High streets, thereby avoiding the on-campus parking charge. You can also take Bus 41 up from Metro Center.

SANTA CRUZ CITY MUSEUM OF NATURAL HISTORY You'll recognize the natural history museum by the huge replica of a whale out front. The museum itself is small but full of information about the Ohlone Native Americans, who originally populated the area, and the seals and sea lions that still do. If you're into honey bees, you can watch thousands encased under glass doing interesting apian things. The museum is on the east side of town, near Pleasure Point—also a great place to watch the surfers do their thing. *1305 E. Cliff Dr., tel. 408/429–3773. Open Tues.–Sat. 10–5, Sun. 11–5. From downtown, walk or drive down E. Cliff Dr. for 2 mi.*

SANTA CRUZ SURFING MUSEUM At Lighthouse Point on West Cliff Drive, there's a tiny exhibit on surfing, from its Hawaiian origins to the present, including an explanation of the modern wet suit. The museum is dedicated to the memory of an 18-year-old surfer who drowned in 1965. Also on display is a surfboard bitten by a great white shark in 1987, testimony to the danger posed by sharks along the coast from Santa Cruz to Pigeon Point. Right outside the lighthouse you can watch the surfers on **Steamer Lane,** considered one of the best surfing spots in California. Look a little farther out and you'll see **Seal Rock,** the summertime home of thousands of barking, shiny, bloblike seals. The path that runs parallel with West Cliff Drive makes for a nice walk, jog, or bike ride. *Mark Abbott Memorial Lighthouse, W. Cliff Dr., tel. 408/429–3429. Open Wed.–Mon. noon–4.*

MYSTERY SPOT If you abhor tourist attractions but feel a strange compulsion to "do" at least one, let this be it. This hilarious little place lies 3 miles north of Santa Cruz in the redwoods and, in the minds of true believers, is at the center of a mysterious force that makes people taller and compels balls to roll uphill, not down. It's a tacky tourist trap to be sure, but its gift shop is filled with one-of-a-kind souvenirs and kitschy knickknacks. Your $3 admission also buys you a "Mystery Spot" bumper sticker. *1953 Branciforte Dr., tel. 408/423–8897. From downtown follow Market St. east for 2½ miles and follow signs. Admission: $3. Open daily 9:30–4:30.*

● ● ● CHEAP THRILLS

Nestled in the redwoods, **Felton, Ben Lomond,** and **Boulder Creek** are quaint towns in a grand setting. All three get a bit crowded on weekends, particularly in summer, but they retain their charm all the same. It will take only 30–45 minutes to travel through all three. On weekends, catch Bus 35 from Metro Center or drive north along Route 9.

FESTIVALS **Cabrillo Music Festival,** held in the summer, has food, live music, and outdoor entertainment. Call the Santa Cruz Civic Auditorium Box Office at 408/429–3444 for more information.

Shakespeare Santa Cruz is served up against the backdrop of beautiful redwoods during a six-week UCSC production of the Bard's works. Held every June–July on campus. Tickets start at $5 and peak at $14. For more information call 408/459–2121.

Fungus Fair. Can you think of 1,001 things to do with fungus? You know—those little mushrooms that cover the forest floor during the rainy season? If you can't, the people at the Fungus Fair will be more than happy to assist you. The fair is held every December at the Santa Cruz City Museum of Natural History (1305 East Cliff Dr., tel. 408/429–3773).

● ● ● AFTER DARK

Much of Santa Cruz's nightlife goes on in the cafés, and tends to end early. Nightlife in the traditional sense is decidedly lacking, and those establishments that do cater to the over-21 crowd check ID's stringently. The journal *Good Times* (free at cafés and bookstores) comes out every Thursday with a listing of upcoming events. Look for happy hours and reduced cover charges, usually on Wednesday or Thursday nights.

BARS AND CLUBS **Boulder Creek Brewing Company** (13040 Rte. 9, tel. 408/338–7882*)* may be a bit yuppie-ish, but it does brew one heck of a pint. Try their Redwood Ale or Texas Tea for starters, then move onto their Guinness-like stout. This place caters to the over-30 crowd, but on weekend nights there are always a few bleary-eyed students sitting in the corner.

The Catalyst (1101 Pacific Ave., tel. 408/423–1336), disparaged by some for its virtual monopoly of the Santa Cruz music scene, features local bands nightly and big-name bands on occasion. Covers range from $1 on Thursday nights to $10 for some of the more major shows.

Front Street Pub (516 Front St., tel. 408/429–8838), one of three microbreweries in the area, has good ciders and its own Lighthouse Amber for $2.50. Bluegrass bands sometimes play on weekends; cover charge is about $2.

Poet and the Patriot Irish Pub (320 Cedar St., tel. 408/426–8620) has lots of smoke in the air (well, lots by Santa Cruz's standards), dart boards on the wall, and Irish beer on tap. For some, including UCSC students and Santa Cruz's "art" crowd, this is paradise. Nearby, the **Kummbwa Jazz Center** (315 Cedar, tel. 408/427–2227) offers jazz and blues shows randomly throughout the year. Call for tickets and scheduling information.

The Red Room (1005 Cedar St., tel. 408/426–2994) is a UCSC institution, a darkly lit and run-down dive that's usually jammed with students. If you get hungry you can always head next door to the **Swan and Heavenly Goose,** an exotic and moderately priced Chinese restaurant.

OUTDOOR ACTIVITIES

The cleverly named **Bike Renting** store (46 Front St., tel. 408/423–9050) has 10-speeds and mountain bikes for $18 per half day. The **Kayak Shack** (on the pier, tel. 408/429–5066) has kayaks for $10 an hour, May–December (it's closed Tuesdays).

Big Basin State Park (take Rte. 9 to Rte. 236, tel. 408/338–6132) and **Henry Cowell State Park** (take Rte. 9 toward Felton, tel. 408/335–4598) have hundreds of hiking and bike trails that meander through the virgin redwoods around Santa Cruz. Go to park headquarters for trail maps (75¢) and permits. Bikes are allowed on designated fire and service roads, but not on hiking trails. At the **Forest of Nisene Marks** (Aptos Creek Rd. exit off Rte. 1, tel. 408/335–9145), southwest of Santa Cruz, you can view the ruins of a Chinese labor camp and hike to the epicenter of the 1989 Loma Prieta earthquake.

The Central Coast Drive

Simone de Beauvoir, Robinson Jeffers, Jack Kerouac, and Henry Miller number among those who've been inspired by Big Sur—the 90-mile stretch of California coastline between Carmel and San Simeon's Hearst Castle. Luckily, Big Sur's dramatic and harsh geography has precluded development; as a result the area is sparsely populated, with only a few gas stations, stores, or restaurants to disturb the serenity of the mountains. The only way to get to Big Sur is on Route 1, a highway carved into the mountains in 1937 by convict labor. It twists its way along the precipitous coastal cliffs and through ponderous redwood forests—the best way to enjoy it, of course, is to take it slowly, pausing at the many turnoffs to take in the awe-inspiring views, or to rove the forests and state parks. Whether you're traveling north or south, you'll have equally picture-perfect panoramas along the way—unless bad weather and fog settle in, which obscure the view and can make the roads extremely dangerous.

The Big Sur coast is accessible by public buses and Greyhound, but most people have their own wheels, undoubtedly the best way to experience the grandeur of California's coastline. The "traditional" drive starts 48 miles south of Santa Cruz in **Monterey,** a heavily touristed and expensive coastal town. You'll pass the towns of **Carmel, Pacific Grove, San Simeon, Morro Bay,** and finally **San Luis Obispo,** 131 miles south of Monterey. In low season you can easily make the drive in under six hours, but summer traffic on Route 1 can be a mess, and will add a good two hours to your driving time. If you can, do the drive during the week or in late fall or early spring, when hotels and motels lop $5–$10 off their prices.

Central Coast

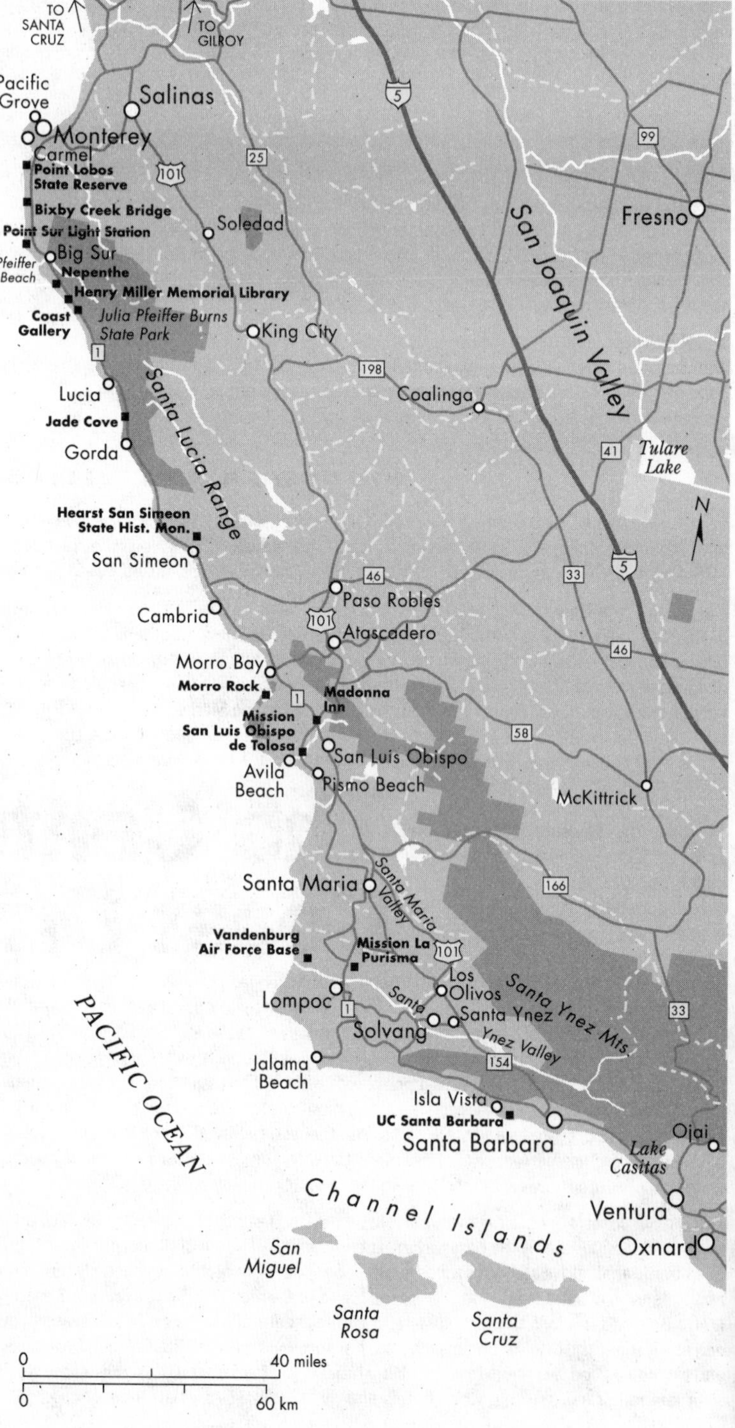

BASICS • • •

AMERICAN EXPRESS You won't find any American Express offices along the coast. However, **Bob McGinniss Travel** is an official AmEx representative. *561 Carmel Rancho Shopping Center, Carmel, tel. 408/624–2724. Open weekdays 9–5.*

FESTIVALS

MONTEREY During the summer, Monterey plays host to the **Monterey Bay Theatrefest** (tel. 408/624–8511), which has free outdoor performances on weekend afternoons in the Custom House Plaza. Call for schedules. In September, look for the **Monterey Bay Jazz Festival** (tel. 408/373–3366), which takes place at the Monterey Fairgrounds. In June, look for a week of live music at the **Monterey Bay Blues Festival.** For more information call 408/394–2652.

SAN LUIS OBISPO **La Fiesta,** held in late May at the Mission Plaza, is the traditional "rite of spring" activity where everyone lets loose to celebrate the city's Spanish heritage. It all begins with a bonfire burning of Old Man Gloom (i.e., winter) and ends with a variety of music and dance performances, and lots of heavy drinking. In late July and early August, the San Luis Obispo **Mozart Festival** puts together recitals, concerts, and lectures about Herr Wolfgang. Performances generally start at $5, but call for more information (tel. 805/543–4580).

TOURIST INFORMATION

BIG SUR **Big Sur Chamber of Commerce** (Box 87, Big Sur 93930, tel. 408/667–2100) can answer questions by phone or mail, but it has no office to visit. It does publish a useful freebie, "Big Sur: A Guide," which you can pick up at the Chambers of Commerce in Monterey, Cambria, or San Simeon, or at one of the little stores along Route 1.

Cambria Chamber of Commerce may be 78 miles south of Big Sur, but for some reason it offers an excellent guide to Big Sur and information regarding camping along the way, useful if you're driving north from Los Angeles. *767 Main St., Cambria 93428, tel. 805/927–3500. Open weekdays 9–5.*

MONTEREY **Monterey Chamber of Commerce,** located downtown, has useful city maps and information about current events. The friendly staff can also help you find a room. *380 Alvarado St., Monterey 93940, tel. 408/649–1770. Open weekdays 8:30–5.*

SAN LUIS OBISPO **San Luis Obispo Chamber of Commerce** provides listings of local accommodations with price ranges and a free pamphlet for the "Heritage Walk" through San Luis Obispo. They also sells maps. *1039 Chorro St., San Luis Obispo 93401, tel. 805/543–1323. Open Tues.–Fri. 9–5, Sat.–Mon. 11–5.*

The **Tri Counties Regional Center** (tel. 805/543–2833) provides useful information for disabled travelers, including a list of hotels and restaurants that are wheelchair accessible in and around San Luis Obispo. The **Women's Resource Center** (1660 Marsh St., San Luis Obispo, tel. 805/544–9313) offers counseling and service information for female travelers.

COMING AND GOING • • •

BY BUS

MONTEREY Greyhound buses travel on U.S. 101 between San Francisco and Los Angeles, with regular service to San Luis Obispo and Monterey via Salinas. In Monterey, the **Greyhound** depot (351 Delmonte Ave., tel. 408/373–4735) is near the bottom of the Municipal Pier. Each day there are four southbound buses to San Luis Obispo ($19), Santa Barbara ($25), and Los Angeles ($25); three northbound buses to Gilroy, San Jose, and San Francisco ($19). The office is open daily 7:30 AM–5 PM, but closed between 12:30 PM and 3:30 PM on the weekend. In the depot are 15 medium-size lockers that cost $1 (in quarters) for 24 hours.

Monterey-Salinas Transit (tel. 408/899–2555) has regular connections down to **Carmel** and **Big Sur** and up to **Salinas** and **Watsonville** from Monterey. Fares range from $1 to $3. All buses arrive and depart from the Monterey **Transit Plaza,** located downtown at the intersection of Tyler and Pearl streets. For Big Sur, take Bus 22. It will drop you outside the Nepenthe restaurant on Route 1.

SAN LUIS OBISPO From the San Luis Obispo **Greyhound** depot (150 South St., tel. 805/543–2121) buses run north along U.S. 101 six times a day and south eight times a day. Fares to both Los Angeles and San Francisco are $28. The station stays open 23 hours a day, closing from 10 to 11 every evening. There are six lockers large enough to hold a backpack as well as 12 smaller ones ($1 for 24 hours). Bus route #3 connects the station to downtown, but you can easily walk the ¼ mile. Motels are within walking distance to the north on Marsh Street (*see* Where to Sleep, *below*).

Green Tortoise (tel. 805/569–1884) stops in San Luis Obispo at the Denny's restaurant on Los Osos Valley Road. Fares to San Francisco and Los Angeles are about $15. Buses to San Francisco pass through San Luis Obispo early Monday morning, and buses to Los Angeles pass through early Saturday morning. Call a week ahead between 8 AM and 8 PM to make reservations.

Bus #7 leaves the San Luis Obispo City Hall for **Morro Bay** four times a day, weekdays only. The last bus is at 5:15 PM, and the fare is $1. There is no bus service to **Avila Beach,** but it's possible to take a public bus to U.S. 101 and Avila Beach Drive and then walk into town, 2 miles down the road. Buses do run from San Luis Obispo to **Pismo Beach** three times a day during the week from City Hall; fare is about 75¢. **Greyhound** also stops in Pismo Beach (Greyhound depot, 890 Price St.).

BY CAR For most of the way you have only two choices: south on Route 1, or north on Route 1. There are no other major highways in the area, and it's nearly impossible to get lost. From Santa Cruz, Route 1 heads south along the coast; once outside San Luis Obispo you can turn onto U.S. 101 to Santa Barbara or Los Angeles.

RENTAL CARS It's almost impossible to enjoy the coast without a car. Even though Greyhound and Amtrak service the area, you'll end up missing most of the scenic beauty of the coast if you're stuck on a cramped bus or train. If you can afford it, you should seriously consider renting a car. Not only will this allow you the freedom to explore the area at your own pace, it may even end up saving you a few dollars—that is, if you're willing to sleep in it for a few nights. In Pacific Grove, near Monterey, try **Rent-A-Wreck** (95 Central Ave., Pacific Grove, tel. 408/373–3356), where you'll find cars for about $110 a week. **EZ Auto Rental** (2040 Del Monte Ave., Monterey, tel. 408/646–1777), in downtown Monterey, has cars for about $95 a week. At last look, **Hertz** (Box 1109, Monterey Peninsula Airport, tel. 415/579–3161) had a $51-a-day rate with unlimited mileage and a free drop off in San Luis Obispo. **USA Rent-A-Car** (2200A Del Monte Ave., Monterey, tel. 408/372–6000) charges about $25 a day with an option to drop the car off in Santa Maria for an extra $25. Rates vary with the season, so call ahead.

BY TRAIN

MONTEREY Amtrak has no station in Monterey, but can get you there by bus ($15) from the train station in San Jose. The bus will drop you at the unstaffed Monterey **Transit Station,** downtown at the intersection of Pearl and Tyler streets. Reservations aren't required; simply show up and pay the bus conductor. There are usually three buses a day that run in both directions.

SAN LUIS OBISPO **Amtrak's** *Coast Starlight* route runs through the **Salinas Depot** (40 Railroad Rd., Salinas, tel. 408/422–7458) in the north and the **San Luis Obispo Depot** (1011 Railroad Ave., at Santa Rosa St., tel. 805/541–0505) in the south. Trains run once a day in each direction. Fares from San Luis Obispo are $30 to Los Angeles, $57 to San Francisco.

HITCHHIKING Hitching is fairly difficult around Monterey, but once you get south on Route 1 your chances of being picked up improve. Meeting someone in a state park parking lot or campground is one strategy. As always, it's better to err on the side of paranoia than to get in the car with the wrong person.

In San Luis Obispo, there's a ride board downstairs at the **Cal Pol University Student Union** (tel. 805/756–1111). You'll see Cuesta College and Cal Poly students hitching in town, but people aren't too keen about picking up people around here, perhaps because there's a California Men's Colony (prison, that is) nearby. It might help to look clean and studentlike with a sign declaring your destination.

WHERE TO SLEEP • • •

AVILA BEACH AND PISMO BEACH Avila Beach has a few small motels but no public campgrounds, although **Avila Hot Springs** (250 Avila Beach Dr., tel. 805/595–2359) offers tent camping for $15 a night. If that's full, campers should head to **Pismo Beach**, where you'll find three public campgrounds.

El Pismo Inn. This teal-blue structure near the pier is a turn-of-the-century hotel cluttered with old furniture and style. Most of the rooms are well-kept and bathed in sunlight, courtesy of the large bay windows. Some rooms even have murals. Rates range from $25 in the off-season to $30 in the summer. *230-40 Poneroy St., Pismo Beach, tel. 805/773–4529. On the main drag near the pier.*

Seaview Motel. The Seaview isn't much to look at, but you get a free Continental breakfast and coffee in the morning. The drab rooms start at $25. *230 Five Cities Dr., off U.S. 101, tel. 805/773–1846. Laundry facilities. Wheelchair access.*

CAMPING Open May through September, **North Beach State Campground** (on Rte. 1 in Pismo Beach) has quiet sites surrounded by trees. Try to get one near the sand dunes. **Oceano Campgrounds** (Pier Ave. and Rte. 1), the first in Pismo Beach to fill up because of its proximity to the sand dunes, charges $14 a night and is open all year. **Pismo Dunes** (Pier Ave.) offers beach camping on soft sand. There are no sites here—simply drive out on the beach and pitch a tent for $5. To make reservations at any of these campsites call 800/444–7275.

BIG SUR Big Sur has more than 1,000 campsites up and down the coast and is an ideal place to camp. If you want to sleep indoors, be prepared to pay handsomely for the privilege. Most hotels (and restaurants and gift shops and grocery stores. . .) in the area charge an arm and a leg because there are plenty of tourists and little competition. There are a few exceptions though, which are listed below.

Big Sur River Inn. The first place you hit coming south, the inn is comfortable and conveniently located near shops, restaurants, and a gas station. The rooms won't win any awards, but they're clean, comfortable and—even better—reasonably priced. Doubles start at $36 and work their way up to $50. *Pheneger Creek, 93920, tel. 800/548–3610. 20 rooms. Reservations advised.*

Deetjen's Big Sur Inn. This place is rustic to the core, which means the electricity could go off at any moment, no phones, no TVs, thin walls, and old bathrooms. However, the atmosphere and the people who run the place are both top-notch. Rooms have down comforters (you'll need them) and interesting old things scattered about. Doubles start at $38. *Route 1, 93920, tel. 408/667–2377. 1 mile south of Nepenthe. 19 rooms, some share bath. Reservations a must.*

CAMPING **Andrew Molera State Park.** The campgrounds are a little less than a mile from the parking lot, but as long as you don't mind shuttling your stuff over a creek and through the woods you'll probably enjoy a stay here. It has a wonderful trail that meanders down to the nearby beach. Beware summer weekends, however, as troops of Cub Scouts and pubescent pre-teens make life here a living hell. All campsites are located in one monster-size field, which means privacy isn't easy to come by. There's no one on duty, so drop your money in the payment box. A ranger comes by around 8 AM to collect the cash and give out tickets to anyone who hasn't paid. *Rte. 1, 21 mi south of Carmel, tel. 408/667–2315. $3 per person. No showers. No reservations. 3-night limit.*

Bottcher's Gap. You'll find these primitive sites by heading south on Route 1 from Carmel for 11 miles, exiting at Palo Colorado Road, and going 8 miles to the road's end. This campground is filled with flies and drunken teenagers in the summer. It's noisy and undeveloped but a good enough place to crash before starting your exploration of the Ventana Wilderness. *Palo Colorado Rd. No showers. Self registration, no phone.*

Julia Pfeiffer Burns State Park. It's crowded with RVs and car-campers, but the grounds are surrounded by huge redwoods and shady oak trees. There are also two hike-in sites for tent campers. All spaces go for $16 a night. *Rte. 1, tel. 408/667–2315. 38 mi south of Carmel. Reservations advised.*

Pfeiffer Big Sur State Park. This is the closest thing to an outdoor hotel. There are more than 300 RV and tent sites in this sprawling campground, most with fire pits and picnic tables. There's also a general store, a laundromat, and hot shower facilities. It's crowded in summer and sites should be reserved. If you're in the mood to ramble, head south along the river that meanders through the park. It eventually dead-ends in an unspeakably beautiful mountain pool, surrounded by 200-foot cliff faces and rocky buttes. It's a semi-treacherous 2-mile hike past the last campsite, but few people know about it. *Rte. 1, tel. 408/667–2315.*

Plaskett Creek. This campground on the east side of Route 1, 9½ miles south of Lucia, has sites for $10. It's often empty during the winter, but reservations are advised in summer. Bring your own food. *Rte. 1, Lucia, tel. 800/444–7275 for reservations. No showers.*

Private campgrounds that are more developed and expensive include **Fernwood Campground** (tel. 408/667–2422); **Lime Kiln Redwoods Campground** (tel. 408/667–2403), and **Riverside Campground and Cabins** (tel. 408/667–2414). All are accessed off Route 1 in Big Sur. Call for more information.

ROUGHING IT It's illegal to park along Route 1 and sleep in you car or van, but many people do it anyway because the area is rarely patrolled. Recently, however, especially near the southern edge of Big Sur closer to San Simeon, some robberies and beatings have occurred. Needless to say, be careful.

CARMEL Carmel is *not* a budget town. Even the beat-up motels price their rooms as if they were lush suites in upscale B&Bs.

The only time when Carmel slashes its prices from absurdly expensive to ridiculously expensive is during the winter.

The Homestead. Right in town, this place fits into the overdone country-inn category—a hotel that goes too far out of its way to be quaint and cozy. However, if you don't mind spending the money, the Homestead is awfully comfortable. Doubles start at $65 in summer, $50 in winter; 4-person cottages are $90. *Lincoln St. and 8th Ave., tel. 408/624–4119. From Route 1 exit at Ocean, follow to Lincoln and turn left. 8 rooms, 4 cottages, some with kitchen. Reservations advised.*

Mission Ranch. Clint Eastwood's other place of business, this ranch boasts farm animals and tennis courts and lies just far enough south of town to have live music at night. Double rooms ($50) and 4- to 6-person private cottages ($95) are available, and both are equally comfortable and atmospheric—almost nauseatingly so. *26270 Dolores St., tel. 408/624–6436. From Route 1 exit and go south on Rio Rd., left onto Lausen Dr. which becomes Dolores. 28 rooms. Reservations advised.*

CAMPING **Saddle Mountain.** This private campground in Carmel Valley is the only one within easy reach of Carmel. There are 50 developed sites at $16 per night. The grounds are peaceful. Bring your own food. *Schutte Rd., tel. 408/624–1617. Take Carmel Valley Rd. off Route 1, turn right at Schutte Rd. Showers available. Reservations advised. Closed Nov.–Mar.*

MONTEREY Monterey is completely void of cheap lodging. There's nothing under $30 a night for one person unless you're traveling mid-June to August, when a temporary youth hostel is open. The city's budget motels are concentrated on Fremont Street (accessible by Buses 9 and 10), which is neither picturesque nor inviting, but it's relatively close to downtown and Cannery Row (10 minutes by car).

UNDER $40 **Motel 6.** Probably the cheapest place on Fremont Street, with vibrating beds (25¢ a minute) and a Gideon Bible in the drawer. It's not sleazy, but it's also not very clean. All rooms have that sanitized-for-your-comfort feel. Single and double rooms average $40 a night, but this will also buy you access to the swimming pool. *2124 Fremont St., 93940, tel. 805/646–8585. Take Bus 8, 9, or 10 to Fremont St.*

Paramont Motel. Eight miles north of Monterey, the Paramont is a clean and comfortable hotel with friendly management who will go out of their way to make you feel at home. Singles and doubles are $33, but no reservations are accepted—you must arrive in the morning and take your chances. *298 Del Monte Blvd., 93940, tel. 408/384–8674. Take Bus 12 to Beach Ave. and walk up Del Monte.*

Stage Coach Motel. The first budget motel you come to on Fremont offers characterless but well-kept rooms, a swimming pool, and a sauna. It's a quiet hotel that frowns upon parties and loud guests. Singles and doubles are both $32 off season, $39 in season. Reservations recommended. *1111 10th St., 93940, tel. 408/373–3622. Take Bus 6 from Transit Plaza to Fremont and Aguaito, walk east 1 block up 10th St.*

Andril's Fire Place Cottages. In Pacific Grove, Andril's rents small cabins among the pines that start at $64 a night in winter and $74 in summer. Most have two beds and rent only by the week, but you may be able to finagle a deal if you only want to stay a few nights. These cabins propose a pleasant break from the motel/hotel rut. Even better, there's a Jacuzzi and spa on the premises. *569 Asilomar Blvd., Pacific Grove 93950, tel. 408/375–0994.*

Del Monte Beach Inn. Across from Del Monte Beach in downtown Monterey, this small bed-and-breakfast offers an affordable escape from the Motel 6s of the world. The rooms are all clean and tastefully decorated in the English Countryside vein. Depending on the room, rates vary from $45 to $75. Two rooms have private baths and a kitchen, the other 16 share four communal bathrooms. *1110 Del Monte Ave., 93940, tel. 800/727–4410. Reservations advised. 1 night's deposit required for all reservations.*

UNDER $80 **Sand Dollar Inn.** It's centrally located four blocks from downtown, has a pool and spa, and serves a free Continental breakfast. Rooms are decorated in pink and blue, and some have fireplaces with fake logs. Rates range from $70 on weekdays and $80 weekends. Check-in is at 3 PM. *755 Abrego St., 93940, tel. 408/372–7551. From the Transit Plaza walk southeast on Munras St., turn left (east) at Fremont St. and right (south) on Abrego St.*

YOUTH HOSTEL The **Monterey Youth Hostel** operates mid-June through August, but its location and prices change from year to year. Sometimes they offer 100 beds at $5 per night, sometimes 19 beds at $12. Call 408/298–0670 for the latest.

CAMPING **Laguna Seca.** Most of the 185 campsites here have RV hookups, but a few undeveloped spaces are reserved for tent campers. None of the sites are very scenic, but at least they're cheap ($12). Popular with "weekend warriors." Reservations advised during the summer. The main office is open daily from 8 AM to 10 PM. *Route 68, tel. 408/755–4899. 9 mi east of Monterey off Route 68. Follow the signs.*

Veteran's Memorial Park Campground. This rather uninspiring campground is five minutes from downtown Monterey—a good location but hardly the great outdoors. Forty primitive sites (no hookups) are doled out on a first-come, first-served basis for $12. Showers are available but bring your own food. *Via Del Rey, tel. 408/646–3865. Take Bus 3 from transit plaza or Route 68 west to Skyline Forest Dr., turn right at the stop sign, drive to bottom of the hill.*

MORRO BAY Motels in Morro Bay are mainly clustered around **Main Street, Morro Bay Boulevard,** and the streets near the water. Nothing is dirt cheap so you may want to camp in **Morro Bay State Park** (tel. 805/772–2560). Take Main Street to State Park Road and follow the signs. There are 129 sites here, but reservations are advised, especially during the summer. Otherwise, try the **Bay Breeze Inn** (1148 Front St., tel. 805/772–5607), which is the cheapest motel near the water. Rooms are $35 during the week, $45 on the weekend. The **Sundown** (648 Main St., tel. 805/772–7381) is a bit farther from the water, but its rooms ($45) are quiet and comfortable. If you're really stuck, try the local **Motel 6** (298 Atascadero Rd., tel. 805/772–5641).

SAN LUIS OBISPO Unfortunately, it looks as if San Luis Obispo's motels and inns are starting to get hip to the high rates other California cities are charging. But compared to some other cities this place is still a deal. Affordable motels are sprinkled around the city with many concentrated on **Monterey Street,** east of Santa Rosa Street. No buses go far enough down Monterey to reach the motels, but you can easily walk to them from Mission Plaza, a half mile away. If you can't get into any of the places listed below, try **Mid-Town Motel** (475 Marsh St., tel. 805/543–4533), near downtown. Rates, which vary by season and number of guests per room, range from $32 for a single to $75 for a double with two beds. A half mile east of downtown, the **Sunbeam Motel** (1656 Monterey St., tel. 805/543–8141) is another good-in-a-pinch establishment, at $28 for a single up to $79 for two people. The **Budget Motel** (345 Marsh St., tel. 805/543–6443), a no-frills sort of place close to the Greyhound station, has singles for $36 and doubles for $50. They also have $58 suites if you're budget-minded and traveling in a convoy.

UNDER $30 **Wineman's Hotel.** This 1930s-era hotel sits in the heart of downtown, a wonderfully archaic place that shouldn't be missed. The rooms feel old—no TV, an ancient telephone—but the price, the atmosphere, and the kindness of the women who run it are unbeatable. Rooms start at $25. There's a rumor this historic hotel will be remodeled (read ruined) in the near future, but for the time being it's San Luis Obispo's best find. *849 Higuera St., tel. 805/543–7465. From Amtrak or Greyhound take Bus 3 to Chorro and Marsh Sts., walk north on Chorro St. and turn east on Higuera St.*

UNDER $40 **Adobe Inn Bed and Breakfast.** This place is a curious mix of southwest pastels and afternoon tea—very comfortable. Room names instead of numbers (e.g. the Prickly Pear Room), and doors that open to the outside, give the Adobe a motel-ish appearance. All rooms are clean and comfortable. Doubles start at $40. *1473 Monterey St., tel. 805/549–0321. All rooms with bath. Reservations advised.*

Motel Inn. Purported to be the first motel in the United States, this place mixes Spanish-style architecture and 1940s-era furniture. Nothing matches and there's plenty of atmosphere. Rooms are a bit musty, but quite clean. Doubles start at $35. *2223 Monterey St., tel. 805/543–4000. From Amtrak or Greyhound take Bus 3 to Santa Rosa and Higuera Sts., walk north on Santa Rosa 1 block, turn onto Monterey. All rooms with bath.*

STUDENT HOUSING **Cal Poly University** offers up their dorm rooms during the summer. Singles fetch $25 and shared rooms $17. All have common bathrooms. The dorms rotate each summer, so call 805/756–1586 for information and reservations.

CAMPING The largest campgrounds are along the beaches west of San Luis Obispo. The **National Forest Campground** at Cerro Alto is a mile off Route 41 between Atascadero and Morro Bay. It has 13 primitive sites and pit toilets, and is a good place from which to explore the nearby mountains. There are no telephones or staff here, and all sites are self-registered. You'll find 14 more undeveloped sites at **El Chorro Regional Park** (tel. 805/549–5200), 5 miles north of San Luis Obispo off Route 1.

● ● ● FOOD

AVILA BEACH AND PISMO BEACH Both of these small coastal cities have the standard beachside tourist restaurants that specialize in fresh seafood. In Avila, the **Olde Port Inn** (Port San Luis at the very end, tel. 805/595–2515, no wheelchair access) has oodles of atmosphere, but dinners are expensive ($9–$17). If you can, try to arrive around lunchtime when many of their same dishes are $3–$7 less. If you've spent your last nickel on an "I Luv Avila Beach" T-shirt, head to the **Avila Grocery and Mercantile** (354 Front

St., tel. 805/595–2098), where you'll find all the makings for a cheap picnic on the beach.

In Pismo Beach, **Chele's Food and Spirits** (198 Pomeroy, tel. 805/773–1020) serves good breakfasts on shell-shaped glass plates for a reasonable $4–$6. People come from miles around to devour seafood and steaks at **McLintock's** (750 Mattie Rd., tel. 805/773–1892), but the place is pricey. If you just want to drink, head for **Harry's Cocktail Lounge** (690 Cypress St., tel. 805/773–1010), which is crowded with Harleys on Sundays.

BIG SUR There aren't many restaurants along the coast between Carmel and San Simeon, but you will come across a few gems in the Big Sur area.

Although they're expensive, almost every restaurant along Route 1 in Big Sur has a stunning view of the coast—worth an extra few dollars.

UNDER $10 **Café Amphora.** Part of the Nepenthe restaurant complex, this café has daily brunch and lunch menus with sandwiches for $6. It's cheaper to eat outside on the deck that's perched on the edge of a huge cliff—great views! If you want to splurge, head inside to the Nepenthe dining room, where pastas and seafood start at $12. *Rte. 1, tel. 408/667–2660. 29 mi south of Carmel. Open weekdays 10–4, weekends 10–5.*

Coast Gallery Café. A casual deli with hot sandwiches ($5–$8) and a great view of the coast; both indoor and outdoor seating. It's behind and upstairs from the Coast Art Gallery. *Rte. 1, tel. 408/667–2301. 33 mi south of Carmel. Open daily 9–5.*

Center Deli. This place has groceries and fairly cheap sandwiches that range from $3–$6. There's no seating, but you can grab a picnic lunch and eat at one of the nearby scenic overlooks. *Rte. 1, tel. 408/667–2225. Next to the Big Sur post office. Open daily 8–9 in summer, 8–8 in winter.*

UNDER $15 **Big Sur River Inn.** This local watering hole is casual and friendly, with poetry readings on Tuesdays and music on weekends. The menu includes grilled fish ($12–$15) and hearty pasta dishes ($10–$15). Breakfasts are decent, but the servings aren't very large. Omelets and egg dishes range from $7–$10. *Rte. 1, Pheneger Creek, tel. 408/667–2700. 24½ mi south of Carmel. Open daily 8:15 AM–8:30 PM.*

CAMBRIA AND SAN SIMEON There's not much to choose from once you hit Cambria and San Simeon. If you see a place that looks good, stop. If you don't, it may be miles before you pass another.

Creekside Gardens Café. A great place for breakfast with omelets ($5) and monster-sized muffins ($2). Outdoor and indoor seating. *2114 Main St., Cambria, tel. 805/927–8646. Open daily 7 AM–2 PM.*

Robin's. Home cooking with an ethnic edge. Both the indoor and outdoor eating areas are surrounded by a thriving garden in the summertime. Try the hot-and-spicy tempeh or the fresh pasta Greco with vegetables, both are $8. Robin's is small, the food is excellent, and the atmosphere peaceful. *4095 Burton Dr., Cambria, tel. 805/927–5007. Off Main St. Open Mon., Wed., Thurs., Fri., Sat. 11–2:30 and 5–9; Sun. 5–9.*

Sebastian's Patio Café. Adjacent to the historic Sebastian General Store, the café offers casual patio dining and hearty lunches that range from burgers to fish-and-chips and large salads, all under $6. Lunch only. The warehouse across the street is rumored to contain some of William Hearst's most fabulous antiques and art works, quietly collecting dust. *442 San Simeon Rd., San Simeon, tel. 805/927–4217. Open May–Oct., 11 AM–3:15 PM.*

CARMEL The proliferation of restaurants in Carmel is an indecisive person's nightmare. There are taverns, tearooms, al frescos, and broilers—everything but a McDonald's, it seems. Unique and expensive are the norms here. If you'd rather picnic go to **Bruno's Market and Deli** (6th and Junipero Aves., tel. 408/624–3821), which specializes in BBQ chicken, ribs, sandwiches, and salads; or **Carmel Village Market** (8th Ave. and Dolores St., tel. 408/624–3476) for groceries and produce.

Friar Tucks. Compared to the rest of Carmel, this place is down to earth. A variety of burgers, salads, and sandwiches in an unpretentious and friendly, pseudo-English atmosphere. Meals start at $5 and work their way up to $9. If you're in the breakfast mood try one of Friar Tuck's outstanding omelets. *5th Ave. and Dolores St., tel. 408/624–4274. Open daily 6:30 AM–2 PM.*

Carmel frowns on businesses having addresses, it's part of the city's so-called "country charm." Essentially it just means you have to search a bit harder to find what you're looking for.

Hog's Breath Inn. Owned by Clint "Dirty Harry" Eastwood, the Hog's Breath is, not surprisingly, one of the more popular spots in town. Fame, though, hasn't ruined this place, and you can dine on excellent seafood or meat lunch dishes for under $10; dinners are under $15. There's a pleasant back patio with outdoor fireplaces and an incredible mural. *San Carlos St. and 5th Ave., tel. 408/625–1044. Reservations advised. Open daily 11:30 AM–3 PM and 5–10 PM. Bar open until 1 AM.*

MONTEREY Monterey has a large selection of hearty seafood and health food restaurants, but unfortunately they're almost all overpriced. To avoid spending a fortune try eating after 4 but before 6:30, when many restaurants and bars run early bird and happy-hour specials. Also ask at your motel for special discount deals they may have with an area restaurant. **Old Monterey Café** (489 Alvarado St., tel. 408/646–1021) serves good coffee and pancake-and-hashbrown breakfasts ($5). **Rappa's** (end of Fisherman's Pier, tel. 408/372–7562) has a pleasant outside patio and a $7 lunch menu. For picnic supplies head to **Troia's Market** (tel. 408/375–9819) at Pacific and Delmonte streets. If you're in the mood for drinks only, the **Monterey Brewing Company** (438 Wave St., tel. 408/375–3634) has a good, dark atmosphere and refreshingly sour beers with names like "Save the Whale Pale Ale" ($2.50). Housed in what appears to be a corrugated-tin shack across from Cannery Row, this place jams with a band most evenings.

UNDER $5 **Red's Donuts.** For cheapo sandwiches and doughnuts, cut over to Red's, which has BLTs and salads for $3. A wild array of pictures bedeck the walls. *433 Alvarado St., tel. 408/372–9761. Open Mon.–Sat. 6 AM–2:30 PM, Sun. 6 AM–12:30 PM.*

UNDER $10 **Rosine's.** If you're sick of the crowds along Monterey's wharf head to Rosine's high-ceilinged, pastel-colored dining room—a quiet place to chomp on a good burger or decent salad for around $6. *434 Alvarado St., tel. 408/375–1400. Open Tues.–Thurs. 7 AM–9 PM, Fri.–Sun. 8 AM–9 PM, Mon. 7 AM–4 PM.*

Toastie's Café. When you walk in you may feel trapped in a dollhouse with all the pink lace this place has, but the fluffy yogurt-and-buckwheat pancakes ($4) and waffles smothered in blueberries ($6) will win you over. *702 Lighthouse Ave., Pacific Grove, tel. 408/373–7543. Open Mon.–Sat. 6 AM–3 PM and 5–9 PM, Sun. 7 AM–2 PM.*

UNDER $15 **Abalonetti.** This outstanding eatery is located at the far end of Fisherman's Wharf. Their specialty is squid, served every which way, but their fresh grilled fish ($9) and homemade seafood ravioli ($9.50) are equally good. Try Abalonetti's cheaper pick-up window next door if you don't want to pay to sit down in the restaurant. *57 Fisherman's Wharf, tel. 408/375–5941. Open daily 11 AM–10 PM.*

Fishwife. Arguably one of the best pasta and seafood restaurants on the peninsula, this place in Pacific Grove is a favorite with locals and travelers in the know. Pastas are all under $10 and fish dishes start at $7. *1996½ Sunset Dr., Pacific Grove, tel. 408/375–7107. Near Asilomar Beach. Open daily 10–10, except Tues.*

MORRO BAY Morro Bay has its share of fish emporiums along the waterfront. The **Fish Shanty** (1245 Embarcadero, tel. 805/772–1277) offers all the fish-and-chips and clam chowder you can eat for $8. The **Hofbrau der Albatross** (571 Embarcadero, tel. 805/772–2411) has an outdoor terrace overlooking the water, and sandwiches and salads from $5–$10. Across from the Hofbrau is the **Sandpiper Continental Café** (570 Embarcadero, tel. 805/772–4975), a good place to grab a cup of fresh-roasted coffee and hear some fish stories. Otherwise, head to **Dorn's** (801 Market St., tel. 805/772–4415), perched on top of a hill overlooking the Embarcadero and Morro Bay harbor. Dorn's is a bit pricey, but its seafood diners ($6–$9) and clam chowder ($3) are excellent.

SAN LUIS OBISPO Places to eat are concentrated in the downtown area, along Higuera Street. Most bars also serve food, and if it's sunny many bars and restaurants offer outside seating. Otherwise, get takeout or buy food from a local grocery store and eat in Mission Plaza on a bench overlooking San Luis Obispo Creek. Nothing in this city is exorbitantly priced, and most dishes are in the $5–$15 range. **San Luis Obispo Donuts** (1057 Monterey St., at the corner of Santa Rosa St.) is open 24 hours and has outdoor tables. **David Muzzio's Market,** on Monterey Street between Chorro and Morro streets, has groceries and a deli counter with sandwiches for $3. If you're looking for a cheap and tasty taco ($2) or veggie burrito ($2.75), head to **Taco's Acapulco** (121 Broad St., tel. 805/545–9466), the best Mexican food stand in town. If you're looking for drinks only, head to **Brubeck's Cellar** (726 Higuera St., tel. 805/541–8688), a snazzy basement club that's popular with "alternative" youngsters. The **SLO Brewing Company** (upstairs at 1119 Garden St., tel. 805/543–1843), a big brick-and-wood microbrewery (try the Garden Alley Amber) also serves pub lunches and sandwiches. For a low-key coffee experience hit up the **Coffee Merchant** (1065 Higuera St., tel. 805/543–6701), a small café with wrought-iron chairs and live music or poetry readings on most nights. House coffee is 90¢ a cup.

UNDER $5 **Del Monte Café.** Near the Amtrak station, this old grocery store was brought back to life and turned into a inexpensive, 50s-style diner—with a menu of the requisite burgers, fries, and other diner-type food. The outdoor patio is popular with Cal Poly students on weekends. One of the best dishes is *huevos rancheros,* a steal at $4. *1901 Santa Barbara St., tel. 805/541–1907. Open daily 7 AM–2 PM.*

Mee Heng Low Chop Suey Shop. San Luis Obispo's oldest Chinese restaurant offers a phenomenal lunch deal—tea, soup, entrée, and (of course) fortune cookie for $4. The dining room doesn't earn high marks in the ambience category, but the reasonably priced and tasty chow meins and chop sueys certainly make up for it. *815 Palm St., tel. 805/543–6627. Across from the Ah Louis store. Open 11:30 AM–9 PM. Closed Wed.*

UNDER $10 **Sebastian's Restaurant and Tavern.** Across from the mission, Sebastian's has cheap lunch pastas and sandwiches in the $5–$9 range. Dinners get more expensive, but the outdoor patio has great views of the mission and the creek. *1023 Chorro St., Mission Plaza, tel. 805/544–5666. Open daily 11 AM–9 PM.*

Woodstock's. This restaurant lost a lot of its ambience when it moved from a cozy, wood-paneled dining room into the ugly gray building it now occupies, but the pizza is still the best around. It's slightly expensive ($16 for a large pizza), but their wheat-crust, deep-dish pizzas are top-rate. *1000 Higuera St. at Osos St., tel. 805/541–4420. Open weekdays 11 AM–1 AM, weekends until 2 AM.*

EXPLORING THE COAST

The following drive is organized along a north–south axis, starting in Monterey, 100 miles south of San Francisco, and working its way south along Route 1 to San Luis Obispo, a surprisingly lively and fun college town 90 miles north of Santa Barbara. You can make the six-hour trip without a stop, but most prefer to get out for a bite to eat and to check out the towns along the way—Carmel, Big Sur, and Morro Bay are among the most popular.

MONTEREY At the south end of the crescent-shaped Monterey Bay, Monterey is one of California's most stunning and well-known oceanfront towns. Unfortunately, this popularity has turned Monterey into one of California's tackiest and most unabashedly commercial seaside resorts. The town has managed to retain a warmth and simplicity, but in recent years a lot of the best sights have degenerated into second-rate tourist traps along the lines of **Cannery Row** and **Fisherman's Wharf**—made famous by Steinbeck in his novels *Cannery Row* and *Sweet Thursday*—which bustle with over-priced gift shops and lackluster restaurants. If a Steinbeck fan, however, you'll probably want to grin and bear it, and enjoy a brief tour of the **Pacific Biological Laboratories** (800 Cannery Row),

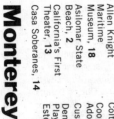

Allen Knight Maritime Museum, **18**
Asilomar State Beach, **2**
California's First Theater, **13**
Casa Soberanes, **14**
Colton Hall, **17**
Cooper-Molera Adobe, **19**
Custom House, **9**
Dennis the Menace Playground/El Estero Park, **23**
Fisherman's Wharf, **10**
Greyhound Bus Station, **15**
Joseph Boston Store, **12**
Larkin House, **16**
Lovers Point, **4**
Monterey Bay Aquarium, **6**
Municipal Wharf, **22**
Pacific Biological Laboratories, **7**
Pacific Grove Museum of Natural History, **5**
Pacific House, **11**
Point Piños Light Station, **1**
Spirit of Monterey Wax Museum, **8**
Stevenson House, **21**
Transit Plaza, **20**
Washington Park, **3**

Monterey

otherwise known to Steinbeck lovers as "Doc's Lab"; and **Kalisa's** (851 Cannery Row), known in Steinbeck's time as the Laida Café—an "institution of commercialized love." Kalisa's has lost much of its charm since the 1930s, but it's still a nice place to grab a cup of coffee. In addition to its historic adobes and 19th-century mission, Monterey's other main attraction is the impressive **Monterey Bay Aquarium** (886 Cannery Row, tel. 408/648–4800), where you'll find a 28-foot-high kelp forest aquarium, a 55,000-gallon sea otter exhibit, and a house-size shark tank—definitely one of Monterey's best attractions.

If you're over 21 and feeling kind of thirsty, head to one of Cannery Row's four wine-tasting rooms. **Bargetto Winery** (700 Cannery Row, tel. 408/373–4053) will let you sip Chardonnay daily from 10:30 to 6 without charge, while the **Paul Masson Museum and Wine Tasting Room** (upstairs from Bargetto, tel. 408/646–5446) offers free drinks and a small exhibit on wine-making and the history of the Masson vineyards.

Getting around Monterey is not difficult. If you take the bike/pedestrian path that runs parallel to the shore you can get from the historic areas of downtown to Fisherman's Wharf and Cannery Row. But because this city is a summertime mecca for thousands of tourists from around the world, both parking and crowds are a serious problem. The most reasonable parking garage in town charges $1 an hour and is located between Alvarado, Franklin, Washington, and Del Monte streets. A map that spotlights affordable public parking areas is available at the **Monterey Peninsula Chamber of Commerce** (380 Alvarado, tel. 408/649–1770).

You'll certainly enjoy a quick tour of Monterey and it's a convenient hub from which to explore California's impressive beaches and redwood forests, but be warned that all this beauty does not come cheaply when you have to find a place to stay after a day of rollicking in the great outdoors (*see* Where to Sleep, *below*). After exploring the beaches and forests, and taking a walk through Monterey to check things out, the cash-strapped might want to avoid the more heavily touristed sites and head for **El Estero Park,** east of downtown at the intersection of Del Monte and Camino Estero. Here you can flop down on the banks of El Estero Lake, rent a pedal boat for $5 (El Estero Boating, tel. 408/375–1484), or play in the funky **Dennis the Menace Playground,** created by cartoonist Hank Ketcham. Otherwise, head south on Route 68 for the **Jacks Peak Regional Park** (tel. 408/647–7795), a day park 10 miles south of Monterey off Olmstead Road that has hiking trails and picnic facilities. Monterey County charges $1 admission to the park during the week and $2 on Fridays, weekends, and holidays.

If you really want to avoid the crowds, head 2 miles west of Monterey to the quiet town of **Pacific Grove,** at the very edge of the peninsula in a dense thicket of gnarled cypresses. Here you'll find the spectacular **Asilomar State Beach** (tel. 408/372–4076), where you can watch the sun set over wild sand dunes and the Pacific. If you're driving from Monterey, take Ocean View Drive west (just west of Cannery Row) and follow it as it bends southward. Also known as the "poor man's 17-mile drive," Ocean View Drive winds past Asilomar Beach and **Lover's Point,** a popular daytime picnic spot and nighttime make-out point. Between October and March in **Washington Park,** at the corner of Pine Avenue and Alder Street, you can glimpse thousands of Monarch butterflies who make their winter homes in the park. If you're into dead butterflies, check out the excellent exhibit at the **Pacific Grove Museum of Natural History** (165 Forest Ave., tel. 408/ 372–4212). Another popular stop in Pacific Grove is the **Point Pinos Light Station** (Ocean View Blvd. at Point Pinos, tel. 408/372–4212), the oldest continuously operating lighthouse on the west coast. It's open weekends from 1 to 4, and has a small museum that's worth a look; admission is free. **17 Mile Drive,** perhaps the area's most famous attraction, takes you from Pacific Grove through **Pebble Beach,** land of golf courses and multimillion-dollar mansions. It's a pleasant drive, but the $8 service charge (payable at the toll gates) is annoying. To get to 17 Mile Drive from Monterey, follow Lighthouse Avenue west until you see the toll gate. A cheerful note: Visitors on foot or bicycle get in for free. If you're getting hungry or tired, Pacific Grove's **Portofino Cafe** (620 Lighthouse Ave., on the lower level of Pacific Grove Plaza, tel. 408/373–7379) is a low-key place that features poetry readings, acoustic music, and various types of mellow entertainment. There's a cover charge at night.

CARMEL Perched on a rocky bluff 8 miles south of Monterey, Carmel is a quiet and affluent beachfront town that doubles as an artists' colony. Don't let Carmel's gorgeous coast or shady beaches fool you, however, because this is a strange place—an aloof bastion of conservatism known for its provincial attitudes and some of the most restrictive laws in the nation. There are no sidewalks, no street lighting, and no mail delivery in residential Carmel-by-the-Sea. Locals enjoy this village setting and have chosen to pick up their mail at the post office, where they hang out and exchange gossip, just like the old days. In addition, high-heeled shoes are against the law (backpackers will find this particularly annoying), downtown establishments do not have street addresses, and no live entertainment is allowed within the local drinking holes or restaurants. Instead, Carmel hosts its live shows in a bring-your-own blanket outdoor forest theater (**The Sunset Cultural Community Center**) with fire pits on each end of the stage. Also interesting is Carmel's self-image: It fancies itself a small and private community, and does its utmost to make sure it stays this way. Yet it's mercilessly invaded daily by tourists hopping from gift shop to art gallery to "quaint" café. Even more bizarre is the fact that Carmel elected Clint "go ahead, make my day" Eastwood as its mayor not so long ago.

He has since stepped down, but Mayor Clint Eastwood proved to be one of the town's most popular tourist attractions, giving Carmel even more of the notoriety and attention it didn't particularly want in the first place.

Your first stop in Carmel should be the downtown area, easily accessed from Route 1, the only major thoroughfare for miles. Here you'll find a parade of gift shops, boutiques, restaurants, and art galleries. The **Carmel Art Association** (on Dolores between 5th and 6th Aves., tel. 408/624–6176) exhibits works by local artists and many pieces inside the small hall are for sale. Carmel's **public beach** is at the end of Ocean Avenue, where you can pick up a game of volleyball or take a nap in the sand, protected from the blistering sun by the groves of cypress trees. A lot of locals dodge this place in favor of the **South Carmel River State Beach,** south of Carmel proper on Route 1, but consider grabbing a supply of wood and some fixin's and having yourself a barbecue on Carmel's public beach—one of the few that permits open fires. Otherwise, head to **Hawk Tower** (26304 Oceanview Ave., tel 408/624–1813), created by poet and sculptor Robinson Jeffers in the 1920s. From the top you get a wonderful view of the coast and of Jeffers' **Tor House,** built in 1918. One of Carmel's most famous personalities, Jeffers built his home from rocks he carried up from the beach himself, creating in the process one of California's most unique and strangely "natural" dwellings. Guided tours ($5) of the house are available by appointment Friday and Saturdays—certainly worth the price of admission. The **Carmel Mission** (Rio Rd. and Lauser Dr., tel 408/624–3600), or "Carmelo," as it's known by locals, is another attractive site worth visiting. It was founded in 1770 by the busy Padre Serra (who is buried here) and includes a stone church, museum, and gardens. Across the street is **Mission Trail Park,** 35 acres of unspoiled nature, where mountain bikes and hiking are permitted.

POINT LOBOS TO POINT SUR Only 3 miles south of Carmel on Route 1 is the **Point Lobos State Reserve** (tel. 408/624–4909), a popular hang out with local sea lions, harbor seals, otters, and migrating whales (December–May). Inside the reserve are miles of hiking trails and scenic overlooks, including the **Seal Lion Point Trail** that leads through a magnificent series of sea coves and tidal pools. If you don't mind hiking an additional mile, park across the street from the reserve's main entrance on Route 1 and walk to the trailheads; otherwise you have to pay $5 to get in. The park is open daily 9 AM to dusk. Three miles past Point Lobos is **Garrapata State Beach.** You can park along the road near the Soveranes Barn to explore the loop trails that go to **Soveranes Point, Soveranes Canyon,** or **Rocky Ridge.** The trail entrance to the point is across the street while the ones for the canyon and the ridge are behind the barn. Some of the trails, which offer views of Salinas Valley and Monterey, sport steep terrain. The point trail is another great place to watch otters frolicking on the offshore rock formations.

Five miles farther south, **Palo Colorado Road** winds its way east from Route 1 for 8 serpentine miles until it ends at **Bottcher's Gap,** where there's a campground run by the U.S. Forest Service (tel. 408/385–5434) (*see* Camping under Where to Sleep, Big Sur, *below*) and a trailhead that leads into the northern edge of the Los Padres National Forest. One of Bottcher's Gap's best trails will take you to **Pico Blanco,** an incredibly rugged and wild mountain peak that the Esselen Native Americans thought of as the top of the world and the site of human creation. You can do some backcountry camping at Pico Blanco; ask at the Forest Service office about good spots.

Back on Route 1, south of where the Palo Colorado Road intersects the highway, is **Bixby Creek Bridge,** a 550-foot concrete span built in 1932. Just before the bridge is the **Old Coast Road,** a circular route that curves inland for 10 miles and meets back up with Route 1 opposite the entrance to the Andrew Molera State Park. If you're the four-wheeling type, you'll like Old Coast Road and its gravel- and mud-plagued inclines; if it hasn't rained for the past few days, it shouldn't be too bad for a regular ol' car, though. This is California at its rugged best—craggy cliffs, majestic redwoods, and views of Little Sur. It's hard to believe this road was the old Route 1. Double back 1½ miles north of the road's base at Andrew Molera to check out the **Point Sur Light Station** (tel. 408/625–4419), built in 1889 to prevent shipwrecks along this foggy and rocky stretch of coast. Tours of the lighthouse are available on weekends for $2. **Andrew Molera State Park** has more than 4,000 largely undeveloped acres with beach access and camping in a meadow. Campers pay $3 per person and $1 per dog. Once the sight of a Monterey Jack cheese factory and a dairy farm, the park is now largely deserted, offering more than 10 miles of hiking and mountain-biking trails. The **Bluff's Trail** that follows the coast is especially striking in spring when all the wildflowers are in bloom. The privately owned **Molera Trail Rides** (tel. 408/625–8664 or 659–0433), located in the campground, offers horseback riding for $50 per day. Call the Park Service (tel. 408/667–2315) for questions concerning the park.

BIG SUR TO SAN SIMEON For the next few miles south of Andrew Molera State Park you'll find yourself in Big Sur, often described more as a philosophy than as specific acreage. Every local defines Big Sur differently, but all agree it includes about 7 miles of scenic Route 1, a small mountain outpost nestled in a stately redwood forest, a few gas stations, an inn, and an occasional restaurant. In the midst of this undefined utopia is **Pfeiffer Big Sur State Park** (tel. 408/667–2171), on the east side of Route 1, 5 miles south of Andrew Molera. The park is one of the most popular campgrounds and hiking spots on the coast, especially during the summer. Trails from here lead up to **Pfeiffer Ridge** and to the 60-foot **Pfeiffer Falls,** at the end of an hour's hike through groves of huge redwoods. Just south of Pfeiffer, on the same side of the highway, lies the **Pine Ridge** trailhead, a favorite with locals. A difficult 6-mile hike inland from here takes you to the **Sykes Hot Springs,** an ideal place for a late-afternoon swim. **Sycamore Road,** 1½ miles south of where Pfeiffer State Park meets Route 1, is unmarked save for a stop sign and a yellow WARNING NARROW ROAD AHEAD sign. If you can find it, however, brave the road for 2 miles and you'll land at **Pfeiffer Beach,** a violently turbulent, wind-swept cove with huge rock formations and an angry ocean that's definitely not suited for swimming. Five miles farther south you'll see **Nepenthe** (tel. 408/667–2345), an expensive restaurant with an extraordinary view (also the last stop of Bus 22 from Monterey). There is a less expensive café next door where you can grab a beer and watch the sun go down.

If you've had your quota of stunning views and scenic overlooks for the day, take a break and head south a few miles from Nepenthe to the **Henry Miller Memorial Library** (tel. 408/667–2574). Located in artist Emil White's home, the library displays assorted Miller artifacts—including all the books Miller gave White—locked away under glass. Library director Jerry Kamstra's book, *Weed: Adventures of a Dope Smuggler* sits alongside an impressive variety of Miller books for sale. Fans of Miller should also stop by the **Coast Gallery** (tel. 408/667–2301), a few miles farther south, where the author's lithographs and paintings are displayed. The gallery's small candle shop is stocked with hundreds of handmade candles.

Back on Route 1, the **Julia Pfeiffer Burns Park** (tel. 408/667–2315) offers camping and a large selection of hiking trails. One of its best trails starts at Route 1 and leads to a bluff with an incredible view of **McWay Creek,** which pours 70 feet down to the ocean. There are also picnic tables here and a few crooked trails that lead down to the beach. Three miles south of Julia Pfeiffer Burn Park is a sign on the right side of the road that reads: ESALEN INSTITUTE–RESERVATIONS ONLY. At the end of the road you'll find the world-famous **Esalen Institute** (tel. 408/667–3000), a one-time, wacked-out hippie colony that specializes in the "exploration of human relationship." Locals tend to scoff, but the institute was one of the first places to introduce Gestalt therapy in the late-'60s. Today, Esalen still attracts people from around the world to its skillfully run workshops and self-help sessions, although its huge gardens, pool, and hot springs are no longer open to the public. To attend a workshop, call the institute for more information.

Once past the institute, be warned—you're almost completely on your own for the next 67 miles heading south. Except for the small town of **Lucia** (23 miles south of Big Sur) and its gas station/restaurant, the **Pacific Valley**—a seemingly endless expanse of rolling grasslands that hug the shore—has few tourist facilities. It's a breathtaking stretch of jagged coast and sprawling beaches, but about the only other thing of interest is **Jade Cove,** a small cliff-encircled beach famous for its large jade deposits. One mile south of the **Pacific Valley Center** gas station (9 miles south of Lucia), the cove is accessible via wooden foot bridges that arch over the barbed wire fence. Hunting for jade is allowed on the beach but not along the cliff walls.

Forty-four miles south of Lucia look for **San Simeon,** a small oceanfront town that's famous for one thing and one thing only: **Hearst Castle,** built in 1919. The Hearst family still owns more than 80,000 acres of land in San Simeon, but the castle designed by Julia Morgan and bank-rolled by publishing magnate William Randolph Hearst—the model for Orson Welles' *Citizen Kane*—was deeded to the state of California after Hearst's death. You can see the massive complex from the highway, but if you're in the mood for a closer inspection you can take one of four tours of the estate. The $14 guided tours last 1½ hours, including bus transportation up the private 5-mile road that leads to the site. Reservations are advised, as tickets sell out quickly. For more information call 800/444–7275. If you want a sneak preview of your tour or cannot afford the castle's steep admission, check out, at no charge, the Smithsonian-esque exhibit at the huge new visitor center at the bottom of the hill. It documents both the history of the Hearst family and the building of the castle. Directly opposite the entrance to Hearst Castle, across Route 1, is a road that leads to the small town of **San Simeon,** where you'll find a quiet public beach and a small pier. Two miles down the road is a strip of motels known as San Simeon Acres.

Not to be missed at the Madonna Inn is the urinal in the men's room, a large waterfall that's activated by lasers (women should knock and look in).

SAN LUIS OBISPO Probably the least-known of the larger central coast towns, San Luis Obispo, surrounded by rocky hills and volcanic peaks, sits 34 miles south of San Simeon, 12 miles inland from the coast. Half the town is made up of students who attend the **California Polytechnic State University** and nearby **Cuesta College,** and in summer the town's population drops dramatically. Downtown, the Chamber of Commerce has a pamphlet detailing four heritage walks, each taking you past buildings that recall different periods of San Luis Obispo's history. The best is the downtown walk, which passes the **Ah Louis Store** (800 Palm St.), built by its namesake in 1884 to serve the needs of the Chinese laborers who helped build the railroads. The store is still open and sells a mishmash of things from the Orient. Southwest of downtown, visible from U.S. 101, is the tacky pink-and-white **Madonna Inn** (100 Madonna Rd., tel. 805/543–3000), a popular hotel where no two of its flamboyant and loudly decorated rooms are alike. The management won't let you visit the **Cave Room** (complete with waterfall) or the **Medieval Room** (complete with a handy suit of armor) unless you have a reservation, but there are postcards in the lobby that detail each one. San Luis Obispo's other main sight is the **Mission San Luis Obispo de Tolosa** (At Chorro and Monterey Sts., tel. 805/543–6850), the fifth-oldest of California's 21 historic missions, built in 1772. Adjacent to the mission is **Mission Plaza,** a small park with grass spots and benches that overlook the San Luis Obispo creek. Across the creek are the restaurants and shops that line **Higuera Street,** the main downtown drag.

In addition to Higuera Street, the downtown attractions are concentrated on **Garden** and **Nipano** streets, where you'll find numerous record stores, restaurants, cafés, and movie theaters. Keep on the look-out for free outdoor concerts in Mission Plaza, usually held on weekend evenings during the summer. This college town has a fairly thriving bar scene, and bars are the primary venues of live music. Your best bet is to pick up a copy of the *New Times*—the free weekly available each Thursday—and check what's on that night. Performances vary from acoustic folk to country dancing, reggae, and rock—all at the same places, but on different nights. For a game of chess and a great cup of coffee head to **Linnea's Café** (1110 Garden St., tel. 805/541–5888), popular with San Luis Obispo's "hipsters." Linnea's also offers acoustic music nightly at 8, usually without a cover. One of the most popular things to do among locals, students, and tourists alike is to visit the Thursday night **Farmers' Market** on Higuera Street from 6 to 9. There's a great selection of fruits and produce, and also live music that's performed up and down the street. An interesting place for music buffs is the **Boo Boo Wax Museum** (978 Monterey St., tel. 805/541–3181), a room full of music rarities, old 45s, and a pop-culture Beatles exhibit that will make your toes curl. The Wax Museum is in the back of Boo Boo Records.

Twelve miles northwest of San Luis Obispo sits **Morro Bay,** a small fishing village easily spotted off Route 1 by its towering **Morro Rock** and the ugly PG&E power plant (look for the three massive smoke pipes). Dubbed *El Morro* by Spanish explorers who believed the seaside edifice resembled helmets worn by Moorish soldiers, Morro Rock is the westernmost in a chain of "seven sisters"—volcanic peaks that stretch south along the coast to San Luis Obispo. Much of Morro Rock's huge face was quarried during the 1950s to build Morro Bay's breakwater, but today the rock has been designated a wildlife refuge for the endangered peregrine falcon and for the other 250 species of migrating birds that visit the city each year. Overlooking the bay at the southern end of town is the **Morro Bay Natural History Museum** (State Park Rd., Morro Bay State Park, tel. 805/772–2694), rife with excellent displays about local marine life and the Native Americans who once lived in the area. Morro Bay has its tourist row—the **Embarcadero**—which runs along the waterfront, full of shell shops, seafood restaurants, and fishing docks. But because Morro Bay is so small, you won't feel like you're in tourist hell here. The easily walked Embarcadero is no more than a mile long, and at sunset it buzzes with activity as fishing trawlers and tuna boats unload the day's catch. However, one of Morro Bay's best attractions is the **Bay Aquarium** (595 Embarcadero, tel. 805/772–7697), where you can feed seals and otters being nursed back to health and tour a small marine-life museum (including a preserved great white shark).

AVILA BEACH AND PISMO BEACH Following the 101 Freeway 12 miles south from San Luis Obispo, the first accessible beach you come to is **Avila Beach** (turn off at San Luis Bay Dr. and follow it to Avila Beach Rd.). Just before you cross into Avila Beach, look for the **PG&E Community Center** (8566 Ontario Rd., tel. 805/546–5232), which has an exhibit detailing the history of the **Diablo Nuclear Power Plant,** located on the outskirts of town. Drop by and listen to what a siren will sound like in the event of a meltdown. A 3½-hour tour of the plant takes you through a simulated control room and the power plant's marine biology lab. Tours are free, but you must call ahead (tel. 805/595–7647) to reserve a space. Continue on Avila Beach Drive and you'll pass **Avila Hot Springs** (250 Avila Beach Dr., tel. 805/595–2359), a developed resort that charges $9 to use its hot mineral baths. Cluttered with beachfront fish shanties and gift shops, Avila Beach also has a wonderfully rickety wooden pier and harbor boardwalk. If the public beach is too crowded, head up **Cave Landing Road** (off Avila Beach Rd. on the way back to U.S. 101) for **Pirates Cove,** one of the few nude beaches in the area. The beach is both dirty and covered with rocks, and extremely isolated. Bring a friend if you can—you never know what kind of freaks are hanging around (women especially should not go alone). On your way back to 101 you may want to detour up **Sea Canyon Drive,** which winds its way north through the hills for about 13 miles until reaching **Los Osos Valley Road.** The drive is beautiful, but the road is unpaved and rocky—perfect for a mountain bike or a 4-wheel drive jeep, miserable for a rental car.

Pismo Beach, perennial destination of that wacky Bugs Bunny ("I knew I shoulda made that left in Albuquerque"), lies a few miles south of Avila Beach off U.S. 101. Famous for its wide beaches and huge sand dunes—part of Rudolph Valentino's *The Sheik* was filmed here—Pismo Beach also used to be the clam capital of the world. Today the clam population has been nearly obliterated by over-fishing and pollution, but you can still take part in a moonlight clam dig during the summer (*see* Outdoor Activities, *below*). Pismo is also the only beachside community in California where autos can be driven on designated parts of the beach—thrilling if you like to see a beach full of cars. Most of the action takes place around the pier downtown, and the streets leading up to it are filled with restaurants, shops, and plenty of tourists.

● ● ● OUTDOOR ACTIVITIES

MONTEREY

BEACHES **Monterey State Beach** (east of the Municipal Wharf) and **Del Monte Beach** (just east of the Naval Postgraduate school) are less spectacular than the beaches of neighboring Pacific Grove and Carmel. Also, you can't swim in Monterey Bay due to dangerous tides, and high winds tend to make beach lounging a chore.

BIKING AND MOPEDS **Bay Bikes** (640 Wave St., above Cannery Row, tel. 408/646–9090) rents mountain bikes for $18 a day. **Monterey Adventures** (1250 Del Monte Ave., tel. 408/373–2696) rents beach cruisers for $15 a day, or $10 for 3 hours. They also rent mopeds for $10 an hour (minimum of two hours) or $40 a day. Driver's license and deposit required.

FISHING AND WHALE WATCHING Contact **Chris' Fishing Trips** (tel. 408/375–5951) or **Monterey Sport Fishing** (tel. 408/372–2203) on Fisherman's Wharf. Both charge $25–$35 for half-day sport-fishing trips. Equipment (tackle, poles, bait) is available for a small additional fee. Both also offer whale-watching trips between December and March when Monterey Bay is filled with migrating whales—a spectacular sight, to say the least.

GOLFING Tee off at the **Pacific Grove Municipal Golf Course** (77 Asilomar Ave., Pacific Grove, tel. 408/375–3456), open to nonmembers year-round. From the course you have an excellent view of Monterey Bay and the Point Pinos Lighthouse. They charge $15 for 18 holes and $8 for 9 holes; reservations taken one week in advance.

KAYAKING Monterey Bay isn't a good place for swimming—it's cold and rocky—but it's a great place to grab a kayak and explore the coast. **Monterey Bay Kayaks** (693 Del Monte Ave., Monterey, tel. 408/373–KELP) offers half-day rentals for $25, which includes instruction for beginners.

Monterey Bay attracts divers from around the world with its vast kelp beds and magnificent underwater terrain.

SCUBA DIVING **Aquarius Dive Shop** (2240 Del Monte Ave. or 32 Cannery Row, both tel. 408/375–1933) offers expensive instruction to beginners and moderately priced equipment rentals for experienced divers; certification and photo ID required. Both Aquarius Dive Shops are located in Monterey. The bluffs and underwater caves off Ocean View Drive are considered the best scuba spots in the area.

CARMEL

BIKING Rent a bike in Carmel and peddle over to Point Lobos, the 17 Mile Drive, or just poke around the town itself. **Bay Bikes** (Lincoln St. and 6th Ave., tel. 408/625–BIKE) rents mountain bikes for $18 a day. If you're in good shape you can ride all the way to Monterey and drop off the bike at their other location (*see above*).

GOLF Put on your checked pants and goofy shoes and head over to the highbrow **Poppy Hills Golf Course** in Pebble Beach (3200 Lopez Rd., tel. 408/625–2035). Of course, you'll have to pay the 17-Mile Drive fee ($8) to get into this public course, but that's part of its aloof appeal. Otherwise, the **Cañada Golf Club** in Carmel Valley (4860

Carmel Valley Rd., 1 mi east of Rte. 1, tel. 408/624–0111) is rated one of California's top 25 public golf courses.

HIKING **Garland Ranch Regional Park** in Carmel Valley offers day hikes along hundreds of trails. Go east off Route 1 on Carmel Valley Road for 7 miles and look for signs directing you to the park.

SCUBA DIVING **Point Lobos State Reserve** (tel. 408/624–4909) allows up to 15 teams on any one day to dive in Whalers Cove among the otters, seals, and sea lions. There's a $6 diving fee plus $5 for parking to drive into the reserve. Reservations can be made through MISTIX (tel. 800/444–PARK). Proof of diver certification is required. If you need to rent equipment contact the Aquarius Dive Shop in Monterey (*see above*).

BIG SUR

BIKING To the dismay of many drivers, lots of people bicycle along Route 1. Cyclists should be fairly experienced and familiar with the narrowness of the highway and the lack of road shoulder. One benefit of cycling is that you often get to camp cheaply at the state parks along the way. If you have a breakdown, contact **Big Sur Mountain Bike and Backpacking Outfitters** (Village Shop 3, Big Sur, tel. 408/667–2468), 24½ miles south of Carmel in the River Inn Village center. The store is often closed, but when open they can provide spare parts and moral support. Bus 22 runs from Monterey to the Nepenthe restaurant, 29 miles south of Carmel, and most buses come equipped with bike racks.

Andrew Molera (tel. 408/667–2315) is the only Big Sur park that offers mountain biking trails. The **Ridge Trail** goes through grass land and oak forests with a view of the Big Sur coastline and climbs 1,200 feet in 2 miles. The **Bob Cat Trail,** accessible from the park's parking lot, parallels the Big Sur River and leads out to Molera Point. Most bike trails in Molera are old fire roads that hikers also use, so stay alert. Another place to go is halfway up **Naciemento Ferguson Road,** south of Lucia off Route 1. Bikes are *not* allowed to the left—the Ventana Wilderness—but on the right side of the road you'll see a few trails.

On Big Sur it's not too hard to feel like you're lost somewhere in a strange land at the beginning of time, surrounded only by virgin redwood forests and untamed natural beauty.

HIKING Big Sur is a hiker's paradise, with miles of trails and endless coastal panoramas. Even better, permits are not required to hike in Big Sur—only if you plan on bringing a camp stove. To get a stove permit, go to **Pfeiffer State Park** (Rte. 1, 26 mi south of Carmel, tel. 408/667–2315). There you can also pick up maps to all the parks and trails. South of Pfeiffer, about a mile down the road on the east side, lies the trail head to **Pine Ridge Trail,** a favorite with locals. After 6 miles of hard hiking you reach the **Sykes Hot Springs,** a natural hot spring where you can soak to your heart's content.

HORSEBACK RIDING Adjacent to Andrew Molera State Park is the privately run **Molera Trail Rides** (tel. 408/625–8664), which has three-hour trips for $50 a person. Most trails meander through the mountains and eventually wind their way towards the beach, where you can have a picnic in the sand before turning back.

SAN SIMEON AND CAMBRIA Not known for its hikes, San Simeon and Cambria both have beaches that allow for a mild hike or nature walk. **San Simeon State Beach,** about 3 miles south of Hearst Castle, is extremely windy at times but usually uncrowded. **Moon Stone Beach,** directly across the highway from Cambria, does not offer much in the way of vigorous hiking, but it's a pleasant beach for a short stroll. If you'd rather tour by bike, **Overland Expeditions** (1920 Main St., Cambria, tel. 805/927–5885) rents 10-speeds and mountain bikes for $18 a day. Surf boards ($15 a day) and body boards ($10 a day) can be procured at the **Cambria Surf Company** (1036 Main St., Cambria, tel. 805/927–8506).

SAN LUIS OBISPO AND MORRO BAY

BIKING Just about everyone has a mountain bike in San Luis Obispo. Locals sometimes ride (and hike) the trails off Los Osos Valley Road or in Montaña de Oro State Park, which allows bikes on a few of its fire roads/trails. A very challenging paved-road ride is up Cuesta Grade, along U.S. 101 north of San Luis Obispo. If you need equipment, **Rent-A-Bike** (tel. 805/543–1144) will actually deliver a 10-speed or mountain bike to your door anywhere in San Luis Obispo and pick it up when you're done. Not bad for $22 a day.

CANOES AND KAYAKING Canoe rentals are available to paddle around the Morro Bay estuary. Head to the **State Park Marina** (tel. 805/772–8796), beside the Bayside Café on State Park Road. Canoes are $6 an hour. **Morro Bay Outfitters** (844 Main St., tel. 805/772–1119) rents both one-person ($35) and two-person ($30) kayaks and also leads guided outings of the harbor.

HIKING This area is full of hikes into the foothills and along the ocean bluffs. The 2-mile **Cerro Alto Trail** will give you a view of the coast and the interior wilderness. Take Route 1 toward Morro Bay until Atascadero, then follow the signs for the Cerro Alto Campground. The trailhead is at the bridge by the ranger station. Otherwise, get a hiking map from the Chamber of Commerce (*see* Basics, *above*). In Morro Bay you can join up with the **Clam Taxi** (tel. 805/772–8085), a guided nature walk that will take you over to the spit of sand in the middle of Morro Bay harbor. Tours leave from the Marina at Embarcadero and Pacific streets every quarter of an hour during the summer.

Montaña de Oro State Park, 12 miles northwest of San Luis Obispo, along Los Osos Valley Road, is one of the nicest parks in the area, with 8,000 acres of largely undeveloped land that turns gold (*montaña de oro:* "mountains of gold") every spring when the park's flowers bloom. Miles of trails wind their way through the park, some of which allow bikes and horses. **Spooners Cove,** once popular with prohibition-era bootleggers, is the most accessible of the numerous coves along the coast. You can buy a trail map of the park for $2 at the **park headquarters** (Pecho Valley Rd., tel. 805/528–0513), located in the Old Spooner Ranch House.

WINDSURFING **Lopez Lake,** considered one of the best windsurfing lakes in California, is about 15 miles south of San Luis Obispo off Route 227. You can rent windsurfing equipment downtown from **Mountain Air Sports** (667 Marsh St., tel. 805/543–1678) for $10–$15 an hour. Call first, however, as Lopez Lake is temporarily closed due to drought conditions.

AVILA BEACH AND PISMO BEACH

BIKING **Pismo Bike Rentals** (500 Cypress St., tel. 805/773–0355) offers beach cruisers for $15 a day and mountain bikes for $25. Most of Pismo's beaches are open to vehicular traffic so don't be afraid to take your bike on the sand.

CLAMMING There aren't as many clams as there once were, but it's still legal to clam on the beach in Pismo and Avila. Clammers need a California State fishing license (obtainable at local sport shops) and a clamming fork (a pitchfork will work, too). Clams must be at least 4½ inches across and there's a limit of 10 per person. Because the clams are buried several hundred feet offshore, the best time to clam is at low tide. Remember that even in summer the water is cold. Boots and gaiters are recommended.

HIKING The **Pismo Dunes Preserve** was once thought to be the center of a powerful and benign energy, an area popular in the 1930s with proto-New Agers and the mystically inclined. You too can experience the power of the dunes if you take a trek among the wildflowers and vegetation. No set trails exist and hikers should be careful not to step on any of the plant life. Look for the preserve on Route 1, just south of town.

HORSEBACK RIDING The **Livery Stable** (1207 Silver Spur Pl., Oceano, tel. 805/489–8100) charges $15 an hour for unguided rides. Head out to the beach and spend the day galloping in the sand.

Santa Barbara

You cross an invisible line as you enter Santa Barbara, a small but noticeable change in attitude that tells you this is no longer "northern" California. Considered the northernmost outpost of "So Cal" (Southern California), Santa Barbara is too wealthy and aloof to fit comfortably with the more genial towns of San Luis Obispo and Monterey, yet it's also too picturesque and relaxed to be seen as an extension of Los Angeles, only 90 miles south. Santa Barbara may be an exceedingly wealthy and conservative community—Ronald Reagan has his ranch here, after all—but the scenery is Riviera-esque in its beauty, and the locals all look as if they do nothing but sit on the beach and tan. There is a scruffier and less daunting contingent of people in town, too, ranging from the mellow U.C. Santa Barbara students to the vagabond homeless, but Santa Barbara works hard to retain its Mediterranean image. Everything here is designed around a Spanish-Moorish theme, with red-tile roofs, wrought-iron gates, and red adobe. Despite the fact that Santa Barbara takes itself much too seriously, it's still one of southern California's most interesting coastal towns, buffered by golden beaches, a historic mission, a few museums, and hundreds of thriving outdoor cafés and restaurants.

BASICS • • •

CURRENCY EXCHANGE They may have a silly name, but the **We Buy Gold and Coins** shop buys and sells foreign currency at a competitive rate. *Corner of Ontare and State Sts., tel. 805/687–3641. Open daily 9:30–5.*

DOCTORS **Santa Barbara Medical Foundation Clinic** is a walk-in clinic that can help you with non-life-threatening medical problems. *215 Pesetas La., tel. 805/964–6211. Open Mon.–Thurs. 8–8, Fri. 8–5, Sat. 9–6, Sun. noon–6.*

LUGGAGE STORAGE The **Greyhound** station has six large lockers and 16 small ones. It's $1 for the first 24 hours. *34 Carillo St., tel. 805/966–3902. Open daily 5:30 AM–2 AM.*

TOURIST INFORMATION The **Visitor Center** stocks brochures, maps, and information on local accommodations. They also have guides to the "Red Tile" walking tour and scenic drives. *1 Santa Barbara St., at Cabrillo Blvd., tel. 805/965–3021. Open weekdays 9–5.*

The **Visitor Information Center** has information on downtown shopping and local budget restaurants. *504 State St., tel. 805/962–2098. Open weekdays 10–5.*

Gay and Lesbian Resource Center (417 Santa Barbara St., tel. 805/963–3636) has information on local gay/lesbian events. They also provide counseling for anyone who just wants to talk.

COMING AND GOING • • •

BY TRAIN Northbound trains on their way to San Luis Obispo ($24), Salinas, San Francisco ($50), Oregon, and Vancouver stop once daily in Santa Barbara's **Amtrak** station (209 State St., tel. 805/963–1015 or 800/872–7245). Southbound trains to Los Angeles ($19) run more frequently. Bus 21 runs from the Amtrak station to the **Transit Center** (1020 Chapala St., at Carillo St., tel. 805/683–3702) in downtown. From here you can walk or take a bus to upper State Street, where some budget hotels are located. No lockers are available in the station, which is open daily 7 AM to 11 PM (the ticket window is closed 1:30 PM–2:30 PM and 6:30–7 PM).

BY BUS Both Green Tortoise and Greyhound stop in Santa Barbara. **Green Tortoise** (tel. 805/569–1884) runs a bus to Santa Barbara from Los Angeles and Ventura on Mondays; and south from San Francisco, Santa Cruz, Salinas, and San Luis Obispo on Saturdays. The bus stops in the parking lot behind Carrows restaurant on Carillo Street. Next to the Transit Center, **Greyhound** (34 Carillo St., tel. 805/966–3962 or

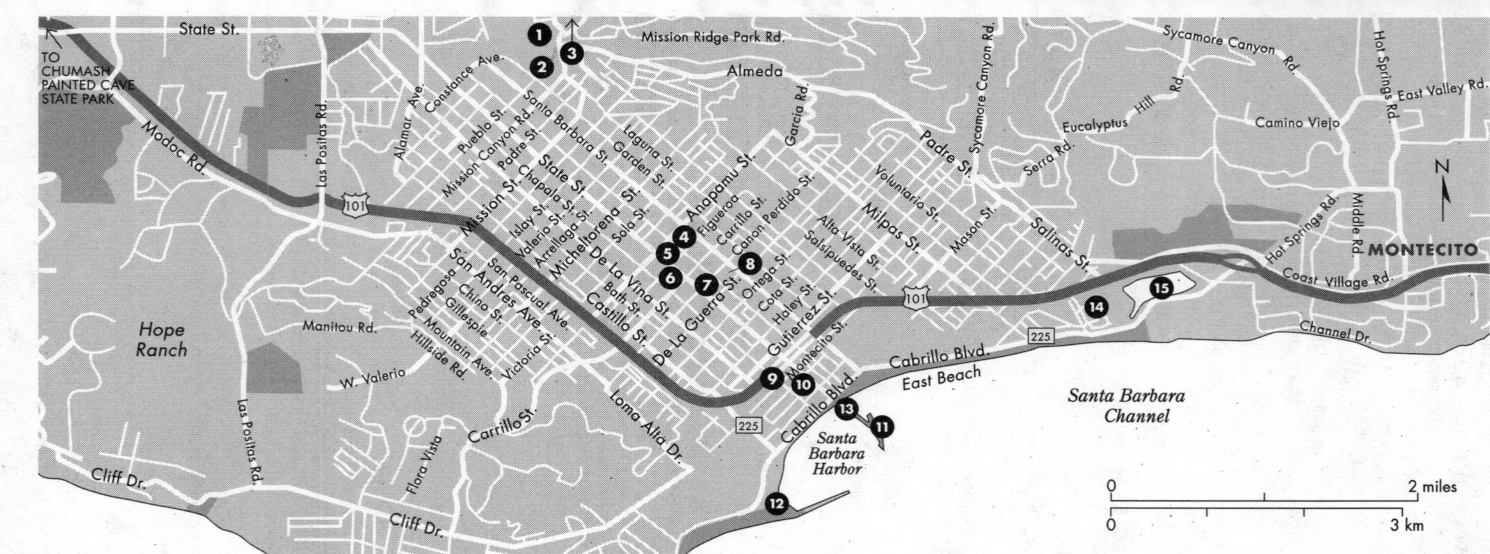

Amtrak Train Station, **10**
Andree Clark Bird Refuge, **15**
Botanic Garden, **3**
Courthouse, **4**
El Presidio State Historic Park, **7**
Historical Museum, **8**
Moreton Bay Fig Tree, **9**
Museum of Art, **5**
Museum of Natural History, **1**
Santa Barbara Mission, **2**
Santa Barbara Yacht Harbor, **12**
Santa Barbara Zoo, **14**
Sea Center, **13**
Stearns Wharf, **11**
Transit Center, **6**

Santa Barbara

805/962–2477) has frequent service to and from Santa Barbara. The fare to San Francisco is $39, to Los Angeles $12.50. The station is open daily 5:30 AM–2 AM. The ticket window, however, closes at 11 PM.

BY CAR **U.S. 101**—which connects Santa Barbara to Los Angeles (95 miles south) and San Luis Obispo (100 miles north)—is the main route to and through the city. Other routes include **Route 154** (San Marcos Pass Road), which leads north out of Santa Barbara to Lake Cachuma and Santa Ymez and eventually rejoins 101 north of Buellton.

GETTING AROUND • • •

The first thing to realize is that the Pacific Ocean is south, not west, and the mountains surrounding Santa Barbara run east–west, *not* north–south. In downtown, the easiest way to orient yourself is by **State Street,** which starts at Stearn's Wharf and runs north through downtown towards Goleta, where it becomes Hollister Avenue. Lower State Street (about the 2000 block and below) and State Street comprise the downtown area where the restaurants, shops, and nightlife spots are most densely concentrated. Streets that cross State Street are specified east or west (example: "East Vanoling" lies to the east of State Street). The beach and Stearn's Wharf are a ¾-mile walk from downtown.

BY BUS All bus routes pass through the **Transit Center** (1020 Chapala St., at Carillo St., tel. 805/683–3702).

BY CAR There are several public parking lots in downtown Santa Barbara, charging roughly $1 each hour. Be prepared for downtown's one-way streets: Santa Barbara, Chapala, Bath, Anacapa, Delavina, and Castillo.

CAR RENTAL **Ugly Duckling Rent-A-Car** (tel. 805/963–9514) has rates starting at $27 a day, or $140 a week. At last look, **Dollar Rent-A-Car** (tel. 800/800–4000) charged $30 a day and $150 a week.

FREE SHUTTLE Free buses run daily along State Street between Stearn's Wharf and Sola Street in downtown and stop every block. Shuttles run Sunday–Thursday 11 AM–5 PM, and Friday–Saturday 10 AM–8 PM. Stops are marked with a round "Santa Barbara Shuttle" sign.

WHERE TO SLEEP • • •

Santa Barbara's Mediterranean climate draws the beach crowd year-round, and the city's hotels and motels are way overpriced. Even worse, there isn't one youth hostel or campground within the city limits. If all you're looking for is access to the beach and proximity to Santa Barbara's shopping, try staying in **Carpenteria,** about 12 miles east. It's less flashy and more family oriented, and motel prices are lower. In Carpenteria try **Casa Del Sol Motel** (5585 Carpulsia Ave., tel. 805/684–4307), whose rates range from $25 for a single to $40 for four people in two double beds. **Motel 6** (4200 Via Real, tel. 805/684–6921) charges anywhere from $30 for a single to $46 for the four people/two double beds arrangement. The **Reef Motel** (4160 Via Real, tel. 805/684–4176) has singles for $36, and doubles for $44 ($46 for four). Otherwise, prepare yourself for an expensive night in Santa Barbara. If you're having trouble finding a place to stay call **Accommodations Santa Barbara** (3344 State St., tel. 800/292–2222), **On the Town** (tel. 805/687–7474), or **Santa Barbara Hot Spots** (tel. 805/564–1637). All offer free listings and price information.

UNDER $45 **California Hotel.** This tall, ancient hotel is one block from the beach and half a block from the train track. When the Amtrak thunders through at 2 AM you may go deaf, but it's the cheapest (and nicest) place in town. Singles are $27, doubles $35. *35 State St., tel. 805/966–7153. Walk 1 block east to State St. from Transit Center.*

Hotel State Street. It's next door to the California Hotel and almost on top of the train tracks (as opposed to half a block away, *see above*). There's lots of noise and no private bathrooms, but it's spotlessly clean and the management is friendly to the extreme. Singles and doubles $35. *121 State St., tel. 805/966–6586.*

Schooner Inn. This place is nice both outside and inside with a pinkish and bluish beachy feel. Rooms are clean and comfortable. Well located downtown. Singles and doubles $30–$40. *533 State St., tel. 805/965–4572. From Transit Center walk east to State St. No reservations. Laundry facilities.*

Sunset Motel. The white-adobe building with a red-tile roof has rooms that are smallish but clean. Within easy walking of downtown. Singles and doubles are $44 with bath. *3504 State St., tel. 805/687–3813. Take Bus 6 or 11 from Transit Center.*

UNDER $125 **Tropicana Inn.** You may choke at the price heading, but if you're sneaky you can fit six people into one of the Tropicana's luxurious, oceanview suites. The management doesn't mind if you do this, but they won't stand for vociferous partyers. This is an older inn that has large, elegant, J. Gatsby-type suites, just two blocks down the street from the beach. Rooms are light pinkish with a lot of solid pine furniture. All suites come with kitchens. *223 Castillo St., tel. 805/966–2219. Between U.S. 101 and Cabrillo Blvd. Take Bus 21 from Transit Center. Continental breakfast in lobby. Pool and spa.*

CAMPING **Cachuma Lake Recreation Area.** Inland over Route 154 (San Marcos pass), this place gets baking hot in the summer. Since there are more than 500 campsites, it can also get congested. There are a grocery store and shower facilities here, but sites are doled out on a first-come, first-served basis. Sites are $12 a night. *Rte. 154, northeast of Santa Barbara, tel. 805/688–8780. Open year-round.*

Carpenteria State Beach. Twelve miles west of Santa Barbara, it has 262 tent and RV spaces. Sites are close together and privacy is a serious problem, but at least the beach is only a Frisbee throw away. Some sites even sit on the sand facing the water. Showers are available and a grocery store/restaurant is within easy walking distance. Crowds are a hassle during the summer and reservations are advised. To reserve, call MISTIX (tel. 800/444–7275). Sites are $16 per night. *U.S. 101, Carpenteria, tel. 805/684–2811. Bus 20 from Transit Center. Open year-round.*

Gaviota State Park. 23 miles west of Goleta off U.S. 101, Gaviota is a somewhat stark and wind-beaten beachside campground with 18 tent spaces and 36 RV hookups. Gaviota is also one of the few state parks not to accept reservations, and all sites are doled out on a first-come, first-served basis. Showers and a grocery store (open in summer only) are nearby. Sites are $16 per night. *U.S. 101, Gaviota exit, tel. 805/968–1033. Open year-round. No reservations.*

Refugio State Beach. Some people claim this is the prettiest campground in the area—surrounded by shady palm trees and lush plant life. It lies a few miles west of El Capitan State beach off U.S. 101, 15 miles west of Goleta. All sites are on the beach. Showers and a grocery store (open in summer only) are on the premises. It's crowded most of the year and reservations are highly recommended; call MISTIX (tel. 800/444–7275). Sites are $14–$16 a night. *U.S. 101, between Gaviota and Santa Barbara, tel. 805/968–1033. Open year-round.*

ROUGHING IT Santa Barbara's mild climate makes sleeping outside an appealing prospect. Most beaches in the area, however, are patrolled at night by unfriendly police officers. You may have better luck in a city park, but as always be wary of the vagabonds and lunatics who roam them at night. You may be able to sleep in your car overnight in Isla Vista (*see* Near Santa Barbara, *below*), where most UCSB students live.

● ● ● FOOD

Most restaurants in this well-to-do resort town are extremely expensive. The food tends to be excellent, but be prepared to pay handsomely for a sit-down dinner. Instead, try one of Santa Barbara's numerous Mexican food stands, popular with UCSB students, where you'll find tasty tacos and burritos at a reasonable price. Most taco joints are located on **Milpas Street,** parallel to and eight blocks east of State Street. Most other restaurants are clustered in downtown along State Street. As a general rule, stay away from the restaurants on Cabrillo Street as they make you pay dearly for their waterfront views. If you're in the mood to splurge, head to **Soho** (21 West Victoria St., tel. 805/965–5497), a small, elegant supper club that offers fresh seafood and pastas. For about $7 you can get a Szechuan salad with grilled prawns, and if you're feeling really extravagant, try the fresh seafood for $16. Soho also serves a Sunday brunch with live jazz. For char-broiled steaks and a heavy dose of Santa Barbara attitude try the semi-expensive **Paradise Café** (702 Anacapa St., tel. 805/962–4416), popular with the more affluent locals. Prices range from $5.95 (soup and salad) to $21.95 (surf and turf). Two **Farmers' Markets** are held in Santa Barbara every week where you can stock up on locally grown produce, flowers, and fish. The first is held on the 500 block of State Street on Tuesdays from 3 to 7 PM, the second at Cola and Santa Barbara streets, Saturdays between 8:30 AM and noon.

UNDER $10 **Esau's Coffee Shop.** The food is standard, but if you're hungry Esau's serves up huge orders of eggs, hash browns, and pancakes to a mixed crowd of surfers and old timers for under $5. *403 State St., tel. 805/965–4416. Open weekdays 6 AM–1 PM, weekends 7 AM–1:30 PM.*

Hector's Mexican Restaurant. Many locals rank Hector's as the number-one eatery in Santa Barbara. Try the soft chicken taco with raisins and pine nuts ($4) or the excellent chile relleno ($5). Everything here, including the tortillas, is made from scratch, and bathed in Hector's homemade sauces. Indoor and outdoor seating available. *7398 Calle Real, Goleta, tel. 805/685–6522. Take Bus 73 from Transit Center. Open 11–2 and 5–9. Closed Mon.*

Sojourner Coffee House. A healthy place to grab a bite. Highlights include homemade soups ($6) and tofu/brown rice plates ($4). The Sojourner doubles as a coffee house popular with UCSB students, a place to play cards, chess, or read a good book without hassle. *134 E. Canon Perdido, tel. 805/965–7922. Near the Presidio 1½ blocks east of State St. Open Mon.–Thurs. 11–11, Fri. 11–midnight, Sat. 5–midnight. Wheelchair access.*

UNDER $15 **De Cedar.** Down the road from the Amtrak station, De Cedar excels at authentic Middle Eastern food, from humus to falafel. It's sometimes packed, sometimes completely empty, but the food is always first-rate. Even better, De Cedar specializes in vegetarian dishes. You can get away with lunch for under $8 and dinner under $12. *231 W. Montecito St., tel. 805/966–1074. Take the free shuttle to the Amtrak station and walk 1 block. Open Tues.–Sun. noon–2:30 and 5:30–10.*

The Palace. The best cajun and creole cuisine in Santa Barbara—perhaps in all southern California. It's classy and upscale, but if you don't mind dressing up a bit you'll get a damn fine, wham-bam whoop-shocker of a meal. Try the cajun popcorn ($5) or any of the fish etouffés ($9–$12). The seafood menu changes on a daily basis, but it's hard to go wrong. If you're really daring, try the cajun martini—guaranteed to sizzle your sinuses and put a spark in your step. *8 E. Cota St., tel. 805/966–3133. Open daily 5:30–10.*

DESSERT/COFFEEHOUSES If you're tired of staring at tanned bodies and neon clothing all day, you'll find the black-leather crowd well represented in Santa Barbara's cafés, most of which are concentrated in downtown.

Green Dragon Art Studio and Espresso Bar. With its organic and decaf espresso drinks, the Green Dragon is the place to indulge with a health-conscious twist. Local artists use the Green Dragon as an informal exhibition space, and there's live music most nights. *22 W. Mission, tel. 805/687–1902. Off State St. Bus 6 or 11, or walk north 11 blocks from Transit Center. Open daily 7 AM–midnight. Wheelchair access.*

Hestia House. This high-ceilinged, airy café attracts both a loud contingent of black-clothed teens and the quiet, nondescript types with heads buried deep in books. House coffee is $1, espresso drinks $2. *1014 State St., near Carrillo St., tel. 805/963–8060. Open weekdays 7 AM–11 PM, weekends 9 AM–midnight. Wheelchair access.*

● ● ● WORTH SEEING

An excellent two-hour walking tour, "Tours Through History," leaves daily from the San Marcos Tour Club (tel. 805/967–9869). For $8 a guide will take you through a six-block-square section of Santa Barbara's historical sites. Otherwise, the visitor center (*see* Basics, *above*) has a self-guided tour map of many of the same sights. One of the city's best attractions is the **Mission Santa Barbara** (Laguna St. at Los Olivos), considered the crown jewel of California's missions. Built in 1786 with the help of local Chumash Native Americans, this Spanish Renaissance structure has come to define the "Santa Barbara" architectural style with its red-tile roof, orange adobe façade, and wrought-iron gates and fixtures. If you visit in May you can catch the *I Madonnari,* a three-day festival at which internationally famous street artists, local artists, and children create elaborate chalk drawings in front of the mission. An entrance fee of $2 is charged to tour the mission but festivals like *I Madonnari* are free. Part modern sculpture garden and part museum, Santa Barbara's **Botanical Gardens** (1212 Mission Canyon Rd., tel. 805/682–4726) offer hundreds of trails and floral specimens for horticultural buffs (admission is $3). Besides the hulking modern sculptures you can also visit the Mission Dam, constructed by the Chumash in 1806. The sweeping branches of the huge **Moreton Bay Fig Tree** (at Montecito and Chapala Sts.) is one of Santa Barbara's most striking sights, transplanted from Australia in the late 1800s. **Stearn's Wharf** (Cabrillo and State Sts.), the oldest operating wharf on the West Coast, has one of the least touristy and beautifully uncluttered piers in California. Next to it are the aquariums and petting pools of the **Sea Center** (tel. 805/962–0885), a small hands-on museum that charges only $2. To the west of Stearn's Wharf is the **Santa Barbara Yacht Harbor** and its artificial breakwater. Walk to the end of the breakwater for an outstanding view of the coast and surrounding areas.

CHUMASH PAINTED CAVE STATE PARK Located in the Los Padres National Forest along San Marcos Pass, this state park houses the faded remains of centuries-old Chumash cave paintings. A locked metal screen keeps you from actually entering the cave, but you can see the colorful animal figures and decorative designs from outside. Afterward, meander along one of the park's numerous hiking trails that crisscross Santa Barbara's chaparral-covered mountains. *Painted Cave Rd., 12 mi northwest of Santa Barbara. Take Route 154 and turn left on Painted Cave Rd. Admission free.*

Built in the 1880s to serve stagecoach passengers on their way to Santa Barbara, the **Cold Springs Tavern** (5995 Stage Coach Rd., tel. 805/967–0066) is still a great place to grab a beer and hang out with the local Harley Davidson crowd. Located off Route 154 at the Stage Coach Road turnoff.

COUNTY COURT HOUSE A 70-foot-tall tower provides a 360° view of the city, and the court house is itself full of ornate murals and elaborate Spanish tile work. You can wander around by yourself or take a free guided tour. *1100 block of Anacapa St., tel. 805/962–6464. Open weekdays 8–5, weekends 9–5. Free tours Tues.–Sat. at 2 PM, Wed. and Fri. at 10:30 AM.*

MUSEUM OF ART French Impressionists and German Expressionists—Monet to Kandinsky—are on display here, in addition to classic Greek and Roman sculptures. East of the art museum, on Anapamu Street, is **Karpeles Manuscript Library,** with original manuscripts by John Steinbeck and others. *1130 State St., tel. 805/963–4364. Walk from Transit Center to State St., then north 2 blocks. Admission: $3; free Thurs. and first Sun. of month. Open Tues.–Sat. 11–5, Thurs. until 9, Sun. noon–5.*

SANTA BARBARA HISTORICAL MUSEUM This place has—what else—historical artifacts from Santa Barbara's past, including an excellent display of Chumash jewelry and pottery. You'll also find some Wild West–era six-shooters and photos. The building itself was made from the clay soil it stands upon. *136 E. De La Guerra St., tel. 805/966–1606. Walk from Transit Center to State St., south on State, east 1 block on De La Guerra. Admission free. Open Thurs.–Sat. 10–5, Sun. noon–5.*

SANTA BARBARA ZOO Considered one of the more attractive zoos in the United States, perhaps because of its garden-like setting, this zoo is home to more than 400 specimens of indigenous and exotic wildlife. It's small, but it's still an excellent place to escape the bustle of Santa Barbara. *500 Los Niños Dr., tel. 805/962–6310. Admission: $4. Take Bus 21 from Transit Center. Open daily 10–5, until 6 in summer.*

CHEAP THRILLS • • •

To catch a live, free concert in the park, head over to **De La Guerra Plaza** between State and Anacapa streets at noon on Fridays. Cozy up to a tree and take a pleasant nap, lulled to sleep by the strains of Big Band music. To watch the rich folks having a good ol' time, make an appearance at the **Santa Barbara Polo and Racquet Club** (337 Foothill Rd., tel. 805/684–8667), east of the city off U.S. 101. In summer catch the Pacific Coast Open polo tournament—the top polo event in the U.S. If you're feeling a bit wacky, hop in your car and make a beeline for **Santa Claus Lane** (U.S. 101, ½ mile west of Carpenteria), one of the strangest "theme malls" in the country. With small shops selling candy and Christmas-oriented items, Santa Claus Lane is a symbol of California's determination to have it all—sun, surf, sand, and Christmas year-round.

FESTIVALS **March:** The Santa Barbara **International Film Festival** lasts 14 days and shows the latest and most off-beat U.S. and foreign films. There are also workshops and seminars. Showings are held in the cinemas on State Street and all performances are open to the public. Call 805/963–0023 for tickets and timetables.

June: Held on the Saturday closest to June 21, the **Summer Solstice Parade** (tel. 805/965–3396) offers Santa Barbara's fringe element a chance to let loose. Even better, no cars or promotional posters are permitted—just processions of people dressed in bizarre costumes.

Summer: Every year thousands of people head to the beach to watch the **Sandcastle and Sculpting Contest** (tel. 805/966–6110), where artists from around the world gather to make the most outlandish sand creations they can dream up. The event is held on different weekends every summer, so call for details.

August: The **Old Spanish Days Fiesta** (tel. 805/962–8101) is a big event—with five days of citywide partying in celebration of Santa Barbara's Spanish and Mexican heritage. Highlights include a carnival, free music, parades, and vociferous street vendors.

October: In unofficial honor of the god of guacamole, the **California Avocado Festival** (tel. 805/684–0038) is held every year in Carpenteria—two fun-filled days of exotic guacomole concoctions tempered with art exhibits and entertainment.

AFTER DARK • • •

Begin with a copy of *The Independent,* the county's free weekly that lists all clubs, movies, and community events.

BARS **The Brewhouse** (202 State St., tel. 805/963–3090) is Santa Barbara's most popular microbrewery, famous for its Anacapa amber porter. On weekend nights there's live music. An historic landmark, **Joe's Café** (536 State St., tel. 805/966–4638) is revered for its deadly stiff drinks and down-home charm. Joe's attracts all sorts, from locals to tourists to UCSB students. **Mel's** (6 W. De La Guerro, tel. 805/963–2211) is something of a dive, but it's filled with some of Santa Barbara's grittiest and most ragged barflies. Wild man Hunter S. Thompson used to hang out in Mel's back booth. Part dance club and part bar, **Zelo** (630 State St., tel. 805/966–5792) is a favorite with hip, black-garbed clubbers, drawn by Zelo's art-deco interior. Zelo's has a full bar and live bands or DJs every night.

MUSIC It may be packed, but **Joseppi's** (434 State St., tel. 805/962–5516) is the place to go for jazz seven nights a week. It's a tiny place with brick and wood, and absolutely no smoking is allowed. The cover charge varies from $1 to $3. For blues and 30s-era jazz, the **Santa Barbara Blues Society** (601 E. Montecito St., tel. 805/966–9355) is calling your name. Most nights you'll find a local jazz band cuttin' a rug inside. The cover charge is generally $6.

For classical music lovers, the **Santa Barbara Symphony's** (214 E. Victoria St., tel. 805/965–6596) season runs October through May. The **Santa Barbara Chamber Orchestra** (Box 90903, tel. 805/564–8887) offers concerts year-round. It's expensive ($19, students $9), but well worth the price if you enjoy top-rate chamber music.

● ● ● OUTDOOR ACTIVITIES

Beach Rentals (8 W. Cabrillo Blvd., tel. 805/963–2524) rents beach cruisers ($5), mountain bikes ($7), tandems ($9), and Rollerblades ($5) by the hour. In addition to the **Cabrillo Bike Path** that runs through downtown and the trails around UCSB, the **Los Padres National Forest** has dozens of mountain bike trails and scenic hikes. The ranger station (6144 Calle Real Colesa, tel. 805/683–6711) has free biking and hiking maps. One of the best sources for information on hiking in the Santa Ynez mountains is **Bike 'N Hike** (1149 Coast Village Rd., tel. 805/969–0719), a small sporting-good store that also rents mountain bikes.

The most popular place along the Santa Barbara Coast to **surf** is at **Rincon Point,** 3 miles south of Carpenteria along Route 1. Surfers also gravitate toward **Refugio State Beach** and **El Capitan State Beach,** located north of Santa Barbara on Route 1. **Sundance Windsurfing** (tel. 805/966–4400) gives three-hour lessons for beginners on summer Saturdays for $45. They also rent surfboards ($15) and wet suits ($10).

Near Santa Barbara

● ● ● ISLA VISTA AND U.C. SANTA BARBARA

It's a bit frightening to see so many drunken people stumbling haphazardly from one party to the next or riding their bikes in intoxicated circles, but it's certainly entertaining.

The University of California at Santa Barbara lies 12 miles west of downtown, perched on the cliffs overlooking the Pacific Ocean. Built in the 1950s, UCSB and the neighboring student town of **Isla Vista** are home to some of California's most laid-back students. Isla Vista (or "IV," as it's known by locals) has a reputation for being a mindless party town that caters to the worst sort of postadolescent behavior, and if you happen to be in town on a weekend night during the school year (September–December and late-January–June), you should check out the party scene. Downtown IV has a decent selection of cafés, bars, and restaurants, as well as easy access to the nearby beaches and scenic overlooks. To get to UCSB take Bus 7, 9, 11, 18, 24, or 25 from the Transit Center, or take U.S. 101 west to Route 217 and follow the signs. Campus tours are available (tel. 805/893–8175) and parking is free on weekends and evenings. Otherwise, a weekday's permit costs $3, purchased from any of the information booths on the roads leading to campus.

● ● ● LOMPOC AND MISSION LA PURISIMA

Fifty-five miles north of Santa Barbara, Lompoc is a quiet military town without much to offer. East of Lompoc off Route 246 is the **La Purisima Mission,** one of the most well-preserved and "authentic" missions in the state. Surrounded by miles of hills and hiking trails, La Purisima is preserved to look as it did in the early 1800s, complete with livestock roaming the grounds and actors performing "living history" scenes. In order to see the mission with its "original inhabitants," contact the **Purisima People Tour** (tel. 805/733–1303), which organizes weekend tours in summer. From Santa Barbara take Route 1 north to U.S. 101 to Route 246 and follow the signs.

SOLVANG • • •

Forty-five miles northwest of Santa Barbara (Route 154 to 246), Solvang bills itself as a 19th-century Danish Towne, teaming with tourist shops, overpriced restaurants, and so-called Dutch bakeries. Originally established in 1911 by Danish immigrants, today the town is a bad Disneyland version of what rural America thinks a Danish village should look like, complete with windmills that double as gas stations and fake cobblestone streets. Unless you're in the mood to buy some Danish cheese, Danish T-shirts, or "I Luv Solvang" mugs, steer clear. A more natural attraction near Solvang are the **Nojogui Falls,** 7 miles southwest on Alisal Road. The falls have temporarily dried up due to California's drought, but normally you'd see a 160-foot waterfall tumbling over a limestone cliff. If you're interested in missions, you might want to stop by the **Mission Santa Ynez** (1760 Mission Dr., tel. 805/688–4814), which has a reconstructed bell tower and original Native American murals.

SANTA YNEZ AND LOS OLIVOS • • •

These old pioneer towns lie along Route 154, 50 miles northwest of Santa Barbara. However, the only thing of interest here today are the wineries that blanket the region's sunbaked fields. **Firestone Vineyard,** one of the largest in California, offers free tours, wine tasting, and a grassy picnic area. *5017 Zaca Rd., tel. 805/688–3940. From U.S. 101 exit at Zaca Station Rd., it's 1½ mi north. Open daily 10–4.*

OJAI • • •

If you follow Route 150 east from Santa Barbara for an hour you'll stumble across Ojai (pronounced "O-hi"), a small but affluent community with lots of orchards and horse ranches. Used as the site of Shangri-la in the 1936 movie *Lost Horizon,* Ojai for some reason attracts a strangely spiritual and mystic crowd. The **Krotona Institute** (tel. 805/646–2653) is a theological-spiritual center with the largest theo-philosophical library on the West Coast. The **Krishnamurti Library** (1130 McAndrew Rd., tel. 805/646–4998), another magnet for New Agers, contains thousands of volumes on spiritual healing, mysticism, and the occult. Both are open to the public. If you're having trouble finding your third eye, head to the nonmystical **Bart's Books** (1302 W. Marlija St., tel. 805/646–3755), an outdoor book stand filled with thousands of used paperbacks. Otherwise, Ojai has a number of restaurants, hotels, and cinemas, but almost everything here is priced beyond the reach of the budget traveler. You may enjoy a quick tour through Ojai if you have a car, but don't strain yourself.

VENTURA AND OXNARD • • •

Located halfway between Santa Barbara and Los Angeles are the unassuming towns of Ventura and Oxnard, two beachside communities that are slowly being engulfed by tract homes and mini-malls. One place that has retained some charm is Ventura's **Main Street** and historic downtown, where you'll find a mission, museums, and endless shops. Stop by the **Visitor's Bureau** (89-L S. California St., tel. 805/1648–2075) for maps and information. The **Mission San Buena Ventura** (225 Main St.) sits next to the most interesting downtown attraction, the **Albinger Archaeological Museum** (113 East Main St., tel. 805/648–5023). This small museum explains how archaeologists go about digging up the earth for clues to ancient cultures, using the mission and its nearby excavation pits as part of its open-air exhibit. Also on display are artifacts from the Native American, Spanish, Mexican, and Chinese settlers who over the centuries have inhabited the area. If you're aching to explore the **Channel Islands,** one of California's least accessible wildlife preserves, **Island Packers** (tel. 805/1142–1393) runs excursions from the Ventura harbor. Day trips start at $34 while overnight trips and transportation for those who want to camp on the islands start at $45. Beside boasting one of the largest populations of brown pelicans in the world, the Channel Islands also contain the ruins of a Paleolithic village, considered by some to be the oldest such settlement known in North

America. Camping on the island is primitive at best; the visitor center at the **Channel Islands National Park Headquarters** (1901 Spinnaker Dr., Ventura Harbor, tel. 805/644–8262) has maps and information. If you need a break, **Shield's Brewing Co.** (corner of Santa Clara St. and Ventura Ave., tel. 805/643–1807), one of Ventura's only microbreweries, has good beer, burgers, and veggie food in the $4–$8 range.

Oxnard, a few miles south of Ventura, is best avoided altogether. There are a few restaurants and tourist shops here but don't think twice about driving straight through this mundane suburb. A bright spot amid all the condos and tract housing is the **Oxnard State Beach Park,** a quiet beach peppered with sand dunes. Take Mairdalay Beach Road from Harbor Boulevard, which parallels the shore.

LOS ANGELES 9

By Victoria Robbins

Los Angeles. The City of Lights. The City of Angels. Aldous Huxley's "City of Dreadful Joy," of freeways, minimalls, movie stars, and broken dreams—a sprawling and smog-filled megalopolis that inspires hate, fear, and disgust, but rarely love. Forty-four Spanish, Native American, and Afro-American settlers founded *El Pueblo de la Reina de Los Angeles* on September 4, 1781, and little could they know that less than 225 years later their peaceful farming community would turn into one of the world's most (in)famous, chaotic, and misunderstood cities. People from all over the world hate L.A., usually without ever having breached its borders. They cull their impression from TV programs, newscasts, big-budget Hollywood films, and the general belief that a city that takes two hours to drive through must, by obligation, be a miserable and charmless wasteland of characterless suburbia and uncultured lunatics who live on the fringe of civilization. Of course they're right, but that's not the point. Los Angeles may be an ugly and unwieldy super-city, but the fact of the matter is that this is precisely what makes L.A. such a great place to explore. Nowhere else in the world will you find such a bizarre and eclectic mix of wealthy business people who drive BMWs, duplicitous producers with their "Let's do lunch" mentality, bleach-blond surf daddies who say "dude" and "tubular" on a regular basis, and the black leather "hip" crowd who roam the streets at night looking for a trashy bar and a game of pool. Of course, don't forget the "I'm an artist" crowd and the "I'm an actor" crowd, as well as the numerous slackers lounging on the beach or roaming the city's streets. When you take everything into consideration, including the diversity of race, religion, culture, and creed, you're left with a city that can't be understood or grasped without contradiction. L.A. may be the sum of its parts, but the truly amazing thing about this city is that you could never experience every part and every type—every seedy twist and turn—of life here, not even if you really wanted to. There's just too much to see, too many people and too many places competing for your attention as you cruise Sunset Boulevard or Melrose Avenue on a Friday night, or as you walk amidst the jumble of street performers and buskers on Venice Beach's boardwalk or on the streets of Downtown.

"Los Angeles may not be the end of the world," locals sometimes say, "but you can certainly see it from here."

What little there is to like in L.A. must be sought out and hunted down. Nothing here is easy, especially if you don't have a car, and to make matters worse you have to be prepared to drive across one town and into another just to get a decent meal or find a good bar. You might expect that L.A. would have organized itself over the years and fallen into some sort of pattern, but in reality it's done nothing of the sort. L.A. is a haphazard and constantly changing city that requires your vigilant attention. If you work at finding things to do and

Los Angeles

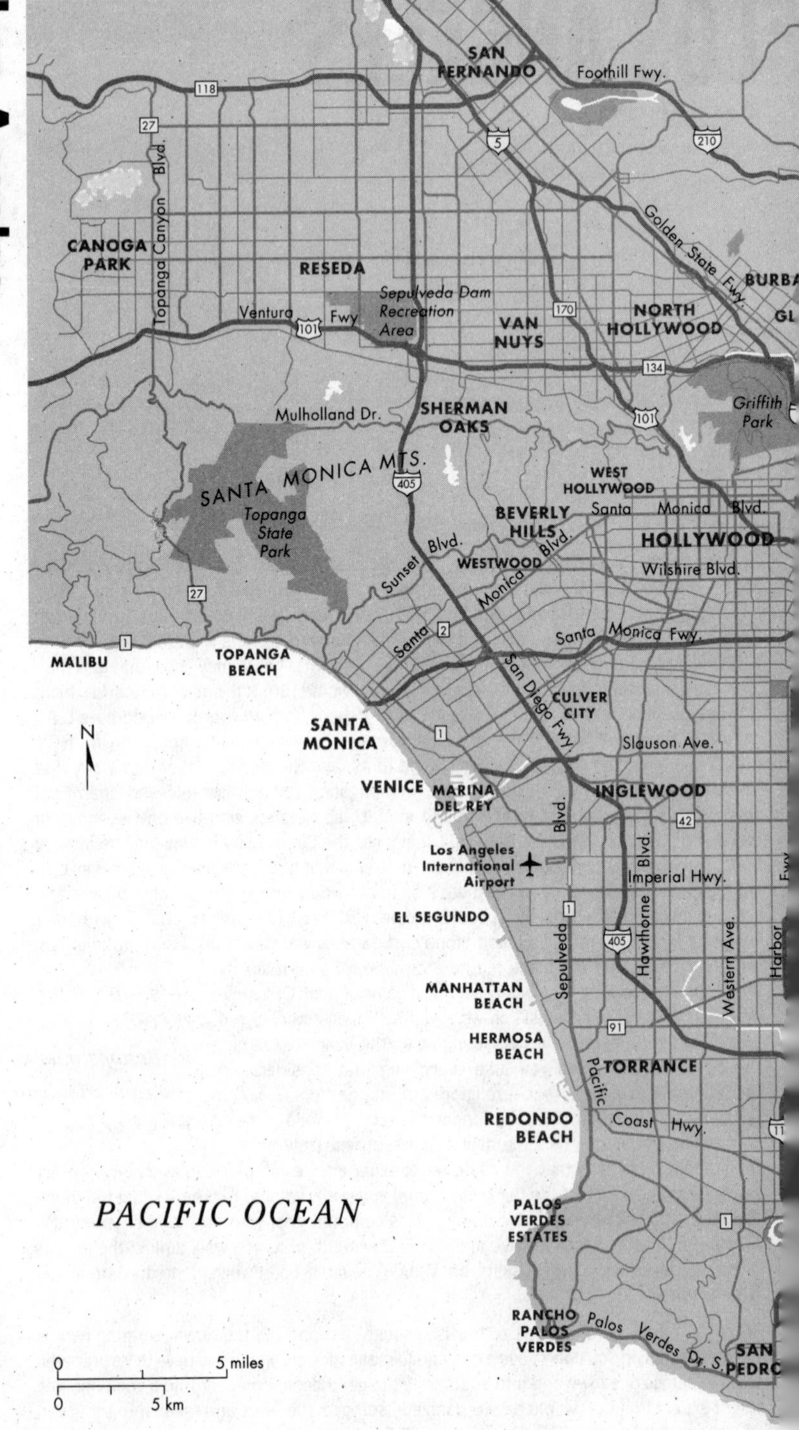

SAN FERNANDO
Foothill Fwy.
118
27
5
210
Topanga Canyon Blvd.
Golden State Fwy.
CANOGA PARK
RESEDA
BURBA
GL
Sepulveda Dam Recreation Area
Ventura
101
Fwy
170
NORTH HOLLYWOOD
VAN NUYS
134
Mulholland Dr.
SHERMAN OAKS
101
Griffith Park
SANTA MONICA MTS.
405
WEST HOLLYWOOD
Topanga State Park
BEVERLY HILLS
Santa Monica Blvd.
HOLLYWOOD
Blvd.
Sunset
WESTWOOD
Monica Blvd.
Wilshire Blvd.
27
Santa
2
Santa Monica Fwy.
1
MALIBU
TOPANGA BEACH
San Diego Fwy.
CULVER CITY
SANTA MONICA
1
Slauson Ave.
N
VENICE
MARINA DEL REY
INGLEWOOD
Blvd.
42
Blvd.
Los Angeles International Airport
Imperial Hwy.
Fwy
1
EL SEGUNDO
405
Sepulveda
Hawthorne
Western Ave.
Harbor
MANHATTAN BEACH
91
HERMOSA BEACH
Pacific
TORRANCE
REDONDO BEACH
Coast Hwy.
PACIFIC OCEAN
PALOS VERDES ESTATES
1
RANCHO PALOS VERDES
Palos Verdes Dr. S.
SAN PEDRO
0
5 miles
0
5 km

Los Angeles

Angeles Crest Hwy.
2
SAN GABRIEL MOUNTAINS
Mt. Wilson
LA CANADA FLINTRIDGE
PASADENA
Foothill Fwy.
210
39
Pasadena Fwy.
110
ALHAMBRA
SAN GABRIEL
EL MONTE
Dodger Stadium
San Bernardino Fwy.
10
MONTEREY PARK
60
Pomona Fwy.
Santa Ana Fwy.
Rosemead Blvd. Fwy.
WHITTIER
72
HUNTINGTON PARK
710
19
DOWNEY
San Gabriel River
42
39
5
COMPTON
Long Beach Fwy.
Riverside Fwy.
91
605
LAKEWOOD
ANAHEIM
710
19
Pacific Coast Hwy.
GARDEN GROVE
San Diego Fwy.
39
55
1
LONG BEACH

places to explore, you will be surprised at how much there is to see; but if you let the city get the better of you or if you expect it to be made easy somehow, you should probably stay on the highway and keep driving when you reach the city limits. Once inside you're on your own, free to explore and discover at your leisure, but you can never forget that life in L.A. happens at break-neck pace. It sounds ridiculous that Angelenos might drive to Malibu for dinner, Venice for drinks, and West Hollywood for a movie, afterward heading to Santa Monica for a snack and finally to the San Fernando Valley for home, but it's true. Such a loop may take a total of four hours, but Angelenos are used to driving long distances in search of the "coolest" nightspot, and visitors to L.A. must be prepared to follow suit if they want to pierce the dark underbelly of this city of freeways and endless suburbs.

For better or for worse—probably for worse—you can never think twice about what you're doing here. This city cannot stand up to scrutiny and your only hope of surviving is to let things awe and dazzle you without question. Like one of Hollywood's big-budget action films, you have to appreciate L.A. for what it is: a glitzy and shallow spectacle that's not meant to enlighten or enrich, but rather simply to entertain. Otherwise, the architecture, the beaches, art galleries, museums, historical sites, and even the people on the streets will seem like a big hoax. There's no doubt that the multi-million dollar homes in Beverly Hills don't fit together with the slum housing in Compton or Watts, or that the homeless in downtown L.A. don't fit with the super-wealthy movie and rock stars who look at Los Angeles as if it were one vast playground, but then no one ever claimed Los Angeles was a rational place. As long as you never forget this—as long as you keep telling yourself Los Angeles isn't supposed to make sense—you'll probably end up growing fond of it and its 10 million inhabitants. Of course, you may end up absolutely abhorring this wasteland of minimalls and fast-food stands, but that's okay, too. In either case, Los Angeles is a city that's hard to feel wishy-washy about.

Basics

AMERICAN EXPRESS **Los Angeles:** *8493 W. 3rd St., Los Angeles 90048, tel. 213/659–1682. Open weekdays 9–7, Sat. 10–6.*

Downtown: *901 W. 7th St., Los Angeles 90017, tel. 213/627–4800. Open weekdays 9–6.*

Beverly Hills: *327 N. Beverly Dr., Beverly Hills 90210, tel. 213/274–8277. Open weekdays 9–6, Sat. 10–5.*

Pasadena: *251 S. Lake Ave., Pasadena 91101, tel. 818/449–2281. Open weekdays 9–5, Sat. 10 AM–12:30 PM.*

DOCTORS AND DENTISTS Call the **Dentist Referral Hot Line** (tel. 310/620–1728) and the **Doctor Referral Hot Line** (tel. 213/483–6122). Both calls are free, and they'll put you in contact with someone in your area.

GAY AND LESBIAN RESOURCES Los Angeles has a large gay and lesbian community. However, gay bashings, general intolerance, and downright hatred are all too common in the City of Angels, and if you need to speak to someone who'll just listen, go to the **Gay and Lesbian Community Services Center.** They also offer information on community events and support groups. *1213 N. Highland Ave., tel. 213/464–7276. Open daily 9–5.*

LUGGAGE STORAGE You can stow your luggage at **Union Station** (800 North Alameda St., tel. 213/624–0171) during the day for $1 per bag, but not overnight. If you have a Greyhound ticket, you can store your bags at the **Greyhound Bus Station** (208 E. 6th St., tel. 213/629–8410) for up to three days for free. If you don't have a ticket, lockers are available for $1 per day, but they must be renewed each day in person. All terminals at **LAX** (the airport) contain lockers for luggage storage, and their rates are usually $1 for 24 hours.

PHARMACIES **Sav-on Drugs** has several 24-hour pharmacies, and a wide selection of pills, ointments, and funny pink liquids. For the nearest location call 800/627–2866.

TELEPHONES In November 1991, the 213 area code that covered most of L.A. was divided up and reorganized. The 213 code still exists, but **310** is now used for the cities of Malibu, the Pacific Palisades, Century City, Brentwood, and Santa Monica, the entire coast down to Long Beach and Catalina Island. Pasadena, Burbank, and San Marino fall under the **818** area code, and Pomona is in the **714** area code. When in doubt dial "0" and ask the operator. For telephone and address information, dial 411 (free from any pay phone).

TOURIST INFORMATION To find out what's going on, pick up a copy of the ***LA Weekly*** or ***Reader***, two great free newspapers available at bookstores, cafés, and supermarkets. Both have extensive listings of movies, plays, live music, and exhibits. The hefty "Calendar" section of the Sunday ***L.A. Times*** also has complete listings.

The Los Angeles Visitor and Convention Bureau is a great place to find information about almost everything L.A. has to offer. Hundreds of free brochures are here for the taking, and detailed maps of L.A. are sold for $2. *Hilton Hotel, 685 Figueroa St., tel. 213/689–8822. Open weekdays 8–5, Sat. 8:30–5.*

The Hollywood office of **The Visitor Information Center** is housed in the **Janes House,** a turn-of-the-century mansion set off the street past a courtyard of shops. They have an excellent hotel and motel guide, as well as lots of free brochures and maps. *6541 Hollywood Blvd., tel. 213/461–4213. Open Mon.–Sat. 9–5.*

RTD Customer Center is the place for anything that has to do with L.A.'s bus lines, including maps, time tables, and bus passes. These people lunch late or something, so don't show up between 2:30 and 3:15 PM, they're closed. *6249 Hollywood Blvd., tel. 213/626–4455. Phone lines open daily 5:30 AM–11:30 PM. Office open weekdays 10–6.*

Trial by Fire: The L.A. Riots of '92

In April 1992, when the Los Angeles policemen accused of the videotaped beating of black motorist Rodney King were acquitted by a mostly white jury, the fuse was lit under a city whose poor race relations had already made it tinder dry. In an almost week-long rampage stemming from the acquittal, predominantly black and Latino rioters burned and looted vast swathes of South-Central Los Angeles. More than 200 people were killed and 1,000 businesses, many minority-owned, were torched. The Korean community, often accused by blacks of discrimination, was particularly hard hit. For many rioters, the rampage was an outlet for pent-up rage after years of hopelessness and discrimination; for others, it was nothing more than an opportunity for self-enrichment, with mass looting of stereos, jewelry, and clothing. A curfew was imposed, and President Bush sent in the army to try and quell the rebellion. The scenes played on TVs across the country to a nation transfixed by the extent of the lawlessness—police shot at by snipers, firefighters attacked by axe-wielding rioters, and soldiers hunkered down in poses last seen in the Gulf War. In a major city, the fabric of society had been rent asunder, and for most of America it became painfully clear just how thin that material is. The question remains whether the country has the will or the know-how to sew up the damage.

COMING AND GOING

BY PLANE **Los Angeles International Airport (LAX),** 17 miles from downtown L.A., near the ocean, serves almost 50 million passengers a year, making it the third-busiest airport in the world. Needless to say, it will seem confusing and downright unfriendly if you're not prepared for it. If it looks a bit chaotic, don't panic—just ask someone for help. And keep in mind that all international terminals (#2, #5, and the Bradley Terminal) have **currency exchange desks** and **tourist information booths** that have information on budget accommodations—they'll even call hostels to find you a bed. They also have a huge amount of reference material on commonly visited spots in L.A. They're usually open weekdays 7 AM–10 PM, and weekends 7 AM–9 PM; you can reach an information line at 310/646–2271.

AIRPORT TRANSIT You have several options. Outside the baggage claim area in each terminal is a **Ground Transportation Information** booth (open daily 8 AM–midnight). If you're in the mood to spend $15 a person, you can always take a shuttle bus. These privately owned buses will take you anywhere in the city 24 hours a day. Taxis are also an option, but they're very expensive (it's $20 to Santa Monica). If you'd rather not spend the money, you can take a public bus (*see* Tourist Information, *above*), although be prepared for the occasional freak or weirdo. For more information on shuttle buses, contact **Super Shuttle** (tel. 310/338–1111) or **Airport Flyer** (tel. 800/344–5755).

BY TRAIN **Union Station** (800 N. Alameda St.) is Los Angeles' only major train station, one block east of Olvera Street in Downtown. **Amtrak** (tel. 800/872–7245) runs regular service from Union Station to cities all over the country including San Francisco ($75, 11 hours), San Diego ($24, three hours), and Chicago ($205, two days). Getting to and from the station is relatively easy—dozens of public buses stop outside. For more information, contact the RTD service center (*see* Tourist Information, *above*).

BY BUS Though **Greyhound** offers decent prices on most of its routes, their Downtown station (208 E. 6th St., tel. 213/629–8400) is an unpleasant place, to put it mildly. If you can, arrange to arrive or depart during daylight hours, when most of the lunatics are still sleeping. Don't worry if you're here late, however, as the waiting room for ticketed passengers is both clean and safe (it's just getting to the room that's kind of creepy). This Greyhound station serves passengers heading all over America and Canada. Over 30 RTD buses stop within a block of the station and the DASH (*see* Getting Around, *below*) Route A stops at Seventh and Los Angeles, at the south side of the station. Call for tickets and timetable information.

Green Tortoise is probably the most interesting and cheapest way to travel in the United States. The back half of each bus is one big mattress, while tables, couches and assorted bunk-type beds make up the front. Their motto is "It's nothing like your last bus ride," and they're not lying. They offer two-week, cross-country trips in the summer, winter trips to Baja, and weekly excursions up and down the California–Oregon coast. They also run an infamous shuttle from Los Angeles to New Orleans during Mardi Gras, popular with friendly drunks and drug addicts. If you don't mind the smell of dirty socks, this is a great way to travel. For complete information, call 800/227–4766 or see Coming and Going in Chapter 1, Basics.

GETTING AROUND

L.A. isn't known for the friendly nature of its drivers, but as long as you avoid people with "Go Ahead, Make My Day" bumper stickers you shouldn't run into trouble.

BY CAR L.A. was built for cars, and its freeway system will take you everywhere. Yes, there are occasional traffic jams, but in general it runs much more smoothly than you'd think. The legal speed limit is 55 miles per hour, but only gray-haired old ladies drive that slowly. However, do watch out for the freeway coppers—known as the CHP (California Highway Patrol)—another bunch that's not known for its friendliness. Every smart Angeleno owns at least one copy of the *L.A. County Thomas Guide*, a voluminous book filled with maps and street indexes. Though you'll inevitably get lost a couple times, don't worry. There are off- and on-ramps and call boxes (emergency telephones)

Los Angeles Freeways

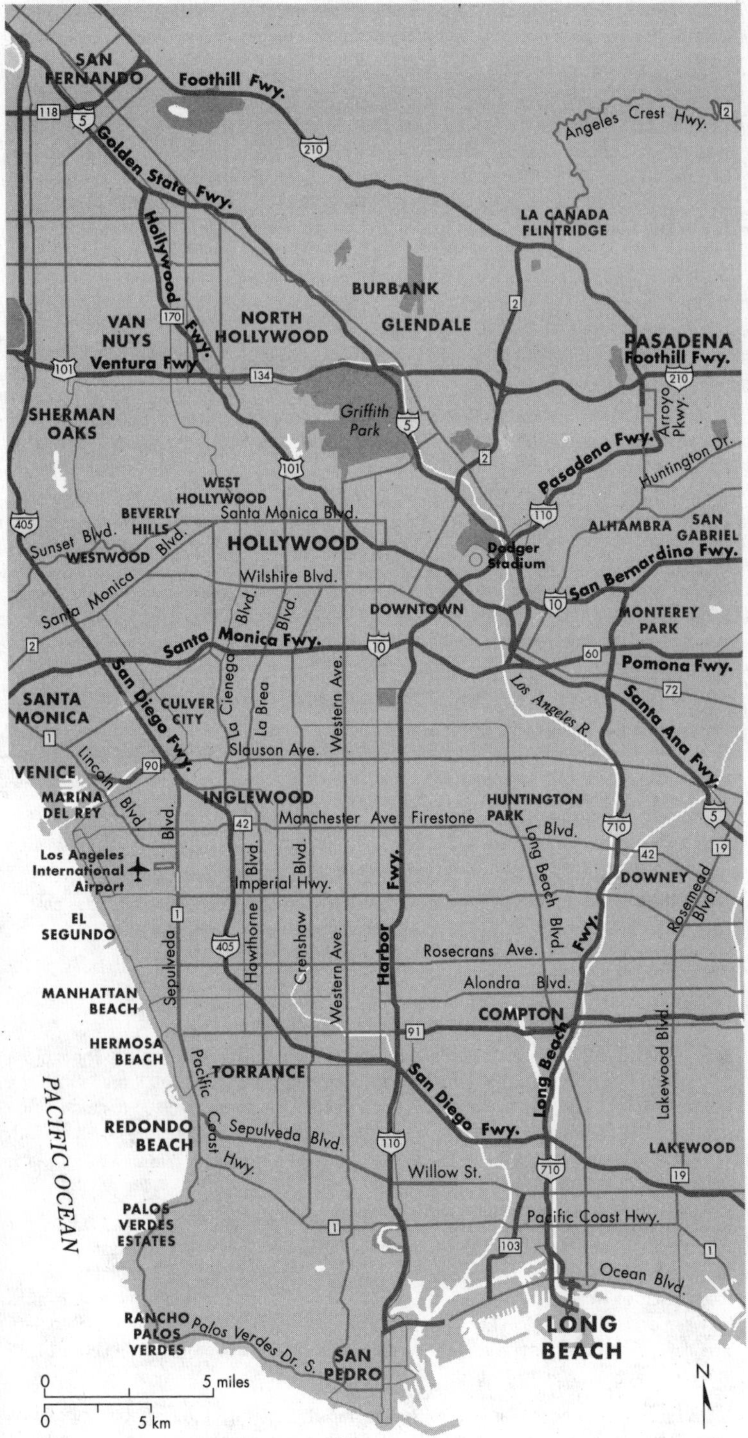

SAN FERNANDO
Foothill Fwy.
118
5
210
Golden State Fwy.
Angeles Crest Hwy.
2
LA CANADA FLINTRIDGE
Hollywood Fwy.
BURBANK
GLENDALE
VAN NUYS
170
NORTH HOLLYWOOD
PASADENA
Foothill Fwy.
101
Ventura Fwy.
134
210
Arroyo Pkwy.
SHERMAN OAKS
Griffith Park
5
2
Pasadena Fwy.
Huntington Dr.
101
WEST HOLLYWOOD
405
BEVERLY HILLS
Santa Monica Blvd.
110
ALHAMBRA
SAN GABRIEL
Sunset Blvd.
WESTWOOD
HOLLYWOOD
Dodger Stadium
San Bernardino Fwy.
Wilshire Blvd.
10
Santa Monica
DOWNTOWN
MONTEREY PARK
2
Santa Monica Fwy.
10
60
Pomona Fwy.
San Diego Fwy.
La Cienega Blvd.
La Brea Blvd.
Western Ave.
Los Angeles R.
72
SANTA MONICA
CULVER CITY
Santa Ana Fwy.
1
Slauson Ave.
Lincoln Blvd.
90
VENICE
MARINA DEL REY
INGLEWOOD
HUNTINGTON PARK
5
42
Manchester Ave.
Firestone Blvd.
710
19
Los Angeles International Airport
Sepulveda Blvd.
Hawthorne Blvd.
Crenshaw Blvd.
Imperial Hwy.
Harbor Fwy.
Long Beach Blvd.
42
DOWNEY
Rosemead Blvd.
EL SEGUNDO
1
405
Western Ave.
Rosecrans Ave.
Long Beach Fwy.
Alondra Blvd.
MANHATTAN BEACH
COMPTON
91
Lakewood Blvd.
HERMOSA BEACH
Pacific Coast Hwy.
TORRANCE
San Diego Fwy.
PACIFIC OCEAN
REDONDO BEACH
Sepulveda Blvd.
110
LAKEWOOD
710
Willow St.
19
PALOS VERDES ESTATES
1
Pacific Coast Hwy.
103
1
Ocean Blvd.
RANCHO PALOS VERDES
Palos Verdes Dr. S.
SAN PEDRO
LONG BEACH
0
5 miles
0
5 km
N

every mile or so. It may take you a while to get used to L.A.'s massive freeway system, but patience and a sense of humor will make the task a bit easier.

RENTING If you plan to spend more than an hour or so in L.A., it's a good idea to rent a car. Though you'll survive on public transit, Los Angeles is too expansive to take in comfortably by bus, and if you don't want to waste nearly half your day waiting at bus stops and making connections, a car is an absolute must. It will give you the freedom to really explore L.A., and it'll allow you to cover more ground in one day than you could cover by bus in three. Rental cars are usually expensive ($25–$40 for daily rentals; $100–$175 per week), but if you don't mind roughing it for a few nights, you might make it up by driving to one of the city's cheaper, outlying hotels. Unfortunately, you usually have to be at least 21 years of age, and drivers under 25 usually have to pay an extra surcharge. All rental companies offer insurance for both foreign and U.S. drivers and collision damage waivers, usually about $9 a day, are a good idea if you can afford it (many credit-card companies offer automatic insurance). Los Angeles has over 200 rental offices—LAX has more than 10 rental desks to choose from—and rates vary according to location.

Alamo Rentals (tel. 800/327–9633) at LAX has rates starting around $26 per day, $99 per week, with unlimited mileage. Drivers must be 21, but those under 25 face an additional charge of $10 per day.

You'll have to badger **Avis** to tell you what office has the cheapest rates. They have branches in **Hollywood** (1548 Cahuenga Blvd., #C, tel. 310/467–0074), **Downtown** (5740 Arba Vitae, tel. 310/215–2826), and at **LAX** (9217 Airport Blvd., tel. 310/646–5600). For more information, call 800/331–1212. Drivers must be 25.

Avon Rent-a-Car (8459 Sunset Blvd., tel. 213/654–5533) starts at $17 a day, $102 a week, with 100 miles per day included. Drivers must be 18; those under 21 pay a $15 charge per day, those under 25, $5 per day.

Budget Rent-A-Car (tel. 800/527–0700) has offices in **Hollywood** (6841 Hollywood Blvd., tel. 213/469–8108), **Downtown** (1256 W. 7th St., tel. 213/483–3307), and at **LAX** (there's an office in every terminal, tel. 310/645–4500). Drivers must be 21; those under 25 pay a $15 charge per day.

Hertz (tel. 800/654–3131) has offices in **Hollywood** (1634 N. La Brea, tel. 213/465–7695), **Downtown** in the Westin Bonaventure Hotel (404 S. Figueroa, tel. 213/629–1498), and at most **LAX** terminals. Drivers must be 25.

Penny Rent-a-Car (12425 Victory Blvd., N. Hollywood, tel. 818/786–1733) has cars at $22 daily, $139 weekly, with 100 miles per day included. Drivers must be 25.

Ugly Duckling (920 S. La Brea, tel. 213/933–0522) has automatics for $25 a day, $129 a week, and sticks for $19 a day, $107 a week, with 100 miles per day included. Drivers must be 21; those under 25 pay a $4 charge per day.

HITCHHIKING L.A. has too many freaks for people to hitchhike safely. Though you may be tempted to save a few dollars by avoiding buses and taxis, you'll probably live a lot longer if you don't hitch. For those with a death wish, the best place to catch a ride is at the bottom of freeway on-ramps. It's illegal, but there are usually a few long-hairs with "San Francisco or Bust" signs who'll keep you company. If you get stopped by the cops, though, they'll escort you off the highway and may even make you appear in court.

BY SUBWAY The city has been spending billions of dollars a year (1 billion per mile!) to connect downtown L.A. with the San Fernando Valley and Long Beach, but it'll be years before it's ready. In the meantime, you can ride the **Blue Line,** the first (and only) installment of what will eventually be a 150-mile system. The line runs for 22 miles between downtown L.A. and Long Beach from 6 AM to 8 PM every 15 minutes, seven days a week. The metro terminal is at Seventh and Flower streets, in Downtown. Tickets are sold at coin-operated machines outside.

BY BUS Referred to as **RTD** (Rapid Transit District), L.A.'s public buses go everywhere in the city, but not quickly. Locals prefer to drive when possible so most buses are rarely crowded, but don't be surprised if you encounter skateboard punks or homeless people. Buses 1–99 serve downtown L.A. All east–west buses are numbered 100–199; north–south buses are 300–399. Fare is $1.10, 25¢ for transfers, usually good for any connecting bus within four hours of purchase. For explicit directions, call the **RTD Customer Center** (*see* Basics, *above*) at 213/626–4455. Bus stops are usually well marked (look for signs that say "RTD"), and between 5 AM and 1 AM you shouldn't have to wait more than 15 minutes. Off-hour service is constantly changing, so ask the driver when the last run is.

DASH (Downtown Area Short Hop) shuttle buses operate primarily in Downtown, although a few make the trip to Hollywood, Pacific Palisades, Westwood Village, Watts and, during the summer, Venice Beach. Call 800/2LA–RIDE for more information.

BY TAXI Taxis are usually not "hailable," which means you have to phone ahead if you want one. They're expensive ($1.80 a mile), but a good idea if you want to go out drinking for the night. Extra charges include: $2 pick-up fee, 50¢ per piece of luggage, and 75¢ for each additional passenger beyond three. Most taxi companies are open 24 hours. The **Independent Cab Co.** (tel. 800/521–8294) is one of the more reputable.

Where to Sleep

Hotels range from the sybaritic and luxurious to the one-room, flea-infested, smelly sort of place where the bed linen is crunchy and yellow. Of course you can always find a nice place if you've got the money, but budget travelers should probably head straight for one of the comfortably casual, reasonably priced hostels. They're usually fairly clean and accommodating, and perhaps the best place in L.A. to meet other travelers. If communal living doesn't appeal you can always try your luck with a chain motel, but even these second-rate establishments are kind of pricey at $25–$35 a night. You might want to look around before making any reservations if you plan on spending more than a few nights here.

HOLLYWOOD

The city of Broken Dreams offers some of the most interesting hotels in L.A. Other than the few along Hollywood Boulevard that rent rooms on an hourly basis (water beds are extra), there's a string of ridiculously priced hotels along Sunset Boulevard, most notably the Chateau Marmont and the Hotel Mondrian (graced with a 60-foot Mondrian painting on the front facade). You should be warned, however, that Hollywood isn't the safest place, and crime can be a problem even in the nice hotels Be careful walking around at night, as muggings are common. Otherwise, Hollywood is great for exploring the dark underbelly of Los Angeles, full of prophets from the 23rd century, homeless university professors who have spoken with God, leather-clad Iron Maiden fans, belligerent drunks, and the usual assortment of riffraff and hooligans who give this city its bizarre, often overwhelming character.

UNDER $50 **Downtown Motel.** The best thing about this place is its location. Hollywood Boulevard, Griffith Park, and Barnsdall Park are all nearby. The rooms are clean and have private baths, and there's a pool in the courtyard. Just don't plan on throwing any parties in your room, as the management isn't exactly pleasant. For some reason, they don't seem to like the under-60 crowd very much. *5601 Hollywood Blvd., tel. 213/464–7191. Singles $38, doubles $38–$42. No wheelchair access, luggage storage.*

OBAN Hotel. This place is run-down. The only thing this seedy hangout has going for it (besides its peculiar name) are laundry machines in the basement. Refrigerators can be rented for $5 a week and you can throw a 7-Eleven burrito in the microwave downstairs, in the hotel office. All rooms have color TV and private baths or showers. *6364 Yucca St., tel. 213/466–0524. Singles $28, doubles $34. Laundry, no wheelchair access, luggage storage.*

UNDER $75 **Farmer's Daughter Motel.** In a quiet location, this motel is a good place to call home when visiting the farmers' market, the L.A. County Museum, and Hancock

Park. The rooms are nice, all with private baths, and there's a pool and sun deck for those blazing hot L.A. afternoons. The motel attracts a large tourist clientele, and several tours of Los Angeles leave from here daily. *115 S. Fairfax near 3rd St., tel. 213/937–3930. For reservations call tel. 800/334–1658. Double $58, $3 extra per person. No wheelchair access, luggage storage.*

Metropolitan Hotel. Conveniently located on Sunset Boulevard, this hotel is a bargain for people traveling in groups of three or more. The lobby is pink-and-black art deco, the management and staff are extremely courteous, and the rooms, each with a view, are modern and spacious. Normally way out of a budget traveler's price range, anyone mentioning *The Berkeley Guides* can get a room with two double beds for $69, including private bath, color TV, and breakfast. If you need a good night's sleep and a place to clean up, the Metropolitan is ideal. *5825 Sunset Blvd., tel. 213/962–5800. Wheelchair access, luggage storage.*

● ● ● PASADENA

Pasadena may not be the most exciting place in the world, but at least it has a reasonable assortment of cheap motels, mostly on East Colorado Boulevard. Pasadena is a long way from LAX and Union Station, but if you have a car and a love for suburbia, Pasadena may be worth the extra miles. All lodging prices go up for the annual Rose Bowl Game, January 1st, the only time of the year it might be difficult to find a place to stay.

UNDER $50 **Hi-Way Host Motel.** The rooms here vary in condition, some being used more often than others, so ask to see one before taking it. All rooms have color TV with HBO, and some have kitchens ($6 extra per day). The staff is friendly and keeps an eye on who comes and goes. There's a $2 charge for each extra person. *3474 E. Colorado Blvd., tel. 818/795–7086. Singles $34, doubles $36, breakfast included. Wheelchair access, luggage storage, pool, kitchen facilities extra.*

Regal Inn Motel. Regal? Not really, but at least the beds don't sag. It's a friendly, mom-and-pop sort of place where cleanliness is still next to godliness, and bathrooms literally sparkle. All rooms have color TV with HBO, and kitchenettes are available at $10 extra per day. $5 flat fee for more than two people in a double. *3800 E. Colorado Blvd., tel. 818/449–4743. Singles $35, doubles $42. No wheelchair access, luggage storage, pool, kitchen facilities extra.*

Siesta Inn. What separates this place from the others is that every room has a phone and an air conditioner—a real plus on 90° summer days. This motel is smaller than most, and quiet. There's a color TV in every room. *2855 E. Colorado Blvd., tel. 818/795–2017. Singles $30, doubles $35. No wheelchair access, luggage storage.*

● ● ● HOSTELS

Hosteling is a cheap alternative to staying in expensive hotels, especially if you're traveling alone. Hostels usually provide such budget-friendly services as laundry rooms, kitchen facilities, and ride boards, and they're also the best place to meet other people traveling in the area. However, if you're looking for privacy, look elsewhere. Most offer only dorm rooms that sleep four to eight people, and showers are usually communal. Most of the city's best hostels are located in Venice Beach, a small oceanside town that's full of roller-skaters, sunbathers, surfers, and weight lifters—the sort of place where people still use the expressions "way cool" and "dude." It's easily reached by public bus from the airport, and the area is well suited to those looking for inexpensive ways to experience the L.A. scene.

Airport Hostel (Interclub Hostel). This place caters to an international clientele, and, strange as it may sound, you must have a passport to stay here. They'll accept a U.S.passport, but foreigners have preference if the hostel is crowded. There's ivy growing all over the red tiled roof, and outside the inner courtyard is a long, wide, shaded balcony overlooking Lincoln Boulevard. The murals covering the Interclub were painted by previous hostelers looking to add their personal touches. Some rooms have four beds,

Hollywood Lodging

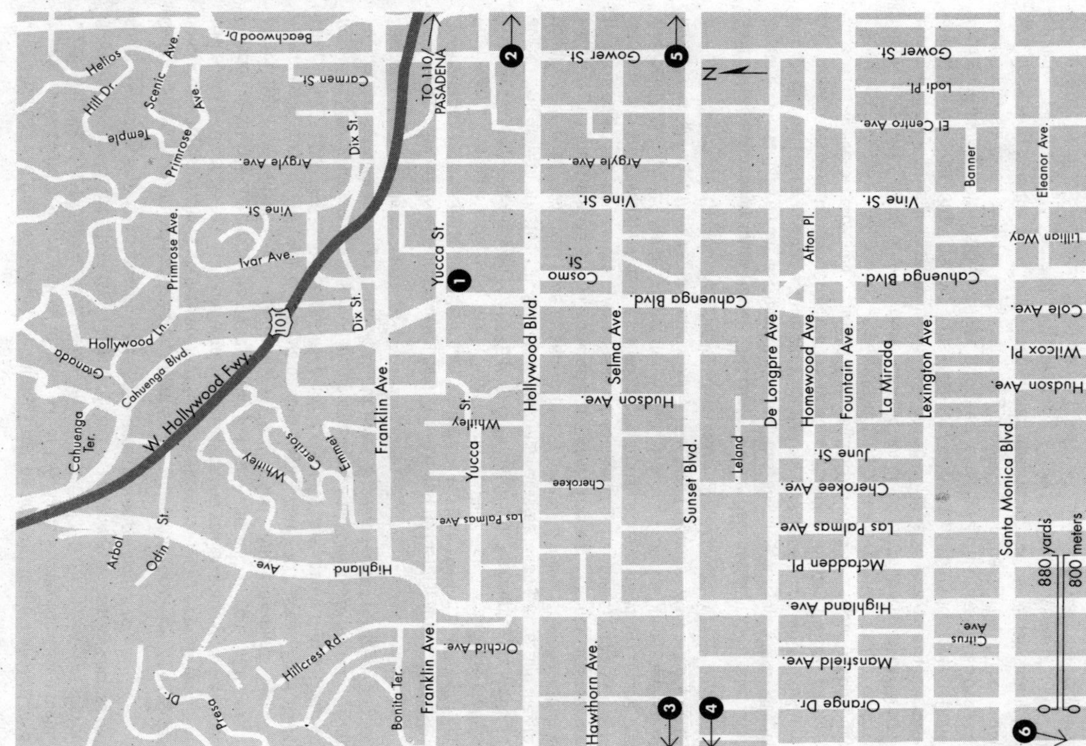

Chateau Marmont, **3**
Downtown Motel, **2**
Farmer's Daughter Motel, **6**
Hotel Mondrian, **4**
Metropolitan Hotel, **5**
OBAN Hotel, **1**

some have six, and there's a 22-bed dormitory. Drinking and smoking are allowed, and there's a ride board if you're looking to head out of L.A. Beds usually run $15 a night; breakfast is $3. *2221 Lincoln Blvd., Venice, tel. 310/305–0250. From LAX take shuttle C to airport bus terminal. Take Santa Monica Bus 3 to Victoria Ave., hostel is across the street. Guest capacity: 74. Laundry, wheelchair access, free parking, kitchen.*

Cadillac Hotel. This Art Deco-style hotel is right up the street from the beach. The regular hotel rooms are expensive, but there are nine hostel-style rooms for four people each that cost about $20 per person. They prefer foreign travelers and you're required to leave your passport at the desk (it can be from the United States). Along with the cost of the room comes use of the common room, sun deck, gym, sauna, and laundry machines. Security is very good. Your mother would approve of your staying here. *401 Ocean Front Walk, Venice, tel. 310/399–8876 or 310/399–1930. From LAX take shuttle C to airport bus terminal. Take Santa Monica Bus 3 to Lincoln and Rose, walk 2 blocks to the ocean, turn left on the boardwalk and go 1 block to the hotel. 9 shared-accommodation rooms. Laundry, no wheelchair access.*

Casa Monica International Guesthouse. Located on a quiet, residential street, this hostel is within easy walking distance of Venice and Santa Monica beaches and the Third Street Promenade. Although rooms are small, they're immaculately clean, and the staff is extremely helpful. Price ranges from $15 to $20. Private rooms for couples are available at $30 a night, with private bath. Breakfast and dinner are free for all guests, and they're usually quite good. You must have a valid ID to stay here, and if you stay longer than a few days you must purchase a $20 membership card. There are kitchen and laundry facilities as well as a music room with piano, a patio, vending machines, and a TV room. Reservations aren't required, but it's a good idea to call ahead, especially during the summer. *1032 7th St., Santa Monica, tel. 310/576–6292. From LAX take shuttle C to airport bus terminal, then Santa Monica Bus 3 to 6th and Wilshire. Walk 1 block north to 7th St. 50 rooms. Laundry, no wheelchair access, luggage storage, kitchen.*

Santa Monica American Youth Hostel. This is perhaps the best hostel in L.A., filled with amenities like laundry machines, huge kitchen facilities, an inner courtyard with a skylight and ivy climbing the walls, and a travel store. Best of all, it's all new and maintained, quite a contrast to its next door neighbor, the Pussycat Adult Movie Theater, the only blemish in an otherwise respectable neighborhood. Between 1887 and 1889, the SMAYH building served as L.A.'s town hall, and fortunately the proprietors haven't done much to destroy the brick and wood charm of this historic building. An American Youth Hostel (AYH) card is required during the peak season (June 1–September 31), although you can purchase one at the front desk if you've lost yours ($25 for Americans; $15 for foreigners). Dorm rooms and doubles both cost $15 a night, and sheet rental is $2. There's also a $5 deposit. No alcohol is allowed on the premises, smoking allowed only in the courtyard. The hostel is a block away from the Third Street promenade. Reservations are necessary during the summer. *1436 2nd St., Santa Monica, tel. 310/393–9913. From LAX take shuttle C to airport bus terminal. Take Santa Monica Bus 3 to 4th and Broadway, walk 2 blocks west to 2nd St., then ½ block north to hostel. 238 beds, all dorm rooms are single sex. 2 AM curfew, laundry, wheelchair access, luggage storage, kitchen facilities.*

Venice Beach Hostel. Although it may look a bit run-down and scary from the outside, this hostel has a seedy charm along the lines of *Barton Fink*, or a bad mystery novel. The halls are dark, the rooms are decrepit, and the plumbing seems to gurgle and groan a lot before churning out a dense stream of brownish-green liquid. To make matters worse, it's located one block from the Venice Beach Boardwalk, not one of L.A.'s safest nighttime haunts. On the lighter side, it's cheap and (not surprisingly) rarely full. You won't live in comfort here, but you'll survive. There's no limit to how long you can stay, but a passport or out-of-state ID is (supposedly) required. Some rooms have private baths and some have kitchen facilities. It's around $11 per night plus a $15 deposit for keys and bedding. You must leave your room between 11 AM and 2 PM for what the management sardonically refers to as "cleaning," but at least there's no curfew. Not recommended for women. *1515 Pacific Ave., Venice, tel. 310/392–6277 or 310/396–0824. From LAX take shuttle C to airport bus terminal. Take Santa Monica Bus 3 north to Lincoln and California. Transfer* *to Santa Monica Bus 2 going west on California to Windward and Pacific. Hostel is on the corner. 17 rooms. No wheelchair access, communal pool table, TV room.*

STUDENT HOUSING • • •

The University of California, Los Angeles (UCLA) has thousands of dorm rooms on campus, but they're not open to visitors. If you have no place to stay, however, you can always head to the campus and look helpless. If you're lucky, some of the students might take pity on you and offer you their floor for the night. There's no guarantee, but with more than 25,000 students there's bound to be someone nice enough to help a weary traveler. You're best chances are between September and December, and mid-January through late May, when classes are in session.

ROUGHING IT • • •

The only way to sleep for free in Los Angeles is to crash out in your car, if you have one. Sleeping on the beaches sounds like a cheap way to see L.A., but the police and roving bands of death squads patrol heavily at night to make sure you don't. Rental cars can be acquired for as little as $25 per day, and you may end up getting a bargain, saving $20 a night by avoiding the city's more expensive hotels. The best places to park overnight are along the beach, either on PCH (Pacific Coast Highway) or on one of the canyon roads that feed PCH. It's illegal, but the police will generally ignore you as long as it's not obvious what you're doing (i.e. don't pitch a tent or light a campfire). Your only other option is to spend the night at the airport. Travelers with early morning flights often sprawl out on the floors and couches, although keep an eye on your luggage as it has a tendency to wander off if not tied to your body.

Food

If you're in L.A. for an extended period of time, there's a brochure put out by KABC (a local radio station) that's worth obtaining. It's called *135 Restaurants Under $10,* by Elmer Dills, a well-known L.A. restaurant reviewer. Send a self-addressed, double-stamped business-size envelope to: 135 Restaurants Under $10, Box A, Hollywood, CA 90027.

DOWNTOWN • • •

Even though Downtown is a bit grimy, there are countless restaurants and food stands scattered throughout the area, most of them quite good. Aside from the myriad highbrow restaurants, you'll find a few gritty hole-in-the-walls loaded with character and good grub. Many of the area's best places to eat were opened in the late '40s and '50s, and you'll be surprised how many of them have survived over the years. The food is predictably greasy and the staff generally rude, but that only adds to the charm of these downtown "greasy spoons."

UNDER $5 **Clifton's Brookdale Cafeteria.** Along with the Original Pantry Café (*see below*), Clifton's is one of L.A.'s last 1930s-era cafeterias, a popular hangout with the under-25 crowd. Besides being the cheapest place around, Clifton's also has an ambience that's hard to beat, including peculiar things like a waterfall, a minichapel, and a wallpaper-simulated redwood forest. There are hundreds of selections on the menu that draw mostly from the Americana category (grilled-cheese sandwiches, hot dogs, burgers, and sundaes), usually for under $5. But if you're really broke, try the macaroni and cheese for $1.09— guaranteed to leave a peculiar greasy taste in your mouth for at least a week. *648 South Broadway, tel. 213/637–1673. Near MOCA and Greyhound Bus station, ½ block up from DASH Route A. Open daily 6 AM–8 PM.*

UNDER $10 **The Itchey Foot.** A favorite with theater goers and business people, this place offers top-notch Italian food at reasonable prices. Two blocks from the Music Center, it's also a good place for drinks and nightcaps, and its small bar is usually filled with artist types and arm-chair philosophers who'd probably be more than willing to talk at length about Los Angeles pop-culture. The extensive menu includes pizza, pasta, sandwiches, and a small but satisfying selection of vegetarian dishes. Of particular note is the pastrami sandwich ($6.20). *801 Temple St. at Figueroa, tel. 213/680–0007. 2 blocks from both DASH routes A and B. Open daily for lunch and dinner until 11:30 PM. Wheelchair access.*

The Yorkshire Grill. In the heart of Downtown, this is a popular luncheon spot with the 9–to–5 crowd. The service is friendly and the sandwiches are big, but between noon and 2 PM you may have to wait for a table. The menu includes over 20 sandwiches, homemade soups, steak and ribs, and salads. Not much style here, but you'll leave satisfied for under $10. *610 W. 6th St., tel. 213/629–3020. Near the L.A. Visitor and Convention Bureau and MOCA. DASH route B stops on W. 6th St. Open Mon.–Sat. 8 AM–9 PM. Wheelchair access.*

Gorky's Café takes its name from Maxim Gorky, the Soviet writer, and it's usually filled with somber poets, has-been (or could-be) musicians, and earnest young men in berets playing chess.

Gorky's Café. Doubling as a gallery and venue for local artists and musicians, Gorky's has become one of the hippest and most pretentious nightspots in Los Angeles. Although there's a rumor that Gorky's may be closing in the near future, for the time being it remains one of the few places in L.A. where you can eat dinner, drink beer, play chess, listen to live music, and socialize with the "Bohemian" crowd, all under the same roof. Gorky's offers a combination of Russian and American dishes served cafeteria style, ranging from stuffed cabbage rolls ($6) to vegetarian lasagna ($5). The food's quite good, although the kitchen usually closes by 10 PM. They also serve excellent but pricey pints of homemade Russian beer. *536 E. 8th St., tel. 213/463–4060. Near the Garment District; take DASH route A to 8th and Los Angeles Sts. and walk east 3½ blocks. Open Sun.–Thurs. 7 AM–10 PM, Wed. and Thurs. 7 AM–11 PM, Fri. and Sat. 7 AM–1:30 AM. Wheelchair access.*

Original Pantry Café. It's a dive, to be sure, but a dive with a reputation for cheap, satisfying food—American cuisine at its best. The Pantry has been operating 24 hours a day, 365 days a year since 1924, and it has the red-vinyl stools, stainless-steel counter tops, and run-down ambience to prove it. Even the waiters and waitresses have names like Vera, Flo, Mel, and Alice. However, if greasy-spoon dining gives you heartburn, you can always head next door to the Pantry's bakery. It costs a bit more than the café, but there's a good selection of breads, pastries, grease-less sandwiches, and soups. *877 South Figueroa St. near 9th St., tel. 213/972–9279. 5 blocks south of the Bonaventure Hotel and the L.A. Visitor and Convention Bureau. DASH route A stops 1 block north. Wheelchair access.*

● ● ● PASADENA

Pasadena has way too many restaurants for a city this size, but hey, that just means more choices for you. Whatever you're looking for, Old Pasadena is a good place to go hunting. The visitor center has a list of over 150 restaurants, with prices.

UNDER $5 **Ernie's Taco Shop.** In a nutshell: fast, cheap, and tasty. Ernie's makes some of the best tacos and *carne asada* burritos in town, all for under $2. It may not look like much from the outside, but this street-side taco joint is top rate. *126 W. Colorado, tel. 818/792–9957. Open weekdays 11–10, weekends 11–midnight.*

UNDER $10 **Birdie's Café.** The theme at Birdie's Café is, not surprisingly, birds—lots of them. In the Great American Tradition, this is the sort of place where theme-style eating takes over every part of the dining experience. The menu is loaded with things like "Egret" (Caribbean-spiced chicken with cranberry-mango chutney), "Japanese Game" (eggplant with gorgonzola, tomatoes, and mushrooms), and "Quail feet" (barbecued spare ribs). Even the drinks have names like Hawk, Pterodactyl, and Black Crow. Luckily, though, the food is excellent, and as long as you don't mind being forced to constantly think about birds (even the toilets are known as "hen" and "rooster"), you'll probably enjoy Birdie's extensive, reasonably priced menu. *17 S. Raymond Ave., tel. 818/449–5884. Open Tues.–Thurs. 7:30 AM–10 PM, Fri.–Sat. 7:30 AM–11 PM, Sun. 7:30 AM–4:30 PM, Mon. 7:30 AM–2 PM.*

Burger Continental. The Burger Continental is part bar, part restaurant, and part belly-dancing venue. Besides cheap pitchers of beer, you'll also find an excellent selection of Middle Eastern dishes (hummus, salads, falafel, couscous) for under $6. There's an informal belly-dancing demonstration most nights, free of charge. Burger Continental is popular with almost everyone in Pasadena, but you'll find the under-25 crowd particularly well-represented here. *535 S. Lake Ave. at California, tel. 818/792–6634. Open daily 6:30 AM–10 PM.*

Crocodile Café. The Crocodile would fit into the characterless and forgettable category if it weren't for its excellent, ethnically influenced food. It's atmosphere is sub-dull, but its blue-corn tostada salads with chicken ($7) and Chinese pot stickers filled with shrimp and vegetables ($5) are savory and filling. *140 S. Lake Ave., tel. 818/449–9900. Between Green St. and Cordova Ave. Open Tues.–Thurs. 11–11, Fri.–Sat. 11–midnight, Mon. 11–10.*

HOLLYWOOD AND WEST HOLLYWOOD • • •

Hollywood—the land of chili dogs, double-chili cheese burgers, and chili fries.

Although Hollywood has a large selection of elegant, up-scale restaurants, some of the best meals in town can be found in a rag-tag series of '50s-style diners, cafés, burger joints, and taco stands along the major boulevards. The grease content is high and the nutrition content low, but these small food stands and drive-thrus can't be beat for taste and, most important in Hollywood, style. As long as you look good while you're eating, nothing else really matters, does it?

UNDER $5 On Sunset Boulevard, head straight for **Carney's** (8351 Sunset Blvd., tel. 213/654–8300), a burger stand that's housed in a train caboose. Their chili has the consistency of cement, but at $1.50 per burger no one seems to mind. On Melrose Boulevard, try **Johnny Rockets** (7507 Melrose Blvd., tel. 213/651–3361), a hip '50s-style dinner that's got chili burgers, fries, ice-cream floats, and a lot of attitude—just look for the row of Harley motorcycles parked in front. But if you want the absolute *best* chili creations in town, **Pink's Hot Dog Stand** (711 N. La Brea, ½ block north of Melrose Ave.) is a must. Popular with many of L.A.'s most (in)famous musicians, Pink's has been serving up first-rate chili dogs for over 20 years. If you're not a fan of chili, head to Hollywood Boulevard and **C.C. Brown's** (7007 Hollywood Blvd.), the reputed birthplace of the hot-fudge sundae.

UNDER $10 **Barney's Beanery.** Half-bar, half-restaurant, Barney's is a magnet for the local hip crowd. Leather jackets and ripped T-shirts are the norm. Barney's has a huge menu, ranging from burgers and fries ($5.50) to pancakes and hash browns ($5). If you're in the mood for a quick game of pool, there are six tables in the middle of the eating area, which sometimes gets annoying when people keep asking you to duck while they take a shot. Both the bar and restaurant are generally packed on weekend nights, and there's a $4 minimum per person for table service after 8 PM. *8447 Santa Monica Blvd. near La Cienega, tel. 213/654–2287. Open daily 10 AM–2 AM.*

Formosa. This small Chinese restaurant specializes in Szechuan cuisine—spicy, pepper-cooked dishes that'll sear the roof of your mouth and clear your sinuses. Most people come to Formosa not for its excellent food, however, but for its decor. There's a small Elvis shrine in the back dining room, and the walls are covered with kitschy photos (many of them autographed) of Hollywood film stars. Formosa is also popular with L.A.'s trendy "in" crowd, and you'll often find a row of custom Harleys parked in front. Formosa's main dining room is no larger than a compact car, so reservations are advised. *12217 Santa Monica Blvd., tel. 310/207–5665. Open weekdays 11:30–9:30, weekends 11:30–10:30.*

UNDER $20 **Campanile.** Campanile is a stuffy eatery popular with the "I want to be an artist" crowd. It offers northern Italian dishes such as basil lamb ($9) and pesto scallops ($8.50). There's both indoor and outdoor seating, pleasant for a semi-formal dinner. *624 S. La Brea at Wilshire, tel. 213/938–1447. Open daily 6 PM–10 PM.*

UNDER $30 **Le Dome.** This is one of those highbrow "Le French" restaurants— the sort of place where the head waiter speaks with a phony accent and calls customers by their first name. However, the food is phenomenal, ranging from roast duck basted in red wine ($18) to scallop and shrimp pasta ($16). If you're in the mood to splurge, Le Dome is the perfect place. Dress is informal, but reservations are advised. *8720 Sunset Blvd., tel. 310/659–6919. 2 blocks west of La Cienega. Open daily 11–10.*

Trumps. Trumps bills itself as an "Exotic American" restaurant, which simply means they offer a mish-mash of odd, one-of-a-kind dishes perfected by their own chefs. If you've ever wondered what chicken with grapefruit ($12) or curried ahi tuna ($14) tastes like, here's your chance. The food at Trumps is exceptionally good, even though it's expensive. Dress is informal, but reservations are advised. The kitchen closes at 10:30 every night, but drinks and hot/cold appetizers are generally served until 1. *8764 Melrose Ave. at Robertson, tel. 310/855–1480. Open Mon.–Sat. 11:45–1AM.*

● ● ● SANTA MONICA AND VENICE BEACH

These two cities have an excellent array of restaurants, bars, and coffee shops. If you're in the mood to explore, take a drive down Wilshire Boulevard, Santa Monica Boulevard, or Main Street, where you'll find a number of both pricey, elegant restaurants and hearty budget ones. New restaurants are constantly opening up, so be adventurous. What may look like a grimy hole-in-the-wall may actually serve some of the best food in the city. If you're anywhere near the beach, be sure to check out both the café and restaurant at the **Rose Café** (220 Rose Ave., tel. 310/399–0711), at the corner of Main Street. You'll find literally hundreds of cheap omelets, burgers, soups, and sandwiches to choose from.

UNDER $10 **Café 50s.** Café 50s is an '80s diner that goes painfully out of its way to recreate the classic American Diner. Crammed floor to ceiling with vintage movie posters, jukeboxes, and old advertisements, it serves standard American cuisine (cheeseburgers, fries, Coca-Cola, and shakes) at reasonable prices. *11623 Santa Monica Blvd., 1 block east of Barrington, tel. 310/479–1955. Open Sun.–Thurs. 9 AM–midnight, Fri.–Sat. 9 AM–1 AM.*

Dem Bones. If you don't like the looks of Café 50s, head next door to this barbecue shack, which serves classic Southern-style spare ribs, pork ribs, and beans, without the attitude of Café 50s. *11619 Santa Monica Blvd., tel. 310/475–0288. Open 11–11.*

The King's Head. Come for pints of Guinness, Bass, Newcastle Brown, and Sam Smith's, along with the best fish-and-chips in L.A. The King's Head has an adjoining bar that's popular with locals and foreign tourists, and after a heavy night of drinking don't be surprised to hear the lads and ladies start a chorus of Irish-English football songs. A complete dinner will run you $7, and pints in the bar range from $2 (domestic) to $3.50 (imported). *116 Santa Monica Blvd. at 3rd St., tel. 310/451–1402. Restaurant open daily 11–11, bar daily 11 AM–2 AM.*

Versailles. Cuban food with hip clientele is the draw of this place. But stick with the basics: though their menu offers a lot of exotic sounding dishes, Versailles's best meals are simple and plain. Try the chicken, bean, and rice plates ($6), dusted with mild Cuban spices. It isn't high on ambience, but it's one of the most popular places in L.A.—and deservedly so. Versailles doesn't accept reservations, so come early—it gets crowded between 7 and 9. *10319 Venice Blvd. at Motor Ave., tel. 310/558–3168. Open daily 11–10.*

UNDER $20 **Eureka.** Eureka specializes in Mediterranean and Thai food—an odd combination of tastes that works amazingly well. Not only do they smoke their own sausages, but they even brew their own beer, a dark, malty concoction that tastes a lot like a smooth porter or stout. Most meals start at $10 and work their way up to $18 or $20, but the lightly spiced sausages and Thai chicken would be bargains at any price. The crowd is eclectic, from business people to poets. *1845 Bundy (enter off Nebraska), tel. 310/447–8000. Open Mon.–Sat. 11 AM–2 PM and 6–10 PM.*

Nanban-Kan. It may not look like much from the outside, but don't let looks deceive you. This is perhaps *the* finest Yakatori house in L.A., which means you'll get hibachi-grilled skewers marinated in a "secret" Nanban sauce. Highly recommended are the skewers of asparagus wrapped in bacon; chicken wings; shrimp; and vegetables. An order of skewers ranges from $1.50 to $3 for two, and it'll take at least four orders to fill you, five to satiate. Nanban-Kan has dining-room seating, but stick with the counter—you'll get a bird's-eye view of the chefs in action. Parking in rear (try the alley behind the restaurant). *11330 Santa Monica Blvd. near Butler, tel. 310/879–0454. Open daily 5:30–11.*

CAFÉS AND COFFEEHOUSES

For years, Los Angeles was criticized for its lack of a focus. Without a town square, a central shopping or pedestrian avenue, L.A. was seen as an unfriendly place where the young, earnest, and socially inclined couldn't just sit down and hang out. Luckily, all that has changed. A number of small coffee houses and cafés (called "coffee houses" if you drive a motorcycle and wear leather; "cafés" if you shop in used-clothes stores and read poetry) have recently sprung up all over the city. Most serve desserts and beer, and some offer a complete range of salads and sandwiches. They're a great place to meet people, and they usually offer (free) a deck of cards, a chess board, or a tacky selection of used paperbacks and L.A. magazines. Coffee tends to be expensive ($1.50–$3), but unlike so many places in L.A., coffee houses and cafés will generally let you sit at a table for as long as you like.

The Bourgeoisie Pig. Don't let the name scare you. This is a wonderfully dark, quirky, art-deco sort of place that's lit mostly with black lights and decorated with the requisite glow-in-the-dark felt paintings. It's too dark to read, but the place is meant for socializing anyway. The Greek sculptures, Roman vases, and idyllic scenes of Apollo, Zeus, and Aphrodite playing on Mount Olympus set the mood for all the hip neoclassicists in the crowd. There's a pool table, but it can take up to an hour to get a turn to shoot. *5931 Franklin near Gower, in West Hollywood, tel. 213/962–6366. Open Tues.–Thurs. noon–2 AM, Fri.–Sun. noon–4 AM.*

Popular with L.A.'s under-30 slackers, the Bourgeoisie Pig is worth a visit if only to see some L.A. mutant culture.

Cacao. Coffee, art, and cramped quarters are what this place is about, unless you're lucky enough to get a pleasant outdoor table in the summer. The work of local artists is showcased on the walls (all for sale), and the crowd tends to be interesting and friendly. Cacao doesn't have a food menu, but it has some great desserts. It's in Santa Monica, two doors up from Café 50s and Dem Bones, and three blocks west of Nanban-Kan (*see* Food, *above*). *11631 Santa Monica Blvd. 1 block east of Barrington. No phone. Open daily 2 PM–midnight.*

The Cinema Café. Movie buffs love this place because they show two movies daily on a 45-inch screen, ranging from *Casablanca* to *The Muppet Movie,* depending on the employees' mood. The café tends to attract an insolent, affected sort of crowd, and sometimes you have to cut the pretentiousness with a knife. If you want to make friends here, make sure you have prepared answers to questions like "what do *you* think about neo-post-anti-abstractionism?" If you can get past the attitude problem, though, the Cinema Café is an interesting, if not amusing place to grab a cup of coffee and enjoy a free movie. In case you left your copy of *Finnegan's Wake* at home, there's also an excellent bookstore across the street. It's in West Hollywood. *7160 Melrose Ave., 1/2 block west of La Brea, tel. 310/939–2233. Open daily 1 PM–3 AM.*

Highland Grounds. This is probably the chicest (i.e., *most* pretentious) café in L.A. at the moment—in case anyone really wants to know. It has an espresso bar, an outdoor patio, live blues most nights, and the sort of people who *really* care about the kind of clothes you're wearing. If you want to make friends, look good. Vintage clothing is a plus, but make sure it's been properly torn and ruffled. *742 N. Highland Blvd. at Willabee, in Hollywood, tel. 213/466–1507. Open daily 8:30 PM–1 AM.*

The Living Room. This café caters mostly to the under-20 crowd, and on weekend nights it's absolutely packed. Even if you can't find a seat, you'll enjoy the decor (quirky art deco) and excellent coffee. Desserts are available. The best time to arrive is after 1 AM, when most of the 16-year-olds on curfew head home. *110 S. La Brea near 1st St., in Hollywood, tel. 213/933–2933. Open Sun.–Thurs. 8:30 AM–2 AM, Fri.–Sat. 8:30 AM–4 AM.*

The Novel Café. If you're in the mood to catch up on your Flaubert or Keats, this is the place to go. The quiet, almost somber crowd sits quietly at their tables, seemingly immersed in deep thought and conversation. There's a complete selection of salads, soups, and sandwiches. It's conveniently located in the middle of Santa Monica, near the beach. *212 Pier Ave. near Main St., tel. 310/396–8566. Open Sun.–Thurs. 7 AM–midnight, Fri.–Sat. 7 AM–2 AM.*

The Pikme-Up. Poetry readings and live blues music on Sunday nights make this a popular place. It's small and quiet, perfect for an evening with a good book. No pretension here. *5437 W. 6th St., tel. 310/939–9706. Open daily 1 PM–1 AM.*

The Sequel/Onyx. Another "artsy" café that's popular with musicians, artists, and poets. It's lively most nights, and there's a good selection of photos and canvases on the wall to keep you occupied if you're not in the mood to play cards or chess with one of the regulars. The Sequel/Onyx serves coffee, teas, and desserts, and it's one block from the **Dresden** bar (*see* After Dark, *below*). *1804 N. Vermont, tel. 213/660–5820. From Hollywood: drive east on Hollywood Blvd., turn left on N. Vermont (1 mi past Vine St.). Open daily 8 AM–1 AM.*

Exploring L.A.

••• DOWNTOWN LOS ANGELES

No other business district in the world has such an eclectic mix of styles and character. Although L.A. has earned itself a reputation for being a violent and charmless sprawling mass of suburbia, downtown L.A. has the appealing feel of a "city"— something you won't often find in this land of freeways and tract housing. Amidst the 50-story office buildings and up-scale restaurants and bars that litter Downtown, you'll find street vendors and the homeless moving comfortably through crowds of business people during lunch hour. A day spent roaming around can take you from the newest skyscrapers to the oldest adobe neighborhoods, from a Chinese temple to the most contemporary of museums. Within a block you can go from a restaurant selling $25 lunches to a thrift store selling 39¢ paperbacks. Downtown L.A. is also an architecture student's field day. In addition to I.M. Pei's **First Interstate World Center** (635 W. 5th St.), check out the **Citicorp Plaza** (725 S. Figueroa St.) with its life-size bronze statue of a headless businessman by Terry Allen. The grid streets are easy to navigate and safe during the day. If you have a car, park on the edge of Downtown and hop on a DASH (Downtown Area Short Hop) shuttle bus or walk it. Daytime traffic is stop-and-go, and downtown parking lots are prohibitively expensive.

CHINATOWN L.A.'s **Chinatown** is bordered by Yale, Bernard, Alameda, and Ord streets, on the outskirts of Downtown. Home to more than 200,000 people, Chinatown looks more like a huge bazaar than anything else, an open-air museum of Asian culture that's alive with all the sights, sounds, and smells you'd expect to find in the city's busiest urban marketplace. Most people from this section of L.A. probably don't even realize they're living in an official "tourist" site, which means you won't feel like you're walking through a make-believe, Disneyland, although there are, of course, the touristy restaurants and gift shops lining North Broadway, the neighborhood's main thoroughfare.

Chinatown's greatest appeal is its people, who move along the city's crowded avenues and crooked alleyways with sacks of chickens or vegetables draped over their shoulders, or sell roasted ducks and fresh produce from wooden carts. And there always seem to be old, toothless men sitting on over-turned crates on the street corners gossiping about something, maybe their grandchildren. Chinatown has a definite L.A. flavor, with wide streets separating the brightly colored pagodas and Chinese markets, and almost every other shop seems to sell some exotic delicacy imported directly from China. The best time

Downtown Los Angeles

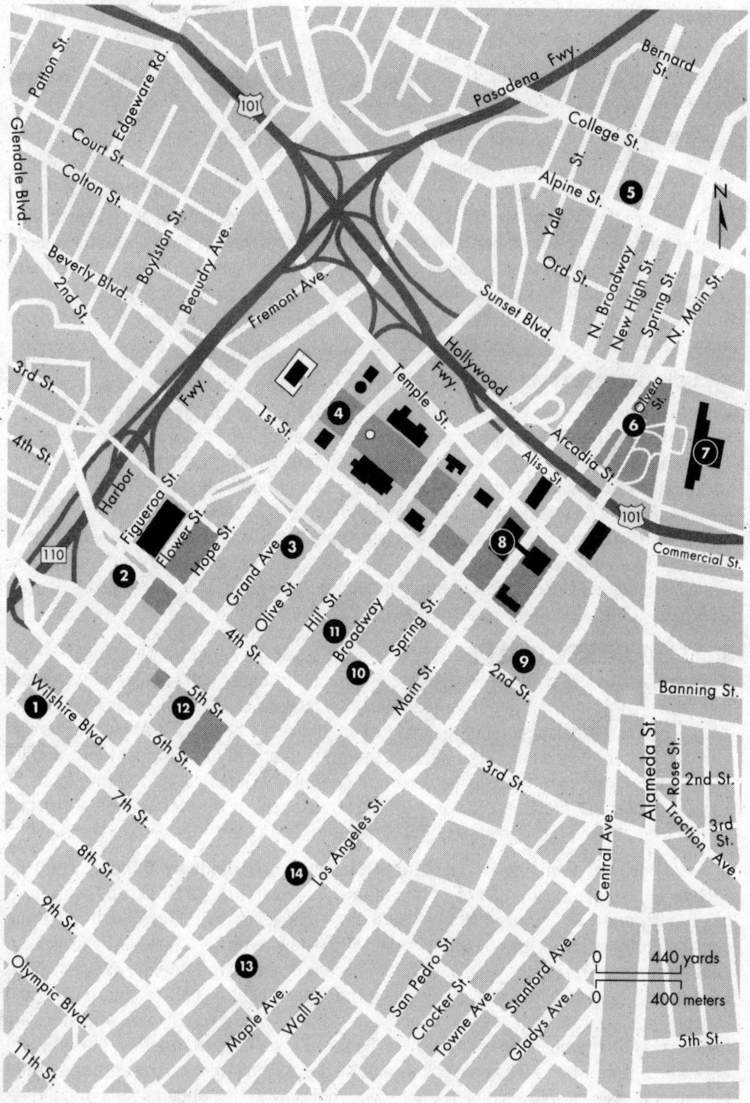

Biltmore Hotel, **12**
Bradbury Building, **10**
Bus Station, **14**
Chinatown, **5**
El Pueblo State Historic Park, **6**
Garmet District, **13**
Grand Central Market, **11**
Greater Los Angeles Visitor and Convention Bureau, **1**
Little Tokyo, **9**
Los Angeles City Hall, **8**
Museum of Contemporary Art, **3**
Music Center, **4**
Union Station, **7**
Westin Bonaventure Hotel, **2**

of year to visit is during the Chinese New Year (usually in February), when a parade of dragons and fireworks swirl through the neighborhood.

Dim sum parlors abound, but it you're looking for great seafood try **Mon Kee's Seafood Restaurant** (679 N. Spring, tel. 213/628–6717).

CITY HALL Los Angeles City Hall, with its striking facade, is the setting for many movies and TV shows, among them *Adam-12* and *Dragnet* ("Just the facts, ma'am."). Tours of the building are given twice daily during the week, and the observation deck on the top floor offers a great view of downtown L.A. (when it's not too smoggy). There's also a decent public cafeteria on the 10th floor, open weekdays from 6:30 AM to 3:30 PM. Even though there's a police station and courthouse just down the street, muggings are quite common in the park that surrounds City Hall, so don't plan on having any picnics here. Stay away at night, too. *200 N. Spring St., tel. 213/485–4423. Free tours weekday mornings at 10 and 11, by reservation only.*

GARMENT DISTRICT The center of L.A.'s thriving clothing business is on Los Angeles Street, between Sixth and Ninth. Although a lot of the stores only sell to wholesalers, you'll find a multitude of places that sell clothes retail at discount prices. There are good deals in the six-story **Cooper Building,** where more than 50 stores offer up-to-date designer fashions for men, women, and children at 25%–75% off. A very dressy wardrobe can be put together here for under $40. Although the Garment District is run down, to be sure, it still retains an aged appeal. You wouldn't want to spend a week here, but the it's good for a three- or four-hour tour, and there are plenty of cheap food stands and coffee shops if you get hungry. *Cooper Building: 860 S. Los Angeles St., tel. 213/622–1139. Open Mon.–Sat. 9:30–5:30, Sun. 11–5.*

GRAND CENTRAL MARKET This is a good place for bemused browsing. Wander through the maze of produce stalls, butcher shops, bakeries, fish stands, and Mexican fast-food stands, and you'll find yourself rubbing elbows with Mexican housewives, chefs from ritzy Santa Monica restaurants, and just about every other kind of Angeleno you can imagine. Recently renovated, the warehouse-size market still has sawdust floors and its 1930s decor. You can find a large selection of fruits, vegetables, and ethnic foods at bargain prices, but most people come for the atmosphere. It is, after all, one of the last of L.A.'s great open-air markets. *317 S. Broadway. Open Mon.–Sat. 9–6, Sun. 10–4.*

Across Broadway from the Grand Central Market is the **Bradbury Building** (304 S. Broadway), a magnificent relic of 19th-century Los Angeles made famous by such films as *Bladerunner* and *Citizen Kane.* Built by George Wyman for a large clothing conglomerate in 1893, the building is one of the few reminders that L.A. was once a beautiful, commercially thriving, and architecturally diverse city. Although its sweatshops have been converted into law offices, the Bradbury's central hall retains its original wrought-iron railings, cage elevators, and five-story, beveled-glass atrium. And stepping inside on a hot afternoon may still give you the sense of walking into another, more distant era—into a time when sewing machines and Model-T Fords were on the cutting edge of technology. Visitors are welcome on weekdays, but only in the lobby.

THE MUSEUM OF CONTEMPORARY ART Come here to see an impressive but quirky collection of American and European art that spans from 1940 to the present. Although there's no lack of wealthy patrons in Los Angeles who are willing to donate or purchase art for the museum, MOCA's general goal is to dazzle you with massive, interactive installations drawn from obscure artists and minor movements. Consequently, you'll find an impressively diverse sampling of all sorts of work, but very few "masterpieces," as defined in the traditional sense. This is no reason to avoid MOCA, as odds are you'll come across something you haven't seen (or even heard of) before. Designed by Arata Isozaki, MOCA's red sandstone building is a work of art in itself, another bastion of modernity that looks somewhat out of place (yet refreshingly so) amidst the sterile office buildings and sprawling freeways that engulf Downtown. When the museum was being built, some of the collection was housed in a stark warehouse called the **Temporary Contemporary** (152 N. Central Ave.). This storehouse became so popular that it has been kept as an alternate exhibit space for the museum. Your ticket admits you to both MOCA and the Temporary Contemporary, and includes free shuttle service between them. *250 Grand Ave., tel. 213/626–6222. Admission: $4, students $2; free Thurs. 5–8. Open Tues.–Sun. 11–6, Thurs. 11–8; closed Mon.*

MUSIC CENTER The Music Center has three performance spaces: the Dorothy Chandler Pavilion, the Mark Taper Forum, and the Ahmanson Theatre. Named for the *L.A. Times'* publisher's widow, who helped finance it, the Dorothy Chandler Pavilion used to play host to the Academy Award ceremonies; today it houses the **L.A. Philharmonic,** the **L.A. Opera,** and the **Joffrey Ballet.** The Mark Taper Forum is a much more intimate venue, seating only 750, and known for presenting experimental and often bizarre theater pieces, some of which eventually end up on Broadway. The Ahmanson Theatre, much larger than the Taper, presents dramas and musical comedies; tickets usually start at $40. Free, hour-long tours of the Music Center are available, but there's very little to see during the day except for the sculpture and fountain by Jacques Lipchitz. The nearest bus stops are on Grand Avenue and First Street. For information on tickets to performances, *see* Theater, *below.* *135 Grand Ave. near First St., tel. 213/972–7211. Tours offered every ½ hr. Mon., Tues., Thurs., Fri. 10–1:30, Sat. 10–noon.*

EL PUEBLO DE LOS ANGELES STATE HISTORICAL PARK Dying for a bag of Mexican jumping beans or a photo of yourself in a velvet sombrero next to a stuffed donkey? Look no further than this state park on **Olvera Street**—a cobble-stone pedestrian avenue lined with Mexican food stands, gift shops, museums, and 19th-century adobe buildings. El Pueblo was built during the mid-18th century when Los Angeles was still a minor settlement governed by Mexico, and today it retains much of its Mexican heritage—a mecca for tourists and Mexican-Americans alike. It's a bit overrun with photo-happy tourists who have never heard of *taquitos* and *carne asada,* but the settlement and its famous Olvera Street have survived intact. If you've never tried a handmade tortilla, head to **La Luz del Dia,** a small sit-down restaurant that offers authentic Mexican cuisine for under $6 a plate. Olvera Street plays host to numerous festivals throughout the year, including the Blessing of the Animals on Easter, *Dia de Los Muertos* (Day of the Dead) in November, and a three-day celebration of Mexican Independence in September. The plaza at the north end of Olvera Street often becomes the stage for folkloric dances on weekends, but even during the week the street is filled with vendors, wandering minstrels, and the glorious smell of home-made *churros* (Mexican doughnuts), burritos, and tortillas. After you're done catering to your worst tourist instincts, visit the **Avila Adobe,** the oldest existing house in Los Angeles, on the plaza facing Olvera Street. Built in 1818, it has recently been converted into a museum (admission free), and its rooms have been faithfully restored. The area is bordered by Alameda, Arcadia, Spring, and Macy streets, in the heart of downtown L.A., and is within easy walking distance of Union Station. *El Pueblo de Los Angeles State Historical Park Visitor Center: Sepulveda House, 622 N. Main St., tel. 213/628–1274. Free 18-min film "Pueblo of Promise" shown at 11 and 2 daily except Sun. Open weekdays 10–3, Sat. 10–4:30. For tours, contact Docent Center, 130 Paseo de la Plaza, tel. 213/628–0605. Free tours given hourly Tues.–Sat. 10 AM–1 PM. For reservations, tel. 213/628–1274.*

UNION STATION Built during the 1940s, it was the first of many public works that helped transform Los Angeles from an underpopulated farming community into an overpopulated metropolis. Hollywood had already made L.A. famous as the movie capital of the world during the 1930s, but Union Station and the Union Pacific train company opened up what was then a barren and inhospitable desert to developers, big business, and heavy industry. Union Station may have faded a bit since then, but with its eclectic mix of Spanish Mission, Moorish, and Art Deco styles, it remains the best example of 1940's architecture in Los Angeles—a rare combination of marble floors, wrought-iron gas lamps, wood panelling, and engraved ceilings that's wonderfully anachronistic. *800 N. Alameda St., just east of Olvera St. on the route of DASH route B.*

Union Station is, simply, one of the last great train stations in the United States.

Philippe's, near Union Station, is an old-style lunch counter where crotchety old women serve tasty, no-frills French-dip sandwiches ($4). It hasn't changed a bit since the 1930s:

There's sawdust on the floor and tarnished photos on the walls—a great place to start or end your trip to L.A.. *1001 Alameda St., tel. 213/628–3781. Open daily 6 AM–10 PM.*

WESTIN BONAVENTURE HOTEL The Westin's dark, glass cylinders tower over Downtown like something from a bad Hollywood space movie. Come here for a great view of L.A. and a fun elevator ride through the roof to a revolving cocktail lounge on the 35th floor. Drinks are expensive but the view is priceless. Take the red elevator. *404 S. Figueroa St., tel. 213/624–1000. Bona Vista lounge open weekdays 3 PM–1 AM, weekends 11 AM–1 AM.*

● ● ● EAST LOS ANGELES

East L.A. has a reputation for being a violent, gang-infested slum that should be avoided at all costs. However, much of East L.A. is actually quite safe, and you'll find a number of sights and monuments that are definitely worth your time. Be careful, of course, especially at night, but as long as you don't drive down the street in a BMW screaming "I'm rich" out the window, you should be okay. In particular, check out the **Los Angeles Contemporary Exhibitions** (1804 Industrial St., tel. 213/624–5650), also known as LACE. Local artists use the space to stage their own shows, giving them the opportunity to get noticed by both the public and L.A.'s art critics. LACE is open 11–5 during the week, and noon–5 on weekends. Also be sure to visit its gift shop, which has an excellent collection of off-beat postcards. The **Museum of Neon Art** (704 Traction Ave., tel. 213/617–1580), also known as MONA, rivals LACE for the title of hippest museum in Los Angeles. Everything here is made from neon, and most pieces are audience interactive.

In **Little Tokyo,** bordered by Temple Avenue, Los Angeles Street, Third Street, and Alameda Avenue, you'll find a group of spotless pedestrian streets overflowing with Japanese restaurants and sushi bars, all reasonably priced. Many business people come to Little Tokyo during their lunch break to take advantage of the best sushi, sashimi, and tempura in town. The **Koyosan Buddhist Temple** (342 E. 1st St., tel. 213/624–1267) is open to the public by appointment only, but on Sunday mornings at 10 you can participate in a service just by showing up. The Sunday service is the only one given in English, and it will give you a chance to explore one of L.A.'s most beautiful temples. **Watts Towers** (1765 E. 107th St., tel. 213/271–9711) is a masterpiece of Los Angeles folk art, a massive cluster of scrap steel and metal wire towers embedded with colored pottery shards and sea shells. Art historians like to compare them to Gaudi's Barcelona cathedrals, but the Watts Towers seem completely unique, a strikingly imaginative work that looms over East L.A. in peculiar majesty.

● ● ● HOLLYWOOD

The first movie made in Los Angeles was filmed in 1910 in a barn at the corner of Sunset and Gower. At that time Hollywood was known as Hollywoodland, and except for the occasional eccentric who lived in Malibu Beach, most of it was populated with fruit-growing farmers and immigrant workers. In less than 40 years, however, Hollywood burgeoned into a hedonistic metropolis, a bombastic super-village that served as a playground for the rich and infamous. But by the time developers decided to remove the last four letters of the Hollywoodland sign in the early 1940s—to make it easier for L.A.'s pool-side culture to pronounce it—the Movie Capital of the World had already begun its slow descent. As the number and quality of Hollywood feature films declined, both because of Cold War blacklisting and imaginative decay, Los Angeles itself fell victim to Hollywood's counterfeit bungalow-and-palmtree culture. By the late 1950s, the plywood streets and back-lot facades of Hollywood's million-dollar film industry had overtaken the city, and in a disastrously short period of time all of Los Angeles had succumbed to Hollywood's glitzy but soulless allure—a superficial mosaic of suburban tract housing and faded glamour.

Hollywood

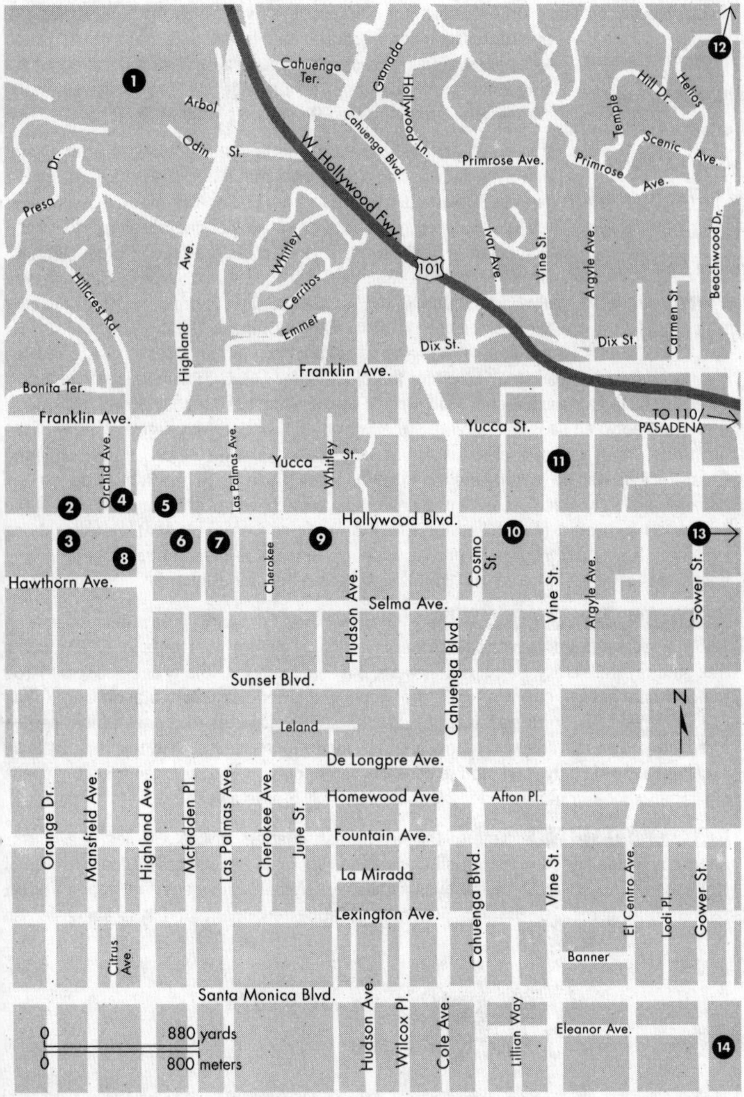

Capitol Records Building, **11**

El Capitan Theatre, **4**

Frederick's of Hollywood, **9**

Hollyhock House, **13**

Hollywood Boulevard Walk of Fame, **10**

Hollywood Bowl, **1**

Hollywood Memorial Cemetery, **14**

Hollywood Movie Costume Museum, **7**

Hollywood Sign, **12**

Hollywood Wax Museum, **5**

Mann's Chinese Theatre, **2**

Max Factor Museum of Beauty, **8**

Motion Picture Coordination Office, **3**

UA Egyptian Theatre, **6**

Today, Hollywood is a stark city within a city that looks good only on film. Filled with prostitutes looking for johns among the tourists, most of Hollywood today is covered in a thick coat of garbage and grime, and about the only stars you'll see aren't on the sidewalk but *in* the sidewalk, memorialized in Hollywood Boulevard's **Walk of Fame**.

Although you may recognize many of the buildings, food stands, and bars along Hollywood Boulevard (often used as a backdrop for films), you'll probably find most of Hollywood pretty bleak, if not downright depressing.

If you can get past the myth and take a good look at what's here, however, you will find a few sights that'll boost your sagging spirits. The 1930s-era **UA Egyptian** and **El Capitan** movie houses have recently been restored, and even the McDonald's along Hollywood Boulevard is worth a quick visit for its art-deco "Golden Arches" (look for Marilyn Monroe's star on the sidewalk outside). If you always thought you and Marlon Brando or Humphrey Bogart wear the same size shoe, head to **Mann's Chinese Theatre** and discover for yourself—it has a famous collection of hand, foot, nose, and even cigar prints outside (be sure to look for the prints of R2-D2, C-3PO, and Darth Vader). If you're in the mood to experience Hollywood's seedier side, head to the "Strip" (Hollywood Boulevard between La Brea and Vine Street) on a Friday or Saturday night. Along with the prostitutes and freaks, there's usually a large crowd of skin heads, long hairs, and Glam-Rockers who do nothing but swill beer and look tough. For a break, head up into the hills behind Hollywood for a walk or a drive. Beachwood Avenue offers a great view of the Hollywood sign atop Mount Lee, and in the windy canyon roads that meander along Hollywood's northern rim you'll find an excellent sample of L.A. architecture, including homes designed by Frank Lloyd Wright, R.M. Schindler, and Richard Neutra.

CAPITOL RECORDS BUILDING When Nat King Cole and Johnny Mercer came up with the idea of building a circular tower shaped like a stack of records in 1950, people thought they were crazy. Perhaps they were, but somebody eventually decided to bankroll their off-beat design, creating for Capitol Records the world's first circular office building (1750 N. Vine St.). Although most of the building is off-limits to tourists, tours can be arranged if you call ahead. There's a small observation deck on the top floor with an excellent view of Hollywood, and in case you're wondering: The red beacon on top spells out "Hollywood" in morse code, 24 hours a day, 365 days a year.

FAIRFAX DISTRICT One of the last Jewish quarters in Los Angeles, the Fairfax district is a small enclave of Jewish-owned and -operated businesses on the outskirts of Hollywood. Though most of the synagogues, butcheries, and delis that made Fairfax famous during the 1940s and '50s have disappeared, many of L.A.'s aging Jewish

They Came, They Swore, They Got the Hell Out

During the 1930s and 1940s, Los Angeles became home to some of America's and Europe's most outstanding scholars and writers. Einstein and Oppenheimer both worked at Pasadena's California Institute of Technology, while F. Scott Fitzgerald, William Faulkner, Bertolt Brecht, and Thomas Mann struggled to make a living in Hollywood as writers, script editors, and playwrights. Most of these men, however, were quickly disillusioned with the Hollywood mentality. Fitzgerald and Faulkner became notorious alcoholics, while Brecht and Mann eventually returned to Europe— impoverished, unappreciated, and disgusted. "I who live in Los Angeles and not London," wrote the German playwright Brecht, who lived in a studio bungalow on 26th Street in Santa Monica, "find, while thinking about Hell, that it must always be still more like Los Angeles."

residents still live here. Fairfax is no Brooklyn, but it's still *the* place in L.A. for kosher food and a good kibitz. Deli fans should head to **Canter's** (419 N. Fairfax Ave.), a '60s-era deli that's popular with local youth and the Hollywood-producer crowd. Canter's is open daily, 24 hours, and their matzo ball soup ($3) and corned beef on rye sandwiches ($5.25) are heavenly. The Fairfax District runs along Fairfax Avenue between Wilshire Boulevard and Third Street.

FREDERICK'S OF HOLLYWOOD Housed in a grey, pink, and purple Art Deco building, flags aflying, Frederick's of Hollywood is legendary for its outrageous lingerie—a good place to pick up a *real* Hollywood gift (it's better than an "I Luv Hollywood" coffee mug). Don't miss the **Bra Museum** in back of the store. Besides its "History of the Bra" display, you may want to take a peek at some of Mr. Frederick's most famous bras, including those worn by Mae West, Madonna, and Cybil Shepard (there's even one of Milton Berle's). The museum was looted during the 1992 riots and several bras were stolen. (What better way to show your rage than to make off with a used brassiere?) Most, if not at all, the bras were later returned—one remorseful man turned in the looted bra to a rather bemused priest. *6608 Hollywood Blvd., tel. 213/466–8506. Admission free. Open Mon.–Thurs. 10–8, Fri. 10–9, Sat. 10–6, Sun. noon–5.*

HOLLYHOCK HOUSE (BARNSDALL PARK) Built in the 1920s, Hollyhock House stands in the middle of Barnsdall Park, a small artist community in the center of Hollywood founded by oil heiress Aline Barnsdall. A luxurious and quirky building that uses both Mayan designs and the Hollyhock flower as decorative motifs, it was designed and built by **Frank Lloyd Wright** (one of the first of his many projects in L.A.). Wright was a perfectionist, and when he agreed to design a house he made sure he had complete and absolute artistic control. Thus everything inside the home, from the furniture to the wall hangings to the small waterfall in the living room, was designed by Wright. Wright was something of an egoist, and there's perhaps no better place to see this than in his Hollyhock design. Mrs. Barnsdall was reportedly 5′ 8″, and it's no coincidence that every doorway in her house is 5' 7"—the "perfect" height of a doorjamb, according to the 5' 6" Wright. Even more peculiar are the Hollyhock House's inwardly sloping walls, built in the shape of an upside down *V* to discourage occupants from hanging non-Wright art in the house. The Hollyhock House is perhaps one of Wright's most interesting designs, and it shouldn't be missed if you're in the neighborhood. *4800 Hollywood Blvd. at Vermont, tel. 213/485–4581. Admission: $1.50. Tours given Tues.–Thurs. 10 AM–1 PM, Sat. and Sun. 12 PM–3 PM.*

HOLLYWOOD BOWL Inspired by a Wright design, the Hollywood Bowl sits nestled in a small canyon at the foot of the Hollywood Hills. On a peaceful summer night, thousands of Angelenos head here for an evening of classical, jazz, or contemporary music, along with a picnic dinner. There are 13 picnic areas surrounding the Bowl, but get here an hour or two early as the picnic sites get crowded. Don't worry if you forget your picnic basket, though; concession stands inside sell everything from pesto chicken to hot dogs, beer, and wine. A meal may run you upwards of $10 with wine, but there's no better place in L.A. to enjoy Bach or Mozart under the stars. The Hollywood Bowl is the summer home of the **Los Angeles Philharmonic** and **Hollywood Bowl Orchestra,** and concerts run nightly during the summer (after sunset it gets cold, so be sure to bring an extra sweater or jacket). Seat prices range from $1 (the stage looks awfully small from here) to $21. If you're on a tight budget, come to the Bowl on a Tuesday, Thursday, or Friday between 9:30 AM and noon and listen to a rehearsal for free. *2301 N. Highland Ave., tel. 213/850–2000. Bowl Bus Shuttle service offered from 13 locations in S. California; also served by RTD Buses 212 and 420. Season runs July– Sept. Wheelchair access.*

Picnics aren't mandatory, but it's become an L.A. tradition to bring a basket of fruit, wine, and sandwiches to the Hollywood Bowl to munch on before a performance.

Next door to the Hollywood Bowl is the **Hollywood Bowl Museum.** It houses a permanent collection of photographs and documents that chart the history of the Bowl, as well as special exhibitions related to performances and guest composers who have conducted here. *Tel. 213/850–2058. Admission free. Open Tues.–Sat. 9:30 AM–4:30 PM, 'til 8:30 PM on concert nights.*

HOLLYWOOD MEMORIAL CEMETERY For the freaks and vampires out there, check out the Hollywood Memorial Cemetery—the final stop on that long road to fame. Although the **Forest Lawn Cemetery** (near the L.A. Zoo) is bigger, the one in Hollywood is more exclusive, and the grounds are peaceful (hardly surprising) and well kept. Hidden among the trees and shrubs are the graves of Mel Blanc, Richie Valens, Jayne Mansfield, Tyrone Power, and Cecil B. De Mille, to name a few. *6000 Santa Monica Blvd., tel. 213/469–1181. Open weekdays 8–5, weekends 9–4.*

HOLLYWOOD MOVIE COSTUME MUSEUM Unlike the Wax Museum (*see below*), this place is a *real* museum, with an interesting collection of costumes and jewelry worn by Hollywood's brightest stars since the 1920s. Most days, the owners hang around and offer guided tours (free) of their displays. Once you get them started, they'll talk for hours about how they tailored the suit Howard Hughes made for Jane Russell, or how they got hold of the shirt Tom Cruise wore in *Risky Business.* Even though it's a small museum geared for the spend-happy tourist (there's a gift counter in the lobby), you'll enjoy this place if you're a film buff. *6630 #D Hollywood Blvd., tel. 213/962–6892. Admission: $5. Open Sun.–Thurs. 10–8, Fri. and Sat. 10–10.*

HOLLYWOOD WAX MUSEUM For those annoyed by the absence of real, live movie stars, the Hollywood Wax Museum offers minimal consolation. Works of art these wax figurines are not. Spend the admission price on a movie, where at least the people move. There are few things more depressing than wandering around the empty halls of this museum at midnight on a Friday night. *6767 Hollywood Blvd. tel. 213/462–8860. Admission: $7.50. Open Sun.–Thurs. 10 AM– midnight, Fri. and Sat. 10 AM–2 AM.*

MANN'S CHINESE THEATER Throngs of tourists climb out of their tour buses to compare the size of their feet and hands with prints left by some 160 celebrities. Built in 1927 by the architects Meyer and Holler, the theater itself looks like a Chinese pagoda that only Hollywood could have dreamed up. The inside is just as elaborate, and if you're looking for a good place to see one of Hollywood's latest releases, head here. TV studios send people to the Mann Theater to give out free tickets for television shows and early cuts of the latest Hollywood action-flick. *6925 Hollywood Blvd., tel. 213/464–8111 for movie information.*

If you go up to any one of the 10 or so people holding a clipboard at Mann's Chinese Theater, you'll likely walk away with a slew of free movie tickets.

MAX FACTOR MUSEUM OF BEAUTY This is another museum dedicated to the history of Hollywood, this time brought to you by Max Factor. You'll be taken on a tour that charts the evolution of movie makeup as well as Max Factor's "creations" for the American Woman ("Oh, she is *so* lovely"). Housed in a former movie studio, this museum also includes the Beauty Calibrator, a machine designed to define that age-old question, "What is beauty?" Perhaps even more peculiar is Max Factor's Kissing Machine—made to test the indelibility of lipsticks after two employees got tired of kissing each other for 40 minutes every morning. The Max Factor Boutique sells Max Factor products at a substantial discount. *1666 Highland Ave. (½ block south of Hollywood Blvd.), tel. 213/463–6668. Admission free. Museum open Mon.–Sat. 10–4, boutique open Mon.–Sat. 9–5.*

MOTION PICTURE COORDINATION OFFICE It may not be an official site, but the Motion Picture Coordination office is the place to go if you're interested in seeing how movies are made. Here you can buy (or just look at) their "shoot sheet," which tells you what is being filmed around town that day. It lists what kind of shoot (eg. film, TV, music video, still photo), who's doing it, when, and where. You may end up driving all over L.A. in search of your favorite movie star, but once you find the set you may be allowed a closer inspection (perhaps even an autograph). Don't push your luck, though: Most sets are guarded by the L.A.P.D., and (as we all know) they're not the friendliest people in town. *6922 Hollywood Blvd., room 602, tel. 213/485–5324. Shoot sheets available after 10:30 AM. You can look at it for free, or purchase it for $1.10. Open weekdays 8–5.*

Donated to L.A. in 1896 by Colonel Griffith J. Griffith, the park and its 4,000 acres of wilderness are one of the last "nature zones" in L.A. Some of the park has been used to house the Observatory, the L.A. Zoo, the Gene Autry Western Heritage Museum, the Greek Theater, golf courses, and tennis courts, but most of it has been protected from developers and left in its (relatively) pristine state. When the hustle and bustle of L.A. becomes too much for you, escape into the tranquility of the park for a hike, bike, or horseback ride (*see* Outdoor Activities, *below*). *Major entrances at Western Ave. at Los Feliz Blvd., Vermont Ave. at Los Feliz Blvd., Hillhurst Ave. at Los Feliz Blvd., and Crystal Springs Dr. near Riverside Dr., where I–5 and the Ventura freeway meet. Ranger station: 4730 Crystal Springs Dr., tel. 213/665–5188. Take RTD Bus 96, 97, or 412 toward the L.A. Zoo. Open daily 6–10.*

GRIFFITH OBSERVATORY Used as the set for *Rebel Without a Cause* and the more recent *Barton Fink,* the copper-domed Griffith Observatory houses the Hall of Science, a planetarium, and a 12-inch telescope. If you're curious to know how much you'd weigh on Mars, head to the Hall of Science, a place built for both kids and adults. There are lots of hands-on exhibits here, and the staff seems to live for answering questions like "What is a rock?" and "How big is space?" The planetarium has two–four shows daily on different celestial themes, as well as a Laserium—a laser art show set to the tunes of bands like Led Zeppelin, U2, and Pink Floyd. If you've never seen a laserium show, it's worth your while, but beware the hordes of red-eyed youths who flock here on Friday and Saturday night—the unofficial meeting place of the "Just Say Yes" crowd. The telescope is open to the public on clear nights after sunset or at 7 PM, whichever is later (except Mondays, September–June). You can get a great view of Los Angeles outside (and on top of) the Observatory. If you feel like hiking, take the path at the far end of the parking lot up to **Mount Hollywood** for a view of L.A. and the San Fernando Valley. *2800 East Observatory Rd., tel. 213/664–1181 or 213/664–1191. By car, enter Griffith Park from Los Feliz Blvd. or Hillhurst, then follow signs. RTD Bus 203 also goes to the Observatory. Admission to the Hall of Science and telescope free. Planetarium tickets $3.50, laserium tickets $6. Open mid-June–first Mon. in Sept., daily 12:30–10 PM; Sept.–mid-June, Tues.–Fri. 2–10 PM, weekends 12:30–10 PM.*

GREEK THEATRE This popular outdoor amphitheater hosts acts from Engelbert Humperdinck to Santana to your MTV favorites. You can see rap, rock, reggae, folk, and country music here throughout the year, so call for information or pick up a copy of the *L.A. Weekly* for listings. Parking is limited and expensive, so get here early or park on Los Feliz Boulevard and then walk up the hill. The theater is surrounded by a large park with picnic tables, the perfect place for a pre-performance snack. *2700 North Vermont Ave., tel. 213/665–5857. Enter Griffith Park at Vermont or Hillhurst off Los Feliz Blvd. Ticket prices and show times vary.*

L.A. ZOO The L.A. Zoo is home to over 2,000 animals surrounded by habitats made to resemble their natural environments. The zoo maintains a collection of over 50 endangered species, and is one of the few zoos in the world to breed successfully the California condor, once numbered at only eight. Check out the koala house, the chimps, gorillas, white tigers, and elephants, and catch one of the twice-daily sea lion feedings. Wear comfortable shoes—the zoo is huge. Tram tours are available, but during the summer lines are long. The best time to visit is during the week, though even then you'll have to compete with hordes of school children on field trips. Food stands and gift shops are located throughout the park; an "I Luv the L.A. Zoo" T-shirt costs $14. *5333 Zoo Dr., tel. 213/666–4650. Located at the intersection of the Golden State Fwy. (I–5) and the Ventura Fwy. (CA 134); use the Los Feliz Blvd. off-ramp. Accessible by RTD bus lines 96, 97, and 412. Admission: $6. Open Sept.–Apr., daily 10–5; May–Aug., daily 10–6.*

On your way to the zoo, stop off at the nearby **Gene Autry Western Heritage Museum,** a wonderful multimedia spectacle—the place to see a robotic Gene Autry singing a lonesome country diddy without a mechanical care in the world. There's also an interesting "Old West Towne" filled with wranglers and gunslingers looking for a brawl at high noon. If you have a warm, fuzzy place in your heart for cowboys and pioneers, this museum is worth the admission price. *4700 Zoo Dr., tel. 213/667–2000. At intersection of Golden State Fwy. and Ventura Fwy. Enter from Fwy. or Griffith Park Dr. Accessible by RTD bus lines 96, 97, 412. Admission: $5.50, students $4. Open Tues.–Sun. 10–5. Wheelchair access.*

TRAVEL TOWN Though anyone over 20 probably hasn't been here for years, most Angelenos have fond memories of a childhood visit to Travel Town, either with parents, school, Cub Scouts, or Brownie Troops. It's not the most exciting sight in L.A., but with its collection of antique cars, railroad steam engines, L.A. trolley cars, and World War II planes, there's something wonderfully sappy about the place. Kids and adults alike can purchase railroad engineer caps from the gift shop and then climb aboard one of Travel Town's well-preserved locomotives. Feel free to yell "All aboard!" Most people do. *5500 West Zoo Dr., tel. 213/662–9678. Take Ventura Fwy. to the Victory Blvd. exit, turn right. Admission free. Open weekdays 10–5, weekends 10–6.*

● ● ● PASADENA

Pasadena has long been an uncomfortable cousin to Los Angeles. Since the city is technically outside the L.A. city limits, it's often looked down on by Angelenos as the boondocks or outback—a place to go if your idea of fun is to sit on the front porch and watch the cars drive by. However, Pasadena doesn't deserve to be dumped on this way, especially since it's home to some of L.A.'s best museums and historic buildings. You can't see a Gutenburg Bible in L.A. because this priceless treasure is kept safe in Pasadena's excellent **Huntington Museum.** Pasadena may not be the liveliest place in the world, but it has a pleasantly provincial, 1950s feel that most of Los Angeles proper lost long ago. Another thing Pasadena has to offer is **Old Pasadena,** a historic neighborhood filled with renovated mansions and 19th-century ranch houses, at the western edge of town. Bordered by Arroyo Parkway, Pasadena Avenue, and Union and Green streets, Old Pasadena is also where young people hang, cruising up and down in their souped-up Camaros on their way to drive-in movies. On New Year's Day, Pasadena is the site of the **Tournament of Roses Parade** and **Rose Bowl** football game, and if you're in town on Thanksgiving (last Thursday in November), check out the **Doo Dah Parade,** a takeoff on the Tournament of Roses in which business executives march with their briefcases in hand, and anyone who wants to can join in. There isn't much public transportation to Pasadena from downtown L.A. or the airport, so without a car the city may be too far out of your reach.

GAMBLE HOUSE The Gamble House was built for David and Mary Gamble (of Proctor and Gamble fame) in 1908 by Pasadena's famous architects **Charles and Henry Greene.** Known for their love of open space and elaborately carved wood, the Greene brothers built this 8,000-square-foot mansion as a winter cottage, at a time when Pasadena was nothing more than a wild prairie of sagebrush and lonesome dirt roads. The tour takes you through bedrooms to hidden alcoves and colorful stained-glass windows. Next door, at 2 Westmoreland Place, is another Greene & Greene house, and behind these houses is **Arroyo Terrace,** a curved street full of Greene & Greene bungalows. However, only the Gamble House gives tours. *4 Westmoreland Pl., tel. 818/793–3334. Just north of the Ventura Fwy. (CA 134). Take Orange Grove Blvd. exit north, take the first left after Walnut St., then the first right onto Westmoreland. Admission: $4, $2 students. Open Thurs.–Sun. noon–3. Tours given several times an hour, last one leaves at 3.*

HUNTINGTON LIBRARY Built on the grounds of Henry E. Huntington's 200-acre estate, the Huntington Library contains an art gallery specializing in 18th-century art (including Gainsborough's "Blue Boy"), a library that proudly displays a Gutenburg Bible, a first folio edition of Shakespeare's works, and a botanical garden. Wear comfortable shoes because you could easily spend hours wandering over the grounds of the immense estate. If you get weary, head off to the Patio Restaurant or go to the tearoom for an old-fashioned English tea. *1151 Oxford Rd., tel. 818/405–2141. For directions call 818/405–2274. Admission: suggested donation of $5, but it's up to you. Library, art* *collections, and gardens open Tues.–Fri. 1–4:30, weekends 10:30–4:30. Restaurant open Tues.–Sun. 1–4.*

NORTON SIMON MUSEUM The Norton Simon Museum contains one of the best collections of art on the West Coast, one that's more traditional than what you'll find at either the Museum of Contemporary Art or the Los Angeles County Museum of Art. You'll find rooms full of Van Gogh, Degas, Manet, Monet, and Rousseau, as well as manicured parks, fountains, and sculpture gardens. Although Norton Simon himself no longer comes around to arrange the displays to his own liking (putting every flower painting he could find into one room, for example, and lavishing it with dozens of fresh tulips), the museum still has a personal, intimate charm. *411 W. Colorado Blvd., tel. 818/449–3730. Near intersection of Foothill (CA 210) and Ventura (CA 134) Fwys. Admission: $4, students $2. Open Thurs.–Sat. noon–6. Wheelchair access.*

PACIFIC ASIA MUSEUM Not only is this one of the few museums in California specializing in Asian and Pacific Basin art, but it's also housed in an amazing building constructed in the Chinese Imperial Palace style, complete with a center courtyard garden and a pond filled with the biggest, ugliest koi fish you've ever seen. Exhibits here include Japanese and Chinese woodworks, illuminated manuscripts, and pottery. *46 N. Los Robles Ave., tel. 818/449–2742. Admission: $3, students $1.50. Gift shop and garden free. Open Wed.–Sun. noon–5. Wheelchair access.*

WEST HOLLYWOOD • • •

This pistol-shaped city is between Hollywood and Beverly Hills and is home to many of L.A.'s best bars, cafés, clubs, and shopping avenues. Though Sunset Boulevard, Melrose Avenue, and Hollywood Boulevard all start in Hollywood, it's only when they cross into West Hollywood that they lose their run-down, grimy look. Most of West Hollywood is filled with exquisite restaurants and lavish shopping boutiques, but if you can navigate your way through these (hopefully by car), West Hollywood is a great place to grab a cheap beer before heading off into the glitzy nightclubs on L.A.'s famous Sunset Strip.

FARMER'S MARKET Farmers' Market used to be *the* place in L.A. to buy food. During the 1930s and '40s it provided most of the West Side with its fresh produce, hauled over the Sepulveda Pass and Laurel Canyon from the orange groves and bean fields in the San Fernando Valley. Today, however, the 150 food stalls and produce counters have been overrun by tourists and copious charmless concession stands. You will find an excellent selection of exotic fruits, homemade candy, cheeses, and fresh-cut meats, but be prepared to pay handsomely for even a small bag of grapes or carrots. Ironically, what used to make Farmers' Market so appealing was its small-town feel, and people made the long drive from Santa Monica or Malibu to pick up cheap *Los Angeles* produce, and because it was a meeting place for local farmers and immigrant workers. Though you can eat pesto lamb and Chicago-style pizza here these days, that's not much of a reason to come; you can do the same elsewhere in L.A. without the hassle and for a lot less money. Farmers' Market does have a pleasant courtyard with outdoor tables, however, and if you like people-watching, you'll certainly get your fill here. *6333 W. 3rd St. at Fairfax, tel. 213/933–9211. Open Mon.–Sat. 9–7, Sun. 10–6.*

LOS ANGELES COUNTY MUSEUM OF ART (LACMA) Located in Hancock Park (remember, this is the park and not the neighborhood with the same name east of here), LACMA is home to a vast collection of art from all over the world. Its permanent holdings consist of everything from pre-Columbian Mexican sculpture to works by Calder, Magritte, David Hockney, numerous artists from the Fauve and Dada circles, and any neo- or post-neo movement you could think of. LACMA really helped put Los Angeles on the world art map, and even the buildings have become well-known works of art. Numerous temporary exhibits and guest lecturers also appear here, so call ahead for current schedules and a listing of shows. Be sure to check out the Japanese art and garden in the Pavilion (one ticket buys you entrance to all LACMA buildings). If you're looking for impressive presents, try the gift shops in the Anderson building or the west wing of the

Japanese Pavilion. *5905 Wilshire Blvd., tel. 213/857–6000 Admission: $5, $3.50 students. Open Tues.–Fri. 10–5, weekends 10–6.*

If you're not exhausted after a visit to LACMA, head next door to the **La Brea Tar Pits** and **George C. Page Museum of the La Brea Discoveries.** Most don't realize it, but L.A. wasn't always a dry, inhospitable desert basin filled with freeways and tract housing. Millions of years ago, it was a lush wetland filled with dinosaurs and pre-historic mammals. When oil was discovered in the 1890s, fossils were found mired in La Brea's underground tar pits, and today these pits have been opened to the public. You can still see animal bones sticking out of the murky tar in the observation area, while inside the museum there's a reconstruction of a wooly mammoth and a hologram of a prehistoric woman whose skeleton was found in the 1950s. Over a million Ice Age Fossils have been found here, and the excavation of La Brea's tar pits is still underway. Budget travelers' tip: admission to the pits is free during the last half-hour, plenty of time for a quick tour of the small museum and observation lounge. *5801 Wilshire Blvd., tel. 213/936–2230. Admission: $5, $2.50 students, free second Tues. of each month and 4:30–5 daily. Open Tues.–Sun. 10–5.*

MELROSE AVENUE Melrose Avenue used to be the hip, "alternative" place to do your shopping—a subculture enclave that offered Doc Martin boots, leather jackets, used clothing, and Dead Kennedy T-shirts at bargain prices. Although you can still find most of these things here, in recent years it has turned into a hangout that caters to L.A.'s not so sub sub-culture. Stores like **Aardvarks** (tel. 213/655–6769), **War Babies** (tel. 213/651–3624), and **American Rag** (on La Brea, ½ block south of Melrose Ave., tel. 213/935–3154) still offer moderately priced new and used clothing, but otherwise most of Melrose's clothing stores have been converted into expensive outlets with little personality. However, if you're looking for art-deco furnishings, hip antiques, or quirky knick-knacks (including inflatable fish, blow-up sex dolls, Virgin Mary telephones, infant Jesus wallpaper, and plastic chili dogs), there are plenty of shops along Melrose Avenue to spend your money in. It's popular with the Hollywood Harley Davidson crowd (i.e., Mickey Rourke look-alikes), and on weekends it's an excellent place for people- and attitude-watching. Most of the avenue closes down around 8 PM, but a few restaurants, '50s-style diners, and hot-dog stands, stay open late into the night. If you've never had a chili dog before, try one at **Pink's** (711 N. La Brea), home of the best greasy chili in town. The Melrose "Strip" is between Fairfax and La Brea.

SUNSET BOULEVARD Sunset Boulevard runs from the beach in Pacific Palisades all the way into Downtown, but "Sunset Strip" is really only between Doheny and Crescent Heights Boulevard, in the heart of West Hollywood. The Strip is peculiar in a lot of ways, for not only does it have some of L.A.'s most famous and popular nightclubs and bars, it also has a large number of elegant boutiques and luxurious hotels and restaurants—an awkward combination of colorful, raucous hangouts and $150-a-night hotel rooms. Friday and Saturday nights is when the Strip really comes alive. Heavy-metal and glam-rock fans flock to the **Whiskey-a-Go-Go,** the **Roxy,** and **Gazarri's** (*see* After Dark, *below*) for a night of cacophony, thrash, and general all-out intoxication, while L.A.'s suit-and-tie crowd head to the **Laugh Factory** and the **Comedy Store** for an expensive evening of stand-up comics and one-liners. Once the nightclubs and bars quiet down—at around 2—**Ben Frank's** (8585 Sunset Blvd., tel. 310/652–8808) 24-hour coffee shop becomes a rowdy see-and-be-seen kind of place, along with the nearby **Carlos n' Charlies** and **Coconut Teaszer**—two after-hours bars filled with yuppie scum (as in die) and (call the police) cocaine freaks. If you're in the mood for a more respectable evening, head to the **Sunset Plaza,** located in the middle of the strip, where you'll find ritzy restaurants and highbrow bars with strict dress codes (i.e., no ripped jeans or Nirvana T-shirts allowed). East of Crescent Heights Boulevard, Sunset continues through Hollywood and Silverlake on its way downtown. Even though this part of the boulevard is less glamorous than the Strip, it has a number of bars, clubs, restaurants, and coffee houses that are worth a visit. If you're a music fan, look in the *L.A. Weekly* for information on concerts at the **Palladium** (6215 Sunset Blvd., tel. 213/962–7600), one of the best rock-music venues in Los Angeles.

The cities of **Beverly Hills, Westwood, Santa Monica,** and **Venice** are loosely known in L.A. as "the Westside," situated roughly between Hollywood and the beach. Home to most of L.A.'s upper-middle class, the Westside is primarily a residential sprawl with few official tourist sites. If you have a car, take a spin through the foothills of the Santa Monica Mountains, in the affluent, exclusive neighborhoods of Beverly Hills and Bel-Air, north of Sunset Boulevard. Though they're notoriously inaccurate, "Star Maps" are available if you want to take a peek at the homes of L.A.'s movie stars, both past and present. Maps are sold by local kids, and usually run $3–$7. **Star Tours** (tel. 213/483–5900) offers a minivan tour of the area, but at $25 a person you'd do better to rent a car.

If you're hungry, head to the **Apple Pan** (10801 W. Pico Blvd.); it was opened in 1947 and the menu hasn't changed one iota since then. They serve up burgers ($2), fries (75¢), and homemade pie ($1.25 a slice). If you're in the mood to shop, head across the street to the **Westside Pavilion,** which has movie theaters, clothing stores, and an over-priced, "international" food court serving take-out meals from around the world.

BEVERLY HILLS Beverly Hills is one of the most exclusive addresses in the world, a place where L.A.'s rich and famous both live and play. It's pretty difficult to get a good look at most of the multimillion-dollar homes hidden behind large hedges and tall gates. But if you head to the **Golden Triangle** (bound by Wilshire and Santa Monica boulevards and Cañon Drive), you'll be able to rub elbows with Beverly Hill's elite along **Rodeo Drive,** perhaps the most aloof (read unabashedly snotty) shopping district in the world. Gucci, Hermès, Cartier, Armani, and Chanel (to name a mere few) all have boutiques along Rodeo Drive, but they may not let you in unless you have an appointment.

If you thought dog psychiatrists and pool men were only a myth, guess again—in Beverly Hills, Mercedes, Jaguars, and Rolls-Royces are the norm, and any house that costs less than $3 million is a good bargain.

SANTA MONICA Santa Monica, the Bay City in Raymond Chandler's *Farewell My Lovely,* is a small beach community that runs between 26th Street and the Pacific Coast Highway (PCH). On the **Santa Monica Pier** (off PCH on the beach) you'll find a few restaurants and an arcade, but be careful at night, as muggings are common. The only other tourist-oriented site is the **Third Street Promenade** (between Broadway and Wilshire)—a pedestrian-only shopping district with clothing stores, coffee houses, and restaurants. For good java and conversation, try the Promenade's **Congo Café.** For a pint of bitter and a plate of L.A.'s best fish-and-chips, head to **The King's Head** (*see* Food, *above*). **Edgemar** (2435 Main St., tel. 310/399–0433), a complex of stores and offices created by architect Frank Gehry, also houses the **Santa Monica Museum of Art.** You'll find local and lesser-known artists exhibiting their work at this small museum that does not yet have a permanent collection. Also look for the **Gallery of Functional Art** in the courtyard. The history of Santa Monica is found within the **Santa Monica Heritage Museum** (2612 Main St., tel. 310/392–8537), which has rooms restored in styles from 1890 to 1930. Modern works by local artists are also exhibited. What happens to airplanes when they get old? They're put out to pasture in Santa Monica's **Museum of Flying** (2772 Donald Douglas Loop North, tel. 310/392–8822), at the Santa Monica Airport. Unbeknownst to most, aerospace is the number one industry in L.A., and Santa Monica used to be home to the Donald Douglas Aircraft Company. The serious aviation buff can come here to see Spitfires, Sopwith Camels, and DC-3s.

VENICE Abbot Kinney was a Los Angeles cigarette manufacturer who had a crazy dream. At the turn of the century he bought up land south of Santa Monica and built himself a replica of Venice, Italy, right down to a scaled-down version of St. Mark's Cathedral and 16 miles of meandering canals. Unfortunately, the canals turned out to be from engineering hell, and the gondolas had a hard time competing with the latest invention in transportation, the automobile. Consequently, almost all the canals got filled in and paved over when the city of Los Angeles annexed Venice in 1925. Of Kinney's original creations, only **Venice Boardwalk** (aka Ocean Front Walk) has survived, crammed with musicians, buskers, artisans, and New Age prophets trying to squeeze a few bucks out of the tourists.

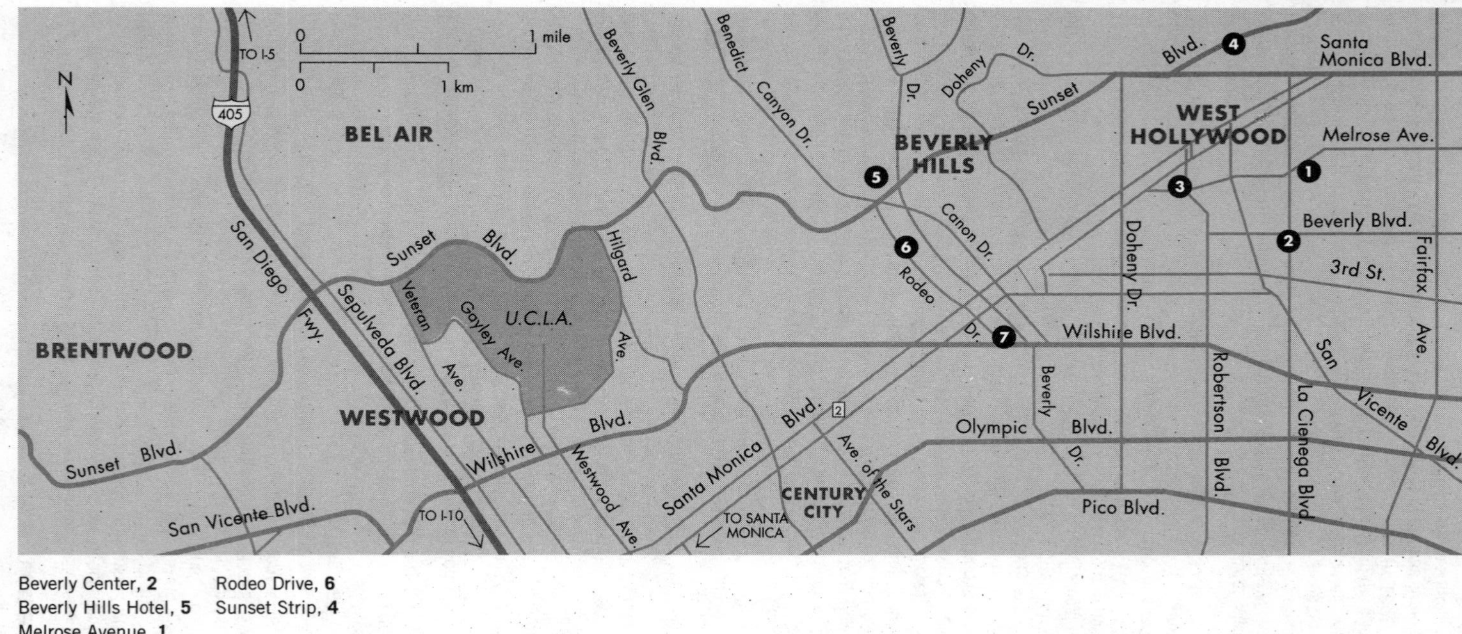

Beverly Center, **2**
Beverly Hills Hotel, **5**
Melrose Avenue, **1**
Pacific Design Center, **3**
Regent Beverly Wilshire Hotel, **7**
Rodeo Drive, **6**
Sunset Strip, **4**

Westside

The '60s and '70s are still very much alive here, and while the hippies still smoke pot on the beach and commune with the ocean, the rebels continue to roller skate up and down the boardwalk, mumbling about conservative politics and Woodstock. Venice Beach embraces the fringe of mainstream society, which makes it one of the few places in Southern California where a three-piece suit looks out of place. In Venice, look for **Muscle Beach,** where bodybuilders from a local gym bring their equipment to work out on the sand. To reach Venice from Santa Monica, head south along Main Street and follow the signs.

WESTWOOD VILLAGE

On the border of U.C.L.A., west of Beverly Hills and north of Wilshire Boulevard, Westwood Village is filled with movie theaters, restaurants, and clothing stores, and is the only place in L.A. where students reign supreme. Though the L.A.P.D. have recently imposed a 10 PM curfew for anyone under 18, it's still lively on weekends when hordes of U.C.L.A. students converge on the town for a night of carousing. With its Italianate buildings and pleasant pedestrian avenues, Westwood is a good place to have Sunday brunch or see a movie (there are over 25 screens within a four-block radius), but don't expect it to change your life. Westwood Village is small, and although **Broxton Avenue,** its main drag, may look nice, there's very little to do here. Unless you want to spend a night drinking beer or margaritas in a charmless bar attached to a charmless restaurant, you'd do better to stop by on your way somewhere else. If you do decide to hang out a while, for a quick bite try **Tommy's** (970 Gayley Ave.), a 24-hour hamburger joint that's world famous for its chili. Also try **Sepi's** (10968 Le Conte, tel. 310/208–7171), a fraternity hangout that sells excellent submarine sandwiches ($3–$5) and keg beer. **Stan's Donuts** (10948 Wayburn, tel. 310/208–8660), across the street from the movie theaters on Broxton Avenue, has the best doughnuts in Westwood; they also have a small lunch counter in the rear serving burgers ($3) and grilled sandwiches.

PACIFIC PALISADES AND MALIBU

From Santa Monica, head north on Pacific Coast Highway toward these two primarily residential communities that hug the coast and cliffs of Santa Monica Bay. Besides the multimillion-dollar homes and fancy restaurants, you'll find one of the best stretches of beach in Los Angeles here. Crowds can be a problem in the summer, but most of Malibu is as rugged and undeveloped as it was 40 years ago when it was home to some of Hollywood's most famous and reclusive movie stars. Malibu still has its share of famous homes and personalities, including Johnny Carson, Sylvester Stallone, Barbra Streisand, Larry Hagman (J.R. Ewing in "Dallas"), the Sheen Family, Bob Dylan, and Sting. If you're the sort of person who enjoys cornering big-name people for an autograph, head to Wolfgang Puck's newest restaurant, **Granita** (23725 W. Malibu Rd., tel. 310/456–0488). It's expensive ($15 appetizers; $30 dinners), but it's popular with L.A.'s bigwigs.

J. PAUL GETTY MUSEUM Nestled in the foothills of the Santa Monica Mountains, the J. Paul Getty Museum houses one of the best classical art collections in the country. J. Paul Getty was perhaps the most generous of L.A.'s early patrons (he left the city a $3-billion endowment in his will), and upon his death his former beachfront estate in Malibu was converted into a museum. It's dedicated to displaying the Greek and Roman sculptures, statues, pottery, and antique jewelry he amassed during his lifetime. The estate, built to resemble the Villa dei Papiri in Pompeii, is itself a work of art—a massive complex of mosaic-lined fountains, marble-covered walkways, and wide, sweeping outdoor patios. Only trees and shrubs which would have been found in southern Italy in the first century AD are allowed to grow here, and even the frescoes found in the main peristyle garden are replicas of ones found in Pompeii and Herculaneum. Currently, the Getty also contains a selection of photographs from the likes of Man Ray, Eugene Atget, and Edward Weston; and canvasses by Van Gogh, Renoir, Gainsborough, and Munch. All the post-Greek and Roman works, however, will be moved to the new complex of buildings currently being built above Sunset Boulevard in Brentwood; completion of the annex is set for 1996. Because parking around the museum is extremely limited, you need to make

Santa Monica and Venice

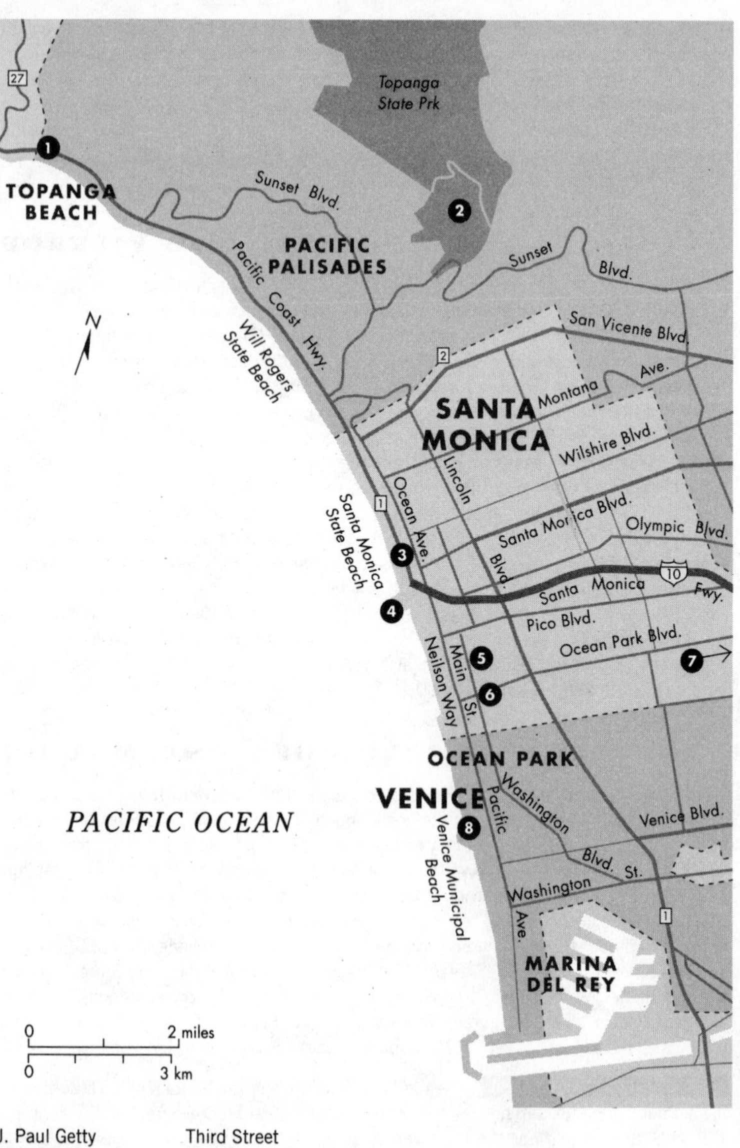

J. Paul Getty Museum, **1**

Museum of Flying, **7**

Santa Monica Heritage Museum, **6**

Santa Monica Museum of Art/ Edgemar/Gallery of Functional Art, **5**

Santa Monica Pier, **4**

Third Street Promenade, **3**

Venice Boardwalk/ Muscle Beach, **8**

Will Rogers State Historic Park, **2**

a parking reservation at least two days in advance, or take a taxi or bus. It's a strange setup, but the museum is free once you pay for parking. Bus 434 stops a half-mile from the museum, but you must obtain a free museum admission pass from the bus driver; no walk-in visitors are allowed in without it. *17985 Pacific Coast Hwy., Malibu, tel. 310/458–2003. Admission free, but parking costs $5. Open Tues.–Sun. 10–5.*

WILL ROGERS STATE PARK Will Rogers was a cowboy, philanthropist, philosopher, journalist, lasso artist, and naturalist. His home in the Santa Monica Mountains has been turned into a museum of southern-Californian cowboy history, along with a collection of artifacts from the Native American tribes who lived in the Malibu–Topanga Canyon area prior to Mexico's occupation of California in the 1600s. With its Navajo rugs, Native American arrowheads, six-shooters, cattle brands, and horse stalls, Will Rogers' house looks more like a quiet country lodge than a museum, and if you want to rent a horse or take a long hike in the gorgeous, undeveloped mountains, this is the place to go. Horses can be rented for under $15 a day, and a number of hiking trails wind their way up into the hills from the estate. *14253 Sunset Blvd., tel. 310/454–8212. RTD Bus 2 stops a half mile away. Open daily 8–6.*

CHEAP THRILLS ● ● ●

For those without four wheels and a mint stereo, your first "cheap thrill" begins when you board an RTD bus—the unofficial meeting place of the mutants, zombies, and other comparable pariahs who give L.A. so much of its personality. Otherwise, cheap excitement ranges from the outlandish (try walking into Gucci on Rodeo Drive and ask to use their bathroom) to the tame (head to Venice Beach's boardwalk and watch the people do their thing). You can always head to Melrose Avenue, Hollywood Boulevard, or Sunset Boulevard for a quick laugh (one look at the glam-rockers outside the Roxy club should send you into hysterics). Otherwise, be creative. In this city of 10 million there's plenty of material for one heck of a strange night.

DODGER STADIUM The L.A. Dodgers can often be found hosting home games between May and September (*see* Spectator Sports, *below*). Angelenos take their teams very seriously, and a night at Dodger Stadium may help reaffirm your belief in the unbearable strangeness of Los Angeles culture. From the singing of the National Anthem to the seventh-inning stretch, baseball at Dodger Stadium is one bewildering spectacle. Seats in the bleachers cost as little as $4 (you'll need a pair of binoculars, though), and there's nothing quite like a Dodger-dog and a beer to soothe the spirits. For information, call the stadium (tel. 213/224–1500) or pick up a copy of the *L.A. Times* sports section.

GRIFFITH PARK Besides the zoo, the observatory, and the Laserium, Griffith Park (*see* Worth Seeing, *above*) has a number of hiking trails and overlooks to keep you occupied for a while. For daytime excitement, grab a picnic lunch and a pair of walkin' shoes and head into the hills for a few hours. Most of the trails are empty during the week, and if Los Angeles is giving you a headache, there's no better place to hide away for an afternoon.

FOREST LAWN MEMORIAL PARKS Forest Lawn is one of L.A.'s largest cemeteries, spread out over expansive hills next to Griffith Park (on the San Fernando Valley side). Besides the requisite gravestones, plastic flowers, and crematoriums, Forest Lawn has a wide collection of ornate private chapels and stone-carved tombstones—some of the most morbid and eerily beautiful art in Los Angeles. Although Forest Lawn used to host wedding services on its grounds, the only people who haunt the graveyard these days are mourners, picnickers, and fans of cemetery art. Visitors are also welcome. *6300 Forest Lawn Dr., tel. 213/254–7251. Open daily 8–5.*

MULHOLLAND DRIVE Mulholland Drive is a windy, hill-top road that runs from Hollywood to Topanga Canyon, traversing the ridge of mountains locally referred to as the "rim" (i.e., toilet rim) between the Westside and the San Fernando Valley. Mulholland offers exceptional views of the Los Angeles area at any time of day, but it's at night that it becomes one big "make-out" scene. Parked along any one of Mulholland's numerous turn-outs and overlooks, you're bound to see cars with steamed-up windows happily bouncing away, and gaggles of distraught youth pounding down a few beers to the tunes of White Snake and Motley Crue. Be careful though: The police have a nasty habit of patrolling the area at night to cut down on drunk driving, and you may end up answering a lot of questions if you look even the slightest bit suspicious. The easiest way to access Mulholland is from the 405 Freeway (I–405; it has its own off-ramp) or from Laurel Canyon or Coldwater Canyon boulevards. These two streets intersect Sunset in West Hollywood; head toward the mountains (north) for Mulholland Drive.

••• FESTIVALS

January: Look for the **Tournament of Roses Parade** and the **Rose Bowl** in Pasadena. In Little Tokyo, the **Oshogatsu Festival** ushers in the Japanese New Year.

February: Mardi Gras is celebrated with a parade on Olvera Street. The **Golden Dragon Parade** marks the Chinese New Year in Chinatown featuring colorful Chinese dancing dragons and lots of illicit fireworks.

March: Drink green beer and try to vomit discreetly at the **St. Patrick's Day Parade** in Century City. The parade doesn't compare with New York's. If this sounds too parochial for you, you can hang around for the annual convention of narcissists, otherwise known as the **Academy Awards,** held downtown. Much like the Academy Awards is the **Blessing of the Animals,** held on Olvera Street. March also marks the **Hollywood Bowl Easter Sunrise Celebration,** as well as the annual **grunion run,** when these small fish leap up onto the beach to mate. The fun lasts until July.

Head to the Nisei Week Japanese Festival in Little Tokyo in July for a look at the culture that is scaring the crap out of Detroit. Maybe Lee Iacocca will turn up to do a little whining.

May: The city's large Mexican population celebrates **Cinco de Mayo** at El Pueblo de Los Angeles Historic Park.

June: The **Gay Pride Festival** gives the city's large gay population a forum in which to showcase their solidarity and their strength.

July: Watch the **Fourth of July Fireworks** along the coast before dawn and after sunset. Held in Echo Park, the **Day of the Lotus Festival** is a celebration of the Pacific Rim cultures. Jazz fans won't want to miss the **Watts Jazz Festival.**

November: Dia de los Muertos (Day of the Dead) is celebrated on Olvera Street.

December: Hollywood Christmas Parade. 'Nuf said.

After Dark

••• BARS

Al's Bar. Around the corner from the Museum of Neon Art, this run-down dive is rife with incredible bar-fly ambience. Thursday's "No talent" open-mike night is one of the best events in late-night Los Angeles. On other nights Al's features live, grungy hard-core music. *305 S. Hewitt St. (East L.A./Downtown border), tel. 213/687–3558 or 213/625–9703.*

Anti-Club. This used to be L.A.'s premier underground club, back in the days when Bauhaus, Sid Vicious (R.I.P.), and the Dickies were still popular. The club still teeters on the cutting edge, but more often than not it plays host to sub-mediocre noise bands and a large crowd of skatebrats. Even so, you'll occasionally find an up-and-coming thrash band on stage, so call ahead. Tickets start at $4. *4658 Melrose Ave., tel. 213/667–9762 or 213/661–3913.*

Barney's Beanery. Janis Joplin partied here the night she died. Once known for having a less-than-kind view of homosexuals, it's changed its attitude in recent years, tolerating, if not embracing, the lifestyle chosen by its residential neighbors. Lots of pool tables and literally hundreds of types of beers here, along with the requisite leathers. It's a hip crowd.

Barney's also serves food (*see* Food, *above*). *8447 Santa Monica Blvd., West Hollywood, tel. 213/654–2287.*

Buffalo Chips and **The Oarhouse.** Don't let the names confuse you: This is basically one bar with two rooms. Wooden carts are suspended from the ceiling, the walls are covered with old dolls, stuffed animals, and other objects that give you the creeps if you stare at them long enough. Not a good place to be during an earthquake, but a great place to be Friday nights at midnight, when they ring in the New Day and give out free champagne. It's a popular place with the tattoo and nose-ring crowd. *2941 Main St., Santa Monica, tel. 310/396–4725.*

Chillers. It's famous for its highly alcoholic, slush puppy-like concoctions mixed in blenders that look like front-loading dryers. If you're daring, try the Pink Panties, Spanish Fly, Zombie, or Cherry Buster. Near the Third Street Promenade, this place attracts an eclectic crowd. *1446 3rd St., tel. 310/394–1993.*

Carry I.D. as it's common to forget your own name after two of Chiller's potent potables.

The Daily Pint. The main bar is packed with serious drinkers, a CD jukebox full of "Best of" albums, and inebriated shuffleboard players. The other room has dart boards, pool tables, and pinball. *2310 Pico Blvd., tel. 310/450–7631.*

The Dresden Room. Make sure to walk through the restaurant section—the interior is stunning—but by all means don't waste your money eating here. Head straight for the bar room instead, otherwise known as Goatee Central. The Italian management isn't quite sure what happened, but the "in" crowd showed up here and took over a couple of years ago. Needless to say, dress in black. There's live piano music most nights. *1760 N. Vermont Ave., Hollywood tel. 213/665–4294.*

Hard Rock Café. Located on the northwest corner of the Beverly Center, just look for the back half of a vintage green Cadillac sticking out of its roof. The Hard Rock offers food, drinks, and music, but no one comes for the food. Most people brave the one- to two-hour lines outside to catch a glimpse of a celebrity chowing down, and see the walls covered with rock-and-roll memorabilia from the likes of the Beatles, Elvis Presley, and Guns N' Roses. It's glitzy and fashionable, but unless you're in the mood to drink $4 beers with an egocentric crowd, go elsewhere. *8500 Beverly Blvd., tel.310/276–7605.*

Kelbo's. A budget traveler's dream come true. Tacky Polynesian decor, probably unchanged since it opened in the '40s. You can sit in huts and drink flaming drinks, if you so choose. More than 100 lamps hang from the ceiling, including several glowing blowfish. The Cocobowl, a small lounge off the main room, has a life of its own, and often hosts live bands on the weekend. *11434 Pico Blvd., West L.A., tel. 310/473–3050 or 310/477–3277.*

King George V. Run by Brits and staffed by Aussies, King George offers both indoor and outdoor seating and a complete food menu (fish-and-chips for $5). It's mostly dead during the week, but on weekend nights it's crammed with pleasure-seeking locals; there's live music occasionally. *301 Santa Monica Blvd., tel. 310/394–9282. Near 3rd St. Promenade.*

McGinty's Irish Pub. In a nutshell: pints of Guinness and Newcastle Brown, darts, and homemade fish-and-chips. Loaded with authentic pub atmosphere and hordes of U.K. exiles. Try to come during the week—it's packed on weekends. *2615 Wilshire Blvd., Santa Monica, tel. 310/453–6220.*

Mom's Saloon. It's popular with frat boys, with sawdust on the floor and a DJ in the corner. Beer comes cheap, and the dance floor usually teems with drunk UCLA freshers. Video games for those who don't feel like dancing. *11777 San Vicente Blvd., Brentwood, tel. 310/820–1516.*

The 35er. Affectionately known as the "thirsty liver," this bar in Pasadena features cheap beer and 50¢ pool games. It's a run-down dive, but it's immensely popular with Pasadena locals. *12 E. Colorado Blvd. (at Fairoaks), tel. 818/356–9315.*

DANCING

Arena. This former ice-making factory is now a large, semi-private dance club that caters primarily to gay men, but all are welcome. There's a $4 cover charge most nights; lots of house music; no live bands. *6655 Santa Monica Blvd., tel. 213/962–4485.*

Club Lingerie. This is the current preferred nightspot of L.A.'s underground dance clubbers. There are two full bars, and live music most nights. The music varies, but generally you'll find good indie bands and a non-Top-40 crowd over 21. *507 Sunset Blvd., Hollywood, tel. 213/466–8557.*

Golden Monkey. Dining upstairs, dancing downstairs. There's usually a line to get in, and bouncers pack a lot of attitude. Music ranges from Paula Abdul remixes to the latest Top-40 hit. No ripped jeans or sneakers allowed, but hair spray and molding mousse are encouraged. *1360 3rd St., tel. 310/576–0553. 21 and over.*

Kingston 12. Reggae music on two dance floors, live music; on weekends. *814 Broadway, Santa Monica, tel. 310/451–4423. 21 and over.*

Mayan. You won't hear much Top-40 music; house music and MTV-ish dance-rock are mode here. It's in a renovated art-deco movie palace in the middle of Downtown, so be careful walking around at night. *1038 S. Hill St., tel. 213/746–4287.*

Shark Club. This huge dance club has DJs and a state-of-the-art lighting system. The crowd is eclectic, and the music verges on MTV/Top-40 dance grooves. *1024 South Grand Ave., tel. 213/747–0999.*

MUSIC

ROCK **Gazzarri's.** Ben "the godfather of rock-and-roll" Gazzarri's face graces the outside, and even though he's passed on, his club still remains one of the best places in L.A. for new bands to "get seen." The Doors, Van Halen, and Guns N' Roses all got their starts here. Today, Gazzarri's specializes in glam-rock and loud metal. *9039 Sunset Blvd., tel. 310/273–6606.*

Roxy. Half the crowd works for record companies, and the other half look like extras from a Guns N' Roses' video. Neil Young, David Bowie, Bruce Springsteen, Pee Wee Herman, Bob Marley, and Prince have all played here, but today you'll mostly find glam-rock and bad metal. *9009 Sunset Blvd., tel. 310/276–2222.*

The Troubadour. Yet another L.A. metal venue. *9081 Santa Monica.*

Whisky A-Go-Go. Everybody who's anybody has played here, including the Kinks, Led Zeppelin, the Who, the Doors, Jimi Hendrix, and the Talking Heads. The term "go-go girls," those foxy women gyrating inside cages, originated here. Now it's rented out by promoters to showcase new local talent. Used in the Oliver Stone movie *The Doors. 8901 Sunset Blvd., tel. 310/652–4202.*

JAZZ **King King.** This is a cozy club with live music that ranges from jazz to hard rock. Big stars sometimes come to see their future competition here. *467 S. La Brea Ave., tel. 310/934–5418.*

St. Mark's. It doubles as a restaurant and jazz bar, and offers live rhythm and blues six nights a week. Cover is $5 during the week, $10 Friday and Saturday nights. *23 Windward Ave., Venice, tel. 310/452–2222.*

CLASSICAL The **Dorothy Chandler Pavilion** (tel. 213/972–7211) offers student rush tickets for the opera ($8) and the philharmonic ($5) an hour before the show. You must have a current student I.D.

If you're not lucky enough to get cheap seats, **Ticketmaster** (tel. 213/480–3232) sells full-price tickets for most **Music Center** (*see* Worth Seeing, *above*) performances. Simply call them, give them a credit card number, and pick your tickets up at the box office. Ticketmaster charges a small fee for this service ($1.50–$4), so buy tickets directly from the box office when you can.

THEATER ● ● ●

There are hundreds of small theaters and playhouses in the L.A. area. You're best bet is to grab a copy of the *L.A. Weekly*, the *Reader*, or the Calendar section of the Sunday *L.A. Times* and see what's on. The **Odyssey Theater Ensemble** (2055 S. Sepulveda Blvd., tel. 310/477–2055) features off-Broadway shows and the works of local playwrights, while the **Japan American Theater** (244 S. San Pedro St., tel. 213/680–3700) features Pacific Rim talent. Otherwise, all three theaters at the Music Center (*see* Worth Seeing, *above*) have cheap seats. The **Mark Taper Forum** (tel. 213/972–7211) offers public rush tickets 10 minutes before curtain for $10. The Mark Taper Forum also presents a cabaret from time to time at the **Itchey Foot** restaurant (*see* Food, *above*). Tickets are $15. **The Ahmanson** reserves the last five rows of the balcony for student tickets, which can be purchased in advance for $16 each (two tickets per student ID). Otherwise, call **Ticketmaster** (tel. 213/480–3232) for tickets.

Groundling Theater. This is where Pee Wee Herman got his start. They put on several different shows a week, some created by the cast, some created with the help of the audience. Tickets usually start around $5. *7307 Melrose Ave., West Hollywood, tel. 310/934–9700.*

Theatre/Theater. "Theatresport," when actors perform improvisational skits with the help of the audience, is big here. The players are extraordinarily witty and funny so if you're in the mood for some low-key laughs, make a bee-line for the place. Seats start at $7. *1713 Cahuenga Blvd., tel. 213/469–9689. Reservations advised. Performances most weekends.*

Outdoor Activities

Other than spending a day on the beach, there are hundreds of things to do outdoors in Los Angeles. Of course smog does pose a serious threat to your health on most days, but, if it's any consolation, it's thinner in the surrounding mountains and hills. If you want to hit the sand, L.A. has over 20 public beaches to choose from. Your best strategy is to start on Pacific Coast Highway in Malibu and drive south along the ocean. You'll reach Venice in under an hour, and get a first-hand look at every beach along the way. One of the more popular is **Leo Carillo State Beach** (tel. 818/706–1310) in Malibu. It's dominated by rocky cliffs and hundreds of tidal pools, and has hidden coves, miles of hiking trails, sea caves, and a campground. For campground reservations, call 800/444–7275.

HORSEBACK RIDING ● ● ●

The **Griffith Park Livery Stables** has horseback riding at reasonable prices. You can show up without a reservation, rent a horse, and immediately set out on Griffith Park trails without a guide, no riding test required. Horses are rented for one or two hours. It's $13 an hour, security deposit required; both English- and Western-style riding available. *480 Riverside Dr., tel. 818/840–8401. At the L.A. Equestrian Center in Burbank between the Golden State and the Ventura Fwys. Take Ventura Fwy., get off on Alameda West, turn left on Main St. Summer hours: weekdays 8 AM–7 PM, weekends 8–4. Winter hours: daily 8–4.*

BIKING ● ● ●

If you're interested in biking in Griffith Park, stop by **Woody's Bicycle World** early to get the best selection of rentals. *3157 Los Feliz Blvd., tel. 213/661–6665. 10-speeds: $10 daily, $30 weekly. Mountainbikes: $15 daily, $45 weekly. Open Mon., Wed., Fri., and Sat. 9–6, Tues. and Thurs. 9–7, Sun. 9–4.*

● ● ● WHALE-WATCHING

Redondo Sport Fishing, on the pier at the Redondo Beach Marina, sends out two boats a day during whale-watching season (December–March). Trips last three hours and cost around $9 per person. Reservations advised. *233 N. Harbor Dr., Redondo Beach, tel. 310/372–2111 or 310/772–2064.*

● ● ● ROLLER-SKATING

Sea Mist Rentals rents bikes, body boards, roller skates, and Rollerblades, offering you several ways to see and be seen on the beachside bike path that stretches between Temescal Canyon and Redondo Beach. Body boards and roller skates are $4 for the first hour, $3 each additional hour. Mountain bikes are $6 for the first hour, $5 each additional hour. Rollerblades and 10-speeds are $5 the first hour, $4 each additional hour. You must leave one form of ID. *1619 Ocean Front Walk, Venice, tel. 310/395–7076. Open weekdays 10–6, weekends 9–7.*

● ● ● SPECTATOR SPORTS

BASEBALL Blue and white are the colors to wear, and bundle up if it's a night game—all the overpriced cups of beer in the world can't keep you warm if the fog rolls in. The **Los Angeles Dodgers** make their home in Dodger Stadium, near downtown L.A. in Chavez Ravine, just off CA 110, between U.S. 101 and I–5. Call 213/224–1500 for ticket information and directions.

BASKETBALL The almost-always-in-the-finals **Los Angeles Lakers** are worshipped in their hometown, but somehow seats are available for most home games. If you're not up to giving your undivided attention to the court, try finding Jack Nicholson in the crowd. He has season tickets and is easily spotted (even though the Lakers play indoors he usually wears sunglasses). The home court is the Great Western Forum in Inglewood and the season runs from October through April. Call 310/419–3182 for ticket information.

ICE HOCKEY Blood, gore, and fights—an **L.A. Kings'** tradition. Ever since the city's only professional hockey club acquired all-star Wayne Gretsky, Angelenos have been flocking to the Forum to cheer on a team that for years had been the joke of L.A.'s professional sport scene. If you like watching a sport where pissed-off players don't wait until after the game to vent their anger, come down to the Forum during hockey season, November–April. For more information, call 310/419–3182.

POLO Will Rogers built a polo field on his grounds so his friends could come over and play a chukker or two and hang around for a barbecue afterwards. The polo field is still in use at **Will Rogers State Park,** and you're invited to come picnic on the sidelines. Games are played Saturday at 2 in the afternoon and Sunday at 10 in the morning, if the field is dry. For more information, call 310/454–8212.

Near Los Angeles

The San Fernando Valley

Ever since the movie *Valley Girl* was released in the early '80s, the San Fernando Valley has basked in the spotlight of dubious international fame. Locals may not be proud that the phrases "oh my gawd," "gag me with a spoon," and "like, fer sure" were first coined here, but, like, most people here don't mind the fact that people from around the world, like, have kind of heard of either the Valley or its infamous shopping mall, the **Galleria** (at the intersection of Ventura and Sepulveda boulevards). To borrow a phrase: totally radical, dude. Colorful lingo aside, the San Fernando Valley has somewhat of an inferiority complex when compared to the wealthier West Los Angeles and the off-color Hollywood, both of which lie on the other side of the Santa Monica Mountains. With more than 3 million people packed into the several cities that form this large jumble of suburbia, the Valley (as it is commonly called) has grown from the quiet orchards and ranchlands it was a mere 40 years ago to an unwieldy, smog-filled, traffic-congested, mall-infested wasteland. Forget the "sub'," this place is the essential "'urbia." Odds are, you'll hate it from the moment you cross over I–405 from Los Angeles proper, but that's okay. Most locals hate it, too. The only reason to make the 30-minute trek to the Valley from Hollywood or Santa Monica is to visit **Magic Mountain, Universal Studios,** or one of the **movie studios** in Burbank (*see* Worth Seeing, *below*). If you're really desperate for something to do, head straight for the **House of Billiards** (14662 Ventura Blvd., tel. 818/501–9923) in Sherman Oaks, one of the Valley's few nighttime diversions. You'll find $4 pitchers and more than 20 pool tables here.

BASICS

TOURIST INFORMATION The San Fernando Valley doesn't have an official visitor's bureau, but each city has a local chamber of commerce. These offices provide brochures and maps of their respective cities, and they'll help you find a cheap place to eat and a decent place to stay—though they won't say a word to promote nonmembers.

Burbank Chamber of Commerce. *200 W. Magnolia Blvd., tel. 818/846–3111. Open weekdays 9–5.*

Sherman Oaks Chamber of Commerce. *14241 Ventura Blvd., tel. 818/906–1951. Open weekdays 9–5.*

Woodland Hills Chamber of Commerce. *21600 Oxnard Blvd., Suite 520, tel. 818/347–4737. Open weekdays 9–4:30.*

COMING AND GOING

BY BUS A number of RTD buses make the trek from the Westside, as Los Angeles proper is known, to the Valley. Call the RTD Customer Service number for specific routes and timetables (tel. 818/781–5090, daily 5:30 AM–11:30 PM). For long-distance travel, **Greyhound** has three stations in the Valley: North Hollywood (11239 Magnolia Blvd.), Glendale (6000 San Fernando Rd.), and San Fernando (1441 Truman Blvd.). Call their general information number (tel. 213/620–1200) for tickets and timetables. Destinations from the Valley include San Diego (4 hours, $35), San Francisco (11 hours, $70), and most other major cities in the United States.

BY CAR Like the rest of Los Angeles, the Valley is a tangle of freeways and wide boulevards jam-packed with cars. Traffic is at its worst between 7 AM–9 AM and 4 PM–7 PM, but even at nonpeak hours the Valley's highways look a lot like parking lots. The main freeways in the Valley are **I–5** (Sacramento to San Diego via Hollywood) and **I–405** (Grapevine to San Diego, via the coast). **U.S. 101** runs east–west through the southern edge of the Valley, connecting Pasadena with Santa Barbara, Monterey, San Francisco, and Oregon. To get to the Valley from the Westside you can take 405 south, or follow **Coldwater Canyon Boulevard, Laurel Canyon Boulevard,** or **Beverly Glen.** These three streets can be accessed from Sunset Boulevard, and all eventually lead to Ventura Boulevard, the Valley's main thoroughfare.

BY PLANE The **Burbank Airport** (2627 Hollywood Way, tel. 818/840–8840) offers service both within and outside California. However, all international flights are handled by LAX. If you don't mind spending the money you can fly essentially anywhere in the United States from Burbank Airport. Rental cars are available at the airport, and **Dollar Rent-A-Car** (tel. 818/846–4471) is one of the cheapest if you're over 21 (they won't rent to anyone younger). If you're under 21, **Easy Rent-A-Car** (tel. 818/841–8888) will rent to you for an additional $5 fee.

AIRPORT TRANSIT **Airport Flyer Express** (tel. 800/244–5155) provides door-to-door shuttle service anywhere in the Valley, but it's expensive. If you're a fan of public transportation (or if you can't afford anything else), RTD offers numerous routes connecting Burbank Airport with the rest of Los Angeles. Call 818/781–5090 for more information.

BY TRAIN **Amtrak** (tel. 800/872–7245) has a small station in Chatsworth, but you should consider making the drive to Union Station in downtown L.A. if you want to take the train; service from the Valley is unpredictable, and most trains leaving from Chatsworth have stopovers in Bakersfield—not a savory place to get stuck for the night.

● ● ● GETTING AROUND

The Valley's main streets are **Ventura Boulevard,** which runs east–west along the southern edge of the Valley, and **Van Nuys Boulevard,** which runs north–south. The **Southern California Rapid Transit District** (tel. 818/781–5890) runs to almost every part of the Valley, but avoid the bus unless you have hours to kill (no joke). The fare is $1.10; to downtown Los Angeles $1.90.

● ● ● WHERE TO SLEEP

To say the Valley is not the most picturesque place in Los Angeles is an understatement—you would be better off staying in Santa Monica or Hollywood. Yet if you're intent on staying here, Burbank has some budget motels. Try the **Bahia** (3400 W. Olive, tel. 818/841–9000) or the **Buena Vista** (2255 N. Buena Vista, tel. 818/848–1600). Otherwise, there are a few cheap motels along Ventura Boulevard near Sepulveda Boulevard, by I–405. They're generally run down and charmless, but they'll do in a pinch.

● ● ● FOOD

There are countless eateries clustered along trendy Ventura Boulevard, on the southern edge of the Valley. **L'Express** (14190 Ventura, Sherman Oaks, tel. 818/990–8683) is popular with the business-lunch crowd, and at night it becomes a swank meeting place for the Valley's middle-age, swinging singles. In Burbank, **Dalt's Grill** (3500 W. Olive Ave., tel. 818/953–7752) offers excellent American and Mexican food for around $10 a plate, and is a favorite with movie-studio types and KROQ (106.7 FM) DJs—the popular radio station broadcasts from next door. The **Sagebrush Cantina** (23527 Calabasas Rd., tel. 818/888–6062) has cheap food (burgers and fries), and live music on Sundays. If you just want a cup of coffee and mellow atmosphere, go to the **Iguana Café** (10943 Camarillo St., North Hollywood, tel. 818/763–7735), popular with the Valley's "artsy" crowd.

UNDER $10 **El Rancho.** This is one of the Valley's most unpretentious Mexican restaurants; it also has really good food. El Rancho doesn't have a tacky mariachi band playing the "Spanish Rose" in the background, nor does it cater to the "Taco Bell is fine with me" mentality. Everything here is prepared from scratch (no pre-fried taco shells or Velveeta!). The small seating area fills up during lunch hour, but otherwise one of El Rancho's 10 or so tables is always open. If you're really hungry try the nachos ($5) or El Rancho's excellent chicken tacos ($3.50). *15030 Ventura Blvd. near Sepulveda Blvd., tel. 818/945–6466. Open Mon.–Sat. 10:30 AM–10 PM, Sun. 10:30 AM–9 PM.*

Mogo's Mongolian Barbeque. Mogo's specializes in all-you-can-eat Mongolian buffets. Essentially, this means you grab a bowl, fill it with meat and vegetables, and then hand it to one of Mogo's chefs. They'll dump it out onto an iron grill (in the middle of the dining room) and cook it as you watch. The food is exceptional, and the beautiful thing is that you can make as many trips to the buffet as you like, sampling different combinations of meats, vegetables, and sauces each time. Lunch buffets start at $5.95; dinner at $7.95. *4454 Van Nuys Blvd. at Ventura Blvd., tel. 818/783–6646. Open Mon.–Sat. 11:30 AM–2 PM and 5–9:30 PM, Sun. 5–9:30 PM.*

Tommy's. Tommy's has made chili burgers into an art form. No one is exactly sure what Tommy's puts into its orange-tinted chili, but the taste is unspeakably good—a combination of peppers, tomatoes, beans, and grease that's capable of healing the sick and fortifying the weak. You may walk away with the worst case of indigestion imaginable, but at least you'll suffer with a smile on your face. Thankfully, Tommy's is open 24 hours a day, 365 days a year. *15745 Roscoe, just west of I–405, tel. 818/893–1715.*

WORTH SEEING ● ● ●

Along with the movie studios in Burbank and North Hollywood, the San Fernando Valley is home to **Six Flags Magic Mountain** (tel. 805/255–4100 or 818/367–5965), which offers some of the scariest roller coasters and water rides in the country. For a mere $25 you'll get the chance to spin upside down six times on the **Viper,** drop 10 stories in under four seconds on **Freefall,** or ride backwards on California's largest roller coaster, the **Colossus.** Magic Mountain is open daily during the summer, only on weekends during the winter. It's off I–5 in Valencia, just north of the Valley. If rides aren't your thing, you might want to head over to the **Tillman Water Reclamation Plant** (5100 Woodley Ave., Van Nuys, tel. 818/989–8175), a sewage treatment facility that treats 45 million gallons of raw waste a day *and* hosts weddings and private parties. Described as the Disneyland of sewage plants, it owes its popularity to Japanese landscape architect Koichi, who designed the center's impressive **Japanese Garden.** Unfortunately, you are not free to meditate amidst the sludge on your own. Reservations are required for the free guided tour. The San Fernando Valley is also home to the **Mission San Fernando Rey De Esparta** (15151 San Fernando Mission Blvd., tel. 818/361–0186), at the northern edge of the Valley between I–405 and I–5. It's small, but its 35-bell carillon casts an enchanting spell over the mission's surrounding gardens.

NBC STUDIOS NBC once gave one of the best studio tours around, but the tours were stopped during the Persian Gulf War for security reasons and NBC has no plans as yet to restart them. However, it's still possible to see tapings of their TV programs, including "The Tonight Show." Either show up at the studio early in the morning for free tickets, or send in a self-addressed stamped envelope with the dates you'll be in Los Angeles. Note: No one under 16 is allowed to watch "The Tonight Show" being taped—apparently Jay Leno is too mature for young audiences. Tapings generally begin around 6 PM. *3000 W. Alameda St., Burbank 91523, tel. 818/840–3537. Ticket counter open weekdays 8–4.*

UNIVERSAL STUDIOS Everyone at Universal Studios is a tourist, and most of them have video cameras to record this fun-filled, action-packed day. Grin and bear it because you'll be here a long time if you want to get your money's worth. This place is second in popularity only to Disneyland, at least in terms of California tourist attractions, and during the summer crowds are a serious problem. The studios comprise over 400 acres, many covered by its main attraction, an hour-long tram ride. The tram takes you through one sound stage after another at a dizzying pace, stopping only long enough for you to get a quick photo before moving on (visitors must stay in the tram at all times). Highlights include an 8.3 earthquake in a simulated San Francisco train station; King Kong wreaking havoc on a burnt-out New York City street; the parting of the Red Sea (really); a tour through the "city" of Amity, where the mechanical Jaws spends his summers; and a quick pass by Alfred Hitchcock's *Psycho* house (it looks ominous on film, but the house is less impressive in person, primarily because Hitchcock built it at 7/8 scale to make Anthony Perkins look more menacing when he stood in the doorway). After the tram ride make your way to the Entertainment Center, where you can watch live-action demonstrations of a "Miami Vice" and wild-west stunt show. You can even take part in a "Star Trek" episode here, thanks to the "magic" of editing. Arrive early to avoid lines, but eat first: All the food stands at Universal are over-priced and not very appetizing. *100 Universal City Plaza, tel. 818/508–9600. Take the Hollywood Fwy. (101) North and exit at Lankershim Blvd., then follow the signs. By bus, take RTD 424 to Lankershim Blvd., then the free shuttle up to the studios. Admission: $24.50. Open daily 7:30 AM–10:30 PM. Ticket office closes at 8 PM. Wheelchair access.*

If you're a glutton for punishment, don't miss the Conan the Barbarian extravaganza, where well-tanned muscle men parade around in their underwear wielding broadswords and grunting a lot.

WARNER BROS. STUDIO Warner Brothers offers a standard tour of its sets and film lots, but unfortunately it's way overpriced. The Warner Bros. tour isn't as glamorous or tourist-oriented as the one at Universal, but you'll get more information on the technical aspects of movie-making, as well as a tour of sets from current TV programs (something you won't find at Universal). Tours generally last two hours, depending on what shows are being taped that day. Call ahead for reservations and program schedules. *4000 Warner Blvd., tel. 818/954–1744. Admission: $24. Tours given weekdays 10 AM and 2 PM. Reservations necessary.*

● ● ● OUTDOOR ACTIVITIES

Along the southern edge of the Valley, the undeveloped **Santa Monica Mountains** provide many areas for day hiking and picnicking. One of the more interesting getaways is the **Paramount Ranch,** a sprawling public park surrounded by rocky hills and golden oak trees (take U.S. 101 west, exit Kanan Rd.; follow it south until Cornell Rd; turn left, follow signs). It was once a movie set (*M*A*S*H* was filmed nearby) and there are still a number of dilapidated, false-front buildings on the site. Topanga Canyon Boulevard also traverses the Santa Monica Mountains, winding through **Topanga Canyon State Park** and ending at Topanga State Beach. If you follow it north you will arrive at **Chatsworth** along the western edge of the Valley. Because of its huge, rocky sandstone formations, Chatsworth was also a movie location. Now it boasts the most popular rock-climbing area in Los Angeles County—**Stony Point,** which is to the east of Topanga Canyon Boulevard, right after the Santa Susanna Pass Road (where, by the way, Charles Manson and friends used to hang out). Information on trails and hikes around the Santa Monica Mountains and the Chatsworth area is available from the **Santa Monica Mountains National Recreation Area** (30401 W. Agoura Rd., Suite 100, Agoura Hills, tel. 818/597–1036).

Palos Verdes and San Pedro

If you're looking for a cheap place to stay in the L.A. area, San Pedro has an excellent hostel that's within a stone's throw of the beach.

Just south of Redondo Beach, the **Palos Verdes Peninsula** rises dramatically—a green-and-gold mass of rolling hills and steep cliffs peppered with extravagant homes and elegant estates. Before becoming a haven for wealthy Angelenos, "PV" (as locals call it) was a vast, treeless ranch owned by José Dolores Sepulveda, whose name still graces one of the longest boulevards in Los Angeles. In 1913, when financier Frank Vanderlip purchased the entire peninsula for $1 million, the pastoral landscape was turned into an exclusive residential community. Since then, PV has blossomed into one of Southern California's most popular planned communities, a conservative and highbrow enclave where the richest of the rich escape the smog, noise, and hassle of Los Angeles. In contrast, **San Pedro,** at the southern edge of the peninsula, is a more humble, working-class neighborhood that's home to the **Los Angeles Harbor,** a major departure point for ferries to Catalina (*see* Catalina, *below*).

The sharp bluffs and cliffs that characterize the Palos Verdes peninsula allow few opportunities for sunbathing on wide, sandy beaches—head toward Redondo if that's what you're looking for. However, PV does have a few secluded coves and small stretches of sand along its rugged coast. It may take a bit of hiking to reach them, but if you don't mind scrambling down a sheer cliff face you could end up on a deserted, picture-perfect patch of beach. **Malaga Cove** is accessible from the Torrance County Beach along Pasco de la Playa. The narrow **Bluff Cove** lies just after Flat Rock Point, accessed by a steep and windy trail from Paseo del Mar. Scuba diving is also a popular activity in PV, and just east of **Royal Palm State Beach** in San Pedro (at Western Ave. and Paseo del Mar) is an underwater diver's trail. A clever idea, the trail is marked by a rope that winds its way through sulphurous hot springs and underwater coves, affording an excellent view of PV's rich kelp beds and colorful marine life. In San Pedro, **Pacific Wilderness and Ocean Sports** (1719 S. Pacific, tel. 310/833–2422) rents scuba gear for about $40 a day.

Palos Verdes, San Pedro, and Long Beach

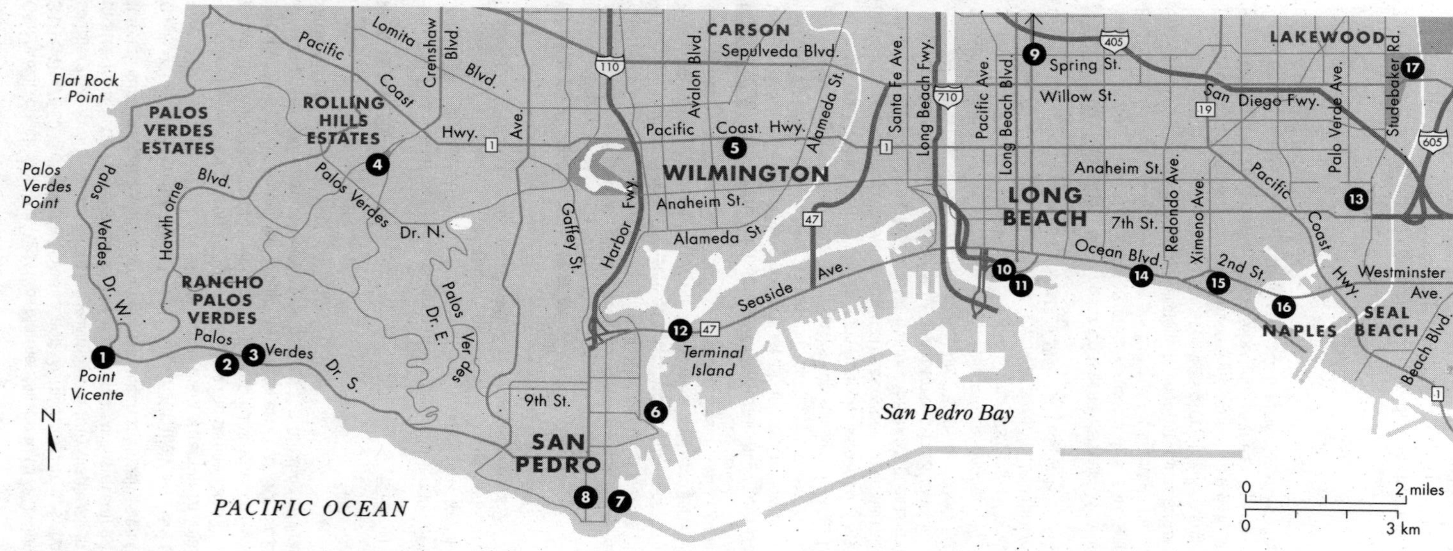

Abalone Cove, **2**
Banning Residence Museum and Park, **5**
Belmont Shore, **15**
Cabrillo Marine Museum, **7**
El Dorado Nature Center, **17**
Korean Friendship Bell, **8**
Museum of Art, **14**
Naples, **16**
Point Vicente Interpretive Center, **1**
Ports O'Call Village, **6**
Rancho Los Alamitos, **13**
Rancho Los Cerritos, **9**
Shoreline Aquatic Park, **11**
Shoreline Village, **10**
South Coast Botanic Gardens, **4**
Vincent Thomas Bridge, **12**
Wayfarers Chapel, **3**

Otherwise, check out the **Cabrillo Marine Museum** (3720 Stephen White Dr., tel. 310/548–7562), off Pacific Avenue and 36th Street. It has the largest collection of southern California marine life in the world, beautifully displayed in aquariums that range in size from 5 to 1,000 gallons. The museum also has evening programs from March through July, when the elusive grunion fish beach themselves on the shore to breed.

Designed by Lloyd Wright, son of Frank Lloyd Wright, the **Wayfarer's Chapel** (5755 S. Palos Verdes Dr., tel. 310/377–1650) is PV's other main attraction: a small church made almost entirely of glass that sits on a bluff overlooking the serene Pacific Ocean. Redwoods have grown up around the structure and, as Wright intended, give it a feel of a natural sanctuary. The chapel's glass panes were only joined together at 30° or 60° angles, the same proportions found in snowflakes, which gives the building a strangely natural, almost familiar feel.

● ● ● BASICS

The **San Pedro Chamber of Commerce** offers a good selection of brochures, maps, and lodging/dining suggestions. They can also help arrange ferry transportation to Catalina or provide you with a list of hiking trails on the Palos Verde Peninsula. *390 W. 7th St., tel. 310/832–7272. 4 blocks east of Gaffey St. Open weekdays 9–5.*

● ● ● WHERE TO SLEEP

Along with its over-priced, second-rate chain motels, the Palos Verdes Peninsula offers one of the nicest youth hostels in Los Angeles County, as well as the opportunity to sleep cheaply in student dorms. There are no outstanding budget hotels in the area, nor are there any outstanding expensive hotels in Palos Verdes. For these sorts of establishments you'll have to head north to L.A. or south to Newport Beach and Laguna.

HOSTELS **San Pedro International AYH-Hostel.** In Angel's Gate Park, with a 260° view of the Pacific, this 70-bed hostel is ideally located in downtown San Pedro and easily reached by public bus. It has comfortable, single-sex rooms (two–six people), a kitchen, a TV room, and a reading room with books and resource listings for budget travelers. In addition, the staff is friendly and there is no lock-out period. This hostel is popular with backpackers and foreign travelers during the summer, and reservations are advised. Rates are $9.25 for members, $12.25 for nonmembers. All guests must have a sleep sack, which can be rented here for $2. Check-out time is 10:30 AM. *3601 S. Gaffey St., Bldg. 613, tel. 213/831–8109. From LAX take Bus 232 to Anaheim St. and Avalon Blvd., catch the southbound 446 to the Angels Gate Park (hostel behind bell). From L.A. Greyhound station take Bus 446 south from 6th and Grand Sts., get off at Angels Gate Park. From Fwy. take CA 110 south to San Pedro, follow to the end, then turn left onto Gaffey St. From Union Station go to Alameda and Macy Sts., take Bus 446 to Angels Gate Park.*

STUDENT HOUSING **Marymount College** rents its student condos to visitors from June 10 through August 10. Unfortunately, most of them are scattered throughout San Pedro (the college provides its own shuttle bus for students during the academic year). Call ahead for reservations and directions to your particular building. Condos vary: Some have harbor views, some have televisions and phones. All rooms, however, have access to bathroom and kitchen facilities. Rooms are rented on a daily or weekly basis; singles start at $35, doubles at $40, and two-bedroom suites (4 person limit) at $59. *30800 Palos Verdes Dr., tel. 213/377–5501. All are furnished with kitchens and linens. TV rental extra. Call for special weekly rate.*

● ● ● FOOD

The Palos Verdes Peninsula offers an incredibly diverse choice of low-priced restaurants. For once, you don't have to avoid the "nice" places if you're short on cash. In San Pedro especially, even the most highbrow places offer meals under $10.

UNDER $10 **The Grand House.** Located in a restored, 1930s-era manor house, the Grand offers exceptional French cuisine priced within the budget traveler's reach. Its menu changes on a daily basis, but you can always find homemade soups and salads for less than $4. Even more important, the Grand House doesn't have that stuffy "Le French Restaurant" feel. Guests are seated either next to the fireplace in the living room, outdoors on a wooden deck, or in the small, cozy, and immensely comfortable dining room. Adjoining the restaurant are some beautifully restored 1930s bungalows, part of the Grand Cottage's bed-and-breakfast. If you're tuckered out after your meal, grab a room ($60) for the night. *809 S. Grand Ave. (at 8th St.), tel. 310/548–1240.*

The Pacific Diner. Locals line up outside this place for hours on weekend mornings, waiting patiently for the Pacific's amazingly tasty omelets ($4) and scrambled eggs ($3.50). The Pacific also serves lunch (burgers and fries), but breakfast is their specialty. Get here early, as one- to two-hour waits are not uncommon. *3821 S. Pacific Ave., tel. 310/831–5334. Open daily 8 AM–1:30 PM.*

Papadakis. Top-rate Greek food and live Greek dancing have made Papadakis one of the most popular restaurants in San Pedro. After a plate of grilled lamb ($7) and some of Papadakis' famous champagne bread, sit back and enjoy a dance by the owner, his wife, his brother, and seemingly everyone else in the Papadakis clan. Two informal performances are held nightly, usually at 6 and 9. Reservations are only accepted for parties of six or more. This is one of San Pedro's finest eateries. *301 W. 6th St., tel. 310/548–1186. Open Mon.–Thurs. 5–9, Fri.–Sat. 5–10, Sun. 5–8.*

Senfuku. This place specializes in sushi and traditional Japanese cuisine. The dining room is somewhat characterless, but the food is excellent and moderately priced. Sushi platters range from $4 to $11, while yakatori and tempura dinners fetch between $5 and $10. *380 W. 6th St., tel. 310/832–5585. Open Mon.–Sat. 5–9:30.*

Long Beach

Just across the **Vincent Thomas Bridge** from San Pedro, Long Beach is an industry-laden seaside resort 30 miles south of downtown Los Angeles. With its towering oil refineries and massive natural-gas processing plants, Long Beach certainly looks like a hideous eyesore that should be bypassed and forgotten. But somehow this city has been able to strike a happy balance between the blight of sprawling industry and appealing seaside charm. Much of Long Beach was built during the '30s when oil was discovered offshore. Though it has since been thoroughly modernized with shopping malls, faceless high rises, and a massive docking complex, downtown Long Beach has maintained an attractive character. Most Angelenos criticize Long Beach for being too residential and suburban, but it offers many of the same diversions found in L.A., without the traffic, congestion, and attitude. Long Beach is also one of southern California's most socially diverse cities, a place where gays, blue-collar workers, conservative business people, and suntanned beach bums co-exist peacefully, at least most of the time.

Broadway Avenue, from Long Beach Boulevard to Redondo Avenue, is a good place to get a feel for the city's funkier side. Downtown Long Beach's art-deco feel is authentic; if you have any doubts check out the terra-cotta detailing and vibrant colors of the **Dr. Rowan Building** (201 Pine St.). Upstairs there's an old jazz joint, **Birdland West,** jammed-packed on weekend nights with blues and '50s jazz fans. Other downtown landmarks include the **Villa Riviera** (800 E. Ocean), a 16-story high rise built in 1929 with an eclectic mix of Gothic, Tudor, French, and Italianate architectural styles. Downtown's other famous landmark is the **Breakers Hotel** (200 E. Ocean), a Spanish Revival–style resort built in 1926. If you enjoy architecture, head to **Belmont Shore,** a small residential community developed in the 1940s, at the East end of Ocean Avenue (Bus 12 stops here). It has some of Long Beach's oldest beach homes and bungalows. Continue to Lingston Drive and make a right onto Second Street (still Bus 12), Long Beach's unofficial boardwalk, a hot spot for bars, cafés, and nightclubs. If you're feeling a bit weary make your way to **Midnite Espresso** (4925 E. 2nd St., tel. 213/439–3978). Their double cappuccino is guaranteed to put bounce back into your step. Across from Belmont Shores are the upscale islands of **Naples,** home to some of Long Beach's wealthiest families. Developed in the early

1900s, Naples is crisscrossed by a series of canals and footbridges that give it a pleasant, Mediterranean feel. You can even rent a gondola (with oarsman!) from **Gondola Getaway** (tel. 213/433–9595). At $50 an hour, though, the gondolas might be best appreciated from a distance.

BASICS

TOURIST INFORMATION **Long Beach Visitor Center.** You'll find maps, tourist brochures, pleasant smiles, and a staff that can help you finds hotels and budget accommodations. Also look for their free "Dining and Restaurant" guide, with over 200 listings in the Long Beach area. *3387 Long Beach Blvd. at Wardlow Rd., tel. 213/426–6773. Just off I–405 at the Long Beach Blvd. exit, follow the signs. Open daily 9–5.*

Long Beach Visitor's Council. Besides maps and transit information, they offer a free guide to attractions, restaurants, and places to sleep. They also have detailed listings of community events and local entertainment. *1 World Trade Center, Suite 300, tel. 213/436–3645 or 800/234–3645. Near the Transit Mall. Open weekdays 8:30–5.*

Traveler's AID. This is a non-profit organization created exclusively for travelers: Besides the usual listings of restaurants and hotels in the Long Beach Area, they'll also help you figure out how to get wherever it is you want to go next. They can even arrange bus, train, and airline tickets for you. In addition to their East Fourth Street office, they have branches at the Long Beach Airport and the Greyhound Bus depot. *947 E. 4th St., tel. 213/432–3485 or 213/432–8169. Open Mon.–Sat. 9–5.*

COMING AND GOING

The easiest way to reach Long Beach is by car. From Los Angeles, simply head south on the I–405 until you see the "Welcome to Long Beach" signs (conversely, from San Diego head north on 405). The **Long Beach Airport** (4100 E. Donald Douglas Dr., tel. 213/421–8293) is served by four airlines: **Alaska** (tel. 800/426–0333), **American** (tel. 800/433–7300), **American West** (tel. 800/247–5692), and **United** (tel. 800/631–1500). All four offer in-state and national flights, but all international traffic is handled by the Los Angeles International Airport (LAX). Public buses marked "downtown" arrive and depart from the Long Beach Airport every half-hour. To reach Long Beach from LAX, take RTD Bus 232 (one-way: $3.50). It'll drop you off at the transit mall downtown, near the Traveler's Aid office (*see above*).

Long Beach's **Greyhound** station (464 W. 3rd St., tel. 213/436–3231) offers service between Los Angeles (45 minutes), San Diego (three hours), and San Francisco (10 hours). But perhaps the easiest way to reach Long Beach from L.A. is on the Metro, via the **Blue Line.** It runs between downtown Long Beach and L.A. every 10–20 minutes. Stops include Long Beach Boulevard, Transit Mall, and First Street. Fares are $1.10 each way, and you can buy tickets from coin-operated vending machines at every stop. Call 213/626–445 or 213/639–6800 for more information.

GETTING AROUND

The **Transit Mall,** on First Street between Long Beach Boulevard and Pacific Avenue, is the main transit hub in Long Beach. Most public buses stop here, and there's an information booth on the plaza that has schedules and bus maps (open weekdays 7:30–4:30, Sat. 10–2). For more information, contact **Long Beach Transit** (1300 Gardenia Ave., tel. 213/591–2301), the city's public bus company. The fare is 75¢, 50¢ for students. Buses usually run from 6 AM to midnight, although there are a few "night owl" lines that run all night. Also look for the **Runabout Shuttle,** a city-operated minivan that runs from Long Beach's Catalina Terminal to the Transit Mall. Shuttles run every five minutes between 7 AM and 6 PM on weekdays, and between 10 AM and 5 PM on weekends. Tickets cost 25¢. Otherwise, you can rent cars for under $15 a day at **Flat Rate Rent-a-Car** in the Golden Sails Hotel (6285 E. Pacific Coast Hwy., tel. 213/433–7283 or 800/432–3058).

WHERE TO SLEEP • • •

The closest hostel is in San Pedro, but Long Beach does have a few budget hotels. Close to the beach and downtown is the **At Ocean Motel** (50 Atlantic Ave., tel. 213/435–8369) with year-round rates that start at $42. Near downtown Long Beach look for the **Belmont Shore Inn** (3946 E. Ocean Blvd., tel. 213/434–6236), near the beach in Belmont Shore. The rooms are clean, and most have kitchens. Rates start at $50. Farther inland is the **Chalet Motel** (1121 E. Pacific Coast Highway, tel. 213/591–3321). Rooms here start at $35 but it's located in a dull part of town and is nearly 3 miles from the coast. Along the **Blue Train Line** north of downtown is the **Hyland Inn** (2471 Long Beach Blvd., tel. 213/440–0401), with rooms that start at $35.

STUDENT HOUSING **Brooks College** rents its double-occupancy dorms to the public between June 1 and September 15. All rooms have shared bathrooms and free linen service, and all visitors are allowed access to the college's dining room, laundry, and pool facilities. Even better, there are over 300 rooms here, so it's rarely full. Doubles start at $10 per night, and dinner costs an extra $6. *4825 E. Pacific Coast Hwy., tel. 213/597–6611. Long Beach Buses 111, 112, and 171 stop right in front of campus.*

FOOD • • •

You'll find a number of budget restaurants nestled around Second street in Belmont Shore. Cheap and greasy are the norm. Look for the **Shorehouse Café** (5271 E. 2nd St., tel. 213/433–2266) and **Hof's Hut** (4828 E. 2nd St., tel. 213/439–4775), two 24-hour coffee shops that cater to the under-30 crowd. If you're a fan of quick, cheap, tasty Mexican food, try **Super Mex** (732 1st St., tel. 310/436–0707). A chicken taco or bean burrito will run you less than $3. For great pizza and cheap beer head to **Marrie's** (649 Broadway Ave., tel. 310/432–6881), a sit-down restaurant that's popular with the natives. Classier, more expensive restaurants can be found around Broadway and the Belmont Pier.

UNDER $10 **Chuck's Coffee Shop.** Right by the Olympic swimming pool and the Belmont Pier, this triangular-shaped coffee shop is famous for one thing—omelets. The most popular is the "Weasel," a chili-and-cheese concoction ($4.50). Chuck's may not have a lot of ambience, but it's the place to come if you're hungry. Their portions are huge. *4120 E. Ocean Blvd., tel. 213/433–9317. Open weekdays 6 AM–3 PM, weekends 7 AM–3 PM.*

System M. Most of the dishes here are pasta-based, ranging from seafood linguini ($6) to broccoli-and-squash lasagna ($5.50), but they also offer a smattering of curried foods (try the chicken), and their potent espresso drinks are guaranteed to put a near-lethal dose of caffeine in your veins. System M doubles as a restaurant and an art gallery, a beacon of "enlightened culture" in suburban Long Beach. *213 Pine Ave. at Broadway, tel. 310/435–2525. Open Tues.–Thurs. 11–10, Fri.–Sat. 11–midnight.*

Upstart Crow Bookstore and Coffeehouse. A selection of simple sandwiches and hearty salads in a quiet and informal atmosphere is what you'll get here—and you can watch the boats in the Shoreline Village Marina from the Upstart's outdoor patio. Choose from over 2,000 new and used titles in the bookstore, then grab a cappuccino at the coffee bar. Even if you're not hungry, this is a good place to wile away the hours. They have live music occasionally. *429 Shoreline Village Dr., tel. 213/437–2088. Open daily 3 PM–midnight.*

UNDER $15 **Panama Joe's Café Bar.** Panama Joe's is best enjoyed during its happy hour, daily from 3 to 7, when tropical drinks (with umbrellas) flow freely down the throats (sans umbrellas) of a progressively social crowd. Panama Joe's also has a large food menu including salads ($5), hamburgers ($7), and locally caught fresh fish. *5100 E. 2nd St., tel. 213/434–7417. Open daily 11 AM–midnight.*

Ragazzi. This is one of Long Beach's finest Italian restaurants and is located on the beach with a beautiful view of the water. Ragazzi has a tremendous selection of pastas, lasagnas, and mouth-watering appetizers (try the mozzarella sticks). If you really want to splurge, try the Pasta Ragazzi ($15), a fettuccine and seafood extravaganza. Ragazzi has both indoor and outdoor seating, but try to get a table outside on the sand. *4020 E. Olympic Plaza, tel. 310/438–3773. Open Tues.–Sun. 5–10.*

Catalina Island

Twenty-two miles off the coast of San Pedro sits this small, year-round beach resort that's perfect for a weekend getaway from the smog, traffic, and bustle of Los Angeles. **Avalon,** Catalina's biggest—and only—city, was originally developed by the Wrigley family of Chicago in 1919, both as a tourist resort and as the spring training ground for their baseball team, the Chicago Cubs. Today, Catalina Island serves as the summer home for some of L.A.'s wealthiest. But it's also a popular destination for sail-boaters and nature-lovers from the mainland, and during the summer its small marina overflows with private yachts, colorful catamarans, and sleek sailboats from around the world.

Cars on the island are allowed only for the 3,600 permanent residents, and even they have a 10-year waiting list to bring one over. You can rent bicycles to explore the 36-mile stretch of hills and beaches along Catalina's northern end, but unfortunately you also need a $50 permit to take your bike outside the mile-long city of Avalon—the island's status as a wildlife preserve makes it a difficult place to explore by bicycle (*see* Tourist Information, *below*). You can probably better explore Catalina on foot, by yourself or with a guided tour. **Inside Adventure Tour** (tel. 310/510–2888) offers a two-hour excursion into Catalina's unpopulated outback for under $10. Look for them on the pier, next to the ferry terminals.

There's enough in Avalon to keep you entertained for a few hours—including bars, restaurants, a public beach, and two movie theaters. Ferries leave from the Los Angeles harbors daily and arrive in Avalon two hours later. Because accommodations on Catalina are expensive, most people stay just for the day. Except for the pleasant view of the Pacific Ocean, there's not much here to detain you.

The **Casino Building,** an art-deco masterpiece built in 1929, is Avalon's most famous attraction. Situated at the end of the pier in the Avalon Harbor, the Casino used to offer legal gambling until the coppers closed it down in the '40s. Ballroom dancing and evening concerts are still occasionally held here; check at the Catalina Chamber of Commerce for schedules. Beyond the Casino overlooking Avalon Harbor, look for Zane Grey's **Old Pueblo House,** recently converted into a hotel. Zane Grey was one of the first naturalists to popularize the plight of Catalina's near-extinct buffalo population, and his film, *The Vanishing America,* prompted the U.S. Department of the Interior to grant Catalina Island the status of a natural wildlife preserve. Just beyond the Pueblo is the **Chimes Tower,** commissioned by Ida Wrigley. It's the only clock tower on the island, and you can hear its bells ringing through the streets every fifteen minutes. One and a half miles southwest of Avalon you'll find the **Wrigley Memorial Gardens** (tel. 213/510–2288), on Avalon Canyon Road, the site of the Wrigley family mausoleum (admission: $1). William Wrigley himself used to be buried here, but his wife Ida moved the body to the mainland when a German U-boat was spotted off the coast of Catalina in 1939. Strangely enough, she thought the Germans had come all this way to steal her dead husband's coffin.

● ● ● TOURIST INFORMATION

Catalina Island Chamber of Commerce. This office has a large selection of maps, sightseeing brochures, and restaurant/hotel guides. They can also make hotel and camping reservations for you. Look for them on Catalina's "pleasure pier" in Avalon Harbor. If you write them in advance, they'll send you a free brochure. *Box 217, Avalon 90704, tel. 310/510–1520. Open summer, daily 8–6; winter, Mon.–Sat. 8–5, Sun. 9–3.*

Los Angeles County Parks and Recreation. If you plan to do any hiking on Catalina, this should be your first stop. Besides offering detailed hiking maps ($1) and trail information, they also issue free camping permits—required by law on Catalina—and $50 bike permits. They also have information on Catalina's beaches and wildlife. *213 Catalina Ave., Avalon, tel. 310/510–0688. Open daily 8:30–1 and 2–4.*

COMING AND GOING • • •

The best way to experience Catalina is to sail over yourself and drop anchor in a secluded cove. Otherwise, **Catalina Cruises** (tel. 213/410–1062 or 800/888–5939) offers the cheapest ferry service from Long Beach, San Pedro, or Redondo Beach. Round-trip tickets cost $27, and the ride takes two hours. The biggest ferry boats have both indoor and outdoor seating, and most offer snacks and sandwiches. The waters around Catalina can get rough, so you may want to bring along some seasickness pills.

GETTING AROUND • • •

Only residents are allowed to have cars on Catalina, but golf carts abound on the island. Take note, however, that it takes at least two hours to reach the far end of the island—and two to get back—and at $30 an hour, golf carts are hardly a bargain. Bicycles are a better bet ($5 an hour), but then again you must obtain a $50 permit to take your bicycle outside Avalon, available at the Los Angeles County Parks and Recreation office (*see* Tourist Information, *above*). Better yet, just grab a lunch and a bottle of water and discover Catalina on your own. From Avalon, follow any road leading away from the beach and blaze your own trail. You'll need a permit to camp (they're free), but otherwise you can hike wherever you like.

WHERE TO SLEEP • • •

Unless you want to camp, think twice before staying here overnight. A hotel will run you at least $50 a night, and they're often booked solid for months. If you're in the mood to splurge, the **Atwater Hotel** (tel. 800/4–AVALON) and the **Bayview** (tel. 310/510–0600) are two of Catalina's nicest hotels, the sort of places where the staff remember your name and greet you with a smile. Both offer ocean-view rooms ($60–$75 a night) and complimentary breakfasts. Camping, on the other hand, is quite cheap ($10 a night). There are five different sites to choose from, and reservations are required at all of them. **Hermit Gulch Campground** (tel. 310/510-8368) is the closest to Avalon, 1 mile west. Otherwise, consult the L.A. county Department of Parks and Recreation (*see* Tourist Information, *above*) for details.

FOOD • • •

All of Catalina's restaurants are in Avalon, the island's main tourist haunt. Most of them are nestled along the beach in Avalon Harbor, offering everything from fresh fish to cheeseburgers. The **Busy Bee** (306 Crescent Ave., tel. 310/510–1983) is one of the more popular hangouts along the waterfront, a reasonably priced, sit-down restaurant with an excellent view of the water. If you're feeling adventurous, try their buffalo burger ($8) or quirky fish quesadilla ($7). If you're on a tight budget, you'll find bread, cheese, fruit, and bottled water at the supermarket on Crescent Avenue.

OUTDOOR ACTIVITIES • • •

In Avalon, **Brown's Bikes** (107 Pebbly Beach Rd., tel. 310/510–0986) rents 10-speeds by the hour ($5) and by the day ($12). If you want to go beyond Avalon, however, you'll need a $50 permit and a helmet, both of which can be gotten at Brown's. Bring your own food and water, as there aren't any tourist facilities outside of Avalon. You can fish without a license from the Avalon Pleasure Pier, but a license (sold at all fishing stores in Avalon) is required for anglers heading to other parts of the island. The **Avalon Boat Stand,** on the pier, rents tackle and arranges half-day and full-day charter boats. Catalina's mountainous terrain is popular with hikers, but permits are required to camp overnight. To obtain one, appear in person at the L.A. County Parks and Recreation office (*see* Tourist Information, *above*) or at the Hermit Gulch campground. Catalina is also very popular with scuba divers and snorkelers. **Catalina Divers Supply** (tel. 310/510–0330) rents gear to experienced divers (certification papers required) year-round. They also organize boating excursions for advanced and novice divers to many of Catalina's rich kelp forests.

ORANGE COUNTY 10

By Michael Rubiano

For some reason, the very words "Orange County" strike terror in the hearts of most Californians. On the coast between Los Angeles and San Diego, Orange County has unfortunately earned itself a bad reputation as a lackluster expanse of suburbia that, at least according to Angelenos, is the dregs of southern California. Orange County is unloved (except for Disneyland), unappreciated, and frankly, avoided whenever possible—more of a place to pass through than a destination in its own right. And yet driving along its windy stretch of the **Pacific Coast Highway** is an eye-opening experience. Here the contradictions of southern California are revealed: the powerful, healing ocean vistas and the scars of commercial exploitation; the appealingly laid-back beach life and the tacky bric-a-brac of the tourist trail.

Orange County definitely has a few things to offer besides tract housing and minimalls, and you'll want to spend some time here discovering the coast, particularly if you're headed south toward San Diego or Mexico. Oil rigs and port facilities line the shore near Long Beach and south Los Angeles, but once you breach Orange County the scenery gives way to pristine stretches of beach and dramatic hillsides. If speed is more important than beauty, the uninspiring **Interstate 5** (I–5) connects Los Angeles with Orange County and San Diego, but otherwise it's worth sticking with the Pacific Coast Highway (PCH). It's often congested with traffic, especially during the summer season, but it's certainly the best way to discover the allure of southern California's golden beaches firsthand. You can easily traverse the Orange County coast in under four hours, and prototypical beach towns like **Newport Beach** and **Laguna Beach** serve as casual stopping points along the route—two cities that tread a fine line between tranquil beach resort and over-developed tourist traps. They're by far the most popular (and overpriced) attractions on PCH, but towns like **Seal Beach, Huntington Beach,** and **San Clemente** (*see* Exploring Pacific Coast Highway, *below*) may be better-suited to those who can't afford $70 hotel rooms and $40 dinners.

Anaheim is about as exciting as static on a radio station, but even after 50 years the Magic Kingdom is one of California's—and perhaps the country's—best-loved attractions.

And, contrary to popular belief, **Disneyland** is not in Los Angeles but in Orange County, encircled by the inland city of **Anaheim.** Besides the ever-popular Disneyland, also look for **Knott's Berry Farm**—another amusing theme park in the city of **Buena Park.** It's true that Orange County is an unwieldy suburbia that lacks any central focus, but it isn't nearly as bad as Angelenos make it out to be. Most of its sights are within easy reach of L.A., so don't be afraid to blaze your own trail through Orange County's unsightly tangle of freeways and suburban sprawl.

Orange County

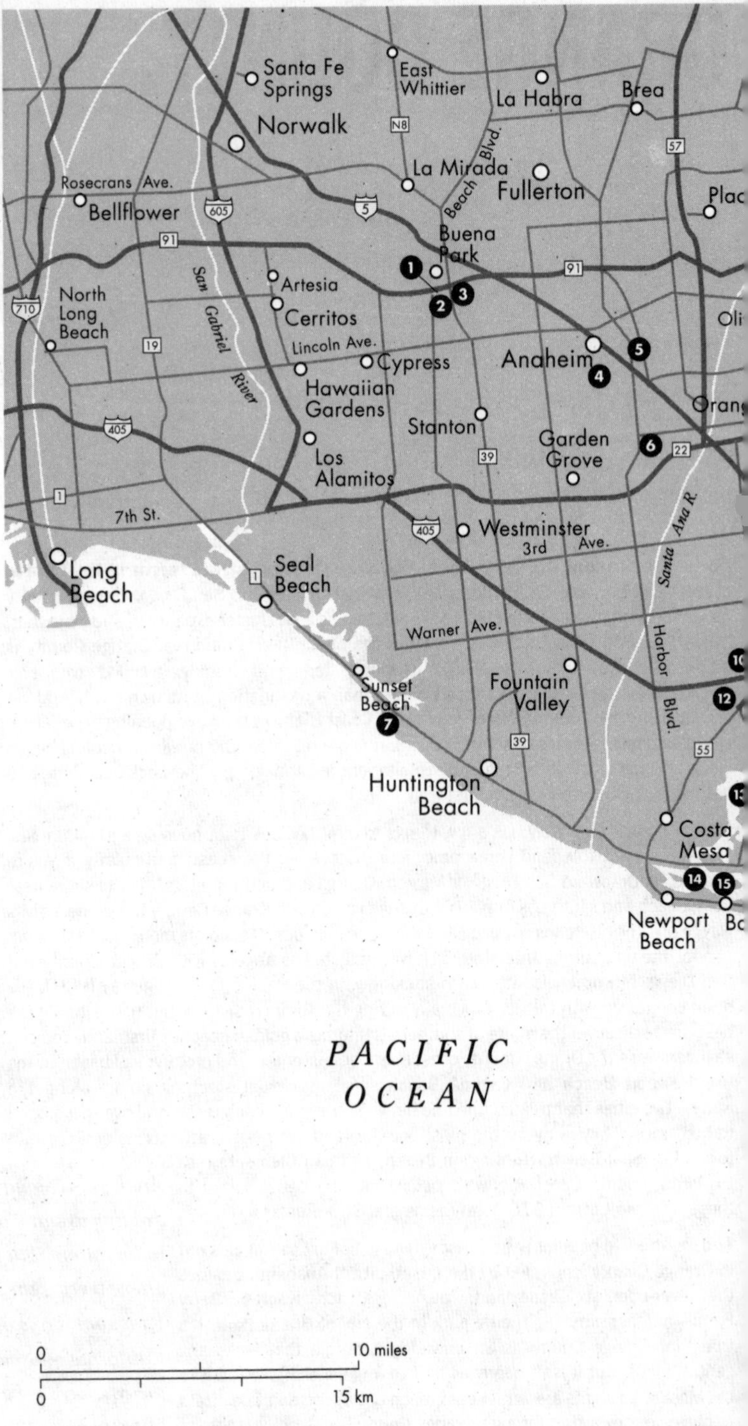

Santa Fe Springs
East Whittier
La Habra
Brea
Norwalk
N8
Beach Blvd.
57
La Mirada
Fullerton
Rosecrans Ave.
Plac
Bellflower
605
5
Buena Park
91
91
1
2
3
San Gabriel River
Artesia
North Long Beach
710
Cerritos
Oli
19
Lincoln Ave.
Anaheim
5
Cypress
4
Hawaiian Gardens
Orang
405
Stanton
Garden Grove
6
22
Los Alamitos
39
1
Santa Ana R.
7th St.
405
Westminster
3rd Ave.
Long Beach
Seal Beach
1
Warner Ave.
Harbor Blvd.
10
Fountain Valley
Sunset Beach
12
7
39
55
Huntington Beach
13
Costa Mesa
14
15
Newport Beach
Bo

PACIFIC OCEAN

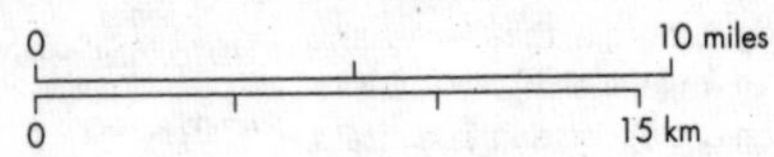

Orange County

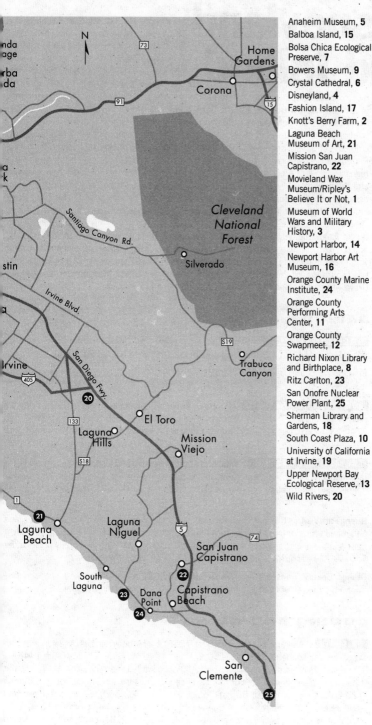

Anaheim Museum, **5**
Balboa Island, **15**
Bolsa Chica Ecological Preserve, **7**
Bowers Museum, **9**
Crystal Cathedral, **6**
Disneyland, **4**
Fashion Island, **17**
Knott's Berry Farm, **2**
Laguna Beach Museum of Art, **21**
Mission San Juan Capistrano, **22**
Movieland Wax Museum/Ripley's Believe It or Not, **1**
Museum of World Wars and Military History, **3**
Newport Harbor, **14**
Newport Harbor Art Museum, **16**
Orange County Marine Institute, **24**
Orange County Performing Arts Center, **11**
Orange County Swapmeet, **12**
Richard Nixon Library and Birthplace, **8**
Ritz Carlton, **23**
San Onofre Nuclear Power Plant, **25**
Sherman Library and Gardens, **18**
South Coast Plaza, **10**
University of California at Irvine, **19**
Upper Newport Bay Ecological Reserve, **13**
Wild Rivers, **20**

Disneyland and Inland

Like apple pie, baseball, and Watergate, Disneyland is a uniquely American phenomenon. Unfortunately, making visitors realize that Orange County doesn't revolve around Disneyland is the biggest task facing local tourist offices. Disneyland is far and away the most popular attraction the county has to offer, but you'll also find other noteworthy attractions nearby. Besides **Knott's Berry Farm,** the oldest theme park in the United States, there's Dr. Schuller's **Crystal Cathedral,** one of the largest churches in the world, built almost completely out of glass. Fans of Richard "I cannot tell a lie" Nixon will also enjoy the strangely named **Richard M. Nixon Library and Birthplace.** More than just a Republican booster club, the Library and Birthplace presents a detailed history of the highs and lows of America's 37th president. Most of these sites are located in **Anaheim** and **Buena Park** off I–5, half an hour from Orange County's coast and one hour south of downtown Los Angeles. Few willingly spend more time than necessary in either of these cities, but they'll do in a pinch if 10 hours at an amusement park has worn you out. Otherwise, don't expect too much from Orange County's inland attractions. Besides the theme parks, the only thing you'll find inland is a ghastly panorama of tedious suburbs and unsightly industry. Accommodations are cheaper here than on the coast, but what you'll save in dollars you'll certainly lose in beauty. If you're looking for a quick escape, head south toward the coast on **Route 39** through **Santa Ana, Westminster,** and **Garden Grove**—three of inland Orange County's most forgettable suburbs.

● ● ● BASICS

AMERICAN EXPRESS **Santa Ana.** *Main Place Mall, 2800 N. Main St., Suite 600, 92701, tel. 714/541–3318. Open weekdays 10–9, Sat. 10–7, Sun. 11–6.*

Brea. *351 S. State College Blvd., 92621, tel. 714/671–6967. Open weekdays 10–6, Sat. 10–3.*

DOCTORS AND DENTISTS Doctors: **Anaheim Memorial Hospital** (1111 W. La Palma, tel. 714/774–1450); **Western Medical Center** (1025 S. Anaheim Blvd., tel. 714/533–6220). Dentists: **Community Clinic of Orange County** (2000 W. Walnut St., tel. 714/541–6545).

TOURIST INFORMATION **Anaheim Area Convention and Visitors Bureau.** Located at the Anaheim Convention Center, this is the best source for maps, restaurant and lodging guides, and information on the nearby amusement parks. *800 W. Katella Ave., tel. 714/999–8999. Open Mon.–Sat. 9–5.*

Buena Park Visitors Bureau. This office has an excellent selection of maps, brochures, and all-around tourist information for the confused traveler. They also offer listings of budget motels in the neighborhood, but be careful: When they say budget they really mean under $40. *7711 Beach Blvd., tel. 714/994–1511. Open Mon.–Sat. 9–5.*

Orange County Transportation District (OCTD). Call for routes, schedules, and bus information for all of Orange County. *Tel. 714/636–7433. Open weekdays 9–5.*

● ● ● COMING AND GOING

BY TRAIN All **Amtrak** (tel. 800/872–7245) trains between Los Angeles and San Diego stop at **Anaheim Station** (2150 E. Katella Ave., 92805, tel. 714/385–1448), a 10-minute drive from Disneyland. The facility is open between 6 AM and 10:30 PM, but it has no luggage storage area or tourist office. Amtrak also serves the **Fullerton Station** (120 E. Santa Fe at Harbor Blvd., 92632, tel. 714/992–0530), which is 6 miles from Knott's Berry Farm and the city of Buena Park. The station is staffed from 6:15 AM to 11 PM, but there are no luggage storage facilities or tourist kiosks. Both stations are connected to the theme parks via public bus: #39 from Anaheim and #99 from Fullerton.

BY BUS The Anaheim **Greyhound Station** (2080 S. Harbor Blvd., tel. 714/635–5060) is only three blocks from Disneyland. Luggage lockers are available for $1 a day, and there's a supermarket and a 24-hour Circle-K minimarket across the street. The station is open 6:30 AM to 6 PM on weekdays; 6:30 AM to 3 PM on weekends. The **Los Angeles RTD** (425 S. Main St., L.A., tel. 213/626–4455) has limited service to Orange County; RTD line #460 goes from downtown Los Angeles to Anaheim, Disneyland, Norwalk, and Knott's Berry Farm for under $3.

BY CAR The easiest way to reach Anaheim is on the **Golden State Freeway,** also known as I–5. There are hundreds of signs once you get within a stone's throw of Disneyland and Knott's Berry Farm. Traffic can be a serious problem during rush hours (7 AM–9 AM and 3 PM–5 PM), but otherwise it shouldn't take you more than one hour by car from downtown L.A., and about 2$^1/_2$ hours from San Diego.

WHERE TO SLEEP

Ample lodging can be found all around Disneyland and Knott's Berry Farm, especially along **Katella Avenue** and **Harbor Boulevard** in Anaheim. However, most hotels and motels are extremely run down and depressing, even though they're priced like top-rate establishments (between $35 and $100 a night). Because of their proximity to the theme parks they're often full, which means they make enough money not to care how shabby or ragged they look. Even worse, you must reserve a room at least one week in advance at these dirt-bag establishments, especially during the summer when hordes of tourists descend. If you need advice, contact the Buena Park Visitors Bureau (*see* Tourist Information, *above*). Otherwise, your only budget option is the city's lone hostel—perhaps the best place to stay in Anaheim if you don't mind communal living.

UNDER $35 **Covered Wagon Motel.** This charmless hole-in-the-wall has little to offer but a bed and four walls. It's one of the cheaper places around, however, and it's directly across the street from Knott's Berry Farm. *7830 Crescent Ave., Buena Park, 90620, tel. 800/535–0033. 20 rooms, all with bath. Reservations advised.*

UNDER $50 **Desert Palm Suites.** Spacious rooms, clean bathrooms, and comfortable beds add up to a decent hotel, but at $50 a night it's way overpriced. It's near Disneyland, however, and sometimes the management runs a $1 shuttle to the amusement park for guests. *631 W. Katella Ave., Anaheim 92802, tel. 714/535–1133.*

Farm de Ville. This place is about as French as "Le House" and "Le Hamburger," but it's across the street from Knott's Berry Farm. For your $50 you'll get a bed, a door, and a toilet, but little else in the way of comfort. Decorated in the "Let's-make-people-gag" style, the Farm de Ville's orange carpets and faded bedspreads are about as charming as roadkill. For convenience, though, it unfortunately earns high marks. *7800 Crescent Ave., Buena Park 90620, tel. 714/527–2201. 130 rooms, all with bath. Reservations advised.*

Magic Carpet/Lamp Motel. Surprise, surprise: another place where your money buys location but little else. Like all hotels in the area, however, it's close to the transportation hubs and Disneyland, and rooms fetch an unsightly $35 during winter; $50 during summer. The only nice thing about this place is free HBO. *1030 W. Katella Ave., Anaheim 92802, tel. 800/843–3145. 81 rooms, all with bath. Reservations advised.*

HOSTELS **Fullerton-Hacienda AYH-Hostel.** For price and location, the Fullerton-Hacienda is your best value. One mile from the Fullerton Station (*see* Coming and Going, *above*), the hostel is served by numerous public buses, and is only a short bus ride away from both Disneyland and Knott's Berry Farm. The hostel's one drawback is that it has only 15 beds: Reservations are a must. There is no lockout period and a late key ($10 refundable deposit) is available if you plan to be out past 11. The hostel also has excellent kitchen facilities. The rate for members is $12, nonmembers pay $15. To reach Disneyland Hotel from here, take OCTD Bus 41 eastbound to Fullerton Station, and transfer to OCTD Bus 43 south. *1700 N. Harbor Blvd., 92635, tel. 714/738–3721. 3 miles north of CA 91 on Harbor Blvd., in Brea Dam Park. From the Fullerton Station take*

Bus 41 westbound to Brea Dam Park. 15 beds. Baths, laundry, wheelchair access, lockers/luggage storage, on-site parking, linen $1.

● ● ● FOOD

There's an abundance of places to eat, ranging from fast-food joints to moderately priced, sit-down restaurants. Once again, however, your dollars will buy location and convenience rather than good food and a comfortable environment. Not surprisingly, most of the restaurants in Anaheim and Buena Park make a lot of money, and they, too, don't really seem to care how good or bad their meals are. If you're headed to the theme parks you should pack a lunch of your own. Most of the restaurants and food stands within the parks are both overpriced and overrated—ranging from $3 ice-cream cones to $15 plates of leathery chicken and cold potatoes. For an innocuous dining experience try one of the local chain restaurants. **Stuart Anderson's Black Angus** (7111 Beach Blvd., tel. 714/670–2012), a state-wide steak house, and the **Baker's Square** (8525 Beach Blvd., tel. 714/828–1450), a coffee shop with burgers and fries, both offer standard food for under $10.

UNDER $10 **Claim Jumper.** Near Knott's Berry Farm, the Claim Jumper specializes in rib and chicken dinners, and for once the food isn't half bad. It's sort of a faceless place where meals are prepared in bulk, but the ribs ($8) are tasty and the chicken ($6.50) is tender. Vegetarians, however, be warned: Except for their table salads and grilled-cheese sandwiches, everything here has some form of meat in it. *7971 Beach Blvd., tel. 714/523–3227. Open weekdays 11–11, weekends 11 AM–midnight.*

Hansa House Smorgasbord. When the Vikings landed in Anaheim, they bought a piece of real estate and opened up this "Swedish" smorgasbord—popular with the all-you-can-eat crowd. Meals are served buffet-style with such "Swedish" favorites as bacon and eggs, sausage, Jell-O, and doughnuts. It may not be the best food in the world, but it *will* fill you up. Breakfast buffets cost $4.95, lunch $5.95, and dinner $9.95. It's near Disneyland. *1840 S. Harbor Blvd., tel. 714/750–2411. Open daily 7–10:30 AM, 11:30 AM–3 PM, and 4:30–9 PM.*

Mrs. Knott's Chicken Dinner Restaurant. Before Knott's Berry Farm was turned into a theme park, it was a chicken ranch and berry farm. Shortly after Mr. Knott cross-bred a raspberry and a loganberry vine in the 1930s to create the first boysenberry plant, his wife baked the first-ever boysenberry pie. Since then, people have been flocking to Mrs. Knott's Restaurant for a slice of homemade pie, and for fried chicken dinners. The restaurant has a cafeteria feel, but the food is actually quite good. It's in the Knott's Berry Farm Marketplace, in the amusement park's parking lot. *8039 Beach Blvd., tel. 714/220–5200. Open Mon.–Sat. 7 AM–10 PM, Sun. 7–7.*

Tiffy's Family Restaurant. A five-minute walk from Disneyland, this coffee shop is quick, cheap, and predictably greasy, and offers the standard selection of burgers and over-priced entrées. It's open late, though, and it's conveniently located. *1060 W. Katella Ave., tel. 714/635–1801. Open daily 6 AM–2 AM.*

● ● ● WORTH SEEING

THE CRYSTAL CATHEDRAL Designed by architect Phillip Johnson, the Crystal Cathedral is a 10,500-glass-pane superstructure that looms over surrounding Garden Grove in peculiar majesty. Home to Dr. Robert Schuller and his *Hour of Power* ministry (one of the most profitable in the country), it looks like something out of a bad science-fiction movie. Its clear-glass ceiling may afford an excellent view of the Garden Grove skyline (smog, tract housing, and minimalls), but it's about as inviting as a jail cell. Inside, you can't help but feel you're being watched on a security camera somewhere, and that a man wearing dark glasses in the parking lot is writing down your license plate number (although what you would expect from a place whose phone number is 54-GLORY?). You're free to inspect the cathedral at your leisure, but you may be followed by one of Dr. Schuller's vigilant sycophants if you don't look respectable enough. Unless you're desperate to see this modern-day Tower of Babel, save your time and buy a postcard from a souvenir shop. *12141 Lewis St., Garden Grove, tel. 714/971–4013 or 714/54–GLORY. Admission free. Usually open for self-guided tours until 4:30. Guided tours Mon.–Sat. 9–3:30, Sun. 1:30–3:30.*

DISNEYLAND Since it opened in 1955, Disneyland has been dazzling generations of children from around the world. All people, it seems, have at least one connection with Disneyland and the Disney Family, be it a song that sticks in your head or a childhood fondness for Mickey Mouse, Peter Pan, Cinderella, or Snow White. If you haven't been here for a few years, not much has changed. **Cinderella's Castle** still stands, the **Pirates of the Caribbean** still sing "A Pirates Life for Me," the **Haunted Mansion** is still looking for it's "1,000th ghost," and, like clockwork, the **Main Street Electrical Parade** goes off without a hitch, day in and day out. Disneyland's newest attractions include **Splash Mountain,** a water-flume journey through swamps, bayous, and raging waterfalls, and **Star Tours,** a flight simulator ride created by George Lucas. If you're not a fan of action-oriented rides, head for Disneyland's traditional favorites, such as the wonderfully sappy **Tom Sawyer's Island, Mr. Toad's Wild Ride,** the **Jungle Boat,** and the **Tiki Room.** *1313 Harbor Blvd., Anaheim, tel. 714/999–4565. Admission: $28 adults, $23 children, children under 3 free. One day admission allows unlimited access to all park rides and attractions. Open (generally) May 11–Aug. 31, daily 8 AM–1 AM; Sept. 1–May 10, weekdays 10 AM–6 PM, Sat. 10 AM–10 PM, Sun. 10 AM–8 PM. Hours vary incredibly so call ahead.*

The busiest times of the year at Disney are during the summer and over holidays, when lines sometimes take as much as two hours to conquer.

Unfortunately, long lines are a problem at all Disneyland attractions. Your best strategy is to visit the popular rides early in the morning or late at night. Besides the rides, Disneyland also has a number of bandstands and music venues, some free, others not. Check at Disneyland's **City Hall** (by the entrance) for concert information and prices. The best restaurant in Disneyland is the **Blue Bayou,** a Cajun and Southern-style eatery in the Pirates of the Caribbean complex. It's crowded, but the mouth-watering cajun chicken ($9) and seafood jambalaya ($10) are certainly worth the wait. Reservations are advised, and they must be made in person. A full dinner will run you about $14.

KNOTT'S BERRY FARM Knott's Berry Farm is the oldest theme park in the United States. What began as a temporary diversion for customers waiting for one of Mrs. Knott's famed chicken dinners has now expanded into five different theme areas spread over 300 acres. It may not have as many action rides or theme lands as Disneyland, but it has an undeniable "down-home" and ranch-house charm that the over-developed and crowded Disneyland lacks. Knott's **Ghost Town,** modeled after an 1880s Old West Mining Town, is a place where you can pan for gold or take a train through a 19th-century gold mine (complete with explosions and cave-ins). **Fiesta Village,** one of the least interesting sections of the park, was built in homage to California's Spanish settlers, complete with miniaturized replicas of the California missions and a number of third-rate Mexican restaurants. About the only thing of interest in Fiesta Village is **Montezuma's Revenge,** a roller coaster that will take you from 0 to 55 mph in less than four seconds. **Wild Water Wilderness,** the most recent expansion, is set in the wild and rugged mountains of California during the early 1900s. **Bigfoot Rapids,** a white-water river ride, is guaranteed to leave you soaking wet. The last area, the **Roaring 20's,** is completely themeless. Though it's meant to be full of ruthless gangsters and boa-draped dames, it's been overrun by thoroughly modern roller coasters like the **Boomerang**—a ride that promises to turn its passengers upside down six times in less than a minute. Needless to say, don't eat any chili dogs before strapping yourself in. *8039 Beach Blvd., Buena Park, tel. 714/220–5200 or 714/827–1776. ½ mi south of CA 91. Admission: $22. Open summer, Sun.–Thurs. 9 AM–11 PM, Fri. and Sat. 9 AM–midnight; winter, weekdays 10–6, Sat. 10–10, Sun. 10–8.*

THE RICHARD NIXON LIBRARY AND BIRTHPLACE This nine-acre tribute to the life and times of the 37th president, built on the grounds of Nixon's childhood home, was opened by presidents Bush, Reagan, Ford, and Nixon on July 19, 1990. The self-guided tour starts with a multimedia exhibit detailing Nixon's prepresidential years.

Next, visitors enter a 293-seat theater to view the film *Never Give Up,* a sappy and self-aggrandizing documentary focusing on Nixon's ability to somehow triumph after each of his many political defeats. The high points of the tour are the videos of the famed 1960 *Kennedy-Nixon Debates* and the "World Leaders" exhibit, littered with gaudy bronze statues of 10 of the 20th century's greatest leaders (at least according to Nixon). The "Presidential Forum," perhaps the silliest display here, allows visitors to "speak" with a smiling Nixon via the magic of video tape. Be sure to ask Nixon how his family is. Finally, don't miss the June 23, 1972, White House tape, which has a Nixon aide suggesting the FBI slow down its investigation of Watergate. Also on display is the pistol Elvis gave Nixon as a token of friendship. After the museum tour, walk through the First Lady's Garden on your way to the farmhouse where Tricky Dick was born. The house contains the original family piano, and there's an audio presentation (narrated by Nixon) that discusses his life as a young boy. *18001 Yorba Linda Blvd., Yorba Linda, tel. 714/993–3393. At intersection of CA 57 and CA 91, follow the signs. Admission: $5. Open Mon.–Sat. 10–5, Sun. 11–5. Free parking available.*

Down the street from the Nixon Library is **Mimi's Café**—wonderful food, great atmosphere, reasonable prices, and huge servings. Try the chicken salad ($6) and the French-dip sandwich ($5). *18342 Imperial Hwy., tel. 714/996–3650. Open daily 7 AM–11 PM.*

ORANGE COUNTY PERFORMING ARTS CENTER Hosting world-class performances by the American Ballet Theater, the L.A. Philharmonic, and even the New York Opera, the Orange County Center for the performing arts is a small island of highbrow culture in lowbrow suburbia. Although performances can cost a small fortune ($30–$70), 20% student discounts are available. Call the ticket office for performance schedules and prices. Outside the complex look for the Noguchi sculpture garden. *600 Town Center Dr., Costa Mesa, tel. 714/556–2787.*

Less than a block away is the **South Coast Plaza,** the "mecca" of malls. With over 270 stores and 8,000 parking spaces, it's one of the largest mall complexes in the country. If these kind of places give you the creeps, however, stay away. At best, the South Coast Plaza is an overgrown monster; at worst, it's a nightmarish reminder of everything that's wrong with modern America. *3333 Bristol St., Costa Mesa, tel. 714/435–2000.*

ANAHEIM MUSEUM Located in the Carnegie Library (1908), this small museum has exhibits on Orange County's prehistory and geological development. There's also a section dedicated to the history of wine-making in the area and a hands-on science gallery filled with flashing lights and buttons that make things go. It's located near the convention center in downtown Anaheim; call ahead for a listing of temporary exhibits. *241 S. Anaheim Blvd. at Broadway, tel. 714/778–3301. Suggested donation: $1.50. Open Wed.–Fri. 10–4, Sat. noon–4.*

BOWERS MUSEUM The Bowers Museum has numerous ethnographic displays from the Americas, the Pacific Rim, and Africa. Exhibitions include Native American arts and crafts, Colombian pottery, traditional African costumes and clothing, and an excellent display of international photography. *2002 N. Main St. near 17th St., Santa Ana, tel. 714/972–1900. Admission free. Open Tues.–Sat. 10–5, Sun. noon–6.*

MOVIELAND WAX MUSEUM In a nutshell: tacky. This so-called museum has more than 250 wax dummies of Hollywood's most famous actors and personalities, from Liz Taylor to John Belushi. Even though most of the displays here look ridiculously fake, this place is inexplicably popular with tourists. Unless you're absolutely desperate for a photo of John Wayne, Gloria Estefan, Humphrey Bogart, or the crew of the *Starship Enterprise,* don't bother. Located down the street from Knott's Berry Farm. *7711 Beach Blvd., tel. 714/522–1155. Admission: $13. Open summer, daily 8 AM–9 PM; winter, daily 9 AM–8 PM.*

Across the street from the Movieland Wax Museum is yet another third-rate tourist trap—**Ripley's Believe It or Not,** a multimedia freak show that has exhibits like "the eight-legged pig" and the "four-eyed man." Save your money. Please. *7850 Beach Blvd., tel. 714/522–7045. Admission: $7. Open daily 9–8.*

AFTER DARK

Orange County isn't known for its exciting nightlife. Except for a few dance clubs and Top-40 hangouts you'll find your options sorely limited. In Irvine, **The Improvisation** (4255 Campus Dr., tel. 714/854–5455) offers live stand-up comedy on a nightly basis, while in Buena Park, the **Medieval Times Dinner and Tournament** (7662 Beach Blvd., tel. 714/521–4740) offers a nightly Arthurian feast and live joust. Be warned, however: A Medieval Times extravaganza is about as touristy as you can get. While knights on horseback compete in medieval games and fight deadly sword battles, you're squashed around an overcrowded table and fed a mediocre meal of roast chicken, potatoes, pastries, and cocktails. To really capture that "medieval" ambience, you're also supposed to eat with your hands and shout violently throughout the meal—a sheer delight at $28.95 per person. Shows start at 7 nightly and last until 9:30. Reservations are required.

BARS AND DANCE CLUBS **Bandstand.** Yee-haw. This club offers live country music Sunday, Tuesday, Thursday, and Friday. Other nights the Bandstand features Top-40 music. The Bandstand has six dance floors and four bars, and most noncountry nights are lively. *1721 S. Manchester, Anaheim, tel. 714/956–1410.*

Crackers. This place specializes in off-the-wall dinner theater *and* late-night dancing. All the waiters and waitresses double as on-stage performers, desperate for large tips, who climb on stage every so often to sing, dance, or tell bad jokes. Dinner costs around $10, and for $2 more you can get hot and heavy on the dance floor with music from Bing Crosby to Madonna. *710 Katella Ave., Anaheim, tel. 714/978–1828. Open daily 11 AM–2 AM.*

Pepper's. This is one of Orange County's most (in)famous pick-up joints. Grab a beer, grab another, and then ask yourself what you're doing here. If you're really in a sour mood, count the number of day-glow T-shirts on the dance floor or the number of convertible VW Rabbits in the parking lot. There's dancing nightly to Top-40 music from 8 PM to 2 AM. The cover charge ranges from $2 to $5, depending on the day of the week; Mondays are free. Pepper's is popular with the under-25 crowd. *12361 Chapman, Garden Grove, tel. 714/740–1333.*

OUTDOOR ACTIVITIES

If inland Orange County is getting on your nerves, hop in your car and head for **Santiago Canyon Road,** a beautiful mountaintop highway that winds through the Cleveland National Forest in the Santa Ana Mountains. Tucked away in the mountains are Modjeska Canyon, Irvine Lake, and Silverado Canyon, of silver-mining lore. The terrain is rugged and peaceful, without one minimall for miles. Baseball fans should head to Anaheim Stadium (tel. 714/634–2000), home of the **California Angels.** Their season runs from April through October, and tickets can be had for under $5. If you prefer a more aggressive spectacle, the **Los Angeles Rams** (tel. 714/937–6767) also call Anaheim Stadium home. Their season runs from August through December, and tickets start at $12.

Pacific Coast Highway

The 50-mile stretch of coast between Seal Beach and San Clemente is fondly known as the "American Riviera," the most scenic and lively stretch of beach anywhere on California's coast. **Seal Beach,** only 10 miles south of Long Beach, is a quirky and uncommercial seaside town with a wonderful 1950s feel to it—the perfect place to begin your coastal odyssey. A little farther south you'll come across **Huntington Beach,** a somewhat trendy enclave filled with bleached-blond surfers and their sun-tanned troupe. The average age here seems to be 18, so if you're looking to let loose and run wild in the sand—welcome to Huntington Beach. **Newport Beach,** one of southern California's most exclusive seaside playgrounds, is just 40 miles south of downtown Los Angeles. The popular summer resort is littered with elegant French restaurants, swank hotels, trendy clothing boutiques, middle-aged millionaires, BMWs with surf racks, and a whole lot of attitude. For all its wealth and affluence, however, Newport is peppered with golden beaches and an undeniable seaside charm—a great place to discover both the tackiness and beauty of California's coast.

Laguna is the highlight of the coast, and if you visit only one city in Orange County let this be it.

If Newport is a seaside Beverly Hills, the hip **Laguna Beach** is the SoHo of the surf. About 60 art galleries peacefully co-exist with the endless volleyball games and parades of people on Laguna's colorful public beach. And in the true spirit of the '60s, when Timothy Leary and his hippie cronies used to hang out in Laguna's fast-food joints, lifestyles here are still best described as "alternative" and "anything goes." If you're in the area during July and August, don't miss the impressive **Pageant of the Masters** (*see* Tourist Information, *below*), one of Laguna's popular summer festivals.

Almost everything along the coast is easily accessed from the Pacific Coast Highway (PCH), and even if you don't have the money to spend on a hotel you can easily make the trek from L.A. to San Diego along PCH in four to five hours. The following drive is organized along a north–south axis, covering **Seal Beach, Huntington Beach, Newport Beach, Corona del Mar, Laguna Beach, San Juan Capistrano,** and **San Clemente.** You may not have time to stop in all of them, but since they nestle against PCH you can decide for yourself which are suited to both your sense of aesthetics and your pocketbook. There's a youth hostel in Huntington Beach if you need a cheap place to crash for the night, but otherwise be prepared to spend upward of $40 for lodging along the coast. Orange County may have some of the best beaches in the world, but a taste of California's laid-back beach life unfortunately doesn't come cheap.

● ● ● BASICS

AMERICAN EXPRESS **Costa Mesa.** South Coast Plaza: *3200 Bristol St., 92626, tel. 714/540–3611. Open weekdays 9–5.*

San Clemente. El Camino Travel Service is an Am Ex representative. *115 S. El Camino Real, Box 127, 92672, tel. 714/492–1191. Open weekdays 8–5:30, Sat. 9–noon.*

DOCTORS AND DENTISTS There are emergency rooms at **Anaheim Memorial Hospital** (1111 W. La Palma, tel. 714/774–1450); **Western Medical Center** (1025 S. Anaheim Blvd., Anaheim, tel. 714/533–6220); **Hoag Memorial Hospital** (301 Newport Blvd., Newport Beach, tel. 714/645–8600); **South Coast Medical Center** (31872 Coast Hwy., South Laguna, tel. 714/499–1311); and **UC Irvine Medical Center** (101 The City Dr., tel. 714/634–6011).

TELEPHONES The area code for the county is **714.** Seal Beach, however, is in the **213** area code.

TOURIST INFORMATION **Huntington Beach Chamber of Commerce.** Besides the usual selection of tourist maps and brochures, this office has a list of the "best & worst" hotels and restaurants in the area, free of charge. *Seacliff Village, 2213 Main St., 92648, tel. 714/536–8888. Open weekdays 9–5.*

Laguna Beach Chamber of Commerce. Stop in for maps and hotel and restaurant listings. They also have information on Laguna's festivals and art exhibitions. *357 Glenneyre, Laguna Beach, 92651, tel. 714/494–1018. Open weekdays 10–5.*

Newport Harbor Chamber of Commerce. The usual: tourist brochures, maps, and sound advice. If you're looking for a cheap, clean place to stay, ask for their list of top lodging choices. *1470 Jamboree Rd., 92660, tel. 714/644–8211. Open Mon.–Sat. 10–4:30.*

Orange County Transportation District (OCTD). Call for routes, schedules, and bus information for all of Orange County. *Tel. 714/636–7433. Open weekdays 9–5.*

San Clemente Tourism Bureau. It doesn't have a lot to offer, but this office can suggest a hotel or restaurant if you're detained for some reason in this lackluster town. *31199 N. El Camino Real, 92672, tel. 714/492–1131. Open weekdays 10–4.*

San Juan Capistrano Visitors Center. It seems hardly worth the effort, but this office can arrange minivan tours of San Juan Capistrano's coastline. *31882 Camino Capistrano, tel. 714/493–1424. Inside the San Juan Capistrano Mission.*

Seal Beach Chamber of Commerce. There's no office, but the staff can suggest lodging and dining options in Seal Beach over the phone. *Tel. 213/700–0179.*

COMING AND GOING • • •

BY TRAIN Between Los Angeles and San Diego, Amtrak's main stopping point is the **San Juan Capistrano Depot** (26701 Verdugo St., tel. 714/496–8181), where you'll also find a top-rate jazz club and restaurant (*see* Food, *below*). Even better, public buses run between this depot, Laguna, and San Clemente hourly between 9 AM and 7 PM, making it a great place to begin your exploration of the coast.

Otherwise, you can stop at the **San Clemente Auxiliary Amtrak Station,** on the beach near the San Clemente AYH Youth Hostel (*see* Where to Sleep, *below*). There's no staff here, nor can you purchase tickets at the station; in fact, the auxiliary depot isn't a station at all but a pick-up and drop-off point for passing Amtrak trains. Passengers who want to leave from here must either already have a ticket in hand or be prepared to pay for one in cash the moment they step on board. Call **Amtrak** (tel. 800/872–7245) for more information. To reach Disneyland or Laguna Beach from here, take OCTD Bus 91 north to the last stop, then 1 north for Laguna; 85 north to Main Street and Santa Ana Boulevard, then 51 north for Disneyland.

BY BUS The **Santa Ana Greyhound Station** (1000 E. Santa Ana Blvd., tel. 714/542–2215) is just off the Santa Ana Freeway, 10 miles north of Newport Beach and the coast. Connections from this station include San Diego, Riverside, Los Angeles, Santa Barbara, San Luis Obispo, and San Francisco. The ticket office is open Monday–Saturday, 7 AM to 8:15 PM. Buses leave hourly throughout the day. To reach the coast from here you'll need to take OCTD Bus 37 to Newport Beach, or a taxi.

The **San Clemente Greyhound Station** (510 Via de la Estrella, tel. 714/848–3050) is open Monday–Saturday 8 AM–6 PM. Four buses run north every day to Santa Ana, L.A., and beyond; they head south three times a day to Oceanside and San Diego. There are luggage lockers and a small food stand here. Public buses leave from the parking lot every hour or so, making the journey to Newport, Huntington Beach, and Laguna for under $3.

BY CAR The scenic Pacific Coast Highway traverses the coast from L.A. to San Juan Capistrano, at which point it merges with I–5. In a perfect world it would take only three hours to travel the entire shoreline, but realists should plan on at least a four- to five-hour ride, especially if you make any stops along the way. If you don't mind driving through Orange County's suburban wasteland, you can always take the **405 Freeway** (I–405) south from L.A. and cross over to the coast on **Route 55** (to Newport Beach) or **Route 133** (to Laguna). This will save some time, but you'll lose out on much of the undeveloped—and most scenic—parts of the coast.

WHERE TO SLEEP • • •

Sad to say, but there are few budget hotels along the Pacific Coast Highway. It's here that the richest of the rich reside; accordingly, lodging rates will be $10–$25 more than in the smaller coast towns and inland cities. Even in the most run-down establishments along PCH you're likely to pay upward of $50 during the summer season, perhaps $40 off-season. Needless to say, camping and hosteling are your only budget alternatives *(see below).*

If you're willing to settle on the outskirts of Newport Beach, you'll find a string of reasonably priced motels ($25–$40) along Newport Boulevard in dreary **Costa Mesa.** Of course, you won't have an ocean view (more likely a view of Route 55), but Costa Mesa is only a 10-minute drive from the beach. The **Tern Inn Motel** (2154 Newport Blvd., tel. 714/548–8173) and the **Marina Gateway Inn** (1680 Superior Ave., tel. 800/345–8015) are probably the best of the bunch, both starting at $30. Otherwise, stay away from the larger beach towns and head for the less popular—and less expensive—outposts south of Laguna, in either San Juan Capistrano or San Clemente. To be sure, nightlife in these towns is dull, but at least you won't have to go into heavy debt for one night's lodging. Once again, stay away from Corona del Mar. Its hotels take American Express, and judging from their prices ($85–$200), you'll need it.

HUNTINGTON BEACH **Huntington Harbor Motor Inn.** It's no bargain, but the Huntington Harbor is the cheapest place on the coast. Musty rooms, all with small, grimy bathrooms, are available on a first-come, first-served basis. Summer rates start at $45; off-season at $35. *16240 PCH, Huntington Beach, tel. 714/846–5561. 18 rooms, all with bath.*

Huntington Shores Motel. This motel is in a safe but very quiet area. The management doesn't tolerate loud parties, nor does it rent to anyone under 21. If this isn't a problem, this place is clean, cozy, and perfectly located. Rooms start at $38, and all have views of the beach, just across the street. Continental breakfast is included. *21002 PCH, tel. 714/536–8861. 50 rooms, all with bath. Heated pool, some rooms with kitchen. Reservations advised 1 month ahead during summer.*

Ocean View Motel. This small, family-run establishment has clean, comfortable rooms for $43. In-room Jacuzzis are available for $15 extra, an option adventurous travelers may find hard to resist. This motel appeals to the summer beach crowd, so make summer reservations two to three weeks in advance. *16196 PCH, tel. 213/592–2700. 29 rooms, all with bath.*

NEWPORT BEACH The only two hotels in Newport under $80 are the **Newport Channel Inn** (6030 W. Coast Hwy., tel. 714/642–3030) at $40 a night, and the **Newport Classic Inn** (2300 W. Coast Hwy., tel. 800/633–3199) at $69 a night. Both are well-maintained, clean, and about 1 mile from the beach. They're popular with the summer beach crowd, and reservations are advised.

LAGUNA BEACH Laguna is the most popular stopover south of Newport, but unfortunately its priced way out of the budget traveler's reach. The **Surf and Sands Hotel** (1555 S. PCH, tel. 714/497–4477) is one of the city's nicest, but a room at this beachfront resort will set you back $110 per night. The **Crescent Bay Inn** (1435 N. Coast Hwy., tel. 714/494–2508) is the cheapest place in town ($40–$60), but the rooms are dirty and run-down. If you want to splurge, the **Capri Laguna** (1441 S. Coast Hwy., tel. 714/494–6533) has clean and sunny beachfront rooms for $65. Even better, it's within walking distance of downtown Laguna. If you're desperate, the **Laguna Reef/Best Western** (30806 S. Coast Hwy., tel. 800/922–9905), on the southern outskirts of Laguna, has generic rooms for $80.

SAN CLEMENTE **San Clemente Motor Lodge.** It's a dump, but if aesthetics and comfort step aside for low prices, this is the place to stay. Besides the youth hostels and campgrounds, this place offers the cheapest lodging in the Laguna Beach area, starting at $30 a night and jumping to $40 on the weekends. The one nice thing about the Motor Lodge is that it's only a 10-minute drive from the beach and 30 minutes to Laguna. *2222 S. El Camino Real, 92672, tel. 714/492–4992. All rooms with bath.*

SAN JUAN CAPISTRANO **Mission Inn.** This place is located near the Mission in San Juan Capistrano, a short two blocks from the Amtrak station. The rooms here are clean and the service is friendly, but be careful walking around at night; it isn't in the best part of town. However, it's the cheapest hotel in town: Double rooms start at $45 during the week; $55 on weekends and summer. *26891 Ortega Hwy., 92675, tel. 714/493–1151. All rooms with bath.*

SEAL BEACH There's not much to choose from, so try the **Radisson Inn** (600 Marina Dr., tel. 310/493–7501), part of an expensive and generic-looking international chain. Comfortable but characterless rooms start at $85 during the summer, $60 off-season. It's near the beach, however, and some rooms have an excellent view of the sea. Otherwise, try the **Golden Sails** (6285 E. Pacific Coast Hwy., tel. 310/596–1631), just across the county line in Long Beach, half a mile from the ocean and 2 miles from Seal Beach's small downtown. Rooms are comfortable and clean, but unfortunately pricey at $60–$70.

HOSTELS **Colonial Inn Youth Hostel.** In Huntington Beach, this privately owned hostel offers 14 semiprivate rooms (with twin beds for couples) and three communal rooms. There's an 11 PM curfew, but a late key is available for $3, plus deposit. Both the rooms and the kitchen facilities are extremely clean. The beach and downtown are a 15-minute ride away, and there are a few restaurants within easy walking distance. Beds are $10 per person, and a photo I.D. of some sort is required. Reservations, especially during the summer, are advised. *421 8th St., Huntington Beach 92648, tel. 714/536–3315. From both the Greyhound station and the Disneyland Hotel take Bus 50 or 50A on Katella, transfer at Beach Blvd. to Bus 29 or 29A toward Huntington Beach. Get off at Main St. (at the beach). The hostel is 2 blocks to your right. 11 PM curfew, common showers, bathroom, and kitchen. Lockout time: daily 9:30 AM–4:30 PM.*

San Clemente Beach AYH-Hostel. The beauty of this hostel is that it provides affordable, clean, and safe indoor lodging only a hop away from a quiet, golden beach. There's even an Amtrak stop nearby, the **San Clemente Auxiliary** (*see* Coming and Going, *above*), where you can catch a public bus to Disneyland or Laguna Beach. However, there isn't much to do in San Clemente, and if you don't have a car you may feel like you're in the middle of nowhere. *230 Av. Granada, San Clemente 92672, tel. 714/492–2848. From the Amtrak stop, walk 5 blocks uphill on Avenida Granada, it's on the right-hand side. 50 bed spaces. 11 PM curfew, laundry, communal kitchen. 9:15 AM check-out.*

CAMPGROUNDS **Bolsa Chica State Beach.** In Huntington Beach, Bolsa Chica's facilities include fire rings, dressing rooms, cold showers, bicycle trails, and a paved ramp for wheelchair beach access. There's even an on-site general store that stocks food and camping supplies. Unfortunately, no tents are allowed—only RVs and car-campers. Reservations are recommended throughout the year. Peak season (mid-May–mid-September) fees are around $16 per space. *18331 Enterprise, Huntington Beach, tel. 714/846–3460. Between Sunset Beach and Huntington Beach on the coast.*

Doheny State Beach. Forget about wasting your money on an expensive hotel; if you have a tent, come straight here. The sites overlook the ocean in Dana Point, nestled among a string of sand dunes and trees. Facilities include fishing areas, swimming, a general store, and food service. During the peak season (March–November), an inland site fetches $16, a beachfront site $21. This campground is popular with backpackers and families on vacation, so call ahead for reservations. *25300 Harbor Dr., Dana Point, tel. 714/496–6172. Near intersection of I–5 and PCH at the entrance to Dana Point Harbor. 121 sites (87 RV or tent spaces and 34 beachfront sites). Special sites available for hikers and bikers.*

Newport Dunes. This privately owned facility is primarily an RV trailer park, but there are a limited number of tent sites for $22 a night. Don't expect the great outdoors, though: The sites are made of cement, and there aren't any trees or grassy knolls around. However, Newport Dunes is only minutes away from Balboa Island and the Peninsula—Newport Beach's liveliest hot spot. There are a few restaurants and stores near the campground, and the beach is only a 10-minute walk away. *1131 Back Bay Dr., Newport Beach, tel. 714/729–3863 or 800/288–0770. Off Jamboree Rd. Reservations advised. Wheelchair access.*

Ronald W. Caspers Wilderness Park. Believe it or not, no one under 18 is allowed to camp here because of the presence of mountain lions. Otherwise, this is a great place for car-campers and RV users. Tents are allowed, but the ground is both uneven and strewn with rocks. Hoards of retired folks seem to flock here, so excessive noise isn't tolerated. All campers must obtain a wilderness-use permit, which is sold on the premises for under $6. Rates are around $10 per vehicle per day. There are numerous hiking trails and scenic walks surrounding the campground, but the beach is a disappointing 3 miles away. *33401 Ortega Hwy., San Juan Capistrano, tel. 714/728–0235 or 714/831–2174. Off CA 74 (Ortega Hwy.) in San Juan Capistrano. 50 developed sites, none with hookups.*

San Clemente State Beach. The developed sites on the beach at San Clemente are open to both tent and RV campers, and additional undeveloped sites are available for those who don't mind sleeping on hilly ground without water hookups or fire rings. Peak-season (March–November) fees are $16, $20 with hookups. Facilities include picnic areas, hiking trails, and fishing. There is no food to be had here so bring your own. *3030 Av. del Presidente, San Clemente, tel. 714/492–3156. At the south end of San Clemente on I–5. 157 developed sites, 72 with hookups. Reservations advised.*

San Onofre State Beach. You may live longer if you avoid this campground. It's administered by Camp Pendleton, 1 mile from the San Onofre Nuclear Power Plant and 3 miles from a missile firing range. If this doesn't bother you, then the campground is much like every other in the area: It's on the beach, sites are open to both RV and tent campers, and there's fishing, hiking, and swimming. Peak season fees start at $16. Reservations recommended year-round. There aren't any stores nearby, so pack your own food. *3030 Av. del Presidente, c/o Pendleton Coast District, San Clemente, tel. 714/492–4872. 3 mi. south of San Clemente on I–5. 221 developed sites (162 for RVs and 59 for tents) with an additional 20 primitive walk-in sites during the summer. Outdoor cold showers available.*

ROUGHING IT Orange County's beaches may look tempting, but almost every nook and cranny has been built upon or bought up by local developers. Even if it looks deserted, odds are someone will ask you to leave if you pitch a tent on a beach. The only way to sleep for free in this area is in your car, but even then you'll be hard pressed to find a parking space where no one will bother you. Your best bet is along PCH, north of Huntington Beach. This part of the coast has the lowest concentration of homes and hotels, and parking is sometimes allowed overnight. Check the signs, because the police will ticket you if you're parked illegally.

● ● ● FOOD

Pacific Coast Highway has a tremendous number of seafood restaurants and steak houses in the $10–$15 range. The views are stunning, and the food is usually top-rate, but unfortunately almost always crowded. Summer weekends are the worst, and reservations are advised in the more snazzy joints. A word to the wise: Avoid Corona del Mar unless your last name is Rockefeller. Its uncrowded beaches are great for an afternoon's stroll, but its restaurants generally start at $15–$20 a person.

HUNTINGTON BEACH All hail **Johnny Rocket's** (300 Pacific Coast Hwy., tel. 714/536–2101)—a budget traveler's dream come true. This '50s-style diner in the **Pierside Pavilion** may not be the classiest place around, but it has a great selection of burgers and fries for under $5—a bargain price on an otherwise expensive stretch of highway. **Louises Trattoria** (302 PCH, at Main St., tel. 714/960–0996) offers tasty Italian dishes in the $8–$12 range with a good view of the ocean. Next door, the **Main Street Bar and Grill** (tel. 714/536–2111) has a large choice of hot sandwiches ($4–$7) and burgers. **Maxwell's** (317 PCH, tel. 714/536–2555) is Huntington Beach's most elegant restaurant. Its fresh seafood dinners are pricey at $12–$20, but its waterfront location and top-rate meals are good for a splurge. Reservations are recommended, and dress is semiformal (i.e., no bathing suits or ripped jeans).

LAGUNA BEACH Even though Laguna's hotels and galleries have "expensive" written all over them, finding a cheap, wholesome meal in Laguna is fairly easy. In the center of town you'll find more than 30 restaurants, ranging from the elegant to the greasy. **Adolfo's Cantina** (858 S. Coast Hwy., tel. 714/497–7883) offers drinks and burgers for under $6, while **Bennie The Bum's Diner** (238 Laguna Ave., tel. 714/497–4786) has a great selection of malts, shakes, and ice-cream sundaes for less than $5. Seafood lovers should head to **Wahoo's Fish Tacos** (1133 S. Coast Hwy., tel. 714/497–0033), a popular local hangout that serves the best—repeat—the best Mexican seafood on the coast. Another local favorite is the **White House** (340 S. Coast Hwy., tel. 714/494–8088), a sit-down restaurant specializing in everything from seafood pastas ($6–$9) to barbecued ribs ($10). After dinner, check out the White House's dance floor—there's live rock and

Top-40 music nightly (Wednesday is reggae night). If you're still stuck for an idea, simply walk along South Coast Highway until you stumble across something that suits your taste. Laguna is fairly small, and you can easily walk from one end of town to the other in under 40 minutes.

NEWPORT BEACH Newport's cheapest eateries are nestled between **Balboa Boulevard** and **Ocean Front Avenue,** one block from the beach and pier. Along with ice-cream parlors and yogurt shops, there's a decent selection of breakfast and burger joints here, and a healthy sampling of the town's bars. The **Daily Grill** (957 Newport Center Dr., tel. 714/644–2223), a slick, black-and-white-tile eatery, is a good place to rub elbows with Orange County's "in" crowd, but don't come here for cheap grub. A run-of-the-mill hamburger goes for $6, and a mediocre cup of coffee fetches a staggering $2. To make matters worse, it's located in the Fashion Island mall, a tedious hangout filled with teenage carousers. It's hokey, noisy, and always crowded, but **The Old Spaghetti Factory** (2110 Newport Blvd., tel. 714/675–8654) is still a budget traveler's nirvana. Nothing on the menu is more than $7, and the portions are huge. Don't expect authentic Italian cuisine, however, because this is pure Americana, popular with senior citizens and families of eight. Reservations are not accepted, so arrive early. The Spaghetti Factory turns into an overcrowded nightmare with lines out the door after 6 PM. They only accept cash, and they're only open between 5 and 10 most nights.

C'est Si Bon (149 Riverside Ave., off PCH, tel. 714/645–0447), a small seaside café, serves one of the best cups of coffee between Newport Beach and Paris. It also has an excellent selection of croissants, baguettes, imported cheeses, and pâté—an ideal place to wile away the hours on a lazy Sunday morning.

SAN CLEMENTE In San Clemente, check out the **Rib Trader** (911 S. El Camino Real, tel. 714/492–6665.). This place features barbecued ribs and chicken for under $10. There's live music every Friday and Saturday night in the bar. Downtown in the Old City Plaza, **R.G. Fish Co.** (111 W. Av. Palizada, tel. 714/366–1005) serves top-rate fresh fish and oysters. It's a bit generic looking, but you can get a hearty meal for under $8. The kitchen closes at 10 PM; its lively bar at 1 AM. For a truly tacky experience, make your way to the **Fisherman's Restaurant** (San Clemente Pier, tel. 714/498–6390), overlooking the water on San Clemente's pier. This standard, family-oriented place has as much ambience as a McDonald's, and it specializes in submediocre fish dinners ($15). It does have a stunning view of the ocean, however, which saves it from the trash heap.

SAN JUAN CAPISTRANO The **Capistrano Depot** (26701 Verdugo St., tel. 714/496–8181) doubles as an Amtrak station and a restaurant/jazz club. White tablecloths, linen napkins, and flowers grace the tables, while guests feast on rack of lamb ($11), prime rib ($9), filet mignon ($12), and scampi ($9). It's a bit expensive, but it's also a great place to splurge, to the strains of live jazz music. For Mexican-spiced seafood, **El Adobe** (31891 Camino Capistrano, tel. 714/493–1163) is calling your name. It's pricey, but there's no better place in town for fish tacos ($6) and homemade seafood chowder ($7). Otherwise, **Sarducci's** (31751 Camino Capistrano, tel. 714/493–9593) has a large selection of pasta, sandwiches, and salads, generally under $8. If you're in downtown San Juan, grab an outside table at Sarducci's and relax with one of their excellent espresso drinks.

SEAL BEACH Start with an Irish pub, fill it with blond beach bums and tanned lifeguards, add a dash of country music and seaside charm, and you'll end up with **Hennessy's Tavern** (140 Main St., tel. 213/598–4419)—one of Seal Beach's most popular hangouts. It has a full dinner menu (grilled chicken $9, steak sandwich $9.95, grilled shrimp $11), but most people prefer to pound down beers and make small talk at the bar. Hennessy's is always packed, but during the week it slows down just enough for a quiet, extremely pleasant meal. Otherwise, head to **Ruby's** (900A Ocean Ave., tel. 213/431–RUBY), a reasonably priced '50s-style diner at the end of Seal Beach's pier. At Ruby's, a hefty burger and side of fries fetches a mere $4.50.

● ● ● EXPLORING PACIFIC COAST HIGHWAY

To explore Orange County's coast you need four things: a car, the Pacific Coast Highway, comfortable walking shoes, and a healthy supply of sun block. PCH serves all the beach towns along the coast; if one seems dull, just hop in your car and head to another. Every 10 miles or so you'll stumble across a new beachfront community with its own unique character, look, and attractions. There's a smattering of restaurants and gas stations up and down the coast, all the way to San Diego. Public buses connect many of the towns along PCH but you should call the OCTD main office (tel. 714/636–7433) for schedules. In general, buses run every half-hour along the coast during summer, every one to two hours during winter, but don't depend on it. Like so many things in southern California, PCH was made for cars, and public buses have a nasty habit of ignoring the region's best sights.

When most coastal cities traded in their beach bungalows for minimalls and condominiums, Seal Beach fought—and continues to fight—against overzealous development.

SEAL BEACH With the blink of an eye you could easily miss this cozy seaside community, just off PCH, 10 miles south of Long Beach and the *Queen Mary.* Even though it has no real "tourist" attractions, Seal Beach has a wonderfully quirky, 1950s beach- town feel to it. Walking down **Main Street** toward the pier you get the sense that locals like their uncommercial streets and beaches just the way they are, even if it means losing out on heaps of tourist money. As a result, Seal Beach retains an unpretentious, backwater appeal, even though it's surrounded on all sides by ultrarich, ultradull, planned communities. Seal Beach is big enough to have a movie theater and its share of restaurants and shops along Main Street, yet for once you won't find a dense jumble of tacky tourist shops and overpriced French restaurants. Orange County's surfers and L.A.'s weekend refugees have recently begun to discover Seal Beach's appeal, but for the moment this quiet beachfront town remains one of southern California's best-kept secrets.

HUNTINGTON BEACH Huntington Beach, 12 miles south of Seal Beach on PCH, is a living museum of southern California beach life. Each September, surfers from around the world converge on the city for its annual surfing competition, held at the **River Jettys**—the unofficial name of its most popular surfing spot. Look for the River Jettys' sign on PCH, 3 miles north of the Wedge (*see below*). Huntington Beach's coast is strikingly beautiful and extremely popular, preferred by Orange County locals because of its nontouristy feel. Most of the people here went to the same schools and eat at the same country clubs, so you may feel a bit like an oddball if you're pale and don't have bleached-blond hair. For the landlubber, **Main Street** has a few restaurants, bars, and shops, while the **Pierside Pavilion,** across the street from the pier, has its share of tacky souvenir shops, clothing boutiques, and movie theaters.

NEWPORT BEACH Newport Beach, 5 miles south from Huntington Beach on PCH, is where the real action takes place on the coast—a 1-mile strip of beach bordered by swank restaurants, rowdy bars, and overpriced gift shops. It's an aloof bastion of high society, yacht clubs, and multimillion-dollar beachfront homes, but luckily it's less conservative than it sounds. Along with its large over-60 community, Newport also has one of the largest concentrations of under-25-year-olds in Orange County. During the summer Newport's beaches are swamped with visitors and locals alike, transforming the city's generally quiet boardwalk into an immensely crowded and colorful promenade.

The best way to explore the city is on foot, starting on the beach and working your way toward Newport's small but cozy downtown, just one block inland from the **Newport Pier.** If you want to blend in with the locals, rent a bicycle or a pair of Rollerblades from any of the shops along the waterfront. Otherwise, head for the **FunZone,** a miniamusement park next to the **Newport Pier**; just look for the old-fashioned Ferris wheel and the penny arcades. From here it's only a five-minute walk to Newport's liveliest night spot—the stretch of beach and bars between **Balboa Boulevard** and **Ocean Front Avenue.** Lunatics may want to check out **the Wedge** (at the end of Balboa Blvd., a 20-minute walk from the pier), one of the most famous—and dangerous—body-surfing breakwaters in the world. Be warned, however: The Wedge is for experienced swimmers only. Waves range anywhere from 8 to 25 feet, and the water is extremely shallow. Even so, the Wedge is the rage among body surfers (no surfboards allowed), and any day of the week you can watch the local surf-heads getting knocked silly by its infamous breakers.

Newport's other main attraction is **Balboa Island,** connected to the mainland by a three-car ferry. You can drive directly to the island via Jamboree Road, but the ferry—one of the few remaining in the state—offers significantly more atmosphere (65¢ per car; 25¢ per passenger); just follow the Balboa Ferry signs from PCH. Ferries leave every 20 minutes and land near the Balboa Pavilion, on Palm Avenue. Once over, there are more than 40 shops and restaurants to explore on the island's main drag, **Marine Avenue.** It's a bit touristy, but even so it has a unique seaside charm that most of California's overdeveloped beach towns lost years ago. Another of the island's many charms is the **Balboa Banana**—a frozen, chocolate-dipped creation that was invented here (so the locals claim) in the 1940s. Look for them in any of the ice-cream parlors along Marine Avenue. The **Victorian Balboa Pavilion** is the architectural jewel of the island. Built in 1902 as a bath and boat house, the pavilion was a haven for the big-band sound of the 1940s. Today, it's the place to go for harbor cruises ($12), deep-sea fishing and whale-watching boats ($15, December—February). Call **Davey's Locker** (309 Palm Ave., Suite C, tel. 714/673–1434) or the **Newport Landing** (309 Palm Ave., Suite F, tel. 714/675–0550) for schedules; both are located inside the pavilion (*see* Outdoor Activities, *below*).

Lido Island, a small but elegant isle in the center of Newport Harbor, boasts some of Orange County's most expensive and outlandish homes. It's a great spot for a walk or a quick drive, and it has an excellent view of the sailboats and catamarans in the channel. There are no tourist facilities, however, and all the beaches are privately owned. If you look like trouble, someone may ask you to leave. To reach Lido Island turn left off PCH at the Via Lido signal and follow it onto the island.

The **Upper Newport Bay Ecological Reserve** (end of Back Bay Dr., tel. 714/640–6746) offers year-round viewing of a protected, natural wetland habitat—home to more than 30 species of indigenous and migratory populations of gulls, geese, blue heron, light-footed clapper rails, and harlequin ducks. Some Newport Beach residents claim the reserve is a waste of good land (i.e., fit for a shopping mall), but luckily the reserve hasn't been built upon or developed—at least not yet. You'll get a good sense here of what the California coast looked like 100 years ago: lush flora and chattery fauna punctuated only by the peaceful rumble of the sea. The road that follows the shore is popular among bicyclists, joggers, and Rollerbladers. From PCH, turn onto Jamboree Road and veer left on Back Bay Drive; follow it to the end.

CORONA DEL MAR Corona del Mar, the "Crown of the Sea," is a small coastal community with an exceptional beach, only 3 miles south of Newport. You can walk clear out into the bay on a rough-and-tumble rock jetty and watch the local fishermen reel in barracuda and perch, or search for starfish and anemones in the tide pools around the breakwater. The town itself stretches for only a few blocks along Pacific Coast Highway, but some of the county's fanciest stores and ritziest restaurants are located here. **Sherman Library and Gardens** (2647 E. Coast Hwy., tel. 714/673–2261), a lush botanical garden and library specializing in Southwest flora, offers a diversion from the sun and sand. Colorful seasonal flowers adorn the grounds, and you can have pastries and coffee in the tea garden. Corona del Mar is off-limits to boats *and* it has two colorful reefs, making it an ideal place for snorkeling and diving. Unfortunately, there's no place that rents gear, so bring your own or stop first in Newport Beach's **Aquatic Center** (*see* Outdoor Activities, *below*). Corona del Mar's golden beaches are ideal for a late-afternoon walk, but past sunset there isn't much to do. Unless you don't mind paying $50 for a suit-and-tie meal in one of the city's fancy restaurants, you're better off stopping here for an hour or two on your way somewhere else.

LAGUNA BEACH Laguna Beach, 17 miles south of Corona del Mar, is home to one of southern California's largest gay communities and one of the state's largest artist colonies. As a result, Laguna has a refreshingly diverse and progressive feel to it. Even though it offers some of the best surfing in the county, don't expect to find too many bleached-blond surf daddies here. Being called conservative, needless to say, is about the worst insult imaginable here. That's not to say that you won't find the upper classes and the BMW crowd well-represented, because you certainly will. Rather, Laguna has somehow managed to maintain a reasonable balance between heavy commercialization and small-town charm and between $100-a-night hotels and unpretentious art galleries.

Laguna is an "alternative" city tailor-made for artists, hippies, and counterculture dropouts, and its residents don't take kindly to fraternity antics or gay-bashing.

If you're in the neighborhood during July and August, make every effort to see the unspeakably beautiful **Pageant of the Masters,** where actors re-create on stage, in stunning detail, some of the world's most famous paintings. If you're into art, also be sure to visit at least one of Laguna's 60 art galleries; or take a quick tour of the **Laguna Beach Museum of Art** (307 Cliff Dr., tel. 714/494–6531), near Heisler Park. Its permanent collection is less than impressive, but some of its temporary shows are quite spectacular, showcasing the works of offbeat and ultramodern artists from the Laguna area. For a truly sublime (i.e., nauseating) experience, make a detour to the **Ritz Carlton** (33533 Ritz Carlton Dr., tel. 714/240–2000), the classiest hotel for miles around. It's become the watering hole of choice for Orange County's elite, and if you're the sort of person who has an answering machine attached to the car phone, you'll feel at home here. Even better, it's also a great place to gawk at the rich and ludicrous; if you're feeling particularly absurd, rent a sports jacket from the concierge (really) and take afternoon tea ($8) in the Ritz Carlton's posh outdoor patio to the strains of live piano music.

At the other end of the spectrum is the **Wild Rivers Water Park,** 12 miles inland from Laguna proper. With over 40 water slides, inner-tube tracks, and high-diving platforms you won't easily get bored here, and on a hot summer day you'll be thankful for a chance to swim in its ice-cold water. At $16 a head, however, it's a bit overpriced. Save your cash and take a dip in the ocean instead. Wild Rivers is very popular with 6- to 16-year-olds, and on most days it's jam-packed with screaming kids trying to cut their way to the front of the line. *8770 Irvine Center Dr., Laguna Hills, tel. 714/768–WILD. Open mid-May– mid-June, weekends 11–5; mid-June–Labor Day, daily 10–8.*

SAN JUAN CAPISTRANO You might think that some of Laguna's progressive appeal would have rubbed off on San Juan Capistrano, only 6 miles to the south, but it's hard to imagine a city as quiet and completely forgettable as San Juan—except, of course, San Clemente (*see below*). San Juan's beaches are pleasant and clean, but for some reason no one bothers much with this small, primarily middle-class community. Groups of surfers sometimes meet on its empty and peaceful beaches at dawn, but otherwise most people see San Juan only from the freeway.

In a sense, however, that's too bad because San Juan does have a few worthwhile attractions. The **Mission San Juan Capistrano** (at the intersection of Camino Capistrano and Ortega Highway, tel. 714/493–1424), founded in 1776 by Father Junipero Serra, was once the major Roman Catholic outpost between Los Angeles and San Diego. Although the original stone church lies in ruins, thanks to an 1812 earthquake, many of the mission's adobe buildings have been restored. Of particular interest is the impressive Serra Chapel, believed to be the oldest building still in use in California. On St. Joseph's Day (March 19) the mission hosts one of the most popular *Fiesta de las Golindrinas* (The Swallows' Festival) celebrations, in anticipation of the return of the swallows from Argentina. Near the mission is the striking **San Juan Capistrano Library** (31495 El Camino Real), built in 1983 by architect Michael Graves. Besides its voluminous library (open to the public), it has a wonderfully peaceful and shaded courtyard with private places for reading. The library is open Monday–Thursday 10–9, Friday and Saturday 10–5.

SAN CLEMENTE The southernmost city in Orange County, San Clemente is probably best remembered as the site of **Casa Pacifica,** the Western White House during the Nixon years. The house, on a massive 25.4-acre estate, is visible from the beach; just look up to the cliffs. Besides Casa Pacifica, however, there isn't much to detain you in San Clemente. Because of its proximity to **Camp Pendleton,** one of the largest military bases in the state, it's overrun with soldiers and army bars and a fair share of flag-waving patriots whose idea of fun is sitting at home with a six-pack watching Persian Gulf reruns on television. San Clemente is only 15 miles south of Laguna Beach on I-5, but in lifestyle, spirit, and appeal it's a world apart. The one nice thing about San Clemente, though, is its beaches: clean, undeveloped, and virtually deserted. If summer crowds are grating on your nerves, make a beeline for San Clemente. There's an excellent campground (*see* Where to Sleep, *above*) on the nearby San Onofre State Beach.

CHEAP THRILLS

The annual **Grunion Run** is a southern California tradition, held every summer along beaches up and down the coast. Locals come out to the beach between 1 AM and 4 AM to catch grunions—small fish that mate on the sand—with their hands. The grunion aren't as punctual as the local tourist offices would like (the "run" occurs anywhere between July and late August), so ask around.

For the cheapest of thrills, take a tour through the **Fashion Island Mall,** one of the largest shopping malls in the United States. It's depressingly commercial and extremely tacky, but it does have countless gourmet-foods shops, restaurants, movie theaters, and big-name department stores (I. Magnin, Neiman Marcus, Robinson's, and the Broadway). Don't miss the **Irvine Ranch Farmers' Market,** on the first level of the Atrium Court, a high-quality specialty gourmet store. *Fashion Island: Newport Center Dr., off PCH in Newport Beach.*

FESTIVALS

HUNTINGTON BEACH In October, join with the locals as they celebrate **Oktoberfest** with German food, music, and—of course—beer. Lots of it. Events are held throughout the city and on the beach, and the Huntington Beach Chamber of Commerce (*see* Tourist Information, *above*) offers a complete listing of Oktoberfest insanity. The **Huntington Beach Summer Surf Championship** is held every July, when the world's top surfers flock to this nationally-televised surf showdown.

LAGUNA BEACH Laguna's many festivals give it a worldwide reputation in the arts community. During July and August, the Sawdust Festival, and the incredibly beautiful Pageant of the Masters take place. The **Pageant of the Masters** (tel. 714/494–1147) is by far Laguna's most impressive event, where live models and carefully orchestrated backgrounds are arranged in striking mimicry of famous paintings. Participants must hold a perfectly still pose while they're on stage and, though you may not realize it at first, every figure in these life-size paintings is alive—from the man in the bathtub in David's *Death of Marat* to the picnickers in Seurat's *Sunday Afternoon on the Island of La Grande Jatte.*

The Waves are Truly "Rad"

San Clemente's beaches would be perfect if it weren't for the San Onofre Nuclear Power Plant, located 3 miles down the coast. This twin-domed power plant is billed as "the safest nuclear station in the world," but it still lends an eerie feeling to the nearby beach, where surfers surf nonetheless. There has never been a reported accident or radiation leak here, but environmentalists claim that even a small leak could render nearly 30% of southern California completely useless and barren—a somber thought to ponder while swimming within view of San Onofre. If you're curious about the station or about nuclear energy in general, the San Onofre Nuclear Information Center (tel. 714/368–1350) is a good place to start. It's located next to the plant, just off PCH. For security reasons, however, walk-in visitors are not allowed; all tours must be arranged in advance over the phone.

It's an impressive effort, requiring hours of training and rehearsal by the 400 or so residents who volunteer each year.

The **Sawdust Festival** (tel. 714/494–3030), which takes place around the same time, is not an event that pays tribute to wood shavings, but a raucous "Auld Tyme Faire" featuring handmade arts and crafts, strolling minstrels, mimes, and hearty tankers of ye olde ale and wine.

Parking for these events may be limited, and it's recommended that you park your car in one of the clearly marked lots along Laguna Canyon Road. They're crowded, but considering how bad Laguna's parking situation is during the summer, they're your best hope. There's a 75¢ shuttle that runs between the lots and the festivals. Admission generally runs between $2 and $4, and advance ticket purchases are advised.

SEAL BEACH Watch world-famous sculptors compete in Seal Beach's **Sandcastle Contest,** held the last weekend of August or the first in September. In late August also look for the **Seal Beach Volleyball Invitational,** when world-class competitors come here for a week of two-person and team volleyball. Call the Seal Beach Chamber of Commerce (*see* Tourist Informaiton, *above*) for exact dates of both events.

● ● ● AFTER DARK

Most of the action in Orange County takes place in Newport Beach, the oceanside playground of lascivious teenagers and tanned surf bums. Be warned, however, that pounding drinks, picking up on people, throwing around sexual innuendos, and drinking constitute the primary nighttime pursuits. If bar-hopping and night- clubbing aren't your style, you can always head to the beach for a stroll at dusk or take a slow drive along the coast.

Some beaches allow barbecues and campfires in designated areas, so find a quiet spot at sunset and build a fire with friends.

BARS **The Cannery.** This is a crowded Newport Beach bar with "karaoke" performances Thursday through Sunday. If you've never seen karaoke, watch out: The bar will play a recording of almost any song you could imagine, minus the vocal tracks, then they'll coax you on stage to sing along. It's a bit ridiculous, but after a few drinks no one seems to mind. Happy hour is on weekdays from 4 to 6:30. Cover charge is $3 Friday and $5 on Saturday. *3010 Lafayette Ave., tel. 714/675–5777. Wheelchair access.*

The Red Onion. This restaurant is part of a state-wide chain—a characterless and rather dull group of eateries that should be avoided when possible. However, this particular one features live music nightly, and over the past years it's become one of the most popular nightspots in the county. It's a meat market, to be sure, but it's usually filled with innocuous intoxicated post-grads out looking for a good time; a good place to socialize with the under-30 crowd. Happy hour is on weekdays from 3 to 6. There's a $5 cover charge on Saturday. *2406 Newport Blvd., Newport Beach, tel. 714/675–2244. Open daily 11 AM–1 AM. Restaurant has wheelchair access, the bar doesn't.*

The Studio Cafe. Jazz lovers should make a beeline for this place. It presents top-rate jazz and blues musicians nightly, and it's mostly filled with people who don't spend 95% of their time at the beach—a rare find in Orange County. Even better, the Studio is definitely not a pick-up joint, which means you don't have to worry about creeps pestering you all evening. The cafe also has a full-service bar and dining room. If you're hungry, try their excellent grilled shrimp platter ($9) or the barbecued ribs ($11). *100 S. Main St., Newport Beach, tel. 714/675–7760. Open daily 11:30 AM–1 AM.*

The Warehouse. If you're looking for a no-frills bar that serves cheap drinks to a lively crowd—look no further. There's live entertainment Thursday–Sunday from 9 to midnight, and it's usually filled with genial, slightly inebriated locals. Happy hour is weekdays from 4:30 to 7:30. Thursday is $2 drink night. The cover charge is $3 on Thursday, $5 on Friday and Saturday. *3450 Via Osporo, Lido Village, Newport Beach, tel. 714/673–4700. Wheelchair access.*

OUTDOOR ACTIVITIES • • •

It doesn't take a genius to realize that the most popular outdoor activity on the coast is beach bumming. From volleyball to paddle ball, from sailing to biking and swimming to sunbathing, there's always something happening at one of the region's numerous beaches. All you need to join in is a towel, a tube of sun block, and perhaps a good book.

BICYCLING/ROLLER-SKATING Bicycling and roller-skating (or, more likely, Rollerblading) are two of the most popular ways to get around, and a beachfront bike path spans the whole distance from Seal Beach to San Diego, with some minor breaks. Most beaches have rental stands, but try the **Laguna Cyclery** (tel. 714/552–1798) in Laguna Beach. It rents bicycles, roller skates, and in-line skates, generally for under $15 a day. For avid bicycle riders, the stretch of coast south of San Clemente is prime terrain. Camp Pendleton welcomes cyclists to use its roads, but don't be surprised if you see a troop helicopter taking off right beside you. With three mountain ranges, five lakes, and 250 miles of roads, this is the country's largest Marine Corps base and maneuvers are held on a regular basis.

FISHING Fishing is allowed from most piers on the coast, but you'll need to pick up a permit ($6) at any local sporting good store. If big game is what you're after, the **Newport Landing** (309 Palm Ave., Suite F, tel. 714/675–0550), located in the Balboa Pavilion (*see* Exploring Pacific Coast Highway, *above*), organizes deep-sea trips. Half-day excursions cost $20, full-day $32 , and for an additional $7 they can provide all necessary equipment.

SCUBA DIVING AND SNORKELING In Newport Beach, the **Aquatic Center** (4537 W. PCH, tel. 714/650–5440) has scuba and snorkel gear. Scuba divers must bring a photo I.D. and certification papers; complete rentals are $50 a day. They also organize group dives along the coast and to Catalina for $55. Call their 24-hour hot line (tel. 714/650–5783) for diving conditions.

SURFING **Bruce Jones Surfboards** (16927 PCH, Sunset Beach, tel. 310/592–2314) rents surfboards for $12 per half-day, $20 full, provided you have a valid photo I.D. and a credit card. Novices get soft boards, so you can learn to surf without getting beaten silly by it. In Dana Point, **Hobie Sorts** (34195 PCH, tel. 714/496–1251) rents surfboards ($20) and body boards ($16).

WHALE WATCHING If you're in the area between January and March, check out the gray whale migration—when herds of gray whales head from Alaska down to Mexico along the California coast. Whale-watching boats leave from both **Davey's Locker** (309 Palm Ave., Suite C, Balboa Island, tel. 714/673–1434) at the Balboa Pavilion (*see* Exploring Pacific Coast Highway, *above*) and **Redondo Sport Fishing** (233 N. Harbor Dr., Redondo Beach, tel. 310/372–2111). Cruises generally last two hours and cost $12–$18.

SAN DIEGO 11

By Michael Rubiano

Lying close to the Mexican border, San Diego enjoys the best weather of any city in America. Cool ocean breezes and more than 300 days of sunshine a year give San Diego a wonderful Mediterranean climate. And like many Mediterranean cities, San Diego moves at a pace that would have New Yorkers beating their heads against the palm trees; Woody Allen couldn't live here if you fed him nothing but valium and horse tranquilizers. But then, it's tough to picture Woody Allen with a neon surfboard tucked under his arm. When most people think of southern California, they conjure up images of surf, sun, and sand (and, if they've watched enough beer commercials, lots of gorgeous blondes); San Diego is one place where this stereotype definitely holds more than an element of truth. The residents of the city spend a great deal of their time outside: Even at night, you'll find a lot of people opting for bonfires on the beach rather than hanging out in nightclubs. And why wouldn't you want to be outside? The city boasts miles of superb beaches, a year-round explosion of flowers and fruits, and—just a few hours' drive inland—pine-covered mountains and empty expanses of desert.

But the future of San Diego is uncertain. A question hovers over the city like an ever-thickening cloud of smog: Will San Diego turn into another Los Angeles? Although the idea of such a transformation may not strike visitors as undesirable, it strikes terror in the hearts of most San Diegans—who give thanks for the huge marine training facility at Camp Pendleton, which insulates the city from the mall sprawl of Orange County to the north. Nonetheless, with one of the highest growth rates of any city in the country and the increasing suburbanization of its outlying areas, San Diego is in real danger of becoming another snarl of concrete, neon, and traffic jams.

The population explosion is fueled both by cold-weather refugees from the eastern states and the continuing influx of Latinos. The border near San Diego is a popular crossing point for thousands of Mexicans and Central Americans entering the United States illegally. Whether they walk down the beach or clamber through holes in the fence, the immigrants are drawn to the United States by the possibility of finding work. They're so numerous that road signs now warn motorists to be on the lookout for families running across the freeways—several people are killed this way each year.

Just 150 years ago, Americans would have been considered the illegal immigrants. But in 1848, after a brief war, Mexico surrendered California to the United States in the Treaty of Guadalupe Hidalgo. During the negotiations, it was a toss-up whether San Diego would fall on the Mexican or American side of the border. Today, the Mexican influence is still very strong, through the architecture, the cuisine—San Diego overflows with *taquerias*—and the sizable Latino population.

San Diego

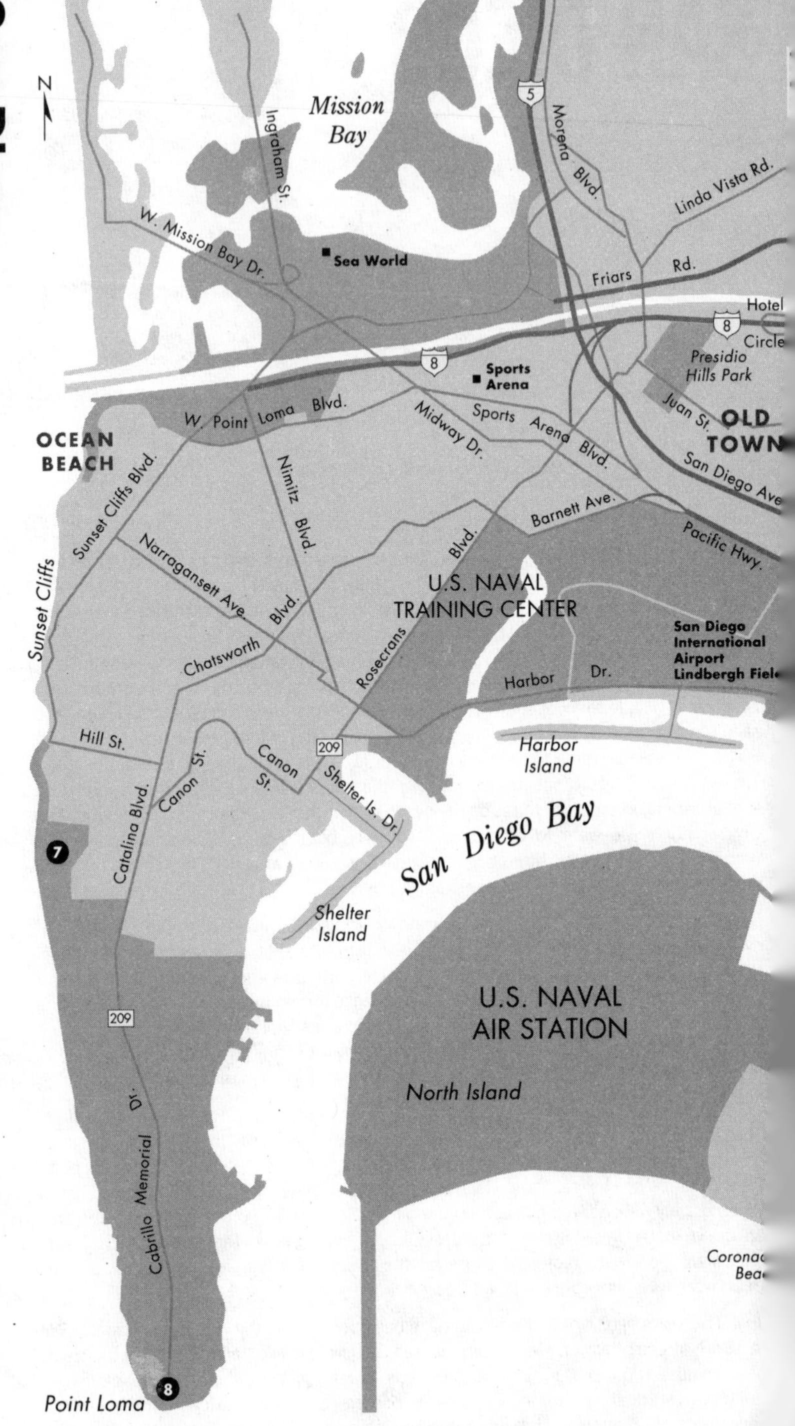

N
Mission Bay
Ingraham St.
Morena Blvd.
Linda Vista Rd.
W. Mission Bay Dr.
Sea World
Friars Rd.
Hotel Circle
Presidio Hills Park
Sports Arena
W. Point Loma Blvd.
Midway Dr.
Sports Arena Blvd.
Juan St.
OLD TOWN
San Diego Ave.
OCEAN BEACH
Sunset Cliffs Blvd.
Nimitz Blvd.
Barnett Ave.
Pacific Hwy.
Narragansett Ave.
Rosecrans Blvd.
U.S. NAVAL TRAINING CENTER
Sunset Cliffs
San Diego International Airport Lindbergh Fiel
Chatsworth Blvd.
Harbor Dr.
Hill St.
209
Harbor Island
Canon St.
Shelter Is. Dr.
Catalina Blvd.
San Diego Bay
7
Shelter Island
U.S. NAVAL AIR STATION
North Island
Cabrillo Memorial Dr.
Corona
Bea
8
Point Loma
5
8

San Diego

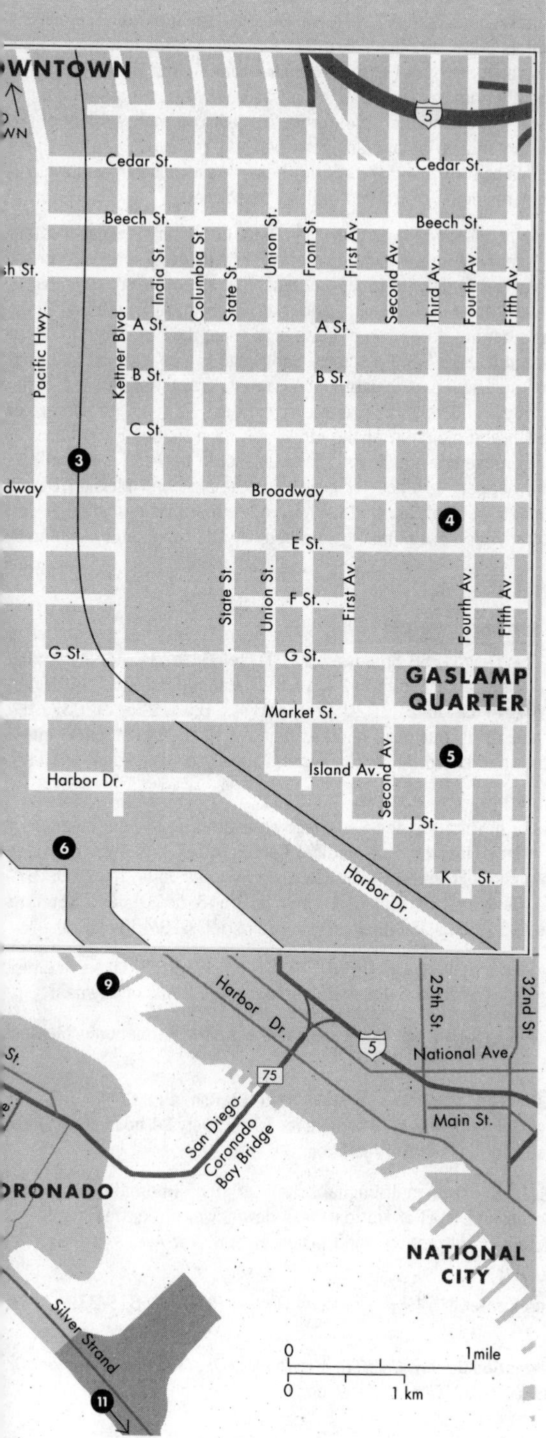

Cabrillo National Monument/Old Point Loma Lighthouse, **8**
Embarcadero, **2**
Gaslamp Quarter Foundation/William Heath Davis House, **5**
Horton Plaza, **4**
Hotel del Coronado, **10**
Old Ferry Landing, **9**
San Diego Maritime Museum, **1**
Santa Fe Depot, **3**
Seaport Village, **6**
Silver Strand State Beach, **11**
Sunset Cliffs Park, **7**

San Diego was taken by force, and much of its economy still relies on force. The city harbors a massive naval base, home to the 11th Naval District. Warships are visible in the bay every day, as are fighters overhead. The navy's Top Gun program, made famous in the movie that stars Tom Cruise, operates out of the Miramar Naval Air Station near La Jolla. If you're from San Diego, all this military activity is a reassuring sight; if you're from northern California, it's just one more symbol of the military-industrial complex gone berserk. You won't find too many people beefing about the military here—it's a conservative town and many residents are retired military personnel.

The Gulf War magnified the enormous political gulf separating southern and northern California: San Francisco and Berkeley proclaimed themselves safe havens for deserters while San Diego nearly drowned in a sea of yellow ribbons.

Despite the enormous growth, San Diego has so far managed to retain its beauty. With the exception of a 7-Eleven every few miles or so, the terrain and the Mexican-influenced architecture conspire to give the city an enduring charm and individualism. Although San Diego has a central downtown of glass high rises, the city doesn't revolve around it. Like San Francisco, San Diego is a collection of distinct communities and neighborhoods that crawl around the hills, canyons, and valleys. At one end you have La Jolla, an enclave of wealth and glamour; at the other, you have Balboa Park, home of many museums and a world-famous zoo; in between are neighborhoods like Hillcrest, the happening place for gays and lesbians, and Mission Bay, a playground for tourists and the site of Sea World. If you're like many visitors, though, you don't give a damn about anything but plunking your body on the beach and listening to the crash of the surf.

Basics

AMERICAN EXPRESS American Express has two offices in San Diego (258 Broadway, 92101, tel. 619/234–4482; Mission Valley Center, Suite 1424, 1640 N. Camino Del Rio, 92108, tel. 619/297–8101) and one in La Jolla (1020 Prospect St., Box 1925, 92037, tel. 619/459–4161). Call ahead as business hours differ. All three accept client mail. Correspondence should be addressed: American Express Travel Service, Attention Client Mail.

EMERGENCIES Major hospitals in the San Diego area all have 24-hour emergency rooms. A brief listing: **Mercy Hospital and Medical Center** (4077 5th Ave., tel. 619/260–7000), **Scripps Memorial Hospital** (9888 Genesee Ave., La Jolla, tel. 619/457–6150), **UCSD Medical Center** (225 Dickinson, tel. 619/543–6400), and **Veterans Administration Hospital** (3350 La Jolla Village Dr., La Jolla, tel. 619/453–7500).

DENTISTS If you need a dentist, call **800/DENTIST,** a dentist-referral service that provides information on types of service, location, and accepted forms of payment.

PHARMACIES A 24-hour pharmacy is located at the **Kaiser Permanente Medical Center** (4647 Zion Ave., tel. 619/528–7770).

LUGGAGE STORAGE The downtown **Amtrak Train Station** and **Greyhound Bus Station** (*see* Coming and Going, *below*) have lockers for $1 for every 24 hours. San Diego International Airport does not have locker facilities.

TOURIST INFORMATION The multilingual staff at the **International Visitor Information Center,** on the first level of Horton Plaza downtown, offers free maps and information on local activities, attractions, and places to stay. *1st Ave. and F St., tel. 619/236–1212. Open daily 8:30–5.*

Balboa Park Information Center. *1549 El Prado, in Balboa Park, tel. 619/239–0512. Open daily 9:30–4.*

Mission Bay Visitor Information Center. *2588 E. Mission Bay Dr., take the Clairemont Dr. exit off I–5 , tel. 619/276–8200. Open daily 9–dusk.*

COMING AND GOING ● ● ●

BY PLANE **San Diego International Airport** (tel. 619/231–5220), commonly known as Lindbergh Field, lies close to downtown. Although the airport does not provide lockers, it's open 24 hours and has restaurants, snack bars, and automated teller machines, as well as a **Traveler's Aid** information desk that's open until 11 PM. Airlines that serve Lindbergh Field include Alaska Airlines (tel. 800/426–0333), America West (tel. 619/560–0727), American (tel. 619/232–4051), British Airways (tel. 800/247–9297), Continental (tel. 800/525–0280), Delta (tel. 619/235–4344), Northwest (tel. 619/239–0488), Skywest (tel. 800/453–9417), Southwest (tel. 619/232–1221), and USAir (tel. 800/428–4322).

AIRPORT TRANSPORT **San Diego Transit Bus 2** (a.k.a. the "30th and Adams" bus) goes from the airport to downtown in about 20 minutes. The fare is $1 and buses leave every 20–30 minutes from 5:30 AM to midnight. The buses drop you off at Third and Broadway downtown, near Horton Plaza, Seaport Village, the Amtrak and Greyhound terminals, and the AYH hostel. In addition, the **Super Shuttle Airport Limousine** (tel. 619/278–8877) can whisk you downtown in about 15 minutes for $6 per person. Super Shuttle runs 24 hours a day. Taxis downtown cost $6–$7, plus tip.

BY TRAIN Eight Amtrak trains travel daily between San Diego and Los Angeles; the first train leaves at 5 AM, the last at 9 PM. The one-way fare to L.A. is $24, $38 round-trip. The **Amtrak Station** (a.k.a. Santa Fe Depot) is centrally located and easily accessible by bus and trolley. The station is open 24 hours, but it's probably not safe enough to crash here. You can store your luggage for a buck (tel. 619/239–9989). A tourist booth offers information on area attractions and trips to Mexico. *1050 Kettner Blvd., at Broadway. For reservations and train schedules, tel. 800/872–7245 or 619/239–9021 for recorded information. Ticket office open 5 AM–9 PM.*

BY BUS The **Greyhound** station (120 W. Broadway, tel. 619/239–9171) is a mess, but at least it's in the heart of the downtown lodging area, just a few blocks east of the train station. You can rent lockers for $1 a day. For those trying to save money, the station is open 24 hours, but your bedfellows are likely to be transients looking for handouts. Several buses leave for L.A. daily—a one-way ticket to L.A. is $13, round-trip is $24.

BY CAR If you arrive by car in San Diego, you'll quickly find these truths to be annoyingly ubiquitous: Parking is a bitch; rush-hour traffic is a bitch; and merging on the freeway can be deadly. In terms of getting in and out of the city, I–5, which runs from the state of Washington all the way to Mexico, passes through the heart of downtown San Diego and terminates in San Ysidro at the U.S.–Mexico border. Farther inland, I–15 acts as the unofficial eastern border of the city, and heads northeast through San Bernardino to Las Vegas. I–8, the main east–west thoroughfare, starts at the Mission Bay area (where the beaches and Sea World are) and travels toward the desert and eventually Tucson.

"Parking is a bitch; rush-hour traffic is a bitch; and merging on the freeway can be deadly."

GETTING AROUND ● ● ●

In San Diego, you don't absolutely need a car to get around although it will save you a lot of time—if you can ever park the damn thing. Balboa Park, the Gaslamp Quarter downtown, Hillcrest, and La Jolla are all easy to explore on foot. In La Jolla, you might want to rent a bicycle as the area is more spread out than downtown. You will definitely need a car, though, to explore the North County coastal cities or if you head inland to Julian and the desert.

Getting around the downtown grid is relatively easy. Streets running north–south are numbered consecutively, starting with First Avenue at the western side of Horton Plaza. East–west streets are named alphabetically, starting with A Street in the north and ending at L Street in the south. There are some exceptions: Broadway is where you would expect to find D Street, Market Street is where H Street should be, and Island Avenue replaces

I Street. North of A, the streets are named alphabetically after trees, starting with Ash Street and ending with Walnut.

BY BUS **San Diego Transit** is cheap and reliable, and it does a good job of covering the city. Instead of fussing with bus maps, call the folks at the **San Diego Transit Information Line** (tel. 619/233–3004; open 5:30 AM–8:30 PM), to find out what buses you need to catch to get where you're going. Otherwise, pick up a bus map at the **International Visitor Information Center** (1st Ave. and F St., tel. 619/236–1212). The fare for regular buses is $1.25, $1.50–$2 for express buses. If you have to switch buses, be sure you get a transfer ticket when you first board. You can buy several types of bus passes at the **Transit Store** (449 Broadway at 5th Ave., tel. 619/234–1060), as well as maps and bus schedules. The $4 **Day Tripper Transit Pass** gives you unlimited use of city buses, the San Diego Trolley, and the San Diego–Coronado Ferry for one day. The **Handicap Pass** ($10) allows disabled passengers to pay only 60¢ for each ride on city and county mass transit.

Sometime in the near future, the Great America Plaza (on Broadway near the waterfront) will become the central depot for the train, bus, and trolley systems, replacing the Santa Fe Depot and other transit centers. When this happens, much of what we say in the Coming and Going and Getting Around sections becomes bunk.

Buses with a wheelchair-lift serve each bus route at least once an hour. In addition, **Dial-a-Ride** provides special services, including pick-up, for qualifying disabled passengers. *In San Diego, tel. 619/533–4671; in North County, tel. 619/726–1111 or 619/436–5632; in Coronado, East County, Imperial Beach, and National City, tel. 619/297–3947; in Chula Vista, tel. 619/425–7433.*

North County Transit District provides service from Oceanside to La Jolla, and inland to Escondido. The fare is 85¢. For route information from coastal cities call 619/722–6283; from inland cities, dial 619/743–6283. Other regional bus companies that serve areas outside the city include **National City Transit** (tel. 619/474–7505) for National City; **Chula Vista Transit** (tel. 619/233–3004) for Bonita and Chula Vista; **The Strand Route** (tel. 619/232–8505) for Coronado, the Silver Strand, and Imperial Beach; and **Northeast Rural Bus System** (tel. 619/765–0145) and **Southeast Rural Bus System** (tel. 619/478–5875) for access to rural county towns.

BY CAR Visitors who buy into the California belief that an automobile is as important as water and oxygen are for human survival can rent one fairly cheaply. No matter whom you rent from, though, avoid driving during rush hour—it's a contradiction in terms. Budget rental companies include **General** (tel. 800/327–7607) and **Alamo** (tel. 800/327–9633). The big rental companies have offices at the airport and in the Hotel Circle. Some rental companies, including **Avis** (tel. 800/331–1212) and **Courtesy** (tel. 619/232–3191), will allow you to drive their cars across the Mexican border, but you must ask permission and purchase Mexican auto insurance.

BY FERRY The **San Diego–Coronado Ferry** leaves from the Broadway Pier on the hour from 10 to 10 daily, and drops you at Coronado's Old Ferry Landing. The fare is $1.60 each way.

BY TAXI The average fare is $1.60 for the first mile, and $1.50 for each additional mile, which is worthwhile if you've got a group of four or five. Some taxi companies accept major credit cards, but call ahead to check. Cab companies include **Co-op Silver Cabs** (tel. 619/280–5555), **Coast Cab** (tel. 619/226–8294), **Coronado Cab** (tel. 619/435–6211), **La Jolla Cab** (tel. 619/453–4222), **Orange Cab** (tel. 619/291–3333), and **Yellow Cab** (tel. 619/234–6161).

BY TROLLEY The shiny red cars of the **San Diego Trolley** (tel. 619/231–8549) are a pleasant way to get around San Diego. The trolley's three different lines begin at the Santa Fe Depot (Kettner Blvd. and Broadway). The **East Line** serves the East County cities of La Mesa, Lemar Grove, and El Cajon. The **Bayside Trolley Line** provides service to the San Diego Convention Center, Seaport Village, and the historic Gaslamp Quarter. The **South Line** should be renamed the "TJ Express," since it leads to the U.S.–Mexico border, where Tijuana is but a hole in the fence away. Trolleys run every 15 minutes from 5 AM to 8 PM, and every 30 minutes until after midnight (whereupon you should check a schedule). Fares range from 50¢ to $2 each way, depending on the distance traveled. Purchase tickets from the vending machines at each station before boarding. For information about trolley passes, *see* Getting Around by Bus, *above*.

Where to Sleep

San Diego has plenty of budget hotels, many of which are easily accessible by public transport. The big question in choosing a place to crash is location: Do you want to be by the beach or would you prefer to be in the center of all the other action? Be aware, though, that the cheapest places may be in relatively deserted areas, so be careful at night and while traveling alone. Few budget motels have wheelchair access, although most youth hostels do; be sure to call ahead to check. San Diego slaps a 9% lodging tax on hotel rooms, and many hotels require a key deposit.

DOWNTOWN • • •

If you don't insist on being near the beach, then stay downtown—it's the happening spot for nightlife and shopping. Not only will you be within spitting distance of Horton Plaza, the Embarcadero, and the Gaslamp Quarter, you'll also be able to reach Balboa Park, the zoo, and Hillcrest easily.

San Diegan teenagers use the terms BFE ("Butt-Fucked Egypt") or "Hell's Half-Acre" to describe places that are out in the boonies. These terms are of course relative, depending on where you are. For example, the residential area south of San Diego is in BFE unless, of course, you live there. For young teenagers though, everywhere is in BFE.

UNDER $25 **Maryland Hotel.** This place in the Gaslamp Quarter is really a retirement home posing as a hotel, and you should only stay here if you're desperate. Consider splurging for a room with a private bathroom unless you want to share with an octogenarian who might drop his dentures in your contact-lens solution. Rooms with bath are $22; with common bath $19; and with no bath $17. Weekly rates also available. *630 F St., tel. 619/239–9243. 2 blocks south of Broadway, and 2 blocks east of Horton Plaza.*

UNDER $35 **Downtown Inn Hotel.** Conveniently located a block east of the Gaslamp Quarter, the Downtown Inn Hotel is mostly a residence hotel. It's also uncomfortable: Beds sag in the middle and the ceiling fans just don't beat the heat. Still, the rates are dirt cheap—so cheap that roaches have decided to check in as well. Some rooms are wheelchair accessible, but they're often rented to long-term customers. *660 G St., tel. 619/238–4100. From Amtrak or Greyhound take an eastbound Broadway bus to 7th Ave. and walk 2 blocks south on 7th St.*

Hotel Churchill. The trolley runs right in front of this hotel, which is about five blocks east of Horton Plaza. The lobby and rooms look as if they were designed by Walt Disney on speed. Check out the Medieval Castle lobby before heading to the Chrome-A-Rama room (this is the place to bring your date if he/she can suck the chrome off a bumper). Perhaps the themes are meant to distract guests from noticing the filth. Rates for rooms with common baths start around $27 for one person and $32 for two. Theme rooms start at $42 (yes, you pay extra for such elegance). *827 C St., tel. 619/234–5186. From Amtrak or Greyhound, take trolley to 8th and C Sts. Laundry facilities.*

La Pensione Hotel. Rooms at this clean residential hotel are quite pleasant, and come complete with a microwave and fridge. Doubles are $29 daily, or $110 weekly. The hotel is six blocks north of Broadway on Columbia Street, close to the Embarcadero. *1654 Columbia St., tel. 619/232–3400. Laundry room, wheelchair access.*

San Diego Lodging

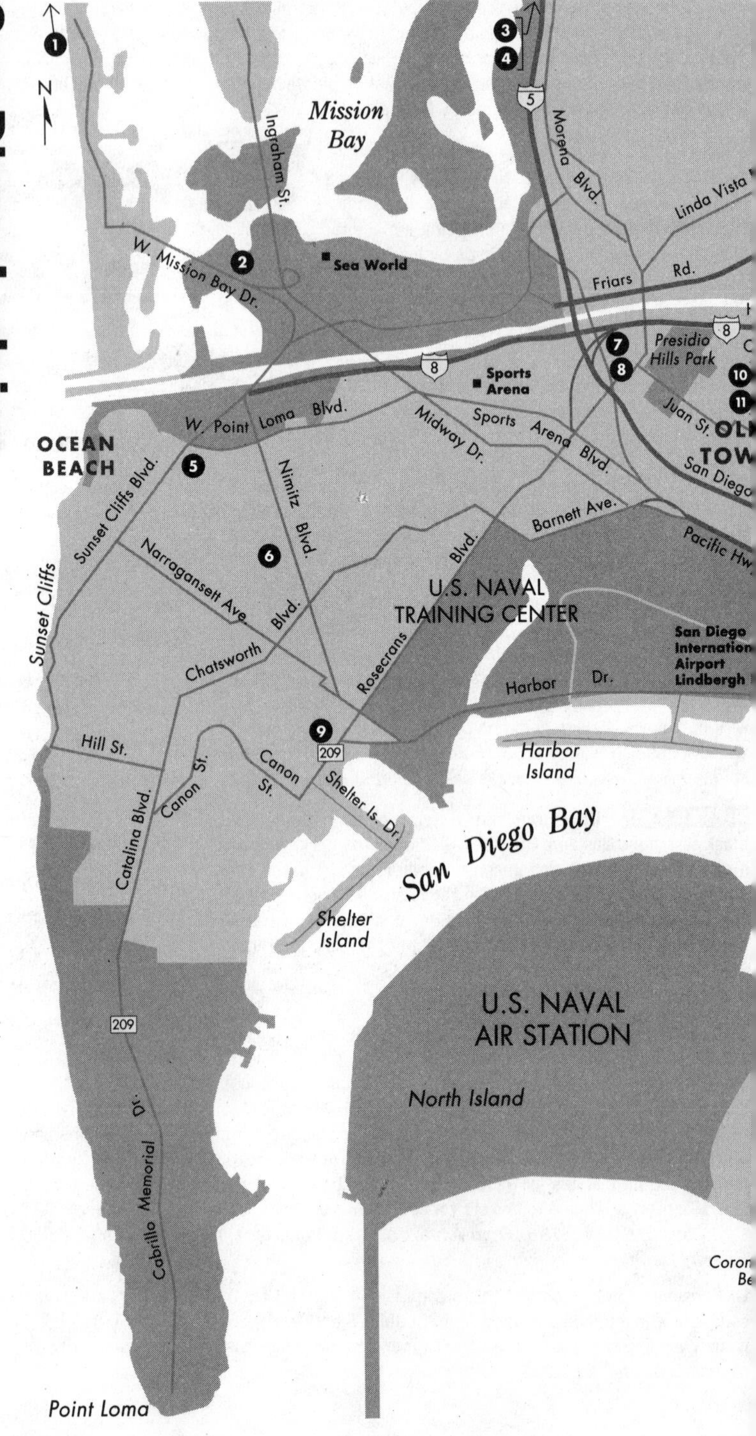

N
Mission Bay
Ingraham St.
Sea World
W. Mission Bay Dr.
Morena Blvd.
Linda Vista
Friars Rd.
5
8
Presidio Hills Park
Sports Arena
W. Point Loma Blvd.
Midway Dr.
Sports Arena Blvd.
Juan St.
San Diego
OCEAN BEACH
Sunset Cliffs Blvd.
Nimitz Blvd.
Barnett Ave.
Pacific Hw
Narragansett Ave.
Blvd.
U.S. NAVAL TRAINING CENTER
San Diego
Airport
Lindbergh
Sunset Cliffs
Chatsworth Blvd.
Rosecrans
Harbor Dr.
Hill St.
209
Harbor Island
Canon St.
Shelter Is. Dr.
Catalina Blvd.
San Diego Bay
Shelter Island
U.S. NAVAL AIR STATION
North Island
Cabrillo Memorial Dr.
Point Loma

San Diego Lodging

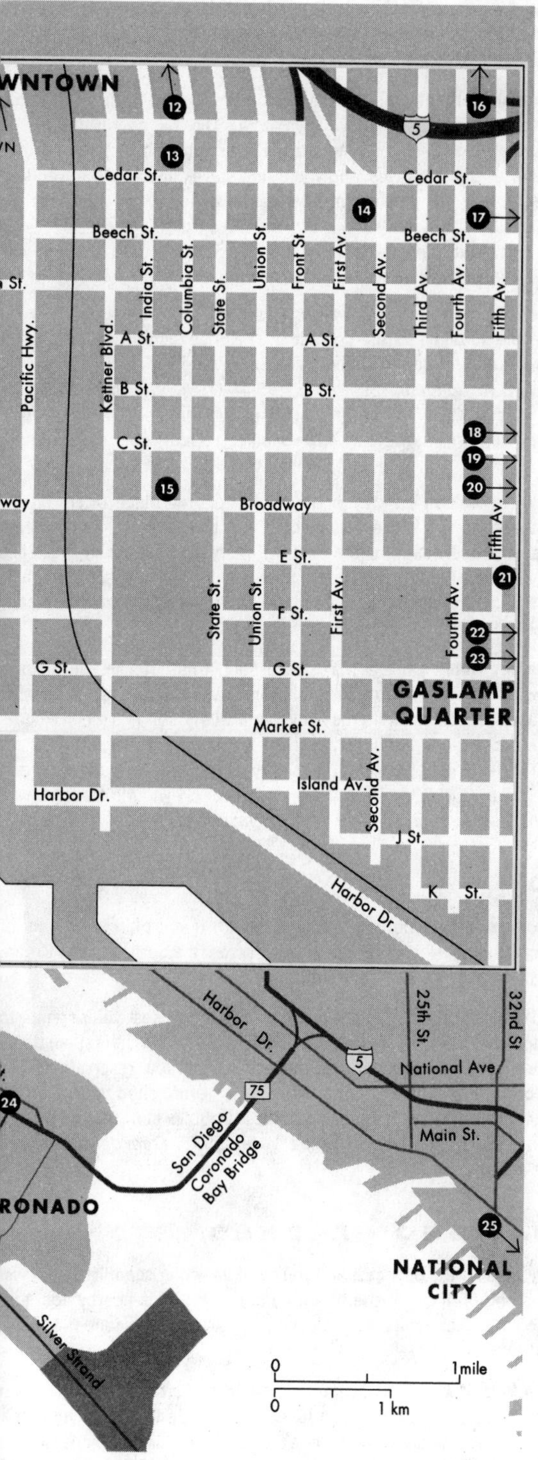

Armed Services YMCA Hostel (AYH), **15**
Campland on the Bay, **1**
Corinthians Suites Hotel, **16**
Dana Inn and Marina, **2**
Downtown Budget Motel, **12**
Downtown Inn Hotel, **23**
Embassy Hotel, **10**
E-Z 8 Motel, **7**
Holiday Motel, **24**
Hotel Churchill, **20**
Imperial Beach Hostel, **25**
Jim's San Diego, **19**
La Pensione Hotel, **13**
La Pensione on Second Avenue, **14**
Maryland Hotel, **22**
Monet's Garden Bed and Breakfast, **11**
Ocean Villa Motel, **5**
Old Town Inn, **8**
Point Loma/Elliot AYH Hostel, **6**
Point Loma Inn, **9**
Siesta Motor Inn, **17**
St. James Hotel, **21**
Trade Winds Motel, **4**
Western Shores Motel, **3**
YWCA Women's Hostel, **18**

La Pensione on Second Avenue. This is the mirror image of the Columbia Street La Pensione, but it lies closer to Horton Plaza. Doubles start at $29 daily, $135 weekly. *1546 2nd Ave., tel. 619/236–9292. Wheelchair access.*

UNDER $50 **Corinthians Suites Hotel.** About seven blocks north of Horton Plaza, this hotel is an inexpensive surprise in the downtown area. The rooms resemble tiny apartments—some people live here permanently. Extras abound, including air-conditioning, refrigerators, and microwaves, and you'll find stoves, laundry, and vending machines in the basement. Low-flying planes make sure you wake up early. Doubles are $40, $150 for a week. *1840 4th Ave., between Elm and Fir Sts., tel. 610/236–1600. From Broadway, walk 8 blocks north on 2nd Ave.; or take Bus 3, exit at 5th and Elm, walk 1 block west to 4th Ave. Wheelchair access, luggage storage.*

Downtown Budget Motel. The hotel is a long walk from the center of downtown and it's pretty noisy, but at $37 for a double it's still a good deal. The price includes a Continental breakfast, and you can make unlimited free local calls. Make reservations if you can, as the hotel is often full. *1835 Columbia St., tel. 619/544–0164, 800/537–9902, or 800/537–2283 in CA. Bus 5, 43, or 105 from downtown to State and Fir Sts., walk 1 block west to Columbia. Airport shuttle service available. Laundry room, wheelchair access.*

Siesta Motor Inn. Closer to Balboa Park than Horton Plaza, this place offers clean, comfortable rooms, and easy access to the trolley about four blocks south. Some rooms come with kitchenettes. Air-conditioning and a pool will help you cool off on those hot summer days and nights, and the laundry facilities may help you to look respectable again. Singles start at around $35, doubles around $41. *1449 9th Ave., at Beech St., tel. 800/748–5604 or 619/239–9113. Take trolley to 8th and C Sts.*

UNDER $60 **St. James Hotel.** Once a real sleaze hole, this hotel in the historic Gaslamp Quarter is now refurbished and respectable. And its location, just two blocks from Horton Plaza and about six blocks from the Greyhound Bus Station, is ideal. Rooms are on the small side and lack air-conditioning, but they're clean and secure. Doubles are $55. You might want to take a cab here at night for safety. *830 6th Ave., between E and F Sts., tel. 619/234–0155 or 800/338–1616. From Amtrak or Greyhound stations walk east along Broadway and turn right on 6th Ave. Laundry facilities.*

● ● ● CORONADO

You may feel a little isolated staying out on Coronado Island. If you plan to do a lot of sightseeing, you're going to spend a lot of time commuting across the Coronado Bay Bridge or riding the ferry. But if you just want to chill out on the beach, go for it.

UNDER $60 **Holiday Motel.** For budget travelers, this is the closest you're going to get to staying at the elite Hotel Del, which is just a short walk away. You can tell all those nattily dressed folks you meet on the croquet field that the Del lost your reservations and you had to stay here. Holiday Motel offers comfortable, newly refurbished rooms, within walking distance of Coronado's Victorian homes and shops. Doubles start around $55 in the summer, $45 in winter. *301 Orange Ave., tel. 619/435–0935. From downtown take Bus 901.*

● ● ● MISSION BAY AND BEACHES

Most visitors like to stay close to the beaches, and you can't go wrong heading here if you want to catch some rays and chill out at the beach bars. Sea World is nearby, too, and Mission Bay Park is a cool place to hang out or ride a bike. The nightlife scene is decent, but not nearly as varied as downtown.

UNDER $50 **Ocean Villa Motel.** Near Ocean Beach and a short drive from Mission Bay Area, this place is nothing fancy, but it does offer peace, quiet, and a pool. Of the few accommodation choices in the immediate area, this is the best value for your money. Rates for up to two people start at $45 in the summer; winter rates are about $10 cheaper. *5142*

West Point Loma Blvd., tel. 619/224–3481. Bus 35 gets you closest to the hotel. Laundry facilities.

Trade Winds Motel. About a mile from the bay and 2 miles from the ocean, this hotel has one redeeming feature: its price. You can be certain the manager didn't attend a Swiss finishing school. When asked what the rates were, the charmer replied "Whatever I feel like charging today." Don't make it easy on the bastard—haggle with him until he drops, or go somewhere else if the price is still too high. Depending on his mood, rates are more than $32, less than $50. *4305 Mission Bay Dr., tel. 619/273–4616. From downtown take Bus 30; no weekend or holiday service by bus.*

Western Shores Motel. The differences between this motel and the Trade Winds next door are that the rates are steadier and the management much friendlier. Doubles in summer are $37; in winter, $34. *4345 Mission Bay Dr., tel. 619/273–1121. From downtown take Bus 30; no weekend or holiday service by bus.*

UNDER $75 **Dana Inn and Marina.** If someone else is footing the bill, stay here; its location and facilities can't be beat. You almost forget you're in San Diego: The rooms resemble rustic cabins, and the hotel's proximity to the bay makes it easy to go for waterside jogs or walks. You definitely pay for the peace and quiet though, and the luxury of lazing by the pool: Doubles start at $70. Sea World is only a 25-minute walk away. *1710 W. Mission Bay Dr., tel. 619/222–6440 or 800/345–9995. Take Bus 34 to W. Mission Bay Dr. and Dana Landing Rd.*

OLD TOWN ● ● ●

The area around Old Town isn't scenic or serene—an interstate freeway ploughs through the area, as do a number of other major roads—and a car is really handy for getting around. Although you can't just walk out of your hotel and find yourself in the middle of loads of fun, the area is reasonably close to Mission Bay and the beaches, as well as downtown, Balboa Park, and Hillcrest. And, of course, there's Old Town itself. A major lodging hot spot in the area is Hotel Circle, along I–8 near the Fashion Valley and Mission Valley shopping centers. Be aware that the prices advertised on the giant signs may not jibe with the price you end up paying; proprietors will frequently tell you that all the cheap rooms are already rented. Wherever you stay in Hotel Circle, try to reserve a room facing away from the freeway.

UNDER $35 **Old Town Inn.** The hotel is near Old Town, but you can' t walk there from the inn without passing beneath a creepy I–5 underpass. The rooms are simple and basic and priced accordingly—around $31 for a single; $3 for each additional person. Don't be caught dead walking through this dark, isolated neighborhood at night. *4444 Pacific Hwy., tel. 619/260–8024 or 800/225–9610. Bus 4 from downtown runs along Pacific Hwy. Wheelchair access.*

E-Z 8 Motel. If you're desperate, this chain has a motel in the Old Town area, complete with a pool, HBO, and air-conditioning. Singles are around $32, doubles $37. *4747 Pacific Hwy., tel. 619/294–2412. Bus 4 from downtown runs along Pacific Hwy. Wheelchair access.*

BFE ● ● ●

UNDER $40 **Point Loma Inn.** In an area dominated by sleazy dives, this place is an oasis. Not only are the rooms newly refurbished, but the management is quite friendly—unusual in an area where most hotels just want your money. Doubles are around $40 in the summer, $38 in the winter. *2933 Fevelon St., at Rosecrans, tel. 619/222–4704. From downtown take Bus 29.*

UNDER $50 **Embassy Hotel.** In a quiet residential area just north of Balboa Park, this hotel is nothing special—it's mainly a residence for senior citizens—but it does offer a respite from the crowded downtown scene. Daily rates for single or doubles start at $40.

3645 Park Blvd., tel. 619/296–3141. From downtown, take Bus 7 through the park. Laundry facilities.

Monet's Garden Bed and Breakfast. Providing home-cooked meals and country-style rooms, this B&B offers a personalized touch about 20 minutes from San Diego. The area itself is dull and somewhat isolated, but the facilities, including giant, fluffy feather beds, make up for it—especially if you plan to spend a lot of time in bed. Prices range from $40 to $65. *7039 Casa La., Lemon Grove, tel. 6610/464–8296. By trolley, take east line to Lemon Grove Depot, then call Dial-A-Ride, tel. 619/234–6160 for a $1 ride to the B&B. 7 rooms.*

HOSTELS

Armed Services YMCA Hostel (AYH). This hostel is something of a Jekyll and Hyde. First the good news: The hostel is conveniently located between the bus and train stations; it's close to the trolley and city buses; and it's within easy walking distance of downtown's major sights and attractions. The bad news: The neighborhood around the hostel is filled with panhandlers and other street life that may make you feel uncomfortable; more importantly, the hostel itself is about as attractive as a public rest room at a gas station—you really don't want to use it but you have no choice. But hell, it's cheap—$10 for members, $13 for nonmembers. The YMCA also offers hotel-like rooms for $20 a day for a single and $32 for a double. *500 W. Broadway, tel. 619/232–1144. 1 block east of Amtrak, 3 blocks west of Greyhound. 10 beds for women, 21 beds for men. Laundry, wheelchair access, lockers.*

Imperial Beach Hostel (AAYH). Closer to Tijuana than to San Diego, this converted fire station is best suited for travelers who want to spend plenty of time at the beach, since there's not much else to do. Trips to downtown San Diego and other San Diego attractions are all-day affairs if you use mass transport. Beds are $9 for members and $14 for nonmembers. *170 Palm Ave., Imperial Beach., tel. 619/423–8039. From downtown, take Bus 901 to Palm and Rainbow, transfer to Bus 933 (westbound) to Palm and Seacoast; or take trolley to Palm City station, transfer to Bus 933. Open 8 AM–10 AM, 5:30 PM–midnight. Open for sign-in at 3:30 PM. 36 beds. Laundry, locker storage, kitchen.*

Jim's San Diego. This place welcomes all travelers who can produce a valid passport. Breakfast is included, and the trolley line runs in front of the hostel. It's somewhat of a walk to get to the downtown attractions, but it's not bad (Horton Plaza is about half a mile, or 10 blocks, west). Beds are $15 a night, $90 a week. *1425 C St., tel. 619/235–0234. Kitchen and laundry facilities, wheelchair access.*

Point Loma/Elliot AYH Hostel. Housed in a spacious building with a large kitchen, common area, and an outdoor patio, this hostel offers lots of peace and quiet. One of the reasons it's so quiet is because it's in what San Diegans refer to as BFE (*see* Information Box, *above*). But the hostel is great if you want to go out and walk or bike. A challenging day's exercise is a bike ride to Sunset Cliffs and Ocean Beach. A nearby supermarket is a definite plus. Beds are $12 for members, $15 for nonmembers. *3790 Udall St., tel. 619/223–4778. From downtown, take Bus 35 to Worden St. and Voltaire St.; Walk 1 block south to Udall St. Office open 7 AM–10 PM. Hostel closed 11 AM–4 PM. 60 beds. Check-in 4 PM–midnight. 2 AM curfew (lock-out), wheelchair access.*

YWCA Women's Hostel. A safe, friendly environment for women travelers, the hostel is a few blocks east of Horton Plaza and other downtown attractions. The trolley runs right in front of the hostel. The hostel has communal kitchens and bathrooms, just like the YMCA. Dorm beds are $9 per night, with an additional $5 for linen rental. Hotel rooms are $17 for a single, $16 per person for a double. *1012 C St., at 10th Ave., tel. 619/239–0355. 12 hostel beds, 33 hotel rooms. Women only. Wheelchair access.*

CAMPGROUNDS • • •

Campland On the Bay. Essentially a cement RV park on the northside of Mission Bay, this campground probably won't make it onto *Wild Kingdom.* If you don't mind a sea of portable trailer homes, the location and available watersports make this a relatively attractive option. Tent sites are $24 a day in the summer, $17.50 in winter. *2211 Pacific Beach Dr., tel. 619/274–6260 or 800/422–9386. Take Bus 30 from downtown. Laundry, wheelchair access, market.*

Food

When it comes to food, San Diego is most widely known for its host of Jack in the Boxes—suitable only for those with steel palates or large quantities of alcohol running through their veins—and for its Mexican food. Focus your attention on the latter. Of the 3 billion *taquerias* in the greater San Diego area, it would not be out of line to say that over two-thirds of these establishments are named some variation of "Roberto's." Among local favorites: **Roberto's, El Roberto's,** and **Aliberto's.** Rumor has it that an old Mexican immigrant started a chain of Mexican restaurants and named each one after a different son. But, then, who gives a rat's ass what they're called when the food tastes this good? Aside from taquerias and fast-food joints, though, it's tough to find good, *cheap* meals in San Diego. Cafeterias do not exist here, and there are relatively few coffee shops or family-style restaurants. The best place to find well-prepared, inexpensive meals are in off-the-beaten-track neighborhoods, such as the Convoy Street district in Kearny Mesa, where you can find virtually every kind of Asian cuisine. Along both Mission Boulevard and Garnet Avenue is a host of little restaurants. Garnet Avenue, which is more popular with the locals as a night spot, offers everything from Peruvian cuisine to Pizzeria Uno. During the day, beach crowds roam Garnet in search of cheap grub before heading back to the surf. The **Farmers' Market** in Horton Plaza receives daily shipments of fresh produce, and the **Farmers' Bazaar** (Corner of 7th Ave. and K St.) features fresh produce, gift and clothing shops, and ethnic restaurants.

DOWNTOWN • • •

The **Gaslamp Quarter** has a number of decent, reasonably priced restaurants. Remember, though, that the downtown restaurant scene consists of a whole lot more than the Gaslamp Quarter. If you don't want to shell out lots of moolah for a sit-down meal, the top floor of **Horton Plaza** is packed with take-out food stalls and restaurants.

UNDER $10 **Little Joe's Restaurant and Pizza House.** Specializing in pizza and pasta dishes, this is one of the cheaper options in the Gaslamp. Little Joe's is hardly ever filled to capacity, but don't tell the waiters that—they like to act as if they just don't have time for you. Don't come here for the decor 'cause there isn't any. *750 5th Ave., tel. 619/234–1320 or 619/234–1350. 3 blocks south of Broadway on Fifty. Open daily 11 AM–3 AM.*

The Old Spaghetti Factory. Offering perhaps the best bargain for Italian food in San Diego, this restaurant serves fresh pasta in a setting that melds the Old World with the Old West. Beside the food, the best part about this place is the lifesize street car in the middle of the restaurant. You can probably eat lunch for under $5, but be prepared to wait for up to two hours for dinner on weekends. *275 5th Ave. at K St., tel. 619/233–4323. Wheelchair access.*

Sushi-Deli. You sit at regular old tables, keep your shoes on, and stare right into the kitchen while you eat, but the beautifully assembled, huge sushi plates and other Japanese dishes will make you float away on a cloud of fish-inspired ecstasy. The sushi combination plate is $4; teriyaki chicken is $3.50. *828 Broadway, tel. 619/231–9597. Wheelchair access.*

UNDER $15 **Kansas City Barbeque.** Napkins ain't gonna cut it after you've finished slobbering over the ribs at this place—ideally, patrons should be washed down with a fire hose. The atmosphere is as appealing as the ribs: If the neon signs, license plates, movie posters, and bar seem a bit familiar it's because scenes from *Top Gun* were filmed here.

Entrées cost $7–$15. *610 West Market St., tel. 619/231–9680. Open daily 11 AM–1 AM. Wheelchair access, but not to the bathrooms.*

● ● ● HILLCREST

Many people overlook the restaurants along Fifth Avenue in Hillcrest, also known as "Restaurant Row." Many of the restaurants are pricey bistros, but there are a few plain, run-down places that serve affordable grub.

UNDER $5 **El Indio Shop.** The Mexican food at all El Indio's three locations is tasty and authentic, it costs under $5, and locals form a line around the block to eat the stuff. The atmosphere leaves something to be desired, but who has time to sightsee when you're snorting down three *taquitos* (little tacos) for just a buck? The India Street branch is off I–5 in an area known as the "India Street Colony," where you'll find a few other budget restaurants. *3695 India St., tel. 619/299–0333; 4120 Mission Blvd., in Mission Beach, tel. 619/272–8226; 409 F St., downtown, tel. 619/239–8151.*

Quel Fromage. Not so much a restaurant as a dessert/coffee house, this establishment serves as a think tank for the "intellectual" set and as a refuge for poets seeking inspiration in their coffee. Mochas, lattes, and other fancy coffees are $1; desserts are around $2. The café becomes busy on Friday and Saturday nights. *523 University Ave., tel. 619/295–1600. Open Sun.–Thurs. 7:30 AM–11 PM, Fri.–Sat. 7:30 AM–midnight. Wheelchair access.*

A Taste of Aloha. In the same building complex as Pasta al Dente, the Taste of Aloha qualifies as a hole in the wall. But the food is satisfying, cheap, and filling. Specialties include Hawaiian and Asian dishes, including teriyaki chicken and beef with rice and salad for $4. *420-D Robinson Ave., at 4th, tel. 619/692–9145. Open Sun.–Thurs. 5 AM–10 PM, Fri.–Sat. 5 AM–midnight.*

UNDER $10 **The Corvette Diner Bar and Grill.** Specializing in malts and burger platters that start around $5, this pseudo-'50s diner features appropriate paraphernalia for that era on the walls, live disc jockeys, and singing waiters and waitresses. It's too bad that neither the Corvette, which sits in the main dining area, nor the food reflects '50s prices. *3946 5th Ave., tel. 619/542–1476. Open Sun.–Thurs. 11–11, Fri.–Sat. 11 AM–midnight. Wheelchair access.*

Kung Food Deli. The deli offers a wide variety of delicious, vegetarian meals, some without dairy or eggs, for $4–$6, as well as smoothies and desserts. Try the restaurant next door for pricier sit-down dinners, or the adjoining New Age shop for advice on out-of-body experiences. A hummus sandwich costs about $4; layered tofu supreme (tofu, spinach, pimentos, and mushrooms with ginger and bell pepper sauce) is $6. *2949 5th Ave., tel. 619/298–9232. Wheelchair access.*

Pasta al Dente. The Old Spaghetti Factory gives you better value and better atmosphere for your money (*see above*), but this is one of the cheaper Italian restaurants in the area. Fettuccine primavera cost $6, ravioli $7. *420-A Robinson Ave., tel. 619/295–2727. 1 block south of University Ave. on 4th Ave. Wheelchair access. Open for lunch and dinner.*

● ● ● OLD TOWN

Restaurant prices are inflated in this touristy area, but Old Town restaurants nevertheless offer culinary authenticity and good atmosphere. The **Bazaar del Mundo** in Old Town State Historic Park has three restaurants that attract long lines each and every weekend: **Casa de Pico** (tel. 619/296–3267), **Hamburguese Restaurant and Cantina** (tel. 619/295–0584) and **Lino's Italian Restaurant** (tel. 619/299–7124). With its large flower-covered patio and wandering mariachis, Casa de Pico is one of the city's most popular margarita spots, although its Mexican food has been sanitized for the American palate.

UNDER $10 **Perry's Cafe/The Breakfast House.** On the fringes of Old Town, Perry's regularly attracts a crowd. It may seem strange to see long lines to get into a place that is isolated, near the highway, and unattractive. But on weekends, people come from far and wide for big, homemade breakfasts that are well under $10. Many breakfasts are under $5: Three pancakes, for example, cost just $2. *4610 Pacific Hwy., tel. 619/291–7121. Open daily 6:30 AM–2 PM.*

UNDER $15 **Casa de Bandini.** In a mansion that was once the center of Old Town's social life, this restaurant is decorated with colorful murals, tapestried chairs, and has a Mexican-Southwest flavor (surprise, surprise). All the locals know this place: Ask them to name a good restaurant in Old Town, and they'll probably mention this one first. Fajita dinner plate is $9, enchilada plates are around $7. *2654 Calhoun St., in Old Town State Historic Park, tel. 619/297–8211. Open summer, Mon.–Sat. 11–10, Sun. 10–10; winter, Mon.–Sat. 11–9, Sun. 10–9. Wheelchair access.*

Old Town Mexican Café. Every night, patrons wait as long as 30 minutes (more on the weekends) to eat here. The place has a lively atmosphere that attracts rowdy groups and amorous couples. The best dishes are those served with freshly made tortillas. Chicken verde enchiladas cost $7.50, and *carne asada* tacos $4. It's easy to dine for less than $10. *2489 San Diego Ave., tel. 619/297–4330. Open for lunch and dinner. Wheelchair access.*

LA JOLLA

Much of La Jolla is overpriced and too expensive for the budget traveler. However, a few places do lurk amid the glitter where you won't blow your budget entirely, just put a leak in it.

UNDER $10 **John's Waffle Shop.** Why do people wake up early on Sunday to stand in line for up to an hour to get into this joint? Because it's good, damn good. The homemade pancakes and waffles melt in your mouth and still leave you enough money to buy that fabulous Cartier letter opener you've always wanted. Three pancakes and two eggs are $4, a ham-and-cheese omelet is $5. You can also get burgers for around $3, but they aren't nearly as satisfying as a complete breakfast. *7906 Grand Ave., tel. 619/454–7371. Open Mon.–Sat. 7–3, Sun. 8–3.*

UNDER $15 **The Spot.** This local favorite serves traditional American cuisine and features deep-dish pizza. Considering the quality of food, the prices are quite reasonable, especially by La Jolla standards. Personal pan pizzas are $6–$7; barbecued ribs and chicken dishes are about $9. *1005 Prospect St., tel. 619/459–0800. Open daily 11 AM–1 AM. Bar open until 2. Wheelchair accessible, but not the bathroom.*

UNDER $20 **Alfonso's of La Jolla.** Wedged between fancy art galleries and expensive shops, Alfonso's sits on La Jolla's main shopping and eating drag. Budget travelers may empty their wallet to eat the Mexican food here, but the restaurant is a prime spot to watch rich folks and wannabes eye one another with disdain over lunch. Stop in at night for a margarita, when these same people set aside their differences long enough to size up one another's tits and assets. Mexican entrees range from $6 to $15. *1215 Prospect St., tel. 619/454–2232. Open Mon.–Thurs. 11–11, Fri.–Sat. 11–midnight, Sun.11–10.*

Exploring San Diego

San Diego is a collection of very different neighborhoods. Within each neighborhood, walking is the most sensible—and cheapest—way to get around, but you'll probably need to hop on a bus or trolley to get from one community to another. If you only have a couple of days, consider spending one of them in central San Diego, checking out downtown, Balboa Park (including the San Diego Zoo), Old Town, and Hillcrest. After that, kick back and chill out. Strung out along the coast, the rest of San Diego's attractions emphasize fun in the sun—beaches, water parks, swimming, and lots of brown bodies. Just pick a beach and enjoy yourself, but leave time for Sea World in Mission Bay and La Jolla, the picturesque "Village" a little farther north.

● ● ● WORTH SEEING

DOWNTOWN AND THE EMBARCADERO Downtown San Diego is one of the few successful California examples of "downtown revitalization," the catch-phrase for the transformation of urban blight into cutesy tourist attractions. Needless to say, urban renovation is not a big favorite among suburban mall developers, whose sole purpose in life is to pave America and play mollifying Muzak to the lobotomized survivors. But with the construction of Horton Plaza, San Diego kept everyone happy by bringing the mall downtown. The marriage of mall culture and urban America has given birth to an area where pawn shops and pool halls co-exist with supper clubs and art galleries.

HORTON PLAZA The center of it all is Horton Plaza, a confection-colored, whimsical monstrosity that looks like it was designed by an architect trapped in his formative years. The unusual architectural style combines the open-air, breezy feeling of a Mediterranean plaza with elements of Early Romper Room—recognizable by the use of large, primary-color shapes and other big objects that don't make any apparent sense. And don't even think of a quick exit—the system of stairways is carefully designed to take you past every major shop before you escape. The mall treats you, in effect, like a rat in a consumer maze. You don't go to Horton Plaza to pick up vacuum-cleaner bags; you go there to play for a few hours, with the ever-present danger of spending hundreds of dollars in its upscale, neon-splashed boutiques. The plaza is named for the San Francisco merchant, Alonzo E. Horton, who bought 960 acres of bay-front land in 1867 for 27.5¢ per acre. *Between Broadway and G St. and 1st and 4th Aves., tel. 619/239–8180. Accessible by all downtown bus routes. Open weekdays 10–9, Sat. 10–6, Sun. 11–6.*

THE EMBARCADERO It's hard to miss the Embarcadero, the section of downtown waterfront that follows the curve of San Diego Bay. Backed by Harbor Drive, the Embarcadero is a good reference point to help you figure out where you are. Otherwise, the Embarcadero's main attraction is its views of the bay and the docked ships, ranging from huge cruise ships to old sailing vessels. The **San Diego Maritime Museum** displays three restored ships. The *Berkeley,* an 1898 riverboat that ferried passengers between Oakland and San Francisco after the 1906 earthquake, serves as the museum headquarters, complete with a gift shop and exhibits on oceanography and naval history. *The Star of India* is a century-old windjammer whose flapping white sails are something of a local landmark. The *Star* made 21 trips around the world in the late 1800s, plying the East Indian trade route, carrying immigrants from Britain to Australia, and loading salmon in Alaska. The *Medea* is a steam yacht once owned by a Scot who used it for fishing trips off Scotland. In World War I, the *Medea* was used to hunt submarines off the English coast. *1306 N. Harbor Dr., at the foot of Ash St., tel. 619/234–9153. Admission: $5. Open daily 9–8.*

A little farther along the Embarcadero, at the intersection of Broadway and Harbor Drive, are the docks for the tour boats that offer rides around the harbor. It's a scene from tourist hell—lots of couples named Herb and Flo, ice cream running down chubby chins, loud T-shirts, and screaming children. **The Original San Diego Harbor Excursions** (tel. 619/234–4111) and **Invader Cruises** (tel. 619/234–8687) offer one- and two-hour trips around San Diego Bay ($10 and $15). You may feel like a tourist, but this is a fun way to see the Naval Air Station, Coronado, and Harbor Island.

SEAPORT VILLAGE **Seaport Village** (849 W. Harbor Dr., at Kettner Blvd., tel. 619/235–4013) is a touristy shopping mall, done up in a melange of styles that range from Cape Cod to adobe. More than 65 specialty shops vie to sell tourists fudge, cookies, nautical kitsch, and expensive souvenirs. If you've seen Fisherman's Wharf in San Francisco or the South Street Seaport in New York, you know the scene. One authentic feature of this place is the **Boardwalk Flying Horses Carousel,** whose handcrafted horses were brought from Coney Island. A ride costs 75¢. Even if you can't stand this kind of tourist show, you may still want to come down for the excellent night views of downtown and the San Diego–Coronado bridge.

While you're in the Seaport Village, visit the **Upstart Crow,** a high-concept bookstore/café with a good section on San Diego history and lots of fancy coffee drinks.

GASLAMP QUARTER Named for the elegant gas lamps (now electric) that line the streets, the Gaslamp Quarter was a flourishing business center in the 19th century and features some of the city's finest Victorian commercial architecture. When the business quarter moved farther west at the turn of the century, the Gaslamp Quarter declined and became the city's seedy underbelly for more than 60 years. Sailors and other assorted fun-seekers wandered the streets in search of hookers or a good poker game. Now that things have been cleaned up by the Gaslamp Quarter Council, the whorehouses and gambling parlors have been replaced by gimmicky cocktail lounges and movie theaters, and a fairly diverse crowd now wanders the neighborhood. During the day, the district offers some of the most eclectic shopping and the best art galleries in the city, and its proximity to Horton Plaza makes it a convenient respite for anyone suffering from pastel overload. The **Gaslamp Quarter Foundation** (tel. 619/233–5227) gives walking tours every Saturday at 11 AM, starting at the William Heath Davis House (410 Island Ave.). Tickets cost $5, $3 for students. Several buildings are of special historical and architectural interest: The **Horton Park Plaza Hotel,** opposite the William Heath Davis House, is the city's first "skyscraper" and a good example of a brothel converted into a respectable establishment; along Fifth Street between Island and Broadway, check out the **Louis Bank of Commerce,** a Baroque Revival building with an oyster bar where Wyatt Earp used to hang out. The section of G Street from Fourth to Tenth avenues is a rapidly growing art district, with lots of new galleries, cafés, bookstores, and boutiques. The **Center City East Arts Association** (tel. 619/235–8255), an umbrella organization for the many galleries and independent artists in the area, hosts frequent open houses and can provide information about specific establishments.

Depending on which of the numerous cafés or bars you visit at night, you're likely to run into large packs of drunken yuppies singing "Louie Louie" or small packs of drunken trend-setters smoking and regularly reapplying their eyeliner.

Stop in at the **Golden Lion Tavern** (801 4th Ave., inside the Golden Lion Building), which features a beautiful stained-glass dome ceiling and mahogany bar, and a lunch crowd that has mastered the art of networking without getting soup on their ties.

BALBOA PARK A refreshing expanse of greenery stradling two mesas that overlook downtown, Balboa Park offers visitors a gorgeous respite from urban San Diego. Its 1,000 acres boast a world-famous zoo, a complex of 13 museums—second only to the Smithsonian in size—and lots of open space in which to cavort. Most of the museums are grouped around **El Prado,** the park's central pedestrian mall, which was built as part of the Panama-California International Exposition of 1915. El Prado acts as the park's spine, with smaller trails forking off into the park. On any given day on El Prado, you'll see lots of strolling families, young skateboarders, and street performers. Many of the museums are housed in big Spanish-Moorish buildings that were also built for the Exposition. Originally intended as temporary structures, the buildings have now endured 75 years of earthquakes and, of course, those bitter San Diego winters. The **Information Center** (tel. 619/239–0512) in the House of Hospitality on El Prado offers general park information as well as the "Passport to Balboa Park," a pass that allows entry to four museums for $9. Many museums give discounts to students with IDs, and the first Tuesday of each month is "Free Tuesday," when one or more museums offer free admission. Balboa Park is within walking distance of downtown and Hillcrest, and several bus routes run through the park (Bus 7 follows Park Boulevard). It's easy to walk from one place to another within the park, but if you're feeling particularly useless you can catch the **Balboa Park Tram,** which runs regularly during the day from the Inspiration Point parking lot off Park Boulevard to all the museums.

SAN DIEGO ZOO The most visited sight in the city, the San Diego Zoo contains 3,900 animals (not counting tourists) covering more than 800 species. The zoo is famous for its botanical collection and its many rare and exotic species, as well as its barless cages designed to simulate the natural habitats of the various critters. It can get tiring walking

Balboa Park

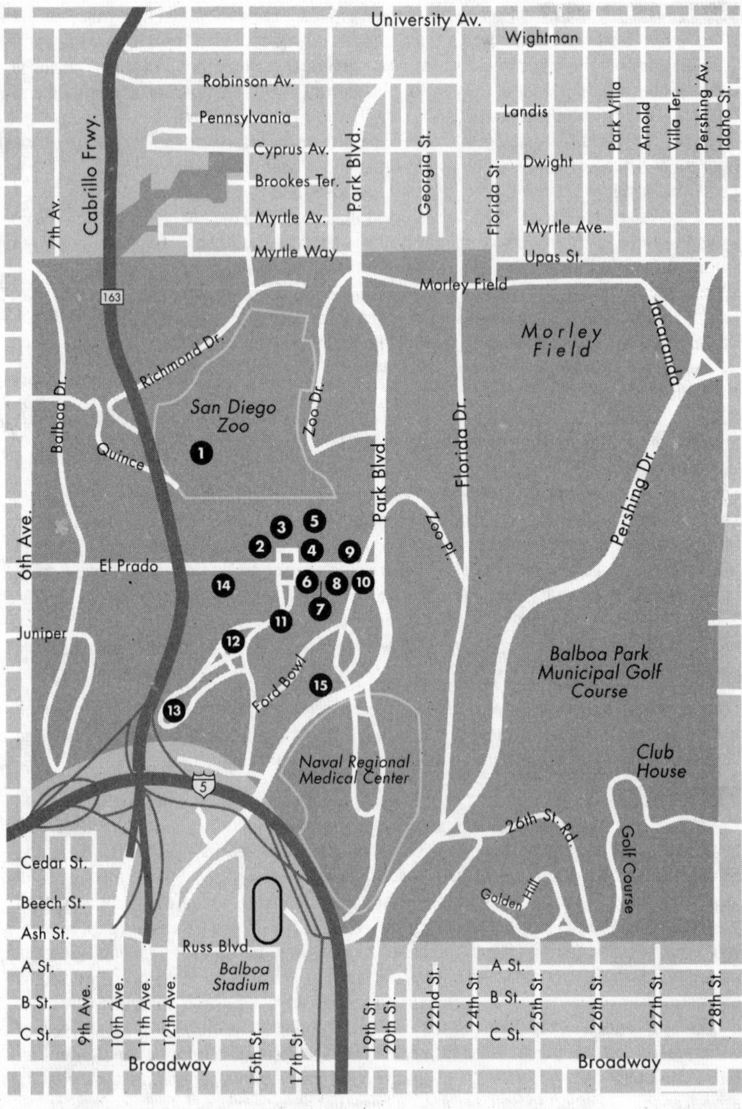

Botanical Building, **5**
Hall of Champions, **7**
House of Pacific Relations, **12**
Museum of Man, **14**
Museum of Photographic Arts, **8**
Natural History Museum, **9**
Park Information Center/House of Hospitality, **6**
Reuben H. Fleet Space Theater and Science Center, **10**
San Diego Aerospace Museum and International Aerospace Hall of Fame, **13**
San Diego Museum of Art, **3**
San Diego Zoo, **1**
Sculpture Garden, **2**
Spanish Village Art Center, **15**
Spreckels Organ Pavillion, **11**
Timken Art Gallery, **4**

around the hilly, 100-acre park, and disabled travelers may have trouble without an electric wheelchair. For an additional $3, you can see most of the zoo from an open-air, double-decker bus, complete with disgustingly cheery tour guide. The **Skyfari tram,** a kind of aerial tramway that carries riders 170 feet above the zoo, is another good way to see the animals, and also offers tremendous views of downtown, the bay, and the ocean. The ride is included in the price of admission. Three special exhibits are worthy of note: **Tiger River,** a collection of 10 exhibits with more than 35 species, is designed to emulate the feeling of a South American jungle. **Sun Bear Forest** contains brooks, waterfalls, and thousands of trees intended to make the bears feel at home. The latest natural habitat, **Gorilla Tropics,** is a simulation of an African rain forest, complete with four aviaries of African birds, six gorillas, thousands of African plants, and even little noises in stereo that sound like the soundtrack from a Tarzan movie. Drop by the **Scripps Flight Cage,** if only to wonder how much newspaper would be needed to line the bottom of this bird home every day. *Tel. 619/234–3153 or 619/231–1515. Admission: $10.75, including Skyfari ride and entry to Chidren's Zoo. Open Labor Day–Apr. 30, daily 9–4; May 1–Labor Day, daily 9–5.*

BALBOA PARK MUSEUMS **Centro Cultural de la Raza.** Along Park Boulevard near Pepper Grove, the cultural center offers changing exhibits of Chicano and Native American art, as well as a permanent collection of Chicano murals. *Tel. 619/235–6135. Admission free. Open Wed.–Sun. noon–5.*

Hall of Champions. If you've held your tongue while some pretentious fart has dragged you through a bunch of galleries oohing and aahing at chocolate-box paintings, get your revenge by taking them to this sports museum. If the curators could put Mickey Mantle's dirty jock strap under glass, they would. As it is, you'll probably have to settle for other sporting memorabilia, including photos and equipment. *Casa de Balboa, tel. 619/234–2544. Admission: $2, students $1. Open Mon.–Sat. 10–4, Sun. 1:30–4:30.*

The Hall of Champions is the museum for couch potatoes and bleacher bums.

House of Pacific Relations (tel. 619/234–0739). Part of the Pan American Plaza developed for the 1935 California-Pacific International Exposition, the House of Pacific Relations consists of a cluster of stucco cottages that represent various foreign countries. The whole thing is done in the most kitschy way possible—you can almost hear strains of "It's a Small World" playing in the background. The House of Pacific Relations sponsors an *Annual Ethnic Food Fair* in May.

Museum of Man. Sitting in the shadow of the California Tower, the museum houses an extensive collection of archaeological and anthropological exhibits that focus on native cultures of the Americas. The "Wonder of Life" exhibit offers an intensive overview of human reproduction, gestation, and birth. The facade of the California Building depicts the history and conquest of California. *Tel. 619/239–2001. Admission: $3. Open daily 10–4:30.*

Museum of Photographic Arts. Also in the Casa de Balboa, this is one of the few museums in the world dedicated solely to photography. MOPA shows the work of both famous and relatively obscure photographers, and exhibits range from the journalistic to the artistic. The museum store sells a plethora of photography books. *Casa de Balboa, tel. 619/239–5262. Admission: $2.50. Open Fri.–Wed. 10–5, Thurs. 10–9.*

Museum of San Diego History. This is a relatively new addition to the Balboa Park museums. Not surprisingly, the focus is solely on San Diego, with a variety of displays that trace the city's history from 1850 to the present. *Casa de Balboa, tel. 619/232–6203. Admission: $4. Open Wed.–Sun. 10–4.*

National History Museum. The museum features a Hall of Desert Ecology, with displays on the plants and animals of southern California and Mexico; and a Hall of Mineralogy, which features a variety of gems, including rose-color tourmaline crystals mined in San Diego County. If you have a dog, tempt him with the museum's collection of dinosaur bones. The Foucault Pendulum, a 185-pound brass ball suspended on a 43-foot cable, demonstrates the rotation of the earth. *Tel. 619/232–3821. Admission: $5, students $4. Open daily 10–4:30, until 5 in summer.*

Reuben H. Fleet Space Theater and Science Center. The Omnimax theater here can simulate a wild roller-coaster ride through the desert, on the space shuttle, along the ocean floor, or inside the human body. It kinda makes you wonder what they'll come up with next. In the evening, listen to rock music and catch the laser show on a giant domed screen in the Laserium—this is a popular pasttime for stoned teenagers. Admission prices include entrance to the science center (admission to the Science Center only is $2), a futuristic playhouse filled with interactive exhibits designed to teach children and adults about scientific principles. *Tel. 619/238–1168. Theater tickets (includes admission to Science Center): $5, students $4; laser shows: $5.50, students $4.40. Open Sun.–Thurs. 9:30–9:30, Fri.–Sat. 9:30 AM–10:30 PM.*

San Diego Aerospace Museum and International Aerospace Hall of Fame. This building is unlike any other in the park. Ford commissioned the building for the 1935 exposition, when sleek, streamlined design was all the rage. A thin line of blue neon outlines the round building at night, making it look like a landlocked UFO. Exhibits about aviation and aerospace pioneers line the rotunda, and a collection of real and replicated aircraft fill the center. *Museum, tel. 619/234–8291; Hall of Fame, tel. 619/232–8322. Admission: $4. Open daily 10–4:30.*

San Diego Automotive Museum. More than 80 vehicles, including horseless carriages, classics, performance and exotic cars, and future protypes are on display at this museum next to the Palisades Building. Some people would say this museum reflects the summit of California culture, but that's crap—yogurt holds that honor (hey, we're Californians, we can say that). *Tel. 619/231–2886. Admission: $3. Open daily 10–4:30.*

San Diego Museum of Art. The museum features a permanent collection of works from the Italian Renaissance, Dutch and Spanish Baroque art, as well as American and Asian art treasures. *Tel. 619/232–7931. Admission: $5, $2 students with ID. Open Tues.–Sun. 10–4:30.*

Spanish Village Art Center. North of El Prado, between the Natural History Museum and the Zoo, this "Spanish village" was built as part of the 1935 exposition. The village houses are now used as arts-and-crafts studios. Artists display their works here on weekends. *Tel. 619/233–9050. Admission free. Open daily 11–4.*

Timken Art Gallery. Next to the Museum of Art, the Timken features European and American works, as well as a collection of Russian icons and French tapestries. *Tel. 619/239–5548. Admission free. Open Tues.–Sat. 10–4:30, Sun. 1:30–4:30. Closed Sept.*

BALBOA PARK GARDENS Built in 1915, the **Botanical Building** is home to more than 500 varieties of tropical and subtropical plants, including a great collection of orchids. When the bloom has gone off your flower, plant yourself on a bench near one of the artificial waterfalls. The **Alcayar Garden,** across El Prado from the Museum of Man, is a replica of the gardens surrounding the Alcayar Castle in Seville, with tiled fountains and flower beds. The **Japanese Friendship Garden,** behind the House of Hospitality, is a tea garden with ponds, benches, and bonsai exhibits. If a tourist knocks over a bonsai in the forest, will anyone hear it? Next to the Simon Edison Center for the Performing Arts is the **Sculpture Garden,** an outdoor exhibit of traditional and modernistic sculptures; the adjoining café serves light meals and coffee. The **Rose Garden,** along Park Boulevard, has more than 2,000 rose plants, most of which bloom in June. Since this is California, though, the plants stay beautiful year-round. The adjacent **Cactus Garden,** a sharp change from the manicured beauty of the Rose Garden, has trails winding around prickly cactus and soft green succulents. **Palm Canyon,** near the Organ Pavilion, has more than 60 varieties of palm trees arranged along a shady bridge.

Old Town San Diego

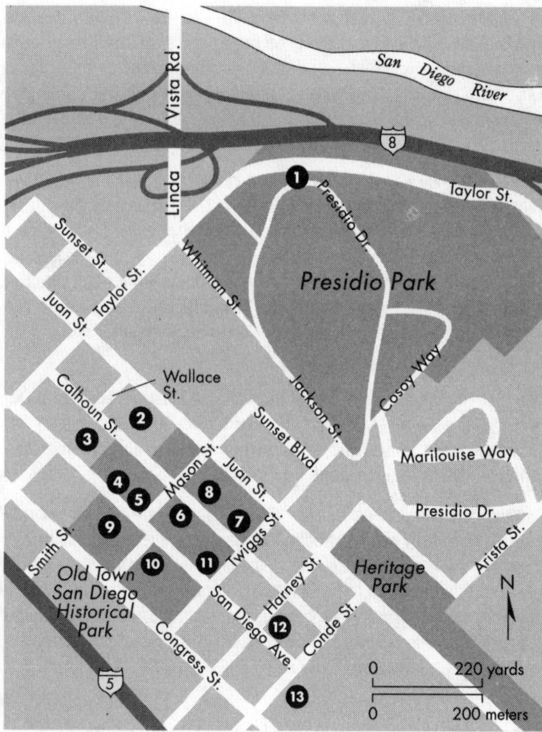

Bazaar del Mundo, **2**
California Plaza, **4**
Junipero Serra Museum, **1**
La Casa de Altamirano (San Diego Union Building), **11**
La Casa de Bandini, **8**
La Casa de Estudillo, **6**
Mason Street Schoolhouse, **9**
Old Adobe Chapel, **13**
Old Town State Historic Park Office, **3**
Robinson-Rose House, **5**
Seeley Stables, **7**
Wells Fargo Museum, **10**
Whaley House, **12**

OLD TOWN

Now a state historic park, Old Town is the birthplace of European California. In 1769, Father Junipero Serra founded the first of a series of California missions on the hill overlooking what is now Old Town, and a small community grew up around it. When the hilltop was made a fortress in 1774 (*see below*), the mission moved 6 miles farther up the San Diego river but the settlers remained in Old Town. After Mexico surrendered California to the United States, new settlers built a number of Yankee-style wood-frame and brick homes in Old Town. Today, Old Town is a living reminder of San Diego's Mexican and early American heritage, albeit a very commercialized one. Although the dirt roads and historical sites have been left untouched by San Diego's rapid development, Old Town has nonetheless undergone change, due largely to a lack of state and local funds. Maintenance for the buildings has been severely cut, as have guided tours and other tourist services. But even without the aid of a tour guide, Old Town's buildings, restaurants, and shops are fun to explore on foot. Located a few miles north of downtown off I–5, the historical park covers a six-block area from Twiggs Street to Wallace Street and from Juan Street to Congress Street, and is closed off to all vehicular traffic. Old Town is served by public Buses 4 and 5 from downtown, and also 6 and 105.

Visitors in wheelchairs may find it difficult to get into the area, and access to some of the buildings is nigh impossible.

OLD TOWN PLAZA Many of the historical sites face Old Town Plaza, the center of the park and a popular gathering point for pooped tourists and starving artists. The **Old Town State Historic Park Headquarters** is in the Robinson Building on the south side of the Plaza. Call the park office to see if they still offer tours. If not, you can still obtain a good booklet for around $2 that provides a brief history and a self-guided tour. *California Plaza at San Diego Ave., tel. 619/237–6770. Open daily 10–5.*

ADOBE BUILDINGS Four adobe buildings remain in Old Town. **La Casa de Estudillo,** built between 1827 and 1830 by the retired commander of the Presidio, is probably the most famous. The home is constructed of logs hauled from the mountains and the beams are secured with rawhide. Check out the cupola on top of the hacienda: The owner came up here to watch bull and bear fights in the plaza. *Across Mason St. from the plaza. Self-guided tours: $2. Open daily 10–5.*

La Casa de Bandini (tel. 619/297–8211) is now a popular restaurant (*see* Food, *above*) and one of the most attractive haciendas in San Diego. Built in 1829 by a Peruvian, Juan Bandini, the house served as the town's social center during Mexican rule. In 1869, Albert Seeley, a big poobah in the stagecoach business, added a second story and turned the place into the Cosmopolitan Hotel. Next door are the **Seeley Stables,** which became the stagecoach stop for Seeley and Wright Stage Lines in 1867. Today the stables house the Roscoe E. Hazard collection of horse-drawn carriages, western paraphernalia, and Indian artifacts ($2 admission).

BAZAAR DEL MUNDO A mercado built in the former Casa de Pico motel, Bazaar Del Mundo (tel. 619/296–3161) claims to be 100% pure Mexican, but it's really just a tourist trap, with lots of souvenir shops, restaurants, and stores selling expensive Latin American handicrafts. The Mexican art of bargaining is unheard of here.

WHALEY HOUSE Outside the historic park area, Whaley House is a two-story brick mansion dating back to 1856. Now fully refurbished in 1800s decor, the house is famous for being haunted. During the 1870s, when the home was used as a courthouse, a fellow named Yankee Jim Robinson was sentenced to hang for stealing a boat. His ghost, which is said to flit around the place, would probably be happier across the street at **El Campo Santo,** an old adobe-walled cemetery where some of the town's colorful characters—gamblers and highwaymen—are buried. *2482 San Diego Ave., tel. 619/298–2482. Admission: $3. Open Wed.–Sun. 10–4:30.*

PRESIDIO PARK A short drive (or a tiring trek) uphill leads to Presidio Park, 40 acres of rolling grassy hills that overlook Old Town. Atop one of the highest hills is the **Junipero Serra Museum,** built on the site of the first California Mission. The mission was moved in 1774 to make way for a fort. The museum has a research library and a collection of artifacts excavated from the Presidio site. *2727 Presidio Dr., tel. 619/297–3258. Admission: $2. Open Tues.–Sat. 10–4:30, Sun. noon–4:30.*

POINT LOMA Acting as a buffer against the temperamental Pacific, Point Loma curves around San Diego Bay and extends south into the sea. If you just stick to Point Loma's main streets, you'd think you had entered the American nightmare—plastic fast-food joints, parking lots, tacky neon signs, and flophouses. Away from the main strips, though, Point Loma is one of San Diego's wealthiest and most established enclaves, and a favorite retirement spot for navy officers. Many of the bayfront homes are nothing less than mansions, and the marinas are packed with expensive yachts. From the bay side you have a terrific view of downtown San Diego, and the point is also a good place to watch the parade of navy ships and aircraft from the U.S. Naval Air Station on North Island.

CABRILLO NATIONAL MONUMENT Perched at the end of the peninsula, the Cabrillo National Monument honors Portugese explorer Juan Rodriguez Cabrillo, the first European to come to San Diego in 1542. As interesting as the monument is the 144-acre park in which it sits. Rugged cliffs and shoreline offer spectacular views of the harbor and coastline, and the park is a prime viewing spot for the migration of the California grey whale from mid-December to mid-March. The visitor center offers films and lectures about the monument, the sea-level tide pools, and the grey whale migration. Also located within Cabrillo National Monument is the **Old Point Loma Lighthouse,** first lit in 1855. The light from its lens was visible for 25 miles, but the geniuses who installed it high up on the cliffs forgot about the fog that often plagues the coast. Since ships' navigators were usually unable to see it the lighthouse closed in 1891, but visitors can still explore the light in its white wooden house. A new lighthouse, much lower on the cliffs, has since replaced it. **Sunset Cliffs Park,** on the western side of Point Loma near Ocean Beach, is one of the prettiest places to watch the fabled California sunset with that fabled California babe or hunk, with the Mamas and the Papas on the stereo. *Tel. 619/557–5450. From downtown, take Bus 2 to Redwood St., transfer Bus 6. Admission: $3 per vehicle, $1 on foot. Open daily 9–5:15.*

MISSION BAY AND SEA WORLD The Mission Bay area of San Diego is a 4,600-acre aquatic park that encompasses trails, beaches, lawns, and the ever-popular Sea World. Certain areas are primarily used by water-skiers, jet skiers, and windsurfers. If you prefer to sunbathe, swim, or model your new bikini, you can hang out on the 27 miles of bayfront beaches or the 17 miles of oceanfront beaches, all of which are free. The park also boasts numerous jogging and biking trails near the water, and grassy areas where people fly kites or throw frisbees (try the Tecolote Shores area for good kite-flying). The beaches near I–5, which are near residential areas, get especially crowded on weekends. The **Mission Bay Visitor Information Center** is an excellent tourist resource for the bay and all of San Diego. *2688 E. Mission Bay Dr., tel. 619/276–8200. Open Mon.–Sat. 9–5:30, Sun. 9:30–5.*

If you don't want to come face to face with a dollop of je ne sais quoi, keep an eye out for signs warning about pollution, particularly on the bay beaches. San Diego has had its fair share of sewage leaks in recent years.

SEA WORLD Sea World is what really brings 'em to Mission Bay. This famous marine park features animal shows, aquarium displays, and petting tanks, as well as the usual gift shops that sell Shamu salt and pepper shakers and the like. Admission prices are steep, but the park is probably the closest you'll get to so many underwater creatures, barring a cameo appearance by Jacques Cousteau. Here, you can see, touch, and feed undersea creatures and watch animal shows starring Shamu, the killer whale. You'll also see whales, dolphins, sea lions, and otters jump over ropes or act in skits with humans. You can't help wondering if these animals ever hang out and reminisce about the days when they used to act like regular old animals. Nearby are huge aquariums where you can see sharks eating slabs of meat or drooling over the little kids tapping on the glass—the effect is similar to watching happy hour at a singles bar. Hop aboard the skyride or skytower for unrestricted views of both the bay and the San Diego skyline. One ride is $1.50. Plan on spending about six hours at the park, but you can come and go as you like. Skip the nighttime fireworks display—it bites. *Sea World Dr., at the western end of I–8, tel. 619/226–3901. Accessible by Bus 9 from downtown or Bus 81. Admission: $23. Open daily 9 AM–11 PM in summer, 9 AM–dusk in winter.*

The first six rows at Sea World are "high-splash" areas where you're guaranteed to ruin your 'do after the first whale makes a crash landing.

BELMONT PARK Nearer the ocean at the end of West Mission Bay Drive, Belmont Park is a hangout for everyone from beer-drinking, sunburned Hell's Angel types to flamboyant disco rollerskaters wearing very tight shorts and strangely pained expressions. More recently it has become a shopping, dining, and recreation area as well. The **Giant Dipper Roller Coaster,** an old-fashioned boardwalk roller coaster, can't compare with the modern screamers (basically, high-speed vomitoriums) but it does make your heart jump; if you're lucky you may even develop a minor case of whiplash. For those who can't hack it, the carousel is George Bush's kind of ride—"kinder and gentler." *Tel. 619/488–0668. Bus 34 from downtown. Roller coaster: $2; carousel: $1. Rides operate Sun.–Thurs. 11–10, Fri.–Sat. 11–11.*

HILLCREST The established center of San Diego's gay community, Hillcrest lies northwest of Balboa Park and within easy walking distance. The neighborhoood offers a growing selection of cafés, bookstores, and bars, as well as shops where you'll find everything from super-strength condoms to sequined evening gowns. Hillcrest extends from Laurel Street north to University Avenue and from Curlew Street east to Park Boulevard, but most of the commercial establishments are concentrated along University Avenue and in the area between Fourth and Sixth near University. **Quel Fromage** (523 University Ave., tel. 619/295–1600) sells coffee drinks and pastries, stocks a large selection of alternative newspapers, and has a bulletin board listing upcoming community events, including readings, music, poetry, and encounter groups. The nearby **Blue Door Bookstore** (3823 5th Ave., tel. 619/298–8610) stocks literature with a gay and lesbian emphasis, although it does carry some mainstream titles as well. On the same street, **Off the Record** (3861 5th Ave., tel. 619/298–4755) stocks a good selection of both new and used records, CDs, and tapes, and the staff can tell you about all kinds of upcoming musical events, both underground and mainstream. The '50s-style **Corvette Diner** (3946 5th Ave., tel. 619/542–1476) will either delight or annoy you with its own DJ, singing waiters and waitresses, '50s memorabilia, the ultimate burger, malts and fries, and the mythical 'Vette. Caution: You will be harassed if you enter this establishment wearing anything other than casual clothing ("Look, it's a suit!"), which is ironic since *everybody* looks like a nerd from the '50s. Hillcrest is accessible from the downtown area by public Buses 1, 3, 11, 16, 25, and 43.

CORONADO When you look out over the water from the Embarcadero, you see Coronado Island, a wealthy suburban enclave that moves at a pace even San Diegans find slow (yes, that slow). If San Diego had royalty, they'd probably occupy the old Victorian homes that proliferate on the island. In the absence of Charles and Di, the island attracts a lot of retirees and stiff military types who love the smell of aviation fuel in the morning—the North Island U.S Naval Air Station takes up the northern tip of the island. If anarchists look hard, they will find all kinds of evil machinations in the cozy relationship of the military and the island's obvious wealth. Whether you want to see the island or stage a sit-in, the easiest way to reach Coronado is on the **Bay Ferry** (tel. 619/234–4111). The 15-minute ride from the B Street Pier to the Old Ferry landing in Coronado is $1.60 each way, and an additional $1.10 for bicycles; ferries leave every hour from 9 AM to 10 PM, except on Friday and Saturday when they run until 11 PM. If you'd prefer to take the limo, you can cross the San Diego–Coronado Bay Bridge instead. Rush-hour traffic may cause delays; spend the extra time reading the crisis phone numbers posted on the bridge to assuage drivers who would rather face death than another California rush-hour hell. The toll into Coronado is $1, but cars with two or more passengers cross for free. The **Coronado Visitor Information Center** (1090 Orange Ave., tel. 619/437–8788 or 800/622–8300) offers brochures on shopping, dining, and lodging.

OLD FERRY LANDING The Old Ferry Landing (tel. 619/435–8895), where the Bay Ferry docks, is Coronado's version of Seaport Village, filled with small shops, restaurants, and other tourist attractions. It differs from its San Diego counterpart only in that it's less crowded and the view across the bay is of the city. It's packaged kitsch and you're best off just using it as a ferry dock. A trackless trolley (tel. 619/437–1861) runs from the nearby Le Meridien Hotel down Orange Avenue, the island's main strip, to the Hotel Del Coronado (*see below*).

HOTEL DEL CORONADO Affectionately referred to as "the Del" by locals, the Hotel Del Coronado is the ultimate example of Victorian architecture. With its tall circular turrets, hand-carved wooden pillars, and sheer size, the Del represents the pinnacle of San Diego affluence and clout. Built in 1888, it has hosted a veritable *Who's Who* of the world's elite, including the Duke of Windsor and several U.S. presidents, and was the backdrop to Marilyn Monroe's *Some Like It Hot.* Explore the hotel at night for maximum effect: After you check out the rich—drinking cocktails and listening to an ivory-tickler—you can run around upstairs looking for poltergeists or Jack Nicholson. Rumor has it that one of the rooms is haunted. *1500 Orange Ave., tel. 619/435–6611. Free guided tours from the lobby on Sat. at 1.*

LA JOLLA With its chichi shops, galleries, and restaurants, La Jolla (pronounced La Hoya) beckons you to park the BMW, toss your beeper away in reckless abandon, and drop a few thousand bucks on a new diamond-studded key ring or some nice gold-plated tweezers. If you left the beemer at home, you can always get there by bus, in which case you should toss your transfer away and drop a few bucks on a Big Mac. In Spanish, La Jolla means jewel, a fitting name for this beautiful community a few miles north of San Diego. Here, the coastline breaks down into a number of coves backed by verdant hillsides that look out over the Pacific. Jewels are expensive, though, and La Jolla is a particularly precious rock. Multimillion-dollar homes are the norm, and you're going to see more ludicrously groomed poodles here than probably anywhere else (except maybe New York's Upper East side). La Jolla is a jet-set community, an enclave of wealth like Santa Barbara, Beverly Hills, and Palm Beach. It's fun to peer into the lives of the rich and neurotic, but you probably can't afford to stay here overnight. As long as the cops don't bust you for loitering, though, you can hang out as long as you like. La Jolla boasts some of San Diego's most beautiful beaches and a whole bunch of free art galleries. Prospect Street, La Jolla's version of Rodeo Drive, offers McDonald's and Haagen-Dazs, as well as restaurants, boutiques, and galleries. On weekends, the leisure set cruises Prospect Street in their convertibles. Girard Avenue, La Jolla's other main thoroughfare, features specialty shops and some even more chic restaurants. La Jolla is accessible by public Buses 30 and 34 from downtown, and is best seen on foot. If you're coming by car on I–5 northbound, take the Ardath Road exit; from I–5 southbound, take the La Jolla Shores Village Drive exit.

The three best places to make out in La Jolla are Mount Soledad, Ellen Browning Scripps Park at La Jolla Cove, and Windansea Beach. But if you're planning to slide into home, bring your own condoms, they're tough to find around here.

MOUNT SOLEDAD Coming north on I–5, take the Ardath Street exit and make a left at the third light to reach the road to Mount Soledad, the highest point in La Jolla. The cross on top of the mountain provides a certain contingent of the populace with a serene place for Easter services, and a younger contingent with a 10-foot reason to feel even guiltier about getting nasty over Mom and Dad's gearshift. On the way up the hill, locals try to find "Midgetville," an area where the houses appear to be normal but are actually diminutive in size. Some teens stand next to every single door up the hill to Mt. Soledad to see if they have found a "dwarf" house.

LA JOLLA COVE The **Ellen Browning Scripps Park** is one of the most popular spots in La Jolla. Forming the western edge of La Jolla Cove, the park is laced by palm-fringed sidewalks where you can see everyone from Bill and Ted look-alikes to captains of industry in their penguin suits. Small beaches appear and disappear with the tides, which have carved small, secluded coves in the cliffs. Some of these cliffs are crumbling and dangerous, but you should be able to pick your way down to the beaches. A great place to watch the sunset is from the long layer of sandstone that stretches out above the waves. While you wait for the sun to punch the time-clock, check out the tidal pools, filled with starfish, anemones, crabs, and small fish.

The most popular beach is at the north end of the cove, which features an underwater preserve for divers and snorkelers. In summer, the water is packed with bodies floating around looking at stuff, and the beaches and lawns disappear under a blanket of sweating, shiny bodies—a good-size oil slick forms every time this lot goes in the water. If you don't get there by noon, forget about parking or staking a place in the sand. The **La Jolla Caves** are at the far northern point of the cove, underneath the La Jolla Cave and Shell Shop (1325 Coast Blvd., tel. 619/454–6080). A trail leads down from the shop into the caves, with some 133 steps down to the largest, Sunny Jim Cave.

SAN DIEGO MUSEUM OF CONTEMPORARY ART Formerly the La Jolla Museum of Contemporary Art, this museum is housed in a remodeled Irving Gill home, and has a collection of post-1950 paintings, sculpture, photography, drawings, and graphic art. Frequent exhibitions of modern furniture and design are also shown. *700 Prospect St., tel. 619/454–3541. Admission: $3, $1 students, free after 5 on Wed. Open Tues., Thurs.–Sun. 10–5, Wed. 10–9. Closed Mon. and 2nd week in Aug.*

SCRIPPS INSTITUTE OF OCEANOGRAPHY The institute showcases more than 20 tanks filled with colorful saltwater fish as well as exhibits on how tides affect the shoreline. An outdoor tidal-pool features starfish, lobsters, corals, and local sea creatures. Unlike at Sea World, the animals here aren't expected to put on a performance, although they do behave like starving actors come feeding time. Paths lead down from the institute to the beaches at La Jolla Shores. The beach north of Scripps Pier is a great spot for tidal pools, where you can find all kinds of marine creepy-crawlies. *8602 La Jolla Shores Dr.,* *tel. 619/534–6933. Suggested admission: $3. Feeding times: Wed. and Sun at 1:30. Open daily 9–5.*

U.C. SAN DIEGO One of the main entrances to the University of California San Diego lies at the intersection of Torrey Pines Road and Genessee Avenue. The campus features eucalyptus trees and lots of buildings in the architectural style known as "brutalism"—harsh, parking garage-like structures that positively ooze post-industrial angst. In keeping with that same theme, one building on campus continuously flashes cryptic messages in huge neon lights, including such memorable one-liners as "Avarice," "Gluttony," "Lust," "Justice," and "Fortitude." It's not clear whether the message board is advocating such behavior or warning students away, but one theory has it that a defrocked Catholic priest was hit by lightning and became fused with the building's electronics.

TORREY PINES STATE RESERVE Farther north along La Jolla's coast is **Torrey Pines State Reserve,** an 887-acre park overlooking the beaches of La Jolla. The reserve is filled with exotic California shrubbery and is home to one of only two groves of Torrey pines in the world. The park has some great hiking trails and picnic spots, with unbelievable views from the cliffs. *Tel. 691/755–2063. Take San Diego County Transit Express #800 from downtown. Admission: $6 per carload. Open daily 9–sunset.*

● ● ● MUSEUMS

The majority of San Diego's museums are in Balboa Park (*see above*), where museum buffs could probably while away weeks at a time. Below are some of the other museums scattered throughout the city.

Firehouse Museum displays antique fire-fighting equipment in the oldest firehouse in San Diego. *At Columbia and Cedar Sts. downtown, tel. 619/232–3473. Open weekends only, 10–4.*

Junipero Serra Museum. *See* Old Town, *above.*

Maritime Museum. *See* Downtown and the Embarcadero, *above.*

Mingei International Museum of World Folk Art. Located in a huge shopping mall with an indoor ice-skating rink, this folk museum exhibits pottery, textiles, and gadgets from all over the globe. *University Towne Center, 4405 La Jolla Village Dr., tel. 619/453–5300. Take Bus 30, 34, 41, 50, or 105 from downtown. Admission: $2. Open Tues.–Sat. 11–5, Sun. 2–5.*

Mission San Diego de Alcala. The first of the 21 California Missions established by Father Junipero Serra, the Mission San Diego de Alcala was originally built on Presidio Hill (near Old Town) in 1769. In 1774, the mission was moved 6 miles up the San Diego River to assure a good water supply. The mission has tape recordings for self-guided tours. Services are held daily in the original mission chapel. The Father Luis Jayme Museum features exhibits of early mission days. *10818 San Diego Mission Rd., tel. 619/281–8449. Bus 43 from downtown, or take I–8 east, exit Mission Gorge Rd. and follow the signs. Open daily 9–5.*

San Diego Museum of Contemporary Art. *See* La Jolla, *above.*

● ● ● BEACHES

San Diego is a beach culture. Head down to the central beaches—Ocean, Pacific, or Mission—to check out the surfers and '60s throwbacks in their natural habitat. Ocean Beach, in particular, is more than just a beach; it's a *community.* It's witnessed the evolution of beach culture from the days when it mirrored Gidget movies, through the increasingly hairy and marijuana-infused days of the '60s, to the present—which everlastingly mirrors America's nightmare decade: the '70s. Even now, AC/DC blasts from car stereos and it's common to see people smoking and rollerskating at the same time. Mission and Pacific beaches cater to a younger crowd that engage in many of the same activities as the older counterparts at Ocean Beach. San Diego's beaches have long been famous, but lately they've been attracting attention for all the wrong reasons. In 1992, San Diego's beaches were, to put it mildly, in deep shit. A leaking sewage pipe dumped millions of gallons of crap into the ocean, forcing bacteria levels to soar. The beaches have been reopened but nothing has been done about sewage from the Mexican side of the border—which is known to contaminate San Diego's most southerly beaches.

Visit Pacific and Mission beaches right after you visit Ocean Beach for a startling revelation about human nature: "The More Things Change, the More They Stay the Same—They Just Wear More Spandex."

SOUTH BAY **Silver Strand Beach State Park.** Connecting Coronado to the mainland, Silver Strand Beach runs from the Del to Imperial Beach. The view from the beach to Point Loma is great, and the long, clean beach is a cool place to have a bonfire at night. The beach got its name from the silver shells found at the water's edge. The water is pretty calm here, so be prepared for lots of families and screaming kids. *Take Bus 901 from downtown.*

Imperial Beach. The Silver Strand ends where Imperial Beach begins. Home of America's largest and longest-running sandcastle competition, the beach attracts a young crowd of surfers and Frisbee players. Unfortunately, this beach and the surrounding area are losing popularity because of increasing crime. *Take Bus 901 from downtown.*

POINT LOMA **Sunset Cliffs.** Beneath the jagged cliffs on the west side of Point Loma, this is one of the most secluded beaches in the city, and is popular with surfers and locals. When the tide's out, check out the tidal pools at the southern end near Cabrillo Point. You can get down to the beach by stairs at the foot of Bermuda and Santa Cruz avenues; otherwise, you have to brave the nasty cliff trails. *Take Bus 35 from downtown.*

NORTHERN SAN DIEGO Violence and crime on Pacific, Mission, and Ocean beaches are on the decline due to new rules banning alcohol from 8 PM to 8 AM, but the beaches still run low on overall aesthetic appeal. Still, droves of funseekers come to these beaches every day to play volleyball, model their tattoos and macramé beachwear, and display the latest roller-skating moves.

Ocean Beach. The area around Ocean Beach supports a well-established mélange of a hippie/me generation/New Age beach community. The northern part of the beach is known as **Dog Beach,** because dogs are allowed to roam free on the sand without a leash—humans had better watch their step. *Take Bus 35 from downtown.*

Mission Beach. The adjoining beaches of Mission and Pacific feature a boardwalk, roller coaster, and endless touristy beach shops. The south end caters more to surfers, swimmers, and volleyball players, and the north end near the roller coaster appeals more to smokers, tokers, and drinkers. *Take Bus 34 from downtown.*

Pacific Beach. Teenagers like to hang out here, which means you'll encounter a surplus of nubile bodies and loud grunge music. *Take local Bus 34 from downtown or express Bus 30.*

LA JOLLA For natural beauty or romantic surroundings, the beaches of La Jolla and the smaller beach towns can't be beaten.

Tourmaline Surfing Park. One of the top surfing beaches in La Jolla, Tourmaline Surfing Park was made famous (along with Windansea Beach) in Tom Wolfe's *The Pumphouse Gang. Take local Bus 34 from downtown or express Bus 30.*

Windansea Beach. Surfing is the big draw during the day, but at night floodlights (together with the lights from luxurious beach homes) illuminate the waves, making the beach a romantic spot to smooch. *Take local Bus 34 from downtown or express Bus 30.*

La Jolla Cove. Low tide at this beach lets you explore the tide pools and the caves. An unexpected high tide will force you to scuba dive for your copy of *Hollywood Wives.* This is a favorite spot for snorkelers, rough-water swimmers, and anyone who appreciates pretty views and spectacular sunsets. *Take local Bus 34 from downtown or express Bus 30.*

La Jolla Shores. One of the most popular, and potentially most crowded beaches in the country, this beach offers fun in the sun to people in their Gaultier swimwear and gold jewelry, as well as other assorted hangers-on. It has a wide sandy beach and relatively calm surf, but parking is a problem. *Take local Bus 34 from downtown.*

Black's Beach. This is the area's unofficial nude beach since nudity was outlawed in the late 1970s. Be careful where you pack your pistol, all you outlaws. The treacherous descent over the cliff trails to the beach is recommended only for the clothed and other hardy souls. Above the beach, hang gliders and sail-planes take off from the Torrey Pines Glider Port. *Take local Bus 34 from downtown or express Bus 30.*

● ● ● CHEAP THRILLS

You can probably buy everything you could ever need for the kitchen, the bath, or your own sick fantasies at **Kobey's Swap Meet,** a big flea market adjacent to the sports arena. Try bargaining; if the proprietor pulls out an Uzi, you know you've gone too far. *3500 Sports Arena Blvd., tel. 619/226–0650. Admission: 50¢ Thurs.–Fri., $1 weekends. Open Thurs.–Sun. 7–3.*

The main road off El Prado, which goes south from the parking lot by the Museum of Art, leads to the **Spreckels Organ Pavilion** (tel. 619/226–0819). Proclaimed to be the "world's largest outdoor musical instrument," the 5,000-pipe organ is played for the public free of charge every Sunday afternoon from 2 to 3. Monday evening concerts are also held during the summer. The concerts are a fun way to relax, but you have to be able to drown out the sounds of landing aircraft to fully appreciate the music.

FESTIVALS Contact the **International Visitor Information Center** (tel. 619/236–1212) to verify events and dates.

Jan. 1: The Annual Penguin Day Ski Fest (tel. 619/276–0830). Similar to the east's "Polar Bear Club," the festival requires you to brave the "antarctic" water of De Anza Cove and ski without a wet suit to earn a "Penguin Patch." Festivities last from 8 to 1 on New Year's Day.

Jan.–Mar.: The best viewing spots for the **Grey Whale Migration** are on harbor cruises (tel. 619/557–5450) or from the Cabrillo National Monument on Point Loma.

Feb.–Mar.: Mardi Gras at Oceanside (tel. 619/757–3651 or 619/757–7380). Jazz, food, and costume parties are the highlights of this annual event.

Feb.–Apr.: Wildflowers Bloom in the Desert. Anza-Borrego Desert State Park is transformed into a rainbow of colors. Call for information (tel. 619/767–5311 or 619/767–4205) because the full bloom lasts only two weeks.

Apr.: Annual San Diego Crew Classic (tel. 619/594–6555 or 619/226–4590). This is a collegiate competition at Crown Point Shores in Mission Bay that attracts more than 2,000 athletes from the United States and Canada.

May: Annual Cinco de Mayo Festival (tel. 619/296–3161). A Mexican celebration, with entertainment and booths in Old Town State Park.

May: Annual Pacific Beach Block Party (tel. 619/483–6666). Join the residents of P.B. at this yearly fiesta, with live music, prizes, arts and crafts, and, of course, food.

June: Annual Campland on the Bay Jazz Festival (tel. 619/581–4200). Major jazz bands perform outdoors.

Mid-June–Early July: Del Mar Fair. San Diego's annual county fair features livestock shows, science projects, garden shows, carnival rides and corn dogs. *Tel. 619/259–1355 or 619/755–1161. Admission: $6.*

June–Sept: Old Globe Festival (tel. 619/239–2255). Features contemporary plays, Shakespearean works, and other classics at the Old Globe Theater in Balboa Park.

July: Over-the-Line Tournament (tel. 619/688–0817). Featuring a game that's a cross between softball and stickball, this weekend-long party attracts more than 1,000 three-person teams.

Aug.: Annual Naval Air Station Miramar Show (tel. 619/537–4082). Headlined by the Blue Angels, the Navy flying team, the show consists of five hours of breathtaking stunts and flying formations right out of *Top Gun.* Admission and parking are free.

Aug.: Annual Sand Castle Days (tel. 619/424–6663). The site of America's largest sandcastle-building event; you can enter your own replica of the Acropolis or the USS *Enterprise.*

Aug.: America's Finest City Week (tel. 619/234–4197). A self-congratulatory week in San Diego featuring parades and concerts.

Sept.: La Jolla Rough Water Swim (tel. 619/456–2100). The largest rough-water swimming competition in the United States takes place at La Jolla Cove.

Oct.: Zoo Founder Day. Everyone is admitted free to the San Diego Zoo (tel. 619/234–3153).

Nov.: Annual San Diego Thanksgiving Dixieland Jazz Festival. Jazz bands from around the United States perform at the Town and Country Hotel (tel. 619/297–5277).

Dec.: Christmas on El Prado (tel. 619/239–0512) features a candlelight procession and carolers, and free admission to all museums.

After Dark

San Diego teenagers head to Tijuana at night, mostly because no one cards them down there, but also because San Diego isn't exactly the most happening of places once the sun sets. Retirees, high-tech researchers, and shaved military types don't make for the kind of scene where young rebels are going to find too many soul mates. For many San Diegans, nightlife is a bonfire on the beach with your baby, a guitar, and a bottle of Night Train. As San Diego continues to grow, though, the city is developing a fairly extensive music scene, a wide variety of bars and cafés, and a tiny underground dance scene whose locations and names change weekly. For listings of events, consult the *Reader,* San Diego's free arts-and-news weekly, which comes out every Thursday and disappears from most newsstands by Friday. Look in 7-Eleven stores, which usually keep them in stock longer than most places. *Revolt in Style* and *Umbrella,* two small underground publications available at trendy cafés and boutiques, also list local events. You can find several gay and lesbian publications throughout Hillcrest.

BARS AND CAFÉS The best bars and cafés are probably in the Gaslamp Quarter and Hillcrest (*see below*), but fun hangouts are scattered throughout the city. A favorite spot in Old Town is **O Hungry's** (2547 San Diego Ave., tel. 619/298–0133). Filled to capacity almost every night, this bar is famous for its foot-tall, half-yard, and one-yard glasses of beer, and zany folk yelling "Más cerveza!" with really bad accents. The surfing set hang out at Belmont Park to look for possible sexual partners, play video games, or ride the roller coaster (*see* Worth Seeing, *above*). Also at Belmont Park is **Club Red Onion** (125 Ocean Front Walk, tel. 619/488–9040), a restaurant/bar that attracts surfers looking to do some dancing. At Pacific Beach, along Garnet Avenue and Mission Boulevard, you'll find a string of nightspots, too. When all else fails, take yourself to **The Turquoise Room** at the **Aztec Bowl** (4356 30th St., ½ block north of El Cajon Blvd., tel. 619/283–3135) for a sureal reminder of what makes this nation tick. Sip a tequila sunrise and take in the cover band's touching rendition of "Sunny" while bowling pins crash in the background.

GASLAMP QUARTER The Gaslamp offers a prime opportunity to sample the most eclectic of San Diego's nighttime offerings. On weekends, packs of people wander from bar to club to café, using alcohol as chum to initiate a sexual feeding frenzy.

Cafe Lulu (419 F St., tel. 619/238–0114). A candlelit, whimsical, postmodern sort of place, Lulu serves expensive espressos and glasses of wine to San Diego's hip kids.

Cafe Sevilla (555 4th Ave., tel. 619/233–5979). One of a growing number of tapas bars in San Diego, Cafe Sevilla is less of a scene than Olé Madrid. As a result, the atmosphere is actually conducive to conversation. If the conversation becomes dull, you can always leap onto a table and dance to the live flamenco guitar.

Java Coffeehouse (837 G St., tel. 619/235–4012). Park your motorcycle wherever it's most visible and come in for a coffee. Special menu offerings include the Bohemian Breakfast (a cup of house coffee, an amaretto cookie, and two cigarettes: $1.75) and coffee drinks for every literary taste, including the Coffee Kerouac, the Kaffe Kafka, and the Café Cocteau.

Olé Madrid (423 F St., tel. 619/557–0146). After 8 on weekends a line forms to get into this tapas bar, and if the guy at the door doesn't approve of the way you're dressed, you may be waiting a long time. Folks oozing the right attitude will discover inside a big replica of Picasso's *Guernica* and a variety of bull-fighting paraphernalia, as well as pitchers of good sangria.

HILLCREST Hillcrest is the center of gay and lesbian life in San Diego, so not surprisingly you're going to find a lot of predominantly gay clubs. But Hillcrest is also the site of several casual bars and cafés that cater to just about everyone.

The Alibi (1403 University Ave., tel. 619/295–0881). The doorwoman's wearing a pink polyester pantsuit and reading *Soap Opera Digest,* Patsy Kline's on the jukebox, and a

Espousing Dada for Next to Nada (Or, What to Do at Night)

Head for one of the city's numerous taquerias, where teenagers hang out on weekend nights with nothing much else to do. To fit right in, order "three rolled with guac" (three rolled tacos with guacamole).

Have a bonfire on the beach. Locals often go to supermarkets or warehouses and "borrow" a pallet—those flat supporting crates that forklifts move stuff around on—to use as firewood. Take the pallet to the beach (either Pacific, Mission, or Ocean Beach), set it on fire, play a heart-rending rendition of "Stairway To Heaven" on the guitar, and break out the rum punch.

Go downtown with $5 in your pocket. With this, you can hit a couple of live music spots (there's no cover charge in most places), have a couple of beers, and gloat at how much fun you're having for only $5. Bring extra if you plan to hit on someone, drink to the detriment of your liver, or sip fancy coffee drinks in trendy cafés.

Attend the Laserium show at the Reuben H. Fleet Space Theater and Science Center with all the 18-year-old red-eyed, long-haired Floyd heads. To fully appreciate this experience you should have an abiding sense of wonder at the enduring social commentary of "Dark Side of the Moon"; recently acquired sight after a lifetime of blindness; or long hair, blood-shot eyes, and a pocketful of illegal substances.

Join the under-21 crowd in Tijuana. Simply take the trolley to the border and walk on into Mexico. Returning could be a problem though, especially if you're intoxicated, have a Spanish surname, or are not a U.S. citizen. Establishments to check out in TJ: Rio Rita's, House, and any place without a cover charge.

casual combination of young, hip kids, and old-time regulars sip tall glasses of beer side by side. This is the ultimate cheap dive, red lights and all.

The Flame (3780 Park Blvd., tel. 619/295–4163). This multiroom women's club features events like salsa night, Monday-night football, and wet T-shirt contests. Lose some cash at one of the pool tables or get down under the two gleaming disco balls.

Soho Tea and Coffee (1045 University Ave., tel. 619/299–7646). This coffeehouse caters to university students and others alternately studying their books and each other. The decor, a charming mix of garage sale meets industrial warehouse, complements the poetry readings and acoustic music that's often staged at night.

LIVE MUSIC

JAZZ In the Gaslamp Quarter, especially in the area near Horton Plaza, you can wander from jazz joint to jazz joint. Two local favorites are **Dick's Last Resort** (345 5th Ave., tel. 619/231–9100), which plays Dixieland jazz from Thursday to Saturday and the blues on Sunday and Monday; and **Croce's Restaurant and Jazz Bar** (802 5th Ave., tel. 619/233–4355), named after the late Jim Croce. There's no cover charge, but a there is $5 minimum on drinks or food. Next door is **Croce's Top Hat Bar and Grille,** which offers nightly rhythm and blues.

ROCK-AND-ROLL **SOMA** (555 Union St., downtown, tel. 619/239–7662). Young, underground bands play here, although a DJ sometimes comes in to play dance music. The cover charge hovers around $5 and the age of the clientele at around 20. The music and dancing can be quite good.

Bodies (528 F St., downtown, tel. 619/236–8988). The rockabilly night spot in town caters to boys and girls with slicked back hair and chunky black shoes. The fun, casual atmosphere is a prime place to experience rockabilly culture, something of a rarity nowadays.

Megalopolis (4321 Fairmount Ave., East San Diego, tel. 619/584–7908). The spot for skateboarders and students from San Diego State, this place features local garage bands, which vacillate wildly in quality. At least the people-watching is good.

DANCING The best way to find out about underground dance clubs is through word of mouth (ask around at Cafe Lulu for tips) or the various alternative publications widely available in Hillcrest and downtown. The **Kansas City Steakhouse** (535 5th Ave., downtown, tel. 619/557–0525) is frequently transformed into a one-night oasis of urban bacchanalia; call or come by to see what's happening.

Club West Coast (12028 Hancock St., tel. 619/295–3724) is a gay club for the seasoned disco veteran only. It's extra loud, extra bright, the music is extra-synthesized, and there's just one too many spinning disco balls.

COMEDY **The Improv** (832 Garnet Ave., tel. 619/483–4520) showcases both local and national comedians. Ticket prices are $8–$10, and you must be over 21. The **Comedy Store** (916 Pearl St., La Jolla, tel. 619/454–9176) has a similar setup, although students with IDs can get two-for-one tickets on Wednesday and Thursday.

Outdoor Activities

BASKETBALL ● ● ●

The best place to join a pick-up game is the **Municipal Gym** in Balboa Park (tel. 619/525–8264). Other good spots for cagers include **Robb Field** (tel. 619/224–7581) in Ocean Beach, the **Mira Mesa Recreation Center** (tel. 619/566–5141), the **University of San Diego** (tel. 619/260–4600), and the **University of California at San Diego** (tel. 619/534–4037).

BIKING

Biking is a big-time sport in San Diego. The **California Department of Transportation** (tel. 619/688–6699) puts out a free map of all county bike paths. Probably the most popular route is Old Highway 101, the coastal road that runs from La Jolla to Oceanside. Easily the most beautiful ride in the city, it hugs the cliffs and beaches all the way. Although the roads are narrow and windy, experienced riders like to follow Lomas Santa Fe Drive in Solana Beach (*see* Near San Diego, *below*) east into beautiful Rancho Santa Fe. For more leisurely rides, Mission Bay, San Diego Harbor, and the Mission Beach boardwalk are all flat and scenic. You can rent bikes all over town for about $20 a day. Try **Alpine Rent A Bike** in Pacific Beach (tel. 619/273–0440), **Hamel's Action Sports Center** in Mission Beach (tel. 619/488–5050), and **California Bicycle** in La Jolla (tel. 619/454–0316).

GOLF

You can rent clubs for a round of golf at the two 18-hole courses at **Torrey Pines Municipal Golf Course** (11480 N. Torrey Pines Rd., La Jolla, tel. 619/570–1234). Considering it's a municipal course, this one's a real beauty, perched on the cliffs overlooking the ocean. **Balboa Park Municipal Golf Course** (Golf Course Dr., tel. 619/235–1184) is a public 18-hole course in the heart of the city. A round costs $33 and you can rent clubs. An okay nine-hole course is **Oceanside Golf Course** (1 Country Club La., Oceanside, tel. 619/433–1360), which also rents out clubs. The greens fee is $10 ($15 on weekends).

JET SKIING

With their high-pitched scream and oily stench, Jet Skis aren't exactly the belles of the beach, but they *are* fun. A good spot to open up the throttle is Mission Bay. If you prefer bouncing the waves, you can launch Jet Skis from most beaches, but some places have special regulations. In the Mission Bay area, you can rent the noisy monsters from **Jet Ski Rentals** (tel. 619/276–9200), but be prepared to pay through the exhaust—it's $30 an hour, with a $100 deposit.

SURFING

Contrary to popular mythology, you need a wet suit if you're going to surf in San Diego any time other than the summer months. If you know what "tubular" really means, you should head for Ocean Beach pier, Tourmaline Surfing Park, and Windansea Beach in La Jolla, South Cardiff State Beach, and Swami's (Sea Cliff Roadside Park) in Encinitas (*see* Near San Diego, *below*). You can rent sticks at **Star Surfing Company** (tel. 619/273–7827) in Pacific Beach, **La Jolla Surf Systems** (tel. 619/456–2777), and **Hansen's Sporting Goods** (tel. 619/753–6595) in Encinitas. Boards cost about $4 an hour, or $17 a day.

Near San Diego

San Diego County is larger than nearly a dozen of the country's states. It stretches from the Pacific coast inland to the sweltering sands of the Anza-Borrego desert. The diversity of terrain is remarkable and it's worth making the effort to get into the rural backcountry or at least up the coast to some of the smaller beach communities.

THE NORTH COAST

The towns along the North Coast offer a glimpse of what San Diego, and southern California in general, were like before freeways and brakelights became such an integral part of the lifestyle and culture. These towns developed separately from one another, and each provides a sense of the enormous diversity that made California what it is today: With its race course and beautiful beaches, **Del Mar** is a playground for the wealthy; **Encinitas**

The San Diego North Coast

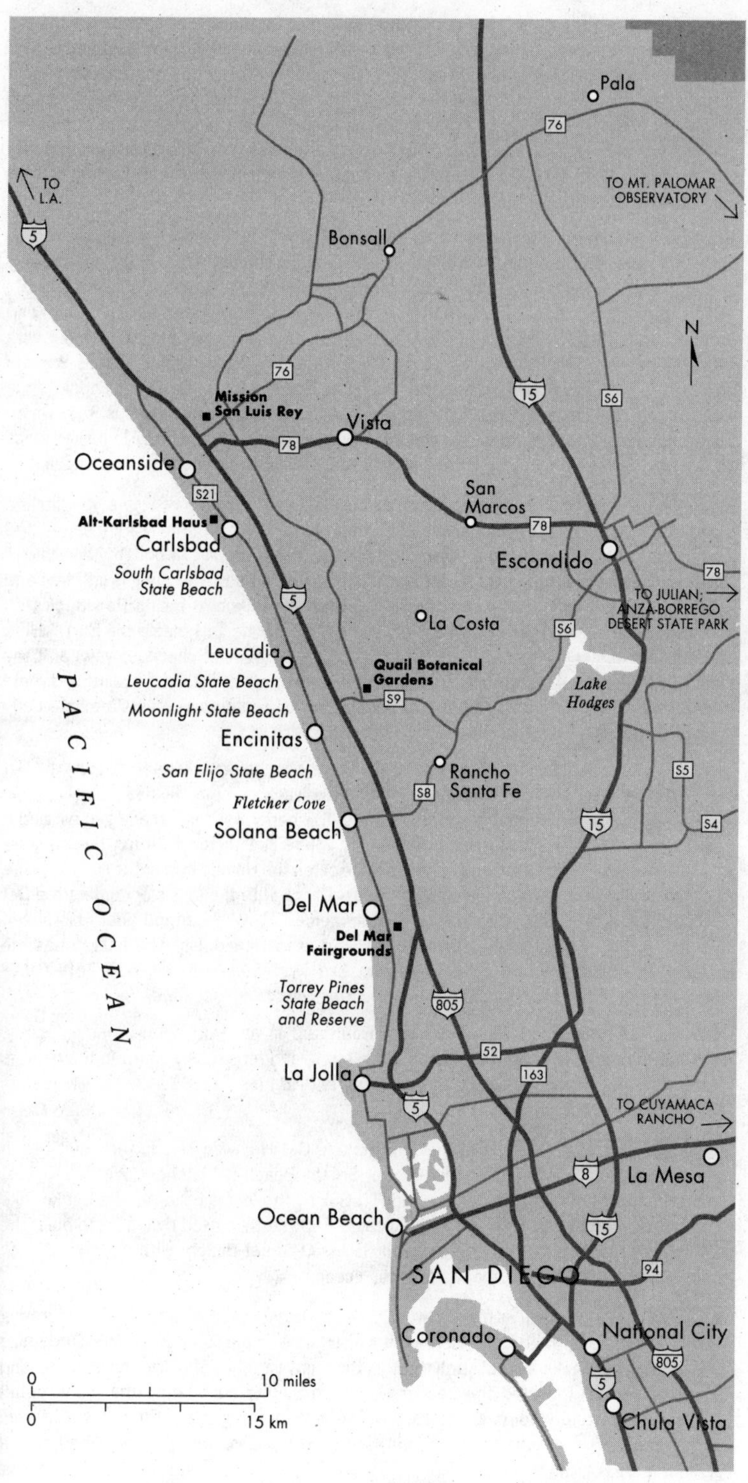
Pala
76
TO MT. PALOMAR OBSERVATORY
TO L.A.
5
Bonsall
N
76
15
S6
Mission San Luis Rey
Vista
78
Oceanside
S21
San Marcos
78
Alt-Karlsbad Haus
Carlsbad
Escondido
South Carlsbad State Beach
78
TO JULIAN; ANZA-BORREGO DESERT STATE PARK
5
La Costa
S6
Leucadia
Quail Botanical Gardens
Leucadia State Beach
S9
Lake Hodges
Moonlight State Beach
PACIFIC OCEAN
Encinitas
Rancho Santa Fe
S5
San Elijo State Beach
S8
Fletcher Cove
15
S4
Solana Beach
Del Mar
Del Mar Fairgrounds
Torrey Pines State Beach and Reserve
805
52
La Jolla
163
5
TO CUYAMACA RANCHO
8
La Mesa
Ocean Beach
15
SAN DIEGO
94
Coronado
National City
805
5
Chula Vista
0
10 miles
0
15 km

and **Solana Beach** are old farming communities; and **Carlsbad** is still rooted in the old Mexican rancheros and the entrepreneurial instinct of John Frazier, who attempted to turn the town into a replica of a German spa. More than anything else, though, the North Coast is known for its wide, beautiful beaches. But as the North Coast's popularity grows, so does its share of problems. Oceanside, for instance, keeps housing prices relatively cheap so military personnel stationed at Camp Pendleton Marine Base can afford to keep roofs over their heads. Unfortunately the cheap accommodations end up also attracting drug dealers and prostitutes.

The quickest way up the North Coast is on I–5, which connects San Diego with Los Angeles. You'll find the cheapest places to sleep along the interstate; you can probably get a room at a Motel 6 for around $30. A far more scenic route is along Old Highway 101, which starts just north of La Jolla and hugs the coastline. If you don't have your own car, **Amtrak** (tel. 619/239–9021 or 800/872–7245) has frequent service to Los Angeles, with stops in Del Mar and Oceanside. Route 800 of the **San Diego County Transit Express** follows I–5 from downtown up the coast as far as Oceanside; if you want to stick to the coastal road, take express Bus 30 as far as La Jolla and change to local Bus 301, which runs to Oceanside. In addition, **Greyhound-Trailways** (tel. 619/239–9171) makes stops at Del Mar, Solana Beach, Encinitas, and Oceanside on its way north to Los Angeles.

DEL MAR If you look like a page from *GQ* or belong on the cover of *Vogue,* you'll blend right in at Del Mar, the southernmost community of North County. Fancy shops and restaurants line Camino del Mar, the area's main drag. Although the town's Mediterranean-style plazas are prohibitively expensive, window-shopping is still free and grabbing a bite won't cost an arm and a leg. Del Mar is known for its **Racetrack** (tel. 619/755–1141) and **Thoroughbred Club,** a.k.a. "Where the Turf meets the Surf." Here the rich and famous wager (no one is tacky enough to say "bet" because you can't say "bet" with your lower jaw thrust forward) on the ponies while discussing political events over a spot of tea. The racing season runs from July to September; meets are held daily except Tuesdays.

The Del Mar Fair is a great place to go with a bunch of corn-dog friends or with a loved one who likes to eat corn dogs.

The Southern California Exposition, commonly referred to as the **Del Mar Fair,** is an annual three-week summer festival that features carnival rides, art exhibits, live performances, arcade games, and a nightly fireworks show. If you're not in town during the summer festival, you may be able to catch the Horse Show or the Holiday Faire held on the same grounds. Check with the locals or contact the **Del Mar Chamber of Commerce** (1401 Camino del Mar, tel. 619/755–4844) to find out exact schedules. The fairgrounds are next to the Racetrack. *Via de la Valle Rd., exit west from I–5, tel. 619/755–1161. Entrance to the fair is about $6 per person. Ride tickets are separate.*

Near the fairgrounds on Jimmy Durante Boulevard is an exotic bird-training facility, **Freeflight.** Visitors are allowed to handle the birds, and remember, a bird in the hand is better than a bird overhead. *2132 Jimmy Durante Blvd., tel. 619/481–3148. Admission: $1. Open daily 9–5.*

SOLANA BEACH A little farther north along Old Highway 101 is the quiet beach community of Solana Beach. A highlight of Solana Beach is **Fletcher Cove,** at the west end of Lomas Santa Fe Drive. It's called Pill Box by the locals because of a bunker-like lifeguard station on the cliffs above the beach. Early settlers used dynamite to blast the cove out of the cliffs. Another pretty spot is the **D Street Beach,** with its long wooden staircase, which offers great views over the ocean.

ENCINITAS Known as the "Flower Capital of the World," Encinitas is an old farming town and a major grower of poinsettias. It's also home of the **Quail Botanical Gardens,** a beautiful place to take a quiet stroll through the many varieties of palms, oaks, ferns, and flowering plants. Disabled travelers may have difficulty negotiating the many uphill pathways. Free guided tours are held every Saturday morning at 10. *Encinitas Blvd., tel. 619/436–3036. Exit east from I–5, turn left on Quail Gardens Dr. Admission free but parking is $1. Open daily 8–5.*

Near the Lagoon along Old Highway 101 are the palm trees of **Sea Cliff Roadside Park.** Locals and the too-cool surfer crowd refer to the beach here as Swami's. We're not sure why, but it might have something to do with the fact that the golden domes of the Self Realization Fellowship are located here. Just north of Encinitas are two of the best beaches along the coast: **Moonlight Beach** (tel. 619/753–5091), a family spot with barbecue pits and picnic areas; and **Leucadia State Beach** (tel. 619/438–3143), a.k.a. "Stonesteps," so named for the stone steps leading from the cliffs to the sand below. Leucadia is popular with swimmers, surfers, and scuba divers.

If you don't think you can make it up the road to the Allstar Inns in Carlsbad, you can always stay at **Image Inns** (607 Leucadia Blvd., tel. 800/992–9330 or 619/944–3800) off I–5. Rooms start at $44 for a single, $49 for a double. If you're camping, you can pitch your tent at **San Elijo State Beach** (tel. 619/753–5091) on Old Highway 101 in Cardiff. The campground has 171 developed sites, with special areas for hikers and bicyclists. Inland sites go for $14, while a view of the beach costs around $19 a day. Peak season is March through November when rates go up to $16 and $21.

CARLSBAD Carlsbad's main attraction is **Alt Karlsbad Haus.** In the basement of this German cottage is a well that put the town on the map. In the 1880s, entrepreneur John Frazier found a spring of mineral water that he claimed bubbled over with healing powers. A man ahead of his time, Frazier marketed and promoted his water to gullible customers. *2802A Carlsbad Blvd., tel. 619/729–6912. Accessible by the Bus 301 from the Oceanside Transit Center. Admission free. Open Mon.–Sat. 10–5, Sun. 1–4:30.*

While you're in Carlsbad, check out the **Sand Bar Cafe** (3878 Carlsbad Blvd., at Tamarack, tel. 619/729–3170). This popular beach watering hole resembles a barn without the hay and the bad smells, but locals like it anyway. They come to dance the night away and listen to live rock bands. Happy hour starts at 4 and goes until 8 (7 on Friday and Saturday). A good, cheap place to crash is **Allstar Inns** (6117 Paseo Del Norte Dr., tel. 619/438–1242), a smaller and cheaper motel chain than Motel 6. Rates here start at $25 plus tax for one person and $29 plus tax for two. The bathrooms are small and the carpets are none too clean, but the prices are the best in town. The **Motel 6** (750 Raintree Dr., off I–5 at Poinsettia La., tel. 619/431–0745) in town has singles for $27 and doubles for $33.

Campers can spread themselves out at **South Carlsbad State Beach** (tel. 619/438–3143), 3 miles south of Carlsbad on Carlsbad Boulevard. The campground has 226 developed sites, with special areas for hikers and cyclists. In summer, expect to pay $16–$21 and reservations are a good idea. Be warned that this campground has a high theft risk. For more information about Carlsbad, contact the **Carlsbad Chamber of Commerce** (5411 Avenida Encinas, tel. 619/931–8400).

OCEANSIDE Although Oceanside is primarily a housing project for Camp Pendleton marines, it does have a few places of interest. Its natural harbor is a great place to try your hand at fishing, sailing, or surfing. If people-watching is more your speed, pick up a lunch at a local restaurant and pull up a plank on the pier. Here you can spend a lazy day watching Mexicans and middle-age white folk trying to catch some dinner. If you can stomach one more mission, head out to **Mission San Luis Rey,** founded in 1798 to help "educate" and convert local Native Americans. The 18th and largest of the missions, San Luis Rey was built as a religious halfway house between San Diego and the San Juan Capistrano Mission. You can explore the mission on a self-guided tour that goes through, among other things, the Old Mission Church and the Madonna Chapel (no, not that one). *4050 Mission Ave., tel. 619/757–3651. Take Mission Ave. east from I–5, or take Bus 303 from the Oceanside Transit Center. Admission: $2. Open Mon.–Sat. 10–4:30, Sun. noon–4:30.*

Motel 6 (1403 Mission Ave., tel. 619/721–6662), off I–5 at the Mission Avenue exit, provides the lowest rates available in Oceanside. It's not the Plaza, but it's clean and you can get a basic room for $33. Otherwise, check out the **Sandman Motel** (1501 Carmelo Dr., tel. 619/722–7661), which has doubles for about $40. It's not very appealing from the outside, but the rooms are decently furnished and quite comfortable. What's more, the beach and the marina are nearby. If you need to know more, contact the **Oceanside Visitor Information Center** (928 N. Hill St., tel. 800/350–7873 or 619/721–1101).

INLAND NORTH COUNTRY

When you get away from the coast, the tourist trappings of fun-in-the-sun California fall away. Much of the land is devoted to farms and ranches, and the region has a bucolic feel very different from the rest of the San Diego area. Closer to the coast, the hills are covered with oak and pine, interspersed with wineries, missions, and freshwater lakes. As you go farther east, the land breaks down into arid desert and scrub. It certainly helps to have a car to get around inland, but—if you've got the time and the patience—you can use the **Northeast Rural Bus System** (tel. 619/765–0145), which provides irregular service between inland towns and Escondido and El Cajon. The bus system is primarily designed to bring residents of small towns to the city on shopping expeditions, but anyone can ride as long as they have the $3.10 fare. Julian and Borrego Springs are among the towns served, but there is no service to Mount Palomar. The buses are actually 14-person minivans, so reservations are essential. If you're elderly or disabled, the bus will pick you up at your door; others wait at designated bus stops.

ESCONDIDO This quiet lake community, 18 miles east of the Pacific and 30 miles north of San Diego, is a subtler, more isolated version of the beach communities that dominate San Diego's North Coast. It's so subtle, in fact, that it's boring. Just how exciting could it be if Lawrence Welk chose the area for his retirement resort? Nevertheless, Escondido serves as a major transport hub for trips inland to Mount Palomar and Julian (*see below*), and the town boasts a major attraction of its own in the **San Diego Wild Animal Park.** The park is more of an enclosure for humans than it is for animals. Opened in 1972 as an extension of the San Diego Zoo in Balboa Park, this 2,100-acre park allows the animals to roam freely in natural-looking habitats with other species normally found in their environments. Humans view the area via a 50-minute, 5-mile trip on the Wgasa Bush Line Monorail. This is the best way to see the different habitats without disturbing any of the animals, which include 41 endangered species. The park is also fun to explore on foot: With plenty of steep hills, the 1¾-mile Kilimanjaro Hiking Trail can prove exhausting. The park also offers daily bird and trained-animal shows. Wild Animal Park is not as "hands-on" as the San Diego Zoo, but remember that the park is more for the animals than it is for the humans, and therein lies its beauty. *Tel. 619/234–6541. Take I–15 north to Via Rancho Parkway and follow the signs. From downtown Escondido, take N.C.T.D. Bus 307. Admission: $14.50, parking $1. Open Sept.–May, daily 9–4; June–Aug., 9–5.*

Escondido is at the intersection of Route 78, which heads east from Oceanside, and I–15, which connects San Diego to Riverside and points north. The **Escondido Transit Center** (700 West Valley Parkway) serves as the hub for **North County Transit District** buses (tel. 619/743–6283) and **Greyhound** (tel. 619/239–9171), both of which offer service from San Diego. The transit center is near an area filled with cheap motels, including a **Motel 6** (509 W. Washington Ave., tel. 619/743–6669) with doubles for about $35. Most of the motels are on Washington Avenue; to get there from the transit center, walk north on Quince Avenue. For more information, contact the **Escondido Convention and Visitors Bureau** (720 North Broadway, tel. 619/745–4741).

PALOMAR OBSERVATORY About 30 miles northeast of Escondido along Route S6 is the Hale Telescope at the Palomar Observatory. With its 200-inch diameter mirror, the telescope remains one of the largest peeping-tom devices in the world. Its range is approximately 1,000,000,000 light years (WOW!) and it's able to photograph corners of the heavens never seen before. The images taken by the telescope are shown at the observatory museum, as is a video explaining the history of the telescope and the pictures of the galaxy that it has taken. *At the north end of Route S6, tel. 619/742–3476. Admission free. Museum open daily 9–4:30, observatory 9–4; disabled access 9:30–2.*

On Route S6, the road leading to the observatory, you'll see two campgrounds. **Fry Creek** (tel. 619/745–2421) has 20 well-shaded sites built into the side of the mountain. The $7 sites are nicely protected from the sun, but disabled travelers won't be able to get there and the toilets are nothing but smelly, raunchy holes in the ground. The **Observatory Campground** (tel. 619/745–2421) has 42 sites, also $7 per night and not accessible to the disabled. The campground is basically a dirt clearing that provides less protection and privacy than Fry Creek. Both campgrounds are open from May 1 to mid-December. At Palomar Mountain, if you turn off onto S7 instead of continuing on S6 to the Observatory, you'll come to **Palomar Mountain State Park** (tel. 619/742–3462 or 619/765–0755). Camping is allowed in the park at **Doane Valley,** which has 31 sites, three of which are accessible to the disabled. The campground has restrooms and showers, and the $14 sites come complete with table, stove, and fire ring. You can make reservations through **Mistix** (tel. 800/444–7275). The **Palomar Mountain General Store** (tel. 619/742–3496), at the intersection of Routes S6 and S7 in Palomar Mountain, really is a *general* store. It sells everything from "art and artifacts to chocolates to groceries and camping supplies to observatory and astronomy-related items." If you're too lazy to cook for yourself, **Mother's Kitchen** (tel. 619/742–4233) next door has inexpensive salads and burgers.

JULIAN A two-hour drive east of San Diego is Julian, one of the last places to see any fertile landscape before the desert. Julian is also one of the few places in southern California where you can witness a true changing of the seasons. At an elevation of 4,220 feet, this quaint little town sees snow during the winter. But people don't come here for the seasons, nor for the town's cute shops and handmade crafts—they come for the homemade pies. As the Eiffel Tower is to Parisians, apple pie is to Julianites. Nothing can compare with the taste, and you will see people ordering two or three at a time.

When you're completely pie-eyed, stagger around the town a bit to burn up some calories. The **Julian Pioneer Museum** (2811 Washington St., tel. 619/765–0227) displays turn-of-the-century paraphernalia such as clothing, toys, Indian artifacts, and stuffed birds. The brewery-turned-museum asks for a $1 donation. Proceeds go to the local women's club, which not only maintains the museum but also sponsors the annual **Wildflower Show,** around Mother's Day, and the **Quilt Show,** around the Fourth of July. Other annual festivals include the **Weed Show** and the **Banjo and Fiddle Contest,** both held during the late summer months. The biggest festival of the year, though, occurs during the first three weekends in October. During this time, the residents of Julian sponsor the **Fall Harvest Festival** and **Apple Days.** As you can no doubt guess, the festivities are marked by apple pies galore!

Surprisingly for a town this size, there are several points of interest besides the museum and festivals. The **Julian Hotel** on Main Street is registered as a national historic landmark, and the **Eagle & High Peak Mines** (follow C St. from the center of town) allow visitors to see the gold mines that made Julian a magnet for get-rich-quick artists. Near Julian, at the intersection of Routes 78 and 79 in Santa Ysabel, is **Dudley's Bakery** (tel. 800/225-3348). People from all over the country (literally) make a beeline here for their pastry and bread. To get to Julian from San Diego, take I-8 east and then 79 north; if you don't have a car, take Route 878 of the Northeast Rural Bus System (*see above*) from Escondido.

Lodging in Julian itself is too expensive for most budget travelers, but you can camp cheaply in nearby Cuyamaca Rancho State Park (*see below*). **William Heise County Park** is another nearby camping option, with 103 sites going for $11 each. Make reservations (tel. 619/565–3600) in the summer months and for the Fall Harvest Festival and Apple Days—three month's notice is not too much. To get to the campground from Julian, follow Route 78 west and then 79 north to Pine Hills Road, a mile or two west of town.

CUYAMACA RANCHO STATE PARK Perhaps the most striking feature of Cuyamaca Rancho State Park is how green it is. A little over an hour's drive east of San Diego and just west of Anza-Borrego Desert State Park, Cuyamaca Rancho is a richly forested area that you would never expect to find among the beaches or deserts of southern California. Over half the park's 25,000 acres are classified as wilderness, which means all vehicles are prohibited in these areas. This preserves the natural beauty of the park and encourages the use of the park's hiking trails, some of which are quite challenging. **Cuyamaca Peak Trail** is a reasonably difficult trail that climbs 3½ miles to the 6,500-foot summit, which has views of both the desert and the ocean on clear days. Also quite tough, the 2-mile **Stonewall Peak Trail** climbs to a height of about 5,700 feet, with views out over the old Stonewall Gold Mine. The difficult **Harvey Moore Trail** is a 9-mile trek that begins $^1/_2$ mile north of the Green Valley campground, goes to the Oceanic East Mesa, and continues through Harper Creek Canyon. For those who don't quite feel up to the challenge, the short and easy **Paso Self-Guided Nature Trail** at the Paso Picacho campground will introduce you to the area's native plants.

Undoubtedly, one of the park's greatest assets is the fact that it's so close to the mountain town of Julian (*see above*). With all its cheap camgrounds, Cuyamaca Rancho is a great place to stay if you can't afford to pay the premium rates of Julian's bed-and-breakfasts or its historic hotel. The money you save can be put to better use, such as buying another of Julian's succulent apple pies! You can make reservations for Cuyamaca Rancho Campgrounds through **Mistix** (tel. 800/444–7275). If you plan on visiting during one of Julian's many festivals, book far in advance. Sites at **Green Valley** (81 sites, some with disabled access) are $12–$14, but the campground doesn't have much privacy nor as many shade trees as the Paso Picacho campground. Prices are the same at **Paso Picacho** (85 sites with no disabled access), a tree-shrouded campground where you can feel a sense of seclusion. **Anoyo Sew** (about 2 miles west of Green Valley) and **Granite Springs** (about 4 miles east of Green Valley) are primitive sites—meaning they are essentially clearings with no facilities—but they're only $3 a night, so who can complain? The easiest way to get to the park from San Diego is to take I–8 east to Route 79 north. If you're using the Northeast Rural Bus System (*see above*), you want Route 878 from Escondido. The park headquarters (tel. 619/765–0755) on Route 79 provides information on trails, camping, and other sights in and near the park.

● ● ● ANZA-BORREGO DESERT STATE PARK

Lying due east of San Diego and covering 600,000 acres of natural desert, this is the largest state park in the United States. Despite the presence of cacti, some bighorn sheep, and other desert wildlife, Anza-Borrego is essentially devoid, with nothing but sand as far as the eye can see. Those who study ecosystems or geology will disagree, but don't undertake the two-hour drive from San Diego unless you're searching for true desolation or you're just dying to build really big sandcastles. Sights worth seeing in the park are just off the main roads on sand and dirt trails. You can drive on these paths, but be advised to use a four-wheel-drive vehicle—you'll get stuck driving anything else. Don't attempt to drive on the trails if the ground is wet or if it looks like rain; flash floods can transpire faster than you can get out of the way.

Font's Point offers breathtaking views of the Borrego Valley and Borrego Badlands, some 3 miles south of Route S22, which passes through Borrego Springs. The **Elephant Tree Discovery Trail** will give you a look at some 10-foot trees with swollen branches and small leaves; to get there, go south on Split Mountain Road where it intersects with 78. The same road leads to **Split Mountain,** a narrow gorge with 600-foot perpendicular walls. The **Narrow Earth Trail,** about 5 miles east of Tamarish Grove off 78, flaunts a visible fault line.

What is really great about the park is that you can pitch a tent anywhere and it won't cost a cent. Be sure to let a park ranger know where you are, especially during the off-peak summer months when the daytime temperature can soar above 120°. If you prefer to set up camp at an established campground, head for **Borrego Palm Canyon,** a mile from the visitor center in Borrego Springs, or **Tamarish Grove,** near the intersection of Routes 78 and S3. Sites start around $10, but are usually half that during the summer. Borrego has showers, Tamarish does not. If camping in the open desert is not to your liking, visit the town of **Borrego Springs.** It's completely surrounded by the park and has a collection of motels (rooms are $40–$45 during the peak winter season), restaurants, and a grocery store. You can reach Borrego Springs by taking Route 78 east into the desert and then going north on Route S3; otherwise, Buses 878 or 879 of the Northeast Rural Bus System (*see above*) will get you there from Escondido.

More information on the park can be obtained from the **Anza-Borrego Desert State Park Headquarters** (200 Palm Canyon Dr., in Borrego Springs, tel. 619/767–4684). The headquarters office offers a series of slide presentations, and the rangers can give you tips on where to camp. To get to the park from San Diego, take I–8 east to Route 79 north to Route 78 east (Route 78 goes west–east and divides the park in half).

PALM SPRINGS AND THE DESERT 12

By Christopher Hallenbeck

Most people who come to the California desert see exactly what they expect: endless miles of nearly naked earth scorched by the sun day after day. From the highway, the desert seems lifeless, even worthless. But with the right temperament and a little familiarity, you can grow to appreciate the stark beauty of this seemingly barren world. Some return to the desert year after year to experience its soulful solitude and discover still more of its hidden natural wonders, whether in the strikingly varied landscape of Death Valley National Monument or among the strange groves of Joshua Tree National Monument. The conditions may be harsh, but the rewards are great.

Others come to the desert to ride out cold winters in sun-drenched resort communities like Palm Springs and Palm Desert. These resorts, complete with truly anonymous golf courses, have sprung up all over the Coachella Valley, supported by a few precious desert oases and the seasonal tourist trade. If you've just arrived in California on the tail of a blizzard, you could certainly do worse than spending a little while lolling around a pool and scoping out celebrities.

Geologically speaking, the California desert is a recent development. Only a few thousand years ago lakes and rivers covered the desert valleys, and animal life flourished. In some ways, this arid land is the ideal place for contemplating the passage of time. While cavorting on the 700-foot sand dunes, take time to remember that these dunes were once the floors of ancient lakes. When the climate was milder, people lived here, too: There's a vast store of prehistoric art, largely petroglyphs (stone etchings), that gives some clues about life back then. You can learn more about the ancestors of today's Native Americans by touring the important Calico Early Man Archaeological Site, where artifacts of the earliest known North Americans are still being unearthed. You'll find souvenirs of the Old West in the empty buildings and abandoned mine shafts that eerily dot the landscape. There's nothing quite like stumbling on a ghost town in a place that seems completely inimical to human life. Modern warfare hasn't passed by without leaving traces either. General Patton's army trained in the desert during World War II, and the tanks and exploding shells have left their marks on the desert floor.

Even though the desert gets little more than a few inches of rain each year, it still manages to support a large web of animal and plant life that has adapted to this bizarrely dehydrated world of dunes, monoliths, and parched scrubland. Look for insects, lizards, iguanas, geckos, burrowing mice, rats, and squirrels. At higher elevations you may even find bighorn sheep.

Despite the fierce climate, parts of the desert have been tamed for human use. Thanks to irrigation from the Colorado River, a great deal of the terrain has been converted into productive farmland, most notably in the Imperial Valley. Where farming is impossible cattle and sheep ranchers manage to eke a living off the land. The presence of nearly 5(different valuable minerals has ensured a long history of mining in the area, unde extraordinarily hostile conditions. Even with the gold and silver mostly gone, the deser continues to supply California with other kinds of power. Hydroelectric power has bee harnessed by the damming of the Colorado, geothermal steam power comes directly fron the desert floor, and windmills taking advantage of the region's low pressure and risin heat supply power to small towns throughout the state.

For the most part, though, California's desert is protected wilderness: undisturbed an undeveloped. The California Desert Conservation Area covers a vast area, stretching fron the coastal mountains in the west to the Nevada and Arizona borders 200 miles east; an from the Mexico border in the south to the Sierra Nevada Mountains 400 miles north. B no means is this huge area homogeneous. Four of North America's greatest desert intersect here, and each has its own climate and wildlife. The Mojave Desert, or Hig Desert, begins over the mountains from Los Angeles and extends north toward the Sierra and east toward the Colorado River, with Death Valley at its northeast corner. Because o its higher elevation, the Mojave has a milder climate than the Sonoran Desert, or Lo Desert, which stretches south to Mexico. The Colorado Desert stretches east of th Sonoran and Mojave into Arizona and Nevada. The Mexican Gran Desierto lies south o the Sonoran.

Palm Springs

This incongruous deser resort community nestled a the foot of 10,831-foot Mt San Jacinto has garnered reputation as a playground for the rich and famous. It became a haven for stars in th 1930s when Ginger Rogers, Humphrey Bogart, and Clark Gable all joined the newl opened Palm Springs Racquet Club. The celebrity contingent is always present, but mos of Palm Springs' growth has come from regular (although, still pretty well-off) people fron cities like Los Angeles and San Diego, attracted by the sunny skies and clean air. Howeve staid it might appear, Palm Springs has also become a popular vacation spot for gays an lesbians from L.A. who frequent a number of popular bars and dance clubs in the area And each spring break the town is besieged by thousands of college students on a part rampage, akin to the scene in the Fort Lauderdale area in Florida. Celebrity mayor Sonn Bono has enacted legislation that he thinks will stop some of the springtime chaos: curfew for those under 18 and a ban on women's bikinis that have less than an inch c material running along the rear. It's not entirely clear how this second law will be enforced

Palm Springs certainly has the right climate for a resort. Even in the dead of winter, th temperature is regularly in the seventies and rarely falls below freezing at night. Th temperature on summer nights is about the same as these winter highs, which are welcome respite from the 100°-plus of summer days. Notwithstanding the fact that thi is the desert, developers have built more than a hundred golf courses. Three times tha many tennis courts dot the Palm Springs landscape, as well as thousands of swimmin pools. The sporting season here runs through winter and spring, when the city hosts severa annual sporting events, like the all-star Skins Game, a pro golf tournament. Perhaps bes known are the major golf and tennis tournaments named after resident celebrities like Bo Hope, Don Drysdale, and Dinah Shore.

Palm Springs is anything but a budget resort: Apparently it's considered bad form to giv a lodging a name with the word "motel"—most hotels, restaurants, and spas cate exclusively to the wealthy. Take a stroll along Palm Canyon Drive to check out the requisit art galleries, or, to see where the real cultural artifacts are found, saunter down El Pase Drive, the ostentatious Rodeo Drive of Palm Springs, past those delightful, little boutique that house the work of designers like Gucci and Yves St. Laurent. Don't despair, though If you really want a few days of good weather in the middle of winter, you can get ther without emptying your wallet by heading to the nearby towns of Desert Hot Springs an Cathedral City.

Palm Springs

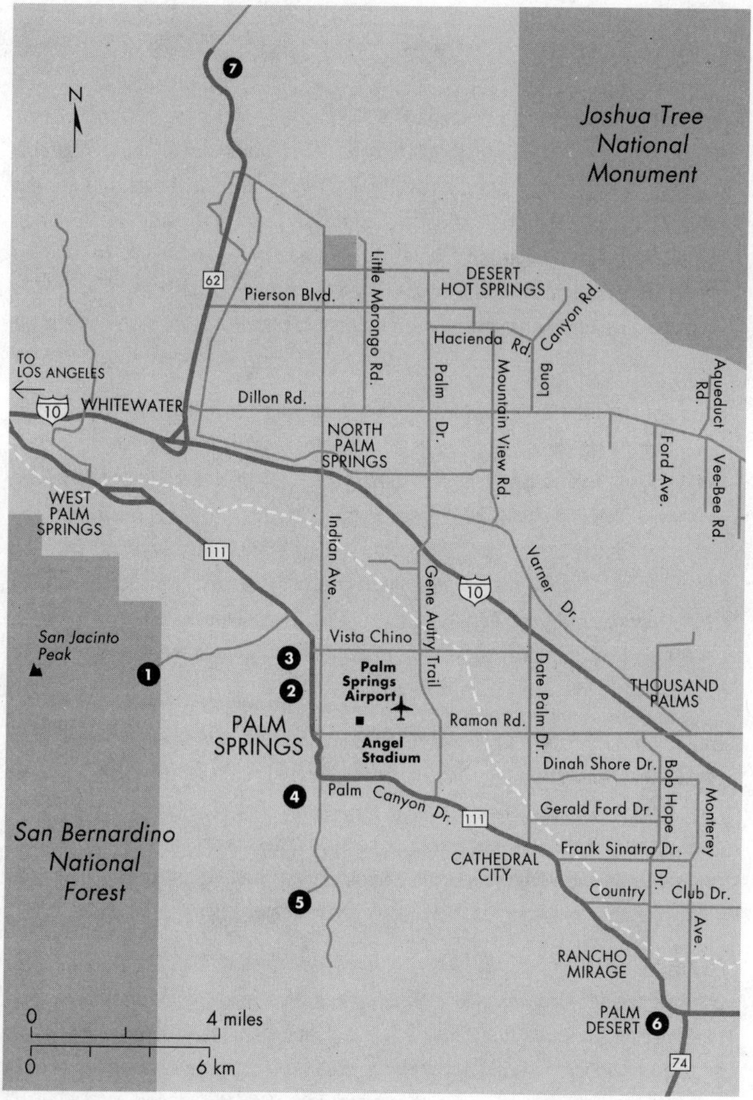

Desert Museum, **3**
Indian Canyons, **5**
Joshua Tree National Monument, **7**
Living Desert Reserve, **6**
Moorten Botanical Garden, **4**
Palm Springs Aerial Tramway, **1**
Village Green Heritage Center, **2**

Desert Survival

The most important thing to remember when traveling in the desert is that human beings cannot survive in such dry heat without a constant supply of water. Take one to two gallons of water per person per day, depending on the season and on whether your plans include strenuous exercise. Don't wait until you're thirsty before taking a gulp—you can become dehydrated before you know it. Avoid using soft drinks, alcohol, or coffee as your liquids as they will only make you more dehydrated. Hikers or anyone going into remote terrain should also carry extra food.

When outdoors in the desert heat (especially during the summer), you must also protect the exterior of your body. Thick-soled shoes are a must as ground temperatures can reach a foot-blistering 200°. Also a hat, sunglasses, and sunscreen should be worn for protection from the sun's rays (the higher SPF the better, that ozone layer's not getting any thicker!). Keep clothed all the time—a sweat-soaked T-shirt, though uncomfortable, may be the only thing slowing the evaporation of your bodily fluids. During the evenings, especially during the winter, temperatures may be near freezing. If you plan to stay overnight in the desert, bring some extra clothes for warmth.

Wait, there's more: Just when you got used to the absence of water, a desert storm could arise without warning and dump thousands of gallons onto the desert floor in less than a minute. Don't linger in low-lying washes and canyons that are subject to periodic flash floods. The desert is also home to rattlesnakes and scorpions—both potentially deadly. They reserve their venom for bothersome annoyances, like you disturbing their resting spot. Although it goes without saying, avoid them.

No, we're not done yet. The desert is filled with hundreds of abandoned mines, many of which have unstable structures and hidden openings. Admire the old buildings and the mine shafts from a safe distance, or proceed at your own risk. In addition to mining, a great deal of military training has taken place in the deserts over the past four decades. If you see something metal glittering in the sun, don't think "souvenir." Think "unexploded shell," leave it plenty of room, and report your findings to a ranger or the local police department.

Whether you're hiking or camping, always let someone know where you're headed. In most wilderness areas and parks you can register at a ranger station before beginning your trip. Notify a friend if you're hiking on unmaintained or private land. Just in case you get stuck or lost while traveling in the desert, bring some sort of signal mirror with you. Even if its reflection doesn't draw some help, it will probably annoy the buzzards.

Much of the area is still owned by a tribe of Native Americans known as the Agua Caliente. A great deal of their roughly 30,000 acres of land is commercial property, making them one of the wealthiest tribes in the country. While you're in Palm Springs, take the time to explore the lush Indian Canyons nearby.

BASICS

TOURIST INFORMATION Your best sources of information are the **Palm Springs Visitor Information Center** (2781 N. Palm Canyon Dr., tel. 619/778–8418), the information desk at the airport, and the **Palm Springs Chamber of Commerce** (190 W. Amado Rd., tel. 619/325–1577).

COMING AND GOING

BY PLANE **Palm Springs Municipal Airport** is served by several major airlines, including **Alaska Air, America West**, **American, American Eagle**, **Continental**, **TWA**, and **United**. The airport is about 2 miles east of the city's main downtown intersection.

BY TRAIN **Amtrak** passenger trains only serve the Indio area, 20 miles east of Palm Springs. For reservations and information, call 800/USA–RAIL. From Indio, bus service westbound is available.

BY BUS **Greyhound** (311 N. Indian Ave., tel. 619/325–2053) serves Palm Springs, with direct service to Los Angeles, $17.60 one way, $33.40 round-trip; the trip takes 3½ hours.

BY CAR Palm Springs is about a two-hour drive east of Los Angeles and a three-hour drive northeast of San Diego. Route 111 leads directly to Palm Canyon Drive, the main thoroughfare in Palm Springs. From Los Angeles take the San Bernardino Freeway (I–10) east to Route 111. From San Diego take I–15 north to the eastbound Pomona Freeway (I–60), which connects to I–10.

GETTING AROUND

Palm Springs proper is pretty easy to navigate. Palm Canyon Drive is the main street running north–south; its intersection with Tahquitz-McCallum is pretty much the center of the action. Heading south, Palm Canyon Drive splits; South Palm Canyon leads to the Indian Canyons and East Palm Canyon takes you to other desert resort communities.

BY BUS **Sunbus** (tel. 619/343–3451) serves the entire Coachella Valley from Desert Hot Springs to Coachella, including Indio. The fare is $1, 25¢ for a transfer. The company also operates the **Sun Trolley**, which runs up and down Palm Canyon Drive from December through mid-May, daily 9 AM–7:30 PM. The fare is 50¢.

BY CAR If you didn't arrive by car, plan on renting one if you intend to stay for more than a day or want to take in any of the sights other than downtown. Try **Avis** (tel. 619/325–1331), **Budget** (tel. 619/327–1404), or **Enterprise** (tel. 619/328–9393). Palm Springs is also served by **Desert Cab** (tel. 619/235–2868).

WHERE TO SLEEP

Admire the luxury resorts from outside (or stroll into the lobbies if you're curious and bold), then check into one of the reasonably priced inns, hotels, or resorts in the surrounding area (a lot of which are really motels, but don't tell anyone we told you that). The price of rooms goes up during the winter, Palm Springs' high season. **Ambassadors Arms Spa** (12921 Tamar Dr., Desert Hot Springs 92264, tel. 619/329–1909) has a Jacuzzi and mineral springs. The 20 units with TV run $32–$42. Take Route 10 past Route 111 to Desert Hot Springs, about 10 miles north of Palm Springs. **Broadview Lodge** (12672 Eliseo Rd., Desert Hot Springs 92240, tel. 619/329–8006) has doubles for $35 year-round. **Budget Inn** (63950 20th Ave., N. Palm Springs 92258, tel. 619/251–1425) is a large motor inn with all the amenities, including a Jacuzzi, sauna, and restaurant. There are 95 units, each $34–$50. **Mira Loma Hotel** (1420 N. Indian Ave., Palm Springs 92258, tel. 619/320–1178) is a cozy, single-story hotel with only 12 rooms. Marilyn Monroe once stayed here and probably swam in the pool. Rooms with refrigerator, TV, and bath cost $45–$55. **Monte Vista Hotel** (414 N. Palm Canyon Dr., Palm Springs 92258, tel. 619/325–5641) has 32 units in the center of town, comfortably equipped with TV, air-conditioning, pool, and Jacuzzi. Rooms range from $50 for a single to around $80 for a suite ($10 less in summer). **Waterfalls Motel** (67495 East Palm Canyon Dr., Cathedral City 92234, tel. 619/328–2616) has doubles that are $44.50 on weekdays and $54.50 on weekends, $5 extra for each additional person. From June through January the rooms go down to $39.50.

● ● ● FOOD

So what if it's a luxury resort? You can still eat cheap. The best place for a wide selection at little cost is the fast-food arcade in the area's biggest mall, the **Palm Desert Town Center**. The arcade is above the **Ice Capades Chalet** (tel. 619/340–4412), a huge indoor ice rink where you can rent skates for $2 (admission $5). You could do worse on a hot summer day. If you want a date or just a snack, check out the **Indian Wells Date Garden and Chocolate Shop** (364 N. Palm Canyon Dr., tel. 619/323–3305) for a date shake or some other chocolate fix. The **Denny's** chain has three 24-hour restaurants along Palm Canyon Drive in Palm Springs and Cathedral City. **Shame on the Moon** (68805 Rte. 111 in Cathedral City, tel. 619/324–5515) is a restaurant popular with gays that serves good Continental-style meals for around $10 (open daily 6–10:30 PM).

● ● ● WORTH SEEING

THE INDIAN CANYONS At this sanctuary owned by Native Americans 5 miles south of downtown Palm Springs, you can see pictographs, bedrock mortar holes, stone houses, and shelters. Sparkling pools and streams meander through the palm-lined canyons, a natural desert oasis. Bands of wild ponies roam through **Murray Canyon**, and **Andreas Canyon** has towering rock faces and dark caves. *End of S. Palm Canyon Dr., tel. 619/327–2714. Admission: $3.25. Open Sept.–June, daily 8–5.*

PALM SPRINGS AERIAL TRAMWAY The tramway's steep, vertical, 1-mile ascent carries you away from the parched desert (it's five minutes from downtown Palm Springs) to the summit of Mt. San Jacinto at an altitude of over 8,500 feet. In the winter, that sometimes means you're traveling from balmy 70° weather to snow. The station house at the top has great views, a snack bar, and a gift shop. Also up here are **San Jacinto State Park** and **San Jacinto State Wilderness**, two separate but contiguous areas with several miles of trails and primitive campgrounds. The **Park Office in Idyllwild** (tel. 619/659–2607; 800/444–PARK for reservations) administers both the park and the wilderness and issues mandatory permits for hiking and camping. Between mid-November and mid-April the **Nordic Ski Center** (tel. 619/327–6002) rents cross-country skis. In January, Mt. Jacinto is the site of the **Moosehead Championship Sled Dog Races**. *Take Tramway Rd. off Rte. 111, Palm Canyon Dr., from N. Palm Springs, tel. 619/325–1391. Cost: $14.95. Trams leave every ½ hour; first trams leave at 10 AM weekdays, 8 AM on weekends and holidays. The last one returns around 9:45 PM; an hour later during daylight savings time.*

THE LIVING DESERT The best of the desert museums, this place has exotic desert animals from California and sample habitats (some with zebras and gazelles) from deserts around the world. A nocturnal exhibit lets you see snakes, owls, and bats at their active best. There are several miles of hiking trails with good desert views and, if you're lucky, the occasional hawk, falcon, coyote, bighorn sheep, lizard, or iguana. *47–900 Portola Ave., Palm Desert, tel. 619/346–5694. 15 mi east of Palm Springs. Admission: $5.50. Open Sept.–mid-June, daily 9–5; closed mid-June–Aug.*

THE OASIS WATERPARK This huge multi-acre water theme park in Palm Springs has water slides, a wave action pool, and beach volleyball. The 7-story-tall slides are thrilling, and the 5-foot swells never stop. Take a break at one of the fast-food stands. *1500 Gene Autry Trail, between Ramon Rd. and East Palm Canyon Dr., tel: 619/325-7873. Admission: $15. Open March 1–Labor Day, daily; Labor Day–Oct., weekends. Closes at dusk.*

DESERT ADVENTURES Based in the Spa Hotel, Desert Adventures (100 N. Indian Dr., Palm Springs 92263, tel. 619/778–1733) offers jeep tours that can take you high into the Santa Rosa Mountains or, better yet, on an exhilarating ride along the San Andreas Fault to see the maze of towering canyons and narrow ravines created by the fault. The two- to four-hour tours begin at $25.

AFTER DARK • • •

Some of the hottest bars in the area are the gay ones. **Daddy Warbucks** (tel. 619/324–1022) and **Rocks** (tel. 619/324–0688) are two popular bars in Cathedral City, with live entertainment and contests (like whipped cream wrestling), usually Wednesday through Sunday. If that's not your speed (i.e., you're looking for a meat market of different persuasion), head for the big model of a volcano outside the **Pompeii Nightclub** (67–339 Rte. 111 at Golf Club Dr., Palm Springs, tel. 619/328–5800) where a predominantly straight clientele discos in the desert. **Zelda's Nightclub and Beachclub** (169 N. Indian Ave., Palm Springs, tel. 619/325–2375) attracts a young crowd for dancing, theme parties, and exotic dancers, both male and female (opens at 8).

OUTDOOR ACTIVITIES • • •

GOLF AND TENNIS The **Palm Desert Resort Country Club** (77–33 Country Club Dr., Palm Desert, tel. 619/345–2791) has an 18-hole course and several tennis and racquetball courts open to the public. Other options include the **Palm Springs Golf Course** (1885 Golf Club Dr., Palm Springs, tel. 619/328–1005) and the **Tennis Center** (1300 E. Baristo Rd., Palm Springs, tel. 619/320–0020). There are also a number of free courts in parks and schools; call **Leisure Service** (tel. 619/323–8272), a city agency, for information.

BALLOON RIDES Both **Fantasy Balloon Flights** (tel. 619/568–0997 or 800/462–2683) and **Sunrise Balloons** (tel. 800/548–9912) offer balloon rides at sunrise or sunset (with champagne to enhance the altitude). Expect to pay $100 and up.

POLO The **Empire Polo Club** (81–800 Ave. 51, Indio, tel. 619/342–3231) gives you that chance you've been waiting for to find out what polo is all about, with year-round polo action on five fields. Every December the club hosts the Stouffer Esmerelda Balloon and Polo Festival, when an armada of hot-air balloons sails across the sky. Another popular polo venue is the **Eldorado Polo Club** (50–950 Madison Blvd., Indio, tel. 619/342–2223), which bills itself as the Winter Polo Capital of the West. Bring a picnic lunch to either club. Admission is free except on Sunday, when it's $5.

Near Palm Springs

CABAZON • • •

Cabazon (on I–10 between Palm Springs and L.A.) is nothing much in itself, but there are some interesting places to stop en route to or from the coast. Most striking is the **Wheel-In**, one of the most unusual truck stops in the United States. About 18 miles northwest of Palm Springs, the Wheel-In has gigantic models of a brontosaurus and a tyrannosaurus looming over the parking lot. One has a marginal prehistoric museum inside, the **Dinosaur Gardens** (tel. 714/849–8309), and a view from the top. It's 50¢ to get in (closed Tuesday). The diner itself serves up hot and hearty truck-stop fare.

Another unlikely sight out in the barren desert is **Hadley's Fruit Orchards**, a huge air-conditioned market filled to capacity with every imaginable type of dried fruit, nuts, and candies—at great prices. No fresh fruit, sorry. *Tel. 714/849–5255. From I–10, take the Apache Trail exit coming from P.S., the Cabazon exit from L.A. Open daily 7–9.*

Also on the Apache Trail, 500 yards past Hadley's, is the **Desert Hills Factory Outlet**, stocked with goods made by Evan-Picone, Bass, Nike, Patagonia, Perry Ellis, Esprit, and many others, on sale anywhere from 30% to 70% off department-store prices. *Open daily 9 AM–8 PM.*

Joshua Tree National Monument

This extraordinary wilderness area covers over a half million acres of land straddling the Mojave and Colorado deserts. The slightly cooler and wetter Mojave, in the northwestern part of the park lies at altitudes of over 3,000 feet. In the southeast is the Colorado, at elevations from 1,000 to 3,000 feet. This is the best place to see towering cacti and thickets of aromatic creosote bushes.

The Joshua tree, after which the monument is named, is actually a large type of yucca. Mormon settlers traveling through the area saw a resemblance between the twisted branches of these trees and images of the prophet Joshua stretching his arms toward the sky. There are no lakes or rivers in the area, but five-fan palm oases have provided water and shade to various Native Americans, prospectors, and a wide array of wildlife. Rising above the desert landscape are mountains of twisted rock and granite monoliths that seem to have dropped from the sky. The strange terrain and various rock faces make Joshua Tree a real treat for hikers and rock climbers.

Despite severe weather and sporadic precipitation, the desert here supports an incredible variety of life. Cactus, yucca, and various desert flowers flourish. You'll be lucky to see any animals, however, since the extreme desert heat makes them nocturnal. Less than six inches of rain fall each year. Average summer temperatures soar over 110°, dropping to between 65°–85° at night. In winter the desert is still dry but much colder; expect temperatures between 30° and 60° during the day and below freezing temperatures at night.

Over a century ago there were mines here with names like Desert Queen and Lost Horse that yielded millions in gold. Today, most of the area is protected, but the mines, now abandoned, remain.

• • • BASICS

TOURIST INFORMATION The shady **Oasis of Mara**, a watering hole for desert travelers, is today the monument's headquarters. The **Oasis Visitor Center** has exhibits, and a half-mile, wheelchair-accessible nature trail that will introduce you to the desert terrain; park rangers will help with backcountry regulations and lists of trails. *Joshua Tree National Monument, 74485 National Monument Dr., Twentynine Palms 92277, tel. 619/367–7511. Open 8 AM–4:30 PM.*

FEES From October through May it will cost you $5 per vehicle, good for seven days. Entrance is free during the summer.

WHEN TO GO Summers are unbearably hot at Joshua Tree, but considerably less crowded than in the spring, when the park can be filled to capacity. Winter and fall are the best times for reasonable weather and relative solitude, but then you'll miss the desert wildflowers blooming in the spring: Take your pick.

WHAT TO PACK Water sources are very limited within the monument, so bring along at least a gallon of water per person per day; you can fill up at the visitor center and at most campgrounds (*see* Desert Safety, *above*).

COMING AND GOING ● ● ●

The monument is 140 miles east of Los Angeles. Take I–10 east to the Twentynine Palms Highway (Route 62), which leads to the two northern entrances, one in the town of Joshua Tree, and the other in the town of Twentynine Palms (where the visitor center is). The south entrance, at Cottonwood Springs, is 25 miles east of Indio, off I–10. It's about an hour from Palm Springs. The only way to get to Joshua Tree without a car is to take **Desert Stage Lines** (tel. 619/367–3581) from Palm Springs to the town of Twentynine Palms, which is 1½ miles from the monument. It's $8.80 one way, $16.75 round-trip and a 1½-hour trip. Considering the size of the monument, though, you're best off with a car.

WHERE TO SLEEP ● ● ●

There are more than 500 camping sites in the monument, and most are free. However, the only ones with water and flush toilets are **Cottonwood** and **Black Rock Canyon**, which charge $6–$10 for camping. All other campsites have picnic tables and pit toilets only, so bring water with you. Fires are permitted at campsite barbecues only, and campers must provide their own wood or charcoal.

Most campgrounds are available on a first-come, first-served basis; you can make reservations at **Black Rock Canyon** through **Ticketron** (tel. 800/452–1111). Ticketron also handles group sites at **Cottonwood, Sheep Pass**, and **Indian Cove**. There are no RV camping sites within the monument, but there's an RV resort in nearby Twentynine Palms—and wouldn't you know?—it's called the **Twentynine Palms RV Resort** (tel. 619/367–3320). Many campgrounds close in summer but you'll have little trouble finding a space at cooler elevations. If you're visiting in the winter or spring, especially on weekends and holidays, arrive early as the campgrounds can fill up quickly.

Backcountry camping is permitted, but you must be at least 500 feet from the nearest trail or day-use area, and a mile from the nearest road. Register at the stations located near the trailheads, and get a copy of the regulations from the visitor center first. Backcountry fires are not allowed.

Here are some of the best campgrounds; there are lots more, many of them nestled in sheltered areas among the boulders.

Black Rock Canyon Campground is close to several trails, making this a convenient place for hikers. The nearby Hi-View Nature Trail and the shorter South Park Peak Trail are ideal for catching great desert views of this mountainous paradise. Some shade is provided by the pinon pines, and it's somewhat cooler because of the elevation. *On Joshua La. off Rte. 62. 100 sites; cost: $10; flush toilets, fresh water; 4,000 feet.*

Cottonwood Campground has no shade, but is near a trail to Cottonwood Spring Oasis. *1 mi east of Cottonwood Visitor Center on access road, 62 sites; cost: $6; flush toilets, fresh water; 3,000 feet.*

Hidden Valley Campground is in an enclosed valley, once used for cattle rustling, that is now popular for rock climbing. A Joshua tree forest provides some shade, and the Barker Dam trail is nearby. *From Quail Springs Rd., follow the 1½-mile winding trail into Hidden Valley. 62 sites; free; 4,200 feet.*

Indian Cove Campground sits among quartz boulders at the north end of the absolutely striking Wonderland of Rocks, a huge expanse of jumbled rock formations. *114 sites; free; 3,200 feet.*

Jumbo Rocks Campground also sits among huge quartz boulders and is near a short nature trail leading to the aptly named Skull Rock. *Take Quail Springs Rd. 15 mi south of Oasis Visitor Center. 130 sites; free; 4,400 feet.*

Ryan Campground has mountain views. A strenuous 3-mile trail leads from here to a 5,470-foot summit that has great vistas of surrounding valleys. *Between Jumbo Rocks and Hidden Valley campgrounds on Quail Springs Rd. 27 sites; free; 4,300 feet.*

Twentynine Palms RV Resort in nearby Twentynine Palms has only RV sites with full hookups, but tent campers can stay here too if they don't mind paying equal fare and being sandwiched between giant motor homes. The $19 price tag includes pool, Jacuzzi, showers, tennis courts, and a sauna. If you're not camping here, you can use the facilities for $5. *Utah Trail and Amboy Rd., Twentynine Palms, tel. 619/367–3320. Heading east on Rte. 62, turn right on Utah Trail for 2 mi to Amboy Rd.*

If you're not into camping try the **Safari Motor Inn** in Joshua Tree (tel. 619/366–311). Both single and double rooms are $32.

EXPLORING JOSHUA TREE NATIONAL MONUMENT

For hikers, climbers, or just about anyone who enjoys a scenic drive, this is the place to be. Roads run through only a fraction of this desert wilderness, but they give you a good sense of the monument's varied scenery: Joshua tree forests, huge granite boulders, desert oases, and abandoned mines. Tell the staff at the visitor center what appeals to you and let them help you plan your time. Many people prefer to visit during the wildflower season from mid-March to mid-May, when the area explodes with color for a few short weeks before the onset of the summer heat.

Rock climbers can arrange for an expedition through **Vertical Adventures in Redondo Beach** (tel. 213/540–6517) or **Wilderness Connections** out of Joshua Tree (tel. 619/366–4745). The hiking here is first rate. Some of the best trails are mentioned in the campsite listings above; the rest of the best are discussed below.

From the **Cottonwood Visitor Center** is a popular 1½-mile trail (one way) to the summit of Mastodon Peak, where the ruins of the **Mastodon Mine** and the **Winona Millsite** are located. The village in the canyon below housed the miners during the 1920s.

A 13-mile dirt road from Yucca Valley to **Covington Flats** will take you through a giant grove of Joshua trees, including the largest specimen in the park. From Covington Flats, you can hike up a relatively difficult 3.8-mile trail to **Eureka Peak** for some magnificent views of the surrounding mountain. As long as the L.A. smog doesn't cloud the sky, you can see all the way from **Key's View** to Signal Mountain in Mexico. You can even see the San Andreas Fault. A small dirt road on the way to Key's View (3½ miles round-trip) leads to the abandoned buildings of one of the area's most famous mines, the **Lost Horse Mine** (which is now fenced off because some over-zealous climber tried to repel down into it!). Drive 8 miles along Utah Trail to the split in the road, take the right branch, and follow the signs; it's about 24 miles from the Oasis Visitor Center.

The 1.7-mile loop to **Skull Rock** from the Jumbo Rocks Campground is one of the nicest short hikes; it's a guided nature trail, good if you're not up to strenuous activity. The **Cholla Cactus Garden**, a painless, ¼-mile nature trail, is also ideal for a leisurely desert stroll. Be sure to wear thick-soled shoes; the barbed cactus spines almost seem to reach out and stick you.

Barker Dam Trail leads to a man-made reservoir a few miles south of the visitor center where you can see Native American mortars and petroglyphs, the only ones open to the public in the monument (others are kept secret because of a rise in vandalism). It's a short trail, only 1.1 miles round-trip. During the summer, the reservoir is more or less a mud pit. From Hidden Valley Campground, drive 1 mile out on dirt road from the bulletin board; follow the signs.

Barstow and the Mojave Desert

As remote as it is, for more than a century Barstow has been a major rail and trade center for the West, with its Santa Fe switchyard still a major employer—more than 700 people work there. Little else attracts people to this scorched slab of desert. (Fort Irwin just northeast of town is home to 4,000 marines in training for desert battle, but they're not exactly here on vacation.) This high desert town is also the halfway point on the four-hour drive between Los Angeles and Las Vegas. On holidays and weekends, some 4,000 people may pass through Barstow in a day, but very few of them do anything more than stretch their legs and apply some more sunscreen.

If you're not in a hurry, stop for awhile and see some of the nearby sights, most of which are truly off the beaten track. The **Eastern Mojave National Scenic Area** in particular is a strange bit of the planet, but there are many other enchanting places in this desert area that people zooming between L.A. and points east will never know about.

BASICS • • •

The **California Desert Information Center** (831 Barstow Rd., Barstow 92311, tel. 619/256–8313) has indoor exhibits on, yes, desert life, and information on unprotected desert areas (where you can do some off-road driving).

The **Barstow Area Chamber of Commerce** (408 E. Fredricks, Box 698, Barstow 92311, tel. 619/256–8617) has info on lodging, restaurants, and nearby activities.

COMING AND GOING • • •

Barstow is halfway between L.A. and Vegas on I–15 (take the Barstow Road exit). It's also the western terminus of I–40, which heads east all the way to North Carolina. Although it's an unlikely destination, Barstow is served by **Amtrak** (N. 1st St., tel. 800/872–7245) and **Greyhound** (120 S. 1st St. at W. Main, tel. 619/256–8757).

WHERE TO SLEEP • • •

If you must stay overnight in Barstow, at least you won't have to pay a lot of money. Try **Travel Inn** (1261 W. Main St., tel. 619/256–8936) or **Economy Inns of America** (1590 Coolwater La. off W. Main St., tel. 619/256–1737). Most of the inns and motels on East Main Street in the center of town cost around $30, and are a bit repugnant. There are pools at many of the hotels, but they're usually drained in the summer, when traffic slows.

FOOD • • •

For some good home-cooking try **Patrick's Family Restaurant** (513 E. Main St., tel. 619/256–7877; closed Tues.) or **Conky's Restaurant** (29836 N. 1st, off Rte. 58, tel. 619/256–8031). The **International House of Pancakes** (1441 E. Main St., tel. 619/256–1020) serves more than flapjacks, is open 24 hours and is wheelchair-accessible. Meals start at around $5. **B Bar B Bingo USA** (2191 W. Main, tel. 619/256–5642) is your best bet for that inimitable truck-stop ambience. This 24-hour restaurant has specials (under $10), salads, plenty of smokers, and a convenience store. It's also wheelchair accessible. And there's always The **Sizzler** (925 Barstow Rd., tel. 619/252–4321) with its massive salad bar, steaks, and seafood. The all-you-can-eat buffet is a good deal (under $7). It's open 11–9:30.

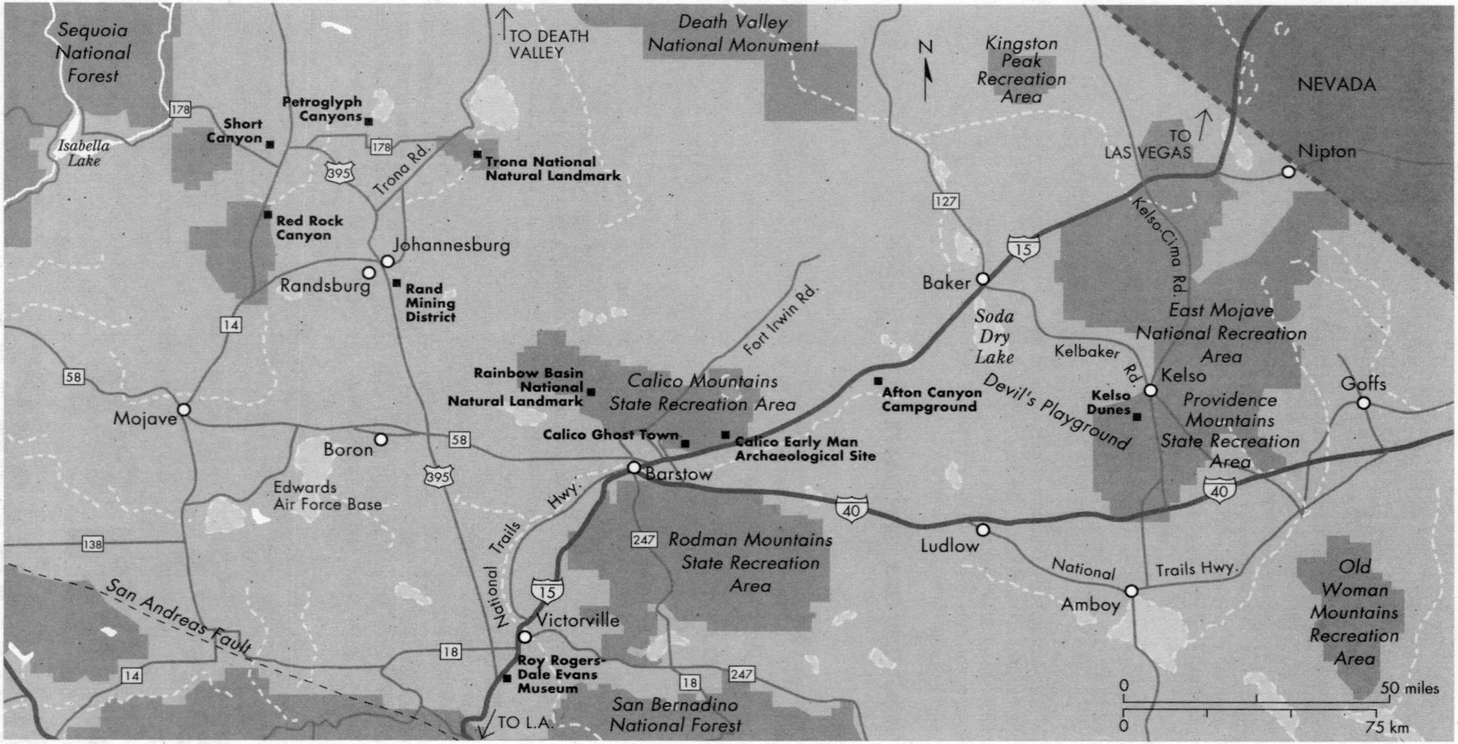

Mojave Desert

Near Barstow

CALICO GHOST TOWN • • •

A hundred years ago, famous lawman Wyatt Earp walked the streets of Calico, a silver-mining boomtown 20 minutes by car from Barstow. Today, the Calico Ghost Town isn't ghost-like at all but a fully restored, 19th-century western town, complete with an old-fashioned ice-cream parlor, general store, shooting gallery, and craft shops. The "ghost town" even has mine tunnels and real railroad cars to explore, and some colorful 19th-century characters roving the streets. It sounds hokey, but it's actually an enjoyable way to spend a couple of hours. The **Calico Hullabaloo** in late-March is highlighted by the **World Tobacco Spitting Championships**. The **National Gunfight Stunt Championships** are during **Calico Days** in early October. Year-round camping is available nearby in a shaded canyon; ask for directions at the ghost town. *Box 638, Yermo 92398, tel. 619/254–2122. About 9 mi northeast of Barstow off I–15. Open daily 7–dusk, shops open 9–5. $4 parking.*

CALICO EARLY MAN ARCHAEOLOGICAL SITE • • •

Here's your chance to take a guided tour of what is perhaps the most significant archaeological find in the United States. More than 200,000 years ago, this site on the shores of ancient **Lake Manix** was a quarry, campsite, and workshop where the earliest-known Americans made tools for cutting, scraping, and drilling. Prior to this discovery, many archaeologists believed that the first people to arrive in North America came less than 30,000 years ago; excavations began in 1964. Noted archaeologist Louis Leakey was director of the project for several years. Stop by if you're interested. *15 mi northeast of Barstow, 2½ mi off I–15 on Minneola Rd., no phone. Donation only. Tours run Wed. 1:30–3:30, Thurs.–Sun. 9:30–11:30 and 1:30–3:30.*

EAST MOJAVE NATIONAL SCENIC AREA • • •

Rock spires, sand dunes, mesas, Joshua trees, mine shafts, and gemstones all weave their spell on the visitor. The scenic area (tel. 619/326–3896) is accessible from either I–15 to the north (it's 60 miles from Barstow) or I–40 to the south. It stretches more than 50 miles east from Baker nearly reaching Route 95. Though huge, the area makes up only 10% of the California Desert Conservation Area's 25 million acres.

You are only supposed to camp in designated sites near the road in the scenic area as there is a lot of private property around and trespassing is an issue (and keep in mind that you must be at least 600 feet from natural water resources). There are also two maintained campgrounds; one of them, the **Hole-In-The-Wall Campground**, has 26 sites next to volcanic rock towers and canyons. The **Midhills Campground**, near the center of the area, also has 26 sites in a woodland area at an elevation of 5,600 feet. *Hole-in-the-Wall: From I–40, drive north of Essex on Essex Rd. to Black Rock Canyon Rd. Cost: $4. Water, pit toilets, grills, RV dump station. Midhills: 2 mi west of Black Canyon Rd. Cost: $4. Picnic tables, water.*

The extraordinary **Kelso Dunes** are a bit of a trek, but well worth the effort. Pristine, and more than 700-feet high, these are the tallest sand dunes in the United States. Wandering around on them is like nothing else. From Baker, on I–15, drive 35 miles south on Kelbaker Road to Kelso; drive 8 miles farther on the same road to a turnoff with a sign for the dunes; then go another 3 miles west on dirt road to parking area. It's a half-mile walk to the dunes. There are no facilities at present although the Bureau of Land Management is working on establishing a visitor center. The dunes cover an incredible 70 square miles, so do remember where you parked.

While in the Eastern Mojave, visit the **Providence Mountains State Recreation Area** and the **Mitchell Caverns Natural Preserve**, 116 miles from Barstow. From the mountains you'll see spectacular views of the desert valleys and dunes below. The underground caves are full of incredible rock and mineral formations. You can expect cool 65° temperatures all year round, a great break from the desert heat. A visitor center is open daily to answer questions. *Tel. 619/389–2281. Take I–40 east from Barstow 100 mi to Essex Rd., then head northwest for 16 mi. Guided tours of the caverns are offered Sept.–June, weekdays at 1:30, weekends and holidays at 1:30 and 3; weekends only during the summer. Tours begin at the visitor center.*

Death Valley National Monument

Seemingly a wasteland in the middle of nowhere with searing summer temperatures and a tendency to be fatal to the ill-prepared, Death Valley lives up to its melodramatic name. Yet, each year, the valley's fierce reputation as one of the lowest and least hospitable places on earth draws thousands of adventurous and/or macabre travelers, who come away moved by its stark beauty and the legends of its crumbling ghost towns.

It all began nearly 3 million years ago when plates under the Earth's crust separated, creating a valley nearly 100 miles long, up to 25 miles wide, and spanning more than 2 million acres. The valley's topography is among the most diverse in the world, ranging from miles of mountains and sand dunes to natural oases and volcanic craters. Scientists can gather an almost complete geological record of the Earth from Death Valley's Ice Age lake beds and vast mineral deposits.

Human history in the valley began around 6000 BC when Native American tribes first camped at Nevares Spring. At the time, the valley floor was covered with water and big game roamed freely. Today, the valley has one of the most severe climates on earth. Less than 5 inches of rain fall every year and the average high temperature in July is a hibachi-like 116°. Birds dropped dead in mid-flight when, on July 10, 1913, the temperature in Furnace Creek reached 134°, the hottest weather ever recorded outside the Sahara Desert (not including ground temperatures, which can heat up to 200°!).

Death Valley's modern era began in 1849 when about 100 emigrant families stumbled onto it in search of a route to California's Gold Country in the Sierra Nevada Mountains. It took these pioneers more than a month to find a passage through the Panamint Mountains lining the valley's western ridge. The tallest of these, Telescopic Peak, towers 2 miles above the valley floor. Eventually, the settlers found a way out, but only after some had perished from the dry heat and many had been forced to abandon their wagons and eat their livestock; hence the name Death Valley. In the years that followed, gold and silver boomtowns like Skidoo and Rhyolite erupted during the valley's short-lived mining era. In 1933 President Hoover declared Death Valley a national monument, and since then it's become a favored destination for hikers, bikers, and others with apocalyptic leanings.

Despite the extreme temperatures and lack of water, a fragile but extensive ecosystem thrives on the desert floor. Over 9,000 species of plants and a wide variety of snakes and lizards have adapted to life in the desert heat. The majority of Death Valley's animals are nocturnal and include rodents like pocket mice, kit foxes, and kangaroo rats. At higher elevations you can sometimes spot jackrabbits and bighorn sheep. Death Valley is also home to over 200 species of birds and, surprisingly, at least three species of fish. The two-inch-long prehistoric desert pupfish has adapted to life in dry salty pools that were huge shimmering lakes millions of years ago.

To travel here in the summer heat you have to be brazen—and at least somewhat masochistic. Best suited are aliens from Mercury and Venus, who will find the scalding temperatures congenial.

Most visitors make the trek through the valley during the cooler months between October and May. Overnight stays should be planned in advance: During the winter (and on holidays) the monument can be crowded, and during the summer many facilities

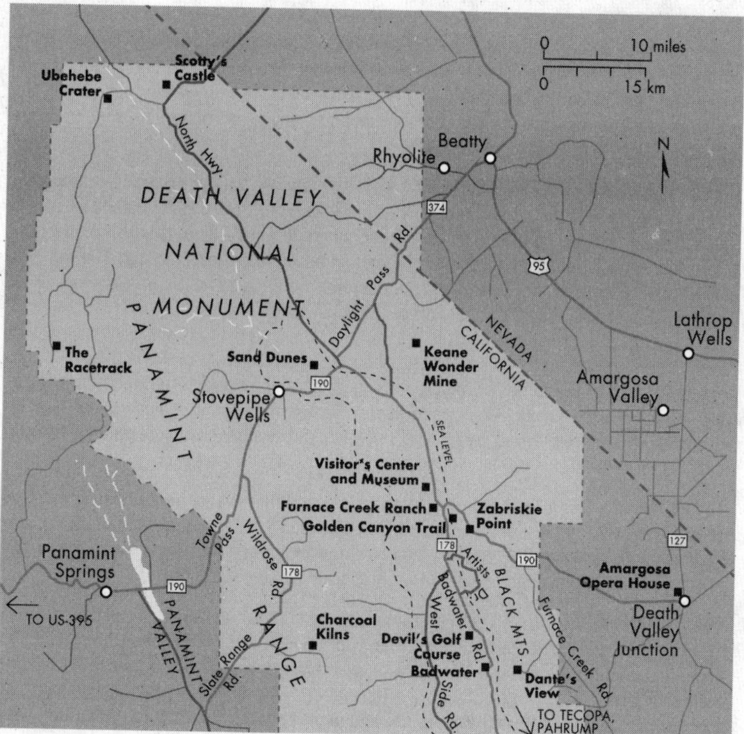

are closed. For a wider range of accommodations, consider staying outside the monument in the nearby communities of Beatty, Shoshone, Death Valley Junction, and Lone Pine. (*see* Near Death Valley, *below*).

Facilities within the monument are limited at any time of year. The center of activity is Furnace Creek, site of the visitor center and Furnace Creek Ranch, where there's lodging, gas, a mini-market, a gift shop, several restaurants, pay showers and laundry, and even an 18-hole golf course. Gas and food, available only at Furnace Creek, Stovepipe Wells Village, and Scotty's Castle (the most limited), are expensive within the monument boundaries.

BASICS • • •

TOURIST INFORMATION **Death Valley Chamber of Commerce** (2 Post Office Row, Tecopa 92389, tel. 619/852–4524) has a wide range of information about food, lodging, and attractions.

Furnace Creek Visitor Center (Death Valley National Monument, Death Valley 92328, tel. 619/786–2331), operated by the National Park Service, is the best starting point for a visit to the valley. Pick up maps, a free "Visitor's Guide," and lists of trails and campsites.

FEES Fees are $5 per vehicle and are valid for seven days. They're collected at the Furnace Creek Visitor Center (*see* Tourist Information, *above*) and the Grapevine Entrance Station, a booth at the valley's northern boundary (open daily 8–5) near Scotty's Castle.

PUBLICATIONS **Death Valley Natural History Association** (Box 188, Death Valley 92328, tel. 619/786–2331) has a complete list of maps and guides that you can order and read before you leave home.

WHEN TO GO The best times to visit are in the fall and spring when the weather is most comfortable. In April and October temperatures average in the mid-70s. In years of relatively heavy rainfall, colorful desert wildflowers bloom during the spring in the mountain passes leading into the valley. Fewer travelers visit the valley floor during the summer when temperatures are unbearably hot and many of the monument's facilities are closed.

FESTIVALS AND SEASONAL EVENTS The **Death Valley '49ers Encampment** (Death Valley '49ers Inc., 534 Cornell Dr., Burbank 91504, tel. 619/786–2331) usually takes place in the second week of November, when descendants of the first pioneers to cross the valley ride in on wagons and horses, dressed in period clothing. The massive encampment features rides, dancing, jamborees, fiddling contests, and enough other amusements to keep several thousand people busy for four days.

WHAT TO PACK

WATER Come prepared. Drinkable water sources are few and far between, so bring at least a gallon of water per person, and keep your water containers filled. It isn't a good idea to take water from the valley springs, but if you do, be sure to boil it or otherwise purify it before drinking.

CLOTHING Bring light-colored, loose-fitting clothing that reflects heat and keeps moisture near the body. Long pants and long-sleeved shirts are preferable. Park rangers also recommend that in the warmer months you wear a hat with a visor, sunglasses, and sturdy thick-soled shoes, since ground temperatures can get mighty hot.

CAR SUPPLIES Fill up with gas before going to Death Valley; stations are few, and the cost is about 30¢ more per gallon than you'll pay at truck stops near the Interstate. Also, check your oil level and tire pressure and bring extra radiator water to soothe an overheated engine. If you're planning on crossing on access roads by four-wheel-drive vehicle, you should also bring a spare tire and jack, a shovel, first-aid kit, food, and, yes, even more water. If your car breaks down, stay with it until someone finds you.

BIKING SUPPLIES A spare tire tube and a set of tools are essential. Bicyclists in Death Valley should follow the same rules as hikers: Dress appropriately for the heat and bring extra food and water.

GENERAL STORES The general stores at **Furnace Creek Ranch** and **Stovepipe Wells** (open daily 7–8) sell groceries, camping goods, cold drinks, and ice at slightly inflated prices. Buy your charcoal or firewood here as collecting wood in the monument is not permitted. Furnace Creek Ranch also runs a 24-hour laundromat on Roadrunner Avenue.

● ● ● COMING AND GOING

BY CAR It's difficult to see Death Valley without wheels. Currently, no public transportation runs through Death Valley. The visitor center at Furnace Creek is the starting point for most excursions. It's a good idea to plan your route in advance to save gas and time (*see* Near Death Valley, *below*).

From Los Angeles, take I–10 east to I–15 north. At Baker, 60 miles northeast of Barstow, take Route 127 north for 84 miles to Death Valley Junction, and then Route 190 north for 30 miles to Furnace Creek Visitor Center. If you're coming from northern California, take Route 99 south to Route 178 near Bakersfield; take Route 178 east to Route 190, which leads into the park and continues to Furnace Creek. From Las Vegas, take Route 95 north from Las Vegas for 85 miles to Amargosa Valley/Lathrop Wells. From here, Route 373 stretches 23 miles south to Death Valley Junction. The visitor center lies 30 miles to the east along Route 190. A scenic shortcut can be taken by turning south off Route 95, 9 miles west of the Nevada Test Site at Mercury, and continuing 26 miles south through the Ash Meadows National Wildlife Refuge (tel. 702/646–3401) in Nevada to Death Valley Junction.

HITCHHIKING Attempting to hitchhike through Death Valley, even in the winter, is only for the foolhardy.

WHERE TO SLEEP ● ● ●

Accommodations within Death Valley National Monument are expensive. The nearby towns of Beatty, Shoshone, Tecopa, Death Valley Junction, and Lone Pine all offer a number of comparable but less pricey options (*see* Near Death Valley, *below*).

UNDER $60 **Stovepipe Wells Village Motel**. This is about as cheap as you're going to find, with single rooms for $50 and doubles for around $60 year-round. *Stovepipe Wells Village, Death Valley 92328, tel. 619/786–2387. Facilities: general store and service station, restaurant, gift shop.*

UNDER $70 **Furnace Creek Ranch**. Roomy cabins, mostly with shower only, are available year round. Prices start at $60 in the summer, and go up to $95 for a deluxe cabin in the winter. Furnace Creek is the most developed area of the valley, and the ranch is smack in the middle, so you won't get lonely here. This is a center for lots of outdoor activities, including swimming and riding. *Box 1, Death Valley 92328, tel. 619/786–2345 or 800/528–6367.*

CAMPGROUNDS There are nine maintained campsites in the monument. All operate on a first-come, first-served basis and accommodate both RVs and tents, with the exception of the Furnace Creek Campground between October and April, when you must make reservations. Fresh water, picnic tables, fireplaces, and flush toilets are also available. The camping is ideal in winter; in summer, the heat will wake you up early. Showers, a swimming pool, and a laundromat are all available for a fee at Furnace Creek Ranch.

NEAR FURNACE CREEK **Furnace Creek**. The entrance lies a half-mile north of Furnace Creek Ranch. For about $8, you can camp near what passes for civilization in these parts. There are many shady spots, and you might get one if you arrive before 8 AM. Reservations are advised. *For reservations, tel. 800/452–1111. 136 sites; $4 service charge.*

Sunset. This site, 1-mile south of the visitor center, primarily accommodates RVs. That's right, it's a big parking lot. *1,000 sites. Cost: $4. Closed May–Oct. No showers, but flush and chemical toilets.*

Texas Spring. Located 1½ miles south of the visitor center off Route 190, Texas Spring is quiet except for the howling coyotes. *93 sites. Cost: $5. Motor home generators prohibited. Closed May–Oct. No showers, but flush toilets; fire rings.*

NEAR STOVEPIPE WELLS **Stovepipe Wells**. It's basically a patch of ground just across from the hotel and gift shop, but there's water and flush toilets. Fires are not permitted. The fee includes pay showers and access to the swimming pool at Stovepipe Wells Motel. *At Stovepipe Wells Village. Cost: $4. Closed May–Oct.*

SUMMER CAMPING During the summer, head for the campgrounds at higher elevations. It's cooler, more wooded, and more isolated than in Furnace Creek.

Emigrant. This small, free campground is 9 miles west of Stovepipe Wells Village at the cool elevation of 2,100 feet. *10 sites. Water and flush toilets available; fires not permitted. Closed May–Sept.*

Mesquite Spring. If you get stuck way up in the north corner of the monument, stay at this shady campground (elevation 1,800 feet) with a natural oasis. *4 mi south of Scotty's Castle; 50 sites. Cost: $5. Water, picnic tables, fireplaces, and flush toilets available.*

Thorndike and Mahogany Flat. Also free, these two sites are located high up at elevations of 7,500 feet and 8,200 feet. *About 8 mi east of Wildrose Campground along rough road, east of Rte. 178 (1 hr. from Furnace Creek). 18 sites. No trailers, campers; tables and fireplaces available, no water. Closed Apr.–Oct.*

BACKCOUNTRY CAMPING During the summer, campers should head for the hills to take advantage of cooler temperatures and mountain breezes. Backcountry camping is permitted at least 1 mile in from maintained roads, 1/4 mile from any water source, and 5 miles from maintained campgrounds. It's a good idea to fill out a backcountry registration form at any ranger station or at the Furnace Creek Visitor Center so that somebody knows where you are.

FOOD

Furnace Creek Ranch offers the widest selection of food within the monument. In addition to the **49ers Coffee Shop** (open 7 AM–9 PM), there's the **Wrangler Steak House**, the **Panamint Pizza Parlor**, and **Senor Coyote's Mexican Restaurant**, all of which have decent meals for under $8, and are open 6 PM–10 PM. The **Corkscrew Saloon**, Death Valley's only bar, stays open to 1 AM, later than anything else in the valley, except the nocturnal animals, and has pool tables, TV, and free hot popcorn! **Scotty's Castle** (*see* Exploring Death Valley, *below*) has a snack bar open 8:30–5:30, that serves spicy fries and good grilled sandwiches. (*For other restaurants in the area, see* Near Death Valley, *below*.)

EXPLORING DEATH VALLEY

With 14 square miles of sand dunes, 200 square miles of jagged salt beds, 11,000-foot peaks, and hills and canyons of startling colors—especially at sunrise and sundown—Death Valley deserves at least a day or two of your time. You can reach the most popular sights from the main roads, and the visitor center can suggest some great hikes and scenic drives.

ORIENTATION PROGRAMS The **Furnace Creek Visitor Center** runs a slide-show orientation every half hour (Mon.–Sat. 8:30–4, Sun. 10–4). Between November and March, park rangers host special evening programs covering ecological, geological, and historical aspects of the valley.

GUIDED TOURS If you don't mind being led around, you can sign up for a guided tour of the valley, beginning at $27, from October to April. Contact the **Furnace Creek Ranch Registration Office** (tel. 619/786–2345, ext. 222).

HIKING The best time to be on the trail is early in the morning and right before sundown, when the sun turns the mountains and sand to a luminous gold, and the heat is less intense. Be prepared (*see* What to Pack, *above*).

GOLDEN CANYON TRAIL "It's dynamite, if you can make it," says a recent visitor. The 5-mile, round-trip trail ends at Zabriskie Point. This moderately strenuous, unmaintained trail climbs over the richly tinted ridges in Golden Canyon. The trailhead is 3 miles south of Furnace Creek, off Highway 190. Get a map at the visitor center before you set out.

KEANE WONDER MINE AND MILL This 2-mile round-trip hike follows a steep trail along the route of an old aerial tramway that ran from the processing mill up to the mine entrance. The tunnels no longer yield gold but promise certain misfortune for anyone who enters them. We've all seen the movie: The rotten timber crumbles, sending our heroes hurtling into the hidden mine shaft below. Don't expect Indiana Jones to rescue you, though. To get to the mine, go about 18 miles north from Furnace Creek on Route 190, then turn onto the cut-off road heading toward Beatty, and continue another 3 miles to the access road. Be careful driving on the rough road, unless you're fond of breaking down in 100° heat.

MOSAIC CANYON An uphill trail winds through the narrows of this canyon, the marble walls of which have been polished smooth by the erosive effects of draining water. The layers of rock built up over millions of years are a geologist's wet dream (non-gender specific, of course). The trail ends 2 miles farther on at the base of a dry waterfall. The farther in you go the more spectacular the views. Mosaic Canyon is located only 1/4 mile west of Stovepipe Wells along Route 190 (it's a 4-mile round-trip).

SALT CREEK INTERPRETIVE TRAIL Fifteen miles north of Furnace Creek, off Route 190, lies a half-mile trail through Salt Creek. This level nature walk is wheelchair accessible and provides glimpses of some of the only fish in Death Valley, subsisting on the plankton and algae that grow in briny ponds which are all that remain of Ice Age lakes.

SAND DUNES Death Valley's dunes tower up to eight stories high and cover more than 10 square miles. The dunes were created when ancient lakes dried up and their sandy bottoms were blown around by the winds. The parking and picnic area for the dunes is marked by a sign off Route 190, about 12 miles north of Stovepipe Wells, toward Scotty's Castle. Four miles to the south, a marker labels the dunes directly parallel to the tallest slopes. You'll want to stop here to take pictures—even amateurs can take magazine-quality photographs, especially in the morning and evening when the dunes cast dramatic shadows. To reach the tallest dunes, hike 1 mile directly from the roadside.

It's an almost mystical joy to wander among the dune's windswept slopes, but don't lose sight of your car. The wind can easily cover your tracks with sand, and then you're, gulp, lost.

TELESCOPE PEAK If you have extra energy and time (about a day's worth), make the 3,000-foot climb from the tallest of the sand dunes to the summit of 12,000-foot Telescope Peak. The strenuous uphill climb affords panoramic views of Death Valley and the High Sierras. In winter you'll need special equipment to finish the last ice-covered mile to the summit.

UBEHEBE CRATER When molten lava under the Earth's crust came in contact with groundwater under the valley floor nearly 3,000 years ago, the subsequent explosions of steam and gas spewed debris for miles around Death Valley. These eruptions created the Crater, a volcano nearly a half-mile wide and 500 feet deep; it's sheer size is awesome, and there's a pretty good view from the rim. The origin of the name "Ubehebe" has been long forgotten, but the Shoshone who still live in the area refer to the crater as "Tem-pin-tta Wo'sah" or "the basket in the rock." The trail down to the bottom of the crater is easy, but remember it takes twice as long to climb back up. Ubehebe Crater is at the northern end of the monument, 5 1/4 miles west of the Grapevine Entrance Station off Route 190.

SCENIC DRIVES AND VIEWS The major attractions in the valley are spread out over hundreds of miles, so you wont be able to see everything unless you stick around for three days or more. The following drive takes in the most spectacular scenery within reasonable distance of the visitor center.

BADWATER-DEVIL'S GOLF COURSE-ARTIST'S DRIVE Begin at **Badwater**, 25 miles south of the visitor center along Route 178. This brackish pool, the remains of an ancient lake, is worth a quick stop, if only so you can say you've visited what's called the lowest place in the western hemisphere: 279.8 feet below sea level—it's marked on an overlooking hill. (Actually, the real lowest point is 282 feet below sea level and about a mile away). Four miles north of Badwater is the aptly named **Devil's Golf Course**, a huge expanse of jagged salt beds that look flat from far away but are really twisted and full of chasms several stories deep. Wear thick-soled shoes if you walk onto the flats—the crystallized salt can easily cut unprotected feet. Continue north 4 more miles before turning off onto **Artist's Drive**, which twists and turns through colorful rock and mineral deposits. The colors are most vibrant at **Artist's Palette**, an overlook about halfway along the drive. The road ends about 5 miles south of the visitor center. There are some great hikes in here, and basically, you can go anywhere you want: Ask at the visitor center for suggestions.

ZABRISKIE POINT-TWENTY MULE TEAM CANYON-DANTE'S VIEW Immortilized by the 1960s Antonioni film of the same name, **Zabriskie Point**, about 4 miles south of the visitor center, is one of the monument's most spectacular spots. At a height of 710 feet, it overlooks a striking badlands panorama of wrinkled, cinnamon-color hills. Nearby, a one-way unpaved drive leads through more mining ruins in **Twenty Mule Team Canyon**, named after the big mule teams that hauled huge borax carts 40 miles across the desert. Thirteen miles south, off Route 190, is a 14-mile paved road that leads through the **Black Mountains** to a scenic lookout at **Dante's View**, 5,000 feet above the valley floor. The bleak landscape below includes the same Devil's Golf Course you saw near Badwater, but from a different perspective. From here the green oasis of **Furnace Creek** can be seen to the north, and on a clear day **Mt. Whitney** is visible on the western horizon (*see* Chapter 7, The Sierra Nevada and San Joaquin Valley). There is a "sleeper" of a trail that heads to **Aguereberry Point** on the opposite side of the valley. Access is via a gravel road, which is sometimes impassable; ask at Furnace Creek for conditions and best route to take.

WORTH SEEING

HARMONY BORAX WORKS AND MUSEUM Along with the adobe ruins of the borax works, you can see the very wagons immortalized in ads for the radio and TV show "Death Valley Days." The 10-ton wagons required the efforts of 20 mules to drag them, often up to 165 miles across the desert to the nearest railroad line in Barstow. Borax is still used for ceramic glazes, porcelain enamel, and in the construction of fiberglass, but it's mined elsewhere these days. The small museum has a lot of artifacts and some photos from the mine's heyday. *Located 2 mi north of Furnace Creek Ranch. Closed in summer.*

If you're driving, make sure that the car is in very good condition and that it has been recently serviced. A spare tire, jack, shovel, and extra radiator water are also essential. If you break down and are unable to repair your car, stay where you are unless you are absolutely sure you can reach help.

SCOTTY'S CASTLE This huge, Spanish-style hacienda in the northern part of the Monument was built as a vacation home by Chicago millionaire Albert Johnson and his wife Bessie in 1924. The hacienda got its name from Walter Scott, a close friend of the family, better known as Death Valley Scotty. Scott used to tell visitors tales of lost gold mines still untouched and unclaimed. The tours through the home are among the most popular attractions in Death Valley. The castle's lavish interiors are worth seeing, but the crowds, especially on the holidays, can be heavy. If you don't want to wait or spend money, take a walk around the castle grounds. *Tel. 619/786–2392. Admission: $6. Open daily 9–5. Tours run about an hour.*

THE WILDROSE CHARCOAL KILNS The kilns, which look like a row of giant hives for monstrous bees, are a set of 10 huge ovens used by miners to turn wood into coal. Miners built the kilns because the area has no natural source of coke (coal subjected to heat), which was needed to process the silver and borax ores. The kilns' average height is just over 25 feet and each stretches almost 10 yards across. You can still smell the resin and creosote left behind in the burning process. The kilns can be reached by driving east on Wildrose Canyon Road from the Wildrose Campground. After 4 miles the pavement ends; you may want to hike the final 1½ miles rather than risk damage to your car.

• • • PARK ACTIVITIES

ALL-TERRAIN VEHICLES Four-wheel drive vehicles can be rented at **Furnace Creek Chevron** (tel. 619/786–2232; open daily 8–5). They're great for getting around on dirt roads, but no off-road driving is permitted in the monument.

BIKING Bicycling is permitted on roads that allow cars, but forbidden off maintained roads or on hiking trails. Be sure to bring extra water, food, tools, and maps, as this could be an ordeal. For a complete list of suggested bike routes, ask at the visitor center. You can rent bicycles at **Furnace Springs Ranch** (tel. 619/786–2345).

HORSEBACK RIDING During the fall, winter, and spring, **Furnace Creek Ranch** (tel. 619/786–2345) offers one- to two-hour guided rides on horseback or in a carriage.

SWIMMING For $2 a day, you can swim at the pools at either **Furnace Creek Ranch** (daily 9 AM–10 PM) or **Stovepipe Wells** (daily 9–9), even if you're not a guest.

Near Death Valley National Monument

BEATTY

Tourists seldom visit the quiet desert town of Beatty, northeast of Death Valley, off Route 374 in Nevada. Denizens of the town admit there isn't much to do here—or rather, there's only one thing, and it's made convenient by Nevada's laws legalizing prostitution. For more information, go to the town's unofficial tourist center, **Bobbie's Pot Shop** (tel. 702/553–2254), a marvelous store in the center of town selling knick-knacks, curios, and guides to the nearby bordellos. Across the street, the official **Visitor Center** provides complete information on lodgings, restaurants, and services. *Box 1235, Beatty, NV 89003, tel. 702/553–2424. Open daily 8–4.*

Lodging and food are substantially cheaper in Beatty than in the nearby monument. If you're hot and tired, you'll welcome the sight of the well-kept **El Portal Motel** (301 Main St., tel. 702/553–2912), with a pool and rooms for $35–$38. The **Stagecoach Hotel and Casino** (Rte. 95, tel. 702/553–2419) may be the closest casino to Death Valley, but you'll probably be more interested in the pool and coffee shop (open daily 6 AM–10 PM). Rooms cost about $30.

RHYOLITE

Rhyolite was once home to over 10,000 people, making it one of the biggest mining towns ever to exist in the United States. It had its own stock exchange and its own opera house, but now it's a ghost town. Stroll down Golden Street, once the busiest street in town, and indulge your penchant for picaresque decay by exploring the deteriorating school, bank, and general store. The mine went bust about 80 years ago. What's left of the town is 4 miles west of Beatty, off Route 374.

DEATH VALLEY JUNCTION

This tiny town in the desert doesn't have a gas station or a restaurant, but it's home to one of the cultural wonders of the West. **Marta Becket's Amargosa Opera House** features a one-woman ballet performance by Marta herself. She was an artist and dancer based in New York until her car broke down in the desert and she decided to stay. Her repertoire of 47 different characters is world famous (almost), as are the painted murals on the walls and ceiling of the opera house. Becket painted the pictures of musicians, bards, clergymen, gypsies, and 16th-century Spanish royalty between 1968 and 1974. From that point on, her notoriety began, well, snowballing. She often plays to sell-out crowds, so call ahead for reservations. *Amargosa Opera House, Box 8, Death Valley Junction 92328, tel. 619/852–4316. Admission: $8 donation. Performances: Nov.–Apr., Fri., Sat., and Mon. at 8 PM; Oct., Dec., and May, Sat. shows only.*

Adjacent to the opera house is the **Amargosa Hotel**, offering rooms for around $42, with a Continental breakfast included. *Box 619, Death Valley Junction 92328, tel. 619/852–4509.*

TECOPA

Pauite Native Americans used to bring their sick to bathe in the healing mineral springs near Tecopa, where the average water temperature hovers somewhere near 108°. If you want to follow the Paiutes' lead, you can enjoy the baths free of charge at **Tecopa Hot Springs Park** (Box 158, Tecopa 92389, tel. 619/852–4264). Park campsites cost around $5.50, RV sites around $7. For a room of your own, try **Delight's Hot Spa** (Box 368, Tecopa 92389, tel. 619/852–4343) where cottages cost under $25 per night; RV's park here for $9. You can get a decent meal at The **Miner's Diner** (tel. 619/852–4222) or the adjacent **Tecopa Trading Post**.

● ● ● PAHRUMP

One of the fastest growing towns in Nevada, Pahrump is a haven for people willing to live anywhere to escape the high cost of city life. It also boasts a number of fireworks dealers and several brothels, which may have helped attract new settlers. Fireworks, including a chicken that lays flaming eggs, can be purchased at any of the stores along Route 160, which runs through this unincorporated town. The brothels, however, are all located outside town. The friendly staff of the **Pahrump Chamber of Commerce** (tel. 702/727–5800) will provide you with all the information you need to enjoy Pahrump's attractions.

Pahrump also has the novelty of being home to Nevada's only winery, **Pahrump Valley Vineyards**, which offers free guided tours. Inside is the excellent restaurant **Tastings**, with dinners for around $20 (lunches $10) and panoramic views of the Amargosa Valley from its tower. *3810 E. Homestead Rd., tel. 702/727–6900. Winery open (and guided tours) daily 10–4:30; restaurant open daily for lunch and dinner.*

LAS VEGAS AND THE GRAND CANYON 13

By Christopher Hallenbeck

Almost everyone reacts the same way when they first lay eyes on Las Vegas, whether from the ground or air. Shimmering in the distance—even during the day—the city grows brighter and brighter as you approach it, eventually turning into street after street of flashing electric lights and frantic commotion. Instantly, you're like a 14-year-old, moved at once by innocent awe and hormones. You may think it's kitschy, you may think it's sleazy, you may think it's corrupt—but suddenly you feel lucky. Then you start gambling. And not just you, but everybody. Standing at a roulette wheel in one of the more than 50 casinos, you may find yourself between a fresh-faced bride whose dress still sports a 7-foot train, and a boneheaded drunk in a pin-striped suit coat and gym shorts who seems overly eager to empty his wallet. The booze is flowing, and if you feel a bit bewildered, that's exactly how you're supposed to feel. Some people grow to cherish their visits to Las Vegas, while others depart in disgust never to return again. If you lose too much money, you can always throw yourself into the Grand Canyon, 300 miles to the east. Most people, though, will be content to dribble in amazement from the rim of what is surely the country's most famous and spectacular attraction.

Las Vegas

Las Vegas has earned its reputation as the ultimate adult playground, a city where everything is done on a grandiose scale. Its dozens of palatial resorts and casinos annually garner billions of dollars in gambling revenues. Competition between the casinos is fierce: Free gifts, cheap food, and even money to gamble with are all available to you if you're willing to investigate. Most of the casinos have elaborately constructed themes and decor, ranging from the tropical island motif at the Tropicana Hotel to the ancient Roman setting at Caesar's Palace. The newest casino in town is the Excalibur, an Arthurian-theme castle with more than 4,000 rooms. Nearly all of these hotels also offer all-you-can-eat buffets ranging from $1 late-night breakfast specials to elegant $20 buffets complete with lobster tails, 12-ounce steaks, and a constant flow of champagne. Each casino claims to provide more for less. The casinos also compete with neon light displays and illuminated billboards, so it's no surprise to visitors that Las Vegas uses more electricity per capita than any other city in the United States. It's especially evident on Fremont Street downtown ("Glitter Gulch") where the traffic lights can easily be lost in this sea of flashing colored bulbs. Las Vegas is also known for its live shows, ranging from female impersonators to magicians to popular talents like Frank Sinatra and Wayne Newton. You'll find that although you're not allowed to wear shorts and tank tops to shows, show girls are clad in "three triangles, three feathers, and butt floss."

Las Vegas

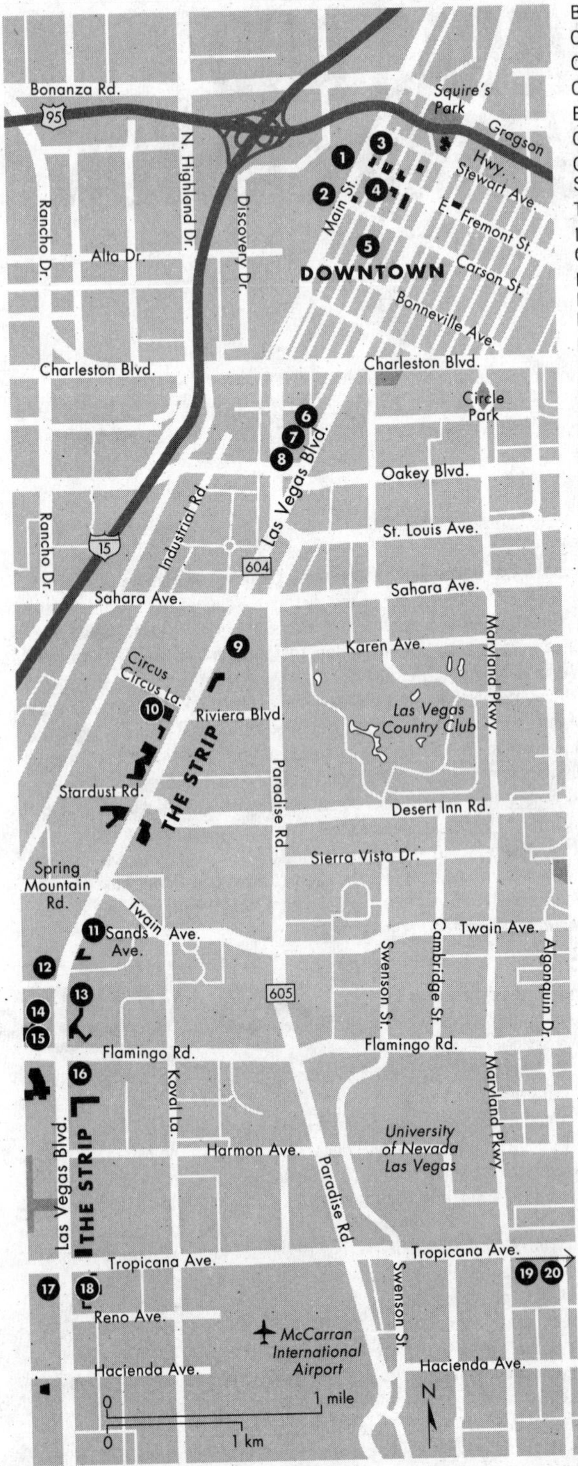

Bally's, **16**
Caesar's Palace, **15**
California Hotel, **3**
Circus Circus, **10**
Excalibur, **17**
Golden Nugget, **4**
Greyhound Bus Station, **2**
The Gun Store, **20**
Imperial Palace Car Collection, **13**
Las Vegas Independent Hostel, **6**
Las Vegas International Hostel, **7**
Liberace Museum, **19**
Mirage, **12**
Omnimax Theatre, **14**
Sand's Hotel, **11**
Tod Motor Hotel, **8**
Tropicana, **18**
Union Station, **1**
Wedding Chapels, **5**
Wet 'N Wild Water Park, **9**

Nevada's liberal laws don't stop at gambling. Las Vegas is home to countless 24-hour liquor stores and strip bars. You can drink anytime you want, although bartenders sometimes get cranky after 3 AM. It's still easier to get married or divorced in Nevada than anywhere else in the country, and your wedding options include drive-through chapels and services performed by Elvis impersonators. Prostitution is legal in some parts of Nevada, but not in Las Vegas. Perhaps that's why there are a dozen pages of "personal entertainers" in the Las Vegas telephone directory.

Whatever else may be going on, gambling is always the bottom line. It's no surprise that nearly every casino has automated tellers and offers credit-card advances. Your traveler's checks are also welcome. For the desperate, a number of check-cashing stores and pawn shops line Las Vegas Boulevard ("the Strip"). In the gambling areas, drinks are inexpensive and often free when you're playing the games. Whether you're making 25¢ bets on craps at the Union Plaza or playing poker at the Mirage with $300 minimums, you'll usually be treated like royalty (especially if you keep tipping the dealers). Legally, you have to be 21 to gamble at a casino, but with a little bit of nerve you can get into a game whatever your age. A surefire way to get carded is to start winning big, but that's hardly likely. The average visitor loses more than $100 on a visit to Las Vegas, and it's not unusual to see people lose thousands in just a few minutes. The spills and chills of high-stakes gambling make quite a spectacle, particularly if you're not the one losing the money.

If you can tear yourself away from the casinos, you may notice that Las Vegas is also a city that sprawls over several square miles and has a population of around 800,000. Nearly half of Nevada's residents live here, feeding off the gambling economy and enjoying more than 300 days of clear, sunny skies a year. Las Vegas is also home to one of the most successful college basketball teams in the nation, the Runnin' Rebels of the University of Nevada at Las Vegas (UNLV). The popular team is a source of civic pride since no professional baseball, basketball, or football teams make their home here. The Thomas and Mack Center where the Rebels play has more seats (60,000) than the university has students.

Temperatures soar over the 100° mark during the summer and usually drop only as low as 50° on the coldest days of winter. The climate, in addition to the 24-hour casinos, makes almost any time ideal for visiting Las Vegas. However, during holidays and weekends the hotels and casinos can be crowded and room prices can double. If you want to save your budget, don't pull into town on Friday or Saturday.

To the east lies 110-mile-long Lake Mead—guidebooks call it a water-sports paradise—created by the construction of Hoover Dam along the Colorado River, just 30 miles south of Las Vegas.

ORIENTATION At one time, the principle center of commerce and tourism was the downtown area on Fremont Street, a five-block strip between the northern end of Las Vegas Boulevard and Main Street, just one block north of the Greyhound Bus station. Also known as Glitter Gulch, Las Vegas's downtown area is still home to many of the city's oldest casinos and is the best place to find budget accommodations. Today, the Strip (Las Vegas Boulevard) runs about 5 miles south from downtown through possibly the most congested glut of resort hotels and casinos in the world. Sharing this route are the pagoda-shaped Imperial Palace, the medieval Excalibur, the Mirage with its towering volcano and tropical pools, and many others. Beyond the Tropicana, the casinos quickly fade into barren desert, with the airport and UNLV farther south off Paradise Road.

Some parts of the city away from the Strip and the downtown area are unsafe for travelers on foot, especially at night. If you're alone, stick to the major tourist areas unless you have a car. Traffic in town is often heavy, but parking at most casinos is free.

BASICS • • •

AMERICAN EXPRESS There's an office with complete financial services inside **Caesar's Palace** (3570 Las Vegas Blvd. S, tel. 702/731–7705). You can cash money orders weekdays 8–5, Saturday 8–2; cash-machine access is available Sunday–Thursday 8–6, Friday and Saturday 8–8.

FOREIGN CURRENCY EXCHANGE **Foreign Money Exchange** (3025 Las Vegas Blvd. S, tel. 702/791–3301) gives American dollars for foreign currency.

DOCTORS AND DENTISTS The **Clark County Medical Society** (tel. 702/739–9989) and the **Clark County Dental Society** (tel. 702/435–7767) will make referrals.

EMERGENCIES The **University Medical Center** (1800 W. Charleston Blvd., tel. 702/383–2000) has a 24-hour emergency facility as well as outpatient services.

LUGGAGE STORAGE Twenty-four-hour lockers are available at the **Greyhound Bus Station** (200 Main St., tel. 702/382–2640) for a small fee. Passengers with Amtrak tickets can store luggage at **Union Station** (1 N. Main St., tel. 702/386–6896) for $1 per bag per day. The **AYH** (youth hostel; 1236 Las Vegas Blvd. S, tel. 702/382–8119) has small outdoor, coin-operated lockers that you can get to round the clock.

MAIL General delivery is available at the **Downtown Postal Station**. *301 E. Stewart, 89125, tel. 702/385–8944. Open weekdays 9–5.*

TELEPHONES The area code for all Nevada is 702. All local calls require a 25¢ deposit.

PHARMACIES **White Cross Drug** is open 24 hours a day at two locations (1700 Las Vegas Blvd. S, tel. 702/382–1733; 953 E. Sahara Ave., tel. 702/735–5189).

TOURIST INFORMATION Many agencies in Las Vegas bill themselves as "official tourist centers" offering hotel reservations, bus tours, and show tickets. These centers are really travel agencies in disguise. Detailed and up-to-date information on shows, buffets, and casinos (as well as substantial discounts on local attractions) can be found in publications like "What's on in Las Vegas" and "Today in Las Vegas," available free in most hotels and gift shops. For advice on the local music scene and alternative shops and service, look for *In* music magazine (tel. 702/732–2328), available in music stores and other local shops that tourists rarely see.

The **Las Vegas Convention and Visitors Authority** provides general information and advice on entertainment and accommodations in town. *3150 Paradise Rd., tel. 702/733–2323. Open weekdays 8–5.*

You've Come a Long Way, Baby

It seems unlikely that nature intended for this little slab of desert to become an oasis for gambling and other polite vices. When the Nevada legislature legalized gambling in 1931, Las Vegas was merely a railroad stop only seven blocks long, although even then prostitution was an integral part of the economy. The construction of Hoover Dam and nearby military installations helped Vegas expand during the Great Depression and World War II. The desert surrounding the city has yielded great mineral deposits and has also been the site for much of the United States' nuclear testing—both factors contributing considerably to Vegas's growth. However, it wasn't until 1946, when mobster Bugsy Siegel and his partners Lucky Luciano and Meyer Lansky opened the Fabulous Flamingo, that Las Vegas began to become a mecca for vacationers. Bugsy eventually got bumped off for his troubles, and somehow that's fitting. In the popular imagination, Las Vegas is the place where it's possible for your crassest dreams to come true, and then kill you. Brush up on your Elvis lore prior to arrival.

The **Las Vegas Chamber of Commerce** (2301 E. Sahara, tel. 702/457–4664) and the **Nevada Commission on Tourism** (tel. 702/486–7234 or 800/638–2328) also give advice and general information.

COMING AND GOING • • •

BY PLANE **McCarran International Airport** (tel. 702/739–5743) is one of the world's few airports with slot machines in the terminal. This large modern facility is 5 miles south of downtown, just east of Las Vegas Boulevard, and is most easily reached via Paradise Road. McCarran is served by several major airlines, including **American** (tel. 800/433–7300), **America West** (tel. 800/247–5692), **Continental** (tel. 702/383–8291), **Delta** (tel. 702/731–3111), **Northwest** (tel. 800/225–2525), **TWA** (tel. 702/385–1000), **USAir** (tel. 800/428–4322), and **United** (tel. 702/385–3222).

AIRPORT TRANSPORT Cabs from the airport to the Strip run about $10; the longer trip downtown costs closer to $15. If you really want to travel to Las Vegas in style, share a limousine for $25 an hour. Call **Lucky 7** (tel. 702/383–5977), **Bell Trans** (tel. 702/735–4428), **Presidential** (tel. 702/736–5577), or pick one up at the terminal.

BY TRAIN **Amtrak** (tel. 800/872–7245) has service to downtown's Union Station (1 N. Main St.), located behind the Union Plaza Hotel and Casino. Passengers can check luggage for $1 a day per bag. Buses to the Strip leave from Fremont Street, one block from the station. Trains bound for Los Angeles and the west leave every morning and trains to Salt Lake City, Chicago, and points east leave every evening.

BY BUS Buses heading across the United States leave from the **Greyhound Bus Station** (200 S. Main St. at Union Plaza, tel. 702/382–2640). Lockers and rest rooms are available for a small price. Buses to the Strip stop on Fremont Street at Union Plaza, two blocks to the left of the station as you exit.

BY CAR Las Vegas is about 300 miles from Los Angeles, Phoenix, and the Grand Canyon; nearly 400 miles from Salt Lake City; and nearly 600 miles from San Francisco. From Los Angeles, take I–10 east to its junction with I–15, near Ontario, and follow I–15 east all the way to Vegas. From northern California, take Route 99 to Bakersfield (or take I–5 to its junction with Route 99, and backtrack north to Bakersfield). From Bakersfield, take Route 58 east to Barstow, and then I–15 east to Las Vegas.

"DRIVE AWAY" If you're hungry for wheels, check out whether there's a car that needs to be delivered where you're going. You'll probably have to pay a refundable deposit of around $250. Don't expect to have your choice of make or model. Try **Auto Driveaway Company** (3355 W. Spring Mountain Rd., tel. 702/252–8904) or look in the yellow pages.

GETTING AROUND • • •

If you're willing to cope with car exhaust and desert heat, walking is the best way to get around the main tourist centers of Las Vegas Boulevard ("the Strip") and Fremont Street ("Downtown" or "Glitter Gulch"), where traffic can be maddening. Lots of pedestrians get mowed down by intoxicated motorists every year, so be careful crossing streets. Buses connect the downtown area and the Strip efficiently, but elsewhere they are limited and don't run all hours. If you want to get out of town, consider renting a car.

BY BUS **Las Vegas Transit** buses (tel. 702/384–3540) cost $1.25. Drivers don't make change, so make sure you have coins on hand. If you plan to use the bus a lot, you can get a commuter card good for 10 rides for $8—a substantial savings. The cards can be purchased from any bus driver, or downtown at the Transportation Center (corner of 3rd and Casino Center). If you're in a wheelchair, bus fare is 55¢ (except when it's $1.25 on the Strip from 7 AM to 10 PM). Most buses are wheelchair accessible. **The Strip Shuttle** (Route 13) runs along the Strip every twenty minutes 8:30 AM–1 AM. Route 6 runs between the downtown area and the Hacienda Hotel at the end of the Strip 24 hours a day, but service slows to once every half-hour 2:45 AM–6 AM. **The Mall Hopper** (Route 14) runs between Las Vegas's three biggest malls Monday–Saturday until around 6 PM, connecting the Boulevard Mall on Maryland Parkway with the Fashion Show Mall on the Strip and the Meadows Mall on Valley View Road. You can also take the **Strip Trolley**, which stops directly at many of the casinos, including Circus Circus, Stardust Mirage, Caesar's, Bally's, and Imperial Palace. The fare is only $1 and the trolley runs daily on the half-hour from 9:30 AM to 2 AM.

TAXIS The basic cab fare is about $1.70 plus $1.40 per mile. It's easy to hail a cab (they wait in front of most hotels), but fares can be expensive if you're not traveling with a group. If you want a taxi and you're not near a hotel, call **Charter** (tel. 702/873–2227), **Desert** (tel. 702/736–8383), **Western** (tel. 702/736–8000), or **Yellow** (tel. 702/873–2227).

RENTAL CARS There are dozens of rental car agencies, so rates are low. Most agencies will rent only to people over 21 and require a cash deposit or a credit card. Most of these companies offer free transportation to and from the airport or your hotel. For the best rates try **American International** (tel. 800/527–0202), **Fairway** (tel. 702/736–1786), **Payless** (tel. 702/739–8488), or **Alamo** (tel. 702/737–3111).

● ● ● WHERE TO SLEEP

There are budget rooms everywhere, especially in the downtown area. Rates are cheapest on weekdays. Expect to pay nearly 50% more on weekends, when vacationers head for Las Vegas in droves and the city often hosts major conventions. Make reservations in advance if you're arriving on Friday or Saturday to avoid a weary round of "no vacancy" signs. If you're going with several friends, consider sharing a room in one of the posh casinos. Squeezing up to nine people into a room designed for four isn't impossible, but the desk clerks in some of the more expensive casinos make you show your room key before allowing you onto the elevator.

UNDER $20 **Downtowner Motel**. The rooms here have refrigerators and VCRs, and there's also free danish and coffee. The area is fairly yucko, but at least the rooms are cheap, with rates ranging from $20 to $50 on weekends. *129 N. 8th St., tel. 702/384–1441 or 800/777–2566.*

Tod Motor Hotel. In its heyday, the Tod was probably a nice hotel; now, it's a bit run down, but the small rooms with big beds are comfortable, and there's a swimming pool to drown your sorrows in after you lose all your gambling money. The hotel is on the Strip, near a number of fast-food joints. Daily rates hover in the $20 range, while the weekly rate of about $90 makes the place popular with people "just passing through." *1508 Las Vegas Blvd. S, tel. 702/427–0022.*

At Circus Circus, one guest reported that she was obliged to fend off the advances of a man trying to entice her with a rubber chicken.

UNDER $35 **Circus Circus**. In *Fear & Loathing in Las Vegas* Hunter S. Thompson hallucinates his way through Circus Circus, but no drugs are needed to make a stay here strange. Everything about the place is immense, including the number of rooms—nearly 3,000! Hordes of weekend visitors block traffic in the street, and block your passage through the casino, while they (and you) gawk at the acrobats who swing on trapezes high above the crowd with bewildering regularity. There's a wedding chapel (gulp!) and a huge RV park ($25–$45 for hook-up) with free shuttle service to the casino. Expect large crowds in the parking lot and at the buffet. *2880 Las Vegas Blvd. S, tel. 702/734–0410 or 800/634–3450. Cable TV, 3 swimming pools, 4 restaurants.*

UNDER $50 **California Hotel**. In the heart of downtown, this hotel has—what else?—a Hawaiian decor. Viva Las Vegas! The hotel's 600 rooms cost less than $50, even on weekends, though the management won't mind if you lose some of the savings to a croupier in a floral shirt. Short of a special deal, this is one of the cheapest casino lodgings you'll find. The casino has lots of $2 tables and 5¢ slot machines. *12 Ogden Ave., tel. 702/385–1222. Valet parking, air-conditioning, cable TV, restaurant, pool in summer.*

UNDER $50 **Caesar's Palace**. The cheapest rooms start at just under $100, but then this kind of, er, decadence just isn't widely available. Haven't you always wanted to loll on a raised circular bed beneath a mirrored ceiling (with the companion of your choice)? Look no further! You can always tell your friends you're doing research on kitsch and, besides, anyone with a low threshold for garishness shouldn't be in Vegas anyway. Stroll down the Appian Way shopping area ("I've always wanted Gucci wrist restrainers") and gaze at the 18-foot white-marble replica of Michelangelo's *David*. You've just obviated the need to visit Rome or Florence, so Caesar's might turn into a big money-saver after all. *3750 Las Vegas Blvd. S, tel. 702/731–7110 or 800/634–6661. Pool, spa, restaurants, arcade.*

HOSTELS The two hostels in town are located on the Strip, three doors apart on the same side of the street. Las Vegas being what it is, the hostels are good places to make friends with drinkers, pot smokers, and drifters (in addition to the occasional innocent abroad).

Las Vegas International Hostel (AYH). Housed on the site of an old motor hotel, the hostel has an attractive lawn with plenty of trees and shade, unlike the rest of Vegas. For the most part, the 16 rooms are clean and spacious. *1236 Las Vegas Blvd. S, tel. 702/382–8119. Hostel members: $8.50, nonmembers: $11.50; $5 key deposit. Office open daily 7–10 AM and 5–11 PM. Check-out time 10 AM. No curfew; laundry.*

Las Vegas Independent Hostel. Only a few doors down from the International Hostel, this well-managed independent hostel offers free lemonade, coffee, and tea, and has the advantage of private rooms. The hostel does honor AYH membership cards. *1208 Las Vegas Blvd. S, tel. 702/385–9955. Members: $8, nonmembers: $10; $2 key deposit. Office open Apr.–Oct., daily 7–10 AM and 3–11 PM; Nov.–Mar., daily 8–10 and 5–11. Check-out time 10 AM. No curfew; laundry.*

CAMPGROUNDS **Las Vegas KOA**. Located about 4 miles from the Strip on several acres along Boulder Highway, the KOA has nearly 80 tent sites and offers a free shuttle to the casinos. A swimming pool, laundry facilities, and a small grocery store are also on the premises. Not exactly the great outdoors, the campgrounds nevertheless are quite pretty, with trees to shade you from the desert sun. *4315 Boulder Hwy., near Desert Inn Rd., tel. 702/451–5527. Cost: $17.95 in winter, $20 mid-May–Sept. for tent sites; $22 for hook-ups year-round.*

FOOD

In recent years, the city has become almost as famous for the bargain buffets offered by casinos as for gambling. All the buffets have huge selections and operate under the philosophy that more for less is better, just so long as some of your savings end up in the casino. You can also save in casino cocktail lounges and bars, where drinks are often less than $2 and huge shrimp cocktails and half-pound hot dogs cost no more than $1.

Few visitors ever venture far from the main tourist areas, but those who do will find a wide selection of inexpensive restaurants (remember that this is a city with 800,000 full-time residents). For the most part, though, Las Vegas's restaurants serve up standard American cuisine. For the real Vegas experience, do it Roman style. Gorge yourself at a buffet, then stick a feather down your throat and do it again.

CASINO BUFFETS Buffet and meal prices change often, so consult the various free tourist guides and casino marquees for up-to-date information. When you do find a great deal, especially the buffets in the newer and more popular casinos, expect to wait in line with hundreds of other tourists with the same idea. The best bargains are available between 11 PM and 6 AM when the casino traffic dies down considerably. Lunch buffets are also good values; many have essentially the same menu as dinner buffets, but cost a few dollars less.

Before you devote yourself to the search for the cheapest meal in Las Vegas, be forewarne that the quality of the food decreases with the price. Even in Vegas, the more you can affor to spend, the better the value for your dollar.

UNDER $5 For the best value, try the **Round Table Buffet** at the **Excalibur**, where n buffet meal costs more than $4, and the selection is immense. Another good bargain i the $2 late-night steak and eggs buffet (11 PM and 6 AM) at the **Golden Nugget**, whic includes a huge steak and all the muffins, potatoes, and cooked-to-order eggs you can ea If you can't wait until 11 for your dinner, the **Prime Rib Room** at the **Lady Luck Casin** downtown opens at 4 PM and serves a complete prime rib dinner with salad and bake potato for about $4.

Breakfast buffets sometimes offer even better all-you-can-eat bargains than the dinners At the **Barbary Coast Casino** on the Strip, a two-egg breakfast with ham, bacon, an sausage costs only $2. But why spend that much when the all-you-can-eat buffet at **Circu Circus** offers nearly 50 breakfast items for $2.29? If that's too steep for you post-gambling budget, $1 will get you a half-pound hot dog at **Slots-A-Fun Casino**, als on the Strip.

UNDER $10 On Sundays at the **Sands Hotel**, the all-you-can-eat smoked salmon prime rib, and champagne dinner is just $10. If you're suspicious, you can watch th cooks preparing the food for "the Feast," a buffet at the **Palace Station** (2411 W. Sahara 1/4 mi west of the Strip) where prices range from $4 for breakfast up to $8 for dinners

RESTAURANTS If you're sick of the casino buffets, there are regular restaurants i many of the casinos and elsewhere around town. **Rainbow's En Restaurant** (1120 E. Sahara Ave., tel. 702/737–0323) serve vegetarian food, including a $6.50 buffet every evening until 9. Ton Roma's in the **Stardust Hotel** (tel. 702/732–6500) serves goo barbecued chicken, shrimp, pork and beef ribs, and homemad onion rings. Dinners starting at $10 begin at 5 PM. Possibly the bes value for Italian food is **Battista's Hole in the Wall** (4041 Audie, te 702/732–1424), which is east of the Strip, off Flamingo Road. Th name is modest enough, but a $10–$15 dinner at this quality Italia restaurant will get you all the wine and cappuccino you can drink and a standing invitation to visit the kitchen. For an exotic mea (around $15), people head to the **Marrakech Restaurant** (4632 S Maryland Pkwy., tel. 702/736–7655), where you eat Moroccan style, sitting on pillows, while an occasional belly dancer leaps over your table.

The food you get at a $2 buffet will satisfy your hunger, but you'll probably be enveloped in an aura of grease for the next several hours and may have to shell out some money for antacids.

●●● WORTH SEEING

Las Vegas's central tourist areas cover many miles, stretching from the Hacienda Hote at the end of the Strip near the airport to downtown Las Vegas nearly 6 miles away. Afte visiting a few casinos, however, you'll probably decide that the biggest difference betwee them is decor; whether you get your drink from a buxom aerialist or an "I Dream of Jeannie clone, the bottom line is gambling. If you have a specific gambling den in mind, drivin may be the quickest way to get there since parking is free at most of them. For mor information about casinos and shows, *see* Entertainment, *below.*

Clark County Southern Heritage Museum. Like the Nevada State Museum in town, thi interesting out-of-town museum on the way to Hoover Dam offers a look at the cultura and political origins of Las Vegas and is packed with historical artifacts. To represen different epochs of Clark County's history, whole houses have been plunked down on th grounds. *1830 S. Boulder Hwy., Henderson, tel. 702/455–7955. Take Boulder Hwy. fro Vegas. Admission: $1. Open daily 9–4:30.*

Ethel M. Chocolate Factory. If you're looking for some free snacks or a brief glimpse c American industry in action, drive south of Las Vegas (about 15 minutes) to the industria community of Henderson. The free 10-minute walking tour of the Ethel M. Chocolat Factory culminates with the free gourmet chocolate of your choice. You can also stro around their 2-acre cactus garden filled with rare and exotic succulents. While you're in town, you can also take the tour of the **Kidd Marshmallow Factory,** where you'll see the whole marshmallow creation process from its start. Don't forget to ask for your free bag of marshmallows. *Chocolate: 2 Cactus Garden Dr., Henderson, tel. 702/458-8864. Take U.S. 95 (the Strip) south, turn left on Sunset Rd. and follow the road to Green Valley Business Park. Open daily 8:30–6. Marshmallows: 8203 Gibson Rd., Henderson, tel. 702/564-5400. From Sunset Rd., turn right on Gibson Ave. and follow it along American Pacific to the factory.*

The Gun Store. Frustrated from a bad night at the craps table? At the Gun Store, you can shoot 50 rounds of ammunition from the pistol or submachine gun of your choice. There are lots of weapons to choose from. You can rent a pistol at the indoor range for under $10; the cost of ammunition varies. The $40 rental fee for a submachine gun includes 50 rounds of ammunition. Consider trying the indoor simulated combat range, where your targets actually fire back. It's an all-American experience, without the usual bloodshed. *2900 E. Tropicana Ave., tel. 702/454–1110. Open daily 9–7.*

Imperial Palace Car Collection. The impressive collection of over 200 rare and exotic cars at the Imperial Palace Hotel and Casino includes cars used by Hitler and Mussolini, affording you a rare chance to study the ashtrays of the dead and fascist. *3535 Las Vegas Blvd. S, tel. 702/731–3311. Admission: $7. Open daily 9:30 AM–11:30 PM.*

Liberace Museum. Until his death a few years ago, Liberace entertained legions of Las Vegas show-goers with some of the purest camp ever concocted. Savage beasts were lulled by his fluid piano playing, blue-haired grandmothers were charmed by his bubbly personality, and most everybody else was moved—whether to awe or mirth is another matter—by his spectacular collection of diamond-studded costumes, wacky pianos, and trademark candelabra. On display are many of the late entertainer's extravagant stage costumes, rare and exotic cars, and pianos, one of which was played by Chopin (though not in Vegas). Look for the studded red-white-and-blue hot pants he wore to celebrate the American bicentennial. Stock up on memorabilia in the gift shop. The admission price may seem steep to the budget traveler, but all profits do go to charity. *1775 E. Tropicana at Maryland Pkwy., tel. 702/798–5595. Admission: $6.50 adults, $3.50 students. Open Mon.–Sat. 10–5, Sun. 1–5.*

Merlin's Magic Motion Rides. At Excalibur (3850 Las Vegas Blvd. S, tel. 702/597–7777), $2 admits you to one of two motorized thrill rides: You watch a movie of an alpine car race or a white water rafting trip while your seat bumps and swivels in a simulation of what's happening on the screen. Hint for thrill seekers: the seats at the end of each row move the most. At busier times—weekends and holidays—expect to wait in line considerably longer than the three-minute duration of the ride. While you're in Excalibur, look for strolling minstrels, dragons, and carnival performers who love to pose for your cameras (expect to be asked for a tip).

"Las Vegas residents used to schedule weekend picnics so they could observe above-ground nuclear testing."

Nevada State Museum and Historical Society. This museum isn't as interesting as the Clark County Southern Heritage Museum, but it does provide a good background on Nevada's flora and fauna and the area's earliest inhabitants. Most intriguing are the well-documented exhibits on the phenomenal growth of Las Vegas in the past 60 years. Gambling isn't the only pastime in Nevada: Las Vegas residents used to schedule weekend picnics so they could observe above-ground nuclear testing. *700 E. Twin Lakes Dr. in Lorenzi Park, tel. 702/486–5205. Admission: $2. Open daily 8:30–4:30.*

Omnimax Theatre. A mammoth dome outside Caesar's Palace houses the Omnimax Theatre, where the already overwhelmed tourist can go for further glutting of the senses. The theater's tiered seats allow everyone an unobstructed view of the towering screen, on which a panoramic nature film is screened. Nearly 100 speakers fill the theater with sound. You'll get dizzy flying through the Grand Canyon and jump at the sight of life-size lava flows. *Caesar's Palace, 3570 Las Vegas Blvd. S, tel. 702/731–7900. Admission: $4.50. Open daily 2–10.*

The Ripley's "Believe It or Not" Museum and Guinness World of Records Museum. These are two other places, besides the Strip, where you can see freaks and unbelievable feats in Las Vegas. Admission prices are a bit steep unless wax figures and this kind of trivia truly excite you. *Ripley's: Four Queens Hotel and Casino, 202 E. Fremont St., tel. 702/385–4011. Admission: $5. Open weekdays 9 AM–11 PM, weekends 9 AM–midnight. Guinness: 2780 Las Vegas Blvd. S, tel. 702/792–0640. Admission: $5.95. Open daily 9 AM–10 PM.*

Wedding Chapels. In Las Vegas, marriage is more than an institution—it's an industry. There are scores of wedding chapels scattered around town, in which thousands of people get married yearly. It couldn't be easier: Under Nevada law, if you're over 18 all you need is identification. Most chapels are open every day, but on holidays like Valentine's Day, lines can stretch around the block. Even celebrities, like basketball player Michael Jordan and actress Bette Midler, get married in Las Vegas chapels. Prices of weddings depend on their extravagance ($50 and up); all the necessary gowns, tuxedos, and limousines can be rented, and you can have the whole shebang videotaped. Licenses can be obtained at the Clark County Marriage License Bureau for $27. Simplified divorces are also available. If none of this is really what you had in mind, there's no harm in only sitting through a ceremony or two—just ask. *Clark County Marriage License Bureau, 200 S. 3rd St., downtown, tel. 702/455–4415. Open weekdays 8–midnight, weekends 24 hrs.*

Wet 'N Wild. During the summer months, locals and tourists alike head for this massive water-oriented amusement park. You can twist and turn through 300 feet of water tubes or plunge eight stories straight down the Der Stuka water slide. There are also many swimming pools, wave pools, rapids, and beach sports (like volleyball). Discount coupons are available in newspaper machines along the Strip and in the free tourist guides. *2601 Las Vegas Blvd. S, tel. 702/734–0088. Admission: $17 per day.*

● ● ● SHOPPING

Most casinos have their own gift shops, and even shopping malls. However, the best selection of Las Vegas memorabilia is available at the **Bonanza Gift Shop** (2460 Las Vegas Blvd. S, tel. 702/385–7359), which claims to be the world's largest. Notable items include inflatable Wayne Newton dolls, used casino dice, and refrigerator magnets. It's open daily until midnight. When you go to the McDonald's next to Vegas World Hotel and Casino (2000 Las Vegas Blvd. S), you can shop at a **McDonald's Boutique** for McDonaldland souvenirs like plastic, purple piggy banks or Ronald McDonald watches. The huge **Western Wear** shop (3235 Las Vegas Blvd. S, tel. 702/369–0336) on the Strip has a huge selection of boots, moccasins, and other leather goods at great prices. Don't buy your film on the Strip or at gift stops if you can avoid it; you'll do much better at **Union Premiums** (1325 E. Flamingo Rd., tel. 702/737–1717).

● ● ● ENTERTAINMENT

SHOWS Las Vegas is renowned for its elaborate and predictably gaudy stage shows featuring popular singers and comics, magicians, and showgirls generally tending toward toplessness. Tom Jones, Wayne Newton, and Frank Sinatra easily sell out all their shows in Las Vegas, and tickets to see the more popular performers run as high as $80 (without tips or drinks). Don't despair, though: For less than $10 you can see shows featuring female impersonators and performing stallions. Consult the free tourist guides for complete listings.

In **Excalibur's King Arthur's Area,** you can take part in a medieval-theme dinner theater with minstrels and "realistic" jousting tournaments. **Bally's Siegfield Room** features a multimedia "Jubilee" with re-creations of a World War I dogfight, the sinking of the *Titanic*, and the usual cast of dancers and showgirls. The talented mimics in "Legends in Concert" help to revive the magic of performers like Elvis, Marilyn Monroe, and Liberace at the **Imperial Palace.** Most popular of all are the illusionists Siegfried and Roy, who make millions a year causing elephants to vanish and levitating their exotic tigers at the **Mirage.**

CASINOS To the first-time visitor, Las Vegas casinos may seem disorienting or intoxicating, or both. The walls are mirrored and bright lights shine from the ceilings, slot and video poker machines are everywhere, and exits seem hard to find. To keep you at **Caesar's Palace,** moving walkways run into the casino past endless blue fountains and Romanesque statues (to return you must walk). Each casino has its own unifying theme and matching decor. The **Tropicana** resembles a tropical island, especially in the pool area, where waterfalls and pools cover more than an acre. The **Mirage** is an amalgamation of strange and unusual sights. Inside rare white tigers and dolphins are on display. Guests file through a lush 60-foot rainforest atrium, while outside a towering volcano erupts every 15 minutes until 1 AM. The Hard Rock Casino is coming soon and will add a rock-and-roll theme to Las Vegas's register of over 35 major casinos. All the casinos are busiest during the evenings, but without any clocks or windows it's truly hard to tell what time of day or night it is. Gambling is a 24-hour pastime in Vegas.

Within the casinos you'll find other, smaller casinos and special gambling areas for craps, blackjack, baccarat, roulette, keno, various forms of poker, and even bingo. If you feel intimidated or confused by the casino games, free lessons are available every morning in many of the casinos including the **Stardust**, the **Sahara**, and **Slots-A-Fun**. (*See* Reno in Chapter 6, The Gold Country, for a brief description of the most popular games). Needless to say, the simplest game in town is working the slot machines, although you may find yourself competing for space with a busload of grandmas from Orange County, each one fiercely territorial about the three machines she's playing. Las Vegas is also a center for sports betting (Bob Stupak, owner of Las Vegas World, bet $1 million on the 1989 Super Bowl and won). At the palatial sports bar, **Thirstbusters** (Sunset and Valley Verde, tel. 702/454–9200), you can follow 15 different sporting events on towering color screens.

Keep an eye out for casino "fun books" available free at many casinos. Inside are coupons good for free gifts, decks of cards, casino dice, and even money to gamble with. If you're looking for the lowest gambling stakes, head for the lamest looking casino. Don't forget to tip—at least if you're winning. Most casino workers are making close to minimum wage and rely on tips to make a decent income (it's considered rude not to throw a few chips the dealer's way).

BARS AND CLUBS **Hard Rock Café**. When you see a six-story neon guitar just east of the Strip, you'll know you've arrived. The cafe doubles as a rock-and-roll museum with dozens of guitars and other musical memorabilia. Prove that you're a member of the international youth culture by queuing up for a souvenir T-shirt just like those sold in other major cities throughout the world. Rock-and-roll is here to stay. *4475 Paradise Rd., tel. 702/733–8400. Open daily: restaurant 11:30 AM–midnight, gift shop 9 AM–midnight.*

Palladium. Did you pack the little black dress? You can wear it to this trendy club with giant video screens and plenty of dance floors. You must be 21 or over. *3665 Industrial Way, tel. 702/733–6366. Cover charge.*

Sam's Town Western Dance Hall. The dancing and music are mainly country and western, thank you, ma'am. *5111 Boulder Hwy., tel. 702/456–7777. 1 mi north of downtown. No cover. Dress: casual.*

Sports Pub. This is a college hangout with pool tables, TVs, and video poker machines. *4440 S. Maryland Pkwy., tel. 702/796–8870. Open 24 hrs.*

Near Las Vegas

LAKE MEAD NATIONAL RECREATION AREA

Six million visitors a year come to this outdoor water sports paradise in the middle of the desert. Created by the construction of Hoover Dam, the lake is incredibly large. Its 115-mile-long shoreline could reach all the way to San Francisco if it were stretched out. The recreation area also includes the nearby Lake Mojave.

You'll have no trouble finding a sandy beach on which to camp in total solitude and privacy. Secluded coves and steep, unexplored canyons ensure that the lake will never seem crowded. Hot summer days are made for swimming, sailing, fishing, and waterskiing. With a little foresight, you can go in with a bunch of friends and rent a houseboat for the cooler nights.

Between the two lakes there are eight marinas with boat-launching facilities. The lakes are full of catfish, rainbow trout, and bass, and fishing licenses can be obtained at most marinas. Some marinas let you camp along the shore where you can be close to comfortable facilities for only $6.

You may want to begin your visit at the **Alan Bible Visitor Center**, (tel. 702/293–8906), which is 4 miles northeast of Boulder City on Route 93 and open daily 8:30–4:30.

If you plan to spend a long time in the area, seriously consider renting a houseboat on Lake Mead or Lake Mojave. Rentals come complete with water slide, microwave, and room for 10. Call **Forever Resorts** (tel. 702/565–7340 or 800/255–5561) at Callville Bay at Lake Mead, or **Cottonwood Cove** (tel. 702/297–1005 or 702/297–1464) at Lake Mojave. Split the cost among friends; rates begin at around $1,375 for three days in summer, or a week in the winter.

Gray Line Bus Tours (tel. 702/384–1234) has buses departing from Las Vegas to destinations such as Hoover Dam, Lake Mead, the Grand Canyon, Laughlin, and the Valley of Fire State Park. Fares start at just over $10.

● ● ● HOOVER DAM

Fifty-six percent of the hydroelectric power generated by Hoover Dam is consumed by the folks in Southern California—only 4% goes to nearby Las Vegas, which at the time of construction was little more than a railway stop. This Depression-era public works project is considered one of the man-made wonders of the world, especially since it was completed on schedule and under budget. Spanning the mouth of Black Canyon, the dam successfully controls the flow of the Colorado River in its intermittent periods of flooding and drought. The dam measures 1,244 feet across, with concrete from 45 to 660 feet thick—at its tallest, it's 70 stories high and at it's widest, it's two football fields thick. *Rte. 993 east of Boulder City, tel. 702/293–8367. Admission: $1. Tours Memorial Day–Labor Day, daily 8–6:45, otherwise, daily 9–4:15.*

Lake Mead Boat Cruises take you right up to the foot of Hoover Dam. The 75-minute tours (around $8) let you see up close the amazing contrast between the lake and its surrounding desert terrain. Tours leave three times daily (twice in the winter) from Lake Mead Marina. *Lake Mead Ferry Service, 1646 Nevada Hwy., Boulder City, tel. 702/293–6180. Take Rte. 93 to Lake Shore Road.*

For background on the building of the dam, see the well-produced "Hoover Dam Movie" at **Desert Sands Pottery, Gifts, and Liquors**. *753 Nevada Hwy., Boulder City, tel. 702/293–1202. Open daily 9–5.*

The **Boulder City/Hoover Dam Museum** gives you an in-depth look at the daily difficulties faced by people building the dam in the 1930s. *444 Hotel Plaza, Box 516, Boulder City, tel. 702/384–5014. Admission: $1. Open daily 9–5.*

● ● ● ELSEWHERE NEAR LAS VEGAS

VALLEY OF FIRE The Valley of Fire State Park earns its name through a combination of desert climate and bizarrely shaped formations of brightly colored sandstone rock. Colors range from burnt orange to bright red to lavender. Fans of "Star Trek" may feel like they've stumbled onto an old set. Trails lead to stands of petrified logs left over from ancient forests, as well as canyons with finely preserved Native American petroglyphs. The park has two campgrounds with tables, fire pits and grills, and rest rooms. The park is near Overton, Nevada, 55 miles from Las Vegas. *Box 515, Overton 89040, tel. 702/397–2088. Take I–15 to Rte. 169 toward Lake Mead and Overton.*

The Lost City Museum in Overton is well worth a visit. Best of all are the submerged pit houses, once the pueblos of Native Americans who lived in the area, which still stand out in front of the museum. The museum also has a remarkable collection of artifacts from surrounding areas, including baskets and pottery. *721 S. Rte. 169, tel. 702/397–2088. Admission: $1. Open daily 8:30–4:30.*

LAUGHLIN The third largest gambling area in Nevada (after Reno and Las Vegas) Laughlin began to flourish in the mid-1960s. The town is nicely situated on the Colorado River, and the first casinos were built to cater to the sun-seeking retirees who had begun invading the area. Now they're frequented by lots of people who like gambling in a relatively unintimidating setting. You can moor your boat along the river and gamble or stuff your face at a buffet. If you come by car, stay at one of the several resort casinos in the area including **Sam's Town Gold River** (2700 S. Casino Dr., tel. 702/298–2242 or 800/835–7903), the **Golden Nugget** (2300 S. Casino Dr., tel. 702/298–1111 or 800/237–1739), and the original **Riverside Resort** (1650 S. Casino Dr., tel. 702/298–2535 or 800/227–3849). Prices rarely exceed $30. To reach Laughlin, take U.S. 95 south from Las Vegas. It's about a 90-minute drive.

The Grand Canyon

Still growing deeper and wider every day (thanks to the Colorado River that runs at its bottom), the Grand Canyon is much more than the world's finest example of erosion. Native Americans inhabiting the canyon region and the surrounding Kaibab Plateau have long likened this breathtaking chasm to a "mountain lying upside down." It's a striking comparison, and an apt one. The canyon covers nearly 1,900 square miles, and for the 275 miles that it snakes through remote northern Arizona, it maintains an average depth of 1 mile and an average width of 10. Every year nearly 4 million travelers come from all over the globe to marvel at its countless buttes, pillars, caves, and scenic views. Especially in the morning and at dusk, when the sun's rays create a dazzling display of changing colors and patterns on the rock, the canyon is, well, grand. No doubt if there really were a mountain that rose as steeply and abruptly from the plateau as the famous canyon falls, it would still find its way onto postage stamps.

The inaccessibility of most of the Grand Canyon serves as a constant reminder of just how vast and unexplored it still is. The tourist centers on the North and South rims lie only 2 miles apart, straight across the gorge, yet a circuitous 215-mile road connects them, and most people visit only one side. The hot, dry summer turns the South Rim into a giant RV park, with hoards of camera-snapping tourists making the area quite unpleasant. If you're coming in summer, you'll have a better chance of finding solitude and serenity on the less popular North Rim, where services are comparable but smaller in scale. The North Rim also has the advantage of being within a few hours' drive of several spectacular national parks and monuments in southern Utah, including Zion and Bryce Canyon, which are praised at least as highly by most visitors as their more famous neighbor.

Spring and fall are the best times to visit the South Rim, when the weather is relatively mild and the crowds are not so heavy. The South Rim is open all year, but its high elevation makes for wet, cold winters. If you're planning a hike down to the canyon floor, don't let snow on the rim stop you. The lower elevations in the canyon rarely get any snowfall. Even if there's a blizzard on the rim, it may be warm and sunny down below. Winters at the North Rim are more severe, forcing the Park Service to close facilities there between November and mid-May. Between 6 and 10 feet of snow may blanket the North Rim during an average winter, making it a great place for cross-country skiing.

From the alpine climate of the rim to the desert climate of the inner gorge, the Grand Canyon supports an intricate web of plant and animal life. Lush forests of spruce, fir, and ponderosa pine blanket the Kaibab Plateau through which the Colorado River has cut its course. At lower elevations, deep within the canyon, pines give way to yucca and cacti, and other desert plants and animals flourish. Hikers occasionally spot such reptiles as lizards and even rattlesnakes during their descent to the canyon floor.

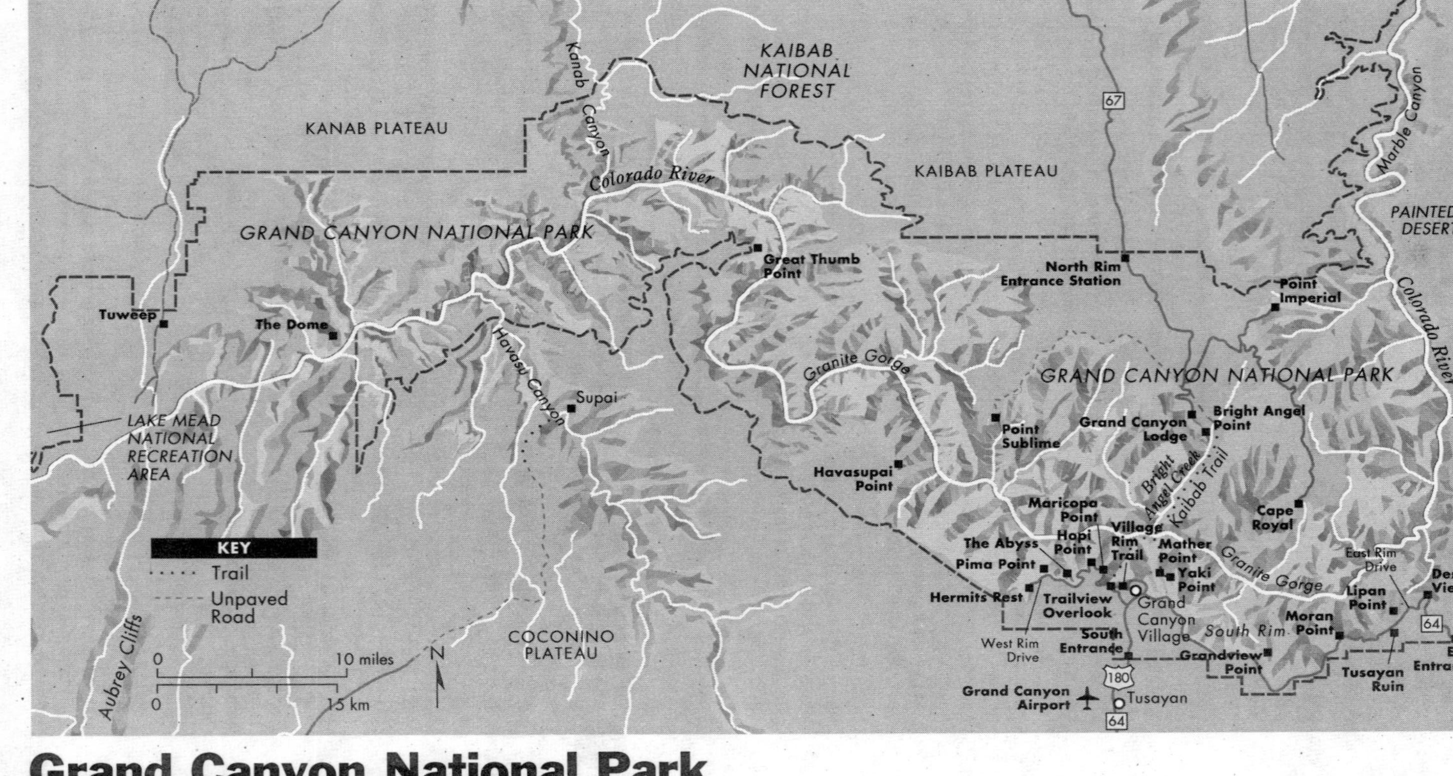

Grand Canyon National Park

The canyon itself is 65 million years old, and the erosion that created it has exposed rock dating back billions of years. As you descend, the rock layers surrounding you get progressively older, like a natural time line of the world's geologic history. The canyon walls contain an unknown number of fossils—this is your chance to encounter a stone fish that swam in the waters of a world very different from our own.

The oldest human artifacts found within the canyon are animal-shaped figurines and arrowheads dating back 4,000 years, but little is known about the people who made them. A great deal more is known about the Anasazi who populated the region 1,500 years ago. Many of their pueblos and other dwellings still stand as a testament to these ancestors of the modern Hopi. The Anasazi gathered food, irrigated and farmed their land, and hunted the plentiful mule deer, bighorn sheep, and mountain lions that still roam the forests and meadows around the canyon. Today, Native Americans still retain much of the canyon and its surrounding areas. The Navajos live to the east, while the Havasupai and Hualapai live on and own much of the land to the south and west of the tourist centers.

From the 360° panorama at the Desert View to the sheer 3,000-foot drop off the canyon rim from the abyss, the Grand Canyon has always been a formidable opponent to human exploration. The original inhabitants of the area knew routes from the rim into the canyon, but no doubt they took their time finding them. The first Europeans to come this way—the party of 16th-century Spanish explorer Francisco Vasquez de Coronado who came west in search of the fabled Seven Cities of Cibola—named the river Rio Colorado or "red river," gazed across the gorge, and turned back in frustration. Few visited the canyon again for nearly 300 years.

Major John Wesley Powell spent three months in 1869 boating a thousand miles down the dangerous Colorado River from Wyoming into present-day Nevada. His group was the first not only to navigate the river, but to make detailed maps of the canyon interior. Powell returned for a second trip in 1872, and his work to unlock the mystery of this seemingly impassable chasm opened the way for exploration, mining, and, more significantly, tourism. The true tourist boom began in 1901 when the Santa Fe Railroad reached the South Rim from Williams, Arizona, shortening the trip to three hours from the 11 it took by horse.

You can still take the train from Williams, but most people today arrive by car or plane. Once you've arrived, you can hike into the canyon on several trails, maintained or unmaintained, and camp on the canyon floor. For the best perspectives from above and below, you have a choice of scenic air tours and Colorado River rafting trips—both well worth the expense. Finally, there's the possibility of riding a pack animal into the canyon, but this one's more for convenience than pleasure. It's hard to travel down a narrow trail reeking of mule manure with a cliff on one side and a sheer drop on the other, and be obliged to place all your trust on an ass.

BASICS • • •

Arizona and Utah are in the Mountain Time Zone, one hour earlier than California and Nevada.

TOURIST INFORMATION For general information, maps, brochures, and brief orientation programs, contact the **Grand Canyon National Park Visitor Center** (Box 699, Grand Canyon 86023, tel. 602/638–7888). It's in Grand Canyon Village (South Rim), 6 miles north of the South Entrance Station and open daily 7:30 AM–8:30 PM. The **Desert View Public Contact Station,** located a half-mile west of Desert View, offers similar services daily 8–6 to visitors entering the park from the east.

For detailed information on lodgings, restaurants, rafting trips, and scenic flights near the South Rim, contact the **Grand Canyon Chamber of Commerce** (Box 3007, Grand Canyon 86023, tel. 602/638–2901). The office, located in Tusayan, 5 miles south of the South Entrance Station, is open daily 9–5. Another valuable source of information is the **Flagstaff Visitor Center** (101 W. Santa Fe Ave., Flagstaff 86001, tel. 602/774–9541 or 800/842–7293), located in downtown Flagstaff, near the Amtrak station. For similar information about the North Rim contact the **Kane County Travel Council** (41 S.100 East, Kanab, UT 84741 tel. 801/644–5033) open daily 9–5. You could also look into Fodor's new book, *National Parks of the West*.

MEDICAL SERVICES The **Grand Canyon Clinic**, located off Center Road between the South Entrance Station and Grand Canyon Village, is open weekdays 8–5:30, Saturday 9–noon. For 24-hour emergency care, call 602/638–2551 or 602/638–2469. The pharmacy (tel. 602/638–2460) here is open weekdays 8:30–5:30.

BANKS **Valley National Bank** in Grand Canyon Village at Mather Center has a 24-hour automated teller machine and will exchange traveler's checks and foreign currency, but not out-of-town checks. It's open weekdays 10–3; and Friday also 4–6.

FEES There's a $10 entrance fee for each car, good for seven days. Bus passengers, hikers, and bikers pay only $4. If you plan to stay longer, a $15 Annual Grand Canyon Passport will allow you to come and go as you please all year long.

PUBLICATIONS The *Grand Canyon Guide* is published seasonally in two editions, one for the North Rim, and one for the South. The guides tell you all you need to know about park activities, regulations, facilities, and ranger programs. Pick up free copies at the entrance stations or at the visitor center in Grand Canyon Village on the South Rim. For a complete listing of maps, trail guides, and other publications you can get by mail, write the **Grand Canyon Natural History Association** (Box 399, Grand Canyon 86023).

GENERAL STORES Prices within the park are considerably higher than in nearby towns. Consider purchasing your groceries and supplies in Flagstaff or Williams, Arizona, before going to the South Rim, or in Kanab, Utah, before heading to the North Rim.

COMING AND GOING

The routes to the North and South Rims are very different, because of a small obstacle separating them—namely, the Grand Canyon itself. There are more options for getting to the South Rim, and consequently, more people using them. The North Rim has always been known for its inaccessibility and, even today, there's no regular public transportation there except from the South Rim. It's offered by the **Trans Canyon Shuttle** (Box 348, Grand Canyon 85023, tel. 602/638–2820), which makes a round-trip daily during the months when the North Rim is open. The five-hour trip costs about $50 one way.

BY CAR

SOUTH RIM The South Rim is almost exactly 500 miles from L.A. From either southern or northern California, take I–40 east from Barstow all the way to Williams, Arizona (322 miles). From Williams, head north 30 miles on Route 64 to Route 180, which will take you the final 30 miles to the South Rim. If you're arriving from the east, take I–40 to Flagstaff, Arizona, and then head north on Route 180.

NORTH RIM To reach the North Rim from either southern or northern California, take I–15 east through Barstow and Las Vegas to southern Utah (about 350 miles from L.A.). Fifteen miles north of St. George, Utah, take scenic Route 9 east through the spectacular Zion National Park. About 50 miles later, Route 9 intersects Route ALT89, which you take south 54 miles through Kanab, Utah, to Jacob Lake, Arizona. From here Route 67 takes you directly to the North Rim.

BY BUS

SOUTH RIM The nearest **Greyhound** depot is in Flagstaff, Arizona (399 S. Malpais La. off Santa Fe Ave., tel. 602/774–4573), which has regular service across the country. L.A. to Flagstaff is about a 12-hour trip and costs $105. **Nava-Hopi Tours, Inc.** (Box 339, Flagstaff 86002, tel. 602/774–5003 or 800/892–8687) provides round-trip service between Flagstaff and the South Rim, for $25. They also have limited service between Flagstaff and Williams for about $15 round-trip (a service they provide to coordinate with train travel, *see below*).

BY TRAIN

SOUTH RIM **Amtrak** (1 Santa Fe Ave., tel. 800/USA–RAIL) makes daily stops in Flagstaff where you can catch a bus to Williams or the South Rim. It's $85 for the 12-hour trip from L.A. to Flagstaff. From downtown Williams, the **Grand Canyon Railway** (518 E. Bill William Blvd., tel. 800/843–8724) winds its way through the wilderness to the historic log depot in Grand Canyon Village. Passengers ride along in a restored steam locomotive from the early 20th century, just as most tourists did before the invention of the automobile. Round-trip fare costs about $47. To reach the depot from I–40, take exit 163 (Grand Canyon Blvd.) for about a half-mile.

BY PLANE

SOUTH RIM The **Grand Canyon Airport**, located near Tusayan, about 10 miles south of the park entrance, is served by several airlines, some offering air tours of the Grand Canyon (*see* Park Activities, *below*). **American West** (tel. 602/638–9544 or 800/247–5692) flies to and from Phoenix and Las Vegas. **Scenic Airlines** (tel. 602/638–2436 or 800/634–6801) and **Air Nevada** (tel. 602/638–2441 or 800/634–6377) also connect with Las Vegas.

From the airport, you can catch the **Grand Canyon–Tusayan Shuttle** (tel. 602/638–2475) or rent a car from **Budget** (tel. 602/638–9560) or **Dollar** (tel. 602/638–2625).

WHERE TO SLEEP

SOUTH RIM Hotels at the South Rim are, in general, expensive and completely booked months in advance. The most reasonable options within the park are the modern **Maswik Lodge** (under $50) or, two blocks away, the rustic **Bright Angel Lodge**, situated right on the rim where rooms without a bath go for under $40. If you feel like splurging, there's **El Tovar Hotel**, a national historic site, which has rooms starting at $100. **Phantom Ranch** at Bright Angel Creek offers the only accommodations below the rim for travelers who are not camping. Keep in mind that this place is accessible only by mule or on foot. The cozy cabins ($55) or dormitory beds ($20) are also available by reservations only. Contact **Grand Canyon National Park Lodges** (Box 699, Grand Canyon 86023, tel. 602/638–2401 or 602/638–2631 for same day reservations) concerning all accommodations within the park.

If you're on a tight budget (and have a car), consider staying in one of the hostels or budget hotels in Flagstaff, 79 miles from the South Rim. The **Twilight Motel** (2010 E. Santa Fe Ave., tel. 602/774–3364) offers simple, no-frills rooms with bath and TV for under $30. The **Western Hill Hotel** (1612 E. Santa Fe Ave., tel. 602/556–0403) has a pool, restaurant, and wheelchair-accessible rooms for under $40.

For a complete listing of accommodations in Flagstaff, call or stop by the **Flagstaff Visitor Center** (101 W. Santa Fe Ave., tel. 602/774–9541 or 800/842–7293), which is open Monday–Saturday 8 AM–9 PM, Sunday 8 AM–5 PM.

HOSTELS The **Weatherford Hotel** is actually a hostel in the heart of historic downtown Flagstaff. They do have three sparse (no TV or phone) hotel rooms, though, at $22 for one person, $24 for two. The rest is dorm-style at $10 a bed. It's directly above **Charly's Pub and Restaurant**, a drinking spot beloved by locals. *23 North Leroux, 86001, tel. 602/774–2731. 1 AM curfew; kitchen.*

The **Dubeau Motel International Hostel**, also in Flagstaff, has both dorm-style ($11) and private rooms ($30). The atmosphere here is casual and breakfast is included in the rate. Perhaps the only drawback is the noise from the huge freight trains that roll by nearly every hour. *19 W. Phoenix Ave., 86001, tel. 602/774–6731. No curfew; store; kitchen.*

The **Grey Hills Inn and Hostel** is on the property of the Grey Hills High School in Tuba City, on the Navajo Reservation 60 miles east of the Grand Canyon. Doubles in the Inn cost $25 (all with shared bath), while hostel accommodations are $10 for AYH members. The rooms are extremely clean and comfortable. *Box 160, Tuba City 86045, tel. 602/283–6271 ext.*

336. Take Rte. 89 from the canyon for 60 mi to Tuba City, go east 10 mi, follow signs. Midnight curfew.

CAMPGROUNDS **Mather Campground** is conveniently located right in Grand Canyon Village, just south of the visitor center. Sites have toilets and water, and showers and laundry services are available at the adjacent Camper Services. The fee is $10 per car per night, $1 per person on foot. For reservations, call 800/365–CAMP (you can reserve up to eight weeks in advance). The nearby **Trailer Village** accommodates motor homes for about $18 per night with full hookups (tel. 602/638–2401 for advance reservations, or 602/638–2531 for same day reservations). Near the East Entrance Station, the **Desert View Campground**, open May to September, operates on a first-come, first-served basis, and has drinking water and toilets; sites are $6.

The U.S. Forest Service maintains the **Ten-X Campground** just 3 miles south of Tusayan, off Route 180. The campground, open May through October, is in a shady forest setting. Sites with picnic tables, water, and toilet cost $7. For reservations, call 602/638–2443

You can also join the kids camping at **Flintstones Bedrock City** (tel. 602/635–2600) at the junction of Route 180 and Route G4 in Valle, 30 miles from South Rim entrance. Tent sites on this barren stretch of gravel are about $15, but there are pay showers, laundry facilities, a snack bar, and the real attraction—a prehistoric theme park dedicated to the Flintstones.

BACKCOUNTRY CAMPING To protect the inner canyon from overcrowding and overuse, backcountry camping is restricted. All hikers wishing to camp below the rim must first get a free permit from the **Backcountry Reservations Office** (BRO) (Box 129, Grand Canyon 86023, tel. 602/638–7888). Permits are limited and reservations are obtained by mail or in person only (you can get them as early as October 1st for anytime the following year). Those of you without reservations can try signing up in person on the waiting list at the BRO near Camper Services the day before your planned hike. To increase the odds, arrive at the office before 8 AM the day before your hike. Whether you have reservations or are hoping to get them, you must arrive at the office by 9 AM the day of your proposed hike or forfeit your place. The BRO is open daily 7–noon and 3–5 in summer; from 8 AM other times.

Inside the rim, you can camp at the **Bright Angel**, **Indian Gardens**, and **Cottonwood** campgrounds, or at a number of other more primitive sites along unmaintained and less traveled trails. For information about the full range of options, consult with staff at the BRO or the visitor center. A free "Hiker's Special" shuttle runs daily between the BRO and the South Kaibab Trailhead, 7:45–11:45 AM.

NORTH RIM The only lodgings close to the canyon are the **Grand Canyon Lodge** (tel. 602/586–7686) at the North Rim itself, and the **Kaibab Lodge** (tel. 602/638–2401) just 5 miles north of the park boundary. Room rates at both lodges start at around $43. The Kaibab Lodge is a winter base for cross-country skiing, and a year-round base for organized hikes and bike tours. The Kaibab also sells and rents camping equipment.

Travelers on a tight budget might have to trek the 90 miles to Kanab, Utah, where there's a wider choice of accommodations and food. The small **Premium Hotel** (99 S. 100 East, Kanab, tel. 801/644–2449) has a dozen rooms with TVs for under $25 a night. The **Sun-N-Sand** (347 S. 100 East, Kanab, tel. 801/644–5050) has a pool, hot tub, and restaurant, with rates starting around $30. The **Parry Lodge** (89 E. Center, tel. 801/644–2601) has rooms named after its most famous guests for $54–$60.

HOSTELS The **Canyonlands International Hostel** is a great place to stay. It has an extensive travel center, and free coffee, tea, and lemonade. Best of all, you can relax in friendly company on the shaded patio. The cost is $8 for AYH members, $10 for nonmembers. *143 E. 100 South, Kanab, UT 84741, tel. 801/644–5554. Office open 8–10 AM or 5–10 PM. Laundry facilities.*

CAMPGROUNDS Primitive camping is available free of charge in the **Kaibab National Forest** as long as Route 67 is open to the North Rim (usually early May through mid-November). Before camping, be sure to stop by at the ranger station in Jacob Lake for additional information and to familiarize yourself with the list of regulations. Call 800/283–CAMP to see if you need reservations. Unfortunately, even though the camping is free, making a reservation through MISTIX (tel. 800/365–CAMP) costs $6.

North Rim Campground inside the park near the canyon's North Rim stays open from May through mid-October. Showers, a laundromat, and a general store are located nearby. The walk-in tent sites are $10 per night. Although some sites are available on a first-come, first-served basis, you're best off making reservations through MISTIX (*see above*).

Jacob Lake Campground is at the junction of Route ALT89 and Route 67. Camping at the nearly 50 sites is $7 a night. Reservations can be made for $6 through MISTIX (tel. 800/283–CAMP). Gas, food, and groceries are available. The nearby Jacob Lake RV Park (tel. 800/283–CAMP), with 80 RV sites and 50 tent sites, is a half-mile south of Jacob Lake.

DeMotte Park Campground (tel. 602/643–7395), 5 miles north of the North Rim Entrance Station, has over 20 tent sites with drinking water and rest rooms for $6 a night. Sites are available on a first-come, first-served basis. You can eat at the nearby Kaibab Lodge.

BACKCOUNTRY CAMPING Hikers spending the night below the rim must first obtain a permit from the North Rim Backcountry Reservations Office located at the North Rim Ranger Station. The same restrictions apply as for the South Rim (*see* Where to Stay, The South Rim, *above*). The North Rim BRO is open daily 7–11, 4–5 during the season.

FOOD • • •

There's nothing notable about the food at Grand Canyon, except for the meals at El Tovar (*see* Where to Sleep, *above*), which are good for splurges only—it's a three-star restaurant. You can basically look forward to an all-American menu of hamburgers, soups, sandwiches, and salads.

SOUTH RIM The best bet for budget travelers is **Babbit's General Store and Deli**, across from the visitors center. It's really a huge supermarket with a wide selection of groceries and supplies (open daily 8–8; the deli closes at 7); there are picnic areas throughout the park where you can enjoy the scenery while refueling. The **Yavapai Cafeteria** near Mather Center has hot sandwiches, plus music and dancing at night (open daily 6 PM–10 PM). For a quick snack, stop at the **Bright Angel Fountain** (open 11–8) for ice cream and sodas. The **Máswik Cafeteria** at the Maswik Lodge is open daily 6 AM–10 PM for breakfast, lunch, and dinner. They have sandwiches, burgers, and the like for $4–$6. The lodge also has a sports lounge (open until 1 AM) for those of you who can't live without civilization.

NORTH RIM Like the South Rim, the North Rim has several restaurants, snack bars, and coffee shops that will satisfy your basic hunger in an uninspiring way. Nearby Kanab really has the best eating options. The **IGA Supercenter Market** in the center of town has a huge selection and the best prices. **Nedra's Too** (Jct. of Rte. 89 and Rte. ALT89, tel. 801/644–5557 or 801/643–7591) makes excellent Mexican dishes for breakfast, lunch, and dinner. Try the open-faced Navajo taco, a delicious local favorite.

EXPLORING THE CANYON • • •

ORIENTATION PROGRAMS

SOUTH RIM The **Visitor Center** (tel. 602/638–7888) in Grand Canyon Village runs free 15-minute slide shows daily on the Canyon's geology, discovery, and development. This is the place to go for information on trails, activities, and facilities. For a more spectacular orientation, visit the Grand Canyon **IMAX Theatre** (tel. 602/638–1203) in Tusayan, just 3 miles south of the park entrance. Here you can have a bird's-eye view of the canyon on a towering 70-foot-high movie screen. Admission to this "budget air and raft tour" is $6.50, with showings daily 8:30–8:30 every hour on the half hour. Another way to learn about the Canyon—if groups don't bother you—is to submit to one of the free ranger-led talks or hikes at the canyon's rim. There are programs from 20 to 90 minutes throughout the day and evening; check the Grand Canyon Guide for schedules.

NORTH RIM The **National Park Service Information Desk** (tel. 601/638–7864) is open daily 8–5 inside the Grand Canyon Lodge. *The Grand Canyon Guide* for the North Rim lists several daily ranger-led programs. If you get to Springdale, Utah (approximately 40 miles from Kanab), visit the **O.C. Tanner Amphitheater** ($4) on a summer evening for a cinematic introduction to the "The Grand Circle" of parks and monuments in southern Utah, including the Grand Canyon.

GUIDED TOURS

SOUTH RIM For information on raft, air, and mule tours of the inner canyon, *see* Park Activities, *below.*

Fred Harvey Transportation Co. (tel. 602/628–2901) has several narrated, wheelchair-accessible bus tours to various locations along the South Rim. The tours range from $8 to $65, and last from 90 minutes to a full day. Tickets are available at the transportation desks at the Maswik and Bright Angel lodges.

Grayline Tours offers several excursions to the Grand Canyon and other scenic locales in northern Arizona. The tours cost just over $30 and originate in Flagstaff. For reservations, contact Nava-Hopi Tours, Inc. (Box 339, Flagstaff 86002, tel. 602/774–5003).

NORTH RIM Bus tours to Point Imperial, Cape Royal, and other scenic viewpoints along the North Rim can be arranged in the Grand Canyon Lodge lobby. For information on North Rim trail rides and Colorado River tours, *see* Park Activities, *below.*

NATURE WALKS

SOUTH RIM The **South Rim Nature Trail** is mostly level and paved, running about 3½ miles between the Yavapai Museum, past the visitor center, out to the overlook at Maricopa Point. From just about anywhere you'll see spectacular views of the inner gorge; you'll also see lots of other people all in search of the ultimate Grand Canyon experience. The problem is, you're always on the outside, looking in, and after a while, the grandeur starts to pale. Sure, take a walk along the rim, but to really experience the canyon, you've got to go down inside, if only a short way. The **West Rim Trail** begins at Maricopa Point. The path becomes dirt here and continues along the rim nearly 8 miles west past Mojave, Pima, and Hopi Points, as well as the sheer walls of the Abyss overlook, before arriving at Hermit's Rest. You'll find few crowds along this walk, and the overlook's most secluded at sunrise and sunset.

NORTH RIM The paved **Bright Angel Point Trail** takes you uphill for a half-mile to a high butte overlooking the inner canyon. If you listen carefully you can hear **Roaring Springs** far below, which supplies water and hydroelectric power to both rims. The trail begins behind the east patio and parking lot of the Grand Canyon Lodge. The **Cape Royal Trail** begins at the Cape Royal parking area, about 25 miles southeast of the lodge. This area is the southernmost point on the North Rim, where you'll get impressive views of the canyon, the Colorado River, and Angel's Window, a huge natural arch. The **Cliff Springs Trail** begins across the road from **Angel's Window Overlook**, just ⅓ mile north of Cape Royal. This 1-mile round-trip trail takes you down a shady ravine, past a ruin, to a rock overhang from whence the spring flows.

LONGER HIKES

SOUTH RIM The **Bright Angel Trail** is the most heavily traveled route to the Colorado River on the canyon floor. The 8-mile trail begins at Bright Angel Lodge at the West Rim interchange. Water is available year round three-quarters of the way down at **Indian Garden Campsite,** and during the summer at rest houses 1½ and 3 miles down. From Plateau Point, 6 miles down and 3,200 feet below the rim, hikers can gaze directly down at the river still 1,000 feet below. A 1½-mile trail along the river connects the **Bright Angel Trail** with the **South Kaibab Trail** and **Bright Angel Creek,** where **Phantom Ranch** and the **Bright Angel Campground** are located.

The descent down the **South Kaibab Trail** is steeper and shorter, 6½ miles, but with no water available on the way. The reward: The views are spectacular. Most people go down South Kaibab and up Bright Angel. For a listing of less heavily traveled (and unmaintained) trails into the inner canyon, consult the visitor center for maps and the Backcountry Reservations Office (*see* Backcountry Camping, *above*) for camping availability.

NORTH RIM The **North Kaibab Trail** is the only maintained trail into the inner canyon from the North Rim. The trailhead begins 2 miles north of the Grand Canyon Lodge and runs over 14 miles to its terminus at the Colorado River. After reaching Roaring Springs, about 9½ miles down, the trail follows Bright Angel Creek directly to the canyon floor. Along the way lies Cottonwood Campground, which is open to backcountry campers and has clean water during the summer. Foot bridges lead to the southern bank of the river. From Roaring Springs, take the 3-mile round-trip detour to Ribbon Falls to see a small waterfall and its emerald pools.

If you want to go down from one rim and up to the other, the Public Affairs Office recommends going down North Kaibab Trail from the North Rim and up Bright Angel. It's 24 miles from the North Rim to the South going this way, just in case you wanted to know.

SCENIC DRIVES AND VIEWS

SOUTH RIM The **West Rim Drive** runs 8 miles west from **Grand Canyon Village** to **Hermit's Rest**. Along this tree-lined, two-lane drive there are several scenic overlooks with panoramic views of the inner canyon. It's closed to automobile traffic in the summer, but you can pick up a free shuttle bus at the West Rim Interchange near the Bright Angel Lodge every quarter hour from 7:30 AM to 6:45 PM. The shuttle stops at all eight scenic viewpoints, making a complete round-trip every 90 minutes. The visitor center has special permits for the disabled.

The **East Rim Drive** also offers some beautiful views of the canyon and the raging Colorado. The 26-mile drive (one way) takes you through the **Painted Desert** (home to the Navajos), past **Lipan Point**—the widest spot in the canyon where you can see every eroded layer (the lowest is the oldest exposed rock on earth), and to the **Tusayan Museum and Ruin** (tel. 602/638–2305) where there are partially intact rock dwellings of the Anasazi, who inhabited the area 1,500 years ago. (*See* Worth Seeing, *below.*)

Hiking in the Grand Canyon

The first thing you should remember while hiking in the Grand Canyon is be careful when you're near the edge. Second, be sure to wear sturdy shoes. And, perhaps most important, before descending along a trail into the inner canyon, prepare yourself to combat the desert climate. The cool breezes and shade that generally protect the rims don't exist in the dry, sun-baked climate of the inner canyon. The further you descend, the hotter it will get. Therefore, bring a gallon of water for each person for every day of hiking.

There are no loop trails into the canyon and back, so remember that you'll have to hike back up the same way you went down. Allow twice as much time for your return trip as you do for the descent. Rangers also recommend that hikers not attempt a trip to the river and back in one day; if you do, carry a flashlight just in case returning to the rim before dark becomes impossible. One final recommendation: bring nose plugs for the Bright Angel and South Kaibab trails. Park rangers are not paid to clean up after the mules.

NORTH RIM The 23-mile drive to **Cape Royal** begins 3 miles north of Grand Canyo Lodge, and leads to the best viewpoints on the North Rim. Along the way, take the detou to **Point Imperial** for views of the eastern end of the canyon.

WORTH SEEING

SOUTH RIM The **Tusayan Museum and Ruin** (tel. 602/638–2305), near the end c the East Rim Drive, 4 miles west of Desert View, is just one of over 2,000 Native America sites in the Grand Canyon. About 30 Anasazi, ancestors of the modern Hopi, lived her eight centuries ago, hunting and farming until drought forced them to move east. Th museum, open daily 8–6, has exhibits about the various tribes who lived in the region ove the past 2,000 years.

The **Yavapai Museum**, a half-mile east of the visitor center, has exhibits about the geolog of the canyon, and the Colorado River that carved it. Go inside for some dizzying views behin huge, protective observation windows. The wheelchair-accessible museum is open daily 8–8

The **Desert View Watchtower**, built in the style of Southwest Native American structure in 1932, stands at 70 feet—the highest point on the South Rim. A stairway inside lead to viewing windows as well as to replicas of petroglyphs, Native American paintings, an a unique Hopi altar. It's at the end of the 25-mile East Rim Drive—and worth the trip fo the spectacular views.

● ● ● PARK ACTIVITIES

MULE AND HORSEBACK RIDES

SOUTH RIM **Fred Harvey** (tel. 602/638–2631) runs mule rides from the South Ri to the bottom of the canyon. Overnight trips including breakfast, lunches, dinner, an lodging at Phantom Ranch costs $255 for one, and about $467 for two.

Apache Stables (Box 158, Grand Canyon 86023, tel. 602/638–2631) offers sho horseback rides along the rim and through the Kaibab National Forest. Rates start aroun $15 and originate at Moqui Lodge in the village of Tusayan.

RAFTING One of the most popular and exhilarating ways to see the Grand Canyon floating on a raft or boat along the sometimes gentle and sometimes raging Colorado Rive Tours are available from over 20 companies in both motorized and oar-controlled boat ranging in length from just one day to extensive and expensive two-week trips. Trips ofte originate near Flagstaff, Page, or Las Vegas, and the price usually includes transportatic to the river. You'll need to make reservations well in advance, specifying whether you war a motorized or oar trip and whether or not you want to ride the rapids. Here's a partial li of rafting companies; for a complete list contact the Grand Canyon Chamber of Commerc (*see* Tourist Information, *above*): **Canyoneers Inc.** (Box 2997, Flagstaff 86003, tel. 602/526 0924 or 800/525–0924); **Fred Harvey Transportation Company** (tel. 602/638–2401 **Hualapai River Trips and Tours** (Box 248, Peach Springs 86434, tel. 602/769–2219 **Wilderness River Adventures** (Box 717, Page 86040, tel. 602/645–3296 602/645–3279).

SCENIC FLIGHTS

SOUTH RIM Equal in popularity to the river tours are the scenic helicopter ar twin-engine airplane tours of the canyon, originating at the Grand Canyon Airport, ju south of Tusayan. These tours offer absolutely the most spectacular views of the inn canyon as well as great picture-taking opportunities (though even on a short, 20-minu flight, you may have to fight from losing your lunch while your tiny plane winds its wa through the breezy canyons). Rates start around $50 for half-hour trips. They're ve popular, so make reservations. Companies offering flights include **Air Grand Canyon** (Bo 3028, Grand Canyon 86023, tel. 602/638–2618); **Grand Canyon Airlines** (Box 303 Grand Canyon 86023, tel. 602/638–2407 or 800/528–2413); **Windrock Aviation** (Bo 1227, Chino Valley 86323, tel. 602/638–9591). Companies offering helicopter fligh include **Airstar Helicopters** (Box 3378, Grand Canyon 86023, tel. 602/638–2622 800/962–3869); **Grand Canyon Helicopters** (Box 455, Grand Canyon 86023, te

602/638–2419 or 800/528–2418); **Kenai Helicopters** (Box 1429 Grand Canyon 86023, tel. 602/638–2412).

NORTH RIM **Grand Canyon AirTours** (Rte. 89S, Kanab, UT 84741, tel. 801/644–2904) offers aerial tours through **Kanab Air** at the Kanab Airport.

CROSS-COUNTRY SKIING

NORTH RIM Although the North Rim is closed during the winter, you can still visit the North Rim Nordic Center at the Kaibab Lodge between December and April. Trails, tours, ski rentals, and instruction are all available. For more information, contact **Canyoneers** (Box 2997, Flagstaff 86003, tel. 800/525–0924).

Near the Grand Canyon

CAMERON AND THE PAINTED DESERT ● ● ●

An hour's drive north of Flagstaff on Route 89 is the **Historic Cameron Trading Post** (Cameron Trading Post, Box 339, Cameron 86020 tel. 602/679–2231). Native Americans have been bringing their crafts to this huge market since 1916. It's an ideal place to buy finely crafted turquoise jewelry, kachina dolls, woven rugs, pottery, baskets, and paintings. There's also a grocery store, a restaurant, and a hotel.

Along the 70 mile stretch of Route 89 to the north of Cameron lies the **Painted Desert**, where Navajo artists sell their crafts directly to passing motorists from roadside stands. The prices are great.

The Painted Desert is an area that lets you step back into the geological mists of time and see trees turned to stone and the results of millennia of erosion that has exposed sandstone in colors of awesome beauty. Reds and yellows predominate, but with clouds and moisture they range from lavender and pink to salmon and purple.

GRAND CANYON CAVERNS AND ROUTE 66 ● ● ●

Between **Kingman** and **Seligman** (70 miles west of Flagstaff), the two-lane Route 66 bends north of I–40 for 90 scenic miles. Route 66 used to be the main route west to California, but has been eclipsed by the multilane I–40. Its no-longer flourishing, almost ghost town-like hotels and washed-out billboards make it look like a souvenir of the 20th century.

About 25 miles west of Seligman is **Grand Canyon Caverns** (Box 108, Peach Springs 86434, tel. 602/422–3223). This unique geologic find consists of huge caverns 21 stories below the Earth's surface filled with stalactites, stalagmites, and other fascinating subterranean rock formations. Simpleminded but amusing 40-minute tours (around $6) are offered daily 10–5.

Index

M

A T-SHIRT FOR YOUR THOUGHTS . . . .

After your trip, you can help make a great book even better! The first 500 respondents whose comments help us most improve future editions will receive an **On the Loose with Berkeley** T-shirt (100% cotton and cool). Just print your name and address clearly and send the completed questionnaire to the address shown below. Entries must be received by January 1, 1994.

Your Name ____________________

Address ____________________

____________________ Zip ____________

Where did you buy this book? City ____________ State ____________

How long before your trip did you buy this book? ____________

Which Berkeley guide(s) did you buy? ____________

Which other guides, if any, did you purchase for this trip? ____________

Which other guidebooks, if any, have you used before? (Please circle)
Fodor's Let's Go Real Guide Frommer's Birnbaum Lonely Planet
Other ____________________

Why did you choose Berkeley? (Please circle as many as apply)
Budget Information More maps Emphasis on outdoors/off-the-beaten-track
Design Attitude Other ____________________

____

If you're employed, occupation? ____________

If you're a student: Name of school ____________ City & State ____________

Age ____________ Male ____________ Female ____________

What magazines or newspapers do you read regularly? ____________

____

How many weeks was your trip? (Please circle) 1 2 3 4 5 6 7 8 More than 8 weeks

After you arrived on your trip, how did you get around? (Please circle one or more)
Rental car Personal car Plane Bus Train Hiking Biking Hitching
Other ____________________

When did you travel? ____________________
Month(s)

Where did you travel? ____________________

____

Did you have a planned itinerary? Yes ____________ No ____________

How much did you spend each day on lodging? (Please circle one)
Under $25 $26–$50 $51–$75 $76–$100 $101–$150 over $150

On transportation?
Under $25 $26–$50 $51–$75 $76–$100 $101–$150 over $150

On food/drink?
Under $25 $26–$50 $51–$75 $76–$100 $101–$150 over $150

The features/sections I used most were (Please circle as many as apply):
Basics Where to Sleep Food Coming and Going Worth Seeing Other

The information was (circle one):
Usually accurate Sometimes accurate Seldom accurate

I would ____ would not ____ buy another Berkeley guide.

These books are brand new and we'd really appreciate some feedback on how to improve them. Please also tell us about your latest find, a new scam, a budget deal, whatever—we want to hear about it.

For your comments:

Send complete questionnaire to The Berkeley Guides, 505 Eshleman Hall, University of California, Berkeley, CA 94720.

Under the auspices of

THE ARBOFILIA ASSOCIATION FOR THE PROTECTION OF TREES, THE BASIC FOUNDATION, AND THE RAINFOREST ACTION NETWORK

For every tree used to produce The Berkeley Guides, we will plant two!

Our rain forests, home to half of all living things on earth, are being destroyed at a rate of 50 acres per minute. At this rate, the rain forests are in danger of disappearing completely in just 50 years.

In addition to using recycled text and cover stock, the Berkeley Guides will help offset this loss by commissioning the planting of 8,000 trees wherever they are most needed via the "Plant an Endangered Tropical Tree Program."

This program is one of the largest reforestation projects of its kind in Central or South America. Over 1,100,000 tropical trees have been planted since 1987. This reforestation project concentrates on planting 400 of some of the most endangered species of tropical hardwood, fruit, and nut trees.

Trees are planted strategically to create a bridge between the National Park and the Central Pacific coast of Costa Rica and the denuded highland rain forest that surrounds this biological preserve. This action secures the future of the wildlife that migrates between the highland and lowland rain forests.

Donations will be made to The Rainforest Action Network (The Basic Foundation PO Box 47012, St. Petersburg, Florida 33743).